Brazil
Handbook

Alex Robinson

66 99

From the moment I arrived at Guararapes airport in Recife ... the living organism that is Brazil laid siege to my sensibilities ... I found myself stimulated as never before, constantly bombarded by the sights, sounds, smells, moods and rhythms of this new world in the tropics.

The Brazilians, by Joseph A Page

Footprint story

It was 1921

Ireland had just been partitioned, the British miners were striking for more pay and the federation of British industry had an idea. Exports were booming in South America – how about a handbook for businessmen trading in that far away continent? The Anglo-South American Handbook was born that year, written by W Koebel, the most prolific writer on Latin America of his day.

1924

Two editions later the book was 'privatized' and in 1924, in the hands of Royal Mail, the steamship company for South America, it became The South American Handbook, subtitled 'South America in a nutshell'. This annual publication became the 'bible' for generations of travellers to South America and remains so to this day. In the early days travel was by sea and the Handbook gave all the details needed for the long voyage from Europe. What to wear for dinner; how to arrange a cricket match with the Cable & Wireless staff on the Cape Verde Islands and a full account of the journey from Liverpool up the Amazon to Manaus: 5898 miles without changing cabin!

1939

As the continent opened up, The South American Handbook reported the new Pan Am flying boat services, and the fortnightly airship service from Rio to Europe on the Graf Zeppelin. For reasons still unclear but with extraordinary determination, the annual editions continued through the Second World War.

1970s

Many more people discovered South America and the backpacking trail started to develop. All the while the Handbook was gathering fans, including literary vagabonds such as Paul Theroux and Graham Greene (who once sent some updates addressed to "The publishers of the best travel guide in the world, Bath, England").

1990s

During the 1990s the company set about developing a new travel guide series using this legendary title as the flagship. By 1997 there were over a dozen guides in the series and the Footprint imprint was launched.

2000s

The series grew quickly and there were soon Footprint travel guides covering more than 150 countries. In 2004, Footprint launched its first thematic guide: *Surfing Europe*, packed with colour photographs, maps and charts. This was followed by further thematic guides such as *Diving the World*, *Snowboarding the World*, *Body and Soul escapes*, *Travel with Kids* and *European City Breaks*.

2009

Today we continue the traditions of the last 88 years that has served legions of travellers so well. We believe that these help to make Footprint guides different. Our policy is to use authors who are genuine experts who write for independent travellers; people possessing a spirit of adventure, looking to get off the beaten track.

Title page: A Bahian woman enjoys the unhurried pace of Salvador's Pelourinho.
Above: Scooping out the water from river boats in Caraíva.

There are few countries as beautiful and vibrant as Brazil. In the Amazon, virgin forest stretches unbroken for more than 2500 km in every direction. The table-top mountains of the interior are covered in medicinal plants and drained by mineral-rich rivers that tumble through gorges and rush over spectacular tiered waterfalls, up to 3 km wide. Thousands of miles of pristine beaches line its coast, some backed by dunes the size of deserts, others by forests of swaying palms. In the Pantanal, the world's biggest wetland, herons and egrets fill the air like butterflies. Tiny cobble and whitewash gold-mining towns contrast with the metropolises of Rio, São Paulo, Salvador and Recife, which offer the most exciting and surprising urban culture in Latin America. But best of all there are the Brazilians, in all their glorious exuberance and diversity. Portugal, France, Ireland, Holland, and Britain all laid claims here and left their cultures to mingle with the indigenous inhabitants; Brazil hosts the most Africans, Arabs and Japanese in the Americas. Consequently, bierfests, sushi, *bauhaus*, rodeos and death metal are as much a part of the culture as bossa nova and football. As yet, the country is undiscovered beyond the clichés, so come before Brazil becomes yet another destination on the exotic travel circuit.

AMAZON

FORTALEZA

BRASÍLIA, GOIÁS & TOCANTINS

RECIFE & THE NORTHEAST COAST

PANTANAL

BAHIA

MINAS GERAIS & ESPÍRITO SANTO

SÃO PAULO

RIO DE JANEIRO

IGUAÇU FALLS & THE SOUTH

Atlantic Ocean

Contents

Planning your trip

ALEX ROBINSON

Botafogo Bay in Rio de Janeiro
with the Pão de Açúcar in
the foreground and the beaches
of Niterói in the distance.

Where to go

The southeast

The highlight of the southeast is **Rio de Janeiro**. No city on earth has a setting to compare: rainforest-covered mountains rise sheer from a bottle-green ocean and a vast wine-glass bay. And Rio clusters and claws at them; its centre climbing over smaller hills and crowding behind crescent gentle coves; its slums clinging to their smooth granite sides. The beaches and music are wonderful, and carnival – which takes place in a stadium, and not in the streets – is one of the world's great spectacles. Rio's ugly and far less courted big sister, **São Paulo**, lies a few hours' bus ride away. Its interminable labyrinths of concrete are unprepossessing at first, but those who find their way into the maze, preferably with a local guide, discover the best nightlife, restaurants, high-end shopping and popular culture in South America. The land-locked state of Minas Gerais is Brazil's literary heartland. Its pastoral landscapes are broken by rocky mountains and dotted with tranquil colonial towns like **Diamantina**, **Ouro Preto** and **Tirandentes**. Minas is infused with a nostalgic lyricism, which inspired Brazil's greatest writer (João Guimarães Rosa), its greatest poet, (Carlos Drummond de Andrade), musician, (Milton Nascimento) and footballer (Edson Arantes do Nascimento or Pele).

Bahia and the northeast

Northeastern Brazil is famous for its beaches and colonial cities. The most popular destination, Bahia, offers the best of both with a string of palm-shaded silvery strands lining its coast and islands, and the largest colonial city in the Americas, **Salvador**. Bahia is the home of capoeira and African Brazilian *candomblé* religion, and Salvador's street carnival is Brazil's most raucous. The state's arid backlands are broken by dramatic, waterfall-covered mountains in the **Chapada Diamantina**. **Recife**, capital of Pernambuco, and its twin city **Olinda**, are almost as pretty as Salvador and have an even livelier cultural scene, with some of the most exciting contemporary Brazilian music and the country's largest street carnival. Travelling to the north coast, there are hundreds of beaches to choose from, some highly developed, others less so. You can swim, surf or ride the dunes in buggies in **Jericoacoara** or **Genipabu**, or kitesurf in the neo-colonial settlement of **Cumbuco**. Then there are the vast dune deserts of the **Lençóis Maranhenses** on the windswept Maranhão coast and the last major city before the mouth of the Amazon, **São Luís**, whose centre is covered in colonial tiles, and whose streets reverberate with some of Brazil's best nightlife.

Opposite page left: Enslaved Africans made the historic centre of Ouro Preto one of the most beautiful in the Americas. **Opposite page right**: The Oficina Brennand in Recife is as bizarre and captivating as the Dalí museum or Gaudí buildings in Catalunya. **Above**: A fisherman pauses for a smoke on a picture-perfect evening in Maragogi.

The centre west

The centre west of Brazil is dominated by the expansive grasslands, table-top mountains and scrub forests of the *cerrado* and the Pantanal wetlands. The *cerrado* comprises South America's most acutely threatened biome, almost as rich in unique flora and fauna as the Amazon and, in the wilds of the **Chapada dos Veadeiros** or **Jalapão**, just as magnificent. The rivers, lakes and grasslands of the **Pantanal** are the best place to see wildlife in the Americas; at the end of the dry season, there are few places on earth where birds can be seen in such astonishing numbers. At the eastern end of the centre west is the country's capital, **Brasília**, carved from the *cerrado* in the 1960s and now a World Heritage Site for its repository of striking modernist architecture.

Northern Brazil

The north of the country is dominated by the **Amazon**, its forest and its tributaries that spread as wide and thin as the blood vessels in a human body. The first Europeans cut their way into the interior of South America in search of an inland sea and an empire rich with gold. And when the river is in full flood its tributaries link through the inundated forest to form what seems like an oceanic labyrinth

of lakes. These are served by sea-going cargo boats that call in at river ports along its length. Some ports are little towns while others, like **Belém**, with its cutting-edge alternative music scene, and **Manaus**, with myriad forest lodges, are home to more than a million people. North of Manaus is the overland route through Boa Vista to Venezuela. The forest stretches north into Colombia at **São Gabriel** and **Tabatinga**, and into Venezuela and the Guianas near **Boa Vista**, and south to the central tablelands of **Mato Grosso**.

Southern Brazil

With its maté-sipping *gaúchos*, beer festivals, squeeze-box tango and blonde-haired, blue-eyed super models, the three states of southern Brazil feel closer to Uruguay, or even Germany, than they do to the rest of Brazil. Most visitors come for the world's most famous waterfalls, **Iguaçu**, on the border with Argentina and Paraguay. But there are canyons and good hiking in the **Serra Gaúcha** mountains in Rio Grande do Sul and the **Serra Graciosa** in Paraná, and beautiful beaches around the laid-back city of **Florianópolis** in Santa Catarina and the tranquil sub-tropical island of **Ilha do Mel**. There's also the world's second-largest beer festival – in the German-Brazilian enclave of **Blumenau**, every October.

Itineraries

One week

Beach and waterfall

Begin in Rio over a weekend and take in the city sights and the nightlife in Lapa. On Monday leave for the beach resort town of Búzios or the pretty colonial port of Paraty, which is surrounded by beautiful beaches, especially near Trindade. Consider taking a trip on the side to the island of Ilha Grande or the rainforests and hiking trails of Itatiatia national park. On Wednesday either take a bus south to Curitiba (via Santos or São Paulo) and take the Serra Verde train to Paranaguá and the Ilha do Mel or return to Rio and fly to the Iguaçu Falls. On Friday fly to São Paulo for a taste of that city's restaurants and nightlife and take a flight home from there.

Carnival hop

Fly into Recife on a Friday for Brazil's best, least expensive and most traditional large carnival and mix with the crowds at the Galo da Madruganda opening ceremony hosted by the great Brazilian percussionist Naná Vasconcelos. Spend Sunday and Monday in Recife/Olinda watching the *maracatu blocos* before flying south to Salvador on Tuesday and spending a few days with the crowds partying in the streets. Fly to Rio for Saturday's champions parade in the Sambódromo; relax on the beach and fly home on Sunday.

Two weeks

Amazon to Recife by beach

Head to the vibrant colonial city of Belém at the mouth of the Amazon, being sure to arrive on a weekend to make the most of the fabulous nightlife. Either spend a few days recovering on the beaches of Marajó island or take a bus or flight south to São Luís, one of Brazil's least known colonial highlights with its fascinating architecture and African culture. After a few days' sightseeing in the city and nearby Alcântara, head for the

Above: Brazil's graffiti, some of the world's best, was exhibited in London's Tate Modern in 2008.
Opposite page: Cacimba do Padre beach on Fernando de Noronha was recently voted one of the top two beaches in Brazil.

Lençóis Maranhenses – a spectacular sand-dune desert on the wild, windy Atlantic. Continue from the Lençóis to Jericoacoara in Ceará for more beautiful beaches and some of the world's best wind- and kite-surfing. Make a brief stop at Fortaleza for some *forró* dancing and do a hop through the smaller beach resorts of Canoa Quebrada and Pipa, in Rio Grande do Norte, before arriving in Olinda and Recife at the weekend. Fly out from Recife.

ALEX ROBINSON

Salvador to Rio by beach

Begin in Salvador, Brazil's first capital, with its impressive historical centre and vibrant African-Brazilian culture. After a few days head to Itacaré, a laid-back surf town to the south, and spend a few days holed up on the beach. Take a long bus journey south to Porto Seguro, where the Portuguese first landed in Brazil and spend a few days here or in the adjacent beach town of Arraial d'Ajuda or, if you feel like a splurge, Trancoso – South America's beach chic capital. Transfer south to Caravelas for a trip to the Abrolhos islands before taking the long journey south to Rio de Janeiro.

Table-top mountains, rainforests, wetlands and beach

Fly into São Paulo and after a day or so in the city take a one-hour flight or a 10- to 14-hour bus ride to Cuiabá and the Pantanal – the best place for wildlife in the Americas. Take a side trip to Cristalino Jungle Lodge in the southern Amazon – one of the finest rainforest lodges in the world – then head to Brasília to see Oscar Niemeyer's modernist fantasy city. From here take a bus north to the wilds of the Chapada dos Veadeiros World Heritage Site to trek, rappel, mountain bike or climb in a landscape of dry forest interspersed with clear-water rivers, canyons and some of the continent's most beautiful waterfalls. Head north to Palmas in Tocantins and visit the forests and waterfalls around that city or take a side-trip into the wild Jalapão table-top mountains. Then fly to Rio or Salvador and the beach.

Colonial cities, waterfalls, wetlands and beach

Fly into São Paulo and take a long bus journey to Campo Grande and the southern Pantanal. Stay either in a *fazenda* near Miranda or take a tour with an agency. Fly or bus it to Iguaçu, which at 3 km wide are the world's most impressive waterfalls. Fly from here to Belo Horizonte and a Friday or Saturday of live music, before visiting some of Latin America's prettiest colonial towns – Ouro Preto, Tiradentes or Diamantina – all with stunning baroque buildings set against a backdrop of rugged mountains. From Minas head to the coast, either at Rio or Salvador.

The Amazon heartland to Rio via the beach or via the wild interior

The Amazon is not a river – it is a hundred thousand rivers, brooks and streams, ranging in colour from coffee with milk to cobalt blue to lemon to black. Begin your journey in the Amazon city of Manaus in a nearby jungle lodge or the Mamirauá reserve. Take a passenger boat downstream to lively Belém at the mouth of the river (preferably at the weekend to experience the nightlife). From here follow 'Amazon to Recife by beach' route (see above), then either continue by bus to Salvador and take a flight to Rio, or fly direct to Rio from Recife. It is also possible to take a far wilder and less travelled road to Rio by heading inland from Belém or São Luís and calling in at Palmas (for the vast *cerrado* wilderness near Jalapão); the waterfall-covered mountains of the Chapada dos Veadeiros; the modernist capital of Brasília; Campo Grande (for the Pantanal); and São Paulo.

Brazil highlights & itineraries

See colour maps in centre of book

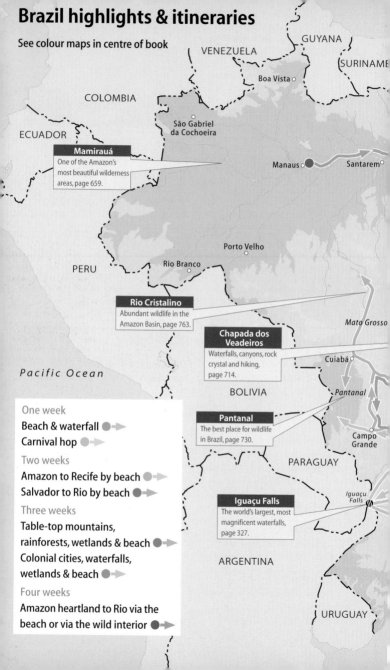

GUYANA

SURINAME

VENEZUELA

Boa Vista ○

COLOMBIA

São Gabriel
da Cochoeira ○

Mamirauá
One of the Amazon's
most beautiful wilderness
areas, page 659.

Manaus ○●━━━ Santarem ○

ECUADOR

Porto Velho ○

PERU

Rio Branco ○

Rio Cristalino
Abundant wildlife in the
Amazon Basin, page 763.

Mato Grosso

**Chapada dos
Veadeiros**
Waterfalls, canyons, rock
crystal and hiking,
page 714.

Cuiabá ○

Pacific Ocean

BOLIVIA

Pantanal

Pantanal
The best place for wildlife
in Brazil, page 730.

Campo ○
Grande

PARAGUAY

One week

Beach & waterfall ●➡
Carnival hop ●➡

Two weeks

Amazon to Recife by beach ●➡
Salvador to Rio by beach ●➡

Three weeks

Table-top mountains,
rainforests, wetlands & beach ●➡
Colonial cities, waterfalls,
wetlands & beach ●➡

Four weeks

Amazon heartland to Rio via the
beach or via the wild interior ●➡

*Iguaçu
Falls*

Iguaçu Falls
The world's largest, most
magnificent waterfalls,
page 327.

ARGENTINA

URUGUAY

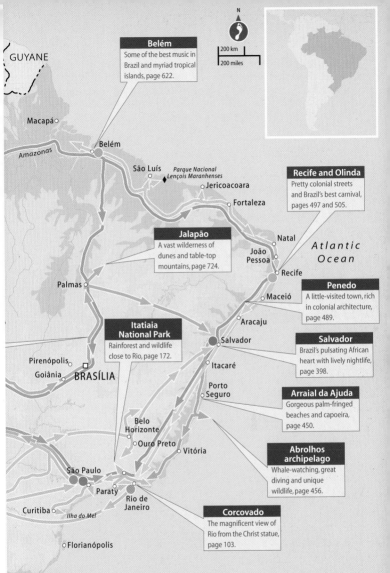

Belém
Some of the best music in Brazil and myriad tropical islands, page 622.

Recife and Olinda
Pretty colonial streets and Brazil's best carnival, pages 497 and 505.

Jalapão
A vast wilderness of dunes and table-top mountains, page 724.

Penedo
A little-visited town, rich in colonial architecture, page 489.

Itatiaia National Park
Rainforest and wildlife close to Rio, page 172.

Salvador
Brazil's pulsating African heart with lively nightlife, page 398.

Arraial da Ajuda
Gorgeous palm-fringed beaches and capoeira, page 450.

Abrolhos archipelago
Whale-watching, great diving and unique wildlife, page 456.

Corcovado
The magnificent view of Rio from the Christ statue, page 103.

N

200 km
200 miles

GUYANE

Macapá

Belém

Amazonas

São Luís

Parque Nacional Lençóis Maranhenses

Jericoacoara

Fortaleza

Natal

Atlantic Ocean

João Pessoa

Palmas

Recife

Maceió

Aracaju

Salvador

Pirenópolis

Goiânia

BRASÍLIA

Itacaré

Porto Seguro

Belo Horizonte

Ouro Preto

Vitória

São Paulo

Paraty

Curitiba

Ilha do Mel

Rio de Janeiro

Florianópolis

Porto Alegre

Relaxing retreats

The luxury spa: Unique Garden

For a serious five-star pampering splurge in the heart of tranquil nature spend a day or a weekend in this state-of-the-art spa in the rainforest-covered Serra da Cantareira mountains outside metropolitan São Paulo. The spa itself has every treatment you could imagine – from thalassotherapy and Watsu to a menu of massages and body wraps that is up there with the best in the world. There's a series of gyms, swimming pools, relaxation areas and a low-calorie gourmet restaurant – all ensuring you return from your stay with a smaller waistline. And accommodation is in individually designed chalets built by post-modernist architect of the moment Rui Ohtake and set in the colourful garden and surrounding sub-tropical forest. See page 212.

The honeymoon splurge: Tauana

This stylish nine-bungalow resort in remote Corumbau, a 15-minute plane ride from Trancoso, or a good three hours overland and by sea, offers the ultimate in romantic and remote eco-chic escapes. The vast wood and palm-thatched cabanas are set in a palm-tree garden wafted by a perennial gentle breeze. All offer an almost private view of the endless, deserted white-sand beach in front of the hotel. The staff are invisible yet the service is superb. There is nothing to do here except integrate with nature and each other: eat fresh fruit and seafood, read, walk along the endless sand, swim in the bath-warm sea and drink a cocktail under the hot sun or a star-filled, tropical sky, and honeymoon in the enormous king-sized beds. See page 460.

On the beach: Mata N'ativa

In less than 10 years, Daniel and Daniela, the owners of this pretty Bahian beach *pousada* have turned their plot of land into a mini garden of Eden, filled with flowering trees, heliconias and humming birds. There's even a little outdoor spa with a jacuzzi overlooking the river. Accommodation is in a series of intimate chalets, the best of which are the duplex suites. Breakfast is wholesome and generous and Daniel's range of light adventure activities in the surrounding forest are great for getting in touch with nature and inner peace. Staying here is a real Walden experience if you want it to be. Yet the beach and Trancoso's romantic Quadrado, with its great restaurants, are just a stroll away. See page 459.

ALEX ROBINSON

Opposite page: An Ofuro bath in one of the massage suites in the Unique Garden Spa.
Above left: The massage room at Bromelias near Paraty in São Paulo overlooks a rainforest stream.
Above right: Casas Brancas, the best hotel in Búzios.

Waterfalls and healing

The Chapada dos Veadeiros table-top mountains just north of Brasília is a wonderful place to relax and recuperate. By day there's hiking in pristine *cerrado* forest, rapelling, canyoning or whitewater rafting, with cooling breaks for a swim in waterfalls as clear and clean as a spring. Many of the trails are littered with rock crystal shards and brilliant white quartzite. And the air is as pure as a mid-ocean breeze. The *chapada* is famous for its rejuvenating energy and many of Brazil's best alternative therapists, reiki practitioners and masseurs have settled in the two tiny towns: Alto Paraíso and São Jorge. See page 714.

Boutique chic: Casas Brancas

This mock-Mykonos Búzios boutique offers peace and quiet in style with stunning bay views and one of Brazil's best hotel spas. It's the perfect place to unwind and dine and to party and pamper – especially during the carnival high season when it can be hard to get the right balance between resting and staying up all night. The best rooms are the upper suites, which have private breakfast terraces with hammocks and comfortable rustic chairs. You could spend the whole day here, gazing out to sea, sipping white wine and taking a break from reading, or daydreaming before a swim in the pool or a massage. Great restaurants, bars, clubs and dozens of beaches are just a short walk away. See page 154.

In the rainforest: Bromelias

Bromelias sits eyrie-like in the lush folds of the Atlantic coastal mountains looking out over the ocean near Paraty. Rooms are in cabins sitting on a hillside in a heliconia-filled garden and there's a sauna and massage spa with Ofuro baths five minutes down the hill next to a rushing mountain stream. The air is filled with tropical birds and butterflies. One of Brazil's best seafood restaurants, Le Gite d'Indaiatiba is a short walk from the hotel. Dining here, accompanied by the music of the rainforest or Olivier and Valeria's impeccable collection of sumptuous jazz is a wonderful experience. Order the red hot *camarões*. See page 183.

Wilderness experiences

Whitewater rafting in Jalapão

Jalapão is one of Brazil's least known and least visited wildernesses offering great hiking, wildlife and perhaps the remotest whitewater rafting in Latin America. There are table-top mountains, vast plains stretching unbroken as far as the eye can see with barely a human being in sight, giant indigo parrots, maned rust-red wolves and puma, plunging canyons and seas of fiery-orange dunes.

Wildlife-watching in the Mamirauá reserve

Bruce Parry may have made it seem remote when he was there for the BBC, but tourists can visit the pristine flooded forests and river villages of Mamirauá too. The wildlife is spectacular – from red-faced uakari monkeys to Amazon manatees and huge black caiman; one of which sleeps right underneath the bedrooms at the floating Uakari Ecolodge.

Horse riding in the Pantanal

There is nowhere better for wildlife in the western hemisphere than the Pantanal. The lakes, rivers and forests of this seasonally flooded wetland cover an area larger than France. And they crawl with wildlife, from packs of hissing spectacled caiman, flocks of 2-m-tall rhea, hunting ocelots, giant otters, anaconda as thick as a wrestler's thigh and more birds than you can imagine. The best way to see them is on horseback – from a Pantanal farm house or *fazenda* – although walking, kayaking or even riding in a jeep are also possible.

Kayaking at Cristalino Jungle Lodge

Nowhere south of Costa Rica offers more exciting or better organized ecotourism than this jungle lodge on the banks of the clear-water Cristalino river in the northern Mato Grosso. The wildlife is superb, with nesting harpy eagles, dozens of primate

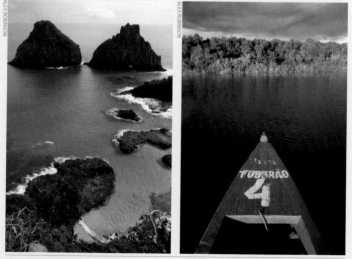

ALEX ROBINSON

Above left: Great snorkelling opportunities in the Baía dos Porces on Fernando de Noronha island.
Above right: Canoeing through the dark water of the Analvilhanas islands on the Amazon's Rio Negro.

species, tapirs and the best bird and butterfly species list in the lowland Amazon. And there's a real chance of seeing big cats too. Jaguars often hunt next to the river bank on the exposed beaches, or snooze on overhanging branches in the early morning sun. One of the best ways to see the reserve is on a kayak paddle down the lazy, winding Cristalino river. Try and leave at dawn for the best chance of seeing wild animals.

Waterfall safaris in the chapadas

Brazil's outback interior is dotted with *chapadas* – time-worn escarpment mountains, as ancient as Africa. They are cut and coursed by dozens of clear- and blackwater rivers that fall and pause in pools and plunge again onto the surrounding plains. The Cachoeira da Fumaça in Bahia's Chapada Diamantina national park drops almost half a kilometre into a deep blue pool, while the Cachoeira do Poço Encantado in Goiás's Chapada dos Veadeiros national park drops over a series of beautiful tiers in pristine *cerrado* forest. And there are scores more besides, in both these parks as well as in the Chapada dos Guimarães in Mato Grosso and in the remoter Chapada das Mesas and Chapada das Mangabeiras in the far northeast.

Top: The *cerrado* forest in the Chapada dos Veadeiros in Goiás drips with gorgeous waterfalls. Above: Red-billed toucan.

Diving in Fernando de Noronha or the Abrolhos archipelago

Brazil's tropical islands are as pretty as any in Southeast Asia and, for now at least, they remain free of Bob Marley theme bars and buzzing mopeds. The wildest and most beautiful are off the coast of northeastern Brazil. Fernando de Noronha looks like a tropical Kerry, with emerald-green water replete with underwater life. The Abrolhos are a string of little rocks off southern Bahia with more whales than the Whitsunday Islands. The diving at both is the best in the Atlantic south of the Caribbean.

Festivals

Recife and Olinda Carnival

Salvador may have the largest traditional street carnival in the world and Rio the most fabulous, but Recife and Olinda host Brazil's most authentic carnival. *Maracatu* drum troupes and *frevo* dancers parade through the streets watched by over a million dancing revellers. The highlight of the carnival is the Galo da Madrugada parade focused on a giant model cockerel. When this leaves from the São José neighbourhood in the city centre carnival officially begins. Recife and Olinda are also famous for their June São João parties – and these can be visited together with those in Caruru or Campina Grande.

Bumba-Meu-Boi in São Luís

A month of festivities in Brazil's other great African-Brazilian city culminate in this drum and sung dance pageant depicting the ritual slaughter of a prize bull, his resurrection by a witch doctor, shaman and Catholic priest, and the rainy season that the magic brings. Bumba-Meu-Boi is also celebrated further north in the Amazon, where it is called Boi Bumba. The biggest party is in Parintins on an island in the middle of the Amazon river – usually at the end of June. The Parintins pageant takes place in a vast purpose-built stadium called the Bumbódromo, and features floats as large as those in Rio Carnaval, costumed dancers and compères. Two teams modelled on Rio's samba schools compete against each other to perform the best show.

Festas Juninhas in Campina Grande and Caruru

In June hundreds of thousands of party pilgrims flock to these desert towns in Paraíba and Pernambuco to drink spiced wine, dress up and dance. The rhythm here is *forró* – a kind of backlands jig powered by staccato accordion and punchy percussion. Caruru

Above: The Boi Bumba celebrations in the Amazon take place on an island in the river.

Left: The Sinhazinha da Fazenda is one of the characters in the Boi Bumba pageant.
Right: Samba drummers at the Rio Carnaval parade in the Sambódromo stadium.

and Campina Grande are arch rivals – and aficionados of both festivals will assure you that theirs is the best. But as the festivals carry on for much of the month (and are at their liveliest on the weekends) it's possible to go to both and make a stop-over on the beach or in Recife/Olinda in between. The Festas Juninhas are celebrated on a smaller scale all over Brazil – from Rio Grande do Sul to Roraima.

New Year's Eve in Rio

The biggest festival of the year in Rio isn't carnival but New Year's Eve, or as it's known locally, Reveillon. It's an overwhelming spectacle. Copacabana beach is packed with well over million people gathered around half a dozen vast sound stages hosted by Rio's biggest stars – such as Jorge Ben and Cidade Negra. The night culminates in a spectacular firework display with a cascade of light pouring off the skyscrapers and erupting off ships in the bay.

Oktoberfest in Blumenau

Bavarian Volksmusik, thousands of Brazilians running around in Lederhosen and Dirndl, huge aluminium tankards of Brazilian Weissbiers with German names like Eisenbahn and Wunderbar and Brazilian dancing to German songs like *Einer geht noch, einer geht noch rein* from 1600 until dawn the next day. It's a truly memorable experience.

Festa do Bonfim, Salvador

Bahia's most colourful festival after Carnaval is held in January and sees thousands of Bahians in traditional Yoruba costumes parade some 8 km from the beachside Church of Conceição da Praia to the beautiful colonial Church of Bonfim. The festival is nominally Catholic but strongly associated with *candomblé*: Our Lord of Bonfim is also Oxalá, father of the Orishas and creator of humankind, thus here are many ancillary celebrations.

When to go

The best time for a visit is from April to June, and August to October. Business visitors should avoid mid-December to the end of February, when it is hot and people are on holiday. In these months, hotels, beaches and transport tend to be very crowded. July is a school holiday month. If visiting tourist centres like Salvador, Rio and the colonial cities in Minas Gerais in the low season, be aware that some tourist sights may be closed for restoration.

In Rio de Janeiro conditions during the winter (May to September) are like those of a north European summer, including periods of rain and overcast skies, with temperatures from 14°C to the high 20s. It is more like a north European autumn in São Paulo and the southern states and it can get very cold in the far south; warm clothing is required as temperatures can change dramatically and it can get cold on high ground anywhere in Brazil, particularly at night. The heaviest rain is from November to March in Rio and São Paulo, and from April to August around Recife (although irregular rainfall causes severe draughts here).

The rainy season in the north and Amazônia can begin in December and is heaviest from March to May, but it is getting steadily shorter, possibly as a result of deforestation. Few places get more than 2 m – the coast north of Belém, some of the Amazon Basin, and a small area of the Serra do Mar between Santos and São Paulo, where the downpour has been harnessed to generate electricity. Summer conditions all over the country are tropical, although temperatures rarely reach 40°C.

The average annual temperature increases steadily from south to north, but even on the equator, in the Amazon Basin, the average temperature is not more than 27°C. The highest recorded was 42°C, in the dry northeastern states. From the latitude of Recife south to Rio, the mean temperature is 23-27°C along the coast, and 18-21°C in the highlands. South of Rio, towards the boundary with Uruguay, the mean temperature is 17-19°C. Humidity is relatively high in Brazil, particularly along the coast. The luminosity is also very high, and sunglasses are advisable.

Brazil

Activity	J	F	M	A	M	J	J	A	S	O	N	D
Wildlife watching in the Pantanal			★	★	★	★	★	★	★	★	★	
Visiting the northern Amazon					★	★	★	★	★	★	★	★
Visiting the southern Amazon		★	★	★	★	★	★					
The best parties and festivals	★	★	★			★						
Hiking in Goiás and Tocantins				★	★	★	★	★	★			
Beach breaks in Rio and the southeast		★	★	★	★	★	★	★	★	★		
Beach breaks in Bahia and the northeast	★	★				★	★	★	★	★	★	★
Surfing and swimming in Florianópolis	★	★	★						★	★	★	★
Kitesurfing and windsurfing in the northeast	★	★				★	★	★	★	★	★	★

Rainfall and climate charts

Rio de Janeiro

Month	Average temperature in °C max-min	Average rainfall in mm
Jan	29 - 23	125
Feb	29 - 23	122
Mar	28 - 22	130
Apr	27 - 21	107
May	25 - 19	79
Jun	24 - 18	53
Jul	24 - 17	41
Aug	24 - 18	43
Sep	24 - 18	66
Oct	25 - 19	79
Nov	26 - 20	104
Dec	28 - 22	137

Porto Alegre

Month	Average temperature in °C max-min	Average rainfall in mm
Jan	31 - 19	89
Feb	31 - 20	81
Mar	28 - 18	99
Apr	26 - 16	104
May	22 - 12	114
Jun	19 - 09	130
Jul	19 - 09	114
Aug	20 - 10	127
Sep	21 - 12	132
Oct	23 - 14	86
Nov	27 - 16	79
Dec	29 - 18	89

Salvador

Month	Average temperature in °C max-min	Average rainfall in mm
Jan	30 - 24	43
Feb	30 - 24	58
Mar	30 - 24	106
Apr	29 - 24	191
May	28 - 23	187
Jun	27 - 22	168
Jul	26 - 22	143
Aug	26 - 22	99
Sep	27 - 22	73
Oct	28 - 23	70
Nov	29 - 23	74
Dec	30 - 24	69

Recife

Month	Average temperature in °C max-min	Average rainfall in mm
Jan	30 - 25	53
Feb	30 - 25	84
Mar	30 - 24	160
Apr	29 - 24	221
May	28 - 23	267
Jun	28 - 23	277
Jul	27 - 22	254
Aug	27 - 22	152
Sep	28 - 23	64
Oct	29 - 24	25
Nov	29 - 24	25
Dec	29 - 25	28

Fortaleza

Month	Average temperature in °C max-min	Average rainfall in mm
Jan	31 - 25	78
Feb	31 - 25	108
Mar	30 - 25	202
Apr	30 - 25	238
May	30 - 25	119
Jun	30 - 24	101
Jul	30 - 24	44
Aug	30 - 24	25
Sep	30 - 25	14
Oct	31 - 25	08
Nov	31 - 26	08
Dec	31 - 26	20

Belém

Month	Average temperature in °C max-min	Average rainfall in mm
Jan	31 - 22	318
Feb	30 - 22	358
Mar	31 - 23	358
Apr	31 - 23	320
May	31 - 23	259
Jun	31 - 22	170
Jul	31 - 22	150
Aug	31 - 22	112
Sep	32 - 22	89
Oct	32 - 22	84
Nov	32 - 22	66
Dec	32 - 22	155

Manaus

Month	Average temperature in °C max-min	Average rainfall in mm
Jan	31 - 24	249
Feb	31 - 24	231
Mar	31 - 24	262
Apr	31 - 24	221
May	31 - 24	170
Jun	31 - 24	84
Jul	32 - 24	58
Aug	33 - 24	38
Sep	33 - 24	46
Oct	33 - 24	107
Nov	33 - 24	142
Dec	32 - 24	203

Brasília

Month	Average temperature in °C max-min	Average rainfall in mm
Jan	26 - 18	127
Feb	26 - 18	129
Mar	26 - 18	146
Apr	26 - 17	91
May	26 - 16	24
Jun	25 - 14	04
Jul	25 - 14	09
Aug	27 - 15	10
Sep	28 - 17	36
Oct	28 - 18	74
Nov	26 - 18	161
Dec	26 - 18	170

Campo Grande

Month	Average temperature in °C max-min	Average rainfall in mm
Jan	31 - 22	142
Feb	31 - 22	114
Mar	32 - 22	104
Apr	31 - 21	69
May	28 - 18	53
Jun	28 - 17	34
Jul	28 - 16	17
Aug	30 - 18	20
Sep	31 - 19	58
Oct	32 - 21	97
Nov	32 - 22	94
Dec	31 - 22	140

ALEX ROBINSON

Sport and activities

Birdwatching

ⓘ **Pantanal Bird Club**, T065-3624 1930, www.pantanalbirdclub.org, is the best for serious birding in the interior. **Serra dos Tucanos**, www.serradostucanos.com.br, is the best in the Atlantic coastal forest. **Birding Brazil Tours**, www.birdingbraziltours.com, has a good reputation, operates out of Manaus and covers the Amazon and the rest of the country. **Focus Tours**, www.focustours.com, specializes in birdwatching and responsible travel. **Ornitholidays**, T01794-519445 (UK), www.ornitholidays.co.uk, is the best company working in Brazil from Europe. Two comprehensive websites are www.worldtwitch.com and www.camacdonald.com.

Brazil has more endemic species than any other country in South America, including the world's rarest bird, Spix's macaw. Habitats range from freshwater wetlands to lowland rainforest, dry *cerrado* and *caatinga*, Atlantic coastal forest, mangrove forest and wet pampa grassland. There are patches of *araucaria* pine forest in the south. None is difficult to get to, but it would be impossible to visit every type of environment in one trip. The system of national parks and protected areas, including those offshore (Abrolhos, Fernando de Noronha), is designed to allow access to Brazil's areas of outstanding beauty. The best time for birding is from September to October as it is quiet, relatively dry and flights are cheapest.

Caving

ⓘ **Sociedade Brasileira de Espeleologia**, www.sbe.com.br. For cave diving, see Scuba diving, page 26.

There are some wonderful cave systems in Brazil, and Ibama has a programme for the protection of the national speleological heritage. National parks such as Ubajara (see page 567) and Chapada Diamantina (page 471) and the state park of PETAR (page 240) have easy access for the casual visitor, but there are also many options for the keen potholer in the states of São Paulo, Paraná, Minas Gerais and the federal district of Brasília.

ALEX ROBINSON

Above: A Tukano fisherman. **Opposite page:** Hang-gliding off the Pedra Bonita in Rio.

Climbing

ⓘ Two useful websites are www.escalada brasil.com and www.rockclimbing.com/ routes/south_and_central_america/brazil.

As Brazil has no mountain ranges of Alpine or Andean proportions, the most popular form of *escalada* (climbing) is rock-face climbing. In the heart of Rio you can see, or join, climbers scaling the rocks at the base of Pão de Açúcar and on the Sugar Loaf itself. Not too far away, the Serra dos Órgãos provides plenty of challenges, not least the Dedo de Deus (God's Finger, see page 163). In the state of São Paulo a good location for climbing is Pedra do Báu near São Bento do Sapucaí, and Brotas is popular for abseiling (rappel). Pedra Branca and the Serra do Cipó are recommended locations in Minas Gerais. Mato Grosso has the Serra do Roncador and there are other good areas in Paraná and Rio Grande do Sul.

Fishing

ⓘ **Amazon Clipper**, www.peacocktrips.com, is far and away the best company in the Amazon (page 669). Lodges like **Barra Mansa**, www.hotelbarramansa.com.br, offer sport fishing in the Pantanal (page 750).

Brazil is great for sport fishing. Officially, the country's fish stocks are under the control of Ibama (www.ibama.org.br) and a licence is required for fishing in any waters. And as states often require permits too it is easiest to organize a trip through an agency. The best areas are the Amazon and Pantanal and the Rio Araguaia. Be aware that many Brazilians do not keep best practice and that rivers are quickly becoming over-fished, especially in the Pantanal, a threat to the world's largest wetland and a unique American biome.

Hang-gliding and paragliding

ⓘ **Associação Brasileira de Vôo Livre (ABVL – Brazilian Hang-gliding Associa tion)**, R Prefeito Mendes de Moraes s/n, São Conrado, Rio de Janeiro, T021-3322 0266, www.abvl.com.br, covers both hang-gliding and paragliding. For a full list of launch sites (and much else besides) see the **Guia 4 Ventos Brasil** site, www.guia4ventos.com.br, which also contains information on launch sites in other South American countries.

There are state associations affiliated with ABVL and there are a number of operators

Above: Whitewater rafting doesn't always go to plan.

offering tandem flights for those without experience. *Rampas* (launch sites) are growing in number. Among the best known is Pedra Bonita at Gávea in Rio de Janeiro, but there are others in the state. Popular *rampas* can also be found in São Paulo, Espírito Santo, Minas Gerais, Paraná, Santa Catarina, Rio Grande do Sul, Ceará, Mato Grosso do Sul and Brasília.

Horse riding

ⓘ **Tropa Serrana**, Belo Horizonte, T031-3344 8986, www.tropaserrana.zip.net. Other operators are listed in relevant chapters.

The Pantanal offers some of the best opportunities for horse riding in Brazil. Almost all the lodges we list offer horse-riding treks into the wetlands – of anything from a few hours to a few days. There are good horse trails in Minas along the routes that used to be taken by the mule trains which transported goods between the coast and the interior. Tours with Tropa Serrana include overnight horse treks and explore many aspects of the Minas Gerais countryside that visitors do not normally see.

Mountain biking

ⓘ **Tamanduá**, www.tamanduaecoturismo. com.br. Other operators are listed in relevant chapters throughout the book.

Brazil is well suited to cycling, both on and off-road. On main roads it is important to obey the general advice of being on the lookout for motor vehicles, as cyclists are very much second-class citizens. Also note that when cycling on the northeastern coast you may encounter strong winds which will hamper your progress. There are endless roads and tracks suitable for mountain biking, and there are many clubs in major cities which organize group rides, activities and competitions. Serra da Canastra in Minas Gerais is a popular area. Tamanduá in São Roque de Minas offer personalized tours and equipment hire.

Rafting

ⓘ **Trópico**, www.tropico.tur.br, and **Korubo Expeditions**, www.korubo.com.br, are recommended. Other operators are listed in relevant chapters throughout the book.

Football nation

Brazilians love football like Indians love cricket and seeing a match live in one of the large cities is an unforgettable experience. The crowd is a sea of waving banners and the noise from the jeers and cheers, drums and whistles is deafening. Football in Brazil is treated with religious reverence. Work is put on hold during an important game. And the country quite literally closes for business during the World Cup.

Brazilians are certain that they are and always will be the best in the world at the sport. German and Italian visitors are afforded token respect; Argentinians, derision; and those from the US, Australia and New Zealand pity. The British should expect mockery. 'Your country invented football' – Brazilians are fond of quipping – 'but we play it'. Brazil may have fared poorly in the last World Cup but they can still justifiably claim to be the best. One popular chant goes *'Tudo o Mundo tenta mais so Brasil e Penta'* (every one tries but only Brazil has won [the World Cup] five times – in

Below: Football is everywhere in Brazil, from beer adverts to graffiti. **Above:** Afternoon football in São Paulo's Ibirapuera Park.

1958, 1962, 1970, 1994 and 2002. They've been runners-up twice, semi-finalists three times and they're the only team to have played in every competition. The best player of all time – as selected by FIFA – is Brazilian: Edson Arantes do Nascimento, aka Pelé, as are the top scorers in history, and the Brazilian national team has been nominated by FIFA as team of the year more than twice as many times as their nearest rivals.

In 2014 the World Cup returns to Brazil – after a 64-year absence. Brazilians will be hoping that they fare better than they did on that occasion. The team had stormed through the competition and were already being hailed as the world champions. When they lost 2-1 to Uruguay, stripped of a title they had already considered theirs, the fans' silence was, in the words of FIFA chairman, Jules Rimet, 'morbid and sometimes too difficult to bear'. The loss became known as the *Maracanaço* (after the Maracanã stadium in Rio where the match was held) – a word which has since become common parlance in Brazil for any kind of tragedy. To see a game in Rio see page 94.

Whitewater rafting started in Brazil in 1992. Trópico, offering trips in São Paulo state (eg on the Juquiá, Jaguarí, Peixe and Paraibuna rivers), in Rio de Janeiro (also on the Paraibuna, at Três Rios in the Serra dos Órgãos), Paraná (Rio Ribeira), Santa Catarina (Rio Itajaí) and Rio Grande do Sul (Três Coroas). There is also good whitewater rafting in the remote Jalapão *chapada* lands with Korubo Expeditions.

Scuba diving

ⓘ **Debouche**, www.dehouche.com. **American/Brazilian Dive Club**, www.mergulho.com, with links to other dive sites in Brazil. **Océan**, www.ocean.com.br, is a dive shop and tour operator, based in Rio de Janeiro state (Rio, Angra dos Reis, Ilha Grande, Arraial do Cabo), which has a **Diving in Brasil** website (Portuguese only).

The best diving in Brazil is the Atol das Rocas; only available through private charter through Debopuche; it's very expensive but completely unspoilt, with visibility up to 40 m and with one of the highest levels of biodiversity in the tropical southern Atlantic. Fernando de Noronha has coral gardens, drop-offs and wrecks which include a 50-m Brazilian navy destroyer with full armament. Visibility is up to 50 m, with both current-free and drift diving. Amongst others, divers see at least two species of turtle, spinner dolphins, more than three species of shark, huge snapper and vast shoals of goatfish and jack. The Abrolhos archipelago offers diving of similar quality, with huge brain corals and, in the Brazilian summer, humpback whale sightings are pretty much guaranteed. Arraial de Cabo is interesting because of the meeting of a southerly cold and northerly warm current and has the best marine life in southeast Brazil.

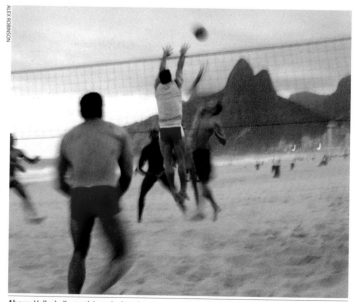

ALEX ROBINSON

Above: Volleyball, or *volei*, on the beach in Ipanema. **Opposite page left**: Surfing is hugely popular in Brazil. **Opposite page right**: According to aficionados, Brazil has the best kitesurfing in the world.

Cave diving can be practised in many of the 200 underwater grottoes such as Bonito, Mato Grosso do Sul, Lapa de São Jorge, 280 km from Brasília, in Chapada Diamantina and Vale do Ribeira located between São Paulo and Paraná.

Surfing

ⓘ **Fluir**, www.fluir.com.br, the country's biggest surf magazine, has information on surfing (in Portuguese). **Brazil Surf Travel**, www.brazilsurftravel.com (in English).

There are good conditions all along the coast. Brazilians love to surf and are well-represented in international competitions, which are frequently held in the country, usually on the beaches near Itacaré in Bahia and on Fernando de Noronha island. Other popular locations include Niterói, Cabo Frio and around, Rio, Ilha Grande, Florianópolis and Ilha de Santa Catarina. For the best surf breaks in Rio, see page 138.

Wind- and kitesurfing

ⓘ Details on companies offering board rental and tuition are listed in relevant chapters throughout the book. For information on kitesurfing in Cambuco, visit www.kite-surf-brazil.com.

There's no better place in the Americas for wind- and kitesurfing than Brazil. The northeast coast receives an almost constant wind for pretty much 365 days of the year and, in the last five years, beach towns like Cumbuco (page 563) and Jericoacoara (page 564) in Ceará have turned from small resorts into world wind- and kitesurf capitals. There is good wind- and kitesurfing around Rio too – especially to the east near Cabo Frio (page 151) and in the city itself. Santa Catarina island (page 351) has several popular windsurfing beaches, while the coast along the Linha Verde (page 465) is ideal for windsurfing, owing to constant fresh Atlantic breezes.

Family travel in Brazil

The heartbeat of Latin America

Brazil is vast. Only four countries – Canada, China, Russia and the United States – are larger. And it's not all Amazon jungle. There are iconic cities, like Rio de Janeiro, São Paulo and Salvador; there's the watery wilderness of the Pantanal, the ground-shaking Iguaçu Falls, a spectacular coastline, carnival, samba, football … Clearly you are going to have to make a few hard choices when it comes to taking the kids to Brazil. Few families will have the time, energy or money to see it all in one go. Travel in the remoter areas can involve a great deal of tedious waiting or very long bus journeys. The good news is that local air passes link many of the main attractions, making it possible to visit two or three regions in a single holiday. A great option is to combine a few active days in the Amazon, the Pantanal or Iguaçu Falls, followed by time out in Rio or at one of the family-friendly resorts along the Atlantic coast near Salvador. The Lençóis Maranhenses, Chapada Diamantina and the Amazon are good options for the more adventurous. See Essentials, page 50, for practical advice on travelling with children.

Rio de Janeiro

Rio's favourite children's attractions are the Sugar Loaf and the Christ statue on Corcovado. Children love going up in the cable cars, on the funicular Trem do Corcovado railway or, for the very lucky, flying around in a helicopter. There are walking trails around the summits of both and cafés and shady areas for when it gets hot. The best child friendly beach is Leblon, which has a special play area for toddlers and younger children, www.baixobebe leblon.com.br. Ipanema and Barra have kiosks selling food and drink and both are closed to traffic on Sundays, as is Copacabana but the water is not clean enough for children. The theme park Terra Encantada has roller coasters, river rapids and a decent zoo.

Iguaçu Falls

The 3-km-wide multi-tiered waterfalls will leave even the most jaded child awe-struck And they lie at the centre of a national park that straddles the border with Argentina. There are very light safari trips into the forests, a little train on the Argentinean side and protected boardwalks out over the river and running around the falls on both sides. Monkeys, coatis and larger parrots and toucans are a common sight and the air is filled with

ALEX ROBINSON

ALEX ROBINSON

Opposite page: Upside-down sunset watching is a popular pastime in Jericoacoara.
Above: The cable car up to the Sugar Loaf.

butterflies. Be sure to take the children to the bird park – where they can feed scarlet macaws peanuts. Boat trips run up to the base of Iguaçu and even under the falls themselves, which is great for older kids but potentially distressing for toddlers.

Bonito and the Pantanal
This pocket-sized resort town on the edge of the Pantanal is a great light adventure destination for children of all ages. The area is pocked with dramatic caves, dotted with tropical forest (divided by safe, short like walking trails) and coursed by dozens of clear-water streams filled with fish. Tourism here is very well organized and caters specifically for kids, who can choose between visiting the caves, floating down streams in a dinghy or swimming with a snorkel and mask, and walking the trails looking for birds and monkeys. There are a number of comfortable, family-friendly *fazendas* a short bus journey away.

Bahian beaches
Bahia offers a great number of resorts, coral islands or remote beach *pousadas* with little more than a pool and a beach.

All are ideal for children. For rock pools head for Boipeba island; where beaches are lapped by a gentle sea that retreats to reveal coral pools at low tie. For long, beautiful beaches cut by little rivers try Trancoso and stay at the Mata N'ativa *pousada* with its little garden. For an all inclusive resort package Praia do Forte eco-resort is hard to beat. It's only 30 km from Salvador airport and whilst the beach is nothing special by Bahian standards it is nested by turtles and there is a turtle monitoring, rescue and and rehabilitation centre where children can see the young reptiles.

The Amazon and further afield
Lodges like Amazon Ecopark just outside Manaus cater for children, have few mosquitoes and provide a very good introduction to the rainforest. The lodge has a tiny island, which is home to rescued and rehabilitated monkeys who are fed bananas every morning. Barreirinhas (for the Lençóis Maranhenses) and Lençóis (for the Chapada Diamantina) both have child-friendly tour operators and hotels.

How big is your footprint?

Sustainable or ecotourism is not just about looking after the physical environment, but also the local community. Whilst it has been slow to catch up with Costa Rica or Ecuador, Brazil now has some first-rate ecotourism projects and the country is a pioneer in urban community tourism in the *favelas*. Model ecotourism resorts in the forest include Pousada Uacari (see page 666) and Cristalino Jungle Lodge (see page 766). Fazenda San Francisco in the Pantanal (see page 749) runs a pioneering jaguar conservation project; REGUA and Serra do Tucanos on the Atlantic coast (see page 168) have done a great deal to protect important birding habitats; and resorts like Mata N'ativa in Trancoso (see page 459) are taking important first steps in beach holiday areas. In the Amazon, Atlantic coast forest and parts of the *cerrado*, access to certain wilderness areas is restricted to scientists. Having a such a low-impact policy over these regions means that their environment is protected from damage or over-use. In much of coastal Brazil, where tourism and property speculation has boomed in the last few years, the impact on local communities is particularly devastating. Some state governments cheerfully exploit the colourful local culture while sharing little of the profit. So rather than staying in a big resort and organizing a tour from back home, seek out smaller locally owned hotels and local indigenous guides. Try to visit projects like the Pataxó Reserve in Jaqueira, Porto Seguro and support the Caiçaras near Paraty.

ALEX ROBINSON

Go green:
▸▸ Within cities, local buses (and in São Paulo) metrôs are fast, cheap and have extensive routes. Try one instead of a taxi, and meet some real Brazilians! Long-distance buses may take longer than flying but they have comfortable reclining seats, some offer drinks, and show up-to-date DVDs. They sometimes have better schedules too.
▸▸ Supermarkets will give you a plastic bag for even the smallest purchases. If you don't need one, let them know – plastic waste is a huge problem – particularly in the northeast. When buying certain drinks, look for the returnable glass bottles.

ALEX ROBINSON

Responsible travel

▸▸ Where possible choose a destination, tour operator or hotel with a proven ethical and environmental commitment – if in doubt, ask.

▸▸ Spend money on locally produced (rather than imported) goods and services, buy directly from the producer or from a 'fair trade' shop, and use common sense when bargaining – the few dollars you save may be a week's salary to others.

▸▸ Use water and electricity carefully – travellers may receive preferential supply while the needs of local communities are overlooked.

▸▸ Learn about local etiquette and culture – consider local norms and behaviour and dress appropriately for local cultures and situations.

▸▸ Protect wildlife and other natural resources – don't buy souvenirs or goods unless they are clearly sustainably produced and are not protected under CITES legislation.

▸▸ Always ask before taking photographs or videos of people.

▸▸ Consider staying in local accommodation rather than foreign-owned hotels – the economic benefits for host communities are far greater – and there are more opportunities to learn about local culture.

▸▸ Make a voluntary contribution to Climate Care, www.co2.org, to help counteract the pollution caused by tax-free fuel on your flight.

Opposite page: There is no rubbish collection in Rocinha *favela*.
Above: Metre-wide Victoria lilies in the Amazon.

Brazil on screen and page

Brazil's first great writer **Joaquim Maria Machado de Assis** (1839-1908), author of *Dom Casmurro*, was a social satirist and modernist from Rio and was among the first African-American writers to find critical acclaim against the odds. **João Guimarães Rosa** vies with Assis for the title of Brazil's most important novelist: Rosa's epic tale of soul-searching in backland Brazil *Grande Sertão: Veredas* (*The Devil to Pay in the Backlands*) has been compared to Joyce's *Ulysses*. Contemporary writers include **Patricia Mello**, famous for her realist *favela* novel *Inferno*, **Darcy Ribeiro** with *O Povo Brasileiro* (*The Brazilian People*) and **Sérgio Buarque de Holanda**'s *Raízes do Brasil* (*Roots of Brazil*), which are invaluable dissections of the Brazilian psyche from a historical perspective. Non-native **John Hemming**'s masterful three-volume history of indigenous Brazil (*Red Gold*, *Amazon Frontier* and *Die if You Must*) and **Joseph Page**'s wonderful introduction to Brazil and its people, *The Brazilians*, are worth a read. See also Background, page 819.

Films to watch

Brazilian cinema thrived in the 1960s with the Cinema Novo movement, whose motto was '*uma câmera na mão e uma idéia na cabeça*' (a camera in the hand and an idea in the head). Directors **Glauber Rocha**, **Nelson Pereira dos Santos** and **Joaquim Pedro de Andrade** emerged and the movement peaked with **Oswaldo Massaini**'s backland epic, *O Pagador de Promessas* (*Keeper of Promises*) which became the first Brazilian film nominated for an Oscar and won the 1962 Palme d'Or. Cinema then suffered under the military regime for nearly three decades, until 1995 when **Fábio Barreto**'s *O Quatrilho* was nominated for an Oscar and heralded a new generation of filmmakers. **Walter Salles** gained recognition with his poignant study of alienation, *Terra Estrangeira* (*Foreign Land*) and an Oscar nomination for his road movie *Central do Brasil* (*Central Station*). **Fernando Meirelles** followed, bursting on the scene with *Cidade de Deus* (*City of God*), a gritty *favela* gangster film shot with virtuoso technique. The 2007 award-winning *Tropa de Elite* (*Elite Squad*) follows a recurring Brazilian theme – exposing relationships between police corruption, poor pay and violence in the *favelas*.

Contents

Footprint features

Essentials

Getting there

Air

Flights into Brazil generally land in São Paulo, which has direct connections with the **USA, Canada, Mexico** and **Central America**, **Europe** and **Asia**, and indirect connections with **Australasia** via Buenos Aires, Santiago or Los Angeles.

Rio de Janeiro, Salvador Belém, Manaus and Recife have connections to the USA and Europe. Many other Brazilian cities have connections to Europe, mostly through Lisbon.

Brazil is connected to Spanish-speaking **Latin America** principally through Rio de Janeiro, São Paulo, Manaus and Brasília. It is connected to the **Guianas** through Belém, Fortaleza, Boa Vista and Macapá. Belém also receives flights from the **Caribbean**.

Charter flights, often at very attractive prices, are available from the USA and Europe. For details see www.netflights.com, www.dialaflight.com, www.charterflights.co.uk, www.edreams.pt or www.edreams.it.

Prices are cheapest in October, November and after Carnaval and at their highest in the European summer and the Brazilian high seasons (generally 15 December to 15 January, the Thursday before Carnaval to the Saturday after Carnaval, and 15 June to 15 August).

Airport information

For most visitors the point of arrival will be **Cumbica International Airport** at Guarulhos in São Paulo (see page 192) or **Tom Jobim International Airport** (also known as **Galeão**) on the Ilha do Governador, 16 km from the centre of Rio de Janeiro (see page 72). Details of other entry airports are given in their respective sections. Make sure you arrive two hours before international flights and it is wise to reconfirm your flight as departure times may have changed. ▶▶ *For airport tax, see page 61.*

International airlines serving Brazil

Aerolíneas, www.aerolineas.com. From Argentina with connections to Europe, Australia, New Zealand and the USA.

Aeroméxico, www.aeromexico.com. From the USA and Mexico via Mexico City to São Paulo.

Aerosur, www.aerosur.com. From Bolivia via Santa Cruz to São Paulo.

Air Canada, www.aircanada.com. From Canada and USA via Toronto to São Paulo.

Air Caraibes, www.aircaraibes.com. From Haiti, Martinique and Paris to Belém.

Air China, www. airchina.com. From China via Beijing to São Paulo.

Air Europa, www.aireuropa.com. From Europe via Madrid to Salvador.

Air France, www.airfrance.com. From Europe via Paris to São Paulo and Rio de Janeiro.

Air Italy, www.airitaly.it. From various Italian airports to Fortaleza.

Alitalia, www.alitalia.com. From Europe via Milan to São Paulo.

American Airlines, www.aa.com. Various non-stop services from key US cities to São Paulo, Rio de Janeiro, Salvador, Recife and Belo Horizonte.

Avianca, www.avianca.com. From Bogotá in Colombia to Rio de Janeiro and São Paulo.

British Airways, www.britishairways.com. From Europe via London to São Paulo and Rio Cabo.

Condor, www.condor.com. From Europe via Frankfurt to Recife and Salvador.

Continental, www.continental.com. From the USA via Newark to São Paulo and Rio.

Copa, www.copaair.com. From Panama City and Havana to Manaus and São Paulo.

Delta, www.delta.com. From various US cities via Atlanta to São Paulo and Rio. Emirates, Middle East via Dubai to São Paulo.

GOL, www.voegol.com.br. From Montevideo, Cordoba and Lima to São Paulo.

Iberia, www.iberia.com. From Madrid to São Paulo and Rio de Janeiro.

JAL, www.jal.co.jp. From Japan via Nagoya and Tokyo to São Paulo.

KLM, www.klm.com. From Europe via Amsterdam to São Paulo.

Korean, www.koreanair.com, Los Angeles and Seoul to São Paulo.

LAN, www.lan.com. From Lima, Santiago to São Paulo and Rio; Lufthansa, Europe via Frankfurt and Munich to São Paulo.

META, www.voemeta.com. From Georgetown (Guyana) and Paramaribo (Surinam) to Belém and Boa Vista.

South African, www.flysaa.com. From Johannesburg to São Paulo.

TAAG, www.taag.aero. From Luanda to São Paulo.

TACA, www.taca.com. From Lima to São Paulo.

TAF, www.taf.com. From Fortaleza, Macapá and Belém to Cayenne.

TAM, www.tam.com.br. From Asunción, Ciudad del Este, Cordoba, Frankfurt, London, Madrid, Miami, Milan, Montevideo, New York, Paris to São Paulo and Rio.

TAME, www.tame.com.ec. From Quito and Guayaquil to Manaus.

TAP, www.tap.pt. From Europe via Lisbon and Porto to Aracaju, Belo Horizonte, Brasília, Cuiabá, Curitiba, Fortaleza, Foz de Iguaçu, Goiânia, João Pessoa, Londrina, Natal, Porto Alegre, Porto Seguro, Porto Velho, Recife, Rio Branco, Rio de Janeiro, São Luís, São Paulo (Congonhas and Guarulhos), Teresina and Vitória – some on a code share basis.

United, www.united.com. From Chicago, Los Angeles, New York, Miami and Washington to São Paulo and Rio.

Varig, www.varig.com. From Bogotá, Buenos Aires and Caracas to São Paulo and Rio.

Verde Airlines, www.flytacv.com. From Lisbon and Boston to Fortaleza via Cape Verde.

VistaPluna, www.pluna.aero. From Montevideo to São Paulo and Rio de Janeiro.

Air passes

TAM, www.tam.com.br, offers a 21-day **Brazil Airpass**, which is valid on any TAM destination within Brazil. The price varies according to the number of flights taken and the international airline used to arrive in Brazil. They can only be bought outside Brazil. One to four flights start at US$529, five flights start at US$679, six flights start at US$839, seven flights start at US$979, eight flights start at US$1119, and nine flights start at US$1259. The baggage allowance is the same as that permitted on their international flights. TAM also operates as part of the **Mercosur Airpass**, which is valid for Brazil, Argentina, Chile, Uruguay and Paraguay using local carriers. It is valid for any passenger with a return ticket to their country of origin, and must be bought with an international flight. The minimum stay is seven days, maximum 45 and at least two countries must be visited. The maximum number of flights is eight. Fares are worked out on a mileage basis and cost between US$295 and US$1195. Children pay a discounted rate for flights and air passes, and under threes pay 10% of the adult rate. Some of the carriers operate a blackout period between 15 December and 15 January.

Baggage allowance

Airlines will only allow a certain weight of luggage without a surcharge; for Brazil this is usually two items of 32 kg but may be as low as 20 kg; with two items of hand luggage weighing up to 10 kg in total. UK airport staff can refuse to load bags weighing more than 30 kg. Baggage allowances are higher in business and first class. Weight limits for internal flights are often lower, usually 20 kg. In all cases it is best to enquire beforehand.

Discount flight agents

Using the web to book flights, hotels and other services directly is becoming increasingly popular. However, cutting out travel agents can end up more costly if you don't know Brazil well as they can often give you valuable money-saving and itinerary tips as well as discount quality hotel bookings and the benefit of their research.

USA and Canada
Air Brokers International, 323 Geary St, Suite 411, San Francisco, CA94102, T01-800-883 3273, www.airbrokers.com. Consolidators and specialists on Around the World and Circle Pacific tickets.
Council Travel, www.counciltravel.com. Branches throughout the USA.
Fly Cheap, T1-800-FLY-CHEAP, www.1800 flycheap.com. Consolidator with discount fares from more than 1000 operators.
STA Travel, 5900 Wilshire Blvd, Suite 2110, Los Angeles, CA 90036, T1-800-777 0112, www.sta-travel.com. Also has branches in New York, San Francisco, Boston, Miami, Chicago, Seattle and Washington DC.
TFI, T800-745 8000, www.lowestprice.com. Offers seats unsold elsewhere on bargain-basement clearing basis.
Travel Hub, T888-AIR-FARE, www.travelhub.com. Consolidator with discount fares from operators country-wide.

Travel CUTS, 187 College St, Toronto, ON, M5T 1P7, T1-800-667 2887, www.travelcuts.com. Specialist in student discount fares, IDs and other travel services. Branches in other Canadian cities.
Travelocity, www.travelocity.com. Online consolidator.

UK and Ireland
Journey Latin America, 12-13 Heathfield Terrace, Chiswick, London W4 4JE, T020-8747 8315, www.journeylatinamerica.co.uk.
STA Travel, 86 Old Brompton Rd, London, SW7 3LH, T020-74376262, www.statravel.co.uk. Branches throughout the UK. Specialists in low-cost student/youth flights and tours. Good for student IDs and insurance.
Trailfinders, 194 Kensington High St, London, W8 7RG, T020-7938 3939, www.trail finders.com. 18 branches in London and throughout the UK. Also one in Dublin and 5 travel centres in Australia.

Australia, New Zealand and South Africa
Flight Centres, www.flightcentre.com.au, www.flightcentre.co.nz, www.flight centre.co.za. Throughout Australia and NZ.
STA Travel, www.statravel.com.au, www.statravel.co.za and www.statravel.co.nz, Throughout Australia, South Africa and NZ.
Travel.com.au Offices throughout Australia.

River

Boats run from Iquitos in **Peru** to Tabatinga in Brazil. Onward travel is then on a five-day riverboat journey (or when they are available, a flight) to Manaus, the capital of the Amazon. This border can also be crossed by land from Leticia in **Colombia**, which is alongside Tabatinga. Security is tight at these borders and Brazilian immigration occasionally refuse to allow entry to Brazil for more than 30 days.

Brazil is connected to **Venezuela** through Puerto Ayacucho, San Carlos de Rio Negro and Cucui/São Gabriel da Cachoeira. The crossing is difficult. Exit stamps should be secured in Puerto Ayacucho. **Wayumi Airlines** flies to San Carlos. From here it is possible to hitch downstream to Cucui and take a bus to São Gabriel. Entry stamps must be secured in São Gabriel. Boats connect São Gabriel with Manaus (five to seven days).

Road

Bus

Argentina is connected to the south of Brazil at Foz de Iguaçu/ Puerto Iguazú (the Iguaçu falls) in Paraná state, Porto Xavier/San Javier on the Uruguay river and Uruguaiana/Paso de los Libres, both in Rio Grande do Sul state.

Bolivia is connected to Brazil at Puerto Quijarro/Corumbá via road and rail, with onward connections to the rest of Bolivia via Santa Cruz.

French Guiana is connected from Cayenne via Oyapock/Oiapoque to Macapá. The road is unpaved in Brazil. It is possible to do a circuit through the Guianas overland from Manaus/Boa Vista to Macapá and onward to Belém, although you will need a visa for Suriname (available in Guyana or Guyane).

Guyana is connected to Brazil at Leticia/Bonfim (by road from Georgetown) and Boa Vista.

Paraguay is reachable via Ciudad del Este/Foz de Iguaçu. Rio de Janeiro and São Paulo can easily be accessed by international buses from Asunción, which has connections with Buenos Aires, Santiago and Montevideo.

Uruguay is connected to the south of Brazil; as of 2008 all crossings go via Bagé where Brazilian immigration is located. From here there are connections to Aceguá for the Uruguayan town of Melo; Jaguarão for Rio Branco and the Uruguayan border; and Barra do Quaraí/Bella Unión, via the Barra del Cuaraim bridge and Quaraí/Artigas.

Venezuela is connected to Manaus via Santa Elena de Uairen/Boa Vista in Roraima state and a good road.

Car

There are agreements between Brazil and most South American countries (check in the case of Bolivia) whereby a car can be taken into Brazil for a period of 90 days without any special documents. For cars registered in other countries, you need proof of ownership and/or registration in the home country and valid driving licence. A 90-day permit is given by customs or at the **Serviço de Controle Aduaneiro** ① *Ministério da Fazenda, Av Presidente Antônio Carlos, Sala 1129, Rio de Janeiro*, and the procedure is straightforward. Keep *all* the papers you are given when you enter, to produce when you leave.

When crossing the border into Brazil, make sure that there is an official who knows about the temporary import of cars. You must specify which border station you intend to leave by, but application can be made to the customs to change this.

Sea

Travelling as a passenger on a cargo ship to South America is not a cheap way to go, but if you have the time and want a bit of luxury, it makes a great alternative to flying. The passage is often only available for round trips.

Shipping agents

Cargo Ship Voyages Ltd, Hemley, Woodbridge, Suffolk IP12 4QF, T01473-736265, www.cargoshipvoyages.co.uk.
Freighter World Cruises, www.freighterworld.com. The largest company in the world devoted to cruises on cargo ships.
Strand Voyages, 1 Adam St, London WC2N 6AB, T020-7766 8220, www.strand travel.co.uk. Booking agents for all routes.

Getting around

Public transport in Brazil is very efficient, but distances are huge. Most visitors will find themselves travelling by buses and planes, except in the Amazon when a boat is often the only way to get around. Train routes are practically non-existent, car hire is expensive and hitchhiking not advisable. Taxis vary widely in quality and price but are easy to come by and safe when taken from a *posto de taxis* (taxi rank).

Air

Because of the size of the country, flying is often the most practical option and internal air services are highly developed. All state capitals and larger cities are linked with each other with services several times a day and all national airlines offer excellent service. Recent deregulation of the airlines has greatly reduced prices on some routes and low-cost airlines offer fares that can often be as cheap as travelling by bus (when booked through the internet). Paying with an international credit card is not always possible online; but it is usually possible to buy an online ticket through a hotel, agency or willing friend without surcharge. Many of the smaller airlines go in and out of business sporadically. **GOL, Oceanair, TAM, TRIP/Total, Varig**, and **Webjet** operate the most extensive routes. Most of their websites (see below) provide full information, including a booking service, although not all are in English.

Domestic airlines

Abaeté, Aeroporto Internacional Deputado Luís Eduardo Magalhães, Salvador, Bahia, T071-3377 2555, www.voeabaete.com.br.

Addey Táxi Aéreo, Aeroporto Internacional Deputado Luís Eduardo Magalhães, Salvador, Bahia, T071-3377 1993, www.addey.com.br.

Aero Star, Aeroporto Internacional Deputado Luís Eduardo Magalhães, Salvador, Bahia, T071-3377 2555, www.aerostar.com.br.

Air Minas, R Petrópolis 20-B, Ribeirão das Neves, Minas Gerais, T0300 210 2112, ww.airminas.com.br.

Cruiser, Aeroporto Bacacheri s/n, Hangar 12, Curitiba, T0300 789 2112, www.aircruiser.com.br.

GOL, R Tamoios 246, Jardim Aeroporto, São Paulo, T0300-789 2121, www.voegol.com.br.

Litorânea, Aeroporto Marechal Cunha Macedo s/n, São Luís, T098-2108 6181, www.voelitoranea.com.br.

META, Av Santos Dumont 100, Aeroporto, Boa, T0300-789 5503, www.voemeta.com.

NHT, R Dona Teodora 503, Porto Alegre, T0300-143 4343, www.voenht.com.br.

Oceanair, Av Prof Vicente Rao, 823, São Paulo, T011-4004 4040/T0300-789 8160, www.oceanair.com.br.

Pantanal Linhas Aéreas, Av Nações Unidas 10989 cj 81, V Olímpia, São Paulo, T0800-602 5888, www.voepantanal.com.br.

Passaredo, R Guatapará 383, Vila Virgínia, Ribeirão Preto, T016-3514 7111, www.voepassaredo.com.br.

Puma, Aeroporto Internacional de Belém, Belém, T0300-789 2527, www.pumaair.com.br.

Rico, Aeroporto Internacional Eduardo Gomes TPS II, Manaus, T092-4009 8333, www.voerico.com.br.

Sete, Praça Capitão Frazão, Hangar Sete, Goiânia, T062-3096 7007, www.voesete.com.br.

TAF, Praça Brigadeiro Eduardo Gomes s/n, Hangar TAF, Fortaleza, T0300-313 2000, www.voetaf.com.br.

TAM, Av Jurandir 856, São Paulo, T011-5582 8811, www.tam.com.br.

TEAM, Av Ayrton Senna 2541, Rio de Janeiro, T021-2117 8300, www.voeteam.com.br.
TRIP and **Total Linhas Aéreas** (operate on a permanent codeshare). TRIP: R Luiz Gama 209, Bonfim, Campinas, www.voetrip.com.br. Total: R dos Hangares 3, Aeroporto da

Pampulha, Belo Horizonte, T0300-789 8747, www.total.com.br.
Varig, Av Alm Silvio Noronha 365 BL C–4, Rio de Janeiro, www.varig.com.br.
Webjet, Praça Antonio Calado 85, bloco 01, Rio, T021-4009 0000, www.webjet.com.br.

Rail

There are 30,379 km of railways, which are not combined into a unified system. Brazil has two gauges and there is little transfer between them. Two more gauges exist for the isolated **Amapá** railway and the tourist-only **São João del Rei** line. Most passenger services have been withdrawn though there are plans to re-introduce train services in the Pantanal, and onward into Bolivia.

River

The main areas where travel by boat is practical (and often necessary) are the Amazon region, along the São Francisco River and along the Atlantic coast. There are also some limited transport services through the Pantanal. ►► *See page 670 for details of river transport in the Amazon.*

Road

The best paved highways are heavily concentrated in the southeast, but roads serving the interior are being improved to all-weather status and many are paved. Most main roads between principal cities are paved. Some are narrow and therefore dangerous; many are in poor condition.

Bus

There are three standards of bus: *Comum*, or *Convencional*, are quite slow, not very comfortable and fill up quickly; *Executivo* are more expensive, comfortable (many have reclining seats), and don't stop en route to pick up passengers so are safer; *Leito* (literally 'bed') run at night between the main centres, offering reclining seats with leg rests, toilets, and sometimes refreshments, at double the normal fare. For journeys over 100 km, most buses have chemical toilets (bring toilet paper). Air conditioning can make buses cold at night, so take a jumper; on some services blankets are supplied.

Buses stop fairly frequently (every two to four hours) at *postos* for snacks. Bus stations for interstate services and other long distance routes are usually called *rodoviárias*. They are frequently outside the city centres and offer snack bars, lavatories, *guarda volume* (left-luggage stores), local bus services and information centres. Buy bus tickets at *rodoviárias* (most now take credit cards), not from travel agents who add on surcharges. Reliable bus information is hard to come by, other than from companies themselves. Buses usually arrive and depart in very good time. Many town buses have turnstiles, which can be inconvenient if you are carrying a large pack. Urban buses normally serve local airports.

Car

Car hire Renting a car in Brazil is expensive: the cheapest rate for unlimited mileage for a small car is about US$65 per day. Minimum age for renting a car is 21 and it's essential to have a credit card. Companies operate under the terms *aluguel de automóveis* or *auto-locadores*. Toll-free numbers for nationwide firms are **Avis**, T0800-558 066 and **Localiza**, T0800-992 000, www.localiza.com.br. Check exactly what the company's insurance policy covers. In many cases it will not apply to major accidents, or 'natural' damage (eg flooding). Ask if extra cover is available. Sometimes using a credit card automatically includes insurance. Beware of being billed for scratches that were on the vehicle before you hired it.

Documents To drive in Brazil you need an international licence. A national driving licence is acceptable as long as your home country is a signatory to the Vienna and Geneva conventions.

Fuel Fuel prices vary weekly and between regions. *Gasolina común* is about US$1.35 per litre with *gasolina maxi* and *maxigold* a little more. *Alcool común; alcool maxi* costs less. Diesel is cheap. There is no unleaded fuel. Fuel is only 85 octane, so be prepared for bad consumption and poor performance and starting difficulties in non-Brazilian cars in winter. It is virtually impossible to buy premium grades of petrol anywhere. With alcohol fuel you need about 50% more than regular gasoline. Larger cars have a small extra tank for 'gasolina' to get the engine started; remember to keep this topped up. Diesel fuel is cheap and a diesel engine may provide fewer maintenance problems. Many cars operate on the Flex system (accepting alcohol and gasoline into the same tank) and natural gas is more widely available in Brazil than any other country in the world.

Insurance Insurance against accident and theft is very expensive. If the car is stolen or written off you will be required to pay very high import duty on its value. The legally required minimum cover for third party insurance is not expensive.

Safety Try to never leave your car unattended except in a locked garage or guarded parking area. Remove all belongings and leave the empty glove compartment open. Also lock the clutch or accelerator to the steering wheel with a heavy, obvious chain or lock. Adult minders or street children will usually protect your car fiercely in exchange for a tip.

Buying a car Any foreigner with a passport can purchase a Brazilian car and travel outside Brazil. A letter in Spanish from your consul explaining your aims and that you will return the vehicle to Brazil can make life much easier at borders and check points. Foreigners do not need the CPF tax document (needed by Brazilians), and the official purchase receipt is accepted as proof of ownership. Don't buy an alcohol-driven car if you propose to drive outside Brazil. It is essential to have an external-intake filter fitted, or dust can rapidly destroy an engine. VW combi vans are cheapest in Brazil where they are made, they are equivalent to the pre-1979 model in Europe. Most other cars are more expensive than their US and European equivalents. If a lot of time is to be spent on dirt roads a 4WD or pick-up is more robust.

Motorcycling

The machine you use should be off-road capable, eg the BMW R80/100/GS for its rugged and simple design and reliable shaft drive. A road bike can go most places an off-road bike can go, at the cost of greater effort. Japanese bikes are easiest to get serviced in Brazil.

Documents International driving licence and bike-registration documents are necessary. Temporary import papers are given on entry, to be surrendered on leaving the country.

Preparation Many roads are rough. Fit heavy-duty front fork springs, the best quality rebuildable shock absorber you can afford (Ohlins, White Power) and lockable luggage such as Krausers (reinforce luggage frames). A large-capacity fuel tank (Acerbis), +300 mile/ 480 km range is essential if going off the beaten track. A washable air filter is a good idea (K&N), also fuel filters and fueltap rubber seals, a good set of trails-type tyres, as well as a high mudguard. Get to know the bike before you go, ask the dealers in your country what goes wrong with it and arrange a link whereby you can get parts flown out to you. If using a fully enclosed chaincase on a chain-driven bike, an automatic chain oiler is a good idea. The **Scott-Oiler** (106 Clober Road, Milngavie, Glasgow G62 7SS, Scotland) has been recommended. Fill it with Sae 90 oil. A hefty bash plate/sump guard is invaluable. A first-class tool kit is a must and if riding a bike with a chain then a spare set of sprockets and an 'o' ring chain should be carried. Parts are few and far between, but mechanics are skilled at making do and can usually repair things.

Safety Try not to leave a fully laden bike on its own. An Abus D or chain will keep the bike secure. A cheap alarm can give you peace of mind. Look for hotels with a courtyard or secure parking and never leave luggage on the bike whilst unattended.

Taxi

Rates vary from city to city, but are consistent within each city. At the outset, make sure the meter is cleared and shows 'tariff 1', except (usually) from 2300-0600, Sunday, and in December when '2' is permitted. Check that the meter is working; if not, fix the price in advance. The **radio taxi** service costs about 50% more but cheating is less likely. Taxis outside larger hotels usually cost more. If you are seriously cheated, note the number of the taxi and insist on a signed bill; threatening to take it to the police can work. **Moto-taxis** are much more economical, but many are unlicensed and there have been a number of robberies of passengers.

Maps

International Travel Maps (ITM), www.itmb.com, publishes an excellent series of travel maps that feature Brazil, including *South America South*, *North East* and *North West* (1:4M), and *Rio de Janeiro* (1:20,000). Also available is *New World Edition*, Bertelsmann, Neumarkter Strasse 18, 81673 München, Germany, *Mittelamerika*, *Südamerika Nord*, *Südamerika Sud*, *Brasilien* (all 1:4M).

    Stanfords ① *12-14 Long Acre, Covent Garden, London, WC2E 9LP, UK, T020-78361321, www.stanfords.co.uk*, sells a wide variety of guides and maps.

    Editora Abril publishes *Quatro Rodas*, a motoring magazine, as well as excellent maps and guides in Portuguese and English from US$15. Its *Guia Brasil* is a type of *Michelin Guide* to hotels, restaurants (not the cheapest), sights, facilities and general information on hundreds of cities and towns in the country, including good street maps. It also publishes a host of other books, including a *Guia das Praias*, with descriptions of all Brazil's beaches, and magazines. All are available at news stands and bookshops all over the country. For information about the *Quatro Rodas* guides, see www.abril.com.br.

Sleeping

There is a good range of accommodation options in Brazil. An *albergue* or hostel offers the cheapest option. These have dormitory beds and single and double rooms. Many are part of the **IYHA**, www.iyha.org. **Hostel world**, www.hostelworld.com; **Hostel Bookers**, www.hostelbookers.com; and **Hostel.com**, www.hostel.com, are useful portals. **Hostel Trail Latin America**, T0131-208 0007 (UK), www.hosteltrail.com, managed from their hostel in Popayan, is an online network of hotels and tour companies in South America. A *pensão* is either a cheap guesthouse or a household that rents out some rooms. A *pousada* is either a bed-and-breakfast, often small and family-run, or sophisticated and often charming small hotel. A *hotel* is as it is anywhere in the world, operating according to the international star system, although five-star hotels are not price controlled and hotels in any category are not always of the standard of their star equivalent in USA, Canada or Europe. Many of the older hotels can be cheaper than hostels. Usually accommodation prices include a breakfast of rolls, ham, cheese, cakes and fruit with coffee and juice; there is no reduction if you don't eat it. Rooms vary too. Normally an *apartamento* is a room with separate living and sleeping areas and sometimes cooking facilities. A *quarto* is a standard room; *com banheiro* is en suite; and *sem banheiro* is with shared bathroom. Finally there are the *motels*. These should not be confused with their US counterpart: motels are specifically intended for very short-stay couples; there is no stigma attached and they usually offer good value (the rate for a full night is called the '*pernoite*'), however the decor can be a little unsettling.

It's a good idea to book accommodation in advance in small towns that are popular at weekends with city dwellers (eg near São Paulo and Rio de Janeiro), and it's essential to book at peak times.

Luxury accommodation

Much of the luxury private accommodation sector can be booked through operators. **Angatu**, www.angatu.com, offers the best private homes along the Costa Verde, together with bespoke trips. **Dehouche**, www.dehouche.com, offers upmarket accommodation and trips in Bahia, Rio and Alagoas. **Brazilian Beach House**, www.brazilianbeachhouse.com, has some of the finest houses in Búzios and Trancoso

Accommodation price codes

LL	over US$200	**L**	US$151-200	**AL**	US$116-150
A	US$81-115	**B**	US$51-80	**C**	US$36-50
D	US$21-35	**E**	US$10-20	**F**	under US$10

Prices include taxes and service charge, but are without meals. They are based on a double room, except in the **E** and **F** ranges, where prices are almost always per person.

but are not so great at organizing transfers and pick-ups. *Matuete*, www.matuete.com, has a range of luxurious properties and tours throughout Brazil. The international luxury travel review and booking service, **Nota Bene**, www.nbreview.com, offers a superb service and the best properties and hotels, but to members only.

Camping
Those with an international camping card pay only half the rate of a non-member at **Camping Clube do Brasil** sites, www.campingclube.com.br. Membership of the club itself is expensive: US$85 for six months. The club has 43 sites in 13 states and 80,000 members. It may be difficult to get into some Camping Clube campsites during high season (January to February). Private campsites charge about US$8-15 per person. For those on a very low budget and in isolated areas where there is no campsite available, it's usually possible to stay at service stations. They have shower facilities, watchmen and food; some have dormitories. There are also various municipal sites. Campsites tend to be some distance from public transport routes and are better suited to people with their own car. Wild camping is generally difficult and a security risk. Never camp at the side of a road; this is very risky.

Homestays
Staying with a local family is an excellent way to become integrated quickly into a city and companies try to match guests to their hosts. **Cama e Café**, www.camaecafe.com.br, organizes homestays in Rio de Janeiro, Olinda and a number of other cities around Brazil. **Couch surfing**, www.couchsurfing.com, offers a free, backpacker alternative.

Quality hotel associations
The better international hotel associations have members in Brazil. These include: **Small Luxury Hotels of the World**, www.slh.com; the **Leading Hotels of the World**, www.lhw.com; the **Leading Small Hotels of the World**, www.leadingsmallhotels oftheworld.com; **Great Small Hotels**, www.greatsmallhotels.com; and the **French Relais et Chateaux group**, www.relaischateaux.com, which also includes restaurants.

The Brazilian equivalent of these associations is the **Roteiros de Charme**, www.roteiros decharme.com.br, with some 30 locations in the southeast and northeast. Whilst membership of these groups pretty much guarantees quality, it is by no means comprehensive. There are many fine hotels and charming *pousadas* listed in our text that are not included in these associations.

Eating and drinking

Food

Only Brazilians consider their cuisine to be up there with the world's best. Mains are generally heavy, meaty and unspiced. Deserts are often very sweet. That said, the best cooking south of the Rio Grande is in São Paulo and Rio, where a heady mix of international immigrants has resulted in some unusual fusion cooking and exquisite variations on French, Japanese, Portuguese, Arabic and Italian traditional techniques and dishes.

Outside the more sophisticated cities it can be a struggle to find interesting food. The Brazilian staple meal generally consists of a slab of fried or barbecued meat, chicken or fish accompanied by rice, black or South American broad beans and an unseasoned salad of lettuce, grated carrot, tomato and beetroot. Condiments are weak chilli sauce, olive oil, salt and pepper and vinegar.

The national dish is a greasy campfire stew called **feijoada**, made by throwing jerked beef, smoked sausage, tongue and salt pork into a pot with lots of fat and beans and stewing it for hours. The resulting stew is sprinkled with fried *farofa* (manioc flour) and served with *couve* (kale) and slices of orange. The meal is washed down with *cachaça* (sugarcane rum). Most restaurants serve the *feijoada completa* for Saturday lunch (up until about 1630). Come with a very empty stomach.

Brazil's other national dish is mixed grilled meat or **churrasco**, served in vast portions off the spit by legions of rushing waiters, and accompanied by a buffet of salads, beans and mashed vegetables. *Churrascos* are served in *churrascarias* or *rodízios*. The meat is generally excellent, especially in the best *churrascarias*, and the portions are unlimited, offering good value for camel-stomached carnivores able to eat one meal a day.

In remembrance of Portugal, but bizarrely for a tropical country replete with fish, Brazil is also the world's largest consumer of cod, pulled from the cold north Atlantic, salted and served in little balls as *bacalhau* (an appetizer/bar snack) or *petisco*. Other national *petiscos* include *kibe* (a deep-fried or baked mince with onion, mint and flour), *coxinha* (deep-fried chicken or meat in dough), *empadas* (baked puff-pastry patties with prawns, chicken, heart of palm or meat), and *tortas* (little pies with the same ingredients). When served in bakeries, *padarias* or snack bars these are collectively referred to as *salgadinhos* (savouries).

The best cooking in Brazil is not national but regional. Bahia offers an African-infused, welcome break from meat, rice and beans further south, with a variety of seafood dishes. Unlike most Brazilians, Bahians have discovered sauces, pepper and chilli. The most famous Bahian dish is *moqueca*, fresh fish cooked slowly with prawns in *dendê* palm oil, coconut milk, garlic, tomatoes, cilantro and chili pepper. A variety served in Espírito Santo, the state south of Bahia, is seasoned with blood-red *urucum* berry and served in a clay pot. Other Bahian dishes include *vatapá* and *caruru*, pastes made from prawns, nuts, bread, coconut milk and *dendê* oil, *xinxim de galinha*, a rich, spicy chicken stew, best without *dendê* oil, and *acarajé,* black-eyed peas or beans squashed into a ball, deep-fried in *dendê* oil and served split in half, stuffed with *vatapá* or *caruru* and seasoned with chilli.

Minas Gerais and **Goiás** are famous for their buffets of stews served over a wood-fired stove and made from a variety of meats and *cerrado* fruits and vegetables like the *pequi*, which is sucked and never bitten; its flesh covers thousands of tiny, razor sharp spines. Minas specialities include *tutu á mineira* made with bacon, egg, refried beans in a paste, and *feijão tropeiro,* herb-infused beans served with *farofa*. A watery, white soft and almost entirely flavourless cheese, *queijo minas* is often served for dessert with ultra-sweet *guava* paste. Some of the most interesting cooking comes form the Amazon. The river fish here are delicious, especially the firm flesh of the *pacu* and *tambaqui*. The *piracururu* is an endangered species and should only be eaten where it is farmed or fished sustainably, from reserves such as **Mamirauá** (see page 659). The most celebrated regional dish in the Amazon is *tacacá no tucupi*, prawn broth cooked in manioc juice and *jambu* leaf. The soup is infused with an alkaloid from the *jambu* that numbs the mouth and produces an energetic rush to the head. There are myriad strange fruits in the Amazon too, many with unique flavours, including the pungent, sweet *cupuaçu*, which makes delicious cakes, and the tart *camu-camu*, a large glass of which holds a gram of vitamin C.

Eating cheaply

The cheapest dish is the *prato feito* or *sortido*, an excellent-value set menu usually comprising meat/chicken/fish, beans, rice, chips and salad. The *prato comercial* is similar but rather better and a bit more expensive. Portions are usually large enough for two and come with two plates. If you are on your own, you could ask for an *embalagem* (doggy bag) or a *marmita* (takeaway) and offer it to a person with no food (many Brazilians do). Many restaurants serve *comida por kilo* buffets where you serve yourself and pay for the weight of food on your plate. This is generally good value and is a good option for vegetarians. *Lanchonetes* and *padarias* (diners and bakeries) are good for cheap eats; usually serving *prato feitos*, *salgadinhos*, excellent juices and other snacks.

The main meal is usually taken in the middle of the day; cheap restaurants tend not to be open in the evening.

Drink

The national liquor is cachaça (also known as *pinga*), which is made from sugar-cane, and ranging from cheap supermarket and service-station fire-water, to boutique distillery and connoisseur labels from the interior of Minas Gerais. Mixed with fruit juice, sugar and crushed ice, *cachaça* becomes the principal element in a *batida*, a refreshing but deceptively powerful drink. Served with pulped lime or other fruit, mountains of sugar and smashed ice it becomes the world's favourite party cocktail, *caipirinha*. A less potent *caipirinha* made with vodka is called a *caipiroska* and with sake a *saikirinha* or *caipisake*.

Some genuine Scotch whisky brands are bottled in Brazil. They are far cheaper even than duty free; Teacher's is the best. Locally made and cheap gin, vermouth and campari are pretty much as good as their US and European counterparts.

Wine is becoming increasingly popular, with good-value Portuguese and Argentinean bottles and some reasonable national table wines such as Château d'Argent, Château

Food and drink glossary

Brazilian dishes

Churrascaria Restaurant with meat barbecue also known as *rodízio*.
Feijoada The national dish, a black-bean and meat stew.
Pão do queijo Brazilian cheesy bread

Bebidas Drinks

água mineral mineral water
água tónica tonic water
café coffee
cerveja beer
chá tea
chocolate quente hot chocolate
leite milk
refrigerante soft drink
suco fruit juice
uísque whisky
vinho wine

Frutas Fruit

abacaxi pineapple
banana banana
coco coconut
laranja orange
limão lime
maçã apple
mamão papaya
manga mango
maracujá passion fruit
melancia watermelon
morango strawberry
uva grape

Carne Meat

bife beef
cabrito kid

cachorro quente hot dog
filé steak
frango chicken
misto quente toasted cheese and ham sandwich
peixe fish
peru turkey
porco pork
presunto ham
salsichas sausages

Legumes Vegetables

alface lettuce
arroz rice
batata potato
cebola onion
cenoura carrot
milho sweetcorn
salada salad
tomate tomato

Others

açúcar sugar
amendoim peanut
bolo cake
iogurte yoghurt
manteiga butter
mostarda mustard
ovo egg
pão bread
pastel pie
pimenta pepper
queijo cheese
sal salt
sanduiche sandwich
sorvete ice-cream

Duvalier, Almadén, Dreher, Preciosa and more respectable Bernard Taillan, Marjolet from Cabernet grapes, and the Moselle-type white Zahringer. A new *adega* tends to start off well, but the quality gradually deteriorates with time; many vintners have switched to American Concorde grapes, producing a rougher wine. Greville Brut champagne-style sparkling wine is inexpensive and very drinkable.

Brazilian beer is generally lager, served ice-cold. Draught beer is called *chope* or *chopp* (after the German Schoppen, and pronounced 'shoppi'). There are various national brands of bottled beers, which include Brahma, Skol, Cerpa, Antartica and the best Itaipava and Bohemia. There are black beers too, notably Xingu. They tend to be sweet. The best beer is from the German breweries in Rio Grande do Sul and is available only there.

Fruit juices or *sucos* come in infinite, delicious variety. *Açaí, acerola, caju* (cashew), *pitanga, goiaba* (guava), *genipapo, graviola* (*chirimoya*), *maracujá* (passion fruit), *sapoti* and *tamarindo* are but a few of the most delicious. *Açaí* acts as a powerful stimulant, particularly when combined with powdered, Amazonian *guaraná* nut. *Vitaminas* are thick fruit or vegetable drinks with milk. *Caldo de cana* is sugar-cane juice, sometimes mixed with ice. *Água de côco* or *côco verde* is coconut water served straight from a chilled, fresh green coconut. The best known of many local soft drinks is *guaraná*, which is a very popular carbonated fruit drink, completely unrelated to the Amazon nut. The best variety is *guaraná Antarctica*. Coffee is ubiquitous and good tea entirely absent.

Shopping

Arts and crafts
Brazil does not offer the variety and quality of arts and crafts you'll find in the Andes. However, good buys include: beautiful bead jewellery and bags made from Amazon seeds; clay figurines from the northeast, especially from Pernambuco; lace from Ceará; leatherwork, Marajó pottery and fabric hammocks from Amazônia (be sure to buy hooks '*ganchos para rede*' for hanging your hammock at home); carvings in soapstone and in bone; *capim-dourado* gold-grass bags and jewellery from Tocantins; and African-type pottery, basketwork and *candomblé* artefacts from Bahia. Brazilian cigars are excellent for those who like mild flavours.

Gold, diamonds and gemstones
Gold, diamonds and gemstones are good buys throughout Brazil and there are innovative designs in jewellery. Buy at reputable dealers (the best value is in Minas Gerais), but cheap, fun pieces can be bought from street traders. There are interesting furnishings made with gemstones, and marble – some of them rather cheesy; and huge slabs of amethyst, quartz and crystal at a fraction of a new age shop price.

Fashion
Brazil has long eclipsed Argentina as the fashion capital of Latin America and São Paulo is its epicentre, hosting the largest fashion show south of New York twice a year at the city's fashion week (www.spfw.com.br). Brazilian cuts, colours and contours are fresh and daring by US and European standards. Quality and variety is very high, from gorgeous bags and bikinis to designer dresses, shoes and denims. In São Paulo the best area for fashion shopping is Jardins (around Rua Oscar Freire) and the **Iguatemi** shopping centre on Avenida Faria Lima, and the city's most exclusive shopping emporium, **Daslu**. In Rio de Janeiro, Ipanema is the place to go for high-end shopping, as well as the **São Conrado Fashion Mall**. ▶ *See Shopping in Rio de Janeiro, page 134, and São Paulo, page 220.*

Herbal remedies
For those who know how to use them, medicinal herbs, barks and spices can be bought from street markets throughout Brazil. Coconut oil and local skin and hair-care products (fantastic conditioners) are better quality and cheaper than in Europe.

Music and instruments

If there is a more musical country on earth than Brazil we are yet to learn of it. Music is as ubiquitous as sunlight in Brazil and browsing through a CD shop anywhere will be sure to result in at least one purchase. See box, page 798, for a list of recommended artists.

Musical instruments are a good buy, particularly Brazilian percussion items. For example, the *berimbau*, a bow with a gourd sound-bell used in *candomblé*; the *cuíca* friction drum, which produces the characteristic squeaks and chirrups heard in samba; and assorted hand drums including the *surdo* (the big samba bass drum); and the *caixa, tambor, repinique* and *timbale* (drums that produce the characteristic Brazilian ra-ta-ta-ta-ta). The most Brazilian of hand drums is the tambourine, a misnomer for the *pandeiro* (which comes with bells), as opposed to the *tamborim* (which comes without). There are many unusual stringed instruments too: the *rabeca* (desert fiddle), the *cavaquinho* or *cavaco* (the Portuguese ancestor of ukulele), the *bandolim* (Brazilian mandolin), with its characteristic pear shape, and many excellent nylon-strung guitars.

Festivals and events

Brazil has festivals all year round with most concentrated in Jun and around Carnaval at the beginning of Lent. This list barely skims the surface.

January

Procissão de Nosso Senhor dos Navegantes, Salvador, Bahia. A big procession and a key event of the *candomblé* calendar. See www.bahia-online.net/festas.
Festa do Bonfim, see www.bahia-online.net/festas, and 6 of the best festivals, page 19.
São Paulo fashion week, São Paulo and Rio de Janeiro. The most important event on the Latin American fashion calendar attended by models and designers from all over the world. See www.spfw.com.br.

February

Festa de Yemanjá, Rio Vermelho, Salvador, Bahia. Dedicated to the *candomblé orixá* (spirit) of the sea and a great place to hear authentic live Bahian bands. See www.bahia-online.net/festas.
Pré-Caju, a pre-carnival carnival in Aracajú, Sergipe 15 days before Salvador carnival and with a similar vibe, though on a far smaller scale. See www.setur.se.gov.br.

February/March

Carnaval, Brazil's biggest festival takes place throughout the country and most famously in Rio's *sambódromo* stadium. For a wild street party head for Salvador; for something more authentic and traditional, Recife; and for a Brazilian crowd entirely free of foreign tourists, try one of the city's in Brazil's interior like Cidade de Goiás, www.vilaboadegoias.com.br/carnaval, or Ouro Preto, www.carnavalouropreto.com.

March

Chocofest, Canela, Serra Gaucha, Rio Grande do Sul. A pre-Easter chocolate-fest with parades, 100,000 visitors and chocolate. See www.canelaturismo.com.br.

April

Festa de Nossa Senhora da Penha, Vila Velha, Vitória, Espírito Santo. A series of spectacular processions celebrating the saint's day of the city's patron. See www.conventodapenha.org.br.
Festa do Açaí, Festa da Castanha and Festa do Cupuaçu, Codajás, Tefé and Presidente Figueiredo, Amazonas. 3 festivals devoted to 3 of the best Amazonian foods: the *açaí* energy berry, *cupuaçu* and the Brazil nut.

Carnaval dates

→ **2009** 21-24 February
→ **2010** 13-16 February
→ **2011** 5-8 February
→ **2012** 18-21 February
→ **2013** 9-12 February

Cuiafolia, the biggest festival of the year in Mato Grosso. The capital, Cuiabá, erupts into a mock-Bahian carnival powered by cheesy Bahian *axé* acts. See www.cuiafolia.com.br.

June
Boi Bumba, Parintins, Amazonas. A huge spectacle re-enacting the Boi story, with 2 competing teams, enormous floats and troupes of dancers. On an island in the Amazon. See www.boibumba.com.
Bumba-Meu-Boi, São Luís, Maranhão, see 6 of the best festivals page 18, and www.saoluisturismo.com.br.
Festas Juninhas (Festas do São João), Campina Grande, Paraíba, Caruru, Pernambuco and throughout Brazil. Brazil's major winter festival when everyone dresses up as a yokel, drinks hot spiced wine and dances *forró*. See 6 of the best festivals, page 18.

July
Anima Mundi, Rio de Janeiro and São Paulo. One of the largest animation festivals in the world; lasts 2 months. See www.animamundi.com.br.
Festa Literária Internacional de Paraty (**FLIP**), Paraty, Rio de Janeiro. The country's premier literary festival attracting big names like Salman Rushdie and Alice Walker. See www.flip.org.br.
Fortal Brazil's largest out of season carnival in Fortaleza powered mostly by Bahian music, but with a few more interesting fringe acts. See www.fortal.com.br.

August
Festa da Nossa Senhora D'Ajuda, Arraial d'Ajuda, Bahia. Festivals and processions celebrating the town's patron saint. See www.arraial-dajuda.com.br.
Festival de Gramado, Gramado, Rio Grande do Sul. Latin America's largest film festival. See www.festivaldegramado.net.
Festa do Peão de Boiadeiro, Barretos, São Paulo state. The biggest rodeo in the world, with a legion of Brazil's cheesiest music stars and legions of cowboys riding bulls. See www.festadopeaode americana.com.br.

October
Brazilian Grand Prix, São Paulo. See www.formula1.com.
Carnoporto, Porto Seguro's huge out of season carnival with all the top cheesy Bahian bands and big crowds. See www.axemoifolia.com.br.
Oktoberfest, Blumenau, Santa Catarina. See 6 of the best festivals, page 19, and www.oktoberfest.com.br.
Jogos dos Povos Indígenas, various locations. Indigenous people from throughout the country gather for the Brazilian equivalent of the Highland games, with wrestling, archery, javelin throwing and general celebrations. See www.funai.gov.br/ indios/jogos/jogos_indigenas.htm.

November
Círio de Nazaré, Belém and throughout Pará and Amazonas states. One of the largest religious celebrations in Brazil. Huge crowds, long precessions and many live music and cultural events. Www.paratur.pa.gov.br.

31 December
Reveillon, New Year's Eve. This is a huge party all over Brazil, and biggest of all on Copacabana beach in Rio. In São Paulo celebrations centre on the city's main Av Paulista, which is lined with sound stages and packed with partygoers.

Essentials A-Z

Accident and emergency

Ambulance T192. **Police** T190. If robbed or attacked, contact the tourist police. If you need to claim on insurance, make sure you get a police report.

Children

Travel with children is easy in Brazil. Brazilians love children and they are generally welcome everywhere. Facilities for children are often better than those back home.

Most restaurants provide children's seats and menus as well as crayons and paper to keep them happy. Children are never expected to be seen but not heard, and are allowed to run around pretty much everywhere.

Some hotels charge a cheaper family rate. Some will not charge for children under 5 and most can provide an extra camp bed for a double room. A few of the more romantic boutique beach resorts do not accept children. If you are planning to stay in such a hotel it is best to enquire ahead. Children under 3 generally travel for 10% on internal flights and at 70% until 12 years old. Prices on buses depend on whether the child will occupy a seat or a lap. Laps are free and if there are spare seats after the bus has departed the child can sit there for free.

Transport can involve long waits in *rodoviárias* (bus stations), but there are usually restaurants and places to sit down. Motion sickness can be treated with Dramin, which comes in dropper bottles (be sure to follow the dose), which is easy to decipher even with little Portuguese. Alternatively bring an international brand such as Kwells from home. 2 glasses of strong *maracuajá* juice act as a weaker natural substitute.

On tours children under 6 usually go free or it may be possible to bargain a discount rate.

Disabled travellers

As in most Latin American countries, facilities are generally very poor, with notable exceptions such as Sugar Loaf in Rio de Janeiro. Problems are worst for those in **wheelchair users**, who will find that ramps are rare, toilets and bathrooms with facilities are few and far between, except for some of the more modern hotels and the larger airports. Public transport is not well geared up for wheelchairs: pavements are often in a poor state of repair or crowded with street vendors requiring passers-by to brave the traffic. Rio and São Paulo metros have lifts and disabled chair lifts at some stations (but not all are operational. Disabled Brazilians obviously have to cope with these problems and mainly rely on the help of others to get on and off public transport and generally move around. Those who are not wheelchair users will find life easier and that Brazilians are usually helpful. Drivers should bring a disabled sticker as most shopping centres and public car parks have disabled spaces.

Disability Travel, www.disabilitytravel.com, is an excellent US site written by travellers in wheelchairs who have been researching disabled travel full-time since 1985. There are many tips and useful contacts (including lists of travel agents on request) and articles, including pieces on disabled travelling through the Amazon. The company also organizes group tours.

Global Access – Disabled Travel Network Site, www.globalaccessnews.com. Provides travel information for 'disabled adventurers' and includes a number of reviews and tips from the public.

Society for Accessible Travel and Hospitality, www.sath.org. Provides some general information, athough there is some specific information on Brazil.

Brazilian organizations include:
Sociedade Amigos do Deficiente Físico,

Ten of the best beaches

Swathes of broad sand 100 km long backed by towering sandstone cliffs; little coves strewn with giant boulders, lapped by an emerald sea and surrounded with virgin rainforest; bays of glass-clear water, tropical islands, vast shifting sand dunes pocked with lakes … Brazil has greatest variety of beaches in South America, and some of the most beautiful in the world.

Ipanema-Leblon, Rio The most glorious stretch of urban sand in the world and the playground of Rio's beautiful people, see page 108.

Ilha Grande, Rio Myriad bays surrounded by rainforest-covered hills and washed by an unfeasibly green sea. Visit, stay with local fishermen and stop Brazil's elite taking the island for themselves, see page 176.

Trindade, Rio Rainforest-covered hills dropping to broad fine sand washed by a bottle-green body-surf sea. Accommodation for backpackers only. For now. See page 181.

Florianópolis and the Ilha de Santa Catarina, Santa Catarina Brazil's favourite surf beaches in bays by the dozen, see page 349.

Itacaré, Bahia Archetypal Bounty bar beaches of white sand, swaying coconuts and sea that varies from pounding surf to gentle lapping turquoise, see page 436.

Trancoso, Bahia The most fashionable in Brazil. Come to see (or skip to avoid) the likes of Leonardo di Caprio in their speedos, see page 452.

Cacimba do Padre, Fernando de Noronha The best surf beach in the South Atlantic with superb diving and snorkelling offshore, see page 522.

Pipa, Rio Grande do Norte Relaxing little low key beach resort town surrounded by beautiful stretches of sand and backed by multi-coloured sandstone cliffs. Come outside the high season, see page 545.

Jericoacoara, Ceará Towering dunes, unforgettable ocean sunrises and sunsets, superb kitesurfing and ugly Italian resorts built without care for the environment, see page 564.

Alter do Chão, Pará White sand, blue water, pink dolphins and a river so wide it looks like a sea, see page 633.

---

www.aibr.com.br/sadef, based in Rio and with associate memberships throughout Brazil; and **Centro da Vida Independente**, Rio, www.cvi-rio.org.br. The publisher **O Nome da Rosa**, R Simão Álvares, 484 Pinheiros, T011-3817 5000, www.nome darosa.com.br, publishes a disabled guide to São Paulo entitled *O Guia São Paulo Adaptada*.

There are a number of specialist and general operators offering holidays specifically aimed at those with disabilities. These include: **Responsible Travel**, www.responsibletravel.com; **CanbeDone**, (www.canbedone.co.uk; and **Access Travel**, (www.access-travel.co.uk, although Brazil was not on their list as of 2008.

Nothing Ventured, edited by Alison Walsh (Harper Collins), has personal accounts of worldwide journeys by disabled travellers, plus advice and listings.

Electricity

Generally 110 V 60 cycles AC, but in some cities and areas 220 V 60 cycles AC is used.

Embassies and consulates

Brazilian embassies and consulates

Argentina C Cerrito 1350, 1010 Buenos Aires, T005411-4515, www.brasil.org.ar.
Australia 19 Forster Cres, Yarralumla, Canberra ACT 2600, T00612-6273 2372, www.brazil.org.au.
Austria Am Lugeck 1/5/15, A-1010 Wien, T00431-512 0631.
Belgium 350 Av Louise, 6ème étage, Boîte 5-1050 Bruxelles, T00322-640 2015.
Bolivia C Capitán Ravelo 2334, Ed Metrobol, Sopocachi, La Paz, Casilla 429, T005912-811 2233.
Canada 450 Wilbrod St, Sandyhill, Ottawa, ON K1N 6M8, T001613-237 1090, www.brasembottawa.org.
Chile C Alonso Ovalle 1665, Santiago, T00562-698 2486, www.brasembsantiago.cl.
Colombia C 93, No 14-20, 8th floor, Aptdo Aéreo 90540, Bogotá 8, T00571-218 0800.
Denmark Ryvangs Alle, 24-2100 Kobenhavn Ø, T00453-920 6478.
France 34 Cours Albert I, 75008 Paris, T00331-4561 6300, www.bresil.org.
Germany Kennedyallee 74-53175 Bonn, T0049228-959 230.
Ireland Harcourt Centre, Europa House, 5th Floor, 41-54 Harcourt St, Dublin 2, T003531-475 6000.
Israel Beit Yachin, 2 Kaplin St, 8th floor, Tel Aviv, T009723-696 3934.
Israel Beit Yachin, 2 Kaplin St, 8th floor, Tel Aviv, T009723-696 3934.
Italy 14 Piazza Navona, 00186 Roma, T003906-683 981, www.ambasciatadelbrasile.it.
Japan 2-11-12 Kita-Aoyama, Minato-Ku, Tokyo 107-8633, T00813-3404 5211, www.braemb.or.jp.
Netherlands Mauritskade 19-2514 HD, The Hague, T003170-302 3959.
New Zealand 19 Brandon St, level 9, Wellington 1, T00644-473 3516.
Norway Sigurd Syrs Gate 4, 1st floor, 0273 Oslo, T0047-2255 2029.

Paraguay C Coronel Irrazábal esq, Av Mariscal López, 1521 Asunción, T0059521-214 466, www.embajadabrasil.org.py
Peru Av José Pardo 850, Miraflores, Lima 100, T00511-421 2759.
Portugal Estrada das Laranjeiras, 1649-021 Lisboa, T003511-2172 48510, www.emb-brasil.pt.
South Africa Hadefields, Block c, 1st floor, 1267 Pretorius St, Hatfield 0083, Pretoria, T002712-426 9400, www.brazil.co.za.
Spain C Fernando El Santo, 6 DP 28010 Madrid, T00341-700 4650.
Sweden Sturgegatan 11, 2 Tr 114 36 Stockholm, T00468-234 010.
Switzerland Monbijouster 68-3007 Berne, T004131-371 8515.
UK 32 Green St, London WIK 7AT, T020-749 0877, www.brazil.org.uk.
USA 3006 Massachusetts Av NW, Washington DC 20008-3699, T001202-238 2700, www.brasilemb.org.
Uruguay Blvd Artigas, 1328, Montevideo, Aptdo Postal 16022, T005982-707 2119, www.brasmont.org.uy.
Venezuela Centro Gerencial Mohedano, 6th floor, C Los Chaguaramos con Av Mohedano, La Castellana, 1060 Caracas, T00582-261 6529.

Gay and lesbian travellers

Brazil is a good country for gay and lesbian travellers as attitudes are fairly liberal, especially in the big cities. Opinions in the interior and rural areas are far more conservative and it is wise to adapt to this. There is a well-developed scene in Rio de Janeiro and São Paulo while Salvador is also a popular destination. Local information can be obtained from the **Rio Gay Guide**, www.riogayguide.com, and in Salvador from the **Centro Cultura**, R do Sodre 45, close to the Museu de Arte Sacra da Bahia, which publishes a guide to the gay scene in the city for US$5.

São Paulo's Pride march (usually in May) is one of the biggest in the world, with more than 2 million people and there are many supporting cultural and musical events and parties. The Rio de Janeiro Pride march (usually Jun) takes place on Copacabana and is the centrepiece of an annual event that includes numerous activities, especially around Carnaval (see page 132 for more details). Other festivals include the nationwide **Mix Brasil festival of Sexual diversity**, www.mixbrasil.uol.com.br.

Health

In large cities Brazil's private medical services are excellent and equal to anything in the UK for general medicine and far better for tropical diseases and dentistry. The greatest disease risks in tropical Brazil are from insect borne infections. The key viral disease is **dengue fever** (see below), which is transmitted by a day-biting mosquito. Bacterial diseases include **tuberculosis (TB)** and some causes of **traveller's diarrhoea**. The parasitic diseases are many, but the 2 key ones are **malaria** and South American **trypanosomiasis** (known as Chagas's Disease). See below for details.

Before you go

Visit your GP/practice nurse or travel clinic at least 6 weeks before your departure for advice on travel risks, malaria and recommended vaccinations. Typically you will need: yellow fever, tetanus-diptheria, hepatitis A and B, typhoid and MMR. Your local pharmacist can also be a good source of readily accessible advice. Make sure you have travel insurance, get a dental check (especially if you are going to be away for more than a month), know your own blood group and if you suffer a long-term condition such as diabetes or epilepsy make sure someone knows or that you have a Medic Alert bracelet/necklace with this information on it.

A-Z of health risks
Bites and stings

This is a very rare event indeed for travellers, but if you are unlucky (or careless) enough to be bitten by a venomous snake, spider, scorpion or sea creature, try to identify the culprit, without putting yourself in further danger (do not try to catch a live snake).

Snake bites in particular are very frightening, but in fact are rarely poisonous; even venomous snakes bite without injecting venom. Victims should be taken to a hospital or a doctor without delay. It is not advised for travellers to carry snake bite anti-venom as it can do more harm than good in inexperienced hands. Reassure and comfort the victim frequently. Immobilize the limb with a bandage or a splint and get the patient to lie still. Do not slash the bite area and try to suck out the poison. This also does more harm than good. You should apply a tourniquet in these circumstances, but only if you know how to. **Do not** attempt this if you are not experienced.

Scorpion fish and some Amazonian cat fish inject venom into bathers' feet when trodden on, which can be exceptionally painful. Wear plastic shoes if such creatures are reported. The pain can be relieved by immersing the foot in very hot water for as long as the pain persists.

Chagas disease

The disease occurs throughout Brazil and affects locals more than travellers. However, travellers can be exposed if sleeping in mud huts. The bug that carries the parasite bites and defecates on an exposed part of skin. You may notice nothing at all or a local swelling, with fever, tiredness and enlargement of lymph glands, spleen and liver. The seriousness of the infection is caused by the long-term effects, which include gross enlargement of the heart and/or guts. Early treatment is required. To prevent the disease, sleep under a permethrin-treated bed net and use insect repellent.

Dengue fever

This is a viral disease spread by mosquitos that tend to bite during the day. The disease is like a very nasty form of the flu with 2-3 days of illness, followed by a short period of recovery, then a 2nd attack of illness. Westerners very rarely get the worst haemorrhagic form of the disease. The symptoms are fever and often intense joint pains, some people also develop a rash. Symptoms last about a week but it can take a few weeks to recover fully. Dengue can be difficult to distinguish from malaria as both diseases tend to occur in the same countries. There are no effective vaccines or antiviral drugs though, fortunately, travellers rarely develop the more severe forms of the disease (these can prove fatal). Rest, plenty of fluids and paracetamol (not aspirin) is the recommended treatment.

Diarrhoea and intestinal upset

Diarrhoea can refer either to loose stools or an increased frequency of bowel movement, both of which can be a nuisance. Symptoms should be relatively short-lived but if they persist beyond 2 weeks, specialist medical attention should be sought. Also seek medical help if there is blood in the stools and/or fever.

Adults can use an anti-diarrhoeal medication such as loperamide to control the symptoms but only for up to 24 hrs. In addition keep well hydrated by drinking plenty of fluids and eat bland foods. Oral rehydration sachets taken after each loose stool are a useful way to keep hydrated. These should always be used when treating children and the elderly.

Bacterial traveller's diarrhoea is the most common form. Ciproxin (Ciprofloxacin) is a useful antibiotic and can be obtained by private prescription in the UK or over the counter in Brazil. Follow the instructions on the packet. If there are no signs of improvement after 24 hrs the diarrhoea is likely to be viral and not bacterial. If it is due to other organisms such as those causing giardia or amoebic dysentery,

different antibiotics will be required. The standard advice to prevent problems is to be careful with water and ice for drinking (see Water, below). Ask yourself where the water came from. If you have any doubts then boil it or filter and treat it. There are many filter/treatment devices now available on the market. Also consider your food. There is a simple adage that says wash it, peel it, boil it or forget it. Also be wary of unpasteurised dairy products, as these can transmit a range of diseases.

Hepatitis

Hepatitis means inflammation of the liver. Viral causes of the disease can be acquired anywhere in the world. The most obvious symptom is a yellowing of your skin or the whites of your eyes. However, prior to this all you may notice is itching and tiredness. Hepatitis B and C are spread through blood and unprotected sexual intercourse, both of which can be avoided. Talk to your doctor about vaccinations.

Leishmaniasis

A skin form of this disease occurs in Brazil. If infected, you may notice a raised lump, which leads to a purplish discolouration on white skin and a possible ulcer. The parasite is transmitted by the bite of a sandfly. Sandflies do not fly far and the greatest risk is at ground level; try to avoid sleeping on the floor. Several weeks' treatment are required under specialist supervision. The drugs themselves are toxic, but if not taken in sufficient amounts recurrence of the disease is more likely. To prevent the disease, sleep above ground, under a permethrin-treated net, use insect repellent and get a specialist opinion on any unusual skin lesions soon after return.

Malaria

Some types of malaria can cause death within 24 hrs and start as something resembling an attack of flu. You may feel tired, lethargic and develop a headache or fever; if left untreated symptoms can develop into fits, followed by coma and then death. Have a low index of suspicion because it is very easy to write off vague symptoms, which may actually be malaria. If you have a temperature, visit a doctor as soon as you can and ask for a malaria test. On your return home, if you suffer any of these symptoms, have a test as soon as possible. Even if a previous test proved negative, this could save your life.

Treatment is with drugs and may be oral or into a vein depending on the seriousness of the infection. Remember **ABCD: Awareness** (of whether the disease is present in the area you are travelling in), **Bite avoidance**, **Chemoprohylaxis** (anti-malarials), **Diagnosis**.

To prevent mosquito bites, wear clothes that cover arms and legs, use effective insect repellents in areas with known risks of insect-spread disease and use a mosquito net treated with an insecticide. Repellents containing 30-50% DEET (Di-ethyltoluamide) are recommended when visiting malaria-endemic areas; effective alternatives include Johnson's Off! (available in Brazil) and Off! Deep Woods. Citronella is also good. The key advice is to guard against contracting malaria by taking the correct anti-malarials and finishing the recommended course. If you are a popular target for insect bites or develop lumps quite soon after being bitten use antihistamine tablets and apply a cream such as hydrocortisone.

Malarial treatment in Brazil is among the best in the world, particularly at the **Hospital Tropical** in Manaus (see page 674); although you will have to pay for this privately.

The principal risk areas for malaria are in states of Acre, Rondônia, Amapa, Amazonas, Roraima and Tocantins, western Maranhão, northern Mato Grosso and Pará (except Belém city). There is also transmission in large urban areas like Porto Velho, Boa Vista, Macapá, Manaus, Santarém and Marabá.

Rabies
Rabies is endemic throughout certain parts of the world so be aware of the dangers of a bite from any animal. Rabies vaccination before travel can be considered but if bitten always seek urgent medical attention – whether or not you have been previously vaccinated – after first cleaning the wound and treating with an iodine-based disinfectant or alcohol.

Sun
Take good heed of advice regarding protecting yourself against the sun. Overexposure can lead to sunburn, sunstroke and, in the longer term, skin cancers and premature skin aging. The best advice is simply to avoid exposure to the sun by covering exposed skin, wearing a hat and staying out of the sun if possible, particularly between late morning and early afternoon. Apply a high-factor sunscreen (at least SPF15) and also make sure it screens against UVB. A further danger in tropical climates is heat exhaustion, or more seriously, heatstroke. This can be avoided by good hydration, which means drinking water past the point of simply quenching thirst. Also, when first exposed to tropical heat, take time to acclimatise by avoiding strenuous activity in the middle of the day. If you cannot avoid heavy exercise it is also a good idea to increase salt intake.

Typhoid fever
This a gut infection that can spread to the blood stream. You get it from someone else's faeces getting into your mouth. A classic example would be the waiter who fails to wash his hands and then serves you a salad. The fever is an obvious feature, occasionally there is a mild red rash on the stomach and often you have a headache. Constipation or diarrhoea can occur. Gut pain and hearing problems may also feature. Antibiotics are required and you are probably best going to hospital. Watch what you eat and the hygiene of the place or those serving your food. There is an effective vaccine, talk to your doctor before you leave.

Underwater health
If you plan to dive make sure that you are fit do so. The **British Sub-Aqua Club**,

www.bsac.com, and **PADI**, www.padi.com, can give advice on health recommendations. Check that any dive company you use is reputable and has appropriate certification from NAUI, www.naui.org, or PADI.

Water

There are a number of ways of purifying water. Dirty water should first be strained through a filter bag and then boiled or treated. Bring water to a rolling boil for several minutes. Products for sterilization generally contain chlorine (eg Puritabs) or iodine (eg Pota Aqua) compounds. There are a number of water sterilizers now on the market available in personal and expedition size. Make sure you take the spare parts or spare chemicals with you and do not believe everything the manufacturers say.

Further information
Websites

Blood Care Foundation (UK), www.blood care.org.uk. A charity that will dispatch certified non-infected blood of the right type to the hospital/clinic where you are being treated.
Communicable Disease Control (USA), www.cdc.gov. A US government site with excellent advice on travel health, has useful disease maps and details of disease outbreaks.
Department of Health Travel Advice, www.doh.gov.uk/traveladvice. An excellent site, also available as a free booklet, the *T6*, from UK post offices. It lists the vaccine advice requirements for each country.
Medic Alert (UK), www.medicalalert.co.uk The foundation that produces bracelets and necklaces for those with medical problems.
NetDoctor (UK), www.netdoctor.co.uk. A general health advice site with a useful section on travel and an 'ask the expert' interactive chat forum.
Public Health Laboratory Service (UK), www.phls.org.uk. Advice on malaria and useful information for those who are pregnant, suffering from epilepsy or planning to travel with children.

Tropical Medicine Bureau, www.tmb.ie. Good collection of general travel health information and disease risks.
World Health Organisation (WHO), www.who.int. Links to the WHO *Yellow Book* on travel advice. This lists the diseases in different regions of the world and makes clear which countries have Yellow Fever Vaccination certificate requirements.

Books and leaflets

Travellers' Health (4th Ed Oxford: Oxford University Press, 2002), Dawood R, editor.
Expedition Medicine (The Royal Geographic Society) Editors David Warrell and Sarah Anderson (ISBN 1 86197 040-4).
The Travellers Good Health Guide, Dr Ted Lankester (ISBN 0-85969-827-0).
Expedition Medicine (The Royal Geographic Society), Editors David Warrell and Sarah Anderson (ISBN 1 86197 040-4).
International Travel and Health, World Health Organisation Geneva (ISBN 92 4 158026 7).

Internet

Brazil is said to be 7th in the world in terms of internet use. Public internet access is so readily available that it is almost pointless to list the locations. There is internet access on every other street corner in even the smallest towns and cities – look for signs saying '**LAN house**' or '**ciber-café**'. The facilities usually double-up as computer games rooms for teenagers. There is usually an hourly charge of around US$2, but you can almost always use partial hours at a reduced rate. More and more hotels offer an internet service to their guests – many in-room wireless; usually free but sometimes at exorbitant rates, while some government programmes even offer free use (notably in Manaus and Cuiaba) in public areas. For a regularly updated list of locations around the world, check www.netcafe guide.com.

Useful slang

que legal	that's great/cool	*mauricinho*	posh, spoilt boy with rich parents
jeito	getting around a problem		
cara	literally 'face', but means bloke/guy	*patricinha*	posh, spoilt girl with rich parents
mano	biker slang for bloke/guy	*descolado*	in fashion/cool
brega	cheesy/tacky		

Language

Brazilians speak Portuguese, and very few speak anything else. Spanish may help you to be understood a little, but spoken Portuguese will remain undecipherable even to fluent Spanish speakers. To get the best out of Brazil, learn some Portuguese before arriving. Brazilians are the best thing about the country and without Portuguese you will not be able to interact beyond stereotypes and second guesses. Language classes are available in the larger cities. **Cactus** (www.cactuslanguage.com), **Languages abroad** (www.languages abroad.co.uk) and **Travellers Worldwide** (www.travellersworldwide.com) are among the companies that can organize language courses in Brazil. **McGraw Hill** and **DK** (*Hugo Portuguese in Three Months*) offer the best teach-yourself books. **Sonia Portuguese** (www.sonia-portuguese.com) is a useful online resource.

Money

Currency

→ *US$1 = R$2.3, £1 = 3.6; €1 = 3.2 (Dec 2008).* The unit of currency is the **real**, R$ (plural **reais**). Any amount of foreign currency and 'a reasonable sum' in reais can be taken in, but sums over US$10,000 must be declared. Residents may only take out the equivalent of US$4000. Notes in circulation are: 100, 50, 10, 5 and 1 real; coins: 1 real, 50, 25, 10, 5 and 1 centavo. **Note** The exchange rate has been fairly volatile recently so check in advance.

Costs of travelling

Brazil is more expensive than other countries in South America. As a very rough guide, prices are about two-thirds those of Western Europe and the USA; though prices vary hugely according to the current exchange rate and strength of the *real*.

Hostel beds are usually less than US$10. Budget hotels with few frills have rooms for as little as US$15, and you should have no difficulty finding a room costing US$25 wherever you are. Rooms are often pretty much the same price whether 1 or 2 people are staying. Eating is generally inexpensive, especially in *padarias* or *comida por kilo* (pay by weight) restaurants, which offer a wide range of food (salads, meat, pasta, vegetarian). Although bus travel is very reasonable, because of the long distances, costs can soon mount up. Internal flights prices have come down dramatically in the last couple of years and some routes work out cheaper than taking a bus – especially if booking through the internet.

ATMs

ATMs, or cash machines, are common in Brazil. As well as being the most convenient way of withdrawing money, they frequently offer the best available rates of exchange. They are usually closed after 2130 in large cities. There are two international ATM acceptance systems, **Plus** and **Cirrus**. Many issuers of debit and credit cards are linked to one, or both (eg Visa is Plus, MasterCard is Cirrus). **Bradesco** and **HSBC** are the 2 main banks offering this service. **Red Banco 24 Horas** kiosks advertise that they take a long

Brazilian etiquette

In his 1941 travel book, *I Like Brazil*, Jack Harding said of Brazilians that "anyone who does not get along with (them) had better examine himself; the fault is his." And perhaps the best writer on Brazil in English, Joseph Page, observed in his 1995 book *The Brazilians* that "cordiality is a defining characteristic of their behaviour. They radiate an irresistible pleasantness, abundant hospitality, and unfailing politeness, especially to foreigners." It is hard to offend Brazilians or to find Brazilians offensive, but to make sure you avoid misunderstandings, here are a few, perhaps surprising, tips.

Public nudity, even toplessness on beaches, is an arrestable offence.

Brazilians will talk to anyone, anywhere. 'Sorry, do I know you?' is the least Brazilian sentiment imaginable and no one ever rustles a newspaper on the metro.

Walks in nature are never conducted in silence. This has led many Brazilians to be unaware that their country is the richest in terrestrial wildlife on the planet.

Drug use, even of marijuana, is deeply frowned upon. Attitudes are far more conservative than in Europe. The same is true of public drunkenness.

When driving it is normal, especially in Rio, to accelerate right up the bumper of the car in the lane in front of you on the highway, hoot repeatedly and flash your headlights. It is considered about as rude as ringing the doorbell in Brazil.

This is the land of red tape. You need a social security number to buy a SIM card and fingerprint ID just to go to the dentist.

Never presume a policeman will take a bribe. And never presume he won't. Let the policeman do the presuming.

Never insult an official. You could find yourself is serious trouble.

Brazilians are very private about their negative emotions. Never moan for more than a few seconds, even with justification – you will be branded an *uruca* (harbinger of doom), and won't get invited to the party.

The phrase 'So para Ingles Ver' ('just for the English to see') is a common expression that means 'to appear to do something by the rule book whilst doing the opposite'.

Never confuse a Brazilian footballer with an Argentinean one.

Brazilians believe that anyone can dance samba. They can't.

Never dismiss a street seller with anything less than cordiality; an impolite dismissal will be seen as arrogant and aggressive. Always extend a polite 'não obrigado'.

Brazilian time Peter Fleming, the author of one of the best travel books about Brazil, once said that "a man in a hurry will be miserable in Brazil." Remember this when you arrive 10 minutes late to meet a friend in a bar and spend the next hour wondering if they've already gone after growing tired of waiting for you. They haven't. They've not yet left home. Unless you specify 'a hora britanica' then you will wait. And wait. And everyone will be mortified if you complain. Nobody does – it would be like getting upset about not being allowed to read the paper over someone's shoulder on the London underground.

list of credit cards in their ATMs, including MasterCard and Amex, but international cards cannot always be used; the same is true of **Banco do Brasil**.

Advise your bank before leaving, as cards are usually stopped in Brazil without prior warning. Find out before you leave what international functionality your card has. Check if your bank or credit card company imposes handling charges. Internet banking is useful for monitoring your account or transferring funds. Do not rely on 1 card, in case of loss. If you do lose a card, immediately contact the 24-hr helpline of the issuer in your home country (keep this number in a safe place).

Exchange

Banks in major cities will change cash and traveller's cheques (TCs). If you keep the official exchange slips, you may convert back into foreign currency up to 50% of the amount you exchanged. The parallel market, found in travel agencies, exchange houses and among hotel staff, often offers marginally better rates than the banks but commissions can be very high. Many banks may only change US$300 minimum in cash, US$500 in TCs. Rates for TCs are usually far lower than for cash, they are harder to change and a very heavy commission may be charged. Dollars cash (take US$5 or US$10 bills) are not useful as alternative currency. Brazilians use *reais*.

Credit cards

Credit cards are widely used, although often they are not usable in the most unlikely places, like tour operators. **Diners Club**, **MasterCard**, **Visa** and **Amex** are useful. Cash advances on credit cards will only be paid in *reais* at the tourist rate, incurring at least a 1.5% commission. Banks in small remote places may still refuse to give a cash advance: try asking for the *gerente* (manager).

Money transfers

Money sent to Brazil is normally paid out in Brazilian currency, so do not have more money sent out than you need for your stay. Funds can ostensibly be received within 48 banking hours, but it can take at least a month to arrive, allowing banks to capitalize on your transfer. The documentation required to receive it varies according to the whim of the bank staff, making the whole procedure often far more trouble than it is worth.

Opening hours

Generally 0900-1800 Mon-Fri; closed for lunch some time between 1130 and 1400. **Shops** Also open on Sat until 1230 or 1300. **Government offices** Mon-Fri 1100-1800. **Banks** Mon-Fri 1000-1600 or 1630; closed at weekends.

Post

To send a standard letter or postcard to the USA costs US$0.75, to Europe US$0.85, to Australia or South Africa US$1. Air mail should take about 7 days to or from Britain or the USA. Franked and registered (insured) letters are normally secure, but check that the amount franked is what you have paid, or the item will not arrive. Aerogrammes are most reliable. To avoid queues and obtain higher denomination stamps go to the stamp desk at the main post office.

The post office sells cardboard boxes for sending packages internally and abroad. Rates and rules for sending literally vary from post office to post office even within the same town and the quickest service is SEDEX. The most widespread courier service is Federal Express, www.fedex.com/br. They are often cheaper than parcel post.

Postes restantes usually only hold letters for 30 days. Identification is required and it's a good idea to write your name on a piece of paper to help the attendant find your letters. Charges are minimal but often involve queuing at another counter to buy stamps, which are attached to your letter and franked before it is given to you.

Safety

Although Brazil's big cities suffer high rates of violent crime, this is mostly confined to the *favelas* (slums) where poverty and drugs are the main cause. Visitors should not enter *favelas* except when accompanied by workers for NGOs, tour groups or other people who know the local residents well and are accepted by the community. Otherwise they may be targets of muggings by armed gangs who show short shrift to those who resist them. Mugging can take place anywhere. Travel light after dark with few valuables and ask hotel staff where is and isn't safe; crime is patchy in Brazilian cities. If the worst does happen and you are threatened, don't panic, and hand over your valuables. Do not resist, and report the crime to the local tourist police later. It is extremely rare for a tourist to be hurt during a robbery in Brazil. Being aware of the dangers, acting confidently and using your common sense will reduce many of the risks.

Certain parts of the country are areas of drug cultivation and should be avoided. These are mentioned where appropriate in the travelling text. All border areas should be regarded with some caution because of smuggling activities. Violence over land ownership in parts of the interior have resulted in a 'Wild West' atmosphere in some towns, which should therefore be passed through quickly. Red-light districts should also be given a wide berth as there are reports of drinks being drugged with a substance popularly known as 'good night Cinderella'. This leaves the victim easily amenable to having their possessions stolen, or worse.

Avoiding cons
Never trust anyone telling sob stories or offering 'safe rooms', and when looking for a hotel, always choose the room yourself. Be wary of 'plain-clothes policemen'; insist on seeing identification and on going to the police station by main roads. Do not hand over your identification (or money) until you are at the station. On no account take them directly back to your hotel. Be even more suspicious if they seek confirmation of their status from a passer-by.

Hotel security
Hotel safe deposits are generally, but not always, secure. If you cannot get a receipt for valuables in a hotel safe, you can seal the contents in a plastic bag and sign across the seal. Always keep an inventory of what you have deposited. If you don't trust the hotel, lock everything in your pack and secure it in your room when you go out. If you lose valuables, report to the police and note details of the report for insurance purposes. Be sure to be present whenever your credit card is used.

Police
There are several types of police: **Polícia Federal**, civilian dressed, who handle all federal law duties, including immigration. A subdivision is the **Polícia Federal Rodoviária**, uniformed, who are the traffic police on federal highways. **Polícia Militar** are the uniformed, street police force, under the control of the state governor, handling all state laws. They are not the same as the Armed Forces' internal police. **Polícia Civil**, also state controlled, handle local laws and investigations. They are usually in civilian dress, unless in the traffic division. In cities, the **Prefeitura** controls the **Guarda Municipal**, who handle security. **Tourist police** operate in places with a strong tourist presence. In case of difficulty, visitors should seek out tourist police in the first instance.

Protecting money and valuables
Apart from the obvious precautions of not wearing jewellery (wear a cheap, plastic, digital watch), take local advice about safety and do not assume that daytime is safer than night. If walking after dark, walk in the road, not on the pavement/sidewalk and do not go on to the beach. Don't take valuables to the beach.

Photocopy your passport, air ticket and other documents, make a record of traveller's cheque and credit card numbers. Keep them separately from the originals and leave another set of records at home. Keep all documents secure; hide your main cash supply in different places or under your clothes. Extra pockets sewn inside shirts and trousers, money belts (best worn below the waist), neck or leg pouches and elasticated support bandages for keeping money above the elbow or below the knee have been repeatedly recommended.

Public transport
When you have all your luggage with you at a bus or railway station, be especially careful and carry any shoulder bags in front of you. To be extra safe, take a taxi between airport/bus station/railway station and hotel, keep your bags with you and pay only when you and your luggage are outside; avoid night buses and arriving at your destination at night.

Sexual assault
If you are the victim of a sexual assault, you are advised firstly to contact a doctor (this can be your home doctor). You will need tests to determine whether you have contracted any STDs; you may also need advice on emergency contraception. You should contact your embassy, where consular staff will be very willing to help.

Women travellers
Most of these tips apply to any single traveller. When you set out, err on the side of caution until your instincts have adjusted to the customs of a new culture. Be prepared for the exceptional curiosity extended to visitors, especially women and try not to overreact. If, as a single woman, you can befriend a local woman, you will learn much more about the country you are visiting. There is a definite 'gringo trail' you can follow, which can be helpful when looking for safe accommodation, especially if arriving after dark (best avoided). Remember that for a single woman a taxi at night can be as dangerous as walking alone. It is easier for men to take the friendliness of locals at face value; women may be subject to unwanted attention. Do not disclose to strangers where you are staying. By wearing a wedding ring and saying that your 'husband'

is close at hand, you may dissuade an aspiring suitor. If politeness fails, do not feel bad about showing offence and departing. A good rule is always to act with confidence, as though you know where you are going, even if you do not. Someone who looks lost is more likely to attract unwanted attention.

Student travellers

If you are in full time education you will be entitled to an ISIC (International Student Identity Card), which is distributed by student travel offices and travel agencies in more than 77 countries. The ISIC card gives you special prices on all forms of transport and access to a variety of other concessions and services. If you need to find the location of your nearest ISIC office contact: **ISIC Association**, Box 15857, 1001 NJ Amsterdam, Holland, T+45-3393 9303, www.isic.org. ISIC cards can be obtained in Brazil from **STB** agencies throughout the country, such as Av Brig Faria Lima 1713, São Paulo, T011-870 0555; also try www.carteirado estudante.com.br. Remember to take photographs when having a card issued.

In practice, the ISIC card is rarely recognized or accepted for discounts outside of the south and southeast of Brazil, but is nonetheless useful for obtaining half-price entry to the cinema. Youth hostels will often accept it in lieu of a IYHA card or at least give a discount, and some university accommodation (and subsidized canteens) will allow very cheap short-term stays to holders.

Tax

Airport departure tax The amount of tax depends on the class and size of the airport, but the cost is usually incorporated into the ticket.
VAT Rates vary from 7-25% at state and federal level; the average is 17-20%.

Telephone

→ *Country code: +55.*

Ringing: equal tones with long pauses.
Engaged: equal tones, equal pauses.

Making a phone call in Brazil can be confusing. It is necessary to dial a 2-digit telephone company code prior to the area code for all calls. Phone numbers are now printed in this way: 0XX21 (0 for a national call, XX for the code of the phone company chosen (eg 31 for Telemar) followed by, 21 for Rio de Janeiro, for example and the 8-digit number of the subscriber. The same is true for international calls where 00 is followed by the operator code and then the country code and number.

Nationwide and international telephone operators and their codes are: **Embratel**, 21 (nationwide); **Telefônica**, 15 (state of São Paulo); **Telemar**, 31 (Alagoas, Amazonas, Amapá, Bahia, Ceará, Espírito Santo, Maranhão, most of Minas Gerais, Pará, Paraíba, Pernambuco, Piauí, Rio de Janeiro, Rio Grande do Norte, Roraima, Sergipe); **Tele Centro-Sul**, 14 (Acre, Goiás, Mato Grosso, Mato Grosso do Sul, Paraná, Rondônia, Santa Catarina, Tocantins and the cities of Brasília and Pelotas); **CTBC-Telecom**, 12 (some parts of Minas Gerais, Goiás, Mato Grosso do Sul and São Paulo state); **Intelig**, 23.

National calls

Telephone booths or *orelhões* (literally – 'big ears' as they are usually ear-shaped, fibreglass shells) are easy to come by in towns and cities. Local phone calls and telegrams cheap.

Cartões telefônicos (phone cards) are available from newsstands, post offices and some chemists. They cost US$2.50 for 30 units and up to US$5 for 90 units. Dial 9, followed by the number, and announce your name and city. Local calls from a private phone are often free. *Acrtões telefônicos internacionais* (International phone cards) are increasingly available in tourist areas and are often sold at hostels.

Mobile phones

Cellular phones are widespread and coverage excellent even in remote areas, but prices are extraordinarily high and users still pay to receive calls outside the metropolitan area where their phone is registered. SIM cards are hard to buy as users require a CPF (a Brazilian social security number) to buy one, but phones can be hired. When using a cellular telephone you do not drop the zero from the area code as you have to when dialling from a fixed line.

Time

Brazil has 4 time zones: Brazilian standard time is GMT-3; the Amazon time zone (Pará west of the Rio Xingu, Amazonas, Roraima, Rondônia, Mato Grosso and Mato Grosso do Sul) is GMT-4, the State of Acre is GMT-5; and the Fernando de Noronha archipelago is GMT-2. Clocks move forward 1 hr in summer for approximately 5 months (usually between Oct and Feb or Mar), but times of change vary. This does not apply to Acre.

Tipping

Tipping is usual, but less costly than in most other countries. In restaurants, add 10% of the bill if no service charge is included; cloakroom attendants deserve a small tip; hairdressers expect 10-15%; porters have fixed charges but often receive tips as well; airport porters should be tipped about US$0.65 per item.

Tour operators

UK

Austral Tours, 20 Upper Tachbrook St, London SW1V 1SH, T020-7233 5384, www.latinamerica.co.uk. Tours to Rio, the Amazon and the northeast.
Condor Journeys and Adventures, 2 Ferry Bank, Colintraive, Argyll PA22 3AR,

T01700-841 318, www.condorjourneys-adventures.com. Tailor-made journeys to standard destinations.

Encounter Overland, 2001 Camp Green, Debenham, Stowmarket, Suffolk 1P14 6LA, T01728-862 222, www.encounter.co.uk. Extended overland trips through the Amazon and throughout South America. Interesting routes.

Explore Worldwide, 1 Frederick St, Aldershot, Hants GU11 1LQ, T01252-760 000, www.exploreworldwide.com. Standard small-group trips to the northeast, Amazon and Rio.

Journey Latin America, 12-13 Heathfield Terr, Chiswick, London W4 4JE, T020-8747 8315, and 12 St Ann's Sq, 2nd floor, Manchester M2 7HW, T0161-832 1441, www.journeylatinamerica.co.uk. Long-established company with excellent escorted tours to some interesting areas like Goiás and the Chapada Diamantina. They also offer a wide range of good-value flight options.

Last Frontiers, Fleet Marston Farm, Aylesbury, Bucks HP18 0QT, T01296-653 000, www.lastfrontiers.com. Imaginative tailor-made tours to some interesting out-of-the-way locations including Fernando de Noronha.

Select Latin America, 3.51 Canterbury Court, 1-3 Brixton Rd, Kennington Park Business Centre, Lonon SW9 6DE, T020-7407 1478, www.selectlatinamerica.co.uk. Quality tailor-made holidays and small group tours.

South American Experience, 47 Causton St, Pimlico, London SW1P 4AT, T020-7976 5511, www.southamericanexperience.co.uk. Standard itineraries with a few more unusual options like the Chapada Diamantina.

Steppes Latin America, 51 Castle St, Cirencester, Glos GL7 1QD, T01285-885 333, www.steppestravel.co.uk. Tailor-made and group itineraries throughout Brazil and Latin America.

Sunvil Latin America, Sunvil House, Upper Square, Old Isleworth, Middlesex,

TW7 7BJ, T020-875 84774,
www.sunvil.co.uk. A good range of
options throughout Brazil, including
some out-of-the-way destinations.
Trips Worldwide, 14 Frederick Place,
Clifton, Bristol BS8 1AS, T0117-311 4400,
www.tripsworldwide.co.uk. Tailor-made
trips throughout South America.
Trivium, T062-212 6232, www.trivium.co.uk.
Highly professional English-run company
based in Goiás, offering general and
specialist botanical tours throughout
the state, especially to the Chapada
dos Veadeiros and to the Atlantic coast
rainforest. Much of the money goes
back into local communities.
Veloso Tours, ground floor, 34 Warple
Way, London W3 0RG, T020-8762 0616,

www.veloso.com. An imaginative
range of tours throughout Brazil
and bespoke options on request.

Wildlife and birding specialists
Ornitholidays, 29 Straight Mile, Romsey,
Hants, SO51 9BB, T01794 519 445, www.ornit
holidays.co.uk. Annual or biannual birding trips
throughout Brazil; usually to the Pantanal,
Atlantic Coast rainforest and Iguaçu.
Reef and Rainforest Tours Ltd, A7 Dart
Marine Park, Steamer Quay, Totnes,
Devon, TQ9 5DR, T01803-866 965,
www.reefandrainforest.co.uk. Specialists
in tailor-made and group wildlife tours.
Trivium (see above), Specialist
botanical tours in conjunction
with the Eden Project.

North America

4starSouth America, T1-800-887 5686, www.4starSouthAmerica.com. Customized or scheduled tours throughout South America. Also has an office in Brazil at Av NS Copacabana 1066/907, Rio de Janeiro, T021-2267 6624.
Brazil For Less, 7201 Wood Hollow Dr, Austin, TX 78731, T1-877-565 8119 (US toll free) or T+44-203-006 2507 (UK), www.brazilforless.com. US-based travel firm with a focus solely on South America, with local offices and operations, and a price guarantee. Good-value tours, run by travellers for travellers. Will meet or beat any published rates on the internet from outside Brazil.
Ela Brasil Tours, 14 Burlington Dr, Norwalk, CT 06851, T203-840 9010, www.elabrasil.com. Excellent bespoke tours throughout Brasil to some very imaginative destinations. Uses only the best and most responsible local operators.

Ladatco Tours, 3006 Aviation Av 4C, Coconut Grove, Florida 33133, USA, T1800-327 6162, www.ladatco.com. Standard tours to Rio, Iguaçu and Manaus for the Amazon.
Mila Tours, 100 S Greenleaf Av, Gurnee, IL 60031-337, T847-248 2111, T800-387 7378 (USA and Canada), www.milatours.com. Itineraries to Rio, Iguaçu and the Northeast.
Tropical Nature Travel, PO Box 5276, Gainesville, Fl 326270 5276, USA, T352-376 3377, www.tropicalnaturetravel.com.

Wildlife and birding specialists

Field Guides, 9433 Bee Cave Rd, Building 1, Suite 150, Austin, Texas 78733, USA, T1-800-7284953, www.fieldguides.com. Interesting birdwatching tours to all parts of Brazil.
Focus Tours, 103 Moya Rd, Santa Fe, NM87508, USA, T505-4664688, www.focus tours.com. Specialists in birdwatching and environmentally responsible travel.

Brazil

Brazil Always Summer Tours, SEPS EQ 714/914, Bloco E, Sala 409, Edificio Talento, Brasilia-DF, CEP 70390-145, T061-3345 4441, www.brazilalwayssummer.com. Tour operator specializing in holidays to Brazil. Services include hotel booking, Rio Carnaval tickets and excellent car rental rates.

Dehouche, T021-2512 3895, www.dehouche.com. Upmarket, carefully tailored trips throughout Brazil.

Manary Ecotours, R Francisco Gurgel, 9067, Ponta Negra Beach, Natal, T084-3204 2900, www.manary.com.br. If ecotourism means wildlife then Manary are not eco at all, but they do offer unusual, exciting tours to the northeastern *sertão,* including the spectacular Serra da Capivara (to see the rock paintings), Cariri and the fossilized dinosaur prints in Paraíba. Very professional service.

Matueté, T011-3071 4515, www.matuete.com. Bespoke luxury options around Brazil including a range of private house rentals.

Open Door Tour Operator, R Alan Kardec, 87, Campo Grande/MS, T067-3321 8303, www.opendoortur.com.br. Specialize in travel to the Pantanal and the Amazon.

Tatur Turismo, Av Tancredo Neves 274, Centro Empresarial Iguatemi, Sala 228, Bloco B, Salvador, 41820-020, Bahia, T071-3114 7900, www.tatur.com.br. Very helpful bespoke Bahia-based agency who can organize tours throughout Brazil, especially in Bahia, using many of the smaller hotels.

Tourist information

The **Ministério do Turismo**, Esplanada dos Ministérios, Bloco U, 2nd and 3rd floors, Brasília, www.turismo.gov.br or www.braziltour.com, is in charge of tourism in Brazil and has information in many languages. **Embratur**, the Brazilian Institute of Tourism, is at the same address, and is in charge of promoting tourism abroad, T061-3429 7777. For information abroad, contact Brazil's representation overseas: France, T+33-1-5353 6962; Germany, T+49-69-9750 3251; Italy, T+39-2-8633 7791; Japan, T+81-8-5565 7591; Portugal, T+351-21-340 4668; Spain, T+34-91-503 0687; UK, T+44-207-7396 5551; USA, T+1-646-378 2126 and T+1-310-341 8394. For information and phone numbers for your country visit www.braziltour.com. Local tourist information bureaux are not usually helpful for information on cheap hotels and it is difficult to get information on neighbouring states. Expensive hotels provide tourist magazines for their guests. Telephone directories (not Rio) contain good street maps.

Other good sources of information are:
LATA, www.lata.org. The Latin American Travel Association, with useful country information and listings of all UK operators specializing in Latin America. Also has up-to-date information on public safety, health, weather, travel costs, economics and politics highlighted for each nation. Wide selection of Latin American maps available, as well as individual travel planning assistance.

South American Explorers, formerly the South American Explorers Club, 126 Indina Creek Rd, Ithaca, NY 14850, T607-277 0488, www.samexplo.org. A non-profit educational organization functioning primarily as an information network for South America. Useful for travellers to Brazil and the rest of the continent.

National parks

National parks are run by the Brazilian institute of environmental protection, **Ibama (Instituto Brasileiro do Meio Ambiente e dos Recursos Naturais Renováveis)**, SCEN Trecho 2, Av L-4 Norte, Edif Sede de Ibama, CEP 70818-900, Brasília, DF, T061-3316 1212, www.ibama.gov.br. For information, contact **Linha Verde**, T0800-618080, linhaverde.sede@ ibama.gov.br. National parks are open to visitors, usually with a permit from Ibama. See also the **Ministério do Meio Ambiente** website, www.mma.gov.br.

Useful websites

www.amcham.com.br American Chamber of Commerce in São Paulo. A good source of information on local markets.

www.brazil.org.uk Provides a broad range of info on Brazilian history and culture from the UK Brazilian embassy.

www.brazil4you.com Comprehensive travel and tourism info on everything from sights to hotels and weather.

www.brazilmax.com Excellent information on culture and lifestyle, the best available in English.

www.braziltourism.org The official tourism website of Brazil, and the best.

www.gringos.com.br An excellent source of information on all things Brazilian for visitors and ex-pats.

www.ipanema.com A quirky, informative site on all things Rio de Janeiro.

www.maria-brazil.org A wonderfully personal introduction to Brazil, specifically Rio, featuring Maria's cookbook and little black book, features and reviews.

www.rainforestweb.org Excellent accurate information on rainforest related issues with detailed comprehensive information on Brazil and extensive links.

www.socioambiental.org Invaluable for up-to-the-minute, accurate information on environmental and indigenous issues.

www.survival-international.org The world's leading campaign organization for indigenous peoples with excellent info on various Brazilian indigenous groups.

www.worldtwitch.com Birding information and comprehensive listings of rainforest lodges.

Visas and immigration

Visas are not required for stays of up to 90 days by tourists from Andorra, Argentina, Austria, Bahamas, Barbados, Belgium, Bolivia, Chile, Colombia, Costa Rica, Denmark, Ecuador, Finland, France, Germany, Greece, Iceland, Ireland, Italy, Liechtenstein, Luxembourg, Malaysia, Monaco, Morocco, Namibia, the Netherlands, Norway, Paraguay, Peru, Philippines, Portugal, San Marino, South Africa, Spain, Suriname, Sweden, Switzerland, Thailand, Trinidad and Tobago, United Kingdom, Uruguay, the Vatican and Venezuela. For them, only the following documents are required at the port of disembarkation: a passport valid for at least 6 months (or *cédula de identidad* for nationals of Argentina, Chile, Paraguay and Uruguay); and a return or onward ticket, or adequate proof that you can purchase your return fare, subject to no remuneration being received in Brazil and no legally binding or contractual documents being signed. Venezuelan passport holders can stay for 60 days on filling in a form at the border.

Citizens of the USA, Canada, Australia, New Zealand and other countries not mentioned above, and anyone wanting to stay longer than 180 days, *must* get a visa before arrival, which may, if you ask, be granted for multiple entry. US citizens must be fingerprinted on entry to Brazil. Visa fees vary from country to country, so apply to the Brazilian consulate in your home country. The consular fee in the USA is US$55. Students planning to study in Brazil or employees of foreign companies can apply for a 1- or 2-year visa. 2 copies of the application form, 2 photos, a letter from the sponsoring company or educational institution in Brazil, a police form showing no criminal convictions and a fee of around US$80 is required.

Extensions

Foreign tourists may stay a maximum of 180 days in any 1 year. 90-day renewals are easily obtainable, but only at least 15 days before the expiry of your 90-day permit, from the Polícia Federal. The procedure varies, but generally you have to: fill out 3 copies of the tax form at the Polícia Federal, take them to a branch of **Banco do Brasil**, pay US$15 and bring 2 copies back. You will then be given the extension form to fill in and be asked for your passport to stamp in the extension. According to regulations (which should be on display) you need to show a return ticket, cash, cheques or a credit card, a personal reference and proof of an address of a person living in the same city as the office (in practice you simply write this in the space on the form). Some offices will only give you an extension within 10 days of the expiry of your permit.

Some points of entry, such as the Colombian border, refuse entry for longer than 30 days, renewals are then for the same period, insist if you want 90 days. For longer stays you must leave the country and return (not the same day) to get a new 90-day permit. If your visa has expired, getting a new visa can be costly (US$35 for a consultation, US$30 for the visa itself) and may take anything up to 45 days, depending on where you apply. If you overstay your visa, or extension, you will be fined US$7 per day, with no upper limit. After paying the fine to Polícia Federal, you will be issued with an exit visa and must leave within 8 days.

Officially, if you leave Brazil within the 90-day permission to stay and then re-enter the country, you should only be allowed to stay until the 90-day permit expires. If, however, you are given another 90-day permit, this may lead to charges of overstaying if you apply for an extension.

Identification
You must always carry identification when in Brazil. Take a photocopy of the personal details in your passport, plus your Brazilian immigration stamp, and leave your passport in the hotel safe deposit. This photocopy, when authorized in a *cartório*, US$1, is a legitimate copy of your documents. Be prepared, however, to present the originals when travelling in sensitive border areas. Always keep an independent record of your passport details. Also register with your consulate to expedite document replacement if yours gets lost or stolen.

Warning Do not lose the entry/exit permit they give you when you enter Brazil. Leaving the country without it, you may have to pay up to US$100 per person. It is suggested that you photocopy this form and have it authenticated at a *cartório*, US$1, in case of loss or theft.

Weights and measures

Metric.

Working in Brazil

Volunteering
The **Task Brasil Trust**, T020-7735 5545, www.taskbrasil.org.uk, is a small UK-based charity set up to help abandoned street children in Brazil. It runs various projects to improve the lives of children and pregnant teenage girls, especially those living on the streets of Rio de Janeiro. You can get involved as a volunteer in Brazil, to help the children with sports, reading and writing, music, art and computer skills. Volunteer at the UK or US offices, or make a donation.

Contents

Footprint features

Rio de Janeiro

At a glance

⊖ **Getting around** Bus, metrô and taxi. Hiring a car is recommended for visiting the more remote areas in Rio state but not for the city.

◉ **Time required** At least 3 days to explore the city; 7-10 days for the city and state.

☀ **Weather** Summer (Dec-Mar) is warm and wet, up to 30°C; winter (Apr-Oct) is dry with blue skies.

✖ **When not to go** Good at any time but wet Dec-Jan. Hotel prices double over New Year and Carnaval.

Don't miss ...

1. Santa Teresa, page 95.
2. Corcovado, page 103.
3. Ipanema and Leblon, page 108.
4. Carnaval, page 132.
5. Parque Nacional da Serra dos Órgãos, page 163.
6. Parque Nacional de Itatiaia, page 172.

N

30 km
30 miles

RIO DE JANEIRO

Atlantic Ocean

São João da Barra
Campos
Lagoa Feia
São Fidelis
Macaé
Rio das Ostras
Barra de São João
Búzios
Cabo Frio
Arraial do Cabo
Araruama
L. de Araruama
Saquarema
Niterói
Neves

Cachoeiro do Itapemirim
Bom Jesus do Itabapoana
Itaperuna
Santo António de Pádua
Itaocara
Novo Friburgo

Ubá
Leopoldina
Rio Novo
Rio Pomba
Juiz de Fora
Matias Barbosa
Três Rios
Parque Nacional Sierra dos Órgãos
Teresópolis
Petrópolis

Prados
Tiradentes
São João del Rei
Barbacena
Santos Dumont
Lima Duarte
Ibitipoca
Conservatória
Valença
Vassouras
Miguel Pereira

Lavras
São Tomé das Letras
Caxambu
Parque Nacional do Itatiaia
Penedo
Visconde de Mauá
Resende
Getulândia
Itaguaí
Japeri
Itaruçu
Muriqui
Mangaratiba
Angra dos Reis
Abraão
Ilha Grande
Aventureiro
Dois Rios
Lopes Mendes
PN da Serra da Bocaina
Paraty

Rio de Janeiro

Rio Paraíba do Sul
Rio Preto

Even those who know nothing else of Brazil will have heard of Rio, its Mardi Gras carnival and its spectacular beach and mountain scenery. What many do not realize is that Rio de Janeiro is a state as well as a city, and that this state boasts beaches, forests and mountains just as beautiful as those in its capital. The southern coast, or Costa Verde, is fringed with emerald-green coves and bays that rise steeply to rainforest-covered hills pocked with national parks. Mountains swathed in coffee plantations sit behind Rio itself, with hill retreats once favoured by the imperial family dotted throughout their valleys and remnants of one of the world's most biodiverse forests covering parts of their slopes. To the northeast of the city lies a string of surf beaches and little resorts, the most celebrated of which is Búzios, a fishing village put on the map by Brigitte Bardot in the late 1960s, which has grown to become a chic little retreat for the state's middle classes.

Rio de Janeiro city

→ *Colour map 4, C3. Phone code: 021. Population: 8 million.*

According to Cariocas – the people of Rio de Janeiro – God made the world in six days and then spent the seventh lying on the beach in Ipanema. For in a city as beautiful as this, they say, only the philistine or the ungrateful would do anything else. Indeed, photographs cannot prepare you for Rio. There is far more to the city than Corcovado capped with Christ or the Sugar Loaf; these are overtures to the grand symphony of the scene. Rainforest-covered boulder mountains as high as Snowdon rise sheer from the sea around the vast Guanabara Bay and stretch to the horizon. Their curves and jags are broken by long sweeping beaches of powder-fine sand pounded by the dazzling green ocean, or by perfect half-moon coves lapped by the gentle waters of the bay. The city clusters around them, climbing over hills and crowding behind beaches and lakes. Its neighbourhoods are connected by tunnels bored through the ancient rock or across winding double-decker highways that cling vertiginously to the cliffs above the fierce Atlantic Ocean.

Against this magical backdrop, the famous Carioca day leisurely unwinds. When the sun is up the middle classes head for the beach, wearing nothing but tiny speedos or bikinis. Here they surf, play beach volleyball or football, or soak up the rays between occasional dips into the waves, with the working day just a brief interruption. When the sun is down, still wearing almost nothing, they head for the botecos (street bars) for an ice-cold draught beer or chope. Then they go home, finally put some clothes on and prepare to go out until the early hours of the morning.

From high on the hills, the other Rio watches over the middle classes. Here lie the favelas – slum cities where the poor and predominantly black communities live. These are Rio's engine of blue-collar work, but also its cultural heart; carnival, samba and Brazilian football were born here. Favelas are at the core of the country's cinema resurgence and the soul of the music of Seu Jorge and Afro-reggae. Brazil's joyful spirit can be felt most strongly in the favelas, alongside its greatest misery and its most shocking violence. ➤➤ *For listings, see pages 115-146.*

Ins and outs

Getting there

Air Rio is served by two airports. **Aeroporto Internacional Tom Jobim** (formerly Galeão and often still called by this name) ① *Ilha do Governador, 15 km north of the city centre*, receives international and domestic flights. There are *câmbios* in the departure hall and on the first floor of international arrivals. The **Banco do Brasil** on the third floor (open 24 hours) has better rates of exchange. There are also ATMs for major Brazilian banks, several of which accept Visa and MasterCard. Duty-free shops are well stocked and open to arrivals as well as departures. There are **Riotur** information booths in the domestic arrivals hall of Terminal 1 (T021-3398 4077, daily 0600-2300), and in the international arrivals hall in Terminal 2 (T021-3398 2245, daily 0600-2400), which provide maps and can book accommodation. **Santos Dumont Airport** ① *in the city centre on Guanabara Bay*, is used for Rio–São Paulo shuttle flights (see Transport, page 141), a handful of other domestic routes, private planes or air taxis. For more information visit www.infraero.gov.br and click on 'aeroportos'.

Taxis can be booked from within the airports or picked up at the stands outside the terminals. Fixed-rate taxis charge around US$30 from Jobim to Copacabana and Ipanema and US$25 to the city centre and Santa Teresa (about half as much from Santos Dumont);

buy a ticket at the counter. Metered taxis cost around US$25 from Jobim to Copacabana, but beware of pirate taxis, which are unlicensed.

There are frequent buses between the two airports, the *rodoviária* (interstate bus station) and the city; the best are the air-conditioned **Real Auto**, T0800-240850, www.realauto onibus.com.br, which leave from outside arrivals at terminals 1 and 2 and run 0500-2400, US$3. There are two routes: *Linha 2018 via Orla da Zona Sul*, runs every 30 minutes, to the Terminal Alvorada bus station in Barra da Tijuca and back again, stopping at the *rodoviária*, Avenida Rio Branco in the centre, Santos Dumont airport, Flamengo, Copacabana, Ipanema, São Conrado and Barra's Avenida das Americas. (This should not be confused with the *Linha 2018 via Linha Vermelha*, which runs a sporadic circular route via Barra and nowhere else of any use to foreign tourists.) *Linha 2145* runs every 25 minutes to Santos Dumont airport and back again, calling at Avenida Rio Branco along the way. Buses can be flagged down anywhere along their route and passengers can request to jump off at any time. There is also a standard Rio bus running along the 2018 line with similar frequency, US$2. See Transport, page 141.

1 Rio de Janeiro Metrô

→ Rio de Janeiro maps
1 Rio de Janeiro metrô, page 73
2 Rio de Janeiro orientation, page 74

Not to scale

Line 1 Line 2

PAVUNA

PENHA

ANCHIETA

Nossa Senhora
da Penha

INHAÚMA

PILARES

JACARÉ

PRAÇA
SECA

AGUA SANTA

MÉIER

TAQUARA

Linha Amarela

GRAJAÚ

JACAREPAGUÁ

Pico da Tijuca

Parque Nacional
da Tijuca

Bom
Retiro

Paulo e
Virginia Grotto

Mayrink
Chapel

Cascatinha
Taunay

Museu Açude

Autódromo

VILA CANOA

Lagoa de
Jacarepaguá

Jacarepaguá

Terra
Encantada

Lagoa
da Tijuca

Pedra Bonita

Bosque da Barra
(Parque Arruda Câmara)

Barra
Shopping

Pedra da
Gávea

Av das Américas

JOÁ

Lagoa
Marapendi

RECREIO DOS
BANDEIRANTES

BARRA DA TIJUCA

Av Ayrton Senna

To Museu Casa do Pontal

Tom Jobim
(Galeão)

MONERO

Ilha do Governador

To Ilha de Paquetá

RIBEIRA

Av Brasil

RAMOS

Ilha do Fundão

Baía de Guanabara

101

Rio-Niterói
Bridge

To Niterói

SÃO
CRISTOVÃO

GAMBOA

Ilha das Cobras

Ilha Fiscal

3

NITERÓI

Quinta da
Boa Vista

Rodoviária
Novo Rio

5

Central

4

Praça 15 de
Novembro

Maracanã
Stadium

Sambódromo

CENTRO

LAPA

Santos Dumont

GLÓRIA

*Enseada
da Glória*

TIJUCA

SANTA
TERESA

6

CATETE

USINA

FLAMENGO

7

URCA

Pão de Açúcar ▲

Corcovado
Christ

Parque Laje

Túnel Rebouças

BOTAFOGO

8

ALTO DA
BOA VISTA

Morro do Leme

9

LAGOA

Jardim
Botânico

COPACABANA

❀
Mesa do
Imperador

❀
Vista
Chinesa

Instituto
Moreira
Salles

Planetário

Lagoa de
Freitas

GÁVEA

LEBLON

IPANEMA

ROCINHA

Morro
Dois Irmãos ▲

10

*Ponta do
Arpoador*

SÃO CONRADO

N

Atlantic Ocean

1 km
1 mile

Bus International and interstate buses arrive at the **Rodoviária Novo Rio** ① *Av Francisco Bicalho 01 at Rodrigues Alves, Santo Cristo, (see Northern Rio map, page 92), T021-3213 1800, www.novorio.com.br*. There is a **Riotur information centre** ① *T021-2263 4857, daily 0700-1900*, which can help with orientation and accommodation. Left luggage costs US$5. There are *câmbios* (cash only) and ATMs. From the *rodoviária* it is best to take a taxi to your hotel or to the nearest metrô station (Metrô Estácio); taxis can be booked at the booth on the ground floor. The metrô runs south as far as Copacabana (Metrô Cantagalo); for Ipanema and Leblon head to Metrô Siqueira Campos and take a taxi from there, or take bus marked 'Metrô-Gávea'.

The **local bus terminal** is just outside the *rodoviária*: turn right as you leave and run the gauntlet of taxi drivers. The bus station attracts thieves, so exercise caution. The air-conditioned **Real** bus (opposite the exit) goes along the beach to São Conrado and will secure luggage. If you need a taxi collect a ticket from the office inside the entrance as this protects against over-charging; a taxi to Flamengo costs approximately US$10.

Getting around

The city is made up of separate districts connected by urban highways and tunnels heavy with traffic, so it's best to use public transport or taxis to get around. An underground railway, the **Metrô** ① *T0800-2595 1111, www.metrorio.com.br, Mon-Sat 0500-2400, Sun and holidays 0700-2300 and 24 hrs during Carnaval*, runs from the outer suburbs of the Zona Norte (not of tourist interest), through the city centre, Glória, Flamengo, Botafogo and as far south as Copacabana. The Metrô-Gávea and Metrô-Barra buses connect at the penultimate station – Siqueira Campos – for Ipanema, Leblon and Barra. **Buses** run to all parts, but should be treated with caution at night, when taxis are a better bet. Buses are usually marked with the destination and any going south of the centre will call at Copacabana and generally Ipanema/Leblon. **Minivans** run from Avenida Rio Branco in the centre as far south as Barra da Tijuca and have the destination written on the window. **Taxis** should always be booked through a hostel or hotel, or caught from a designated taxi *posto*; the name of the *posto* should be written in navy blue on the side of the taxi. Avoid freelance taxis hailed in the street or those without a taxi rank inscription. Santa Teresa is reached by **tram** which leaves from the Largo da Carioca, near the metrô station and the cathedral, passing over the Lapa viaduct and running along all the main streets in Santa Teresa and eventually reaching either Dois Irmãos or Paula Mattos at the far end of Santa Teresa (see page 95).

Best time to visit

Rio has one of the healthiest climates in the tropics, with trade winds keeping the air fresh. June, July and August are the coolest months, with temperatures ranging from 22°C (18°C in a cold spell) to 32°C on a sunny day at noon. December to March is hot and humid, with temperatures of 32-42°C. October to March is the rainy season; the annual rainfall is about 1120 mm. **Carnaval** is a movable feast, running for five riotous days from the Friday afternoon before Shrove Tuesday to the morning hangover of Ash Wednesday.

Tourist information

Riotur ① *Praça Pio X, 119, 9th floor, Centro, T021-2271 7000, www.riodejaneiro-turismo. com.br and www.rio.rj.gov.br/riotur*, is the city's government tourist office. There are also booths or offices in **Copacabana** ① *Av Princesa Isabel 183, T021-2541 7522, Mon-Fri 0900-1800*, and **Copacabana Posto Seis** ① *Av Rainha Elizabeth 36 at NS de Copacabana, T021-2513 0077, Mon-Fri 0900-1800*. The helpful staff speak English, French and German and can provide good city maps and a very useful free brochure. There are further information stands at **Corcovado** ⓘ *R Cosme Velho 513, T021-2258 1329 ext 4, on the upper and lower levels of the elevator*, and at the international airport and Novo Rio bus station. There is also a free telephone information service, *Alô Rio*, in Portuguese and English, T0800-2285 5000 or T021-2252 8080 (from outside Rio).

The state tourism organization is **Turisrio** ⓘ *R da Ajuda 5, 6th floor, Centro, T021-2215 0011, www.turisrio.rj.gov.br, Mon-Fri 0900-1800*. The private sector **Rio Convention and Visitors Bureau** ⓘ *R Visconde de Pirajá 547, suite 610, Ipanema, T021-2259 6165, www.rio conventionbureau.com.br*, also offers information and assistance in English. **Embratur** ⓘ *R Uruguaiana 174, 8th floor, Centro, T021-2509 6017, www.braziltour.com*, provides information on the whole country.

Guidebooks *Trilhas do Rio*, by Pedro da Cunha e Menezes (Editora Salamandra, second edition), US$22.50, describes walking trips around Rio. For a light-hearted approach to living in Rio, see *How to be a Carioca*, by Priscilla Ann Goslin. Danusia Barbara's *Restaurantes do Rio* (Senac Rio) is a widely respected gastronomic guide. Casa da Palavra publishes a series of architectural guides to Rio, *Guia da Arquitetura*, in Portuguese and English. Many hotels provide guests with a useful free tourist booklet, *Guia do Rio*, which is published quarterly and has the most up-to-date listings.

Maps The *Guia Quatro Rodas – Rio* map book is the only completely comprehensive street map and is essential if you are driving. It can be bought at most newsstands.

Newspapers and magazines Advertisements in the classified sections of dailies *O Globo* and *Jornal do Brasil* proffer apartments for rent and other such services. Both have entertainments pages too; *O Globo* has a travel section on Thursday; the *Jornal do Brasil's Programa* on Friday is an essential 'what's-on' magazine. Even better is the Rio supplement to *Veja*, a weekly news magazine. *Caro Amigos*, http://carosamigos.terra.com.br, is Brazil's most influential centre-left magazine.

Websites www.brazilmax.com is by far the best site, with very useful and incisive cultural information, events listings and articles in English on the whole country. www.ipanema.com has practical information about Rio. www.samba-choro.com.br has information about carioca music, venues and new releases. www.guiadasemana.com.br is an excellent entertainment site, with cinema, theatre and restaurant listings (in Portuguese). There are internet cafés throughout the city and 90% of hotels and hostels offer internet access.

Background

The coast of Rio de Janeiro was first settled about 5000 years ago. When the Europeans arrived, the indigenous inhabitants belonged to the Tupi or Tupi-Guarani, Botocudos, Puri and Maxacali linguistic groups. Tragically, no indigenous people in this region survived the European incursions.

The Portuguese navigator, Gonçalo Coelho, landed at what is now Rio de Janeiro on 1 January 1502. Mistaking the Baía de Guanabara (the name the local people used) to be the mouth of a great river, they called it the 'January River'. But the bay wasn't settled until 1555 when the French, under the Huguenot Admiral Nicholas Durand de Villegagnon, occupied Lage Island. They later transferred to Seregipe Island (now Villegagnon), where they built the fort of Coligny. The fort has been demolished to make way for the Escola

Naval (naval college), and the island itself, since the narrow channel was filled up, has become a part of the mainland. Villegagnon set up a colony as the starting point for what he called Antarctic France.

In 1559-1560, Mem de Sá, the third governor of Brazil, mounted an expedition from Salvador to attack the French, who were supported by the indigenous Tamoio. The Portuguese succeeded in capturing the French fort and putting an end to Antarctic France, but did not colonize the area until 1567 when they transferred their settlement to the Morro de São Januário. This is generally considered the date of the founding of the city of São Sebastião do Rio de Janeiro, so called in honour of the Portuguese prince who would soon assume the throne.

Though constantly attacked by local indigenous groups, the new city grew rapidly and when King Sebastião divided Brazil into two provinces, Rio was chosen as capital of the southern captaincies. Salvador became sole capital again in 1576, but Rio again became the southern capital in 1608 and the seat of a bishopric. There was a further French incursion in 1710-1711 as a result of the tension between France and Portugal during the war of Spanish Succession, and because of the flow of gold out of Minas Gerais through Rio. Rio de Janeiro was by now becoming the leading city in Brazil. Not only was it the port out of which gold was shipped, but it was also the focus of the export/import trade of the surrounding agricultural lands. On 27 January 1763, it became the seat of the viceroy. After independence, in 1834, it was declared capital of the empire and remained so for 125 years.

The shaping of a city

When the Portuguese royal family fled to Brazil in 1808, the ideas that were brought over from Europe started a major transformation of the city. True, works to beautify and clean up the place had been undertaken when the city acquired viceregal status, but the remodelling that occurred in the early 19th century was on a different scale (see Fine art and architecture on pages 796 and 801). The city also expanded, growing north into São Cristóvão and Tijuca and south through Glória, Catete, Flamengo and Botafogo. The prosperous coffee barons and business class built their mansions and the imperial court was the centre of the nation's attention. The decline of the coffee trade in Rio de Janeiro state and the proclamation of the Republic did not affect the city's dominance as political, economic and cultural heart of Brazil.

Growth continued into the 20th century and one of the most significant acts was the construction of a monumental new boulevard through the middle of the commercial district. The 33-m-wide Avenida Central, later renamed Avenida Rio Branco, was driven through the old city's narrow streets in 1904-1905 as the principal means of access in Rio. Meanwhile, the city continued to expand outwards: north into industrial zones; south around the coast; and inland, up the hills, mainly in the form of *favelas* (slums).

When, in 1960, the nation's capital was moved to Brasília, Rio went into decline, especially the commercial centre, and began to suffer badly from poor urban planning decisions and too many high-rise buildings. However, in the late 1990s, the mayor of the city, Luiz Paulo Conde, embarked on a massive programme of regenerating the centre through remodelling and attracting residents to neglected districts. As an architect and urbanist, he brought a social vision that encompasses the improvement of *favelas* and a plan to clean up the south of the city as far as Leblon.

In December 1997 a new 25-km expressway, the Linha Amarela, was opened from the Ilha do Fundão, near the international airport, to Barra da Tijuca, cutting the journey time to Barra by more than half.

Central Rio and Lapa

Hot and sweaty central Rio spreads back from Guanabara Bay in a jumbled grid of streets between Santos Dumont airport and the Jesuit Mosteiro São Bento. It dates from 1567, but much of its architectural heritage has been laid waste by successive waves of government intent on wiping out the past in favour of dubious and grandiose visions of Order and Progress. Nevertheless it remains the centre of Rio's history as well as the city, with some distinguished colonial buildings, Manueline follies and elaborate neoclassical facades huddled together under totalitarian blocks of flats and Le Corbusier-inspired concrete. All watch over a mass of cars and a bustle of people: business suits on lunch, beggars, skateboarders dressed in would-be New York oversized jeans and baseball caps, street performers and opportunists looking to snatch a purse. It can all feel a bit hectic and bewildering. But don't give up. There is plenty to explore here and a wealth of air-conditioned havens in which to escape for respite and a coffee.

The greatest concentration of historic buildings is in the south of the centre, near Santos Dumont airport and around **Praça 15 de Novembro**, from where Rio de Janeiro grew in its earliest days. Here you'll find most of the museums, some of the city's more beautiful little churches and colonial buildings such as the **Paço Imperial** and the **Palácio Tiradentes**. More colonial buildings lie at the centre's northern extremity around the Morro de São Bento. These include the finest baroque building in Rio, the **Mosteiro de São Bento**, and the city's most imposing church, **Nossa Senhora da Candelária**.

The city's main artery is the **Avenida Presidente Vargas**, 4.5 km long and more than 90 m wide, which divides these northern and southern sections. It begins at the waterfront, splits around the Candelária church, then crosses the Avenida Rio Branco in a magnificent straight stretch past the **Central do Brasil** railway station. Vargas is dissected by two important arterial streets. **Avenida Rio Branco**, nearest to the sea, was once lined with splendid ornate buildings, which were quite the equal of any in Buenos Aires. These have largely been razed to the ground but a few remain around **Cinelândia. Avenida 31 Março**, further to the west beyond the railway station, leads to the **Sambódromo** and the Carnaval district. Some of the better modern architecture is to be found along Avenida República do Chile, including the conical 1960s **Catedral Metropolitana de São Sebastião**.

Ins and outs

For Praça 15 de Novembro, Largo do Carioca, Cinelândia and Lapa take the metrô to Carioca in Cinelândia. For Candelária and São Bento take the metrô to Uruguiana. For the Cidade Nova and Sambódromo take the metrô to Praça Onze. Opening times for churches, museums and public buildings change frequently. All museums close during Carnaval.

Praça 15 de Novembro and the imperial palaces

Originally an open space at the foot of the Morro do Castelo – a hill which has now been flattened – the Praça 15 de Novembro (often called Praça Quinze) has always been one of the focal points in Rio de Janeiro. Today it has one of the greatest concentrations of historic buildings in the city. Having been through various phases of development, the area underwent major remodelling in the late 1990s. The last vestiges of the original harbour, at the seaward end of the *praça*, were restored. Avenida Alfredo Agache now goes through an underpass, creating an open space between the *praça* and the seafront and giving easy access to the ferry dock for Niterói. The area is well illuminated and clean

③ Rio de Janeiro centre

Eating 🍴
Adega Flor de Coimbra 3 E4

Café da Moda & Folic 2 C4
Confeitaria Colombo 8 C4

Republique 4 C2
Bar Luiz 1 C4

To Rodoviária

Av Perimetral

Praça Mauá

Morro de São Bento

Mosteiro de São Bento

Lad J Home

Do Acre Bento Cons Saraiva

Dom Gerardo

B do Bragança

Rangel

M Neiva

Visc de Inhaúma

R Candelária

Visc de Itaboraí

Cais dos Mineiros

Ilha das Cobras

Rio de Janeiro maps
2 Rio de Janeiro orientation, page 74
3 **Rio de Janeiro centre, page 80**
4 Praça 15 de Novembro, page 82

Baía de Guanabara

To Ilha Fiscal

Daemon

Teófilo Otóni

Santa Rita

Candelária

1 de Março

Mercado

Andradas

Museu de Farmácia Antônio Lago

Miguel Couto

Alfândega

Buenos Aires

Do Rosário

Ouvidor

Praça 15 de Novembro

Paço Imperial

Ferry Dock

Uruguaiana

NS do Rosário e São Benedito dos Pretos

Real Gabinete Português e Leitura

São Francisco de Paula

Quitanda

Carmo

Av Presidente Kubitschek

Av Alfredo Agache

Camões

Teatro João Caetano

7 de Setembro

Gonçalves Dias

Rod Silva

Da Assembléia

São José

dom Manoel

Teatro

Carioca

Av Rio Branco

Av Nilo Peçanha

E Braga

Praça Rui Barbosa

Museu da Imagem e do Som

Museu Histórico Nacional

Ordem Terceira de São Francisco da Penitência

Largo da Carioca

Carioca

Av Presidente Antônio Carlos

Praça do Expedicionário

Largo de Misericórdia

Convento de Santo Antônio

Alm Barroso

Av M G Aranha

Debret

Av General Justo

Av República do Chile

Av 13 de Maio

Museu Nacional de Belas-Artes

Av Porto Alegre

Palácio Gustavo Capanema

Santa Luzia

S Luzia

Av Mal Câmara

Catedral Metropolitana de São Sebastião

Prof T Gama

Theatro Municipal

Praça Floriano

Biblioteca Nacional

Pedro Lessa

Av México

Churchill

Roosevelt

To Santos Dumont Airport

Tram Terminus

Alvin

Sen Dantas

Cinelândia

Av Pres Wilson

Arcos da Lapa

Av República do Paraguai

Evaristo da Veiga

Marrecas

Praça Mahatma Gandhi

Av Beira Mar

Sílvio Romero

Escola da Música da Universidade Federal do Rio de Janeiro

Passeio Público

tex de Freitas

Av Augusto Severo

Av Infante D Henrique

Museu de Arte Moderna

Convento de Santa Teresa

Joaquim

Sala Cecília Meireles

Parque do Flamengo

4

6

LAPA

5

To Botafogo

6

Sabor Saúde **7** C5

Bars & clubs 🍸
Rio Scenarium **6** D3

and the municipality has started to stage shows, music and dancing in the *praça*. At weekends an antiques, crafts, stamp and coin fair (Feirarte II) is held 0900-1900. The rather modest colonial former royal palace, **Paço Imperial** ⓘ *on the southeast corner of Praça 15 de Novembro, T021-2533 4407, www.pacoimperial.com.br, Tue-Sun 1200-1800*, is one of the centre's landmarks. It was built in 1743 as the residence of the governor of the Capitania and was made into the royal palace when the Portuguese court moved to Brazil. After independence it became the imperial palace. It fell into disuse in the mid-20th century to be resurrected as a temporary exhibition space and arts centre. There's often something interesting on display here, and two decent air-conditioned café-restaurants, the **Bistro** and **Atrium**, provide respite from the heat. Just north of the palace is the **Chafariz do Mestre Valentim**, or Chafariz do Pirâmide; a fountain designed by the famous sculptor.

Beside the Paço Imperial, across Rua da Assembléia, is the grand neoclassical **Palácio Tiradentes** ⓘ *T021-2588 1411, Mon-Sat 1000-1700, Sun and holidays 1200-1700, guided visits by appointment only, T021-2588 1251*. It was named in honour of the former dentist (*tiradentes* means teeth puller), Joaquim José da Silva Xavier, who is often seen as the symbolic father of Brazilian independence, and who was held prisoner here and executed nearby. The building itself was constructed between 1922 and 1926 and is now the state legislative assembly. A **statue of Tiradentes** by Francisco de Andrade stands in front.

④ **Praça 15 de Novembro**

➡ Rio de Janeiro maps
2 Rio de Janeiro orientation, page 74
3 Rio de Janeiro centre, page 80
4 Praça 15 de Novembro, page 82

Eating ⓣ
Albamar **5** C3
Bar des Artes **4** C3

Cais do Oriente **3** B2

Bars & clubs ⓝ
Mercado **1** B3

Largo da Misericórdia and the museums

There is a cluster of interesting little museums south of Praça XV on the way to Santos Dumont airport that can be reached by the Largo da Misericórdia, which runs immediately south of the Palácio Tiradentes. At the end of the *largo* is the **Ladeira da Misericórdia**; the oldest street in Rio and now just a severed stump on the side of the grand Santa Casa da Misericórdia hospital. This hill was once crowned by a magnificent monastery and fort that watched out over the bay. Next door to the hospital, in a series of handsome buildings, is the **Museu Histórico Nacional** ① *Praça Marechal Âncora, T021-2550 9224, www.museuhitoriconacional.com.br, Tue-Fri 1000-1730, Sat and Sun 1400-1800, US$3, free on Sun*. This is one of the city's more distinguished museums, with a collection of magnificent carriages, historical treasures, colonial sculpture and furniture, maps, paintings, arms and armour, silver and porcelain. It also retains a rampart from that first fort that crowned the former Morro do Castelo hill from the 1603 until the 20th century. The building was once the war arsenal of the empire, and was partly constructed in 1762 (this part is called the 'Casa do Trem'). The **Museu da Imagem e do Som (MIS)** ① *Praça Rui Barbosa 1, T021-2262 7653, Mon-Fri 1100-1700, www.mis.rj.gov.br, free, visits by appointment only*, houses a collection of cinema images, photos of Rio and of Carioca musicians, and recordings of popular music including early *choro* by artists including Jacob do Bandolim. There are booths for listening to music and a small cinema for watching the 16 mm and 35 mm film archive. At the time of writing, the museum was open only on Tuesdays and Fridays due to refurbishment in early 2009.

Travessa do Comércio and the Carmelite churches

North of Praça XV, the **Travessa do Comércio** and its continuation to the left, the **Rua do Ouvidor**, are reached via the **Arco do Teles** directly across from the palace. The arch is all that remains of an 18th-century construction, now incorporated into a modern building, and the two streets give an idea of how most of Rio must have looked in the 19th century. Little bars and restaurants line the streets and are very lively after 1800. These include the **Arco Imperial**, where Carmen Miranda lived between 1925 and 1930 (her mother kept a boarding house). There are also some interesting bookshops and one of Brazil's prettiest little baroque churches, **Nossa Senhora da Lapa dos Mercadores** ① *R do Ouvidor 35, T021-2509 2239, Mon-Fri 0800-1400*. This began life as a street oratory erected in a blind alley by market vendors who traditionally petitioned Our Lady of Lapa for help in hard times; it became a church in 1750, was remodelled in 1869-1872 and has now been fully restored.

The busy thoroughfare of Rua 1 de Março cuts across the top of Praça XV and Rua Ouvidor and is littered with Carmelite churches, all of them worth a quick look. The most famous is at the northwestern corner of the *praça*: **Nossa Senhora do Carmo da Antiga Sé** ① *R 1 de Março at R 7 de Setembro 14, T021-2509 2239, Tue-Thu 0900-1700, Sat 1100-1700*, has one of the finest baroque interiors in Rio and occupies the site of the original founding Carmelite chapel, which stood here between 1590 and 1754. The current church dates from 1761. After the arrival of the Portuguese court in 1808 it became the designated Royal Chapel and subsequently the city's first cathedral – between 1900 and 1976. The crypt allegedly holds the remains of Pedro Alvares Cabral, the European discoverer of Brazil; a claim disputed by the town of Santarém in Portugal. Just north of this church and right in front of the end of Rua Ouvidor is the **Igreja da Ordem Terceira do Monte do Carmo** ① *R 1 de Março s/n, Mon-Fri 0800-1400, Sat 0800-1200*. This was built in 1754, consecrated in

1770 and rebuilt in the 19th century. It has strikingly beautiful portals by Mestre Valentim (see Fine Art and Sculpture, page 796), the son of a Portuguese nobleman and a slave girl. He also created the main altar of fine moulded silver, the throne and its chair and much else. At the rear of the old cathedral and the Igreja da Ordem Terceira do Monte do Carmo, on Rua do Carmo, is the **Oratório de Nossa Senhora do Cabo da Boa Esperança**; one of the few remaining public oratories from the colonial period in Rio.

Candelária and around

Rio's most imposing church lies on an island in a sea of traffic some 500 m north of Praça XV. The mock-Italianate **Igreja de Nossa Senhora da Candelária** ① *Praça Pio X, T021-2233 2324, Mon-Fri 0730-1600, Sat 0800-1200, Sun 0900-1300*, has long been the church of 'society Rio'. Celebrities still gather here in the marble interior for the city's most prestigious weddings. The church is modelled on the Basílica da Estrela in Portugal. The tiles in the dome are from Lisbon, the marble inside is Veronan and the heavy bronze doors were commissioned from France. All were shipped across at vast expense in the late 18th century, during an era when even though such materials were readily available in Brazil at similar quality and far lower prices, snob value demanded that they be imported. The church was built on the site of a chapel founded in 1610 by the Spaniard Antônio Martins Palma who arrived in Rio after surviving a terrible storm at sea. He erected the chapel in homage to Nuestra Señora de Candelária, the patron saint of his home, La Palma island in the Canaries.

There are a number of cultural centres near the church. The **Centro Cultural Correios** ① *R Visconde de Itaboraí 20, T021-2253 1580, www.correios.com.br, Tue-Sun 1200-1900, free*, in a smart early 20th-century building with a little private park, is a good stop for an air-conditioned juice or coffee. It has a theatre, a 1000-sq-m concert hall and spaces for temporary exhibitions and cultural events, and a postage stamp fair on Saturdays. Just opposite, with entrances on Avenida Presidente Vargas and Rua 1 de Março 66, is the **Centro Cultural Banco do Brasil (CCBB)** ① *R 1 de Março 66, T021-3808 2020, www.bb.com.br/cultura, Tue-Sun 1000-2100*, in a fine early 19th-century neoclassical building with a beautiful glass domed roof. The centre hosts many of the city's large and distinguished art shows, including some excellent photographic exhibitions. It also has an arts cinema, library, multimedia facilities and lunchtime concerts (around US$5). The restaurant is air-conditioned and the food respectable. At the corner of Rua Visconde de Itaboraí (No 253) and Avenida Presidente Vargas, just opposite Candelária, is the **Casa França-Brasil** ① *R Visconde de Itaboraí 78, T021-2253 5366, www.casafrancabrasil.com.br, Tue-Sun 1000-2000*, a Franco-Brazilian cultural centre designed by one of the key players in the 19th-century French cultural mission to Rio, Grandjean de Montigny. It holds temporary exhibitions exploring the long relationship between the two countries. The newest of the cultural centres near Candelária is the **Espaço Cultural da Marinha** ① *Av Alfredo Agache, on the waterfront, T021-2104 6025, www.sdm.mar.mil.br/espaco.htm, Tue-Sun 1200-1700, free*. This former naval establishment, built on a jetty over the bay, now contains museums of underwater archaeology and navigation. *Galeota*, the boat used by the Portuguese royal family for sailing around the Baía de Guanabara is kept here and a Second World War submarine and warship, the *Bauru* (not to be confused with the sandwich of the same name), is moored outside. The museum is very popular with Brazilian children and is crowded at weekends.

Just offshore, but connected to the mainland by a causeway to Ilha das Cobras, is the **Ilha Fiscal** ① *T021-2104 6992, boats leave Thu-Sun at 1300, 1430 and 1600, closed 1 Jan,*

Carnaval, Holy Week and Christmas. It was built as a customs house at the emperor's request, but he deemed it too beautiful, and said that it should be used only for official parties. Only one was ever held – a masked ball hosted by the viscount of Ouro Preto in honour of the crew of the Chilean warship, *The Admiral Cochrane*, five days before the republic began. It is now a museum, linked with the Espaço Cultural da Marinha. The island is passed by the ferry to Niterói.

Mosteiro de São Bento

The **Praça Mauá**, which lies north of Avenida Presidente Vargas, marks the end of Centro and the beginning of the port zone. Many of the empty warehouses here are used as workshops by the samba schools for the construction of their beautiful carnival floats. The area would be unremarkable were it not for the **Mosteiro de São Bento** ① *R Gerardo 68, T021-2516 2286, www.osb.org.br, daily 0700-1730, free, guided tours Mon-Sat 0900-1600; modest dress, no shorts; taxi from the city centre US$6,* whose sober Brazilian baroque façade sits on a promontory looking out over the bay. It is widely publicized as a World Heritage Site, which it is not. But of all the city's colonial buildings this is the most worth visiting, both for its magnificent interior and for its significance as the most important Benedictine monument outside Europe. The church began life in 1586 with a group of monks who arrived in Rio from Salvador and it grew to become the most powerful monastery in the city. It preserves a lavish gilt baroque interior but is very poorly lit (the church charges an absurd US$5 to put on all of the electric lights). However, in the gloom it is possible to make out that not an inch remains unadorned. The three doors sculpted by Father Domingos da Conceição, which give access to the nave, and the sculptures of St Benedict, St Escolastica and Our Lady of Monserrat are particularly remarkable. The last, which is also by Domingos de Conceição, has painted birds' eggs for eyes. The painting is as wonderful as the carving; particularly the panels in the Blessed Sacrament chapel by Inácio Ferreira Pinto and *O Salvador*, the masterpiece of Brazil's first painter, Frei Ricardo do Pilar, which hangs in the sacristy. The enormous candelabra are attributed to Mestre Valentim, Rio's most celebrated church artisan, and are made from solid silver especially imported from Peru and the mines of Potosí in Bolivia at a price higher than Brazil's own gold. The monastery's library (open to men only) preserves a number of priceless religious manuscripts alongside 200,000 other books.

São Bento can be reached either by a narrow road from Rua Dom Gerardo 68, or by a lift whose entrance is at Rua Dom Gerardo 40. Both routes lead to a *praça* with tall trees, but arriving in the lift is more magical as you are whisked from the heat and bustle of the dock area to an oasis of calm, which sets the mood beautifully for a wander around the monastery buildings. If you would rather walk, the monastery is a few minutes from Praça Mauá, turning left off Avenida Rio Branco; Rua Dom Gerardo 68 is behind the massive new RBI building. Every Sunday at 1000 there is a Latin Mass with plainsong. Arrive an hour early to get a seat. On other days, Mass is at 0715 and the monks often sing at vespers.

Largo da Carioca and around

This higgledy-piggledy street of colonial churches, modern buildings and street stalls sits between Rua da Carioca and the Carioca metrô station about 1 km south of Praça XV along Rua da Assembléia. There is a variety of interesting sights here within a very small area. The **Convento de Santo Antônio** ① *T021-2262 0129, Mon, Wed, Thu, Fri 0730-1900, Tue 0630-2000, Sat 0730-1100 and 1530-1700, Sun 0900-1100, free,* the second oldest in Rio, sits on a little hill off the Largo da Carioca. You will often see single women here gathered to pray: there are many more women than men in Brazil and St Anthony is traditionally a provider of husbands. The church interior is baroque around the chancel, main altars and two lateral altars, which are devoted to St Anthony, St Francis and the Immaculate Conception respectively. The beautiful sacristy is decorated with *azulejos* (tiles) and adorned with paintings depicting scenes from St Anthony's life. Many members of the Brazilian imperial family are buried in the mausoleum. Separated from this church only by a fence of iron railings is one of Rio's least-known baroque jewels: the little church of the **Ordem Terceira de São Francisco da Penitência** ① *T021-2262 0197, Mon-Fri 0900-1200 and 1300-1600, free*, which was built between 1622 and 1738. It has a splendid gilt interior by Francisco Xavier de Brito, who is largely credited with introducing baroque to Brazil and who was probably Aleijadinho's teacher in Ouro Preto. There's a also a fine panel depicting the glorification of St Francis by Caetano da Costa Coelho Behind the church is a tranquil catacomb-filled garden.

A couple of streets north, at the end of Rua do Ouvidor and dominating the square that bears its name, is the twin-towered **Igreja de São Francisco de Paula** ① *Largo São Francisco de Paula, Mon-Fri 0900-1300, free*, with some fine examples of Carioca art including carvings by Mestre Valentim, paintings by Vítor Meireles and murals by Manuel da Cunha. Across the Largo de São Francisco and on the corner of Rua Uruguaiana 77 and Ouvidor is the **Igreja de Nossa Senhora do Rosário e São Benedito dos Pretos** ① *T021-2224 2900, Mon-Fri 0700-1700, Sat 0700-1300, free*. Since the 17th century this church has been at the centre of African Christian culture in Rio. During the 19th century it was the site of an elaborate festival that recreated scenes from the courtly life of the king of Congo. A king and queen were crowned and they danced through the nearby streets followed by long parades of courtiers in fancy dress; a precursor perhaps for Carnaval. It was here that the announcements for the final abolition of slavery were prepared. The church once had a fabulous gilt interior but this was sadly destroyed in a fire in 1967. Next to the church is a small museum devoted to slavery in Brazil, whose collection of instruments of subjugation speaks starkly of life for black people in the last Western country to abolish the slave trade.

The **Real Gabinete Português de Leitura** ① *R Luís Camões 30, T021-2221 3138, www.realgabinete.com.br, Mon-Fri 0900-1800, free*, sits just to the north of Largo São Francisco de Paula on Rua Luís de Camões. This is one of the city's hidden architectural treasures and one of the best pieces of mock-Manueline architecture in Brazil. Manueline architecture is usually described as Portuguese Gothic and takes its name from King Manuel I who ruled Portugal between 1495 and 1521. It is unlike any other European Gothic style, drawing strongly on Islamic and nautical themes – a lavish fusion of Islamic ornamentalism and sculpted seaweeds, anchors, ropes and corals, typified by the Cristo monastery in Tomar and the Mosteiro dos Jerônimos in Lisbon. The modest exterior of the Real Gabinete, which was designed by Portuguese architect Rafael da Silva e Castro in 1880, was inspired by the façade of Jerônimos. It is decorated with statues of Camões, Henry the Navigator, Vasco da Gama and Pedro Álvares Cabral, who claimed Brazil for Portugal. More interesting, however, is the magnificent reading hall built around the oldest central steel structure in Rio. Towering arches decorated with Islamic flourish ascend via coiled wooden ropes to an elaborate painted ceiling with skylights from which a massive iron chandelier is suspended. There are some 120,000 books in the library's collection, many of them very rare. The magnificent belle-époque coffee house, **Confeitaria Colombo**, is a short walk to the east, at Rua Gonçalves Dias 32 (see Eating, page 122).

Praça Tiradentes and the cathedral

One long block behind the Largo da Carioca and São Francisco de Paula is **Praça Tiradentes**, old and shady, with a **statue to Dom Pedro I** carved in 1862 by Luís Rochet. The emperor sits on horseback shouting his famous 1822 declaration of independence, the Grito de Ipiranga: 'Liberty or Death'. The **Teatro João Caetano** sits on the northeastern corner of the *praça* and is named after a famous 19th-century actor. Prince Dom Pedro first showed the green and yellow Brazilian flag in the original building, which was an important venue for meetings discussing Brazilian independence. The current theatre was constructed in 1920 after the original had fallen into disrepair. Two canvases by one of the city's most celebrated artists, Emiliano Di Cavalcanti, hang on the second floor. Just north of the *praça*, in a handsome salmon pink colonial building, is the **Centro de Arte Hélio Oiticica** ① *R Luís de Camões 68, Mon-Fri 1000-1800*, named after another famous Carioca artist and now a smart contemporary art exhibition space with six galleries, a good art bookshop and an air-conditioned café. Important national and international artists exhibit here. Shops in nearby streets specialize in selling goods for *umbanda*, the Afro-Brazilian religion. The **Catedral Metropolitana de São Sebastião** ① *Av República do Chile, T021-2240 2669, www.catedral.com.br, daily 0700-1900, Mass Mon-Fri 1100, Sun 1000*, lies just south of the Praça Tiradentes and the Largo da Carioca; bordering Cinêlandia to the east and Lapa to the south. It is an oblate concrete cone fronted by a decorative ladder and replete with rich blue stained glass, which looks like a modernist Mayan temple. The design could be mistaken for a Niemeyer, but is in fact by another Brazilian Le Corbusier disciple, Edgar de Oliveira da Fonseca, with heavy modernist statues and panels by Humberto Cozzi. It's best to visit in the late afternoon when the sunlight streams through the immense monotone stained-glass windows. There is a small sacred art museum in the crypt, which has a handful of relics including Dom Pedro II's throne and the fonts used for the baptizing of imperial Brazilian babies. The *bonde* (tram) to Santa Teresa leaves from behind the cathedral, the entrance is on Rua Senador Dantas (see page 95). Soon after leaving the station the tram traverses the Arcos da Lapa offering wonderful views.

One of the city's quirkier museums lies only a short walk from the cathedral. The **Museu de Farmácia Antônio Lago** ① *R dos Andradas 96, 10th floor, T021-2263 0791, www.abf.org.br/museu.html, Mon-Fri 1430-1700 by appointment only via email abf@abf.org.br, US$2*, is a reproduction of a 17th-century Brazilian apothecary's shop, complete with Dr Jekyll cabinets and rows of dubious-looking herbal preparations in glass and porcelain vessels.

Cinelândia and Avenida Rio Branco

The area around Praça Floriano was the liveliest part of the city in the 1920s and 1930s when Hollywood hit Brazil. All of the best cinemas were situated here and their popularity became so great that the *praça* was named after them. Today **Cinelândia** remains lively, especially at the end of the week, owing to its proximity to the city's nightlife capital, Lapa. The 30-m-wide **Avenida Rio Branco**, which bisects Cinelândia, is the financial heart of the city. Lined by an untidy mishmash of modernist and art deco skyscrapers it was built at the turn of 20th century under the 'tear it down' regime of Mayor Pereira Passos. Rio once had long stately avenues that rivalled the best of Buenos Aires but only clusters have survived. Although it has seen better days, the **Theatro Municipal** ① *Praça Floriano, T021-2262 3935, www.theatromunicipal.rj.gov.br, Mon-Fri 1300-1700, bilingual guided tours by appointment T021-2299 1667*, remains a splendid piece of French-inspired, lavish neoclassical pomp. The tour is worth it to see front of house and backstage, the

The fall and rise of Lapa

In the belle époque, Lapa's colonial streets were the Bohemian heart of Rio and lined with bars and dance halls which were the haunt of artists and intellectuals like Di Cavalcanti. However, after the war they fell into decay and disrepute and only the dangerous walked here. For decades Lapa festered, until in the 1980s a series of performance artists in love with the memory of the area braved Lapa and the neighbourhood slowly began to revive. Others followed them and a small alternative community began to form. Art and antiques dealers moved in. Then came tango and samba clubs and a handful of restaurants. Today Lapa is once more the heart of Bohemian Rio and many of its decaying colonial houses are now renovated and freshly painted, but enough remain for Lapa to retain a slightly edgy, Havanesque feel. Come here for a great night out and a window on the panoply and polyphony of modern Rio. Arrive at around 2100 whilst it is still relatively quite, take a streetside table under the arches at anyone of the crumbling colonial cafes along Avenida Mem da Sa, order an absinthe and wait. Little by little characters from every walk of Rio life enter the living stage – down at heel *favela* couples drunk and stumbling, Patricinhas dressed in Zoomp's ultra expensive casual, capoeira artists, jugglers, old men in blazers with hula hoops round their necks, befuddled tourists, towering transvestites in lycra shorts the size of a glove. As their numbers increase to boiling point they become a throng, unable to keep apart from each other, moving in Brownian Motion past the doors of numerous gradually waking clubs; past the thump and thud of techno, the staccato whir of *forró* and the hip swing of samba. Once the clubs have really got going, leave your table and join the throng – to dance to any music of your choice and become for a night ... a Carioca.

decorations and the machine rooms – a luxuriously ornate temple to an early 20th-century Carioca high society. On either side of the ostentatious colonnaded façade are rotundas, surmounted by cupolas. The muses of poetry and music watch over all, alongside an imperial eagle, wings outstretched and poised for flight. The interior is a mock-European fantasy of Carrara-marble columns, crystal chandeliers and gilt ceilings fronted by a vast sweeping, *Gone With the Wind* staircase. The stage is one of the largest in the world. The theatre was designed by Francisco de Oliveira Passos, son of the contemporaneous city mayor, who won an ostensibly open architectural competition together with French architect Albert Guilbert.

Opposite, on the other side of Avenida Rio Branco, is the newly refurbished **Museu Nacional de Belas-Artes** ① *Av Rio Branco 199, T021-2240 0068, www.mnba.org.br, Tue-Fri 1000-1800, Sat and Sun 1400-1800, free.* Fine art in Rio and in Brazil was, as a whole, stimulated by the arrival in 1808 of the Portuguese royal family. In 1816 the Academia de Belas-Artes was founded by another Frenchman, Joaquim Lebreton. This building was constructed 1906-1908 to house the national gallery and contains the best collection of art in the country. This includes depictions of Brazil by European visitors such as Dutchman Frans Post and Frenchman Jean-Baptiste Debret, and the best of 20th-century Brazilian art by important names such as modernist and social realist Cândido Portinari, Emiliano Di Cavalcanti (famous for his iconographic images of black Cariocas at a time when racism was institutionalized in Rio), Tarsila do Amaral (founder of the first major school of Brazilian Art, *antropofagismo*, which strongly influenced *tropicália*) and the brutalist art deco sculptor Victor Brecheret. Another gallery contains further works by foreign artists and the temporary exhibition hall houses many of Rio de Janeiro's most important international exhibitions.

Another of Cinelândia's stately neoclassical buildings is the **Biblioteca Nacional** ① *Av Rio Branco 219/239, T021-2262 8255, Mon-Fri 0900-2000, Sat 0900-1500, free*, an eclectic Carioca construction, this time with a touch of art nouveau. The library is fronted by a stately engaged portico supported by a Corinthian colonnade. Inside is a series of monumental staircases in Carrara marble. The stained glass in the windows is French. The first national library was brought to Brazil in 1808 by the Prince Regent, Dom João, from a collection in the Ajuda Palace in Lisbon. Today the library houses more than nine million items, including a first edition of the *Lusiad of Camões*, a 15th-century Moguncia Bible and Book of Hours, paintings donated by Pedro II, scores by Mozart and etchings by Dürer.

Nearby, in the former Ministry of Education and Health building, is the **Palácio Gustavo Capanema** ① *R da Imprensa 16, off the Esplanada do Castelo, at the junction of Av Graça Aranha and R Araújo Porto Alegre, just off Av Rio Branco, T021-2220 1490, by appointment only, Mon-Fri 0900-1800*. Dating back to 1937-1945, it was the first piece of modernist architecture in the Americas and was designed by an illustrious team of architects led by Lúcio Costa (under the guidance of Le Corbusier) and included a very young Oscar Niemeyer – working on his first project. Inside are impressive murals by Cândido Portinari, one of Brazil's most famous artists, as well as works by other well-known names. The gardens were laid out by Roberto Burle Marx who was responsible for many landscaping projects throughout Rio (including the Parque do Flamengo) and who worked with Costa and Niemeyer in Brasília.

Lapa → *See map, page 96.*

Only a decade ago Lapa, which lies just south of the cathedral on the edge of Cinelândia, was a no-go area; tawdry and terrifying, walked only by prostitutes, thugs and drug addicts chasing the dragon in the crumbling porticoes of the colonial and art nouveau buildings. The area can still feel a little edgy, especially on weekdays after dark. But it has undergone an unimagined renaissance. This was once the Montmartre of Rio; the painter Di Cavalcanti wrote poetically of wandering its streets at night on his way home to Flamengo, past the little cafés and ballrooms and the rows of handsome town houses. Now the cafés are alive once more, spilling out onto the streets, and the ballrooms and town houses throb with samba and electronica. Opera is once more performed in the concert halls of the Escola de Música, and the area's once notorious thoroughfare, Rua do Lavradio, is now lined with smart little restaurants and clubs, playing host to one of the city's most interesting bric-a-brac and antiques markets on Saturdays. ➡ *See Bars and clubs, page 127.*

Although the area is best just for a cautious wander after 2000 at the end of the week, or for the Saturday market, there are a few interesting sights. The most photographed are the **Arcos da Lapa**, built in 1744 as an aqueduct to carry water from Santa Teresa to the Chafariz da Carioca, with its 16 drinking fountains, in the centre of the city. The aqueduct's use was changed at the end of the 19th century, with the introduction of electric trams in Rio. Tracks were laid on top of the arches and the inaugural run was on 1 September 1896. The tram is still in use today and is one of the city's most delightful journeys; it leaves from behind the Catedral de São Sebastião and runs to Santa Teresa, see page 95.

Bars huddle under their southern extremity on Avenida Mem de Sá, one of Rio's most popular nightlife streets. Street performers (and vagrants) often gather in the cobbled square between the *arcos* and the cathedral. There are a number of moderately interesting buildings off this square. The eclectic baroque/neoclassical **Escola da Musica da Universidade Federal do Rio de Janeiro** ① *R do Passeio 98, open officially just for performances*, has one of the city's best concert halls. A stroll away is the bizarre baroque façade of another prestigious classical concert hall, the **Sala Cecília Mereilles** ① *Largo da Lapa 47*. More picturesque are the mosaic-tiled **Ladeira do Santa Teresa** stairs, which wind their way steeply from the square and from the back of Rua Teotônio to Santa Teresa. These are much beloved of music video directors and fashion photographers who use them as a backdrop to carefully produced gritty urban scenes. The steps are tiled in red, gold and green and bordered by little houses, many of which are dishevelled and disreputable but wonderfully picturesque. Be vigilant here.

North of Avenida Mem de Sá is **Rua do Lavradio**. This was one of urban Rio's first residential streets and is lined with handsome 18th- and early 20th-century town houses. These are now filled by samba clubs, cafés, bars and antiques shops. Any day is good for a browse and a wander, and on Saturdays at the end of the month there is a busy antiques market, live street tango, no cars and throngs of people from all sections of Carioca society. Some of the houses here were once grand. Number 84 once belonged to the marquis who gave the street its name. Further along is what was once Brazil's foremost Masonic lodge, the imposing **Palácio Maçônico Grande Oriente do Brasil**, which tellingly has had as its grand masters King Dom Pedro I and one of the country's most important Republican politicians, José Bonifácio Andrada e Silva.

Central do Brasil railway station

Central do Brasil or **Dom Pedro II** railway station, as it is also known, once served much of the country but now serves only Rio. This brutal 1930s art deco temple to progress was one of the city's first modernist buildings and was made famous by the Walter Salles film *Centro do Brasil* (Central Station). The film's thronging crowd scenes were set here. For similar shots come with your camera in the morning or evening and watch hundreds of thousands of people bustle in and out of trains leaving for the northern and western parts of Rio.

Gamboa, Cidade Nova and the Sambódromo

In the early 20th century, after the Paraguayan war and the abolition of slavery but before the warehouses were built in **Gamboa**, this northern dockland area was known as 'Little Africa' due to the high number of resident Bahian immigrants. With them, the African-Bahian rhythms of the *candomblé* religion were introduced into the Carioca community and the next generation spawned a host of famous local musicians that included Donga, Chico da Baiana and João de Baiana.

The streets and back yards of Gamboa became the birthplace of a new music: samba, born of Angolan *semba* rhythms fused with European singing styles and instruments. Donga and João da Baiana used to gather on the Pedra do Sal stairs close to the Praça Mauá to play and hold impromptu music and samba dance parties. Later the dance was incorporated into an alternative Mardi Gras festival as a counterpart to the ballroom dances of the white elite. Street parade clubs were formed by another young Carioca, Hilário Jovino Ferreira. Their structure was copied later by the much larger samba schools that still produce the Carnaval parades today.

The story of Carnaval

Rio's story, and that of the world's most famous carnival is a tale of two cities: the European and the African. In the early 20th century the city was a prudish place, dominated by a stuffy elite, who enclosed themselves in mock-French palaces and mansions around the city's beautiful coves. The other Brazil was (and remains), poor and marginalized and clinging to the hills. Its people visited European Rio only to work at the quays where their African forefathers had been unloaded in crates a generation before.

The Mardi Gras carnival was a European affair. In homage to European balls, the Portuguese and their ancestors danced behind closed doors and masks to the fashionable rhythm of the time, polka. But black Brazil would not be excluded. Its people took the Portuguese instruments and polka dance steps out of Rio's ballrooms and into their *favela* shanty towns. Here they were fused with the West African rhythm of *maracatú*, frenetic with percussive hand-held *timpani* and resonating to the deep visceral throb of the *zabumba* drum. Over the top the Africans sung laments to their poverty and celebrations of the essential joys of life. These were echoed by a sung chorus. As the celebrations developed, the revellers began to dress in ever more elaborate costumes and dance and march in discrete *blocos* or individual parades. These were often themed according to the African tribal group from which the celebrants came and were led by a king and queen. In Pernambuco, whose carnival is the most traditional of all in Brazil, the *blocos* are still referred to as nations.

In the 20th century the celebrations had evolved into a fully-blown carnival which soon eclipsed the masked balls of the elite. And the Carnaval music became a particular style all its own – *samba*. By the end of the Second World War the *favela* carnivals had expanded into the streets of the city itself to become Rio's Carnaval. The *blocos* became *samba* schools, who spent an entire year preparing the carnival performance and making floats and costumes. Later even the middle and upper classes of Rio became involved and came to identify themselves with the African-Brazilian culture their ancestors had so despised.

Carnaval today is a multi-million dollar enterprise, sponsored by the gaming industry and featuring the stars of Brazil's equivalent of Bollywood – *TV Globo*. The top samba schools compete in front of crowds of hundreds of thousands and a board of judges, who mark them with Olympic precision according to a series of distinct categories.

In 2008 the city government inaugurated a theme park, **Cidade de Samba (Samba City)** ① *R Rivadávia Corréa 60, Gamboa, T021-2213 2503, www.cidadedosambarj.com.br, Tue-Sat 1000-1900*, to celebrate samba and bring the administrative and production centre of a number of the larger schools together in one location. Schools from the **Liga Independente das Escolas de Samba (LIESA)** now have a permanent carnival production centre of 14 workshops, each of them housed in a two-storey building. Visitors can watch floats and costumes being prepared or watch one of the year-round carnival-themed shows. Although it feels corporately controlled and its atmosphere cannot compare to a visit to a samba school such as **Primeira Estação de Mangueira** (see page 133), which lies at the centre of its own neighbourhood rather than a tourist park, Samba City is an interesting alternative to the US-style theme parks that proliferate in Brazil.

Carnaval itself is centred closed to Gamboa in the **Cidade Nova**. Oscar Niemeyer's 650-m stadium street, the **Sambódromo** ① *R Marquês de Sapucaí s/n, metrô Central or metrô Praça Onze, Cidade Nova, T021-2502 6996, Mon-Fri 0900-1700*, was purpose-built for the annual parades. ⏵ *See box, page 132.*

Nearby, **Praça Onze** is today the terminus of the city's main thoroughfare, Avenida Presidente Vargas. But it was once a square and an established meeting place for *capoeristas* whose acrobatic martial art to the rhythm of the *berimbau* and hand clap inspired much Carnaval choreography. A replica of the head of a Nigerian prince from the British Museum, erected in honour of **Zumbi dos Palmares**, sits on Avenida Presidente Vargas itself. Zumbi was a Bantu prince who became the most successful black slave emancipator in the history of the Americas, founding a kingdom within Brazil in the 19th century. The **Centro de Memória do Carnaval** ① *Av Rio Branco 4, 2nd floor, T021-3213 5151, www.liesa.com.br, visits by appointment only*, is a research centre and preserves one of the largest repositories of international and Brazilian carnival images, documents and publications in the world.

⑤ Northern Rio

> **⏵ Rio de Janeiro maps**
> **2** Rio de Janeiro orientation, page 74
> **5** Northern Rio, page 92

Northern Rio

Cemitério dos Ingleses

Over the Morro da Providência, between the Estação Dom Pedro II and the bay, is the **Cemitério dos Ingleses** ⓘ *R da Gamboa 181*. The cemetery, the oldest in Rio, was granted to the British community by Dom João, Regent of Portugal, in 1810. Catholics who could afford a burial were laid to rest inside their churches (see the numbers on the church floors, marking the graves), but the British in Rio, being non-Catholic, were not allowed to be buried in the religious establishments. There are other interesting cemeteries in Rio, notably **O Cemitério São João Batista** ⓘ *R Real Grandeza, Botafogo, T021-2539 7073*, where many of the city's most famous are buried, including Machado de Assis, Heitor Villa-Lobos, Carmen Miranda, Santos Dumont, Clara Nunes and Tom Jobim. The grand sculptures and mansion-sized mausoleums, many by Brazil's most celebrated sculptors, contrast with the concrete boxes and plastic flowers of the lower middle classes.

Nossa Senhora da Penha

The church of **Nossa Senhora da Penha** ⓘ *Largo da Penha 19, T021-2290 0942, www.santuariodapenhario.com.br, Tue-Sun 1000-1600*, is one of the most important pilgrimage centres in the whole country, especially for black Brazilians. It sits on an enormous rock, into whose side 365 steps have been carved. Pilgrims ascend these on their knees during the festival month of October. The church in its present form dates from the early 20th century, but it was modelled on an early 18th-century chapel and a religious building has been on this site since the original hermitage was built in 1632. There are great views from the summit.

To get there take the metrô to Del Castilho. Leave the station to the left, walk down the passageway and catch microbus (micro-ônibus) No 623 labelled 'Penha-Shopping Nova América 2' to the last stop. Get off at the shopping centre, in front of Rua dos Romeiros, and walk up that street to the Largo da Penha from where there are signposts to the church.

Maracanã stadium

① *T021-2566 7800, daily 0900-1700 (0800-1100 on match days); guided tour of the stadium from Gate 16 (in Portuguese, daily 1000-1600, US$4), and of the museum (US$0.50). Take the metrô to Maracanã station on Linha 2, one stop beyond São Cristóvão. Bus Nos 238 and 239 from the centre, 434 and 464 from Glória, Flamengo and Botafogo, 455 from Copacabana, and 433 and 464 from Ipanema and Leblon all go to the stadium. Trips to football matches can be organized through www.bealocal.com.*

According to Brazilians, Maracanã is the largest sports stadium in the world. However, Indianapolis in the USA and Strahov stadium in Prague, Czech Republic, are both larger and have seen bigger crowds. Nonetheless, the stadium is huge and was attended by the largest crowd ever to see a football match in 1950 when Brazil lost to Uruguay in front of more than 200,000 spectators. More importantly, it is the Mount Olympus of the country's football gods. This is where Pelé scored his 1000th goal in 1969. His feet, as well as those of Ronaldo and other Brazilian stars, are immortalized in concrete outside the stadium. Even if you're not a football fan, matches are worth going to for the spectators' samba bands and the adrenalin-charged atmosphere – especially a local or Rio-São Paulo derby, or an international game. There are three types of ticket: *cadeiras* (individual chairs), the most expensive; *arquibancadas* (terraces), good for watching the game but don't sit between rival groups of fans; or *geral* (standing), the cheapest, not recommended and not safe. Prices vary according to the game, but it's more expensive to buy tickets from agencies than at the gate; it is cheaper to buy tickets from club sites on the day before the match.

Don't take valuables or wear a watch and take special care when entering and leaving the stadium. The rivalry between the local clubs Flamengo and Vasco da Gama is intense, often leading to violence, so it is advisable to avoid their encounters. If you buy a club shirt or favour, don't be tempted to wear it on match day: if you find yourself in the wrong place, you could be in trouble.

Quinta da Boa Vista

① *Take the metrô to São Cristóvão and follow signs to Quinta da Boa Vista, a 5-min walk. Beware of muggings on weekdays; don't take valuables.*

About 3 km west of Praça da República (beyond the Sambódromo) is the Quinta da Boa Vista, the emperor's private park from 1809 to 1889. The **Museu Nacional** ① *T021-2254 4320, www.ufrj.br/museu, Tue-Sun 1000-1600, US$3,* is housed in the former imperial palace. The building is crumbling and the collections dusty and poorly displayed. Only the unfurnished throne room and ambassadorial reception room on the second floor reflect past glories. In the entrance hall is the famous Bendegó meteorite, found in the state of Bahia in 1888; its original weight, before some of it was chipped, was 5360 kg. Besides several collections of foreign pieces (including Peruvian and Mexican archaeology, Graeco-Roman ceramics and Egyptian mummies), the museum contains collections of Brazilian indigenous weapons, costumes, utensils and historical documents. There are also frowsty collections of stuffed birds, beasts, fish and butterflies.

Also in the park is the **Jardim Zoológico** ① *Av Dom Pedro II, T021-3878 4200, www.rio.rj.gov.br/riozoo, Tue-Sun 1000-1630, US$5.* The zoo is in the northeastern corner of the park. It has a collection of 2100 animals, most of which are kept in modern, spacious enclosures, and there is an important captive breeding programme for golden-headed and golden lion tamarins, spectacled bears and yellow-throated capuchin monkeys. The aviary is impressive and children can enjoy a ride in a little train through the park.

Santa Teresa

A tram ride from the cathedral to Santa Teresa over the Arcos de Lapa viaduct is an unmissable Rio experience. The old yellow trams clatter up the winding, hilly streets lined with pretty colonial houses and lavish mansions towards the forested slopes of Tijuca national park, leaving in their wake sweeping views of Guanabara Bay and the Sugar Loaf. Along the way they pass the **Largo do Guimarães** and the **Largo das Neves**, little *praças* of shops and restaurants that feel as if they belong clustered around a village green rather than in a large city. For nowhere in this city of distinct neighbourhoods is more of a world unto itself than Santa Teresa. The neighbourhood has a strong community identity forged by one of the highest concentrations of artists, writers and musicians in the city, who congregate in bars like **O Mineiro** on the Largo dos Guimarães or **Bar Porto das Neves** on the Largo das Neves. At weekends the lively nightlife spills over into clubs like **Espírito Santo** (see page 127) and then into neighbouring Lapa which is only a five-minute taxi ride away. Those who can bear to be away from the beach often find staying in Santa Teresa a far more culturally rewarding experience than the southern suburbs and there are many excellent options.

A sense of separation is reflected not only in the suburb's geography, but also its history. In 1624, Antônio Gomes do Desterro chose the area both for its proximity to Rio and its isolation, and erected a hermitage dedicated to Nossa Senhora do Desterro. The name was changed from Morro do Desterro to Santa Teresa after the construction in 1750 of a convent of that name dedicated to the patroness of the order. The convent exists to this day, but it can only be seen from the outside.

Ins and outs

Getting there and around The best way to visit Santa Teresa is on the traditional open-sided **tram**, the *bondinho*. This can be caught from the terminus next to the Catedral Metropolitana or from Cinelândia: take the metrô to Cinelândia station, go to Rua Senador Dantas then walk along to Rua Profesor Lélio Gama (look for **Banco do Brasil** on the corner); the station is up this street. Take the Paula Mattos line; the fare is US$0.40 one way. Bus Nos 206 and 214 run between Avenida Rio Branco in the centre and Santa Teresa. At night, take a taxi (about US$7 to the centre or Ipanema). In recent years, Santa Teresa has had a reputation for crime, however, the area is much more heavily policed nowadays. Be vigilant with your camera and be particularly wary after dark. Steer clear of any steps that lead down the hill and on Rua Almirante Alexandrino or at the Tijuca end of Largo dos Guimarães.

Sights

Santa Teresa is best explored on foot: wander the streets to admire the colonial buildings or stop for a beer in a little streetside café and marvel at the view. The better colonial houses, most of which are private residences, include the **Casa de Valentim** (a castle-like house in Vista Alegre), the tiled **Chácara dos Viegas** in Rua Monte Alegre and the **Chalé Murtinho**. This was the house in which Dona Laurinda Santos Lobo held her famous artistic, political and intellectual salons at the turn of the 20th century. The house was in ruins until it was partially restored and turned into a cultural centre called **Parque das Ruínas** ⓘ *R Murtinho Nobre 41, daily 1000-1700*. It has superb views of the city, an exhibition space and an open-air stage (live music on Thursday). Next door is the **Chácara do Céu**, or **Museu Castro Maya** ⓘ *R Murtinho Nobre 93, T021-2507 1932, www.museu castromaya.com.br, Wed-Mon 1200-1700, US$1*, housed in the former home of the Carioca millionaire and art collector, Raymundo Ottoni de Castro Maya. It has a wide range of works by modern painters, including Modigliani and important Brazilian like Di Cavalacanti. There are wonderful views out over Guanabara Bay. To get to both the Chácara and the Parque das Ruínas take the Santa Teresa tram to Curvelo station, walk

⑥ Glória, Santa Teresa & Lapa

➡ Rio de Janeiro maps
2 Rio de Janeiro orientation, page 74
6 Glória, Santa Teresa and Lapa, page 96

200 metres
200 yards

N

Sleeping	Mama Ruisa 5 D4	Eating
Casa Áurea 1 D3	Novo Mundo 6 D6	Adega do Pimenta 1 D4
Catete Hostel 3 D6	Rio Hostel 7 C4	Aprazível 9 D3
Glória 2 D6		Bar do Arnaudo 5 D3
Inglês 4 D6		Espírito Santa 3 D4

along Rua Dias de Barros, following the signposts to Parque das Ruínas. There are also superb views from the **Museu Casa de Benjamin Constant** ⓘ *R Monte Alegre 225, T021-2509 1248, Wed-Sun 1300-1700*, the former home of the Carioca military engineer and positivist philosopher who helped to found the Republic.

Glória, Catete and Flamengo

The city centre is separated from Copacabana and the other ocean beaches by a series of long white-sand coves that fringe Guanabara Bay and which are divided by towering rocks. The first of the coves is the **Enseada da Glória**, fronting the suburb of the same name and sitting next to the Santos Dumont airport. Avenida Infante Dom Henrique, a broad avenue lined with an eclectic mix of grand houses and squat office blocks, leads from here to what was once the city's finest beach, **Flamengo**, a long stretch of sand separated from the rest of southern Rio by the Morro da Viúva (widow's peak). The suburb of **Catete** lies just behind Flamengo. These three areas were once the heart of recreational Rio; the posing-spots of choice for the belle-époque middle and upper classes and perhaps the most coveted urban beaches in the world. These days the water is polluted and swimming ill-advised, but the suburbs are pleasant for a stroll.

Ins and outs

Bus No 119 from the centre or No 571 from Copacabana serve the neighbourhoods, as does the metrô. The centrepiece of the three suburbs are the gardens of the Parque do Flamengo, on Avenida Infante Dom Henrique, reached from metrô Glória, Catete, Largo de Machado or Flamengo. Closed to traffic on Sunday. Be careful after dark.

Sights

Before the pollution became too much, Burle Marx, Brazil's 20th-century Capability Brown, designed the **Parque do Flamengo**, a handsome stretch of waterfront to separate

7 Catete & Flamengo

Sleeping	Inglês 4 A5	Único 11 A5
Catete Hostel 2 A4	Novo Mundo 5 A5	Windsor Flórida 1 A5
Imperial 3 A4	Paysandú 7 B5	

300 metres
300 yards

Avenida Infante Dom Henrique from the city's most glorious beach, and gave it ample shade with a range of tropical trees and stands of stately royal palms. The gardens stretch from Glória through to the Morro da Viúva at the far end of Flamengo; they were built on reclaimed land and opened in 1965 to mark the 400th anniversary of the city's founding. The lawns and promenade are favourite spots for smooching lovers, especially at sundown. There are children's play areas too and a handful of monuments and museums. These include the impressive postmodern **Monumento aos Mortos da Segunda Guerra Mundial** ① *Av Infante Dom Henrique, Tue-Sun 1000-1700 for the crypt museum; beach clothes and flip flops not permitted*, the national war memorial to Brazil's dead in the Second World War. The gently curved slab is supported by two slender columns, representing two palms uplifted to heaven and guarded by soldiers from the adjacent barracks. In the crypt are the remains of the Brazilian soldiers killed in Italy in 1944-1945. At the far northern end of the Parque do Flamengo is the **Museu de Arte Moderna** ① *Av Infante Dom Henrique 85, T021-2240 4944, www.mamrio.com.br, Tue-Sun 1200-1700, last entry 1630, US$4*, another striking modernist building with the best collection of modern art in Brazil outside São Paulo. Works by many well-known Europeans sit alongside collections of Brazilian modern and contemporary art including drawings by Cândido Portinari and etchings of everyday work scenes by Gregório Gruber.

The beautiful little church on the Glória hill, overlooking the Parque do Flamengo, is **Nossa Senhora da Glória do Outeiro** ① *T021-2225 2869, Tue-Fri 0900-1200 and 1300-1700, Sat and Sun 0900-1200, guided tours by appointment on the 1st Sun of each month*. Built 1735-1791, it was the favourite church of the imperial family and Dom Pedro II was baptized here. The building is polygonal, with a single tower. It contains some excellent examples of the best *azulejos* (tiles) in Rio and its main wooden altar was carved by Mestre Valentim. Next door is the small **Museum of Religious Art** ① *T021-2556 6434, same hours as church*.

Behind Glória and Flamengo is the rather down-at-heel suburb of Catete, which is dotted with museums. The best of these is the **Museu da República** ① *R do Catete 153, T021-3235 2650, www.museudarepublica. org.br, Tue, Thu, Fri 1200-1700, Wed 1400-1700, Sat, Sun and holidays 1400-1800, US$4, free Wed and Sun*, the former palace of a coffee baron, the Barão de Nova Friburgo. The palace was built 1858-1866 and, in 1887, it was converted into the presidential seat, until the move to Brasília. The ground floor of this museum consists of the sumptuous rooms of the coffee baron's mansion. The first floor is devoted to the history of the Brazilian republic. You can also see the room where former president Getúlio Vargas shot himself. Behind the museum is the **Parque do Catete**, which contains many birds and monkeys and is a popular place for practising Tai Chi.

➡ **Rio de Janeiro maps**
2 Rio de Janeiro orientation, page 74
7 Catete and Flamengo, page 98

Eating 🍴
Alcaparra **2** A5
Lamas **11** B4

The **Museu do Folclore Edison Carneiro** ⓘ *R do Catete 181, T021-2285 0441, Tue-Fri 1100-1800, Sat and Sun 1500-1800, free*, houses a collection of amusing but poorly labelled small ceramic figures representing everyday life in Brazil, some of which are animated by electric motors. Many artists are represented and displays show the way of life in different parts of the country. There are also fine *candomblé* and *umbanda* costumes, religious objects, displays about Brazil's festivals and a small but excellent library, with helpful staff who can help find books on Brazilian culture, history and anthropology. Flash photography is prohibited.

The **Museu Carmen Miranda** ⓘ *Parque Brigadeiro Eduardo Gomes (Parque do Flamengo), Flamengo, T021-2299 5586, Tue-Fri 1100-1700, Sat and Sun 1300-1700, US$1*, has more than 3000 items related to the famous Portuguese singer forever associated with Rio, who emigrated to Brazil as a child and then moved to Hollywood. The collection includes some of her famous gowns, fruit-covered hats, jewellery and recordings. There are occasional showings of her films.

8 Urca, Botafogo & Cosme Velho

Sleeping 🛌   Tupiniquim Hostel **1** *C3*   Eating 🍴

Botafogo, Urca and Pão de Açúcar (Sugar Loaf)

Pão de Açúcar, or the **Sugar Loaf**, looms over the perfect wine-glass bay of **Botafogo**, the next of the Guanabara Bay coves after Flamengo. Huddled around the boulder's flanks is the suburb of **Urca**, home to a military barracks and the safest middle-class houses in Rio. Remnant forest, still home to marmosets and rare birds, shrouds the boulder's sides and a cable car straddles the distance between its summit, the **Morro de Urca** hill and the houses below, making one of the continent's most breathtaking views easily accessible. Urca and Botafogo have a few sights of interest and make convenient bases with decent accommodation and restaurant options, particularly in the lower price ranges.

Ins and outs

Botafogo has a metrô station. Buses that run between Copacabana and the centre stop in Botafogo, so take any bus marked 'Centro' from Copacabana or 'Copacabana' from the centre. Bus No 107 (from the centre, Catete or Flamengo) and No 511 from Copacabana (No 512 to return) take you to Urca and the cable-car station for the Sugar Loaf. Alternatively, walk 10 minutes northeast from behind the Rio Sul shopping centre to the cable-car station, which lies on Praça General Tiburcio, next to the Rio de Janeiro federal university. The rides themselves go up in two stages, the first to the summit of Morro da Urca, the smaller rock that sits in front of the Sugar Loaf, and the second from there to the top of the Sugar Loaf itself. Allow at least two hours for your visit.

> ➡ **Rio de Janeiro maps**
> 2 Rio de Janeiro orientation, page 74
> 8 Urca, Botafogo and Cosme Velho, page 100

Pão de Açúcar (Sugar Loaf)

The western hemisphere's most famous monolith rises almost sheer from the dark sea to just under 400 m, towering over Botafogo beach and separating Guanabara Bay from the open Atlantic Ocean. The views from the top, out over Copacabana, Ipanema and the mountains and forests of Corcovado and Tijuca are as unforgettable as the view from New York's Empire State Building or Victoria Peak in Hong Kong. The **cable car** ① *Av Pasteur 520, Praia Vermelha, Urca, T021-2461 2700, www.bondinho. com.br, daily 0800-1950, US$20, every 30 mins*, runs to the top where there are extensive paths, plentiful shade and snack bars. Come early for the clearest air, best views and smallest crowds.

Raajmahal **6** *C3*

The essential Rio beach kit

To get the best out of Rio dress as the locals do – become a *Carioca*. Leave your sense of shame and your board shorts, in the hotel and go out in search of the essential Carioca uniform. The first thing you will need is a *sunga*, a tiny piece of square lycra used barely to cover the essentials, or, if you are a woman a bikini, which although even smaller is not, contrary to popular belief, a 'dental floss' thong. The most fashionable places for these are in Ipanema or the fashion mall in São Conrado (see page 137). The next

essential is a *canga* – a sarong of the kind ubiquitous in Asia; which is used as a wrap, towel and beach mat, easily found in boutiques on any main street in Rio, like Visconde de Pirajá in Ipanema. You will then need a *frescobol kit* – a wooden racket and a rubber ball to hit back and forth across the sand and a pair of *Havaianas* – Brazilian flip flops. Both are available for next to nothing in the supermarket. A tanned, perfect body and small white poodle (for women) and pair of cheap sunglasses (for men) complete the outfit.

Paths up and around the Sugar Loaf There is more to Sugar Loaf than the views from the top. The surrounding rocks hide secluded little beaches, remnant forest and small colonial suburbs well worth seeing. The best place to begin is at **Praia Vermelha**, the beach to the south of the rock where there is a simple restaurant, the **Círculo Militar da Praia Vermelha** (no sign) with wonderful views. The walking track, **Pista Cláudio Coutinho** ① *daily 0700-1800*, runs from here along the waterfront around the foot of the rock. You'll see plenty of wildlife at dawn, especially marmosets and colourful tanagers, along with various intrepid climbers scaling the granite. About 350 m from the beginning of the Pista Coutinho is a turning to the left for a path that winds its way up through the forest to the top of **Morro de Urca**, from where the cable car can be taken for US$10. You can save even more money by climbing the **Caminho da Costa**, a path to the summit of the Pão de Açúcar. Only one stretch of 10 m requires climbing gear; wait at the bottom of the path for a group going up. You can then descend to Morro de Urca by cable car for free and walk the rest of the way down. There are 35 rock-climbing routes up the boulder. The best months for climbing are April to August. ⏵ *For climbing clubs, see Activities and tours, page 138.*

Botafogo

The Funai-run **Museu do Índio** ① *R das Palmeiras 55, T021-2286 8899, www.museudo indio.org.br, Mon-Fri 0900-1730, Sat and Sun 1300-1700, US$2.50, free on Sun, 10-min walk from Botafogo metrô or bus No 571 from Catete*, preserves some 12,000 objects from more than 180 Brazilian indigenous groups, including basketry, ceramics, masks and weapons as well as 500,000 documents and 50,000 photographs. Very few are on display and the museum's few rooms are mostly devoted to information panels and short film shows. The garden includes a Guaraní *maloca* and there is a small, well-displayed handicraft shop and a library of ethnology.

The **Museu Villa-Lobos** ① *R Sorocaba 200, T021-2266 3845, www.museuvillalobos. org.br, Mon-Fri 1000-1730, free*, is a block east of the Museu do Índio. Such was the fame and respect afforded to Latin America's most celebrated composer (see box, page 148) that the museum was founded just one year after his death in 1960. Inside the fine 19th-century building is a collection of his personal objects including instruments, scores, books and recordings. The museum has occasional concerts and temporary shows and supports a number of classical music projects throughout Brazil.

The **Dona Marta viewpoint**, which sits in the forest immediately above Botafogo and is connected by road to Corcovado, offers the best views of the Sugar Loaf in the city. Do not visit after 1730 as robbers from the nearby *favelas* frequent the roads.

Christ statue at Corcovado and Cosme Velho

Few famous sights in the world live up to the high expectations overexposure has placed on them. The view from **Corcovado mountain** is one of them. Come, if you can, for dusk. Almost a kilometre above the city and at the apex of one of the highest pinnacles in Tijuca forest stands **O Redentor** – Christ the Redeemer – lit in brilliant xenon and with arms open to embrace the urban world's most breathtaking view. At his feet to the west are a panoply of bays, fringed with white and backed by twinkling skyscrapers and the neon of myriad street lights. To the east as far as the eye can see lie long stretches of sand washed by green and white surf. And in front and to the south, next to the vast ocean beaches, is the sparkle of Niterói watched over by low grey mountains and connected to Rio by a 10-km-long sinuous bridge that threads its way across the 10-km expanse of Guanabara Bay. As the light fades, the tropical forest at Christ's back comes to life in a chorus of cicadas and evening birdsong loud enough to drown even the chatter of a thousand tourists.

At the base of the mountain is the sleepy suburb of **Cosme Velho**, leafy and dotted with grand houses, museums and a little artist's corner called the Largo do Boticario. The two are linked by a 3.8-km railway, opened in 1884 by Emperor Dom Pedro II.

Ins and outs

There are several ways to reach the top of Corcovado. A cog railway and a road connect the city to the mountain from the suburb of Cosme Velho. Both are on the northern side of the Rebouças tunnel, which runs to and from the Lagoa. From the upper terminus of the **cog railway** ⓘ *R Cosme Velho 513, T021-2558 1329, www.corcovado.com.br, daily every 30 mins 0830-1830, 10 min-journey, US$8 one-way, US$15 return*, there is a climb of 220 steps to the top or you can take the newly installed escalator, near which there is a café. Mass is held on Sunday in a small chapel in the statue pedestal. There is a museum at the station with panels showing the history of the statue and the railway.

To get to the cog railway station take a taxi or bus to Cosme Velho and get off at the station. **Buses** are as follows: from the centre or Glória/Flamengo bus No 180; from Copacabana bus Nos 583 or 584; from Botafogo or Ipanema/Leblon bus Nos 583 or 584; from Santa Teresa take the micro-ônibus. **Taxis**, which wait in front of the station, also offer tours of Corcovado and Mirante Dona Marta and cost around US$25.

If going **on foot**, take bus No 206 from Praça Tiradentes (or No 407 from Largo do Machado) to Silvestre, where there is a station at which the train no longer stops. It is a steep 9-km walk from here to the top, along a shady road. Take the narrow street to the right of the station, go through the gate used by people who live beside the tracks and continue to the national park entrance. Walkers are not usually charged entrance fees. Allow a minimum of two hours (up to four hours depending on fitness).

By **car**, drive through Túnel Rebouças from the Lagoa and then look out for the Corcovado signs before the beginning of the second tunnel and off to your right. Ignore the clamour of the touts at the beginning of the Corcovado road. They will try to convince you that the road is closed in order to take you on an alternative route and charge a hefty fee. If going by car to Corcovado, the entrance fee is US$2.20 for the vehicle, plus US$2.20 for each passenger. If you are coming down after dark try to go in company or at weekends when more people are about.

Almost all the hotels, even the hostels, offer organized **coach trips** to Corcovado, which usually take in Sugar Loaf and Maracanã as well. These offer a fairly brief stop on the mountain and times of day are not always the best for light. **Helicopter tours** are available though these leave from the Sugar Loaf or the Lagoa.

Cosme Velho
The **Museu Internacional de Arte Naif do Brasil** (MIAN) ⓘ *R Cosme Velho 561, on the same street as the station for Corcovado, T021-2205 8612, www.museunaif.com.br, Tue-Fri*

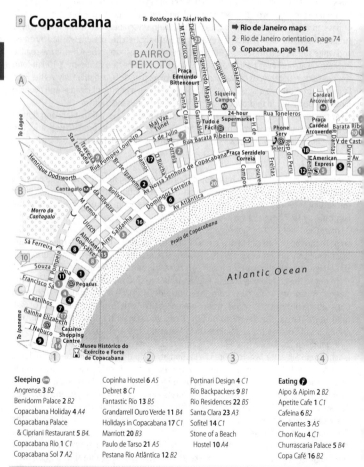

9 **Copacabana**

➡ Rio de Janeiro maps
2 Rio de Janeiro orientation, page 74
9 Copacabana, page 104

Sleeping
Angrense 3 *B2*
Benidorm Palace 2 *B2*
Copacabana Holiday 4 *A4*
Copacabana Palace
  & Cipriani Restaurant 5 *B4*.
Copacabana Rio 1 *C1*
Copacabana Sol 7 *A2*

Copinha Hostel 6 *A5*
Debret 8 *C1*
Fantastic Rio 13 *B5*
Grandarrell Ouro Verde 11 *B4*
Holidays in Copacabana 17 *C1*
Marriott 20 *B3*
Paulo de Tarso 21 *A5*
Pestana Rio Atlântica 12 *B2*

Portinari Design 4 *C1*
Rio Backpackers 9 *B1*
Rio Residences 22 *B5*
Santa Clara 23 *A3*
Sofitel 14 *C1*
Stone of a Beach
  Hostel 10 *A4*

Eating
Aipo & Aipim 2 *B2*
Apetite Cafe 1 *C1*
Cafeina 6 *B2*
Cervantes 3 *A5*
Chon Kou 4 *C1*
Churrascaria Palace 5 *B4*
Copa Café 16 *B2*

1000-1800, weekends 1200-1800, US$3.20, is one of the most comprehensive museums of naïf and folk paintings in the world with a permanent collection of 8000 works by naïf artists from 130 countries. The museum also hosts several thematic and temporary exhibitions through the year. Parts of its collection are often on loan around the world. There is a coffee shop and a souvenir shop where you can buy paintings, books, postcards and T-shirts. Courses and workshops on painting and related subjects are also available.

The **Largo do Boticário** ① *R Cosme Velho 822*, is a pretty, shady little square close to the terminus for the Corcovado cog railway and surrounded by 19th-century buildings. It offers a glimpse of what the city looked like before all the concrete and highways. That the square exists at all is thanks to concerned residents who not only sought to preserve it but were also instrumental in rebuilding and refurbishing many of the buildings, using rubble from colonial buildings demolished in the city centre. Many of the doors once belonged to churches. The four houses that front the square are painted different colours (white, pale blue, caramel and pink), each with features picked out in decorative tiles, woodwork and stone. Many artists live here and can often be seen painting in the courtyard.

Copacabana and Leme

Copacabana, which is called Leme at its northern end, epitomizes Rio both for better and for worse. Like the city as a whole, it is breathtakingly beautiful from afar and a little ugly close to. At first sight it looks magnificent. The beach is a splendid broad sweeping crescent of fine sand stretching for almost 8 km, washed by a bottle-green Atlantic and watched over by the **Morro do Leme** – another of Rio's beautiful forest-covered hills. Behind it is a wide neon- and argon-lit avenue lined with high-rises, the odd grand hotel and various bars, restaurants and clubs. The tanned and toned flock all around in little bikinis, *sungas* and colourful beach wraps, playing volleyball on the sand and jogging along the wavy black and white dragon's tooth pavements, while others busk, play capoeira and sell their wares. But, like much of Brazil, the devil is in the detail and up close Copacabana is a lot less appealing. The sand may be clean enough but those bottle-green waves are far from it. Many of the bars and hotels are tatty and tawdry,

Rio's sun worshippers

Ipanema and Copacabana are the most famous beaches in the world and there can surely be no people more devoted to lazing in the sun than Cariocas. But it wasn't always so. In the 19th century Brazilians would only go near sea water if they had been ordered to do so by a doctor. Even then it would only be for a quick dip at the beginning or the end of the day when the sun was weak. A tan was regarded as unhealthy and a sign of being lower class; to actually sit in the sun was a serious breach of social propriety.

All this began to change when the famous French actress Sarah Bernhardt came to Rio in 1886 to star in *Frou Frou* and *The Lady of the Camelias* at the São Pedro theatre. During her time off she caused a scandal, appalling the great and the good by travelling to then distant Copacabana, throwing on a swimsuit, sunbathing and even swimming in the sea. By the turn of the 20th century others had begun to follow suit, and by 1917 going to the beach had become sufficiently fashionable that the city established strict rules and regulations to govern sun worship. People were permitted to bathe only between 0500-0800 and 1700-1900, had to wear appropriate dress and be quiet and discreet; failure to do so resulted in five years in prison. Official attitudes only began to change in the 1920s with the building of the Copacabana Palace and the arrival of more foreigners who ignored Rio's prudishness and convinced Cariocas to begin to enjoy the beach.

some of them frequented by a Pattaya-type crowd of young, thin Cariocas and fat older foreigners looking to buy more than a drink. And at night Copacabana can be dangerous. Soliciting is rife and muggings are not uncommon.

Ins and outs

Buses are plentiful and cost US$0.40; Nos 119, 154, 413, 415, 455 and 474 run between the city centre and Avenida Nossa Senhora de Copacabana. If you are going to the centre from Copacabana, look for 'Castelo', 'Praça XV', 'E Ferro' or 'Praça Mauá' on the sign by the front door. 'Aterro' means the expressway between Botafogo and downtown Rio (not open on Sunday). From the centre to Copacabana is easier as all buses in that direction are clearly marked. The 'Aterro' bus takes 15 minutes. Numerous buses run between Copacabana and Ipanema; the two beaches are connected by Rua Francisco Otaviano or Rua Joaquim Nabuco, immediately west of the Forte de Copacabana. Copacabana has metrô stations a few blocks inland from the beach at Cardeal Arcoverde, Siqueira Campos and Cantagalo.

Sights

Copacabana has always been a beach and beyond it there are no sights of any note. The area exploded in population after the construction of the **Túnel Velho** (Old Tunnel) in 1891 and the **New Tunnel** in the early 20th century and has been growing, mostly upward, ever since. Streets are lined with high-rise flats that huddle together even on the seafront, crowding around the stately neoclassical façade of the **Copacabana Palace** hotel, which was the tallest building in the suburb until the 1940s.

Copacabana – what's in a name?

Copacabana is most famously a beach in Brazil. However, it is also a beach in New South Wales, a nightclub in New York, a small town in Bolivia and a song by Barry Manilow. All of these, one might think owe their name to Brazil's Copacabana. But it is not so. Copacabana is an Inca word meaning beholder of the blue horizon or beholder of the precious stone. The original Copacabana was a port for the islands of the Sun and the Moon on the shores of Lake Titicaca, endowed with spiritual significance for the Inca people. These islands were the mythical navel of the world and the birthplace of the Inca nation and the sun deities with which they are associated. As far as we know, the Incas never made it to Rio, and certainly were not responsible directly for naming Rio's Copacabana. For this we must thank the Virgin Mary. Sleight of hand from either the church or the Inca people themselves, who often used syncretism to preserve the heart of their spiritual practices led to the Bolivian Copacabana being transformed from an Inca shrine to a Christian one. In 1576, after surviving a storm on the lake, fishermen commissioned Francisco Yupanque, a direct descendant of the Inca nobility to carve a statue in homage to Our Lady whom they credited with having rescued them. The statue, which had strong Inca features was placed inside a purpose built church in the town of Copacabana, which was renamed Nuestra Señora de Copacabana. It quickly became a pilgrimage centre, especially for sailors and copies of the Inca Virgin were often carried on voyages between Spain and the New World. In the 17th century a boat sailing from Spain to South America came into great difficulties during a storm in the Atlantic. The sailors prayed to an image of Nuestra Señora de Copacabana that they had in their possession and, like those Inca fishermen, they were saved. Their captain promised to build a chapel to the Virgin when he reached land, and he did so in Rio de Janeiro. The Chapel, Nossa Senhora de Copacabana and the original image left their by the ship's captain stood at the far end of Copacabana on the Arpoador until 1914 when it was razed to the ground to make way for the Forte de Copacabana.

Apart from New Year's Eve, when the whole suburb becomes a huge party venue and bands play along the entire length of the beach, Copacabana is a place for little more than landscape and people-watching. It's possible to swim in the sea when the current is heading out from the shore, but otherwise not advisable. The best way to enjoy the area is to wander along the promenade from *posto* (lifeguard post) to *posto*, perhaps stopping to enjoy a coconut at one of the numerous beachfront snack bars, and noting the different crowd at each one. Everyone looks at everyone in Rio so don't be afraid to subtly stare.

At the far end of the beach is the **Museu Histórico do Exército e Forte de Copacabana** ① *Av Atlântica at Francisco Otaviano, www.fortecopacabana.ensino.eb.br, Tue-Sun 1000-1600, US$2*, a museum charting the history of the army in Brazil through the colonial, imperial and republican periods, with cases of military artefacts and panels in Portuguese on campaigns such as the one fought at Canudos against Antônio Conselheiro. There are good views out over the beaches from the fort and a small restaurant.

Ipanema and Leblon

Like Copacabana and Leme, Ipanema and Leblon are essentially one long curving beach enclosed by the monolithic Dois Irmãos rocks at the western end and the Arpoador rocks to the east. And, like Copacabana and Leme, they have few sights beyond the sand, the landscape and the beautiful people. Comparisons, however, end there. Ipanema and Leblon are as fashionable and cool as Copacabana is grungy and frenetic. If Copacabana is samba, then Ipanema is bossa nova: wealthy, sealed off from the realities of Rio in a neat little fairy-tale strip of streets and watched over by twinkling lights high up on the flanks of the Morro Dois Irmãos. They look so romantic that it is easy to forget that they come from the world's largest *favela*.

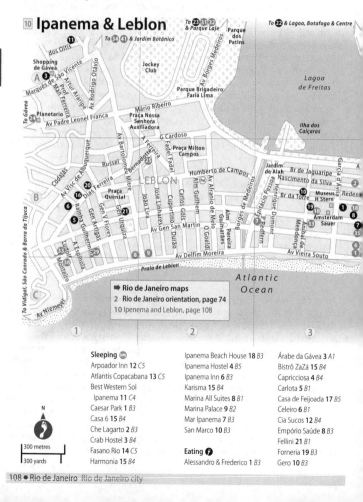

Rio de Janeiro maps
2 Rio de Janeiro orientation, page 74
10 Ipanema and Leblon, page 108

Sleeping
Arpoador Inn **12** C5
Atlantis Copacabana **13** C5
Best Western Sol
Ipanema **11** C4
Caesar Park **1** B3
Casa 6 **15** B4
Che Lagarto **2** B3
Crab Hostel **3** B4
Fasano Rio **14** C5
Harmonia **15** B4

Ipanema Beach House **18** B3
Ipanema Hostel **4** B5
Ipanema Inn **6** B3
Karisma **15** B4
Marina All Suites **8** B1
Marina Palace **9** B2
Mar Ipanema **7** B3
San Marco **10** B3

Eating
Alessandro & Frederico **1** B3

Árabe da Gávea **3** A1
Bistrô ZaZá **15** B4
Capricciosa **4** B4
Carlota **5** B1
Casa de Feijoada **17** B5
Celeiro **6** B1
Cia Sucos **12** B4
Empório Saúde **8** B3
Fellini **21** B1
Forneria **19** B3
Gero **10** B3

Closeted and cosseted though it may be, these are the beach suburbs in which to base yourself whilst in Rio. Almost all of the city's best restaurants and bars are here (and in the suburbs of Gávea and Lagoa, which lie behind). The streets are fairly clean and usually walked by nothing more dangerous than a small white poodle; there is plenty of reasonable accommodation, which doesn't rent by the hour at the lower end of the market; and the sea is good for swimming.

Ins and outs
There is no metrô in Ipanema or Leblon. The destination for buses is clearly marked but, as a rule of thumb, any buses heading east along the seafront go to Copacabana or if going west to Barra da Tijuca, and those going inland will pass by the Lagoa or Gávea.

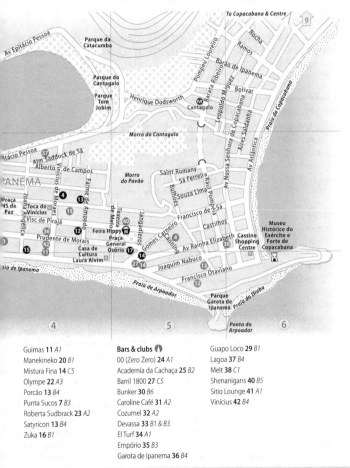

Guimas **11** A1
Manekineko **20** B1
Mistura Fina **14** C5
Olympe **22** A3
Porcão **13** B4
Punta Sucos **7** B3
Roberta Sudbrack **23** A2
Satyricon **13** B4
Zuka **16** B1

Bars & clubs ⬤
00 (Zero Zero) **24** A1
Academia da Cachaça **25** B2
Barril 1800 **27** C5
Bunker **30** B6
Caroline Café **31** A2
Cozumel **32** A2
Devassa **33** B1 & B3
El Turf **34** A1
Empório **35** B3
Garota de Ipanema **36** B4

Guapo Loco **29** B1
Lagoa **37** B4
Melt **38** C1
Shenanigans **40** B5
Sitio Lounge **41** A1
Vinícius **42** B4

Sights

Like Copacabana, Ipanema and Leblon are places for people-watching. A half-day wandering around Ipanema/Leblon followed by a half-day wandering Copacabana/Leme can be most interesting. The crowds are quite different. While Copacabana attracts a real cross-section of Rio society, Ipanema and Leblon are predominantly haunts of the fashionable peacocks, who strut along the beachfront promenade, especially around **Posto Nove**. Beyond the people and the breathtaking landscape, there is little to see here but plenty to do, especially for avid consumers. Shopping is best on and around Garcia D'Avila and at the **Feira Hippy** (see Markets, page 136), where you will find everything from high-quality Brazilian designer swimwear to seed bracelets and T-shirts with pictures of Bob Marley. Those seeking culture but unwilling to leave the beach should head for the **Casa de Cultura Laura Alvim** ① *Av Vieira Souto 176, T021-2247 6946*, comprising an arts cinema, art galleries (temporary exhibitions), workshop spaces and a bookshop. If it is pouring with rain you could watch diamonds being cut and set at the **Museus H Stern** ① *R Garcia D'Avila 113, T021-2106 0000*, or **Amsterdam Sauer** ① *R Garcia D'Avila 105, T021-2512 1132*, or hang out in the **Garota de Ipanema**, the bar where the *Girl from Ipanema* was written in the late 1950s (see Bars and clubs page 129).

Gávea, Lagoa and Jardim Botânico

Just inland from Ipanema and Leblon, nestled under the forested slopes of Corcovado and the Tijuca national park and spread around the picturesque saltwater lagoon of Lagoa Rodrigo de Freitas, are these three mainly residential suburbs. There are a few sights of interest and all have lively top-end nightlife. **Gávea** tends to attract the young and wealthy, while the 30-somethings dine in the restaurants in **Lagoa** overlooking the lagoon and go out to clubs in **Leblon** or to the exclusive **Jockey Club**. ⇥ *See Bars and clubs, page 129.*

Ins and outs

Buses from the centre are marked 'Gávea', or for the Jardim Botânico, Leblon, Gávea or São Conrado 'via Jóquei'. Bus Nos 571 and 170 from the centre go to the Jardim Botânico or No 172 from Flamengo or Botafogo. Bus No 584 runs between Jardim Botânico and Copacabana. Bus Nos 176 and 178 run from the centre and Flamengo and bus Nos 591 and 592 from Copacabana go to the planetarium.

Lagoa de Freitas

The Lagoa is another of Rio de Janeiro's unfeasibly beautiful natural sights and has long been admired. Darwin and German naturalists Spix and Martius mention it in their accounts. It is best seen in the early evening when thick golden sunlight bathes the rainforest-clad slopes of the **Serra da Carioca**, which rise high above it to reach their spectacular pinnacle with the distant xenon-white statue of Christ.

Like Copacabana and Guanabara Bay, it could be even more beautiful if only it were looked after a little better. The canal that links the lake to the sea is far too narrow to allow for sufficient exchange of water; pollution makes it unsafe for swimming and occasional summer algal blooms have led to mass fish deaths.

The lake is surrounded by a series of parks. Immediately next to it is the **Parque Tom Jobim** and contiguous are **Brigadeiro Faria Lima**, **Parque do Cantagalo** and **Parque das Taboas**. All have extensive leisure areas popular with roller skaters and volleyball players.

The favelas

Brazil's reputation as a violent country comes almost exclusively from the gun fights against the police and the inter-gang wars which take place in the slums of Rio de Janeiro, São Paulo, Belo Horizonte, Salvador and other big cities. Such slums are known as *favelas* in Portuguese and although visits to are offered on organized tours, many are highly dangerous – closed communities where strangers enter in peril of their life; like the *favela* so shockingly portrayed in the multi award winning film, *Cidade de Deus* (City of God). The film was no exaggeration: Brazil's *favela*-driven crime statistics speak for themselves. A study undertaken in 2002 by British anthropologist, Luke Dowdney, in conjunction with Brazilian non-governmental organizations working in Rio's slums found that in the 14 years to that date almost 4000 under 18-year-olds were killed by firearms in Rio. Many died in inter-gang wars. Many were shot indiscriminately by the police. This compares with just under 500 children killed in the fighting between Palestinians and Israelis in the same period. The study also estimated that there were between 5000-6000 armed children in the city.

For some years now there has been a stand-off between the drug gangs and their child soldiers and the police and Rio's streets have been relatively safe for tourists. But in mid-2004, after three police officers were shot (one in front of his wife), the city police announced a knee jerk offensive called Operation Maximum Pressure, where 850 officers were sent to target drug gangs within the *favelas* themselves. Although many were arrested and large quantities of guns recovered the police as ever shot first and asked questions later. Rancour grew, and the operations targeted many *favelas* which until that point had been relatively peaceful. After the macho deputy state governor, Luiz Paulo Conde announced plans to build 3-m-high concrete walls around Rocinha and Vidigal (which sit between Leblon and São Conrado), gang members took their fight to the streets of Copacabana, exchanging gunfire with the police on the Avenida Atlântica near Arpoador. Even after international condemnation from Amnesty International and complaints from the mayor, Conde refused to back down. The wall was not for social exclusion, he said, but to mark off territory and to protect Tijuca forest from the drug traffickers. Despite his remonstrations building has not yet begun. But all is not bad news. Even though the federal and state governments use little more than intimidation and brute force against the urban poor, more enlightened individuals, like the wife of the culture minister, Rosa Gil, and musicians like Grupo Afro Reggae in Rio and organizations like the Rudolph Steiner Monte Azul project in São Paulo are making a real difference by bringing education and the hope of work to the young urban poor. Crime statistics where they are working have shown a marked decrease. As yet government bodies have shown little interest in following their example, preferring the vote winning iron fist approach.

There are live shows and *forró* dancing in the **Parque dos Patins** and kiosks serve a variety of food from Arabic to Japanese. Nearby is the **Parque Carlos Lacerda** ① *Av Epitacio Pessoa, daily 0800-1900*, an open-air art gallery with sculptures by local artists in a landscaped park shaded by ornamental trees.

Jardim Botânico (botanical gardens)

① *R Jardim Botânico 1008, T021-3874 1808, www.jbrj.gov.br, daily 0800-1700, US$2.*
These extensive 137-ha gardens protect 70,000 rare vascular plants and are home to 140 species of birds, and butterflies including the brilliant blue morphos. There are stately stands of 40-m-high royal palms, large tropical ficus and ceiba trees and pau brasil, from which the country gets its name. Giant Amazonian victoria regia lilies cover many of the ponds and there are views up to Corcovado through the trees. The gardens were founded in 1808 by the king, Dom Joao VI, as a nursery for European plants and new specimens from throughout the world. When the electric tram line arrived in this part of the city, housing and industries soon followed, but the gardens, then as now, remained a haven of peace. There is a herbarium, an aquarium and a library as well as the **Museu Botânico**, housing exhibitions on the conservation of Brazilian flora, and the **Casa dos Pilões**, the first gun-powder factory in Brazil. A new pavilion contains sculptures by Mestre Valentim. Many improvements were carried out before the 1992 Earth Summit, including a new *orquidario*, an enlarged bookshop and a smart café. Birdwatchers can expect to see rarities including the social flycatcher, great and boat-billed kiskadees, cattle tyrants, sayaca, palm and seven-coloured (green-headed) tanagers as well as over 20 different kinds of hummingbird, roadside hawks, laughing falcons and various toucans and parakeets. There are marmosets in the trees.

Less than 1 km from the gardens is the little-visited **Parque Laje** ① *R Jardim Botânico 414, daily 0900-1700, free*, which is more jungle-like than the Jardim Botânico and has a series of small grottoes, an old tower and lakes, as well as the **Escola de Artes Visuais** (visual arts school) housed in a large colonial house in the grounds.

The **Planetario** ① *R Padre Leonel Franco 240, Gávea, www.rio.rj.gov.br/planetario, by appointment, free*, has a sculpture of the Earth and Moon by Mário Agostinelli. On Wednesday evenings at dusk, in clear weather, astronomers give guided observations of the stars. At weekends there are shows for children at 1630, 1800 and 1930. There are occasional *chorinho* concerts on Thursday or Friday.

The **Instituto Moreira Salles** ① *R Marquês de São Vicente 476, Gávea, T021-3284 7400, www.ims.com.br, Tue-Fri 1300-2000, Sat and Sun 1300-1800, free*, is a cultural centre in a modernist mansion with gardens landscaped by Burle Marx. There are exhibition halls for photographic shows and an auditorium for concerts and films.

Rough paths lead to the summit of the flat-topped **Pedra da Gávea** and to magnificent views. Hang-gliders fly to the beach at São Conrado from the **Pedra Bonita** behind the Pedra da Gávea. ▸▸ *See Activities and tours, page 138.*

Barra da Tijuca and beyond

This rapidly developing district, modelled on Miami, is one of the city's principal middle-class residential areas. It focuses on a 20-km sandy beach that is renowned for its surfing, especially at its far westernmost end: **Recreio dos Bandeirantes**. There are countless bars and restaurants, concentrated at both ends, as well as campsites, motels and hotels. Budget accommodation tends to be self-catering.

Ins and outs

Buses from the city centre to Barra are Nos 175 and 176; from Botafogo, Glória or Flamengo take No 179; from Leme Nos 591 or 592; and from Copacabana via Leblon No (45 minutes to one hour). A taxi from the centre costs US$25 (US$35 after 2400) or US$15 from Ipanema. A comfortable bus, **Pegasus**, goes along the coast from the Castelo bus terminal to Barra da Tijuca and continues to Campo Grande or Santa Cruz, or take the free 'Barra Shopping' bus. Bus No 700 from Praça São Conrado goes the full length of the beach to Recreio dos Bandeirantes.

Sights

The **Bosque da Barra/Parque Arruda Câmara** ① *junction of Av das Américas and Av Ayrton Senna, daily 0700-1700,* preserves the vegetation of the sandbanks that existed on this part of the coast before the city took over. The **Autódromo** (motor-racing track) is behind Barra and the Lagoa de Jacarepaguá, in the district of the same name. The Brazilian Grand Prix was held here during the 1980s before returning to Interlagos, São Paulo.

Terra Encantada ① *Av Ayrton Senna 2800, T021-2430 9800, www.terra-encantada. com.br, Thu-Sun 1000-2300,* is a 300,000-sq-m theme park in Barra whose attractions are based on the different cultural heritages of Brazil: indigenous, African and European. Among the attractions are roller coasters, river rapids, a cinema and shows. Rides close at 2200 and on the main street restaurants, bars and nightspots open.

A bit further out is the **Museu Casa do Pontal** ① *Estrada do Pontal 3295, Recreio dos Bandeirantes, T021-2490 3278, www.museucasadopontal.com.br, Tue-Sun 0930-1700.* Located in a little wood near Recreio dos Bandeirantes beach, this is one of the finest collections of Brazilian folk art in the country. There are over 5000 works by more than 200 artists from 24 different Brazilian states, accumulated French designer Jacques van de Beuque over a 40-year period. Recommended.

Parque Nacional da Tijuca

① *Daily 0600-2100, see map page 74.*

Corcovado is situated within Tijuca national park; one of the largest areas of urban rainforest in the world. It is a haven for city-weary Cariocas, as well as for some 200 species of birds, numerous small mammals and primates and hundreds of species of endangered Atlantic coast rainforest plants. The forest has a number of natural springs, many of which have been diverted through bamboo channels to form natural showers – be sure to bring swimming gear. There is plenty of shade and the views from the various vantage points are almost as impressive as those from Corcovado.

The vegetation in the Parque Nacional da Tijuca is not primary; most is natural regrowth and planned reforestation. It is a testament to what humans can do to regenerate lost forest. The first Europeans to arrive in the area cut down trees for use in construction and as firewood. The lower areas were cleared to make way for sugar plantations. When coffee was introduced to Rio de Janeiro in 1760 further swathes were cut down for *fazendas.* But the deforestation destroyed Rio's watershed and in 1861, in one of the world's first conservation projects, the imperial government decided that Tijuca should become a rainforest preserve. The enormous task of reforesting the entire area was given to an army major, Manuel Gomes Archer, who took saplings from other areas of Atlantic forest and replanted Tijuca with native trees and a selection of exotics in fewer than 13 years. The names of the six slaves who did the actual manual work is not known. Reforestation was continued by Tomas de Gama. In 1961 Tijuca was joined to several other patches of remnant forest to form a national park of 3300 ha.

Ins and outs

To get to the park entrance, take bus No 221 from Praça 15 de Novembro, No 233 ('Barra da Tijuca') or No 234 from the *rodoviária* or No 454 from Copacabana to Alto da Boa Vista.

There is no public transport within the park and the best way to explore is by trail, tour, bicycle or car. If hiking in the park other than on the main paths, a guide may be useful if you do not want to get lost. Contact the **Sindicato de Guías**, T021-267 4582.►► *See Hiking, page 138.*

Sights

One of the best walks is to the **Pico da Tijuca** (1022 m). Views from the top are wonderful and the walk offers the chance to see plenty of animals. Allow two to three hours. To get to the trailhead enter the park at **Alto da Boa Vista** and follow the signposts (maps are displayed) to **Bom Retiro**, a good picnic place (1½ hours' walk). At Bom Retiro the road ends and there is another hour's walk up a fair footpath to the summit (take the path from the right of the Bom Retiro drinking fountain, not the more obvious steps from the left). The last part consists of steps carved out of the solid rock. There are several sheer drops at the summit which are masked by bushes – be wary. The route is shady for almost its entire length. The main path to Bom Retiro passes the **Cascatinha Taunay** (a 30-m waterfall) and the **Mayrink Chapel** (1860). Panels painted in the Chapel by **Cândido Portinari** have been replaced by copies and the originals will probably be installed in the Museu de Arte Moderna. Beyond the chapel is the wonderful little restaurant **Os Esquilos**, which dates from 1945. Allow at least five hours for the walk.

Other viewpoints include the **Paulo e Virginia Grotto**, the **Vista do Almirante**, the **Mesa do Imperador** and the **Vista Chinesa** (420 m), a Chinese-style pavilion with a view of the Lagoa Rodrigo de Freitas, Ipanema and Leblon. **Museu Açude** ⓘ *Estrada do Açude 764, Alto da Boa Vista, T021-2492 2119, www.museuscastromaya.com.br, Thu-Sun 1100-1700, Sun brunch with live music 1230-1700,* is in the former home of tycoon Castro Maia with some impressive murals and *azulejos* (tiles).

Ilha de Paquetá

Paquetá Island, the second largest in Guanabara Bay, is noted for its gigantic pebble-shaped rocks, butterflies and orchids. Its name means 'many shells' in Tupi, but it has also been called the Ilha dos Amores. The only real reason to come here is for the wonderful views but there are a few historical buildings on the island including the **house of José Bonifácio**, a Cariocan anti-slavery campaigner, and the newly refurbished **Solar D'El Rei**, which houses a library. At the southwest tip is the interesting **Parque Darke de Mattos**, with beautiful trees, lots of birds and a lookout on the Morro da Cruz. The island has several beaches, but the water is none too clean. The only means of transport are bicycles and horse-drawn carriages (many have harnesses which cut into the horse's flesh). Neither is allowed into the Parque Darke de Mattos. A tour by *trenzinho* (tractor), costs US$1.25, or just wander around on foot (quieter and free); bicycles can also be hired. The island is very crowded at weekends and on public holidays, but is usually quiet during the week.

Ins and outs

Paquetá Island can be visited by ferry services that leave more or less every two hours from the boat terminal at Praça 15 de Novembro. **Boats**, T021-2533 7524, run 0515-2300 (from 0710 on Sunday and holidays), US$1, one hour. **Hydrofoils**, T021-3397 0656, run hourly 1000-1600, or 0800-1630 at weekends, US$4 (more expensive at weekends), 20 minutes.

Western Rio

Almost half of the municipal area of Rio de Janeiro is in what is referred to as the **Zona Oeste** (the West Zone). On the coast, this stretches from Barra da Tijuca past a whole succession of surf beaches such as **Prainha** and **Grumari** (very attractive, rustic beach bars), not accessible by public transport, but attracting heavy traffic at weekends. Further west still are the **Barra de Guaratiba** and **Pedra de Guaratiba** beaches and, finally, those at **Sepetiba**. This stunning coastal road (the start of the Costa Verde highway) is becoming obliterated by executive housing developments, so visit soon.

Sítio Roberto Burle Marx ① *Estrada da Barra de Guaratiba 2019, Barra de Guaratiba, T021-2410 1171, daily 0930-1330, by appointment only*, was, from 1949 to 1994, the home of the great Roberto Burle Marx (1909-1994), world famous as a landscape designer and artist. His projects achieved a rare harmony between nature, architecture and man-made landscapes. He created many schemes in Brazil and abroad; in Rio alone his work includes the Parque do Flamengo, the pavements of the Avenida Atlântica in Copacabana, Praça Júlio de Noronha in Leme, the remodelling of the Largo da Carioca, the gardens of the Museu Nacional de Belas-Artes and of the Biblioteca Nacional and the complex at the Santa Teresa tram station near the Catedral Metropolitana.

Covering 350,000 sq m, the estate contains an estimated 3500 species of plants, mostly Brazilian. It is run now by the **Instituto do Patrimônio Histórico e Artístico Nacional (IPHAN)** and one of its main aims is to produce seedlings of the plants in its collection. Also on view are Burle Marx's collection of paintings, ceramics, sculptures and other objets d'art, plus examples of his own designs and paintings. The library houses 2500 volumes on botany, architecture and landscape design.

◉ Rio de Janeiro listings

Hotel and guesthouse prices
LL over US$200 **L** US$151-200 **AL** US$116-150
A US$81-115 **B** US$51-80 **C** US$36-50
D US$21-35 **E** US$10-20 **F** under US$10

Restaurant prices
††† over US$20 †† US$8-20 † under US$8

◒ Sleeping

The best places to stay in Rio are **Santa Teresa**, or **Ipanema** and the Arpoador: the former for nightlife, culture and easy access to Lapa, the Sambódromo and carnival; the latter for the beach. Ipanema is probably the safest area of any in the city. Those looking for hotels with charm and personality will find Rio unremarkable. With a few notable exceptions those in the higher and mid-range bracket are a mix of anonymous business chain towers and fading leftovers from the 1970s, complete with period decor. Those at the lower end are almost invariably dubious hot-pillow establishments in equally dubious areas. Backpackers, however, are well catered for. Searches on sites such as www.hostels.com or www.hostelworld.com will yield almost 50 options and numbers are increasing every month. There are far too many for us to list them all here, so we have only included our favourites.

All accommodation is considerably pricier over New Year and Carnaval. Reserve well in advance, especially budget accommodation.

Self-catering apartments This is a popular form of accommodation in Rio, available at all price levels. In **Flamengo** furnished apartments for short-term let, accommodating up to 6, cost US$300 per month. In **Copacabana**, **Ipanema** and **Leblon** prices start at about US$25 a day (US$500-600 a month) for a simple studio, up to US$2000 a month for a luxurious residence sleeping 4-6. Heading south past **Barra da Tijuca**, virtually all the accommodation available is self-catering. Renting a small flat, or sharing a larger one, can be much better value than a hotel room.

Blocks consisting entirely of short-let apartments can attract thieves, so check the (usually excellent) security arrangements; residential buildings are called *'prédio familiar'*. Higher floors (*'alto andar'*) are quieter.

'Apart-Hotels' are listed in the *Guia 4 Rodas* and **Riotur**'s booklet. Agents and private owners advertise under *'Apartamentos – Temporada'* in publications like *Balcão* (twice weekly), *O Globo* or *Jornal do Brasil* (daily); advertisements are classified by district and size of apartment: *'vagas e quartos'* means shared accommodation; *'conjugado'* (or *'conj'*) is a studio with limited cooking facilities; *'3 quartos'* is a 3-bedroom flat. There should always be a written agreement when renting.

Homestays

A range of luxurious private homes throughout Rio and Rio state is offered by www.angatu.com and www.brazilian beachhouse.com.

L-AL Cama e Café, R Paschoal Carlos Magno 5 at R Monte Alegre, T021-2224 5689, T021-9638 4850 (mob, 24 hrs), www.camaecafe.com and www.riohomestay.com. One of the best accommodation options in Rio with a range of more than 50 homestay deals

in Santa Teresa, Cosme Velho and Ipanema from the simple to the luxurious. Included in these are Mestre Valentim's mock neo-Gothic castle and Ronnie Biggs's former home. Homestays are very good value and provide the opportunity to get to know locals and see Rio from the inside. Mixing with your host is at the guest's discretion. Rooms can be treated as impersonally as those in a hotel, or guests can fit in as part of the household. **Cama e Café** work hard to match guests with hosts who share similar interests.

Santa Teresa *p95, map p96*
LL Mama Ruisa, R Santa Cristina 132, T021-2242 1281, www.mamaruisa.com. French-run boutique hotel with carefully casual public spaces and 4 simply decorated, elegant hard wood and whitewash rooms decorated in a modern French colonial style and named in homage to French artistic icons. Also has a pool and sweeping views.
B-D Casa Áurea, R Áurea 80, T021-2242 5830, www.casaaurea.com.br. Tranquil, friendly, arty hostel and boutique hotel in a colonial house in a Santa Teresa backstreet. All rooms vary in shape, size and colour and they and the public spaces, which include a large garden patio, are decorated with tasteful art and craftwork. 5 languages spoken, attracts an interesting crowd and close to the restaurant areas.
B-E Rio Hostel, R Joaquim Murtinho 361, T021-3852 0827, www.riohostel.com. One of Rio's best small hostels. clinging to the side of

a hill, it has spectacular views of the centre and is on the doorstep of the city's best nightlife. Doubles and dorms are simple but well kept and overlook the city or the little pool. Carina, the friendly owner, has an inexplicable love of Jamie Oliver as well as all things British and Australian. Excellent facilities and services such as internet, kitchens, lockers, tours and a shuttle service. There is a new branch in Ipanema.

Glória, Catete and Flamengo
p98, maps p96 and p98

Primarily residential areas between the centre and Copacabana, with good bus and metrô connections. Glória, Catete and Flamengo lie next to a park landscaped by Burle Marx and a beautiful beach lapped by a filthy sea.

LL Glória, R do Russel 632, Glória, www.hotel gloriario.com.br. A stylish and elegant 1920s hotel, closed for refurbishment at the time of writing but due to re-open in high luxury in 2010. Check the website for details.

L Novo Mundo, Praia Flamengo 20, Catete, T021-2105 7000, www.hotelnovomundo-rio.com.br. Standard 4-star rooms in an art deco building with suites with balcony views of the Sugar Loaf.

L Windsor Flórida, Ferreira Viana 71/81, Catete, T021-2195 6800, www.windsor hoteis.com. Business-oriented hotel with a well-equipped business centre, one of the city's largest convention centres, bars (for private hire), a restaurant and modestly decorated no-nonsense modern rooms.

B Imperial, R do Catete 186, Catete, T021-2556 5212, www.imperialhotel.com.br. One of the city's very first grand hotels, built in the late 19th century. Rooms are divided between the old building and the new annexe. The latter has modern US-style motel rooms, which are better equipped but have enclosed views. There is a pool, sauna and gym.

B Inglês, R Silveira Martins 20, Glória, T021-2558 3052, www.hotelingles.com.br. Conveniently located near the metrô and in front of the Museu da República gardens.

The better rooms have been refurbished and have a/c and there's a pleasant public balcony overlooking the park.

B Paysandú, Paysandú, R Paissandú 23, Flamengo, T021-2558 7270, www.paysandu hotel.com.br. Old art deco tower next to the Palacio da República and Flamengo gardens, with spartan rooms but helpful staff, good location, tours available. **C** for a single.

B-C Único, R Buarque de Macedo 54, Catete, T021-2205 9932. Pleasant, sunny rooms in a labyrinth of corridors. Check the mattresses; some are spongy. Better-value doubles than many of the hostels.

B-D Catete Hostel, R do Catete 92, casa 1, Catete, T021-3826 0522, www.catetehostel. com.br. Simple rooms and dorms in concrete and formica, all a/c and with en suite. Breakfast included. 24-hr reception and check-in.

Camping

If travelling with a trailer, you can park at the **Marina Glória car park**, where there are showers and toilets, a small shop and snack bar. Pay the guards to look after your vehicle. See also www.camping-club.com.br.

Botafogo and Urca *p101, map p100*

B-D El Misti Hostel, Praia de Botafogo 462, casa 9, Botafogo, T021-2226 0991, www.elmistihostel.com. A converted colonial house with 6 dorms, shared bathrooms, kitchen and internet, capoeira classes and tour service. Popular with party-goers.

B-D Sun Rio Hostel, R Praia de Botafogo 462, casa 5, Botafogo, T021-2226 0461, www.sun riohostel.com.br, next door to **El Misti**. A/c dorms, doubles and en suites, all very well kept and clean. Shared kitchen, internet, bike rental and tours organized. Friendly owner Daniela is very welcoming.

C-D Tupiniquim Hostel, R São Manoel 19, at R da Passagem, Botafogo, T021-2244 1286, www.tupiniquimhostel.com.br. Small-scale hostel in a pretty little town house offering a range of interesting volunteer activities alongside the standard facilities. Friendly staff.

Copacabana p105, map p104

Once *the* place to stay in Rio but now increasingly sleazy. Ipanema is a better option. Many hotels charge about 30% more for a sea view, but some town-side upper rooms have good views of the mountains.

LL Copacabana Palace, Av Atlântica 1702, T021-2548 7070, www.copacabana palace.com.br. Rio's grande dame remains the city's only world-class large hotel, a mantle it has worn since first being made famous by Ginger Rogers and Fred Astaire, who filmed *Flying down to Rio* here. Pictures of them and hundreds of other famous faces adorn the upper gallery, in classy, understated black and white. Rooms are quiet, spacious and comfortable, with superb beds, effortless service, and conservative and rather European decor. The hotel restaurant, **Cipriani**, is of a similar high standard to its celebrated sister restaurants in Venice and New York.

LL Marriott, Av Atlântica 2600, T021-2545 6500, www.marriott.com. Rio's newest top-end business hotel with 245 guest rooms specifically designed for the business traveller, an executive floor, 12 meeting rooms and a whole gamut of other business services.

LL Pestana Rio Atlântica, Av Atlântica 2964, T021-2548 6332, www.pestana.com. The best option in Copacabana after the **Palace**, with spacious bright rooms and a rooftop pool and terrace with sweeping views. Part of the well-managed Portuguese **Pestana** group. Very high standards. Highly recommended.

LL Sofitel, Av Atlântica, 4240, T021-2525 1232, www.sofitel.com. One of the best beachfront options in the city, at the safer Arpoadoar end of Copacabana and with easy walking access to Ipanema. The hotel has large, airy modern rooms (the best are on the upper floors, with wonderful views over the beach), a sauna, pool and a French restaurant, **Le Pré Catelan**, with one of the best kitchens in the city.

L-AL Copacabana Rio, Av N S de Copacabana 1256, T021-2267 9900, www.copacabanario hotel.com.br. Quiet, efficiently run 1970s tower with simple but well-maintained standard 3-star rooms, a little pool and generous breakfasts. Safe area at the Ipanema end of the beach a block from the sand.

L-AL Grandarrell Ouro Verde, Av Atlântica 1456, T021-2542 1887, www.dayrell.com.br. One of the better small hotels in Copacabana with spacious well-decorated rooms and a decent restaurant. Good for families.

L-AL Portinari Design, R Francisco Sá 17, T021-3222 8800, www.hotelportinari.com.br. Comfortable mock-boutique suites in a great location at the Arpoador end of Copacabana. Decent breakfast with a view on the top floor, internet and a little spa. Good service.

AL Benidorm Palace, R Barata Ribeiro 547, T021-2548 8880, www.benidorm.com.br. Modern rooms decked out in light wood in a tower fully renovated in 2007. The best and quietest are at the back and have small marble bathrooms. Facilities include a sauna and internet in the lobby.

AL-A Copacabana Sol, R Santa Clara 141, T021-2549 4577, www.copacabanasolhotel. com.br. Newly refurbished. Tiled, a/c rooms with cable TV, Wi-Fi, safes and en suite bathrooms with marble commodes and showers. Good value.

A Atlantis Copacabana, Av Bulhões de Carvalho 61, T021-2521 1142, atlantishotel@ uol.com.br. Fading Arpoador hotel in a quiet, safe street very close to the beach. Small rooftop pool, sauna, and the best hotel rates in the area so close to the beach.

A Debret, Av Atlântica 3564, T021-2522 0132, www.debret.com. Bright, spacious, modern seafront rooms in pastel colours and with separate ante rooms; others are a little dark.

A Hotel Angrense, Travessa Angrense 25, T021-2548 0509, www.angrensehotel.com.br. Well-kept basic a/c rooms in a little art deco block on a quiet street; 24-hr reception, English-speaking staff, reliable tour agency and good carnival rates.

A Santa Clara, R Décio Vilares 316, T021-2256 2650, www.hotelsantaclara.com.br. Bright, newly refurbished rooms a few blocks back from the beach. Well maintained, discreet and good value, at the lower end of this price range.

B-E Copinha Hostel, R Felipe de Oliveira 11, T021-2275 8520, www.copinhahostel.com.br. Clean, well-run little lemon-yellow hostel with a range of a/c dorms and doubles in white tile and with en suites. 24-hr reception, kitchen, cable TV and transport services.

B-E Stone of a Beach hostel, R Barata Ribeiro 111, Copacabana, T021-3209 0348, www.stoneofabeach.com.br. Very popular and well-run hostel with spacious, clean dorms and doubles, a lovely pool and bar on the terrace and one of the best ranges of tours in Rio, including surf classes. Excellent English spoken.

D-E Rio Backpackers, Travessa Santa Leocádia 38, on the corner of R Pompeu Loureiro between Barao de Ipanema and R Bolivar, T021-2236 3803, www.riobackpackers.com.br.

Self-catering apartments

Copacabana Holiday, R Barata Ribeiro 90A, T021-2542 1525, www.copacabana holiday.com.br. Recommended, well-equipped small apartments from US$500 per month, minimum 30-day let.

Fantastic Rio, Av Atlântica 974, apt 501, Leme, T021-2543 2667, http://fantasticrio. vilabol.uol.com.br. All types of furnished accommodation from US$20 per day. Good service, contact Peter Corr.

Holidays in Copacabana, Av Atlântica 4066, apt 605, T021-2513 0281. A/c apartments to rent, all are near the beach and have a phone and maid service; English, French, German spoken. All apartments owned by the agency, prices from around US$60 per flat. No sign on the door; ask the *porteiro* to ring for Yvonne.

Paulo de Tarso, Av Princesa Isabel 236, apt 102, T021-2542 5635, pauldetarso@ig. com.br. Apartments near the beach from US$25 per person. Several languages spoken, very helpful.

Rio Residences, Av Prado Júnior 135, apt 508, T021-2541 4568, cell T021-9605 2912. Swiss-run, includes airport transfer.

Ipanema and Leblon *p108, map p108*

LL Best Western Sol Ipanema, Av Vieira Souto 320, Ipanema, T021-2625 2020, www.bestwestern.com. Part of the US group and world's largest chain, with the usual hotel catalogue rooms. Popular with agencies and business travellers.

LL Caesar Park, Av Vieira Souto 460, Ipanema, T021-2525 2525, www.caesar-park.com. Anonymous chain hotel with mock 19th-century flourishes in a beachfront tower. Some rooms have beach views. Decent service includes beach patrol and child-minding. Pool, sauna, restaurant and business facilities.

LL Fasano Rio, Av Vieira Souto 80, Ipanema, T021-3896 4000, www.fasano.com.br. This Philippe Starck-designed luxury hotel in the tasteful Paulistano hotel chain is by far the best in Ipanema and, aside from **La Suite** in Barra da Tijuca, the best in Rio. The superior **Fasano Al Mare** restaurant serves delicious Italian seafood. There's a spectacular rooftop terrace, pool, fitness centre, sauna and massage, a good bar with live music, and limousine service for airport transfers.

LL Marina Palace and Marina All Suites, Av Delfim Moreira 630 and 696, Ipanema, T021-2294 1794, www.hotelmarina.com.br. 2 towers of 1980s vintage almost next door to each other. The former has smart, modern but standard 4-star rooms, a rooftop pool and occasional discount rates over the internet, the latter is a luxury boutique with designer suites and is favoured by the likes of Giselle Bundchen. By international standards it is shabby, but it has an excellent and fashionable sea view restaurant and bar which is great for breakfast and a light lunch or dinner.

B San Marco, R Visconde de Pirajá 524, Ipanema, T021-2540 5032, www.sanmarco hotel.net. Newly renovated 2-star with simple rooms and a free *caipirinha* for every internet booking. Price includes breakfast. 2 blocks from beach. Recommended.

AL-A Arpoador Inn, Francisco Otaviano 177, Ipanema, T021-2523 0060, www.arpoadorinn.com.br. One of the best deals on the seafront. Well maintained, with off-season special offers. Recommended.

AL-A Ipanema Inn, Maria Quitéria 27, behind Caesar Park, Ipanema, T021-2523 6092, www.ipanemainn.com.br. A popular package tour and small business hotel less than 100 m from the beach. Good value and location.

AL-A Mar Ipanema, R Visconde de Pirajá 539, Ipanema, T021-3875 9190, www.maripanema. com. Simple, smart, modern rooms a block from the beach. The front rooms can be noisy.

L-AL Cama e Café, see Santa Teresa, page 116.

B-E Casa 6, R Barão da Torre 175, casa 6, Ipanema, T021-2247 1384, www.casa6 ipanema.com. French-owned B&B in 2 town houses on a street filled with hostels, 3 blocks from the beach. Good long-stay rates. Small rooms with en suites are decorated in wood and tile and are fan-cooled.

B-E Che Lagarto, R Barão de Jaguaripe 208, Ipanema, T021-2247 4582, www.chel agarto.com. Bright-red party hostel with young staff and a terrace with views of Corcovado. Dorms and doubles.

B-E Crab Hostel, R Prudente de Morais 903, Ipanema, T021-2267 7353, www.crab hostel.com.br. Party hostel a block from the beach in a side street behind a set of steel doors. Tiny indoor pool, sauna, cable TV, dorms and rooms, some with en suites.

B-E Harmonia, R Barão da Torre 175, casa 18, Ipanema, T021-2523 4905, www.hostel harmonia.com. 3 blocks from beach, doubles or dorms, kitchen facilities, English, Spanish, German and Swedish spoken, good internet, very popular, welcoming and helpful.

B-E Ipanema Beach House, R Barão da Torre 485, Ipanema, T021-3203 3693, www.ipanema house.com. Great little hostel with very friendly staff, pool, internet, outdoor bar, continental breakfast, a range of dorms and doubles and 24-hr check-in.

B-E Ipanema Hostel, R Canning, casa 1, Ipanema, T021-2287 2928, www.riohostel ipanema.com. Sister hostel to the friendly and welcoming **Rio Hostel** in Santa Teresa with a range of small rooms and dorms, a tour operator, internet and a lively crowd.

B-E Karisma, R Barão da Torre 177, Ipanema, T021-2523 1372. Tranquil little hostel 3 blocks from the beach, small but well-kept dorms and pokey doubles, all up a steep flight of stairs. English spoken, lockers, internet and kitchen.

Gávea p110

LL La Maison, R Sergio Porto 58, T021-7812 5836, www.lamaisonario.com. Rio's only other decent boutique hotel, also run by the French owners of **La Suite**, sits in a period town house on a quiet backstreet in this residential suburb. The bright spacious rooms are tastefully decorated in primary colours and there are wonderful views of Corcovado from the open-sided breakfast area and the little pool. The beach is a taxi ride away.

Barra da Tijuca and beyond *p112*
Spectacular settings, but isolated and
far from centre.
LL La Suite, R Jackson de Figueiredo, 501, Joá,
T021-2484 1962, fxdussol@hotmail.com.
Rio's only boutique hotel of distinction with 8
individually themed and exquisitely designed
rooms perched like an eyrie over an exclusive
beach in Rio's wealthiest small suburb. The
rooms, the restaurant and the pool offer
magical views. Pelé is a neighbour and the
restaurant is run by Ludmila Soeiro, a former
chef at one of Rio's best restaurants, **Zuka**.
LL Sheraton, Av Niemeyer 121, Vidigal
(a suburb between Leblon and São Conrado),
T021-2274 1122, www.sheraton-rio.com.
One of the **Sheraton's** poorer hotels –
a 1970s slab of concrete in painful need of
restyling and refurbishing. Wonderful beach
views though and a decent pool area.

Camping
Camping Clube do Brasil, reservations:
Av Sen Dantas 75, 29th floor, Centro, CEP
20037-900, T021-2210 3171. There are 2
beach sites at Barra da Tijuca. The first is at
Av Sernambetiba 3200, T021-2493 0628
(bus No 233 from centre, or No 702/703 from
the airport via the southern suburbs, US$5),
a long way from the centre, with sauna, pool,
bar, café, US$12 (half price for members).
During Jan and Feb it is often full and
may be restricted to members only.
   There's a simpler site at Estrada do Pontal
5900, T021-2437 8400. Lighting, café, good
surfing, US$6. Both have trailer plots.

🍴 Eating

There are many restaurants in Rio and very
few good ones. With the arrival of decent
food from São Paulo in the 1990s things have
been improving, especially in **Leblon**. But it is
important not to be taken in by appearances
or hotel concierges. Expect to pay at least
US$30 per person in the better restaurants.
At the cheaper end of the spectrum, Rio lacks
that almost ubiquitous Brazilian institution,
the corner bakery. Cariocas generally wolf
down their breakfast and snacks on foot at
streetside bars so a decent sit-down breakfast
that isn't mock-French in appearance (and
price) can be hard to find. But there are plenty
of stand-up juice booths serving fruit juices
made from as many as 25 different fruits from
orange to *açaí* and carrot to *cupuaçu*, all of
which are wonderful. You can eat a filling
lunch for an average US$5 per person, less
if you choose the *prato feito* (US$1.50-6),
or eat in a place that serves food by weight
(starting at about US$10 per kg).

Central Rio and Lapa
p79, maps p80 and p82
Restaurants in the business district are
generally only open for weekday lunch.
Many *lanchonetes* in this area offer good
cheap meals. The **Travessa do Comércio** has
many extemporaneous street restaurants
after 1800, especially on Fri, and is always
buzzing with life. **R Miguel Couto** (opposite
Santa Rita church) is called the 'Beco das
Sardinhas' because on Wed and Fri in
particular it is full of people eating
sardines and drinking beer.
   There are several Arabic restaurants on
Av Senhor dos Passos, which are also open
Sat and Sun. In addition to those listed there
are plenty of cafés, including a few chic new
options on **R Lavradio in Lapa**, where the
lively monthly Sat antiques market is held.
🍴 Adega Flor de Coimbra, R Teotônio
Regadas 34, Lapa, T021-2224 4582. *Chope*
and reliable Portuguese food, including
excellent *bacalhau* and sardines in olive oil.
This little restaurant bar, founded in 1938,
was the home of the Carioca painter Cândido
Portinari and was once a haunt of Rio's
left-wing intelligentsia who would gather
here to discuss political theory over a glass of
chilled French wine. Now the eclectic crowd
is decidedly capitalist, mostly young after-
workers and is particularly lively on Fri.
🍴 Albamar, Praça Marechal Âncora, 184,
Centro, T021-2240 8378. A long-established

Rio seafood restaurant as popular with politicians and businessmen as it has been ever since its opening 70 years ago in the old Mercado Municipal. Getúlio Vargas, Juscelino Kubitschek, Fernando Henrique Cardoso and almost all the other Brazilian presidents have dined here on dishes such as *bacalhau* with oysters and whiting fillet à la albamar, which have been on the menu for as long as anyone can remember. Great views out across Guanabara Bay.

ᵀᵀᵀ **Cais do Oriente**, R Visconde de Itaboraí 8, Centro, T021-2233 2531, www.caisdo oriente.com.br. Wonderful restaurant with a range of different spaces, each with its own atmosphere: from a formal Portuguese-style belle-époque dining room to an informal palm-shaded open-air patio and a terrace with live music. The menu by French chef Alex Giraud is similarly varied with a broad selection of fusions and Mediterranean, Brazilian and oriental dishes.

ᵀᵀᵀ **Eça**, Av Rio Branco 128, T021-2524 2300, www.hstern.com.br/eca. Rio city centre's best business lunch from Frederic de Maeyer – a classically trained chef who once cooked in the Michelin-starred L'Escalier du Palais Royale in Brussels.

ᵀᵀᵀ **Republique**, Praça da República 63, 2nd floor, Centro, T021-2532 9000. A long-established Rio favourite, now newly refurbished by the architect Chico Gouveia (whose decoration is based on the colours of the French flag), serving daring and ambitious South American fusion cooking by distinguished Rio chef Paulo Carvalho.

ᵀᵀ **Bar Luiz**, R da Carioca 39, Centro, T021-2262 6900. For 117 years this little bar in one of the few remaining colonial houses in the city centre has been at the heart of Rio life. Almost every Carioca you can name from Di Cavalcanti and Tom Jobim to Ronaldo and Chico Buarque has at one time or another formed part of the lively throng which gathers here on weekday evenings and most particularly on Fri and Sat to drink the famous *chope* and eat tapas. During the day it is a great place

for a quiet snack and a respite from the heat and busyness of the city.

ᵀᵀ **Café da Moda**, Loja Folic, R Gonçalves Dias 49, 3rd floor, Centro, T021-2222 0610, www.folic.com.br. An a/c café devoted to the narrow waistline and located within the **Folic** shop. Salads are named after famous models: Gisele Bündchen, Kate Moss, Claudia Schiffer and so on, with more macho options for men, such as Zulu, which comprises buffalo mozzarella, maize, tomato, croutons, lettuce and a garnish of marjoram. Light meals without fashionable names also available.

ᵀᵀ-ᵀ **Bar das Artes**, Paço Imperial, Praça XV de Novembro 48, Centro, T021-2215 5795. Neat, clean and peaceful café on the ground floor of the Paço Imperial (formerly the royal palace) in the busy centre of Rio. Salads, sandwiches, light meals and desserts such as strawberry strudel.

ᵀᵀ-ᵀ **Confeitaria Colombo**, R Gonçalves Dias 32 (near Carioca metrô station), Centro, T021-2232 2300, www.confeitariacolombo.com.br. Afternoons only during the week. The only remaining belle-époque Portuguese coffee house in Rio, serving a range of café food, cakes, pastries and light lunches. The *feijoada colonial* on Sat is accompanied by live *choro*.

ᵀ **Sabor Saúde**, R da Quitanda 21, Centro, T021-2252 6041. Breakfast and lunch only. Vegetarian and wholefood including sandwiches (whose contents you can compile yourself), quiches, pastries, salads and light dishes such as grilled salmon with rosti.

Santa Teresa p95, map p96

ᵀᵀᵀ **Aprazível**, R Aprazível 62, T021-3852 4935. Decent but unspectacular Brazilian dishes and seafood with one of the best restaurant views in the city: tables are outdoors in a tropical garden overlooking Guanabara Bay. This is a good Sun lunch spot when they have occasional *choro* and samba.

ᵀᵀ **Adega do Pimenta**, R Almte Alexandrino 296. Mon and Wed-Fri 1130-2200, Sun 1100-1800. A very small German restaurant in the Largo do Guimarães with excellent sausages, sauerkraut and cold beer.

Rio's best restaurants

Confeitaria Colombo (Centro) and **Alessandro and Frederico** (Ipanema), café culture, pages 122 and 125.
Carême Bistrô (Botafogo) for French, page 123.
Cipriani (Copacabana) for Italian, page 124.
Carlota (Leblon) for intimate dining, page 125.
Gero (Ipanema) and **Bar d'Hotel** (Leblon) for people-watching, page 125.
Satyricon (Ipanema) for seafood, page 125.

Ψ Bar do Arnaudo, Largo do Guimarães, R Almte Alexandrino 316, T021-2252 7246. A modest-looking restaurant decorated with handicrafts but serving generous portions of wonderful northeast-Brazilian cooking. Try the *carne do sol* (sun-dried beef, or jerky) with *feijão de corda* (brown beans and herbs), or the *queijo coalho* (a country cheese, grilled).

Ψ Espírito Santa, R Almte Alexandrino 264, T021-2508 7095. Closed Mon. Lunch only Tue, Wed, Sun. Upstairs is a chic Mediterranean restaurant with a view. Downstairs is a funky weekend basement club. Great cocktails.

Ψ Jasmim Manga, Largo dos Guimarães 143, T021-2242 2605. A pretty little cyber café with decent coffee and a nice view over the square.

Ψ Sobrenatural, R Almte Alexandrino 432, T021-2224 1003. Simple, elegant seafood served by sexagenarian career waiters in bow ties. The huge dining room is always lively with chatter.

Glória, Catete and Flamengo
p98, map p96 and p98

There are many cheap and mid-range eating places on **R do Catete**, all fairly similar.

ΨΨΨ Alcaparra, Praia do Flamengo 144, Flamengo, T021-2557 7236. Elegant traditional Italian/Portuguese restaurant overlooking the sea. A long-established favourite of senior politicians and business people who often ask for the *bacalhau*.

Ψ Lamas, R Marquês de Abrantes 18A, Flamengo, T021-2556 0799. This famous café brasserie with its conservative decor of white tablecloths and dark wood has been serving steaks, *bacalhau* and draught *chopp* to the Rio intelligentsia since 1874. It is still a wonderful place to see the city's movers and shakers and gives a real sense of how European the city once was.

Ψ Estação República, R do Catete 104, Catete, T021-2225 2650. A choice of more than 40 dishes, from soups and sushi to salads and stews, in this pay-by-weight restaurant housed in the Palácio do Catete.

Botafogo and Urca *p101, map p100*

There are many cheap and mid-range options in the **Botafogo Praia** shopping centre.

ΨΨΨ Carême Bistrô, R Visconde de Caravelas, 113, Botafogo, T021-2537 5431. An elegant and intimate little restaurant serving some of the best French bistro food in Rio. The original chef Christophe Faivre, who created much of the menu, worked at Guy Savoy in Paris. He has since been replaced by his once-junior chef Flavia Quaresma who continues to produce house favourites such as *coq au vin*, and by Argentinian executive chef Guillermo Martín Lusardi who has created a delicious new degustation menu. Respectable wine list.

ΨΨΨ Miam Miam, General Goes Monteiro 34, Botafogo, T021-2244 0125, www.miam miam.com.br. Closed Mon. The most fashionable of Rio's alternative fashion set sip *caipirinhas* here. Frequent visitors include Bebel Gilberto and Adrianna Calcanhotto – both names on the Brazilian music scene. Decoration is retro chic with 1950s and 1960s lounge furniture from the **Hully Gully** antique shop in Copacabana's Siqueira

Campos mall and cartoons in homage to cult 1970s Carioca cartoonist, Carlos Zéfiro. Food is light Mediterranean but people come here for the crowd and the cocktails before moving on to Lapa.

⌗ Raajmahal, R General Polidoro 29, Baixo Botafogo, T021-2542 6242, www.raaj mahal.com.br. One of the few restaurants in Brazil offering authentic Indian food with a huge menu including a range of vegetarian dishes such as *mater paneer*.

⌗ Yorubá, R Arnaldo Quintela 94, Botafogo, T021-2541 9387. Evenings only except weekends, closed Mon, Tue. Rio's favourite Bahian restaurant, and several times voted the best in the city by *Veja* magazine. The menu comprises usual run of Bahian food from *acarajé* (beans fried in dendê palm oil) to *vatapá* (fish or chicken with coconut milk, shrimps, peanuts, dendê palm oil and chilli) alongside more unusual dishes such as chicken in ginger sauce with cashew nut rice.

Copacabana *p105, map p104*

There are stand-up bars selling snacks all around Copacabana and Ipanema. There are plenty of open-air restaurants along **Av Atlântica**, none of which can be recommended for anything but the view.

⌗⌗⌗ Cipriani, Copacabana Palace (see page 118). The best hotel restaurant for formal dining, with a chef from the Hotel Cipriani in Venice. Very good seafood and Italian fare.

⌗⌗⌗ Copa Café, Av Atlântica 3056, T021-2235 2947. A French bistro run by São Paulo chef Cássio Machado with light food and fabulous mini burgers with Dijon mustard. Very popular with Carioca celebrities like Caetano Veloso. DJ after dinner in the evenings at weekends.

⌗⌗⌗ La Fiorentina, Av Atlântica 458a, Copacabana, T021-2543 8395, www.la fiorentina.com.br. The best Italian in Copa is famous for its *espaguete com frutos do mar* (seafood spaghetti), served in a light prawn marinade. The bar is a very popular meeting spot for middle class locals and the wine list is reasonable for Rio.

⌗⌗⌗ Mala e Cuia, R Barata Ribeiro 638, T021-2545 7566. *Comida mineira* at another of the restaurants in this recommended chain.

⌗⌗⌗ Siri Mole and Cia, R Francisco Otaviano 90, T021-2233 0107. Excellent Bahian seafood and Italian coffee in elegant a/c surroundings. At the upper end of this price bracket.

⌗⌗⌗-⌗⌗ Churrascaria Palace, R Rodolfo Dantas 16B, T021-2541 5898, www.churrascaria palace.com.br. Copa's answer to **Porcão** or **Esplanada Grill** with 20 different kinds of barbecued meat served in plush surrounds, under a/c and at your table with buffet salads to accompany.

⌗⌗ Chon Kou, Av Atlântica 3880, T021-2287 3956. A traditional Chinese restaurant which also offers an extensive sushi menu. Japanese is far more popular than Chinese in Brazil a/c with piped music; sit upstairs for good views over Copacabana beach. A welcome change from most other options in this area.

⌗⌗ Kilograma, Av NS Copacabana 1144, T021-3202 9050, www.kilograma.com.br. Open on weekends and holidays. A pay-per-weight meat barbecue with a huge buffet choice and good-value fixed lunch menu.

⌗⌗-⌗ Aipo and Aipim, Av Nossa Senhora de Copacabana 391b and 920 in Copacabana, and R Visconde de Pirajá 145 in Ipanema, T021-2267 8313. Plentiful tasty food sold by weight at this popular chain.

⌗⌗-⌗ Eclipse, Av NS de Copacabana 1309, T021-2287 1788, www.eclipse.com.br. Spruce, well-run and very popular 24-hr restaurant offering good value *prato feito* lunches and a generous range of meats, pastas, snacks and sandwiches served in the cool interior or on streetside tables.

⌗ Apetite Cafe, R Souza Lima 78, T021-2247 3319. One of Copa's few bakery cafes. Offers a range of breakfasts, respectable coffee, snacks, options for kids and an a/c interior for when it gets too hot.

⌗ Cafeina, C Ramos 44, T021-2547 8651. Very popular breakfast spot with good coffee, tasty pastries and other snacks and ice cold juices.

⌗ Cervantes, Barata Ribeiro 07-B at Prado Júnior 335B. Stand-up bar or sit-down a/c restaurant, open all night, queues after 2200. Said to serve the best sandwiches in town. A local institution.

♥ **La Tratoria**, Av Atlântica, opposite **Hotel Excelsior**. Good service and Italian food, very reasonable. Recommended.

♥ **Temperade**, Av NS de Copacabana 1243, T021-2267 1149. Open evenings and holidays. A/c, good-value pay-by-weight food, with mains and a huge range of very sweet desserts.

♥ **Traiteurs de France**, Av NS de Copacabana 386. Delicious French tarts and pastries.

Ipanema and Leblon p108, map p108

♥♥♥ **Alessandro and Frederico**, R Garcia D'Ávila 134, loja D, Ipanema, T021-2521 0828. Upmarket café with decent café latte and breakfasts. Great juice bar next door.

♥♥♥ **Bar D'Hotel**, Marina All Suites (see Sleeping, page 120). Light but very well-flavoured fish dishes served to people with tiny waists in casual designer cool surrounds. Very good cocktails. The best for breakfast or lunch with a beach view.

♥♥♥ **Bistrô ZaZá**, R Joana Angélica 40, Ipanema, T021-2247 9101. Hippy chic pseudo-Moroccan/French restaurant that attracts a mix of tourist and bohemian Zona Sul Cariocas. Good fish dishes and cocktails and good fun. Evenings are best for intimate dining when the tables are lit by candles.

♥♥♥ **Capricciosa**, R Vinícius de Moraes 134, Ipanema, T021-2523 3394. The best pizzeria in town and a lynchpin in the TV and fashion scene – the famous and wealthy gather here to gossip and catch up. Queues can be long.

♥♥♥ **Carlota**, R Dias Ferreira 64, Leblon, T021-2540 6821. The best of many on a street lined with restaurants and bars. Great unpretentious Mediterranean food in an elegant, casual all-white dining room.

♥♥♥ **Forneria**, R Aníbal de Mendonça 112, Ipanema, T021-2540 8045. Paulistano restaurateur Rogerio Fasano's latest elegant eating-space in Rio serves supreme burgers in pizza dough and cooked in a wood-fired oven, and other superior bar snacks. Usually full with an elegant after-beach crowd.

♥♥♥ **Gero**, R Aníbal de Mendonça 157, Ipanema, T021-2239 8158. Tasty Italian fare with excellent fish served to TV *Globo novella* stars and the like in a beautiful minimalist space.

♥♥♥ **Manekineko**, R Dias Ferreira 410, Leblon, T021-2540 7641. Rio's best Japanese with a large menu of superb traditional dishes and Japanese, European and South American fusion. The intimate dining area, comprising a corridor of low-lit booths, is always packed.

♥♥♥ **Porcão**, Barão de Torre 218, Ipanema, T021-2522 0999. One of the city's best *churrascarias* serving all manner of meat in unlimited quantities for a set price.

♥♥♥ **Satyricon**, R Barão da Torre 192, Ipanema, T021-2521 0627. The best seafood in Rio, especially the squid. Lively crowd in a large dining room which precludes intimacy. A favourite with businessmen, politicians and Ronaldo. Avoid Sat when there is a buffet.

♥♥♥ **Zuka**, R Dias Ferreira 233, Leblon, T021-3205 7154. One of the most fashionable restaurants in Rio with an exciting and eclectic fusion of everything – French and Japanese, American fast food and Italian – all presented on huge rectangular plates and in a carefully designed modern space.

♥♥ **Casa da Feijoada**, Prudente de Morais 10, Ipanema, T021-2523 4994. Serves excellent *feijoada* all week. Generous portions.

♥♥ **Celeiro**, R Dias Ferreira 199, Leblon. Superior salads and buffet food, which has been consistently voted the best in the city by the magazine, *Veja*.

♥♥ **Cia Sucos**, R Farme de Amoedo at Visconde de Pirajá 183b, T021-3247 0795. One of the largest range of juices in Rio including uniquely South American and Brazilian fruits such as *seriguela*, *mangaba*, *umbu* and *cupuaçu*.

♥♥ **Fellini**, R General Urquiza 104, Leblon, T021-2511 3600, www.fellini.com.br. The best pay-by-weight restaurant in the city with a large range of delicious Brazilian and international dishes, salads and quiches. Plenty of options for vegetarians. Funky website.

♥♥ **New Natural**, R Barão da Torre 173, T021-2226 7317. One of Ipanema's

most popular vegetarian and wholefood restaurants with a large range of hot dishes and desserts served per kilo. There's an adjacent natural products shop next door and the restaurant offer home delivery.
♥♥ **Punta Sucos**, R Maria Quitéria 70a, T021-2247 2518. A favourite Carioca pre- and post-beach pit-stop offering a huge range of tropical juices and snacks such as *açai na tigela* (mushed açai berries with guarana syrup).
♥ **Empório Saúde**, R Visconde de Pirajá 414, Ipanema, T021-2522 1494. Closed Sun and evenings. A large variety of vegetarian comfort-cooking from quiches to stews in a wholefood shop inside a shopping gallery. Good value.

Gávea, Lagoa and Jardim Botânico p110
Gávea is the heartland of trendy 20-something Rio. The neighbourhoods of Jardim Botânico and Lagoa appear at first sight to offer unlimited exciting upmarket dining opportunities. But the restaurants are mostly mutton dressed up as lamb. They look great, cost loads and serve dreadful food. Here are a very few exceptions:
♥♥♥ **Olympe**, R Custódio Serrão 62, Lagoa, T021-2539 4542. The Troisgros family were founders of nouvelle cuisine and run a 3 Michelin-star restaurant in Roanne. Claude Troisgros' cooking fuses tropical ingredients with French techniques, exemplified by the roasted quail filled with *farofa* and served with raisins, pearl onions and a sweet and sour *jabuticaba* sauce.
♥♥♥ **Roberta Sudbrack**, Av Lineu de Paula Machado 916, Jardim Botânico, T021-3874 0139, www.robertasudbrack.com.br. Roberta was the private chef for President Henrique Cardoso and cooked for all the visiting international dignitaries who dined with him during his term of office. She is celebrated for her European-Brazilian fusion cooking and won *Veja*'s coveted chef-of-the-year award in 2006.
♥♥ **Árabe da Gávea**, Gávea shopping mall, R Marquês de São Vicente 52, T021-2294 2439. By far the best Arabic restaurant in Rio.

♥♥ **Guimas**, R José Roberto Macedo Soares, Baixo Gávea, T021-2259 7996. An old favourite for *Globo* actors and low-key celebrities, serving salt Portuguese food in a homely dining room or on the outside veranda on check tablecloths. Very crowded with fashionable under-30s after 2200 on Mon and towards the end of the week.
♥♥ **Mistura Fina**, Av Rainha Elisabeth 769, Ipanema, T021-2523 1703, www.mistura fina.com.br. See Bars and clubs, page 129.

⚫ Bars and clubs

Rio nightlife is young and vivacious. **Lapa** is a current hotspot at weekends, once down-at-heel and still not entirely safe but undergoing a great renaissance, with a string of clubs along Mem de Sá and Lavradio with dance steps from samba and *forro* to techno and hip-hop. Similarly busy, even on Sun and Mon, is **Baixa Gávea**, where beautiful 20-somethings gather around Praça Santos Dumont.

Wherever you are in Rio, there's a bar near you. Beer costs around US$1.50 for a large bottle, but up to US$5 in the plusher venues, where you are often given a card that includes 2 drinks and a token entrance fee. A cover of US$3-7 may be charged made for live music, or there might be a minimum consumption charge of around US$3, sometimes both. Snack food is always available. **Copacabana**, **Ipanema** and **Leblon** have many beach *barracas*, several open all night. The seafront bars on Av Atlântica are great for people-watching; but avoid those towards **Leme** as some may offer more than beer.

Clubs on and around Rio's beaches are generally either fake Europe, eg **Melt** and **Bunker** (although decent DJs like Marky play here), or fake US, eg **Nuth** and **00**. Santa Teresa has the most interesting bohemian bars and is a good place to begin a weekend night before heading down the hill to Lapa, Rio's capital of nightlife, with a plethora of samba venues undergoing a steady renaissance. See also Samba schools, page 132.

What night where?

Monday Baixo Gávea, around Praça Santos Dumont with dancing pretty much limited to **Cozumel**, nearby in the Jardim Botânico. **Empório** in Ipanema has live music.

Tuesday **Devassa** in Leblon is busy on Tuesdays and **Bom Bar** down the road has an oriental night.

Wednesday **Clan Café** in Cosme Velho have live music. **Bunker** in Copacabana is good for dancing.

Thursday Pretty much anywhere is busy. The **Melt** club in Leblon has its busiest night, Lapa begins to get busy and all of the bars in Leblon have a decent crowd.

Friday Lively anywhere. **Mistura Fina** (Lagoa), **Clan Café** (Cosme Velho) usually have an interesting live jazz, MPB or bossa nova act. **Club Six** in Lapa has its busiest dance music night.

Saturday Much the same as Friday and the best night for Lapa and any of the samba clubs there, especially the **Rio Scenarium**, or the **Bom Bar** and **Sítio Lounge** in Leblon. **Nuth** in Barra da Tijuca is always heaving.

Sunday Generally quiet, though Baixo Gávea is always busy and there are often live acts at **Melt** (Leblon); **00** (Gávea) has a gay night.

Central Rio, Lapa and Santa Teresa

p79 and p95, maps p80, p82 and p96

Lapa, Santa Teresa and increasingly, the city centre, have Rio's most interesting, bohemian nightlife and shouldn't be missed if you are in Rio over a weekend. Ideally come early on a Sat for the afternoon market and live street tango on **R Lavradio**, eat in Santa Teresa and sample the bars on the **Largo dos Guimarães** and the **Largo das Neves** before returning to Lapa for live samba or funk. Although it is easy to walk between the 2 *bairros*, never walk alone. Always be wary of pickpockets.

Bar do Goiabeira, Largo das Neves 13, Santa Teresa, T021-2232 5751. One of several restaurant bars on this pretty little square. This and all the others attract an arty crowd after 2100, especially on the little streetside tables. Decent *petiscos* and a range of aromatic vintage *cachaças*.

Bar do Mineiro, R Paschoal Carlos Magno 99, Santa Teresa, T021-2221 9227, 100 m from Largo dos Guimarães. Rustic *boteco* opening right onto the street and with hundreds of black-and-white photos of Brazilian musicians displayed on the white-tiled walls. Attracts a busy, arty young crowd at weekends, downing Minas *petiscos* and bottled beer.

Carioca da Gema, Av Mem de Sá 79, Centro, near **Rio Scenarium**, T021-2221 0043, www.barcariocadagema.com.br. One of the longest established samba clubs and daytime cafés in Lapa, with the cream of the live bands and, if you arrive early, sit-down tables. Great little pre-show pizza restaurant upstairs.

Circo Voador. See Music, page 130. One of the best venues in Rio.

Club Six, R das Marrecas 38, Lapa. Huge pounding European/NYC dance club with everything from hip-hop to ambient house. A grungy old dance hall where transvestites gossip on the stairs and bands play Gafieira or dance hall samba. Caetano Veloso's son, Moreno (who invented the new love of dance hall samba in Rio), sometimes plays here with his band **Orquestra Imperial**. If you're a samba lover and 20- or 30-something at heart, this is the place to be. Few tourists, so far …

Clube dos Democráticos, R do Riachuelo 91, T021-2252 4611, www.clubedos democraticos.com.br

Dama da Noite, R Gomes Freire 773, Lapa. Samba, *chorinho* and crêpes on the patio.

Espírito Santa, R Almte Alexandrino 264, Largo do Guimarães, Santa Teresa, T021-2508 7095, www.espiritosanta.com.br. Faux-Amazonian restaurant with a Buddha

Pedro Luís e A Parede recommends

Pedro Luís and his band play some of the most exciting new samba in Rio, integrating the style with other Brazilian rhythms, modern electronica and indie. They play live in Rio regularly and you can check them out on www.plap.com.br. Here are Pedro's recommendations for what to do in Rio: **Circo Voador,** www.circovoador.com.br and **Fundição Progresso,** T021-2220 5070, www.fundicao.org, are arts and music centres with concert halls, where some of the city's most exciting new performers and film-makers showcase their talents. The Circo runs a lot of social projects too and is in a beautiful location beneath the Arcos de Lapa. The **Espaço Cultural Municipal Sérgio Porto,** R Humaitá 163, Humaitá, T021-2266 0896, is another arts space with two galleries and a theatre where you can see everything from live music to alternative poetry or performance art – all from some of the freshest and most innovative performers in the city.

on the bar and a lively basement club where every Sat DJ Zod plays the best in Rio funk and West African dance. The bar manager, Adriana, makes superb cocktails. Ask her for one of her special *caipirinhas*.
Mercado, R do Mercado 32, Centro, T021-2221 2327, www.mercado32.com.br. Closed weekends. In the heart of the centre in a converted 19th-century building, this little restaurant and bar offers live *MPB* on most nights during the week and live *chorinho* every Thu from 2030.
Nuth Centro, R da Quitanda 51 at 7 de Setembro, www.nuthcentro.com.br. Brings Barra's cheesy take on Miami's bare-midriffed, buff-bodied, plastic boobed club culture to the city centre. Wonderful for people watching. Men should wear a medallion. Take a taxi; the area is nocturnally sketchy.
Rio Scenarium, R do Lavradio 20, Lapa, T021-3852 5516, www.rioscenarium.com.br. 3-storey samba and dance club in a beguilingly spacious colonial house used as a movie prop storage facility by *TV Globo*. Overflowing with Brazilian exuberance and people of all ages dancing furiously, to samba and assorted Euro and Lusitanian club sounds, and the bizarre backdrop of a 19th-century apothecary's shop or mannequins wearing 1920s outfits. Arrive after 2300.

Sacrilégio, Av Mem de Sá 81, Lapa, next door to **Carioca da Gema.** T021-2507 3898. Samba, *chorinho*, *pagode* and occasional theatre. Close to many other bars.
Semente, R Joaquim Silva 138, Lapa, T021-2242 5165. Mon-Sat from 2200, US$2.50 cover, minimum consumption US$2. Popular for samba, *choro* and salsa. Book at weekends. Great atmosphere. Recommended.
The Week, R Sacadura Cabral 154, Zona Portuária, T021-2253 1020, www.the week.com.br. The most popular dance club of choice as this book went to press. Heaving with a mostly gay crowd and with state-of-the-art dance spaces, DJs and sound systems. Don't expect any Brazilian sounds; it's strictly international here.

Glória, Catete and Flamengo
p98, maps p96 and p98.
Look out for the frequent free live music at the **Marina da Glória** and along Flamengo beach during the summer.

Botafogo and Urca *p101, map p100*
Casa de Matriz, R Enrique de Novais 107, Botafogo. Great grungy club with a bar, Atari room, small cinema and 2 dance floors. Full of Rio students.
Porão, under the Anglican church hall, R Real Grandeza 99, Botafogo. British ex-pats meet here on Fri nights.

Copacabana, Ipanema and
Leblon p105 and p108, maps p104 and p108

There is frequent live music on the beaches of Copacabana and Ipanema, and along the **Av Atlântica** throughout the summer, especially around New Year.

Academia da Cachaça, R Conde de Bernadotte 26-G, Leblon, with another branch at Av Armando Lombardi 800, Barra da Tijuca. The best *cachacas*, great *caipirinhas* and traditional Brazilian dishes. Good on Fri.

Bar D'Hotel, Marina All Suites, Ipanema (see page 120). The well-dressed and tanned drink the excellent house cocktails here at the cool long bar before dining on light Mediterranean fare. Beach views. Good for sunset in smart casual.

Barril 1800, Av Vieira Souto 110, Ipanema. Pleasant place to watch the sunset with a cold glass of *chope* beer in hand. Highly recommended.

Bip Bip, R Almte Gonçalves 50, T021-2267 9696. *Botequim* bar that attracts a crowd of jamming musicians every Tue.

Bom Bar, R General San Martin 1011, Leblon. A downstairs bar and an upstairs club; packed after 2300, especially on Sat.

Bunker, R Raul Pompéia 94. European-style dance club where the likes of DJs Marky and Patife play. Busy Wed-Sat; gets going around 0200. The queues have become a party in themselves – at the bar next door.

Clandestino, R Barata Ribeiro 111, T021-3209 0348. A cavernous little cellar bar attracting a lively young crowd who dance to soul, Rio funk and occasional live acts. Busiest on Fri.

Devassa, Av General San Martin 1241, Leblon, and Visconde de Pirajá 539, www.devassa.com.br. A 2-floor pub/bar/ restaurant that is always heaving with the Ipanema middle-class. Brews its own beer.

Empório, R Maria Quitéria 37, Ipanema. Street bar that attracts the hordes. Mon is the busiest night.

Garota de Ipanema, R Vinícius de Moraes 49, Ipanema. Where the song *Girl from Ipanema* was written. Now packed with foreigners on the package Rio circuit listening to bossa.

For the real thing head to **Toca do Vinícius** on a Sun afternoon (see page 131).

Guapo Loco, R General San Martin 1011, Leblon. A swish downstairs bar and an upstairs club attracting a smart, clubby 18-25 crowd. Packed after 2300, especially Sat.

Melt, R Rita Ludolf 47, Leblon, T021-2249 9309, www.melt-rio.com.br. Downstairs bar and upstairs sweaty club. Occasional performances by the cream of Rio's new samba funk scene – usually on a Sun. Always heaving on Thu.

Mistura Fina, Av Rainha Elisabeth 769, Ipanema, T021-2523 1703, www.mistura fina.com.br. A brand new venue for the famous Rio jazz, bossa and MPB club, which has played host to names from Tom Jobim to Liza Minelli. Dinner, a cool bar, ocean views and great music.

Shenanigans, R Visconde de Pirajá 112, Ipanema. Obligatory mock-Irish bar with Guinness and Newcastle Brown. Not a place to mix with the locals.

Vinícius, R Vinícius de Moraes 39, Ipanema, 2nd floor. Mirror image of the **Garota de Ipanema** with slightly better acts and food.

Gávea, Lagoa and Jardim Botânico p110

Bar Lagoa, Av Epitácio Pessoa 1674, Lagoa. Attracts an older arty crowd on weekdays.

Caroline Café, R JJ Seabra 10, Jardim Botânico, T021-2540 0705, www.caroline cafe.com. Popular with Rio's young and good-looking middle classes. Kicks off after 2100. Also serves food.

Clan Café, R Cosme Velho 564 (in front of the Corcovado train station), T021-2558 2322. Closed Sun and Mon. Great little sit-down *choro* and samba club almost unknown to tourists, with live music and decent bar food.

Cozumel, Av Linu de Paula Machada 696, Jardim Botânico, Praça Santos Dumont 31. Gets going at 2300. No T-shirts; very much a rich-kid party place.

El Turf (aka **Jockey Club**), opposite the Jardim Botânico, Praça Santos Dumont 31. Opens at 2200, gets going at 2300; you may have to wait to get in at the weekend if you arrive after 2400. No T-shirts allowed. Very much a Rio

rich-kid singles and birthday-party place; another branch in **Rio Sul** shopping centre.
Sitio Lounge, R Marques de São Vicente 10, Gávea. The nearest thing Rio has to a lounge bar. Good for a chilled out Sat night.
00 (Zero Zero), Av Padre Leonel Franca 240, Gávea. Mock-LA bar/restaurant/club with a small outdoor area. Currently the trendiest club in Rio for Brazil's equivalent of 'sloanes' or 'valley girls'. Gay night on Sun.

Barra da Tijuca p112
Nuth, R Armando Lombardi 999, www.nuth. com.br. Barra's slickest club; very mock-Miami and frequented by a mixed crowd of rich-kid surfers, footballers (including Romario) and women with surgically enhanced beauty. The music is a mix of tacky Brazilian and Eurotrash with occasional samba funk live acts.
Pepe, Posto 2, Barra da Tijuca beach. One of a string of very popular beach bars frequented by toned, tanned surfers.

⊙ Entertainment

Rio de Janeiro p72
Cinema
There are cinemas serving subtitled Hollywood fare and major Brazilian releases on the top floor of almost all the malls. The normal seat price is around US$3. Discounts on Wed and Thu (students pay half price any day of the week). Alternative and art-house films are shown in the following theatres:
Centro Cultural do Banco do Brasil, R Primeiro de Março 66, Centro, T021-808 2020. One of Rio's better arts centres with the best of the art films and exhibitions from fine art to photography (Metrô Uruguaiana).
Cinemateca do MAM, Infante Dom Henrique 85, Aterro do Flamengo, T021-2210 2188. Cinema classics, art films, roving art exhibitions and a good café with live music. Views of Guanabara Bay from the balconies.
Estaçao Ipanema, R Visconde de Pirajá 605, Ipanema. European art cinema, less-mainstream US and Brazilian releases.

Horse racing
Jockey Club Racecourse, by the Jardim Botânico and Gávea, meetings on Mon and Thu evenings and Sat and Sun 1400, entrance US$1-2, long trousers required, tables can be booked. Take any bus marked 'via Jóquei'. Betting is by tote only.

Live music
Many young Cariocas congregate in Botafogo for live music. There are free concerts throughout the summer along the Copacabana and Ipanema beaches, in Botafogo and at the parks: mostly samba, reggae, rock and MPB (Brazilian pop). There is no advance schedule; information is given in the local press. Rio's famous jazz, in all its forms, is performed in lots of enjoyable venues too, see www.samba-choro.com.br for more information.
Canecão, R Venceslau Brás 215, Botafogo, T021-2295 3044. A big, inexpensive venue for live concerts most nights, and a taste of some purely local entertainment on Mon.
Centro Cultural Carioca, R do Teatro 37, T021-2242 9642, www.centrocultural carioca.com, for advance information, 1830-late. This restored old house with wraparound balconies and exposed brick walls is a dance school and music venue that attracts a lovely mix of people. Professional dancers perform with musicians; after a few tunes the audience joins in. Thu is impossibly crowded; Sat is calmer. Bar food available. US$3 cover charge. Highly recommended.
Circo Voador, R dos Arcos, Lapa, T021-2533 0354, www.circovoador.com.br. Lapa's recuperation began with this little concert hall under the arches. Some of the city's best smaller acts still play here – including Seu Jorge who first found fame playing with *Farofa Carioca* at the Circo.
Praia do Vermelha, Urca. Bus No 511 from Copacabana. Residents bring musical instruments and chairs onto the beach for an informal night of samba 2100-2400. Free.
Rhapsody, Av Epitácio Pessoa 1104, Lagoa, T021-2247 2104. Piano-bar restaurant with a mix of Brazilian and Diana Kraal-style crooning.

Toca do Vinícius, R Vinícius de Moraes 129C, Ipanema. Rio's leading bossa nova and *choro* record shop has concerts from some of the finest performers every Sun lunchtime.

See also Bars and clubs, page 126.

Theatre

There are about 40 theatres in Rio, presenting a variety of classical and modern performances in Portuguese. Seat prices start at about US$15; some children's theatre is free. For information on particular performances, check in *Veja* at weekends, or ask at the tourist office.

✪ Festivals and events

Rio de Janeiro *p72*

Carnaval

Tickets → *See also box, page 132.*

The Sambódromo parades start at 1900 and last about 12 hrs. Gates open at 1800. There are *cadeiras* (seats) at ground level, *arquibancadas* (terraces) and *camarotes* (boxes). The best boxes are reserved for tourists and VIPs and are very expensive or by invitation only. Seats are closest to the parade, but you may have to fight your way to the front. Sectors 4, 7 and 11 are the best spots (they house the judging points); 6 and 13 are least favoured (being at the end when dancers might be tired) but have more space. The terraces, while uncomfortable, house the most fervent fans

and are tightly packed; this is the best place to soak up the atmosphere but it's too crowded to take pictures. Tickets start at US$40 for *arquibancadas* and are sold at travel agencies as well as the Maracanã Stadium box office (see page 94). Tickets should be bought as far as possible in advance; they are usually sold out before Carnaval weekend but touts outside can often sell you tickets at inflated prices. Samba schools have an allocation of tickets which members sometimes sell, if you are offered one of these check the date. Tickets for the champions' parade on the Sat following Carnaval are much cheaper. Many tour companies offer Rio trips including Carnaval, but tickets are at inflated prices.

Sleeping and security

Be sure to reserve accommodation well in advance. Virtually all hotels raise their prices during Carnaval, although it is usually possible to find a reasonably priced room. Your property should be safe inside the Sambódromo, but the crowds outside can attract pickpockets; as ever, don't brandish your camera, and only take the money you need for fares and refreshments (food and drink are sold in the Sambódromo). It gets hot, so wear shorts and a T-shirt.

Taking part

Most samba schools will accept a number of foreigners and you will be charged upwards of US$125 for your costume as your money

Carnaval

Carnaval in Rio is as spectacular as its reputation suggests – a riot of colour, flamboyance and artistry unrivalled outside Brazil. On the Friday before Shrove Tuesday, the mayor of Rio hands the keys of the city to *Rei Momo*, the Lord of Misrule, signifying the start of a five-day party. Imagination runs riot, social barriers are broken and the main avenues, full of people and children wearing fancy dress, are colourfully lit. Areas throughout the city such as the Terreirão de Samba in Praça Onze are used for shows, music and dancing. Spectacularly dressed carnival groups throng around the Sambódromo (Oscar Niemeyer's purpose-built stadium, see page 90) strutting, drumming and singing in preparation for their parade. And there are *blocos* (parades) throughout the city, in neighbourhoods such as Santa Teresa and Ipanema. It can be ghostly quiet in the southern beach zones during this time.

Unlike Salvador which remains a wild street party, Rio's Carnaval is a designated parade, taking place over a number of days and contained within the Sambódromo stadium. Alongside the parade are a number of *bailes* (parties) held within designated clubs, street shows like those held around Praça Onze.

There are numerous samba schools in Rio, which are divided into two leagues before they parade through the Sambódromo. The 14 schools of the *Grupo Especial* parade on Sunday and Monday while the *Grupos de Acesso* A and B parade on Saturday and Friday respectively. There is also a *mirins* parade (younger members of the established schools) on Tuesday. Judging takes place on Wednesday afternoon and the winners of the groups parade again on the following Saturday. Tickets to these winners' parades are always easy to get hold of even when all others are sold out.

Every school comprises 2500-6000 participants divided into *alas* (wings) each with a different costume and parading on or around five to nine *carros alegóricos* (beautifully designed floats). Each school chooses an *enredo* (theme) and composes a samba that is a poetic, rhythmic and catchy expression of the theme. The *enredo* is further developed through the design of the floats and costumes. A *bateria* (percussion wing) maintains a reverberating beat that must keep the entire school, and the audience, dancing throughout the parade. Each procession follows a set order with the first to appear being the *comissão de frente*

helps to fund poorer members of the school. You should be in Rio for at least 2 weeks before Carnaval. It is essential to attend fittings and rehearsals on time, to show respect for your section leaders and to enter into the competitive spirit of the event. For those with the energy and the dedication, it will be an unforgettable experience.

Rehearsals

Ensaios are held at the schools' *quadras* from Oct onwards and are well worth seeing. It is wise to go by taxi, as most schools are based in poorer districts.

Carnaval shows

Tour agents sell tickets for glitzy samba shows, which are nothing like the real thing. When buying a Carnaval DVD, make sure the format is compatible (NTSC for USA or most of Europe; PAL for the UK, region 4).

Samba school addresses and parties

Samba schools hold parties throughout the year, especially at the weekends. These are well worth visiting. See websites for details.
Acadêmicos de Salgueiro, R Silva Teles 104, Andaraí, T021-2238 5564, www.salgueiro.com.br.

(a choreographed group that presents the school and the theme to the public). Next comes the *abre alas* (a magnificent float usually bearing the name or symbol of the school). The *alas* and other floats follow as well as *porta bandeiras* (flag bearers) and *mestre salas* (couples dressed in 18th-century costumes bearing the school's flag), and *passistas* (groups traditionally of mulata dancers). An *ala of baianas* (elderly women with circular skirts that swirl as they dance) is always included as is the *velha guarda* (distinguished members of the school) who close the parade. Schools are given between 65 and 80 minutes and lose points for failing to keep within this time. Judges award points to each school for components of their procession, such as costume, music and design, and make deductions for lack of energy, enthusiasm or discipline. The winners of the *Grupos de Acesso* are promoted to the next higher group while the losers, including those of the *Grupo Especial*, are relegated to the next lowest group. Competition is intense and the winners gain a monetary prize funded by the entrance fees.

The Carnaval parades are the culmination of months of intense activity by community groups, mostly in the city's poorest districts. Rio´s *bailes* (fancy-dress balls) range from the sophisticated to the wild. The majority of clubs and hotels host at least one. The **Copacabana Palace**'s is elegant and expensive whilst the **Scala** club has licentious parties. It is not necessary to wear fancy dress; just join in, although you will feel more comfortable if you wear a minimum of clothing to the clubs, which are crowded, hot and rowdy. The most famous are the **Red and Black Ball** (Friday) and the **Gay Ball** (Tuesday) which are both televised. Venues for these vary.

Bandas and *blocos* can be found in all neighbourhoods and some of the most popular and entertaining are: **Cordão do Bola Preta** (meets at 0900 on Saturday, Rua 13 de Maio 13, Centro); **Simpatia é Quase Amor** (meets at 1600 on Sunday, Praça General Osório, Ipanema) and the transvestite **Banda da Ipanema** (meets at 1600 on Saturday and Tuesday, Praça General Osorio, Ipanema). It is necessary to join a *bloco* in advance to receive their distinctive T-shirts, but anyone can join in with the *bandas*. The expensive hotels offer special Carnaval breakfasts from 0530. **Caesar Park** is highly recommended for a wonderful meal and a top-floor view of the sunrise over the beach.

Beija Flor de Nilópolis, Pracinha Wallace Paes Leme 1025, Nilópolis, T021-2791 2866, www.beija-flor.com.br.
Imperatriz Leopoldinense, R Prof Lacê 235, Ramos, T021-2270 8037, www.love-rio.com/imperatriz.
Mocidade Independente de Padre Miguel, R Coronel Tamarindo 38, Padre Miguel, T021-3332 5823, www.mocidade.com.
Portela, R Clara Nunes 81, Madureira, T021-3390 0471, www.gresportela.com.br.
Primeira Estação de Mangueira, R Visconde de Niterói 1072, Mangueira, T021-2567 4637, www.mangueira.com.br.

Unidos da Viradouro, Av do Contorno 16, Niterói, T021-2717 7540, www.databrasil.com/viradouro.
Vila Isabel, Boulevard 28 de Setembro, Vila Isabel, www.gresunidosdevilaisabel.com.br.

Transport

Taxis to the Sambódromo are negotiable and will find your gate, the nearest metrô is Praça Onze and this can be an enjoyable ride in the company of costumed samba school members. You can follow the participants to the *concentração*, the assembly and formation on Av Presidente Vargas, and mingle with them while they queue to enter the Sambódromo. Ask if you can take photos.

Useful information

Carnaval week comprises an enormous range of official and unofficial contests and events, which reach a peak on the Tue. **Riotur's** guide booklet and website gives concise information on these in English. The entertainment sections of newspapers and magazines such as *O Globo*, *Jornal do Brasil*, *Manchete* and *Veja Rio* are worth checking. Felipe Ferreira's guide to the Rio Carnaval, *Liga Independente das Escolas de Samba do Rio de Janeiro*, www.liesa.com.br, has good explanations of the competition, rules, the schools, a map and other practical details.

Other festivals

20 Jan The festival of São Sebastião, patron saint of Rio, is celebrated by an evening procession, leaving Capuchinhos church in Tijuca and arriving at the cathedral of São Sebastião. On the same evening, an *umbanda* festival is celebrated at the *Caboclo* monument in Santa Teresa.

Jun The Festas Juninas are celebrated throughout Brazil. In Rio they start with the festival of Santo Antônio on 13 Jun, when the main event is a Mass, followed by celebrations at the Convento do Santo Antônio and the Largo da Carioca. All over the state, the festival of São João is a major event, marked by huge bonfires on the night of 23-24 Jun. It is traditional to dance the *quadrilha* and drink *quentão*, *cachaça* and sugar, spiced with ginger and cinnamon, served hot. The Festas Juninas close with the festival of São Pedro on 29 Jun. Being the patron saint of fishermen, his feast is normally accompanied by processions of boats.

Oct This is the month of the feast of Nossa Senhora da Penha (see page 93).

30 Dec Less hectic than Carnaval, but very atmospheric, is the festival of Yemanjá when devotees of the *orixá* of the sea dress in white and gather at night on Copacabana, Ipanema and Leblon beaches, singing and dancing around open fires and making offerings. The elected Queen of the Sea is rowed along the seashore. At midnight small boats are launched as offerings to Yemanjá. The religious event is dwarfed, however, by a massive New Year's Eve party, called **Reveillon** at Copacabana. The beach is packed as thousands of revellers enjoy free outdoor concerts by big-name pop stars, topped with a lavish midnight firework display. It is most crowded in front of the Copacabana Palace Hotel. Another good place to see the fireworks is at the far end of the beach in front of R Princesa Isabel, famous for its fireworks waterfall at about 0010. Many followers of Yemanjá now make offerings on 29 or 30 Dec and at Barra da Tijuca or Recreio dos Bandeirantes to avoid the crowds and noise of Reveillon.

○ Shopping

Rio de Janeiro *p72*
Arts and crafts

La Vereda, R Almirante Alexandrino 428, Santa Teresa, T021-2507 0317. Colourful arty little boutique filled with crafts, from illuminated *favela* models to textiles, toys and paintings.

Bookshops

Da Vinci, Av Rio Branco 185, lojas 2, 3 and 9. All types of foreign books, *Footprint* available.
Folha Seca R do Ouvidor 37, T021-2507 7175. Arty little bookshop tucked away next to NS de Lapa church and with a good range of Brazilian photography and art books difficult to find elsewhere.
Livraria da Travessa, R Visconde de Pirajá 572, Ipanema, T021-3205 9002. Classy little bookshop with broad selection of novels, magazines and guidebooks in English. Great café upstairs for a coffee while you read.
Saraiva, R do Ouvidor 98, T021-2507 9500. A massive (megastore) bookshop which also includes a music and video shop and a café; other branches in **Shopping Iguatemi** and **Shopping Tijuca**.

Camping equipment

On R 1 de Março, north of Av Pres Vargas, are
military shops which sell jungle equipment
such as hammocks, mosquito nets and
clothing, eg **Casa do Militar**, No 145 and
London, No 155; you can also buy the
Brazilian flag in any size you want here.
Malamada, R da Carioca 13. Recommended
for rucksacks.

Fashion

Fashion is one of the best buys in Brazil, with
a wealth of Brazilian designers selling clothes
of the same quality as European or US famous
names at a fraction of the price. Rio is the best
place in the world for buying high-fashion
bikinis. The best shops in Ipanema are on
Garcia D'Ávila and R Nascimento Silva, which
runs off it. This is where some of the best
Brazilian designers such as **Andrea Saletto** and
Rosana Bernardes, together with international
big-name stalwarts like **Louis Vuitton** and
Cartier, and Brazil's classiest jeweller, **Antonio
Bernardo**. Most of the international names,
together with all the big Brazilian names like
Lenny (Brazil's best bikinis), **Alberta**, **Salinas**,
Club Chocolate and so on, are housed in the
São Conrado Fashion Mall.

In addition to those listed below, there
are some little shops on Aires Saldanha,
Copacabana (1 block back from beach),
which are good for bikinis and cheaper
than in the shopping centres.

Andrea Saletto, R Nascimento Silva 244,
Ipanema, T021-2522 5858, and in the fashion
mall, loja 211, T021-3225 4235. One of the
most sophisticated labels in Rio – elegant
and low-profile style, classical cuts and
the use of light and tropical fabrics:
cotton, linen and silk.

Blue Man, São Conrado Fashion Mall.
Tiny bright bikinis beloved of those with
perfect bodies.

Bum Bum, R Visconde de Pirajá 351,
Ipanema, T021-2287 9951, www.bumbum.
com.br. Together with **Rosa Cha**, one of
the most internationally renowned bikini
designers, tiny and beautifully cut.

Carlos Tufvesson, R Nascimento Silva 304,
Ipanema, T021-2523 9200, www.carlos
tufvesson.com. Brazil's latest bright young
star who received a standing ovation for his
collection at the Barra fashion week in Rio.
Sensual evening-wear in high-quality fabric.

Casa Turuna, Av Passos 77, T021 2509 3908,
www.casaturuna.com. The places to buy
your Carnaval costumes in or out of carnival
season, together with samba skirts, masks
and general pageantry. Open since 1915.

Lenny, R Visconde de Pirajá, 351, Ipanema,
T021-2287 9951, and in the **São Conrado
Fashion Mall**. Lenny Niemeyer is widely
regarded as Brazil's most sophisticated
bikini designer.

Maria Bonita, R Aníbal de Mendonça 135,
Ipanema, T021-2540 5354. Impeccably cut,
elegantly simple, sophisticated women's
wear in high-quality fabrics. One of the
oldest labels in Rio de Janeiro.

Saara is a multitude of little shops along
R Alfândega and R Senhor dos Passos (between
the city centre and Campo Santana), where
clothing bargains can be found (especially jeans,
kanga beach wraps and bikinis); it is known
popularly as 'Shopping a Céu Aberto'.

Salinas, R Visconde de Pirajá 547, Ipanema,
T021-2274 0644, and fashion mall, T021-
2422 0677. Very highly regarded Brazilian
bikinis: small, exquisitely made with great
attention to detail and using only the best
fabrics, in a variety of contemporary styles
from hand crochet and beading to reversibles
in multiple colour combinations.

Jewellery

Only buy precious and semi-precious stones
from reputable dealers. There are several
good jewellery shops at the Leme end of
Av NS de Copacabana.

Amsterdam Sauer, R Garcia D'Ávila 105. Have
10 shops in Rio and others throughout Brazil,
plus St Thomas (US Virgin Islands) and New
York; they offer free taxi rides to their main shop.

Antônio Bernado, R Garcia d'Ávila 121,
Ipanema, T021-2512 7204, and in the **São
Conrado Fashion Mall**. Brazil's foremost

jeweller who has been making beautifully understated pieces with contemporary designs for nearly 30 years. Internationally well known but available only in Brazil. **H Stern**, R Visconde de Pirajá 490 and R Garcia d'Ávila 113, Ipanema. 10 outlets, plus branches in major hotels throughout the city (as well as elsewhere in Brazil and worldwide). **Mineraux**, Av NS de Copacabana 195. For mineral specimens rather than cut stones. Belgian owner.

Markets

The **Northeastern market** takes place at the Centro Luiz Gonzaga de Tradições Nordestinas, Campo de São Cristóvão, www.feiradesaocristovao.org.br with music and magic, on Fri from 1800, Sat 0800-2200 and Sun 0800-1200 (bus No 472 or 474 from Copacabana or centre). There's a Sat **antiques market** on the waterfront near Praça 15 de Novembro, 1000-1700. Also on Praça 15 de Novembro is **Feirarte II**, Thu and Fri 0800-1800. **Feirarte I** is a Sun open-air handicrafts market (everyone calls it the **Feira Hippy**) at Praça Gen Osório, Ipanema, 0800-1800, touristy but fun: items from all over Brazil. **Babilônia Feira Hype** is held every other weekend at the Jockey Club 1400-2300. This lively and popular market has lots of stalls selling clothes and crafts, as well as massage and live music and dance performances. A **stamp and coin market** is held on Sun in the Passeio Público. There are **markets** on Wed 0700-1300 on R Domingos Ferreira and on Thu, same hours, on Praça do Lido, both Copacabana. Praça do Lido also has a **Feir arte** on Sat and Sun 0800-1800. There is an **artesania market** nightly by the Othon Hotel, near R Miguel Lemos: one part for paintings, one part for everything else. There's a **Sunday market** on R da Glória, colourful, cheap fruit, vegetables and flowers; and an early-morning food market, 0600-1100, R Min Viveiros de Castro, Ipanema. Excellent **food and household goods markets** take place at various places in the city and suburbs (see newspapers for

times and places). **Feira do Livro** is a book market that moves around various locations (Largo do Machado, Cinelândia, Nossa Senhora da Paz – Ipanema), selling books at 20% discount.

Music

Arlequim Música, Paço Imperial, Praça XV de Novembro 48, loja 1, T021-2220-8471, www.arlequim.com.br. A good selection of high quality Brazilian music and film in a shop housed in the Paço Imperial. The Livraria Imperial bookshop occupies the same space and sells used books.
Modern Sound, R Barata Ribeiro 502D, Copacabana, T021-2548 5005, www.modernsound.com.br. For one of the best selections of Brazilian music in the city. Live performances most weekday nights from small, classy acts like the Bossa Jazz Trio and Delia Fischer.
Toca do Vinícius, R Vinícius de Moraes 129C, Ipanema. Specializes in bossa nova books, CDs and souvenirs, doubles as a performance space.

Photography

Flash Studio, R Visconde de Pirajá 156. For processing, expensive.
Honório, R Vinícius de Moraes 146E. Stocks lithium batteries.
Mecánica de Precisão, R da Conceição 31, shop 202. Good.
One Hour Foto, in the Rio Sul and Barra shopping centres. Recommended.
T Tanaka Cia Ltda, Av Franklin Roosevelt 39, of 516, T021-2220 1127. Nikon camera repairs.

Shopping centres

Rio Sul, at the Botafogo end of Túnel Novo, has almost everything the visitor may need. It has been refurbished and is convenient and very safe. Some of the services available are: **Telemar** (phone office) for international calls at A10-A, Mon-Sat 1000-2200; next do or is Belle Tours Câmbio, A10. There is a post office at G2. A good branch of **Livraria Sodiler** is at A03. Entertainment includes the **Fun Club** nightclub on the 4th floor, open all night, very young crowd; live music at the **Terraço**; the Ibeas **Top Club** gym; and a cinema. Eating places include fast food restaurants, 2 branches of **Kotobuki** sushi bar (another branch on the road to Praia Vermelha, recommended) and **Chaika** for milkshakes, ice creams and sandwiches (4th floor, original branch on Praça NS da Paz, Ipanema). A US$5 bus service runs as far as the Sheraton passing the main hotels, every 2 hrs between 1000 and 1800, then 2130. **São Conrado Fashion Mall**. The best designers and an excellent restaurant at the **Clube Chocolate** shop.

Other shopping centres, which have a wide variety of shops and services, include: **Shopping Cidade Copacabana**, R Siqueira Campos, www.shoppingcidade copacabana.com.br; **Shopping Botafogo Praia**, Praia de Botafogo 400, T021-3171 9559, www.botafogopraiashopping.com.br; **Norte Shopping** (Todos os Santos); **Plaza Shopping** (Niterói); **Barra** in Barra da Tijuca.

▲ Activities and tours

Rio de Janeiro *p72*
Boat trips
Several companies offer trips to **Ilha de Paquetá**, and day cruises, including lunch, to **Jaguanum Island**, and a sundown cruise around **Guanabara Bay**.
Saveiros Tour, R Conde de Lages 44, Glória, T021-2224 6990, www.saveiros.com.br. Tours in sailing schooners around the bay and down the coast, also 'Baía da Guanabara Histórica' historical tours.

Cycling
Rio Bikers, R Domingos Ferreira 81, room 201, T021-2274 5872. Tours (hire available).

Diving
Squalo, Av Armando Lombardi 949-D, Barra da Tijuca, T/F021-2493 3022, squalo1@hot mail.com. Offers courses at all levels, NAUI

and PADI training facilities, also snorkelling and equipment rental.

Driving tours and personal drivers
Dehouche (see Tour operators, page 139). Luxury tours around Rio city and state in top end a/c saloon cars. Very good English.
José de Oliveira Lima Filho, T021-9243 1208. Ex-driver for the US secret service in Rio. Has access to exclusive addresses and private parties. Expensive.
Madson Araujo, T021-9395 3537, www.tour guiderio.com. Bespoke personal tours of the Rio city sights and trips into Rio de Janeiro state. Full details on the comprehensive website. Many languages spoken.
Otávio Monteiro, T021-8835 1160 or T021-7841 4799, om2brasil@hotmail.com. Good-value driver and personal tours will go anywhere in Rio or the state. Reliable, good English.
Roz Brazil, T024-9257 0236, www.roz brazil.com. Some of the best drive and light walking tours around Petrópolis, Teresópolis and the Serra dos Órgãos with British Brazilian Rosa Thompson, who has been living in the area for decades. Pick-ups from Rio.

Football coaching
Pelé da Praia, R Garcia D'Avila, Ipanema, T021-9702 5794, www.peledapraia.com.br. Football and volleyball coaching from a real Cariocan character who has been working on Ipanema beach for many years.

Golf
Gávea Club, São Conrado, T021-3399 4141. 18 holes.
Itanhangá Golf Club, Jacarepaguá. 18-hole and 9-hole courses, visitor cards from Av Rio Branco 26, 16th floor.

Gymnasiums
There are hundreds of excellent gyms and sports clubs; most will not grant temporary (less than 1 month) membership: big hotels may allow use of their facilities for a small deposit.

Rio's best surf breaks

BB Beach Break; **PB** Point Break; **RB** Reef Break; **SB** Shore Break; **R** Right and **L** Left.
Wave heights are given in feet. For further information see *Footprint Surfing the World*.

Arpoador Breaks next to the rocks, gets good, the beach is illuminated making night surfing possible, BB, L, 1-8 ft.
Barra da Guaratiba Rivermouth, perfect and powerful waves in the right conditions, B, L, 2-5 ft.
Barra da Tijuca 18-km beach with sand banks, closes out when big, BB, R&L.
Canto de Leblon On a big swell a wave breaks next to the rocks, gets good.
Copacabana Posto 5, needs a big swell and the water can be dirty, SB, R&L.
Forte BB, R&L, 1-4 ft.
Grumari BB, R&L, 1-7 ft.
Ipanema Hollow, not much shape, BB, R&L, 1-5 ft.
Leblon Hollow next to the breakwater, BB, R&L, 1-5 ft.
Macumba Small waves, BB, R&L, 1-4 ft.
Quebra Mar Next to the breakwater, hollow in the right conditions, BB, L, 1-7 ft.
Pepino Sometimes a good hollow left can break next to the rocks on the left side of the beach. Hang gliders land here, BB, R&L, 1-6 ft.
Prainha Wild and good, BB, R&L, 1-8 ft.
Recreio dos Bandeirantes Breaks by a rock a few metres from shore, on both sides and in different directions; can handle some size when other spots close out, BB, R&L, 2-8 ft.
São Conrado BB, R&L, 1-5 ft.

Hang-gliding and paragliding

Delta Flight, T/021-3322 5750, T021-9693 8800, www.deltaflight.com.br. Hang-gliding rides above Rio from Pedra Bonita mountain with instructors licensed by the Brazilian Hang-gliding Association. 19 years of experience and equipment is renewed every year. Contact Ricardo Hamond.
Just Fly, T/F021-2268 0565, T021-9985 7540 (mob), www.justfly.com.br. Tandem flights with Paulo Celani (licensed by the Brazilian Hang-gliding Association), pickup and drop-off at hotel included, flights all year, best time of day 1000-1500 (5% discount for *Footprint* readers on presentation of book at time of reservation).
Rejane Reis, Exotic Tours, (see Tour operators, page 140), arranges hang-gliding, paragliding, microlight flights, walks and other activities.

Ruy Marra, T021-3322 2286, or find him at the beach. Paragliding from Leblon beach with Brazilian paragliding champion (US$75).
Ultra Força Ltda, Av Sernambetiba 8100, Barra da Tijuca, T021-3399 3114; 15-min tandem hang-gliding flights.

Hiking and climbing

Clube Excursionista Carioca, R Hilário Gouveia 71, room 206, T021-2255 1348, www.carioca.org.br. Recommended for enthusiasts, meets Wed and Fri.
Diogo Monnerat, T021-9916 9944, diogo.monnerat@gmail.com. Rock-climbing on the Sugar Loaf and hikes around Rio de Janeiro, including Tijuca and Pedra da Gávea.
ECA, Av Erasmo Braga 217, room 305, T021-2242 6857. Personal guide US$100 per day, owner Ralph speaks English.

Rio Hiking, T021-2552 9204 and T021-9721 0594, www.riohiking.com.br. Hiking tours around Rio city and state, including the Pedra da Gávea, Tijuca Park, Itatiaia and the Serra dos Órgãos and various city tours, including Santa Teresa. Run by friendly and fun Carioca mother and son team who speak excellent English.

Horse riding
See also **Rio Hiking**, above.
Sociedade Hípico Brasileiro, Av Borges de Medeiros 2448, T021-2527 8090, Jardim Botânico.

Parachuting
Several other people offer tandem jumps; check that they are accredited with the **Associação Brasileira de Vôo Livre**.
Barra Jumping, Aeroporto de Jacarepaguá, Av Ayrton Senna 2541, T021-3325 2494, www.barrajumping.com.br. Tandem jumping (*vôo duplo*).

Rafting
See **Rio Hiking**, above, for trips on the Paraibuna and Macaé rivers (both around 2 hrs from Rio).

Sailing
Federação Brasileira de Vela e Motor, R Alcindo Guanabara 15, room 801, Centro, T021-2220 3738. For information.
Federação de Vela, Praça Mahatma Gandhi 2, 12th floor, T021-2220 8785. For information.

Sea kayaking
See also **Rio Hiking**, page 139, for a variety of sea-kayaking tours.
Clube do Rio de Janeiro, Av Pasteur, Urca, T021-2295 4482. Yachting.

Surfing
For the state of the waves on the beaches in and around Rio de Janeiro, see box, page 138. See also **Rio Hiking**, page 139, for surf lessons on Barra, Grumari and Prainha.

Contact **Associação Brasileira de Bodyboard**, T021-2274 3614; **Federação de Bodyboard do Estado do Rio de Janeiro**, T021-2256 5653; **Federação de Surf do Estado do Rio de Janeiro**, T021-2287 2385; **Organização dos Surfistas Profissionais do Rio de Janeiro**, T021-2493 2472.

Swimming
On all Rio's beaches you should take a towel or mat to protect you against sandflies. In the water stay near groups of other swimmers. There is a strong undertow.

Tour operators
Adrianotour, T021-2208 5103. For guided tours, reservations and commercial services. English, French, German and Spanish spoken.
Be A Local, T021-9643 0366, www.bea local.com. The best of the *favela* tours with walking trips around Rocinha and money going towards community projects; trips to *baile funk* parties at weekends and to football matches.
Buggy Tour, T021-2220 2043, www.dolores buggytour.com. Beach buggy tours of Rio with a real Carioca character, Dolores. Good English, Spanish, Italian and French.
Cultural Rio, R Santa Clara 110/904, Copacabana, T021-3322 4872 or T021-9911 3829 (mob), www.culturalrio.com.br. Tours escorted personally by Professor Carlos Roquette, English and French spoken, almost 200 options available.
Dehouche, T021-2512 3895, www.dehouche.com. Luxury tailor-made tours throughout Brazil and Rio de Janeiro, including the best private flats, excursions to islands near Angra and the opportunity of driving a Ferrari around the Grand Prix circuit.
Fábio Sombra, T021-2295 9220, T021-9729 5455 (mob), fabiosombra@ hotmail.com. Offers private and tailor-made guided tours focusing on the cultural aspects of Rio and Brazil.

Favela Tour, Estr das Canoas 722, bl 2, apt 125, São Conrado, T021-3322 2727, T021-9989 0074 (mob), www.favelatour.com.br. Safe, interesting guided tours of Rio's *favelas* in English, French, Spanish, Italian, German and Swedish. For the best attention and price call Marcelo Armstrong direct rather than through a hotel desk.

Guanatur Turismo, R Dias da Rocha 16A, Copacabana, T021-2548 3275. Sells long-distance bus tickets.

Helisight, R Visconde de Pirajá 580, loja 107, Térreo, Ipanema, T021-2511 2141, www.helisight.com.br. Daily from 0900. Helicopter sightseeing tours. Prices from US$50 per person for 6-7 mins from Morro de Urca or the Lagoa over Sugar Loaf and Corcovado, to US$150 per person for 30 mins over the city.

Marlin Tours, Av NS de Copacabana 605, of 1204, T021-2548 4433, bbm.robin@

openlink.com.br. Recommended for hotels, flights and tours, English spoken.

Metropol, R São José 46, T021-2533 5010, www.metropolturismo.com.br. Cultural, eco, and adventure tours to all parts of Brazil.

Rejane Reis, Exotic Tours, T021-3322 6972, www.exotictours.com.br. Unusual trips throughout Rio such as *candomblé*, rafting or hikes up to the Pedra da Gávea. Cultural and *favela* tours. Good English spoken.

Rio by Jeep, T021-3322 5750, T021-9693 8800, www.riobyjeep.com. 5-hr tours in open or closed jeeps with local guides showing Rio from 3 perspectives: gorgeous beaches, historical downtown and Tijuca national park. Contact Ricardo Hamond.

Santa Teresa Tour, T021-2507 4417, www.santateresatour.com. Historical tours around the neighbourhood run by **Rio Hiking** (see Hiking, page 139) in a community support project along with people from the local *favelas*. Daily walks and tram tours from Lapa into Santa Teresa, usually departing from the Largo dos Guimarães or Lapa at 0930 daily. Book ahead.

Turismo Clássico, Av NS de Copacabana 1059/805, T021-2523 3390, classico@infolink. com.br. Organized trips to samba shows cost US$50 including dinner; good, but it's cheaper to go independently. Recommended.

Volleyball classes

For more general information and other schools see www.voleinapraia.com.br.

Escola de Vôlei da Leticia, Ipanema beach in front of R Farme de Amoedo, T021-9841 3833 and T021-2239 9679. Adult classes in Portuguese, Tue-Fri 0800-0900 and Mon-Fri 1900-2000. Run by Letícia Pessoa who has been working on Ipanema since 1995.

Escola de Vôlei do Renato, Copacabana beach in front of R Hilário de Gouvea, T021-9955 7480, www.voleinapraia.com.br. Adult classes Mon-Fri 1900-2100, adult and 8-12 year olds Mon-Fri 0730-0930. Run by Renato França who has been working on the beach for 12 years.

Safety and favela tourism

Rio has a reputation for being violent and unsafe and though it can be so you are unlikely to encounter problems if you follow a few basic rules. These all boil down to common sense and not attracting attention to yourself. Enquire where is and where is not safe at your hotel or hostel – violence and thieves are almost always localized. Dress modestly and if possible like a local; flip-flops (not trekking sandals), locally bought shorts and a T-shirt or polo shirt. Keep expensive jewellery and watches out of sight. Carry a photocopy of your passport and leave the original and other valuables in the hotel safe box. Carry ready money in a pocket and a reserve in a money belt and wear your camera where it cannot be seen or keep it in a scruffy bag. Be especially careful after dark in the city centre and on quiet areas of Copacabana beach – never walk on the sand alone after dark. If you are mugged anywhere in Rio do not offer resistance and report the crime to the police or tourist police immediately. But bear in mind that Brazilians are generally the friendliest and most accommodating of people and although there is a great deal of violence in Rio, most of it is restricted to the *favelas* – which can be extremely dangerous, see box, page 111.

There has been a growth in *favela* tourism in recent years and there are even *pousadas* opening in some of the *favelas*.

Favela tours when conducted by reputable operators (see page 139) are pretty safe and illuminating and we strongly recommend them. The best companies have a relationship with the locals, permission to be there and visit only areas they know to be relatively safe. Beyond this, however, we are under no illusions about the dangers of *favelas*. Never enter a *favela* on your own or without someone you know very well and trust and bear in mind that a stay in a *favela pousada* will require that you do so. Violence in *favelas* is not a myth. To give some concrete examples: in the 14 years to 2003, when a UNESCO report was published on violence in Brazil; some 4000 under-18-year-olds were killed by firearms in Rio; almost all of them in the *favelas*. This compares with just under 500 killed in fighting between Palestinians and Israelis in the whole of Israel over the same period. And the numbers are not falling. According to the latest available statistics as of 2006, between 1979 and 2003 homicides in under 25 year olds in Brazil increased by 742.9% and more people died of gunfire in the country than in conflicts such as the Gulf War, the First and the Second Intifadas, the dispute between Israel and Palestine and the conflicts in Northern Ireland, both in terms of absolute figures and in annual averages.

⊖ Transport

Rio de Janeiro *p72*

Air

See Ins and outs, page 72, for airport information. Metered taxis cost around US$25 from Copacabana to Jobim international airport. Buses to the airport 0500-2400 run from the *rodoviária*, Av Rio Branco in the centre, Santos Dumont airport, Flamengo, Copacabana, Ipanema, São Conrado and Av das Americas or the Terminal Alvorada bus station in Barra da Tijuca, US$3. Contact **Real Auto**, T0800-240850, www.realauto onibus.com.br, for information. As well as international connections, Rio de Janeiro has flights to all the country's major airports, some via **São Paulo**, **Brasilia** or **Salvador**. The best deals on flights within Brazil are available through: **GOL**, www.voe gol.com.br; **Oceanair**, www.oceanair.com.br; and **TAM**, www.tam.com.br.

There is a shuttle flight between Santos Dumont airport and **São Paulo** (Congonhas airport, US$150 single, US$300 return). The shuttle operates every 30 mins throughout the day from 0630-2230. Sit on the right- hand side for views to São Paulo, the other side coming back, book flights in advance.

Airline offices

Aerolíneas Argentinas, R São José 70, 8th floor, Centro, T021-2292 4131, airport T021-3398 3520. **Air France**, Av Pres Antônio Carlos 58, 9th floor, T021-2532 3642, airport T021-3398 3488. **Alitalia**, Av Pres Wilson 231, 21st floor, T021-2292 4424, airport T021-3398 3143. **American**, Av Pres Wilson 165, 5th floor, T0800-703 4000. **Avianca**, Av Pres Wilson 165, offices 801-03, T021-2240 4413, airport T021-3398 3778. **British Airways**, airport T021-3398 3889. **Iberia**, Av Pres Antônio Carlos 51, 8th and 9th floors, T021-2282 1336, airport T021-3398 3168. **Japan Airlines**, Av Rio Branco 156, office 2014, T021-2220 6414. **KLM**, Av Rio Branco 311A, T021-2542 7744, airport T021-3398 3700. **LAB**, Av Calógeras 30A, T021-2220 9548. **Lan Chile**, R da Assembléia 92, of 1301, T021-2222 0972 or T0800-554 9000, airport T021-3398 3797. **Lufthansa**, Av Rio Branco 156D, T021-2217 6111, airport T021-3398 5850. **Oceanair**, www.oceanair.com.br, **RioSul/Nordeste**, Av Rio Branco 85, 10th floor, T021-2507 4488 (has an advance check-in desk in Rio Sul Shopping). **Swissair**, Av Rio Branco 108, 10th floor, T021-2297 5177, airport T021-3398 4330. **TAM**, www.tam.com.br, and **TAP**, Av Rio Branco 311-B, T021-2210 1287, airport, T021-3398 3455. **United**, Av Pres Antônio Carlos 51, 5th floor, T0800-245532. **Varig**, Av Rio Branco 277G, T021-2220 3821 information, T0800-997000 bookings; airport T021-3398 2122. Most staff speak English.

Bus
Local

There are good services to all parts of the city, but buses are very crowded and not for the aged and infirm during rush hours. Buses have turnstiles which are awkward if you are carrying luggage. Hang on tight, drivers live out Grand Prix fantasies. At busy times allow about 45 mins to get from Copacabana to the centre by bus. The fare on standard buses is US$0.40 and suburban bus fares are US$0.75. Bus stops are often not marked. The route is written on the side of the bus, but it's hard to see until the bus has actually pulled up at the stop.

Private companies, including **Real**, **Pegaso** and **Anatur**, operate a/c *frescão* buses, which can be flagged down practically anywhere. They run from all points in Rio Sul to the city centre, *rodoviária* and the airports. Fares are US$1.50 (US$1.80 to the international airport).

City Rio, T0800-258060, is an a/c tourist bus service with security guards, which runs between all the major parts of the city. Bus stops, marked by grey poles, are found where there are concentrations of hotels. Good maps show what places of interest are close to each bus stop. Timetables change frequently. Hotels can provide the latest information on when the buses run.

Long distance

Rio's interstate bus station, the **Rodoviária Novo Rio** (see Ins and outs, page 76), www.novorio.com.br, is just north of the city centre and can be reached by buses: M94 and M95, Bancários– Castelo, from the centre and the airport; Nos 136, 172, *rodoviária–Glória–Flamengo–Botafogo*; Nos 127, 128, 136, *rodoviária–Copacabana*; No 170, *rodoviária–Gávea–São Conrado*; Nos 128, 172, *rodoviária– Ipanema–Leblon*. The area around the bus station is not safe after dark and you should beware of thieves at any time. Take a taxi to or from the nearest metrô station (Estácio or Praça Onze) or to your hotel. **Riotur** has a booth in the bus station that can help with hotel reservations and point you to the taxi bookings stand.

Buses run from Rio to every state capital and many smaller cities in all parts of the country from Belém in the far north to Porto Alegre and the Uruguay border in the far south. There are departures to major destinations, such as São Paulo, more than every hour. It is advisable to book in advance in high season and weekends. Travel agencies throughout the city sell tickets as do many hostels. Otherwise turn up at least 90 mins before your bus leaves to buy a ticket. Timetables, companies and platform information and the most up to date prices are available on www.novorio.com.br; type your destination into the box provided.

Most street travel agents and hostels sell *passagens de onibus* (interstate bus tickets), or will direct you to a company that does so. Agencies include **Dantur Passagens e Turismo**, Av Rio Branco 156, subsolo loja 134, T021-2262 3424/3624; **Guanatur**, R Dias da Rocha 16A, Copacabana, T021-2235 3275; **Itapemirim Turismo**, R Uruguaiana 10, loja 24, T021-2509 8543, both in the centre; and an agency at R Visconde de Pirajá 303, loja 114, Ipanema. They charge about US$3 for bookings.

Within Rio state
To **Niteroi**, No 996 Gávea–Jurujuba; No 998 Galeão–Charitas 740-D and 741 Copacabana–Charitas; 730-D Castelo–Jurujuba, US$1.50, all run between Rio and Niterói.

To **Búzios**, 4 buses leave daily from Rio's *rodoviária* (US$15, 2½ hrs). Go to the **1001** counter, T022-2516 1001 for tickets. You can also take any bus from Rio to the town of **Cabo Frio** (these are more frequent), from where it's 30 mins to Búzios and vice versa. Buying the ticket in advance is only necessary on major holidays.

To **Petrópolis**, buses leave the *rodoviária* every 15 mins throughout the day (US$8) and every hour on Sun. A/c buses leave

hourly (after 1100) from Av Nilo Peçanha. The journey takes 1½ hrs. Sit on the left-hand side for the best views.

To **Angra dos Reis**, buses run at least hourly from the *rodoviária* with **Costa Verde**, some direct; several go through Copacabana, Ipanema and Barra then take the *via litoral*, sit on the left, US$10, 2½ hrs. You can flag down the bus in Flamengo, Copacabana, Ipanema, Barra da Tijuca, but it may well be full at weekends. To link up with the ferry to Ilha Grande be sure to catch a bus before 1000.

International
To **Asunción**, 1511 km via **Foz do Iguaçu**, 30 hrs (**Pluma**), US$70. To **Buenos Aires** (**Pluma**), via **Porto Alegre** and **Santa Fe**, 48 hrs, US$100 (book 2 days in advance). To **Santiago de Chile**, (**Pluma** US$135, or **Gen Urquiza**), 70 hrs.

Car
Service stations are closed in many places on Sat and Sun. Road signs are notoriously misleading in Rio and you can end up in a *favela* (take special care if driving along the Estr da Gávea to São Conrado as it is possible to unwittingly enter Rocinha, Rio's biggest slum).

Car hire
There are many agencies on Av Princesa Isabel, Copacabana. A credit card is virtually essential for hiring a car. Recent reports suggest it is cheaper to hire outside Brazil; you may also obtain more comprehensive insurance this way. **Avis**, Antônio Carlos Jobim international airport, T021-3398 5060, Santos Dumont airport, T021-3814 7378, Av Princesa Isabel 150A and B, Copacabana, T021-2543 8481; **Hertz**, international airport, T021-398 4338, Av Princesa Isabel 273-A, Copacabana, T021-2275 7440; **Interlocadora**, international airport, T021-3398 3181; **Localiza**, international airport and Santos

Dumont airport, T0800-992000, Av Princesa Isabel 150, Copacabana, T021-2275 3340; **Nobre**, Av Princesa Isabel 7, Copacabana, T021-2541 4646; **Telecar**, R Figueiredo Magalhães 701, Copacabana, T021-2235 6778.

Car repairs

Kyoso Team Mecânico Siqueira Campos, at the entrance to the old tunnel, T021-2255 0506. A good mechanic who enjoys the challenge of an unusual car. Recommended.

Distances and journey times from Rio

Juiz de Fora, 184 km (2¾ hrs); **Belo Horizonte**, 434 km (7 hrs); **São Paulo**, 429 km (6 hrs); **Vitória**, 521 km (8 hrs); **Curitiba**, 852 km (12 hrs); **Brasília**, 1148 km (20 hrs); **Florianópolis**, 1144 km (20 hrs); **Foz do Iguaçu**, 1500 km (21 hrs); **Porto Alegre**, 1553 km (26 hrs); **Salvador**, 1649 km (28 hrs); **Recife**, 2338 km (38 hrs); **Fortaleza**, 2805 km (48 hrs); **São Luís**, 3015 km (50 hrs); **Belém**, 3250 km (52 hrs).

Ferry

Every 10 mins ferries and launches cross Guanabara Bay for **Niterói** from the 'Barcas' terminal at Praça 15 de Novembro. The journey takes 20-30 mins and costs US$2. Catamarans (*aerobarcas*) also leave every 10 mins but take just 3 mins and cost US$4. Fares are halved between 0700 and 1000. The slow, cheaper ferry gives the best views. From Niterói, ferries and catamarans return to Rio de Janeiro from the terminal at Praça Araribóia.

Metrô

See page 76 and map page 73. The metrô provides a good service; it is clean, a/c and fast. It operates 0600-2300, Sun 1400-2000; closed holidays. The fare is US$0.50 single; multi-tickets and integrated bus/metrô tickets are available. Substantial changes in bus operations are taking place because of the extended metrô system; buses connecting with the metrô have a blue-and-white symbol in the windscreen. **Line 1** operates between the inner

suburb of Tijuca (station Saens Peña) and Arcoverde (Copacabana), via the railway station (Central), Glória and Botafogo.

Line 2 runs from Pavuna, passing Engenho da Rainha and the Maracanã stadium, to Estácio.

Taxi

See also Ins and outs, page 72. The fare between Copacabana and the centre is around US$12. Between 2300-0600 and on Sun and holidays, 'tariff 2' is used. Taxis have red number plates with white digits (yellow for private cars, with black digits) and have meters. Smaller ones (mostly Volkswagen) are marked TAXI on the windscreen or roof. Make sure meters are cleared and on 'tariff 1', except at those times mentioned above. It is safest to use taxis from *pontos* – taxi ranks that are abundant throughout the city. *Ponto* taxis have the name of the *ponto* painted on the outside, indicating which *ponto* they belong to. Radio taxis are safer but almost twice as expensive, eg **Cootramo**, T021-2560 5442; **Coopertramo**, T021-2260 2022; **Centro de Táxi**, T021-2593 2598; **Transcoopass**, T021-2560 4888. Luxury cabs are allowed to charge higher rates; **Inácio de Oliveira**, T021-2225 4110, is a reliable taxi driver for excursions; he only speaks Portuguese. Recommended. **Grimalde**, T021-2267 9812, has been recommended for talkative daytime and evening tours; English and Italian spoken, negotiate a price.

Train

Buses marked 'E Ferro' go to the train station. There are suburban trains to **Nova Iguaçu**, **Nilópolis**, **Campo Grande** and elsewhere.

Tram

See also Ins and outs, page 72 and Santa Teresa, page 95. The last remaining tram runs from near the Largo da Carioca (there is a museum open Fri only 0830-1700) across the old aqueduct (Arcos) to Dois Irmãos or Paula Mattos in **Santa Teresa**; a historical and interesting journey, US$0.40.

❶ Directory

Rio de Janeiro *p72*

Banks

Bradesco, R Buenos Aires 286, Centro, T021-2224 5319; **Banco do Brasil**, Av Mal Floriano 114 Centro, T021-2514 8988; **Bradesco**, Av NS de Copacabana 1018 A, Copacabana, T021-2522 1332; **Banco do Brasil**, Av NS de Copacabana 1274, Copacabana, T021-2523 1441; **Bradesco**, R Visconde de Pirajá 102 B lj A, Ipanema, T021-2522 2611; **Banco do Brasil** (R Joana Angélica 124, Ipanema, T021-2522 1442; **Banco do Brasil**, International Airport Antonio Carlos Jobim, T021-3398 3015.

Currency exchange Most large hotels and reputable travel agencies will change currency and TCs. Copacabana (where rates are generally worse than in the centre) is full of *câmbios* and there are also many on Av Rio Branco. **American Express**, Av Atlântica 1702, loja 1, T021-2548 2148, Mon-Fri 0900-1600, Av Pres Wilson 231, 18th floor, Centro, and at Antônio Carlos Jobim international airport, T021-3398 4251 (VIP room 1st floor), good rates (T0800-785050 toll-free); **Câmbio Belle Tours**, Rio Sul Shopping, ground floor, loja 101, parte A-10, Mon-Fri 1000-1800, Sat 1000-1700, changes cash. In the gallery at Largo do Machado 29 are **Câmbio Nick** at loja 22 and, next door but one, **Casa Franca**.

Cultural centres

American Library, União Cultural Brasil-Estados Unidos, R Col Oscar Porto 208; **Centro Brasileiro Britânico**, R Ferriera de Araújo 741, Pinheiros, T021-3039 0567; **Centro Cultural Fiesp**, Av Paulista 1313, Tue-Sun 0900-1900, foreign newspapers and magazines. **Goethe-Instituto**, R Lisboa 974, Mon-Thu 1400-2030.

Dentist

Amílcar Werneck de Carvalho Vianna, Av Pres Wilson 165, suite 811, English-speaking; **Dr Mauro Suartz**, R Visconde de Pirajá 414, room 509, T021-2287 6745, speaks English and Hebrew, helpful.

Embassies and consulates

Argentina, Praia de Botafogo 228, T021-2553 1646. Very helpful over visas, 1130-1600; **Australia**, Av Presidente Wilson, T021-3824 4624. Mon-Fri 0900-1300, 1430-1800; **Austria**, Av Atlântica 3804, T021-2522 2286; **Canada**, R Lauro Müller 116, T021-2543 3004; **Denmark**, Praia do Flamengo 66, T021-2558 6050; **France**, Av Pres Antônio Carlos 58, T021-2210 1272; **Germany**, R Pres Carlos de Campos 417, T021-2553 6777; **Israel**, Av NS de Copacabana 680, T021-2548 5432; **Netherlands**, Praia de Botafogo 242, 10th floor, T021-2552 9028 (Dutch newspapers here and at KLM office on Av Rio Branco); **Paraguay**, same address, 2nd floor, T021-2553 2294, visas US$5; **Sweden**, **Finland** and **Norway**, Praia do Flamengo 344, 9th floor, T021-2553 5505; **Switzerland**, R Cândido Mendes 157, 11th floor, T021-2221 1867; **UK**, Praia do Flamengo 284, 2nd floor, T021-2553 3223 (consular section direct line), F2553 6850, consular section is open Mon-Fri 0900-1230 (consulate 0830-1700), metrô Flamengo, or bus No 170, the consulate issues a useful *Guidance for Tourists* pamphlet; **Uruguay**, Praia de Botafogo 242, 6th floor, T021-2553 6030; **USA**, Av Pres Wilson 147, T021-22927117, Mon-Fri 0800-1100, passports 1330-1500.

Immigration

Federal Police, Praça Mauá (passport section), entrance on Av Venezuela, T021-2291 2142. To renew a 90-day visa, US$45. Renew at least a week before your visa runs out and allow 4 hrs for the bureaucratic process of queuing and form filling.

Internet

Internet cafés are easy to find throughout the city. There are several places in **Rio Sul** shopping centre, Botafogo; many on Av NS de Copacabana, and others on R Visconde de Pirajá, Ipanema. **Phone Serv**, Av NS de Copacabana 454, loja B, US$3 per hr internet, telephone service. **Tudo é Fácil** has 3 branches in Copacabana: R Xavier da Silveira 19; Av Prado Júnior 78; and R Barata Ribeiro

396. Well organized, with identification cards so once registered you can bypass the front desk, telephone booths and scanners, US$2 per hr, discounts for extended use.

Language courses

Instituto Brasil-Estados Unidos, Av Copacabana 690, 5th floor, 8-week course, 3 classes a week, US$150, 5-week intensive course US$260, good English library at same address; **IVM Português Prático**, R do Catete 310, sala 302, US$18 per hr for individual lessons, cheaper for groups, helpful staff, recommended; **Cursos da UNE** (União Nacional de Estudantes), R Catete 243, include cultural studies and Portuguese classes for foreigners.

Laundry

Fénix, R do Catete 214, loja 20; **Laundromat** at Av NS de Copacabana 1216; **Lavanderia**, Visconde de Pirajá 631A, Ipanema, T021-2294 8142; **Lavlev Flamengo**, RC de Baependi 78, or R das Laranjeiras 43, L28. In **Rio Sul** there are self-service launderettes such as **Lavelev**, about US$7 for a machine, including detergent and drying, 1 hr. There are also laundrettes at: R Buarque de Macedo 43B, Catete; R Voluntários da Patria 248, Botafogo; and Av Prado Júnior 63B, Copacabana.

Medical services

Hospital Miguel Couto, Mário Ribeiro 117, Gávea, T021-2274 6050, has a free casualty ward. **Hospital Municipal Rocha Maia**, R Gen Severiano 91, Botafogo, T021-2295 2295/2121, near Rio Sul shopping centre, a good public hospital for minor injuries and ailments; free, but there may be queues; **Policlínica**, Av Nilo Peçanha 38, for diagnosis and investigation. **Saúde de Portos**, Praça Mcal Âncora, T021-2240 8628/8678, Mon-Fri 1000-1100, 1500-1800. For vaccinations; vaccination book and ID required.

Post

The **Central Post Office** is on R 1 de Março 64, at the corner of R do Rosário. Also at Av NS de Copacabana 540 and many other locations. All handle international post. There is a post office at Antônio Carlos Jobim international airport; **Federal Express**, Av Calógeras 23 (near Santa Luzia church) T021-2262 8565, is reliable

Poste Restante at Correios, Av NS de Copacabana 540 and all large post offices (letters held for a month, recommended, US$0.10 per letter);

Students

Student Travel Bureau, Av Nilo Peçanha 50, SL 2417, Centro, T/F021-2544 2627, and R Visconde de Pirajá 550, loja 201, Ipanema, T021-2512 8577, www.stb.com.br, has details of travel, discounts and cultural exchanges for ISIC holders.

Telephone

International telephone booths are blue. International calls can be made at larger **Correios**, eg Av NS de Copacabana 540; larger **Embratel** offices also have telex and fax; at the airports and the Novo Rio *rodoviária*; at R Dias da Cruz 192, Méier-4, 24 hrs, 7 days a week; in Urca, near the Pão de Açúcar cable car; at Praça Tiradentes 41, a few mins' walk from metrô Carioca; at R Visconde de Pirajá 111, Ipanema; and at R do Ouvidor 60, Centro.

Telephone numbers often change in Rio de Janeiro and other Brazilian cities. If in doubt, phone **Auxilio à Lista**, T102, which is the current daily updated directory of telephone numbers. This number can be used all over the country, but if you want to find out a Rio phone number from outside Rio, dial the city code 021, then 121. Note that these services are in Portuguese, so you may need to seek assistance from a hotel receptionist or similar. For further details on Brazil's telephone system, see Essentials, page 62.

Toilets

There are very few public toilets in Rio de Janeiro, but shopping centres, many bars and restaurants (eg McDonald's) offer facilities. Just ask for the *banheiro*.

East of Rio de Janeiro

Rio de Janeiro state is one of Brazil's smallest, but it is packed with great things to see. East of Rio the country gets drier and looks more Mediterranean. The coast, which is lined with fabulous beaches for hundreds of kilometres, is backed by a long series of saltwater lakes and drifting sand dunes. Most visitors ignore Niterói, the city immediately opposite Rio across Guanabara Bay, despite the fact is has ocean beaches as good as or better than Rio's. Instead, they head straight for the surf towns around Cabo Frio or the fashionable little resort of Búzios, which has good beaches and lively summer nightlife. ⤷ *For listings, see pages 153-159.*

Niterói ⊕⊖❼❸▲⊖⓿ ⤷ *pp153-159. Colour map 4, C3.*

Cariocas are rude about everywhere, but they are especially rude about their neighbour across Guanabara Bay. The only good thing about Niterói, they say, is the view it has of Rio de Janeiro. As a result few visitors make it here. However, its ocean beaches are less polluted and far less crowded than Rio's and the views from them across the bay, especially at sunset, are wonderful. Oscar Niemeyer's Museu de Arte Contemporânea, a flying-saucer-shaped building perched on a promontory in Niterói is one of his very best buildings. There is no reason to stay overnight in Niterói but the city is well worth visiting as a day trip or on the way to Búzios.

Ins and outs

Getting there Ferries and launches to Niterói leave from the 'Barcas' terminal at Praça 15 de Novembro in central Rio. Boats run every 10 minutes and the journey takes 20-30 minutes, US$2. *Aerobarcas* (catamarans) take just three minutes and cost US$4. Fares are halved from 0700 to 1000. Boats arrive at the Praça Araribóia terminal in Niterói.

Bus Nos 996 Gávea–Jurujuba, 998 Galeão–Charitas, 740-D and 741 Copacabana–Charitas, 730-D Castelo–Jurujuba, US$1.50, all run between Rio and Niterói. If you are driving, the bridge across Guanabara Bay is well signposted. There is a toll of US$4.

Getting around To get to the ocean beaches from Niterói, take bus Nos 38 or 52 from Praça General Gomes Carneiro or a bus from the street directly ahead of the ferry entrance, at right angles to the coast road. For Jurujuba take bus No 33 from the boat dock; sit on the right-hand side, it's a beautiful ride.

Tourist information Contact **Neltur** ① *Estrada Leopoldo Fróes 773, São Francisco, T021-2710 2727, www.neltur.com.br.*

Sights

Surrounded by long curved walkways, the space-age building of the **Museu de Arte Contemporânea** ① *Mirante da Praia da Boa Viagem, T021-2620 2400, www.macniteroi. com.br, Tue-Sun 1100-1800, US$2.50, free Wed,* is rapidly becoming the most famous work by Brazil's celebrated disciple of Le Corbusier, Oscar Niemeyer. It is in a fabulous location, sitting above a long bach with a sweeping view across Guanabara Bay to Rio as a backdrop. The building itself looks like a Gerry Anderson vision of the future; one can almost imagine *Thunderbird 1* taking off through its centre. The main gallery is a white circle of polished concrete perched on a low monopod and sitting in a reflection pool. It is

Villa-Lobos – Rio's greatest musical son

One of the many contradictory beauties of Brazil is that whilst the country as a whole is entrenchantly institutionalized and socially stratified, its best music has always burst forth spontaneously from the various roots of Brazil, and been loved by all. Gilberto Gil says in one song that it comes from "beneath the soil at our feet"; the feet of Bahia. African feet. Marlui Miranda celebrates it as indigenous, Hermeto Pascoal and Egberto Gismonti as bursting from Nature. And none of these composers, revered though they are throughout Brazil, move within set traditions – their music defies labels. This attitude to music within Brazil is as much a product of the vision of one man as it is a lucky fluke. Heitor Villa-Lobos, the country's most distinguished composer once famously stated: "one foot in the academy and you are changed for the worst". He went on to change the academy; founding a system of education, still used today which fused classical training with a love and appreciation for popular and traditional musical forms.

Like so many other great Brazilian musicians from Djavan to Tom Jobim, Villa-Lobos began his musical career in Rio's cafes. You could have seen him at the turn of the 19th century playing cello in places like **Bar Luiz** in the city centre. He then secured a place in the Rio Symphony Orchestra, where he played under the Strauss's baton, and where he began to compose. His early concerts enchanted Cariocas and by 1923, he had attracted enough official favour to win a government grant to study in Paris; a considerable amount of money at that time. Here he met and became friends with Milhaud, was strongly influenced by Satie and composed many of his most famous works – like the *Bachianas Brasileiras*, which re-invented and Brazilianized baroque music. On his return to Brazil Villa-Lobos founded the Conservatório Nacional de Canto Orfeónico and the Brazilian Academy of Music, where he invented and instilled his much revered system of musical education.

Villa-Lobos was a magnetic personality and a Carioca through and through. Julian Bream, the foremost European interpreter of his guitar music remembers him as 'larger than life, quite extraordinary. He didn't seem to be a composer. He wore loud checked shirts, smoked a cigar, and always kept the radio on, listening to the news or light music or whatever.' He was famous for his anecdotes which were told with a cigar in one hand and a glass of brandy in the other. These were full of unlikely accounts of encounters with tribes of cannibalistic *indígenas* and giant snakes, met on his numerous travels throughout the Amazon and North East, in search of Nature and traditional folk music.

His music too is idiosyncratic; anecdotal; visual and thoroughly Brazilian. *Bachianas Brasileiras* and *Little Caipira Train* are celebrations of daily Brazilian life. *Green Mansions* and *Saudades das Selvas Brasileiras* (*Longing for the Brazilian Forest*) are dedications to the beauty of the natural landscape. He even wrote a series of *choros*; a musical style which fused Portugal and Africa and which would later produce Samba. He died, on November 17, 1959, in his beloved Rio de Janeiro. His house is now a museum, see page 102.

reached by a coiling, serpentine ramp which meets the building on its second storey. The exhibitions comprise seasonal shows and a permanent collection of Brazilian contemporary art of all disciplines. The top level is devoted to temporary displays and the intermediate to the permanent collection. Niemeyer overcomes the problem of the unsuitability of a curved space for the exhibition of art by using an inner hexagonal core enclosed by flat screen walls. More difficult to overcome is that the glimpses of the stunning panorama of Rio through the gaps in the hexagon are far more captivating than most of the art. The building is worth seeing at dusk when it is lit; the sky above the streetlights of Rio is light peacock blue infused with lilac and the distant figure of the Corcovado Christ shines brilliant xenon-white over the dark mass of mountains.

Many buildings associated with the city's period as state capital are grouped around the **Praça da República**. None are open to the public. The city's main thoroughfare, Avenida Ernâni do Amaral Peixoto, runs from the *praça* and is lined with buildings similar to Avenida Presidente Vargas in Rio. At the end of the avenue is the dock for Rio, a statue of the indigenous chief, Araribóia, and **Bay Market Shopping Centre**.

Perched on a rocky promontory at the mouth of Guanabara Bay, the 16th-century **Fortaleza Santa Cruz** ① *Estrada General Eurico Gaspar Dutra, Guanabara Bay, T021-2710 7840, daily 0900-1600, US$1.50, compulsory guided tour in Portuguese only*, is still used by the Brazilian military and is the most important historical monument in Niterói. As well as the usual range of cannon, dungeons and bulwarks the tour includes a visit to gruesome execution sites and a little chapel dedicated to Saint Barbara. The statue of the saint inside was originally destined for Santa Cruz dos Militares in Rio. However, unlike most Cariocas, the saint obviously prefers Niterói: any attempts to move her image from here have allegedly been accompanied by violent storms.

Beaches
The beaches closest to the city centre are unsuitable for bathing (Gragoatá, Vermelha, Boa Viagem, das Flechas). The next beaches along, also in the city and with polluted water, have more in the way of restaurants, bars and nightlife and some of the best views in the whole country, especially at sunset and sunrise. **Icaraí** is the smartest district, with the best hotels and good nightlife. Together with **São Francisco** and **Charitas**, there are good views out across the bay to Rio. The road continues round the bay, past Preventório and Samanguaiá to **Jurujuba**, a fishing village at the end of the No 33 bus route. About 2 km from Jurujuba along a narrow road are the attractive twin beaches of **Adão** and **Eva** beneath the Fortaleza Santa Cruz with more lovely views of Rio across the bay. These beaches are often used for *candomblé* (Brazilian-African spirit religion) ceremonies.

Piratininga, **Camboinhas**, **Itaipu** and **Itacoatiara**, four fabulous stretches of sand, are the best in the area, about 40 minutes from Niterói through picturesque countryside. Buses leave from the street directly ahead of the ferry entrance, at right angles to the coast road. The undertow at Itacoatiara is dangerous, but the waves are popular with surfers and the beach itself is safe. Itaipu is also used by surfers.

Costa do Sol ⊖🅿♨🅰⊖🅘 ⇥ *pp153-159*.

To the east of Niterói lies a series of saltwater lagoons, the **Lagos Fluminenses**. Two small lakes lie behind the beaches of Piratininga, Itaipu and Itacoatiara, but they are polluted and ringed by mud. The next lakes, **Maricá** and **Saquarema**, are much larger; although they are still muddy, the waters are relatively unpolluted and wildlife abounds in the scrub and bush around the lagoons. This is a prime example of the *restinga* (coastal swamp and forest) environment. The RJ-106 road runs behind the lakes en route to Cabo Frio and Búzios, but an unmade road goes along the coast between

Itacoatiara and Cabo Frio, giving access to the many long, open beaches of Brazil's Costa do Sol. The whole area is perfect for camping.

Maricá → Colour map 4, C3. Phone code: 022. Population: 60,500.

The 36-km Itaipu–Açu road, with many wild, lonely stretches, leads to Maricá, a sleepy fishing village with sand streets, on its own lagoon. There is good walking in the **Serra do Silvado**, 14 km away on the road to Itaboraí. Between Maricá and Saquarema are **Ponta Negra** and **Jaconé**, both surfing beaches. Information is available from the **tourist office** ① *Av Ver Francisco Sabino da Costa 477, www.marica.rj.gov.br.*

Saquarema → Colour map 4, C3. Phone code: 022. Population: 44,000.

Saquarema is a fishing and holiday village, known as the centre for surfing in Brazil. Its cold, open seas provide consistent, crashing waves of up to 3 m. Frequent national and international championships take place here, but beware of strong currents. The lovely white church of **Nossa Senhora de Nazaré** (1675) is on a green promontory jutting into the ocean. Local legend has it that on 8 September 1630, fishermen, saved from a terrible storm, found an image of the Virgem de Nazaré in the rocks. A chapel was founded on the spot and subsequent attempts to relocate the Virgin (as when the chapel was falling into disrepair) resulted in her miraculously returning to the original site. For **tourist information**, see www.saquarema.rj.gov.br.

Araruama → Colour map 4, C3. Phone code: 022. Population: 66,500.

The **Lagoa Araruama** (220 sq km), is one of the largest lakes in Brazil and is famous for its medicinal mud. The salinity is high, the waters calm and almost the entire lake is surrounded by sandy beaches, making it popular with families looking for unpolluted bathing. The constant breeze makes the lake perfect for windsurfing and sailing. The major industry of the area is salt, and all around are saltpans and wind pumps used to carry the water into the pans. The town itself is at the western end of the lake on the inland shore, 116 km from Rio.

At the eastern end of the lake, also inland, is **São Pedro de Aldeia**, which has a population of 55,500 and, despite intensive development, still retains much of its colonial charm. There is a lovely **Jesuit church** built in 1723, and a **tourist office** ① *Ton Av São Pedro, www.araruama.rj.gov.br.*

Arraial do Cabo → Colour map 4, C4. Phone code: 022. Population: 21,500.

This rather ugly little salt-industry town near Cabo Frio is considerably less busy than the resort at Cabo Frio a little to the north, and provides access to equally good beaches and dunes. The lake and the ocean here are divided by the Restinga de Massambaba, a long spit of sand mostly deserted except for the beaches of **Massambaba** and **Seca**, at the western end, and **Grande** in the east at Arraial do Cabo town itself. Arraial has lots of other small beaches on the bays and islands that form the cape, round which the line of the coast turns north, including the long, busy stretch at **Anjos**, **Praia do Forno** and **Prainha**. Excursions can be made by boat around the islets and by jeep or buggy over the sand dunes.

Ins and outs A very steep road connects the beaches of Itaipu and Itacoatiara with RJ-106 (and on to Bacaxá and Araruama) via the village of Itaipu-Açu. Most maps do not show a road beyond Itaipu-Açu; it is certainly too steep for buses. An alternative to the route from Niterói to Araruama through the lagoons is further inland than the RJ-106, via Manilha, Itaboraí and Rio Bonito on the BR-101 and RJ-124; this is a fruit-growing region.

Diving and adventure sports While Arraial is not a dive destination of international quality in its own right, it is one of the best in Brazil and there are a number of sites of varying difficulty with caverns and swim-throughs that are well worth exploring. Cold and warm currents meet here just off the coast and the marine life is more abundant than almost anywhere else on mainland southern Brazil. Expect to see schools of tropical and subtropical reef fish such as batfish and various tangs and butterfly fish, the occasional turtle, colonies of gorgonians and beautiful (though invasive) soft corals probably brought here on oil tankers from the Indo-Pacific. Dolphins are frequent visitors. The best visibility is between November and May. Water temperature is always below 20°C. The little town is also establishing itself as an adventure sports destination with activities including dune boarding, parachuting, kite surfing and kayaking available. ►► *See Activities and tours, page 158.*

Excursions **Praia do Farol**, on Ilha do Cabo Frio, is one of Brazil's best beaches, with sand dunes and crystal-clear water. The **tourist office** ① *T022-2620 5039, www.arraialdocabo-rj.com.br/zarony.html*, is at Praça da Bandeira. ►► *See Activities and tours, page 158.*

Cabo Frio ●❷❹▲❸❻ ►► *pp153-159. Colour map 4, C4.*

→ *Phone code: 022. Population: 127,000.*

This busy tourist town, 168 km from Rio, is a popular middle-class Brazilian seaside resort, which overflows at the weekend with Cariocas. Although the town itself is very touristy, there are some attractive white-sand beaches, some with dunes and good surf and windsurfing, and accommodation nearby. Bring mosquito repellent.

Cabo Frio vies with Porto Seguro for the title of Brazil's first city. The navigator Amerigo Vespucci landed here in 1503 and returned to Portugal with a boatload of *pau brasil*. Since the wood in these parts was of better quality than that further north, the area subsequently became the target for loggers from France, the Netherlands and England. The Portuguese failed to capitalize on their colony here and it was the French who established the first defended settlement. Eventually the Portuguese took it by force but it was not until the second decade of the 17th century that they planned their own fortification, the **Forte São Mateus** ① *daily 0800-1800*, which was started in 1618 on the foundations of the French fort. It is now a ruin at the mouth of the Canal de Itajuru, with rusting cannons propped up against its whitewashed ramparts. The canal connects Lagoa Araruama with the ocean.

The town beach, **Praia do Forte**, is highly developed and stretches south for about 7.5 km to Arraial do Cabo, its name changing to **Praia das Dunas** (after the dunes) and **Praia do Foguete**. These waters are much more suited to surfing. North of the canal entrance and town is the small under-developed beach of **Praia Brava** (popular with surfers and naturists) and the wine-glass bay of **Praia das Conchas**, which has a few shack restaurants. Next is **Praia do Peró**, 7 km of surf and sand on the open sea with a small town behind it and cheap accommodation. The best dunes are at Peró, Dama Branca (on road to Arraial) and the Pontal dunes at Praia do Forte.

Ins and outs The **airport** ① *Estrada Velha do Arraial do Cabo s/n, T022-2647 2399*, receives flights, in high season only, from Rio, Belo Horizonte and Sao Paulo, Ribeirão Preto and Uberlândia. The **tourist office** ① *Av Contorno 200, Praia do Forte, T022-2647 1689, www.cabofrio.tur.br or www.cabofrio.rj.gov.br*, is in the large orange building.

➤ *Phone code: 022. Population: 18,000.*

Búzios is the principal resort of choice for Carioca and Mineira upper middle classes searching for their idea of St Tropez sophistication. When it was discovered by Brigitte Bardot in 1964 it was little more than a collection of colonial fishermen's huts and a series of pristine beaches hidden beneath steep hills covered in maquis-like vegetation. Now there are strings of hotels behind all of those beaches and the huts have become lost within a designated tourist village of bars, bikini boutiques and restaurants, most of which are strung along the pretty little main street, **Rua das Pedras**. Bardot sits here too – cheesily immortalized in brass, and subsequently in tens of thousands of pictures taken by the troops of cruise line passengers who fill Búzios's streets in high season. St Tropez this is not, but it can be fun for twenty-somethings who are single and looking not to stay that way. The beaches are beautiful and there are a few romantic hotels with wonderful views.

Ins and outs

Getting there Four buses leave daily from Rio's *rodoviária* (US$8, 2½ hrs). Tickets can be bought from the **1001** counter, T022-2516 1001. You can also take any bus from Rio to the town of Cabo Frio (these are more frequent), from where it's 30 minutes to Búzios. Buying the ticket in advance is only necessary on major holidays. The Búzios *rodoviária* is a few blocks' walk from the centre. Some *pousadas* are within 10 minutes' walk, eg **La Coloniale** and **Brigitta's**, while for others you'll need to take a local bus (US$0.50) or taxi. The buses from Cabo Frio run the length of the peninsula and pass several *pousadas*. The journey by car along the BR-106 takes about 2½ hours from Rio. Traffic back to Rio can be appalling on Sunday nights and during the peak holiday season.

Tourist information The main **tourist office** ⓘ *Manguinos, Pórtico de Búzios s/n, T022-2633 6200, T0800-249999, 24 hrs*, is at the entrance to town on the western edge of the peninsula. It has helpful staff, some of whom speak English. There's another office at ⓘ *Praça Santos Dumont, T022-2623 2099*, in the centre of Búzios town, which is more limited. For most of the hotels and services on the peninsula check www.buzios online.com.br or www.buzios.rj.gov.br. Maps are available from hotels and tourist offices.

Beaches

During the daytime, the best option is to head for the beaches, of which there are 25. The most visited are **Geribá** (many bars and restaurants; popular with surfers), **Ferradura** (deep-blue sea and calm waters), **Ossos** (the most famous and close to the centre), **Tartaruga** and **João Fernandes**. The better surf beaches, such as **Praia de Manguinhos** and **Praia de Tucuns**, are further from the town centre. To help you to decide which beach suits you best, you can join one of the local two- or three-hour schooner trips, which pass many of the beaches, or hire a beach buggy (available from agencies on Rua das Pedras or through most hotels and hostels). These trips cost around US$10-15 and can be arranged through **Escuna Queen Lory**, T022-2623 1179.

For Sleeping and Eating price codes and other relevant information, see pages 42-47.

◉ **Sleeping**

Niterói *p147*

AL-A Icaraí Praia, R Belisário Augusto 21, T021-2710 5030, www.icaraipraia hotel.com.br. Plain rooms in a faded 1980s beachfront tower.

AL-A Tower Hotel, Av Almte Ari Parreiras 12, Icaraí, T021-2612 2121, www.towerhotel. com.br. Niterói's smartest hotel (3-star) with ordinary, rather faded rooms, an indoor pool, sauna and reasonable business facilities.

B Pousada Suba and Veja, R Mal Raul Albuquerque (Mirante de Piratininga), Km 18, T021-2619 0823. Wonderful views out over one of the most beautiful beaches on the Costa do Sol. Bar, restaurant, pool and sauna.

Camping

Piratininga, Estr Frei Orlando Km 2, T021-2609 4581.

Maricá *p150*

B Pousada Colonial, Ponta Negra, T/F022-2748 1707. Simple suites and bungalows, with breakfast.

B Solar Tabaúna, Ponta Negra, T022-2648 1626. Similar to the **Colonial** but with a pool.

Saquarema *p150*

B Pousada Pedra d'Água Maasai, Trav de Itaúna 17, Praia de Itaúna, T/F022-2651 1092, www.maasai.com.br. Good little beachfront hotel with 18 apartments, pool, sauna and a reasonable seafood restaurant.

C Pousada do Holandês, Av Vilamar 377, Itaúna beach. Many languages spoken by Dutch owner and his Brazilian wife. Good meals – follow the signs, or take a taxi, from Saquarema. Recommended.

C-D Pousada Canto da Vila, Av Min Salgado 52, T022-2651 1563, www.pousada canto davila.com.br. 14 little rooms and 2 larger ones. Overlooking the beach. Pokey but well maintained.

D-E Garota de Itaúna, Av Oceânica 165, Itaúna, T022-2651 2321. Very simple rooms next to the beach and a good seafood restaurant.

D-E Ilhas Gregas, R do Prado 671, Itaúna, T022-2651 1008. Youth hostel with a pool, sauna, bar and restaurant.

Camping

Itaúna's, R dos Tatuís 999, access from Av Oceânica, T022-2651 1711.

Araruama *p150*

A Enseada das Garças, R José Costa 1088, Ponta da Areia, about 5 km from São Pedro de Aldeia, T022-2621 1924, www.roteirosde charme.com.br. Beautiful little hotel over-looking the sea with access to good walking trails.

A Ver a Vista, R São Sebastião 400, São Pedro de Aldeia, T022-2665 4721, www.veravistahotel.com.br. Small apartment hotel with a sauna, bar and swimming pool.

C Pousada do Peu, RJ-132, Km 12, T022-2665 3614. Basic, popular with families.

E Praia do Sudoeste, R Pedro Américo, Lt 27, T022-2621 2763. Youth hostel with simple rooms, available in high season only.

Camping

Camping Clube do Brasil, RJ-106, Marica Km 81.5, Ponte dos Leites beach.

Camping da Colina, RJ-106, Km 108, Praia da Teresa, São Pedro de Aldeia, T022-2621 1919. Not much shade.

Arraial do Cabo p150

A Pousada Nautillu's, R Marcílio Dias 100, T022-2622 1611, www.pousadanautillus.com. Medium-sized *pousada* with a pool, sauna, bar and restaurant. Recommended.

B Pousada dos Atobás, R José Pinto Macedo 270, T022-2622 2461, www.pousada dosatobas.com.br. Small newly built hostel with a pool, sauna and bar.

C Orlamar, Av Beiramar 111, Recanto da Prainha, T/F022-2622 2410, www.pousada orlamar.com. Literally on the beach, with car access only at low tide. Reasonable restaurant and bar.

Camping

Camping Clube do Brasil, Praia dos Anjos, T022-2622 1023. Crowded beach. Plenty of places to eat along the beach.

Cabo Frio p151

AL-B La Plage, R das Badejos 40, Peró, T022-2647 1746, www.redebela.com.br. Cheaper in low season. Newly refurbished with fully equipped suites; those upstairs have a sea view, excellent for families. Right on the beach, services include pool and bar, à la carte restaurant, hydromassage, sauna, 24-hr cyber café, garage.

B Othon Sítio do Portinho, R Cnel Ferreira 281, T022-2644 9264, www.pousadasitiodo portinho.hpg.com.br. Cheaper in low season. A good *pousada* set in gardens in this residential suburb. Very nice a/c rooms and all the usual facilities, including pool and bar. You can get to Portinho district from Av Excelsior or along the canal (go under the bridge). For all **Othon** hotels see www.hoteis-othon.com.br.

B-C Pousada Água Marinha, R Rui Barbosa 996b, Centro, about 4 blocks from Praia do Forte, T022-2643 8447, p.aguamarinha@ uol.com.br. Cheaper in low season. Plain white rooms with comfortable beds, a/c, fan, TV, frigobar, breakfast, pool and parking. Good choice in the centre.

C-E Pousada São Lucas, R Goiás 266, Jardim Excelsior, T022-2645 3037 (formerly a youth hostel). 3 mins from the *rodoviária*.

Price is for double room with TV. Also has dorms with hot shower, breakfast and fan (a little cheaper in low season).

E Albergue da Juventude São Lucas, R Goiás 266, Jardim Excelsior, 3 mins from the *rodoviária*, T022-2645 3037. IYHA youth hostel. Price per person.

E Albergue Internacional da Juventude de Muxarabi, R Leonor Santa Rosa 13, Jardim Flamboyant, T022-2643 0369. Youth hostel. Price per person.

E Albergue Peró, R Coutrin 13, Peró, T022-2644 3123, www.perohostel.com.br. IYHA youth hostel, a stroll from the Peró beach with bike rental, restaurant, dorms and doubles.

E Albergue Praia das Palmeiras, Praia das Palmeiras 1, T022-2643 2866. Youth hostel.

Camping

Camping Clube do Brasil, Estr dos Passageiros 700, 2 km from town, T022-2643 3124.

Camping da Estação, Estr dos Passageiros 370, T022-2643 1786.

Dunas do Peró, Estr do Guriri 1001, T022-2629 2323. Small *pousada* with a campsite on Praia do Peró.

Búzios p152

The best rooms on the peninsula are not on the beaches but are those with a superb view, on the Morro do Humaitá hill, 10 mins' walk from the town centre; hire a beach buggy. Prior reservations are needed in summer, during holidays such as Carnaval and New Year's Eve, and at weekends. For cheaper options and better availability, try Cabo Frio.

Several private houses rent rooms, especially in summer and holidays. Look for the signs: '*Alugo quartos*'.

LL-L Casas Brancas, Alto do Humaitá 8, T022-2623 1458, www.casasbrancas.com.br. Far and away the best hotel in Búzios: a series of rooms perched on the hill in mock-Mykonos buildings with separate terraces for the pool and spa areas. Sweeping views over the bay. Wonderfully romantic at night when it is lit by candlelight. If you can't afford to

stay, come for dinner. The **Abracadabra** next door is owned by Casas Brancas and is similar though cheaper and less stylish.
LL-L El Cazar, Alto do Humaitá 6, T022-2623 1620. Next door to Casas Brancas and almost as luxurious, though a little darker inside. Beautiful artwork on the walls and central-Asian kelims on the ipe wood floors. Tasteful and relaxing.
L-AL Pousada Byblos, Alto do Humaitá 14, T022-2623 1162, www.byblos.com.br. Wonderful views out over the bay and bright, light rooms with tiled floors and balconies.
AL Pousada Pedra da Laguna, R 6, lote 6, praia da ferradura, T/F022-2623 1965, www.pedradalaguna.com.br. Spacious rooms, the best with a view, 150 m from the beach. Part of the Roteiros do Charme group (see page 43).
A Pousada Hibiscus Beach, R 1 No 22, quadra C, Praia de João Fernandes, T022-2623 6221, www.hibiscusbeach.com. A peaceful spot, run by its British owners, overlooking Praia de João Fernandes, 15 pleasant bungalows, a/c, satellite TV, garden, pool, light meals available, help with car/buggy rentals and local excursions. One of the best beach hotels.
A-B Brigitta's Guest House, R das Pedras 131, T/F022-2623 6157, www.búzios online.com.br/brigitta. Beautifully decorated little *pousada* where Bardot once stayed, with just 4 rooms on the main street. Its delightful

restaurant, bar and tea house overlooking the water are worth a visit.
A-B Casa da Ruth, R dos Gravatás, Geribá, T022-2623 2242, www.búziosturismo. com/casadaruth. Simple mock-Greek rooms in lilac overlooking the beach and pool.
C-E Praia dos Amores, Av José Bento Ribeiro Dantas 92, T022-2623 2422, www.buzios turismo.com/auberge. IYHA, not far from the bus station, next to Praia da Tartaruga and just under 1 km from the centre. About the best value in Búzios.
C-E Ville Blanche, R Manoel T de Farias, 222, T022-2623 1840. A hostel and hotel right in the centre in the street parallel to R da Pedras with a/c dorms for up to 10, and light-blue tiled doubles with fridges, en suites and a balcony. Can be noisy.

Camping and Chalets
E Country Camping Park, R Maria Joaquina Justiniano 895, (off Praça da Rasa), Praia Rasa, Km 12, T022-2629 1155, www.buzios camping.com.br. Chalets and a well-run shady campsite 1 km from the beach.

🍴 Eating

Niterói *p147*
🍴 **Marius**, Pref Sílvio Picanço 479, Charitas, T021-2610 1111. Excellent *churrascaria* (grilled meat barbecue), seafood, European

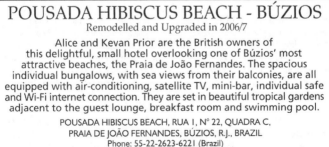

and Brazilian cooking in a restaurant overlooking the sea. Decent wine list.

Da Carmine, R Matriz de Barros 305, Icaraí, T021-3602 4988. Decent Italian seafood and pasta and a respectable wine list.

La Sagrada Familia, R Domingues de Sá 325, Icaraí, T021-2610 3556, www.la sagradafamilia.com.br. The best restaurant in Niterói, varied menu and reasonable wine list and housed in a beautiful colonial building.

Saquarema p150

Le Bistrô, Av São Rafael 1134, Itaúna. The best restaurant in the area with good seafood.

Tem Uma Né Chama Teré, on the main square. Decent Brazilian standards and fish.

Araruama p150

Don Roberto, Av Getúlio Vargas 272, São Pedro de Aldeia, T022-2621 3913. Wood-fired pizzas.

O Pirata, RJ-106 Amaral Peixoto 16, São Pedro de Aldeia. A varied menu including reasonable seafood.

Arraial do Cabo p150

Todos os Prazeres, R José Pinto Macedo, T022-2622 2365. Closed Mon and Wed off season. A decent varied menu of Franco-Brazilian fusion.

Cabo Frio p151

The neat row of restaurants on Av dos Pescadores are worth a browse for good-value seafood and pasta. They have French-style seating on the pavement under awnings.

Picolino, R Mcal F Peixoto 319, T022-2643 2436. In a nice old building, very smart, mixed menu of seafood and a few international dishes.

Gaijin, R José Bonifácio 28, T022-2643 4922. Reasonable Japanese food in generous portions.

Hippocampo, R Mcal F Peixoto 283, next door but one, T022-2645 5757. One of the better seafood restaurants with good *robalo* (bass) and *badejo* (whiting).

Chico's, Av Teixeira e Souza 30, upstairs in Centro Comercial Víctor Nunes da Rocha, town centre, T022-2645 7454. Clean, smart, does breakfast, self-service, some more expensive dishes. On the ground floor is the **Coffee Shop.** More a stand than a shop, cheap; but better coffee in **Branca.**

"In" Sônia, Av dos Pescadores 140, loja 04. Good service and tasty fish, many dishes offered for 2 people.

Tonto, Av dos Pescadores, next door to "In" Sônia, T022-2645 1886 for delivery. Also serves pizza and has a bar, too.

Branca, Praça Porto Rocha, in the centre of town. Per kilo lunch 1100-1700, also fast food, pizza after 1800, coffee, pastries and cakes, good. A large, popular place.

Chez Michou, Av dos Pescadores. Closed Mon. For crêpes (as in **Rio Sul** shopping centre in Rio de Janeiro). Upstairs are a number of bars and nightclubs, eg **Eleven**, above San Francisco restaurant, and others.

Búzios p152

See also **Casas Brancas**, page 154 (fine views and romantic dining) and **Brigitta's**, page 155 (funky seafood bistro). There are many restaurants on and around R das Pedras and one of the charms of Búzios is browsing this street. The cheaper options tend to be off the main drag. There are plenty of beachside *barracas* (palapas) all over the peninsula serving the usual beans, rice and chips combinations outside of the low season.

There are a few other very cheap places on Praça Santos Dumont, off R das Pedras, and a small supermarket a couple of doors away from **La Prima.**

Acquerello, R das Pedras 130, T022-2623 2817. Smart a/c seafood and Italian restaurant with a reasonable wine list. The best on the street.

Satyricon, Av José Bento Ribeiro Dantas 500, Praia da Armação (in front of Morro da Humaitá), T022-2623 1595. Búzios's most illustrious restaurant specializing in Italian seafood. Decent wine list.

Moqueca Capixaba, R Manoel de Carvalho 116, Centro, T022-2623 1155. Bahian seafood, with dishes cooked in coconut or dendê oil.
Banana Land, R Manoel Turíbio de Farias 50, T022-2623 0855. Cheap and cheerful per kilo buffet.
Chez Michou, R das Pedras, 90, Centro, T022-2623 2169. An open-air bar with videos, music and dozens of choices of pancakes accompanied by ice-cold beer. Always busy.
La Prima, Av Manuel Turibo de Farias. Homely, sandwiches and self-service food; doubles as a bakery.

🎵 Bars and clubs

Búzios *p152*
In season, nightlife in Búzios is young, beautiful and buzzing. Out of season it is non-existent. Most of the bars and the handful of clubs are on R das Pedras. These include **Guapo Loco**, a bizarrely shaped Mexican theme-bar and restaurant with dancing. **Privilege**, Av José Bento Ribeiro Dantas 550, R Orla Bardot, Búzios's main club and one of Brazil's best European-style dance clubs with pumping techno, house and hip-hop, and 5 rooms, including a cavernous dance floor, sushi bar and lounge. **Ta-ka-ta ka-ta**, R das Pedras 256, is strewn with motorbike parts and has its walls covered completely with graffiti. The Dutch owner obstinately refuses to say where he comes from. There are plenty of others including lively options such as **Bar do Zé**, R das Pedras 382, T022-2623 4986 and **Alexo**, next door.

✳ Festivals and events

Niterói *p147*
Mar-May Festa do Divino, a festival that traditionally begins on Easter Sun and continues for the next 40 days, in which the *bandeira* (banner) *do Divino* is taken around the local municipalities. The festival ends at Pentecost with sacred and secular celebrations.

24 Jun São João, lots of parades, *forró* dancing and barn-dance costumes.
22 Nov Founding of the town. Parades, concerts and dancing.

Saquarema *p150*
Mar-May Festa do Divino, see Niterói, above.
8 May Founding of the town. Dancing, concerts and plenty of drinking.
29 Jun Festival of São Pedro, at the end of the Festas Juninas.
7 Sep Nossa Senhora de Nazaré, the town's patron saint's day.

Araruama *p150*
16 May Founding of the town.
29 Jun São Pedro, patron saint day of São Pedro de Aldeia.

Arraial do Cabo *p150*
13 May Founding of the town.
May/Jun Corpus Christi.

🛍 Shopping

Búzios *p152*
Many of Brazil's fashionable and beautiful come here for their holidays and Búzios is therefore a good place to pick up the kind of beach clothes and tropical cuts that they would wear. Although seemingly expensive these clothes are a fraction of what you would pay for labels of this quality in Europe, the US or Australia. Shopping is best on R das Pedras. Aside from the boutiques, there is little else of interest beyond the expected range of tourist tack shops. Of the boutiques the best are as follows:
Allegra, R das Pedras. Sexy light dresses, skirts, T-shirts and tops.
Bum Bum Ipanema, R das Pedras 321, T022-2623 4139. Bright young bikinis in gorgeous cuts.
Farm, R das Pedras 233, T022-2623 7477. Elegant and cool beachwear and light clothes for women.

Lenny, R das Pedras 233, T022-2623 3745. The most à la mode bikinis – from the point of view of Brazilians.

Salinas, R das Pedras. Beautifully crafted bikinis and beachwear. Together with **Rosa Chá**, the most à la mode – from the point of view of foreigners.

Tenda, R das Pedras. A little boutique with the pick of Brazilian designers including the supermodels' bikini choice – **Rosa Chá**.

Tepo, R Manoel Turíbio de Farias 202D (parallel to R das Pedras), T022-2623 7140. Upmarket indigenous arts and crafts, jewellery and fashion.

▲ Activities and tours

Niterói *p147*
Rio Cricket Associação Atlética (RCA), R Fagundes Varela 637, T021-2717 5333. Bus No 57 from the ferry.
Rio Sailing Club (late Clube de Niterói), Estr Leopoldo Fróes 418, lote 338, T021-2610 5810. Bus No 33 marked 'via Fróes'.

Arraial do Cabo *p150*
Deep Trip, Av Getulio Vargas 93, Praia Grande, Arraial do Cabo, T022-2622 1800, www.deeptrip.com.br. The only PADI-affiliated dive operator in Arraial, with a range of courses and dive trips.
Gas, Av Litoranea 80, Praia Grande, T022-9956 1222, www.arraialdocabo-rj.com.br/gas. Various adventure sports including dune boarding, parachuting and kayak surfing. Runs dive trips but is not PADI accredited.
K-Kite School, R da Alegria 15, T022-2662 9465, www.kkite.hpg.ig.com.br. Windsurfing and kitesurfing, and lessons.

Trips to Ilha do Cabo Frio
Barco Lindo Olhar, T022-2647 4493, ask for Vadinho or Eraldo in the town's main marina.
Zarony tours, Marina dos Pescadores, 2nd pier on Praia dos Anjos, T022-2622 5837, www.arraialdocabo-rj.com.br/zarony.html.

Cabo Frio *p151*
Planeta Costa Azul, Square Shopping, loja 21, T022-2645 2023, www.planetacostado sol.com.br. For flights and local packages.

Búzios *p152*
Malizia, R das Pedras, T022-2623 2022. Money exchange, car hire and other services.
Mister Tours, R Germiniano J Luís 3, Centro, T022-2623 2100.

☉ Transport

Niterói *p147*
Boat Ferries and launches run between the terminal at Praça Araribóia in Niterói and the 'Barcas' terminal at Praça 15 de Novembro in **Rio de Janeiro** every 10 mins (15-20 mins, US$2). There are also catamarans (*aerobarcas*) every 10 mins (3 mins, US$4; US$2 0700-1000. The slow, cheaper ferry gives the best views.
Bus Buses running between Niterói and **Rio de Janeiro** include No 996 Gávea–Jurujuba, No 998 Antônio Carlos Jobim international airport–Charitas, No 740-D and No 741 Copacabana–Charitas, No 730-D Castelo–Jurujuba, US$0.60-0.75.

Saquarema *p150*
Bus To **Rio de Janeiro** (Mil e Um, 1001), every 2 hrs 0730-1800, 2 hrs, US$3.40.

Arraial do Cabo *p150*
Bus To **Rio de Janeiro**, US$6.

Cabo Frio *p151*
Air Flights in high season to **Rio de Janeiro**, **Belo Horizonte**, **Sao Paulo**, **Ribeirão Preto**, and **Uberlândia** with GOL, www.voe gol.com.br, or **Total**, www.total.com.br.

Bus
Local Salineira and Montes Brancos run the local services. US$0.75 to places such as **Búzios**, **São Pedro da Aldeia**, **Saquarema**, **Araruama**, **Arraial do Cabo**; US$0.50 for

closer destinations. The urban bus terminal is near Largo de Santo Antônio, opposite the BR petrol station.

Long distance The *rodoviária* is 2 km from the centre. Buses to **Rio de Janeiro** every 30 mins, 2½ hrs, US$8.To **Búzios**, from the local bus terminal in the town centre, every hour, US$1. Útil to **Belo Horizonte** US$20. Unifac to **Belo Horizonte**, **Juiz da Fora**, **Petrópolis**. Macaense runs frequent services to **Macaé**. To **São Paulo**, at 2100, US$22.60.

For the route from Cabo Frio to **Vitória** either take Macaense bus to **Macaé** (5¼ hrs), or take **1001** to **Campos** (3½ hrs, US$5.60), and change. **1001** stops in Campos first at the **Shopping Estrada** *rodoviária*, which is the one where the bus connection is made, but it's outside town (US$3 taxi to the centre, or local bus US$0.35). The **1001** then goes on to the local *rodoviária*, closer to the centre, but there are no long-distance services from that terminal. Shopping Estrada *rodoviária* has a tourist office, but no cheap hotels nearby. Aguia Branca buses to **Vitória** at 0900 and 1900, US$8.10, 3 hrs 40 mins.

Búzios *p152*

Beach buggies A popular way to get around the cobbled streets of Búzios. Buggy rental available at **Malízia**, T022-2623 2022 or **Rent Buggy**, T022-2623 6421.

Bus The Búzios *rodoviária* is a few blocks' walk from the centre. **1001**, T021-2516 1001, to **Rio de Janeiro** US$8, 2½ hrs (be at the bus terminal 20 mins before departure), 4 departures daily. Buses running between the *rodoviária* Novo Rio in **Rio de Janeiro** and **Cabo Frio** stop at Búzios and are more frequent. Cabo Frio is a 30-min journey from Búzios. Buying the ticket in advance is only recommended on major holidays.

Car

By car via the BR-106 takes about 2½ hrs to **Rio de Janeiro** and can take far longer on Sun nights and on Brazilian public holidays.

⊙ Directory

Niterói *p147*
Banks Banco 24 Horas, Niterói Shopping, R da Conceição 188; Bradesco, R Gavião Peixoto 108. **Internet** O Lido Cyber C@fé, Av Rui Barbosa 29, loja 124, São Francisco. **Laundry** Lavlev, R Pres Backer 138. **Medical services** Universitário Antônio Pedro, Av Marques do Paraná, T021-2620 2828.

Saquarema *p150*
Banks Bradesco, Rod Amaral Peixoto 83.

Araruama *p150*
Banks Bradesco, Av São Pedro 120, São Pedro de Aldeia.

Arraial do Cabo *p150*
Banks Bradesco, R Sen Macedo Soares 44, Ponta Negra. Unibanco, R Dom Pedro, will not change cheques and has no ATM.

Cabo Frio *p151*
Banks Banco do Brasil, Praça Porto Rocha 44, the only bank with exchange, *câmbio* 1100-1430; Bradesco, Av Assunção 904, has Visa ATM; HSBC, Av Assunção 793, has ATM for AmEx, Visa/Plus, MasterCard/Cirrus. **Internet** Aç@i, Av João Pessoa, near R Casemiro de Abreu, US$0.75 per 30 mins, older machines, not always open; Cyber Mar, Nunes da Rocha, Av Teixeira e Souza 30, new, a/c, minimum US$1.50 for 30 mins, US$2.20 per hr, daily 0800-2000; Cyber Tel, Praça Porta Rocha 56, T022-2649 7575, in gallery next to Banco do Brasil. Only 3 machines, but good and fast, US$2 per hr.

Búzios *p152*
Banks There are banks and money exchanges on R das Pedras; Banco do Brasil, R Manuel de Carvalho 70, Centro, T022-2523 2302. **Internet** Búzios@internet, Av J B Ribeiro Dantas 97, close to Shopping One, US$1.20 per 30 mins.

Inland resorts and coffee towns

The mountain resorts of Petrópolis, Teresópolis and Nova Friburgo are set high in the scenic Serra do Mar behind Rio. All three are lovely mountain retreats with accommodation in charming fazendas (coffee estates). The imperial city of Petrópolis retains many of its original buildings and boasts what is perhaps Brazil's finest museum. This is a beautiful area and is becoming increasingly popular for walking, as well as horse riding and other activities. The resorts were originally established because the cool mountain air offered a respite from the heat of Rio and from yellow fever and other diseases that festered in the unhealthy port in the 19th century. They also provided the routes that brought first gold, then coffee from the interior to the coast. ➤➤ *For listings, see pages 167-170.*

Petrópolis ⊜⊘⊛⊗⊕▲⊕⊙ ➤➤ *pp167-170. Colour map 4, C3.*

→ *Phone code: 024. Population: 290,000.*

Emperor Pedro I, who tired of the sticky summer heat in Rio, longed for a summer palace in the cool of the Atlantic coast mountains but abdicated before he could realize his dream. When the new emperor, Pedro II, took the throne, he soon approved plans presented by the German architect Julius Friedrich Köler for a palace and a new city, to be settled by immigrants. The result was Petrópolis. The city was founded in 1843 and in little over a decade had become a bustling Germanic town and an important imperial summer retreat. The emperor and his family would spend as much as six months of each year here and, as he had his court in tow, Köler was able to construct numerous grand houses and administrative buildings. Many of these still stand – bizarre Rhineland anomalies in a neotropical landscape.

Ins and outs

There are buses from the *rodoviária* in Rio every 15 minutes throughout the day and every hour on Sundays. The journey takes about 1½ hours, US$8. Sit on the left-hand side for best views and bring travel sickness pills if you are prone to nausea on winding roads. Return tickets are not available, so buy tickets for the return journey on arrival in Petrópolis. The main **tourist office** ① *Praça da Liberdade, Mon-Sat 0900-1800, Sun 0900-1700*, is at the far southwestern end of Avenida Koeler. It has a list of tourist sights and hotels, a good, free, colour map of the city, and a useful pamphlet in various languages. Some staff are multilingual; all are helpful.

Sights

Three rivers dominate the layout of Petrópolis: the **Piabanha**, **Quitandinha** and the **Palatino**. In the historic centre, where most of the sites of tourist interest are to be found, the rivers have been channelled to run down the middle of the main avenues. Their banks are planted with flowering trees and the overall aspect is unusual in Brazil; you quickly get a sense that this was a city built with a specific purpose and at a specific time in Brazil's history.

Petrópolis's main attraction is its imperial palace. The **Museu Imperial** ① *R da Imperatriz 220, T024-2237 8000, Tue-Sun 1100-1730, last entry 1700, US$4, under 6s free, expect long queues on Sun during Easter and high season*, is Brazil's most visited museum and is so well kept you might think the imperial family had left the day before, rather than in 1889. It's modest for an emperor, neoclassical in style and fully furnished, and is worth a visit if just to see the Crown jewels of both Pedro I and Pedro II. The palace gardens in front are filled with little fountains, statues and shady benches. Descendants of the original family live in a house behind the palace. Horse-drawn carriages wait to be hired outside the gate; not all the horses are in good shape.

Opposite the Museu Imperial is the handsome **Palácio Amarelo** ① *Praça Visconde de Mauá 89, T024-2291 9200, Tue-Sun 0900-1800, US$1*, built in 1850 as the palace of another Brazilian baron and now the Câmara Municipal (town hall). The twin shady *praças* **dos Expedicionários** and **Dom Pedro II** (which has a pigeon-covered statue of the emperor) lie opposite each other at the junction of Rua do Imperador and Rua da Imperatriz, 100 m south of the Museu Imperial (left as you leave the museum). A small **market** is held here on Sundays and there are a handful of cafés and restaurants.

At the northern end of Rua da Imperatriz (turn right out of the museum and follow the river as it curves left along Avenida Tiradentes) is the Gothic revival **Catedral de São Pedro de Alcântara** ① *R São Pedro de Alcântara 60, T024-2242 4300, Tue-Sun 0800-1200 and 1400-1800, free*, where Emperor Pedro II, his wife Princesa Teresa, Princesa Isabel and Count D'Eu are entombed in mock-European regal marble. This lies at the end of the city's most impressive avenue, **Avenida Koeler**, which is lined with mansions built by the imperial and republican aristocracy. Among them are the neoclassical **Palácio Rio Negro** ① *Av Koeler 255, T024-2246 9380, Mon 1200-1700, Wed-Sun 0930-1700, US$1.50, under 6s free, multilingual guides*, built in 1889 by the Barão do Rio Negro as the summer retreat of Brazilian presidents, and the **Casa da Princesa Isabel** ① *Av Koeler 42, outside visits only*, the former residence of Dom Pedro II's daughter and her husband the Count D'Eu.

Avenida Koeler ends at the **Praça da Liberdade** (formerly known as Praça Rui Barbosa) where there are cafés, goat-drawn carts for children and very photogenic views of the cathedral. A further 100 m west of the *praça* (away from Avenida Koeler) is the **Museu Santos Dumont** ① *R do Encanto 22, T024-2247 3158, Tue-Sun 0930-1700, US$1.50, free for*

Petrópolis

Sleeping 😴
Casablanca Centre **3**
Casa Comércio **5**
Othon Riverside Parque **4**
Pousada da Alcobaça **2**
Solar do Império **1**
York **8**

Eating 🍴
Cantina Bom Giovanni **1**

Casa d'Ángelo **2**
Falconi **3**

under 6s. The summer home of Alberto Santos Dumont, who Brazilians claim was the first man to fly an aeroplane, was designed in 1918 as a mock-Alpine chalet. Santos Dumont called it 'the enchanted one', and it is a delightful example of an inventor's house. Steps to the roof lead to an observation point and are carefully designed to allow visitors only to ascend right foot first. His desk doubled up to become his bed. The alcohol-heated shower is said to be the first in Brazil.

The city has a handful of other interesting buildings. The **Casa de Rui Barbosa** ① *Av Ipiranga 405, private residence*, was the home of the Bahian media mogul and writer who was instrumental in abolishing slavery in Brazil. The **Casa de Petrópolis** ① *Av Ipiranga 716, outside visits only*, is a magnificent Gothic folly set in formal French gardens and was built in 1884 by José Tavares Guerra, the grandson of the founder of industrialization in Brazil, the Barão de Mauá. Taking centre stage in the Praça da Confluência is the **Palácio de Cristal**, which was commissioned and built in France following London's great exhibition, when such palaces were all the rage in Europe. It opened to great aplomb, fell into disrepair in the 20th century and is now the home of weekend concerts and shows.

Some 10 km from the centre, on the way to the BR-040 to Rio, is the **Palácio Quitandinha** ① *Av Joaquim Rolla 2, T024-2237 1012, Tue-Sun 0900-1700, US$2.50*, a vast mock-Bavarian edifice that was built in 1944 to be the largest casino in South America. The lake in front of the building is in the shape of Brazil. Further out of town still is the **Orquidário Binot** ① *R Fernandes Vieira 390, T024-2248 5665, Mon-Fri 0800-1100 and 1300-1600, Sat 0700-1100*. This nursery has one of the best collections of Brazilian orchids in the state and is well worth visiting even if you don't intend to buy.

Teresópolis ◉🕖❄️🏛️🅾️ ›› *pp167-170. Colour map 4, C3.*

→ *Phone code: 021. Population: 140,000.*

At 910 m this is the highest city in the state of Rio de Janeiro. It was the favourite summer retreat of Empress Teresa Cristina and is named after her. Development in recent years has destroyed some of the city's character, but most visitors use the town as a base for visiting the Serra dos Órgãos, which lie nearby.

Because of its altitude and the relatively cool temperatures, the area was not exploited by the early colonists since they could not grow the tropical crops that were in demand in Europe. The existence of *fazendas* in the region was first documented in the early 19th century, the best known being that of George March, an Englishman. In order to accommodate a constant stream of visitors, March added lodgings to his farm; not long after other landowners followed suit. Before taking the name of the empress, the parish was called Santo Antônio de Paquequer.

Ins and outs

Numerous buses run between Teresópolis and Rio's *rodoviária* daily. Eight buses a day run between Teresópolis and Petrópolis. Information is available from the **Secretaria de Turismo** ① *Praça Olímpica, T021-2742 3352, ext 2082*, and **Terminal Turístico Tancredo Neves** ① *Av Rotariana, T021-2642 2094, www.teresopolis.rj.gov.br*, at the entrance to town from Rio. There are very good views of the serra from here.

Sights

The **Colina dos Mirantes** is a 30-minute steep climb from Rua Jaguaribe (2 km from the centre; an inexpensive taxi ride), and offers sweeping views of the city and surroundings.

Around the town are various attractions, such as the Sloper and Iaci lakes, the Imbui and Amores waterfalls and the **Fonte Judith**, which has mineral-rich water, and is accessed from Avenida Oliveira Botelho, 4 km southwest. Just off the road to Petrópolis is the **Orquidário Aranda** ① *5 km from the centre, Alameda Francisco Smolka, T021-2742 0628.*

The road to Nova Friburgo (see page 164) is known as the **Vale das Hortaliças** because it passes through a zone where vegetables and flowers are cultivated. There is an interesting rock formation called **A Mulher de Pedra**, 12 km out of Teresópolis on this road.

Serra dos Órgãos ⊜▲↠ *pp167-170.*

These mountains near Teresópolis, named after their strange rock formations, which are said to look like organ pipes, preserve some of the most diverse stretches of Atlantic coast forest in the state of Rio de Janeiro. The wildlife, plant and birdwatching here are excellent, as are the walking and rock climbing. The best way to see the park is on foot. A number of trails cut through the forest and head up into the alpine slopes, including the ascent of the **Dedo de Deus** (God's Finger); a precipitous peak that requires some climbing skills. Other trails lead to the highest point in the park, the **Pedra do Sino** (Bell Rock), 2263 m, a three- to four-hour climb up a 14-km path. The west face of this mountain is one of the hardest climbing pitches in Brazil. Other popular walks include the **Pedra do Açu trail** and paths to a variety of anatomically named peaks and outcrops: O Escalavrado (The Scarred One), O Dedo de Nossa Senhora (Our Lady's Finger), A Cabeça de Peixe (Fish Head), A Agulha do Diabo (The Devil's Needle) and A Verruga do Frade (The Friar's Wart).

Serra dos Órgãos

Ins and outs

If you have a car, a good way to see the park is to do the Rio–Teresópolis–Petrópolis– Rio road circuit, stopping off for walks in the forest. This can be done in a day. The park has two ranger stations, both accessible from the BR-116: the **Sede** (headquarters, T/F021-2642 1070) is closer to Teresópolis (from town take Avenida Rotariana), while the **Sub-Sede** is just outside the park proper, off the BR-116. By the Sede entrance is the Mirante do Soberbo, with views to the Baía de Guanabara. Both the Sede station and the Mirante can be reached on the bus marked 'Mirante do Soberbo', which leaves every half an hour from the Teresópolis *rodoviária* and city centre.

Anyone can enter the park and hike the trails from the Teresópolis gate, but if you intend to climb the Pedra do Sino, you must sign a register (those under 18 must be accompanied by an adult and have permission from the park authorities). Entrance to the park is US\$2, with an extra charge for the path to the top of the Pedra do Sino. For information, contact the Rio de Janeiro branch of **Ibama**, T021-2231 1772.

Flora and fauna

The park belongs to the threatened *Mata Atlântica* coastal rainforest, designated by **Conservation International** as a global biodiversity hot spot and the preserve of what are probably the richest habitats in South America outside the Amazonian cloudforests. There are 20- to 30-m-high trees, such as paineiras (floss-silk tree), ipês and cedros, rising above palms, bamboos and other smaller trees. Flowers include begonias, bromeliads, orchids and quaresmeiras (glorybushes). The park is home to numerous rare and endemic birds including cotingas, the rarest of which is the grey-winged cotinga, guans, tanagers, berryeaters and trogons. Mammals include titi and capuchin monkeys, all of the neo-tropical rainforest cats including jaguar and oceleot, tapir and white collared peccary. Reptiles include the sapo-pulga (flea-toad), which at 10 mm long vies with the Cuban pygmy frog as the smallest amphibian in the world.

Nova Friburgo and around ●❶❸❸❶ ⟩⟩ *pp167-170. Colour map 4, C3.*

→ *Phone code: 024. Population: 175,000.*

This town, standing at 846 m in a beautiful valley with excellent walking and riding, is a popular resort during the summer months. It was founded by Swiss settlers from Fribourg, the first families arriving in 1820. Apart from tourism, Nova Friburgo has an important textile industry, specializing in lingerie, and also produces cheeses, preserves, sweets and liqueurs. Information is available from the **Centro de Turismo** ① *Praça Demerval Barbosa Moreira, T024-2523 8000, ext 236.*

A cable car, US\$5, from Praça dos Suspiros goes 650 m up the **Morro da Cruz**, for a magnificent view of the rugged country. Most of the interesting sites are in the surrounding countryside, so a car may be necessary to see everything. About 10 km northeast are the **Furnas do Catete**, an area of forest, caves, waterfalls and rock formations, one of which is called the **Pedra do Cão Sentado** (The Seated Dog); there is a small entry fee. Other natural attractions are the **Pico da Caledônia** (2310 m) 15 km southwest, and the **Véu de Noiva waterfall**, 9 km north.

The district of **Lumiar**, 34 km southeast, has beautiful scenery, waterfalls, natural swimming pools and good canoeing in the Rio Macaé and Rio Bonito. These two rivers meet at a point called **Poço do Alemão**, or Poço Verde, 4.5 km south of Lumiar.

Towns in the coffee zone

Although coffee no longer dominates this part of Brazil as it did in the 19th century, there are still many reminders of the wealth of this trade. It is apparent in the towns of **Vassouras** and **Valença**, and especially in the *fazendas*, which were the homes and production headquarters of the coffee barons. Today, many of these plantations have been incorporated into a rural, cultural and historic tourist circuit. The train journey from Miguel Pereira has spectacular views of this mountainous terrain.

Background

The coffee zone covered the valley of the Rio Paraíba do Sul and neighbouring hills and valleys. Before railways were built in the second half of the 19th century, mule trains carried the coffee from the interior to the coast on roads such as the Estrada do Comércio from Minas Gerais, through Valença and Vassouras, to the town of Iguaçu. At the end of the 19th century, the abolition of slavery, the exhaustion of the land and lower international prices for coffee caused the collapse of the coffee trade. The towns had to adapt to new economic activities or die, but many of the *fazendas* remain and, although not easy to get to, are worth the effort to visit. *Fazendas: As Casas Grandes Rurais do Brasil* (by Fernando Tasso Frajoso Pires, Abbeville Press), is a beautiful book about these magnificent houses.

Miguel Pereira → *Colour map 4, C3. Phone code: 024. Population: 24,000.*

This town, 113 km north of Rio de Janeiro, has an excellent mountain climate. In the mid-19th century the area was entirely given over to coffee; other industries were introduced when a railway branch line reached here in the late 19th century. The town was named after a doctor who, in the 1930s, promoted the region for holidays away from the coast. About 3 km from town on the road to Rio is the **Lago do Javari**, a popular recreational spot. Mountain roads through the Serra do Mar head east to Petrópolis (see page 160) and Vassouras (see below), but ask about their condition before using either of them. For tourist information, visit **Setur** ⓘ *Av Manuel Guilherme Barbosa 375, T024-2484 1616.* There are a few cheap hotels in town and a number of mid-range options stretched along the main road and in the countryside on the outskirts.

Vassouras and around 🖂🌐🎭🔆🎬🌀 ›› *pp167-170. Colour map 4, C3.*

→ *Phone code: 024. Population: 32,000.*

It is hard to believe that the small town of Vassouras was once one of the most important cities of the Brazilian empire. During the coffee boom in the 19th century, it was surrounded by coffee farms whose owners became immensely rich. These coffee barons acquired noble titles and, as their power increased, they built enormous, opulent town houses in Vassouras. The majority of these buildings are still there, surrounding the beautiful main **Praça Barão de Campo Belo**. Emperor Pedro II visited the city several times.

In 1875 the railway station was opened in Vassouras, allowing the local farmers to send their produce directly to Rio de Janeiro. But the town went into decline when the coffee boom ended. For many years it had almost no economic activity, except for some cattle ranching and small-scale agriculture. Now it has a university and is being rediscovered by the tourist industry. It still retains its small-town calm, but the reminders of its golden past mix with the student nightlife in the bars along a street called, unofficially, 'The Broadway'.

Sights

The best way to explore Vassouras is on foot. Starting at the *rodoviária*, walk as far as the **Estação Ferroviária**, the former railway station. Recently restored, it is now the headquarters of the Universidade de Vassouras. Continue straight on to the **Praça Barão de Campo Belo**, where you will find the most important old houses and public buildings, all dating from the 19th century. Note the neoclassical influence. One of these old 'baronial' houses is now the **Casa da Cultura** ① *R Custódio Guimarães 65, on the left-hand side of the square*, a municipal cultural centre that has tourist information and temporary exhibitions of local art and folklore. Ask if you can go upstairs. On the second floor, at the top of some of the internal walls, look for where the paint has peeled and you can see the 19th-century method of house construction: a frame of interwoven wood and bamboo covered with clay.

At the top end of the main *praça* is the church of **Nossa Senhora da Conceição**, the most important in the city, completed in 1853 in neoclassical style. Behind the church is the small **Praça Sebastião Lacerda**, surrounded by huge fig trees. Allegedly there is one fig tree for each of the rich coffee barons who lived in Vassouras in the last century. Keep on walking until you come to the cemetery. A visit is recommended; most of the wealthiest men of Brazil's second empire are buried here. Rich mausolea decorated with Italian and Portuguese marble sculptures show the competition among the families. Two of the most important clans are represented: the Teixeira Leite family and the Correa e Castro family. On the grave of Monsenhor Rios, a Catholic priest who died in 1866, a strange purple flower blooms every year in November on the Day of the Dead. Its intense smell is reminiscent of rotting flesh. Scientists have studied it, but have reached no conclusion as to what it is. The flower vanishes after a few days and the small bush lives on until January or February. It is now protected by a small iron fence and a number of miracles are reported to have occurred there.

Back at Praça Barão de Campo Belo, on Rua Barão de Vassouras, is the **Palacete do Barão do Ribeirão**, the former residence of a coffee baron, later converted into the town's court. It is currently closed for restoration as it has been badly attacked by termites. Turn right and at the end of Rua Dr Fernandes Junior you will find the fascinating **Casa da Hera museum** ① *No 160, T024-2471 2342, Wed-Sun 1100-1700*, an old country house covered with ivy, which belonged in the 19th century to one of the richest men in the town, Joaquim Teixeira Leite. After his death the house was inherited by his daughter, Eufrásia Teixeira Leite, who lost interest in the coffee business. She went to Paris, living a life of parties and luxury for many years. After she died in 1930 the house was made into a museum, in accordance with her will. All the furniture, decoration and architecture is original, from the golden years of coffee. The wide variety of imported tapestries, pianos and porcelain contrasts with the very rough building materials: a fantastic portrait of life in the 1850s. On some Sundays, depending on the number of visitors, tea is served in a traditional way, to recreate the atmosphere of the old coffee *fazendas*.

Because Vassouras is a university centre, it has more variety than other towns of a similar size. The action is concentrated in Rua Expedicionário Oswaldo de Almeida Ramos, but you won't need to pronounce that: simply ask for the Broadway and everybody will direct you to the right place. Here there are enough bars and open-air restaurants to suit all tastes and budgets.

Another possibility is a guided visit to the food technology centre at the **Senai**, close to the main *praça*. Here students learn how to process fruit, vegetables, meat and also how to work in a brewery. Most of the hotels can arrange a weekend guided visit.

Excursions from Vassouras

As yet, Vassouras lacks a well-developed tourist infrastructure. There is a lot to see around the city, especially the old *fazendas*, but they are only just starting to open to the public. The majority of them are privately owned and can only be visited with a prior appointment. The bigger hotels can arrange guided tours with transport at weekends. During the week, the only option is to go by car, as some of the *fazendas* are a long way away, down dirt roads. The best *fazendas* in the vicinity are: **Santa Mônica**, **São Fernando**, **Paraíso** and **Oriente**. More information can be obtained from the **Casa da Cultura** or from the **Secretaria de Turismo** ① *Municipalidade, Praça Barão de Campo Belo, T024-2471 1367*.

Valença and Conservatória

Like Vassouras, **Valença** is a historical monument and its history follows much the same pattern, with wealth from the coffee trade followed by some small-scale industry and agriculture. There are a number of *fazendas* nearby and, in the town, a faculty of medicine. Information is available from the **Secretaria de Turismo** ① *T024-2442 0102*.

About 35 km from Valença is **Conservatória**, another town in the coffee zone. Although it did not become as wealthy as Vassouras or Valença, it still has some fine 19th-century houses and is much more peaceful. In Conservatória, local farm produce can be bought, as well as blankets, macramé (a knitwork technique using knots) and crochet work. A local custom is the serenade through the streets; serenaders meet at the **Museu da Seresta** ① *R Osvaldo Fonseca*, on Friday and Saturday. This region can also be reached via the Japeri turning on the BR-116, a beautiful mountain drive. The **Secretaria de Turismo** ① *T024-3438 1188*, is in the centre of town and can advise on stays in *fazendas*. There are a few moderate and cheap hotels in town.

⊚ Inland resorts and coffee towns listings

For Sleeping and Eating price codes and other relevant information, see pages 42-47.

⊜ Sleeping

Petrópolis *p160, map p161*
Good budget accommodation is hard to find, but bargaining is possible Mon-Fri.
LL Locanda della Mimosa, Alameda das Mimosas, Vale Florido, T024-2233 5405, www.locanda.com.br. A 6-room *pousada* in a terracotta Palladian villa in the mountains near town, overlooking a little pool. The owner is one of the finest chefs in Brazil, see page 169.
LL Solar do Império, Av Koeler 276, T024-2103 3000, www.solarimperio.com.br. A luxury boutique hotel with period furniture in a converted mansion opposite the Palácio Rio Negro. Excellent spa and restaurant.
L Pousada da Alcobaça, R Agostinho Goulão 298, Correas, T024-2221 1240, www.pousada

daalcobaca.com.br. In the **Roteiros de Charme** group (see page 43). Delightful, family-run large country house set in flower-filled gardens leading down to a river, with pool and sauna. Worth stopping by for tea on the terrace, or for dinner at the restaurant. Recommended.
A Othon Riverside Parque, R Hermogéneo Silva 522, Retiro, 5 mins from the centre, T0800-248011, T024-2231 0730, www.hoteis-riverside.com.br. Mock-colonial hotel with a nice outdoor pool set in attractive gardens with views of the surrounding countryside. The helpful owner can arrange tours.
B Casablanca Centre, R General Osório 28, T024-2242 2612, www.casablancahotel.com.br. Old 1960s block, reasonable rooms and restaurant. Somewhat faded.
B York, R do Imperador 78, near the *rodoviária*, T024-2243 2662, www.hotel york.com.br. Convenient package-tour hotel with faded 1980s rooms, decent breakfast.

C Casa Comércio, R Dr Porciúncula 56, opposite the *rodoviária*, T024-2242 3500. One of the cheapest options. Clean but simple with shared baths or en suites. Linked to a tour agency, www.rioserra.com.br/trekking, which offers trips in the surrounding mountains.

Camping
Associação Brasileira de Camping and YMCA, Araras district. Space can be reserved through Rio **YMCA**, T024-2231 9860.

Teresópolis *p162*
Many cheap hotels on R Delfim Moreira.
L Fazenda Rosa dos Ventos, Km 22 on the road to Nova Friburgo, T021-2742 8833, www.hotelrosadosventos.com.br. Part of the **Roteiros do Charme** chain. One of the best hotels in inland Rio with a range of chalets in 1 million sq m of private forest and with wonderful views. Excellent restaurant.
C Várzea Palace, R Sebastião Teixeira 41, T021-2742 0878. Simple hotel with very friendly staff. Highly recommended.
D-E Recanto do Lord Hostel, R Luiza Pereira Soares 109, Centro-Artistas, T021-2742 5586, www.teresopolishostel.com.br. Family-oriented hostel with rooms and dorms, kitchen, cable TV and barbecue area. Breakfast included. Tours, treks and climbing in the mountains can be organized. Book in advance for Jan and Feb. Camping is permitted beside the hostel.

Camping
Quinta de Barra, R Antônio Maria 100, Km 3 the road to Petrópolis, T021-2643 1050.

Serra dos Órgãos *p163, map p163*
Ibama has some hostels, US$5 full board, or US$3 first night, US$2 thereafter, a bit rough.
L Reserva Ecológica de Guapi Assu (REGUA), Cachoeiras de Macacu-RJ, T021-2745 3998, www.regua.co.uk. A British-run conservation NGO and ecotourism project focused on a large main house with several rooms, set in primary rainforest. Expert guided walks into the reserve, in one of the richest areas in the state for birds, mammals and orchids.

L Serra dos Tucanos, Caixa Postal 98125, Cachoeiras do Macacu, T021-2649 1557, www.serradostucanos.com.br. One of the best wildlife and birdwatching lodges in Brazil with excellent guiding, equipment and accommodation in a comfortable lodge set in the Atlantic coastal rainforest.

Camping
Two sites in the Sub-Sede part, one close to the museum, the other not far from the natural swimming pool at Poço da Ponte Velha; one site in the Sede part. The Sede has a restaurant and the Sub-Sede a *lanchonete*.

Nova Friburgo *p164*
AL Bucsky, 5 km on the road to Niterói, T021-2522 5052. Meals, tours and guided walks.
AL Pousada do Riacho, Estr Nova Friburgo Km 8, Cardinot, T021-2522 2823, www.pousada doriacho.com. Charming upmarket **Roteiros do Charme** hotel with extensive gardens and surrounded by gentle mountains.
A Fazenda São João, 11 km from **Garlipp** (same ownership) up a side road, T021-2542 1304. Riding, swimming, sauna, tennis, hummingbirds and orchids. The owner will meet guests in Nova Friburgo or even in Rio.
A Garlipp, Muri, 8 km south, Km 70 from Rio, T/F021-2542 1173. German-run chalets.
B Fabris, Av Alberto Browne 148, T021-2522 2852. Central, with plain en suite rooms with TVs hot showers. Large breakfast buffet.
C-D Maringá, R Monsenhor Miranda 110, T021-2522 2309. Standard but with a very good breakfast. Recommended.

Camping
Camping Clube do Brasil has sites on the Niterói Rd, at Caledônia (7 km out, T021-2522 0169) and Muri (10 km out, T021-2542 2275).
Fazenda Sanandu, 20 km out on the same road. Private campsite.

Vassouras *p165*
AL Santa Amália, Av Sebastião Manoel Furtado 526, T/F024-2471 1897, close to the *rodoviária*. In a very pleasant and quiet park, pool, sauna,

volleyball and football pitches, one of the best in town, negotiate rates during the week and low season (Mar-Jun, Aug-Nov).
B Gramado da Serra, R Aldo Cavalcanti 7, T/F024-2471 2314. Bar, restaurant, pool, sauna.
B Mara Palace, R Chanceler Dr Raul Fernandes 121, T024-2471 1993. In a house built in 1870, fully and tastefully preserved, swimming pool, bar, sauna, sports, nice atmosphere and good service, owner can arrange visits to *fazendas*.
C-D Pousada Bougainville, T024-2471 2451. Modest little guesthouse, breakfast included.
D Pousada Veredas, T024-2471 2728. Basic but with helpful staff and breakfast included.

🍴 Eating

Petrópolis *p160, map p161*
Bakeries and cheap eateries by the *rodoviária*.
🍴🍴🍴 **Locanda della Mimosa**, Alameda das Mimosas, Vale Florido, T024-2233 5405, www.locanda.com.br. One of the best in Brazil, with fusion cooking with a focus on game. Danio Braga was 4 times *Quatro Rodas* chef of the year. The 3000-bottle wine cellar includes heavyweights like 1990 Château Haut-Brion.
🍴 **Cantina Bom Giovanni**, R do Imperador 729, T024-2242 5588. A 1st-floor simple, canteen-style Italian restaurant. Justifiably popular for self-service lunch and dinner.
🍴 **Casa d'Ángelo**, R do Imperador 700, by Praça Dom Pedro II. A traditional, long-established teahouse, self-service food. Also a bar at night.
🍴 **Falconi**, R do Imperador 757, T024-2242 1252. Traditional restaurant with rustic elegance that has been serving Italian food since 1914. Pasta and pizza for US$3. Recommended.

Teresópolis *p162*
There is a good café in the ABC supermarket.
🍴🍴🍴 **Da Irene**, R Tte Luís Meireles 1800, T021-2742 2901. Very popular upmarket Russian restaurant. Reservations necessary.
🍴🍴 **Bar Gota d'Água**, Praça Baltasar da Silveira 16. A little bar, simple fish dishes and *feijoada*.
🍴🍴 **Taberna Alpina**, Duque de Caxias 131. Excellent German cuisine.

Nova Friburgo *p164*
Many restaurants offer European cuisine, reflecting the people who settled in the area. Also Brazilian food, pizzas and *confeitarias*.
🍴🍴🍴 **Chez Gigi**, Av Euterpe Friburguense 21, T024-2523 0107. Excellent Brazilian-French fusion cooking with dishes such as duck's breast in *jabuticaba*, pear and damson sauce.
🍴🍴 **Auberge Suisse**, R 10 de Outubro, T024-2541 1270. Fondue, *roschti* and other Swiss options alongside very good steak.

Vassouras *p165*
The best quality and value restaurants are in the centre, on The Broadway.

🎉 Festivals and events

Petrópolis *p160, map p161*
16 Mar Foundation day.
Jun Bohemia Beer Festival. Brazil's earliest beer dates from 1853 and was originally brewed in the city. Although production has been moved to Rio, the festival is still celebrated here.
29 Jun São Pedro de Alcântara, the patron saint of Petrópolis.

Teresópolis *p162*
May Festa das Colônias.
13 Jun Santo Antônio, the town's patron saint.
29 Jun São Pedro, celebrated with fireworks.
7 Jul Foundation day.
15 Oct Santa Terezinha.

Nova Friburgo *p164*
May Maifest festival, celebrated all month.
16 May Founding of Nova Friburgo.
24 Jun São João Batista, patron saint's day.

Vassouras *p165*
Feb/Mar Carnaval is one of the best in the region, with its own samba schools and balls.
Jun Santo Antônio, São Pedro and São João are celebrated with traditional parties.
8 Dec The feast of Nossa Senhora da Conceição, the city's patron saint, is celebrated with a Mass and procession.

O Shopping

Petrópolis *p160, map p161*
R Teresa, southeast of the centre, is where the textile industry exhibits its wares. In common with Itaipava, it draws buyers from all over the country and is a good place to find high-quality knitwear and bargain clothes. Closed Mon morning and Sun.

▲ Activities and tours

Petrópolis *p160, map p161*
Rio Serra, T024-2235 7607, www.rioserra. com.br/trekking. Horse riding, trekking, whitewater rafting and a range of trips into the scenic mountain area, multilingual guides.
Roz Brazil, T024-9257 0236, www.roz brazil.com. Some of the best drive and light walk tours around Petrópolis, Teresópolis and the Serra dos Órgãos with British Brazilian Rosa Thompson, who has been living in the area for decades. Pick-ups from Rio.
Verticalia, T024-9387 2572, www.alaya.com.br. Tree-based adventures with zip lines and canopy obstacle courses (adults/children over 5).

Serra dos Órgãos *p163, map p163*
Tours are available through the tourist office or the IYHA Recanto do Lord in Teresópolis. See also **Roz Brazil**, above.
Focus Tours (see page 65), www.focus tours.com. Birdwatching trips.
Lazer Tours, T024-2742 7616. Tours of the park are offered by Francisco (find him at the grocery shop on R Sloper 1). Recommended.

⊙ Transport

Petrópolis *p160, map p161*
Bus Buses run to **Rio de Janeiro** every 15 mins throughout the day (US$8), Sun every hour, 1½ hrs. Sit on the right-hand side for best views. Ordinary buses arrive in Rio at the *rodoviária*; a/c buses run hourly and arrive at Av Nilo Peçanha, US$4. Book your return journey as

soon as you arrive in Petrópolis. Bus to **Niterói**, US$4.50; to **Cabo Frio**, US$10. To **Teresópolis**, 8 a day, US$3. To **São Paulo** daily at 2330.

Teresópolis *p162*
Bus The *rodoviária* is at R 1 de Maio 100. Buses to **Rio de Janeiro** Novo Rio *rodoviária* every 30 mins. Book your return journey as soon as you arrive in Teresópolis. Fare US$3.60. From Teresópolis to **Petrópolis**, 8 a day, US$3.

Nova Friburgo *p164*
Bus Bus station, Ponte da Suadade, T024-2522 0400. To **Rio**, every hr, 2 hrs, US$4.

Vassouras *p165*
Bus Buses to **Rio**'s Novo Rio *rodoviária* with Normandy, every 1½ hrs 0615-2030, 2 hrs, US$6.50. More during summer and holidays.

⊙ Directory

Petrópolis *p160, map p161*
Banks Banco do Brasil, R Paulo Barbosa 81; Banco 24 Horas ATM is by the Varig office at R Mcal Deodoro 98. Travel agents with *câmbios*; BKR, R Gen Osório 12; **Goldman**, R Barão de Amazonas 46 (between Praça da Liberdade and the university); Vert Tur, R 16 de Março 244.
Internet Compuland, R do Imperador opposite Praça Dr Sá Earo, US$1.50 per hr. **Post office** R do Imperador 350 in the Palácio dos Correios. **Telephone** R Mcal Deodoro, just above Praça Dr Nelson de Sá Earp, no fax.

Teresópolis *p162*
Banks Cash/TCs at Teretur, Trav Portugal 46.
Internet Cott@ge Cybercafe, R Alfredo Rebello Filho 996, 2nd floor, US$3 per hr.

Nova Friburgo *p164*
Banks Bradesco, Praça Demerval Barbosa Moreira.

Vassouras *p165*
Banks Banco do Brasil, R Caetano Furquim, in the centre, has an ATM but no *câmbio*.

West of Rio de Janeiro

Towns to the west of Rio are mostly spread along the ugly Rio–São Paulo motorway known as the Via Dutra. None are appealing. But the mountains that watch over them preserve important tracts of Atlantic coast rainforest, particularly around Itatiaia. This is one of the best places close to Rio for seeing wild animals and virgin rainforest and is the country's oldest protected area. The little mock-Alpine resort of Visconde de Mauá sits in the same mountain chain a little further towards São Paulo, although the forest here is less well preserved. » For listings, see pages 173-174.

Serra da Mantiqueira ⬤🅟🅕🅖 » *pp173-174.*

This lush mountain range separates Rio de Janeiro and from Minas Gerais state and is one of few remaining areas with extensive *Mata Atlântica* (Atlantic coastal rainforest) in southeastern Brazil. It is dotted with pretty little towns and national and state parks.

Penedo → *Colour map 4, C3. Phone code: 024. Population: 8000. Altitude: 600 m.*
The small town of Penedo, 175 km from Rio, attracted Finnish settlers in the 1930s who brought the first saunas to Brazil. There is a Finnish museum, a cultural centre and Finnish dancing on Saturdays. This popular weekend resort also provides horse riding and swimming in the Portinho River. There are five buses a day from Resende. There is a **tourist office** ⓘ *Av Casa das Pedras, T024-3351 1876*, and plenty of mid-range and cheap hotels in town.

Visconde de Mauá → *Colour map 4, C3. Phone code: 024. Altitude: 1200 m.*
About 33 km beyond Penedo (part of the road is unpaved) is the charming small village of Visconde de Mauá in the **Serra da Mantiqueira**. In the early 20th century Swiss and German immigrants settled in the town, which is popular with tourists today. The surrounding scenery is lovely, with green valleys, clear rivers, wild flowers and opportunities for good walks and outdoor activities. Many places offer acupuncture, shiatsu massage and macrobiotic food and there is a hippy feel to the crafts on sale. Horses can be hired in Visconde de Mauá from Berto (almost opposite Vendinha da Serra), or Pedro (Lote 10) and many places in Maringá arrange riding. The **Rio Preto** is good for canoeing and there is an annual national event (dates change; check in advance). The **tourist office** ⓘ *T024-3387 1283*, is closed out of season.

Three other small hill towns are nearby: **Mirantão**, at 1700 m, with semi-tropical vegetation; **Maringá**, just across the state border in Minas Gerais and a delightful two-hour walk; and **Maromba**. On the way to Maromba is the **Mirante do Posto da Montanha**, a lookout with a view of the Rio Preto, which runs through the region and is the border between Rio de Janeiro and Minas Gerais states. Also in Minas Gerais, 6 km upriver from Maringá but on a different road, are the **Santa Clara falls** (turn off before Maromba). Between Visconde de Mauá and Maringá is a natural pool in the river (turn left before crossing the bridge). After Maromba follow the signs to **Cachoeira e Escorrega**, a small waterfall and waterslide with a cold natural swimming pool, a 2-km walk. A turning off this road leads to another waterfall, the **Cachoeira Véu da Noiva**.

Although served by buses from both São Paulo and Rio, *pousadas* are spread out and the area is best visited with a car. For **tourist information**, the website www.guia maua.com.br lists many of the hotels and restaurants and gives a good overview of the area (in Portuguese but with pictures).

Parque Nacional de Itatiaia ⊕🚻▲⊙ ➤ *pp173-174. Colour map 4, C3.*

Deep valleys shrouded in pristine rainforest hiding rocky clear-water rivers and icy waterfalls. Little winding trails through a whole swathe of different ecosystems, watched over by some of world's rarest birds and mammals. Hotels and guesthouses to suit all budgets from which to explore them. And all within easy reach of Rio or São Paulo.

Itatiaia is a must for those who wish to see Brazilian forest and animals and have a restricted itinerary or limited time. This 30,000-ha mountainous park is Brazil's oldest. It was founded in 1937 to protect Atlantic coast rainforest in the Serra de Mantiqueira mountains, and important species still find a haven here, including jaguars and pumas, brown capuchin and black-faced titi monkeys. This is good hiking country with walks through subtropical and temperate forests, grasslands and *paramo* to a few peaks just under 3000 m. The best trails head for Pedra de Taruga, Pedra de Maçã and the Poranga and Véu de Noiva waterfalls. The Pico das Agulhas Negras and Serra das Prateleiras (up to 2540 m) offer good rock climbing. There is a **Museu de História Natural** ① *Tue-Sun 1000-1600*, near the park headquarters with a depressing display of stuffed animals from the 1940s.

Ins and outs

Getting there and around Itatiaia lies just off the main São Paulo–Rio highway, the Dutra. A bus marked '504 Circular' runs from Itatiaia town run four times a day (variable hours) to the park, calling at the hotels in town and stopping at **Hotel Simon** (see Sleeping, page 173). The bus can also be caught at Resende, at the crossroads before Itatiaia. Through tickets to São Paulo or are sold at a booth in the large bar in the middle of Itatiaia main street.

The best way to see the park is to hire a car. There is only one way into the park from Itatiaia town and one main road within it – which forks off to the various hotels, all of which are signposted.

Tourist information Entry per day is US$10 per car. Basic accommodation in cabins and dormitories is available in the village strung along the road leading to the park. There are some delightful options inside the park but they are more expensive. Avoid weekends and Brazilian holidays if wildlife watching is a priority. Information and maps can be obtained at the **Administração do Parque Nacional de Itatiaia (park office)** ① *Estrada Parque Km 8.5, www.ibama.gov.br/parna_itatiaia*. Information can also be obtained from **Ibama** ① *T024-33521461 for the local headquarters, or T021-3224 6463 for the Rio de Janeiro state department*. The **Administração do Parque Nacional de Itatiaia** operates a refuge in the park, which acts as a starting point for climbs and treks. Information on trekking can be obtained from **Clube Excursionista Brasileira** ① *Av Almirante Barroso 2, 8th floor, Rio de Janeiro, T021-2220 3695*.

Flora and fauna

The park is particularly good for birds. It has a list of more than 350 species with scores of spectacular tanagers, hummingbirds (including the ultra-rare Brazilian ruby, with emerald wings and a dazzling red chest), cotingas (included the black and gold cotinga, which as far as we are aware has never been photographed) and manakins. Guans squawk and flap right next to the park roads.

The vegetation is stratified by altitude so that the plateau at 800-1100 m is covered by forest, ferns and flowering plants (such as orchids, bromeliads, begonias), giving way on the higher escarpments to pines and bushes. Higher still, over 1900 m, the distinctive rocky landscape has low bushes and grasses, isolated trees and unique plants adapted to high winds and strong sun. There is also a great variety of lichens.

Engenheiro Passos → *Phone code: 024. Population: 3500.*
Further along the Dutra highway (186 km from Rio) is the small town of Engenheiro Passos, from which a road (BR-354) leads to São Lourenço and Caxambu in Minas Gerais (see page 303). By turning off this road at the Registro Pass (1670 m) on the Rio-Minas border, you can reach the **Pico das Agulhas Negras**. The mountain can be climbed from this side from the **Abrigo Rebouças** refuge at 2350 m, which is manned all year round; US$2.50 per night, take your own food.

◉ West of Rio de Janeiro listings

For Sleeping and Eating price codes and other relevant information, see pages 42-47.

● Sleeping

Visconde de Mauá *p171*
There are many *fazendas, pousadas* and chalets in the vicinity, but very little budget accommodation.
LL Fronteira, Estr Visconde de Mauá-Campo Lindo, Km 4, T024-3387 1219. A *Roteiros de Charme* hotel (see page 43). Huge cabins with tiny private gardens set in a forested garden with wonderful views. Sauna, pool and a good restaurant and bar.
C-D Encanto, on the road to Maringa, Km 7, T024-3387 1155, www.guiamaua.com.br/encanto. 7 chalets in woodland and a sauna. Popular with 20- and 30-somethings.
C-D Fazenda Boa Vista, Vale das Flores, on the road to Maringa, Km 15, T024-9998 3614, www.fazendaboavista.com.br. Great views, a pool and a range of organized activities. The simple chalets sit in a private rainforest reserve. Minimum 2-day stay.
C-D Sitio Portal da Travessia, on the road to Maringa, Km 7, T024-3387 1154, www.portaldatravessia.com.br. 6 chalets next to a mountain stream and with a spring-water natural pool. The range of activities include hikes and horse riding.

Camping
Barragen's, Maringá, T024-3387 1354. One of several campsites in the area.

Parque Nacional de Itatiaia *p172*
A Hotel Donati, T024-3352 1110, www.hoteldonati.com.br. One of the most delightful hotels in the country – mock-Swiss chalets and rooms, set in tropical gardens visited by animals every night and early morning. A series of trails leads off from the main building and the hotel can organize professional birding guides. Decent restaurant and 2 pools. Highly recommended.
A Hotel Simon, Km 13 on the road in the park, T024-3352 1122, www.hotelsimon.com.br. A 1970s concrete block with *Hawaii Five 0* decor at the top of the park by the trailhead for the higher walks to Agulhas Negras and Três Picos. Great views from the fading rooms.
B Pousada do Elefante, Km 12, 15 mins' walk back downhill from **Hotel Simon**. Good food, swimming pool, lovely views, may allow camping.
B-C Hotel Cabanas de Itatiaia, T024-3352 1252. Magical views from these comfortable but rather ridiculous Swiss chalets on the hillside. Pool and good restaurant too.
C-D Cabanas da Itatiaia, T024-33521152, www.hotelcabanasitatiaia.com.br. Price per person in these simple chalets in secondary forest overlooking a stream in the lower reaches of the park. The sister hotel, opposite (**Aldeia dos Passaros**), has a pool. Both share facilities and are very friendly and helpful. Great breakfasts, good off-season rates and a riverside sauna.

D Hotel Alsene, at 2100 m, 2 km from the side entrance to the park, take a bus to São Lourenço and Caxambu, get off at Registro, walk or hitch from there (12 km). Very popular with climbing and trekking clubs, dormitories or camping, chalets available, hot showers, fireplace, evening meal after everyone returns, drinks but no snacks.
E Ipê Amarelo, R João Maurício Macedo Costa 352, Campo Alegre, T/F024-3352 1232. **IYHA** youth hostel.

Camping
Camping Clube do Brasil site is entered at Km 148 on the Via Dutra.

Engenheiro Passos *p173*
Around Engenheiro Passos there are many *fazenda* hotels.
L Fazenda Villa Forte, 1 km from town, T/F024-3357 1122. With meals, bar, sauna, massage, gym and other sports facilities.
A Fazenda Palmital, Km 11, BR-354 towards Caxambu, T/F024-3357 1108. Chalets on the edge of the national park, arranged around a lake in a garden and with a waterfall nearby. Facilities include a pool, sauna, horse riding and a play area for kids.

Eating

Visconde de Mauá *p171*
Everywhere in town shuts at about 2200.
Gosto com Gosto, R Wenceslau Brás, Mineiro. Self-service Minas Gerais dishes that are heavy on meat and flavour.
Bar do Jorge. Café.

Parque Nacional de Itatiaia *p172*
The hotels in the park all have restaurants. **Hotel Donati** and **Cabanas de Itatiaia**, the latter with a view, have the best (see Sleeping, above).

Via Park, 1441 Estr Parque, Itatiaia town, 4 km before the park entrance, T024-9268 7934. Delicious trout with Brazilian accompaniments, in super-generous portions.

Bars and clubs

Visconde de Mauá *p171*
Adega Bar, open till 2400, live music and dancing (Sat only).
Forró da Marieta for *forró* dancing.

Activities and tours

Parque Nacional de Itatiaia *p172*
Wildlife guides
Ralph Salgueiro, T024-3351 1823, www.ecoralph.com; and **Edson Endrigo**, T024-3742 8374, www.avesfoto.com.br, offer birdwatching trips in Itatiaia and throughout Brazil, English spoken.

Transport

Visconde de Mauá *p171*
Bus From Visconde de Mauá to **Resende**, 2 hrs, at 0830 and 0900, returning from Resende at 1500 and 1630, US$5. Direct bus to/from **Rio de Janeiro**, Cidade de Aço, 2 daily, 3½ hrs, US$7.

Parque Nacional de Itatiaia *p172*
Bus Bus '504 Circular' to/from **Itatiaia town** 4 times daily, picks up from **Hotel Simon** in the park and stops at **Resende** (at the crossroads before Itatiaia) and hotels in town.
Itatiaia town has bus connections with **São Paulo** and **Rio de Janeiro** and it's possible to buy through tickets from the middle of the main street.

Costa Verde

The Rio de Janeiro–Santos section of the BR-101 is one of the world's most beautiful highways, hugging the forested and hilly Costa Verde southwest of Rio. The Serra do Mar mountains plunge down to the sea in a series of spurs that disappear into the Atlantic to reappear as a cluster of islands offshore. The most beautiful of these is Ilha Grande: an 80,000-ha mountain ridge covered in rainforest and fringed with wonderful beaches. Beyond Ilha Grande, further down the coast towards São Paulo, is one of Brazil's prettiest colonial towns, Paraty, which sits surrounded by long white beaches in front of a glorious bay of islands. Seen from the harbour in the morning light, this is one of Brazil's most photographed sights. ▶▶ *For listings, see pages 182-188.*

Ins and outs

The BR-101 is paved all the way to Santos (see page 226), which has good links with São Paulo. Buses from Rio run to Angra dos Reis, Paraty, Ubatuba, Caraguatatuba and São Sebastião, where it may be necessary to change for Santos or São Paulo. Hotels and *pousadas* have sprung up all along the road, as have expensive housing developments, though these have not spoiled the views. The drive from Rio to Paraty should take four hours, but it would be better to break the journey and enjoy some of the attractions. The coast road has lots of twists and turns so, if prone to motion sickness, get a seat at the front of the bus to make the most of the views.

Mangaratiba → *Phone code: 021. Population: 25,000.*

About 22 km down the coast, this fishing village is halfway between Rio and Angra dos Reis. It stands on a little bay within the Baía de Sepetiba and in the 18th century was a port for the export first of gold, later coffee, and for the import of slaves. During the coffee era, it was the terminus for the Estrada São João Marcos highway from the Rio Paraíba do Sul. Mangaratiba's beaches are muddy, but the surroundings are pleasant and better beaches can be found outside town. These include **Ibicuí** (2 km) and **Brava** (between Ibicuí and Saí) to the east, at the head of the bay **Saco**, **Guiti** and **Cação**, and further west **São Brás**. There are numerous hotels in town. Boats run to Ilha Grande several times a day. Times vary according to the season but the last usually departs around 1400. ▶▶ *See Ins and outs, page 177.*

Angra dos Reis and around ⬤✴▲⬤⬤ ▶▶ *pp182-188. Colour map 4, C3.*

→ *Phone code: 024. Population: 120,000.*

The vast bay of Angra dos Reis is studded with more lush islands than there are days in the year. Some are the private playgrounds of Carioca playboys. Others are media islands, owned by magazines devoted to the cult of the Brazilian celebrity, and permanently twinkling with camera flashes. A few are thronged with bikinis and board shorts in high season and pulsate to *forró* and samba beats. And many are as wild and unspoilt as they were when the Portuguese arrived 500 years ago. Yachts and speedboats flit across the bay, ferrying their bronzed and smiling cargo between the islands and beaches. In between, they dock at floating bars and restaurants for an icy *caipirinha* or catch of the day, and at night to dance or be lulled by the gentle sound of bossa nova.

Angra town itself is scruffy and down at heel – little more than a jumping-off point to the private islands and to Ilha Grande – but it's an increasingly popular destination for international travellers. This is a result of the migration of the wealthy out of Rio and their acquisition of beaches and property from the local fishermen, whose families now live in the *favelas* that encrust the surrounding hills (see box, page 177).

Angra was once a pretty colonial town like Paraty further along the coast, and several buildings remain from its heyday. Of particular note are the church and convent of **Nossa Senhora do Carmo**, built in 1593 on Praça General Osório, the **Igreja Matriz de Nossa Senhora da Conceição** (1626) in the centre of town and the church and convent of **São Bernardino de Sena** (1758-1763) on the Morro do Santo Antônio. On the Largo da Lapa is the church of **Nossa Senhora da Lapa da Boa Morte** (1752) and a **Museum of Sacred Art** ① *Thu-Sun 1000-1200, 1400-1800.*

On the Península de Angra, west of the town, is the **Praia do Bonfim**, a popular beach; offshore is the island of the same name, on which the **hermitage of Senhor do Bonfim** (1780) is located. Some 15 km east are the ruins of the **Jacuecanga seminary** (1797).

Angra is connected to Rio and Paraty by regular buses, to Ilha Grande by ferry and fishing boat, and to Ilha do Gipóia by fishing boat. The **tourist office** ① *Av Julio Maria, T024-3365 2041, www.angra-dos-reis.com, www.angra.rj.gov.br,* is just behind the Cais de Santa Luiza quay. The websites have more information than the office.

Ilha Grande 😊🕐▲😊🕐 *pp182-188. Colour map 4, C3.*

→ *Phone code: 021.*

Ilha Grande is a mountain ridge covered in tropical forest protruding from the emerald sea and fringed by some of the world's most beautiful beaches. There are no cars and no roads, just trails through the forest, so the island is still relatively undeveloped. With luck it will remain so, as much of Ilha Grande forms part of a state park and biological reserve, and cannot even be visited.

That the island has so much forest is largely a fluke of history. The island was a notorious pirate lair in the 16th and 17th centuries and then a landing port for slaves. By the 20th century it was the site of an infamous prison for the country's most notorious criminals, including the writer Graciliano Ramos (see Literature, page 794); whose

Abraão

Sleeping
Ancoradouro 1
Aqua Rio Hostel 2
Che Lagarto Ilha Grande Hostel 6
Colibri 3

Emilia Ecocamping 4
Estalagem Costa Verde 10
Farol dos Borbas 5
IYHA Albergue Holandes 7
Porto Girassol 8
Pousada Cachoeira 9

Eating
Corsário Negro 1
Lua e Mar 2

200 metres
200 yards

The caiçaras

Brazilians of mixed Indian, African and Portuguese race living on the coast and leading traditional lives fishing and hunting are known as *caiçaras*. Until the 1970s almost all the beaches and islands between Rio de Janeiro and Santos were home to caiçara communities. But then the Rio to Santos main highway was constructed and floods of visitors began to pour in. With them came developments – for luxury private houses, hotels and condominiums like Laranjeiras – which is home to members of Brazil's wealthy and allegedly highly corrupt elite. *Caiçara* communities were bought off for pittance or forced from their land with threats of violence or even death. And an entire way of life and knowledge of the Atlantic coast forest, strongly rooted in indigenous traditions is in danger of being entirely lost. All the *favelas* in Angra dos Reis bear the name of a different beach on Ilha Grande or the beaches and islands around the bay. Nowadays there are *caiçara* communities only on a few isolated stretches between Rio and Santos – like the Ponta da Joatinga peninsula south of Paraty and Aventureiros beach in Ilha Grande. Many think that carefully managed, sensitive ecotourism will help protect them and spread the story of their plight, which is little known even within Brazil.

Memórias do Cárcere relate his experiences. The prison closed in 1994 and is now overgrown. Since then Ilha Grande has been a well-kept Brazilian secret, and is gradually becoming part of the international backpacker circuit.

Ins and outs

Fishing boats and ferries (**Barcas SA**, T021-2533 7524), leave from Angra dos Reis and Mangaratiba taking two hours or so to reach Vila do Abraão, the island's only real village. From Angra they only leave in the morning and early afternoon and must be chartered (US$60-100 per boat; it is usually possible to get a group together in high season). The weather is best from March to June and the island is over-run during the Christmas, New Year and Carnaval periods. There is a helpful **tourist office** on the jetty at Abraão. Further information and pictures can be found at www.ilhagrande.com. Be wary of undercover police searching for backpackers smoking cannabis on Ilha Grande's beaches.

Beaches and walks

The beach at **Abraão** may look beautiful to new arrivals but those further afield are far more spectacular. The two most famous are: **Lopes Mendes**, a long stretch of sand on the eastern (ocean side) backed by flatlands and patchy forest; and **Aventureiro**, fringed by coconut palms and tropical forest, its powder-fine sand pocked with boulders and washed by a transparent aquamarine sea. Lopes Mendes is two hours' walk from Abraão. Aventureiro is over six hours, but it can be reached by boat. A few fishermen's huts and *barracas* provide food and accommodation here but there is no camping. Good beaches closer to Abraão include the half-moon bay at **Abraãoozinho** (15 minutes' walk) and **Grande das Palmas**, which has a delightful tiny whitewashed chapel (one hour 20 minutes' walk). Both lie east of the town past **Hotel Sagu**. There are boat trips to **Lagoa Azul**, with crystal-clear water and reasonable snorkelling, **Freguesia de Santana** and **Saco do Céu**.

There are a couple of good treks over the mountains to **Dois Rios**, where the old jail was situated. There is still a settlement of former prison guards here who have nowhere to go. The walk is about 13 km each way, takes about three hours and affords beautiful scenery and superb views. Another three-hour hike is to **Pico do Papagaio** (980 m) through forest; it's a steep climb for which a guide is essential, however, the view from the top is breathtaking. **Pico da Pedra d'Água** (1031 m) can also be climbed.

Paraty ⊜🌴🍴🏛️❄️🌐⚓🔺⛵🔆 ➤➤ pp182-188. Colour map 4, C2.

→ Phone code: 024. Population: 30,000.

Paraty is one of Brazil's prettiest colonial towns and one of Rio de Janeiro state's most popular tourist destinations. It is at its most captivating at dawn, when all but the dogs and chickens are sleeping. As the sun peeps over the horizon the little rectilinear streets are infused with a rich golden light, which warms the whitewash and brilliant blue-and-yellow window frames of the colonial town houses and the façades of the Manueline churches. Brightly coloured fishing boats bob up and down in the water in the foreground and behind the town the deep green of the rainforest-covered mountains of the Serra da Bocaina sit shrouded in their self-generated wispy cloud. The town was founded in the 17th century as a gold port and most of its historic buildings date from this period.

At the weekend Paraty buzzes with tourists who browse in the little boutiques and art galleries or buy souvenirs from the indigenous Guarani who proffer their wares on the cobbles. At night they fill the numerous little bars and restaurants, many of which, like the *pousadas*, are owned by the bevy of expat Europeans who have found their haven in Paraty and who are determined to preserve its charm. During the week, especially off season, the town is quiet and intimate, its atmosphere as yet unspoilt by the increasing numbers of independent travellers.

The town's environs are as beautiful as Paraty itself. Just a few kilometres away lie the forests of the **Ponta do Juatinga Peninsula**, fringed by wonderful beaches, washed by little waterfalls and still home to communities of Caiçara fishermen who live much as they have done for centuries. Islands pepper the bay, some of them home to ultra-rare animals such as the tiny golden lion tamarin monkey, which is found nowhere else. The best way to visit these destinations is on a boat trip with one of the town's fishermen from the quay.

Ins and outs

The *rodoviária* is at the corner of Rua Jango Padua and Rua da Floresta. There are direct bus connections with Rio and São Paulo several times daily, and with a number of destinations along the coast. Taxis charge a set rate of US$4 from the bus station to the historic centre, which is pedestrianized and easily negotiable on foot. Staff at the **Centro de Informações Turísticas** ⓘ *Av Roberto Silveira, near the entrance to the historic centre, T024-3371 1266,* are friendly and helpful and some speak English. There is a good town map in the *Welcome to Paraty* brochure, www.eco-paraty.com. More information is available at www.paraty.com.br. The wettest months are January, February, June and July. In spring, the streets in the colonial centre may flood, but the houses remain above the waterline. ➤➤ *See Transport, page 188.*

Sights

In keeping with all Brazilian colonial towns, Paraty's churches were built according to social status and race. There are four churches in the town, one for the 'freed coloured men', one for the blacks and two for the whites. **Santa Rita** (1722), built by the 'freed coloured men' in elegant Brazilian baroque, faces the bay and the port. It is probably the most famous picture postcard image of Paraty and houses a small **Museum of Sacred Art** ① *Wed-Sun 0900-1200, 1300-1800, US$1.* **Nossa Senhora do Rosário e São Benedito** ① *R do Comércio, Tue 0900-1200,* (1725, rebuilt 1757) built by black slaves, is small and simple; the slaves were unable to raise the funds to construct an elaborate building. **Nossa Senhora dos Remédios** ① *Mon, Wed, Fri, Sat 0900-1200, Sun 0900-1500,* is the town's parish church, the biggest in Paraty. It was started in 1787 but construction continued until 1873. The church was never completely finished as it was built on unstable ground; the architects decided not to add weight to the structure by putting up the towers. The façade is leaning to the left, which is clear from the three doors (only the one on the right has a step). Built with donations from the whites, it is rumoured that Dona Geralda Maria da Silva contributed gold from a pirate's hoard found buried on the beach. **Capela de Nossa Senhora das Dores** ① *Thu 0900-1200* (1800), is a chapel facing the sea. It was used mainly by wealthy 19th-century whites.

There is a great deal of distinguished Portuguese colonial architecture in delightful settings. **Rua do Comércio** is the main street in the historic centre. It was here that the

Paraty

100 metres
100 yards

Sleeping 🛏
Camping Beira-Rio **14**
Camping Clube
  do Brasil **15**
Casa do Rio **1**

Coxixo **2**
Morro do Forte **13**
Pousada Arte
  Colonial **10**
Pousada Capitão **5**
Pousada da Careca **11**
Pousada do Corsário **6**
Pousada do Ouro **7**
Pousada do Sandi **8**

Pousada Mercado
  do Pouso **9**
Pousada Pardieiro **4**
Solar dos Gerânios **12**

Eating 🍴
Bartolomeu **1**
Café Paraty **2**
do Hiltinho **4**

Dona Ondina **11**
Merlin O Mago **13**
Punto di Vino **5**
Sabor da Terra **6**
Thai Brasil **7**

Bars & clubs 🍸
Coupé **8**
Dinho **9**

prominent traders lived, the two-storey houses having the commercial establishments on the ground floor and the residences above. Today the houses are occupied by restaurants, *pousadas* and tourist shops.

The **Casa da Cadeia**, close to Santa Rita Church, is the former jail, complete with iron grilles in the windows and doors. It is now a public library and art gallery.

On the northern headland is a small fort, **Forte do Defensor Perpétuo**, built in 1822, whose cannon and thick ruined walls can be seen. From the fort there are good views of the sea and the roofs of the town. It's about 15 minutes' walk from the centre. To get there, cross the Rio Perequê Açu by the bridge at the end of the Rua do Comércio; climb the small hill, which has some attractive *pousadas* and a cemetery, and follow the signs. Also here is the **Museum of Arts and Popular Traditions** ① *Wed-Sun*, in a colonial-style building. It contains carved wooden canoes, musical instruments, fishing gear and other items from local communities. On the headland is the gunpowder store and enormous hemispherical iron pans that were used for extracting whale oil, which was used for lamps and to mix with sand and cement for building.

Boat trips and beaches

The most popular trip, and highly recommended, is a five-hour **schooner tour** around the bay for swimming (US$15, lunch is an optional extra). Smaller boats are available for US$10 an hour or US$20 for three hours. Many beautiful beaches are visited.

Praia do Pontal is the town beach, five minutes' walk from the historic centre: cross the bridge and turn right along the river. The water and sand are not very clean but the handful of *barracas* under the trees are a nice place to hang out. **Praia do Jabaquara** is about 20 minutes away on foot: cross the bridge and continue straight up the hill. There are a few *barracas* here and the sand is cleaner, but the water tends to be muddy.

There are other beaches further from town, many of which make worthwhile excursions. Scruffy **Boa Vista** is just south of town and beyond this (reachable only by boat) are, in order, the long, broad and clean stretches of **Praia da Conçeicao**, **Praia Vermelha** and **Praia da Lula**, all of which have simple restaurants and are backed by forest and washed by gentle waves. The **Saco da Velha**, further south still, is small and intimate, protected by an island and surrounded by rainforested slopes.

The small town of **Paraty Mirím**, is 17 km away and has a vast sweeping beach with a Manueline church built on the sand and some ruined colonial buildings. It is reached by boat or by four buses a day (three on Sunday) and has simple restaurants and places to camp. Fishing boats leave from here for other islands and beaches including the **Praia do Pouso da Cajaíba**, which has lodgings of the same name, and the spectacular sweep at **Martim do Sá**. The **Saco do Mamanguá** is a long sleeve of water that separates the Ponta da Juatinga and Paraty Mirím, which has good snorkelling.

Caminho do Ouro (Gold Trail) → *www.caminhodoouro.com.br.*

This partly cobbled trail through the mountains was built by slaves in the 18th century to bring gold down from Ouro Preto before transporting it to Portugal. Recently restored, it can be visited, along with the ruins of a toll house, on foot or horseback as a day trip. Tours leave at 1000 from the **Teatro Espaço** ① *R Dona Geralda 327, T024-3371 1575*.

There are several *cachoeiras* (waterfalls) in the area, such as the **Cachoeira da Penha**, near the church of the same name. It is 10 km from town on the road to Cunha; take a local bus from the *rodoviária*, US$1, there are good mountain views on the way. The tourist office and travel agencies have details on the waterfalls and hikes.

A recommended excursion is to **Fazenda Murycana** ① *T024-3371 3930 for tours and information*, an old sugar estate and 17th-century *cachaça* distillery with original house and waterwheel. You can taste and buy the different types of *cachaça*; some are aged in oak barrels for 12 years. Try the *cachaça com cravo e canela* (with clove and cinnamon). There is an excellent restaurant and horse riding is available but English is not spoken by the employees. Mosquitoes can be a problem at the *fazenda*, take repellent and don't wear shorts. To get there, take a 'Penha/Ponte Branca' bus from the *rodoviária*, four a day; alight where it crosses a small white bridge and then walk 10 minutes along a signed, unpaved road. There is a good chance of hitching a lift back to Paraty.

Trindade ●● ↠ *pp182-188. Colour map 4, C2.*

Ramshackle little Trindade (pronounced *Tringdajee*) may not be as beautiful in its own right as Paraty but its setting, sandwiched between rainforested slopes and emerald sea, is equally spectacular. And, unlike Paraty, it has a long, broad beach. The town has long been a favourite hang-out for young middle-class surf hippies from São Paulo and Rio, who come here in droves during the holiday period. It is now also finding its place on the international backpacker circuit and it's easy to see why. The beach is spectacular, the *pousadas* and restaurants cheap and cheerful, and there are a number of campsites. Sadly there is no sewage treatment and when the town is full, foul black water flows onto the sand. There are plenty of unprepossessing restaurants along the town's main drag, **Avenida Principal**. All serve the usual 'beans and rice and chips' combinations. Avoid coming here during Christmas, New Year, Carnaval and Easter.

Ins and outs Trindade is 30 km south of Paraty. It is reached by a steep, winding 7-km road branching off the Rio–Santos road (BR-101). Buses that run between Paraty and Ubatuba all pass the turning to Trindade and will drop you or pick you up here. Ask for 'Patrimonio' or 'Estrada para Trindade'. In high season there are vans from here to Trindade (US$2). In low season you'll have to hitch or walk; cars pass regularly. Be wary of carrying any drugs – the police at the turn-off post are very vigilant and searches are frequent. Tourist information is available at the booth at the entrance to town (no English spoken) or through the Paraty website, www.paraty.com.br and tourist office. Trindade has no banks.

Around Trindade

Beyond Trindade and the upmarket condominium at **Laranjeiras** there is a series of beaches. **Sono** is a long, sweeping stretch of sand backed by *barracas*, some of which have accommodation to rent. Sanitation is a problem, however. **Ponta Negra** is a little *caiçara* village, beautifully situated in a cove between rocky headlands. It has its own beach, simple but elegant homestay accommodation, fishing-boat trips and organized treks into the surrounding forest, which is rich in birdlife and full of waterfalls. It is possible to climb to the highest peak on the peninsula for views out over the Paraty area. The community is traditional and conservative; visits should be arranged in advance through village leaders. ↠ *See Sleeping, page 185.*

Ins and outs Sono and Ponta Negra are reached from the Sono trailhead, which lies at the end of the bus route to Trindade/Laranjeiras. The path is easy to find and follow. Allow 1½ hours for Sono and three hours for Ponta Negra. There are several buses a day to Trindade and the trailhead from Paraty. ↠ *See Transport, page 188.*

For Sleeping and Eating price codes and other relevant information, see pages 42-47.

◉ Sleeping

Angra dos Reis and around *p175*
Only stay in Angra town if you miss your bus or boat. There are a few cheap hotels near the port and main *praça*.
L do Frade, on the road to Ubatuba, Km 123 BR-101, 33 km from Angra, T024-3369 2244. Luxury hotel on the Praia do Frade with bar, restaurants, sauna and sports facilities.
AL Pestana, Estr Do Contorno 3700, Km 13, T024-3367 2754, www.pestanahotels.com.br. A range of bungalows on a forested hillside overlooking an emerald-green sea. Very pretty, peaceful and secluded with a decent open-sided restaurant and bar overlooking the water and excellent service.
B Caribe, R de Conceição 255, T024-3365 0033. Central and well kept, a good option.
E-C IYHA Angra Hostel, Praça da Matriz 152 at R do Comércio, T024-3364 4759. A block back from the boat dock for Ilha Grande and next to the Igreja Matriz. Clean, well run, with internet, lockers, dorms and doubles. The cheapest option for the early boat. Maps of Angra provided.

Ilha Grande *p176, map p176*
Accommodation on the island is in *pousadas* at Vila do Abraão or camping nearby. It is possible to hire a fisherman's cottage on Aventureiro Beach, which can be reached by the *Maria Isabel* or *Mestre Ernani* boats (T021-3361 9895 or T021-9269 5877) that leave from the quay in front of the BR petrol station in Angra dos Reis. Alternatively boats can be chartered direct from Angra dos Reis (2-3 hrs). There is a handful of upmarket options in isolated locations reachable only by boat.

Vilo do Abraão
Reservations are only necessary in peak season or on holiday weekends.

B Ancoradouro, R da Praia 121, T024-3361 5153, www.ancoradouro.ilhagrande.com. Clean, simple rooms with en suite in a beach-front building, 10 mins' walk east of the jetty.
B-C Farol dos Borbas, Praia do Abraão, T024-3361 5866, www.ilhagrande tour.com.br. 1 min from the jetty. Simple, well-maintained, fan-cooled rooms with tiled floors and breakfast tables and chairs. The best have balconies. The worst have no windows. Boat trips organized.
C Porto Girassol, R do Praia 65, T024-3261 5277, portogirasol@ilhagrande.com. Simple rooms in a mock-colonial beach house, 5 mins' east of the jetty.
C-E Aqua Rio Hostel, Town Beach, Abraão, T024-3361 5405, www.aquario.ilha grande.com. Party hostel on a peninsula overlooking the beach. Dorms, scruffy rooms, a large, relaxing bar area, seawater pool and great ocean views.
C-E Che Lagarto Ilha Grande Hostel, Town Beach, Abraão; book through the website www.chelagarto.com. Large beachside party hostel with well-kept dorms, doubles, bar and tours including trail walking and kayaking.
C-E IYHA Albergue Holdandes, R Assembleia de Deus, T024-3361 5034, www.holandes.com.br. Book ahead. Dorms, doubles and 4 little chalets in the forest on the edge of town. Breakfast included, laundry and advice on boats and tours. Good atmosphere.
C-E Pousada Cachoeira, 12-min walk from centre, T024-3361 5083, www.cachoeira.com. Price per person. Great little *pousada* full of character, with small rooms in chalets in a forest garden. Run by a German-Brazilian couple; English spoken. Good breakfast.
D Colibri, R da Assembléia 70, T024-3361 5033, www.colibriresort.com. Smart little Swedish-owned resort with rooms decorated with a personal touch and an outdoor breakfast area. Tours around the island offered.
D Estalagem Costa Verde, R Amâncio Felicio de Souza 239a, ½ a block behind the church,

T024-3104 7490, www.estalagemcosta
verde.com.br. Bright hostel with light,
well-maintained rooms decorated with
a little thought. Great value.

Camping Emilia Ecocamping, R Amâncio
F de Souza 18, T024-3361 5094, www.eco
camping.com.br. Hot showers, lockers, fridges,
communal living area with table tennis,
a campsite with lots of shade and cabins
(**E** per person).

Outside Vila do Abraão
See also **Angatu** in Paraty, below.
LL-L Sitio do Lobo, T024-2227 4138,
www.sitiodolobo.com.br. An architect-
commissioned house converted into a small
boutique hotel and sitting on an isolated
peninsula with its own little dock. The views
are marvellous: emerald sea, rainforest,
mountains in the distance, fiery red sunsets.
The best rooms are the suites; the others
overlook the pool but are boxy. Access
to the rest of the island is only by boat.
The restaurant serves the best food
on the island.
AL-A Sankay, Enseada do Bananal (1 hr by
boat from Angra or Abraão), T024-3365 1090,
www.pousadasankay.com.br. A beautiful
little *pousada* perched on a peninsula with
wonderful views. Simple rooms with brick or
stone walls. The best is the *Cavalo Marinho*
(Seahorse) suite. Sauna and bar. Dinner
included. Used for much of the year by
Body and Soul Adventures.

Paraty *p178, map p179*
There are many options in Paraty and
2 beautiful places in the hills nearby.
Also browse www.paraty.com.br/frame.htm.
LL Angatu, T011-3872 0945,
www.angatu.com. The very best private
houses in the region, including Prince João
de Orleans e Braganza's waterfront home
and luxury villas on the surrounding islands.
All come with your own yacht and, if you
choose, guides and tours around the
bay and to Ilha Grande.

L Bromelias Pousada and Spa, Rodovia
Rio–Santos, Km 562, Graúna, T/F024-3371
2791, www.pousadabromelias.com.br.
An Asian-inspired spa *pousada* with its own
aromatherapy products and a range of
massage treatments. Accommodation is
in tastefully decorated chalets perched on
a hillside forest garden overlooking the sea
and islands. Pool, sauna and restaurant.
L Pousada do Ouro, R Dr Pereira (or da Praia)
145, T/F024-3371 1311, www.pousada
ouro.com.br. Near Paraty's eastern waterfront
and built as a private home with a fortune
made on the gold route. Plain rooms in an
annexe and suites in the main building.
The tropical garden houses an open-air
poolside pavilion. Pictures of previous
guests such as Mick Jagger, Tom Cruise
and Linda Evangelista adorn the lobby.
L Pousada do Sandi, Largo do Rosário 1, T024-
3371 2100, www.pousadadosandi.com.br.
The most comfortable in town set in an
18th-century building with a grand lobby,
comfortable mock-colonial rooms and a
very good adjoining restaurant and pool area.
Superior breakfast, parking and excellent
tours organized through www.angatu.com.
L Pousada Pardieiro, R do Comércio 74, T024-
3371 1370, www.pousadapardieiro.com.br.
Tucked away in a quiet corner, with a calm,
sophisticated atmosphere. Attractive colonial
building with lovely gardens, delightful rooms
facing internal patios and a little swimming
pool. Always full at weekends. No children
under 15.
AL Hotel Coxixo, R do Comércio 362,
T024-3371 1460, www.hotelcoxixo.com.br.
A converted colonial building in the heart
of the 17th-century town, which has been
turned into a temple to its Brazilian movie-
star owner, Maria Della Costa. Black-and-
white pictures of her from the 1950s adorn
every corner. Rooms are decked out in
Catholic kitsch. The best rooms in the hotel
and in Paraty are the plush colonial suites.
A-B Le Gite d'Indaitiba, Rodovia Rio–Santos
(BR-101) Km 562, Graúna, T024-3371 7174,
www.legitedindaiatiba.com.br. French-

owned *pousada* with one of the best restaurants in southeastern Brazil. Carefully designed stylish chalets set in gardens on a hillside overlooking a mountain stream. Sweeping views of the sea and bay of islands and a 2-m-wide spring water swimming pool.

A-B Morro do Forte, R Orlando Carpinelli, T/F024-3371 1211, www.pousadamorrodo forte.com.br. Lovely garden, good breakfast, pool, German owner Peter Kallert offers trips on his yacht. Out of the centre. Recommended.

B Pousada Capitão, R Luiz do Rosário 18, T024-3371 1815, www.paraty.com.br/ capitao. Converted colonial building, close to the historic centre, swimming pool, English and Japanese spoken.

B Pousada do Corsário, Beco do Lapeiro 26, T024-3371 1866, www.pousadadocorsario. com.br. New building with a pool and its own gardens, next to the river and 2 blocks from the centre. Simple, stylish rooms, most with hammocks outside. Highly recommended.

B Pousada Mercado do Pouso, Largo de Santa Rita 43, T/F024-3371 1114, www.paraty com.br/mercadodepouso. Historic building close to waterfront decked out in lush wood, good sea views. Family atmosphere, no pool.

B-C Pousada Arte Colonial, R da Matriz 292, T024-3371 7231, www.paraty.com.br/ artecolonial. One of the best deals in Paraty. A beautiful colonial building in the centre decorated with style and a personal touch by its French owner, with artefacts and antiques from all over the world. Friendly, helpful and with breakfast. Highly recommended.

B-F Misti Chill Hostel and Pousada, R Orlando Carpinelli, 3-Praia do Pontal, T024-3371 2545, www.mistichill.com. Beachfront accommodation from dorms to private rooms with a/c.

C-D Solar dos Gerânios, Praça da Matriz, T/F024-3371 1550, www.paraty.com.br/ geranio. Beautiful colonial family house on main square in traditional rustic style that is a welcome antidote to the more polished *pousadas*. Rooms have lovely wooden lattice balconies – ask for the corner one which has 2. Very reasonably priced, English spoken. Warmly recommended.

D-E Casa do Rio, R Antônio Vidal 120, T024-3371 2223, www.paraty.com.br/ casadorio. Youth hostel in a little house with riverside courtyard and hammocks. There's a kitchen and price includes breakfast. Trips by jeep or on horseback to waterfalls, mountains and beaches. Dorms a little crowded.

D-E Pousada do Careca, Praça Macedo Soares, T024-3371 1291. Simple rooms. Those without street windows are musty.

Camping

Camping Beira-Rio, just across the bridge, before the road to the fort.

Camping Clube do Brasil, Av Orlando Carpinelli, Praia do Pontal, T024-3371 1877. Small, good, very crowded in Jan and Feb, US$8 per person.

Praia Jabaquara, T024-3371 2180.

Trindade p181

Expect no frills in Trindade.

D Chalé e Pousada Magia do Mar, T024-3371 5130. Thatched hut with space for 4. Views out over beach.

D Pousada Marimbá, R Principal, T024-3371 5147. Simple colourful rooms and a breakfast area.

D-F Ponta da Trindade Pousada and Camping, T024-3371 5113. Simple fan-cooled rooms and a sand-floored campsite with cold showers and no electricity.

Around Trindade p181

C-D Ponta Negra homestays, Ponta Negra, contact **Teteco**, T024-3371 2673, teteco@paratyweb.com.br, or Cauê, francocvc@hotmail.com.

🍴 Eating

Ilha Grande p176, map p176

Aside from **Sito do Lobo** (guests only, see Sleeping, above), food on the island is fairly basic: fish, chicken or meat with beans, rice and chips. There are plenty of restaurants serving these exciting combinations in Abraão. We list the very few better options.

🍴🍴🍴 Lua e Mar, Abraão, on the waterfront, T024-3361 5113. A few more adventurous fish-based options than the other restaurants.

🍴🍴 Corsário Negro, R da Vila, T024-3361 5321. The best in Abraão with good seafood, vegetarian food and excellent *caipirinhas*. The owner is a mine of information about the island and is fascinating to chat to.

Paraty p178, map p179

The best restaurants in Paraty are in the historic part of town and are almost as good as you will find in Rio or São Paulo. Watch out for surreptitious cover charges for live music, which are often very discreetly displayed. The less expensive restaurants, those offering *comida a quilo* (pay by weight)

and the fast-food outlets are outside the historic centre, mainly on Av Roberto Silveira.

Paraty's regional specialities include *peixe à Parati* (local fish cooked with herbs and green bananas), served with *pirão* (a mixture of manioc flour and the sauce that the fish was cooked in). Also popular is the *filé de peixe ao molho de camarão* (fried fish fillet with a shrimp and tomato sauce). There is plenty of choice in Paraty so have a browse. Also see **Le Gite d'Indaitiba**, page 183.

🍴🍴🍴 Bartolomeu, R Samuel Costa 179, T024-3371 5032. Argentinian steaks, fish (including good ceviche) and great cocktails from ex-*Elite* fashion model-turned-gourmet cook, Deborah Cortes.

🍴🍴🍴 do Hiltinho, R Mcal Deodoro 233, historical centre, T024-3371 1432. Decent seafood, including local dishes.

🍴🍴🍴 Merlin O Mago, (next to **Hotel Coxixo**), R do Comercio 376, historic centre, T024-3371 2157, www.paraty.com.br/merlin.htm. Franco-Brazilian cooking in an intimate dining room/bar, by a German dance bleu chef and illustrious photojournalist. Decent wine list. Highly recommended.

🍴🍴🍴 Punto Di Vino, R Mcal Deodoro 129, historical centre, T024-3371 1348. The best for seafood in town; owned and run by a Neapolitan who catches his own 'catch of the day'. Great wood-fired pizza, live music and an excellent selection of wine.

🍴🍴🍴 Thai Brasil, R Dona Geralda 345, historic centre, T024-3371 0127, www.thaibrasil.com.br. Beautiful restaurant decorated with handicrafts and furnished with hand-painted chairs and tables. The cooking comprises well-executed Thai standards without spices (Brazilians yelp in pain at the sight of a chilli).

🍴🍴 Café Paraty, R da Lapa and Comércio, historic centre. Open 0900-2400. Sandwiches, appetizers, light meals, also bar with live music nightly (cover charge). A local landmark.

🍴🍴 Catimbau, Baía de Paraty, T024-33711847. A restaurant and bar sitting between 2 giant boulders on a tiny island in the bay. It is run by ex-Hollywood line producer and local fisherman Caca and his Dutch wife Mimi and serves simple but very fresh seafood accompanied by ice-cold beer or *caipirinhas*. Can be visited by request on any bay tour.

† **Dona Ondina**, R do Comércio 2, by the river, historic centre. Closed on Mon, Mar and Nov. Family restaurant with well-prepared simple food. Good value.

† **Vila Verde**, Estr Paraty–Cunha, Km 7, T024-3371 7808, www.vilaverde paraty.com.br. It's worth a stop off here on the way to or from the waterfalls, the Caminho Douro or Cunha. The restaurant serves light Italian and its open sides overlook a tropical garden that attracts numerous morpho butterflies, humming birds and tanagers.

† **Kontiki**, Ilha Duas Irmãs, T024-999 9599, www.paraty.com.br/kontiki.htm. Daily 1000-1500 and Fri and Sat for dinner. A tiny island, 5 mins from the pier where a small speed boat runs a (free) shuttle service. Wonderful island setting; ordinary food. Reservations recommended.

† **Sabor da Terra**, Av Roberto Silveira, next to Banco do Brasil. Closes 2200. Reliable, if not bargain-priced self-service food.

🍸 Bars and clubs

Paraty *p178, map p179*
The best way to sample Paraty's nightlife is to wander its handful of streets.
Bar Coupé, Praça da Matriz. A popular hang-out with outside seating. Good bar snacks and breakfast.
Bar Dinho, Praça da Matriz at R da Matriz. Good bar with live music at weekends, sometimes mid-week.
Umoya, R Comendador José Luiz. Video bar and café, live music at weekends.

🎭 Entertainment

Paraty *p178, map p178*
Dance
As well as the Dança dos Velhos, another common dance in these parts is the *ciranda*, in which everyone, young and old, dances in a circle to songs accompanied by guitars.

Theatre
Teatro Espaço, R Dona Geralda 327, T024-3371 1575, ecparati@ax.apc.org. Wed, Sat 2100, US$12. This world-famous puppet show should not be missed. The puppets tell stories (in mime), which are funny, sad, even shocking, with incredible realism. The short pieces (lasting 1 hr) are works of pure imagination and emotion and a moving commentary on the human condition.

🎉 Festivals and events

Angra dos Reis and around *p175*
New Year Festa do Mar, boat processions.
5 Jan Folia dos Reis, the Three Kings, culmination of a religious festival that begins at Christmas.
6 Jan Founding of Angra dos Reis.
May Festa do Divino and, on the 2nd Sun, the Senhor do Bonfim maritime procession.
Jun As elsewhere in the state, the Festas Juninas are celebrated.
8 Dec Festival of Nossa Senhora da Conceição.

Paraty *p178, map p179*
Feb/Mar Carnaval, hundreds of people cover their bodies in black mud and run through the streets yelling like prehistoric creatures (anyone can join in).
Mar/Apr Semana Santa (Easter Week) with religious processions and folk songs.
Mid-Jul Semana de Santa Rita, traditional foods, shows, exhibitions and dances.

Aug Festival da Pinga, the *cachaça* fair at which local distilleries display their products and there are plenty of opportunities to over-indulge.
Sep (around the 8th) Semana da Nossa Senhora dos Remédios, processions and religious events.
Sep/Oct Spring Festival of Music, concerts in front of Santa Rita Church.
31 Dec New Year's Eve, a huge party with open-air concerts and fireworks (reserve accommodation in advance).

○ Shopping

Paraty *p178, map p179*
Shopping here is by and large a disappointment. There are many shops but most sell the kind of tack you'd find in any tourist town in the world; key rings, fridge magnets, cheesy T-shirts and so on. The best items are fine art (which tends to be overpriced), and artisan ware: fish trays, small wooden canoes and boats. The Guarani people sell their arts and crafts on the R da Matriz. Paraty *cachaça* is some of the best in the state, although it can't compare with bottles from Minas.

▲ Activities and tours

Angra dos Reis and around *p175*
See **Angatu**, under Paraty, below.

Ilha Grande *p176, map p176*
Boat trips
These are easy to organize on the quay in Abraão on Ilha Grande.

Scuba diving
Ilha Grande Dive, R da Praia s/n, Vila do Abraão, T021-3361 5512, igdive@bol.com.br (next to the *farmacia* on the seafront). Offers trips around the entire bay.

Paraty *p178, map p179*
Angatu, T011-3872 0945, www.angatu.com. The best private tours and diving around the bay in luxurious yachts and motor cruisers, with private entries to the exclusive island parties. Also offers private villa rental in and around Paraty (see Sleeping, page 183). Book well ahead. Highly recommended.
Antígona, Praça da Bandeira 2, Centro Histórico, T/F024-3371 1165, www.anti gona.com.br. Daily schooner tours, 5 hrs, bar and lunch on board. Recommended.
Paraty Tours, Av Roberto Silveira 11, T/F024- 3371 1327, www.paraty tours.com.br. Good range of trips. English and Spanish spoken.
Rei Cigano, contact through **Bartolomeu** restaurant (see Eating, page 185), or ring Tuca T024-7835 3190, thiparaty@ hotmail.com. Day excursions and overnights or even expeditions along the Brazilian coast in a beautiful 60-ft sailing schooner with cabins.
Soberana da Costa, R Dona Geraldo 43, in **Pousada Mercado do Pouso**, T/F024-3371 1114, see Sleeping, page 184. Schooner trips. Recommended.

○ Transport

Angra dos Reis and around *p175*
Bus Costa Verde buses run at least hourly to the *rodoviária* in **Rio de Janeiro**, some are direct, others take the *via litoral* and go through Barra, Ipanema and Copacabana, US$10, 2½ hrs. Sit on the right for the best views. Busy at weekends. There are also regular buses to and from **São Paulo**, **Paraty**, **Ubatuba** and the São Paulo coast.

Ferry Ferries run to **Ilha Grande**, see the timetable on page 188. Fishing boats will also take passengers for around US$5 per person before 1300 or when full. Boat charter costs around US$60-100.

Ferry times to Ilha Grande

	Monday-Thursday	Friday	Weekends and holidays
Mangaratiba–Abraão	0730	0730, 2200	0800
Abraão–Mangaratiba	0930, 1400	0930, 1400	1000
Angra–Abraão	1115, 1600	1115, 1600	1330
Abraão–Angra	1800	1800	1730

Monday to Friday: US$3.50 (one way); weekends and holidays: US$9 (one way).
For further information contact T021-4004 3113, T0800-704 4113, www.ilhagrande.org.

Ilha Grande *p176, map p176*
Bicycles Can be hired and tours arranged;
ask at *pousadas*.

Ferry Ferries run between Ilha Grande and
Angra dos Reis. See Angra dos Reis and
the timetable, above.

Paraty *p178, map p179*
Bus On public holidays and in high season,
the frequency of bus services usually increases.
Costa Verde runs 9 buses a day to **Rio de
Janeiro** (241 km, 3¾ hrs, US$8.10). To **Angra
dos Reis** (98 km, 1½ hrs, every 1 hr 40 mins,
US$4); 3 a day to **Ubatuba** (75 km, just over
1 hr, São José company, US$4), **Taubaté**
(170 km) and **Guaratinguetá** (210 km); 2 a day
to **São Paulo**, 1100 and 2335 (304 km via **São
José dos Campos**, 5½ hrs, US$8.50 (Reunidas
book up quickly and are very busy at
weekends), and **São Sebastião**.

Taxi Set rate of US$4 for trips within
the historic centre.

Trindade and around *p181*
Paraty–Ubatuba buses all pass the turning
to Trindade and will pick you up from here.
In high season there are vans from Trindade
to the turning (US$2). In low season you'll
have to hitch or walk. Frequent cars pass and
hitching here is normal. There are 4 or 5 direct
buses a day which also call in on **Laranjeiras**
for the trailhead to **Sono** and **Ponta Negra**.

🅞 Directory

Angra dos Reis and around *p175*
Banks There are several banks in town,
with ATMs and money-changing facilities.
These include **Banco 24 Horas**, R do
Comércio 250, and **Bradesco**, R do
Comércio 196.

Ilha Grande *p176, map p176*
Banks Only open at weekends.

Paraty *p178, map p179*
Banks Banco do Brasil, Av Roberto
Silveira, just outside the historic centre, ATM.
Exchange 1100-1430, ask for the manager.
Internet Connections are plentiful, but
are slow and expensive. Paraty Cyber
Café, Av Roberto Silveira 17. Friendly,
0900-2300, coffee and snacks served.
US$3 for 30 mins. **Laundry** Paraty Wash,
Shopping Martins, loja 15, opposite the
bus station. **Medical services** Hospital
Municipal São Pedro de Alcântara (Santa
Casa), Av Dom Pedro de Alcântara,
T024-3371 1623. **Post office** R da Cadeia
and Beco do Propósito, Mon-Sat 0800-1700,
Sun 0800-1200. **Telephone** International
calls can be made from Praça Macedo Soares,
opposite the tourist office. Local and
long-distance calls can be made from
public phones; buy phone cards from
newspaper stands in the centre.

Contents

Footprint features

At a glance

⊖ **Getting around** Metrô, city bus and long-distance bus. Taxi is the only option for some journeys. Car hire recommended for the coast.

◉ **Time required** 2-3 days for the city; preferably over a weekend for nightlife. 5-7 days to visit the city and parts of state.

☀ **Weather** Warm and wet summer (Oct-Mar) on the coast; drier inland with blue skies. Cool winter (Apr-Sep) with blue skies. Temperatures can drop to below 10°C during a cold front.

✕ **When not to go** Jan-Feb is very wet.

★ **Don't miss ...**
1 MASP, page 206.
2 Oscar Niemeyer buildings, page 207.
3 São Paulo restaurants, page 212.
4 São Paulo nightlife, page 215.
5 Ilhabela, page 233.
6 Cananéia and Ilha do Cardoso, page 241.

Atlantic Ocean

N

50 km
50 miles

São Paulo is as famous for its ugliness as Rio is for its beauty. But while Rio looks marvellous from a distance and less than perfect close to, São Paulo is the opposite. Restaurants, shops, hotels and nightlife here are infinitely better than in Rio. And, while wandering and browsing in plush neighbourhoods such as Jardins, it is even possible to forget that few cities in the world have quite so much relentless concrete punctuated with quite so few green spaces; or have rivers quite so disgracefully polluted as the Tietê. Marlene Dietrich perhaps summed it up when she said – "Rio is a beauty – but São Paulo; ah … São Paulo is a city."

Indeed, São Paulo is more than a city. It is also a state a little larger than the UK; and while most of its interior is dull agricultural hinterland, its coast is magnificent; just as beautiful as Rio de Janeiro's but far less visited by international tourists. The northern beaches are long and glorious and pounded by some of South America's finest surf. Brazil's largest island, which is every bit as pristine and romantic as Ilha Grande, lies a short boat ride off shore. The beaches further south are less beautiful but far wilder; behind them, stretching into the neighbouring state of Paraná, are the largest expanses of primary forest on Brazil's Atlantic coast.

São Paulo city

→ *Colour map 5, A5. Phone code: 011. Population: 18-20 million. Altitude: 850 m.*
São Paulo is vast and can feel intimidating on first arrival. But this is a city of separate neighbourhoods, only a few of which are interesting for visitors, and once you have your base it is easy to negotiate. São Paulo is the intellectual capital of Brazil. Those who don't flinch at the city's size and leave, who are instead prepared to spend time (and money) here, and who get to know Paulistanos, are seldom disappointed and often end up preferring the city to Rio. Nowhere in Brazil is better for concerts, clubs, theatre, ballet, classical music, all-round nightlife, restaurants and beautifully designed hotels. You will not be seen as a gringo in São Paulo, and the city is safer than Rio if you avoid the centre after dark and the outlying favelas (which are impossible to stumble across). ▶▶ *For listings, see pages 210-225.*

Ins and outs

Getting there

Air São Paulo is the cheapest and the principal entry point to Brazil and is one of the key entry points to South America. All international flights (except a handful to Bolivia) and many of the cheapest internal flights arrive at **Guarulhos airport** ⓘ *Guarulhos, 25 km northeast of the city, T011-6445 2945*, officially known as **Cumbica**. There are plenty of banks and money changers in the arrivals hall open daily 0800-2200. There is a post office on the third floor of Asa A. Tourist information, including city and regional city maps and copies of the entertainment section from the Folha de São Paulo newspaper with current listings, is available from **Secretaria de Esportes e Turismo (SET)** ⓘ *ground floor of both terminals, Mon-Fri 0730-2200, Sat, Sun and holidays 0900-2100*. Airport taxis charge US$50 to the centre and operate on a ticket system: go to the second booth on leaving the terminal and book a co-op taxi at the *Taxi Comum* counter; these are the best value. **Emtu** buses run every 30 minutes to Praça da República, Paulista, the bus station and Congonhas airport, US$10, 30-45 minutes, 0500-0200. Buy a ticket at the booth in domestic arrivals.

The domestic airport, **Congonhas** ⓘ *Av Washington Luiz, 7 km south of the centre, 5 km from Jardins, T011-5090 9000*, is used for the Rio–São Paulo shuttle (about 400 flights a week US$150 single, US$300 return) and some other domestic services including Salvador, Belo Horizonte and Vitória. A taxi to the city centre or Jardins costs about US$20.

Bus Most buses arrive at the **Tietê rodoviária** ⓘ *5 km north of the centre, T011-2223 7152, www.passagem-em-domicilio.com.br (with details of bus times and prices in Portuguese)*. Left luggage costs US$4 per day per item. You can sleep in the bus station after 2200 when the guards have gone; showers US$4. There is a metrô with connections throughout the city, US$1, and buses to the centre (less safe), US$0.80. Taxis to Jardins cost US$15, US$20 at weekends. Buses from the São Paulo state coast and Paraná arrive at **Barra Funda** ⓘ *T011-3666 4682, www.passagem-em-domicilio.com.br*, while buses from Minas Gerais arrive at **Bresser** ⓘ *T011-6692 5191*. Buses from Santos and the coast arrive at **Jabaquara** ⓘ *T011-5581 0856*. All are connected to the centre by metrô. ▶▶ *See Transport, page 223.*

Train Railways are being privatized and many long-distance passenger services have been withdrawn. São Paulo has four stations but the only one useful for tourists is **Estação da Luz** ⓘ *Metrô Luz, T0800-550121*, which receives trains from the northwest and southeast of São Paulo state and connects with the tourist train from Paranapiacaba to Rio Grande de Serra.

Arriving late at night

São Paulo's international airport, Cumbica in Guarulhos, has 24-hour facilities (for food, banking and of course taxis) in case you arrive late at night or in the early hours of the morning. It is a long drive from the airport to the city and the a/c bus to Praça da República does not operate between 0200 and 0500 and the service to Avenida Paulista does not run from 2315 to 0645. A taxi to the centre of the city will cost around US$50.

Congonhas airport, which is connected to most of Brazil's major cities, is in the city centre. Although there are no 24-hour services there are hotels across the road from the terminal (via the footbridge) and most areas in and around the centre are a maximum of US$10 taxi ride away.

Getting around

Bus Bus routes can be confusing for visitors and slow due to frequent traffic jams. However, buses are safe, clean and only crowded at peak hours. Maps of the bus and metrô system are available at depots, eg Anhangabaú. All the *rodoviárias* (bus stations) are on the metrô, but if travelling with luggage, take a taxi.

Metrô The best and cheapest way to get around São Paulo is on the excellent metrô system (see map, page 194), which is clean, safe, cheap and efficient; though rather limited in its coverage. The first metrô in Brazil, it began operating in 1975 and has two main lines intersecting at Praça da Sé: **north–south** from Tucuruvi to Jabaquara; and **east–west** from Corinthians Itaquera to Barra Funda, both operate 0500-2400. A third runs **west–south** from Vila Madalena to Imigrantes via Avenida Paulista, and operates 0600-2200. Stations are well policed and safe. A single journey costs US$1; US$8 for a book of 10 tickets. A combined bus and metrô ticket costs US$2; useful for getting to Congonhas airport.

Taxi Taxis display their tariffs in the window (starting at US$4) and have meters. Ordinary taxis are hailed on the street or at taxi stations such as Praça da República. Radio taxis are more expensive but less hassle. ▸▸ *See Transport, page 224, for recommended companies.*

Orientation

At the heart of the city, the **Centro Histórico** is a place to visit but not to stay. Most of the historical buildings and former beauty are long gone, but its pedestrianized streets are fascinating and gritty, with lively markets and a cluster of interesting sights lost in the concrete and cobbles. For a birds' eye view of the city, head to the lookout platform at the top of the Banespa Tower at dusk. The commercial district, containing banks, offices and shops, is known as the **Triângulo**, bounded by Ruas Direita, 15 de Novembro, São Bento and Praça Antônio Prado, but it is rapidly spreading towards the Praça da República.

Immediately southwest of the Centro Histórico is the city's grandest and most photographed skyscraper-lined street, **Avenida Paulista**. The Museo de Arte de São Paulo (MASP), the best art gallery in the southern hemisphere, is here. North of Avenida Paulista is the neighbourhood of **Consolação**, centred on tawdry Rua Augusta but undergoing a Renaissance at the cutting edge of the city's underground live music and nightlife scene. South of Avenida Paulista is the neighbourhood of **Jardins**. This is the city's most affluent inner neighbourhood with elegant little streets hiding Latin America's best restaurants and designer clothing boutiques. There are plenty of luxurious hotels and some budget options.

Next to Jardins, 5 km south of the centre, the **Parque do Ibirapuera** is the inner city's largest green space, with running tracks, a lake and live concerts. Like Brasília, it is a repository of historically important Oscar Niemeyer buildings, many of which are home to interesting museums. The adjoining neighbourhoods of **Vila Mariana** and **Paraíso** have a few hotel options and great live music at SESC Vila Mariana.

Situated between Ibirapuera and the river, **Itaim, Moema** and **Vila Olímpia** are among the nightlife centres of São Paulo with a wealth of streetside bars, ultra-chic designer restaurants and European-style dance clubs. Hotels tend to be expensive as these areas border the new business centre on Avenida Brigadeiro Faria Lima and Avenida Luís Carlos Berrini, in the suburb of **Brooklin**. **Pinheiros and Vila Madalena** are less chic, but equally lively at night and with the funkiest shops.

Best time to visit

São Paulo sits on a plateau at around 800 m and the weather is temperamental, influenced by the city's altitude and by the sea, whose cold or warm air is pushed up by the coastal mountains. Rainfall is ample and temperatures fluctuate greatly. Summer temperatures vary between 20° and 30°C, occasionally peaking into the high 30s or even 40s. Winter temperatures fluctuate between 15° and 25°C, occasionally dropping to below 10° when a cold front comes up from the Atlantic. The winter months (April-October) are also the driest, with minimal precipitation in June and July. Christmas and New Year are wet. When there are thermal inversions, air pollution can be troublesome.

1 Sao Paulo metrô

➡ **São Paulo maps**
1 São Paulo metrô, page 194
2 São Paulo orientation, page 196
3 São Paulo centre, page 200
4 Avenida Paulista and Jardins, page 205

Tourist information

There are tourist information booths with English-speaking staff in international and domestic arrivals (ground floor) at **Cumbica airport** (Guarulhos). There are also tourist information booths in the **bus station** and in the following locations throughout the city: **Praça da Luz** ① *in front of the Pinacoteca cafe, daily 0900-1800*; **Av São João** ① *Av São João 473, Mon-Fri 0900-1800*; **Avenida Paulista** ① *Parque Trianon, T011-3251 0970, Sun-Fri 0900-1800*; and **Avenida Brig Faria Lima** ① *opposite the Iguatemi shopping centre, T011-3211 1277, Mon-Fri 0900-1800*. An excellent map is available free at these offices.

Editora Abril publishes maps and the excellent *Guide to São Paulo – Sampa*. For cheap travel, *Viajar Bem e Barato*, is available at news-stands and bookshops throughout the city.

Websites The best website in English is www.brazilmax.com. www.guiasp.com.br has comprehensive entertainment listings in Portuguese, but is readily understandable. Also see http://vejasaopaulo.abril.com.br for entertainment, restaurants and general information in Portuguese.

Background

The history of São Paulo state and São Paulo city were much the same from the arrival of the Europeans until the coffee boom transformed the region's economic and political landscape. According to John Hemming (*Red Gold*, see Books page 819), there were approximately 196,000 indigenous inhabitants living in what is now São Paulo state. Today their numbers have been vastly diminished and of the few who survived, some live in villages within São Paulo itself and can be seen selling handicrafts in the centre.

The first official settlement in the state was at São Vicente on the coast, near today's port of Santos. It was founded in 1532 by Martim Afonso de Sousa, who had been sent by King João III to drive the French from Brazilian waters, explore the coast and lay claim to all the lands apportioned to Portugal under the Treaty of Tordesillas.

In 1554, two Jesuit priests from São Vicente founded São Paulo as a *colégio* (a combined mission and school) on the site of the present Pátio de Colégio in the Centro Histórico. The Jesuits chose to settle inland because they wanted to distance themselves from the civil authority, which was based in Bahia and along the coast. Moreover, the plateau provided better access to the indigenous population who they hoped to convert to Catholicism. Pioneers seeking to found farms followed in the Jesuits' wake and as the need for workers on these farms grew, expeditions were sent into the interior of the country to capture and enslave the indigenous people. These marauders were known as *bandeirantes* after the flag wielder who ostensibly walked at their head to claim territory. Their ignominious expeditions were responsible for the opening up of the country's interior and supplying the indigenous slave trade. A statue by one of Brazil's foremost modernist sculptors, Victor Brecheret, sits on the edge of Ibirapuera in homage to the *bandeirantes* (see box, page 228). In a sense, the *bandeirantes'* success in discovering gold led to the demise of São Paulo in the 18th century. The inhabitants rushed to the gold fields in the *sertão*, leaving São Paulo to fall to ruin and fall under the influence of Rio de Janeiro. The relative backwardness of the region lasted until the late 19th century when the coffee trade spread west from Rio de Janeiro. Landowners became immensely rich. São Paulo changed from a small town into a financial and residential centre. Exports and imports flowed through Santos and the industrial powerhouse of the country was born. As the city boomed, industries and agriculture fanned outwards to the far reaches of the state.

2 São Paulo

➡ São Paulo maps
1 São Paulo metrô, page 194
2 **São Paulo orientation, page 196**
3 São Paulo centre, page 200
4 Avenida Paulista and Jardins, page 205

SESC Pompéia

Av Mq de São Vicente

Barra
Funda

Esta
Bar
Fund

Av Ma

Matarazzo

Av Pompéia

Cerro Cora

Av Sumaré

Vila
Madalena

VILA MADALENA

Sumaré

Av Pedroso de Moraes

Av Dr Arnaldo

Clínicas

Av Paulo Vi

Luís Murat

Henrique Schaumann

Fradique Coutinho

JARDINS

Av das Nações

Prof Melo

Museu de Arte
Contemporânea
(MAC)

Av Frederico Herman Jr

Av Brig Faria Lima

Pedroso de Morais

Av Rebouças

Rio pinheiros

Av Marginal do Rio Pinheiros

dos Pinheiros

Av Brasil

Av da
Universidade

Av Afranio

Peixoto

CIDADE
UNIVERSITÁRIA

PINHEIROS

Av Rebouças

Instituto
Butantã

Alvarenga

Marques

Av Vital Brasil

Av Eusabio
Matoso

Av Colombia

Groenlândia

Av 9 de Julr

SP-270

Av Francisco Morato

Av das Nações Unidas

Av Brig Faria Lima

4

Iguatemi
Shopping
Centre

Av Lineu de P Machado

Av Magalhães de Castro

Jóquei
Clube

Av Cidade Jardim

Av dos Tajuras

Daslu
Department
Store

Shopping
Cidade Jardim

R Eng O Americano

Av Juscelino Kubitschek

ITAIM

VILA

Sleeping 🛏
Blue Tree Towers 1
Grand Hyatt São Paulo 2
Praça de Árvore IYHA 3
Unique 4

N

1 km
1 mile

Av Magalhães de Castro

Luís Carlos
Berrini

Av dos Bandeirantes

To Morumbi &
Parque Burle Marx

To New Business
District & Brooklin

To 2 & Morumbi Shopping Centre

To Ibirapuera Shopping
Centre & Congonhas Airport

Between 1885 and the end of the century the boom in coffee and the arrival of large numbers of Europeans transformed the state beyond recognition. By the end of the 1930s more than a million Italians, 500,000 Portuguese, nearly 400,000 Spaniards and 200,000 Japanese had arrived in São Paulo state. It is the world's largest Japanese community outside Japan and their main contribution to the economy of São Paulo has been in horticulture, raising poultry and cotton farming, especially around cities such as Marília. Significant numbers of Syrian-Lebanese arrived too, adding an extra dimension to the cultural diversity of the city.

Much of the immigrant labour that flooded in during the early years of the 20th century was destined for the coffee *fazendas* and farms. Others went to work in the industries that were opening up in the city. By 1941 there were 14,000 factories and today the city covers more than 1500 sq km – three times the size of Paris.

Centro Histórico

São Paulo's city centre was once one of the most attractive in South America. English visitors in the 19th century described it as being spacious, green and dominated by terracotta-tiled buildings. There were even parrots and sloths in the trees. Today they are long gone and the centre is dominated by towering (and rather ugly) buildings, broken by a handful of interesting churches and cultural centres, and criss-crossed by narrow pedestrian streets. These are lined with stalls selling everything from shoes to electronics, second-hand goods and bric-a-brac, throughout the week. The best way to explore the area is by metrô and on foot, but don't stay after dark as the area is unsalubrious.

Praça da Sé and around → *Metrô Sé.*

The best place to begin a tour is at the **Praça da Sé**, an expansive square shaded by tropical trees and dominated by the hulking Catholic **Catedral Metropolitana** ① *Praça da Sé, T011-3106 2709, Mon-Sat 0800-1800, Sun 0830-1800, free.* This is the heart of the old city and has been the site of Brazil's largest public protests. Crowds gathered here in the late 1980s to demand the end to military rule. And, in 1992, they demanded the impeachment and resignation of the new Republic's second elected president, Fernando Collor – the first in a seemingly never-ending series of corrupt leaders who in 1990 had frozen the country's savings accounts and personally pocketed millions. The *praça* is always busy with hawkers, beggars, shoeshiners and business men rushing between meetings. Evangelists with megaphones proselytize on the steps of the cathedral – a symbol of the war between Christians for the souls of the poor that dominates contemporary urban Brazil. The *praça* is a great spot for street photography though be discreet with your camera and check that you aren't followed after taking your shots. Like São Paulo itself, the cathedral is more remarkable for its size than its beauty and is an unconvincing mish-mash of neo-Gothic and Renaissance. A narrow nave is squeezed uncomfortably between two monstrous 97-m-high spires beneath a bulbous copper cupola. It was designed in 1912 by the inappropriately named engineer Maximiliano Hell, inaugurated in the 1950s and fitted with its full complement of 14 towers only in 2002. The interior is bare but for a few stained glass windows designed in Germany and capitals decorated with Brazilian floral motifs.

There are a few other sights of interest around the *praça*. Next door to the cathedral itself and housed in a 1930s art deco building is the **Conjunto Cultural da Caixa** ① *Praça da Sé 111, T011-3107 0498, Tue-Sun 0900-2100, US$2,* a gallery that hosts art and photography exhibitions and has a small banking museum with colonial furniture, on one of its upper floors. Two minutes' walk immediately to the west of the cathedral, squeezed between ugly modern buildings at the end of Rua Senador Feijó, is the **Igreja da Ordem Terceira de São Francisco** ⓘ *Largo de São Francisco 133, T011-3106 0081, daily 0730-2000, free*. This is one of the city's oldest churches, preserving a modest baroque interior (parts of which date to the 17th century) painted in celestial blue. It is quiet and meditative inside. The exterior is largely an 18th-century excrescence. The church is often referred to as 'O Convento de São Francisco' after a beautiful baroque convent that stood here until the 1930s. It was demolished along with vast swathes of the old colonial centre.

Pátio do Colégio and around → *Metrô Sé.*

The site of the founding of São Paulo can be reached by walking north from the bottom of the Praça da Sé (farthest from the cathedral) along Rua Santa Teresa and to the Praça Pátio do Colégio. Here lies the **Pátio do Colégio and Museu de Anchieta** ⓘ *Praça Pátio do Colégio, T011-3105 6899, www.pateodocollegio.com.br, Mon-Fri 0800-1700, US$3, free on the last Sun of the month*. Jesuit priests, led by 18-year-old Padre José de Anchieta arrived here in 1554, when the area was a tiny clearing on a hill in the midst of a vast forest. They made camp and instructed their domicile indigenous Guarani to construct a simple wattle and daub hut. They inaugurated the building with a celebration of Mass on 25 January 1554, the feast of the conversion of São Paulo. Their simple hut took the saint's name, the 'Colégio de São Paulo de Piratinga'. The hut became a school for converted *indígenas* seduced from the forests around. The school became a church and the church gave its name – São Paulo – to a settlement for *bandeirante* slaving raids into the Brazilian interior. In 1760, the Jesuits were expelled from the city they founded, for opposing the *bandeirantes* and their indigenous slave trade. But the Pátio do Colégio (as the complex of buildings came to be known) remained, becoming the palace of the fledgling province's Portuguese colonial captains general, and then of its Brazilian imperial governors. The church's tower fell down in 1886, and shortly after the whole building, but for one piece of wattle and daub wall, was demolished. The Jesuits didn't return to São Paulo until 1954 but they had long memories and immediately set about building an exact replica of their original church and college, which is what stands today. Most of the buildings are occupied by the **Museu Padre Anchieta**. This preserves, amongst other items, a modernist and not altogether sympathetic painting of the priest, by Italian Albino Menghini, bits of his corpse (which is now that of a saint after Anchieta was canonized by Pope John Paul II), a 17th-century font used to baptize the *indígenas* and a collection of Guaraní art and artefacts from the colonial era.

The exhibition spaces, cultural centres and concert halls of the **Centro Cultural Banco do Brasil** ⓘ *R Álvares Penteado 112, T011-3113 3651, www.bb.com.br/appbb/portal/bb/ctr/sp/index.jsp, Mon-Fri 0900-1800, free except for exhibitions*, can be reached by turning immediately west from the front of the Pátio do Colégio along Rua do Tesouro and then right for a block along Rua Álvares Penteado. These are housed in an attractive art deco building with a pretty glass ceiling. Many of the galleries are contained within the banks original vaults, some of which retain their massive iron doors.

Mosteiro do São Bento and around → *Metrô São Bento.*

The most beautiful of all the churches in São Paulo is the Benedictine Basilica de Nossa Senhora de Assunção, known as the **Mosteiro São Bento** ⓘ *Largo São Bento, T011-3228 3633, www.mosteiro.org.br, Mon-Fri 0600-1800, Sat and Sun 0600-1200 and 1600-1800,*

Latin Mass with Gregorian chant Sun 1000; Latin vespers Mon-Fri 1725, Sat 1700, free.
Benedictines arrived on this site in 1598, shortly after the Jesuits and, like them, proceeded to proselytize the indigenous people. Despite their long history in the city the monastery is a modern church dating from the 1920s. It was designed by Munich-based architect Richard Bernal in homage to the English Norman style. Its façade is strikingly similar to Southwell cathedral in Nottinghamshire, though with added Rhineland roofs and baroque revival flourishes. But few visit São Bento for the exterior. The church preserves a striking Beuronese interior painted by Dom Adelbert Gresnicht, a Dutch monk of the Order. The style is named after techniques developed by Benedictines in the monastery of Beuron in southwest Germany in the late 19th and early 20th centuries. It finds much inspiration in Byzantine art and is characterized by compressed perspective and iconic, almost exaggerated colours. São Bento is one of the finest Beuronese churches in the world. The

③ São Paulo centre

Sleeping 🛏
Formule 1 **4**

Gran Corona **1**
Itamarati **2**

Othon Palace **3**

stained glass (and much of the statuary) is also by Dom Adelbert. Most of the windows show scenes from the life of St Benedict with the most beautiful, at the far end of the nave, showing Our Lady ascending to heaven guided by the Holy Spirit in the form of a dove. The church has Brazil's finest organ which is given its own festival in November and December every year. And with this being a Benedictine monastery, there is of course a temple to commerce: the shop sells delicious sweets home-made by the monks in their bakery.

Immediately in front of the monastery, at the corner of Avenida São João and Rua Libero Badaró, is the **Edifício Martinelli (Martinelli Building)** ① *Av São João 35, not open to the public*. This was the city's first skyscraper and, when it was built, looked out over a sea of terracotta roofs and handsome tree-lined avenues. The building is reminiscent of New York's upper east side but is by no means as distinguished: while colonial São Paulo was unique and beautiful, the buildings that replaced it looked tawdry and crowded next to the New York it longed to imitate.

To Estação da Luz (500m)

Eating ●
Terraço Italia 3

Around the corner is another architectural pastiche, the **Edifício Banespa (Banespa Tower)** ① *R João Bricola 24, T011-3249 7180, 1000-1700, US$4*, looking a bit like a wan Empire State Building small enough to collapse under the weight of King Kong. The view from the observatory is best experienced at dusk when the chaos of multi-storey concrete is set against a smog-filled purple sky and the vast highways are lit by a thousand paralysed cars. The city stretches far and wide, over the polluted black gutter of the Tietê and to every distant horizon. On its fringes are the vast *favelas* and new neighbourhoods with infant skyscraper flats.

Praça da República → *Metrô República*
There are a few interesting sites here. Most notable is the **Edifício and Terraço Itália** ① *Av Ipiranga 344, T011-3257 6566, www.traccoitalia.com.br, US$5*, a rather unremarkable restaurant in the city's tallest building with a truly remarkable view from the observation deck. Arrive half an hour before sunset for the best balance of natural and artificial light, and bring a tripod. The skyscraper immediately in front of the *terraço* is Oscar Niemeyer's **Edifício Copan** ① *Av Ipiranga 200, not open to the public though some visitors are allowed to go to the terraço at the discretion of security*, built in 1951 in a spate of design by the

architect, which also included the nearby **Edifício Montreal** ① *Av Ipiranga at Cásper Líbero*, and the **Edifício Califórnia** ① *R Barão de Itapetininga*.

From the corner of Praça da República, a 10-minute walk southeast along Rua 24 de Maio, brings you back into the main part of the city centre and Metrô Anhangabaú, via the ugly, wedding-cake **Teatro Municipal Opera House** and the **Viaduto do Chá** steel bridge riding over the small, dirty Vale de Anhangabaú park and the Avenida 23 de Maio and 9 de Julho highways.

Luz and north of the centre

Luz → *Metrô Luz or Metrô Tiradentes.*

Some of São Paulo's finest museums are to be found a few kilometres north of the city centre in the neighbourhood of Luz. The area is dominated by two striking 19th- and early 20th-century railway stations, the **Estação da Luz** ① *Praça da Luz 1, T0800-550121 for information on suburban trains*, and **Estação Julio Prestes** ① *Praça Julio Prestes 51*. The former marked the realization of a dream for O Ireneu Evangelista de Sousa, the Visconde de Mauá, who was Brazil's first industrialist. A visit to London in the 1840s convinced de Sousa that Brazil's future lay in rapid industrialization – a path he followed with the founding of an ironworks employing some 300 workers from England and Scotland. It made him a millionaire and in 1854 he opened his first railway, designed and run by the British. It linked Jundiaí, in the heart of the São Paulo coffee region, with Santos on the coast via what was then the relatively small city of São Paulo. The grandness of the Estação de Luz station, which was completed in 1900, attests to the fact that the city quickly grew wealthy by exploiting its position at the railway junction. By the time the Estação Julio Prestes was built, Britannia no longer ruled the railways. This station was modelled on Grand Central and Penn in New York. In 1999 the enormous 1000-sq-m grand hall was converted into the **Sala São Paulo** ① *Praça Julio Prestes 51, T011-3337 5414, for details of shows see www.guiasp.com.br or look in a copy of Veja*, the city's premier classical music venues and home to Brazil's best orchestra, the Orquestra Sinfônica do Estado de São Paulo.

The city's finest collection of Brazilian art lies 100 m from the Estação da Luz in the **Pinacoteca do Estado** ① *Praça da Luz 2, T011-3224 1000, www.pinacoteca.org.br, Tue-Sun 1000-1800 (last entry at 1730), US$3, excellent museum shop and café*. Here you will find works by Brazilian artists from the colonial and imperial eras, together with paintings by the founders of Brazilian modernism, such as Lasar Segall, Tarsila do Amaral, Candido Portinari and Alfredo Volpi. The gallery also contains sculpture by Rodin, Victor Brecheret and contemporary works by artists such as the Nipo-Brazilian painter Tomie Ohtake. The excellent photography gallery in the basement displays some of the world's greatest black-and-white photographers, many of whom are from Brazil. The museum overlooks the Parque da Luz, a green space dotted with modernist sculpture. Take care in this area after dark.

The Pinacoteca's sister gallery, the **Estação Pinacoteca** ① *Largo General Osório 66, T011-3337 0185, daily 1000-1730, US$2, free on Sat*, is just over 500 m west of the Pinacoteca along Rua Mauá, next to the Estação Julio Prestes. It houses 200 of the country's finest modernist paintings from the archive of the Fundação José e Paulina Nemirovsky, including further key pieces by Tarsila do Amaral, Emiliano Di Cavalcanti, Portinari Anita Malfatti, Victor Brecheret and Lasar Segall. International art includes Chagall, Picasso and Braque. There is an excellent air-conditioned café.

Black and white photography

One of the legacies of Brazil's love affair with France is an enduring tradition of beautifully observed and masterfully printed black-and-white documentary photography. Its most famous exponent, Sebastião Salgado, has won numerous international awards including the prestigious World Press Photo prize. But he is the tip of a large iceberg whose bulk is made-up of photographers little published outside of Brazil. José Bassit and Thiago Santana have both documented the rich tapestry of religious life that has changed little in centuries in the country's poor and arid interior. Claudia Andujar focuses on the Amazon and has produced remarkable, intimate and deeply touching images of the lives of the indigenous people and rural poor who live there, including series of double- or triple-exposed dream-like images portraits where faces and bodies mix with the landscape like an Australian aboriginal wall painting. The best places to see Brazilian photographic art are on the ground floor of the **Pinacoteca**, Praça da Luz 2, T011-3229 9844; the **Galeria Vermelho**, R Minas Gerais 350, Higienópolis, T011-3257 2033, www.galeriavermelho.com.br; and the **Íma Foto Galería**, R Fradique Coutinho 1239, Vila Madalena, T011-3816 1290, www.imafotogaleria.com.br.

Luz's other excellent museum is the **Museu de Arte Sacra** ① *Av Tiradentes 676, 400 m north of the Pinacoteca, next to Metrô Tiradentes, T011-3227 7687, http://artesacra. sarasa.com.br, Mon-Fri 1000-1700, Sat and Sun 1000-1900, US$2.* Housed in a functioning Conceptionist monastery, parts of which date from 16th century, it is a haven of peace. Displays include works by many of Brazil's masters, including Francisco Xavier de Brito who brought baroque to Brazil, his pupil, Aleijadinho, who carved Minas Gerais's most exquisite churches, Mestre Valentim, who was responsible for some of the finest work in Rio's churches, and paintings by Mestre (Manoel da Costa) Athayde, one of the country's most important 19th-century artists. There is also a haunting Afro-Brazilian São Bento (with blue eyes) and an extraordinarily detailed 18th-century Neapolitan nativity crib comprising almost 2000 pieces; it is the most important of its kind outside Italy.

Bom Retiro → *Metrô Luz.*

The district of Bom Retiro used to be a centre for industry, but since the 1960s the factories have been replaced by shops and small businesses. The streets of Jose Paulino and 25 de Marco are packed with bargain clothing stores and wholesalers, and it is one of the city's best areas for budget shopping. ▸▸ *See Shopping, page 220.*

Further afield, the **Memorial da América Latina** ① *Av Mário de Andrade 664, next to Metrô Barra Funda, T011-3823 9611, www.memorial.org.br, Tue-Fri 0900-2100, Sat 0900-1800, Sun 1000-1800, free,* was designed by **Oscar Niemeyer** and built in March 1989. Inside, under a glass floor, is a relief map of Central and South America. As well as a permanent exhibition of handicrafts from all over Latin America, there is a photo library, books, magazines, newspapers and films shown on video.

A few blocks west is **SESC Pompeia** ① *R Clélia 93, www.sescsp.org.br,* an arts complex, which together with SESC Vila Mariana showcases some of the best medium-sized musical acts in the city – names like João Bosco, CéU and Otto. It is a vibrant place, with a theatre, exhibitions, workshops, restaurant and café, as well as areas for sunbathing and watching television.

The revolution will not be bossa nova

Forget bossa, electronica, MPB, samba funk and the rest. The most exciting musical movement in Brazil by far is Brazilian rap. Don't for a minute think it is imitation USA. This is genuine protest music poured out in a range of Brazilian styles and infused not only with anger and outrage but also with hope and the possibility of real change. It is irresistibly funky, thick with the rhythms of samba, *maracatu*, capoeira, and samba rock. And unlike the cosy middle-class *tropicalismo* of Caetano Veloso it comes from the heart of the country – from the innumerable, innumerate majority, the marginalized of the urban shantytowns or *favelas*.

Rappers from Brazil's vast poor underclass use music to declaim their country's great social divide, its racial injustice and corrupt politicians. They sing of living conditions that make Detroit's 8 Mile look like Rodeo Drive. In the words of Racionais MC's:

60% of youth in the poor suburbs without criminal records have already suffered police violence; three of every four people killed by the police are black; in Brazilian Universities only 2% of students are black; every four hours, a young black person dies violently in São Paulo.

Solidarity born out of this increased awareness has led to the formation of community organizations or crews who dedicate themselves to various art forms from MC poetry to graffiti and dance and increasingly to community service work. Community projects like Grupo Afro Reggae in Rio and A Casa do Hip-Hop in São Paulo now function in most *favelas* and peripheral poor areas in Brazil's big cities offering educational workshops, classes, free concerts, and libraries. They are succeeding where government has failed – bringing many young people out of the drug trade into music.

Avenida Paulista, Liberdade and Jardins

Liberdade → *Metrô Liberdade.*

Liberdade was the first centre for the Japanese community in São Paulo; a city with more ethnic Japanese than any outside Japan. It lies directly south of the Praça da Sé but can easily be reached on foot. There are all manner of Asian shops selling everything from woks to *manga* and the streets are illuminated by lights designed like Japanese lanterns. A market selling Asian produce and food is held every Sunday in the Praça da Liberdade and there are many excellent Japanese restaurants.

The **Museu da Imigração Japonesa** ① *R São Joaquim 381, 3rd floor, T011-3209 5965, www.nihonsite.com/muse, Tue-Sun 1330-1730, US$3,* in the Japanese-Brazilian cultural centre is a modern, well-kept little museum with exhibitions telling the story of the Japanese migration to Brazil, including reconstructions of early Japanese Brazilian houses, artefacts and information panels. All are in Portuguese.

Avenida Paulista → *Metrô Vergueiro or Paraíso for the southeastern end of Paulista.*

Southwest of the Centro Histórico, **Avenida Paulista**, is lined by skyscrapers and is thick with six lanes of cars. It is one of São Paulo's classic postcard shots and locals like to compare it to Fifth Avenue in New York. In truth, it's more commercial and lined with functional buildings, most of which are unremarkable individually and awe-inspiring as a whole.

The avenue was founded in 1891 by the Uruguayan engineer Joaquim Eugênio de Lima, who wanted to build a Paulistano Champs-Élysées. After he built a mansion on

Avenida Paulista, many coffee barons followed suit and by the early 20th century, Paulista had become the city's most fashionable promenade. The mansions and the rows of stately trees that sat in front of them were almost all demolished in the 1940s and 1950s to make way for ugly office buildings, and in the 1980s these were in turn demolished as banks and multinationals established their headquarters here.

4 Avenida Paulista & Jardins

Sleeping 🛏

Emiliano **1** B2
Fasano **2** B2
Formule 1 **3** C3
George V **4** B2
Golden Tulip Park
  Plaza **5** C2
Ibis São Paulo Paulista **6** B3
Landmark Residence **8** B2
L'Hotel **7** C3
Paulista Garden **9** C2
Pousada Dona Zilah **10** B2
Pousada dos
  Franceses **11** C3

Renaissance **12** B3
Transamérica Ópera **13** B2
Unique & Skye Bar **14** C2

Eating 🍴

A Mineira **1** C3
Baalbeck **2** B2
Balneário das Pedras **3** A1
Charlô Bistro **5** B2
Cheiro Verde **6** B2
DOM **7** B2
Figueira Rubaiyat **16** B1
Fran's Café **8** C3
Gero **9** B1
Jun Sakamoto **10** A1

Kayomix **11** B2
La Tambouille **24** C1
Mani **25** B1
MASP **13** B3
Massimo **14** B3
Namesa **15** B2
Sattva **17** B2
Sujinho **18** A3

Bars & clubs 🍸

Balcão **21** A2
Finnegan's Pub **22** A1
Outs **23** B3
Studio SP **24** B3

500 metres (approx)
500 yards (approx)

The highlight of Avenida Paulista is the **Museu de Arte de São Paulo (MASP)** ① *Metrô Trianon-MASP, Av Paulista 1578, T011-3251 5644, www.masp.uol.com.br, Tue-Sun 1100-1800, US$5*. This is the most important gallery in the southern hemisphere, preserving some of Europe's greatest paintings. If it were in the US or Europe it would be as busy as the Prado or the Guggenheim, but here, aside from the occasional noisy group of schoolchildren, the gallery is invariably deserted. Even at weekends, visitors can stop and stare at a Rembrandt or a Velazquez at their leisure. France gets star-billing, with 11 Renoirs, 70 Degas, and a stream of works by Monet, Manet, Cezanne, Toulouse-Lautrec and Gauguin. Renaissance Italy is represented by a Raphael Resurrection, an impeccable Bellini and a series of exquisite late 15th-century icons. The remaining walls are adorned with paintings by Bosche, Goya, Van Dyck, Turner, Constable and many others, cherry-picked from post-War Europe.

On Sunday, an antiques fair is held in the open space beneath the museum (see Shopping page 220). Opposite MASP is the **Parque Tenente Siqueira Campos** ① *R Peixoto Gomide 949 and Av Paulista, daily 0700-1830*, also known as Parque Trianon, covering two blocks on either side of Alameda Santos. It is a welcome, luxuriant, green area located in what is now the busiest part of the city. The vegetation includes native plants typical of the *Mata Atlântica*. Next to the park is the smaller Praça Alexandre de Gusmão.

Consolação → *Metrô Consolação.*
Consolação, off the northeastern end of Avenida Paulista, is emerging as the edgiest and most exciting nocturnal neighbourhood in São Paulo. Until a few years it was home to little more than rats, sleazy strip bars, street-walkers and curb-crawlers, but now it harbours a thriving alternative weekend scene. Its untidy streets are lined with grafitti-scrawled shop fronts, the deep velvet-red of open bar doors, go-go clubs with heavy-set bouncers outside and makeshift street bars. On Fridays and Saturdays from 2200 a jostle of hundreds of young Paulistanos down bottles of cooler-fresh Bohemia beer at rickety metal tables. And lines of sharply dressed and well-toned 20- and 30-somethings queue to enter a gamut of fashionable bars, clubs and pounding gay venues, including one of Brazil's most exciting underground venues: **Studio SP** (see Bars and clubs, page 216).

Jardins → *Metrô Consolação.*
Immediately west of Paulista, an easy 10-minute walk from Consolação Metrô along Rua Haddock Lobo, is the plush neighbourhood of Jardins. There are no sights of note but this is by far the most pleasant area to stay in São Paulo. It is also the best place for shopping and has excellent casual and fine dining.

South of Jardins

There are no direct metrô stations for Ibirapuera but Metrô Ana Rosa is a 15-minute walk east of the park: turn right out of the station and walk due west along Avenida Conselheiro Rodrigo Alves and Avenida Dante Pazzanese. Any bus to DETRAN (the Driver and Vehicle licensing building, labelled in huge letters) stops opposite Ibirapuera.

Parque do Ibirapuera
The **Parque do Ibirapuera** ① *entrance on Av Pedro Álvares Cabral, daily 0600-1730*, was designed by architect Oscar Niemeyer and landscape artist Roberto Burle Marx for the city's fourth centenary in 1954. It is the largest of the very few green spaces in central São Paulo and its shady woodlands, lawns and lakes offer a breath of fresher air in a city that

Oscar Nieymeyer in São Paulo

São Paulo is home to many impressive buildings by South America's most important modernist architect, Oscar Niemeyer. Many have only opened to the public in the last few years.

→ **Auditório Ibirapuera** (Parque Ibirapuera), a stunning door-wedge shape with a sinuous portal entrance.

→ **Bienal buildings** (Parque Ibirapuera), home of Fashion Week and the Art Bienal; the serpentine walkways are fabulous.

→ **Edifício Copan** (Centro/Consolação), a tower built as a swirling wave.

→ **Ibirapuera museums and walkways** (Parque Ibirapuera), minimalist blocks with vast interior spaces linked by classic Niemeyer curving walkways.

→ **Memorial da América Latina** (Barra Funda), a gargantuan concrete wave between towering rectilinear monoliths.

→ **The Oca** (Parque Ibirapuera), a bright white concrete half-dome, in homage to indigenous communal houses.

→ **Sambódromo do Anhembi** (Anhembi), the stadium venue for São Paulo carnival built right after Rio's.

has only 4.6 sq m of vegetation per inhabitant. The park is also home to a number of museums and monuments and some striking Oscar Niemeyer buildings that were designed in the 1950s but are still being built today. These include the **Oca** ① *Portão 3, open for exhibitions*, a brilliant white polished concrete dome, built in homage to an indigenous Brazilian roundhouse. It stages major international art exhibitions and has an auditorium shaped like a giant wedge. The **Bienal buildings** ① *Portão 3, open for exhibitions*, are also by Niemeyer and house the city's flagship fashion and art events: the twice yearly **São Paulo fashion week** and the **Art Biennial**, the most important events of their kind in the southern hemisphere.

A **sculpture garden** separates the Bienal from the Oca; this garden is watched over by **O Museu de Arte Moderna (MAM)** ① *Portão 3, T011-5549 9688, www.mam.org.br, Tue, Wed, Fri 1200-1800, Thu 1200-2200, Sat and Sun 1000-1800, US$2*. This small museum showcases the best Brazilian contemporary art in temporary exhibitions. There is always something worth seeing and the gallery has an excellent restaurant. MAM is linked by a covered walkway to the **Museu Afro-Brasil** ① *Portão 10, T011-5579 0593, www.museuafrobrasil.com.br, Wed-Sun 1000-1800, free*, which lies inside Niemeyer's spectacular, stilted **Pavilhão Manoel da Nobrega** building and devotes more than 12,000 sq m to a celebration of black Brazilian culture with regular films, music, dance, and theatrical events.

A few hundred metres to the west of here, on the shores of the artificial lake, the **Planetário e Museu de Astronomia (Planetarium)** ① *Portão 10, T011-5575 5206, Sat and Sun 1200-1800, US$5*, was restored in 2006 and is now one of the most impressive in Latin America. Shows are in Portuguese.

Less than 100 m to the south, is the **Pavilhão Japonês** ① *Portão 10, T011-5573 6453, Sat and Sun 1000-1700, free except for exhibitions*. The building and gardens were designed in strict adherence to Japanese aesthetic principles, and materials were imported from Japan. The pavilion on the lower floor has an exhibition space devoted to Japanese-Brazilian and Japanese culture and a traditional Japanese tearoom upstairs.

The park also has a running track, football pitches and hosts regular concerts on Sundays. Those seeking something quieter on a Sunday can borrow a book from the portable library and read it in the shade of the **Bosque da Leitura** or 'reading wood'. Bicycles can be hired in the park (US$3 per hour).

Ibirapuera also has a few monuments of note. **O Monumento as Bandeiras**, which sits on the northern edge of the park, is a brutalist tribute to the marauding and bloodthirsty slave traders or *bandeirantes* who opened up the interior of Brazil. It was created by Brazil's foremost 20th-century sculptor, Victor Brecheret. The **Obelisco aos Héroes de 32**, on the eastern edge of the park, is a monumental Cleopatra's needle built in honour of the Paulistano rebels who died in 1932 when the dictator Getúlio Vargas crushed resistance to his Estado Novo regime.

Itaim, Vila Olímpia and Moema
Business mixes with pleasure in these plush neighbourhoods south of Jardins and near Ibirapuera park. By day they are filled with office workers; by night, especially at weekends, hundreds of street bars and clubs are busy with partying Paulistano professionals.

Brooklin and the New Business District
Brooklin's Avenida Engenheiro Luís Carlos Berrini has taken over from Avenida Paulista as the business centre of the new São Paulo. Many of the larger companies banks and international corporations now have their South American headquarters here, making this the best place to stay for business.

Parque do Estado (Jardim Botânico)
This large park housing the botanical and zoological gardens is 15 km south of the centre at **Água Funda** ① *Av Miguel Estefano, T011-3031 3687*. The **Jardim Botânico** ① *T011-5584 6300, Wed-Sun 0900-1700*, has a vast garden esplanade surrounded by magnificent stone porches, with lakes and trees and places for picnics, and a very fine orchid farm worth seeing during the flowering season (November to December). More than 19,000 different kinds of orchids are cultivated. There are orchid exhibitions in April and November. The astronomical **observatory** nearby is open to the public on Thursday afternoons. Howler monkeys, guans and toco toucans can be seen here towards the end of the day. To get there take the metrô to São Judas on the Jabaquara line, then take a bus.

Burle Marx Park ① *Av Dona Helena Pereira de Moraes 200, Morumbi, daily 0700-1900*, was designed by the famous landscape designer Burle Marx. It is the only place in the city where you can walk along trails in the *Mata Atlântica* (Atlantic rainforest).

West of Jardins

Vila Madalena and Pinheiros → *Metrô Madalena.*
Vila Madalena and neighbouring Pinheiros are São Paulo's East Village, Notting Hill or Prenzelauerburg. Streets are crammed with bars, restaurants and an array of the city's freshest designer labels, clambering over the steep hills and buzzing with young and arty middle class Paulistanos. Galleries such as **Choque Cultural**, www.choque cultural.co.uk, sell work by the city's increasingly famous grafitti artists. Rhythms pound out of myriad music venues, and the area attracts the rich and famous: Seu Jorge lives and drinks in Vila Madalena, as does leading avant garde musician, Max de Castro (see box, page 215).

Cidade Universitária
Instituto Butantã/Butantã Snake Farm and Museum ① *Av Dr Vital Brasil 1500, T011-3726 7222, Tue-Sun 0845-1615, US$1*, on the university campus is one of the most popular tourist attractions in São Paulo. The snakes are milked for their poison six times a day and

the antidotes made from the venom have greatly reduced deaths from snakebite in Brazil. The centre also deals with spider and scorpion venom, has a small hospital and is a biomedical research institute. Visitors are not likely to see the venom being milked, but there is a museum of poisonous animals, which is well organized and educational, with explanations in Portuguese and English. To get there from Praça da República take the bus marked 'Butantã' or 'Cidade Universitária' (Nos 701U or 792U) along Avenida Paulista, and ask to be let out at Instituto Butantã.

In the Prédio Novo da Reitoria, the **Museu de Arte Contemporânea (MAC)** ① *T011-3091 3039, www.mac.usp.br/mac, Tue-Sat 1200-1800, Sun 1000-1800, free*, has an important and beautifully presented collection of Brazilian and European modern art, with pieces by Braque, Picasso, Modigliani, Matisse and Tarsila do Amaral. Also in the university is the **Museu de Arqueologia e Etnologia (MAE)** ① *R Reitoria 1466, T011-3812 4001*, with a frowsty and ill-kept collection of Amazonian and ancient Mediterranean material.

On the west bank of the Rio Pinheiros, just southeast of the campus, is the palatial **Jockey Club de São Paulo** ① *Av Lineu de Paula Machado 1263, T011-3811 7799*, a racecourse in the Cidade Jardim area. Race meetings are held on Monday and Thursday at 1930 and on weekends at 1430. The racecourse is easily accessible by bus from Praça da República.

East of Jardins

Parque da Independência
In the suburb of Ipiranga (a Tupi-Guarani word meaning 'red clay'), 5.5 km southeast of the city centre, the **Parque da Independência** contains the famous **Monumento à Independência** to commemorate the declaration of Brazilian Independence. Beneath the monument is the **imperial chapel** ① *Tue-Sun 1300-1700*, containing the tomb of the first emperor, Dom Pedro I, and Empress Leopoldina. The monument was the second to be built to commemorate the centenary of Independence in 1922. The little house of **Casa do Grito** ① *Tue-Sun 0930-1700*, is a replica of the house where Dom Pedro I spent the night before his famous Cry of Ipiranga, 'Independence or Death', which declared Brazil's separation from Portugal (see Background, page 778). At the time when Independence was declared, Ipiranga was outside the city's boundaries, in an area where bricks were made, on the main trade route between Santos and São Paulo.

The **Museu Paulista** ① *www.mp.usp.br, Tue-Sun 0900-1645, US$1*, is housed in a huge palace at the top of the park. The original building, later altered, was the first monument to Independence. The museum contains old maps, traditional furniture, collections of old coins, religious art and rare documents, and has a department of indigenous ethnology. Behind the museum is the **Horto Botânico/Ipiranga Botanical Garden** ① *Tue-Sun 0900-1700*, and the **Jardim Francês**, designed as a garden for plant study, now a recreational area. There is a light and sound show on Brazilian history in the park on Wednesday, Friday and Saturday at 2030. To get there, take either bus No 478P (Ipiranga–Pompéia for return) from Ana Rosa, or take bus No 4612 from the Praça da República.

Excursions from São Paulo

Santo Amaro Dam (Old Lake) and Interlagos
The **Brazilian Grand Prix** is staged at Interlagos, www.faspnet.com.br, overlooking a vast artificial lake set in remnant forest. Information on races is available from the tourist office or visit www.guiasp.com.br. See also box, page 219.

Paranapiacaba

This tiny 19th-century town, nestled in the cloudforest of the Serra do Mar about 50 km southeast of São Paulo, was built by English railway workers who constructed the São Paulo–Santos railway. Almost all of the houses are made of wood and many look like they belong in suburban Surrey. There is a small railway museum and a handful of little *pousadas* and restaurants. It is easily visited in a day trip from São Paulo.

Suburban trains leave from the Estação da Luz every 15 minutes for Rio Grande da Serra (Line 10 – the turquoise line), US1.50, 55 minutes. From Rio Grande da Serra station, bus No 424 runs to Paranapiacaba hourly during the week, every 30 minutes at weekends. The journey is around one hour. A tourist train is due to start running hourly from Estação da Luz on Sundays from 2009.

Embu

This colonial town, 28 km southwest of São Paulo, has become a centre for artists and craftsmen. The town is on a hill, surrounded by industry and modern developments. The centre is quite small; many of the old houses are brightly coloured and most contain arts, furniture, souvenir or antiques shops. To get to Embu take a São Paulo–Pinheiros bus from Clínicas, which follow the main highway (40 minutes, US$0.80). Alight at Largo 21 de Abril in Embu. To return to São Paulo, walk up Rua da Matriz from 21 de Abril, turn left down Avenida Junior, then left again on Rua Solano Trindade to a junction where the buses stop.

Campos do Jordão → *Colour map 5, A6. Phone code: 012. Population: 38,000.*

This tacky mountain resort between Rio de Janeiro and São Paulo, 1628 m high in the Serra da Mantiqueira, is full of very ugly mock-Alpine hotels set in denuded hills. Although it is popular with Paulistanos there is little reason to come here except perhaps for the classical music and dance festivals in June and July. Walking is far better in Itatiaia or Visconde de Mauá. The **tourist office** ① *T011-3664 3525, www.camposdojordao.tur.br*, is in the alpine-looking gateway to the city, the **Portal da Cidade**. There are plenty of hotels and restaurants on and around the main street and banks with ATMs and money-changing services. Regular buses run to and from São Paulo.

◉ São Paulo listings

Hotel and guesthouse prices
LL over US$200 **L** US$151-200 **AL** US$116-150
A US$81-115 **B** US$51-80 **C** US$36-50
D US$21-35 **E** US$10-20 **F** under US$10

Restaurant prices
††† over US$20 †† US$8-20 † under US$8

⊜ Sleeping

São Paulo has the best hotels in Latin America and by far the best in Brazil. There are designer hotels that Ian Shrager would be proud of including business towers that combine all the requisite facilities with an almost personal touch. However, rooms are expensive and while there are some reasonable budget options they are not in the best locations. Sampa (as São Paulo is affectionately known) is a place where you have to spend money to enjoy yourself. The best places to stay are **Jardins** (the most affluent area) and **Paulista** (close to one of the business centres). Business travellers will find good hotels on **Faria Lima** and **Av Luís Carlos Berrini** (in the new centre in the south of the city). Some of the better hostels are in seemingly random locations or are in the seedy centre, which is an undesirable place to be at night.

Centro Histórico *p198, map p200*

AL Othon Palace, R Líbero Badaró 190, T011-3291 5000, www.othon.com.br. The only business hotel of quality in the Triângulo; in a 1950s heritage building.

A Gran Corona, Basílio da Gama 101, T011-3214 0043, www.grancorona.com.br. An old-fashioned but fairly well-kept hotel recently refurbished and with internet in every room. In a small street just off Praça da República.

C-D Itamarati, Av Dr Vieira de Carvalho 150, T011-3474 4133, www.hotelitamarati.com.br. A long-standing cheapie popular with budget travellers. The rooms are simple white cubes with little more than a bed and the whole building has seen better days.

D Formule 1, Av São João 1140, Centre, just off Praça da República, T011-6878 6400, www.accor.com.br. The safest and most salubrious deal in the city centre. A range of modern, functional and anonymous little a/c boxes. Take breakfast elsewhere unless you're fond of hydrogenated vegetable fats.

Av Paulista and Jardins *p204, maps p196 and p205*

LL Emiliano, R Oscar Freire 384, T011-3069 4369, www.emiliano.com.br. Together with the **Fasano** and **Unique**, these are best suites in the city: bright, light and beautifully designed with attention to every detail. No pool but a relaxing small spa. Excellent Italian restaurant, location and service.

LL Fasano, R Vittorio Fasano 88, T011-3896 4077, www.fasano.com.br. One of the world's great hotels, which looks like a modernist gentleman's club designed by Armani. There's a fabulous pool and the best formal haute-cuisine restaurant in Brazil. The lobby bar is a wonderful place to arrange a meeting. Excellent position in Jardins.

LL L'Hotel, Av Campinas 266, T011-2183 0500, www.lhotel.com.br. Part of the **Leading Hotels of the World** group, with a series of suites decorated with mock-European paintings and décor, in emulation of the mock-European look of Upper East Side New York hotels. The St Regis this is not,

but it's comfortable, offers good service and is a convenient base for Paulista.

LL Renaissance, Alameda Santos 2233 (at Haddock Lobo), T011-3069 2233, www.marriott.com. The best business hotel off Av Paulista with standard business rooms, a good spa, gym, pool and 2 squash courts. There are excellent business and conference facilities including a full business centre, secretarial services and airline booking.

LL Unique, Av Brigadeiro Luís Antonio 4700, Jardim Paulista, T011-3055 4700, www.hotel unique.com. The most ostentatiously designed hotel in the country: an enormous half moon on concrete uprights with curving floors, circular windows and beautiful use of space and light. The bar on the top floor is São Paulo's answer to the LA Sky Bar and is filled with the beautiful and famous after 2130.

LL-AL George V, R Jose Maria Lisboa 1000, T011-3088 9822, www.george-v.com.br. Proper apartments of 60-180 sq m, with living rooms, fully equipped kitchens (with dishwashers and washing machines), huge bathrooms, closets and comprehensive business services. Shared facilities include sauna, indoor pool and modern gym. Special deals available on the website.

A Golden Tulip Park Plaza, Alameda Lorena 360, T011-3058 4055, www.parkplaza.com.br. Modern tower with apartments of 30 sq m, spa and well-equipped gym. Good value.

A Transamérica Ópera, Alameda Lorena 1748, T011-3062 2666, www.transamerica flats.com.br. Conservatively decorated but elegant and well-maintained modern flats of 42 sq m in a tower between the heart of Jardins and Av Paulista. At the bottom end of this price range.

B Landmark Residence, Alameda Jaú 1607, T011-3082 8677, www.landmark residence.com.br. Spacious apartments with hotel catalogue furnishings and a shared gym, gardens and modest business centre. Good location.

B-C Ibis São Paulo Paulista, Av Paulista 2355, T011-3523 3000, www.accorhotels.com.br. Great value.

Modern, business-standard rooms with a/c in a tower right on Av Paulista. Cheaper at weekends. Online reservations.

C Formule 1, R Vergueiro 1571, T011-5085 5699, www.accorhotels.com.br. Another great-value business-style hotel, with a/c apartments big enough for 3 (making this an **E** option for those in a group). Right next to Paraíso Metrô in a safe area.

C Paulista Garden, Alameda Lorena 21, T/F011-3885 8498, www.paulistagardenhotel.com.br. Small, simple rooms with a/c, cable TV and fridges. Close to Ibirapuera Park.

C Pousada Dona Zilah, Alameda Franca 1621, Jardim Paulista, T011-3062 1444, www.zilah.com. Little *pousada* in a renovated colonial house with plain but well-maintained rooms and common areas decorated with thought and a personal touch. Excellent location, bike rental and generous breakfast included. Triple rooms available (**D**).

D-F Pousada dos Franceses, R dos Franceses 100, Bela Vista, T011-3262 4026, www.pousadadosfranceses.com.br. Price per person. A plain little *pousada* 10 mins' walk from Brigadeiro Metrô, with dorms, doubles and singles. Free internet, TV room and breakfast included.

South of Jardins *p206, map p196*
Cogonhas and the airport
This area lies south of the centre and Ibirapuera next to Congonhas airport and Brooklin.

D ACE Hostel, R Gastão da Cunha 253, Congonhas airport, T011-5034 2472, www.bedandbreakfast.com.br. Friendly pocket-sized hostel in a brightly painted residential house. Services include TV, DVD and movies, broadband internet, kitchen, laundry book exchange and pick-up. Tours of São Paulo available.

E-F Praça da Árvore IYHA, R Pageú 266, Saúde, T011-5071 5148, www.spal bergue.com.br. 2 mins from Praça da Arvore Metrô. Well-kept *pousada* in a quiet back street. Friendly and helpful. kitchen, laundry and internet service. Overpriced.

Brooklin and the New Business District *p208, map p196*
This is São Paulo's new business capital. Most hotels are to be found on Av Brigadeiro Faria Lima and Av Luís Carlos Berrini.

LL-L Grand Hyatt São Paulo, Av das Nações Unidas 13301, T011-6838 1234, www.saopaulo.hyatt.com. A superb business hotel close to Av Luís Carlos Berrini, which successfully fuses corporate efficiency and requisite services with designer cool. Spa, pool, state-of-the-art business centre and marvellous views from the upper-floor suites.

AL-L Blue Tree Towers, Av Brigadeiro Faria Lima 3989, Vila Olímpia, T011-3896 7544, www.bluetree.com.br. Modern business hotel with discreetly designed rooms and excellent service. Ideally positioned for Faria Lima's business district and the restaurants and nightlife of Vila Olímpia and Itaim. Pool, massage, gym, sauna and well-equipped business centre.

Excursions from São Paulo *p209*
LL Unique Garden Spa, Estrada 3500, Serra da Cantareira, T011-4486 8724, www.unique garden.com.br. The über-cool style of hotel **Unique** (see page 211) transposed into a natural setting of the Serra da Cantareira subtropical forest, 40 mins north of São Paulo. The buildings are equally impressive, with Ruy Ohtake's iron-grey post-industrial half-moon replaced with a series of Frank Lloyd Wright inspired post-modernist bungalows. The spa treatments are wonderful. Shuttles can be organized through hotel **Unique**.

🍴 Eating

Those on a budget can eat to their stomach's content in per kilo places or, if looking for cheaper still, in *padarias* (bakeries). There is one of these on almost every corner. They all serve sandwiches such as *Misto Quentes*, *Beirute's* and *Americanos* – delicious Brazilian burgers made from decent meat and served with ham, egg, cheese or salad. They always have good coffee, juices, cakes and *almoços* (set lunches) for a very economical price. Most have a designated seating area, either at the *padaria* bar or in an adjacent room; you aren't expected to eat on your feet as you are in Rio. Restaurants in São Paulo are safe on the stomach. Juices are made with mineral or filtered water.

Centro Histórico *p198, map p200*
Restaurants in the old centre tend to be open during lunchtime only; there are many *per* kilo options and *padarias*.
Terraço Italia, Av Ipiranga 344, T011-3257 6566. Average and overpriced Italian restaurant but with the best views in the city. Come for a coffee, although there's a minimum charge of US$10.
Café da Pinacoteca, Pinacoteca Museum, Praça da Luz 2, T011-3326 0350. Portuguese-style café with marble floors and mahogany balconies. Great coffee and cakes.

Liberdade *p204*
Gombe, R Tomas Gonzaga 22, T011-3209 8499. Renowned for grilled tuna and various noodle dishes.
Sushi Yassu, R Tomas Gonzaga 98, T011-3209 6622. The best of Liberdade's traditional Japanese restaurants. Excellent sushi/sashimi combinations.

Av Paulista and Jardins *p204, map p205*
Charlô Bistro, R Barão de Capanema 440 (next to **DOM**), Jardins, T011-3088 6790, with another branch at the high-society set **Jockey Club**, Av Lineu de Paula Machado 1263, Cidade Jardim, T011-3034 3682. One of the premier VIP and old family haunts in the city. Run by a scion of one of the city's establishment families. Decked out in tribute to a Paris brasserie and with food to imitate.
DOM, R Barão de Capanema 549, Jardins, T011-3088 0761. Jardin's evening restaurant of the moment. Alex Attala has won the coveted *Veja* several times. Contemporary food, fusing

Brazilian ingredients with French and Italian styles and served in a large open modernist dining room to the sharply dressed.
Fasano, Fasano Hotel (see Sleeping), R Fasano, T011-3896 4077, www.fasano.com.br. Long regarded as the best restaurant for gourmets in São Paulo. A huge choice of modern Italian and French cooking, modelled on the best of Milan from chef Salvatore Loi. An intimate space in a magnificent room where diners have their own low-lit booths and are served by flocks of black-tie waiters. Exemplary wine list. Formal dress.
Figueira Rubaiyat, R Haddock Lobo 1738, T011-3063 3888. The most interesting of the **Rubaiyat** restaurant group, with steaks prepared by Argentinian chef, Francis Mallman. Very lively for lunch on a Sun and remarkable principally for the space: open walled, light and airy and under a huge tropical fig tree.
Gero, R Haddock Lobo 1629, T011-3064 0005. Fasano's version of a French bistro, but serving pasta and light Italian food. Ever-so-casual design by architect Aurelio Martinez Flores and an evening clientele that includes some of the best-known faces in São Paulo high society. Be prepared for a long wait at the bar alongside people who are there to be seen. No reservations.
La Tambouille, Av 9 de Julho 5925, Jardim Europa, T011-3079 6276. The favourite Franco-Italian restaurant of the city's old money society. Chef Andre Fernandes' signature dishes are the saffron linguini with fresh mussels and prawn sauce and the brie ravioli with rocket and pinoli infused with white truffles. Excellent wine list.
Massimo, Alameda Santos 1826, Cerqueira César, Jardins, T011-3284 0311. One of São Paulo's longest-established Italian restaurants serving northern Italian food to the city's politicians and business executives. Credit cards not accepted, despite the costly price.
A Mineira, Alameda Joaquim Eugenio de Lima 697, Jardins, T011-3283 2349. Self-service Minas food by the kilo. Lots of choice. *Cachaça* and pudding included in the price.

♚♚♚ **Baalbeck**, Alameda Lorena 1330, Jardins, T011-3088 4820. Lebanese cooking vastly superior to its setting. Great falafel.

♚♚♚ **Fran's Café**, Av Paulista 358, and all over the city. Open 24 hrs. The Brazilian equivalent of **Starbuck's**, but with decent, strong, richly flavoured coffee and a menu of light eats.

♚♚♚ **Kayomix**, R da Consolação 3215, Jardins, T011-3082 2769. Brazilian-oriental fusions such as salmon taratare with shimeji and shitake.

♚♚♚ **Namesa**, R da Consolação 2967, Jardins, T011-3088 7498. Great little gourmet snacks such as wild boar pâté with pistachio pesto, created by the chef from **DOM**.

♚♚♚ **Restaurante do MASP**, Av Paulista 1578, T011-3253 2829. In the basement of the museum (see page 206), reasonably priced standards such as lasagne and stroganoff, often accompanied by live music.

♚♚♚ **Sattva**, R da Consolação 2904, Jardins, T011-3083 6237. Light vegetarian curries, stir fries, salads and pastas.

♚♚♚ **Sujinho**, R da Consolação 2068, Consolação, T011-3256 8026. South American beef in large portions. Other carnivorous options available.

♚ **Cheiro Verde**, R Peixoto Gomide 1413, Jardins, T011-289 6853 (lunch only). Hearty vegetarian food, such as vegetable crumble in gorgonzola sauce and wholewheat pasta with buffalo mozzarella and sundried tomato.

Itaím, Vila Olímpia and Moema
p208, map p196

These areas, south of the centre, have ultra-trendy restaurants with beautiful people posing in beautiful surroundings. We include only a handful of the best.

♚♚♚ **348 Parrilla Porteña**, R Comendador Miguel Calfat, 348, Vila Olímpia, T011-3849 2889. An Argentinian restaurant with the best steak in the country from the choicest cuts available only on export from Buenos Aires. The *ojo del bife* cuts like brie and collapses in the mouth like wafered chocolate. The accompanying wines are equally superb, especially the 2002 Cheval dos Andes. Great, unpretentious atmosphere.

♚♚♚ **Boo**, R Viradouro 132, Itaim Bibi, T011-3078 7477. Opposite **Kosushi**, with a carbon-copy crowd, Luso-Asian cooking and a beautiful garden setting.

♚♚♚ **Buddha Bar**, Villa Daslu, Av Chedid Jafet 131, Vila Olímpia, T011-3044 6181. Fashionable São Paulo's current favourite restaurant is a vast, clubby space dominated by a massive mood-lit Buddha sitting above Daslu's new flagship department store. The food is Brazilian-Asian-light Mediterranean fusion by award-winning chef Bel Coelho who has been causing a stir in São Paulo kitchens since she apprenticed with Laurent Suaudeau at the tender age of 17. Since then she's graduated from New York's Culinary Institute of America, worked in two more of São Paulo's finest kitchens (the **Fasano** and **DOM**), for Gordon Ramsay and most recently at the 2-star Michelin Celler de Can Roca in Girona. Bel recommends her *robalo crocante com pupunha assada e molho de castanha de caju* (crispy bass with roasted pupunha palm berry and Brazil nut and cashew sauce).

♚♚♚ **Kinoshita**, R Jacques Félix 405, Vila Nova Conceição, T011-3849 6940, www.restaurantekinoshita.com.br. Tsuyoshi Murakami offers the best menu of traditional cooked or Kappo cuisine in Brazil, dotted with creative fusion dishes in a Nobu vein. His cooking utilizes only the freshest ingredients and includes a sumptuous degustation menu with delights such as tuna marinated in soya, ginger and garlic, served with ponzo sauce and garnished with Kaiware (sprouted daikon radish seeds). Murakami trained in the ultra-traditional 100-year-old **Ozushi** restaurant in Shambashi Tokyo, **Shubu Shubu** in New York and **Kyokata** in Barcelona.

♚♚♚ **Kosushi**, R Viradouro 139, Itaim Bibi, T011-3167 7272. The first of São Paulo's chic Japanese restaurants, which began life in Liberdade and is now housed in a beautifully designed Asian modernist space. The rich and famous come here to be seen. Great sushi combinations.

♚♚♚ **Parigi**, R Amauri 275, Itaim, T011-3167 1575. One of the premier places to be seen; celebrity couples come here for intimate

Max de Castro recommends

Max de Castro (www.myspace.com/maxdecastro) is São Paulo's most exciting avante garde musician. His 2005 album *Max De Castro* is a classic and no one knows the city better. Here are his personal recommendations for visitors wanting to get a taste of the real São Paulo:

→ Visit the **Galeria Choque Cultural** (see page 208). For me this is the most interesting place in the city. Originally a graffiti gallery, it supports our avant garde and post-modern artistic movements (graffiti, design, sculpture) and showcases street art and the most sophisticated modern artistic developments.

→ **Hang out in Vila Madalena.** This is the city's most interesting neighbourhood, with independent fashion shops, great bars and wonderful restaurants.

→ Go to a **Roda de Samba**, a traditional samba circle. The *samba de vela* (www.sambadavela.com.br) is very lively and has produced many new artists and composers since in began in 2000. The show begins when a candle is lit in the centre of the circle. Extemporaneous *sambistas* play until it goes out.

→ On the last Sunday of every month you can catch the *samba da laje* (www.overmundo.com.br/agenda/samba-da-laje) in Vila Santa Catarina. The women of the **Senhora Generosa** community gather here to make a delicious *feijoada*, which only costs around US$3. Then the famous samba show starts as it has for the last 10 years, with the men on the drums and the women from the community singing.

---

public-view Franco-Italian dining. The menu also has classical French dishes such as *coq au vin*. Attractive dining room, beautifully lit, and decked out in lush dark wood.

Vila Madalena and Pinheiros *p208*
The streets of Vila Madalena are lined with restaurants and cafes – many on Aspicuelta and Girassol. Pinheiros has some of the finest fine dining restaurants in the city.
♔♔♔ **Balneário das Pedras**, R Lisboa 191, Pinheiros, T011-3082 4344. Ex-formula one driver Pedro Paulo Diniz and celebrity chef Cássio Machado seem to be vying with each other to produce the most effortlessly relaxed but designer-crafted eatery in São Paulo. Machado is the latest to throw down the gauntlet with this retro 1970s lounge-bar-cum-rustic-chic restaurant designed by Juarez Puig. It's a gourmand's address, just down the road from Jun Sakamoto's celebrated sushi house, but the crowd is far from foodie: models and preening playboys sipping sake caipirinhas on the faux-jaguar skin sofas or glancing at each other over their three-sauce tuna and prawn

confit with bergamasca polenta in the tinkling heliconia-filled garden restaurant out back.
♔♔♔ **Jun Sakamoto**, R Lisboa 55, Pinheiros, T011-3088 6019. Japanese cuisine with a French twist. Superb fresh ingredients, some of it flown in especially from Asia and the USA. The dishes of choice are the degustation menu and the duck breast teppaniyaki.
♔♔♔ **Mani**, R Joaquim Antunes 210, Pinheiros, T011-3085 4148. Superior light Mediterranean menu, which utilizes Brazilian ingredients and perfectly complements the waistlines of the celebrity crowd. Daniel Redondo and partner Helena Rizzo have worked in Michelin-starred restaurants in Europe.

🟠 Bars and clubs

→ *See Music and dance central colour section.*
São Paulo has more nocturnal panache than Rio. There is great live music on most nights of the week. Large concert venues such as the **Pacaembu Stadium** host the likes of U2 or Ivete Sangalo. Medium-sized venues such

as **Credicard Hall**, are played by acts such as Caetano Veloso, Gilberto Gil and Chico Buarque. Smaller venues include **SESC's** (cultural centres with excellent concert halls), and are found in Vila Mariana and Pompéia. They host smaller, classy artists like Otto, Naná Vasconcelos, João Bosco and Seu Jorge. It is also worth checking out **Bourbon Street**, **Urbano** and **Grazie a Dio** for emerging acts such as Tutti Baê and Mombojó.

DJs like Marky and the sadly deceased Suba have made the São Paulo club scene world famous. Marky is resident DJ at the **Lov.E Club** (see under Vila Olímpia). Fri's biggest party is **Vapour at the Prime Club** (see below). Other fashionable spots include **30Hz at Jive**, Alameda Barros 376, Higienópolis on Sat, T011-3824 0097, and **The Bass**, R Vitória 810, City Centre, T011-3337 1915, on Sun.

The city is dotted with bars serving cold lager beer or *chope* (pronounced 'chopee'). Almost all serve food and many have live music. You won't have too much difficulty finding one, especially if you head to Vila Madalena, Itaim or Vila Olímpia. Beer and snacks are also available at the bar in any *padaria* (bakery).

Av Paulista and Jardins *p204, map p205*
Jardins has a few bars, the most famous of which are in the better hotels.
Bar Balcão, R Doutor Melo Alves 150, T011-3063 6091. After-work meeting place, very popular with young professionals and media types who gather on either side of the long low wooden bar, which winds its way around the room like a giant snake.
Barretto, in the Fasano Hotel (see Sleeping). A rather conservative atmosphere with heavy dark wood, mirrors and cool live bossa jazz. The crowd is mostly the Cuban cigar type with a sprinkling of the tanned and toned, in figure-enhancing designer labels.
Emiliano Bar, Emiliano Hotel (see Sleeping). Similar crowd to **Skye** but despite its popularity, it can feel like a sterile corridor rather than an intimate space. DJs play on Fri nights.

Finnegan's Pub, R Cristiano Viana 358, Pinheiros, T011-3062 3232, www.finnegan. com.br. One of São Paulo's Irish bars; every city has one. This one is actually run and owned by an Irishman and is very popular with ex-pats.
Skye, the rooftop bar at the **Unique Hotel** (see Sleeping). Another fashionable spot with a definite door policy. The views of glistening skyscrapers pocked by patches of green and red tile are wonderful.

Consolação *p206*
Clube Royal, R Consolação 222, T011-3129 9804, www.royalclub.com.br. The latest funk and rare groove club on the young and need-to-be-seen alternative São Paulo circuit is decorated as only a Brazilian club could be – as a faux English pub with 'Picasso-inspired retro-erotic cubism' in a bright Brazilian *tropicália* of colours.
Outs, R Augusta 486, T011-6867 6050, www.clubeouts.com. One of the bastions of the alternative, more rock-orientated scene with a mix of DJs playing everything from UK indie to bizarre Brazilian rock-groove-samba fusions, *mangue beat* and death metal reggae from the Amazon.
Studio SP, R Augusta 591, T011-3129 7040 www.studiosp.org. A show hall on the neighbourhood's main thoroughfare. Turning up for the support act (usually before 2200) means getting in for free to see the main show. Both are invariably a diversion; with a mix of great underground acts. Bands like Trash pour Quatro (www.trashpour4.com) offer *bossa nova* re-workings of kitsch classics like *Material Girl*, in the spirit of Berk and the Virtual Band. Singers like Andreia Dias (www.andreia dias.com.br) offer smoky, seductive electronica mixed with lilting Brazilian rhythms. And they intersperse with harder *mangue beat* acts like Mombojo from Pernambuco (www.mombojo.com.b) who thrash out energetic rap rock powered by pile-driver *maracatu* rhythms or riot *carimbó-samba* metal from Amazonians Madame Saatan (www.myspace.com/madamesaatan).

Vila Madalena and Pinheiros *p208*
Vila Madalena and adjacent Pinheiros lie just
northeast of Jardins. A taxi from Jardins is
about US$7; there is also a metrô station, but
this closes by the time the bars get going.
These suburbs are the favourite haunts of São
Paulo 20-somethings, more hippy chic than
Itaim, less stuffy than Jardins. This is the best
part of town for live Brazilian music and
uniquely Brazilian close dances such as *forró*;
as opposed to international club sounds. It can
feel grungy and informal but is buzzing. The
liveliest streets are **Aspicuelta** and **Girassol**.
A Marcenaria, R Fradique Coutinho 1378,
T011-3032 9006, www.amarcenaria.com.br.
This is the bar of choice for the young, single
lovers of Brazilian rock who gather here from
2130; the dance floor fills up at around 2300.
Bambu, R Purpurina 272, Vila Madalena,
T011-3031 2331, www.bambubrasi
bar.com.br. A kind of backland desert jig
called *forró* has everyone up and dancing
in this slice of mock-Bahia, with live
northeastern accordion and *zabumba*
drum bands in the front room and a hippy
middle-class student crowd downing
industrial strength *caipirinhas* out back.
Casa de Francisca, R José Maria Lisboa 190
at Brigadeiro Luís Antônio, T011-3493 5717,
www.casadefrancisca.blogspot.com. Emerging
acts Luz Marina and her partner Maurício
Oliveira (www.myspace.com/luzmarinaluz) –
play at this smoky, little café bar on a quiet
side street. Luz plays a kind of folk meets
psychedelia reminiscent of fellow São
Paulo songstress and Latin Grammy Award
nominee CéU (www.ceumusic.com).
DiQuinta, R Baumann 1435, T011-5506 0100,
www.diquinta.com.br. Mainstream medium-
sized acts like exciting Cuban-Brazilian bolero-
meets-bossa newcomer Marina de la Riva
(www.marinadelariva.com.br) or samba funk
stalwarts Tutti Baê (www.tuttibae.com.br),
Clube do Balanco (clubedobalanco.uol.com.br)
and Funk Como le Gusta (www.funkcomole
gusta.com) play here and at other venues in
Vila Madalena like Grazie o Dio. This club is
one of the few to be busy on a Thu night.

Grazie a Dio, R Girassol, 67, T011-3031 6568,
www.grazieadio.com.br. The best bar in Vila
Madalena to hear live music – there's a
different band every night with samba on
Sun. Great for dancing. Always packed.
Mood, R Teodoro Sampaio 1109, T011-3060
9010. Euro-style club with the latest sounds
and DJs like Mau Mau and Felipe Venancio.
Posto 6, R Aspicuelta 644, Vila Madalena,
T011-3812 7831. An imitation Rio de Janeiro
boteco with attractive crowds and backdrop
of bossa nova and MPB. Busy from 2100.
Tocador de Bolacha, R Patizal 72, T011-3815
7639, www.tocadordebolacha.com.br. Classic
samba, bossa nova and rock discs adorn the
walls at this cosy little bar, and table mats for
the bar food are album covers in plastic sleeves.
Chorinho (a kind of Brazilian ragtime) and
samba bands play in the tiny back room from
Wed night and there's always an eclectic crowd,
from stoned students to swinging 60 year olds.
Urbano R Cardeal Arcoverde 614, Pinheiros,
T011-3085 1001, www.urbano.com.br. São
Paulo's premiere dance club, modelled on
a London club with a lounge bar area, huge
dancefloor and a combination of live bands
and DJs. Popular with musicians and creative
industry 20- and 30-somethings.
Vapour at the Prime Club, R dos Pinheiros
783, Pinheiros, T011-308 7466. Big party on Fri.

Itaím, Vila Olímpia and Moema
p208, map p196
This area, just south of Ibirapuera and north
of the new centre, is about US$10 by taxi
from Jardins and US$15 from the Centre,
but well worth the expense of getting here.
It is packed with street-corner bars, which are
great for a browse. The bars here, although
informal, have a style of their own, lively
and varied crowds and decent service. The
busiest streets for a bar wander are **R Atilio
Inocenti** near the junction of Av Juscelino
Kubitschek and Av Brigadeiro Faria Lima,
Av Hélio Pellegrino and **R Araguari**,
which runs behind it.
Bourbon Street, R dos Chanés 127, Moema,
T011-5095 6100, www.bournbonstreet.

com.br. Great little club with acts like funkster Tutti Bae and international acts like BB King.

Café de la Musique, Av Presidente Juscelino Kubitschek 1400, Itaim T0 11-3079 5588, www.cafedelamusique.com.br. Spaces in this übercool dance club owned by celebrity lothario Alvaro Garnero are decked-out by three of São Paulo's most reknowned designers; Naomi Campbell is a regular.

Columbia, R Estados Unidos 1570. Lively. **Hell's Club** downstairs. Opens 0400, techno, wild.

Disco, R Professor Atílio Inocennti 160, Itaim, T011-3078 0404, www.clubdisco.com.br. One of the city's plushest high society discos and a favourite with leading socialites and models, especially during fashion week. The decor is by Isay Weinfeld who designed the Fasano, and the music standard Eurotrash and US club sounds.

Liquid Lounge, Av Hélio Pellegrino 801, Vila Olímpia, T011-3849 5014, www.liquid lounge.com.br. Pulsing European-style dance club with a smart bar area. Always busy.

Na Mata Café, R da Mata 70, Itaim, T011-3079 0300, www.namata.com.br. Popular flirting and pick-up spot for 20- and 30-something rich kids who gyrate in the dark dance room to a variety of Brazilian and European dance tunes and select live bands.

Brooklin and the New Business District

Lotus, Av das Nações Unidas 12599, Brooklin Novo, T011-3043 7130, www.lotussp.com.br. Only 400 are allowed into this jewel-box space that's a sister-club to the New York Lotus. It looks like a film set from a latter day Clockwork Orange and they're all Brazilian 'A' list so make sure you get your concierge to book for you.

Further afield

The Week, R Guaicurus 324, Lapa, T011-3872 9966, www.theweek.com.br. All 6000 sq m of this cavernous split-level progressive trance club are heaving, especially the lush VIP room at the fashionable Babylon party on Sat nights. When it gets too sweaty there's a pool, so pack your trunks.

⊕ Entertainment

São Paulo *p192, maps p196, p200 and p205*
For listings of concerts, theatre, museums, galleries and cinema visit www.guiasp.com.br, or look in the *Guia da Folha* section of *Folha de São Paulo*, and the *Veja São Paulo* section of the weekly news magazine *Veja*.

Art galleries

Casa da Fazenda, Morumbi, exhibits in 19th-century house. **Espaço Cultural Ena Beçak**, R Oscar Freire 440. **Galeria São Paulo**, R Estados Unidos 1456.

Cinema

Entrance is usually half price on Wed; normal seat price is US$3 in the centre, US$5-6 in R Augusta, Av Paulista and Jardins. There is no shortage of multi-screen cinemas in the city showing the latest releases, eg **Belas Artes**, R da Consolação 2423. There are also cine clubs, eg **Cine SESC**, R Augusta 2075; **Espaço Unibanco**, R Augusta 1470/1475, and cinemas at the **Museu da Imagem e do Som**, **Centro Cultural Itaú** and **Centro Cultural São Paulo**.

Theatre

The **Teatro Municipal Opera House**, see page 202, is used by visiting theatrical and operatic groups, as well as the City Ballet Company and the Municipal Symphony Orchestra who give regular performances. There are several other first-class theatres: **Aliança Francesa**, R Gen Jardim 182, Vila Buarque, T011-3259 0086. **Itália**, Av Ipiranga 344, T011-3257 9092. **Paiol**, R Amaral Gurgel 164, Santa Cecília, T011-3221 2462. Free concerts at **Teatro Popular do Sesi**, Av Paulista 1313, T011-3284 9787, Mon-Sat 1200, under MASP.

⊛ Festivals and events

São Paulo *p192, maps p196, p200 and p205*
Throughout the year there are countless anniversaries, religious feasts, fairs and exhibitions. To see what's on, check the local

The Brazilian Grand Prix

Motor racing has had a long and distinguished history in Brazil and the first race day at Interlagos took place on 12 May 1940. The first Brazilian Grand Prix was held here in 1972 and Emerson Fittipaldi drove to victory in front of a home crowd in 1973 and 1974. The following year another Brazilian, José Carlos Pace (after whom the track is officially named Autódromo José Carlos Pace), was first to cross the chequered flags.

During the 1980s the Grand Prix race was held at the Jacarepaguá racetrack in Rio where the outspoken Nelson Piquet won twice in 1983 and 1986 with some of the fastest lap times seen on this track.

The race returned to the improved track Interlagos during the 1990s, and the legendary Aryton Senna won here in 1991 and 1993. After his tragic death in 1994, as a result of mechanical failure, Brazilian viewing figures for motor racing fell drastically but picked up with the success of Rubens Barrichello.

Today, there are a number of very capable Brazilians driving for the Formula One teams including in 2008, Nelsinho Piquet (Renault) and Felipe Massa (Ferrari). Massa has a good record at Interlagos. He won the Grand Prix in 2006, came in second in 2007 and won again in 2008, missing out on the championship to British rival Lewis Hamilton by one point, much to the crowd's dismay.

The Brazilian Grand Prix is usually the last race of the season, held in October or November. The race consists of 72 laps of the 4292-km circuit for a total distance of 309.024 km. Approximately 55,000 people attend, in addition to millions watching around the world. The training session takes place on Friday morning; the time trial on Saturday morning and the race itself on Sunday afternoon with warm ups and the drivers' parade in the morning.

Tickets can be bought from the racetrack during the whole week or by contacting ABN Amro Bank on T011-5507 2500 from abroad and T0800-170200 inside Brazil. Minimum ticket price is US$100 rising to US$350 depending on the viewing sector. Sectors A and G are uncovered and the cheapest, whilst sector D is covered, provides a better view and is more expensive. Tickets for the training sessions are cheaper and can be bought from 0700 on the day from the box office at the circuit. VIP hospitality is readily available but at a high price.

There is no parking for private vehicles at the racetrack, but park and ride facilities (US$5) are available on Saturday from Shopping SP Market, Avenida das Nações Unidas 22540, and on Sunday from Hipermercado, Avenida das Nações Unidas 4403 and Shopping Interlagos, Avenida Interlagos 2255. There are also buses (Saturday-Sunday) from Praça da República, between Rua do Arouche and Rua Marquês de Itu (295), from Praça Com Lineu Gomes at Congonhas airport and from Rua dos Jequitibás in front of the Jabaquara bus station (189). All buses have coloured stickers to indicate which drop-off point they serve. Further information about the Grand Prix in English can be obtained from www.gpbrasil.com, www.gpbrasil.com.br or www.formula1.com.

---

press or the monthly tourist magazines. Fashion week is in the **Bienal Centre** (Bienal do Ibirapuera) in Ibirapuera Park, Parque do Ibirapuera, T011-5576 7600

25 Jan Foundation of the city.

Feb Carnaval. *Escolas de samba* parade in the Anhembi Sambódromo. During Carnaval most museums and attractions are closed.
Jun Festas Juninas and the Festa de São Vito, the patron saint of the Italian immigrants.

Sep Festa da Primavera.
Oct Formula One grand prix at Interlagos.
Dec Christmas and New Year festivities.

O Shopping

São Paulo *p192, maps p196, p200 and p205*
Books and music
Livrarias Saraiva and Laselva are found in
various shopping malls and at airports, sell
books in English. FNAC, Av Paulista 901
(at Paraíso metrô), Praça Omaguás, 34,
Pinheiros, www.fnac.com.br.

Clothing and accessories
If upper crust São Paulo shops and sips coffee
in Jardins, the rest of the city buys its wares in
the contiguous area of Bom Retiro (see page
203). There are Brazilian guidebooks devoted to
shopping here. At first sight the neighbourhood
is relentlessly urban: ugly concrete with rows of
makeshift houses converted into hundreds of
shops selling a bewildering array of clothing.
Much of it is trash and during the week
wholesale stores may specify a minimum
number of items per buyer. But a few hours
browsing will yield clothing bargains to rival
those in Bangkok. Many of the outfitters
manufacture for the best mid-range labels in
São Paulo, including those in Shopping
Ibirapuera (see below). The best shopping
is on and around R José Paulino – a street
with more than 350 shops. The best day to
come is Sat from 0800, when most items
are sold individually.

Av 25 de Março (Metrô São Bento) in the
city centre offers a similarly large range of
costume jewellery, toys and small decorative
items (best on Sat 0800-1430) and the
neighbourhood of Brás stocks cheaper but
lower quality items. For more information
see www.omelhordobomretiro.com.br.

Fashion boutiques
São Paulo is one of the new hot spots on the
global fashion circuit and is by far the most
influential and diverse fashion city in South
America. The designers based here have
collections as chic as any in Europe or North
America, but at a fraction of the price. Best
buys include smart casual day wear, bikinis,
shoes, jeans and leather jackets. *Havaiana* flip
flops, made famous by Gisele Bundchen and
Fernanda Tavares, are around 10% of the
price of Europe. The best areas for fashion
shopping are Jardins (around R Oscar Freire)
and the Iguatemi shopping centre (Av Faria
Lima). The city's most exclusive shopping
emporium is Daslu, see below.

Adriana Barra, R Peixoto Gomide 1801,
casa 5, Jardins, T011-3064 3691. Elegantly
whimsical clothing in beautiful fabrics
displayed in an artsy little boutique.

Ale Ribeiro, R Tupi 564, T011-3667 2323. One
of the newest of São Paulo's emerging group
of exciting women designers with lush jersey
wrap dresses and tops. Has worked for Carlos
Miele and Daslu's amongst others.

Alexandre Herchcovitz, R Haddock Lobo
1151, T011-3063 2889. The most famous
Brazilian designer, using brightly coloured
materials to create avant garde designs
strongly influenced by European trends.

Andre Lima, R Dr Cardoso de Mello 474,
Vila Olímpia, T011-3849 3444. Another
bright new star on the São Paulo fashion
scene. André grew up in the Amazon and
his collections are light, tropical and sensual.

Fause Haten, Alameda Lorena 1731, Jardins,
T011-3081 8685. One of Brazil's most
internationally renowned designers who
works in plastic, lace, leather, mohair and
denim with laminate appliqués, selling through,
amongst others, Giorgio Beverly Hills.

Forum, R Oscar Freire 916, Jardins T011-
3085 6269, www.forum.com.br. A huge white
space attended by beautiful shop assistants
helping impossibly thin 20-something
Brazilians squeeze into tight, but beautifully
cut jeans and other fashion items.

Hotel Lycra, R Oscar Freire 1055, Jardins, T011-
3897 4401, www.hotellycra.com. A favourite
shopping spot for the Jardins teenybopper
set who park their expensive open-top
18th birthday presents outside and pop in

to browse the collection from a rotating selection of young, new Brazilian designers. **Iodice**, R Oscar Freire 940, T011-3085 9310, and **Shopping Iguatemi**, T011-3813 2622, www.iodice.com.br. Sophisticated and innovative knitwear designs sold abroad in boutiques like **Barney's NYC**.

Lenny, Shopping Iguatemi, T011-3032 2663, and R Escobar Ortiz 480, Vila Nova Conceicao, T011-3846 6594, www.lenny.com.br. Rio de Janeiro's premier swimwear designer and Brazil's current favourite.

Mario Queiroz, R Alameda Franca 1166, T011-3062 3982, www.marioqueiroz.com.br. Casual and elegant clothes with a strong gay element, for 20-something men.

Ricardo Almeida, Daslu and Shopping Iguatemi, T011-3812 6947. One of the few Brazilian designers who styles for men. His clothes are a range of dark suits and slick leather jackets aimed at would-be bit-part actors from *The Matrix*.

Ronaldo Fraga, R Aspicuelta 259, Vila Madalena, T011-3816 2181, www.ronaldo fraga.com. Fraga's adventurous collection combines discipline with daring, retaining a unified style across the sexes yet always surprising and delighting with its off the wall creativity. His VW Beetle clogs and hand-made light cotton, one-of-a-kind blusa devore off-the-shoulder tops are coveted fashion items among young Paulistano creatives and the intimate little homey boutique is a delight to browse in. Great kids collections too.

Rosa Chá, R Oscar Freire 977, T011-3081 2793, and **Shop X76**, Shopping Iguatemi, T011-3032 3078. The world's best fashion label in designer swimwear. Beautifully cut bikinis in top-quality materials.

UMA, R Girassol 273, T011-3813 5559, www.uma.com.br. Raquel Davidowicz offers rails of sleek contemporary cuts set against low-lit, cool white walls with a Japanese-inspired monochrome minimalism mixed with colourful Brazilian vibrancy.

Victor Hugo, R Oscar Freire 816, T011-3082 1303. Brazil's most fashionable handbag designer.

Walter Rodrigues, R Natingui 690/696, Vila Madalena, T011-3031 8562. Haute couture for women, renowned for evening gowns that are fluid, sensual and very much inspired by the belle époque.

Zoomp, R Oscar Freire 995, T011-3064 1556, **Shopping Iguatemi**, T011-3032 5372, www.zoomp.com.br. **Zoomp** have been famous for their figure-hugging jeans for nearly 3 decades and have grown to become a nationwide and now international brand.

Handicrafts

São Paulo has no handicrafts tradition but some items from the rest of Brazil can be bought at **Parque Tte Siqueira Campos/Trianon** on Sun 0900-1700.

Casa dos Amazonas, Av Jurupis 460.

Ceará Meu Amor, R Pamplona 1551, loja 7. Good-quality lace from the northeast.

Galeria Arte Brasileira, Av Lorena 2163, galeria@dialdata.com.br. Good value.

Sutaco, República metrô station. Handicrafts shop promoting items from the state of São Paulo, Tue-Fri 1000-1900, Sat 1000-1500; there is a showroom at R Augusta 435.

Jewellery

Many shops sell precious stones.

Amsterdam Sauer, has outlets at Av São Luís 29, hotels **Maksoud Plaza** and **Sheraton**, shopping centres Iguatemi, Morumbi, and at the international airport.

H Stern, Praça da República 242, R Augusta 2340, R Oscar Freire 652 and at Iguatemi, Ibirapuera, Morumbi, Paulista and other shopping centres, hotels **Hilton**, Sheraton and **Maksoud Plaza**, and at the international airport.

Markets

The best bric-a-brac market in São Paulo takes place on **Praça Benedito Calixto**, Pinheiros every Sat. Stalls in the square and in the surrounding streets sell arts, crafts, CDs, T-shirts and second-hand goods. There is live *choro* and *samba* music and good food. There are many stylish arts and crafts and fashion shops around **Praça Benedito Calixto**. The 'Hippy

Fair' that used to take place in Praça da República was moved to Tiradentes Metrô station but is not nearly as lively or colourful. **Oriental Fair**, Praça de Liberdade Sun 1000-1900, is good for Japanese snacks, plants and some handicrafts, very picturesque, with remedies on sale, tightrope walking, gypsy fortune tellers, etc. Below the Museu de Arte de São Paulo, an **antiques market** takes place Sun 1000-1700. **Av Lorena**, which is one of the upmarket shopping streets off R Augusta in Jardins, has an open-air market on Sun selling fruits and juices. There is a flea market on Sun in **Praça Don Orione** (main square of the Bixiga district). The **Ceasa flower market**, Av Doutor Gastão Vidigal 1946, Jaguaré, Tue and Fri 0700-1200, should not be missed.

Photography
Cine Camera Service, R Conselheiro Crispiniano 97, 2nd floor, www.namba.com.br. For repairs to Canon and other makes.

Shopping malls and department stores
For more information on shopping malls see www.brasilcontact.com/thinks/brazil_saopaulo-ondecomprar.html.
Daslu, Av Chedid Jafat 131, T011-3841 3000, www.daslu.com.br. This temple to snobbery is worth visiting if only for anthropological reasons. It is the fashion store of choice for South America's high society and it's not uncommon for customers to fly in from Argentina or Mato Grosso on private planes and spend up to US$50,000 in a single shopping spree. Collections include that of **Daslu** itself, alongside up and coming Brazilian names like **Juliana Jabour**, **Cris Barros**, www.crisbarros.com.br, and **Raia de Goeye** www.raiadegoeye.com.br and big name international designers. These sit alongside boutiques selling everything from high-class wines to beautiful coffee-table books.
Shopping Cidade Jardim, Av Magalhães de Castro 12000, T011-3552 1000, www.cidadejardimshopping.com.br. The city's newest upmarket mall is a vast, neoclassical edifice with a lush tropical garden in its interior and towering skyscraper apartment blocks above. It is filled with Brazilian names like **Carlos Miele** (in an 8000-sq-ft space whose store has undulating lines inspired by the curves of the human body) and **Osklen**, whose casual beach and adventure clothes look like Ralph Lauren gone tropical and are aimed at a similar yacht- and-boardwalk crowd. International names include **Hermes** and there is a branch of **Daslu**, which unlike their store across the river, has changing rooms. There's a spa at the mall, too, as well as a branch of the informal Italian bistro **Nono Ruggero** and an outpost of the popular upmarket Brazilian-Japanese chain **Kosushi**.
Shopping D, Av Cruzeiro do Sul 1100, Canindé, T011-3311 9333. Some 320 shops with many clothes in the middle to low price ranges. On the edge of the city near the river.
Shopping Iguatemi, Av Brigadeiro Faria Lima 2232, www.iguatemisaopaulo.com.br. Another top end shopping mall just south of Jardins with a healthy representation of most of Brazil's foremost labels – some of these shops are detailed above.
Shopping Ibirapuera, Av Ibirapuera 3103, www.ibirapuera.com.br. A broad selection of mid-range Brazilian labels and general shops including toy and book shops.

▲ Activities and tours

São Paulo *p192, maps p196, p200 and p205*
Football
The most popular local teams are Corinthians, Palmeiras and São Paulo who generally play in the Morumbi and Pacaembu stadiums.

Golf courses
The following courses are within half an hour's drive from the centre.
São Fernando Golf Club, Estr de Cotia, Km 29. There is a lakeside club at Km 50 on the Santos road with 18 holes.
São Paulo Golf Club, Praça Dom Francisco Souza 635, Santo Amaro. 18 holes in beautiful surroundings.

Tour operators

São Paulo has several large agencies offering tours around the country.

Ambiental Viagens e Expedições, www.ambiental.tur.brGood for trips to less well known places throughout the country like Jalapão. English and Spanish spoken, helpful.

Matueté, R Tapinás 22, Itaim, T011-3071 4515, www.matuete.com. Luxury breaks throughout Brazil and city tours, including personal shopping. Ask for Camilla. English spoken.

Tropico Turismo, T011-4025 9281, www.tropico.tur.br. Adventure day trips around São Paulo including rappelling, zip-lines and canopy walking, whitewater rafting and hikes. English spoken. Well-organized.

◒ Transport

São Paulo *p192, maps p196, p200 and p205*
Air

See also Ins and outs, page 192.

Guarulhos international airport (**Cumbica**), operates services to all parts of the world and much of Brazil. The cheapest internal flights are with GOL, www.voegol.com.br, and Oceanair, www.oceanair.com.br. To get to the airport, Emtu buses run every 30 mins from Praça da República 343 (northwest side, corner of R Arouche) 0530-2300, and from Tietê *rodoviária*, US$6.50, 30-45 mins. Buses also run from Bresser bus station and there are buses from Jabaquara bus terminal, without luggage space, usually crowded. Taxi fares from the city to the airport are US$35-40. Rush-hour traffic can easily turn this 30-min journey into an hour. Varig has its own terminal for international flights, adjoining the old terminal and shared with only a handful of other airlines.

Congonhas domestic airport, is used for flights within Brazil including the shuttle flight with **Rio de Janeiro** (Santos Dumont airport, US$80-150 single, depending on availability). The shuttle services operate every 30 mins throughout the day from 0630-2230. Sit on the left-hand side for views to Rio de Janeiro, the other side coming back, book flights in advance. To get to Congonhas airport, take an Emtu bus the centre or a taxi, US$20.

Airline offices Aerolíneas Argentinas, Araújo 216, 6th floor, T011-3259 0319 (Guarulhos airport 6445 3806). **Alitalia**, Av São Luís 50, T011-3257 1922 (6445 3791). **American Airlines**, Araújo 216, 9th floor, T0800-703 4000 or T011-3214 4000 (6445 3808). **British Airways**, Av São Luís 50, 32nd floor, T011-3145 9700 (6445 2021). **GOL**, T0300-115 2121, www.voegol.com.br. **Iberia**, Araújo 216, 3rd floor, T011-2507 6711. **JAL**, Av Paulista 542, 2nd floor, T011-3251 5222 (6445 2040). **Lufthansa**, R Gomes de Carvalho 1356, 2nd floor, T011-3048 5868 (6445 2220). **Oceanair**, Av Washington Luís 7059, Av Washington Luís 7059, Santo Amaro, T011-2176 1000. **Rio-Sul**, R Bráulio Gomes 151, T011-5561 2161. **TAM**, R da Consolação 247, 3rd floor, T0300-123 1000 (24 hrs), or T011-3155 6700. **TAP**, Av São Luís 187, T011-3255 5366. **United**, Av Paulista 777, 9-10th floor, T011- 3145 4200/T0800-162323, T011-6445 3283. **Varig**, T011-4003 7000, Guarulhos T011-6445 3117, Congonhas T011-5091 2215.

Bus

There are 4 bus terminals: Tietê, Barra Funda, Bresser and Jabaquara. All are connected to the metrô system.

Tietê rodoviária This is the main bus station and has a convenient metrô station. Unfortunately the only way to the platforms is by stairs which makes it very difficult for people with heavy luggage and almost impossible for those in a wheelchair. Tietê handles buses to the interior of São Paulo state, to all state capitals and international destinations. To **Rio**, 6 hrs, every 30 mins, US$12.50 (*leito* US$25), special section for this route in the *rodoviária*, request the coastal route via Santos (*via litoral*) unless you wish to go the direct route. To **Florianópolis**, 11 hrs (US$100, *leito* US$120). To **Porto Alegre**, 18 hrs, US$150 (*leito* US$180). To **Curitiba**,

6 hrs, US$70. To **Salvador**, 30 hrs, US$120 (*leito* US$150). To **Recife**, 40 hrs, US$140-160. To **Campo Grande**, 14 hrs, US$60. To **Cuiabá**, 24 hrs, US$100. To **Porto Velho**, 60 hrs (or more), US$125. To **Brasília**, 16 hrs, US$80 (*leito* US$90). To **Foz do Iguaçu**, 16 hrs, US$70. To **São Sebastião**, 4 hrs, US$20 (ask for 'via Bertioga' if you want to go by the coast road, a beautiful journey but few buses take this route).

International connections Buses to Uruguay include: **Montevideo**, via Porto Alegre, cold a/c at night, plenty of meal stops, bus stops for border formalities, passengers disembark only to collect passport and tourist card on the Uruguayan side. Buses to Paraguay include: **Asunción** (1044 km), 18 hrs with **Pluma** (US$150, *leito* US$180), **Brújula** (US$120) or **RYSA** (US$180), all stop at **Ciudad del Este** (US$80, US$110 and US$130 respectively, **Pluma** *leito* US$150). Cometa del Amambay runs to **Pedro Juan Caballero** and **Concepción**. To **Buenos Aires** (Argentina), **Pluma**, 36 hrs, US$200. To **Santiago** (Chile), **Pluma** or **Chilebus**, 56 hrs, US$200, **Chilebus**, poor meals, but otherwise good, beware over-booking.

Barra Funda (Metrô Barra Funda), to cities in southern **São Paulo state** and many destinations in Paraná, including **Foz do Iguaçu** (check for special prices on buses to **Ciudad del Este**, which can be cheaper than buses to Foz). Buses run to **Cananéia** daily at 0900 and 1430, 4 hrs. Alternatively go via **Registro** (buses hourly), from where there are 7 buses daily to Cananéia and regular connections to **Curitiba**.

Bresser (Metrô Bresser), for Cometa (T011-6967 7255) or Transul (T011-6693 8061) serving destinations in Minas Gerais. **Belo Horizonte**, 10 hrs, US$60, 11 a day (*leito* US$80), 9 a day with Gontijo. Translavras and Util also operate out of this station. Prices are given under destinations. See www.passagem-em-domicilio.com.br for more information including bus times and the latest prices.

Jabaquara (at the southern end of the metrô line), is used by buses to **Santos**,

US$3.60, every 15 mins, taking about 50 mins, last bus at 0100. Also serves destinations on the southern coast of São Paulo state.

Car hire
The major names all serve São Paulo and have offices at the airports.

Taxi
Taxis display cards of actual tariffs in the window (starting price US$4). There are ordinary taxis, which are hailed on the street, or at taxi stations such as Praça da República, radio taxis and deluxe taxis. For **Radio Taxis**, which are more expensive but involve fewer hassles, **Central Radio Táxi**, T011-6914 6630; **São Paulo Rádio Táxi**, T011-5583 2000; **Fácil**, T011-6258 5947; **Aero Táxi**, T011-6461 4090; or look in the phone book; calls are not accepted from public phones.

Trains
Estação da Luz (Metrô Luz), runs 8 trains a day to connect with the tourist train from **Paranapiaçaba** to **Rio Grande da Serra**, US$1.

❶ Directory

São Paulo *p192, maps p196, p200 and p205*
Banks Banking hours are generally 1000-1600, although times differ for foreign exchange. **Banco do Brasil** will change cash and TCs and will advance cash against Visa. All transactions are done in the foreign exchange department of any main branch (eg Av São João 32, Centro), but queues are long. **Banespa**, R Duque de Caxias 200, Centro, or Praça da República 295, accepts Visa, TCs and cash. **Citibank**, Av Ipiranga 855, or Av Paulista 1111, open 1100-1500. **MasterCard**, R Campo Verde 61, 4th floor, Jardim Paulistano, cash against card. There are many *câmbios* on or near Praça da República. Most travel agents on Av São Luís change TCs and cash at good rates, but very few are open on Sat. **Amoretur**, Praça da República 203, will change TCs. **Avencatur**, Av Nações

Unidas 1394, Morumbi, changes TCs, euro, good rates. **Coraltur**, Praça da República 95. **Interpax**, Praça da República 177, loja 13, changes cash (many currencies) and TCs, Mon-Fri 0930-1800, Sat 0930-1300. **Cultural centres** For cultural articles related to São Paulo and Brazil in general, check out the **Instituto Cultural Itaú**, www.ici.org.br. **Alliance Française Theatre**, see under Theatre, page 218. **American Library**, União Cultural Brasil-Estados Unidos, R Col Oscar Porto 208. **Centro Brasileiro Britânico**, R Ferriera de Araújo 741, Pinheiros, T011-3039 0567. **Centro Cultural Fiesp**, Av Paulista 1313, Tue-Sun 0900-1900, has foreign newspapers and magazines. **Goethe-Instituto**, R Lisboa 974, Mon-Thu 1400-2030. **Embassies and consulates** **Argentina**, Av Paulista 1106, T011-3284 1355 (0900-1300), very easy to get a visa here. **Australia**, R Tenente Negrão 140, T011-3849 6281. **Bolivia**, R Honduras 1447, T011-3081 1688, (0900-1300). **Canada**, Av Nações Unidas 12901, T011-5509 4343 (0900-1200, 1400-1700). **France**, Av Paulista 1842, 14th floor, T011-3287 9522, (0830-1200). **Germany**, Av Brigadeiro Faria Lima 2092, T011-3814 6644, (0800-1130). **Ireland**, Av Paulista 2006, 5th floor, T011-3287 6362, (1400-1700). **Israel**, Av Brig Faria Lima 1713, T011-3815 7788. **New Zealand**, Av Campinas 579, T011-3288 0700. **Paraguay**, R Bandeira Paulista 600, 15th floor, T011-3849 0455, (0830-1600). **Peru**, R Votuverava 350, T011-3819 1793, (0900-1300). **South Africa**, Av Paulista 1754, T011-3285 0433. **UK**, Av Paulista 37, 17th floor, T011-3287 7722, consulad@uol.com.br. **Uruguay**, Av Santos 905, T011-3284 0998, (1000-1600). **US**, R Padre João Manuel 933, T011-3081 6511, (0800-1700). **Venezuela**, R Veneza 878, T011-3887 4583, (0900-1130). **Immigration** Federal Police, Marginal Tietê, (1000-1600) for visa extensions. **Internet** Av Paulista 1499, conj 1001, Metrô Trianon, (1100-2200), English spoken,

second-hand books. **Kiosknet**, Shopping Light, 4th floor, R Cel Xavier de Toledo 23, opposite Teatro Municipal, T011-3151 3645, US$2.50 per hr. **O Porão**, R Tamandaré 1066, near Vergueiro metrô station. **Saraiva Megastore**, Shopping El Dorado, US$3. **Language courses** The official **Universidade de São Paulo** (USP) is situated in the Cidade Universitária (buses from main bus station), beyond Pinheiros. They have courses available to foreigners, including a popular Portuguese course. Registry is through the **Comissão de Cooperação Internacional**, R do Anfiteatro 181, Bloco das Colméias 05508, Cidade Universitária, São Paulo. Other universities include the **Pontifical Catholic University** (PUC), and the **Mackenzie University**. Both these are more central than the USP, Mackenzie in Higienopolis, just west of the centre, and PUC in Perdizes. Take a taxi to either. Both have notice boards where you can leave a request for Portuguese teachers or language exchange, which is easy to arrange for free. Any of the *gringo* pubs are good places to organize similar exchanges. **Laundry** Chuá Self Service, R Augusta 728, limited self-service, not cheap. **Di-Lelles**, R Atenas 409, pricey. **Medical services** Hospital das Clínicas, Av Dr Enéias de Carvalho Aguiar 255, Jardins, T011-3069 6000. Hospital Samaritano, R Cons Brotero 1468, Higenópolis, T011-3824 0022. Recommended. Both have *pronto-socorro* (emergency services). Contact your consulate for names of doctors and dentists who speak your language. **Emergency and ambulance:** T192. Fire: T193. **Post office** Correio Central, Praça do Correio, corner of Av São João and Prestes Máia, T011-3831 5222. Booth adjoining tourist office on Praça da República, Mon-Fri 1000-1200, 1300-1600, for letters and small packages only. **Telephone** Embratel, Av São Luís 50, and Av Ipiranga 344. For the international operator dial T000111, for international collect calls dial T000107. Red phone boxes are for national calls, blue ones for international phone calls.

The coast of São Paulo

São Paulo's coast is packed at the weekend (when the city dwellers leaves for the beach) and deserted during the week. There are many beautiful beaches to choose from: some backed by rainforest-covered mountains and all washed by a bottle-green warm Atlantic. The best are along the northernmost part of the state coast, the Litoral Norte, around Ubatuba, and along the Litoral Sul near Cananéia. There are beautiful islands too including Brazil's largest, Ilhabela, and her wildest, Ilha do Cardoso. The dividing point between the Litoral Norte and Litoral Sul is the historic city of Santos; made most famous by Pelé (there's a museum devoted to him), and dotted with a few interesting buildings and museums in a spruced-up, attractive colonial city centre. ▸▸ *For listings, see pages 242-248.*

Santos and São Vicente ⬤🏨⊛🍴⬤ ▸▸ *pp242-248. Colour map 5, A6.*

→ *Phone code: 013. Population: 418,000.*

The Portuguese knew how to choose a location for a new settlement. **Santos** stands on an island in a bay surrounded by towering mountains and extensive areas of lowland mangrove forest – a setting equally as beautiful as that of Salvador or Rio. When it was dominated by colonial houses, churches and clean white-sand beaches Santos itself must have been one of Brazil's most enchanting cities. But in the 20th century an evil reputation for yellow fever and industrial pollution from nearby Cubatão left the city to decay and it lost much of its architecture along with its charm. Contemporary Santos, however, is getting its act together. The old colonial centre has been tidied up and Scottish trams ferry tourists past the city's sights. These include a series of colonial churches and the Bolsa do Café – a superb little museum whose café-restaurant serves the most delicious espresso in Brazil. Santos is also Pelé's home and the city he played for almost all his career. Santos FC has a museum devoted to the club and to Pelé and it is easy to attend a game.

On the mainland, **São Vicente** is, to all intents and purposes, a suburb of Santos, having been absorbed into the conurbation. It was the first town founded in Brazil, in 1532, but nowadays it is scruffy and with very few sights of interest but for the rather dilapidated colonial church, the Matriz São Vicente Mártir (1542, rebuilt in 1757) in the Praça do Mercado. The Litoral Sul (see page 238) begins after São Vicente.

Background

Santos is one of Brazil's oldest cities and has long been its most important port. The coast around the city is broken by sambaqui shell mounds that show the area has been inhabited by humans since at least 5000 BC (see page 772). When the Portuguese arrived, the Tupinikin people dominated the region. However, the first settlements at neighbouring São Vicente (1532) were constantly under attack by the Tamoio who were allies of the French. The French were defeated at Rio in 1560 and the Tamoio massacred soon after.

By the 1580s Santos was a burgeoning port with some 400 houses. The first export was sugar, grown as cane at the foot of the mountains and on the plateau. By the late 19th century this had been replaced by coffee, which rapidly became Brazil's main source of income. The city was connected to São Paulo and the coffee region by the British under the guidance of Barão Visconde de Mauá, and the city grew wealthy. The seafront was lined with opulent coffee mansions and the centre was home to Brazil's most important stock exchange, the Bolsa do Café.

Santos

Centro detail

Gonzaga detail

N

600 metres
600 yards

Sleeping 🛌
Atlântico **1**
Gonzaga Flats **2**
Mendes Plaza **4**
Natal **5**

Parque Balneário &
Old Harbour Restaurant **6**
Pousada do Marquês **7**

Eating 🍴
Café Paulista **4**
Pier One **1**
Point 44 **2**
WTC **3**

The bandeirantes

Reviled in some quarters for their appalling treatment of Indians, revered in others for their determination and willingness to withstand extreme hardship in the pursuit of their goals, the *bandeirantes* are an indispensable element in the formation of Brazil.

The Portuguese knew that South America held great riches; their Spanish rivals were shipping vast quantities back to Europe from Peru. They also knew soon after setting up their colonies on the Atlantic side of the continent that Brazil was not readily yielding equivalent wealth. Legends proliferated of mountains of precious stones, golden lakes and other marvels, also of terrifying places, all in the mysterious interior. Regardless of the number of expeditions sent into the *sertão* which returned empty-handed (or failed to return at all), there was always the promise of silver, emeralds or other jewels to lure the adventurous beyond the coast.

The one thing that Brazil had in abundance was Indians. Throughout the colony there was a demand for slaves to work the plantations and farms and the indigenous population satisfied the need for labour. This was especially true in the early 17th century when Portugal temporarily lost its African possession of Angola, from which it sent many slaves to Brazil.

The men who settled in São Paulo, both the Europeans and those of mixed parentage, the *mamelucos*, proved themselves expert at enslaving Indians. Without official sanction, and certainly not blessed by the Jesuits, these adventurers formed themselves into expeditions which would leave São Paulo, often for years at a time, to capture slaves for the internal market. The Guaraní Indians who had been organized into *reducciones* by the Jesuits around the Río Paraguay were the top prize and there developed an intense rivalry between the *bandeirantes* and the Jesuits. The priests regarded the Paulistas as murderous and inhumane; the slavers felt they had some justification in attacking the missions because they were

---

In the 1980s, the hinterland between the sea and mountains became the site of one of South America's most unpleasant industrial zones. The petrochemical plants of Cubatão were so notorious that they were referred to in the press as the 'The Valley of Death'. Santos and around was said to be the most contaminated corner of the planet, with so much toxic waste undermining the hills that the whole lot threatened to slip down into the sea. In the late 1980s, a spate of mutant births in Cubatão eventually prompted a clean-up operation, which is said to have been largely successful.

Ins and outs

Getting there Santos is served by regular buses from São Paulo as well as towns along the Litoral Norte and Litoral Sul such as Curitibia, Rio de Janeiro and Florianópolis. Buses arrive at the **rodoviária** ① *Praça dos Andrades, T013-3219 2194*, close to the colonial centre. Those from São Paulo also stop at Ponta da Praia and José Menino, which are nearer to the main hotel district in Gonzaga. A taxi to Gonzaga from the bus station costs about US$5; all taxis have meters.

Getting around The best way to get around the centre of Santos is by the newly restored Victorian trams, which leave on guided tours (daily, except Monday, 1100-1700) from in in Spanish territory and, in the 17th century, the entire western boundary of Brazil was in dispute.

This was one side of the coin. The other was that the bandeirantes were incredibly resourceful, trekking for thousands of kilometres, withstanding great hardships, travelling light, inspired not just by the desire to get rich, but also by a fierce patriotism. They certainly did show barbaric treatment to the Indians, but the enthusiasm that inspired the slave drives combined well with the desire to demystify the sertão, to uncover its riches. It was this which fuelled the prospecting expeditions after Angola had been recaptured in 1648. The bandeirantes trekked into Minas Gerais, Goiás and Mato Grosso looking for precious metals. Through their efforts, the Minas Gerais gold rush began. They were also enlisted by governors in the northeast to wage war on Indians and they were involved in the destruction of the quilombo at Palmares).

The principal effect of the expansionist spirit of the bandeira movement was that the interior of Brazil was explored. In the bandeirantes' footsteps came settlers and cattle herders who took over the lands that had been emptied of their Indian population. Although Indians were exploited as labour and became a source of income for the Paulistas, they also intermarried with the Europeans. The mixed-race mamelucos and even Indians themselves took part in the bandeiras, hastening the miscegenation process which became so evident throughout Brazil. Portuguese control of territory was extended by the bandeirantes' journeys. In their later phase, these journeys also filled Portugal's coffers because much of the wealth derived from the discovery of gold was sent back to Europe.

To find out more, read John Hemming, Red Gold (chapters 12 and 13); and Richard M Morse (editor), The Bandeirantes.

front of the Prefeitura Municipal on Praça Visconde de Mauá. The tram passes most of the interesting sights, including the azulejo-covered houses on Rua do Comércio, the Bolsa do Café and some of the oldest churches. Local buses run from the colonial centre and rodoviária to the seafront – look for Gonzaga or Praia on their destination plaque. Bus fares within Santos are US$0.60; to São Vicente US$0.90.

Orientation The centre of the city is on the north side of the island. Due south, on the Baía de Santos, is **Gonzaga**, São Paulo's favourite beach resort where much of the city's entertainment takes place. Between these two areas, the eastern end of the island curves round within the Santos Channel. At the eastern tip, a ferry crosses the estuary to give access to the busy beaches of Guarujá and Praia Grande. The city has impressive modern buildings, wide, tree-lined avenues, and wealthy suburbs.

Tourist information There are **SETUR** offices at the rodoviária, at Praía do Gonzaga on the seafront (in a disused tram, very helpful, lots of leaflets), and next to the British railway station on Largo Monte Alegre. The **Orquidário Municipal** ① T0800-173887, www.santos. sp.gov.br, has limited opening hours. Although poverty is apparent the city is generally safe but it is wise to exercise caution at night and near the port.

Sights

The heart of the colonial centre is **Praça Mauá**. The surrounding streets are very lively in the daytime, with plenty of cheap shops and restaurants. The most interesting buildings are to be found here and all can be visited by tram. The most impressive is the **Museu do Café** ① *R 15 de Novembro 95, T013-3219 5585, www.museudocafe.com.br, Tue-Sat 0900-1700, Sun 1000-1700, US$2*, housed in the old Bolsa Oficial de Café. Its plain exterior hides a grand marble-floored art deco stock exchange and museum, with a café serving some of the best coffee and cakes in South America. The building was once open only to wealthy (and exclusively male) coffee barons who haggled beneath a magnificent stained-glass skylight, depicting a bare-breasted Brazil – the *Mãe Douro* – crowned with a star in a tropical landscape populated with tropical animals and perplexed *indígenas*. The skylight and the beautiful neo-Renaissance painting of Santos that decorates the walls of the exchange is by Brazil's most respected 19th-century artist, Benedito Calixto, who was born in Santos. One of the few remaining coffee baron mansions the, **Fundação Pinacoteca** ① *Av Bartolomeu de Gusmão 15, T013-3288 2260, www.pinacoteca.unisanta.br, Tue-Sun 1400-1900, free*, on the seafront, is now a gallery housing some of his paintings, most of them landscapes, which give some idea of the city's original beauty.

Santos has a few interesting and ancient colonial churches. Only the **Santuário Santo Antônio do Valongo** ① *Marquez de Monte Alegre s/n, Tue-Sun 0800-1700, guided tours most days after 1000, in Portuguese only*, is regularly open to the public. Its twee mock-baroque interior is from the 1930s, but the far more impressive original 17th-century altarpiece sits in the Franciscan chapel to the left of the main entrance. The statue of Christ is particularly fine. Next door to the church is the British-built terminus of the now defunct Santos–São Paulo railway, which serves as a small museum. The tourist office sits above it.

On Avenida Ana Costa there is an interesting monument to commemorate the brothers Andradas, who took a leading part in the movement for Independence. There are other monuments on Praça Rui Barbosa to Bartolomeu de Gusmão, who has a claim to the world's first historically recorded airborne ascent in 1709; in the Praça da República to Brás Cubas, who founded the city in 1534; and in the Praça José Bonifácio to the soldiers of Santos who died in the Revolution of 1932.

Brazil's iconic football hero, Pelé, played for Santos for almost all his professional life, signing when he was in his teens. **Santos Football Club** ① *R Princesa Isabel 77, Vila Belmiro, T013-3257 4000, http://santos.globo.com, Mon 1300-1900, Tue-Sun 0900-1900, US$3, for tours of the grounds call T013-3225 7989*, has an excellent museum, the Memorial das Conquistas, which showcases not only Pelé (with his kit, boots and other assorted personal items on display), but the history of the club. Its collection of gold and silver includes several international championship trophies. Pelé still lives in the city and can sometimes be seen at matches. It is possible to see Santos play; details available on their website.

Monte Serrat, just south of the city centre, has at its summit a semaphore station and look-out post which reports the arrival of all ships in Santos harbour. There is also an old church, **Nossa Senhora da Monte Serrat**, where the patron, Our Lady of Montserrat, is said to have performed many miracles.

The top can be reached on foot or by **funicular**, which leaves every 30 minutes (US$6). Seven shrines have been built on the way up and annual pilgrimages are made by the local people. There are fine views.

In the western district of José Menino is the **Orquidário Municipal** ① *Praça Washington, orchid garden Tue-Sun 0900-1700, bird enclosure 0800-1100, 1400-1700, US$0.50*. The flowers bloom from October to February and there is an orchid show in November. Visitors can wander among giant subtropical and tropical trees, amazing orchids and, when the aviary is open, meet macaws, toucans and parrots. The open-air cage contains hummingbirds of 20 different species and the park is a sanctuary for other birds.

Beaches

Santo has 8 km of beaches stretching round the Baía de Santos to those of São Vicente at the western end. From east to west they are **Ponta da Praia**, below the sea wall and on the estuary, no good for bathing, but fine for watching the movements of the ships. Next are **Aparecida**, **Embaré**, **Boqueirão**, **Gonzaga** and **José Menino** (the original seaside resort for the merchants of Santos). São Vicente's beaches of **Itararé** and **Ilha Porchat** are on the island, while **Gonzaguinha** is on the mainland. The last beach is **Itaquitanduva**, which is in a military area but may be visited with authorization. In all cases, check the cleanliness of the water before venturing in (a red flag means it is too polluted for bathing).

Excursions from Santos

The small island of **Ilha Porchat** is reached by a bridge at the far end of Santos/São Vicente bay. It has beautiful views over rocky precipices, of the high seas on one side and of the city and bay on the other. At the summit is **Terraço Chopp** ① *Av Ary Barroso 274*, a restaurant with live music most evenings and great views. On summer evenings the queues can be up to four hours, but in winter, even if it may be a little chilly at night, you won't have to wait.

Litoral Norte ●●❀●●① ↦ *pp242-248.*

The resorts immediately north of Santos – Guarujá, Praia Grande and Bertioga – are built-up and none too clean. It becomes more beautiful at Camburi, the southernmost beach of São Sebastião province, named after the historical town that sits in front of Ilhabela, an island fringed with glorious beaches. Further north, Ubatuba, borders the state of Rio de Janeiro and has dozens of beautiful stretches of golden sand backed by forest-covered mountains.

Camburi, Camburizinho and Maresias → *Phone code: 012.*

Beyond Boracéia are a number of beaches, including Barra do Una, Praia da Baleia and **Camburi**. The latter is the first beach in São Sebastião province and is surrounded by the *Mata Atlântica* forest. It has a long stretch of sand with some surf, many *pousadas* and two of the best restaurants in São Paulo state. The best place for swimming is at **Camburizinho** (though you should avoid swimming in the river which is not clean). You can walk on the Estrada do Piavu into the *Mata Atlântica* to see vegetation and wildlife; bathing in the streams is permitted, but use of shampoo and other chemicals is forbidden. About 5 km from Camburi is **Praia Brava**, 45 minutes' walk through the forest. The surf here is very heavy, hence the name. Camping is possible.

The road continues from Camburi, past beaches such as **Boiçucanga** (family-orientated with many *pousadas*) to **Maresias**, which is beloved of well-to-do Paulistas who come here mostly to surf. It has some chic *pousadas* and restaurants and tends to be younger and less family orientated than Camburi.

São Sebastião → *Colour map 5, A6. Phone code: 012. Population: 59,000.*

From Maresias it is 21 km to São Sebastião, which was once as attractive as Paraty and still retains a pretty colonial centre. Ferries leave from here for the 15-minute crossing to **Ilhabela** (see page 233), the largest offshore island in Brazil, which is shrouded in forest on its ocean side and fringed with some of São Paulo's best beaches.

The city was founded at the time when Brazil's rainforest stretched all the way from the coast to the Pantanal, and all the land north to Rio de Janeiro was ruled by the indigenous Tamoio and their French allies. The settlement was initially created as an outpost of the indigenous slave trade and a port from which to dispatch armies to fight the French and claim Rio for the Portuguese crown. After this was achieved and the Tamoio had been massacred, São Sebastião grew to become one of Brazil's first sugar-exporting ports and the hinterland was covered in vast fields of cane tilled by the enslaved *indígenas*. When the number of local slaves became depleted by the lash and disease, the city became one of the first ports of the African slave trade.

Ins and outs São Sebastião is served by regular buses from Ubatuba and Santos and is also connected to São Paulo. Ferries (for cars as well as passengers), US$2 from Ilhabela run 24 hours a day (see page 247) and take 15 minutes. The **tourist office** ① *daily 1000-1700, www.prefeituradesaosebastiao.com.br*, lies on the waterfront one block towards the sea from Praça Major João Fernandes. Staff are very helpful and can provide maps and information on ferries to Ilhabela and beaches in the entire São Sebastião province. The city is far cheaper for accommodation than Ilhabela.

Sights São Sebastião's remaining colonial streets are in the few blocks between the shoreline and the Praça Major João Fernandes, which is dominated by the **Igreja Matriz** ① *daily 0900-1800*. Although this retains remnants of its original 17th-century design, this is predominantly a 19th-century reconstruction devoid of much of its original church art.

São Paulo coast

However, the newly refurbished **Museu de Arte Sacra** ⓘ *one block south of the praça, R Sebastião Neves 90, T012-3892 4286, daily 1300-1700, free*, in the 17th-century chapel of São Gonçalo, preserves a number of 16th-century statues found in cavities in the wall of the Igreja Matriz during its restoration in 2003.

The city has a few sleepy streets of Portuguese houses, fanning out from the square, and a handful of civic buildings worth a quick look before the ferry leaves for Ilhabela. The most impressive is the **Casa Esperança** ⓘ *Av Altino Arantes 154, not open to the public although they often let visitors in on request*, on the waterfront. It was built from stone and wattle and daub glued together with whale oil, and then whitewashed with lime from thousands of crushed shells collected on the beaches of Ilhabela. The interior has some peeling 17th-century ceiling paintings.

Ilhabela (Ilha de São Sebastião)
→ *Colour map 5, A6. Phone code: 012. Population: 21,000 (100,000 high season).*
Ilhabela is Brazil's largest oceanic island and one of its prettiest. It is wild enough to be home to ocelots, and the lush forests on its ocean side (80% of which are protected by a state park) drip with waterfalls and are fringed with glorious beaches. Its centre is crowned with craggy peaks, often obscured by mist: **Morro de São Sebastião** (1379 m), **Morro do Papagaio** (1309 m), **Ramalho** (1285 m) and **Pico Baepi** (1025 m). Rainfall on the island is heavy, about 3000 mm a year, and there are many small biting flies known locally as *borrachudos*.

The island is considered the 'Capital da Vela' (capital of sailing) because its 150 km of coastline offers all types of conditions. The sheltered waters of the strait are where many sailors learn their skills and the bays around the coast provide safe anchorages. There are, however, numerous tales of shipwrecks because of the unpredictable winds, sudden mists and strange forces playing havoc with compasses, but these provide plenty of adventure for divers. There are over 30 wrecks that can be dived, the most notable being the *Príncipe de Asturias*, a transatlantic liner that went down off the Ponta de Pirabura in 1916.

Ins and outs There are good transport connections with the mainland. **Litorânea** buses from São Paulo connect with a service right through to Ilhabela town. Ferries run day and night and leave regularly from the São Sebastião waterfront, taking about 20 minutes; free for pedestrians, cars US$1 weekdays, US$10 at weekends. It is very difficult to find space for a car on the ferry during summer weekends. A bus meets the ferry and runs to Ilhabela town and along the west coast. Try to visit during the week when the island feels deserted and avoid high season (December to February) at all costs. Hotels and *pousadas* are expensive; many people choose to stay in São Sebastião instead. For information contact the **Secretaria de Turismo** ① *R Bartolomeu de Gusmão 140, Pequeá, T012-3472 1091, www.ilhabela.sp.gov.br.* ▶▶ *See Transport, page 247.*

Sights Most of the island's residents live on the sheltered shore facing the mainland, along which are a number of upmarket *pousadas*. Swimming is not recommended on this side of the island within 4 km of São Sebastião because of pollution. Watch out for oil, sandflies and jellyfish on the sand and in the water.

About 20 minutes north of the ferry terminal is the main population centre, **Vila Ilhabela**. The village has some pretty colonial buildings and the parish church, **Nossa Senhora da Ajuda e Bom Sucesso**, dates from the 17th century and has been restored. There are restaurants, cafés and shops. Four kilometres north of Ilhabela, **Pedras do Sino** (Bell Rocks) are curious seashore boulders which, when struck with a piece of iron or stone, emit a loud bell-like note. There is a beach here and a campsite nearby.

From Vila Ilhabela, the road hugs the coast, sometimes high above the sea, towards the south of the island. An old *fazenda*, **Engenho d'Água**, a few kilometres from town in a grand 18th-century mansion (not open to the public), gives its name to one of the busiest beaches. About 10 km further, you can visit the old **Feiticeira** plantation. It has underground dungeons, and can be reached by bus, taxi, or horse and buggy. A trail leads down from the plantation to the beautiful beach of the same name.

On the south coast is the fishing village of **Bonete**, which has 500 m of beach and can be reached either by boat (1½ hours), or by driving to Borrifos at the end of the road, then walking along a a rainforest-covered trail for three hours – a beautiful walk.

Much of the Atlantic side of the island is protected by the **Parque Estadual de Ilhabela**. There is a dirt road across to the east of the island, but it requires a 4WD. A few kilometres along this road is a turning to the terraced waterfall of **Cachoeira da Toca** (US$4). Set in dense jungle close to the foot of the Baepi peak, the cool freshwater pools are good for bathing and attract lots of butterflies. The locals claim that there are more than 300 waterfalls on the island, but only a few of them can be reached on foot; those that can are worth the effort. There is a 50-km return trek from Vila Ilhabela over the hump of the island down towards the Atlantic. The route follows part of the old slave trail and requires a local guide as it negotiates dense tropical forest. It takes at least two days.

Some of the island's best beaches are on the Atlantic side of the island and can only be reached by boat. **Praia dos Castelhanos** is recommended. At the cove of **Saco do Sombrio** English, Dutch and French pirates sheltered in the 16th and 17th centuries. Needless to say, this has led to legends of hidden treasure, but the most potent story about the place is that of the Englishman, Thomas Cavendish. In 1592 he sacked Santos and set it on fire. He then sailed to Saco do Sombrio where his crew mutinied, hanged Cavendish, sank their boats and settled on the island.

São Sebastião & Ilhabela

Beaches ○

Armação **2**
Arrastão **48**
Arrozal **6**
Barraqueçaba **57**
Cabras **17**
Castelhanos **33**
Caveira **37**
Centro **52**
Cigarras **46**
Curral **23**
Deserta **50**
Enchovas **27**
Engenho d'Água **13**
Enseada **45**
Eustáquio **35**

Feiticeira **20**
Figueira **32**
Fome **42**
Grande (Ilhabela) **22**
Grande (São Sebastião) **54**
Guaecá **58**
Guanxuma **36**
Itaguaçu **14**
Itaquanduba **15**
Jabaquara **43**
Julião **21**
Mercedes **9**
Olaria **47**
Pacuíba **44**
Pedra do Sino **5**
Pedra Miúda **18**

Pequeá **12**
Perequê **16**
Pinto **3**
Pitangueiras **55**
Poço **40**
Ponta Azeda **4**
Ponta da Cabeçuda **34**
Ponta da Pirabura **30**
Ponta das Canas **1**
Ponta da Sela **25**
Ponta da Sepetiba **26**
Ponta do Boi **29**
Ponta do Diogo **28**
Ponta do Lobo **41**
Ponta Grossa **39**
Pontal da Cruz **49**

Portinho **19**
Porto Grande **51**
Preta **53**
Saco do Indaiá **10**
Saco Grande **31**
Serraria **38**
Siriúba **7**
Timbó **56**
Veloso **24**
Viana **8**

→ *Phone code: 012. Population: 67,000.*

This is one of the most beautiful stretches of the São Paulo coast and has been recognized as such by the local tourist industry for many years. In all, there are 72 beaches of varying sizes, some in coves, some on islands. Surfing is the main pastime, of which it is said to be capital, but there is a whole range of watersports on offer, including sailing to and around the offshore islands. The **Tropic of Capricorn** runs through the beach of Itaguá, just south of the town.

The commercial centre of Ubatuba is at the northern end of the bay by the estuary, by which the fishing boats enter and leave. A bridge crosses the estuary, giving access to the coast north of town. A small jetty with a lighthouse at the end protects the river mouth and this is a pleasant place to watch the boats come and go. The seafront, stretching south from the jetty, is built up along its length, but there are hardly any high-rise blocks. In the commercial centre are shops, banks, services, lots of restaurants (most serving pizza and fish), but few hotels. These are mainly found on the beaches north and south and can be reached from the Costamar bus terminal.

Ins and outs

The road from São Sebastião is paved, so a journey from São Paulo along the coast is possible. Ubatuba is 70 km from Paraty (see page 178). There are regular buses from São Paulo, São José dos Campos, Paraibuna, Caraguatatuba, Paraty and Rio de Janeiro. The beaches are spread out over a wide area, so if you are staying in Ubatuba town and don't have a car, you will need to take one of the frequent buses. Taxis in town can be very expensive. ⏩ *See Transport, page 248.*

The **tourist office** ① *Av Iperoig opposite R Prof Thomaz Galhardo*, is on the seafront. The area gets very crowded at carnival time as Cariocas come to escape the crowds in Rio. There is a small airport from which stunt fliers take off to wheel and dive over the bay. In summer 10-minute panoramic flights and helicopter rides over Ubatuba are offered from US$15.

Background

This part of the coast was hotly contested between the local indigenous population and the Portuguese. The Jesuits José Anchieta and Manuel Nóbrega came to the village of Iperoig, as it was called in 1563, to put a stop to the fighting; the former was even taken hostage by the locals during the negotiations. A cross on the Praia do Cruzeiro (or Iperoig) in the centre commemorates what the town proudly claims to have been the first peace treaty on the American continent. The colonists eventually prevailed and the town of Vila Nova da Exaltação da Santa Cruz do Salvador de Ubatuba became an important port until Santos overtook it in the late 18th century. In the 20th century its development as a holiday resort was rapid, especially after 1948 when it became an Estância Balneária. The shortened name of Ubatuba derives from the Tupi-Guarani, meaning 'place of ubas', a type of tree used for making bows and canoes. Cariocas disparagingly refer to it as Uba 'chuva' – as it can rain heavily here at any time.

Sights

Ubatuba has a few historic buildings, such as the **Igreja da Matriz** on Praça da Matriz, dating back to the 18th century. It has only one tower, the old 19th-century prison, which now houses the small historical museum. Other interesting buildings include: **Cadeia Velha** on Praça Nóbrega; the 18th-century **Câmara Municipal** on Avenida Iperoig; and the **Sobrado do Porto**, the 19th-century customs house at Praça Anchieta 38, which contains **Fundart** (the Art and Culture Foundation). Mostly, though, it is a modern, functional town. In the surrounding countryside there are *fazendas* which are often incorporated into the *trilhas ecológicas* (nature trails) along the coast.

The **Projeto Tamar** ① *R Antonio Athanasio da Silva 273, Itaguá, T012-3432 6202*, is a branch of the national project which studies and preserves marine turtles. The **Aquário de Ubatuba** ① *R Guarani 859, T012-3432 1382, Fri-Wed 1000-2200*, has well-displayed Amazon and Pantanal species including caimans and piranhas.

Beaches

The only place where swimming is definitely not recommended is near the town's outflow between Praia do Cruzeiro and Praia Itaguá. The sand and water close to the jetty don't look too inviting either. The most popular beaches are **Praia Tenório**, **Praia Grande** and **Praia Toninhas** (4.5 km, 6 km and 8 km south respectively). Condominiums, apartments, hotels and *pousadas* line these beaches on both sides of the coast road. Of the municipality's 72 beaches, those to the south are the more developed although the

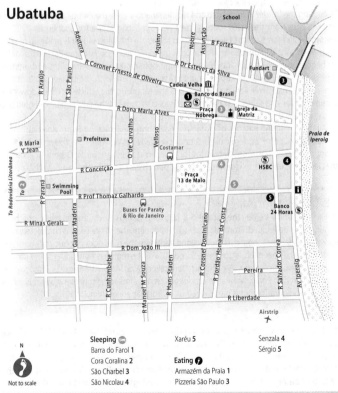

Ubatuba

Sleeping
Barra do Farol **1**
Cora Coralina **2**
São Charbel **3**
São Nicolau **4**

Xaréu **5**

Eating
Armazém da Praia **1**
Pizzeria São Paulo **3**

Senzala **4**
Sérgio **5**

N
Not to scale

further you go from town in either direction, the less built up they are. Boogie boards can be hired at many of the beaches, or you can buy your own in town for around US$5.

Saco da Ribeira, 13 km south, is a natural harbour that has been made into a yacht marina. Schooners leave from here for excursions to **Ilha Anchieta** (or dos Porcos), a popular four-hour trip. On the island are beaches, trails and a prison, which was in commission from 1908 to 1952. The **Costamar** bus from Ubatuba to Saco da Ribeira runs every half an hour (US$0.85) and will drop you at the turning by the **Restaurante Pizzeria Malibu**. It's a short walk to the docks and boatyards where an unsealed road leads to the right, through the boatyards, to a track along the shore. It ends at the **Praia da Ribeira** from where you can follow the track round a headland to the beaches of **Flamengo**, **Flamenguinho** and **Sete Fontes**. It's a pleasant stroll (about one hour to Flamengo), but there is no shade and you need to take water. Note the sign before Flamengo on one of the private properties: "*Propriedade particular. Cuidado c/o elefante!*".

Parque Nacional Serra da Bocaina
① *Permission to visit must be obtained in advance from Ibama in São José do Barreiro, the nearest town, T012-3117 2183/88. There are hotels and trekking agencies here, including Vale dos Veados, Estr da Bocaina, Km 42, T012-3577 1194.*

Straddling the border of São Paulo and Rio de Janeiro states, the Parque Nacional Serra da Bocaina rises from the coast to its highest point at **Pico do Tira** (or Chapéu) at 2200 m, encompassing three strata of vegetation. Up to 1000 m the forest is mainly made up of large trees such as *maçaranduba* (milk, or cow trees), *jatobá* (courbaril), cedar and *angelim* (angely). Between 1000 m and 2000 m the predominant varieties are pines and myrtles. Higher than this, the landscape is more grassy and open, with bromeliads, orchids and lichens. The main river flowing through it is the **Mambucaba**, which cascades down the mountainsides in a series of waterfalls. Trails lead to some of the falls and an old gold trail leads through the park (a three or four-day hike).

All the remaining patches of *Mata Atlântica* along the Linha Verde provide habitat for some of Brazil's rarer endemic birds. A book such as Nigel Wheatley's *Where to Watch Birds in South America* has more details for those interested in rare birds. Otherwise, contact specialists locally and, where necessary, ask permission to birdwatch on private land.

Litoral Sul ●●● ⇝ *pp242-248.*

Unlike the Linha Verde, the Litoral Sul between Santos and Cananéia has not been continuously developed. From São Vicente to Itanhaém, the whole coast is completely built up with holiday developments, but beyond Itanhaém the road does not hug the shore and a large area has been left untouched. Some 80% of the region is now under some form of environmental protection. An organization called **SOS Mata Atlântica** ① *R Manoel da Nóbrega 456, São Paulo, www.sosmatatlantica.org.br*, aims to help preserve what is left of the coastal vegetation but is part owned by a large paper company.

Itanhaém → *Phone code: 013. Population: 72,000.*
Itanhaém lies 61 km south of Santos. Its pretty colonial church, **Sant'Ana** (1761) on Praça Narciso de Andrade, and the **Convento da Nossa Senhora da Conceição** (1699-1713, originally founded 1554), on the small hill of Morro de Itaguaçu, are reminders of the Portuguese dedication to converting the *indígenas* to Catholicism. Also in the town is the **Casa de Câmara e Cadeia**, but the historic buildings are quite lost amid the modern

development. The beaches here are attractive, but like those at Mongaguá and Praia Grande, several stretches are prone to pollution. Excursions can be made by boat up the **Rio Itanhaém**. Frequent buses run from Santos, an hour away. There are several good seafood restaurants along the beach, hotels and camping.

Peruíbe → *Colour map 5, A5. Phone code: 013. Population: 52,000.*

Some 31 km further down the coast, there are more beaches at Peruíbe, but some fall within the jurisdiction of the Estação Ecológica Juréia-Itatins (see below). While the beach culture has been well developed here with surfing, windsurfing, fishing and so on, a number of 'alternative' options have recently flourished. The climate is said to be unusually healthy owing to a high concentration of ozone, which helps to filter out harmful ultraviolet rays from the sun. UFO watchers and other esoterics claim that it is a very mystical place. Local rivers have water and black mud proven to contain medicinal properties. And the neighbouring ecological station is a major draw now that ecotourism has become big business in São Paulo state. Peruíbe's history dates back to 1530 when the village of Abarebebê was founded; about 9 km northeast of here, the ruins can be visited, with its church built of stone and shells. There is a **Feira do Artesanato** ① *Av São João, Sat and Sun 1400-0100 (1400-2300 in winter).*

Buses connect the town with Santos, for São Paulo. For information, contact the **Secretaria de Turismo** ① *R Nilo Soares Ferreira 50, T013-3455 2070.* You may have to ask permission in the **Departamento da Cultura** ① *Centro de Convenções, Av Sã João 545, T013-3455 2232,* to visit Abarebebê and other sites. Also at this address is the **Secretaria Estadual do Meio Ambiente** ① *T013-3457 9243,* for information on the **Estação Ecológico Juréia-Itatins**.

Estação Ecológico Juréia-Itatins

① *For permission to visit the ecological station, contact the Secretaria Estadual do Meio Ambiente, address above, or the Instituto Florestal (DRPE), R do Horto 931, São Paulo, T011-3952 8555. See map page 240.*

Peruíbe marks the northernmost point of the Estação Ecológico Juréia-Itatins, 820 sq km of protected *Mata Atlântica*. The four main ecosystems are *restinga*, mangrove forest, *Mata Atlântica* and the vegetation at about 900 m on the Juréia mountains. Its wildlife includes many endangered species including rare flowers and other plants. There are deer, jaguar, monkeys, dolphins, alligators and birds, including the yellow-headed woodpecker and toucans. Human occupation of the area has included sambaqui, builders, *fazendeiros* and present-day fishing communities who preserve an isolated way of life.

The ecological station was founded in 1986. Tourism is very carefully monitored and only certain areas are open to the public. These are: the **Núcleo Itinguçu**, 18 km from Peruíbe, which contains the Cachoeira do Paraíso (Paradise Falls) and other pools and waterfalls; **Vila Barra do Una**, a fishing village with a 2-km beach, camping and places to eat, 25 km from Peruíbe; and **Canto da Praia da Juréia** at the extreme southern end, 38 km from Iguape, with 7 km of beach and all the coastal ecosystems.

Hikers can walk the 4-km **Trilha do Arpoador** and the 5-km **Trilha do Imperador**, but both need prior reservation and numbers are limited; similarly for the **Despraiado mountain bike trail**. Trips can be made, with authorization, up the **Rio Guaraú** (8 km from Peruíbe) and the **Rio Una do Prelado** (25 km from Peruíbe). Other places of interest are **Vila do Prelado**, which was a stop on the Imperial São Vicente-Iguape post route (electric light was only installed in 1995), and the **Casa da Farinha**, where manioc flour is made, 28 km from Iguape.

Iguape and Ilha Comprida → *Colour map 5, A5. Phone code: 013. Population: 28,000.*

At the southern end of the ecological station is the town of Iguape, founded in 1538. In the early days of its existence, ownership of the town was disputed between Spain and Portugal because it was close to the line drawn by the Pope marking their respective territories in the 'New World'. Typical of Portuguese architecture, the small **Museu Histórico e Arqueológico** ① *R das Neves 45, Tue-Sun 0900-1730*, is housed in the 17th-century Casa da Oficina Real de Fundição. There is also a **Museu de Arte Sacra** ① *Praça Rotary, Sat and Sun 0900-1200, 1330-1700*, in the former Igreja do Rosário. The main church, the **Basílica de Bom Jesus**, is a mid-19th-century construction. Information is available from **Prefeitura Municipal** ① *R 15 de Novembro 272, T013-3841 1626*.

The main attractions for tourists are yachting, fishing and half a dozen beaches. Excursions include the ruined *fazenda* of **Itaguá**. Handicrafts include items made from wood and clay, basketware and musical instruments.

Opposite Iguape is the northern end of the **Ilha Comprida** with 86 km of beaches, some of which are disappointing. This **Área de Proteção Ambiental** is not much higher than sea level and is divided from the mainland by the Canal do Mar Pequeno. The northern end is the busiest and on the island there are hotels, a supermarket and some good restaurants; the fresh fish is excellent.

Caverns of the Vale do Ribeira and PETAR (Caverna do Santana) → *Colour map 5, A5.*

This cave system, 40 km from Eldorado, west of the BR-116, forms one of the largest concentrations of caverns in the world. Among the best known is the 8-km Gruta da Tapagem or **Caverna do Diabo** (Devil's Cave) ① *Mon-Fri 0800-1100, 1200-1700, Sat, Sun*

Estação Ecológica Juréia-Itatins

and holidays 0800-1700, US$2. It is as huge as a cathedral with well-lit formations in the 600 m that are open to the public.

Some 43 km north of the Caverna do Diabo is the **Parque Estadual Turístico do Alto Ribeira (PETAR)**, www.petaronline.com.br, which includes three groups of caves. The Núcleo Santana, contains the Cavernas de Santana (5.6 km of subterranean passages and three levels of galleries), Morro Preto and Água Suja, plus a 3.6-km ecological trail to the waterfalls in the Rio Bethary, and the Núcleo Ouro Grosso. This section of the park is 4 km from the town of Iporanga. Iporanga is the most convenient town for visiting all the caves; it is 64 km west of Eldorado Paulista, 42 km east of Apiaí, on the SP-165, 257 km southwest of São Paulo. The third group, Núcleo Caboclos, near the town of Apiaí.

Ins and outs The nearest towns to the caves are Iporanga and Apiaí; buses run to both from the Barra Funda *rodoviária* in São Paulo or you can take a bus to Registro and change there. If coming to Iporanga from Curitiba, change buses at Jacupiranga on the BR-116 for Eldorado Paulista. Most people who visit the caves use their own transport and there is little transport infrastructure for those who come without a car. However the **Pousada Quiririm** (see Sleeping, page 244), 3 km from PETAR, rents boats and can organize trips into the caves with advance notice.

Registro → *Phone code: 013. Population: 49,000.*

A suitable stopping place for visiting the caves area is Registro on the BR-116, in the heart of the tea-growing region, populated mainly by Japanese-Brazilians. There are a number of cheap hotels around the corner from the *rodoviária* (including **Brasília**, Rua Brasília) and banks with ATMs.

Cananéia → *Colour map 5, A5. Phone code: 013.*

The 18th-century façades of the little port town of **Cananéia** stand, gradually decaying, at the heart of the wildest region in southeastern Brazil. Extensive mangrove wetlands, lowland forests and porpoise-filled estuaries surround the town on all sides. Rising up behind them are the rugged, rainforest-covered mountains of the Serra do Mar, which stretch all the way into neighbouring Paraná. The white sands of **Ilha do Cordoso** are accessible by boat, and the long broad beaches of **Boqueirão Sul**, southern Ilha Comprida, are just five minutes by ferry across the little brackish river that fronts the town.

Although this is one of the country's oldest cities (it was one of Martim Afonso de Souza's landfalls), Cananéia lacks the twee charm and tourist facilities of its cousins, Morretes to the south and Paraty to the north. The 17th-century **Igreja de São João Batista** has plants growing out of its belltower and the façades of its colonial buildings are crumbling in the humidity. The only time of year that sees many visitors is Carnaval and New Year. This is a town with an *Under the Volcano* atmosphere; it feels like the end of the line. *Pousadas* open their doors at whim. Restaurants are limited to fish, beans and rice served on plastic tables by friendly waiters. However, for those seeking out-of-the-way places, herein lies its appeal.

Ins and outs Cananéia can be easily visited on the way from São Paulo or Santos to Curitiba. At least two buses a day run to those destinations from the little *rodoviária*, a block west of the central Praça Martim Afonso de Souza.

Car and passenger ferries leave every 30 minutes from in front of the *praça* for the beach at Boqueirão Sul in southern Ilha Comprida. It takes about an hour to walk from the ferry dock to the beach. A few simple *pousadas* line the way. It is also possible to take boats all the way to Ilha do Mel in Paraná (see page 325).

Ilha do Cardoso

The densely wooded Ilha do Cardoso is a Reserva Florestal e Biológica. **Marujá**, the only village on the island, is tiny and has no electricity. There are some very rustic *pousadas* and restaurants and camping is allowed at designated places, but the island is otherwise uninhabited. There are lots of idyllic beaches, where spectacled caiman can be spotted lazing on the virtually untouched white sand. The best place for surfing is **Moretinho**.

There are three daily ferry services from Cananéia, the journey takes four hours (the ticket office as it Rua Princesa Isabel, T013-3841 1122). Boats run tours from the docks for around US$7 per person in high season and at weekends. Launches can be hired for about US$70 for a full day at other times. Alternatively, drive 70 km along an unpaved road, impassable when wet, to **Ariri**, from where the island is 10 minutes by boat.

Ins and outs Speedboats to Ilha Cardoso must be chartered in Cananéia (US$60-80 for up to five people). *Escunas* (larger boats) generally leave daily in the morning for the fishing community of Marujá and more regularly at weekends and during the high season (US$7 each way).

◉ The coast of São Paulo listings

For Sleeping and Eating price codes and other relevant information, see pages 42-47.

● Sleeping

Santos *p226, map p227*
Discounts up to 50% during low season. There are many cheap hotels near the Orquidário Municipal a few blocks from the beach.
A Mendes Plaza, Av Floriano Peixoto 42, a block from the beach in the main shopping area, T013-3208 6400, www.mendes plaza.com.br. A large, newly refurbished 1970s business-orientated hotel with 2 restaurants and a rooftop pool.
A Parque Balneário Hotel, Av Ana Costa 555, Gonzaga, T013-3289 5700, www.parque balneario.com.br. The city's 5-star hotel, with full business facilities and a rooftop pool overlooking the beach. Close to the shops and restaurants. Recently renovated.
A-B Atlântico, Av Pres Wilson 1, T013-3289 5961, www.atlantico-hotel.com.br. A/c rooms in a newly renovated, well-kept 1930s hotel

on the seafront. All rooms have TV; the best are in the upper floors with sea views. There's a decent business centre, sauna, bar and restaurant.
A-B Gonzaga Flats, R Jorge Tibiriça 41, Gonzaga, T013-3289 5800, www.gonzaga flat.tur.br. Apartments in a 1990s block, all with kitchenettes and small sitting rooms with sofa beds. Space for up to 4 people.
C-D Hotel Natal, Av Mal Floriano Peixoto 104, Gonzaga T013-3284 2732, www.hotel natal.com.br. Fan-cooled or a/c apartments with or without bathrooms. Cable TV.
C-D Pousada do Marquês, Av Floriano Peixoto 202, Gonzaga, T013-3237 1951, www.pousadadomarques.com.br. Very simple en suite rooms with fan and cable TV.

Camburi, Camburizinho and Maresias *p231*

A Camburyzinho, Estr Camburi 200, Km 41, Camburizinho, T012-3865 2625, www.pousada camburizinho.com.br. 30 smart rooms around a pool with a bar and beach service.

B Piccolo Albergo, R Nova Iguaçu 1979, Maresias, T012-3465 6227, www.piccolo albergo.com.br. 5 smart chalets in a forest setting near a waterfall. With sauna and a natural swimming pool.

B Pousada das Praias, R Piauí 70, Camburizinho, T012-3865 1474, www.pousadadaspraias.com.br. Pleasant little beachside *pousada* with a pool and sauna.

São Sebastião *p232, map p235*

The city itself is not particularly desirable so only stay here if you have to, otherwise it's best to head for Ilhabela. There are a few cheap places near the main *praça* and *rodoviária*.

C-E Roma, Praça João Fernandes 174, T012-3892 1016, www.hotelroma.tur.br. Simple but well-maintained rooms around a fig-tree filled courtyard. The simplest are a little scruffy. Includes breakfast.

Camping

Camping do Barraqueçaba Bar de Mar de Lucas, near the beach about 6 km south of São Sebastião. Hot showers, English spoken, cabins available. Recommended.

Ilhabela *p233, map p235*

There are a number of moderate and cheap hotels on the road to the left of the ferry.

LL-L Maison Joly, R Antonio Lisboa Alves 278, Morro do Cantagalo, T012-3896 1201, www.maisonjoly.com.br. Exquisite little *pousada* perfect for couples. Each cabin is tastefully decorated in its own style and has a wonderful view out over the bay. Great restaurant and pool. Private, intimate and quiet. No children allowed.

L-AL Barulho d'Agua, R Manoel Pombo 250, Curral, Km 14, T012-3894 1406, www.barulho dagua.com.br. Intimate little cabins set in rainforest next to a clear river. Very romantic.

A Ilhabela, Av Pedro Paulo de Morais 151, Saco da Capela. T012-3896 1083, www.hotel ilhabela.com.br. One of the larger *pousadas*, orientated to families and with a well-equipped but small gym, pool, restaurant and bar and good breakfast. Recommended.

A Porto Pousada Saco da Capela, R Itapema 167, T012-3896 2255, www.sacodacapela.com.br. 18 carefully decorated cabins set in a rocky forest garden on a steep hill. Good pool and breakfast.

B Pousada dos Hibiscos, Av Pedro Paulo de Morais 714, T012-3896 1375, www.pousada doshibiscos.com.br. Little group of cabins set around a pool with a sauna, gym and bar. Nice atmosphere. Recommended.

B Vila das Pedra, R Antenor Custodio da Silva 46, Cocaia, T012-3896 2433, www.viladas pedras.com.br. 11 chalets in a forest garden. Tastefully decorated and a very nice pool.

C Canto Bravo, Praia do Bonete, T012-9766 0478. Set on a secluded beach 1½ hrs' walk (or 20-min boat ride) from Ponta de Sepituba. Modest and elegantly decorated cabins and excellent simple breakfast and lunch (included in the price).

C-D Tamara, R Jacob Eduardo Toedtli 163, Itaquanduba, T012-3896 2543, www.pousada-tamara.com.br. 17 *cabañas* with a/c around a small pool.

E Ilhabela, Av Col José Vicente Faria Lima 1243, Perequê, T012-3472 8468, hostelling@ iconet.com.br. IYHA hostel. Price per person.

Camping

In addition to **Pedra do Sino**, there are campsites at **Perequê**, near the ferry dock, and at **Praia Grande**, a further 11 km south.

Ubatuba *p236, map p237*

Very cheap accommodation is hard to come by and at all holiday times no hotel charges less than US$20.

B São Charbel, Praça Nóbrega 280, T012-3432 1090. Very helpful and comfortable, on the busy main square. The advertised rooftop 'pool' is, in reality, a tiny plunge pool.

C São Nicolau, R Conceição 213, T012-3432 5007. A 3-min walk from the bus station, convenient for the town beach restaurants and services. A/c rooms have a TV and fridge. Well run and looked after, with a good breakfast.

C Xaréu, R Jordão Homem da Costa 413, T012-3432 1525. 3-min walk from the bus station,

convenient for the town beach restaurants and services. Pretty rooms with wrought-iron balconies in a pleasant garden area. Good value, excellent breakfast. Recommended.
D Barra do Farol, R Dr Félix Guizard Filho 6, T012-3432 2019. Homely, motel-style rooms close to seafront.
E Cora Coralina, Rod Oswaldo Cruz Km 89, near Horto Florestal, T011-3258 0388. IYHA hostel. Simple dorms/doubles. Friendly, helpful.
E JS Brandão, R Nestor Fonseca 173, Jardim Sumaré, near the Tropic of Capricorn sign south of town, T012-3432 2337. Price per person. IYHA hostel. Pleasant staff, modest accommodation but clean and well kept.

Beach hotels
L Recanto das Toninhas, Praia das Toninhas, T012-3842 1410, www.toninhas.com.br. Part of the *Roteiros de Charme* group (see page 43). Elegant *cabañas* with sea views set around a very pretty pool with a full range of services and activities, including a sauna, restaurant, bar, tennis court and excursions.
AL Refúgio do Corsário, Baia Fortaleza, 25 km south of Ubatuba, T012-3443 9148. A clean quiet hotel on the waterfront with full board and a range of activities including sailing and swimming. Very relaxing.
AL Saveiros, R Laranjeira 227, Praia do Lázaro, 14 km from town, T012-3842 0172, www.hotel saveiros.com.br. Pretty little *pousada* with a pool and a decent restaurant. English spoken.
A Solar das Águas Cantantes, Estr Saco da Ribeira 253, Praia do Lázaro, Km 14, T012-3442 0178, www.ubatuba2000.com.br/solar. A mock-Portuguese colonial house replete with *azulejos* and set in a shady tropical garden. The restaurant is one of the best on the São Paulo coast and serves excellent seafood and Bahian dishes.
B-C Rosa Penteado, Av Beira-Mar 183, Praia de Picinguaba, T012-3833 8998, www.ubatuba site.com.br/atelierrosapenteado. 4 pretty beachside *cabañas* decorated with paintings and objects made by the owner. The price includes a very good breakfast and dinner.

E Maurício, Av Abreu Sodré 607, north of town, near Praia do Perequê-Açu. Cheap rooms in a private house. Laundry service.

Camping
Camping Clube do Brasil, Lagoinha, 25 km from town, T012-3443 1536; also at Praia Perequê-Açu, 2 km north, T012-3432 1682. There are about 8 other sites in the vicinity.

Peruíbe *p239*
A Piero Al Mare, R Indianópolis 20, Praia Orla dos Coqueiros, T013-458 2603. Modest, plain rooms with breakfast and a restaurant.
B-C Waldhaus, R Gaviotas 1201, Praia do Guaraú, T013-3457 9170. Small hotel in a pleasant setting with friendly staff, a/c or fan-cooled rooms and a restaurant.
C-D Vila Real, Av Anchieta 6625, T013-3458 2797. Basic but well looked after and with good staff.

Iguape and Ilha Comprida *p240*
The northern part of Ilha Comprida is reached from Iguape. The southern part of Ilha Comprida is closer to Cananéia. There are hotels in the southern end too, reachable from Cananeia. All those listed here are in Iguape.
B Silvi, R Ana Cândida Sandoval Trigo 515, T013-3841 1421, silvihotel@virtualway.com.br. Simple, but pleasant and with friendly staff.
C Solar Colonial Pousada, Praça da Basilica 30, T013-3841 1591. A range of rooms in a converted 19th-century house.
D Veleiro, Av Beira Mar 579, T013-3895 2407. Modest but well maintained. Recommended.

Camping
There is a campsite at **Praia da Barra da Ribeira**, 20 km north, and wild camping is possible at **Praia de Juréia**, the gateway to the ecological station.

Caverns of the Vale do Ribeiro *p240*
B-C Pousada Quiririm, Rodovia Antonio Honório da Silva, Km 156, 6 Bairro da Serra - Iporanga, www.pousadadoquiririm.com.br.

Pretty litte *pousada* with chalets set in a sub-tropical garden overlooking the forest. Organizes trips to the caves. Full board. Book ahead, especially at weekends.
C Pousada das Cavernas, Iporanga, T015-3556 1168 or T011-3543 3082. Pleasant, simple with breakfast.
D Pousada Rancho da Serra, Iporanga, T015-3556 1168 or T011-3588 2011. Friendly staff who can offer advice about caving.
E Youth hostel, near the Caverna do Diabo, Província de Tokushima, Parque Estadual da Caverna do Diabo, Km 43, SP-165, Eldorado Paulista.

Camping
Camping in **PETAR**, US$3 per person, 3 sites.

Cananéia and Ilha do Cardoso
p241 and p242
There are a few cheap hotels in Cananéia town and other more expensive options across the water (2 mins on ferry and about 30-min walk) on the southern end of Ilha Comprida (see page 240). R Tristã Lobo lies a few blocks inland from the *praça* and runs parallel to the shoreline.
B-C Pousada de Pedrino, R Tristão Lobo 49, Cananéia historical centre, T013-3851 1368. Simple a/c motel-like rooms with tiled floors and TVs and a small restaurant. No sign outside the hotel. R Tristão Lobo lies 2 blocks inland from the main *praça*.
C-D Pousada do Sossego, Praia do Marujá, Ilha do Cardoso, T013-3852 1141, www.cananet.com.br/sossego. Simple rooms in shacks right on a pristine, lonely stretch of beach. The *pousada* can organize trail walks, boat trips and fishing.
C-D Pousada Ilha do Cardoso, Praia do Marujá, Ilha do Cardoso, T013-3852 1613. A little concrete house near the beach and on the edge of the fishing village, with terraces and breakfast included.
D-E Villa São João Baptysta, R Tristã Lobo 289, T013-3851 1587. A small, charming family *pousada* in a converted 18th-century house. Simple but welcoming.

🍴 Eating

Santos *p226, map p227*
🍴 **Old Harbour**, Av Ana Costa 555, in the Parque Balneário Hotel, T013-3289 5700. Traditional Brazilian fare with daily lunch buffets and a hearty *feijoada* on Sat lunch.
🍴 **Pier One**, Av Almirante Saldanha da Gama, Ponta da Praia. Good evening option in a restaurant perched over the water next to the Ponte Edgard Perdigao bridge. Very good *meca santista* – a local fish speciality served with banana, manioc flour and bacon – and live music at weekends.
🍴 **WTC**, R 15 de Novembro 111/113, Centro Histórico, T013-3219 7175. A business man's club housed in a handsome 19th-century building. Popular with local bigwigs. One of the best restaurants in the city with a Mediterranean-influenced menu.
🍴-🍴 **Point 44**, R Jorge Tibiriçá 44. Great lunchtime buffet with enormous choice of *churrascaria*, in a large bustling dining room. Bar snack menu, live music Tue-Sat evening and dancing on Tue, Thu and Sat.
🍴 **Café Paulista**, Praça Rui Barbosa 8 at R do Comércio, Centro Histórico, T013-3219 5550. A Santos institution. Founded in 1911 by Italians, this place has been serving great Portuguese dishes such as *bacalhau*, and bar snacks (such as *empada camarão*), and coffee.

Camburi, Camburizinho and Maresias *p231*
There are numerous cheap and mid-range restaurants with bars and nightclubs in Camburi, Camburizinho and Maresias.
🍴 **Manacá**, R do Manacá, Camburizinho, T012-3865 1566. Closed Mon and Wed. The best restaurant on the São Paulo coast and one of the best in the state, with French cooking techniques with Brazilian, Asian and seafood ingredients. Specialities include sole in orange and ginger sauce, puréed potato and wasabi. Very romantic setting, in a tropical rainforest garden reached by a candlelit boardwalk. Come for dinner. Worth a special trip.

São Sebastião *p232, map p235*
¶ **São Sebastião bar and restaurant**,
Praça Major João Fernades 278, diagonally
opposite the Igreja Matriz, T012-3892 4100.
Generous *pratos feitos*, fish and chicken
and great juices. Very good value.

Ilhabela *p233, map p235*
There are cheap places in the town, including
a decent *padaria* (bakery) and snack bars.
¶¶¶ **Pizzabela**, Hotel Ilha Deck, Av Alm
Tamandaré 805, Itaguassu, T012-3896 1489.
Paulistanos consider their pizza the best in
the world. This is one of the few restaurants
outside the city serving pizza, São Paulo-
style. Expect lots of cheese. Nice surrounds.
¶¶¶ **Viana**, Av Leonardo Reale 1560, Praia do
Viana, T012-3896 1089. The best and most
expensive restaurant on the island, with
excellent seafood and light Italian dishes.
Good wine list. Book ahead.

Ubatuba *p236, map p237*
There is a string of mid-range restaurants
along the seafront on Av Iperoig, as far
as the roundabout by the airport.
¶¶¶ **Giorgio**, Av Leovigildo Dias Vieira
248, Itaguá. Sophisticated Italian
restaurant and bar.
¶¶¶ **Solar das Águas Cantantes**,
(see Sleeping). Very good seafood
and Bahian restaurant in elegant surrounds.
¶¶ **Pizzeria São Paulo**, Praça da Paz de Iperoig
26. Undeniably chic gourmet pizzeria in
beautifully restored building. Owned by
a young lawyer who brings the authentic
Italian ingredients for the gorgeous pizzas
from São Paulo every weekend.
¶¶ **Senzala**, Av Iperoig. Established 30 years
ago, this Italian has a lovely atmosphere. Don't
miss the seafood spaghetti. Recommended.
¶ **Armazém da Praia**, R Cel Ernesto de
Oliveira 149, opposite the post office.
Open for lunch only. Pretty, family-
run self-service.
¶ **Sérgio**, R Prof Thomaz Galhardo 404.
Open for dinner, weekends only. Serving
ice-cream, pizza and, at weekends, *feijoada*.

⊛ Festivals and events

Santos *p226, map p227*
Throughout the summer there are many
cultural, educational and sporting events.
26 Jan Foundation of Santos.
Mar/Apr Good Fri.
Jun Corpus Christi; Festejos Juninos.
8 Sep Nossa Senhora de Monte Serrat.

São Sebastião *p232, map p235*
20 Jan Festival of the Patron Saint,
featuring *congadas*, a song and dance
derived from slaves from the Congo.

Ilhabela *p233, map p235*
There are sailing weeks and fishing
contests throughout the year; dates
change annually.
Feb Carnaval.
May Ilhabela is rich in folklore and legends.
Its version of *congada* is famous, particularly
at the Festival of São Benedito.
28 Jun São Pedro, with a maritime procession.
1st week of Jul Santa Verônica in Bonete.
Sep The town's anniversary.

Ubatuba *p236, map p237*
Feb Carnaval.
End Jun São Pedro.
Jul Festa do Divino Espírito Santo.
Sep Ubatuba is known for its handicrafts
(carved wood, basketware) and it holds
an annual Festa da Cultura Popular.
28 Oct Ubatuba's anniversary.

Peruíbe *p239*
18 Feb Founding of Peruíbe.
Jun Festival do Inverno.
Oct Mês das Missões.

Iguape and Ilha Comprida *p240*
Throughout the year there are various
sporting and cultural events.
Jan/Feb Summer festival in Iguape.
Feb Carnaval on Ilha Comprida.
Mar/Apr Semana Santa.
Jun Corpus Christi.

The biggest rodeo in the world

The world's biggest annual rodeo, the Festa do Peão Boiadeiro, is held during the third week in August in Barretos, some 115 km northwest of Ribeirão Preto. The town is completely taken over as up to a million fans come to watch the horsemanship, enjoy the concerts, eat, drink and shop in what has become the epitome of Brazilian cowboy culture. There are over 1000 rodeos a year in Brazil, but this is the ultimate. The stadium, which has a capacity for 35,000 people, was designed by Oscar Niemeyer and the wind funnels through the middle, cool the competitors and the spectators. Since the 1950s, when Barretos' rodeo began, the event grew slowly until the mid-1980s when it really took off.

Tours from the UK are run by **Last Frontiers**, Fleet Marston Farm, Aylesbury, Bucks HP18 0QT, T01296-658650, www.lastfrontiers.co.uk.

Aug The month of the pilgrimage of Senhor Bom Jesus de Iguape.
3 Dec Iguape's anniversary.

❸ Transport

Santos *p226, map p227*
Bus To **São Vicente**, US$0.90. For most suburbs buses leave from Praça Mauá, in the centre of the city. Heading south, several daily buses connect Santos to **Peruíbe**, **Iguape** and **Cananeia** for **Ilha Comprida** and **Ilha do Cardoso**.

There are buses to **São Paulo** (50 mins, US$3.60) approximately every 15 mins, from the *rodoviária* near the city centre, José Menino or Ponta da Praia (opposite the ferry to Guarujá). Note that the 2 highways between São Paulo and Santos are sometimes very crowded, especially at rush hours and weekends. To **Guarulhos/Cumbica airport**, Expresso Brasileiro at 0600, 1330, 1830, return 0550, 0930, 1240, 1810, US$20, allow plenty of time as the bus goes through Guarulhos, 3 hrs. TransLitoral from Santos to **Congonhas airport** then to Guarulhos/Cumbica, 4 daily, US$12, 2 hrs. To **Rio de Janeiro**, Normandy, several daily, 7½ hrs, US$40. To Rio along the coast road is via **São Sebastião** (US$10, change buses if necessary), **Caraguatatuba** and **Ubatuba**.

Taxi All taxis have meters. The fare from Gonzaga to the bus station is about US$15. Cooper Rádio táxi, T013-3232 7177.

São Sebastião *p232, map p235*
Bus 2 buses a day to **Rio de Janeiro** with Normandy, 0830 and 2300 (plus 1630 on Fri and Sun), can be heavily booked in advance, US$30 (US$10 from Paraty) 6½ hrs; 12 a day to **Santos**, via Guarujá, 4 hrs, US$11; 11 buses a day also to **São Paulo**, US$15, which run inland via **São José dos Campos**, unless you ask for the service via **Bertioga**, only 2 a day. Other buses run along the coast via **Maresias**, **Camburi** or north through **Ubatuba**. Last bus leaves at 2200.

Ferry Free ferry to **Ilhabela** for foot passengers, see below.

Ilhabela *p233, map p235*
Bus A bus runs along the coastal strip facing the mainland. **Litorânea** runs buses from Ilhabela town through to **São Paulo** (office at R Dr Carvalho 136) but it is easiest to reach the island by taking a bus from São Paulo to São Sebastião across the water and then the ferry across to Ilhabela.

Ferry The 15- to 20-min ferry to **São Sebastião** runs non-stop day and night. Free for foot passengers; cars cost US$1 weekdays, US$10 at weekends.

Ubatuba *p236, map p237*
Bus There are 3 bus terminals.
Rodoviária Costamar, R Hans Staden and R Conceição, serves all local destinations.

The *rodoviária* at R Prof Thomaz Galhardo 513, for **São José** buses to **Paraty**, US$2.25, some **Normandy** services to **Rio de Janeiro**, US$9 and some **Itapemirim** buses.

Rodoviária Litorânea is the main bus station. To get there, go up Conceição for 8 blocks from Praça 13 de Maio, turn right on R Rio Grande do Sul, then left into R Dra Maria V Jean. Buses go to **São Paulo**, 3½ hrs, frequent, US$8, **São José dos Campos**, US$6, **Paraibuna**, US$5, **Caraguatatuba**, US$2.

Iguape and Ilha Comprida *p240*
Bus Buses run from Iguape to **São Paulo**, **Santos** or **Curitiba**, changing at Registro.

Ferry A continuous ferry service runs from Iguape to Ilha Comprida (free but small charge for cars); buses run until 1900 from the ferry stop to the beaches. From Iguape it is possible to take a boat trip down the coast to **Cananéia** and **Ariri**. Tickets and information from **Dpto Hidroviário do Estado**, R Major Moutinho 198, Iguape, T013-3841 1122. It is a beautiful trip, passing between the island and the mainland.

Caverns of the Vale do Ribeiro *p240*
Bus Buses from Apiaí run to the Barra Funda *rodoviária* in **São Paulo**, US$22. If heading to **Curitiba**, take the bus from Iporanga to Jacupiranga on the BR-116 and change.

Cananéia and Ilha do Cardoso
p241 and p242
Bus Buses run twice daily from Cananéia to **São Paulo** (Barra Funda). Alternatively go via **Registro** (from where there are buses hourly to Barra Funda).

ⓘ Directory

Santos *p226, map p227*
Banks Open 1000-1730. ATMs in Santos are very unreliable and often out of order. Visa ATMs at Banco do Brasil, R 15 de Novembro 195, Centro and Av Ana Costa, Gonzaga. Many others. **Embassies and consulates** France, R General Câmara 12, sala 51, T013-3219 5161. **Germany**, R Frei Gaspar 22, 10th floor, T013-3219 5092. UK, R Tuiuti 58, 2nd floor, T013-3219 6622. **Immigration** Polícia Federal, Praça da República. **Internet** F hop, Shopping Parque Balneário. US$3 per hr. **Laundry** Av Mcal Floriano Peixoto 120, Gonzaga, self-service, wash and dry US$5. **Medical services** Ana Costa, R Pedro Américo 42, Campo Grande, T013-3222 9000; Santa Casa de Misericórdia, Av Dr Cláudio Luiz da Costa 50, Jabaquara, T013-3234 7575. **Post office** R Cidade de Toledo 41, Centro and at R Tolentino Filgueiras 70, Gonzaga. **Telephone** R Galeão Carvalhal 45, Gonzaga.

Ilhabela *p233, map p235*
Banks Bradesco, Praça Col Julião M Negrão 29 in Vila Ilhabela.

Ubatuba *p236, map p237*
Banks There is a Banco 24 Horas next to the tourist office and an HSBC ATM at 85 R Conceição. The Banco do Brasil in Praça Nóbrega does not have ATMs. **Internet** Chat and Bar, upper floor of Ubatuba Shopping. US$3 per hr, Mon-Sat 1100-2000. **Post office** R Dona Maria Alves between Hans Staden and R Col Dominicano. **Telephone** On Galhardo, close to Sérgio restaurant.

Contents

Footprint features

Minas Gerais & Espírito Santo

At a glance

◉ **Getting around** Buses and internal flights for Diamantina and the north.

◉ **Time required** 5-7 days for the southern colonial towns, Belo Horizonte and Diamantina.

☼ **Weather** Summer (Apr-Oct) is hot and dry; winter (Oct-Mar) is hot and wet. Cold fronts can cause temperature drops at any time.

✕ **When not to go** Dec-Jan are the wettest months.

★ **Don't miss ...**
1 Ouro Preto and Congonhas do Campo, pages 263 and 274.
2 Tiradentes, page 277.
3 Parque Nacional da Serra do Cipó, page 290.
4 Diamantina, page 291.
5 Pedra Azul, page 309.

The inland state of Minas Gerais ('General Mines'), was once described as having a heart of gold and a breast of iron. The state was founded solely to provide precious metals for the imperial coffers. As the gold-mining camps grew and prospered they became towns of little cobbled streets crowned with opulent Manueline churches. Many of the towns are well preserved and these, and the rugged forested hills around them, are the principal reasons to visit.

Espírito Santo, immediately to the east of Minas, is less visited. But although its coastline is not as pretty as that of Bahia to its north, it is far less developed. Beaches here can be almost deserted but for the visiting turtles. The state's interior is rugged, swathed in coffee and eucalyptus and dotted with giant granite rocks even larger than those to the south in Rio de Janeiro. The most famous and striking is Pedra Azul, which is on the main highway between Espírito Santo and Minas.

Minas Gerais

The state of Minas Gerais is a little larger than France and almost as mountainous. In the south the land rises to over 2700 m on the border of Itatiaia national park in Rio, and in the east, to 2890 m at the Pico da Bandeira in the Caparaó national park. Both these areas of highland are part of the chain of forest-clad mountains that forms the escarpment, which cuts Minas Gerais off from the coastal lowlands of the states of Rio de Janeiro and Espírito Santo. The north of Minas is a dry and desolate region known as the sertão, protected by the large national park, Grande Sertão Veredas, which contains significant areas of cerrado forest and the groves of buriti palms (veredas), which give the park its name. Some of the country's rarest and most intriguing animals, such as the maned wolf and giant anteater, live here. The foremost of the colonial towns are Tiradentes, Ouro Preto and Diamantina. Many of these have churches decorated with carvings by the country's most celebrated sculptor, Aleijadinho. The state capital, Belo Horizonte, has few attractions but good transport links.

Background

Like the Spanish, the Portuguese looked to their colonies for easy money. Outside the Jesuit reduction cities, there were never plans to invest in empire, only to exploit the land and the local people as ruthlessly as possible. At first it was wood that attracted the Portuguese, and then indigenous slaves for the cane plantations that stretched along the northern coast. But it was the ultimate in rich pickings that led to colonial Brazil becoming more than a coastline empire. In 1693, whilst out on a marauding expedition, a Paulista bandeirante found *ouro preto* – gold made black by a coat of iron oxide – in a stream south of modern Belo Horizonte. When news reached home, an influx of adventurers trekked their way from São Paulo through the forests to set up makeshift camps along the gold streams. These camps developed into wealthy towns such as Ouro Preto and Mariana. Later, with the discovery of diamonds and other gemstones, a captaincy was established and named, prosaically, 'General Mines'.

The wealth of Minas was reflected in its streets and in the baroque churches, whose interiors were covered in gold plate and decorated with sculptures by the best artisans in Brazil. And with the wealth came growing self-importance. The Inconfidência Mineira (see box, page 272), the most important rebellion in colonial Brazil, began in Ouro Preto in the late 18th century under a group of intellectuals educated in Portugal who were in contact with Thomas Jefferson and English industrialists. The Inconfidência never got beyond discussion but it was decided that the only non-aristocratic member of the group, José Joaquim da Silva, would be in charge of taking the governor's palace, occupied by the hated Visconde of Barbacena, who was responsible for levying the imperial taxes. Da Silva was derisively known as Tiradentes (the tooth puller) by his compatriots. Today he is the only Inconfidênte rebel that most Brazilians can name and he is celebrated as a folk hero – one of the common people who dared to challenge the powerful elite, and who was cruelly martyred as a result.

After Brazil changed from an empire into a republic, Minas Gerais vied for power with the coffee barons of São Paulo and, in the 20th century, produced two Brazilian presidents. Juscelino Kubitschek, an establishment figure chosen by the electorate as the best alternative to the military, opened up Brazil to foreign investment in the 1960s, and founded Brasília. Tancredo Neves also opposed the Brazilian military, was elected to power in 1985. A few days before his inauguration, he died in mysterious circumstances. His last words were reportedly "I did not deserve this". He was replaced by José Sarney, a leading figure in the Brazilian landowning oligarchy.

Belo Horizonte

→ *Colour map 4, B3. Phone code: 031. Population: 5 million.*

The capital of Minas Gerais, Belo Horizonte, is the third largest city in Brazil. Although moderately attractive it offers little in the way of sights, beyond a handful of museums and parks. Most travellers come here to change bus on the way to Ouro Preto or Tiradentes, or to find work as an English language teacher. The bustling modern skyscraper-filled centre sits in a bowl circled by dramatic mountains, which regularly trap pollution as the city strains under ever-increasing tides of rural migration. The city is pocked with hills that rise and fall in waves of red-tiled houses, tall apartment blocks and jacaranda- and ipe-lined streets. These are clogged with cars, particularly during the rush hour, a situation that has led the municipal government to introduce an efficient integrated public transport system linking the bus and metrô networks, in imitation of Curitiba in Paraná.
▸▸ *For listings, see pages 258-262.*

Ins and outs

Getting there
International and many national flights land at **Tancredo Neves International Airport**, more commonly referred to as **Confins** ① *39 km north of Belo Horizonte, T031-3689 2700, www.infraero.gov.br.* A taxi to the centre costs US$50. Buses from Confins, either *executivo* (from the exit, US$15), or the comfortable normal bus (**Unir**, from the far end of the car park, hourly, US$5), go to the *rodoviária*. The domestic airport is at **Pampulha** ① *9 km north of the centre, T031-3490 2000.* Blue bus No 1202 to the city centre leaves across the street from the airport (25 minutes, US$1.50), passing the *rodoviária* and the cheaper hotel district. Interstate buses arrive at the *rodoviária* next to Praça Rio Branco at the northwest end of Avenida Afonso Pena. The bus station is clean and well organized with toilets, a post office, telephones, left-luggage lockers (US$2, open 0700-2200) and shops. ▸▸ *See Transport, page 261.*

Getting around
The city has a good public transport system. **Red** buses run on express routes and charge US$1.50; **yellow** buses have circular routes around the Contorno, US$1; **blue** buses run on diagonal routes charging US$1.50. Some buses link up with the regional overground metrô. At present, the metrô is limited to one line and covers a limited portion of the north and west of the city and few areas of interest to tourists. However there are plans to extend the service to Pampulha airport and the centre, US$0.90.

Orientation
Belo Horizonte centres on the large Parque Municipal in the heart of downtown Belo Horizonte and on the broad main avenue of Afonso Pena. This is constantly full of pedestrians and traffic, except on Sunday morning when cars are banned and part of it becomes a huge open-air market. Daytime activity is concentrated on and around the main commercial district on Avenida Afonso Pena, which is the best area for lunch. At night, activity shifts to Savassi, southwest of the centre, which has a wealth of restaurants, bars and clubs.

Best time to visit
Central Minas enjoys an excellent climate (16-30°C) except for the rainy season (December to March); the average temperature in Belo Horizonte is 21°C.

Tourist information

The municipal office, **Belotur** ① *R Pernambuco 284, Funcionários, T031-3220 1310, www.turismo.mg.gov.br, www.belotur.com.br; also on Parque Municipal, at the airports and rodoviária*, has lots of useful information and maps. The free monthly *Guía Turística* lists events and opening times. The tourism authority for Minas Gerais, **Turminas** ① *Praça Rio Branco 56, T031-3272 8573, www.turminas.mg.gov.br/intminas.html*, is very helpful; its *Gerais Common Ways* booklet has facts. **Ibama** ① *Av do Contorno 8121, Cidade Jardim, T031-3337 2624*, has information on national parks. The website www.belohorizonteturismo.com.br is also useful.

As in any large city, watch out for sneak thieves in the centre and at the bus station. The Parque Municipal is not safe after dark, so it is best not to enter alone.

① Belo Horizonte orientation & Pampulha

➡ **Belo Horizonte maps**
1 Belo Horizonte orientation and Pampulha, page 254
2 Belo Horizonte centre, page 255

Sleeping 🛏
Ouro Minas Palace **3**

Sights

Although dotted with green spaces like the **Parque Municipal** ① *Tue-Sun 0600-1800*, and a few handsome buildings such as the arts complex at the **Palácio das Artes** ① *Afonso Pena 156*, central Belo Horizonte has few sights of interest beyond a handful of small museums. The **Museu Mineiro** ① *Av João Pinheiro 342, T031-3269 1168, Tue-Fri 1000-1700, Sat and Sun 1000-1600*, houses religious and other art in the old senate building, close to the centre. There is a section dedicated specifically to religious art, with six

Belo Horizonte centre

➡ **Belo Horizonte maps**
1 Belo Horizonte orientation and Pampulha, page 254
2 Belo Horizonte centre, page 255

Sleeping 🛌
Best Western Sol Belo Horizonte **12**
Continental **1**
Dayrell Minas **3**
Esplanada **2**
IYHA Chalé Mineiro **4**
Le Flamboyant Flats **6**
Liberty Palace **5**
Mercure **11**
O Sorriso do Lagarto Hostel **7**
Othon Palace **8**
São Salvador **9**
Villa Emma Flats **10**

Eating 🍴
A Cafeteria **1**
Café da Travessa **2**
Café Tina **3**
Dona Derna **4**
Kauhana **5**
La Traviata **6**
Sushi Beer **7**
Taste Vin **8**
Vecchio Sogno **9**

pictures attributed to Mestre Athayde (see pages 265-267), exhibitions of modern art, photographs and works by *naïf* painters. Also of interest are the woodcarvings by Geraldo Teles de Oliveira (GTO). The **Museu Histórico Abílio Barreto** ① *Av Prudente de Morais 202, Cidade Jardim, T031-3277 8861, Tue, Wed, Fri, Sun 1000-1700, Thu 1000-1200*, is in an old *fazenda* which has existed since 1883, when Belo Horizonte was a village called Arraial do Curral d'el Rey. The *fazenda* now houses antique furniture and historical exhibits. To get there, take bus No 2902 from Avenida Afonso Pena.

Pampulha

The city's most interesting attraction by far is the suburb of Pampulha: a complex of Oscar Niemeyer buildings set around a lake in formal gardens landscaped by Roberto Burle Marx. The project was commissioned by Juscelino Kubitschek in the 1940s, when he was governor of Minas Gerais and a decade before he became president. Some see it as a proto-Brasília, for this was the first time that Niemeyer had designed a series of buildings that work together in geometric harmony. It was in Pampulha that he first experimented with the plasticity of concrete; the highlight of the complex is the **Igreja São Francisco de Assis** ① *Av Otacílio Negrão de Lima, Km 12, T031-3441 9325, daily 0800-1800*. This was one of Niemeyer's first departures from the orthodox rectilinear forms of modernism and one of the first buildings in the world to mould concrete, with its series of parabolic waves running together to form arches. Light pierces the interior through a series of louvres and the curves are offset by a simple free-standing bell tower. The outside walls are covered in *azulejo* tiles by Candido Portinari, Brazil's most respected modernist artist. These were painted in a different style from his previous social realism, as exemplified by pictures such as *O Mestiço*. The building provoked a great deal of outrage because of its modernist design. One mayor proposed its demolition and replacement by a copy of the church of Saint Francis in Ouro Preto.

There are a number of other interesting Niemeyer buildings on the other side of the lake from the church. With its snaking canopy leading up to the main dance hall, the **Casa do Baile** ① *Av Octacílio Negrão de Lima 751, Tue-Sun 0900-1900, free*, is another example of his fascination with the curved line. There are wonderful views out over the lake. People would dance here and then take a boat to the glass and marble **Museu de Arte de Pampulha (MAP)** ① *Av Octacílio Negrão de Lima 16585, T031-3443 4533, www.comarte virtual.com.br, Tue-Sun 0900-1900, free*, which was then a casino set up by Kubitschek. Today it houses a fine collection of Mineira modern art and more than 900 works by national artists.

Just 700 m south of the lake are the twin stadia of **Mineirão** and **Mineirinho**, clear precursors to the Centro de Convenções Ulysses Guimarães in Brasília, which was designed by Niemeyer's office though not the architect himself. Mineirão is the second largest stadium in Brazil after the Maracanã in Rio, seating 92,000 people.

Around Belo Horizonte ●●● ›› pp258-262.

Caves

The hilly countryside around Belo Horizonte is honeycombed with some of Brazil's most beautiful caves. The best and most famous is the **Gruta de Maquiné** ① *120 km from Belo Horizonte, off the BR-040/ MG-231, daily 0800-1700, US$5*, near the town of **Cordisburgo**. The cave has six chambers open to visitors; these are well lit and encrusted with beautiful speleological formations. It's best to come at the beginning or end of the day, and avoid the weekend when there are crowds. Cordisburgo has a handful of hotels and was the home of Brazil's most celebrated modern writer, João Guimarães Rosa, the author of the great Minas

Gerais epic *Grande Sertão: veredas*. The **Casa Museu de Guimarães Rosa** ⓘ *Av Padre João 744, Tue-Sun 0800-1700*, is dedicated to the writer and housed in his former home. It preserves many of Guimarães Rosa's original manuscripts.

Less than 40 km to the south (and some 80 km northwest of Belo Horizonte) is the town of **Sete Lagoas**, near the **Gruta Rei do Mato** ⓘ *T031-3773 0888, 0800-1700*, where prehistoric inscriptions and cave paintings have been found. The **Gruta de Lapinha** ⓘ *Tue-Sun 0900-1700, US$2 entry to caves and archaeological museum*, is 36 km north of the city.

Ins and outs Cordisburgo and the Gruta Maquiné are served by three buses daily from Belo Horizonte (2½ hours). Sete Lagoas, which has accommodation, is served by three buses daily (1½ hours) and Gruta Lapinha by four buses (one hour).

Parque Natural de Caraça

This remarkable reserve sits in the heart of the Serra do Espinhaço mountains about 120 km east of Belo Horizonte and is perhaps the best place in South America for seeing maned wolf. The park ranges in altitude from 720 m to 2070 m. The lower areas are rich in Atlantic forest while the higher areas support *cerrado*, grassland and other mountain habitats. There are lakes, waterfalls and rivers. Since the early 1980s, the monks have been leaving food for maned wolves on the seminary steps, and at least four can usually be seen in the every evening. Other endangered mammals in the park include southern masked titi monkeys, which can often be spotted in family groups, tufted-eared marmosets and brown capuchin monkeys. Birdlife includes various toucans, guans and hummingbirds (such as the Brazilian ruby and the white-throated hummingbird), various tanagers, cotingas, antbirds, woodpeckers and the long-trained and scissor-tailed nightjars. Some of the bird species are endemic, others are rare and endangered.

The trails for viewing the different landscapes and the wildlife are marked at the beginning and are quite easy to follow, although a guide (available through the seminary) is recommended.

The **seminary buildings** and the church are beautifully set in a shallow valley 1220 m above sea level and surrounded on three sides by rugged mountains that rise to 2070 m at the Pico do Sol. The name Caraça means 'big face', so called because of a hill that is said to resemble the face of a giant who is looking at the sky. This can be best appreciated by climbing up to the cross just above the church. The church itself has a painting of the Last Supper attributed to Mestre Athayde (see pages 265-267) with a trompe l'oeil effect. The eyes of Judas Iscariot (the figure holding the purse) seem to follow you as you move. Part of the seminary has been converted into a hotel, which is the only place to stay in the park (see Sleeping, page 259). It is also possible to stay in **Santa Bárbara**, 25 km away on the road to Mariana, which has a few cheap hotels, and hitchhike to Caraça.

Ins and outs The park is open 0700-2100; if staying overnight you cannot leave after 2100. Entry to the park costs US$5 per vehicle. Santa Bárbara is served by 11 buses a day from Belo Horizonte (fewer on weekends). There is also a bus service to Mariana, a beautiful route, via Catas Altas, which has an interesting church and a *pousada* belonging to the municipality of Santa Bárbara. To get to the park, turn off the BR-262 (towards Vitória) at Km 73 and go via Barão de Cocais to Caraça (120 km). There is no public transport to the seminary. Buses go as far as Barão de Cocais, from where a taxi is US$12. Book the taxi to return for you, or hitch (which may not be easy). The park entrance is 10 km before the seminary. The alternative is to hire a guide from Belo Horizonte, which costs about US$75 including transport and meals.

For Sleeping and Eating price codes and other relevant information, see pages 42-47.

⊜ Sleeping

Belo Horizonte *p253, maps p254 and p255*
There are cheap options near the *rodoviária* and on *R Curitiba*, but many of these hotels are hot-pillow establishments; you will have a more comfortable stay in one of the youth hostels. You can spend the night in the *rodoviária*, but only if you have an onward ticket (police check at 2400).

L Ouro Minas Palace, Av Cristiano Machado 4001, T031-3429 4001 (toll free T0800-314000), www.ourominas.com.br. The most luxurious hotel in the city with palatial suites, including several for women only on the top floors. Excellent service, a pool, sauna, gym with personal trainers and good business facilities. Not central but within easy reach of the centre and airports.

AL Dayrell Minas, R Espírito Santo 901, T031-3248 1000, www.dayrell.com.br. One of the best and most central business hotels, with a very large convention centre and full business facilities, fax and email modems in the rooms. Rooftop pool. Not much English spoken.

AL Liberty Palace Hotel, R Paraíba 1465, Savassi, T031-2121 0900, www.liberty palace.com.br. Recently opened business hotel right in the heart of the Savassi restaurant district. Standard 1990s business rooms with spacious marble bathrooms, 24-hr room service, IDSL in all rooms and a well-appointed business centre.

AL Othon Palace, Av Afonso Pena 1050, T031-3247 0000, www.hoteis-othon.com.br. A 1980s chain hotel with a rooftop pool, good service and an excellent location in the centre opposite the Parque Municipal. Rooms on lower floors can be noisy.

A Best Western Sol Belo Horizonte, R da Bahia 1040, T031-3311 1300, www.hotel solbh.com.br. Well-renovated 1990s business hotel in the centre with a pool, sauna and

respectable service. Recently taken over by the **Best Western** group.

B Le Flamboyant flats, R Rio Grande do Norte 1007, Savassi, T031-3261 7370, www.clan.com.br. Well-maintained 1980s flats with a pool. Separate sitting rooms with TVs, and kitchens with cookers. Some have 2 bedrooms.

B Mercure, Av Do Contorno 7315 (Santo Antonio), T031-3298 4100, www.accorhotels. com.br. The newest of the city's business hotels with a good pool, sauna, gym and rooms decked out in standard business attire. A few kilometres from the centre.

C Esplanada, Av Santos Dumont 304, T031-3273 5311. An upmarket cheapie with bright en suite rooms with soap and towels provided and generous breakfasts. Triples available for little more than doubles; prices are negotiable.

C Villa Emma flats, R Arturo Toscanini 41, Savassi, T031-3282 3388, www.clan.com.br. The cheapest option in Savassi. Spacious flats in need of a lick of paint, with 2 bedrooms, separate living areas and a kitchen. Internet access in some rooms.

D Continental, Av Paraná 241, T031-3201 7944, www.hotelminascontinental.com.br. Central, quiet, with small interior rooms newly renovated with modern fittings. Recommended.

D São Salvador, R Espírito Santo 227, T031-3222 7731. Small well-kept rooms, the best of which are the triples with en suites. Reasonable breakfast and a public telephone. One of many similar cheapies in the area.

D-E O Sorriso do Lagarto hostel, R Padre Severino 285, Savassi, T031-3283 9325, www.osorrisodolagarto.com.br. Simple little hostel in a converted town house with kitchen, internet and fax service, breakfast, lockers, washing machines and a living area with DVD player. With a branch in Ouro Preto.

E-F IYHA Chalé Mineiro, R Santa Luzia 288, Santa Efigênia, T031-3467 1576, www.chale mineirohostel.com.br. Attractive and well maintained, with dorms and doubles, a small pool and shared kitchen, TV lounge and telephones. Towels and bed linen are extra. To get here take bus No 980 from the *rodoviária*.

Parque Natural de Caraça *p257*
AL-B Santuário do Caraça, reservations: Caixa Postal 12, Santa Bárbara, T031-3837 1939, www.overmundo.com.br/guia/ santuario-do-caraca. This on-site hotel has reasonable rooms, the restaurant serves good food from farms within the seminary's lands, lunch 1200-1330. No camping is permitted.

🍴 Eating

Belo Horizonte *p253, maps p254 and p255*
Mineiros love their food and drink and Belo Horizonte has a lively café dining and bar scene. **Savassi** overflows with bohemian streetside cafés, bars and restaurants and is the best place in the city for a food browse. There is a lively, cheap street food market on **R Tomé de Souza**, between Pernambuco and Alagoas every night around 1900-2300: think Bangkok with Minas food and buzzing bars. **Pampulha**, on the outskirts, has the best of the fine-dining restaurants, which are well worth the taxi ride. There are plenty of cheap per kilo restaurants and *padarias* near the budget hotels in the centre. Seriously cheap *comida mineira* is served in the restaurants around the *rodoviária*, *prato feito* US$1.50.
Aurora, R Expedicionário Mário Alves de Oliveira 421, São Luís, T031-3498 7567. Closed Mon and Tue. One of the best restaurants in the city, in a garden setting next to the Lago da Pampulha. Imaginative menu with dishes fusing Mineira and Italian techniques and making use of unusual Brazilian fruits. Respectable wine list.
Taste Vin, R Curitiba 2105, Lourdes, T031-3292 5423. Decent, if a little salty mock-French food. Celebrated for its soufflés and provençale seafood. The respectable wine list includes some Brazilian options. Recipient of the *Veja* best restaurant award 2007/2008.

Vecchio Sogno, R Martim de Carvalho 75 and R Dias Adorno, Santo Agostinho, under the Assembléia Legislativo, T031-3292 5251. Lunch only on Sun. The best Italian in the city with an inventive menu fusing Italian and French cuisine with Brazilian ingredients. Excellent fish. Good wine list.
Xapuri, R Mandacaru 260, Pampulha, T031-3496 6198, www.restaurant exapuri.com.br. Closed on Mon. *Comida mineira*, great atmosphere, live music, very good food, expensive and a bit out of the way but recommended.
Dona Derna, R Tomé de Souza, Savassi, T031-3223 6954. A range of restaurants in one. Upstairs is Italian fine dining with excellent dishes and a respectable wine list. Downstairs on weekdays is traditional Italian home cooking and by night a chic pizzeria called **Memmo**.
La Traviata, Av Cristovão Colombo 282, Savassi, T031-3261 6392. An atmospheric little Italian with a terrace overlooking the dragon's tooth pavements of Cristovão Colombo. The menu is strong on meat and fish with reasonable pasta and pizzas. Modest wine list, good-value house bottles.
Kauhana, R Tomé de Souza, Savassi, T031-3284 8714. Tasty wood-fired pizzas, both savoury and sweet, in an array of flavours. Pleasant open-air dining area.
Sushi Beer, R Tomé de Souza, Savassi, T031-3221 1116. A large open-air dining area overlooked by a long bar and with a lively crowd and good atmosphere. Food ranges from superior per kilo Minas and Japanese food to meats and pizzas. Respectable range of beers and whiskies.
A Cafeteria, Av Cristovão Colombo 152, Savassi, T031-3223 9901. Salads, great sandwiches in pitta bread and a range of mock-Italian standards served to a lively young crowd and accompanied by live music most nights. One of several café-bars on the corner of Colombo and Albuquerque.
Café da Travessa, Av Getúlio Vargas 1405 at Praça Savassi, T031-3223 8092. Great little café-bookshop. Dishes range from rosti to Brazilian tapas, pasta and wraps. Pizza

Érika Machado recommends

Érika is one of Brazil's great emerging talents, famous for her quirky, catchy pop songs with inventive lyrics – a kind of Mineira version of Lily Allen. Here she tells what she likes to do most in her home city, Belo Horizonte. Hear her music at www.erikamachado.com.br.

→ The **Museu de Arte Contemporânea Inhotim**, www.inhotim.org.br, isn't exactly in B H but it's really worth going to see. I worked there for seven months with the artist Adriana Varejão and it was sensational. Inhotim's a natural park with a contemporary art museum that showcases the work of more than 80 artists and with an archive of around 350 pieces.

→ The best restaurant in the world is **Xapuri** (see page 259), it's amazing! Here you'll find the best Minas food. It's in Pampulha where all the great Niemeyer buildings are and near the Guanabara historical park, www.parque guanabara.com.br/historia.asp. Every Friday there's an MC duel here under the Viaduto de Santa Tereza; it's an open mike and entry is free. See http://duelodemcs.blogspot.com.

→ Another artistic movement that's less urban but equally great is the *candomblé da Serra do Cipó*, in the national park (see page 290) and carried out by *quilombo* communities (Africans who escaped from slavery).

upstairs. Good coffee and a tasteful choice of books and Brazilian CDs. Breakfast till late.

❦ **Café Tina**, Av Cristovão Colombo 336, Savassi, T031-3261 5068. Closed Mon. Bohemian café in a 19th-century town house serving soups, risottos and delicious puddings to an arty young crowd.

🅝 Bars and clubs

Belo Horizonte *p253, maps p254 and p255*
Bars
There are plenty of bars around Tomé de Souza in Savassi, where a young and arty crowd spills out onto the street, and the beer and *caipirinhas* are cheap and plentiful. Always lively are **Bar do James**, Vargas at Tomé de Souza and **Koyote**, R Tomé de Souza 1012.

Clubs
Clube da Esquina acts play at the city's theatres. Look out for information on www.guiadasemana.com.br and follow the link for Belo Horizonte.

A Obra, R Rio Grande do Norte 1168, Savassi, T031-3215 8077, www.aobra.com.br.

The leading alternative music venue in the city. Great for the best new Minas acts such as Érika Machado (see above).

🅔 Entertainment

Belo Horizonte *p253, maps p254 and p255*
Cinema
Belo Horizonte is a good place to watch high-quality Brazilian and foreign films. There are many art cinemas and cineclubs in the centre such as the **Espaço Unibanco**, R Guajajaras 37.

Theatre
Belo Horizonte has at least a dozen theatres, including **Teatro Alterosa**, Av Assis Chateaubriand 499, Floresta, T031-3237 6610; **Teatro da Cidade**, R da Bahia 1341, T031-3273 1050; and **Teatro Marília**, Av Alfredo Balena 586, Centro, T031-3222 4445. The city prides itself on its theatre and dance companies (look out for the *Grupo Galpão*); don't expect to find many shows in any language other than Portuguese. See the local press for details.

❀ Festivals and events

Belo Horizonte *p253, maps p254 and p255*
Maundy Thu Corpus Christi.
15 Aug Assunção (Assumption).
8 Dec Conceição (Immaculate Conception).

◑ Shopping

Belo Horizonte *p253, maps p254 and p255*
Bookshops
Acaiaca, R Tamóios 72. Good for dictionaries.
Daniel Vaitsman, R Espírito Santo 466, 17th floor, T031-3222 9071. English-language books.
Livraria Alfarrábio, R Tamóios 320, T031-3271 3603. Used foreign-language books.
Livraria Van Damme, R das Guajajaras 505, T031-3226 6492. Brazilian and Portuguese.

Gems and jewellery
Manoel Bernardes, Av Contorno 5417, Savassi, T031-3225 4200. Attractive jewellery. Very reasonable prices.

Markets
Mercado Central, Av Augusto de Lima 744. Large and clean, open every day until 1800 selling arts, crafts and bric-a-brac. There is a Sun handicraft fair on **Av Afonso Pena**. Hippies still sell their wares on **R Rio de Janeiro**, 600 block, each evening. A flower market is held at Av Bernardo Monteiro, near Av Brasil, every Fri 1200-2000. Also here on Sat is a food and drinks market.

Music
Cogumelo, Av Augusto de Lima 399, T031-3274 9915.

▲ Activities and tours

Belo Horizonte *p253, maps p254 and p255*
Caving
Grupo Speleo, at the Universidade Federal de Minas Gerais, has the most experience in visiting out-of-the-way caves.

Ecotourism and adventure sports
Associação Mineira dos Organizadores do Turismo Ecológico (Amo-Te), R Monte Verde 125, Lípio de Melo, T031-3477 5430, oversees ecotourism in the state of Minas Gerais. This includes trekking, riding, cycling, rafting, jeep tours, canyoning, national parks and *fazendas*. For companies that arrange special-interest tours, speak to **Amo-Te** first.

Horse riding
Tropa Serrana, T031-3344 8986, T031-9983 2356 (mob), tropaserrana@hotmail.com. Recommended.

Tour operators
Ametur, R Alvarengo Peixoto 295, loja 102, Lourdes, T/F031-3292 1976. Information on *fazendas* that welcome visitors and overnight guests.
Master Turismo (American Express representative), R da Bahia 2140, T031-3330 3655, www.masterturismo.com.br, at Sala VIP, Aeroporto de Confins and Av Afonso Pena 1967, T031-3330 3603. Very helpful.
Ouro Preto Turismo, Av Afonso Pena 4133, grupo 109, Serra, T031-3221 5005. Recommended.
Revetur, R Espírito Santo 1892, 1st floor, Lourdes, T031-3337 2500. Recommended.

● Transport

Belo Horizonte *p253, maps p254 and p255*
Air
Confins A taxi to Trancredo Neves International Airport from the centre costs US$40. Buses run every 30 mins 0415-2300 from the *rodoviária*: *convencional linha 5250* (US$3), *executivo* (US$11) www.conexaoaeroporto.com.br, taking 40-60 mins.

Belo Horizonte has connections with **São Paulo** and **Rio de Janeiro** and several Brazilian cities with GOL, www.voegol.com.br, **Oceanair**, www.oceanairlines.com, and TAM, www.tam.com.br. There are international flights to **Paris**

(TAM), **Lisbon** (TAP), **Buenos Aires** (TAM), **Miami** (TAM) and **Panama City** (COPA), with connections throughout the Americas. **Pampulha** Almost all the *convencional* services (see above) also stop at the domestic airport (25 mins, US$1) double check before you board. From Pampulha there are shuttle services to several cities including **Rio de Janeiro**, **Salvador** and **São Paulo**. Airlines serving the airport include: Air Minas, www.airminas.com.br, Passaredo, www.voepassaredo.com.br, TRIP/Total, www.voetrip.com.br, Varig, www.varig.com, and Webjet, www.webjet.com.br.

Bus

For information on the bus station and local buses, see Ins and outs, page 253. For bus routes, companies, prices and times see www.rodoviariadebelohorizonte.com.

To **Rio** with Cometa, T031-3201 5611 and Util, T031-3201 7744 (6½ hrs, US$50 and *leito* US$70). To **Vitória** with São Geraldo, T031-3271 1911 (US$40 and *leito* US$50). To **Brasília** with Itapemirim, T031-3291 9991, and Penha, T031-3271 1027 (10 hrs, 6 a day including 2 *leitos*, only 1 leaves in daylight at 0800, US$50, *leito* US$65). To **São Paulo** with Cometa and Gontijo, T031-3201 6130 (10 hrs, US$40). To **Foz do Iguaçu** (22 hrs, US$70). To **Salvador** with Gontijo (24 hrs, at 1900 daily, US$60), and São Geraldo (at 1800). São Geraldo also goes to **Porto Seguro** (17 hrs, direct, via Nanuque and Eunápolis, US$60). To **Recife** with Gontijo (2000, US$100); to **Fortaleza** (US$110); to **Natal** (US$110. To **Belém** with Itapemirim, US$120). To **Campo Grande** with Gontijo (at 1930) and Motta (3 a day), T031-3464 0480, US$50, a good route to Bolivia, avoiding São Paulo. All major destinations served. For buses within Minas Gerais, see under each destination.

Car hire

All the major companies have offices at Confins airport and in the city.

Around Belo Horizonte *p256*
Lakes and grottoes

Buses (**Útil**) to the **Gruta de Lapinha** leave Belo Horizonte daily at 1015 and 1130, returning 1600, also Mon at 1830 (1¼ hrs, US$3.25 one way). Half-hourly bus service **Belo Horizonte–Lagoa Santa** (US$2). Bus **Lagoa Santa–Lapinha** every 30 mins. The local bus stop for Lagoa Santa is 2 km downhill from the Lapinha caves. To **Gruta de Maquiné**, several buses daily with Irmãos Teixeira (2¼ hrs, US$8).

🛈 Directory

Belo Horizonte *p253, maps p254 and p255*
Banks Banco do Brasil, R Rio de Janeiro 750, Av Amazonas 303. Visa ATM at Bradesco, R da Bahia 947. **Citibank**, R Espírito Santo 871. Changing TCs is difficult, but hotels will change them for guests at a poor rate. **Embassies and consulates** Austria, R José Américo Cançado Bahia 199, T031-3333 5363. Denmark, R Paraíba 1122, 5th floor, T031-3286 8626. France, R Pernambuco 712A, T031-3261 7805. Germany, R Timbiras 1200, 5th floor, T031-3213 1568. Italy, Av Afonso Pena 3130, 12th floor, T031-3281 4211. Netherlands, R Sergipe 1167, loja 5, T031-3227 5275. UK, R dos Inconfidêntes 1075, sala 1302, Savassi, T031-3261 2072, britcon.bhe@terra.com.br. USA, R Timbiras 1200, 7th floor, T031-213 1571. **Immigration** Polícia Federal, R Nascimento Gurgel 30, T031-291 0005. For visa extensions. To get there take bus No 7902 from the corner of R Curitiba and Av Amazonas and get off at the Hospital Madre Teresa. **Internet** Internet Café Club, R Fernandes Tourinho 385, Plaza Savassi, US$5 per hr. There are numerous others throughout the city. **Medical services** Mater Dei, R Gonçalves Dias 2700, T031-3339 9000. Recommended. **Post office** Av Afonso Pena 1270. Poste restante is behind the main office at R de Goiás 77. The branch on R da Bahia is less slow. **Telephone** Av Afonso Pena 1180, by the *correios*, daily 0700-2200.

Colonial cities near Belo Horizonte

Streets of whitewashed 18th-century houses with deep-blue or yellow window frames line steep and winding streets leading to lavishly decorated churches with Manueline façades and rich gilt interiors. Behind lies a backdrop of grey granite hills and green forests, still filled with tiny marmoset monkeys and flocks of canary-winged parakeets. The colonial gold-mining towns of southern Minas are the highlights of any visit to the state: islands of history and remnant forest in an otherwise dull agricultural landscape. Most lie south of Belo Horizonte and many people choose to visit them on the way to or from Rio. However, they make a far more charming and restful base than Belo Horizonte and we would recommend spending your time here, with just a quick stop in the capital on the way north or south. ▸▸ *For listings, see pages 283-289.*

Ins and outs

The cities fall into three groups: south of Belo Horizonte (Ouro Preto, Mariana, Congonhas do Campo, São João del Rei and Tiradentes); east (Sabará and Caeté); and north (Diamantina and Serro). All of the southern towns are on the main Rio highway (Ouro Preto being the closest to the state capital and São João del Rei the furthest from it). The towns to the east are on the main highway to Espírito Santo. Those to the north are a longer journey from Belo Horizonte, off the inland route to Bahia.

The most famous of the towns is **Ouro Preto**. It can be visited in a day trip from Belo Horizonte, however one day is not enough and the town is a much more interesting and pleasant place to stay than the capital. **Mariana** is easy to see in a day trip from Ouro Preto. The spectacular Aleijadinho church in **Congonhas do Campo**, further south, requires only a few hours to visit and is now reachable by a new highway. There is no need to stay overnight. **Tiradentes**, further south still, is the prettiest, best-preserved and most visited of all the cities but feels somewhat touristy and twee. Nearby, **São João del Rei** is more decrepit but very much a real city. They are linked at weekends by a 30-minute steam train ride and daily by frequent buses. **Sabará** and **Caeté**, to the east of the capital, can be visited as an easy day trip from Belo Horizonte or on the way to Espírito Santo. **Diamantina** and **Serro** are far to the north, on one of the routes to Bahia from Belo Horizonte, and are easiest to see as a stopover en route to Bahia.

Ouro Preto 🚌🚗⊗🅿️⛰️🍴🛏️ ▸▸ *pp283-289. Colour map 4, C3.*

→ *Phone code: 031. Population: 67,000. Altitude: 1000 m.*

Ouro Preto, named after the black iron oxide-coated gold that was discovered here by the adventurer Antônio Dias, was one of the first of the Minas gold towns to be founded. As a former state capital, it became the wealthiest and most important town in the region. Although it now has a hinterland of ugly blocks of flats and crumbling *favelas*, it preserves some of the most significant colonial architecture in Brazil and remains, at heart, an 18th-century city of steep church-crowned hills, cobbled streets, *azulejos*, plazas and fountains. In homage to its historical importance Ouro Preto becomes the capital of Minas Gerais once again every year for one day only, on 24 June. The modern city bustles with young Brazilians studying and partying at the various local universities and has a thriving café and nightlife scene. Sadly the historic centre, once closed to traffic, is now thick with buses and cars, which is taking its toll on some of the beautiful buildings.

Milton Nascimento – the voice of Minas

Milton Nascimento is the most influential Brazilian singer and composer not to have come out of Bahia or Rio. He has produced some of Brazil's most haunting music, been nominated for a Grammy and had songs covered by almost as many artists as Paul McCartney.

Milton grew up in rural Minas in a town like many others – lost in a landscape of lush green hills and cattle pasture and where life focussed on the *praça* and local church. He was raised by his stepmother who'd once sung in a choir conducted by Villa-Lobos, and who exposed him to religious music from an early age.

Catholicism came to underlie both his musical style and lyrical themes, which were expressed most memorably on a string of ground breaking 1970s albums. The music on these is unique, with rich choral harmonies, jazz interludes and sweetly melancholic melodies interplaying with Afro-Brazilian rhythms and sound effects. Lyrics poetically exalt the day to day life of the oppressed. And Milton's golden voice soars over the top.

You'll hear Milton's songs throughout Ouro Preto. If you are tempted to buy one of his records, opt for *Clube de Esquina*, his 1972 classic.

Ins and outs

Getting there Ouro Preto's **rodoviária** ① *R Padre Rolim 661, T031-3559 3225*, is 1 km north of Praça Tiradentes. A 'circular' bus runs from the *rodoviária* to Praça Tiradentes, US$0.40. Taxis charge exorbitant rates. There are frequent bus connections with Belo Horizonte and daily buses to Rio and São Paulo as well as other cities throughout Minas, including Congonhas, with some buses passing through Conselheiro Lafaiette.
➤ *See Transport, page 288.*

Tourist information The **tourist office** ① *Praça Tiradentes 41, T031-3559 3269, www.ouro preto.org.br, 0800-1800*, has details of accommodation in *casas de família*, *repúblicas* and other places. It also has leaflets showing the opening times of sights, which change frequently, and can organize a local guide from the **Associação de Guias de Turismo** (**AGTOP**) ① *R Padre Rolim s/n, T031-3551 2655, Mon-Fri 0800-1800, Sat and Sun 0800-1700, little English spoken*, which has its own office opposite the bus station. Cássio Antunes is a recommended guide.

Praça Tiradentes and around

The city has a number of churches and chapels as well as some excellent examples of *chafariz* (public fountains), *passos* (oratories) and stone bridges. The best place to start exploring the city is the central **Praça Tiradentes**, where you'll see a **statue of Tiradentes**, the leader of the Inconfidêntes (see box, page 272). Another Inconfidênte, the poet Tomás Antônio Gonzaga, lived at Rua Cláudio Manoel 61 near the São Francisco de Assis church, and was exiled to Africa. Most Brazilians know his poem based on his forbidden love affair with the girl he called *Marília de Dirceu*. Visitors are shown the bridge and decorative fountain where the lovers held their trysts. The house where she lived, on the Largo Marília de Dirceu, is now a school.

On the north side of Praça Tiradentes is a famous **Escola de Minas** (**School of Mining**). It was founded in 1876, is housed in the fortress-like Palácio dos Governadores (1741-1748) and includes the **Museu de Mineralogia e das Pedras** ① *No 20, Mon, Wed-Fri*

1200-1645, Sat and Sun 0900-1300, US$1.50, which has displays of rocks, minerals, semi-precious and precious stones from all over the world. Just north of the *praça*, towards the *rodoviária*, is the church of **Nossa Senhora das Mercês e Misericórdia** (1773-1793).

On the south side of the *praça*, next to Carmo church, is the **Museu da Inconfidência** ① *No 139, T031-3551 1121, Mon-Fri 0800-1800, US$1.50*, a fine historical and art museum in the former Casa de Câmara e Cadeia, containing drawings by Aleijadinho and the Sala Manoel da Costa Athayde.

West of Praça Tiradentes

The church of **Nossa Senhora do Carmo** ① *R Brigadeiro Mosqueira, Tue-Sun 1300-1700, entry is shared with Nossa Senhora do Pilar*, built 1766-1772, was planned by Manoel Francisco Lisboa, and both his son and Mestre Athayde worked on the project. It was a favourite church of the aristocracy. The best of the city's museums is housed in an annexe of the church, the modern and well-appointed **Museu do Oratório** ① *T031-3551 5369, daily 0930-1200, 1330-1730*. Inside is a selection of exquisitely crafted 18th- and 19th-century prayer icons and oratories, many of them with strong indigenous design and some disguised as bullet cases. On the opposite side of the road, the **Teatro Municipal** ① *R Brigadeiro Musqueiro, daily 1230-1800*, is the oldest functioning theatre in Latin America, built in 1769.

A block north of the theatre, **Casa Guignard** ① *R Conde de Bobadela 110, T031-3551 5155, Tue-Fri 1200-1800, Sat, Sun and holidays 0900-1500, free*, displays the paintings of Alberto da Veiga Guignard. Further west, just before the river, the **Casa das Contas** ① *R São José 12, T031-355 1444, Tue-Sat 1230-1730, Sun and holidays 0900-1500, US$0.50*, built 1782-1784, houses a museum of money and finance on its upper storeys. Far more interesting is the damp, dark basement where slaves were formerly housed. In colonial Preto a slave's life was literally worth less than a chicken: swapping an African Brazilian for poultry was considered a good deal.

Following Rua Teixeira Amaral across the river, the church of **São José** was begun in 1752, but not completed until 1811; some of the carving is by Aleijadinho. Up on the hill, **São Francisco de Paula** ① *0900-1700*, was started in 1804, making it the last colonial church in Ouro Preto. Further west, on the Largo do Rosário, the church of **Nossa Senhora do Rosário** dates from 1785, when the present church replaced a chapel on the site. It has a curved façade, which is rare in Brazilian baroque. The interior is more simple than the exterior, but there are interesting side altars.

One of the city's grandest churches, **Nossa Senhora do Pilar** ① *just north of R do Pilar, Tue-Sun 0900-1100 and 1200-1700*, was attended by the Portuguese upper classes. The ceiling painting by João de Carvalhães features a trompe l'oeil effect – as you walk to the front of the church the lamb appears to move from one side of the crucifix to the other – a symbol of the resurrection. Manoel Lisboa, Aleijadinho's father, was responsible for all the carving except the heavily gilded work around the altar, which is by Francisco Xavier de Brito. The **museum** in the church vaults is one of the best in Minas, preserving some stunning gold and silver monstrances and some of Xavier de Brito's finest sculptures, including a wonderful image of Christ.

East of Praça Tiradentes

A block southeast of Praça Tiradentes, on the Largo São Francisco is the grand **São Francisco de Assis** ① *Largo de Coimbra, Tue-Sun 0830-1150, 1330-1640, US$2; the ticket also permits entry to NS da Conceição, keep your ticket for admission to the museum*, considered to be one of the masterpieces of Brazilian baroque. Built 1766-1796,

Aleijadinho worked on the general design and the sculpture of the façade, the pulpits and many other features. The harmonious lines of the exterior and the beauty of the interior are exceptional; the church feels like a model of Catholic reverence and propriety. It is far from it. Aleijadinho was a mulatto – as were Mestre Athayde's wife and children – and as such they were prohibited from entering white churches like São Francisco, from eating any meat other than offal, ears and trotters and they had no rights in civil society. Mulatto sculptors were not even considered to be artists; they were referred to as artisans or *artistas de sangue sujo* (artists of dirty blood). The church is full of subtle criticisms of the Portuguese encoded in the art by Athayde and Aleijadinho. The model for the Virgin (depicted in the highest heaven, surrounded by cherubs and musicians and saints

Ouro Preto

To Rodoviária & Belo Horizonte

Sleeping		
Brumas **11**	Pousada do Mondego **5**	Pousada São Francisco
Colonial **1**	Pousada dos	de Paula **8**
Grande **13**	Bandeirantes **4**	Pousada Solar de NS
	Pousada Itacolomi **7**	do Rosário **2**

Augustine, Hieronymous, Gregory and Ambrosius), is said to have been Mestre Athayde's mulatto wife. She has her breasts showing, open legs and her face shows African traces; all of which can only be noticed with careful attention and all of which would have been anathema to the Portuguese. The *Last Supper* painting in the sanctuary replaces the apostles with Portuguese feeding on meat and being attended to by Brazilian servants. And Aleijadinho's *Sacred Heart of Jesus* near the altar has its hands and feet cut into quarters in a reference to the fate that befell Tiradentes at the hands of the Portuguese. A **museum** at the back of the church has a small selection of paintings of serious-looking saints and a fountain by Aleijadinho depicting Blind Faith holding up a banner saying "such is the path to heaven". In the largo outside São Francisco is a handicraft market.

To Cachoeira das Andorinhas & Zen Buddhist Monastery

Serra de Ouro Preto

R Cons Quintiliano

To Mariana

R Camilo de Brito
R Barão dos Camargos

Bus to Mariana

Escola de Minas/ Museu de Mineralógia

Bradesco

Statue of Tiradentes

Praça Tiradentes

Chafariz do Passo de A Dias

Bernardo de Vasconcelos

R Cláudio Manoel

Largo do Coimbra

Handicraft

R Antônio Dias

NS da Conceição

Mina do Chico Rei

R Dom Silvério

Museu da Inconfidência

R Manoel Cabral

Largo São Francisco

R Carlos Tomás

São Francisco de Assis

Largo de Musicista José dos Anjos Costa

R Felipe dos Santos

R Alfredo Baeta

Alagoas

Lovers' Bridge

R da Conceição

To Igreja de Santa Efigênia

NS das Mercés e Perdões

R das Mercés

Chafariz de Marília

Solar das Lajes **12**

Eating 🍴
Adega **1**

Deguste **4**
Forno de Barro **5**
Le Coq D'Or **6**
Pasteleria Lampião **5**

Racism under the Portuguese

To Brazilians under the shackles of Portuguese colonial rule, Tiradentes was far more than a failed revolutionary. He was a hero who had risen from the oppressed classes to dare to stand up against the tyrannical Portuguese rule and was revered as a saint and martyr after his death. Under the Portuguese the black, indigenous and mixed race majority were regarded as lower than animals. Little of the wealth from the mines ever reached Brazilian hands and whilst the Portuguese and their religious and lay brotherhoods lived in luxurious opulence, the Brazilians who tore the gold from the hills were poor and oppressed. Slaves were forced to sleep in dark, damp dungeon-like quarters under the houses of their masters – like those in the **Casa dos Contos** museum in Ouro Preto – and there value was literally less than a chicken, for which they were readily exchanged. They were prohibited from eating meat or poultry and were allowed only offal and scraps – thrown together with beans into *feijoada* stews. Anyone with a noticeable trace of African or indigenous blood was forbidden from mixing with Portuguese. Not only were they required to attend separate churches; they were forbidden from passing in front of the spire of the white church as it would cause offence to God. The mulatto artists and their sympathizers, like Aleijadinho and Mestre Athayde (whose wife was a black Brazilian), also experienced prejudice and were known as 'artistas de sangue sujo' or artists with dirty blood; relegated to the level of craftsmen rather than true fine artists. They in turn used their ecclesiastical art as a form of disguised political and social protest. Many of the paintings and sculptures replace prophets, saints or Christ himself with Tiradentes. Aleijadinho's Christ crucified is symbolized by a medal showing severed hands and feet around a gold heart on the tabernacle of the church of **São Francisco de Assis** in Ouro Preto and the medal of the church of the same name in São João del Rey – a reference to Tiradentes who was hung drawn and quartered by the Portuguese. Mestre Athayde's *Last Supper* painting in São Francisco de Assis, Ouro Preto depicts drunken and decadent Portuguese feasting on meat and wine with a servant in attendance, and his masterpiece – the painting on the ceiling of the same church – replaces the normally white virgin Mary with a mixed race Brazilian woman, thought to have been modelled on his wife.

South of here, the church of **Nossa Senhora das Mercês e Perdões** ① *R das Mercês, Tue-Sun 1000-1400*, (1740-1772), was rebuilt in the 19th century. Some sculpture by Aleijadinho can be seen in the main chapel.

Further east, **Nossa Senhora da Conceição** ① *Tue-Sat 0830-1130, 1330-1700, Sun 1200-1700*, was built in 1722 and is the parish church of Antônio Dias (one of the original settlements that became Vila Rica de Albuquerque). It is heavily gilded and contains Aleijadinho's tomb. It has a **museum** devoted to him but with very few of his pieces. Be sure to see the exquisite miniature crucifixion on the basement floor. Across the river, the **Mina do Chico Rei** ① *R Dom Silvério, 0800-1700, US$1.50*, is not as impressive as some other mines in the area, but is fun to crawl about in and has a restaurant attached. The Chico Rei was supposedly an African king called Francisco, who was enslaved but bought his freedom working in the mine.

On the eastern edge of town, **Santa Efigênia** ① *Ladeira Santa Efigênia and Padre Faria, Tue-Sun 0800-1200*, built 1720-1785, has wonderful panoramic views of the city. This was a church used by black Brazilians only and the gilt that lines the interior is said to have been made from gold dust washed out of slaves' hair. Manuel Francisco Lisboa (Aleijadinho's father) oversaw the construction and much of the carving is by Francisco Xavier de Brito (Aleijadinho's mentor).

Around Ouro Preto

The town is dominated by a huge cross, easily reached from the road to Mariana, which affords lovely views of the sunset; but don't go alone as it's in a poor district.

The **Cachoeira das Andorinhas**, a waterfall north of town, is reached by taking a bus to Morro de Santana and then walking 25 minutes. To walk all the way takes 1½ hours. Near the waterfall it is possible to visit the **Zen Buddhist monastery** ① *apply in advance to Mosteiro Zen Pico de Rajos, Morro de São Sebastião, Caixa Postal 101, 35400-000, Ouro Preto, T031-3961 2484.* Excursions of 2½ hours are arranged at 0830 and 1430 visiting many cultural and ecological sites of interest.

Parque Estadual de Itacolomi and the **Estação Ecológica do Tripuí** are protected areas close to the city. The former (a three-hour walk from the centre, cars prohibited) includes the peak of Itacolomi, which the first gold prospectors used as a landmark, the source of the Rio Doce as well as endangered wildlife and splendid views. Tripuí is in the valley where the first gold was found; it protects a rare flatworm, *Peripatus acacioi*. It can also be reached on foot, or the bus to Belo Horizonte will drop you near the entrance.

Minas da Passagem

① *T031-3557 5000, www.minasdapassagem.com.br, Mon and Tue 0900-1700, Wed-Sun 0900-1730, visits should be booked in advance.*

The world's largest gold mine open to the public lies mid-way between Ouro Preto and Mariana. Its gloomy passages and clunking machinery date from 1719. A 20-minute guided tour visits the old mine workings and underground lake (take bathing suit). There is a waterfall too, the **Cachoeira Serrinha**, where swimming is possible; walk 100 m towards Mariana then ask for directions. There is also the opportunity to pan for gold on the tour. Note that some signs say 'Mina de Ouro', omitting 'da Passagem'.

The nearest town to the mine is **Passagem de Mariana**. The bus stops at the edge of town by the **Pousada Solar dos Dois Sinos**, which has a church behind it. Tours can be organized from hotels or agencies in town.

Mariana 🚍🌐🏤🛏️ ›› *pp283-289. Colour map 4, C3.*

→ *Phone code: 031. Population: 47,000. Altitude: 697 m.*

Mariana is the oldest of the colonial mining towns in Minas Gerais, founded by *bandeirantes* a few years before Ouro Preto, on 16 July 1696. At first, when it was little more than a collection of huts, it was called Arraial de Nossa Senhora do Carmo. But by 1711 it had become the town of Vila de Nossa Senhora do Carmo, and by the mid-18th century it had grown to be the most important administrative centre in the newly created Capitania de São Paulo e Minas do Ouro. Its name was changed to Mariana in honour of the wife of Dom João V, Dona Maria Ana of Austria. It retains many fine colonial buildings, most of them constructed in the second half of the 18th century. The artist Mestre

Athayde was born here, as was the Inconfidênte Cláudio Manuel da Costa. The town was declared a national monument in 1945.

Unlike its more famous neighbour, Ouro Preto, in whose shadow the town tends to sit, Mariana has remained a working mining centre. For many years the **Companhia do Vale do Rio Doce** (**CVRD**), the state mining company, had major operations here and provided a great deal of assistance for the restoration of the colonial heritage. Since CVRD's concentration on its new investments at Carajás, and its subsequent privatization, there have been doubts about its commitment to mining in Mariana and to the town itself.

Ins and outs

Getting there Buses from Ouro Preto and Belo Horizonte stop at the new *rodoviária*, out of town on the main road, then at the **Posto Mariana**, before heading back to the centre at Praça Tancredo Neves. Many buses seem to go only to the *posto* (petrol station) above the town, but it's a long walk from the centre. A bus from the *rodoviária* to the centre via the *posto* and Minas da Passagem costs US$0.40. ▸▸ *See Transport, page 289.*

Tourist information The **tourist office** ⓘ *Praça Tancredo Neves, T031-3557 9044, www.mari ana.mg.gov.br*, can organize guides and has a map and free monthly booklet, *Mariana Agenda Cultural*, packed with information. **Mariana Turismo** ⓘ *R Direita 31*, is also helpful.

Sights

The historic centre of the town slopes gently uphill from the river and the **Praça Tancredo Neves**, where buses from Ouro Preto stop. The first street parallel with the Praça Tancredo Neves is Rua Direita, which is lined with beautiful, two-storey 18th-century houses with tall colonial windows and balconies. The **Casa do Barão de Pontal** ⓘ *R Direita 54, Tue 1400-1700*, is unique in Minas Gerais, with its balconies carved from soapstone.

Rua Direita leads to the **Praça da Sé**, on which stands the cathedral, **Basílica de Nossa Senhora da Assunção**. Before Vila de Nossa Senhora do Carmo became a town, a chapel dating from 1703 stood on this spot. In various stages it was expanded and remodelled until its completion in 1760. The portal and the lavabo in the sacristy are by Aleijadinho and the painting in the beautiful interior and side altars is by Manoel Rabello de Sousa. Also in the cathedral is a wooden German organ (1701), made by Arp Schnitger, which was a gift to the first diocese of the Capitania de Minas do Ouro in 1747. It was restored in 1984 after some 50 years of silence. Concerts are held in the cathedral including regular **organ concerts** ⓘ *Fri 1100 and Sun 1200, US$7.50*, see the local press for details.

Turning up Rua Frei Durão, on the right is the **Museu Arquidiocesano** ⓘ *R Frei Durão 49, Tue-Sun 0900-1200, 1300-1700, US$1.50*, which has fine church furniture, a gold and silver collection, Aleijadinho statues and an ivory cross. On the opposite side of the street is the **Casa da Intendência/Casa de Cultura** ⓘ *R Frei Durão 84, 0800-1130, 1330-1700*, which holds exhibitions and has a museum of music. The ceilings in the exhibition rooms are very fine; in other rooms there are *esteiro* (flattened bamboo) ceilings.

The large **Praça Gomes Freire** was where horses would be tied up (there is an old drinking trough on one side) and where festivals were held. Now it has pleasant gardens. On the south side is the **Palácio Arquiepiscopal**, while on the north side is the **Casa do Conde de Assumar**, home of the governor of the capitania from 1717 to 1720; it later became the bishop's palace.

Praça Minas Gerais has one of the finest groups of colonial buildings in Brazil. In the middle is the **Pelourinho**, the stone monument to justice at which slaves used to be beaten. The fine **São Francisco church** ⓘ *daily 0800-1700,* built 1762-1794, has pulpits, a fine sacristy and an altar designed by Aleijadinho, and paintings by Mestre Athayde, who is buried in tomb No 94. The statue of São Roque is most important as he is the patron saint of the city (his day is 16 August). Among Athayde's paintings are the panels showing the life of St Francis, on the ceiling of the right-hand chapel. The church is one of the most simple in Mariana but, in terms of art, one of the richest. There is a small exhibition of the restoration work funded by CVRD.

Mariana

To Railway Station (disused),
Prefeitura Municipal &
Ginásio Poliesportivo

To Nossa Senhora do Rosário

R do Carmo

Av Getúlio Vargas

RA Guimarães

R 16 de Julho

Buses to
Ouro Preto

R Antônio Olinto

Praça
Tancredo
Nevés

Terminal
Turístico

Av S Furtado

R Frei Durão

R Santana

Buses from
Ouro Preto

R Josafá

R Macedo

Casa do Barão
de Pontal

Praça
da Sé

R Direita

Mariana
Turismo

Cathedral

Casa da
Câmara e Cadéia

Praça
Minas
Gerais

São
Francisco

Museu
Arquidiocesano

Casa de
Intendência

Capela de
Santana

R Catete

Pelourinho

Casa do
Conde de
Assumar

Trav São Francisco

NS do
Carmo

R Dom Silvério

R Silva Jardim

R Barão de Camargo

Praça
Gomes
Freire

Palácio
Arquiepiscopal

R do Seminário

R do Seminário

Colégio
Providência

R Cônego Rego

R Dom Viçoso

Seminário
Menor

Arquiconfraria

R Das Mercês

R Bicentenário

To Main Highway,
Rodoviária,
Minas de
Passagem,
Ouro Preto &
Belo Horizonte

Main Route
into Town

São Pedro
dos Clérigos

To Highway

To Highway

N

Not to scale

Sleeping
Central 1
Faísca 2

Pousada do Chafariz 4
Pousada Solar
dos Corrêa 3

Providência 5

Eating
Panela de Pedra 1

Tiradentes and the Inconfidência Mineira

In the last quarter of the 18th century, Vila Rica de Nossa Senhora do Pilar do Ouro Preto was a dynamic place. Gold had brought great wealth to the city and this was translated into fine religious and secular buildings. Much of the artistry that went into these constructions and their decoration was home-grown, such as the genius of O Aleijadinho (see page 274). In conjunction with this flowering of the arts an intellectual society developed. And yet all this went on under the heavy hand of the Portuguese crown, which demanded its fifth share (the *quinto*), imposed punitive taxes and forbade local industries to operate. While the artists and artisans could not travel and had to seek inspiration in what was around them, the intellectuals were often from families who sent their young to Europe to further their education. So, when the gold yields began to decline and the Portuguese demands became even more exorbitant, some members of society began to look to Europe and North America for ways to free Minas Gerais from the crown.

One side of the argument was the view of the governor, the Visconde de Barbacena, who refused to admit that the mines were exhausted and that poverty was beginning to affect the community. As far as he was concerned, there was no gold because it was being smuggled out of the captaincy and there was no economic problem, just a large unpaid debt to the Portuguese crown. On the other side was the idea, as expressed by the French poet Parny, that Brazil was a paradise on earth, with everything except liberty. The Jesuit Antônio Vieira, who lived in the previous century, put it thus: "the cloud swells in Brazil and it rains on Portugal; the water is not picked up from the sea, but from the tears of the unfortunate and the sweat of the poor, and I do not know how their faith and constancy has lasted so long."

In the late 1780s a group of people began to have secret discussions on how to resolve the intolerable situation. It included the poets Cláudio Manuel da Costa, Tomás Gonzaga and Ignacio de Alvarenga, the doctors Domingos Vidal Barbosa and José Alvares Maciel, Padres Toledo and Rolim and the military officers Domingos de Abreu Vieira, Francisco de Paula Freire de Andrade and José de Resende Costa. Into this group came Joaquim José da Silva Xavier, a junior officer, who was born at the Fazenda de Pombal near São João del Rei in about 1748.

At right angles to São Francisco is **Nossa Senhora do Carmo** ① *daily 1400-1700*, built 1784, with steatite carvings, Athayde paintings, and chinoiserie panelling. Some consider its exterior to be the most beautiful in Mariana. Unfortunately this church was damaged by fire in 1999. Across Rua Dom Silvério is the **Casa da Cámara e Cadéia** (1768), once the Prefeitura Municipal. It is a superb example of civic colonial construction.

On Rua Dom Silvério the **Colégio Providência** at No 61 was the first college for boarding students in Minas Gerais. Also on this street is the **Igreja da Arquiconfraria** and, nearing the top of the hill, the **Chafariz de São Pedro**. On the Largo de São Pedro is the church of **São Pedro dos Clérigos**, founded by Manuel da Cruz, first bishop of the town (1764), one of the few elliptical churches in Minas Gerais. It is unadorned, although there is a painting by Athayde, *A Entrega do Menino Jesus a Santo Antônio*. The cedar altar was made by José Pedro Aroca. Look for the cockerel, carved in memory of the biblical verses about St Peter betraying Christ before the cock has crowed three times. Ask to see the view from the bell tower.

Introduction

Brazil is one of the world's great musical countries, and your travels here will be accompanied by a rich and varied soundtrack. Brazilians dance to, or play, a bewildering array of musical styles, which are unique to their country – from the lilting flow of bossa nova, to the funk of samba, or the up-close and intimate *forró* jigs of the northeastern desert. There's always a live band on somewhere, any night of the week, no matter how small the town, and it seems that everyone plays something, whether it's a guitar, a bow and arrow-shaped twanging *berimbau*, a drum or a mandolin. And they generally play it with the dexterity they play football.

Brazilian music has very little in common with that of the rest of Latin America. No one has heard of the Buena Vista Social Club or Shakira, and the locals dance neither tango nor salsa. Music here comes from a more diverse set of roots than the rest of the continent: from half a dozen West African nations; from the wistful melancholy of Portuguese folk, whose mood is altogether different from that of Spain; from the calls and trance choruses of the forest *indígenas*; and from Galician Celtic dances and German campfire songs. Brazilians add to this an unfailing musical curiosity, which scours the world for new sounds and which crosses generations and transcends trends. In Brazil, people love music for its own sake not because it's in vogue. Music you might say, is always in fashion here, but fashion is never in music.

Previous page: Seu Jorge, international film actor, style icon and the foremost samba funk singer in Brazil. **Above:** Nelson da Rabeca (see page 488) in his living room in Marechal Deodoro, Alagoas.

Above: Rio's Clube dos Democráticos is one of the best places in Brazil for live big band or gafieira samba.

Rio: samba and the boys from Ipanema

If you've heard one Brazilian tune it's likely to be either the joyful, summery chorus of *Mas que Nada* or a lift-music version of *The Girl from Ipanema*. Both songs come from Rio de Janeiro and from a time before men had walked on the moon. *Mas que Nada* is a **samba** – the country's most ubiquitous and enduring music style, and the sound of Rio carnival. Samba was born in the poor, black district of Gamboa in the early 20th century (see page 90) and it comes in many forms, from the big drum troupes whose chorus of *tambores* and giant *surdo* bass drums can fill a stadium, to quieter, acoustic sung samba. But it is invariably best heard live, and preferably in Rio de Janeiro itself (see pages 126-130 for a list of venues). Despite its age, samba lives on and remains very popular with young Brazilians, particularly as **samba soul** and **samba funk** (also known as Rio samba, whose most famous exponent is **Seu Jorge**) and in its close-danced beach-and-barbecue form, **pagode**. Both samba and pagode are also dance styles, characterized by fast feet and leg movements with stiff upper body and hips. They are incredibly tricky to master. For the first half of its life, samba was working class, poor and black. But in the 1950s its rhythms were adopted by a group of young, nerdy, white middle-class boys from Ipanema and Copacabana. Musicians like the conservatory-trained **Antônio Carlos (Tom) Jobim**, the poet and diplomat **Vinícius de Moraes**, and Bahian émigré **João Gilberto** began to play a kind of samba on the acoustic guitar or piano, which they accompanied with witty lyrics and more complex chord progressions drawn from French impressionist composers and a jazzier Brazilian musical style called **choro** (which is still popular today). Few of these new samba singers could

ALEX ROBINSON

Above: Nowadays bossa nova is more popular abroad than it is in Brazil. Rio session musicians *Os Ipanemas* are one of the most popular acts in Europe. **Opposite page:** Locals gather to dance samba on weekend nights at the Rio Scenarium club in Lapa, Rio de Janeiro.

sing and their breathy, almost spoken vocal style became a trademark of the their sound, which was christened the new wave or **bossa nova**.

Bossa nova became internationally famous when its soft sound was adopted by a series of US 'cool jazz' musicians in the 1960s. The foremost of these was the saxophonist **Stan Getz** who in 1964 released one of the best-selling jazz albums of all time, *Getz/Gilberto*, with João Gilberto. It included a single version of Tom Jobim and Vinícius de Moraes' *The Girl from Ipanema* (with English lyrics vastly inferior to Vinícius'). This rocketed into the billboard chart and João's wife, **Astrud Gilberto**, who sang the song, was propelled to stardom. Her success defined and continues to define the Brazilian vocal style in the minds of foreigners: light, happy and invariably female. It also stimulated an exodus of musicians from Brazil, which included a Carioca session pianist called **Sergio Mendes**.

He repeated Astrud's success with a popular samba song by Carioca singer Jorge Ben – *Mas Que Nada*. Bossa largely died in Brazil in the 1970s, and it can be hard to hear it beyond the tourist bars, but it lived on in the USA as jazz-bossa and hotel lobby music, and was resurrected in Europe in the new millennium with Bebel Gilberto's club chill-out room re-recordings of her father João's music. Her sound is slowly beginning to filter back to Brazil's club and cocktail bar scene today.

Essential CDs
Choro: anything by Pixinguinha
Samba: Bezerra da Silva, *O Partido Alto da Samba*
Bossa nova: Elis Regina and Tom Jobim, *Elis e Tom*
Rio funk: Seu Jorge, *America Brasil*
Rio soul: Tim Maia, *O Melhor de Tim Maia*
Pagode: Zeca Pagodinho, *Ao Vivo MTV*

Brazil's other great musical capital city is Salvador. From the late 1960s to the 1980s, this most African of Brazilian cities produced some of Brazil's most creative and exciting musicians. Choro, samba and bossa nova were all acoustically driven. When the Beatles and Hendrix rose to global stardom in the 1960s and even Dylan picked up an electric guitar, there was something of a revolution in Brazil. Conservatives wanted to keep the country's music 'authentic' and unpolluted by foreign influences. Liberals, spearheaded by a group of avant garde musicians from Bahia led by **Tom Zé**, **Gilberto Gil** and **Caetano Veloso**, and a São Paulo trio called **Os Mutantes**, embraced electric instruments and psychotropic drugs and took Brazilian music in a new electric direction. This was christened **tropicália** after a fusion of the words tropical and psychedelia. The seeds of *tropicália* blew from Bahia over the whole of Brazil to produce myriad musical fruits, fusions of rock, soul, funk and Brazilian rhythms. Collectively these came to be known as **MPB**, or Música Popular Brasileira.

Naná Vasconcelos from Recife (see page 500) has consistently been voted the best percussionist in the world by *Down Beat* magazine. He opens the Recife/Olinda Carnaval.

Acoustic music lived on in Bahia after *tropicália*. The late 1970s saw the emergence of a string of heavily percussive bands focused around drum troupes and called **blocos afros**. These were cultural organizations associated with Salvador carnival and rooted in the ritual music of the African Brazilian spirit religion of *candomblé*, traditional **Samba de Roda** (sung in a ring of people and accompanied only by percussion), and the martial art dance of **capoeira**. Bands like **Olodum**, **Ilê Aiyê** and Carlinhos Brown's **Timbalada** (see page 425) promoted African-Brazilian issues and solidarity through their music. Seeing them up close in the streets of Salvador, with dozens of drummers playing together in perfect syncopated unison, is an incredibly powerful experience. But even the drums of the *blocos afros* are being drowned out by Bahia's most popular music, **axé**, which sounds a little like salsa sexed-up, fused with rock and roll and overdosing on speed. It's energetic but shallow, with slushy lyrics and little sophistication. It's also relentlessly commercial and it's sweeping through the carnivals and clubs of the northeast leaving musical variety and the more traditional musical styles in its wake. Salvador is sadly not at its best musical moment as this book goes to press (see box, page 406). For a list of what to hear where, see pages 423-425.

Essential CDs
Tropicália: various artists, *Tropicália Panis e Circenses*; Caetano Veloso, *Bicho*; Gilberto Gil, *Parabolicamará*; Tom Zé, *Fabrication Defect*
Blocos afros: Olodum, *20 Anos*; Carlinhos Brown, *Alfagamabetizado*
Samba de roda: Mariene de Castro, *Abre Caminho* (see page 425)

ALEX ROBINSON

The rhythms of the African-indigenous Brazilian martial art dance of capoeira have strongly influenced Brazilian music in general, especially in Bahia.

Recife and São Luís: back to Africa and into the mangroove

Salvador's crown as the musical capital of the northeast has, at least for now, passed to São Luís, the new centre of African-Brazilian music, and Recife, where the spirit of *tropicália* lives on as *mangue beat*. On a Saturday night in the colonial centre of São Luís, large groups gather in impromptu bands to play the local equivalent of samba, **cacuriá**. Women dance and swirl in flowing dresses, and everyone is sucked into the throng. The city is at its liveliest

Essential CDs
Cacuriá: Dona Teté, *O Divino Cacuriá de Dona Teté*
Brazilian reggae: Tribo de Jah, *Essencial*
Mangue beat: Nação Zumbi, *Afrociberdelia*; Mundo Livre S/A, *Samba Esquema Noise*
Siba: *Fuloresta de Samba*

during the **Bumba-Meu-Boi** festivals, which have their own costumed dances (see pages 18 and 607) and it preserves a strong connection with the Caribbean through **reggae**, which is played in many of the small bars in the city centre.

Recife in Pernambuco state is more avant garde and intellectual. At weekends, the smoky bars of the old city centre vibrate to the guitars, drums, desert fiddles and electrified accordions of experimental bands and singers, whose sound is a fusion of the **maracatu** rhythms of African Pernambuco, with folk sounds from the arid backlands and international rock influences from bands like Nick Cave and the Bad Seeds, and British Sea Power (see page 499). There's a great diversity of sound, but the scene as a whole emerged as **mangue beat** in the 1990s. This was a deliberate attempt to re-discover Pernambuco's African and poor rural majority and re-articulate their heritage in a modern context. It was led by the charismatic singer **Chico Science** and his band **Nação Zumbi** (see page 684), **Fred Zeroquatro**, lead singer of **Mundo Livre S/A** (see page 515), and rootsier **Mestre Ambrósio**. Chico died in a car crash in 1997 but Mundo Livre and Mestre Ambrósio's lead singer, **Siba**, can be heard at carnival time. Their legacy and spirit lives on.

Opposite page: Fred Zeroquatro of Mundo Livre S/A from Recife – one of the founders of the *mangue beat* movement. **Top:** An *aparelhagem* techno-brega club night in Belém.
Middle: Banda Glória playing at the Aldeia Turiassu in São Paulo.
Bottom: Moreno Veloso, Domenico Lancelotti and Alexandre Kassin of Maís 2 – one of the freshest new bands from Rio.

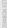

The rest of northeastern Brazil is dominated by **forró**, a kind of punchy jig originally driven by triangle, accordion and a deep bass drum, but now usually played by a full band. Popular wisdom says that the name derives from a Brazilianized pronunciation of 'for all' and comes from the 'for all' dances held for railway workers by their British bosses in the early 20th century. In reality, the dance is probably far older, dating from the 19th century. At this time, dance hall floors in the *sertão* were made of baked mud and, in order for them not to get dusty, people would drag their feet as they danced. The name probably comes from an abbreviation of *forrobodó* meaning 'dragged feet'. *Forró* is party music, and the biggest parties of all are the **Festas Juninhas** (see pages 18 and 535) in the *sertão* backlands in Caruru, Pernambuco and Paraíba in June, when hundreds of thousands gather to dance at breakneck speed, yet so close that they are literally entwined. You can do the same at any time of year, though, in the beach bars in Maceió, Fortaleza and half a dozen other little resorts. But get a Brazilian to show you the dance steps first or you'll feel like a rugby player dancing ballet.

Above: *Forró* is danced at the Festas Juninhas celebrations in Campina Grande, Paraíba.
Opposite page: MPB singer Maria Rita, the new face of intelligent Brazilian pop.

Essential CDs

Forró: Sivuca, *Cabelo do Milho*; Mel com Terra, *Forró Mel com Terra*; Elba Ramalho, *Flor de Paraíba* ; Dorivã, *Taquarulua*

Brazilian pop: rodeo crooning and spangly skirts

As in any country, the music visitors are most frequently exposed to is chart pop, and in Brazil it's no better than anywhere else. And no worse. But unlike almost everywhere else, it is home grown. Brazilian pop loosely falls into two styles: up tempo *axé* carnival music and its variants; and a kind of romantic crooning, *sertanejo*. The former originates largely from Bahia and Para and is generally sung by scantily clad, supremely energetic, muscular divas like Ivete Sangalo or Joelma from Banda Calypso. They front a band of precisely choreographed session musicians and even more scantily clad dancers. Lyrics are crass and cheesy, and the music as basic as the Spice Girls. But the shows are supremely professional and they attract crowds of hundreds of thousands, as does *sertanejo*. But here the singers are male duos with mullet haircuts, usually dressed in checked shirts and stetsons, who sing desperately cheesy romantic power ballads about 'grande amor'. Videos are often intercut with shots of prize bulls and rodeos.

The Amazon: surf guitar and carimbó rock

There's only one place in the Amazon for music – Belém. The city pounds to the springy West-Africa-meets-the-Caribbean rhythm of **carimbó** and strums to the psychedelic sixties Dick Dale surf twang of **guitarrada**. A night out on the town is unforgettable and quite unlike anywhere else in the world. At the weekend *aparelaghem* parties, DJs housed in giant space-pod sets as large as a truck and covered in shimmering flashing lights, play pounding techno-*guitarrada* or techno-*brega* to warehouse-sized crowds of revellers. Psychedelic *carimbó*-reggae bands

made up of 20 year olds and fronted by 70-year-old rockers in dark glasses and satin suits, play in sweaty clubs on the riverside, sharing a stage with surf guitar bands or red hot power metal samba bands fronted by a wispy woman with dreadlocks and tattoos. There's nowhere else like it anywhere, even in Brazil. Come here for the Círio festival if you can and dive in.

Essential CDs
Carimbó: Curimbó de Bolso, *Cantação Amazônida*
Techno-guitarrada: Pio Lobato, *Technoguitarrada*
Guitarrada: Guitarradas do Pará
Amazon metal: Madam Sataan, *Madam Sataan*
Carimbó psychedelia: Coletivo Radio Cipo, *Formigando na Calcada do Brasil*
Surf pyschedelic pop: La Pupuña, *The Shark Side of the Moon*

Top: Mestre Laurentino of Coletivo Rádio Cipó, the self-proclaimed oldest rocker in the world.
Above: Coletivo Rádio Cipó, one of many bands making Belém one of Brazil's most exciting musical cities.

Minas Gerais: Milton Nascimento and metal from the mines

The state of Minas is Brazil's lyrical, reflective heart. Many of the country's finest poets and writers grew up in its pretty villages of whitewashed sugar-cube houses and colonial bell towers set in rolling hills. Many associate the Minas sound with Milton Nascimento and his band, the **Clube da Esquina**. Clube da Esquina formed as a loose association of like-minded musicians in 1970s Belo Horizonte, and together they forged a new Brazilian musical style whose influence has spread far beyond their country. Herbie Hancock, Wayne Shorter and Stevie Wonder are admirers of Milton Nascimento and the great French modern jazz and classical composer, Lionel Belmondo, has called him as important a composer as Ravel. Unlike much Brazilian music, the Clube da Esquina sound is textural and melodic rather than rhythmic and dancy, owing more to folk and church music than samba and bossa nova. Soaring, melancholy vocal lines interplay with sweeping, rich harmonies, the chants of Africa and indigenous Brazil, and catholic choral lines, children's voices, gentle acoustic guitar, mandolin, the orchestra, a distant organ or drum, a ringing bell tower … all rising and falling with the dynamic breadth of a Villa-Lobos or Vaughan Williams tone poem. Above this rich, pastoral landscape of sound, Milton's voice soars in golden baritone or searing falsetto telling hundreds of stories of Minas Gerais, of Brazil itself, of its marginalized and

Milton Nascimento, one of the towering greats of international music (see page 264).

Essential CDs
Clube da Esquina: Milton Nascimento, *Clube da Esquina*; *Clube da Esquina II*
Modern Minas: Erika Machado, *No Cimento*; Uakti and Philip Glass, *Aguas da Amazonia*

innocent, its slaves, serfs and *indígenas*, woven together with deeply personal impressions and reflections from Milton's own life. Although his legacy lives on in a hundred singer-songwriters who play in the bars and theatres of Belo Horizonte, Minas continues to produce some of Brazil's most individual voices: the all-instrumental band **Uakti** who build their own unique percussion instruments and play a kind of mesmerizing minimalist trance on them, collaborating with composers like Philip Glass; **Érika Machado** (see page 260) who sings beautifully crafted, catchy pop with quirky, witty lyrics; **Proa**, a kind of new-wave indie electronica; and Brazil's most commercially successful band, **Sepultura**, who play some of the world's most driving, exciting virtuoso death metal.

Street musicians gather for an impromptu jam in Vila Madalena, one of São Paulo's many musical neighbourhoods.

São Paulo: the avant garde

Everything from the Brazilian musical continent comes together in São Paulo. It is Brazil's nexus, its default capital where the talent gravitates in search of money. On any night anywhere you can hear a bizarre *carimbó*-metal act from Belém, Recife *mangue beat*, an off-the-wall Mineiro songwriter, cowboy ballads from Goiás or some old-school samba. Yet the city has its own sound too, a kind of avant garde art rock samba formulated by one of Brazil's great unsung musical geniuses, **Itamar Assumpção**. Itamar was the Zappa of Brazil, a supremely odd, witty, individual musical and lyrical voice who gathered a group of immensely talented musicians around him in the 1980s and performed strings of famously bizarre, theatrical shows. His work inspired numerous other mavericks such as baroque music-hall samba rockers, **Karnak**, and the electronica pioneer, **Max de Castro** (see page 215). Together their sound became known as **vanguarda**. São Paulo has also produced many of Brazil's internationally famous DJs, notably **Patife** and **Marky**, both of whom had a predilection for drum 'n' bass.

Essential CDs

Avant garde: Itamar Assumpção, *Preto Bras*; Karnak, *Karnak*; Max de Castro, *Max de Castro*

Club: DJ Patife, *Cool Steps*

Brazilian instruments glossary

Atabaque: the Brazilian equivalent of the conga drum
Bandolim: Brazilian pear-shaped mandolin
Tambor: a tight-skinned samba drum
Repinique: a tight-skinned samba drum
Surdo: a deep, booming samba drum
Reco reco: a friction percussion instrument that looks like a cheese grater
Cavaquinho: a four-stringed miniature Portuguese guitar
Caxixi: a little basket full of pebbles or beads used in capoeira and general percussion
Cuica: a friction drum whose call sounds like a crying monkey
Xequere: a gourd or wooden shell enclosed in a basket of beads, used in samba and *maracatu*
Tamborim: a small hand-held drum
Pandeiro: a small-hand held drum with bells on the edge (tambourine in English)
Zabumba: a deep sonorous drum used in *forró*
Violão: a guitar
Timbal: a clear high-tone drum used in Bahian music and most famously by Carlinhos Brown
Rocar : a series of little plate bells in a metal frame
Berimbau: a bow-shaped twanging percussion instrument used in capoeira
Gongue: a metal bell used in *maracatu*

Above: Berimbaus, Xequeres, Timbales and other assorted percussion instruments for sale in the streets of Salvador. **Next page:** Carioca MPB singer Marisa Monte playing live at the Barbican in London.

He was also a dentist and became known by the nickname Tiradentes – tooth-puller. Already dissatisfied with the way the army had treated him, by failing to promote him among other things, in 1788 he was suspended from active duty because of illness. The subsequent loss of pay roused him further. In trying to get reinstated he met Freire de Andrade and Alvares Maciel and later conversations prompted him to tell them of his idea of an uprising against the Portuguese. The Inconfidência grew out of these types of meeting, some planning action, others the future political and economic organization of a new, independent state.

The conspirators worked to gain support for their cause, but one soldier they approached, Coronel Joaquim Silverio dos Reis, used the information he had been given to betray the cause. The governor received reports from other sources and began to build up a picture of what was going on. Tiradentes was the first to be arrested, at the beginning of May 1789, in Rio de Janeiro. It seems that the plotters at this time still had no clear idea of what their ultimate aim was, nor of the importance of their attitudes. They never got the chance anyway because all were arrested soon after Tiradentes. They were imprisoned and kept incommunicado for two years while the case against them was prepared. Tiradentes was singled out as the most important member of the group and, under questioning, he did not disabuse his captors, taking full responsibility for everything. A defence for the Inconfidêntes was prepared, but it almost totally ignored Tiradentes, as if he were being made a scapegoat. It made no difference, though, because the defence lost; 11 Inconfidêntes were sentenced to death in November 1791. Soon afterwards the authorities in Brazil read out a surprising letter from the queen, Dona Maria I, commuting the death sentence for 10 of the conspirators to exile in Portugal or Africa. The 11th, Tiradentes, was not spared. On 21 April 1792 he was hanged and his body was quartered and his head cut off, the parts to de displayed as a warning against any similar attempts to undermine the crown. Even though Tiradentes would never have been freed, one of the astonishing things about the queen's letter was that it was dated 18 months before it was brought to light.

The **Capela de Santo Antônio**, wonderfully simple and the oldest in town, is some distance from the centre on Rua Rosário Velho. Overlooking the city from the north, with a good viewpoint, is the church of **Nossa Senhora do Rosário** ① *R do Rosário,* dating back to 1752, with work by Athayde and showing Moorish influence.

Outside the centre to the west, but within easy walking distance, is the **Seminário Menor**, now the Instituto de Ciencias Históricas e Sociais of the federal university.

South of the river, Avenida Getúlio Vargas leads to the new **Prefeitura Municipal**. It passes the **Ginásio Poliesportivo** and, across the avenue, the **railway station**. This is a romantic building with a clock tower, but it is rapidly falling into disrepair.

Around Mariana

The small village of **Antônio Pereira**, 24 km north of Mariana, is where imperial topaz is mined. Tours can be made of an interesting cave with stalactites. Local children will show you around for a small fee. ⇥ *See Transport, page 289.*

O Aleijadinho

Brazil's greatest sculptor, Antônio Francisco Lisboa (1738-1814) was the son of a Portuguese architect and a black slave woman and was known as O Aleijadinho (the little cripple). A debilitating disease – probably leprosy – left him so badly maimed that he was forced to work on his knees and later on his back with his chisels strapped to his useless hands. Like Mestre Athayde and many other Mineira baroque artists his art was political. He was strongly sympathetic with the Inconfidêntes movement and was probably a friend of Tiradentes. Many of his sculptures contain subtle references to Tiradentes's martyrdom and veiled criticisms of the Portuguese. His most remarkable works are the haunting, vivid statues of the prophets in Congonhas (which are so lifelike that they almost seem to move), and the church decoration in Ouro Preto.

Congonhas do Campo ●❶❷❸ ▶▶ pp283-289. Colour map 4, C3.

→ Phone code: 031. Population: 42,000. Altitude: 866 m.

In the 18th century, Congonhas was a mining town. Today, in addition to the business brought by the tourists and pilgrims who come to the sanctuary, it is known for its handicrafts. There is little need to stay in Congonhas as the town's main sight, Aleijadinho's beautiful church and chapel-lined stairway, can be seen in a few hours between bus changes. Leave your bags at the information desk in the bus station.

Ins and outs

Getting there The rodoviária is 1.5 km outside town; a bus to the centre costs US$0.40. In town, the bus stops in Praça JK from where you can walk up Praça Dr Mário Rodrigues Pereira, cross the little bridge, then go up Rua Bom Jesus and Rua Aleijadinho to the Praça da Basílica. A bus marked 'Basílica' runs every 30 minutes from the rodoviária to Bom Jesus, 5 km, US$0.45. A taxi from the rodoviária will cost US$5 one-way, US$10 return including the wait while you visit the sanctuary.

Tourist information Fumcult ① in the Romarias, T031-3731 1300 ext 114, acts as the tourist office and is very helpful. On the hill are a tourist kiosk, souvenir shops, the Colonial Hotel and Cova do Daniel restaurant. There are public toilets on the Alameda das Palmeiras.

O Santuário de Bom Jesus de Matosinhos

① Tue-Sun 0700-1900. No direct bus from Congonhas do Campo or Rio to the sanctuary; change at the town of Conselheiro Lafaiete, from where there is a frequent service, US$1.

The great pilgrimage church and its Via Sacra dominate the town. The idea of building a sanctuary belonged to a prospector, Feliciano Mendes, who promised to erect a cross and chapel in thanks to Bom Jesus after he had been cured of a serious illness. The inspiration for his devotion came from two sources in Portugal, the cult of Bom Jesus at Braga (near where Mendes was born) and the church of Bom Jesus de Matosinhos, near Porto. Work began in 1757, funded by Mendes' own money and alms he raised. The church was finished in 1771, six years after Mendes' death, and the fame that the sanctuary had acquired led to its development by the most famous architects, artists and sculptors of the time as a Sacro Monte. This involved the construction of six linked chapels, or pasos

Santuário de Bom Jesus de Matosinhos

Room of Miracles

Igreja de Bom Jesus de Matosinhos

Adro dos Profetas (Terrace of the Prophets)

Capela da Colocação na Cruz (The Nailing on the Cross)

Capela da Flagelação e da Coroação de Espinhos (The Flagellation & Crowning with Thorns)

Capela do Carregamento da Cruz (The Carrying of the Cross)

Alameda das Palmeiras

To Romarias

Capela da Prisão do Cristo (The Taking of Christ)

Capela do Monte das Oliveiras (The Mount of Olives)

Capela da Ceia (The Last Supper)

Adro dos Profetas detail

N
Not to scale

Sleeping
Colonial & Cova do Daniel Restaurant 1

Prophets
Abdias 1

Amós 2
Baruc 3
Daniel 4
Ezequiel 5
Habacuc 6
Isaías 7
Jeremias 8
Joel 9
Jonas 10
Naum 11
Oséias 12

(1802-1818), which lead up to a terrace and courtyard before the church.

There is a wide view of the country from the church terrace, below which are six small chapels set in an attractive sloping area with grass, cobblestones and palms. Each chapel shows scenes with life-size Passion figures carved by Aleijadinho and his pupils in cedar wood. In order of ascent they are: the chapel of the Last Supper; the chapel of the Mount of Olives; the chapel of the betrayal of Christ; the chapel of the flagellation and the crowning with thorns; the chapel of Jesus carrying the Cross; and the chapel of Christ being nailed to the Cross.

On the terrace stand the 12 prophets sculpted by Aleijadinho 1800-1805; these are thought of as his masterpieces. Carved in soapstone with a dramatic sense of movement, they constitute one of the finest works of art of their period in the world. Note how Aleijadinho adapted the biblical characters to his own cultural references. The prophets are sculpted wearing leather boots, as all important men in his time would have done. Daniel, who entered the lion's den, is represented with the artist's own conception of a lion, never having seen one himself: a large, maned cat with a face rather like a Brazilian monkey. Similarly, the whale that accompanies Jonah is an idiosyncratic interpretation. Each statue has a prophetic text carved with it. The statues "combine in a kind of sacred ballet whose movements only seem uncoordinated; once these sculptures cease to be considered as isolated units, they take on full significance as part of a huge composition brought to life by an inspired genius." (*Iberian-American Baroque*, edited by Henri Stierlin) The beauty of the whole is enhanced by the combination of church, Via Sacra and landscape over which the prophets preside.

Inside the church, there are paintings by Athayde and the heads of four sainted popes (Gregory, Jerome, Ambrose and

Augustine) sculpted by Aleijadinho for the reliquaries on the high altar. Other artists involved were João Nepomuceno Correia e Castro, who painted the scenes of the life and passion of Christ in the nave and around the high altar, João Antunes de Carvalho, who carved the high altar, and Jerônimo Félix and Manuel Coelho, who carved the crossing altars of Santo Antônio and São Francisco de Paula. Despite the ornate carving, the overall effect of the paintwork is almost muted and naturalistic, with much use of blues, greys and pinks. Lamps are suspended on chains from the mouths of black dragons. To the left of the church, through the third door in the building alongside the church, is the Room of Miracles, which contains photographs and thanks for miracles performed.

Up on the hill, the Alameda das Palmeiras sweeps from the **Hotel Colonial** round to the **Romarias**, a large, almost oval area surrounded by buildings. This was the lodging where the pilgrims stayed. It now contains the **Espaço Cultural** and tourist office, as well as workshops, the museums of mineralogy and religious art, and the **Memória da Cidade**.

Of the other churches in Congonhas do Campo, the oldest is **Nossa Senhora do Rosário**, Praça do Rosário, built by slaves at the end of the 17th century. The **Igreja Matriz de Nossa Senhora da Conceição**, in Praça 7 de Setembro, dates from 1749; the portal is attributed to Aleijadinho, while parts of the interior are by Manuel Francisco Lisboa. There are also two 18th-century chapels, **Nossa Senhora da Ajuda**, in the district of Alto Maranhão, and the church at **Lobo Leite**, 10 km away.

Tiradentes

Sleeping		
Ponto do Morro **1**	Pousada do Largo **4**	Pouso das Gerais **10**
Porão Colonial **2**	Pousada do Laurito **5**	Solar da Ponte **9**
Pousada do Alferes **3**	Pousada Mãe d'Água **6**	
Pousada do Arco Iris **11**	Pousada Maria Bonita **7**	**Eating**
	Pousada Três Portas **8**	Aluarte **1**

Tiradentes ⊕⊘⊘▲⊕⊖ → pp283-289. Colour map 4, C3.

→ Phone code: 032. Population: 6000.

Aside from Ouro Preto, Tiradentes is the most visited of the Minas colonial towns. Its winding, hilly streets lined with carefully restored baroque Portuguese churches and neat whitewashed cottages huddle around the Santo Antonio river, beneath the rugged hills of the Serra de São José. Inside are art galleries, restaurants, souvenir shops and *pousadas*, all busy with tourists even during the week. Horse-drawn carriages clatter along the cobbles and at weekends a steam train towing Pullmans full of delighted children puffs its way slowly below the mountains to the pretty colonial town of **São João del Rei** (see page 279).

Ins and outs

Tiradentes and São João del Rei lie within less than 30 minutes of each other and buses leave every 30 to 40 minutes. Tiradentes is the more twee; São João is uglier but more of a real town. Tiradentes has a far greater choice of accommodation. São João has better bus connections with Rio, São Paulo, Belo Horizonte, Mariana and Ouro Preto. The **tourist office** ① *R Resende Costa 71*, is in the *prefeitura*.

R Silvio Vasconcelos

R de Moraes

R dos Inconfidentes
10

R Henrique Diniz

Antônio Carvalho

Rio Dos Moraes

To Train Station & São João del Rei

Praça da Estação

Estalagem **2**
Maria Luisa Casa de Chá **7**
Quartier Latin **6**
Quinto de Ouro **4**
Theatro da Vila **3**

Virados do Largo **5**

Walking tour - -▶- -

Sights

A suggested walking tour is as follows. From the main *praça*, **Largo das Forras**, take Rua Resende Costa up to the Largo do Sol, a lovely open space where you'll find the simple church of **São João Evangelista** ① *Wed-Mon 0900-1700*. Built by the *Irmandade dos Homens Pardos* (mulattos), it has paintings of the four Evangelists and a cornice painted in an elaborate pattern in pink, blue and beige. Beside the church is the **Museu Padre Toledo**, the house of this leader of the Inconfidência Mineira, which is now a museum protecting some handsome colonial furniture and a painted roof depicting the Five Senses. The **Casa de Cultura** in the row of 18th-century houses on Rua Padre Toledo, which leads from Largo do Sol to the Igreja Matriz de Santo Antônio, is protected by the same organization.

The **Igreja Matriz de Santo Antônio** ① *daily 0900-1700, US$1, no photography*, first built in 1710 and enlarged in 1736, contains some of the finest gilded woodcarvings in the country. The main church is predominantly white and gold. Lamps hang from the beaks of golden eagles. The symbols on the panels painted on the ceiling of the nave are a mixture of

Old Testament and medieval Christian symbolism (for instance the phoenix, and the pelican). A carved wooden balustrade separates the seating in the nave from richly carved side chapels and altars. The principal altar is also ornately decorated, as are the walls and ceiling around it. The church has a small but fine organ brought from Porto in the 1790s. The upper part of the reconstructed façade is said to follow a design by Aleijadinho. In front of the church, on the balustrade which overlooks the main street and the town, are also a cross and a sundial by him.

From Santo Antônio, it is well worth taking a detour up to the **Santuário da Santíssima Trindade**. The chapel itself is 18th century while the Room of Miracles associated with the annual Trinity Sunday pilgrimage is modern.

Heading back down past Santo Antônio along Rua da Câmara, you come to the **Casa da Câmara e Antigo Fórum**. Here the road divides, the left-hand street, Jogo de Bola, leads to the Largo do Ó (which rejoins the main street), while Rua da Câmara goes to the crossroads with Rua Direita. At this junction is the **Sobrado Ramalho**, said to be the oldest building in Tiradentes. It is believed to be where the gold was melted down, and contains many soapstone carvings. It has been beautifully restored as a cultural centre.

Before taking Rua Direita back to Largo das Forras, carry straight on towards the river and cross the bridge to the magnificent **Chafariz de São José** (public fountain), installed in 1749. The water is brought by a stone aqueduct from springs in the forest at the foot of Serra São José. It is still used for drinking, washing and watering animals.

Rua Direita has some interesting old buildings. The charming **Nossa Senhora do Rosário** ① *Praça Padre Lourival, Wed-Mon 1200-1600, US$0.50*, has fine statuary and ornate gilded altars. On its painted ceiling colonnades rise to heaven; two monks stand on a hill and the Virgin and Child are in the sky. Other ceiling panels depicting the life of Christ are in poor shape. The church contains statues of black saints, including São Benedito, patron saint of cooks; in one of the statues he is holding a squash. The church dates from 1727, but building by the 'Irmandade dos Pretos Cativos' (black slave brotherhood) began as early as 1708.

Opposite Praça Padre Lourival, is the **Antiga Cadeia** (18th-19th century) which now contains the **Museu de Arta Sacra**. Rua Direita meets the Largo das Forras at the **Prefeitura Municipal**, a two-storey building with an extra room under the roof. It now houses the tourist, post and phone offices.

If you have any energy left, there are other churches and chapels in the town, including the **Igreja de Bom Jesus da Pobreza**, on the Largo das Forras. Across the river, the 18th-century **Nossa Senhora das Mercês** ① *Largo das Mercês, Sun 0900-1700*, has an interesting painted ceiling and a notable statue of the Virgin. On the grassy Morro de São Francisco is the small chapel of **São Francisco de Paula** (mid-18th century).

Excursions from Tiradentes

The **steam trains** ① *Fri-Sun and holidays, 1000 and 1415 from São João del Rei, returning from Tiradentes at 1300 and 1700, US$8*, which run on the 76-cm gauge track between São João del Rei and Tiradentes (13 km) have been in continuous operation since 1881 – a testament to the durability of the rolling stock and locomotives made by the Baldwin Company of Philadelphia. The maximum speed is 20 kph. To get to the railway station from the centre of the village you have to cross the river and head out of town on the Rua dos Inconfidêntes. Follow this road until it becomes the Rua Antônio Teixeira Carvalho, which carries on to the bridge over the Rio das Mortes. On the opposite bank is a small park and the station. For the railway museum at the railway station in São João del Rei, see page 281.

A recommended walk from Tiradentes is to the protected forest on the **Serra de São José**. The easiest access is from behind the Chafariz, where a black door in the wall is opened at 0730 (Wednesday to Sunday). In just five minutes you are in the forest following the watercourse, where monkeys and birds can be seen. Alternatively, you can walk up into the **Serra** from behind the Mercês Church; ask for directions. It is recommended that you take a guide if you wish to walk along the top of the Serra.

There is a good one- or two-hour walk from Tiradentes to the **Balneário de Águas Santas**, which involves crossing the Serra. At the *balneário* is a swimming pool, a lake and a *churrascaria*, **Senzala**. A map can be obtained from the **Solar da Ponte**, or ask locally for directions (taxi US$15). On the way you pass **Parque Frei Mariano Vellozo**, which contains the Cachoeira do Mangue falls. It is busy at weekends and can be reached by car on the old road to São João.

São João del Rei ⊜⊘⊕⊛⊜⊜⊕ ‣ *pp283-289. Colour map 4, C3.*

→ *Phone code: 032. Population: 79,000.*

São João del Rei lies at the foot of the Serra do Lenheiro, astride what once must have been a winding little stream. This has now sadly been transformed into a concrete gutter with grass verges. Eighteenth-century bridges cross the stream leading to streets lined with colonial buildings and plazas with crumbling churches, the most interesting and best preserved of which is the church of **São Francisco**. The town feels far less of a tourist museum piece than nearby Tiradentes. There is a lively music scene here, with two renowned orchestras and an annual arts festival in July, and the bars are filled with locals rather than tourists waiting for their coach. There is a good view of the town and surroundings from **Alto da Boa Vista**, where there is a **Senhor dos Montes** (Statue of Christ).

São João del Rei is famous as the home of Tiradentes and of Tancredo Neves. The former was born in the **Fazenda de Pombal**, about 15 km downstream from Tiradentes on the Rio das Mortes. After his execution, the *fazenda* was confiscated. It is now an experimental station owned by Ibama. Tancredo Neves, to whom there is a memorial in the town, was the man who would have become the first civilian president of Brazil after the military dictatorships of the mid-20th century, had he not mysteriously died before taking office.

Ins and outs

The *rodoviária*, 2 km west of the centre, has a telephone office, toilets, luggage store, *lanchonetes* and a tourist office. São João is a good base for visiting Tiradentes (or vice versa); less than 30 minutes away by bus or an hour away at weekends via one of Brazil's most memorable steam train rides.

Many streets and squares seem to have more than one name, which can be a little confusing, but as the town centre is not large, it is hard to get lost. One such street crosses the Ponte da Cadeia from Rua Passos; it has three names: Rua da Intendência, Manoel Anselmo and Artur Bernardes. The **Secretaria de Turismo** ① *in the house of Bárbara Heliodora, T032-3372 7338, open 0900-1700*, provides a free map.

Sights

The Córrego do Lenheiro, a stream with steep grassy banks, runs through the centre of town. Across it are two fine, stone bridges, **A Ponte da Cadeia** (1798) and **A Ponte do Rosário** (1800), as well as several other modern bridges. Both sides of the river have colonial monuments, which are interspersed with modern buildings. On the north side are many streets with pleasant houses, but in various states of repair. **Rua Santo Antônio** has many single-storey eclectic houses from the imperial period, which have been restored and painted. **Rua Santo Elias** has several buildings all in the same style. Behind the church of Nossa Senhora do Pilar (see below), the **Largo da Câmara** leads up to **Mercês church**, which has quite a good view. Throughout the city you will see locked portals with colonial porticos. These are *passinhos*, shrines that are opened in Holy Week. They can be seen on **Largo da Cruz** and **Largo do Rosário**.

São Francisco de Assis ① *Praça Frei Orlando, Tue-Sun 0830-1700, US$1*, built 1774, is one of the most beautiful churches in Brazil. Although often attributed to Aleijadinho, it was designed and decorated by two almost completely undocumented artists, Francisco de Lima Cerqueira and Aniceto de Souza Lopes (who also sculpted the Pelourinho in the Largo da Câmara). The magnificent but modest whitewash and stone façade sits between

São João del Rei

Sleeping		Eating
Aparecida 1	Ponte Real 5	611 4
Beco do Bispo 6	Pousada Casarão 3	Chafariz 3
Brasil 2	Pousada São Benedito 7	Churrascaria Ramón 1
Lenheiro Palace 4	Sinha Batista 8	Quinto do Ouro 2

two cylindrical bell towers and is decorated with an ornately carved door frame and a superb medal of St Francis receiving illumination. The *praça* in front is shaped like a lyre and, in the late afternoon, the royal palms cast shadows that interconnect to form the lyre's strings. The six carved altars inside have been restored, revealing fine carving in sucupira wood. Their artistry is wonderful and the three pairs of altars mirror each other, each pair in a different style (note the use of pillars and the different paintings that accompany each altar). The overall shape of the nave is elliptical, the gold altar has spiralling columns and an adoring St Francis kneels atop.

The cathedral, **Basílica de Nossa Senhora do Pilar** ① *R Getúlio Vargas (formerly R Direita), daily 1000-1600*, was built in 1721, but has a 19th-century façade which replaced the 18th-century original. It has rich altars and a brightly painted ceiling (Madonna and Child in the middle, saints and bishops lining the sides). Note the androgynous gold heads and torsos within the eight columns set into the walls either side of the main altar. There is a profusion of cherubs and plants in the carving. This abundance and angelic innocence contrasts with the suffering of the Passion and the betrayal of the Last Supper (two pictures of which are before the altar), all common themes in Brazilian baroque. In the sacristy are portraits of the Evangelists.

The **Memorial Tancredo Neves** ① *R Padre José Maria Xavier 7, Wed-Fri 1300-1800, weekends and holidays 0900-1700, US$1*, is a homage to the man and his life. A short video on São João del Rei is shown. It also holds exhibitions and has a bookshop.

The **Museu Ferroviário (Railway Museum)** ① *Av Hermílio Alves 366, T032-371 8004, US$0.50*, is well worth exploring. The museum traces the history of railways in general and in Brazil in brief. There is an informative display of the role of Irineu Evangelista de Souza, Barão de Mauá, who was a pioneer of both industry and the railways following his visit to England in 1840. The locomotive that ran on the first railway from Rio de Janeiro to the foot of the Serra do Mar was called 'A Baronesa' after his wife. The railway to São João, the Estrada de Ferro Oeste de Minas, was not a success, but it was instrumental in the development of the region. In the museum is an 1880 Baldwin 4-4-0 locomotive from Philadelphia (No 5055) and a 1912-1913 VIP carriage, both still used on the steam journey to Tiradentes. Outside, at the end of the platforms are carriages and a small Orenstein and Koppel (Berlin) engine. You can walk along the tracks to the round house, where there are several working engines in superb condition, an engine shed and a steam-operated machine shop, still working. It is here that the engines get up steam before going to couple with the coaches for the run to Tiradentes. On days when the trains are running, you can get a good, close-up view of operations even if not taking the trip. Highly recommended. For the steam train to Tiradentes, see page 278.

Sabará ●❶❸● → *pp283-289. Colour map 4, B3.*

→ *Phone code: 031. Population: 116,000.*

Some 23 km east of Belo Horizonte is the colonial gold-mining (and steel-making) town of Sabará. The town is strung along the narrow steep valleys of the Rio das Velhas and Rio Sabará. Since the late 17th century, the Rio das Velhas was known as a gold-bearing river and a community soon grew up there. By 1702 it was the most populous in Minas Gerais. In 1711, the name Villa Real de Nossa Senhora da Conceição de Sabará was given to the parish and in 1838 it became the city of Sabará.

Ins and outs

There are regular buses from Belo Horizonte, US$0.75, 30 minutes. If travelling by car, there is a road, mostly unpaved, that runs to Sabará from Ravena on the BR-381 Belo Horizonte–Vitória highway, which crosses the hills and is a pleasant drive. Tourist information is available from the **Secretaria de Turismo** ① *R Pedro II 200, T031-3671 1522*. *Passeio a Sabará*, by Lúcia Machado de Almeida, with splendid illustrations by Guignard, is an excellent guide to the town.

Sights

There are a number of old churches, fountains, rambling cobbled streets and simple houses with carved doors of great interest. From the bus terminus, walk up Rua Clemente Faria to Praça Santa Rita, where there's a large *chafariz* (fountain). The square adjoins Rua Dom Pedro II, which is lined with beautiful 18th-century buildings. They include the **Solar do Padre Correa** ① *R Dom Pedro II 200*, (1773) now the Prefeitura, a mansion with a rococo chapel and *salão nobre* (main reception room); the **Casa Azul** ① *R Dom Pedro II 215*, (1773), now the INSS building, with a chapel and a fine portal; and the **Teatro Municipal**, former opera house, built in 1770 and the second oldest in Brazil. It has a superb interior, with three balconies, a carved wooden rail before the orchestra pit, wooden floors and *esteiro* (flattened, woven bamboo) ceilings.

At the top of Rua Dom Pedro II is the Praça Melo Viana, in the middle of which is **Nossa Senhora do Rosário dos Pretos** ① *Tue-Sun 0800-1100, 1300-1700*, left unfinished at the time of the slaves' emancipation. Behind the façade of the building are the chancel, sacristy (both 1780) and the first chapel (1713). There is a museum of religious art in the church. To the right of the church is the **Chafariz do Rosário**. Also on the *praça* are the ornate Fórum Ministro Orozimbo Nonato and two schools. From Praça Melo Viana, take Rua São Pedro to the church of **São Francisco** (1781); beyond the church is the **Chafariz Kaquende**.

In Rua da Intendência is the museum of 18th-century gold mining, the **Museu do Ouro** ① *Tue-Sun 1200-1730, US$1*. It contains exhibits of gold extraction, as well as religious items and colonial furniture. The building itself is a fine example of colonial architecture. Sources disagree as to its date of construction, but the general view is that it was before 1730. Originally the foundry, it became the Casa da Intendência in 1735. For most of the 19th century it was abandoned and became the gold museum in 1945.

Another fine example of civil colonial architecture is the **Casa Borba Gato** ① *R Borba Gato 71*, so called because tradition has it that it belonged to the famous *bandeirante*, Manoel de Borba Gato, one of the first to settle on the Rio das Velhas, but exiled from the region after the murder of the king's representative, Rodrigo de Castel Blanco in 1682. The building currently belongs to the Museu do Ouro.

On Rua do Carmo is the church of **Nossa Senhora do Carmo** ① *US$1, leaflet provided*, (1763-1774), with doorway, pulpits and choir loft by Aleijadinho and paintings by Athayde. From the ceilings, painted blue and grey and gold, religious figures look down surrounding the Virgin and Child and the Chariot of Fire. In the chancel, the Ten Commandments in blue work have a distinctly Moorish air, what with the tents and the night-time scenes.

Similar in style externally is the **Capela de Nossa Senhora do Pilar**, which is beside the municipal cemetery and in front of a large building with blue gates and doors.

Nossa Senhora da Conceição ① *Praça Getúlio Vargas, free*, (1720), has a lot of visible woodwork and a beautiful floor. The carvings have a great deal of gilding, there are painted panels, and paintings by 23 Chinese artists brought from Macau. The clearest Chinese work is on the two red doors to the right and left of the chancel.

Let them eat queca

In the 18th and 19th century many British railway workers and miners came and settled in Minas and their legacy can still be seen today. Indeed many of the habits thought to be quintessentially Minas Gerais by other Brazilians are obviously English to European eyes. Mineiras are famous throughout Brazil for saying 'Why so?' when perplexed. Mock Tunbridge-ware inlaid boxes and desks can be found in many traditional Minas homes. And at tea time, near Christmas many older Mineiras eat 'queca'…. Identical to British fruit cake: rich, sweet and inlaid with crystallized fruit and introduced to Minas by the bored wives of English miners who settled in Nova Lima. It is traditionally accompanied by cups of weak, milky tea.

Nossa Senhora do Ó, built in 1717 and showing unmistakable Chinese influence (paintings in need of restoration), is 2 km from the centre of the town at the Largo Nossa Senhora do Ó. To get there, take the local bus marked 'Esplanada' or 'Boca Grande'.

If you walk up the **Morro da Cruz** hill from the **Hotel do Ouro** to a small chapel, the **Capela da Cruz**, or Senhor Bom Jesus, you can get a wonderful view of the whole region. Look for beautiful quartz crystals while you are up there.

Excursions from Sabará

Some 25 km from Sabará and 60 km from Belo Horizonte is **Caeté**. The town, originally called Vila Nova da Rainha, has several historical buildings and churches. On the Praça João Pinheiro are the **Prefeitura** and **Pelourinho** (both 1722), the **Igreja Matriz Nossa Senhora do Com Sucesso** ⓘ *daily 1300-1800*, (1756, rebuilt 1790) and the **Chafariz da Matriz**. Also on the *praça* is the **tourist information office** ⓘ *Casa da Cultura, T031-3651 1855*. Other churches are **Nossa Senhora do Rosário** (1750-1768), with a ceiling attributed to Mestre Athayde, and **São Francisco de Assis**. The **Museu Regional** ⓘ *R Israel Pinheiro 176, Tue-Sun 1200-1700*, in the house of the Barão de Catas Altas, or Casa Setecentista, contains 18th- and 19th-century religious art and furniture. The house itself is a fine example of 18th-century civic architecture, with two floors and an interior patio. From Caeté you can go to the **Serra da Piedade** mountains.

⊙ Colonial cities near Belo Horizonte listings

For Sleeping and Eating price codes and other relevant information, see pages 42-47.

⊜ Sleeping

Ouro Preto *p263, map p266*
Many hotels will negotiate lower prices off season. Ask at the tourist office for reasonably priced accommodation in *casas de família*. Avoid touts who greet you off buses and charge higher prices than those advertised in hotels; it is difficult to get hotel rooms at weekends and holiday periods. Rooms can be booked through www.ouropretotour.com or www.ouropreto.com.
AL Grande Hotel, R das Flores 164, Centro T031-3551 1488, www.hotelouropreto. com.br. One of a handful of gorgeous Niemeyer hotels dotted throughout Minas, newly restored and with views over the city.
A Pousada do Mondego, Largo de Coimbra 38, T031-3551 2040, www.mondego.com.br. Beautifully kept colonial house in a fine location by São Francisco Church, room rates vary according to view, small restaurant, Scotch bar, popular with groups. Recommended (a **Roteiros de Charme** hotel,

see page 43), the hotel runs a *jardineira* bus tour of the city, 2 hrs, minimum 10 passengers, US$15 for non-guests.

A Pousada Solar de NS do Rosário, Av Getúlio Vargas 270, T031-3551 5200, www.hotelsolardorosario.com.br. Fully restored historic building with a highly recommended restaurant, bar, sauna, pool; all facilities in rooms.

B Luxor Pousada, R Dr Alfredo Baeta 16, Praça Antônio Dias, T031-3551 2244, www.luxorhoteis.com.br. Converted colonial mansion, no twin beds, comfortable and clean but spartan, good views, restaurant good but service slow.

C Pousada Casa Grande, R Conselheiro Quintiliano 96, T/F031-3551 4314, www.hotelpousadacasagrande.com.br. A large colonial town house with 21 smart, but simply appointed rooms with polished wooden floors, en suites and some with views out over the city.

D Colonial, Trav Padre Camilo Veloso 26, close to Praça Tiradentes, T031-3551 3133, www.hotelcolonial.com.br. A little colonial house with 14 rooms. All are well maintained. Some are distinctly smaller than others so it is worth looking at a few. Decor is modest, with furniture sitting on a polished wooden floor.

D Pousada Itacolomi, R Antônio Pereira 167, T031-3551 2891, www.pousadaita colomi.com.br. Small but well kept with good rates for the 3-room apartments. Recommended. Next door to the Museu da Inconfidência.

D Pousada Nello Nuno, R Camilo de Brito 59, T031-3551 3375, www.pousadanello nuno.com.br. The cheaper rooms have no bath. The friendly owner, Annamélia, speaks some French. Highly recommended.

D Pousada Tiradentes, Praça Tiradentes 70, T031-3551 2619, www.pousadatiradentes op.com.br. The rooms are spartan but well kept and moderately comfortable. Each has a TV, fridge. Conveniently located.

D Pouso Chico Rei, R Brig Musqueira 90, T031-3551 1274, www.pousodo chicorei.com.br. A fascinating old house

with Portuguese colonial furnishings, very small and utterly delightful, book in advance (room No 6 has been described as a 'dream').

D Solar das Lajes, R Conselheiro Quintiliano 604, T/F031-3551 3388, www.solardas lajes.com.br. A little way from the centre but with an excellent view and a pool. Well run.

E Pousada dos Bandeirantes, R das Mercês 167, T031-3551 1996, www.hotelpousada bandeirantes.com.br. Behind the São Francisco de Assis Church and offering beautiful views.

E Pousada São Francisco de Paula, R Pe José Marcos Pena 202, next to the São Francisco de Paula church, T031-3551 3456, www.pousadasaofranciscodepaula.com.br. One of the best views of any in the city; from the rooms or from a hammock in the garden. Services and facilities include the free use of a kitchen, multilingual staff, excursions. The hostel has 8 rustic rooms including a dormitory, which come with or without a simple breakfast, private or communal bathrooms. Full breakfasts and snacks are available, 100 m from the *rodoviária*. Recommended.

F Brumas, R Pe José Marcos Pena 68, T031-3551 2944, www.brumashostel.com.br. 150 m downhill from *rodoviária*, just below São Francisco de Paula church. Dormitory, kitchen and laundry and superb views. Don't walk down from the bus station after dark.

Student hostels

During holidays and weekends students may be able to stay at the self-governing hostels, known as *repúblicas* (described as very welcoming, 'best if you like heavy metal music' and 'are prepared to enter into the spirit of the place'). The *prefeitura* has a list of over 50 *repúblicas* with phone numbers, available at the **Secretaria de Turismo**. Many are closed between Christmas and Carnaval.

Camping

Camping Clube do Brasil, Rodovia dos Inconfidêntes, Km 91, 2 km north, T031-3551 1799. Quite expensive but very nice.

Mariana *p269, map p271,*
Most of these hotels are housed in colonial buildings. Further details can be found on www.mariana.mg.gov.br.
C Faísca, R Antônio Olinto 48, T031-3557 1206. Up the street from the tourist office. Suites and rooms, breakfast included.
C Pousada Solar dos Corrêa, R Josefá Macedo 70 and R Direita, T/F031-3557 2080. A restored 18th-century townhouse with spacious a/c rooms.
D Pousada do Chafariz, R Cônego Rego 149, T031-3557 1492, www.pousadado chafariz.hpg.com.br. A converted colonial building with parking, breakfast and a family atmosphere. Recommended.
D Providência, R Dom Silvério 233, T031-3557 1444. Has use of the neighbouring school's pool when classes finish at noon.
D-E Central, R Frei Durão 8, T/F031-3557 1630. A charming but run-down colonial building on the Praça Gomes Freire. Recommended but avoid the downstairs rooms.

Congonhas do Campo *p274*
E Colonial, Praça da Basílica 76, opposite Bom Jesus, T031-3731 1834. Good and comfortable but noisy, breakfast extra, cheaper without bath. Fascinating restaurant, **Cova do Daniel**, downstairs is full of colonial handicrafts and good local food.
E Freitas, R Marechal Floriano 69, T031-3731 1543. Basic, with breakfast, cheaper without bath.

Tiradentes *p277, map p276*
Prices drop in the more expensive hotels Sun-Thu. www.tiradentesturismo.com.br has details and pictures of many of the *pousadas*.
AL Solar da Ponte, Praça das Mercês, T032-3355 1255, www.roteirosdecharme/sol.htm. The atmosphere of a country house, run by John and Anna Maria Parsons, the price includes breakfast and afternoon tea, only 12 rooms, fresh flowers, bar, sauna, lovely gardens, swimming pool, light meals for residents only. Highly recommended (it is in the **Roteiros de Charme** group, see page 43).

B Pousada Mãe D'Água, Largo das Forras 50, T032-3355 1206. One of the larger *pousadas*, with an outdoor pool set in a small garden, sauna, pool room and a/c rooms. Price includes breakfast.
B Pousada Três Portas, R Direita 280A, T032-3355 1444. Charming central hotel in a restored town house with 8 rooms and a suite. Facilities include a heated indoor pool, sauna and room service. Great for couples.
B-C Pouso das Gerais, R dos Inconfidêntes 109, T032-3355 1234, www.pousodasgerais. hpg.com.br. Spotless, fresh fan-cooled rooms with parquet flooring, desk, TV and marble basins in the bathrooms. Central, quiet, pool and breakfast included. Recommended.
C Hotel Ponto do Morro, Largo das Forras 2, T032-3355 1342. A central motel, just off the main square. Avoid the darker, lower rooms.
C Porão Colonial, R dos Inconfidêntes 447, T032-3355 1251. Pleasant, though a little out of town. With a pool, sauna and parking.
C Pousada Maria Bonita, R Antônio Teixeira Carvalho 134, T/F032-3355 1227, www.idasbrasil.com.br. A motel with a pool and a garden full of gnomes leading down to the river. About 10 mins out of town, near the station. At the weekend the price includes breakfast, lunch and an evening snack.
C-D Pousada do Arco Iris, R Frederico Ozanan 340, T032-3355 1167. The best of a string of *pousadas* in houses on this stretch of road just out of town. Swimming pool, popular, family run, 5 rooms only. Price includes breakfast. Book ahead.
D Pousada do Alferes, R dos Inconfidêntes 479, T032-3355 1303. Simple but central on the main shopping street close to the square.
D Pousada do Largo, Largo das Forras 48, T/F032-3355 1219. With a pool, sauna and rooms with Brazilian TV.
D Pousada do Laurito, R Direita 187, T032-3355 1268. Central, cheap and good value. Very popular with international backpackers.

São João del Rei *p279, map p280*
B Lenheiro Palace, Av Pres Tancredo Neves
257, T/F032-3371 8155. Modern hotel with
good facilities, parking, cheaper in low
season, teahouse, breakfast.
C Ponte Real, Av Eduardo Magalhães 254,
T/F032-3371 7000. Modern, comfortable,
sizeable rooms, good restaurant.
C-D Beco do Bispo, Beco do Bispo 93, 2 mins
west of the São Francisco church, T032-3371
8844, www.becodobispo com.br. The best in
town. Well-kept, bright a/c rooms, hot
showers, cable TV, a pool, convenient location
and a very helpful English-speaking staff.
Organizes tours. Highly recommended.
D Aparecida, Praça Dr Antônio Viegas 13,
T032-3371 2540. Unillustrious but centrally
located by the bus and taxi stop, with a
restaurant and *lanchonete*.
D Pousada Casarão, Ribeiro Bastos 94,
opposite São Francisco church, T032-3371
7447. Housed in a delightful converted
mansion. The decent-sized rooms have firm
beds. Also a games room with a pool table.
E Brasil, Av Pres Tancredo Neves 395,
T032-3371 2804. In an old house full of
character, on the opposite side of the
river from the railway station, cheap.
Recommended but basic, no breakfast.
E Pousada São Benedito, R Mcal Deodoro
254, T032-3371 7381. Price per person.
Basic, with shared rooms and bathrooms.
E Sinha Batista, R Manock Anselmo 22, T032-
3371 5550. The best of the cheaper options.
With largish rooms in a colonial building
conveniently located by the central canal.

Sabará *p281*
B Del Rio, R São Francisco 345, T031-3671 3040.
Standard 3-star rooms. Reasonable service.
C Solar das Sepúlvedas, R da Intendência
371, behind the Museu do Ouro, T031-3671
2708. Grandiose, popular with Brazilian
families and with a pool.
E Hotel do Ouro, R Santa Cruz 237, Morro
da Cruz, T031-3671 5622. Rooms with
en suite bathrooms, hot water, breakfast
and a marvellous view, great value.

🍴 Eating

Ouro Preto *p263, map p266*
Try the local firewater, *licor de jaboticaba*,
made from a sweet Brazilian tropical fruit.
🍴🍴🍴 **Le Coq D'Or**, R Getúlio Vargas 270 (next to
the Rosário church), T031-3551 5200. Brazilian-
French fusion cooking in a smart dining room
with live music. One of the city's best.
🍴🍴 **Adega**, R Teixeira Amaral 24, T031-3551
4171. 1130-1530. Vegetarian smorgasbord,
US$5, all you can eat. Highly recommended.
🍴🍴 **Beijinho Doce**, R Direita 134A, Café Gerais,
124 R Direita. Decent *bacalhau* and steak,
delicious pastries, lousy coffee. Try the truffles.
🍴🍴 **Café e compania**, R São José 187, T031-
3551 0711. Closes 2300. Very popular, *comida
por kilo* at lunchtime, good salads and juices.
🍴🍴 **Deguste**, R Coronel Alves 15, T031-3551
6363. Large portions, good value.
🍴🍴 **Pasteleria Lampião**, Praça Tiradentes.
Good views at the back (better at lunchtime
than in the evening).
🍴🍴 **Taverna do Chafariz**, R São José 167, T031-
35512828. Good local food. Recommended.
🍴 **Forno de Barro**, Praça Tiradentes 54.
Decent Mineira buffet with varied plates
and sweet puddings. Generous portions.
🍴 **Vide Gula**, R Sen Rocha Lagoa 79a. Food by
weight, friendly atmosphere. Recommended.

Mariana *p269, map p271*
🍴🍴 **Engenho Nôvo**, Praça da Sé 26. Bar at
night, English spoken. Recommended.
🍴🍴 **Mangiare della Mamma**, D Viçoso 27.
Italian. Recommended.
🍴🍴 **Tambaú**, R João Pinheiro 26. Regional food.
🍴 **Panela de Pedra**, in the Terminal Turístico.
Serves food by weight at lunchtime.

Congonhas do Campo *p274*
🍴 **Estalagem Romaria**, 2 mins from Hotel
Colonial in the Romarias. Good restaurant
and pizzeria, reasonable prices.

Tiradentes *p277, map p276*
There are many restaurants, snack bars
and *lanchonetes*. your fancy.

¶¶¶ Estalagem, R Min Gabriel Passos 280, T032-33551144. Excellent and generous traditional Mineira meat dishes.

¶¶¶ Quartier Latin, R São Francisco de Paula 46, Praça da Rodoviária, T032-3355 1552. French-trained cordon bleu chef with a menu of French-inspired, Italian and seafood. Salads are made from their own organic vegetables. Respectable wine list. Good but expensive.

¶¶¶ Quinto de Ouro, R Direita 159. Mineira and international dishes. Recommended.

¶¶¶ Theatro da Vila, R Padre Toledo 157, T032-3355 1275. A gourmet restaurant with Italian, French and Brazilian fusion cooking and an excellent wine list. Good views out over the little garden and performances in summer in the restaurant's garden theatre.

¶¶¶ Virados do Largo, Largo do Ó, T032-3355 1111. The best Mineira restaurant in town together with **Estalagem**.

¶¶ Aluarte, Largo do Ó 1, T032-3355 1608. Bar with live music in the evening, nice atmosphere, US$4 cover charge, garden, sells handicrafts. Recommended.

¶ Maria Luisa Casa de Chá, Largo do Ó 1, diagonally opposite **Aluarte**, T032-3355 1502. Tea, cakes and sandwiches in an arty Bohemian atmosphere. Great for breakfast.

São João del Rei p279, map p280

¶¶¶ Churrascaria Ramón, Praça Severiano de Resende 52. One of the better *churrascarias*, generous portions, plenty of side dishes.

¶¶¶ Quinto do Ouro, Praça Severiano de Resende 04, T032-3371 7577. Tasty and well-prepared regional food at reasonable prices. Said to be the best Mineira cooking in town.

¶¶ Chafariz, R Quintino Bocaiuva 100, T032-3371 8955. The best per kilo restaurant with a huge choice and plenty of vegetarian options.

¶ Restaurant 611, R Getúlio Vargas 145. Cheap but excellent Mineira cooking. Eat all you like for US$2. Plenty of choice. A local favourite.

Sabará p281

¶ Cê Que Sabe, R Mestre Caetano 56. Mineira and other Brazilian fare. Recommended.

⊕ Entertainment

São João del Rei p279, map p280
Music
São João del Rei has 2 famous orchestras which play baroque music. In colonial days, the music master not only had to provide the music for Mass, but also had to compose new pieces for every festival. All the music has been kept and the Ribeiro Bastos and Lira Sanjoanense orchestras preserve the tradition. Both have their headquarters, rehearsing rooms and archives on R Santo Antônio (Nos 54 and 45 respectively). The **Orquestra Ribeiro Bastos** plays at Mass every Sun in São Francisco de Assis at 0915 and Fri 1900 at the Matriz do Pilar, as well as at many religious ceremonies throughout the year (eg Holy Week). The **Orquestra Lira Sanjoanense**, which is said to be the oldest in the Americas (founded in 1776), plays at Mass in Nossa Senhora do Pilar at 1900 every Thu and on Sun in Nossa Senhora do Rosário at 0830 and Nossa Senhora das Mercês at 1000, as well as on other occasions. It is best to check at their offices for full details. There are similar orchestras in Prados and Tiradentes, but the latter is not as well supported as those in São João.

⊕ Festivals and events

Ouro Preto p263, map p266
Many shops close during Holy Week and on winter weekends.
Feb Carnaval attracts many people.
Mar/Apr Ouro Preto is famous for its **Holy Week** processions, which actually begin on the Thu before Palm Sun and continue (but not every day) until Easter Sun. The most famous is that commemorating Christ's removal from the Cross, late on Good Fri.
Jun Corpus Christi and Festas Juninas.
Jul The city holds the Festival do Inverno da Universidade Federal de Minas Gerais (UFMG), the 'Winter Festival', about 3 weeks of arts, courses, concerts and exhibitions.
8 Jul Anniversary of the city.

15 Aug Nossa Senhora do Pilar, patron saint of Ouro Preto.
12-18 Nov Semana de Aleijadinho, a week-long arts festival.

Mariana *p269, map p271*
Feb Carnaval
Mar/Apr Traditional Holy Week celebrations.
29 Jun São Pedro.
Jul Mariana shares some events of Festival do Inverno da UFMG with Ouro Preto.

São João del Rei *p279, map p280*
Feb Carnaval is lively and popular here and going through a bit of a renaissance.
Apr Semana Santa.
15-21 Apr Semana da Inconfidência.
May/Jun Festival do Inverno, with many cultural events.
Jul FUNREI, the university (on R Padre José Maria Xavier), holds Inverno Cultural.
Aug First 2 weeks, Nossa Senhora da Boa Morte, with *novena barroca* (baroque music).
12 Oct Nossa Senhora do Pilar, patron saint of the city.
8 Dec Founding of the city.

Sabará *p281*
25 Dec-6 Jan Folia de Reis.
Jun Festas Juninas and Festival da Cachaça.
Oct 2nd Sun. Festival of Nossa Senhora do Rosário, the patron saint.

○ Shopping

Ouro Preto *p263, map p266*
Buy soapstone carvings at roadside stalls rather than in the cities; they are much cheaper. Many artisans sell carvings, jewellery and semi-precious stones in the Largo de Coimbra in front of São Francisco de Assis Church. Also worth buying is traditional cookware in stone, copper or enamelled metal.

Gems and jewellery
Gems are not much cheaper from freelance sellers in Praça Tiradentes than from the shops. If buying gems on the street, ask for the seller's credentials.
Gemas de Minas, Conde de Bobadela 63. One of the city's better jewellers.
Videmaju, R Conselheiro Santana 175. Vincente Júlio de Paula, a professor at the School of Mines, sells stones at very good prices.

Tiradentes *p277, map p276*
Art galleries
Fernando Pitta, Beco da Chácara, T/F032-355 1475. Produces fascinating paintings, mixed media and sculpture, worth a visit.
Oscar Araripe, R da Câmara. Paintings of Tiradentes and other local scenes in bright colours, popular and commercial.

São João del Rei *p279, map p280*
The pewter factory, Av Leite de Castro 1150, T032-3371 8000, 10 mins' walk from the *rodoviária*, 0900-1800. Run by Englishman John Somers and his son Gregory, is worth a visit for both its exhibitions and its shop. The nearby town of Resende Costa (30 km north) is known for its textile handicrafts.

▲▲ Activities and tours

Ouro Preto *p263, map p266*
Yoga centre, down an alley between Nos 31 and 47 (Cine Teatro Vila Rica), Praça Alves de Brito, T031-3551 3337. Offers shiatsu and Kerala massage.

Tiradentes *p277, map p276*
For horse-riding treks, contact John Parsons at the Solar da Ponte, see page 285.

⊖ Transport

Ouro Preto *p263, map p266*
Bus There are 11 buses a day to/from **Belo Horizonte**, 2 hrs, Pássaro Verde, US$10. Day trips are possible; book your return journey to Belo Horizonte early if returning in the evening; buses get crowded. To **Mariana**,

buses run from the Escola de Minas near Praça Tiradentes every 30 mins, US$2, all passing **Minas da Passagem** (buses also leave from Ouro Preto *rodoviária*).

There is a bus to **Rio**, Útil at 0705, 1715 and 2000 (US$50, 12 hrs; from Belo Horizonte or Juiz de Fora, 8 hrs); to **Brasília** at 1830 (12 hrs); to **Vítoria** at 2100 (8 hrs). There are also Útil buses to **Conselheiro Lafaiete**, 3-4 a day via Itabirito and direct services to **Congonhas do Campo** via the new Caminho de Ouro highway. Other Útil services to **Rio**, **Barbacena**, **Conselheiro Lafaiete** and **Congonhas** go via Belo Horizonte. Direct buses to **São Paulo**, 3 a day with Cristo Rei (10 hrs, US$45). Gontijo go to **Salvador** via **Belo Horizonte**.

Mariana *p269, map p271*
Bus Buses to **Ouro Preto** can be caught by the bridge at the end of R do Catete, every 30 mins, US$0.60, all passing **Minas da Passagem**. There is a bus to **Belo Horizonte** (via Ouro Preto), US$10, 2¼ hrs. Buses for **Santa Bárbara** (near Caraça) leave from the *rodoviária*.

Around Mariana *p273*
Bus There are 3 buses a day from Mariana to **Antônio Pereira**, Mon-Fri, 0800, 1200, 1445, plus 1100, 1750 and 2100 on Sat.

Congonhas do Campo *p274*
Bus A bus marked 'Basílica' runs every 30 mins from the *rodoviária* to **Bom Jesus**, 5 km, US$1. A taxi from the *rodoviária* will cost US$5 one way, US$10 return including the wait while you visit the sanctuary.

Buses run to **Belo Horizonte**, 1½ hrs, US$4, 8 times a day. To **São João del Rei**, 2½ hrs, US$5, tickets are not sold until the bus comes in. To **Ouro Preto** or **Rio**, buses go via Belo Horizonte, Murtinho or Conselheiro Lafaiete. There is a frequent bus service to **Conselheiro Lafaiete**, US$2.

Tiradentes *p277, map p276*
Bus Last bus back to **São João del Rei** is 1815, 2230 on Sun.

Taxi Around town there are pony-drawn taxis; ponies can be hired for US$5/hr.
A taxi to **São João del Rei** costs US$15.
Train See page 278 for the train between Tiradentes and **São João del Rei**.

São João del Rei *p279, map p280*
Bus Buses to **Rio**, 5 daily with **Paraibuna** (3 on Sat and Sun), 5 hrs, US$40. **Cristo Rei** to **São Paulo**, 8 hrs, 5 a day (also to Santos), and Translavras, 4 a day (also to Campinas), US$14. **Belo Horizonte**, 3½ hrs, US$20. To **Juiz de Fora**, US$15, at least 8 a day with Transur. Frequent service to **Tiradentes** with Meier, 8 a day, 7 on Sat, Sun and holidays, US$3; on the return journey to São João, the bus stops outside the railway station before proceeding to the *rodoviária*.

Sabará *p281*
Bus To/from **Belo Horizonte** with Viação Cisne, US$0.75, 30 mins, from separate part of Belo Horizonte *rodoviária*.

Directory

Ouro Preto *p263, map p266*
Banks Banco 24 Horas, Praça Alves de Brito, next to Correios with a Visa ATM; **Banco do Brasil**, R São José 189, good rates, also for TCs; **Bradesco**, corner of Sen Rocha Lagoa and Padre Rolim, opposite the Escola de Minas with a Visa ATM. **Internet** There are many around town, eg **Point**, R Xavier da Veiga 501A, language school and cultural centre. **Post office** Praça Alves de Brito.

Tiradentes *p277, map p276*
Post office and telephone Combined office on Largo das Forras in the Prefeitura Municipal, R Resende Costa 71. It closes at 1200 for lunch.

São João del Rei *p279, map p280*
Banks Bradesco, Av Hermílio Alves 200, next to the Theatro Municipal, has an exchange, 1000-1600 and a Visa cashpoint.

Northern and western Minas Gerais

The population thins out in Northern Minas and as it stretches into the sertão backlands and the state of Bahia, the landscape gets ever more arid. Water mostly comes from the river São Francisco, a blue streak cutting through the beiges and browns of the semi-desert. Few tourists, however, get further than the colonial mining town of Diamantina, recently declared a World Heritage Site and every bit as pretty as its more famous contemporaries to the south. There are extensive tracts of beautiful cerrado forest towards the border with Goiás, parts of it protected by the Serra do Cipó and Grande Sertão Veredas national parks. Western Minas is less visited still, yet there are some beautiful stretches of forest in the Serra da Canastra, which can be visited on the way to or from Mato Grosso or Goiás. ►► For listings, see pages 296-298.

Parque Nacional da Serra do Cipó ● ►► pp296-298.

① Information from Ibama in Belo Horizonte, T031-3291 6588, www.ibama.gov.br.
The Serra do Cipó, 100 km northeast of Belo Horizonte, protects 33,400 sq km of important *cerrado* and gallery forest, which provide a home for ultra-rare bird species like *cipo canastero* and grey-backed tachuri. Endangered mammals are also found here, including one of the more wimpy carnivores, the maned wolf, looking like a giant fox with overly long legs, which hunts small grassland rodents with its feet. There are also masked titi and brown capuchin monkeys and a number of endemic carnivorous plants. The walks that cut through the park pass through some of the most beautiful rugged grassland country in the state, leading to waterfalls and strands of tropical forest.

Ins and outs
At least eight buses daily run from Belo Horizonte along the MG-010 to Serra do Cipó town. There are *pousadas* all along the MG-010 and the bus will stop at them on request. The road through the park has been newly paved and runs through Conceição do Mato Dentro (36 km) and Serro (99 km) and on to Diamantina. *Pousadas* can organize guides for the park. There is excellent walking and many trails. For tourist information see the websites: www.guiaserradocipo.com.br, www.serradocipoturismo.com.br and www.serra docipo.com, all of which have details of tour operator and accommodation.

The route to Diamantina ● ►► pp296-298. Colour map 4, B3.

Conceição do Mato Dentro and the Tabuleiro waterfall → Phone code: 038.
A newly paved road climbs into the hills from Serra do Cipo town to **Conceição do Mato Dentro**, a sleepy 17th-century town nestled in the rugged folds of the **Serra do Espinhaço**. These mountains run from Central Minas all the way up to the Chapada Diamantina in Bahia and beyond. The surrounding countryside has well-preserved *cerrado* forest and bushland and is gushing with waterfalls. The most spectacular of all is Brazil's third tallest waterfall, the **Cachoeira do Tabuleiro**, Conceição, a sliver of water that plunges some 273 m from a *cerrado*-covered escarpment into a crystal-clear pool. The waterfall lies in the **Parque Natural Municpal Ribeirão do Campo** (Parque do Tabuleiro), which preserves the falls and around 3000 ha of *cerrado*. There are some 1700 species of vascular plants here, including 150 very rare orchids, alongside similar bird species to the Serra do Cipó,

Serro

This unspoiled colonial town sits on the banks of the Rio Jequitinhonha in the heart of lush hilly dairy farm country dotted with *cerrado* forest and waterfalls. The town preserves many pretty, crumbling churches and leafy squares and the locals make some of the best Minas Gerais cheese, *queijo mineiro*, in Brazil. This watery, milky putty is adored by all Brazilians (though foreigners often wonder what all the fuss is about) and is traditionally eaten with guava jam. Serro makes a good stop-off on the route south or north. It receives very few visitors and you will feel like a curiosity. There are a few buildings worth visiting. The prettiest church is **Santa Rita**, on a hill in the centre of town, reached by a long line of steps. On the main Praça João Pinheiro, by the bottom of the steps, is the arcaded **Nossa Senhora do Carmo**, with original paintings on the ceiling and in the choir. The town has two large mansions: **Barão de Diamantina** ⓘ *Praça Presidente Vargas*, is in ruins, but **Barão do Serro** ⓘ *R da Fundição, Tue-Sat 1200-1700, Sun 0900-1200*, across the river, is beautifully restored and used as the town hall and Casa de Cultura. There are old mine entrances in the hillside behind the courtyard. The **Museu Regional Casa dos Ottoni** ⓘ *Praça Cristiano Ottoni 72*, is an 18th-century house now containing furniture and everyday objects from the region. The Ottoni brothers, who were born here, were prominent naval officers turned politicians in the 19th century. The even sleepier and prettier villages of **São Gonçalo do Rio das Pedras** and **Milho Verde** are a short bus ride away in the surrounding hills and are well worth a visit.

Ins and outs

Conceição do Mato Dentro and Serro are served by at least eight buses daily from Belo Horizonte, via the Serra do Cipó, on a newly paved road. Both towns also have bus connections with Diamantina several times daily. There are plenty of accommodation options. For information on Conceição and the Tabuleiro waterfall contact the **Secretária do Turismo** ⓘ *Conceição do Mato Dentro, T031-3868 2423/2431, www.conceicaodomato dentro.com.br*. Their office lies in the centre and the town is tiny. The park itself should be visited with a guide, available through the Secretária or hotels in the town. Expect to pay around US$30 for a half-day round-trip with a guide and an additional US$5 to enter the park. Take walking shoes, swimming gear and water. For information on Serro, São Gonçalo and Milho Verde, contact the **Secretária de Turismo** ⓘ *Chácara do Barão do Serro, T038-3541 1368 ext 234, www.serro.mg.gov.br*.

Diamantina ⬤🔵🟠🟢⚫🔺⬤🔵 ▶ *pp296-298. Colour map 4, B3.*

→ *Phone code: 038. Population: 48,000. Altitude: 1120 m.*

Diamantina, a UNESCO World Heritage Site and northern Minas's prettiest colonial town, sits nestled in rugged hills 300 km north of Belo Horizonte. The town's churches are less spectacular than those in Ouro Preto or São João del Rey, but the city has a wonderful architectural unity and is better preserved and less touristy.

The *cerrado* forests that swathe the countryside around the town are home to some of the rarest birds and mammals on the continent. The recently opened São Gonçalo do Rio Preto state park, 45 km from Diamantina, is the best base from which to explore them. Regular flights from Belo Horizonte to Diamantina have made visiting far easier than it used to be; it is now possible to continue overland from the town to Bahia.

Ins and outs

Getting there The **airport** ⓘ *a few kilometres from town, T038-3531 9176*, receives three flights a week from Belo Horizonte or Pampulha with **Trip**, www.voetrip.com.br. A taxi to the centre costs US$7. The **rodoviária** ⓘ *3 km east of the centre, T038-3531 9176*, has regular bus connections with Belo Horizonte and the Serra do Cipó. Diamantina is connected to Brasília through Curvelo, and Araçuaí and Itaubim from Porto Seguro in Bahia. Taxis are expensive. Excursions in the area can be organized through **Real Receptivo**. There are numerous car hire companies, including **Localiza**. ▸▸ *See Activities and tours, and Transport, page 298.*

Tourist information The **tourist office** ⓘ *Casa de Cultura, Praça Antônio Eulálio 53, 3rd floor, T038-3531 1636, www.diamantina.mg.gov.br*, is friendly and helpful and provides pamphlets and a reliable map, as well as information about church opening times, buses and local guides. The website www.diamantina.com.br is a very useful alternative (in Portuguese), and lists hotels and tour operators.

Background

Like Minas's other colonial towns, Diamantina owes its existence and colonial finery to mining wealth, in this case diamonds, which were first discovered here in 1728. The settlement became known as Arraial do Tijuco and grew rapidly into a city. As the city's wealth increased, so did the feelings of resentment at the Portuguese tyranny. The majority black and mixed-race population were treated as subhuman. They were considered of such low birth that they were banned from walking in front of façades of the white churches as it would be an affront to God. They remained largely in poverty, leading many of the citizens to sympathise with the Inconfidêntes (see page 272). One local priest, José da Silva de Oliveira Rolim (Padre Rolim), joined the movement.

Sights

Diamantina is easily manageable on foot; the city centre is compact and there are plenty of little street-side cafés and bars. The best place to start exploring is the **Praça Guerra** (Praça do Sé) which is dominated by the towering 1930s cathedral. The most interesting church, **Nossa Senhora do Carmo** ⓘ *R do Carmo, Tue-Sat 0800-1200, 1400-1800, Sun 0800-1200*, is a short walk west along Rua Carmo Quitanda. It is most remarkable for its beautiful interior paintings, carried out by José Soares de Araujo, a former bodyguard from Braga in Portugal. Many of the city's churches are painted by him, but this is by far his finest work. The Carmelites are said to have been founded before the time of Christ by the prophet Elijah, who is depicted on the magnificent ceiling, ascending to heaven in a chariot of fire, and brandishing a sword on one of the side altars. Another ceiling painting shows the patron saint and founder of the Third Order of Mount Carmel, the 12th-century English saint, St Simon Stock, receiving a scapular from the Virgin. The placing of the church tower at the back of the building was ostensibly to please Chica Silva, the black slave of Padre Rolim. In an era when black Brazilians were valued less than chickens she achieved liberty, married the wealthy diamond merchant João Fernandes de Oliveira and became the most influential woman in the city, living in luxury with him and their 14 children in a house overlooking the Praça Lobo de Mesquita. The house is now a museum, the **Casa de Chica da Silva** ⓘ *Praça Lobo Mesquita 266, free*.

Just south of Nossa Senhora do Carmo is the church of **Nossa Senhora do Rosário dos Pretos** ⓘ *Largo Dom Joaquim, Tue-Sat 0800-1200 and 1400-1800, Sun 0800-1200,* designated for the black underclass who were not permitted to attend mass at Nossa Senhora do Carmo. Its simple interior has a magical meditative silence. Outside is an original 18th-century public fountain, the Chafariz do Rosário where water pours from the mouths of distinctly African faces.

Diamantina has a number of other interesting small museums worth exploring. The **Museu do Diamante** ⓘ *R Direita 14, Tue-Sat 1200-1730, Sun 0900-1200, US$1*, in the house of Padre Rolim houses an important collection of the materials used in the diamond industry, together with some beautiful 18th- and 19th-century oratories and icons and the iron collars that were once fitted to the slaves that worked the mines.

The **Biblioteca Antônio Torres** ⓘ *R Quitanda 48, Mon-Fri 1400-1700*, is a smart 18th-century townhouse, which is also known as the **Casa Muxarabie** after the enclosed Moorish balcony on one of the windows.

Diamantina

Sleeping 🛏
Dália **1**
Montanhas de Minas **5**
Pousada do Garimpo
 & Restaurant **2**
Pousada Dona Daizinha **6**
Pousada dos Cristais **7**
Pousada Ouro de Minas **4**

Relíquias do Tempo **8**
Santiago **9**
Tijuco **3**

Eating 🍴
Caipirão **1**
Cantina do Marinho **2**
Grupiara **3**

Recanto do Antônio **4**
Sisisi **5**

Bars & clubs 🍸
Apocalipse Point **6**
Café a Baiuca **7**
Espaço B **8**

Behind the 18th-century building that now houses the **Prefeitura Municipal** (originally the diamond administration building) at Praça Conselheiro Matta 11, is the **Mercado Municipal** or **dos Tropeiros** (muleteers) ① *Praça Barão de Guaicuí*. It was built in 1835 as a residence and trading house before being expanded and has wooden arches. The **Casa da Glória** ① *R da Glória 297*, is the city's most photographed building. Two houses on either side of the street are connected by a covered corridor-bridge. This was once part of a convent school and the girls would laugh and flirt through the small windows. It is now part of a university.

President Juscelino Kubitschek, the founder of Brasília, was from Diamantina and his house is now a **museum** ① *on the outskirts of town, R São Francisco 241, Tue-Sun 1000-1200 and 1400-1800, US$2.* Try and be in the city for the regular **Vesperata** festivals when groups of musicians serenade passers-by from the city's numerous balconies, especially around the Praça Guerra; a tradition that began in the 17th century.⤍ *See Festivals and events, page 298.*

Excursions from Diamantina

There is a good walk along the **Caminho dos Escravos**, the old road built by slaves between the mining area on Rio Jequitinhonha and Diamantina. A guide is essential and not expensive; ask at the Casa de Cultura. Beware of snakes and thunderstorms.

About 9 km from town is the **Gruta de Salitre**, a big cave with a strange rock formation. There are no buses, but it is a good walk and you can find some interesting minerals along the way. Ask the tourist office for directions, or take a taxi. Closer to the town is the **Cachoeira da Toca**, a 15-m waterfall, which is good for swimming.

Along the riverbank it is 12 km on a dirt road to **Biribiri**, a pretty village with a well-preserved church and an abandoned textile factory. It also has a few bars and is popular and noisy at weekends. About halfway there are swimming pools in the river; opposite them, on a cliff face, are red animal paintings of unknown age and origin. There is some interesting plant life along the river and beautiful mountain views.

The sleepy little town of **São Gonçalo do Rio Preto**, which sits next to a beautiful mountain river, is famous for its traditional festivals. It lies some 60 km from Diamantina on the edge of the **Parque Estadual de São Gonçalo do Rio Preto** – an area of stunning, pristine *cerrado* filled with flowering trees and particularly rich in birdlife. There are *pousadas* in São Gonçalo and *cabañas* in the park (reachable by taxi). Guides are also available.

The far north ☉ ⤍ *pp 296-298.*

Pirapora → *Colour map 4, B3. Phone code: 038. Population: 50,000.*
North of Três Marias is this terminus for boat journeys on the Rio São Francisco. The cutting down of trees, in part as fuel for the boats, and the low rainfall in recent years, has reduced the river's flow. The town itself is a tourist attraction because of the falls in the river, which make for excellent fishing. The fishermen use punt-like canoes. The sandy river beaches are used for swimming. The riverboats' grotesque figureheads, *carrancas*, are made in the workshops of **Lourdes Barroso** ① *R Abaeté 390.*

São Francisco → *Colour map 4, A3. Phone code: 038. Population: 50,000.*
Between Pirapora and Januária is the colonial fishing town of São Francisco, with many attractive houses and a good handicraft market in the town hall. Of the two remaining wood-burning stern-wheel boats (allegedly built for Mississippi services in the 1860s and

imported from the USA in 1922 to work on the Amazon) one, the *Gaiola*, was restored for services on the Rio São Francisco. The town is popular during **Semana Santa**, **Festas Juninas** and has a carnival in July.

Rio São Francisco

Brazil's other great river cuts a deep blue course through the desert backlands of Minas and Bahia before plunging through dramatic gorges in Alagoas and pouring into the bottle-green Atlantic. There are pretty colonial towns dotted along its entire length, many of them completely lost in time. Passenger services on the river from Minas have been discontinued but masters of cargo boats in the port may permit passage. There are regular stops at **Januária** (famous for Brazil's reputed best *cachaça*) and **Bom Jesus da Lapa** in Bahia. The latter is a pilgrimage centre with a church built in a grotto inside a mountain, but it's a very poor town. There are hotels and a choice of bars on the river beach.

Western Minas Gerais and the Serra da Canastra ●● » pp296-298.

Parque Nacional da Serra da Canastra

South of Araxá is the Serra da Canastra national park, in which the Rio São Francisco rises. It is a cool region (May and June average 18°C), comprising two ranges of hills, the Serra da Canastra and the Serra das Sete Voltas, with the Vale dos Cândidos between. The altitude ranges from 900 m to 1496 m; the lower vegetation is mostly grassland, rising to high-altitude plants on the uplands. Animals include the maned wolf, the great anteater, armadillos and deer. Birds that can be seen include rheas, owls, seriema, king vulture and the diving duck. There are also other birds of prey, partridges and tinamous. Besides the source of the Rio São Francisco (6.5 km from the São Roque park entrance), visitors can see the two parts of the **Dasca d'Anta waterfall**.

Ins and outs Gates close at 1800. The park has a **visitor centre** just inside the park, at the São Roque de Minas entrance. There are three other entrances: Casca d'Anta, São João Batista and Sacramento. The park is best reached from Piumhi, on the MG-050, 267 km southwest of Belo Horizonte (this road heads for Ribeirão Preto in São Paulo). From Piumhi you go to São Roque de Minas (60 km). Information is available from **Ibama** ① *Av do Contorno 8121, Cidade Jardim, Belo Horizonte, T031-3291 6588 ext 119/122; or from Caixa Postal 01, São Roque de Minas, T031-3433 1195.*

Uberaba and around → *Colour map 4, B1. Phone code: 034. Population: 240,500.*

From Araxá, the BR-262 heads 120 km west to Uberaba, also in the Minas Triangle on the Rio da Prata, and 485 km from São Paulo. It is an important road junction on the direct highway between São Paulo and Brasília and serves a large cattle-raising district. At the beginning of April each year, the Rural Society of the Minas Triangle holds a famous cattle and agricultural exhibition at Uberaba.

Between Uberaba and Ponte Alta (31 km east on the BR-262) is **Peirópolis**, which is an incredibly important paleontological site, with dinosaur remains and eggs. The **Centro de Pesquisas Paleontológicas** (**Museu do Einossauro**) ① *T034-3972 0023, Mon-Fri 0800-1800, Sat and Sun 1100-1700,* is 23 km east of Uberaba, at Km 784.5. The prosperous city of Uberlândia about 100 km north of Uberaba is a major transport hub. There are hotels near the *rodoviária* if you get stuck here.

For Sleeping and Eating price codes and other relevant information, see pages 42-47.

◉ Sleeping

Parque Nacional da Serra do Cipó *p290*
LL Toucan Cipó, booked exclusively through www.dehouche.com as part of a tour. A British-owned luxury *fazenda* in pristine *cerrado* forest cut by clear-water streams. Very rich in bird and mammal life.
AL-A Cipó Veraneio, Rodovia MG-10, Km 95, Jaboticatubas, www.cipoveraneiohotel.com.br. Comfortable a/c rooms with cable TV, fridges and en suites in terraces of stone cabins next to the road that cuts through the park. The hotel has a pool, sauna, very good tour operator and a *cachaça* distillery just up the road, which produces some of Minas's finest.

Camping
Camping Véu da Noiva, Km 101, Santana do Riacho, T031-3201 1166, www.guia serradocipo.com.br/acm. Pretty little campsite in a forest grove near a waterfall and Swiss-style chalets (from **D** per person).

Conceição do Mato Dentro and the Tabuleiro waterfall *p290*
B-C Pousada da Gameleira, R Eloi Chaves 78, Tabuleiro, T031-3868 2337, www.pousadadagameleira.com.br. A rustic farmhouse set in the countryside near the park, with blocky a/c rooms set along corridors. The hotel organizes and runs land rover and walking tours.
C-D Pousadinha Adentro, R Dr Basílio Santiago 55, T031-3868 1294, T031-9714 6134 (mob). 3 little spruce suites, with shared balconies in a pretty little house in the town centre. Generous breakfast and a friendly family owner.
D Hotel Cuiabá, Av Bias Fortes, 17, centro, T031-3868 1413. A very simple town house right in the centre of Conceição, with 6 bare double rooms some with en suites.

E-F Bromelia, R Principal 72, Tabuleiro, T031-9683 9284, ask for Zaide. Very simple concrete house near to the park with boxy tiled rooms a little larger than a bed. Friendly owner and breakfast included. More expensive in high season.

Serro *p291*
B Pousada Vila do Príncipe, R Antônio Honório Pires 38, T/F038-3541 1485. Very clean, in an old mansion containing its own museum. The artist Mestre Valentim is said to have been born in the slave quarters.
C-D Pousada Mariana, Praça Floriano Peixoto 44, T031-3541 1569. A small town hotel with basic a/c and fan-cooled rooms run by a local family. There are other cheap hotels nearby.

Diamantina *p291, map p293*
Rooms are usually half price for those travelling alone. Unless otherwise stated, all are within 10 mins' walk of the centre.
AL Tijuco, R Macau do Melo 211, T038-3531 1022, www.hoteltijuco.com.br. A wonderful Niemeyer design that looks like a building from Thunderbird island. The large rooms have been refurbished whilst staying true to the original 1960s kitsch. The best rooms are at the front with balconies and glorious views.
A Pousada do Garimpo, Av da Saudade 265, T/F038-3531 2523, www.pousadado garimpo.com.br. Plain well-kept rooms in a smart hotel on the outskirts of town, a taxi ride from the centre. There's a pool, sauna and a restaurant serving some of the city's best Minas cooking from celebrated chef, Vandeka.
A Relíquias do Tempo, R Macau de Baixo 104, T038-3531 1627, www.pousada reliquiasdo tempo.com.br. Cosy wood-floored rooms with en suites in a pretty 19th-century house just off Praça JK. Public areas are decorated like a colonial family home. Breakfasts are generous.
B-C Hotel Montanhas de Minas, R da Romana 264, T038-3531 3240, www.grupo

montanhasdeminas.com.br. Spacious rooms
with stone floors and en suites, some
with balconies. Decent breakfasts.
C Dália, Praça JK (Jota-Ka) 25, T038-3531
1477, www.hoteldalia.com.br. Well-kept
rooms with solid beds, parquet floors and
large bathrooms. Ask to see several rooms
as some are musty.
C-D Hotel Santiago, Largo Dom João 133,
T038-3431 3407, www.diamantinanet.com.br/
hotelsantiago. Plain, small but spruce rooms
with en suites. Reasonable breakfast.
C-D Pousada dos Cristais, R Joga da
Bola 53, T038-3531 3923, www.diamantina
net.com.br/pousadadoscristais. A range of
simple, large rooms in white, with wooden
floors. Situated on the edge of town with
views out across the mountains.
C-D Pousada Ouro de Minas,
R do Amparo 90A, T038-3531 2306,
www.grupomontanhasdeminas.com.br.
Simple well-kept rooms with stone
floor rooms with tiny bathrooms in
a converted colonial house.
C-E Pousada Dona Daizinha, R Direita
131, T038-3531 1351. Simple wood-floor
rooms in a colonial house; some with
space for up to 5. Very good breakfast
and friendly service.

Camping
Wild camping is possible near the
waterfall just outside town.

Pirapora *p294*
C Canoeiras, Av Salmeron 3, T038-3741
1933. Used by river-tour parties.
C Pirapora Palace, Praça Melo Viana 61,
7 blocks west and 1 block south of the
rodoviária, T038-3741 3851. Ask for a
room on the garden, safe.
E Daila, Praça JK 13. With breakfast, no bath.
E Grande, R da Quitanda 70. With bath,
but without breakfast.

São Francisco *p294*
B Hotel Green Fish, R Min Hermenegildo
de Barros 560, T/F038-3631 1106.

Uberaba *p295*
There are numerous places to stay in town,
visit www.hoteis-pousadas.com.br/uberaba
for details.

🍴 Eating

Diamantina *p291, map p293*
🍴🍴 **Cantina do Marinho**, R Direita 113,
T038-3531 1686. This formal restaurant
decorated with bottles of wine and attended
by black-tie waiters is celebrated for its
salmão provençale and *bacalhau*.
🍴🍴 **Grupiara**, R Campos Carvalho 12,
T038-3531 3887. Decent regional cooking,
a convivial atmosphere and good-value
per-kilo options at lunch.
🍴 **Caipirão**, R Campos Carvalho 15,
T038-3531 1526. Minas cooking with a
lunchtime buffet cooked over a traditional
wood-fired clay oven and evening
à la carte.
🍴 **Recanto do Antônio**, Beco da Tecla 39,
T038-3531 1147. Minas food and decent
steak served in a chic rustic dining room
in a colonial house.
🍴 **Sisisi**, Beco da Mota 89, T038-3531 3071.
Pasta, Minas cooking and a very good-
value *prato feito* at lunchtime.

🍸 Bars and clubs

Diamantina *p291, map p293*
Apocalipse Point, Praça Barão de
Guaicuí 78, T038-3531 9296. *Sertaneja*
music, *axe* and live music upstairs.
Lively at weekends with a 20- and
30-something crowd.
Café a Baiuca, R da Quitanda. Coffee bar
by day with old men reading the paper,
and by night a funky little bar with
music DVDs and a crowd spilling
out onto the street.
Espaço B, R Beco da Tecla. A bookshop-
café serving crêpes and draught beer to
an arty crowd until the small hours.

☺ Festivals and events

Diamantina *p291, map p293*
During the famous **Vesperatas**, musicians and singers serenade from balconies along the colonial streets and drum troupes and bands parade along them. Twice a month always on a Sat.
Feb Carnaval is said to be very good here.
May-Jun Corpus Christi.
13 Jun Santo Antônio.
Jul 50 days after Pentecost, O Divino Espírito Santo, is a major 5-day feast.
12 Sep O Dia das Serestas, the 'Day of the Serenades', for which the town is famous; this is the birthday of President Juscelino Kubitschek, who was born here.
Oct First half of the month, Festa do Rosário.

▲ Activities and tours

Diamantina *p291, map p293*
There are a few tour operators in the city, but they come and go like the wind and none are firmly established. The tourist office can help organize trips to São Goncalo do Rio Perto and the surrounding area.
Diamantina Tur, Praça do Garimpeiros 616, T038-8801 1802. City tours, adventure activities (rappelling and trekking) and trips to nearby natural attractions and Biri Biri. From US$8 per person per day.
Real Receptivo, R Campos Carvalho 19, loja 12, T038-3531 1636. City tours and trips to nearby natural attractions. From US$8 per person per day for groups of 4 or more.

☺ Transport

Diamantina *p291, map p293*
Air There are 3 weekly flights to **Belo Horizonte** (Pampulha airport) with Trip, www.voetrip.com.br.

Bus There are 6 buses a day to **Belo Horizonte** (5 hrs) US$20, via Curvelo (for connections to Brasília, 10 hrs), with Pássaro Verde. There are daily buses to **Montes Claros**, with daily connections here for **Brasília** and **Parque Nacional Grande Sertão Veredas**. For the **Serra do Cipó** take the bus to Serro (2 daily) and change for Santa Ana do Riacho and the Serra do Cipó. There is one bus per day to **São Gonçalo do Rio Preto**.
If en route to Bahia, there are 2 daily buses to **Araçuaí** (4 hrs) from here *combis* and buses run to **Itaobim** (US$4, 2 hrs) from where there are connections to **Vitória da Conquista** (US$5.50, 4 hrs) and on to **Porto Seguro** and other destinations in Bahia. (If you get stuck in Araçuaí there is a **Pousada Tropical** opposite the *rodoviária*, T038-3731 1765, with bath, clean, cheap and friendly.) The BR-116 passes interesting rock formations at Pedra Azul (see page 309) before crossing the border with Bahia.

Uberaba *p295*
Bus To **Belo Horizonte**, US$35 (*leito* US$30), 7 hrs with onward connections to **Goiânia**, **Riberão Preto**, **São Paulo** and **Brasília**.

❶ Directory

Diamantina *p291, map p293*
Banks There is a Banco do Brasil and a Bradesco, in the centre.

Eastern and southern Minas Gerais

The border area between Minas and Espírito Santo is the most rugged part of the state. Marked by the ridges of the Serra do Caparaó mountains, it is home to some of the country's highest peaks and covered with eucalyptus plantations and remnant Mata Atlântica forest. It remains an important centre for semi-precious stone processing and crystal carving. The two principal towns, Governador Valadares and Teófilo Otôni, are on the BR-116 inland Rio–Salvador road, and both have good connections with Belo Horizonte. ▸▸ *For listings, see pages 304-306.*

Caratinga Biological Station

ⓘ *US$15 per person per day, payable only in reais. Trips can be arranged through Focus Tours, www.focustours.com, see page 65.*

The privately owned Caratinga Biological Station, set in 880 ha of mountainous, inland Atlantic forest, is protected by a conscientious family and **Conservation International**. The reserve is home to four rare primates: half of the world's northern muriquis (*Brachyteles hypoxanthus*), a sub-species of woolly spider monkeys, which are the largest primates in the Americas and one of the most critically endangered; the brown (or black-capped) capuchin; the brown howler monkey and the buffy-headed marmoset (a sub-species of tufted eared marmoset). Also at the station are brown-throated three-toed sloths and one of the largest inventories of birds outside the Andean regions of the Amazon – 217 species at last count. The primates and many of the birds are easily seen.

Parque Estadual do Rio Doce

ⓘ *T031-3822 3006, or phone the Instituto Estadual de Florestas T031-3330 7013. Access is by the BR-262 or 381, from which you have to turn off onto dirt roads to get to the park.*

The Parque Estadual do Rio Eoce is 248 km east of Belo Horizonte in the municipalities of Dionísio, Timóteo and Marliéria. Between 230 m and 515 m above sea level and covering almost 36,000 ha, this is one of the largest tracts of *Mata Atlântica* in southeast Brazil. As well as forest there are a number of lakes, on which boat trips are possible, besides swimming and fishing. The park is home to a great many birds and animals. There is an information centre, a campsite 6 km into the park and trails that have been marked out for hiking.

Parque Nacional Caparaó ●● ▸▸ *pp304-306.*

This is one of the most popular parks in Minas, with good walking through strands of Atlantic rainforest, *paramo* and to the summits of three of Brazil's highest peaks, **Pico da Bandeira** (2890 m), **Pico do Cruzeiro** (2861 m) and the **Pico do Cristal** (2798 m). Wildlife is not as plentiful as it is in Caratinga as the park has lost much of its forest and its floral biodiversity. However, there are still a number of Atlantic coast primates here, such as the brown capuchins, together with a recovering bird population.

From the park entrance (where a small fee has to be paid) it is 6 km on a poorly maintained road to the car park at the base of the waterfall. From the hotel, jeeps (US$20 per jeep) run to the car park at 1970 m (2½ hours' walk), then it's a three- to four-hour walk to the summit of the Pico da Bandeira, marked by yellow arrows. There are plenty of camping possibilities all the way up, the highest being at **Terreirão** (2370 m). It is best to visit during the dry season (April to October), although it can be quite crowded in July and during Carnaval.

Ins and outs

The park is 49 km by paved road from Manhuaçu on the Belo Horizonte–Vitória road (BR-262). If you have your own transport, drive from the BR-262, go through Manhumirim, Presidente Soares and Caparaó village, then 1 km further to the **Hotel Caparaó Parque**. There are bus services from Belo Horizonte (twice a day), Ouro Preto or Vitória, to Manhumirim, 15 km south of Manhuaçu. From Manhumirim, take a bus direct to Caparaó, or to Presidente Soares (7 km), then hitch 11 km to Caparaó. ▶▶ *See Transport, page 306.*

To contact the park write to Caixa Postal 17, Alto Jequitibá, or telephone T255, via the operator on 101-PS 1, Alto do Caparaó. **Ibama** ① *T031-291 6588 ext 119/122, www.ibama. com.br*, also has information.

Towards southern Bahia → *Phone code: 033. Population: 127,500.*

Situated 138 km north of Governador Valadares, **Teófilo Otoni** is popular with dealers of crystals and gemstones, and has the best prices in the state. There are various hotels (see Sleeping, page 304). Regular buses arrive from Belo Horizonte and travel on to Porto Seguro via **Nanuque**, where it is possible to break the Belo Horizonte–Salvador journey, with accommodation near the *rodoviária*.

Parque Florestal de Ibitipoca ⊜▲⊚ ▶▶ *pp304-306.*

→ *Altitude: 1760 m.*

This park is 85 km from **Juiz de Fora**, the largest city in southwestern Minas (with plenty of hotels, lively nightlife and good transport, see www.pjf.mg.gov.br). The park is rich with wildlife, including maned wolf and there are quartzite-encrusted caves, interesting rock formations, waterfalls, rivers, many different types of vegetation, orchids, bromeliads, cacti and lots of lichens and flowers, such as purple *quaresmeiras*. Evidence suggests that the land was once under the sea. More recently it was on the *bandeirantes'* trails (see box page 272). A little gold was found, but it was mostly mica that was extracted; there is quartzite everywhere you look.

Ibitipoca preserves birds and animals, including monkeys, which you are likely to hear rather than see. The French botanist Auguste St-Hilaire visited the area in 1822. To see all that the park has to offer takes about four days. There are a number of trails of varying length; on the longest be prepared for stretches of up to eight hours (take water and protection against the sun). It's possible to stay overnight (see Sleeping, page 304).

The nearest village, **Conceição de Ibitipoca**, is one of the oldest in Minas Gerais. Its church was built in 1768 and has original paintings on the ceiling. There is a statue of São Sebastião and a separate bell tower. The key for the church is at **Ibiti-Bike**. Mass is held once a month. Modern buildings in the village give it a messy look, but the park is definitely worth visiting. There are various places to eat in the village and the local speciality is *pão de canela* (cinnamon bread). Hand-dyed and woven bedspreads and handicrafts in wood are also made in the village.

Ins and outs

The park is open daily 0800-1600; entry costs US$2. By unpaved road it is 27 km from Lima Duarte to Conceição de Ibitipoca. The road is rough and difficult in the wet, but in the dry season especially, ordinary cars can make it. From Conceição it is a 3-km walk (or hitchhike) to the park. Take a bus from Juiz da Fora to Lima Duarte and from there to Ibitipoca.

São Tomé das Letras ⊜❼▲⊜❻ ⇢ pp304-306. Colour map 4, C2.

⇢ Phone code: 035. Population: 6750.

São Tomé das Letras, 35 km from Três Corações, is a beautiful hilltop town which is very popular at weekends. The streets were once lined with houses made of local stone, giving the town a distinctive architectural identity, but its popularity as a tourist destination has seen many of these replaced or overshadowed by ugly concrete buildings and São Tomé is sadly beginning to lose its charm.

Rock paintings found in caves nearby have been dated to about 2000 BC. Inscriptions in the caves have lent the town a mystical reputation, attracting new-age travellers. Many believe it is a good vantage point for seeing UFOs (some claim that the inscriptions are extraterrestrial in origin), and that there are places with special energies. The **Carimbado cave** is rich in myths and legends, such as that its passages lead to an underground civilization and that its powers form an energy source linked to Machu Picchu in Peru.

The Shangri-lá rapid, which is a beautiful spot, is also called the **Vale do Maytréia**. The shops reflect this atmosphere and the hotels are classified by UFOs instead of stars. Whatever you think of it, São Tomé is certainly an unusual place.

Ins and outs

There are three daily buses (two on Sunday) from Três Corações, 1½ hours (the first 30 minutes is on a paved road); take the one that leaves Três Corações at dawn to see the mist in the valleys. If driving to the town, take care at the unsigned road junctions. After the pavement ends, at the next main junction, turn right.

At 1291 m it is one of the five highest places in Brazil. The average maximum temperature is 26°C and the minimum is 14°C. The rainy season is October to March. There is a **tourist office** ① R José Cristiano Alves 4, for information.

Background

A quarry town since the beginning of the 20th century, there is evidence of the industry everywhere you look. Settlement in colonial times dates from the mid- to late-18th century when the *bandeirantes* from São Paulo moved into this area, displacing the indigenous inhabitants. Even before the 20th-century 'alternative' arrivals, the hill acquired the following legend: at the end of the 18th century, an escaped slave hid in a cave for a long time. A finely dressed man appeared, asking him why he was living there. On hearing the slave's story, the man gave him a message on a piece of paper which, on presentation to his master, would earn the slave forgiveness. The slave duly did as the man said and the master, impressed by the writing and the paper, went to the cave to seek the mysterious man for himself. He found no one, but instead a statue of São Thomé (St Thomas). The master therefore built a chapel at the site, which was replaced by the Igreja Matriz in 1784, now standing beside the cave. The inscriptions, in red, can just about be seen in the cave; they are the 'Letras' of the town's name.

Sights

The town is almost at the top of the hill. Behind it are rocky outcrops on which are the **Pyramid House**, the **Cruzeiro** (cross) at 1430 m, with good 360-degree views, the **Pedra da Bruxa** and paths for walking or, in some parts, scrambling.

The bus stops at the main *praça*, where there is the frescoed 18th-century **Igreja Matriz** beside the fenced cave. A second church, the 18th-century **Igreja das Pedras** (Nossa Senhora do Rosário) is on a *praça* to the left as you enter town (Rua Ernestina Maria de Jesus Peixoto). It is constructed in the same style as many of the charming old-style buildings, with slabs of the local stone laid on top of each other without mortar.

Tours from São Tomé das Letras

In the surrounding hills are many caves: **Sobradinho**, 12 km; **Carimbado**, 5 km; **Gruta do Feijão**, a short walk from town; **Gruta da Bruxa**, 6 km. Seven waterfalls are also close by, including: **Cachoeira de Eubiose**, 4 km; **Véu de Noiva**, 12 km; **Paraíso**, near Véu de Noiva; **Vale das Borboletas da Lua**, 8 km; and **do Flávio**, 6 km. There are also rapids such as **Shangri-lá**, 17 km, and **Vale dos Gnomos**, near the Vale das Borboletas. Some of these places make a good hike from the town, but you can also visit several in a day on an organized tour. ▶ *See Activities and tours, page 306.*

Towns and spas of southwestern Minas ●●●● ▶ *pp304-306.*

A group of popular spas are easily reached by road from Rio de Janeiro and São Paulo. Most of the hydro resorts lie south of the Dutra Highway (BR-381, Belo Horizonte–São Paulo). These are Cambuquirá, Lambari, São Lourenço and Caxambu, south of the town of Três Corações, which also gives access to the centre of São Tomé das Letras. Further west and north, on the Minas/São Paulo border is the much larger resort of Poços de Caldas. Some 240 km southwest of Belo is the huge lake formed by the Furnas Dam. It can be seen from the BR-381 road to São Paulo.

Tres Corações → *Colour map 4, C2. Phone code: 035. Population: 64,000.*

The modern city of Tres Corações is a convenient place for making connections to the spas but is desperately uninteresting. It is, however, the birthplace of Pelé, the legendary football star, to whom there is a statue in Praça Coronel José Martins.

The spas of Minas Gerais & São Paulo

The *rodoviária* is beside the old railway station where a steam engine is on show (the railway is used but there is no passenger traffic). At Avenida Getúlio Vargas 154 is the **Casa de Cultura Godofredo Rangel** (Departamento de Turismo e Cultura and Library). **Praça Odilon**, on Rua de Andrade, has a post office and **Banco do Brasil** (but no exchange facilities). From Praça Martins, Avenida Julião Arbex leads steeply uphill to a statue of Christ on top of a chapel on Praça Monsehnor Fonseca.

Hydro resorts 😊😊 ▸▸ *pp304-306.*

Cambuquirá → *Phone code: 035. Population: 13,000. Altitude: 946 m.*
Some 20 km south of Três Corações by paved road, Cambuquirá's **Parque das Águas** is a hilly town with a pleasant atmosphere. Horse-drawn taxis ferry visitors around. Nearby *fazendas* sell *cachaça*.

Lambari → *Phone code: 035. Population: 19,000. Altitude: 900 m.*
This is another hilly town, 27 km south of Cambuquirá. The **Parque das Águas** ① *daily 0600-1800*, has seven mineral springs and mineral water swimming pools on Praça Conselheiro João Lisboa. There are boat trips on the **Lago Guanabara** and to **Ilha dos Amores**. The resort has a casino.

São Lourenço → *Phone code: 035. Population: 35,000. Altitude: 850 m.*
São Lourenço, 60 km southeast of Lambari, is easily accessible from Rio de Janeiro (five or six hours by bus) or São Paulo (six or seven hours by bus), and is useful as a junction but is fairly dull in its own right. There is a splendid park with tennis, boating, swimming, a flying field and fishing. Its rich mineral waters are used in the treatment of various medical complaints. The famous carbo-gaseous baths are unique in South America and can be found at **Parque das Águas** ① *Praça Brasil, daily 0800-1700.*

Caxambu → *Phone code: 035. Population: 21,000. Altitude: 900 m.*
The waters at Caxambu, 31 km northeast of São Lourenço, are used for treating stomach, kidney and bladder diseases, and are said to restore fertility (the Parque das Águas is closed on Monday). The waters seemed to work for Princess Isabel, daughter of Dom Pedro II, who produced three sons after a visit. The little church of **Santa Isabel da Hungária** (1868) stands on a hill as a thanks offering. The surrounding mountains and forests are very beautiful and there is a view over the city from **Morro Caxambu**, 1010 m.

Poços de Caldas 😊🌀❀😊 ▸▸ *pp304-306. Colour map 4, C2.*

→ *Phone code: 035. Population: 124,000.*
The city is right on the São Paulo state border, some 150 km north of the hydro resorts around Lindóia. Sited at 1180 m on the crater of an extinct volcano in a mountainous area, it has an excellent climate. The resort, a traditional honeymoon centre, has thermal establishments for the treatment of rheumatic, skin and intestinal diseases (you need a local doctor's certificate to use these facilities; ask at the resort for recommendations). Venetians from Murano settled here and established a crystal-glass industry.

Ins and outs   Poços de Caldas is 272 km from São Paulo, 507 km from Rio and 510 km from Belo Horizonte. The *rodoviária* is 3 km from the centre and receives buses from Rio de Janeiro and São Paulo. A monorail runs down main avenue, Avenida Francisco Sales, to the cable car station.

Excursions from Poços de Caldas

From Poços de Caldas it is possible to visit the **Véu das Noivas** with its three waterfalls illuminated at night; the tall statue of **Cristo Redentor** at 1678 m, which can be reached by cable car and is popular with hang-gliders; **Pedra Batão**, an 80-m granite rock; and the Japanese teahouse at the **Recanto Japonês**.

◉ Eastern and southern Minas Gerais listings

For Sleeping and Eating price codes and other relevant information, see pages 42-47.

● Sleeping

Parque Nacional Caparaó *p299*
B-C Caparaó Parque, 2 km from the park entrance, 15 mins' walk from the town of Caparaó, T032-3747 2559, www.caparao parquehotel.com.br. In a spectacular location right next to a series of rainforest-swathed mountain ridges and with hiking and other adventure activities organized.

Towards Southern Bahia *p300*
There are several hotels (**C**) in Teófilo Otoni.
D Pousada Tio Miro, R Dr Manoel Esteves 389, T033-3521 4343. Relaxed atmosphere. Recommended.

Parque Florestal de Ibitipoca *p300*
C Estrela da Serra, R Olga Silva Oliveira s/n, Centro, Conceição da Ibitipoca, T032-3281 8188. A simple standard town hotel with a range of fan-cooled and a/c rooms and advice on getting into the park. The price includes breakfast and dinner; lunch costs US$10.

Camping
Ibiti-Lua, in the park itself, is a campsite for 50 tents, with toilets, showers, restaurant/bar and car park.

São Tomé das Letras *p301*
There are lots of *pousadas* and rooms to let all over town. Streets are hard to follow because their names can change from one block to the next; numbering is also chaotic.
C-E Rancho Paraíso, 8 km on the road to Sobradinho, T035-3237 1342. Basic lodging, campsite, restaurant, garden and trekking.
D Pousada Arco-Iris, R João Batista Neves 19, T/F035-3237 1212. Rooms and chalets, sauna, swimming pool.
E Fundação Harmonia, on the road to Sobradinho (4 km), Bairro do Canta Galo, T035-3237 1280. Cheap and cheerful, price per person. The community emphasizes principles for a healthy lifestyle, for mind and body, 'new age', workshops, massage, excursions, veggie food (their shop is on the main *praça*).
E Hospedaria dos Sonhos I, R Gabriel Luiz Alves. Price per person. Clean, with bath, no TV, restaurant, shop, groups accommodated.
E Mahã Mantra, R Plínio Pedro Martins 48, T035-3989 5563. IYHA hostel.
E Pousada Baraunas, R João Cristiano Alves 19, T035-3346 1330. Basic youth hostel with dorms and double. Price per person.
E Pousada Novo Horizonte, R João Cristiano Alves 10. Price per person. Simple rooms, friendly staff, information on local attractions.
E Sonhos II (do Gê), Trav Nhá Chica 8, T035-3237 1235. Price per person. Very nice, restaurant, swimming pool, sauna, television in rooms. Recommended.

Tres Corações *p302*

There are other, more basic hotels near the *rodoviária*.

C Cantina Calabreza, R Joaquim Bento de Carvalho 65, T/F035-3231 1183. Pool, sauna, has a reasonable restaurant, **Italo-Brasileira**, and a takeaway service.

E Avenida, Av Getúlio Vargas 55. Very basic, older and more decrepit than the **Capri**.

E Capri, Av Getúlio Vargas 111, not far from the bridge across the river, T035-3231 1427. With or without bath, simple but okay, TVs in the more expensive rooms.

Hydro resorts *p303*

As well as those listed there are many others in all price ranges.

B Emboabas, Av Jorge Amado 350, São Lourenço, T035-3332 4600. Standard plain town hotel with a restaurant.

B Parque Hotel, R Américo Werneck 46, Lambari, T035-3271 2000. Central, standard town hotel with plain rooms.

C Itaici, R Dr Jos dos Santos 320, Lambari, T/F035-3271 1366. Simple, anonymous but centrally located.

C Pousada Canto do Sabiá, about 3 km out of Caxambu, BR-354 towards Itamonte, T035-3341 3499. This charming *pousada* has chalets and serves excellent breakfast.

D Santos Dumont, Av Virgílio de Melo Franco 400, Cambuquirá.

Camping

Fazenda Recanto das Carvalhos, BR-460 towards Pouso Alto, 10 km from Lambari, T035-3332 2098.

Poços de Caldas *p303*

There are many others in the **B** range, but very few under US$50 a night.

B Novo Hotel Virgínia, R Minas Gerais 506, T035-3722 2664. Simple standard town hotel with a/c and fan-cooled rooms.

B Palace, Praça Pedro Sanches, T035-3722 3636. Old-fashioned but well run, with sulphur baths. Good.

Eating

São Tomé das Letras *p301*

There are many other restaurants and bars in town.

††††† O Alquimista, R Capt Pedro Martins 7. Closed Mar-Jun and Aug-Nov. The best in town, with a decent menu of Minas dishes.

†† das Magas, R Camilo Rosa. A varied menu of Minas and pasta dishes. Good lasagne.

† Padarias Bom Dia, opposite the bus stop on the main *praça*. Pleasant bakery with a range of cheap lunches and sandwiches.

† Veranda Pôr-do-Sol, R Plínio Pedro Martins, *comida caseira*. Pizza. Brazilian home-cooking including a range of Minas dishes and pizzas.

† Ximama, Martins at the corner of G L Alves. Simple pizza restaurant with generous lashings of cheese on the toppings.

Tres Corações *p302*

†† Xodó Quinta da Bock, Av Getúlio Vargas, opposite the Cantina Calabreza, just up from **Hotel Capri**, open-air restaurant serving beer.

††-† Pizzeria Jardins, 1st floor, Av Getúlio Vargas 363, beyond the *praça*. Cheap, good *executivo* menu and other dishes, popular.

Poços de Caldas *p303*

There are plenty of restaurants and all the good hotels have dining rooms. Local specialities are smoked cheese, sausages, sweets and jams (try squash and coconut).

Festivals and events

Poços de Caldas *p303*

Feb Carnaval.

1-13 May São Benedito.

Aug 2nd half of the month. The **Festa UAI** of popular *mineira* music and dance, foods and handicrafts.

▲ Activities and tours

Parque Florestal de Ibitipoca *p300*
Serra do Ibitipoca, R Braz Bernardino 105,
loja 212, Braz Shopping, Juiz de Fora.
Runs tours to the park.

São Tomé das Letras *p301*
Tours to the caves, waterfalls and rapids
surrounding the town can be arranged.
To the waterfalls Flávio, Eubiose, Paraíso
and Véu de Noiva, US$50; Shangri-lá, US$70;
Vale das Borboletas, Gruta do Carimbado
and Ladeira do Amendoim (a slope on which
cars appear to run uphill when in neutral,
like the one in Belo Horizonte), US$50,
T035-3237 1283 or enquire at the
Néctar shop on R José Cristiano Alves.
  The tourist office has a list of accredited
guides for both ecotourism and adventure
tourism: Departamento de Turismo,
Cultura E Proteção ao Patrimônio,
R José Cristiano Alves 04, T035-3237
1461, www.visitesaothome.com.br.

◎ Transport

Parque Nacional Caparaó *p299*
Bus There are direct services to
Manhumirim, 15 km south of Manhuaçu,
US$1, from where there are connections to
Belo Horizonte (twice a day with Pássaro
Verde), **Ouro Preto** or **Vitória**. Or hitch the
11 km to **Presidente Soares** and take a
bus to Manhumirim from there (several
daily, 7 km).

Parque Florestal de Ibitipoca *p300*
Bus From Ibitipoca, take a bus to **Lima
Duarte**, 2 daily; then from there to **Juiz da
Fora** with Frota Nobre (8 daily, US$10).

São Tomé das Letras *p301*
Bus To **Três Corações**, 3 daily buses
(2 on Sun), US$7, 1½ hrs.

Tres Corações *p302*
Bus There are 3 daily buses (2 on Sun) to
São Tomé das Letras, US$7, 1½ hrs (the
first 30 mins is on a paved road); take the
one that leaves Três Corações at dawn
to see the mist in the valleys. To **Belo
Horizonte**, Gardénia, 4 a day (3 on Sun),
US$35, 5½ hrs, roadworks permitting. To **São
Paulo**, Transul, 7 a day, US$50. Beltour runs
buses to **Rio de Janeiro**; Cristo Rei to **Santos**.

Hydro resorts *p303*
Bus São Lourenço and Caxambu have
frequent, numerous buses to **São Paulo**, **Rio**
and **Belo Horizonte**. São Paulo-**Três Corações**
bus (**Gardênia**) passes through Cambuquira,
US$21. 4 buses a day from Bresser station in
São Paulo to **Lambari**, US$21.

Poços de Caldas *p303*
Bus To **Rio**, 8 hrs, US$50; to **São Paulo**,
4½ hrs, US$35.

❶ Directory

São Tomé das Letras *p301*
Bank There is a **Bradesco** in the main *praça*.
Post office In the group of buildings at
the top right of the *praça*, facing the Gruta
São Tomé.

Espírito Santo

Sandwiched between Rio de Janeiro, Minas Gerais and Bahia, the coastal state of Espírito Santo is relatively unknown, except by Mineiros heading for the coast for their holidays. It has many beaches, but they are overshadowed by those of its northern and southern neighbours. There are a number of nature reserves and turtle-breeding grounds in Espírito Santo, and European immigration has given the towns a distinctive atmosphere. The state capital, Vitória, is also the main industrial and commercial centre. People here are known as Capixabas, after a former tribe.

The state has a hot, damp seaboard with a more-or-less straight, low coastline and long beaches open to the Atlantic. The south is mountainous and dotted with vast granite boulders even larger than Sugar Loaf in Rio. The most spectacular is Pedra Azul. The slopes are covered with pine plantations and remnants of Mata Atlântica rainforest. The coast is covered with restinga scrub and grassland. The north of the state is flat and dominated by vast eucalyptus plantations which run down to the long coastal sand dunes. ⏩ *For listings, see pages 311-314.*

Background

Espírito Santo was one of the original captaincies created by the Portuguese in the 16th century, but their colony was very precarious in its early days. During the struggle for supremacy, the son of Mem de Sá (the governor in Bahia) was killed, but, as elsewhere, the invaders eventually prevailed, though not as successfully as in many of the other captaincies, as the Portuguese were only able to gain a foothold on the coastal plains. When the focus of attention moved to the mines in Minas Gerais in the 18th centuries, the state became strategically important. Initially it was not on the gold exporting route, but after iron mining began a trail from Belo Horizonte to Vitória was created. This remains one of the major economic corridors in the country.

Vitória ⏺️🅰️🅱️🅲️ ⏩ *pp311-314. Colour map 4, C5.*

→ *Phone code: 027. Population: 266,000.*

The town of Vitória is beautifully set on an island, its entrance second only to Rio's. The beaches are just as attractive, but smaller, and the climate is less humid. Five bridges connect the island with the mainland. Vitória dates from 1551 and takes its name from a battle won by the Portuguese over the local indigenous people. There are a few colonial remnants, but it is largely a modern city and port. The upper, older part of town, reached by steep streets and steps, is much less hectic than the lower harbour area which suffers dreadful traffic problems. A rail connection westwards to Minas Gerais provides transport for export of iron ore, coffee and timber. Port installations at Vitória and nearby Ponta do Tubarão have led to some beach and air pollution.

Ins and outs

Aeroporto Das Goiabeiras ① *10 km north of the city centre, Av Fernando Ferrari s/n, T027-3235 6300*, has connections with Belo Horizonte, Brasília, Rio de Janeiro, Salvador and São Paulo amongst others. From the airport, a taxi to the centre costs US$25, or take bus No 212. The *rodoviária* is 15 minutes' walk west of the centre.

Information is available from **Cetur** ① *Av Princesa Isabel 54, T027-3322 8888, also at the airport T027-3327 8855 and rodoviária*, with friendly staff and a free map; or **Instituto Jones dos Santos Neves** ① *Av Marechal Campos 310, Edif Vitória Center, T027-3322 2033 ext 2215.*

Sights

On Avenida República is the huge **Parque Moscoso**, an oasis of quiet, with a lake, play-ground and tiny zoo. Other parks are the **Morro da Fonte Grande**, with good views from the 312-m summit, and the **Parque dos Namorados**, 6 km from the centre at Praia do Canto. Two islands reached by bridge from Praia do Canto are **Ilha do Frade** and **Ilha do Boi**.

Colonial buildings still to be seen in the city are the **Capela de Santa Luzia**, Rua José Marcelino in the upper city (1551), now an art gallery; the church of **São Gonçalo**, Rua Francisco Araújo (1766) and the ruins of the **Convento São Francisco** (1591), also in the upper city. In the **Palácio do Governo**, or **Anchieta**, on Praça João Climaco (upper city), is the tomb of Padre Anchieta, the 16th-century Jesuit missionary and one of the founders of São Paulo. The **Catedral Metropolitana** was built in 1918 and stands in Praça Dom Luís Scortegagna. The **Teatro Carlos Gomes**, on Praça Costa Pereira, often presents plays as well as holding jazz and folk festivals.

Vila Velha, reached by a bridge across the bay, has an excellent beach, but is built up and noisy: take a bus from Vitória marked Vilha Velha. Visit the ruined, fortified monastery of **Nossa Senhora da Penha**, on a hill above Vila Velha; the views are superb. The Dutch attacked it in 1625 and 1640. There is also a pleasant ferry service to Vila Velha.

Vitória

Beaches

Urban beaches such as **Camburi** can be affected by pollution (some parts of it are closed to bathers), but it is quite pleasant, with fair surf. South of the city is Vila Velha (see above), but for bigger waves go to **Barra do Jucu**, which is 10 km further south.

There is a hummingbird sanctuary at the **Museu Mello Leitão** ① *Av José Ruschi 4, T027-3259 1182, Tue-Fri 0800-1200, 1300-1700*, a library including the works of the hummingbird and orchid scientist, Augusto Ruschi. Hummingbird feeders are hung outside the library. Also in the municipality is the **Dr Augusto Ruschi Biological Reserve** (formerly the Nova Lombardia National Biological Reserve), a forest rich in endemic bird species, including several endangered hummingbirds, Salvadori's antwren, cinnamon-vented Piha, russet-winged spadebill, Oustalet's tyrannulet, rufous-brown solitaire and hooded berryeater. Before visiting, permission to visit must be obtained from **Ibama** ① *Av Marechal Mascarenhas de Moraes 2487, Caixa Postal 762, Vitória ES, CEP 29000, www.ibama.gov.br.*

Coastal mountains ● ⇥ *pp311-314.*

Mountains separate Vitória from Minas. These were once covered in lush Atlantic coastal rainforest, which now survives only in isolated patches and has been replaced by pine and coffee plantations. The road to Minas is nonetheless picturesque, climbing steeply off the coastal plain and winding its way around the hills and through steep valleys. Many of the towns here were settled by Germans and Swiss and their alpine heritage lives on in a curiously kitsch way: the temperature never drops below freezing, but the tourist chalets are built with long sloping roofs that look like they could fend off a ton of snow. Some customs brought over in the 1840s by the first German and Swiss settlers, are loosely preserved in the villages of **Santa Leopoldina** and **Domingos Martins**, both around 45 km from Vitória, less than an hour by bus (two companies run to the former, approximately every three hours). Domingos Martins (also known as Campinho) has a Casa de Cultura with some items of German settlement. Santa Leopoldina has an interesting **museum** ① *Tue-Sun 0900-1100, 1300-1800*, covering the settlers' first years in the area. **Santa Teresa**, which lies beyond them, is a favourite weekend retreat for people from Vitória. It is linked to Santa Leopoldina by a dirt road.

Whilst these towns are moderately interesting, the only real reason to break the journey between Vitória and Minas is to see **Pedra Azul**, www.pedraazul.com.br, a giant granite mountain that juts out of the nearby hills and changes colour from slate blue to deep orange as the day passes. Although surrounded by pine plantations it preserves a little indigenous forest around its flanks, and the state park in which it sits is good for a day's light walking.

South of Vitória ●●●●● ⇥ *pp311-314.*

Cachoeiro do Itapemirim is a busy city straddling both banks of the fast-flowing Rio Itapemirim. **Cachoeira Alta**, with a natural swimming pool, is 38 km away on the road to Castelo. The countryside south of Vitória is flat and uninteresting, broken only by fields of sugar cane and the occasional granite mountain looming over the plain. The beaches that dot the coast are less beautiful than those in the north of the state and considerably less beautiful than those in neighbouring Rio. The most popular are those at **Guarapari**, some 50 km south of Vitória on the coast road. The town gets very crowded at holiday times, especially mid-December to the end of February when Mineiros flood down from Belo

Horizonte. The sand here is mildly radioactive but if the Casa de Cultura in town is to be believed, the radiation is good for the health. Plenty of Capixabas and Cariocas seem to agree, as they come here to cure everything from rheumatism to backache. There are many hotels and plenty of cheap seafood restaurants in town and by the beach.

A little further south is the far quieter village of **Ubu** and, 8 km beyond, **Anchieta**, which has a small estuarine river much beloved of water birds. Boatmen from the Colônia da Pesca charge about US$20 for a short trip along the river. Close by is **Iriri**, a small village in a beautiful setting with two beaches, Santa Helena and Inhaúma. There are a few hotels. Five kilometres beyond is **Piúma**, a calm, little-visited place, renowned for its craftwork in shells, a skill that has been passed down through generations of craftsmen and women. The name derives from the indigenous word *pium*, meaning mosquito. The resort town of **Marataízes** is the last before the border with Rio de Janeiro state.

North of Vitória 😊🔴🟢 »» pp311-314.

Santa Cruz
The ES-010 road follows the coast from Vitória north to the mouth of the Rio Doce. It passes beaches such as Manguinhos and Jacaraípe, and the town of Nova Almeida before reaching Santa Cruz, 60 km north of the state capital. The town, at the mouth of the Rio Piraquê-Açu, depends economically on cellulose factories, which have been the subject of an international outcry over child labour. It is a simple place, with few facilities. The coast around Santa Cruz, called **Aracruz**, has several good beaches, mostly undeveloped, uncrowded and tranquil.

Turtle beaches
The **Reserva Biológica Comboios** ① *44 km north of Santa Cruz, contact Ibama, Av Marechal Mascarenhas 2487, Caixa Postal 762, CEP 29000, Vitória, T027-3264 1452, www.ibama.com.br,* is designed to protect the marine turtles that frequent this coast. This long stretch of sand backed by *restinga* on the Brazilian seaboard is prime nesting ground, and three species of turtle come here to lay their eggs: the leatherback, the green (*araunã*) and the *cabeçuda*. **Regência**, at the mouth of the Rio Doce, 65 km north of Santa Cruz, is part of the reserve and has a regional base for **Tamar**, the national marine turtle protection project. On the north shore of the mouth of the Rio Doce is **Povoação**, which also has an office of **Tamar** ① *Caixa Postal 105, CEP 29900-970, Lagoa do Monsorá, Povoação, www.tamar.com.* Regência is popular with sailors, anglers, divers and surfers.

Linhares and Sooretama reserves → *Colour map 4, B5.*
The town of **Linhares**, 143 km north of Vitória on the Rio Doce, has good hotels and restaurants but is otherwise dull. However, it is a convenient starting place for visiting the turtle beaches. Besides the one at the mouth of the Rio Doce (see above), there is another **Tamar** site at **Ipiranga**, which is 40 km east of Linhares by an unmade road.

Linhares is close to two other nature reserves. The **Linhares Reserve** ① *permission from the director must be obtained to visit, T027-3374 0016,* owned by **CVRD** (the former state-owned mining company, now privatized), is possibly the largest remaining lowland tract of Atlantic forest. There is very good birdwatching in the reserve and specialities include red-billed curassow, minute hermit, rufous-sided crake, blue-throated (ochre-cheeked) parakeet, black-billed scythebill and black-headed berryeater.

The **Sooretama Biological Reserve** ① *45 km north of Linhares, 65 km south of Conceição da Barra, on the BR-101,* protects tropical Atlantic rainforest and fauna. It contains several bird species not found in the Linhares Reserve, and much of the wildlife is rare and endangered. Both Sooretama and Linhares have orchids apparently not found anywhere else. Sooretama has been protected since 1969. With year-round tropical humidity, vegetation here is dense with ancient trees reaching over 40 m in height. Two rivers, the Barra Seca and the Cupido, cross the reserve and, together with Lagoa Macuco, provide marshlands, which attract migratory birds as well as numerous resident flocks. The reserve is strictly monitored by Ibama and is not open to the public, but drivers and cyclists can cut across it by road.

São Mateus, 88 km north of Linhares, is another unillustrious but inoffensive inland town, which is another base for **Tamar** ⓘ *T027-3761 1267, www.tamar.com.* It is 13 km from good beaches at **Guriri**.

Conceição da Barra → *Colour map 4, B5. Phone code: 027. Population: 25,500.*

The most attractive beaches in Espírito Santo are around Conceição da Barra, 261 km north of Vitória. It is an organized town that welcomes visitors. Many people come in summer and for **Carnaval**, otherwise it is quiet. Viewed from its small port, the sunsets are always spectacular. **Corpus Christi** (early June) is celebrated with an evening procession for which the road is decorated with coloured wood chips. The town has an office for **Tamar** ⓘ *Caixa Postal 53, Conceição da Barra, T027-3762 1124, www.tamar.com.*

Itaúnas

Itaúnas, 27 km north of Conceição, is an interesting excursion (it has some *pousadas* and a small campsite). The small town has been swamped by sand, and has been moved to the opposite riverbank. There is now a fantastic landscape of 30-m-high dunes, coastal swamp land (with numerous capybara) and deserted beaches. From time to time, winds shift the sand dunes enough to reveal the buried church tower. The theory is that the sudden encroachment of the sands in the 1970s was caused by massive deforestation of the surrounding area. The coast here, too, is a protected turtle breeding ground; for information contact **Tamar** in Conceição da Barra (see above). Buses run here three to four times a day from Conceição da Barra. The town is very popular in high season with middle-class Mineiros and Paulistanos who regard it as less spoilt than Trancoso and the other once laid-back resort towns of southern Bahia.

The beach of **Meleiras**, 3 km south, is accessible only on foot or by boat and is one of a number of pleasant trips. It is 12 km long and offers fabulous diving and fishing. **Guaxindiba**, 3 km north, is partially developed, with hotels and restaurants, but the natural vegetation is still intact. It is possible to drive all the way along dirt roads into Bahia if you have a 4WD.

◉ Espírito Santo listings

For Sleeping and Eating price codes and other relevant information, see pages 42-47.

◉ Sleeping

Vitória *p307, map p308*
There are a string of adequate but scruffy hotels opposite the *rodoviária* and plenty of others in the beach areas: **Camburi** to the

north, **Vila Velha** to the south, both about 15 mins from city centre. Accommodation is very easy to find here except in high season.
AL Senac Ilha do Boi, R Bráulio Macedo 417, Ilha do Boi, T027-3345 0111, www.hotelilhado boi.com.br. The most luxurious in town with its own marina, bay views and restaurant and pool.
A Best Western Porto do Sol, Av Dante Michelini 3957, Praia de Camburi, 7 km from

the centre, T027-3337 2244. A beachside hotel built in the 1980s, with a restaurant, pool, sauna and bar.

B Pousada da Praia, Av Saturnino de Brito 1500, Praia do Canto, T/F027-3225 0233. Ordinary little hotel near the beach. Pool.

C Avenida, Av Florentino Avidos 347, T027-3223 4317. Adequate but undistinguished rooms with a/c and a decent breakfast. Recommended.

C Vitória, Cais de São Francisco 85, near Parque Moscoso, T027-3223 0222. Basic hotel with a reasonable restaurant. Recommended but look at a variety of rooms before committing yourself.

D Europa, 7 de Setembro, T027-3323 0108, at the corner of Praça Costa Pereira. Hotel and restaurant, noisy but cheap. Offers advice on nearby veggie restaurants.

D-E Cidade Alta, R Dionísio Rosendo 213, T027-3222 1855. Cheap little fan-cooled boxes opposite the cathedral in the heart of the city centre. The area can be a little sketchy at night.

E IYHA Príncipe Hostel, Av Dario Lourenço de Souza 120, Ilha do Príncipe, T027-3322 2799, hotelp@terra.com.br. The IYHA youth hostel, housed in a big blocky former budget hotel near the *rodoviária*.

Coastal mountains *p309*

C Pousada Peterle, Estr Pedra Azul, Domingos Martins, T027-3248 1171, www.pousadapeterle.com.br. Spacious mock-Swiss chalets set in a little garden with views of the rock. No restaurant but generous breakfast.

South of Vitória *p309*

There are plenty of hotels and *pousadas*. The most popular beach is **Castelhanos** and its extension **Guanabara**, which separates Anchieta from Ubu. Castelhanos has more *palapas*. Gunanbara is quieter. Both have calm waters.

AL Flamboyant, Km 38, Rod do Sol, Guarapari, T/F027-3229 0066, www.hotelflamboyant.com.br. *Fazenda* hotel with fishing and horse riding. Good internet rates for weekends and longer stays in low season.

A Thanharu Praia, R Jovina Serafim dos Anjos, Praia de Castelhanos, between Anchieta and Ubu, T/F028-3536 1246, www.thanharu.com.br. A big Costa del Sol-style concrete block of a beachside hotel with a pool and sauna. Popular with families and on one of the livelier beaches.

A-B Porto do Sol, Av Beira Mar 1, Praia do Morro, Guarapari, T027-3161 7100, www.hotelportodosol.com.brl. Mediterranean-style village on a rocky point overlooking a calm beach, pool, sauna.

A-B Praia Costa Azul, Iriri, T028-3534 1599. A standard, uninspiring beach hotel with rooms gathered around a pool. Lodging in private houses is also possible. A regular bus runs from Guarapari.

B Pontal de Ubu, R Gen Oziel 1, Praia de Ubu, T028-3536 5065, www.hotelpontaldeubu.com.br. Popular family hotel with a pool, saunas, bike rental and organized activities.

B-C Monte Aghá Pousada Haras, R das Castanheiras, Piúma, T028-3520 1363. *Fazenda* hotel with horse riding.

B-C Pousada da Meméia, R Manuel Alves Abrantes, Iriri, T028-3534 1534, www.pousadamemeia.com.br. A range of rooms in a medium-sized *pousada* with a bar and sauna.

C Costa Sul, R Getúlio Vargas 101, Guarapari, T027-3261 2942. Basic, friendly, clean and good breakfast. Much beloved of Brazilians and mosquitoes.

C-D Alto da Praia, Av Estr Dos Cancelas 111, Alto da Praia, Marataízes, T028-3532 3630, www.altodapraia.com.br. Small *pousada* with a/c rooms and a pool.

C-D Coqueiros Praia, Av D Helvécio 1020, Praia dos Namorados, Iriri, T028-3534 1592, www.coqueirospraiahotel.com.br. Small but very well-kept and intimate little beachside *pousada* with a/c rooms and a play area for kids.

C-D Dona Judith, Av Lacerda de Aguiar 353, Marataízes, T028-3532 1436. Basic but friendly.

E Guarapari Hostel, Av F, quadra 40, Guarapari, T027-3261 5210. Simple IYHA hostel at Guarapari popular with students.

Camping
Marataízes, Praia do Siri, 9 km south of Marataízes, T027-3325 2202. Municipal site.
Praia de Itapessu, R Antônio Guimarães s/n, quadra 40, Guarapari, T027-3261 0475. Turn left out of the *rodoviária*, then right and right again, past **Pousada Lisboa**, 2 blocks, across a dual carriageway (Av Jones de Santos Neves), 1 block to the campground, US$10 with good breakfast. Recommended.

Santa Cruz *p310*
There are *pousadas* at Praia Formosa, 3 km south of town, and campsites at Barra do Sahy, Praia do Putiry and Formosa beaches.
B Pousada dos Cocais, Praia de Sauê, T/F027-3250 1515. With a restaurant and a pool.
C Coqueiral Praia Park, Praia do Coqueiral, 6 km along the road to Barra do Riacho, T027-3250 1214. A/c rooms with TVs and a restaurant, pool, pretty location.
D Pousada das Pedras, Praia dos Padres, T027-3250 1716. Basic but friendly with plain rooms.

Linhares and Sooretama reserves *p310*
B-D Reserva Natural da Vale do Rio Doce, BR-101, Km 120, T027-3371 9797, www.cvrd.com.br/linhares. Beautiful location within the reserve. Great for birds and wildlife. With a bar, sauna and simple but pleasant rooms.
B-D Virgínia, Av Gov Santos Neves 919, Linhares, T/F027-3264 1699. Modern building with a range of rooms at different prices. Good if you get stuck in town.

Conceição da Barra *p311*
There are plenty of beach hotels to choose from here and you will have no problem finding one after a short browse, as long as it is not high season.
C Pousada Gandia, Av Atlântica 1054, (Praia de Guaxindiba), T/F027-3762 1248. Small *pousada* with simple rooms, a pool, baby sitting services and helpful staff.
C Praia da Barra, Av Atlântica 350, T/F027-3762 1100, www.hotelpraiadabarra.com.br. Simple and friendly 50-room *pousada* with a/c or fan, a pool and sauna.

D Caravelas, Av Dr Mário Vello Silvares 83, a block from the beach, T027-3762 1188. Basic with shared bathrooms and a light breakfast. Recommended.
E Pousada Pirámide, next to the *rodoviária*, T027-3762 1970. The owner, Lisete Soares, speaks English, good value, 100 m from beach. Recommended.

Camping
Camping Clube do Brasil, Rod Adolfo Serra, Km 16, T027-3762 1346. Site with full facilities.

Itaúnas *p311*
There are numerous attractive little *pousadas* on and around the town's grassy main square.
C Pousada Bem Te Vi, R Adolpho Pereira Duarte 41, T027-3762 5012, www.pousada bemtevi.com. One of the few *pousadas* in town with a pool, with a range of modern rooms organized around a courtyard; all with a/c or fans, TVs, fridges and breakfast.
C Pousada Cambucá, just off Praça Principal, T027-3762 5004, www.portonet.com.br/cambuca. Wooden-floored rooms, some with balconies and a decent seafood restaurant.
C-D Casa da Praia, R Dercílio Fonseca, T027-3762 5028, www.casadapraiaitaunas.com.br. Simple *pousada* close to the beach.

🍴 Eating

Vitória *p307, map p308*
Moqueca capixaba, a seafood dish served in an earthenware pot, is the local speciality. It is a variant of the *moqueca*, which is typical of Bahia.
🍴🍴🍴 **Lareira Portuguesa**, Av Saturnino de Brito 260, Praia do Canto, T027-3345 0329. Portuguese, expensive.
🍴🍴 **Mar e Terra**, opposite the rodoviária. Good food, live music at night.
🍴🍴 **Pirão**, R Joaquim Lírio 753, Praia do Canto. Regional food.
🍴 **Lavacar**, Praia Camburi. One of many similar on this beach, serves food and has live music.

South of Vitória p309
�* **Peixada do Garcia**, Av Magno Ribeiro
Muqui, Guarapari. Respectable seafood.
⚤ **Peixada do Menelau Garcia**,
Av Mário Neves, Guarapari. More
respectable seafood.

Conceição da Barra p311
There are plenty of simple seafood restaurants
town and some basic *palapas* on the beach.
⚤ **Tia Teresa**, R Dr Mário Vello Silvares 135.
Brazilian food, self-service, good value.

⊖ Transport

Vitória p307, map p308
Air Bus 212 runs between the airport city
centre waterfront and the rodoviária. Flights
to **Belo Horizonte** (Confins airport), **Brasília**,
Curitiba, **Rio de Janeiro**, **São Paulo**, **Natal**,
Fortaleza and **Salvador** amongst others.
   Airline offices TAM, Av Fernando
Ferrari 3055, Goiaberas, T027-3327 0868.

Bus To **Rio**, 8 hrs, US$35 (*leito* 45). To **Belo
Horizonte**, US$25 (*leito* 35). To **Salvador**,
18 hrs, US$45; to **Porto Seguro** direct 11 hrs
with lots of stops, US$25 (also *leito* service);
alternatively, take a fast bus to Eunápolis,
then change for Porto Seguro and other
destinations on the Bahia coast. For
Caravelas the **Abrolhos islands** in
Bahia, change at Teixeira de Freitas.

Car hire Several including a **Localiza**
at the airport.

South of Vitória p309
Bus There are regular buses to **Gurarpari**
from Vitoría and onward from here to the
other resorts down the coast. The **Alvorada**
bus company has a separate *rodoviária* from
Itapemirim/Penha, Sudeste, São Gerardo and
others. They are close together, 15 mins' walk
from the city centre or US$10 by taxi. **Penha**
tickets are sold at **R-Tur Turismo**, in the centre
at R Manoel Severo Simões and R Joaquim da
Silva Lima, where air tickets, free brochures,
maps, and hotel addresses can also be
obtained. To **Vitória**, 1 hr with **Sudeste**, US$8.
To **Rio** with **Itapemirim**, 2 a day, US$35.

Linhares and Sooretama reserves p310
Bus Frequent buses from Vitória. Most
Bahia-bound buses stop at Linhares.

Itaúnas p311
Bus Bus from the *padaria* in Conceição
da Barra at 0700, returns 1700.

⊕ Directory

Vitória p307, map p308
Banks Bradesco, Banco do Brasil and
other major banks throughout the city.

South of Vitória p309
Banks Banco 24 Horas, Praça do Coronado,
Praia da Areia, Guarapari; Banco do Brasil,
R Joaquim da Silva Lima 550, Guarapari;
Bradesco, R Henrique Coutinho 901,
Guarapari; **Banco do Brasil**, Av Lacerda
de Aguiar 356, Marataízes.

Iguaçu Falls & the south

At a glance

◉ **Getting around** Buses and internal flights. Car hire a possibility.

◉ **Time required** 2 days for Iguaçu, 5 days for Iguaçu and Ilha do Mel or Florianópolis. 7-10 days for 3-4 destinations.

◐ **Weather** Varies across this large region. Summer (Oct-Mar) tends to be warm and dry; winter (Apr-Sep) is cool and wet. Nov is best for Iguaçu, when the falls are fullest. It can freeze in the mountains Jun-Jul.

✕ **When not to go** In Jun-Aug the sea is cold.

★ **Don't miss ...**
1 Serra da Graciosa, page 321.
2 Ilha do Mel and the Parque Nacional de Superagüi, pages 325 and 326.
3 Iguaçu Falls, page 327.
4 Florianópolis, page 349.
5 Praia do Rosa, page 362.
6 São Miguel das Missões, page 383.

Southern Brazil is famous first and foremost for one sight: Iguaçu. These are the world's mightiest and grandest waterfalls, surrounded on all sides by lush subtropical forest, stretching for almost 3 km, and falling in a thunderous two-tier curtain from a height almost twice that of Niagara. But although Iguaçu is undoubtedly the highlight, it would be a shame to rush in and out of southern Brazil without seeing anything else. There are many other spectacularly beautiful natural sights: toy trains winding their way through jagged, verdant mountains to some of the largest stretches of lowland coastal forest in South America; bays studded with islands, each of which is home to different and often unique fauna; the crumbling ruins of Jesuit monasteries; and, of course, miles of glorious beaches.

The feel of the south is very different to the rest of Brazil; towns are more European and made up of settlers from the Ukraine, Germany and Italy. In Joinville and Blumenau an archaic Bavarian dialect is still widely spoken and there is an annual *bierfest*. Buses run on time, streets are relatively clean and people don't talk much. Things change again in the border country with Argentina and Uruguay, which retains an insular and macho *gaúcho* culture that seems to have more in common with the Argentine pampas than Brazil.

Paraná

Paraná is most famous for the Iguaçu Falls, the largest and most magnificent waterfalls in the Americas. No guidebook can do justice to the spectacle and they are a must on any itinerary to Brazil. Besides Iguaçu, Paraná has a great deal to offer those in search of pristine nature: the largest area of coastal rainforest in Brazil swathes the mountains of the northern coast, while little beach-fringed islands, such as Ilha do Mel, sit a short way offshore. Both are easily reached from the neat and tidy capital, Curitiba, on one of the continent's most impressive railway journeys. The interior of the state is dotted with villages and towns founded by the European settlers that flocked here at the end of the 19th century.

The area of what is now Paraná was neglected by the Portuguese until the beginning of the 17th century when gold was discovered. The region fell under the control of São Paulo, but there was no great success in the extraction of gold, partly because of a lack of indigenous labour (they had all been sent elsewhere or had died of disease). As soon as the precious metal was discovered in Minas Gerais, the mines shut down in Paraná. Instead, the colonists turned to agriculture and cattle-raising and, in the 18th and 19th centuries, the state was dominated by fazendeiros and drovers. Until 1853, the area was controlled from São Paulo. When the new province was created, cattle and maté-growing were the most important activities, but with the coming of the railways at the end of the 19th century, timber became equally significant.

When it became apparent in the second half of the 19th century that the province of Paraná would not develop without a major increase in the population, an official immigration policy was launched. The Italians were the first, but later settlers came from all over Europe and, since the start of the 20th century, from Japan, Syria and the Lebanon. ▸▸ For listings, see pages 336-348.

Curitiba ⬛🚋🚗🏊🚠🅿️⛰️🅰️🚆🅾️ ▸▸ pp336-348. Colour map 5, A4.

➔ Phone code: 041. Population: 1.6 million. Altitude: 908 m.

Paraná's capital is famous in Brazil for its civic planning and quality of life. It is said to be one of the three cleanest cities in Latin America. In outlying areas 'Ruas da Cidadania' (citizenship streets), have been built so that local people can avoid travelling to the centre. These throng with activity and provide municipal services, child care and leisure activities. The first and most famous of these was built at Boqueirão in 1995, but the one at Rua da Cidadania da Matriz, next to the Praça Rui Barbosa transport terminal, is more central and has 20 computer terminals for free access to the internet.

However, few visit Brazil to see well-planned cities. The main reason to stay longer than a quick change of bus or train is the recently opened Oscar Niemeyer museum: a stunning modernist building that looks like a giant eye. This can happily be seen in a few hours between transport connections. Curitiba also marks the start of one of South America's most spectacular railway journeys: to Morretes and the Baía de Paranaguá via the Serra da Graciosa mountains.

Ins and outs

Getting there **Afonso Pena airport** ① *18 km south of the city centre, T041-3381 1515,* receives international flights from Paraguay and Argentina and has direct connections with São Paulo, Rio de Janeiro, Porto Alegre and other state capitals. There are car rental booths, banks with international ATMs and cafes along with buses (US$1) and taxis (US$15) to the centre. International and interstate buses arrive at the combined bus and

Sete Quedas waterfall

In the far northwest of the state, also on the Rio Paraná, were the tremendous waterfalls known in Brazil as Sete Quedas (Seven Falls), and in Spanish Latin America as the Salto de Guaíra. They were drowned by the filling of the lake behind the Itaipu Dam in 1982. The 1978 *South American Handbook* described Sete Quedas thus: "The great river, nearly 5 km wide, hurls itself through the rocky gorges of the falls with a tremendous roar. Rocky islands between the falls are connected by wooden suspension bridges; the whole area can warrant a whole day. Many of the falls are from 30 to 40 m high. This is the most enormous volume of falling water in the world; it is double Niagara's."

railway station, the **Rodoferroviária** ① *Av Alfonso Camargo, www.rodoviariaonline. com.br*, where there are restaurants, banks, shops, phones, a post office, pharmacy, tourist office and other public services. The website has timetables and prices. Trains run along the Serra Verde between Curitiba and Paranaguá (see box, page 346).

Getting around Within the city there is an integrated transport system with several types of bus route; pick up a map in one of the tourist booths for details. The 'Transport–City Circular–Linha Turismo' circles the major transport terminals and points of interest in the city centre and costs US$7 for five stops. ▸▸ *See Transport, page 345.*

Tourist information The main office is in the **Instituto Municipal de Turismo/Curitiba Turismo** ① *R da Glória 362, 1st floor, T041-3250 7729, Mon-Fri 0800-1200 and 1400-1800.* There is also an office at the **rodoferroviária** ① *Av Presidente Afonso Camargo 330, T041-3320 3121, Mon-Fri, 0800-1800, Sat 0800-1400*, and a **tourist booth** ① *T041-3324 7036, daily 1000-1800*, on the 24-hour street, Rua 24 Horas.

Background

The city was founded on 19 March 1693 as Vila Nossa Senhora da Luz dos Pinhais on the spot that is now Praça Tiradentes. For many years it was little more than a pit stop for cattle herders on their way between Rio Grande do Sul and the cities to the north. But in 1842 it was elevated to the rank of city and given the name of Curitiba and, in 1853, it was made the state capital. It received waves of Italian, German and eastern-European immigrants in the late 19th and 20th centuries, which led to the state's distinctive European identity, and rapid deforestation.

Sights

The city has extensive open spaces and some attractive modern architecture. There is a good panoramic view from the glass observation deck of the telecommunications tower, **Torre Mercês**, built by Telepar and so is also known as the **Telepar Tower** ① *R Jacarezinho, corner of R Professor Lycio Veloso 191, T041-3322 8080, Tue-Fri 1230-2030, Sat and Sun 1030-2030, US$1.50.* The 110-m tower stands at an elevation of 95 m above sea level. There is a map of the city on the floor so that you can locate key sites.

The commercial centre is the busy Rua 15 de Novembro, part of which is a pedestrian area called **Rua das Flores**. Since urban planning first began in 1720, the Rua das Flores has been a focus for street life and street entertainment and is now perennially decorated with flowers and trees, and lined with benches, cafés, restaurants, cinemas and shops. At its southern end, the **Boca Maldita** is particularly lively and a popular meeting place.

On Praça Tiradentes is the **cathedral** ① *R Barão do Serro Azul 31, T041-3324 5136*, built in neo-Gothic style and inaugurated in 1893 (restored in 1993). Behind the cathedral, near Largo da Ordem, is a pedestrian area with a flower clock and old buildings. It is very atmospheric in the evening when it is illuminated by old gas lamps. City centre bar and nightlife is concentrated here. There is an art market on Sunday morning in **Praça Garibáldi**, beside the attractive Rosário church.

Museums worth visiting include the **Museu Paranaense** ① *Praça Generoso Marques, Palácio São Francisco, R Kellers 289, T041-3304 3300, www.pr.gov.br/museupr, Tue-Fri 0930-1730, Sat and Sun 1100-1500*, which has temporary shows and concerts in the garden on Sunday, alongside a collection of ethnological and historical material, and the **Museu de Arte Contemporânea** ① *R Desembargador Westphalen 16, Praça Zacarias, T041-3222 5172, Tue-Fri 0900-1900, Sat and Sun 1400-1900*, which showcases Brazilian contemporary works, with an emphasis on artists from Paraná.

Curitiba

Not to scale

Sleeping 😴
Bourbon & Tower **1**
Del Rey **5**

Deville Express **4**
Deville Rayon **6**
IYHA Curitiba Eco-hostel **7**
IYHA Hostel Roma **2**
Kings **13**
Lumini **18**

Mercure Curitiba Centro **3**
Nova Lisboa **15**
Parati **19**
Slaviero Braz **8**
Slaviero Palace **10**
Tourist Universo **12**

Eating 🍴
Baviera **11**
Boulevard **10**
Durski **6**
Green Life **9**
Happy Rango **1**

Unlike most Brazilian cities, Curitiba has plenty of green spaces. The most popular is the **Passeio Público** ⓘ *closed Mon*, in the heart of the city, with three lakes, each with an island, and a playground. About 4 km east of the *rodoferroviário*, the **Jardim Botânico Fanchette Rischbieter**. This has a fine glass house, again with domes, curves and lots of steel, inspired by the Crystal Palace in London. The gardens are in French style and there is also a **Museu Botânico** ⓘ *R Ostoja Roguski (Primeira Perimetral dos Bairros), T041-321 8646.* It can be reached by the orange Expreso buses from Praça Rui Barbosa.

Near the shores of Lagoa Bacacheri, on the northern edge of the city, is one of Brazil's many hidden quirks: an **Egyptian temple** ⓘ *R Nicarágua 2453.* The temple is devoted to the Rosicrucian cult: a 19th-century offshoot of Theosophical occultism that has taken hold in Brazil alongside many other arcane religions. This is surely the only country on Earth where Rosicrucians advertise themselves with car bumper stickers. Visits can also be arranged to the Brazilian centre of the Rosicrucians; take the Santa Cândida bus to Estação Boa Vista, then walk.

Museu Oscar Niemeyer (MON)

ⓘ *3 km north of the centre, R Marechal, Hermes, T041-3350 4400, www.museuoscar niemeyer.org.br, Tue-Sun 1000-1830, US$2.*

The Museu Oscar Niemeyer was designed by, and is devoted to, the famous Brazilian modernist architect who designed Brasília and was a disciple of Le Corbusier, together with other Para- nanese artists. The stunning principal building is shaped like a giant eye and the whole museum serves as a gallery for diverse shows, which in the past have ranged from Picasso drawings to modern Japanese art. An underground passage, also lined with a range of (always high quality) exhibits and photographs links the eye to a sculpture garden.

Curitiba to Paranaguá
⊕⊕▲⊕ⓒ ▶▶ *pp336-348.*

Serra da Graciosa and Parque Nacional Marumbi

When the first European ships arrived at Paraná in the mid-16th century, they would have been daunted by the prospect of conquering the lands of southern Brazil. From the sea, the thickly forested and steep crags of the **Serra da Graciosa** must have seemed an insurmountable wall fortifying the continent from the coast. But in a cruel twist of fate, it was native trails cutting

Mister Sheik **5**
Saccy **3**
Salmão **7**

London Pub **14**
The Farm **13**
Tuba's **12**

Bars & clubs ⚫
Fire Fox **4**

through the mountains that led to inland Paraná being colonized. After the paths were discovered, the Portuguese forced African slaves to pave them with river stones. Miners and traders were soon dragging mules laden with gold, silver, textiles and *herva maté* up and down the mountains. As trade grew, the port at Paranaguá became the most important south of Santos and little towns of whitewashed churches and smart Portuguese buildings like Morretes and Antonina grew up along the trails. In 1885 the routes were busy enough to merit the construction of a railway, which wound its way around the slopes, across rushing rivers and through the forest to the sea.

Ins and outs

Two roads and a railway run from Curitiba to Paranaguá. The railway journey remains the most spectacular in Brazil, cutting through numerous tunnels, crossing dizzy viaducts (especially imported from Belgium), offering sudden views of deep gorges and high peaks and waterfalls before arriving at the sea. Near Banhado station (Km 66) is the waterfall of **Véu da Noiva**, and from the Marumbi station at Km 59 you can reach the Marumbi mountain range. For timetables, see box page 346.

The principal trail (Estrada Da Graciosa) between Curitiba and Paranaguá is now a spectacular cobbled road that runs for 15 km through the mountains and the Marumbi national park. There are fire grills, shelters and camping at the various rest stops. You can also hike the original mule trail, which follows the road and passes the rest stops; trails leave from just outside Morretes railway station and are well signposted. Take food, water and plenty of insect repellent.

The Serra da Graciosa Marumbi national park has recently opened up to guided trekking, rock climbing and light ecotourism. Companies like **Calango Expedições**, www.calangoexpedicoes.com.br, and the Florianópolis-based travel company, **Brazil Ecojourneys**, www.brazilecojourneys.com, offer tours. There is good climbing and hiking in the park. ➤➤ *See Activities and tours, page 344.*

Around Curitiba

Morretes, Antonina and around → *Colour map 5, A5.*

Morretes was founded in 1721 and is one of the prettiest colonial towns in southern Brazil. A parade of whitewashed Portuguese colonial buildings with painted window frames straddle the pebbly river, and church spires stick up from a sea of red-tiled roofs against the backdrop of the deep-green forest-swathed hills.

The **Estrada da Graciosa** road passes through Morretes, and there are numerous daily buses from Curitiba and Paranaguá. The train stops here too, for a lunch break. There are a handful of *pousadas* and numerous restaurants serve the local speciality, *barreado* (meat stew cooked in a clay pot), which was originally served a day in advance of **Carnaval** in order to allow women to escape from their domestic cooking chores and enjoy the party. The **tourist office** ① *T041-3462 1024 or see www.morretes.pr.gov.br*, is by the river.

The town itself is tiny and easily negotiated on foot. A series of walks lead from the town into the Serra da Graciosa mountains. The most popular trails run to the **Salto dos Macacos** and **Salto da Fortuna waterfalls**, which take between three and four hours there and back from town. Walks can be organized through **Calango Expedições**. ▶▶ *See Activities and tours, page 344.*

Antonina, just 14 km from Morretes, is almost as picturesque and sits on the Bahia do Paranaguá. It was once an important port town but is now sleepy and little visited, except during the lively **Carnaval**. It can be reached by local bus from Morretes.

Paranaguá and around ⊖❼❼❸❶ ▶▶ *pp336-348. Colour map 5, A5.*

→ *Phone code: 041. Population: 128,000.*

After the endless lorry parks and the messy dual carriageway leading into the town, the centre of Paranaguá, 268 km south of Santos, comes as a pleasant surprise, especially around the waterfront. Colonial buildings decay quietly in the heat and humidity, some are just façades encrusted with bromeliads; and fishermen get quietly drunk in little *botiquines*.

There's not much to do in the town but stroll along the cobbles and while away the time in the interesting city museum, housed in a formidable 18th-century **Jesuit convent** ① *R 15 Novembro 575, T041-423 2511, www.proec.ufpr.br, 0800-1200, 1400-1800, US$1*, which showcases aspects of the city's interesting past. Other attractions include a 17th-century fountain, the church of **São Benedito**, and the shrine of **Nossa Senhora do Rocio**, 2 km from town. The town is more remarkable for what lies on its doorstep: the **Ilha do Mel** and **Baía do Paranaguá**, see page 324.

Ins and outs

Tourist information is available from **Posto de Informações Turísticas da Paraná Turismo** ① *at the dock, Estação Náutica, R General Carneiro 258 and Nestor Victor, T041-3425 4542, www.paranagua.pr.gov.br, 1100-1700*. The office provides free maps and boat schedules, and has toilets and left-luggage facilities.

Background

Before it became Paranaguá, the region was an important centre of indigenous life. Colossal shell middens, called *sambaquis* (see the Museu Arqueológico do Sambaqui in Joinville, page 360) have been found on the surrounding estuaries, protecting regally adorned corpses. The mounds can be as high as a two-storey building and date from between 7000 and 2000 years ago. They were built by the ancestors of the *tupinguin* and *carijo* people who were here when the first Europeans arrived. The bay's outer islands were initially claimed and occupied by the Spanish (who thought they had reached the coast near Potosí in Bolivia, thousands of miles inland, when they first saw the Serra da Graciosa). But in the late 16th century a *bandeira* expedition under Heiliodoro Eobano found gold in Paranaguá. When the Portuguese realized the importance of the area, they beat the Spanish off the land and fortified the southern end of Ilha do Mel, establishing a port at Paranaguá.

Excursions from Paranaguá

Matinhos, 40 km south, is a medium-sized Mediterranean-style resort, invaded by surfers in October for the Paraná surf competition. About 8 km further south is **Caiobá**, at the mouth of a bay, the other side of which is **Guaratuba**, which is less built up than Caiobá. The ferry between the two towns is frequent and is a beautiful crossing (free for pedestrians, US$1.50 for cars). Each of these towns has a few hotels but most close in winter; there is camping at Matinhos and Guaratuba.

Parque Nacional Vila Velha

On the road to Ponta Grossa is Vila Velha, now a state park, 97 km from Curitiba, 10 km from Ponta Grossa. The sandstone rocks have been weathered into fantastic shapes, although many have been defaced by thoughtless tourists. Nearby are the **Lagoa Dourada**, surrounded by forests, and the **Furnas**: three waterholes, the deepest of which has a lift (US$1, not always working) that descends almost to the level of the lake. The park office is 300 m from the highway and the park a further 1.5 km. You can camp in the church grounds or put your tent up in a disused campground, which is now overgrown and has no facilities. Allow all day if visiting all three sites (unless you hitch, or can time the buses well; it's a lot of walking).

Ins and outs The park is open 0800-1900. Tickets cost US$3.50 to see the stones and US$2 to visit the crater lakes and Lake Dourada; tickets also include entrance to the Furnas. To get there, purchase tickets from the **Princesa dos Campos** bus company in Curitiba on a bus heading towards Ponta Grossa and ask the driver to let you out at Parque Estadual de Vila Velha. The journey takes about 1½ hours. The last bus back is at 1600 and stops outside the park along the main road; return tickets can be purchased on board the bus (US$5).
▶▶ See Transport, page 347.

Baía de Paranaguá ⊜🕖⊜ ▶▶ *pp336-348.*

The Baía de Paranaguá is one of Latin America's biodiversity hotspots and the best place on the Brazilian coast to see rare rainforest flora and fauna. Mangrove and lowland subtropical forests, islands, rivers and rivulets combine to form the largest stretch of Atlantic coast rainforest in the country. The area protects critically endangered species like the black-faced lion tamarin, which was only discovered in 1990, and the red-tailed Amazon parrot (which despite its name is only found here), alongside a full gamut of South American spectaculars including jaguars. Most of the bay is protected by a series of national and state parks (see Parque Nacional de Superagüi, page 326), but it is possible to visit on an organized tour from Paranaguá (or with more difficulty from **Guaraquecaba** on the northern side of the bay). The **BARCOPAR boatman's cooperative** ① *Associação dos Proprietários de Barcos de Turismo e Transporte do Estado do Paraná, R General Carneiro 32, Paranaguá, T041-3425 6173, www.barcopar.com.br,* offers a range of excellent trips in large and small vessels ranging from two hours to two days and from US$15 per person to US$100.

Ilha do Mel → *Colour map 5, A5.*

Ilha do Mel is a weekend escape and holiday island popular with Paraná and Paulista surfers, 20-something hippies and day-tripping families. There are no roads, no vehicles and limited electricity. Outside of Carnaval and New Year it is a laid-back little place. Bars pump out Bob Marley and *maranhão* reggae; spaced-out surfers lounge around in hammocks; and bare-footed couples dance *forró* on the wooden floors of simple beachside shacks. Much of the island is forested, its coastline is fringed with broad beaches and, in the south, broken by rocky headlands. Its location in the mouth of the Bahía de Paranaguá made it strategically important to the Portuguese in the 18th century. The lighthouse, **Farol das Conchas**, was built in 1872 to guide shipping into the bay. The cave of **Gruta das Encantadas** is surrounded with myths and legends about mermaids, enchanting all who came near.

The island divides into two sections connected by a spit of sand at the **Nova Brasília** jetty, the principal port of arrival. The rugged eastern half, where most of the facilities are to be found, is fringed with curving beaches and capped with a lighthouse. The flat, scrub forest-covered and balloon-shaped western half is predominantly an ecological protection area. Its northern side is watched over by the **Fortaleza Nossa Senhora dos Prazeres**, a fort

Ilha do Mel

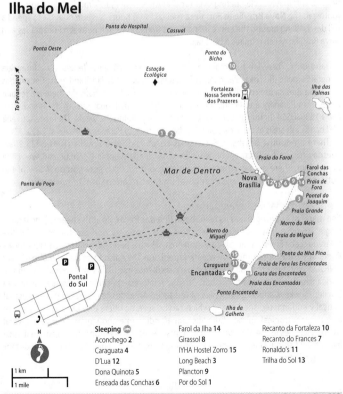

Sleeping 🛌
Aconchego **2**
Caraguata **4**
D'Lua **12**
Dona Quinota **5**
Enseada das Conchas **6**

Farol da Ilha **14**
Girassol **8**
IYHA Hostel Zorro **15**
Long Beach **3**
Plancton **9**
Por do Sol **1**

Recanto da Fortaleza **10**
Recanto do Frances **7**
Ronaldo's **11**
Trilha do Sol **13**

built in 1767 on the orders of King José I of Portugal, to defend what was one of the principal ports in the country. In 1850, a British warship captured three illegal slave-trading ships, giving rise to a battle known as **Combate Cormorant**. The view from the 20th-century gun emplacements on the hill above the fort is the best on the island.

The best surf beaches are **Praia Grande** and **Praia de Fora**, both about 20 minutes' walk from the Nova Brasília jetty. **Fortaleza** and **Ponta do Bicho** on the north shore are more tranquil and are safe for swimming; they are about 45 minutes' walk from the jetty or five minutes by boat. **Farol** and **Encantadas** are the liveliest and have the most accommodation, restaurants and nightlife. However, Encantadas has become somewhat polluted, with the cesspits overflowing into open sewers in the wet.

Walking on Ilha do Mel A series of well-signposted trails lead throughout Ilha do Mel and its coast. The most walked are as follows: the **lighthouse trail from Farol beach** (20 minutes), which is paved but steep; the views are wonderful. The **Nova Brasília to Encantadas trail** (three hours) offers a series of beautiful views, paths through the forest and stretches of semi-deserted beach. However, once you reach the end of the trail, you will either have to return the same way or take a boat taxi around the rocks back to Nova Brasília. This involves clambering over rocks at the end of Praia Grande; take appropriate footwear. The **Nova Brasília to Fortaleza trail** takes 1½ hours. It is also possible to spend a full day walking around the entire island (apart from the stretch between Encantadas and Nova Brasília, which requires a boat taxi).

Ins and outs There are two main routes. From Paranaguá, large ferries leave from Rua General Carneiro (Rua da Praia) in front of the tourist information kiosk and run to Encantadas and Nova Brasília (twice daily, one hour 40 minutes, US$6). Alternatively, there are regular buses from Paranaguá to Pontal do Sul, from where a small boat runs to the island, daily 0800-1800, US$4 (hourly at weekends, less frequently during the week). There are souvenir and handicraft stalls at the ferry point. The last bus back to Paranaguá leaves at 2200.

There are tourist booths at Encantadas beach and Nova Brasília (T041-3426 9091, Tuesday to Sunday 0800-1800). See also www.ilhadomelonline.com.br and www.ilha domel.com. There are no shops on the island so stock up before you go. Many of the hotels have internet access and there are a few internet cafés. ▸▸ See Transport, page 347.

Parque Nacional de Superagüi

The island of **Superagüi** and its neighbour, **Ilha das Peças**, lie at the heart of the largest single stretch of Atlantic Coast rainforest in the country and are the focus for the Guaraqueçaba Environmental Protection Area, which is part of the **Nature Conservancy's Parks in Peril Programme**, www.parksinperil.org. They also form a national park and UNESCO World Heritage Site. Many endangered endemic plants and animals live in the park, including hundreds of orchids, Atlantic rainforest-specific animals such as brown howler monkeys and large colonies of red-tailed Amazons (a parrot on the 'red list' of critically endangered species and which can be seen nowhere else but here). There are also rare neotropical animals here like jaguarundi, puma and jaguar. There are several Guarani villages in the area; other inhabitants are mostly of European descent, making a living from fishing. There is superb swimming from deserted beaches, but watch out for stinging jellyfish.

Ins and outs Access to the park and accommodation can be arranged through the village on Superagüi beach, just north of Ilha do Mel. Boats run from Paranaguá on Saturday at 1000 (arriving 1400) and return on Sunday at 1530 (two stops en route), US$10 one way. Private boats from Praia da Fortaleza on Ilha do Mel run if the weather is good. Contact **Ibama** ① *on the island, 2 km out of the village T041-3252 0180*, for information and commercially organized tours. It is possible to use the route through Superagüi as an alternative route from Paraná into São Paulo state.

Iguaçu Falls ○⊘ ›› pp336-348. Colour map 5, A2.

→ *Phone code 045, www.fozdoiguaçu.pr.gov.br.*

Foz do Iguaçu, or Las Cataratas del Iguazú as they are known in Spanish, are the most overwhelming and spectacular waterfalls in the world. Situated on the Rio do Iguaçu (meaning 'big water' in Guaraní), which forms the border between Argentina and Brazil, they are made up of no less than 275 separate waterfalls. The Paraguayan city of Ciudad del Este is just a few kilometres away but Paraguay does not own territory at the falls themselves.

The most spectacular part is the **Garganta do Diabo** (Devil's Throat), the mouth of a 28-km-long gorge that stretches downstream to the Alto Río Paraná. It is best visited from the Argentine side (see Ins and outs, below, and page 331).

Viewed from below, the water tumbles and roars over the craggy brown cliffs, framed by verdant rainforest encrusted with bromeliads, orchids, begonias and dripping ferns. A seemingly perpetual rainbow hovers over the scene and toco toucans, flocks of parakeets, caciques and great dusky swifts dodge in and out of the vapour whilst a vast number of butterflies dance over the forest walkways and lookouts.

Ins and outs

The town nearest the falls is also, confusingly, called Iguaçu – or to give it its full name – Foz de Iguaçu. Around 80% of the falls lie in Argentina, which offers the most spectacular views and the best infrastructure. There are national parks protecting extensive rainforest on both sides. Transport between the two parks is via the Ponte Tancredo Neves, as there is no crossing at the falls themselves.

The **Brazilian park** offers a superb panoramic view of the whole falls and is best visited in the morning (four hours is enough for the highlights) when the light is better for photography. The **Argentine park** (which requires at least half a day) is great value and includes a railway trip in the entrance fee as well as offering closer views of the individual falls. To fully appreciate the forest, with its wildlife and butterflies, you need to spend a full day and get well away from the visitor areas. Both parks can, if necessary, be visited in a day, starting at about 0700. However, in the heat, the brisk pace needed for a rapid tour is exhausting. Sunset is best from the Brazilian side.

The busiest times are holiday periods and on Sunday, when helicopter tours are particularly popular. Both parks have visitor centres, though the information provided by the Argentine centre is far superior to that in the Brazilian centre. Tourist facilities on both sides are constantly being improved.

There are many advantages to staying in Foz do Iguaçu town and commuting to the Argentine side; it has, for example a much bigger choice of hotels and restaurants. Whichever side you decide to stay on, most establishments will accept reais, pesos or dollars. Cross-border transport usually accepts guaraníes as well.

A useful guidebook is *Iguazú, The Laws of the Jungle* by Santiago G de la Vega, Contacto Silvestre Ediciones (1999), available from the visitor centre.

Getting to the falls from Brazil Buses leave Foz do Iguaçu town from the **Rodoviária Terminal Urbana** ① *Av Juscelino Kubitschek, 1 block from the infantry barracks*. The grey or red **Transbalan** service runs to the falls every half an hour 0530-2330, past the airport and **Hotel Tropical das Cataratas** (40 minutes, US$0.80 one way, payable in reais only). Return buses run 0800-1900. The bus terminates at the visitor centre, where you must pay the entrance fee and transfer to the free park shuttle bus, which leaves every five minutes 0830-1900. If driving, cars must be left in the visitor centre car park. Taxis from Foz do Iguaçu charge US$7 one way or US$30 for return trip, including waiting (negotiate in advance). Many hotels organize tours to the falls, which have been recommended in preference to taxi rides.

Getting to the falls from Argentina **Transportes El Práctico** buses run every hour from the Puerto Iguazú bus terminal, stopping at the park entrance to buy entry tickets and continuing to Puerto Canoas. Fares US$5 return to the visitor centre (cars US$3), a further US$0.50 to Puerto Canoas, payable in pesos, dollars, guaraníes or reais. The first bus leaves

◻ Iguaçu Falls orientation

Sleeping 🛏	IYHA Paudimar
Hostel Natura **1**	Campestre **1**
	Suiça **2**

at 0740, the last is at 1940, and the last return is at 2000, journey time 30 minutes. Buses are erratic, especially when wet, even though the times are clearly indicated. There are fixed rates for taxis, US$15 one-way, up to five people. A tour from the bus terminal, taking in both sides of the falls, costs US$40.

Clothing In the rainy season when water levels are high, waterproof coats or swimming costumes are advisable for some of the lower catwalks and for boat trips. Cameras should be carried in a plastic bag. Wear shoes with good soles, as the rocks can be very slippery in places.

Background

The Caiagangue people originally inhabited the region, but the first European visitor to the falls was the Spaniard Alvaro Núñez Cabeza de Vaca in 1541. He nearly fell off one of the waterfalls on his search for a connection between the Brazilian coast and the Río de la Plata, and named them the Saltos de Santa María (Santa Maria waterfalls). Though the falls were well known to the Jesuit missionaries, they were largely forgotten until the area was explored by a Brazilian expedition sent out by the Paraguayan president, Solano López, in 1863.

➡ **Iguaçu Falls maps**
▌ Iguaçu Falls orientation, page 328
2 Iguaçu Falls, page 330
3 Foz do Iguaçu, page 333

Parque das Aves

Rio Iguaçu Superior

Circuito Inferior
Argentine Visitor Centre
Brazilian Visitor Centre
Circuito Superior
Isla San Martín
Iguaçu Falls
Garganta do Diabo
Floriano Falls
To Porto Canoas

Parque Nacional Iguazú

To Bernardo de Yrigoyen

To Airport

Parque Nacional Foz do Iguaçu (Brazil)

The Brazilian national park was founded in 1939 and designated a World Heritage Site by UNESCO in 1986. The park covers 185,262 ha on the Brazilian side and 67,000 ha on the Argentinian side, extending along the north bank of the Rio Iguaçu, then sweeping northwards to Santa Tereza do Oeste on the BR-277. The subtropical rainforest benefits from the added humidity in the proximity of the falls, creating an environment rich in flora and fauna. Given the massive popularity of the falls, the national parks on either side of the frontier are surprisingly little visited.

Fauna The parks on both sides of the falls are replete with wildlife and are a haven for birders. The most common mammals seen are coatis, which look like long-nosed racoons and squeakily demand food from visitors; do not be tempted as these small animals can be aggressive. There are other mammals here too, including jaguar, puma, ocelot and margay, which can occasionally be seen along the park roads just before and after dawn. They are wary of humans, although in 2003 a jaguar broke into the Parque das Aves (see page 332) and ate the zoo's prize caiman. Most frequently encountered are little and red brocket deer,

2 Iguaçu Falls

➡ Iguaçu Falls maps
1 Iguaçu Falls orientation, page 328
2 **Iguaçu Falls, page 330**
3 Foz do Iguaçu, page 333

Entrance to
Brazilian Park

Central Station

Visitor
Centre ②

Entrance to
Argentinian Park

Sendero Verde

Waterfall Station

Rio Iguaçu Inferior

Parque Nacional
Foz do Iguaçu

Macuco Safari

BRAZIL

Rod das Cataratas

Circuito
Inferior

Circuito
Superior

Isla San Martín

Three
Marie's
Port

ARGENTINA

Visitor
Centre

*Rio Iguaçu
Inferior*

*Rio Iguaçu
Superior*

*Garganta
do Diabo*

Boardwalk

Ruta 12

Devil's
Canyon
Station

To Porto Canoas

N

400 metres
400 yards

Waterfalls 〰

Duas Irmãs (Two Sisters) **1**
Pequena (Small) **2**
Ramírez **3**
Bossetti **4**
Bernabé Méndez **5**
Mbiguá **6**
Adão e Eva (Adam & Eve) **7**
San Martín **8**
Escondido **9**
Rivadavia **10**
Lanousse **11**
Alvar Núñes **12**
Dois Mosqueteiros
  (two Musketeers) **13**
Belgrano **14**
Três Mosqueteiros
  (three Musketeers) **15**
Mitre **16**
Peñón **17**
Santa Maria **18**
Floriano **19**
Deodoro **20**
Benjamin Constant **21**
Unión **22**

Sleeping 🛏
Sheraton Internacional
Iguazú Resort **2**

Tropical das Cataratas **1**

white-eared opossum, *paca* (which look like large dappled guinea pigs) and a subspecies of the brown capuchin monkey. Other mammals include white-lipped peccary, bush dog and southern river otter. The endangered tegu lizard is common. Over 100 species of butterflies have been identified, among them the electric blue morpho, the poisonous red and black heliconius and species of papilionidae and pieridae.

The birdlife is especially rewarding. Five members of the toucan family can be seen: toco and red-breasted toucans, chestnut-eared araçari, saffron and spot-billed toucanets. From the bamboo stands you may see spotted bamboo wren, grey-bellied spinetail, several antshrikes and short-tailed ant-thrush. In the forest you might see rufous-thighed kite, black-and-white hawk-eagle, black-fronted piping-guan, blue ground dove, dark- billed cuckoo, black-capped screech-owl, surucua trogon, rufous-winged antwren, black- crowned tityra, red-ruffed fruitcrow, white-winged swallow, plush-crested jay, cream- bellied gnatcatcher, black-goggled and magpie tanagers, green-chinned euphonia, black- throated and utlra-marine grosbeaks, yellow-billed cardinal, red-crested finch. (Bird and mammal information supplied by Douglas Trent, **Focus Tours**; see Essentials, page 65.)

The falls All cars and public buses stop at the visitor centre, where there are souvenir shops, a **Banco do Brasil** ATM and *câmbio* (1300-1700), a small café and car park. If possible, visit on a weekday when the walks are less crowded. The centre is open daily 0800-1700 and there is a 10 reais (US$3) car-parking fee, payable only in Brazilian currency. This includes a transfer to the free park shuttle bus.

The first stop on the shuttle bus is the **Macuco Safari**, US$33 (bookable through most agencies, which may charge a premium for transfers). The safari takes one hour 45 minutes, leaving every 15 minutes, and visits the forest near the falls, with an option to take a boat to the edge of the falls themselves.

The second stop is the **Cataratas Trail** (starting from the hotel of the same name, non-residents can eat at the hotel, midday and evening buffets). This 1.5-km paved walk runs part of the way down the cliff near the rim of the falls, giving a stupendous view of the whole Argentine side of the falls. It ends up almost under the powerful **Floriano Falls**; from here an elevator used to carry visitors to the top of the Floriano Falls but has not been functioning recently; a path adjacent to the elevator leads to Porto Canoa. A catwalk at the foot of the Floriano Falls gives a good view of the **Garganta do Diabo**.

The **Porto Canoas** complex, with its snack bar, toilets, souvenir shops and terraces with views of the falls, was completed in 2000 after some controversy. Its restaurant serves a US$12 buffet. Highly recommended for a memorable meal.

Parque Nacional Iguazú (Argentina) → *International phone code + 54.*
Created in 1934, the park extends over an area of 67,620 ha, most of which is covered by the same subtropical rainforest as on the Brazilian side. It is crossed by Route 101, a dirt road that runs southeast to Bernardo de Yrigoyen on the Brazilian frontier. Buses operate along this route in dry weather, offering a view of the park.

Fauna You would have to be very lucky to see jaguars, tapirs, brown capuchin monkeys, collared anteaters and coatimundi. As in Brazil, very little of the fauna in the park can be seen around the falls; even on the nature trails described below you need to go in the early morning and have luck on your side. Of the 400 species of birds, you are most likely to spot the black-crowned night heron, plumed kite, white-eyed parakeet, blue-winged parrolet, great dusky swift, scale-throated hermit, suruca trogon, Amazon kingfisher, toco toucan, tropical kingbird, boat-billed flycatcher, red-rumped cacique, and the colourful purple-throated euphonia.

The falls The park is open daily 0800-1900. Entry costs US$5, payable in pesos or dollars (not reais). Guests at **Hotel Sheraton** should pay and get tickets stamped at the hotel to avoid paying again. The visitor centre includes a museum of local fauna and an auditorium for slide shows (available on request, minimum of eight people). It also sells a good guide book on Argentine birds. Food and drinks are available in the park but are expensive, so it is best to take your own. There is a **Telecom** kiosk at the bus stop.

A free train service leaves every 20 minutes from the visitor centre, departing for the start of two sets of walkways, both taking about an hour. The 'Circuito Inferior' or **Lower Trail**, leads down very steep steps to the lower falls and the start of the boat trip to Isla San Martín (see below). The easy 'Circuito Superior', **Upper Trail**, follows the top of the falls, giving panoramic views. The **Sendero Verde** path, taking about 20 minutes from near the visitor centre, leads to the start of the Upper and Lower trails. A second train route takes visitors to the start of an easy walkway that leads just over 1 km to the **Garganta del Diablo** (Devil's Throat). A visit here is particularly recommended in the evening when the light is best and the swifts are returning to roost on the cliffs, some behind the water.

Below the falls, a free ferry leaves regularly, subject to demand, and connects the Lower Trail with **Isla San Martín**. A steep path on the island leads to the top of the hill, where there are trails to some of the less-visited falls and rocky pools (take bathing gear in summer).

Activities and tours A number of activities are offered, both from the visitor centre and through agencies in Puerto Iguazú (Argentina), see page 344. On clear nights the moon casts a blue halo over the falls. During the full moon, there are sometimes night-time walking tours between the **Hotel Sheraton** and the falls (or from the **Hotel Tropical das Cataratas** on the Brazilian side, see page 339). Mountain bikes and boats can also be hired at US$3 per hour. For serious birdwatching and nature walks with an English-speaking guide, contact the **Pantanal Bird Club**, page 768.

Foz do Iguaçu and around ⊙●●⊙⊙▲⊙● » pp336-348. Colour map 5, A2.

→ *Phone code: 045. Population: 260,000.*

The proximity of the falls have made Foz the third most visited town in Brazil. It has no attractions of its own but is only 28 km from the falls and although there are some upmarket hotel options, the town has a greater range of cheap accommodation and restaurants.

From the town it is possible to visit a number of beaches on the shores of **Lake Itaipu** (see Itaipu Dam, page 334); the closest are at **Bairro de Três Lagoas** (Km 723 on BR-277), and in the municipality of **Santa Terezinha do Itaipu** (US$2.50), 34 km from Foz. The leisure parks have grassy areas with kiosks, barbecue sites and offer fishing as well as bathing. It is also possible to take boat trips on the lake.

The bird park, **Parque das Aves** ⓘ *Rodovia das Cataratas Km 16, US$10,* is well worth visiting. It contains rare South American (and foreign) birds including various currasows, guans, parrots, macaws and toucans. These are housed in large aviaries through which you can walk, with the birds flying and hopping around you. There is also a butterfly house. The bird park is within walking distance of the **Hotel San Martín**. The IYHA Paudimar Falls Hostel (see Sleeping, page 340) offers a discount for its guests. The national park bus stops here, 100 m before the entrance to the falls.

Ins and outs

Getting there Foz do Iguaçu's **Aeroporto Internacional de Cataratas** ① *Rodovia BR-469, Km16.5, T045-3521 4200*, is 12 km from the town centre and receives flights from, Belém, Brasília, Curitiba, Macapá, Manaus, Rio de Janeiro and São Paulo. The airport has a **Banco do Brasil**, a **Bradesco** and a *câmbio*, car rental offices, a tourist office and an official taxi stand. Taxis cost US$18 to the town centre (US$20 from town to airport). **Transbalan** (Aeroporto/ Parque Nacional) buses run to town, US$1 but don't permit large amounts of luggage (backpacks okay); they run every 20 minutes 0700-1900 and every hour 1900-2200. Many hotels run minibus services for a small charge. From the airport buses run to

③ Foz do Iguaçu

➡ Iguaçu Falls maps
1 Iguaçu Falls orientation, page 328
2 Iguaçu Falls, page 330
3 Foz do Iguaçu, page 333

Sleeping
Athenas 1
Baviera 2
Foz do Iguaçu 4
Foz Plaza 14
Foz Presidente 8
Foz Presidente II 5
IYHA Paudimar Falls Hostel 13
Luz 6
Mercure Grand Internacional Foz 12
Pousada da Laura 7
Pousada Evelina Navarrete 15
Rafain Centro 9
San Remo 11
Suiça 3
Tarobá 10

Eating
Atos 13
Bier Garten 1
Bufalo Branco 3
Cabeça de Boi 12
Café Laurent 14
City Caffé 4
Marias e Maria 5
Oficina do Sorvete 6
Rafain 2
Tropicana 11
Ver o Verde 15
Zaragoza 7

Bars & clubs
Alquimia 17
Armazém 8
BR3 9
Capitão 10
Oba! Oba! 16

Border essentials: Brazil–Argentina

Foz do Iguaçu (Brazil)–Puerto Iguazú (Argentina)

It takes about two hours to get from Foz to the Argentine falls, very tiring when the weather is hot. From October to February Brazil is one hour ahead of Argentina.

Immigration If entering Argentina only for the day, there is no need to obtain a Brazilan exit stamp but you must visit Argentine immigration, so take your passport. The city bus between Foz do Iguaçu and Puerto Iguazú therefore only stops and waits at the Argentine border post, not the Brazilian one. If you are crossing from one country to the other for an extended period and need stamps from both, then you can ask the bus driver for a 'transfer' so that you can get off at the Brazilian border post and get on the next bus without paying again. There are money exchange facilities beside the Argentine immigration.

Transport Buses marked 'Puerto Iguazú' run every 20 minutes from the Terminal Urbana in Foz do Iguaçu, crossing the frontier bridge; 30 minutes' journey (three companies, US$2.50). To get to the Argentine side of the falls without going into Puerto Iguazú, get off the bus from the frontier bridge at the first traffic lights and cross the road for the bus to the falls. Taxis run from Foz do Iguaçu to the border, waiting at immigration, US$10; US$45 to Hotel Sheraton Iguazú.

Note Be sure you know when the last bus departs from Puerto Iguazú for Foz (usually 1900); last bus from Foz 1950. If visiting the Brazilian side for a day, get off the bus at the Hotel Bourbon, cross the road and catch the bus to the falls, rather than going into Foz and out again. Combined tickets to Puerto Iguazú and the falls cost more than paying separately.

cities throughout southeastern Brazil and to Asunción in Paraguay. The rest of Argentina can easily be reached from Puerto Iguazú just across the border.

The **Foz do Iguaçu Rodoviária** ① *Av Costa e Silva, 4 km from centre on road to Curitiba, T045-3522 3633*, receives long-distance buses. There is a tourist office, **Cetreme** desk for tourists who have lost their documents, *guarda municipal* (police) and luggage store. Buses to the centre cost US$1. Buy onward tickets on arrival if possible as seats get booked up well in advance. There is also a local bus station, **Terminal Urbana**, in the centre of town.

Tourist information The **Secretaria Municipal de Turismo** ① *Praça Getulio Vargas 69, Centro, T045-3521 1461, www.fozdoiguacu.pr.gov.br, daily 0700-2300*, is very helpful, as is the 24-hour **tourist helpline** ① *T045-3521 1125*. There are tourist booths at the *rodoviária*, T045-3522 1027, daily 0700-1900 and airport, T045-3521 4276 open for all arriving flights, with a free map and bus information. *Triplice Fronteira* is a local newspaper with street plans and tourist information. Avenida Juscelino Kubitschek and the streets south of it, towards the river, once had a reputation for being unsafe at night but the situation is improving.

Itaipu Dam → *Colour map 5, A2.*
① *Visitor centre, T045-3520 6999, www.itaipu.gov.br, tours are free but in groups only; 6 tours daily Mon-Sat, the first at 0800, the last at 1500; 'technical' visits can also be arranged. Buses marked 'Usina Itaipu' run from Foz do Iguaçu's Terminal Urbana, US1.50.*
The Itaipu Dam, on the Río Paraná, is the site of the largest single power hydroelectric power station in the world built jointly by Brazil and Paraguay. Construction of this

massive scheme began in 1975 and it came into operation in 1984. The main dam is 8 km long, creating a lake that covers 1400 sq km. The height of the main dam is equivalent to a 65-storey building, the amount of concrete used in its construction is 15 times more than that used for the Channel Tunnel between England and France. The Paraguayan side may be visited from Ciudad del Este. Both governments are proud to trumpet the accolade, 'one of the seven wonders of the modern world' (the only one in South America), which was given to it by the American Society of Civil Engineering in *Popular Mechanics* in 1995. Whatever your views on the need for huge hydroelectric projects, it is worth visiting Itaipu to gain a greater understanding of the scale and impact of such constructions.

The **Ecomuseu de Itaipu** ① *Av Tancredo Neves, Km 11, T045-520 5813, Tue-Sat 0900-1100, 1400-1700, Mon 1400-1700*, and **Iguaçu Environmental Education Centre** ① *free with guide, recommended*, are geared to inform about the preservation of the local culture and environment, or that part of it which isn't underwater. A massive reforestation project is underway, and over 14 million seedlings have already been planted. Six biological refuges have been created on the lakeshore.

If it's sunny go in the morning as the sun is behind the dam in the afternoon and you will get poor photographs. The visitor centre has a short video presentation (ask for the English version) with stunning photography and amazing technical information. The spillways are capable of discharging the equivalent of 40 times the average flow of the Iguaçu Falls. If you are lucky, the spillways will be open. After the film and a brief visit to the souvenir shop where an English guidebook is available, a coach will take you to the dam itself. As it crosses the top, you get a stomach-churning view of the spillways and really begin to appreciate the scale of the project.

To get to Itaipu, the 'executive' bus and agency tours are an unnecessary expense. Buses No 110 or 120 from Terminal Urbana (stand 50 Batalhão) go every 13 minutes to the public relations office at the main entrance (US$0.40).

☽ *The dam's 18 turbines have an installed capacity of 12,600,000 kw and produce about 75 billion kwh a year, providing 80% of Paraguay's electricity and 25% of Brazil's.*

Ciudad del Este (Paraguay) ●🏦🏧🏨🏪 ≫ *pp336-348.*

→ *International phone code + 595. Phone code: 061. Population: 140,000.*

Described as the biggest shopping centre in Latin America, Ciudad del Este attracts Brazilian and Argentine visitors in search of bargain prices for electrical goods, watches, perfumes, etc. Founded as Ciudad Presidente Stroessner in 1957, the city grew rapidly during the construction of the Itaipú hydroelectric project. Dirty, noisy, unfriendly and brashly commercial, it is worth a visit just for the people-watching, but be careful with valuables and be particularly cautious after dark.

The Paraguayan side of the **Itaipú Hydroelectric Project** ① *Mon-Sat 0730-1200, 1330-1700, Sun and holidays 0800-1200, 1330-1630, free guided tours include a film show (in several languages) 45 mins before bus tours, check times in advance and take your passport*, can be visited. Buses run from Rodríguez y García, outside the terminal, to the visitor centre. On the way to Itaipú is **Flora y Fauna Itaipú Binacional** ① *0830-1030, 1330-1630*, with animals and plants rescued from the area when the dam was built. It is about 2 km from the visitor centre on the road back to Ciudad del Este.

Cascada de Monday (Monday Falls), where the Río Monday drops into the Paraná Gorge 10 km south of Ciudad del Este, is a worthwhile trip; there is good fishing below the falls. Return fare by taxi US$20.

Border essentials: Brazil–Paraguay

Foz do Iguaçu (Brazil)–Ciudad del Este (Paraguay)

The Ponte de Amizade/Puente de Amistad (Friendship Bridge) over the Río Paraná, 6 km north of Foz, leads straight into the heart of Ciudad del Este. It's also possible to cross by ferry. Note that Paraguay is one hour behind Brazil.

Transport Buses marked 'Cidade-Ponte' leave from the Terminal Urbana in Foz do Iguaçu, to the Ponte de Amizade, US$0.75. There is an hourly passenger ferry service from Porto de Lanchas and Porto Guaíra to Salto del Guayra on the Paraguayan side, US$0.50, and an hourly car ferry from Porto Guaíra (US$4 for car with two people). The car ferry runs until 1830 (Brazilian time). For transport from Ciudad del Este, see page 347.

Immigration Paraguayan and Brazilian immigration formalities (open until 1700) are dealt with at opposite ends of the bridge. A large new customs complex has been built at the Brazilian end of the bridge. The area is intensively patrolled for contraband and stolen cars; ensure that all documentation is in order.

Guaíra (Brazil)–Saltos del Guairá (Paraguay)

Another crossing to Paraguay is at Guairá, at the northern end of the Itaipu lake. It is five hours north of Iguaçu by road and can be reached by bus from Campo Grande and São Paulo. Ferries cross to Saltos del Guairá on the Paraguayan side.

Paraná listings

For Sleeping and Eating price codes and other relevant information, see pages 42-47.

Sleeping

Curitiba *p318, map p320*
General information can be found on the websites: www.ondehospedar.com.br/pr/curitiba.php and www.cmoraes.com.br/webhotelshtml/curitiba.shtml. There are good hotels southeast of the centre in the vicinity of the *rodoferroviária*, but the cheaper ones are seedy and close to the wholesale market, which operates noisily throughout the night.

LL Bourbon & Tower, R Cândido Lopes 102, T041-3322 4600, www.bourbon.com.br. One of the better modern hotels in the centre with a mock old-fashioned charm engendered by wood panelling and fake period furniture. Rooms have jacuzzis. Business facilities.

AL-A Deville Rayon, R Visconde de Nacar 1424, T041-2108 1100, www.deville.com.br.

Central, refurbished in 2008, a good option for business travellers. All the expected services including pool, saunas, well-equipped gym and travel agency. Good online promotions.

A Mercure Curitiba Centro, R Emiliano Perneta 747, T041-3234 1212, www.mercure.com.br. Standard business hotel in the centre with large rooms – most with separate living area, a pool and business centre.

A-B Del Rey, R Ermelino de Leão 18, T/F041-2106 0099, www.hoteldelrey.com.br. Central, upmarket yet relaxed, refurbished, large rooms and suites, a good restaurant and gym. Good-value online rates.

A-B Deville Express, R Amintas de Barros 73, T041-3322 8558, www.deville.com.br. In the city centre with a bar, small modest restaurant. All rooms a/c with fridge.

A-B Slaviero Palace, R Sen Alencar Guimarães 50, T041-3017 1000, T0800-3704 3311, www.hotelslaviero.com.br. The best of the 2nd-grade business hotels in the centre. Anonymously decorated but with a business centre and airport transfer.

B Slaviero Braz, Av Luís Xavier 67, T041-3017 1000, www.hotelslaviero.com.br. Refurbished hotel in a 1940s building preserved as 'Patrimonio Histórico'. Large rooms, handsome public areas and business facilities.

C-D Kings, Av Silva Jardim 264, T041-3022 8444, www.kingshotel.com.br. Modern, secure and well-maintained apartment hotel with very attractive monthly rates.

C-D Lumini, R Gen Carneiro, T041-3264 5244, www.hotellumini.com.br. Good a/c apartment hotel in a quiet street.

C-D Parati, R Riachuelo 30, T041-3223 1355, www.hotelparati.com.br. Well-maintained flats with kitchenettes in an anonymous 1980s block next to the Federal University of Paraná, near the centre. Breakfast included.

D Nova Lisboa, Av 7 de Setembro 1948, T041-3264 1944, www.pandalocacoes.com/novalisboa. A very simple small hotel near the rodoviária, housed in an ugly concrete building above a shop. Price includes breakfast, cheaper without.

D Tourist Universo, Praça Gen Osório 63, T041-3322 0099. On one of the city's most attractive squares, in centre. Very smart for price, sauna and pool. Intimate, excellent value.

D-F IYHA Curitiba Eco-hostel, R Luiz Tramontin 1693, Campo Comprido, T041-3029 1693, www.curitibaecohostel.com.br. A new hostel with all services. Situated in the Tramontina borough and set in attractive gardens with their own sports facilities. The lowest rates are per person.

D-F IYHA Hostel Roma, R Barão do Rio Branco 805, T041-3224 2117 or T041-3322 2838, www.hostelroma.com.br. Smart hostel with 110 beds in single-sex dorms. All have private bathrooms. TV room, fax, internet and a member's kitchen. Breakfast included. The lowest rates are per person.

Camping

Camping Clube do Brasil, BR-116, Km 84, 16 km in the direction of São Paulo, T041-3358 6634.

Morretes, Antonina and around p323

For information see www.morretes.com.br.

LL-A Santuário Nhundiaquara, www.nhundiaquara.com. A range of chalets set around a tinkling stream in 400 ha of private rainforest under the Pico do Marumbi. They range from super-luxurious mock-Alpine malocas with plunging roofs to simpler rooms in annexes. Kids are welcome and there's a lovely, if chilly, spring-water swimming pool.

A-B Pousada Graciosa, Estrada da Graciosa Km 8 (Porto da Cima village), T041-3462 1807, www.pousadagraciosa.com. Simple but comfortable wooden chalets set in rainforest some 10 km north of Morretes. Very peaceful and green but no children under 12.

C Pousada Cidreira, R Romulo Pereira 61, T041-3462 1604, www.morretes.com.br/pousadacidreira. Centrally located with characterless but clean rooms, most with balconies and all with TV and en suites. Some rooms have space for 3. Breakfast included.

C-D Atlante, Praça Coronel Macedo 266, 14 km from Morretes in Antonina. Large, frowsty rooms in a converted colonial mansion house in the town centre, all fan-cooled or a/c and with terraces. Good breakfasts.

C-D Hotel Nhundiaquara, R General Carneiro 13, Morretes, T041-3462 1228, www.nundia quara.com.br. A smart whitewashed building beautifully set on the river whose exterior appearance and excellent restaurant belie the hotel's small, plain but recently painted rooms. With breakfast.

Paranaguá p323

For information see www.paranagua.pr.gov.br.

AL Hotel Camboa, R João Estevão (Ponta do Caju), T041-3423 2121, www.hotel camboa.com.br. Family resort with tennis courts, large pool, saunas, trampolines, restaurant and a/c rooms. Out of town near the port. Book ahead.

AL São Rafael, R Julia Costa 185, T041-3423 2123, www.sanrafaelhotel.com.br. Business hotel with plain tiled rooms, a business centre, restaurants, pool and jacuzzis in the en suites.

D Hotel Ponderosa, R Pricilenco Corea 68 at 15 Novembro, a block east and north of the boat dock, T041-3423 2464. Tiled rooms with en suites, some rooms have a sea view.

D Pousada Itibere, R Princesa Isabel 24, 3 blocks east of the boat dock, T041-3423 2485. Very smart spartan rooms with polished wood floors, some with sea views. Friendly service from the Portuguese owner.

Camping
Arco Iris, Praia de Leste, on the beach, 29 km south of Paranaguá, T041-3458 2001.

Excursions from Paranaguá p324
There are 4 campsites and a few other cheap *pousadas* in Matinhos.
B Praia e Sol, R União 35, Matinhos, T041-3452 1922. Recommended *pousada*.

Ilha do Mel p325, map p325
For information see www.ilhadomel online.com or www.pousadasilhadomel. com.br. All rooms are fan-cooled unless otherwise stated.

You can rent a fisherman's house on Encantadas – ask for **Valentim's Bar**, or for Luchiano. Behind the bar is **Cabanas Dona Maria**, shared showers, cold water; food available if you ask in advance. Many *pousadas* and houses with rooms to rent (shared kitchen and living room). Shop around, prices from about US$10 double, low season, mid-week.

A-B Enseada das Conchas, Farol, T/F041-3426 8040, www.pousadaenseada.com.br. With 4 individual theme decorated rooms with associated colours: Amanhecer (morning) in light gold, *Mata Atlântica* (Atlantic rainforest) in green, Azul do Mar (sea blue) and Luz do Sol (sunlight) in burnished orange. Set in a lush garden overlooking the sea. Lots of rescued cats. Great breakfast.

B Long Beach, Praia Grande, T041-3426 8116, www.lbeach.cjb.net. The best on this beach with comfortable chalets for up to 6 with en suites. Very popular with surfers. Book in advance.

B-C Caraguata, Encantadas, T041-3426 9097 or T041-9998 7770, www.caraguata-ilhadomel.com.br. A/c en suites in wood with fridge and Monet prints on walls. Very close to the jetty.

C Dona Quinota, Fortaleza, T041-3423 6176. 3 km from Nova Brasília, right on the beach. Little blue-and-cream cottages with polished wood floors and en suites. Price includes breakfast and supper. **Dona Clara** next door is very similar in yellow instead of blue.

C Por do Sol, Nova Brasília, T041-3426 8009, www.pousadapordosol.com.br. Simple but elegant en suite rooms in grey tile and wood around a garden shaded by sombrero trees. A large deck with hammock-strewn *cabañas* sits next to the beach. Includes breakfast.

C-D Aconchego, Nova Brasília, T041-3426 8030, www.cwb.matrix.com.br/daconchego/. 10 scrupulously clean rooms in a house behind an expansive beachside deck strewn with hammocks. Public TV and breakfast areas. Charming. Includes breakfast.

C-D Girassol, T041-3426 8006, www.ilha domelgirassol.com.br. Wooden rooms with en suites in a little bougainvillea and fruit tree garden. Very close to jetty. Includes breakfast.

D Plancton, Farol at Fora, T/F041-3426 8061, www.pousadaplancton.com.br. A range of wooden buildings in a hummingbird filled garden. Rooms for 5 split over 2 levels. Wood and slate-tiled en suites. Clean, fresh. Italian food available in high season.

D Recanto da Fortaleza, Ponta do Bicho, T041-3275 4455, www.ilhadomel pousada.com.br. The best of the 2 next to the fort. Basic cabins with en suites and tiled floors. Free pick-up by boat from Nova Brasília (ring ahead), bike rental. Price includes breakfast and dinner.

D Recanto do Frances, Encantadas, T041-3426 9105, www.recantodofrances.com.br. 5 mins from Prainha or Encantadas. French-owned and full of character, with each chalet built in a different style to represent

a different French city. Good crêpe restaurant. With a sister *pousada* nearby
D Ronaldo's, Encantadas, T041-3426 9019. Simple rooms with private bathrooms. Friendly owner.
D-E D'Lua, Farol, T041-3426 8031. Basic and surfer-hippy with a very friendly new-age owner, Jo.
D-E Farol da Ilha, Nova Brasília, T041-3426 8017. Plain wood and terracotta-tiled dorms and double rooms in a garden. Surfboards for rent. Price includes generous breakfast.
D-E IYHA Hostel Zorro, Encantadas, T041-3426 9052, www.hostelzorro.com.br. A party hostel overlooking the beach. Small but clean wooden rooms and dorms, and all the usual facilities.
D-E Trilha do Sol, Farol, T041-3426 8025. Simple wooden rooms with en suites.

Camping

There are mini campsites with facilities at **Encantadas**, **Farol** and **Brasília**. Camping is possible on the more deserted beaches (good for surfing). If camping, watch for the tide, watch possessions and beware of the *bicho de pé*, which burrows into feet (remove with a needle and alcohol) and the *borrachudos* (discourage with **Autan** repellent).

Iguaçu Falls *p327, map p328 and p330*
Brazil

The best hotels with the most modern facilities and the easiest access to Iguaçu are all near the falls. There is little here for budget travellers. Sleeping in your car inside the park is prohibited. You can camp at the **Paudimar IYHA**, but it's pretty cold and damp in winter.
LL Hotel Tropical das Cataratas, directly overlooking the falls, 28 km from Foz, T045-3521 7000, www.hoteldascataratas.com.br. The only hotel within the park on the Brazilian side is a mock-belle époque building with slightly frayed rooms, grand public areas and a poolside garden visited by numerous birds, butterflies and, at dawn, small mammals. The hotel is right next to the falls offering by far the easiest access and the best chance to beat the crowds. The food is adequate, as good as any in town, but hardly dazzling. Non-resident evening diners will be in the park after it closes and must take a taxi back to town.
C-F Hostel Natura, Rodovia das Cataratas Km 12.5, Remanso Grande, T045-3529 6949, www.hostelnatura.com (near the Paudimar). Rustic hostel with a small pool set in fields pocked with large ponds and on the road to the park. Public areas include a pool table, TV lounge and a small kitchen. Rooms are fan-cooled and the hostel can arrange visits to the falls. Their website has detailed instructions for how to reach them including bus times and a map.
C-F IYHA Paudimar Campestre, Rodovia das Cataratas Km 12.5, Remanso Grande, near airport, T045-3529 6061, www.paudimar.com.br. Youth hostel with spotless single-sex dorms, pool, communal kitchen, football pitch, camping. The gardens are visited by birds and small mammals. From the airport or town take the Parque Nacional bus (0525-0040) and alight at the Remanso Grande bus stop, by **Hotel San Juan**, then take the free shuttle bus (0700-1900) to the hostel, or walk the 1200 m from the main road. Breakfast included. Tours arranged. There's a **Paudimar** desk at the *rodoviária*. Only IYHA members in high season when the hostel gets very busy. Low prices are per person.

Argentina

Camping is possible at **Camping Puerto Canoas**, 600 m from Puerto Canoas, with tables, but no other facilities, the nearest drinking water is at the park entrance.
AL Sheraton Internacional Iguazú Resort, Parque Nacional Iguazú, www.starwood.com. A 1970s wedge of concrete built on the opposite side of the falls from the **Hotel das Cataratas**. Views are spectacular, especially out over the pool from the room balconies on the upper storey. But the falls are a 20-min walk from the hotel. Well maintained, well run. Babysitting service available.

Foz do Iguaçu *p332, map p333*

Many hotels offer excursions to the falls. In a bid to get their commission, touts may tell you the hotel of your choice no longer exists, or offer you room rates below what is actually charged. In high season (eg Christmas-New Year) you will not find a room under US$15, but in low season there are many good deals.

LL-L Mercure Grand Internacional Foz, R Alm Barroso 2006, T045-3521 4100, www.internacionalfoz.com.br. The only 5-star hotel in the region with excellent business and conference facilities. Spacious but very standard upmarket hotel rooms and services. Recently refurbished after being taken over by the **Mercure/Accor** group.

AL-A Rafain Centro, Mcal Deodoro 984, T/F045-3523 1213, www.rafaincentro.com.br. The smart and upmarket communal areas and attractive pool area belie the rather well-worn rooms.

B Baviera, Av Jorge Schimmelpfeng 697, T045-3523 5995, www.hotelbavieraiguassu. com.br. A mock-Bavarian folly with a chalet-style exterior. On the main road, central for bars and restaurants. The rooms look as if they haven't been renovated since the 1980s.

B Foz do Iguaçu, Av Brasil 97, T045-3523 4455, www.hotelfozdoiguacu.com.br. Another vast and gloomy 1970s hotel with faded rooms. With large breakfasts included in the price.

B Foz Plaza Hotel, R Marechal Deodoro 1819, T/F045-3521 5500, www.fozplaza.com.br Serene and well-refurbished 1980s hotel with a restaurant and a bar, swimming pool, fitness centre, sauna and a games room.

B Foz Presidente, R Xavier da Silva 1000, T/F045-3572 4450, www.fozpresidente hoteis.com.br. Restaurant, pool, with breakfast, convenient for buses. Brighter and more modern than most of Foz's offerings. Recommended.

B Foz Presidente II, R Mcal Floriano Peixoto 1851, T045-3523 2318, www.fozpresidente hoteis.com.br. Smaller and a little more expensive than its sister hotel (with whom it shares leisure areas), but also with pool, bar and restaurant.

B Suíça, Av Felipe Wandscheer 3580, T045-3525 3232, www.hotelsuica.com.br. Old 1970s hotel with rather dark tile-floor rooms and a pool. Helpful Swiss manager. The extensive facilities include a fitness centre, gym, play area for kids and several pools.

C Luz, Av Costa e Silva Km 5, near *rodoviária*, T045-3522 3535, www.luzhotel.com.br. Well-kept but bog standard small 1980s hotel with a buffet restaurant. Rooms have a/c and Brazilian TV. Recommended.

C-D Pousada Evelina Navarrete, R Irlan Kalichewski 171, Vila Yolanda, T/F045-3574 3817, www.pousada evelina.com.br. Lots of tourist information, internet, well-maintained dorms, doubles and singles (some with a/c) and good breakfast. English, French, Italian, Polish and Spanish spoken. Helpful staff with lots of useful tourist information and organized walks. The *pousada* is near Av Cataratas on the way to the falls; take a bus to Parque Nacional from the bus station and ask to be let off after 3.5 km, near the **Chemin** supermarket. R Irlan Kalichewski is down the hill, 3 blocks towards the city on the left. Warmly recommended.

C-D Tarobá, R Tarobá 1048, T045-3523 9722, www.hoteltaroba.com.br. Good value. Clean with plain-tiled a/c rooms, a tiny indoor pool and helpful staff. Recommended.

D-F IYHA Paudimar Falls Hostel, R Antônio Raposo 820, T045-3028 5503, www.paudimarfalls.com.br. Despite its name, the companion hostel to the **Paudimar** near the falls, is in the centre of town. It has similar facilities, with doubles, cramped dorms, pool and the usual hostel services.

D-F Pousada da Laura, R Naipi 671, T045-3572 3374. Secure and run by the enthusiastic Laura who speaks some Spanish, English, Italian and French.

The hostel has a kitchen, laundry facilities and en suites and is a good place to meet other travellers. Good breakfast.

E Athenas, R Almte Barroso 2215 on corner of Rebouças, T045-3574 2563. Good value, special rates for backpackers, some rooms with shared bath, fan, breakfast extra, beers sold.

E San Remo, R Xavier da Silva 563 at Taroba, T045-3523 1619, roberto_171@hotmail.com. Scrupulously clean though small rooms with TVs and writing desks. All-you-can-eat breakfast. English, Spanish and Hebrew spoken. In-house travel agency.

Camping

E Pousada Internacional, R Manencio Martins 21, Vila Yolanda, T045-3529 8183, www.campinginternacional.com.br. US$10 per person (half price with International Camping Card), pool, clean basic cabins. Park vehicle or put tent away from trees in winter in case of heavy rainstorms. The food here is poor and the refectory closes at 2300.

Ciudad del Este (Paraguay) p335
The international dialling code for Paraguay is +595. Accommodation is generally expensive.

A Convair, Adrián Jara y García, T061-500342. Comfortable business-style hotel with cheaper rooms without bath.

B Panorama Inn, Pampliega at Eusebio Alaya, T061-500110. A modern, corporate hotel with anonymous hotel catalogue rooms, breakfast and reasonable service.

C Munich, Fernández y Miranda, T061-500347. Standard town block with a/c rooms, parking and breakfast.

D Austria (also known as **Viena**), Fernández 165, above restaurant, T061-500883. With good breakfast and a/c, Austrian family, views from upper floors. Warmly recommended.

E Caribe, Emiliano Fernández, facing Austria. A/c rooms with hot-water showers set in a nice garden, helpful owner. Recommended.

Eating

Curitiba p318, map p320

Hot sweet wine is sold on the streets in winter to help keep out the cold. There are a couple of *lanchonetes* in the market which is close to the *rodoferroviária*. Also good meals in the bus station.

Boulevard, R Vol da Pátria 539 (centre), T041-3224 8244. Closed on Sun. The city's most celebrated restaurant serving a mix of French, Italian and Brazilian cooking to a smart crowd. Reasonable wine list.

Baviera, Alameda Augusto Stellfeld, Av Dr Murici (centre), T041-3232 1995. Open 1830-0100. A Curitiba institution, established over 30 years and serving pizza in an intimate beer cellar setting. Delivery service.

Durski, R Jaime Reis, 254 (centre), T041-3225 7893. Good Eastern European food, including a locally celebrated and lavish banquet of pâtés, borcht, *platzki*, filled pasties and a variety of meat dishes.

Green Life, R Carlos de Carvalho 271 (centre), T041-3223 8490. Open for lunch only. Vegetarian buffet restaurant.

Happy Rango, Av Visconde de Nacar 1350, near R 24 Horas. Open 24 hrs. Brightly lit, basic corner joint selling fast food and pizzas.

Mister Sheik, Av Vicente Machado 534. Arabic fast food in pitta with salad, popular for deliveries. Recommended.

Saccy, R São Francisco 350, at Mateus Leme. Pizza, tapas and a popular bar with live music, see Bars and clubs, page 343.

Salmão, R Emiliano Perneta 924, T041-3225 2244. Open until 0100. Restaurant in historic house, delicious fish and pizza, often special promotions, live music every night. Short taxi ride from centre.

Morretes p323

Armazém Romanus, R Visc do Rio Branco 141, T041-3462 1500. Family-run restaurant with the best menu and wine list in the region. Dishes made from home-grown ingredients include excellent *barreado* and flambéed desserts.

Madalozo, R Alm Frederico de Oliveira 16, overlooking the river, T041-3462 1410. Good *barreado* and generous salads.
Terra Nossa, R XV Novembro 109, T041-3462 2174. *Barreado*, pasta pizzas and fish. Middle of the road but generous portions and a small wine list. From R$25 for a 2-person *prato da casa*.

Paranaguá *p323*
The choice here is poor.
Danúbio Azul, R XV Novembro 95, T041-3423 3255, www.restaurantedaxcnubioazul.com.br. The best in town with a range of fish and chicken dishes, pastas and pizzas; all in enormous quantities. 1 block back from the sea at the east end of town.
Divina Gula, R XV Novembro 165, T041-3422 2788. Open until 1400 only. Seafood buffet and *feijoada* at weekends. 3 blocks east of the Ilha do Mel dock.
Restaurant Rosa, R Praia 16, T041-3423 2162. Cheap but decent seafood, good risotto. A block west of the Ilha do Mel dock.

Ilha do Mel *p325, map p325*
Many *pousadas* also serve food, some only in season (Christmas to Carnaval). Many have live music or dancing (especially in high season). Things kick off after 2200.
Fim da trilha, Prainha (Fora de Encantadas), T041-3426 9017. Spanish seafood restaurant. One of the best on the island.
Colmeia, Farol, T041-3426 8029. Snacks, crêpes, good cakes and puddings.
Mar e Sol, Farol, T041-3426 8021, www.restaurantemaresol.com. Huge portions of fish and chicken, all with chips and rice. Also a small selection of more adventurous dishes like bass in shrimp sauce.
Recanto do Frances, Encantadas. French crêpes and Moroccan cous cous.
Toca do Abutre, Farol. Live music and the usual huge portions of fish or chicken with rice, beans and chips.
Zorro, Encantadas. One of several cheap fish, beans and rice restaurants on the seafront, shaded by palapas. *Forró* dancing at night.

Iguaçu Falls *p327, map p328 and p330*
Brazil
Tropical das Cataratas, the nearest dining to the falls themselves (see Sleeping).

Foz do Iguaçu *p332, map p333*
Bufalo Branco, R Rebouças 530, T045-3523 9744, superb all-you-can-eat *churrasco*, includes *filet mignon*, salad bar and dessert. Sophisticated surroundings and attentive service. Highly recommended.
Cabeça de Boi, Av Brasil 1325, T045-3523 2100. *Churrascaria* with live music and a buffet, coffee and pastries also.
Rafain, Av das Cataratas, Km 6.5, T045-3523 1177. Closed Sun. Set price for excellent buffet with folkloric music and dancing (2100-2300); touristy but very entertaining. Out of town, take a taxi or arrange with travel agency. Recommended.
Zaragoza, R Quintino Bocaiúva 882, T045-3574 3084. Large and upmarket, for Spanish dishes and seafood. Respectable wine list. Recommended.
Atos, Av Juscelino Kubitschek 865, T045-3572 2785. Lunch only. Per kilo buffet with various meats, salads, sushi and puddings.
Bier Garten, Almirante Barroso 550. Bustling pizzeria and *choperia*.
Tropicana, Av Juscelino Kubitschek 228. All-you-can-eat pizza or *churrascaria* with a salad bar, good value.
Café Laurent, Av Jorge Schimmelpfeng 550, T045-3574 6666. Smart student café serving decent tea, coffee, cakes and pies.
City Caffé, Av Jorge Schimmelpfeng 898. Stylish café open daily 0800-2330 for sandwiches, Arabic snacks and pastries.
Marias e Maria, Av Brasil 50. Good *confeitaria*.
Oficina do Sorvete, Av Jorge Schimmelpfeng 244. Daily 1100-0100. Excellent ice creams, a popular local hang-out.
Ver o Verde, R. Almirante Barroso 1713, T045-3574 5647. Lunch only. Buffet vegetarian food with some white meat and fish. Great value.

Ciudad del Este (Paraguay) *p335*
Most restaurants close on Sun. Cheaper restaurants can be found along García and in the market.

¶¶ **Coreio**, San Blas 125. Good Korean food.
¶¶ **Hotel Austria/Viena** (see Sleeping). Good Austrian food in large portions.
¶ **Mi Ranchero**, Adrián Jara. Good food, service and prices, well known.

🅞 Bars and clubs

Curitiba *p318, map p320*
A cluster of bars at the square of Largo da Ordem have tables and chairs on the pavement, music which tends to be rock, and bar food: **Fire Fox**, Av Jaime Reis 46, flanked by **Tuba's** and **The Farm**. **London Pub**, São Francisco 350, São Francisco. Recommended. **R 24 Horas** is an indoor street with very similar, functional bars and cafés, open 24 hrs.
Saccy, R São Franscisco, 350, corner with Mateus Leme, 12. Pizza, tapas and lively bar with live music.

Foz do Iguaçu *p332, map p333*
Most bars double as restaurants and are concentrated on Av Jorge Schimmelpfeng for 2 blocks from Av Brasil to R Mal Floriano Peixoto. Wed-Sun are best nights; the crowd tends to be young.
Alquimia, Av Jorge Schimmelpfeng 334, T045-3572 3154. Open 2400-0500. Popular nightclub, attached, US$3.
Armazém, R Edmundo de Barros 446, intimate and sophisticated, attracts discerning locals, good atmosphere, mellow live music, US$1 cover. Recommended.
BR3, Av Jorge Schimmelpfeng corner with Av Brasil. Open until 2400. Modern.
Capitão Bar, Av Jorge Schimmelpfeng 288 and Almte Barroso, T045-3572 1512. Large, loud and popular, nightclub attached.
Oba! Oba!, Av das Cataratas 3700, T045-3574 2255 (Antigo Castelinho).

Live samba show Mon-Sat 2315-0015. Very popular, US$9 for show and includes 1 drink.
Rafain, Av das Cataratas Km 6.5. With floor show and food, see page 342.

🅔 Entertainment

Curitiba *p318, map p320*
Best to look in the newspaper for music and what's on in the bars, clubs and theatres. *Gazeta do Povo* has an arts and what's on section called *Caderno G*.

Cinema
Tickets are usually US$4-5 Mon-Thu, US$6-8 at weekends. There are cinemas at: **Shopping Center Água Verde**, T041-3242 8741; **Shopping Crystal**, R Comendador Araújo 731, T041-3323 3061; **Shopping Curitiba**, Praça Oswaldo Cruz 2698, T041-3326 1412; **Shopping Novo Batel**, T041-3222 2107.

Foz do Iguaçu *p332, map p333*
Casinos
Organized tours to casinos (illegal in Brazil) over the border in Paraguay and Argentina take 3 hrs.
Casino Iguazú, Ruta 12 Km, 1640, Puerto Iguazú (Argentina), T3757-498000. Weekdays 1800-0500, 24 hrs weekends. Restaurant on site.

Cinema
Boulevard, Av das Cataratas 1118, T045-523 4245. Large complex open from 1700 and all day Sun. Also bowling, games rooms and bingo.

🅕 Festivals and events

Curitiba *p318, map p320*
Feb Ash Wed (half-day).
Mar/Apr Maundy Thu (half-day).
8 Sep Our Lady of Light.

○ Shopping

Curitiba *p318, map p320*
Curitiba is also good for clothes and shoes.

Bookshop O Livro Técnico, Shopping Itália, R João Negrão and Mcal Deodoro.
Jewellers H Stern jewellers at Mueller Shopping Centre.

Souvenirs and handicrafts
Feira de Arte e Artesanato, Praça Garibáldi, Sun 0900-1400. Lojas de Artesanato, Casa de Artesanato Centro, R Mateus Leme 22, T041-3352 4021. Lojas de Artesanato 'Feito Aquí', Dr Muricy 950, international airport and Shopping Mueller. Try Lojas Leve Curitiba, at several locations, R 24 Horas, Afonso Pena airport, Ópera de Arame, Jardim Botânico, Memorial de Curitiba. There is also an art market at Praça Rui Barbosa.

Foz do Iguaçu *p332, map p333*
Av Brasil is the main shopping street.
Bookshop Kunda Livraria Universitária, R Almte Barroso 1473, T045-3523 4606. Guides and maps of the area, books on the local wildlife, novels, etc in several languages, including French and English.

Souvenirs and handicrafts Tres
Fronteiras, Rodovia das Cataratas, Km 11. Large shop on road to falls, frequent stop on tours. Chocolates, and huge selection of crafts and jewellery, some of it overpriced.

Ciudad del Este *p335*
Prices are decidedly high for North American and European visitors. The leather market is well worth a visit, be sure to bargain. Don't buy perfume at tempting prices on the street, it's only coloured water. Make sure that shops that package your goods pack what you actually bought. Also watch the exchange rates if you're a short-term visitor from Argentina or Brazil.

▲▲ Activities and tours

Curitiba *p318, map p320*
Tour operators
BMP Turismo (American Express), R Brig Franco 1845, T041-3224 7560.

Serra da Graciosa and Morretes
p321 and p323
Tour operators
Calango Expedições, Praça Rocha Pombo s/n, Estação Ferroviária, Morretes, T/F041-3462 2600, www.calangoexpedicoes.com.br.
Brazil Ecojourneys, Estrada Rozália Paulina Ferreira 1132, Armação, Florianópolis, T048-3389 5619, www.brazilecojourneys.com.

Parque Nacional Iguazú
(Argentina) *p331*
Tour operators
The following are based in Puerto Iguazú. Aventura Náutica is a journey by launch along the lower Río Iguazú, US$15. Safari Náutico, a 4-km journey by boat above the falls, US$15. Gran Aventura, an 8-km ride through the jungle, with commentary on the flora and fauna in English and Spanish, followed by a boat trip on the rapids to the Devil's Throat, US$33. This trip is longer and better value than the Macuco Safari on the Brazilian side. The full day combines Safari Náutico with Aventura Náutica, US$30 (5 hrs), or US$45 with Gran Aventura (7 hrs).

Foz do Iguaçu *p332, map p333*
Guides
Recommended guides include: Chiderly Batismo Pequeno, R Almte, Barroso 505, Foz, T045-3574 3367; Ruth Campo Silva, STTC Turismo, Hotel Bourbon, Rodovia das Cataratas, T045-3574 3849 (American Express); Wilson Engel, T045-3574 1367. Friendly, flexible.

Helicopter tours
Helicopter tours over the falls leave from the Hotel das Cataratas, US$60 per person, 10 mins. Booked through any travel agency

or direct with **Helisul**, T045-3523 1190. Apart from disturbing visitors, the helicopters are also reported to present a threat to some bird species which are laying thinner-shelled eggs. As a result, the altitude of the flights has been increased, making the flight less attractive.

Tour operators
Beware of touts at the bus terminal who often overcharge for tours (they have been known to charge double the bus station price) and airport and be sure that the park entrance fees of around US$15 and all the transfer fees are included in the price. There are many travel agents on Av Brasil and in larger hotels. Most do not accept credit cards.
Acquatur, Av das Cataratas 3175, T045-3523 9554, www.acquaturturismo.com.br. Offer full range of tours in executive cars with bilingual guides and airport transfers.
Jaha Iguassu, Av República Argentina 926, T045-3572 4158 www.jahaiguassu.bio.br. Backpacker-orientated tours, hotel bookings and connections through to Rio, the Pantanal and the Amazon.
Macuco Safari, T045-3523 6475, www.macucosafari.com.br. Boat and forest tours suitable for all ages. Make sure you bring a waterproof bag for your camera.

⊖ Transport

Curitiba *p318, map p320*
Air
Two types of bus run from the *rodoferroviária* to the airport, making several stops along the way: **Aeroporto Executivo**, daily 0500-2330, 20 mins, US$5; regular city bus, 40 mins, US$1.75. There are daily flights to **Rio de Janeiro** and **São Paulo**, and connections to **Fortaleza**, **Foz do Iguaçu**, **Florianópolis** (and cities in the interior of Paraná), the **Pantanal**, **Amazon**, **Mato Grosso**, as well as to **Argentina**, **Chile** and **Uruguay**.
Airline offices Gol, T0300-3789 2121, www.voegol.com.br. NHT, www.voe nht.com.br. Oceanair, T0300-3789 8160,

www.oceanair.com.br. **Passaredo** www.voe passaredo.com.br. **Pluna** www.fly pluna.com. **TAM**, R Ermelino Leão 511, T041-3219 1200, www.tam.com.br, also at airport, T041-3236 1812. **Trip**, at airport, T041-3381 1710. **Varig**, T041-4003 7000, www.varig.com.br, at airport, T041-3381 1607. **Webjet**, T0300-3210 1234, www.webjet.com.br.

Bus
See also Ins and outs, page 319. For detailed timetables of buses from Curitiba see www.rodoviariaonline.com.br.
Local There are several route types on the integrated transport system; pick up a map for full details. There are 25 transfer terminals along the exclusive busways and trunk routes, allowing integration between all the different routes. **Express** are red, often articulated, and connect the transfer terminals to the city centre, pre-paid access, they use the 'tubo' bus stops. **Feeder** are orange conventional buses that connect the terminals to the surrounding neighbourhoods. **Interdistrict** green conventional or articulated buses run on circular routes, connecting transfer terminals and city districts without passing through the centre. **Direct** or **speedy** silver grey buses use the 'tubo' stations (3 km apart on average), to link the main districts and connect the surrounding municipalities with Curitiba. **Conventional** yellow buses operate on the normal road network between the surrounding municipalities, the Integration Terminals and the city centre. **City circular** white minibuses, **Linha Turismo**, circle the major transport terminals and points of interest in the traditional city centre area. US$3.50 (multi-ticket booklets available), every 30 mins from 0900-1700, except on Mon. First leaves from R das Flores, narrow street in front of McDonald's. 3 stops allowed.
Long distance Frequent buses to **São Paulo** (6 hrs, US$40) and **Rio de Janeiro** (12 hrs, US$60). To **Foz do Iguaçu**, 10 a day, 10 hrs, US$50; **Porto Alegre**, 10 hrs, US$50; **Florianópolis**, every 2 hrs, 4½ hrs, US$35;

Serra Verde train timetable

For a description of the journey, see Curitiba to Paranaguá, below.
Curitiba–Paranaguá From Curitiba the train leaves daily at 0815, stopping at Marumby at 1035, Morretes at 1115 and arriving at Paranaguá at 1215. A litorina service runs at weekends, leaving Curitiba at 0915.
Paranaguá–Curitiba Monday to Friday from Morretes at 1500, stopping at Marumby at 1540 and Curitiba at 1800. At weekends the train runs from Paranaguá at 1400, stopping at Morretes at 1600, Marumby at 1640 and reaching Curitiba at 1900.

Blumenau, 4 hrs, US$25, 7 daily with Penha/ Catarinense; good service to most towns in Brazil. Pluma bus to **Buenos Aires** and to **Asunción**. TTL runs to **Montevideo**, 26 hrs, 0340 departure (*semi-cama*).

Car hire Interlocadora, at the airport, T041-381 1370. **Localiza**, at the airport and Av Cândido de Abreu 336, T041-3253 0330.

Ferry Ferries from R Gen Carneiro (R da Praia) in front of the tourist information kiosk run to **Ilha do Mel**, at 0930 and 1500 (1 hr 40 mins, US$4). Alternatively, go to the small harbour in Paranaguá and ask for a boat to Ilha do Mel, US$15 one-way (no shade). Make sure the ferry goes to your chosen destination (Nova Brasília or Encantadas are the most developed areas).

Train Passenger trains to **Paranaguá**, see below.

Curitiba to Paranaguá p321
Train For current train times see the box, above. There are 2 trains running on the line from Curitiba to **Morretes** and **Paranaguá**.
The **Litorina** is a modern a/c railcar with on-board service and bilingual staff, which stops at the viewpoint at the Santuário da Nossa Senhora do cadeado and Morretes. Hand luggage only. Tickets can be bought 2 days in advance and cost US$63 one-way to Morretes (3 hrs) and a further US$47.50 for the return leg to Curitiba. The ticket includes a drink and sandwich. The windows don't open and are scratched, so not ideal for photos.

The **Trem Classe Convencional**, runs daily to Morretes, with a stop at Marumbi on the mountain, and continues to Paranaguá at weekends only, buy tickets 2 days in advance, *turístico*, US$26.50 (US$18 back), *executivo* US$42 (US$27 back), an *econômico* fare (US$14/US$11) is available from the ticket office only, best about 2 weeks in advance. 4 hrs to Paranaguá.

Schedules change frequently; delays are to be expected. Check times in advance with **Serra Verde Express**, T041-3323 4007, www.serraverde express.com.br. Tickets sold at the *rodoferroviária*, Portão 8, 0700-1830 (till 1200 on Sun). Sit on the left-hand side on the way from Curitiba. On cloudy days there's little to see on the higher parts. The train is usually crowded on Sat and Sun. Many travellers recommend returning by bus (1½ hrs, buy ticket immediately on arrival, US$6.50), if you do not want to stay 4½ hrs. A tour bus meets the train and offers a tour of the town and return to Curitiba. Serra Verde Express also gives information about trips by car on the Estrada de Graciosa and sells various packages to the coast.

Morretes p323
Bus The Paranaguá–Antonina bus stops at Morretes, 11 daily: to **Paranaguá**, US$4, to **Antonina** US$5. 12 daily to **Curitiba** US$10.

Paranaguá p323
Bus All operated by Graciosa. To **Curitiba**, US$3, many 1½ hrs (only the 1500 to Curitiba takes the old Graciosa road); direct to **Rio** at 1915, 15 hrs, US$23. 8 buses a day to **Guaratuba** (US$1, 2 hrs), **Caiobá** and **Matinhos**. The buses to Guaratuba go on the ferry, as do direct buses to Joinville, 0740, 1545.

Car hire Interlocadora, T041-3423 4425.

Parque Nacional Vila Velha p324
Bus Take a bus from Curitiba to the national park, not to the town 20 km away. Ask the bus driver where you should get off. **Princesa dos Campos** bus from Curitiba at 0730 and 0930, 1½ hrs, US$5.65 (return bus passes park entrance at 1600); it may be advisable to go to **Ponta Grossa** and return to Curitiba from there. Last bus from Vila Velha car park to Ponta Grossa at 1800. Bus from Vila Velha at 1310, 1610 and 1800, US$1, 4.5 km to turn-off to Furnas (another 15-min walk) and Lagoa Dourada (it's not worth walking from Vila Velha to Furnas because it's mostly uphill along the main road).

Ilha do Mel p325, map p325
Ferry See Ins and outs, page 326. Boats run from Encatadas and Nova Brasília to **Paranaguá** and **Pontal do Paraná** (Pontal do Sul). The last bus from Pontal do Paraná to Paranaguá leaves at 2200.

Foz do Iguaçu p332, map p333
Air Daily flights to **Rio**, **São Paulo**, **Curitiba** and other Brazilian cities.
  Airline offices Rio Sul, R Jorge Sanways 779, T045-3574 1680, freephone T0800-992994. **TAM**, R Rio Branco 640, T045-3523 8500 (offers free transport to Ciudad del Este for its flights, all cross-border documentation dealt with). **Varig**, Av Juscelino Kubitschek 463, T045-3523 2111. **Vasp**, Av Brasil 845, T045-3523 2212.

Bus For transport to the falls and crossing into Argentina, see page 328 and box page 334.

To get to the long-distance bus station a few kilometres outside of town, take any bus that says '*rodoviária*'. To **Curitiba**, Pluma, Sulamericana, 9-10 hrs, 3 daily, paved road, US$15; to **Guaíra** via Cascavel only, 5 hrs, US$10; to **Florianópolis**, Catarinense and Reunidas, US$28, 14 hrs; Reunidas to **Porto Alegre**, US$30; to **São Paulo**, 16 hrs, Pluma US$30, *executivo* 6 a day, plus 1 *leito*; to **Rio** 22 hrs, several daily, US$38. To **Asunción**, Pluma, RYSA (direct at 1430), US$11.

To **Buenos Aires** (Argentina), there is a bus direct from Foz (Pluma daily 1200, US$46). It is cheaper to go to **Posadas** via Paraguay. To **Asunción** (Paraguay), Pluma (0700), RYSA (direct at 1430, 1830), from *rodoviária*, US$16.50 (cheaper if bought in Ciudad del Este).

Car hire Avis, airport, T045-3523 1510. Localiza at airport, T045-3529 6300, and Av Juscelino Kubitschek 2878, T045-3522 1608. Unidas, Av Santos Dumont, 1515, near airport, T/F045-3339 0880.

Taxi Only good value for short distances when you are carrying all your luggage.

Ciudad del Este (Paraguay) p335
Air To **Asunción**, Arpa, 3 flights Mon-Sat, 1 on Sun. Also **TAM** daily en route to São Paulo.
  Airline offices TAM, Edif SABA, Monseñor Rodríguez.

Bus The terminal is on the southern outskirts. Bus No 4 from the centre goes there, US$0.50 (taxi US$3.50). Many buses (US$17.50 *rápido*, 4½ hrs, at night only; US$10 *común*, 6 hrs) to and from **Asunción**. Nuestra Señora and Rysa are recommended. To **Encarnación** (for Posadas and Argentina), along a fully paved road, frequent, 3 hrs, US$7.50 (cheaper than via Foz do Iguaçu).
  To Brazil International bus from outside the terminal to the new long-distance terminal (*rodoviária*) outside Foz. Local buses from the terminal run along Av Adrián Jara and go to the city terminal (Terminal

Urbana) in **Foz** every 15 mins, 0600-2000, US$0.65. Most buses do not wait at immigration, so disembark to get your exit stamp; walk across the bridge (10 mins) and obtain your entry stamp; keep your ticket and continue to Foz on the next bus free. Paraguayan taxis cross freely to Brazil (US$20), but it is cheaper to walk across the bridge and then take a taxi, bargain hard. You can pay in either currency.

To Argentina Direct buses to **Puerto Iguazú**, frequent service by several companies from outside the terminal, US$2, you need to get Argentine and Paraguayan stamps (not Brazilian); the bus does not wait so keep your ticket for the next bus.

Directory

Curitiba *p318, map p320*
Banks Bradesco, R 15 de Novembro, Visa ATM. Plus or Cirrus-associated credit cards can be used at Citibank, R Mcal Deodoro 711, or at Buenos Aires 305 near Shopping Curitiba. **Credicard**, R Saldanha Marinho 1439, Bigorrillo. Cash with MasterCard. **Diplomata**, R Pres Faria 145 in the arcade. **Transoceânica**, R Mcal Deodoro 532, English and German spoken. **Triangle Turismo Travel**, Praça Gen Osório 213. Cash and TCs.

Morretes *p323*
Banks Banco do Brasil, does not officially change money, but friendly staff will sometimes do so. It has an ATM.

Paranaguá *p323*
Banks Banco do Brasil, Largo C Alcindino 27. **Bradesco**, R Faria Sobrinho 188. **Câmbio**, R Faria Sobrinho. For cash.

Foz do Iguaçu *p332, map p333*
Banks There are plenty of banks and travel agents on Av Brasil. Banco do Brasil, Av Brasil 1377 has ATM. High commission for TCs. **Bradesco**, Av Brasil 1202. Visa ATMs. **Banco 24 Horas** at Oklahoma petrol station, Visa ATMs.

HSBC, Av Brasil 1151, ATM. **Embassies and consulates** Argentina, Travessa Eduardo Bianchi 26, T045-3574 2969 (Mon-Fri 1000-1430). **France**, R Federico Engels 48, Villa Yolanda T045-3574 3693. **Paraguay**, Bartolomeu de Gusmão 480, T045-3523 2898. **Internet** Throughout the town eg at Boulevard, Av das Cataratas 1118, T045-3523 4245. Café Internet, R Rebouças 950, T/F045-3523 2122, US$1.50 per hr; also phone, fax and photocopying. Ask for fastest machine, Mon-Sat 0900-2300 and Sun afternoon. Café Pizzanet, R Rio Branco, 412, corner with Av Juscelino Kubitschek, US$2 per hr. Pizzeria, fax, phone, photocopier. Zipfoz.com, R Barão do Rio Branco 412, corner with Av Juscelino Kubitschek. Smart, a/c, US$1.50 per hr. **Laundry** Londres Lavanderia, R Rebouças, 711, only US$1.50 per kg, open Sat. **Medical services** There is a free 24-hr clinic on Av Paraná, 1525, opposite Lions Club, T045-3573 1134. Few buses so take taxi or walk (about 25 mins). **Post office** Praça Getúlio Vargas 72. **Telephone** Telepar on Edmundo de Barros.

Ciudad del Este (Paraguay) *p335*
Banks Local banks open Mon-Fri 0730-1100. Dollars can be changed into reais in town. Banco Holandés Unido, cash on MasterCard, 5% commission. Several exchange houses: Cambio Guaraní, Monseñor Rodríguez, changes TCs for US$0.50. Branch on Friendship Bridge has good rates for many currencies, including dollars and reais. Tupi Cambios, Adrián Jara 351. Cambios Chaco, Adrián Jara y Curupayty. *Casa de câmbio* rates are better than street rates. Money changers (not recommended) operate at the bus terminal, but not at the Brazilian end of the Friendship Bridge. **Embassies and consulates** Brazil, C Pampliega 337, corner of Pai Perez, T061-5615 0984. **Telecommunications** Antelco, Alejo García and Pai Pérez, near the centre on the road to the bus terminal.

Santa Catarina

The state of Santa Catarina is famous above all for its beaches, especially those around the cities of Florianópolis and Laguna. These are among the most beautiful in southern Brazil, and have the best surf in the country. The state is also famous for its beautiful people who, defying the national stereotype, are often tall, blonde and blue-eyed. For this was an area that saw much northern-European immigration in the 19th and 20th centuries. The Portuguese from the Azores settled along the coast, the Germans moved along the Itajaí Valley, the Italians headed for the south and into Rio Grande do Sul, while in the north there are Ukrainians, Japanese, Africans, Hispanics and Indians. Immigrant communities still give a unique personality to a number of the state's towns and districts, as each group maintains its traditions and festivals, its architecture, food and language or accent. German and Ukrainian are spoken as much as Portuguese, and every year one million people visit the Oktoberfest in Blumenau. The vast majority of people today can trace their family to these ethnic origins.

As well as each region having its own distinctive culture, Santa Catarina also has its own climate and scenery. The highlands, just in from the coast, are among the coldest in Brazil and are covered in remnant aracauria pine forest, a tree related to the Chilean monkey puzzle. Except for the summer months of January and February, Santa Catarina's beaches are pleasant and uncrowded. The best months to visit are March, April and May before the water gets too cold for swimming. ▸▸ *For listings, see pages 364-372.*

Florianópolis and around 🌐🍴🏨🎿⭐🌊🅿️▲🚌🛏️🚕 ▸▸ *pp364-372. Colour map 5, B5.*

→ *Phone code: 048. Population: 345,000.*

Halfway along the coast of Santa Catarina is the state capital Florianópolis, founded in 1726 as the gateway to Ilha de Santa Catarina. The natural beauty of the island, beaches and bays make it a magnet for holidaymakers in summer. The southern beaches are good for swimming, the eastern ones for surfing (but be careful of the undertow) and many visitors choose to stay here rather than in the city centre. 'Floripa' is accepted as a shortened version of Florianópolis, with the people known as 'Floripans', although they like to call themselves 'Ilhéus', or islanders.

Ins and outs

Getting there International and domestic flights arrive at **Hercílio Luz airport** ⓘ *Av Deomício Freitas, 12 km south of town, T048-3236 0879.* There are car hire booths, shops, cafés and a small tourist information office in the airport. Aeroporto/Corredor Sudoeste buses run between the airport terminal and the **local rodoviária** ⓘ *city centre, R Antônio Luz 260, Forte de Santa Bárbara, T048-3324 1415,* every 20 minutes until midnight. A taxi to the city costs around US$20.

The main bus station **Rita Maria rodoviária** ⓘ *15 mins' walk from the centre, Av Paulo Fontes 1101, T048-3212 3100,* is served by buses from all major cities in the south and southeast, with frequent connections to Curitiba, Porto Alegre, São Paulo, Rio and Santos. There are also buses between the city and Joinville, Blumenau, Gramado, Foz do Iguaçu and connections to Uruguay and Argentina. ▸▸ *See Transport, page 371.*

Getting around The city is fairly small and compact, quite hilly, but easy and safe to walk around. Standard buses, and more expensive yellow microbuses, run to nearly every important point on the island. There are buses to the eastern and southern beaches (beaches and sights like Joaquina, Lagoa, Lagoa do Peri and Pantano do Sul) from the local *rodoviária* on Rua Antônio Luz 260. Buses to the north of the island leave from another local

Florianópolis

Sleeping 🛌
Blue Tree Towers **7**
Bristol Castelmar **1**
Central Sumaré **2**
Faial **3**
Farol da Ilha **4**
Florianópolis Palace **6**
Hi! Hostel **5**
Pousada Pau de Canela **8**

Valerim Center **9**

Eating 🍴
Café das Artes **2**
Cía Lanches **1**
Kayskidum **8**
Lindacap **4**
Macarronada Italiana **11**
Mirantes **10**

O Mercador **9**
Papparella **5**
Toca da Garoupa **7**
Trapiche **3**
Vida **6**

Bars & clubs 🍸
Box 32 **3**

rodoviária on Rua Francisco Tolentino immediately in front of the long-distance *rodoviária*. There are also *combis* to the beaches leaving from Praça 15 de Novembro in the city centre.

Tourist information The main tourist office is **SETUR** ① *R Tenente Silveira 60, Centro, T048-3952 7000, www.visitefloripa.com.br, Mon-Fri 0800-1700*. There are also information booths in the **rodoviária** ① *T048-3223 2777*, at the **airport** ① *Mon-Fri 0700-1800, Sat and Sun 0800-1800*, and in the **Mercado Público** ① *3rd booth along from R Arcipreste Paiva, T048-3244 5822, Mon-Fri 0800-1200, 1330-1800, Sat and Sun 0800-1200*. All have maps and some pamphlet information in English. Useful websites include www.guiafloripa.com.br.

Sights

Florianópolis is a pleasant, clean, safe and well-organized city linked to the mainland by a picturesque little suspension bridge. It has few sights but is a good base for exploring the Ilha de Santa Catarina, which has many fine beaches. The 19th-century port area, the **Alfândega** ① *R Conselheiro Mafra, T048-3224 6082, Mon-Fri 0900-1900, Sat 0900-1200*, and **Mercado Público** ① *R Conselheiro Mafra T048-225 3200, Mon-Fri 0600-1830, Sat 0600-1300, fish stalls on Sun*, have been restored and now house cafés, shops and little arts and crafts stalls. The **Catedral Metropolitana** ① *Praça 15 de Novembro*, was built in 1773 on the site of the first chapel erected by the founder of the city, Francisco Dias Velho. Inside is a life-size sculpture in wood of the flight into Egypt, originally from the Austrian Tyrol.

There are a few museums to while away a rainy day. The **Forte Sant'Ana** (1763) houses a **Museu de Armas Major Lara Ribas** ① *beneath the Ponte Hercílio Luz, T048-229 6263, Mon 1400-1800, Tue-Sun 0830-1200, 1400-1800, free*, with a collection of guns and other items, mostly post Second World War. The **Museu Histórico de Santa Catarina** ① *Praça 15 de Novembro, T048-3028 8091, Tue-Fri 1000-1800, Sat, Sun and holidays 1000-1600, US$1.50*, in the 18th-century Palácio Cruz e Souza, has a lavish interior with highly decorated ceilings and contains furniture, documents and objects belonging to governors of the state. The **Museu de Antropólogia** ① *T048-3331 8821, Mon-Fri 0900-1200, 1300-1700*, at the Universidade Federal de Santa Catarina Campus, has a dusty collection of stone and other archaeological remains from the indigenous cultures of the coast. It is also possible to visit the former home of Imperial Brazil's foremost propaganda painter, **A Casa Victor Meirelles** ① *R Victor Meirelles 59, T048-3222 0629, Tue-Fri 1300-1800, US$1*. The Catarinense painter was responsible for various apotheoses of colonization, such as *Primeira Missa no Brasil* (the First Mass in Brazil) and the war against the Dutch in Pernambuco, *A Batalha de Guararapes*.

There is a look-out point at **Morro da Cruz** (take the **Empresa Trindadense** bus, US$1, which waits for 15 minutes then returns; or walk back).

Ilha de Santa Catarina ⊖⊘⊙⊙ ›› *pp364-372.*

Santa Catarina island is often referred to as Florianópolis or Grande Florianópolis. It is fringed with some 42 beautiful beaches; all are easily accessible and many offer accommodation. In general, the north is more heavily visited and has the bulk of the resorts and busiest beaches, whilst the south and east are somewhat quieter. The most popular surf beaches are at **Praia Mole**, and **Joaquina** in the north and **Barra da Lagoa** to the east. **Campeche** and the southern beaches offer more peace and quiet, and the **Lagoa de Conceição** just east of Florianópolis city has windsurfing and lively nightlife. Surfing is prohibited 30 April-30 July because it is the breeding season of the *tainha* (flathead mullet), a popular table fish.

Ins and outs

Almost all the beaches on the Ilha de Santa Catarina are easily reached by standard public buses (US$1.25), air-conditioned *executivo* buses, or *colectivos* (minivans), which run regularly. Buses to the eastern and southern areas (such as Joaquina, Lagoa, Lagoa do Peri and Pantano do Sul) leave from the local *rodoviária* on Rua Antônio Luz 260. Buses to the north of the island leave from another local *rodoviária* on R Francisco Tolentino immediately in front of the long-distance *rodoviária*. There are also *combis* to the beaches leaving from Praça 15 de Novembro in the city centre. Schedules are available from the tourist office (see page 351) and there is a full timetable on www.pmf.sc.gov.br/portal/pmf/horarioonibus. The temperature in the north of the island can differ from the south by several degrees.

Northern and central Ilha de Santa Catarina

Santo Antônio de Lisboa Heading north from Florianópolis on the SC 401 highway, **Santo Antônio de Lisboa** is the first town of any size that you come to, after about 10 km. The main beach here is **Sambaqui**, a calm bay named after a huge shell midden once discovered here, and now used more for oyster cultivation than for swimming. The town has a few sights of interest though and is one of the oldest settlements on the island, founded by fishermen from the Azores in the 18th and 19th centuries. There's a little art gallery, the **Casa Açoriana** ⓘ *R Cônego Serpa 30, Santo Antônio de Lisboa, T048-3235 1262, Sun and Mon 1000-1900, Tue-Sat 1000-2200*, which displays works from some 50 local artists, together with objects remembering the Azores. There are some pleasant cafés and restaurants on the waterfront and a handful of places to stay. Santo Antônio is sometimes called the 'city of bees' and honey is sold everywhere; some of the best is available in the apiary museum, **Museo da Apicultura**.

To get to Santo Antônio, take **Trindadense** bus No 331, or any bus going north, to the turn-off to the village on the way to Sambaqui beach (fare US$1.25).

Jurerê and Canasvieiras Beyond Santo Antônio, the island becomes increasingly commercial; around **Ponta Grossa**, **Jurerê**, **Canasvieiras** and, in the far north, **Ponta das Canas**. Together these resort towns make a mini-conurbation of hotels and services, clustered behind some of the islands' prettiest, if most heavily developed, beaches: Praia do Forte, Praia Jurerê, Praia Canasvieras and Praia Ponta das Canas. **Praia do Forte** is overlooked by the **Forte São José da Ponta Grossa** ⓘ *US$2*, a beautifully restored colonial fort with a small museum about its history. The latter three all offer good windsurfing and buzzing in-season beach and bar life. There are plenty of hotel options here.

Praia Brava and the north east A half-hour walk of the far end of Ponta das Canas beach brings you to the first ocean beach, **Praia Brava**, which is backed by condominiums, sometimes polluted but good for surfing. Just south of here, is **Praia dos Ingleses** (bus No 602), which gets its name from an English ship that sank in 1700. The area is urban, popular with families and with many lively bars in high season. Dunes separate this beach from **Praia Santinho**, where Carijó inscriptions can be seen on the cliffs. Both Ingleses and Santinho have decent surfing. A 2-km trail continues south from Santinho to **Praia do Moçambique**, a glorious 8-km stretch of golden sand backed by an environmental protection area, the **Parque Florestal do Rio Vermelho**, which has some of the best surfing on the island.

Lagoa da Conceição The far end of Praia do Moçambique, near the cape, is known as Praia da Lagoa after **Lagoa da Conceição**, which lies less than a kilometre inland to the east, separating the Atlantic coast from Florianópolis city. This is a good place to stay with frenetic bar and nightlife in season. The lake and coastline are forested, pocked with dunes and offer great windsurfing and fishing. The town of Lagoa da Conceição has a pretty 18th-century church, **Nossa Senhora da Conceição** (1730). It also has a market on Wednesday

Ilha de Santa Catarina

and Saturday. Hang-gliding and paragliding can be organized from here or through the efficient English-speaking **Brazil Ecojourneys** ① *Estrada Rozália Paulina Ferreira 1132, T048-3389 5619, www.brazilecojourneys.com*. From the Centro da Lagoa on the bridge there are regular boat trips to **Costa da Lagoa**, which run around the lake stopping at various points (Monday to Friday until 2130, weekends and holidays until 1830; check when you buy your ticket, US$4 return). The service is used mostly by the local people who live around the lake and have no other form of public transport. The ride is spectacular and there is a charming restaurant to greet you at the end of a thirsty journey. A recommended meal is the *tainha* (local mullet) with salad, chips and an abundance of rice.

Barra da Lagoa, Praia Mole and around Immediately east of the lake and south of Praia Moçambique, **Barra da Lagoa** is a pleasant fishing village and beach, lively in the summer season, with plenty of good restaurants and a popular youth hostel. You can walk across the wooden suspension bridge to a restaurant overlooking the bay, a spectacular setting for a meal. It is reached by **Transol** bus No 403 (every 15 minutes from Terminal Urbano, 55 minutes, US$1.25). The same bus goes to the beaches immediately to the south at **Mole**, which is a soft-sand beach, good for walking and with championship surfing. In season, it has some of the liveliest beach and nightlife with a 20-something crowd. **Joaquina**, immediately to the south of Mole and served by the same bus, has some of the best surfing on the island; championships are held here in January. There is sandboarding on the towering powdery dunes that separate the beach from the Lagoa da Conceição.

Southern Ilha de Santa Catarina
Campeche **Praia do Campeche**, 30 minutes by bus (**Pantano do Sul** or **Costa de Dentro**) from Florianópolis is one of the most popular places to stay in the island. It has long been a hippy and new age hang-out, perhaps initially in homage to the French writer Antoine de Saint-Exupéry, author of *Le Petit Prince*, who visited here several times in the 1920s when he was working as a pilot of Ligne Latécoère. The tiny town's main street is named after his book. There are several beaches around Campeche. **Praia da Armação** is the busiest, with many bars and restaurants overlooking a powdery surf beach. From here there are trips offshore to the **Ilha do Campeche** (US$10), an island with a fine white-sand beach broken by boulders, scrubby subtropical forest and good diving. It is protected by the **Instituto de Património Histórico Nacional (IPHAN)** because of the myriad petroglyphs, paintings and inscriptions that pepper the islands' rocks.

Armação, Lagoa do Peri and the far south The beaches immediately to the south of Campeche are called **Morro das Pedras** and **Armação**. Both have good surfing, especially the north end of Armação, which is considered one of the most challenging surf spots on the island. Armação village was an important whaling centre in the 19th and early 20th centuries. A few hundred metres inland from Armação beach is the **Lagoa do Peri**, a protected area and the largest stretch of freshwater on the Santa Catarina coast.

After Armação town look for a bar by the roadside called **Lanchonette e Bar Surf**. Just before the bar there is a road to the left. Walk up a red clay path and after about 200 m you should see a path (unsignposted) on the left, leading up into the hills. A steady walk of up to two hours will lead you over two *montes* (hills) with a fabulous view over **Praia da Lagoinha de Leste**. This beach rarely gets crowded, even in the summer months. Camping is permitted and if you don't fancy the walk, you can pay one of the fishermen to take you from the Azorean fishing village of **Pantano do Sul**, immediately to the south. This is an unspoilt, relaxed spot with a long, curved beach and lovely views across to the Três Irmãs islands. There are several *pousadas*, bars and restaurants, though not much nightlife. For **Praia dos Naufragados**, at the southern tip of the island, take a bus to Caieira da Barra do Sul and walk for an hour through fine forests. From the lighthouse and fishing village, it's possible to visit the small island of **Forte Nossa Senhora da Conceição**, just offshore You can take a boat trip with **Scuna Sul** (see Activities and tours, page 370) from Florianópolis.

Ribeirão da Ilha and the southwest

A trail (or boat ride, US$25) leads from the village of dos Naufragados to **Caieiras do Sul**, which is connected to Florianópolis city on the SC401 road. The beach here is lapped rather than pounded by waves as it is the first southern beach round from the cape. Heading north on the SC401 is the village of **Tapera do Sul**, surrounded by mangroves. The road leads on to the pretty Azorean fishing village of **Ribeirão da Ilha**. This is the best preserved of all Florianópolis's 18th-century settlements, with streets of colourful low houses topped with terracotta tile and fronted by rather unprepossessing concrete cobbles. The village is one of the most popular places in southern Brazil to eat oysters with the local producer, **Ostravagante**, being the only one in the state to have the federal seal of approval for oyster farming. There are many oyster restaurants in town and many buses for the 27-km return ride to Florianópolis city.

North of Florianópolis (mainland) ⊕⊕ » *pp364-372. Colour map 5, B5.*

Porto Belo and around → *Phone code: 047. www.portobelo.com.br.*

The coast north of Florianópolis is dotted with resorts. They include **Porto Belo**, a fishing village on the north side of a peninsula settled in 1750 by Azores islanders, with a calm beach and a number of hotels and restaurants. Around the peninsula are wilder beaches reached by rough roads: **Bombas**, **Bombinhas** (both with the same sort of accommodation as Porto Belo), **Quatro Ilhas** (quieter, good surfing, 15 minutes' walk from Bombinhas), **Mariscal** and, on the southern side, **Zimbros** (or Cantinho). Many of the stunning beaches around Bombinhas are untouched, accessible only on foot or by boat. Its clear waters are marvellous for diving.

Southwest of Porto Belo, reached by turning off the BR-101 at Tijucas and going west for 30 km, is **Nova Trento**, a small town in a valley first colonized by Italians and still showing heavy Italian influence. The local cuisine includes cheese, salami and wine such as you might find in Italy; there are several Italian restaurants and wine producers where you can buy *vinho artesanal*. There is a good view of the Tijucas valley and as far as the sea (on a clear day) from the **Morro da Cruz**, at 525 m. West of Porto Belo is **Praia de Perequê**, with a handful of hotels on the long beautiful beach.

Itapema, 60 km from Florianópolis, is another former fishing village on a wide sweep of sandy beach now dominated by tourism. In high season the town accommodates around 300,000 visitors. The **Plaza Itapema Resort e Spa**, T047-3368 2222, is all-inclusive and the best such establishment on this part of the coast. Around the headland are several smaller and quieter beaches, **Praia Grossa** being one of the best, with good surf.

Camboriú → *Colour map 5, B5. Phone code: 047. Population: 42,000.*

Some 80 km north of Florianópolis is Camboriú, once beautiful, but now the most concentrated urban development on Brazil's southern coast. From 15 December to late February it is very crowded and expensive, and in low season it is popular with retired people. A few kilometres south, at **Lojas Apple**, there is **Parque Cyro Gevaerd**, a museum (archaeology, oceanography, fishing, local arts and crafts), zoo and aquarium; and **Meia Praia**, which is quieter and cleaner than Camboriú. A *teleférico* (cable car) has been built to **Praia Laranjeiras**, previously deserted (US$13 return from Barra Sul shopping centre to Laranjeiras via *Mata Atlântica* station). Between Itajaí and Camboriú is the beautiful, deserted and rough beach of **Praia Brava**. Note that from mid-July to mid-August it can be chilly.

The resort is served by direct buses from Florianópolis, Joinville and Blumenau. International buses from Uruguay to São Paulo pass through here. There are a huge number of modern hotels (four-star or less), and aparthotels. From March to November it is easy to rent furnished apartments by the day or week. Turning up and finding a room is straightforward.

Itajaí and around → *Colour map 5, B5. Phone code: 047. Population: 135,000.*

At the mouth of the Rio Itajaí-Açu, some 94 km up the coast from Florianópolis, is the most important port in Santa Catarina. It has thriving fishing and ship-building industries and is the centre of a district largely colonized by Germans and Italians, although the town itself was founded by immigrants from the Azores.

Despite the port, tourism is heavily promoted and in summer the population triples. Itajaí celebrates a **Marejada Festival** in October in honour of Portugal and the sea (see Festivals and events, page 370). For tourist information, contact the **Centro de Promoções Itajaí Tur** ① *T047-3348 1080.*

Porto Belo beaches

Sleeping	Blumenauense Praia **2** Pousada Zimbros **3**
Baleia Branca **1**	Porto Belo **1**

The local beaches are **Atalaia**, **Geremias** and **Cabeçudas** (within walking distance, quiet and small), but within the municipality there is also **Praia do Morcego**, which is considered a health resort because of the high mineral content of the water. There is also a cave here, the **Caverna do Morcego**, about which there are many myths and legends.

About 50 km southwest of Itajaí is the **Caverna de Botuverá**, which you enter through a dripping tunnel that can flood in the wet season. The first gallery is like a cathedral, with stalactites and rock formations including 'the organ', and the guide will play a sort of tune for you. Not all the galleries are fully explored. Pillars of 20 m have been found; each metre of rock taking 10,000 years to form. To get to Botuverá, take the road to Brusque off the BR-101, where there is a tourist office that can give you directions and other details.

Penha → *Population: 15,000.*

About 20 km north of Itajaí is Penha, another resort along the BR-101, with a broad, curved sandy beach with rocky headlands at either end, offering smaller coves for swimming, surfing and fishing. The town was founded by Portuguese fishermen in the 18th century and fishing is still important as anywhere else along the coast. Tourism took off in the 1970s and during the high season the population rises to 100,000. Its major claim to fame is the **Beto Carrero World**, one of the largest theme parks in the world, on Praia de Armação. Penha even offers themed shopping. At **Shopping Temático**, on Avenida Eugênio Krause, you can visit different countries in different ages. There are several festivals and events in Penha (see page 370) as well as hotels, *pousadas* and camping.

Other resorts north of Itajaí include **Piçarras**, with sandy beaches interspersed with rocky headlands (ideal for fishing, several hotels), and **Barra Velha**, with a good, cheap hotel, **Hotel Mirante**, which has a restaurant, and two more expensive hotels.

Blumenau ⊕⊖ ⇥ *pp364-372. Colour map 5, B4.*

→ *Phone code: 047. Population: 262,000.*

Blumenau is in a prosperous district settled mostly by Germans. A clean, orderly city with some almost caricatured Germanic architecture, the *enxaimel* design (exposed beams and brickwork) typifies some of the more famous buildings such as the **mayor's residence**, the **Molemann Shopping Centre**, built to resemble a medieval German castle, and the **Museum of the Colonial Family** ⓘ *Av Duque de Caxias 78, Tue-Fri 0900-1700, Sat 0900-1200 and 1400-1630, Sun mornings only, US$1.15*, the German immigrant museum, dating back to 1868.

The first Germans to arrive were the philosopher Herman Bruno Otto Blumenau and 16 other German explorers, who sailed up the river in 1850. Work began on building schools, houses and the first plantations; the city soon became a notable textile centre. Today, high-tech and electronics industries are replacing textiles as the town's economic mainstay. There is a helpful **tourist office** ⓘ *R 15 de Novembro, on the corner of R Ângelo Dias.*

Sights of interest include the **German Evangelical Church**, and the houses of **Dr Bruno Otto Blumenau** and of **Fritz Müller**. The latter two are now **museums** ⓘ *both 0800-1200 and 1330-1730, free*, and are worth a visit. Müller, a collaborator of Darwin, bought the Blumenau estate in 1897 and founded the town. **Museu Ervin Kurt Theichmann** ⓘ *R 15 de Novembro 791, T047-3387 0282*, has sculptures. The **Museu da Cerveja** ⓘ *Praça Hercílio Luz, 160, T047-3326 8380*, examines the history of the region's breweries and the origins of **Oktoberfest**. Just out of town, the **Museu Pomerano** ⓘ *Rodovia SC 418, Km 3, T047-3387 0477*, tells the story of the colonial family.

Excursions from Blumenau

The **Parque Ecológico Spitzkopf** ① *R Bruno Schreiber 3777, Progresso, T047-3336 5422, US$2.75*, makes a pleasant day-trip for hiking. It has very pleasant walks through the forest, including a 5.5-km trail passing waterfalls and natural pools up to the Spitzkopf Peak at 936 m, from where you get a wonderful view of the region. If you are not into hiking up hills, there are paths around the lower slopes which will take you half a day. To get there, take the 'Garcia' bus from Avenida 7 de Setembro via Rua São Paulo to Terminal Garcia, then change to 'Progresso' until the end of the paved road, US$0.80 each bus. Then walk 1.5 km to the park entrance, There's a small zoo and cabins to rent (German spoken).

From the riverside road opposite the *prefeitura* in Blumenau, you can take a bus past rice fields and wooden houses set in beautiful gardens to **Pomerode**, 33 km north of Blumenau. There's an interesting **zoo** ① *R Hermann Weege 160, US$5.50*, founded in 1932 and the oldest in the state, which houses over 600 animals of different species. Next door, **Schornstein** is a restaurant with its own microbrewery, serving excellent German food. There is a **tourist office** ① *R 15 de Novembro, T047-3387 2627*, and the **Associação dos Artistas e Artesãos de Pomerode** ① *next door to the prefeitura municipal*, has exhibitions of local arts and crafts and a shop. The north German dialect of Plattdeutsch is still spoken here and there are several folkloric groups keeping alive the music and dance of their ancestors: Alpino Germânico, Pomerano, Edelweiss and Belgard. Shooting and hunting is also traditional in the area and there are 16 **Clubes de Caça e Tiro**, which are active at all festivities. The men compete for the title of '*Rei do Tiro Municipal*' in July and the women compete for the '*Rainha do Tiro Municipal*' in November.

A half-day excursion to **Gaspar** (15 km) allows you to visit the cathedral, **Igreja Matriz São Pedro Apóstolo**, set high above the river. To get here take a **Verde Vale** bus from the stop outside the huge supermarket on Rua 7 de Setembro in the centre of Blumenau (for tickets, see Transport page 371). There are four water parks in Gaspar with water slides and other amusements. Two of the best are; **Parque Aquático Cascanéia** ① *R José Patrocínio dos Santos, T047-3397 8500*, with chalets, parking, restaurants; and on the same street, **Cascata Berlim** ① *T047-9991 4898/0779*, with camping facilities, a natural pool and a restaurant.

Further west along the Rio Itajaí–Açu, around Ibirama, the river is good for whitewater rafting. You can take a break between rapids to bathe in the waterfalls.

Blumenau to Iguaçu

An alternative to taking a direct bus from Florianópolis or Blumenau to Iguaçu, is to travel through rich and interesting farming country in Santa Catarina and Rio Grande do Sul, stopping at the following places. **Joaçaba** is a town of German immigrants, in the centre of the Vale do Contestado; for information call T047-3522 3000. **Erexim** has a strong *gaúcho* influence. **Iraí**, a town with thermal springs, is situated in an Italian immigrant area and is good for semi-precious stones. From any of these places you can go to Pato Branco and Cascavel and then to Foz do Iguaçu.

Two hours from Joaçaba is **Treze Tílias**, a village where 19th-century Tyrolean dialect is still spoken and the immigrant culture is perfectly preserved. It was settled in 1933 by a group led by Andreas Thaler, who had been the Austrian minister of agriculture. Dairy farming is the main economic activity and children are taught German and Portuguese in school. The style of architecture has been lifted straight from the Alps and the city prides itself on being in the mountains, with all the associated romanticizing of European mountain life found in such resorts throughout Brazil. It may get a bit chilly but it never

Blumenau's Oktoberfest

In 1983, Blumenau suffered a great flood. After its destructive impact, the idea was born to introduce a German-style 'traditional' Oktoberfest beer-festival to motivate people to reconstruct the city. The festival celebrating German music, beer and the German way of life was started in 1984 here, and was expected to become the second largest in the world after Munich's (bands come from Germany for the event). It is the second largest street party in Brazil, after Carnaval. It is set next to the São Francisco de Assis National Park and usually held in the first half of October. During the day the narrow streets are packed around the Molemann Shopping Centre, which is where many locals like to begin their festivities before the Oktoberfest Pavilion opens. The centre contains a mixture of bars, live music and, of course, *chopp*. At 1900 the doors open and you will find four decorated pavilions, each holding different events from drinking competitions to the 'sausage Olympics', all accompanied by non-stop traditional German music. The cultural pavilion holds traditional dress and cake-making competitions, as well as getting the audience involved in the singing, which grows steadily worse as the evening rolls on. There is also a fun fair and folk dancing shows. Food around the stalls is German and half a litre of *chopp* will cost you around US$2. Brazilian popular bands are slowly being introduced, much to the disapproval of the older inhabitants. Visitors report it is worth attending on weekday evenings but weekends are too crowded. It is repeated, but called a 'summer festival', in the three weeks preceding Carnaval.

snows. The major festivity of the year is the four-day **Tirolerfest** in October, celebrating the customs of the Tirol, with food, sculpture and art. There's **tourist office** ⓘ *Praça Andreas Thaler 25, T/F047-3537 0176*, and buses run to and from Joaçaba and Blumenau.

São Francisco do Sul → *Phone code: 047. Population: 27,000.*
At the mouth of the Baia de Babitonga, São Francisco do Sul is the port for the town of **Joinville** (see below), 45 km inland at the head of the Rio Cachoeira. It is the country's third oldest city (Binot Paulmier de Gonneville landed here in 1504), after Porto Seguro in Bahia and São Vicente in Rio de Janeiro. The colonial centre has over 150 historical sites and has been protected since 1987. An interesting, **Museu Nacional do Mar** ⓘ *R Babitonga, Centro Histórico, T047-3444 1868, Tue-Fri 1000-1800, Sat and Sun 1000-1900, US$1.75*, reflects Brazil's seafaring history. The **cathedral**, Nossa Senhora da Graça (1719), still has its original walls made with sand, shells and whale oil. The **Museu Histórico de São Francisco do Sul** ⓘ *R Coronel Carvalho*, is in the 18th-century Cadeia Pública. There is a **tourist information** desk in the cinema behind the *prefeitura*. Not far from the historical centre is the modern port. **Petrobrás** has an oil refinery here.

There are about 13 excellent beaches nearby, such as **Ubatuba**, **Enseada** (which has good nightlife, hotels, pensions and three campsites), **Prainha** (surf championships are held here) and **Cápri**. Quieter waters can be found at **Ingleses**, **Figueiras**, **Paulas** and **Calixtos** but, being in the bay, the sea is polluted. A ferry crosses the Baia de Babitonga from Bairro Laranjeiras, 8 km from the centre, to Estaleiro, 30 minutes. The historic town of **Vila da Glória**, 6 km from Estaleiro, can be visited. For schooner trips contact T047-3974 7266. Take mosquito repellent.

➔ *Phone code: 047. Population: 430,000. www.joinville.sc.gov.br.*

The state's largest city lies 2 km from the main coastal highway (BR-101), within a two-hour drive of Curitiba and Florianópolis. Joinville is known as the 'city of the princes' for its historical connections with royalty. It is also nicknamed the 'city of flowers', and even 'Manchester Catarinense'. The large German population gives it a distinctly European feel, and the city is well-ordered, attractively maintained and easy to navigate on foot.

Ins and outs

Ins and outs **Lauro Carneiro de Loyola airport** ① *13 km from the city centre*, receives flights from São Paulo; a taxi from the airport to the centre costs US$10. Joinville is connected by bus to the larger cities in the south and south east of Brazil. The **rodoviária** ① *2.5 km outside the town, south exit, T047-3433 2991*, has regular bus services to the centre.

Tourist information   You can find information on the city on www.portaljoinville.com.br. There is a **tourist office** ① *corner of Praça Nereu Ramos with R do Príncipe, T047-3433 1511*, and information is also available from **Promotur** ① *Centreventos, Av José Vieira 315, sala 20, T047-3453 2633, www.promotur.com.br.*

Sights

The **Museu Nacional da Imigração e Colonização** ① *R Rio Branco 229, Tue-Fri 0900-1700, Sat and Sun 1100-1700, www.museunacional.com.br*, has a collection of objects and tools from the original German settlement and other items of historical interest. **Arquivo Histórico de Joinville** ① *Av Hermann August Lepper 650, T047-3422 2154, Mon-Fri 0830-1200, 1330-2000*, houses a collection of documents dating from the town's foundation.

The **Museu Arqueológico do Sambaqui** ① *R Dona Francisca 600, T047-3422 5626, Tue-Sun 0900-1200, 1400-1800*, has a collection dating back to 5000 BC, with an exhibition devoted to the life of the indigenous people who built the sambaqui shell mounds along the south coast of Brazil. There are also two archaeological reserves: **Sambaqui do Rio Comprido**, carbon dated to 2865 BC, and **Sambaqui Morro do Ouro**.

The Alameda Brustlein, better known as the **Rua das Palmeiras**, is an impressive avenue of palm trees, leading to the **Palácio dos Príncipes**. The trees were planted in 1873 by Frederico Brustlein with seeds brought in 1867 by Louis Niemeyer. The **railway station** ① *R Leite Ribeiro, T047-3422 2550*, dates from 1906 and is a fine example of the German style of architecture; the **Mercado Municipal** ① *Praça Hercílio Luz*, is in the *enxaimel* style. At the other end of the spectrum, the **cathedral**, on Avenida Juscelino Kubitscheck at Rua do Príncipe, is futuristic with spectacular windows recounting the story of man. The **Cemitério dos Imigrantes** ① *R 15 de Novembro 978, Mon-Fri 1400-1730*, is interesting; the attached **Casa da Memória do Imigrante** has information on the town's history, with audiovisual and documentary displays.

The **Parque Zoobotânico** ① *R Pastor Guilherme Rau 462, T047-3433 1230, Tue-Sun 0900-1800, 15 mins' walk in the direction of Mirante*, is a good zoo and park, with many local species of birds and animals and a children's park. From here it is 25 minutes' walk to the **Mirante** for a beautiful view of the town and the bay. The tower on the top is at an altitude of 250 m and you can walk up a spiral staircase on the outside for a panoramic view. An **orchid farm** ① *R Helmuth Fallgatter 2547, opposite the Terminal de Integração Tupy, Boa Vista, 0800-1200, 1330-1800*, is open to the public for sales or just to look around.

At **Expoville**, 4 km from the centre on BR-101 (continuation of 15 de Novembro), is an exhibition of Joinville's industry, although it is used for many other exhibitions and festivals as well. The new, multi-functional **Centreventos Cau Hansen** has been built to house sporting activities, shows, festivals, conferences and other events. It is home to the first Bolshoi Ballet School outside of Moscow. The tiled mural around the entrance, by Juarez Machado, depicts a circus. There are some 600 industries in the manufacturing park, many of which are substantial exporters.

Joinville

Sleeping	Mattes 5	Trento Queijos
Anthurium Parque 1	Tannenhof 9	e Vinhos 5
Blue Tree Towers 7		Tritão 6
Flor do Brasil 6	Eating
Ideal 2	China 2
Joinville Palace 3	Pinheiro 3
Joinville Tourist 4	Sopp 4

N

200 metres
200 yards

Excursions from Joinville

You can take a boat trip on the **Príncipe de Joinville III** ① *from Lagoa Saguaçú, Bairro Espinheiros, 9 km from the centre, T047-3455 0824, departs 1000, returns 1600, US$40 per person including lunch*, past 14 islands to São Francisco do Sul. Stops include the **Museu Nacional do Mar**, the port, lunch at a fish restaurant, Ilha da Rita and Ilha das Flores.

The festival of **São João** in June can be seen best in Santa Catarina at **Campo Alegre**, the first town on the road inland to Mafra. There are bonfires, a lot of (German) folk dancing, and large quantities of local specialities, *quentão* (spiced red wine) and *pinhões* (giant 3-cm-long pine nuts). It is a beautiful climb on the road from the BR-101 to Campo Alegre.

South of Florianópolis ●● ➤ *pp364-372.*

The **Parque Estadual da Serra do Tabuleiro**, just south of the BR-282, is the largest protected area in Santa Catarina, covering 87,405 ha, or nearly 1% of the state. Apart from its varied and luxuriant flora, which is home to many birds and animals, it is also important to Florianópolis for its water supply. There is a small **reserve** ① *park office, near Paulo Lopes, Km 252, BR-101, daily 0800-1700*, where animals and birds previously in captivity are rehabilitated before returning to the wild.

Continuing south, two beaches worth a stop are **Pinheira** and **Guarda do Embaú**, which you get to by crossing a river in a canoe. The surfing is excellent here; Guarda in particular is a favourite spot of surfers from Rio and São Paulo (except during the fishing season 15 May-15 July). **Garopaba**, 89 km south of Florianópolis, is a village of 11,000, which swells to 100,000 during the holidays. Its indigenous Carijó name 'Y-Gara-Paba' means 'much water, many fish and many hills'. There is a simple colonial church and a sandy coast.

Silveira, 3 km east, is considered one of Brazil's finest surfing spots. Swimming can be risky, though, because of the surf and sudden drops in the ocean floor. There is good fishing for *tainha*, lobster, anchovy and other varieties. **Praia do Rosa**, 18 km south, is a 3.5-km beach with good swimming, fishing, diving and pleasant coastal walks. It is also one of Brazil's prime whale-watching sites, with southern right whales coming to the bay to calve between June and November. The headquarters of the **Baleia Franca** project is **Pousada Vila Sol e Mar** ① *Estrada Geral da Praia do Rosa, Ibirapuera, T048-3355 6111, www.vidasolemar.com.br, whale-watching trips cost US$45 per person Mon-Fri, US$75 Sat and Sun*, which has cabins for rent and a youth hostel (see Sleeping, page 367). Dolphin-watching and birdwatching trips are available year round.

Laguna ➔ *Colour map 5, B4. Phone code: 048. Population: 48,000.*

The small fishing port of Laguna in southern Santa Catarina (124 km south of Florianópolis), founded in 1676, was a focal point of defence against Spanish invasions and still retains vestiges of its turbulent past. These days Laguna serves mainly as a holiday resort, perched between the ocean and a chain of three lakes. In 1839, Laguna was the capital of the Juliana Republic, a short-lived separatist movement led by Italian idealist Guiseppe Garibáldi. At that time he met a devoted lover, Ana Maria de Jesus Ribeiro, who followed him into battle, was taken prisoner, escaped and rejoined Garibáldi at Vacaria. Their first son, Menotti, was born in Rio Grande do Sul, but the family moved to Montevideo in 1841, where they lived in poverty. They later moved to Argentina and then to Italy, where they fought for the unification of the peninsula. Ana Maria (or Anita) died near Ravenna in 1849 while they were fleeing to Switzerland from the Austrian army. She became a heroine in both Brazil and Italy and there are monuments to her in Rome, Ravenna, Porto Alegre, Belo Horizonte,

Florianópolis, Juiz da Fora, Tubarão and Laguna. At Laguna is the **Anita Garibáldi Museum**, containing documents, furniture and her personal effects.

Laguna's well-preserved historic centre boasts many attractive colonial buildings but lacks good accommodation. Resort-style hotels, popular with families, can be found at **Mar Grosso**, Laguna's beach. This heavily developed stretch of sand is 2 km from the centre, but you'll find nicer beaches and dunes 16 km away (accessible by ferry and road) at **Cavo de Santa Marta**.

Also from Laguna, it's possible to take a bus to **Farol**; a beautiful ride that involves crossing the mouth of the Lagoa Santo Antônio by ferry (10 minutes) – look out for fishermen aided by *botos* (dolphins). Here is a fishing village with good surf, deserted beaches and a lighthouse, the **Farol de Santa Marta**. This is the largest lighthouse in South America with the third largest view in the world. It was built by the French in 1890 of stone, sand and whale oil. Guided tours are available (taxi, US$10, not including ferry toll). There are countless inexpensive *pousadas* in the village, as well as several campsites.

Serra Geral ⬤ ⟫ *pp364-372.*

This spectacular mountain range some 170 km south of Florianópolis rises steeply from the southern Santa Catarina coast near Praia Grande, ascending from sea level to almost 2000 m in just over 20 km. It is cut by dozens of majestic canyons formed when the African and American plates pulled apart ripping great gashes in the hills. Each of these canyons has its own microclimate, ranging from verdant and mossy to dry and cool. The canyons and the rugged, semi-wild country that surrounds them offers some of the best hiking in southern Brazil. The *serra* is protected by two contiguous national parks: Parque Nacional Aparados da Serra and Parque Nacional de Serra Geral.

In the wet season, the canyons are lush with an abundance of ferns, lichens and mosses and in the misty mornings it's common to hear the eerie roar of red howler monkeys. Birds and butterflies are abundant, including spectaculars like the red-breasted toucan, endemics like the vinaceous Amazon (a chunky green parrot with a bloody beak) and rarities like the red-legged seriema, which looks a little like a wispy secretary bird in scarlet tights. Mammals include howler and brown capuchin monkeys, ocelot, grey foxes, agouti, paca and armadillos.

Parque Nacional Aparados da Serra
ⓘ *T054-3251 1262, open year-round Wed-Sun 0900-1700, US$6.50 plus US$2.50 for a car.*
This park is famous for its much-photographed **Itaimbezinho canyon**, some 8 km long and 720 m deep and fringed with subtropical forest. Two waterfalls cascade 350 m into a stone plunge pool in the base that spills over into the silver sliver of the Rio do Boi, which winds its narrow way along the canyon bottom. A steep rocky path leads to river from the canyon rim, but it's a tough, hair-raising walk that shouldn't be undertaken lightly – or without a guide. It's also possible to do a three-day trek along the banks of the Rio Boi itself, or a series of hikes along the upper rim of the canyon and ultimately to the beach at Praia Grande, around 20 km away.

Parque Nacional da Serra Geral
ⓘ *T054-3251 1320, open year-round daily 0800-1800, free.*
This park has a similar landscape to Aparados da Serra but even deeper gorges. The most impressive are Malacara and Fortaleza; the latter an astounding 1170 m deep. There are spectacular views to the coast from the top of both and wild, remote hiking.

Ins and outs If you plan to hike in the *serra* it is best to go on an organized trip with **Brazil Ecojourneys**, http://brazilecojourneys.com. However, it is possible to visit independently. The most convenient base is **Cambará do Sul**, www.cambaradosul.tur.br. The Aparadas da Serra park entrance is 18 km from Cambara and there are numerous *pousadas*, some of which organize trips into the mountains. The best time to visit is June to August when skies are clear but it can be very cold; temperatures on the high peaks fall well below zero and it can even snow. Rain is heaviest in April, May and September.

Cambará do Sul can be reached from Praia Grande, Caxias, São Francisco de Paula, São José dos Ausentes and Porto Alegre (the latter bus is very slow). Buses run from the *rodoviária* in Cambará do Sul, T054-3251 1567, with **Consórcio São Marcos/União**, to Criciúma stopping at the entrance to the park (30 minutes, US$2), and leaving Monday to Saturday at 0945 and an additional bus on Monday, Wednesday and Saturday at 1145. There is no bus on Sunday. To return, flag down the bus to Cambará from Praia Grande which passes the park entrance daily between 1745 and 1815.

West of Florianópolis ●●● ►► *pp364-372.*

From Florianópolis, the BR-282 heads west to Lages. About 12 km along are the hot springs at **Caldas da Imperatriz** (41°C) and **Águas Mornas** (39°C). The latter are open to the public Monday to Friday morning only. Both have good spa hotels (see page 368).

Lages and around → *Colour map 5, B4. Phone code: 049. Population: 160,000.*
The area around Lages is particularly good for 'rural tourism', with lots of opportunities for hiking, horse riding, river bathing and working on a farm. The weather can get really cold in winter and even the waterfalls have been known to freeze. Many of the local *fazendas* are open for visitors and offer accommodation. This is *gaúcho* country and you will get *gaúcho* hospitality, culture and food.

● Santa Catarina listings

For Sleeping and Eating price codes and other relevant information, see pages 42-47.

● Sleeping

Florianópolis *p349, map p350*
The following hotels are in Florianópolis city. Many visitors to Florianópolis prefer to stay on the beaches, see Ilha de Santa Catarina, below.
L Blue Tree Towers, R Bocaiúva 2304, next to Shopping Beiramar, T048-3251 5555, www.bluetree.com.br. Very smart, well-equipped modern business hotel. Good restaurant, pool, gym and sauna.
AL-A Pousada Pau de Canela, Rio Taveres 606, T048-3338 3584, www.pousada

paudecanela.com.br. Well-located *pousada* with 10 personalized rooms, restaurant, bar and swimming pool.
B Bristol Castelmar, R Felipe Schmidt 1260, T048-3225 3228, www.bristolhoteis.com.br. Standard 1980s business hotel with a restaurant, pool and sauna. There are great views from the upper-floor rooms.
B Faial, R Felipe Schmidt 603, T048-3225 2766, www.hotelfaial.com.br. Comfortable and traditional with simple rooms and a good restaurant.
B Florianópolis Palace, R Artista Bittencourt 14, T048-3224 9633, www.floph.com.br. Once the best hotel in town, now a 1970s throwback but with a decent pool, sauna and large a/c rooms. Recommended.

C Farol da Ilha, R Bento Gonçalves 163, T048-3225 2766, www.hotelfaial.com.br. Well-kept 1990s hotel with 35 a/c rooms, owned by the hotel **Faial**. Convenient for the bus station.

C Valerim Center, R Felipe Schmidt 554, T048-3225 1100. Functional 2-star with large rooms, hot water and hard beds.

C-D Central Sumaré, R Felipe Schmidt 423, T048-3222 5359. Clean and friendly, good value but some rooms are significantly better than others so look at several. Breakfast included. More expensive with bath.

E Hi! Hostel, R Duarte Schutel 227, T048-3225 3781, www.floripahostel.com.br. Price per person. IYHA hostel, breakfast included, cooking facilities, clean, some traffic noise, very friendly, will store luggage. Recommended. Prices rise Dec-Feb; more expensive for non-members. They also have a branch in Canasvieiras, see below.

Ilha de Santa Catarina *p351, map p353*

L Lexus Beira Mar, R Antônio Prudente de Morais, 814, T048-3266 0909, www.hotel lexus.com.br. 1- and 2-bed studio flats on the beach, with breakfast. Friendly.

L-A Porto Ingleses, R das Gaivotas 610, Praia dos Ingleses, T048-3269 1414, www.porto ingleses.com.br. Small resort with a pool, play area for kids, restaurant and beach service. All accommodation has a/c and is spacious.

AL-A Hotel São Sebastião da Praia, Av Campeche 1373, Praia de Campeche, T048-3338 2020, www.hotelsaosebastiao.com.br. Resort hotel on a splendid beach. Offers good deals on stays of 2 nights or more.

AL-A Vila Tamarindo, Av Campeche 1836, Praia do Campeche, T048-3237 3464, www.tamarindo.com.br. Friendly eco-lodge offering a range of alternative therapies and activities. Rooms and suites, some with jacuzzi and/or sea view.

A Pousada 32, on the beach, Barra da Lagoa, T/048-3232 4232, www.pousada32.com.br. Comfortable apartments with kitchen, sleeping 4-7.

B Pousada dos Tucanos, Estr Geral da Costa de Dentro 2776, near Pântano do Sul, T048-3237 5084. English, French, Spanish spoken, spacious bungalows in garden setting. Excellent organic food. Very highly recommended. Take bus to Pântano do Sul, walk 6 km or telephone and arrange to be picked up by German owner.

C Bangalôs da Mole, Rodovia Jornalista Manoel de Menezes 1005, Praia do Mole, T048-3232 0723, www.bangalos damole.com.br. Modern tile-roof cabins tucked away from the beach on a little headland; some with kitchenettes and decks with a view.

C Pousada Floripaz, Estr Geral (across hanging bridge at bus station), Barra da Lagoa, T048-3232 3193. Safe, family-run and with helpful owners. Boat and car tours. Recommended. Book in advance.

C-D Barratur, R Felipa Benta Ramos 18, Barra da Lagoa, T048-3232 3000. Brightly painted beach chalets, the largest of which sleep up to 6, good value.

D Pousada Zilma, R Geral da Praia da Joaquina 279, Lagoa da Conceição, T048-3232 5161. Quiet, safe and simple with helpful staff. Recommended.

D-E The Backpackers Sharehouse, Estr Geral, Barra da Lagoa (across hanging bridge, opposite **Pousada Floripaz**), T048-3232 7606, T048-3232 7606. This large, busy hostel is in a prime location and offers free surfboard rental as well as cable TV.

D-E Hi Hostel Canasvieiras, R Dr João de Oliveira 517, esq Av das Nações, Canasvieiras, T048-3266 2036, www.floripahostel.com.br. Open 15 Dec-15 Mar. IYHA hostel, 2 blocks from sea with well-kept dorms and doubles.

E-F Albergue do Pirata, Pântano do Sul, www.alberguedopirata.com.br. Doubles and dorms with breakfast in natural surroundings with lots of trails.

Camping
Camping Clube do Brasil, São João do Rio Vermelho, north of Lagoa da Conceição, 21 km

out of town; also has sites at Barra da Lagoa, Lagoa da Conceição, Praia da Armação, Praia dos Ingleses and Praia Canasvieiras.

Wild camping is allowed at **Ponta de Sambaqui** and the beaches of **Brava, Aranhas, Galheta, Mole, Campeche, Campanhas** and **Naufragados**.

'Camping Gaz' cartridges from **Riachuelo Supermercado**, on R Alvim and R São Jorge. **Camping Fortaleza da Barra Barra**, Estrada Geral da Barra da Lagoa 3317, T048-3232 4235. Basic facilities but clean site. Helpful owner, will hold valuables.

Porto Belo and around *p355, map p356*
Lots of campsites around the peninsula.
LL Ponta dos Ganchos, 30 mins' drive north of Florianópolis, just south of Porto Belo, Governador Celso Ramos, T048-3262 5000, www.pontadosganchos.com.br. One of the most luxurious resorts in Brazil; isolated on its own steep peninsula with bungalows tucked away on the higher slopes. The best are almost 100 sq m with sweeping (private) views out over the Atlantic. Good restaurant and excellent service. Pick-up service from Florianópolis airport.
A-B Baleia Branca, Av Nena Trevisan 98, Porto Belo, T047-3369 4011, www.hotelbaleia branca.com.br. 12 chalets in a garden with pools, pool, sauna and camping area.
B Hotel Pousada Zimbros, Estrada Geral Zimbros s/n, T047-3369 3225. Cheaper off-season, on beach, sumptuous breakfast, restaurant. Highly recommended.
B Porto Belo, R José Amâncio 246, Porto Belo T047-3369 4483. IYHA. Lots of apartments, most sleep 4-6, good value for a group.
C-D Blumenauense Praia Hotel, Av Sen Atílio Fontana, Praia do Perequê, T047-3369 8208. Simple rooms with en suites and breakfast. On the beach.

Itajaí and around *p356*
B Grande, R Felipe Schmidt 198, T047-3348 0968. Classic 1940s hotel, looking a bit frayed.
B-C Marambaia Cabeçudas, Praça Marcos Konder 46, Praia de Cabeçudas, 6 km out

of town, www.maramabaiahotel.com.br. Modern resort hotel with a pool and gym. Comfortable though anonymous rooms.

Blumenau *p357*
B-C Glória, R 7 de Setembro 954, T047-3326 1988, hotelgloria@hotelgloria.com.br. Modern resort hotel with a pool and gym. Comfortable though anonymous rooms.
C Herrmann, Floriano Peixoto 213, T047-3322 4370. One of the oldest houses in Blumenau, rooms with or without bath, good breakfast, German spoken.
D-E Grün Garten Pousada, R São Paulo 2457, T047-3323 4332, www.grungarten.com.br. Price per person. Good hostel with dorms and doubles, 15 mins' walk from *rodoviária*.

Excursions from Blumenau *p358*
A-AL Fazzenda Park Hotel, Estrada Geral do Gasparinho 2499, Gaspar, T047-3397 9000, www.fazzenda.com.br. Swimming pool, fishing, walking and riding.
C Pousada Max, R 15 de Novembro 257, Pomerode, T047-3387 3070. Also a good option.
C Schroeder, R 15 de Novembro 514, Pomerode, T047-3387 0933. A good option.
D Pousada Ecológica Spitzkopf, R Bruno Schreiber 3777, T047-3336 5422. Beautiful, clean and extremely quiet, with pool, heating and a bar, but no restaurant.

Joinville *p360, map p361*
L Tannenhof, R Visc de Taunay 340, T/F047-3433 8011, www.tannenhoff.com.br. 4-star, pool, gym, traffic noise, excellent breakfast, restaurant on 14th floor.
L Anthurium Parque, R São José 226, T047-4009 6299, www.anthurium.com.br. In a colonial building, once home to a bishop, good value, English spoken, pool, sauna, part of the **Roteiros de Charme** hotel group, see page 43.
A Blue Tree Towers, Av Juscelino Kubitschek, 30, T047-3841 7444, www.bluetree.com.br. Smart business hotel with very good service and facilities.

Spick and span modern rooms. Sauna, gym and an excellent restaurant and bar.
B-C Joinville Palace, R do Príncipe 142, T047-3433 6111, www.joinvillepalace hotel.com.br. Simple a/c rooms with heating and TV. Visa accepted.
C Joinville Tourist, R 7 de Setembro 40, T047-3433 1288, www.touristhotel.com.br. Smart though anonymous 3-star with a pool, bar and restaurant.
D Ideal, R Jerônimo Coelho 98, T047-3422 3660. Simple, well kept and convenient for the *rodoviária* municipal.
D-E Mattes, 15 de Novembro 801, T047-3433 9886. Simple but with good service and facilities and a big breakfast. More expensive rooms have cable.
E Flor do Brasil, opposite bus station. Basic but clean rooms with ceiling fan, TV and private bath.

South of Florianópolis *p362*
L Pousada Vila Sol e Mar, Estrada Geral da Praia do Rosa, Ibirapuera, T048-3355 6111. The *pousada* has cabins for rent, with kitchen, TV, restaurant, sushi bar, tennis, surf school. Dolphin-watching and birdwatching trips are available year round. There's also a youth hostel, **Dinda Rosa**, which is popular with surfers – book in advance in high season.
A Morada do Bouganvilles, Estr Geral do Morro, Praia da Rosa, T048-3355 6179. Luxurious chalets in a bougainvillea-filled garden with a small pool and a bar.
A Pousada da Lagoa, R Rosalina de Aguiar Lentz 325, Garopaba, T/F048-3254 3201, www.pousadadalagoa.com.br. Comfortable countryside *pousada* with an outdoor pool, reasonable restaurant and bar and a series of trails running into the environs.
A Quinta do Bucanero, Estr Gerald a Rosa, Praia da Rosa, T048-3355 6056, www.bucanero.com.br. Closed Jun-Jul. Tastefully decorated luxury resort with private access to the beach. Set in lush vegetation in a protected area with a range of activities from horse riding to boat trips available. No children.

E Albergue da Juventude Dinda Rosa, Estr Geral do Rosa s/n, Praia da Rosa, T048-3355 6614, www.dindarosa.com.br. Busy hostel with its own (expensive) convenience store. Price per person.
E Praia do Ferrugem, Estr Gerals do Capão, Garopaba, T048-3254 0035. IYHA youth hostel. Price per person.

Camping
4 km south of Florianópolis, there is a camping site with bar at **Praia do Sonho**. Beautiful, deserted beach with an island fort nearby.

Laguna *p362*
B Flipper, Av Senador Gallottti 680, Mar Grosso, T048-3647 0558, www.flipper hotel.com.br Resort hotel with large rooms, pool, and friendly staff. Good for families.
C Turismar, Av Rio Grande do Sul 207, T048-3647 0024. A simple 2-star with a view out over Mar Grosso beach.
D Beiramar, 100 m from **Recanto**, opposite Angeloni Supermarket, T048-3644 0260. Clean, TV, rooms with view over lagoon.
D-E Recanto, Av Colombo 17, close to bus terminal. With breakfast. Modern but basic. Cheaper without private bath. The hotel owns snack bar next door.

Serra Geral *p363*
L Parador Casa da Montanha, Estr Parque Nacional, T054-3504 5302, reservations T054-9973 9320, www.paradorcasada montanha.com.br. 7 cabins up a precarious dirt road and perched in the edge of a canyon. A have stunning, dizzying views. Very beautiful. Full board included in the price and optional excursions into the park on horseback or foot. Minimum stay 2 days.
C-E Pousada Itaimbeleza, Rodoviária, Cambará do Sul, T054-3251 1365, www.itaimbezinho.tur.br. A range of rooms in 2 properties: one in the town near the *rodoviária* (with plain motel like rooms with or without a/c and/or bathroom) and the other rustic log cabins with room for up to 4 in the countryside and on the edge of the

park. Children under 7 stay free, there's a pool and breakfast and advice on tours.

West of Florianópolis p364
L Aguas Mornas Palace Hotel, R Coronel Antônio Lehmkuhl 2487, Águas Mornas, T048-3245 7015, www.aguasmornaspalace hotel.com.br, at the springs. Well-maintained luxury spa with a range of treatments.
AL Caldas da Imperatriz, SC 432, Rodovia Princesa Leopoldina Km 4, Caldas da Imperatriz, Santo Amaro da Imperatriz, T048-3245 7088, www.hotelcaldas.com.br. A grand, old-fashioned European spa built in 1850 under the auspices of Empress Teresa Cristina, originally with public baths. All meals are included in the price.

Lages and around p364
A Grande, R João de Castro 23, T/F049-3222 3522. Standard 3-star town hotel.
D Rodeio, T049-3223 2011. One of 3 similar hotels near the *rodoviária* with rooms with or without bath and a good breakfast.

Fazendas near Lages
All on working farms. Prices include all meals.
A Fazenda Aza Verde, Antiga BR-2, Soroptimista 13, T049-3222 0277. Horses, fishing, boats, games room, heating, pool.
A Fazenda Ciclone, BR-116, Km 276, localidade Vigia, T049-3222 3382. Horses, fishing, table tennis, billiards, river beach.
A Fazenda do Barreiro, Rod SC 438, Km 43, T049-3222 3031. Games room, library, horses, pool, fishing, boats, TV.
A Fazenda Dourado Turismo Rural, Estr Lages-Morrinhos Km 14, T049-3222 2066/ T049-9982 2094. Simple but comfortable a/c chalets surrounding a grassy lawn and in the edge of Araucária pine forest. With restaurant, pool and live music at weekends.
A Fazenda Nossa Senhora de Lourdes, R Aristiliano Ramos 565, T049-3222 0798. Pool, games room, library, horses, fishing, good walking.
A Fazenda Rancho do Boqueirão, BR-282, Km 4, Saída São José do Cerrito, T049-3226

0354. Heating, TV, library, games room, pool, horses, bicycles, good walking, fishing.
A Fazenda Refúgio do Lago, Rod SC 438, Km 10, Pedras Brancas, T049-3222 1416. Pool, games room, library, horses, shooting, fishing, boats, river beach.

🍴 Eating

Florianópolis p349, map p350
Take a walk along R Bocaiúva, east of R Almte Lamego, to find the whole street filled with Italian restaurants, barbecue places.
♦♦♦ Toca da Garoupa R Alves de Brito 178, just off R Bocaiúva. The city's best seafood restaurant housed in a rustic-chic wood slat house.
♦♦ Lindacap, R Felipe Schmidt 1162, T048-3222 4002. Closed Mon; Sun lunch only. Fish, chicken and meat *pratos* as well as seafood, smart, good buffet.
♦♦ Macarronada Italiana, Av Beiramar Norte 2458. Good, comfortable, upmarket Italian, with a decent pizzeria next door. In front of the Blue Tree Towers hotel.
♦♦ O Mercador, Box 33/4 Mercado Público. Excellent self-service specializing in fish and seafood, tables outside on cobbled street. Recommended.
♦♦ Papparella, Almte Lamego 1416. Excellent and enormous pizzas thick with cheese.
♦♦ Trapiche, Box 31, Mercado Público. Self-service fish and seafood, tables on pavement.
♦♦ Vida, R Visc de Ouro Preto 298, next to Alliance Française. Decent vegetarian set meals and pay by weight.
♦ Café das Artes, at north end of R Esteves Junior 734. Nice café, excellent cakes.
♦ Cía Lanches, Ten Silveira e R Trajano, downstairs, and, in Edif Dias Velho, Av R Felipe Schmidt 303. A wide selection of juices and snacks.
♦ Kayskidum, Av Beiramar Norte 2566. *Lanchonete* and crêperie, very popular.
♦ Mirantes, R Alvaro de Carvalho 246, Centro, with other branches on R Branco and a *churrascaria* on R 7 de Setembro.

Buffet self-service, good value food with a set menu for less than US$5 per kilo.

Ilha de Santa Catarina *p351, map p353*
♥♥ Ponta das Caranhas, Estr Geral da Barra da Lagoa 2377. Good seafood and chicken dishes in a romantic waterside setting with outdoor seating.
♥♥-♥ Oliveira, R Henrique Veras, Lagoa da Conceiçao. Excellent traditional seafood in pleasant surrounds. Closed Tue.

Joinville *p360, map 361*
The **Müeller Shopping** has a good food hall.
♥♥♥ Pinheiro, R Rio Branco 299, T047-3422 9090. Fish and shrimp dishes.
♥♥ Chimarrão, R Visconde de Taunay 343, T047 3027 7632. Good *churrascaria* serving many types of meat, *rodizio*-style.
♥♥ China, R Abdon Batista 131, opposite the cathedral, T047-3422 3323. Eat in or home-delivery service for oriental food.
♥♥ Sopp, R Mcal Deodoro 640, on corner with R Jaraguá, T047-3422 3637. Eclectic menu incorporating German, Brazilian and Japanese dishes. Good chopp.
♥♥ Trento Queijos e Vinhos, R 15 de Novembro 2973, T047-3453 1796. Traditional Italian with reasonable pastas and pizza.
♥♥-♥ Biergarten, R Visconde de Taunay 1183, T047 3423 3790. Good-quality German meals, snacks and beers at this combination restaurant and bar.

◐ Bars and clubs

Florianópolis *p349, map p350*
To find out about events and theme nights check the **Beiramar Shopping Centre** for notices in shop windows, ask in surf shops or take a trip to the University of Santa Catarina in Trindade and check out the noticeboards. The newspaper *Diário Catarinense* gives details of bigger events, eg **Oktoberfest**.

The **Mercado Público** in the centre, which is alive with fish sellers and stalls, has a different atmosphere at the end of the

day when hard-working locals turn up to unwind. However, this area is not particularly safe at night and most bars and restaurants are closed by 2200. The stall, **Box 32**, is good for seafood and has a bar specializing in *cachaça*, including its own brand. **Restaurant Pirão** overlooks the market square with a quieter view and live Brazilian music on Tue, Thu and Fri. **Empórium**, Bocaiúva 79, is a shop by day and popular bar at night.

You may need a car to get to other clubs and bars or the hot spots at the beaches.
Café Cancun, Av Beiramar Norte, T048-3225 1029. Wed-Sun from 2000, US$5. Bars, restaurant, dancing, sophisticated.
Café Matisse, Av Irineu Bornhausen 5000, inside the Centro Integrade de Cultura, www.cafematissefloripa.com.br. A colourful little café decorated with impressionist prints and art by local artists and which plays hosts to live bands and DJs.
Ilhéu, Av Prof Gama d'Eça e R Jaime Câmara, US$5. Bar open until early hours, tables spill outside, very popular with locals, fills up quickly, venue for live music rather than a disco (tiny dancefloor).

Ilha de Santa Catarina *p351, map p353*
Throughout the summer, the beaches open their bars day and night; during the rest of the year the beginning of the week is very quiet. The beach huts of **Praia Mole** invite people to party all night (bring a blanket), while **Club Seven** (in the Boulevard) and **L'Equinox Bar** (Joaquina) attract serious clubbers **Seven** offers theme nights and is very popular with surfers. Any bars are worth visiting in the Lagoon area, although Barra da Lagoa becomes quiet after nightfall, even in high season. Around the Lagoa the Brazilian phrase *'qualquer lugar é lugar'* (any place is the place to be) perfectly captures the laid-back beach mood. Other clubs and bars generally require a car: **Latitude 27**, near Praia Mole, good for live music, **Ilhéus Bar** (Canasvieiras) and the popular **Ibiza** nightclub in Jureré, which has house and techno DJs inside, live music outside.

🎭 Entertainment

Florianópolis *p349, map p350*
Cinema The cinema at **Shopping Centre Beiramar** has international films with subtitles.
Music Free live music every Sat morning at the marketplace near the bus terminal.

🎉 Festivals and events

Florianópolis *p349, map p350*
Easter Farra de Boi (Festival of the Bull). It is only in the south that the bull is actually killed on Easter Sun. Despite being controversial, the festival arouses fierce local pride and there is much celebration. The Portuguese brought the tradition of the bull, which has great significance in Brazilian celebrations.
Dec-Jan The island dances to the sound of the Boi-de-Mamão, a dance that incorporates the puppets of Bernunça, Maricota (the Goddess of Love, a puppet with long arms to embrace everyone) and Tião, the monkey.

Itajaí *p356*
Oct Marejada is held in honour of the sea, in the Centro de Promoções Itajaí Tur, where there are musical and folkloric festivities, a pavilion for dancing and shows, and a pavilion for food (with lots of different ways of preparing *bacalhau* and masses of seafood).

Penha *p357*
Feb Seafood festival and Carnaval
May/Jun Festa do Divino. A procession and crowning of the Emperor.
24-29 Jun Festa de São João e São Pedro. A tradition from the Azores.

Blumenau *p357*
Oct Oktoberfest, see box page 359.

Joinville *p360, map p361*
May Fenatiro, the annual festival for the 2000 members of the local shooting clubs.
Jul Joinville hosts one of the largest dance festivals in the world; around 4000 dancers

stay for 12 days and put on shows and displays, ranging from jazz and folklore to classical ballet, seen by some 30,000 spectators in a variety of locations.
Oct Fenachopp, beer festival.
Nov Annual flower festival, mostly orchids, disappointing, US\$1.50 entry.

🛍 Shopping

Florianópolis *p349, map p350*
Shopping Centre Beiramar is the largest mall with the usual range of fashion (with plenty of surf wear), music and assorted shops. There are many smaller shopping malls dotted around the resorts. Bargain hunters are better off bartering in the family-run businesses at the Mercado Público. Here, Casa da Alfândega, has a good selection of crafts and souvenirs.

⛰ Activities and tours

Florianópolis *p349, map p350*
Brazil Ecojourneys, Estrada Rozália Paulina Ferreira 1132, Armação, Florianópolis, T048-3389 5619, T048-9111 6366 (mob), www.brazilecojourneys.com. One of the most efficient operators in southern Brazil. Trips around Santa Catarina, with hiking in the Serra and Paraná and Rio Grande do Sul and numerous activities around Florianópolis from trail-walking to para and hang-gilding, surfing and sandboarding.
Scuna Sul, T048-3222 1806, www.scuna sul.com.br. Very popular boat trips around the Ilha de Santa Catarina from US\$7.50.

Excursions from Blumenau *p358*
Activities include parapenting, a jeep club (www.jeepclubedeblumenau.com.br), horse riding, and swimming pools with water slides. Ask at the tourist office for details.
Parque das Nascentes, 20 km from the city, T047-3335 1863, www.parquedas nascentes.com.br, US\$2.25. Offers waterfalls, pleasant trails and camping.

⊕ Transport

Florianópolis *p349, map p350*
Air
To get to the airport take a **Ribeiroense** bus 'Corredor Sudoeste' from Terminal Urbano. Flights to **São Paulo** (Congonhas), **Rio de Janeiro**, **Porto Alegre** and **Curitiba**.

Airline offices Aerolíneas Argentinas, R Tte Silveira 200, 8th floor, T048-3224 7835. **GOL**, T0300-3789 2121, www.voegol.com.br. **Nordeste/Rio Sul**, Jerônimo Coelho 185, sala 601, T048-3224 7008, airport T048-3236 1779. **Oceanair**, T0300-3789 8160, www.oceanair.com.br. **TAM**, at airport, T048-3236 1812, www.tam.com.br. **Varig**, Av R Branco 796, T048-3224 7266.

Bus
Local There are 3 bus stations for routes on the island, or close by on the mainland: **Terminal de Ônibus Interurbano** between Av Paulo Fontes and R Francisco Tolentino, west of the Mercado Público; **Terminal Urbano** between Av Paulo Fontes and R Antônio Luz, east of Praça Fernando Machado; and a terminal at **R Silva Jardim** and R José da Costa.

Yellow microbuses (**Transporte Ejecutivo**), starting from the south end of Praça 15 de Novembro, charge US$2.50 depending on the destination. Normal bus fares cost from US$1.40.

Long distance International buses and those to other Brazilian cities leave from the *rodoviária* **Rita Maria** on the island, at the east end of the Ponte Colombo Machado Salles.

Regular daily buses to **Porto Alegre** (US$16, 7 hrs), **São Paulo**, 9 hrs (US$23.75, *leito* US$36.25), **Rio de Janeiro**, 20 hrs (US$31 *convencional*, US$42 executive, US$55 *leito*); to **Foz do Iguaçu** (US$22, continuing to **Asunción** US$30). To **São Joaquim** at 1145, 1945 with **Reunidos**, 1815 with **Nevatur**, 5-6 hrs, US$9.30; to **Laguna** US$5.25. No direct bus to Corumbá, change at Campo Grande.

To **Montevideo** (Uruguay), US$52, daily, by TTL. **Buenos Aires** (Argentina), US$55, **Pluma**, buses very full in summer, book one week in advance.

Car hire
Auto Locadora Coelho, Felipe Schmidt 81, vehicles in good condition. **Interlocadora**, T048-3236 0179, at the airport, rates from US$40 a day before supplements. **Localiza** at the airport, T048-3236 1244, and at Av Paulo Fontes 730, T048-3225 5558.

Porto Belo and around *p355, map p356*
Bus To **Florianópolis**, several daily with **Rainha**, US$5, fewer at weekends, more frequent buses to **Tijucas**, **Itapema** and **Itajaí**, all on the BR-101 with connections. **Catarinense** runs several buses daily to **Blumenau**, US$5.50. Local buses run from Porto Belo to the beaches on the peninsula.

Blumenau *p357*
Bus Coletivos Volkmann (T047-3395 1400), run to **Pomerode**, roughly every 40 mins, check schedule at the tourist office, *rodoviária* or www.turismovolkmann.com.br. Also several buses daily with **Catarinense** and **Reunidos**, 40 mins, US$2.50. Regular buses with Catarinense to **Curitiba**, US$13-18, **Florianópolis**, US$15, and **Joinville** US$9. Timetables and fares at www.cata rinense.net twice daily from Blumenau to **Porto Alegre** with Penha/Itapemirim, 10 hrs, US$50/45.

Excursions from Blumenau *p358*
There are buses from Pomerode to **Jaraguá do Sul**, **Joinville**, **São Bento do Sul**, **Florianópolis**, **São Paulo**, **Curitiba** and other local places with **União**, **Reunidas**, and Catarinense.

São Francisco do Sul *p359*
Bus The bus terminal is 1.5 km from the centre. Bus to the centre (Terminal Municipal), 'Rodoviária' runs Mon-Fri only, or 'Dom Pedro II' every 40 mins at weekends. There is 1 direct bus daily to **Curitiba** with

Penha (www.penha.locaweb.com.br)
and 2 daily with **Catarinense**
(www.catarinense.net), US$10, 3 hrs.

Joinville *p360, map p361*
Air The airport is 13 km from the city;
a taxi from the centre costs US$10. **GOL**
and **TAM** fly to **São Paulo**.
    Airline offices TAM, T047-3433 2033.
Varig/Rio Sul, R Alexandre Dohler 277,
T047-3433 2800.

Bus Regular buses run to the *rodoviária*
is 2.5 km outside the town, south exit. To
Blumenau, US$3, 2¼ hrs. To **Porto Alegre**,
1½ hrs US$15, with **Santo Anjo da Guarda**;
same company goes to **Florianópolis**, 5 daily
(2 hrs, US$25); to **Tubarão**, every hour with
Alvorada (US$3, 30 mins). To **Farol** with
Lagunatur or **Auto Viação São José**, 8 buses
a day Mon-Fri, 3 on Sat, 2 on Sun (US$5.50),
a beautiful ride.

Car hire **Interlocadora**, R do Príncipe 839,
T047-3422 7888. **Localiza**, R Blumenau 1728,
T047-3433 9393, or at the airport T047-3467
1020. **Olímpia**, R 9 de Março 734, T047-
3433 1755.

Laguna *p362*
Bus To **Porto Alegre**, US$21½ hrs,
with **Santo Anjo Da Guarda**; same company
goes to **Florianópolis**, 2 hrs, US$12, 5 daily;
to **Tubarão**, every hour with **Alvorada**,
50 mins. To **Farol** with **Lagunatur** or **Auto
Viação São José** (8 buses a day Mon-Fri,
3 on Sat, 2 on Sun, US$2.50, a beautiful ride).

Lages *p364*
Bus The bus station is 30 mins' walk
southeast of the centre. To **Florianópolis**,
6-8 buses daily on the direct road (BR-282),
5 hrs, US$22; twice daily to **Caxias do Sul**,
4 hrs, US$15.

🛈 Directory

Florianópolis *p349, map p350*
Banks **Açoriano Turismo**, Jaime Câmara
106, T048-224 3939, takes Amex. Money
changers on R Felipe Schmidt outside BESC.
Banco do Brasil, Praça 15 de Novembro,
exchange upstairs, 1000-1500, huge
commission on cash or TCs. Lots of ATMs
downstairs. **Banco Estado de Santa Catarina**
(BESC), *câmbio*, R Felip, Schmidt e Jerônimo
Coelho, 1000-1600, no commission on TCs.
ATM for MasterCard/Cirrus at **Banco Itaú**,
Shopping Centre Beiramar (not in the centre,
bus Expresso). **HSBC**, ATM, R Felipe Schmidt
376, corner with R Álvaro de Carvalho.
Lovetur, Av Osmar Cunha 15, Ed Ceisa
and **Centauro Turismo**, same address.
Embassies and consulates Chile,
R Alvaro de Carvalho 267, 6th floor,
Edif Mapil, T048-3223 3383. France, Alliance
Française, T048-3222 7589 (Fri 0900-1200).
Spain, R Almte Alvim 24, Casa 9, T048-
3222 1821. Uruguay, R Prof Walter de Bona
Castela 26, T048-3234 4645 (0800-1200,
1400-1800). **Internet** Moncho, Tiradentes
181. **Language schools** Step 1 Idiomas,
R Joe Collaço 99, Córrego Grande, T048-
3233 6605, www.step1.com.br. Portuguese
classes for foreigners with short and
longer-term courses. **Laundry** Lav e Lev,
R Felipe Schmidt 706, opposite Valerim
Plaza. **Post office** Praça 15 de Novembro 5.
Telephone Praça Pereira Oliveira 20.

Joinville *p360, map p361*
Banks There are Bradesco and Banco
do Brasil banks in the city. **Internet**
Biernet Bar, R Visconde de Taunay 456,
and numerous others. **Medical
services** 24-hr pharmacies: Drogaria
Catarinense, Filial Boa Vista, in front of
the Hospital Regional, T047-3437 2355,
or Filial São João, Av Getúlio Vargas 1343,
T047-3422 7691. **Farmacia Catarinense**,
R 15 de Novembro 503, T047-3422 2318.

Rio Grande do Sul

Brazil's southernmost state regards itself as different from the rest of the country and has long been lobbying for independence. Its people identify more with Uruguay and Argentina and, like their counterparts on the pampas, refer to themselves as gaúchos.

The scenery is different too. An escarpment, in places over 1000 m high, runs down the coastal area as far as Porto Alegre providing escape from the summer swelter. The state capital is the most industrialized and cosmopolitan city in the south and tops the country's 'urban quality of life' rankings. All along the coast, the green hills of Rio Grande do Sul are fringed by sandbars and lagoons, forming one of the world's longest beaches. On the border with Santa Catarina in the north is the remarkable Aparados da Serra national park, where there is often snow.

In southern Rio Grande do Sul, the grasslands stretch as far as Uruguay to the south and more than 800 km west to Argentina, and are scattered with the remains of Jesuit missions. This is the distinctive land of the gaúcho (cowboy) and the herders are regularly seen in traditional garb. In restaurants, steaks the size of Texas are the order of the day; look out for local specialities such as 'comida campeira', 'te colonial' and 'quentão'. ▶▶ *For listings, see pages 385-394.*

Background

The first people to settle in the area were pioneer farmers, and the traditional dress of the *gaúcho* (pronounced ga-oo-shoo in Brazil) can still be seen: the flat black hat, *bombachas* (baggy trousers) and poncho. The indispensable drink of the southern cattlemen is *ximarão* (*mate* without sugar, also spelt *chimarrão*). The *gaúcho* culture has developed a sense of distance from the African-influenced society further north. Many people will tell you they have more in common with Uruguayans or Argentines than Brazilians – apart from when it comes to football. Today, there are many millions of cattle, sheep and pigs, and the state produces some 75% of all Brazilian wine.

Since 1999, the state government has implemented a radical consultative scheme whereby people in all 497 municipalities jointly decide school, road and other infrastructure spending. The 'participatory budget', pioneered for more than a dozen years in Porto Alegre, is widely supported and has attracted international acclaim. For more information visit www.estado.rs.gov.br.

Porto Alegre 🔲🔗🔖🌸🔘🔺🔖🔗 ▶▶ *pp385-394. Colour map 5, B3.*

→ *Phone code: 051. Population: 1,361,000.*

Situated at the confluence of five rivers and freshened by over a million trees, Porto Alegre is one of Brazil's more pleasant cities. Culturally rich, ethnically diverse and progressive, it is the capital of the southern frontier and the hub of trade with Argentina and Uruguay. It is a good base for exploring the rest of Rio Grande do Sul's natural beauty and historical sites. The capital of Rio Grande do Sul is where cowboy culture meets the bright lights. Though it is the biggest commercial centre south of São Paulo, it is friendly and manageable on foot.

Ins and outs

Getting there International and domestic flights arrive at **Salgado Filho airport** ① *R Severo Dullius 90010, 8 km from the city, T051-3358 2000.* There are regular buses to the bus station and a metrô service to the city centre. International and interstate buses arrive at the **rodoviária** ① *Largo Vespasiano Júlio Veppo, Av Mauá with Garibáldi, T051-3286 8230, www.rodoviaria-poa.com.br*, an easy walk from the city centre. There are good facilities, including a post office and long-distance telephone service until 2100. ▶▶ *See Transport, page 391.*

Porto Alegre

Sleeping 🛏
América **14**
Blue Tree Millennium Flat **1**
Comfort Inn **5**
Conceição Center **2**
Continental **3**
Elevado **13**
Embaixador **4**
Lancaster **6**
Minuano **15**
Palácio **7**
Plaza São Rafael **8**
Porto Alegre Residence **10**
Ritter **9**
Uruguay **11**

Eating 🍴
Al Dente **1**
Café do Cofre **9**
Chopp Stübel **5**
Galpão Crioulo **2**
Ilha Natural **3**
Koh Pee Pee **6**
Portoalegrense **8**
Wunderbar **4**

Getting around *Lotação* (first-class minibuses), painted in a distinctive orange, blue and white pattern, stop on request. They are safer and more pleasant than normal buses and cost about US$1.60. The **Trensurb metrô** ① *T051-2129 8477, www.trensurb.com.br, single journey US$1.10*, runs from the southern terminal at the Mercado Público (station beside the market), as far north as Sapucaia do Sul. The second station serves the *rodoviária*, and the fifth station serves the airport (10 minutes). A good way to get your bearings in the city is to take the **Linha Turisma** ① *buses leave from Travessa do Carmo 84, Cidade Baixa, T051-3212 3464, portoalegre@turismo.prefpoa.com.br, US$5, reservations necessary*, a popular open-top tourist bus around the city.

Best time to visit Standing on a series of hills and valleys on the banks of Lake Guaíba, Porto Alegre has a temperate climate for most of the year, although temperatures often exceed 40°C at the height of summer and drop below 10°C in winter.

Tourist information For general information contact the **Secretaria do Turismo** ① *T0800-517686, www.portoalegre.rs.gov.br/turismo*. Also helpful are the **Central de Informações Turísticas** ① *R Vasco da Gama 253, Bom Fim, T051-3311 5289, daily 0900-2100*, and **Setur** ① *Borges de Medeiros 1501, 10th floor, T051-3228 5400, also at the airport and rodoviária*, which provides free city maps. There are free guided walks on Sunday at 1500 or 1600 from Praça da Alfândega or on Saturday from Praça da Matriz, T0800-517686. Contact the tourist office, or ask in the Mercado Público. The state tourism website is www.turismo.rs.gov.br.

Maps Army maps (1:50,000) of Rio Grande do Sul's trekking regions (Canela, Parque Nacional de Aparados da Serra) are available at **Junta Servicio Militar** ① *Prefeitura Municipal, R Prof E Castro 850, T051-3223 3611*. These maps are not available in rural areas.

Safety Avoid the area around the bus terminal at night, and the market area in Praça 15 de Novembro becomes dangerously deserted after around 2100. Thefts have been reported in Voluntários da Pátria and Praça Parcão.

Sights

The older residential part of the town is on a promontory, dominated previously by the **Palácio Piratini** (governor's palace) and the imposing 1920s metropolitan **cathedral** on the **Praça Marechal Deodoro** (Praça da Matriz). Also on, or near, this square are the neoclassical **Theatro São Pedro** (1858), the **Solar dos Câmara** (1818), now a historical and cultural centre) and the **Biblioteca Pública**, but all are dwarfed by the skyscraper of the **Assembléia Legislativa**. Down Rua General Câmara from Praça Marechal Deodoro is the **Praça da Alfândega**, with the old customs house, the **Museu de Arte de Rio Grande do Sul**, the old post office and the Banco Meridional. A short walk east from here, up Rua 7 de Setembro, is the busy **Praça 15 de Novembro**, where the neoclassical **Mercado Público** sells everything from religious artefacts to spice and meat. You'll find plenty of good cafés, here, and the pavement bars outside are busy at lunch-times and during 'happy hour'. Opposite the market is the bar/restaurant **Chalé da Praça XV**, a Bavarian-style building dating back to 1874. This is a very popular meeing spot and its outdoor seats are perfectly placed for people watching.

Do not miss the pedestrianized part of **Rua dos Andradas** (Rua da Praia). It is the city's principal outdoor meeting place, the main shopping area, and by around 1600 it is jammed full of people. Heading west along Rua dos Andradas, you pass the pink **Casa de Cultura Mário Quintana** in the converted **Hotel Majestic** (see Entertainment, page 390). A little further along is a wide stairway leading up to the two high white towers of the church of **Nossa Senhora das Dores**, the only National Heritage graded church in the city. Many tall buildings in this part of the city rise above the fine, sometimes dilapidated, old houses and the streets are famous for their steep gradients. On the banks of Lake Guaíba, the **Usina do Gasômetro** is Porto Alegre's answer to London's Tate Modern. Built 1926-1928 as a thermoelectric station, it was abandoned in 1974 before being converted to showcase art, dance and film in 1992. Its 117-m chimney has become a symbol for the city. There is a café in the bottom of the chimney, and the sunset from the centre's balcony is stunning. In the **Cidade Baixa** quarter are the colonial **Travessa dos Venezianos** (between Ruas Lopo Gonçalves and Joaquim Nabuco) and the **house of Lopo Gonçalves** ① *R João Alfredo 582*, which houses the **Museu de Porto Alegre Joaquim José Felizardo** ① *Tue-Sun 0900-1200 and 1330-1800, free*, with exhibits about the city's history.

The **Museu Júlio de Castilhos** ① *Duque de Caxias 1231, Tue-Sun 0900-1700*, has a permanent collection on the history of Rio Grande do Sul state, as well as temporary exhibits. The **Museu de Arte do Rio Grande do Sul** ① *Praça Senador Florêncio (Praça da Alfândega), Tue 1000-2100, Wed-Sun 1000-1700, free*, is interesting. It specializes in art from Rio Grande do Sul, but also houses temporary exhibitions. **Museu de Comunicação Social** ① *R dos Andradas 959, T051-322 44252, Mon-Fri 1200-1900*, in the former *A Federação* newspaper building, deals with the development of the press in Brazil since the 1920s.

Parks

Porto Alegre is well endowed with open spaces. Many of the trees are of the flowering varieties, such as jacarandas and flamboyants. There are seven parks and 700 squares in the city, of which the most traditional is **Parque Farroupilha** (Parque Redenção), a fine park near the city centre. It has a triangular area of 33 ha between Avenida Osvaldo Aranha, Avenida José Bonifácio and Avenida João Pessoa, and contains a lake, mini-zoo, amusement park, bicycle hire, the Araújo Viana auditorium and a monument to the Second World War. On Sundays there is a *feira* of antiques and handicrafts at the José Bonifácio end, where locals walk, talk and drink *chimarrão*, the traditional *gaúcho* drink. **Parque Moinhos de Vento** is popular for jogging and has a replica of a windmill in the middle of the park; there used to be several working mills here, which gave the *bairro* its name. The riverside drive, Avenida Edvaldo Pereira Paiva, around Parque Maurício Sirotsky Sobrinho, is closed to traffic on Sunday for cycling, skating, jogging and strolling. **Marinho do Brasil** is another large park between the centre and the *zona sul*, where there are lots of sporting activities. The **botanic gardens** ① *R Salvador França 1427, zona leste, US$1.50, Tue-Sun 0800-1700, take bus No 40 from Praça 15 de Novembro to Bairro Jardim Botânico*, are a short bus ride from the city centre and well worth a visit. The interesting **Museu de Ciéncias Naturais** is also housed in the garden's grounds.

The 5-km-wide **Lake Guaíba** lends itself to every form of boating and there are several sailing clubs. Two boats run trips around the islands in the estuary: **Cisne Branco** ① *T051-3224 5222, www.barcocisnebranco.com.br, several sailings daily, from 1 hr, US$8*, from Cais do Porto, near Museu de Arte de Rio Grande do Sul; and **Noiva do Caí** ① *T051-3211 7662, several on Sun, some mid-week, 1 hr, US$1.90, check winter schedules*, from the Usina do Gasômetro. Jet-skiers jump the wake of the tour boats. **Ipanema beach**, on the southern banks of the river, has spectacular sunsets. You can see a good view of the city, with glorious sunsets, from the **Morro de Santa Teresa** (take bus No 95 from the top end of Rua Salgado Filho, marked 'Morro de Santa Teresa TV' or just 'TV').

Around 30 km north of Porto Alegre on the BR-116 is the very good **Parque Zoológico** ① *BR-116, Parada 41, Tue-Sun 0830-1700, US$2.50*, set in 780 ha and home to more than 2000 animals, birds and reptiles.

Tramandaí north to Torres ➜ *Phone code: 051. Population: 31,000.*

The main beach resorts are east and north of the city. Heading east along the BR-290, 112 km from Porto Alegre, is **Osório**, a pleasant lakeside town with a few hotels. From here it is 18 km southeast to the rather polluted beach resort of **Tramandaí**. The beaches here are very popular, with lots of hotels, restaurants and seaside amenities. Extensive dunes and lakes in the region provide an interesting variety of wildlife and sporting opportunities. The beach resorts become less polluted the further north you travel, and the water is clean by the time you reach **Torres**.

Just inland, the BR-101 heads north from Osório to Florianópolis and beyond. A series of lakes separates the road from the coastal belt, but there is another road running all along the coast from Tramandaí to Torres and the border with Santa Catarina. Between the two towns are the resorts (heading south to north) of **Atlântida do Sul**, **Capão da Canoa**, **Arroio Teixeira** and **Arroio do Sal** (Casa da Sogra serves good food). At **Capão da Canoa** there is surfing at Atlântida beach, while the **Lagoa dos Quadros**, inland, is used for windsurfing, sailing, waterskiing and jet-skiing.

Torres and around
➜ *Colour map 5, B4. Phone code: 051.*

Torres is a well-developed resort, with a number of beaches, high-class hotels and restaurants, as well as professional surfing competitions and entertainment. There is a lively club scene during the holidays. There is no lack of cheap places to stay, but from Christmas to Carnaval rooms are hard to find. ➤ *See Festivals and events, page 390.*

Torres gets its name from the three huge rocks, or towers, on the town beach, **Praia Grande**. Some 2 km long, the beach is safe for swimming and there is surf near the breakwater. Fishing boats can be hired for a trip to **Ilha dos Lobos**, a rocky island 2 km offshore, where sea lions spend the winter months. Dolphins visit **Praia dos Molhes**, north of town, year round, and southern right whales en route to Santa Catarina can

Porto Alegre coast

occasionally be seen in July. On the edge of Rio Mampituba, which marks the state boundary, the beach is good for net fishing and has restaurants.

About 2 km south of Torres, past rocky little Prainha, is **Cal** (camping is possible at **Paradise Dunas**, December to February only), popular with surfers. A further 2 km south, passing the Praia da Guarita leisure development, is **Itapeva**, with a campsite open year round. The water here is calm, okay for swimming and there is good dune trekking in the **Parque da Guarita**. There are bars and cafés and a **tourist office** ① *R Rio Branco 315, Torres, T051-3664 1219/ T051-3626 1937.*

South of Tramandaí → *Phone code 051.*

A paved road runs south from Tramandaí (mostly prohibited to trucks) along the coast to **Quintão**, giving access to many beaches. One such beach is **Cidreira**, 26 km south of Tramandaí; it is not very crowded and has **Hotel Farol** on the main street. A bus from Porte Alegre costs US$3.40. A track continues to charming **Mostardas** and along the peninsula on the seaward side of the Lagoa dos Patos to São José do Norte, opposite Rio Grande (see Excursions from Rio Grande, page 382). There is accommodation in **Palmares do Sul** (across the peninsula from Quintão) and Mostardas. The latter also has a Banco do Brasil and good pizzeria (Rua Luís Araújo 941, closed Monday). About 30 km south of Mostardas is **Tavares**, with a barely passable hotel (**F**) in the *praça*.

Mostardas makes a good base for visiting the **Lagoa do Peixe national park** ① *information at Praça Luís Martins 30, Mostardas, T051-3673 1464*, one of South America's top spots for migrating birds. Flamingos and albatrosses are among the visitors. There is free access to the park, but there is no infrastructure. From Mostardas you can hop off the bus (daily at 1045) that passes through the northern end of the park on its way to the beach, where there are basic hotels and restaurants. The main lake, which has the highest bird concentration, is about 20 km from both Mostardas and Tavares.

Serra Gaúcha ⊜❼▲❸❻ ›› pp385-394.

Some of the Serra Gaúcha's most stunningly beautiful scenery is around the towns of Gramado and Canela, 130 km north of Porto Alegre. There is a distinctly Swiss/Bavarian flavour to many of the buildings in both towns. In spring and summer the flowers are a delight, and in winter there are frequent snow showers. December is the busiest month for tourism, with Brazilian and Argentinian families flocking here in droves to see the genuinely impressive Christmas displays.

This is excellent walking and climbing country among hills, woods, lakes and waterfalls. The Rio Paranhana at Três Coroas, 25 km south of Gramado, is well known for canoeing, especially for slalom. Local crafts include knitted woollens, leather, wickerwork and chocolate.

Gramado → *Colour map 5, B4. Phone code: 054. Population: 28,600.*

At 850 m above sea level, Gramado provides a summer escape from the 40°C heat of the plains. The town lies on the edge of a plateau with fantastic views. It is clean and full of Alpine-style buildings making it feel like a Swiss Disneyworld. Famous for its chocolate, Gramado survives almost entirely through tourism. Its main street, Avenida Borges de Medeiros, is full of kitsch artisan shops and fashion boutiques. In the summer, thousands of *hortênsias* (hydrangeas) bloom. Among its parks are **Parque Knorr** and **Lago Negro**, and **Minimundo** ① *T054-3286 1334, Tue-Sun 1300-1700*, a collection of miniature models such as European castles. About 1.5 km along Avenida das Hortênsias heading towards Canela is the **Prawer chocolate factory** ① *Av das Hortênsias 4100, T054-3286 1580, www.prawer.com.br, Mon-Fri 0830-1130 and 1330-1700*, which offers free tours of the truffle-making process and free tastings. Opposite is the **Hollywood Dream Car Automobile Museum** ① *Av das Hortênsias 4151, T054-3286 4515, 0900-1900, US$8*, which has an excellent collection of American gas-guzzlers dating back to a 1929 Ford Model A and Harley-Davidson motorbikes from 1926. For a good walk or bike ride into the valley, take the dirt road Turismo Rural 28, 'Um Mergulho no Vale' (A Dive into the Valley), which starts at Avenida das Hortênsias immediately before the (the Brazilian Environment Ministry) chocolate factory. There are two **tourist information offices** ① *Av das Hortênsias (Pórtico), T054-3286 1418*, and ① *Praça Maj Nicoletti/Av Borges de Medeiros 1674, T054-3286 1475, www.gramadosite.com.br*.

Canela and around → *Colour map 5, B4. Phone code: 054. Population: 33,600.*

A few kilometres along the plateau rim, Canela has been spared the plastic makeover of its neighbour and offers more affordable sleeping and eating options. The painted wooden buildings provide a certain downtown charm. Canela is surrounded by good parks and is developing as a centre of adventure tourism, with rafting, abseiling and trekking on offer. There's a **tourist office** ① *Laga da Fama 227, T054-3282 2200, www.canelaturismo.com.br*.

Just outside Canela is the **Mundo à Vapor** ① *RS 235, Rodovia Canela–Gramado T054-3282 1115, daily 0915-1700, US$5*, an interesting museum dedicated to steam power. The main attraction is the dramatic reconstruction of the famous 1895 rail disaster in Montparnasse, Paris. Kids and adults clamour to have their picture taken alongside a giant steam train that appears to have burst through the front of the building.

Canela is surrounded by beautiful parks, including **Parque Caracol** ① *T054-3278 3035, 0830-1800, US$4.50*. Here, you'll find the Rio Caracol, a spectacular 130-m-high waterfall, which emerges from thick forest and tumbles like dry ice from an overhanging elliptical escarpment. Just outside the park is **Parque do Teleférico** ① *www.canelatelerifico.com.br*, where you can take a 20-minute ski lift ride over the trees, canyons and falls (US$10). The falls are east-facing, so photography is best before noon. A 927-step metal staircase leads to the plunge pool. If cycling, there is an 18-km circular route continuing on to **Parque Ferradura** (along a 4-km spur), where there is a good view into the canyon of the Rio Cai. From the Ferradura junction, turn right to continue to the national forest **Floresta Nacional** ① *T054-3282 2608, 0800-1700, free*, run by Ibama, with woodland walks. From here, the dirt road continues round to Canela. Another good hike or bike option is the 4-km dirt track southeast of Canela past **Parque das Sequóias to Morro Pelado**. At over 600 m, there are spectacular views from the rim edge.

Army maps (1:50,000) are available from military posts in Caxias do Sul and Porto Alegre. The urban department in Canela's prefeitura municipal, Rua Dona Carlinda, and the environmental lodge in Parque Estadual do Caracol have copies available for viewing only.

South of Porto Alegre ⊙❶❷❸❹ » *pp385-394. Colour map 5, C3.*

Pelotas → *Phone code: 053. Population: 323,200.*

Pelotas, Rio Grande do Sul's second largest city, was founded in the early 19th century and grew rich on the *charque* (dried beef) trade. On the BR-116, 271 km south of Porto Alegre, it lies on the banks of Rio São Gonçalo, which connects the Lagoa dos Patos with the Lagoa Mirim. The heyday was 1860-1890 and its early colonial architecture enhances the city's air of being stuck in a time warp. It is sleepy yet prosperous, with much typically Brazilian charm. It has an array of shops in the pedestrianized town centre, and pleasant parks with lots of green spaces. There is a 19th-century cathedral, **São Francisco de Paula**, and, as testament to British settlers of the time, the Anglican church **Igreja Episcopal do Redentor**, a couple of blocks from the main square on Rua XV de Novembro. The tree-lined Avenida Bento Gonçalves offers a pleasant escape from the summer heat. Pelotas is famous for its cakes and sweets; try some of the preserved fruits from the many small confectioners.

Ins and outs The **airport** ① 8 km from the town centre, receives flights from Porto Alegre. The *rodoviária* is out of town, with a bus every 15 minutes to the centre. There's no official tourist information centre but **Terrasul** ① *R Gen Neto 627, T053-3227 9973, www.terra sulpelotas.com.br*, has local maps and can organize good-value city and regional tours. Recommended.

Excursions from Pelotas

Within a radius of 60 km (about an hour's drive), there are numerous excursions to the farms of settlers of German descent in the hilly countryside (for example Cerrito Alegre and Quilombo), where you can find simple and clean accommodation, with cheap, good and plentiful food.

West of town, the **Lagoa dos Patos** is very shallow; at low tide it is possible to walk 1 km out from the shore. During heavy rain, saltwater entering the lake brings with it large numbers of crabs, which are a local delicacy. Fishermen are generally happy to take tourists out on sightseeing or fishing trips for a small fee (it's best to go in a group). **Praia do Laranjal** is full of local beach houses and there are several friendly bars. **Barro Douro** is very green with a campsite but no beach. It's the site of a big local festival for *Iemanjá* on 1-2 February; well worth visiting. From Pelotas, take a Ze3 bus (or taxi US$30).

South of Pelotas, on the BR-471, is the **Taim Water Reserve** ① *information from Ibama in Porto Alegre, T051-3225 2144, www.ibama.gov.br*, on the Lagoa Mirim. The road cuts the reserve in two and capibaras, killed by passing traffic, are sadly a common sight along the route. Many protected species, including black-necked swans and the quero-quero bird, migrate to the Taim for the breeding season. There are no facilities. About 5 km from Taim there is an **ecological station** with a small museum of regional animals; there is some accommodation for scientists or other interested visitors, however, most visitors stay in Rio Grande, 80 km away, or in Pelotas.

Rio Grande → *Colour map 5, C3. Phone code: 053. Population: 186,500.*

At the entrance to the Lagoa dos Patos, 274 km south of Porto Alegre, is Rio Grande, founded in 1737. The city lies on a low, sandy peninsula, 16 km from the Atlantic Ocean. Today it is the distribution centre for the southern part of Rio Grande do Sul, with significant cattle and meat industries.

During the latter half of the 19th century, Rio Grande was an important centre. It has lost much of its importance but is still notable for the charm of its old buildings. The **Catedral de São Pedro** dates from 1755-1775. The **Museu Oceanográfico** ① *2 km from the centre on Av Perimetral, T053-3231 3496, daily 0900-1100, 1400-1700*, has an interesting collection of 125,000 molluscs. To get there take bus No 59 or walk along the waterfront. At Praça Tamandaré is a small zoo. There is a **tourist office** at the junction of Rua Duque de Caxias and Rua Gen Becaler.

Border essentials: Brazil–Uruguay

As from 2008 the border at Chuí was closed and all crossings into Uruguay now go via Bagé where Brazilian immigration is located. Before crossing into Uruguay, you must visit Brazilian Polícia Federal in Bagé to get an exit stamp; if not, the Uruguayan authorities will send you back.

Public transport to these crossings is from Bagé. Bagé is not connected to Porto Alegre by regular bus; it may be better to book crossings through an agency in Porto Alegre as they will know the current situation regarding how to get the exit stamp and link this with transport, see page 391. **Brazil Ecojourneys** in Florianópolis also provides reliable information, see page 370.

Barro do Quaraí (Brazil)–Bella Unión (Uruguay)
This is the most westerly crossing in Rio Grande do Sul, and is via the Barra del Cuaraim bridge, near the confluence of the Uruguai and Quaraí rivers. Bella Unión has three hotels and a campsite in the Parque Fructuoso Rivera; the Brazilian consulate is at Calle Lirio Moraes 62, T055-3739 2054. There are onward buses to Salto and Montevideo.

Quaraí (Brazil)–Artigas (Uruguay)
The crossing from Quaraí to Artigas is in a cattle-raising and agricultural area. The Brazilian consulate is at Calle Lecueder 432, T055-8642 2504. Artigas has hotels, a hostel and campsites. Buses run from the border to Salto and Montevideo.

Santana do Livramento (Brazil)–Rivera (Uruguay)
Santana do Livramento is the main town in this area. Its twin Uruguayan city is Rivera. All one need do is cross the main street to Rivera, but by public transport this is not a straightforward border. The town has hotels and a youth hostel and Banco do Brasil (Avenida Sarandí). The *rodoviária* is at General Salgado Filho and General Vasco Alves. To Porto Alegre, two daily, seven hours, US$20; three daily to Urugaiana (four hours, US$10), services also to São Paulo and other destinations.

Aceguá (Brazil)–Melo (Uruguay)
60 km south of Bages, 59 km north of the Uruguayan town of Melo.

Jaguarão (Brazil)–Río Branco (Uruguay)
The most easterly border crossing is from Jaguarão to Río Branco via the 1.5-km Mauá bridge across the Rio Jaguarão. The police post for passport checks is 3 km before the bridge; customs is at the bridge.

Excursions from Rio Grande
Cassino is a popular seaside town with hotels and shops, 24 km from Rio Grande via a good road. There are several beaches within easy reach of Cassino, but they have no facilities. A wrecked ship remains on the shore where it was thrown by a storm in 1975. Travelling south, the beaches are, in order: **Querência** (5 km), **Stela Maris** (9 km), **Netuno** (10 km), all with surf.

The *barra* (breakwater), 5 km south of Cassino, through which all vessels entering and leaving Rio Grande must pass, is a tourist attraction. Barra–Rio Grande buses, from the east side of Praça Ferreira, pass the *superporto* where there is very good fishing. The coastline here is low and straight, lacking the bays found to the north of Porto Alegre. One attraction is railway flat-cars powered by sail (agree the price in advance); the railway was built for the construction of the breakwater.

Across the inlet from Rio Grande, the little-visited settlement of **São José do Norte** makes a pleasant trip. Founded in 1725 and still mostly intact, the village depends on agriculture and crab fishing. There are only three hotels and a good campsite, **Caturritas**, T053-3238 1476, in pine forests 5 km from the town. There are also several long beaches. Ferries (departing every half-hour, 30 minutes) link São José with Rio Grande; there are also three car ferries daily, T053-3232 1500. Information is available from the **tourist office** ① *R General Osório 127*.

Bagé and the border with Uruguay

There are *pousadas* and cheap guest houses in Bagé. See www.bage.rs.gov.br for more information on the town. Getting to and from Bagé is a struggle, although this will surely change with the closing of the Brazilian side of the border at Chuí. Currently the only bus connections are via Pelotas, Cassino and Santana do Livramento. → See Transport, page 393.

Western Rio Grande do Sul ●▲●●● → *pp385-394*.

The southern interior of the state is the region of the Real Gaúcho, well-worth visiting for the ruined Jesuit missions set up in the 18th century to protect the indigenous Guarani and convert them to Christianity. They are World Heritage Sites and their story inspired Roland Joffe's landmark film, *The Mission*.

Passo Fundo → *Colour map 5, B3. Phone code: 054. Population: 168,500.*

Northwest of Porto Alegre by 328 km is Passo Fundo, regarded as 'the most *gaúcho* city in Rio Grande do Sul', so much so that the town's square boasts a statue of a *maté* gourd and bombilla. There is an international *rodeio* in December. The town has several hotels in the A-B category.

Santo Ângelo and the Jesuit Missions → *Colour map 5, B2. Phone code: 055.*

Santo Ângelo is a pleasant town with the best infrastructure for visiting the missions. It has a missionary museum in the main square where there is a **cathedral** with a hideous fresco of missionaries indoctrinating the indigenous population. The only considerable Jesuit remains in Brazilian territory are the very dramatic ones at **São Miguel das Missões**, some 50 km from Santo Ângelo. At São Miguel, now a World Heritage Site, there is a church (1735-1745) and small **museum** ① *0900-1800, entrance to the ruins US$2.50.* A *son et lumière* show in Portuguese is held daily, in winter at 2000, and later in summer, although the timing depends on how many people there are. The show ends too late to return to Santo Ângelo and there are one or two options for accommodation (see Sleeping, page 387). It is difficult to find a good place to eat in the evening; although there is a reasonable pizzeria next to the *rodoviária* or you could try a snack bar for hamburgers. *Gaúcho* festivals are often held on Sunday afternoons, in a field near the mission (follow the music).

Border essentials: Brazil–Argentina

Porto Xavier (Brazil)–San Javier (Argentina)
From Santo Angelo it is a four-hour bus ride to the border town of Porto Xavier and an easy crossing (short ferry ride across the Río Uruguay) into Argentina. For exit and entry stamps, visit the federal police at the ferry stations on either side. The five-minute crossing (US$3.75) takes passengers to San Javier, from where there are regular buses, via Posadas, to Iguazú. From the Argentinean ferry station it is a short bus or taxi ride to the town centre, with cashpoints, shops, and the *rodoviária*.

Uruguaiana (Brazil)–Paso de los Libres (Argentina)
It is also possible to cross the border through Uruguaiana, a cattle centre 772 km from Porto Alegre, and its twin Argentine town of Paso de los Libres in the extreme west. A 1400-m bridge over the Rio Uruguay links the two cities.

Brazilian immigration and customs are at the end of the bridge, five blocks from the main *praça*. Buses connect the bus stations and centres of each city every 30 minutes. If you have to disembark for visa formalities, the next bus will pick you up without extra charge. Buses run from Uruguaiana via Barra do Quaraí/Bella Unión (US$4.50) to Salto and Paysandú in Uruguay. Exchange and information is available in the same building. Exchange rates are better in the town than at the border. There are a number of cheap and mid-range hotels in town. A taxi or bus across the bridge is about US$3.50.

Porto Xavier and the Argentine missions
You can continue into Argentina to see the mission ruins at San Ignacio Miní and Posadas by getting a bus from Santo Ângelo (0600, 0900, 1300,1545, 1930) to the quiet border town of **Porto Xavier** (four hours, US$10), on the Rio Uruguay. Buses also run to Porto Xavier from Porto Alegre (one daily), and Santa Maria.

Salto do Yucumã
Between November and April, the Rio Uruguay overflows along its east bank for over 1800 m, creating the world's longest waterfall. The 12-m-high Salto do Yucumã is in the 17,000-ha **Parque do Turvo**. Its isolation (530 km northwest of Porto Alegre on the Argentine border) means few tourists visit. Accordingly it is a wildlife haven with over 220 bird species and 34 mammal species (12 threatened). The nearest town, **Derrumbadas**, 4 km from the park and has an **information point** ① *T054-3551 1558, ext 228*. Lemon extract production is an important local industry.

For Sleeping and Eating price codes and other relevant information, see pages 42-47.

● **Sleeping**

Porto Alegre *p373, map p374*
Hotels in the area around R Garibáldi and Voluntários da Patria between Av Farrapos and *rodoviária* are overpriced and many rooms are rented by the hour.
L Plaza São Rafael, Av Alberto Bins 514, T051-3220 7000, www.plazahoteis.com.br. Recently refurbished 1970s luxury hotel with excellent service and business facilities including laptop computer rental and 2 free internet lines in each room. Gym and sauna. Less anonymous than the city's US chain hotels (there is a **Sheraton** in town).
L-AL Blue Tree Millennium Flat, Av Borges de Medeiros 3120, Praia de Belas. Smart mini-apartments with microwave, study and breakfast bar. The rooftop pool, gym and bar have stunning sunset views. Recommended.
AL Continental, Largo Vespasiano Júlio Veppo 77, T051-3211 2344, www.hoteis continental. com.br. Reasonable business hotel with a pool, gym and with good weekend discount rates. Recommended.
A Porto Alegre Residence, R Des André da Rocha 131, T051-3225 8644. Large rooms. Recommended.
B Comfort Inn, R Loureiro da Silva 1660, Cidade Baixa. T051-2117 9000. Good-value 3-star hotel with gym, Wi-Fi, breakfast. Handy for Cidade Baixa nightlife
B Embaixador, R Jerônimo Coelho 354, T051-3215 6600, www.embaixador.com.br. Comfortable 4-star with gym, sauna and an unexciting restaurant. Weekend discounts.
B Hotel Rishon, R Dr Flores 27, Centro, T051-2228 1387. Rooms with cable TV, fridge, microwave, breakfast included, central.
B Ritter, Lg Vespasiano Júlio Veppo 55, opposite the *rodoviária*, T051-3228 4044, www.ritterhoteis.com.br. 4-star and 3-star wings, English, French, German spoken, bar,

small pool, sauna. Decent restaurant, good service. Recommended.
C Conceição Center, Av Sen Salgado Filho 201, T051-3225 7774, www.hoteisconceicao. com.br. Simple but respectable town hotel with plain but well-kept a/c rooms with fridges. Has a cheaper (**D**) sister hotel, see website for details.
C Lancaster, Trav Acelino de Carvalho 67, T051-3224 4737. Central, quiet, a/c rooms and a restaurant.
D Elevado, Av Farrapos 65, T051-3224 5250, www.hotelelevado.com.br. Big rooms, noisy at the front, microwave and coffee-making facilities, good value.
D Palácio, Av Vigário José Inácio 644, T051-3225 3467. Centrally located, with hot water, family rooms and a safe. Recommended.
E América, Av Farrapos 119, T/F051-3226 0062, www.hotelamerica.com.br. Friendly, great value, large rooms with sofas, quiet rooms at back, laundry service, good breakfast, garage. Highly recommended.
E Minuano, Av Farrapos 31, T/F051-3226 3062. Small immaculate rooms, and parking.
E Uruguay, Dr Flores 371. Simple fan-cooled rooms. Recommended.

Camping
Praia do Guarujá, 16 km out on Av Guaíba.

Beaches around Porto Alegre
p378, map p378
A Solar da Barra, R Plínio Kroeff 465, Mampituba, near Torres, T051-3664 1811. Low-season discounts. 2 pools, one of which is thermal, sauna, children's playground.
B Beira-Mar, Av Emancipação 521, Tramandaí beach, T051-3661 1234. Pleasant but simple hotel with a thermal pool and sports facilities.
B Napoli, Av Paraguassu 3159, Capão da Canoa, T/F051-3665 2231. Simple beach *pousada* (**C** low season).
B-C Pousada Brisa do Mar, R Júlio de Castilhos and R Borges de Medeiros, Torres, T051-3664 2019. Good breakfast. Recommended.

C Alvorada, Arroio Teixeira, on the beach, T051-3622 1242. Open Dec-Mar. Good facilities, café.

C Ibiama, R Dr Mário Santo Dani 1161, Osório beach, T/F051-3663 2822. Simple rooms and breakfast.

C Kolman, R Sepé 1800, Capão da Canoa, T051-3625 2022/2021. Standard family beach hotel with a pool.

D Hotel Costa Azul, Av José Bonifácio 382, Torres, T/F051-3664 3291. Friendly and close to the *rodoviária*, with breakfast.

D São Jorge, F Amaral 19, Tramandaí beach, T051-3661 1154. Quiet, simple, recommended.

E São Domingos, R Júlio de Castilhos 875, Torres, T051-3664 1865. IYHA youth hostel, clean, closed out of season. Price per person.

E Tramandaí, R Belém 701, Tramandaí beach, T051-3228 3802. IYHA youth hostel with dorms and doubles. Price per person.

Camping

Marina Park, RS-389, 7 km, Capão da Canoa, T051-3301 6150.

Pinguela Parque, BR-101, 22 km, Osório beach, T051-3628 8080.

Praia de Itapeva, 5 km, Torres, T051-3605 5112.

South of Tramandaí *p379*

D Hotel Farol, on the main street, Cidreira. With bath.

E Hotel Mostardense, R Bento Conçalves 200, Mostardas, T051-3673 1368. Good.

Gramado *p379*

LL-A Gramado Parque, R Leopoldo Rosenfeldt 818, T/F051-3286 2588. Beautiful lakeside location, plush suites with all mod cons, good breakfast.

LL-A Ritta Höppner, R Pedro Candiago 305, T051-3286 1334, www.rittahoppner.com.br. Luxurious, well-appointed and spacious bungalows. The most expensive have private mini-pools. Friendly, good breakfasts. Afternoon tea included in price. German owners also run Mini Mundo theme park and guests have free entrance.

AL Serra Azul, R Garibáldi 152, T054-3295 7200, www.serraazul.com.br. Sauna, massage, tennis and 2 pools, one of which is thermal.

A Chalets do Vale, R Arthur Reinheimer 161 (off Av das Hortênsias at about 4700), T054-3286 4151, chaletsdovale@via-rs.net. 3 high-quality chalets in lovely wood setting, 2 double beds, kitchen, TV. Good deal for groups of 4 or families. Recommended.

A Estalagem St Hubertus, R da Carriere 974, Lago Negro, T/F051-3286 1273, www.sthubertus.com. Part of the **Roteiros de Charme** group, see page 43.

A-B Pousada Bella Terra, Av Borges de Medeiros 2870, T054-3286 3333, www.pousada bellaterra.com.br. Good central location, friendly, comfortable accommodation.

B Pequeno Bosque, R Piratini 486, located in wood close to Véu da Noiva waterfall, T051-286 1527. Simple but pleasant and with a good breakfast.

B Pousada Zermatt, R da Fé 187, Bavária, T/F051-3286 2426. Simple and plain accommodation but recommended.

C Luiz, Sen Salgado Filho 432, T054-3286 1026. Pleasant rooms, friendly service and a good breakfast.

C Pousada Pertuti, Av Borges de Medeiros 3571, T054-3286 2513. Good breakfast, use of kitchen, friendly. Recommended.

D Dinda, R Augusto Zatti 160, T055-3286 1588. Basic but one of the cheapest in town.

E Gramado Hostel, Av das Hortênsias 3880, T054-3295 1020. Good HI hostel with dorm beds, doubles and family rooms. 24-hr internet, parking, breakfast. Nice grounds.

Camping

Camping Gramado, R Venerável 877-B, Av Central, T054-3286 2615.

Canela and around *p380*

AL Laje de Pedra, R das Flores 272, T051-3012 7240. Resort hotel with 3 restaurants, pool, thermal pool, sauna, tennis.

A Vila Suzana Parque, R Col Theobaldo Fleck 15, T054-3282 2020. Chalets, heated pool, attractive.

C **Canela**, R Ernesto Dorneles 333, T054-3282 8410. Breakfast, English-speaking staff. Recommended.
C **Pousada das Sequóias**, R Godofredo Raymundo 1747, T054-3282 1373, http://www.sequoias.com.br. Pretty forest cabins in national park, 2 km from city centre.
D **Pousada Schermer**, Travessa Romeu 30, T054-3282 1746. Basic backpacker accommodation but very friendly, well kept and highly recommended.
E **Pousada do Viajante**, R Ernesto Urbani 132, behind *rodoviária*, T054-3282 2017. Youth hostel offering dorms and doubles with kitchen facilities. Recommended.

Camping
Camping Clube do Brasil, 1 km from waterfall in Parque do Caracol, 1 km off main road (signposted), take bus for Parque Estadual do Caracol, 8 km from Canela. Excellent honey and chocolate for sale. Highly recommended.
Sesi, R Francisco Bertolucci 504, camping and smart cabins in lovely parkland setting, 2.5 km outside Canela, T/F054-3282 1311. Restaurant, clean, barbeque facilities. Helpful staff. Highly recommended.

Pelotas *p380*
A-B **Manta**, R Gen Neto 1131, T053-225 2411, www.hoteismanta.com.br. Blocky 1970s hotel with a pool, restaurant and bar. The best in town though somewhat frayed.
D **Aleppo Hotel**, R Gen Osório 708, T/F053-3225 3950. Bright, clean and big rooms and breakfast. Recommended.
D **Motel Mediterâneo**, Av Presidente João Goulont 5473, T053-3271 4746. About 150 m from the *rodoviária*. Recommended if arriving late.

Rio Grande *p381*
B **Atlântico Rio Grande**, R Duque de Caxias 55, T/F053-3231 3833, www.hoteis atlantico.com.br/riogrande. Standard town hotel with a/c rooms. Good value.

B **Europa**, R Gen Neto 165, main square, T053-3232 8133. Conveniently located in the centre of town with a range of a/c rooms.
D **Paris**, R Mcal Floriano Peixoto 112. An old colonial building. Charming. Recommended.

Excursions from Rio Grande *p382*
A **Atlântico**, Av Rio Grande 387, Cassino, T053-3236 1350. Clean, refurbished and with special rates for students.
B **Marysol**, Av Atlântica 700, Cassino, T053-3236 1240. Friendly, simple *pousada* near the beach.

Bagé and the border with Uruguay *p383*
B-C **Pousada do Sobrado** T053-3242 2713 www.pousadadosobrado.com.br. Rooms in a gorgeous converted colonial ranch house (and an ugly modern brick annexe), decorated with heavy antique furniture. The ranch is in the countryside outside town.
C-D **Obinotel**, Av 7 de Setembro 901, T053-3242 8211, www.redeversare.com.br. An old 1960s 2-star in the centre of town with a restaurant and large, rather frayed rooms.

Santo Ângelo and the Jesuit Missions *p383*
A **Maerkli**, Av Brasil 1000, Santo Ângelo, T055-3312 2127. Pleasant but basic 1980s hotel.
C **Hotel Barichello**, Av Borges do Canto 1567, São Miguel das Missões, T055-3381 1272. Nice, clean and quiet. It also has a restaurant, *Churrasco*, for lunch.
C **Turis Hotel**, R Antônio Manoel, 726 Centro T055-3313 5255. Good-value rooms with a/c and fridge. Good breakfast. Internet access, good cheap, pizzeria on the terrace on the main square. Recommended. The hotel is about 5 mins' walk from the ferry at the end of the main street.
C-E **Pousada das Missões**, next to the ruins, São Miguel das Missões, T055-3381 1030, pousada.missoes@terra.com.br. Very good youth hostel. Private rooms with a/c and TV, lovely grounds with pool, friendly. Highly recommended.

D-E Hotel Nova Esperança, Trav Centenario 463, Santo Ângelo, T055-3312 1173, behind the bus station. Simple, reasonably well maintained but with no breakfast.

Porto Xavier and the Argentine missions p384

D Rotta, Av Mal Fl Peixoto 757, near the *praça*. Plain rooms with or without a/c, and/or TV, bath, very good breakfast.

Salto do Yucumã p384

There are several cheap hotels in the area.
C-D Hotel Imperial, Av Jn Castilhos 544, Três Passos, 28 km from the park, T055-3522 2135. Standard small town hotel, breakfast included.

In Tenente, 16 km from the park are:
F Hotel Avenida, beside the petrol station, T055-3551 1859; and **F Hotel Iucuma**, R Tapulas 271, T055-3551 1120.

⦿ Eating

Porto Alegre p373, map p374

Gaúcho cooking features large quantities of meat, while German cuisine is also a strong influence. *Campeiro* (regional farm food), now a dying art, uses plenty of rice, vegetables, and interesting sauces. Vegetarians might try some of the *campeiro* soups and casseroles and growing number of alternative or natural restaurants, otherwise stick to Italian restaurants or *churrascaria* salad bars.

Apart from the many good restaurants, much of the tastiest food can be found in street stalls and cheap *lancherias*; the central market along the *praça* is lined with them.
♯♯♯ Galpão Crioulo, Av Loureiro da Silva (Parque da Harmonia also known as Maurício Sirotsky Sobrinho, Cidade Baixa), T051-3226 8194. Open1130-1600, 1900-0100. Good *churrascaria* with a show and dancing.
♯♯♯ Koh Pee Pee, R Schiller 83, T051 3333 5150. Mon-Sat 1930-2400. Sophisticated restaurant serving excellent Thai cuisine. Seafood dishes are especially good.

♯♯♯ Portoalegrense, Av Pará 913, São Geraldo, T051-3343 2767. Closed Sun. The best carnivore restaurant in the city with excellent beef steak and a respectable wine list.
♯♯ Al Dente, R Mata Bacelar 210, T051-3343 1841. Mon-Sat 1900-2400. Wonderful home-made pastas of every variety, and a staggering array of sauces to choose from. Romantic atmosphere, recommended.
♯♯ Chopp Stübel, R Quintino Bocaiúva 940, Moinhos de Vento, T051-3332 8895. Mon-Sat 1800-0030. One of the best in the city for reasonably priced German food. Recommended.
♯♯ Le Bon Gourmet, Av Alberto Bins 514 (in **Plaza São Rafael** hotel). Mon-Sat 1900-2300. Steaks, pasta and fine fish dishes. The 24-hr **514 Bar** is at the back of hotel lobby.
♯♯ Wunderbar, R Marquês do Herval 598, Moinhos de Vento, T051-3222 4967. Open 1830 until the last diner leaves. Popular and very friendly German restaurant and bar which is always very busy. Recommended.
♯ Café do Cofre, R Siqueira Campos 1125, T051-3227 8322. Lunch only. Good light meals, including salads and sushi.
♯ Ilha Natural, R Gen Câmara 60, T051-3224 4738. Lunch only Mon-Fri. Self-service, cheap.
♯ Nova Vida Restaurant Alternativo, Av Borges de Medeiros 1010. Mon-Sat 1100-1500. Good vegetarian. Also at Demetrio Ribeiro 1182.
♯ Restaurant Majestic and **Café Dos Cataventos**, Casa de Cultura Mário Quintana, R dos Andrades 736. 2 snack and *almoco* restaurants – the latter in the courtyard and the other on the roof. Both serve good drinks, snacks and meals. Fantastic rooftop sunsets.

Gramado p379

There's no lack of choice with plenty of decent, if pricey, restaurants along Av Borges de Medeiros.
♯♯♯ Bella du Valais, Av das Hortensias 1432 T054-3286 1744, expensive but very good Swiss cuisine, including wonderful fondues.
♯♯♯ Churrascaria Patrão Velho, Av das Hortênsias 4759, T054-3286 0823. Very good meat and side dishes. Recommended.

Restaurante Hakone, R Garibaldi 271, T654-3286 1403. One of very few moderately priced places to eat in Gramado. Good fixed-price lunchtime buffet and evening *rodizio* of pizza, pasta, salad and soup.

Canela *p380*

Empório Canela, Felisberto Soares 258, T054-3031 1000. Pleasant bistro with a good range of soups, pastas and traditional campeiro dishes. Decent wine list and *petiscos*.
Café Canela, Praça Joã Correa 7, T054-3282 4422. Good meat and cheese dishes.
Parati Lanches, Praça Joã Correa 97. Daily 0800-2400. Traditional watering hole with pool tables.

Pelotas *p380*

El Paisano, R Mcal Deodoro 1093, T053-3227 1507. Closed Mon, opening hours vary seasonally. Legendary Uruguayan steak.
Lobão, Av Bento Gonçalves 3460, T053-3225 6197. Standard barbecue *churrascaria*, plenty of side dishes.
Mama Pizza, R Gen Osório 720. Good affordable pizza run by **Hotel Manta**.

Rio Grande *p381*

Blue Café, R Luís Loréa 314. Open 0830-1930 (Fri until 2300 Fri). Expresso machine and good cake. Jazz/blues music on Fri.
Barrillada Don Lauro, R Luís Loréa 369, T053-3233 2037. Uruguayan steak in pleasant restaurant.
Rio's, R Val Porto 393, T053-3231 1180. Vast but good *churrascaria*.

Bars and clubs

Porto Alegre *p373, map p374*
There are many classy bars, cafés and bistros in the pleasant **Moinhos de Vento**, the city's richest suburb (a US$6 taxi ride from downtown). Most of the activity is centered around the streets Padre Chaves and Fernando Gomes.

On weekend nights, thousands head for the Cidade Baixa and spill out of the bars and clubs along **R da República** and **José do Patrimonio**
Bar do Beto, Av Venâncio Aires 876, Cidade Baixa, T051-3332 0063. Open 1700-0300, serves food too.
Bar do Goethe, R 24 de Outubro 112, Moinhos de Vento, T051-3222 2043, www.bardogoethe.com.br. Excellent range of artesan beers and good German snacks.
Bar do Nito, Av Cel Lucas de Oliveira 105, Moinhos de Vento, T051-3333 4600. Popular music bar.
Bar Perimetral, Av Loureiro da Silva 1696, Cidade Baixa. T061-3211 2422. Hugely popular beer and snack bar, packed at weekends. Mon-Thu 1800-1200, Fri-Sun 1800 until last customer.
Cult, R Gen Lima e Silva 806, Cidade Baixa, T051-3221 6299. Open 2000-late, also serves good food. Music ranges from jazz to rock.
Doce Vício, R Vieira de Castro 32. 3 floors with games room, bar and restaurant, Tue-Sun 1830-0230.
Dr Jekyll, Travessa do Carmo 76, Cidade Baixa, T051-3226 9404. Nightclub open from 2200, closed Sun.
Fly, R Gonçalvo de Carvalho 189. Wed-Mon 2100-0200. Predominantly male, attractive gay bar with art exhibition, sophisticated.
Opinião, R. José do Patrocínio 834, Cidade Baixa T051-3211 5668, www.opiniao. com.br Tue-Sat 2200 until the last customer leaves. Long-standing favourite with fashionable 20-somethings, with rock DJs and regular live music. Great cocktails and good *petiscos*.
Ossip, Av Republica 677 (corner with João Afredo). Pleasant wine bar.
Restaurant Majestic, R dos Andradas 736. Don't miss a sunset drink here, on the roof of **Casa de Cultura Mário Quintana**.
Sergeant Pepper's, Dona Laura 329, T051-3331 3258. Closed Mon. Bar with live music Thu-Sat.

Tortaria, R Fernando Gomes 114, Moinhas de Vento, T051-3395 5599. Serving well-kept *chopp* alongside delicious cakes, this popular spot is open until 0100 and makes a good starting point for a night's bar hopping.

Trivial, R Dona Laura 78, Rio Branco, T051-3346 7046, www.trivialbar.com.br. Bar open from 2100.

Zelig, R Sarmento Leite 1086, Cidade Baixa, T051-3286 5612, www.zelig.com.br. Open from 2000 until the last customer leaves. Off-beat restaurant, bar and exhibition space. Good, diverse menu and DJs covering a broad musical spectrum. Very busy Sun.

Entertainment

Porto Alegre p373, map p374

Casa de Cultura Mário Quintana, R dos Andradas 736, T051-3221 7147. Tue-Fri 0900-2100, Sat-Sun 1200-2100. A centre for the arts, exhibitions and theatre.

Theatro São Pedro, Praça Mcal Deodoro, T051-3227 5100. Tue-Fri 1200-18.30, Sat and Sun 1600-1800. Theatre with regular free concerts, art gallery, café.

Usina do Gasômetro, Av Pres João Goulart 551, T051-3212 5979. Tue-Sun 0900-2200. Art gallery with displays by young artists.

Festivals and events

Porto Alegre p373, map p374

2 Feb The main event is the festival of Nossa Senhora dos Navegantes (*Iemanjá*), whose image is taken by boat from the central quay in the port to the industrial district of Navegantes.

Sep Semana Farroupilha celebrates *gaúcho* traditions with parades in traditional style, its main day being 20 Sep. The **Carnaval** parade takes place in Av A do Carvalho, renamed Av Carlos Alberto Barcelos (or Roxo) for these 3 days only, after a famous carnival designer.

Oct-Nov Each year a month-long **Feira do Livro** (book festival) is held in Praça da Alfândega. See www.feiradolivro-poa.com.br for details.

Torres p378

Apr Ballooning festival.

16 Sep Independence day celebration, when a cavalcade of horses arrives in town from Uruguay.

Gramado p379

Aug Festival of Latin American cinema.

Shopping

Porto Alegre p373, map p374

Bookshops

Idiomas, Galeria Central Park, R Mostardeiro 333, Mon-Fri 0900-1200, 1400-1830, Sat 0930-1230, closed Sun.

Livraria Londres, Av Osvaldo Aranha 1182. Used books in English, French and Spanish and old *Life* magazines.

Prosa i Verso, Galeria Av Center, R Mostardeiro 120, T051-3222 2409. Mon-Sat 0930-1800.

Saraiva Megastore, Shopping Praia de Belas.

Siciliano, R dos Andradas 1273 and other branches.

Jewellers

H Stern, jewellers at the shopping centre Iguatemi and international airport.

Markets

There is a **street market** (leather goods, basketware) near the central post office. Sun morning **handicraft and bric-a-brac market** (plus sideshows), Av José Bonifácio (next to Parque Farroupilha).

Shopping centre

The **Praia de Belas** shopping centre, is among the largest in Latin America. US$5 taxi ride from town.

▲ Activities and tours

Porto Alegre *p373, map p374*
Swimming Forbidden from the beaches near or in the city because of pollution – except for **Praia do Lami**, in the south of the city, which has been cleaned up. Beaches in Belém Novo and Ipanema are okay too.

Tour operators
Caminhos Rurais is a cooperative with an extensive online directory of wine tasting, horse riding and hiking tour operators. Their website, www.caminho esrurais.com.br, lists operators of wine tasting, horse riding and walking tours.

See also the 'Turismo' section in *Zero Hora* classifieds (Tue) for tour company adverts.
Porto Brasil, R Hilario Ribeiro 202, Moinhos de Vento, Porto Alegre, T051-3025 2626, www.portobrasil.com.br. Sells air and bus fares and can help with general travel queries.
Rota Cultural, Av Do Forte 1281, Porto Alegre, T051-3348 1649, www.rota cultural.com.br. Agency running eco trips into rural Rio Grande do Sul. Also organizes boat and air tours.

Beaches around Porto Alegre
p378, map p378
Marcelo and Saraia Müller, Blue Beach Tur, Av Silva Jardim 257, Torres T/F051-3664 3096, bluebeach@terra.com.br. Boat trips up Rio Mampitumba, abseiling, trekking, and visits to Parque Nacional Aparados da Serra/Geral. Recommended.

Canela and around *p380*
Atitude, Av Osvaldo Aranha 391, T054-3282 6305, www.atitude.tur.br. Rafting, waterfall abseiling, and trips to Aparados da Serra National Park. Recommended.
Black Bear Adventure, R Ernesto Riegel 713, Gramado, T054-9939 7191, www.black bearadventure.com.br. Rafting, waterfall abseiling, climbing and trekking tours.

Santo Ângelo and the Jesuit Missions *p383*
Caminho das Missões, R Marquês do Herval 1061, T055-3331 29632, www.caminhodas missoes.com.br. 3- to 13-day 'pilgrimages' (80-180 km) between the various ruins. Also organizes bike tours and trips to Foz do Iguaçu. Open to all beliefs.

☉ Transport

Porto Alegre *p373, map p374*
Air
See also Ins and outs, page 373. Regular buses run from the bus station to the airport; or take the metrô. There are international flights to Uruguay and Argentina as well as internal connections with **Curitiba**, **São Paulo**, **Rio de Janeiro** and **Florianópolis**.

Bus
There are 2 sections to the *rodoviária*; the ticket offices for interstate and international destinations are together in 1 block, beside the municipal tourist office (very helpful). The intermunicipal (state) ticket offices are in another block; for travel information within the state, ask at the very helpful booth on the station concourse.

To **Rio**, US$80, 24 hrs (Itapemirim www.pluma com.br); **São Paulo** (Itapemirim, www.itapemerim.com.br), *leito* US$67 (18 hrs), standard US$56; **Brasília** (Real Expresso) www.real expresso.com.br, US$110, 34 hrs; **Uruguaiana** (Pluma), US$17.50, 8 hrs; Florianópolis, US$30-60, 7 hrs with **Santo Anjo** (take an *executivo* rather than a *convencional*, which is a much slower service); **Curitiba** (Itapemirim), standard US$40 coastal and *serra* routes, 12 hrs; **Rio Grande**, US$25 every 2 hrs from 0600, 4 hrs. **Foz do Iguaçu**, *leito* US$70, standard US$35 (Unesul, www.unesul.com.br). To **Cascavel** in Paraná for connections to Campo Grande, Cuiabá and Porto Velho, 4 daily, US$45, 12 hrs (Unesul). To **Jaguarão** on the

Uruguayan border at 2400, US$22, 6 hrs. To **Florianópolis** *leito* US$49, standard US$24.

International buses Take your passport and tourist card when purchasing international bus tickets. To **Montevideo** (Uruguay), with TTL, www.ttl.com.br, *executivo* daily 2030 US$80; *leito* Fri only at 2100, US$80.

To **Asunción** (Paraguay) with Unesul at 1900, Tue, Fri, 18 hrs via Foz do Iguaçu, US$40.

To **Santiago** (Chile), with Pluma 0705, Tue and Fri, US$135.

There are bus services to **Buenos Aires** (Argentina) with Pluma, US$68, 19 hrs (depending how long the border takes), daily at 1805, the route is via Uruguaiana, Paso de los Libres, Entre Ríos and Zárate. For **Misiones** (Argentina), take the 2100 bus (not Sat) to Porto Xavier on the Río Uruguay, 11 hrs, US$36-45, get your exit stamp at police station, then take a boat across to San Javier, US$3.50, and go to Argentine immigration at the port, then take a bus heading to Posadas.

Car Good roads radiate from Porto Alegre, and Highway BR-116 is paved to **Curitiba** (746 km). In summer, visibility can be very poor at night owing to mist, unfenced cows are a further hazard. The paved coastal road to **Curitiba** via **Itajaí** (BR-101), of which the first 100 km is the 4-lane Estrada General Osório highway, is much better than the BR-116 via Caxias and Lajes. The road to **Uruguaiana** is entirely paved but bumpy.

Car hire Allocar, R 25 de Julho 102, T051-3337 1717, www.allocar.com.br. Bazzoni, T051-3325 2913, www.bazzoni.com.br. **Hello Rent a Car**, T051-3342 2422, www.hello car.com.br. At airport and delivers to hotels. Milhas, R Pereira Franco 400, T051-3337 2223. Pontual, Av Pernanbuco 1700, São Geraldo, T051-3342 2282.

Beaches around Porto Alegre *p378, map p378*
Bus To **Tramandaí**, 5 a day, US$3.50. To **Osório–Mostardas/Tavares**, daily at 1600, US$4.40. To **Torres**, 9 a day, US$6; **Tramandaí** daily at 1300 and 1700, **Osório** daily at 0630, 1100, 1300 and 1830.

South of Tramandaí *p379*
Bus There are 3 buses a week from Mostardas and Tavares to **São José do Norte** (130 km) via **Bojuru** (leaving Mostardas 0630 and **Tavares** 0700 Sun, Wed, Fri, 5 hrs, US$4.50). If travelling northwards from **São José do Norte**, the bus leaves 0800 on Tue, Thu and Sat. There is also a daily bus from both **Tavares** and São José do Norte to **Bojuru**, where there is a basic hotel. The road south of Tavares is called the **Estrada do Inferno**. Car drivers should carry a shovel and rope. 4WD only after rains.

Taxi For local transport from Mostardas, try José Carlos Martins Cassola, T051-3673 1186, or Itamar Velho Sessin, T051-3673 1431.

Gramado *p379*
Bus Buses to **Canela**, 10 mins, run every 20 mins. Several daily buses to **Porto Alegre** US$10-14.

Canela and around *p380*
Bus To **Parque Estadual do Caracol**, from outside **Parati Lanches**, Praça Joã Correa, 0800, 1200, 1730 (returning at 1220, 1800), US$1.30. Several daily to **Caxias do Sul**, 2 hrs, US$2. Every 2 hrs to **São Francisco de Paula**, US$2.60. (Take the 0800 for the connection to Cambará for **Parque Nacional de Aparados da Serra**.) To **Florianópolis**, it is quickest to go via Porto Alegre (US$11).

Bike hire From Pousada das Sequóias or **Pousada Casa Rosa**, R Gov Flores da Cunha 150, T054-3282 2400.

Pelotas *p380*
Air The airport is 8 km from the centre. Mon-Fri flight to **Porto Alegre** (1530, US$60) with NHT, www.voenht.com.br.
Bus Frequent daily buses to **Porto Alegre**, 244 km (US$18, 3-4 hrs, paved road); **Rio Grande** (US$4.50, 1 hr). TTL bus services (Montevideo–Porto Alegre) depart daily at 2400, US$70. To **Buenos Aires** via **Uruguaiana** (0710, 2030, US$40). From Bagé, where there is a police post, the Uruguayan company **Núñez** runs buses 3 times a week to **Melo**, via Aceguá. Good direct road northwest to **Iguaçu** via **São Sepé**, **Santa Maria** and **São Miguel** mission ruins. **Santa Maria** (5 daily, US$8.80, 4 hrs) and **Santa Ângelo** (daily at 0805, US$16, 8 hrs).

Taxi Radio Taxi Princesa, T053-3225 8466. Recommended.

Rio Grande *p381*
Boat There's a boat trip across mouth of Lagoa dos Patos, to the pleasant village of **São José do Norte**, every hour from Porto Velho.

Bus To **Pelotas**, every 30 mins (1 hr, 56 km, US$1.75); to **Santa Vitória**, 220 km; to **Porto Alegre**, 5 a day, US$10, 4 hrs; to **Itajaí**, 14 hrs, US$15. All buses to these destinations go through Pelotas. Bus tickets to **Punta del Este** or **Montevideo** (daily 2330) at *rodoviária* or Benfica Turismo, Av Silva Paes 373, T054-3232 1807.

Bagé and the border with Uruguay *p383*
The only current bus connections to and from Bagé are as follows: through **Pelotas** and **Cassino** (on the route Bage–Terminal Cee–

Pinheiro Machado–Pelotas–Cassino) on Sun and Mon leaving Cassino at 0700 and 2000 respectively, 5 hrs); through Cassino and Pelotas (on the route Santanado Livramento–Ipamaroti–Dom Pedrito–Ferraria–Bagé–Vila Operaria–Pinheiro Machado–Pelotas–Cassino), leaving on Sun at 1800 from Cassino, 4-5 hrs; and through **Torres** and **Tramandai** (on the Livramento–Dom Pedrito–Bagé–Tramandai–Capao Da Canoa–Arroio Do Sal–Torres route), leaving Torres at 1930 on Sun, 5 hrs.
   To Uruguay To **Montevideo** (COT, Cynsa, both on Av Brasil between Olivera and Artigas, or **Rutas del Sol**, on L Oliveria), US$13, 5 hrs.

Santo Ângelo and the Jesuit Missions *p383*
Bus To **Porto Alegre**, 5 *convencional* daily, 6 hrs, US$32. To **São Miguel**, 0715, 1100, 1530, 1700 (Sat 1000, 1330, Sun 0930, 1830), 1 hr, US$2. To **Foz do Iguaçu**, via Cascavel, 1930, 13 hrs, US$21.

Salto do Yucumã *p384*
Bus There are 4 buses daily from **Três Passos** to Santo Ângelo. 2 daily **Tenente Portela**–Santo Ângelo.

O Directory

Porto Alegre *p373, map p374*
Banks Banco do Brasil, Uruguai 185, 9th floor, (1000-1500), good rates for TCs. Bradesco, Praça Sen Florência. Visa machine. Citibank, R7 de Setembro 722, T051-3220 8619, exchange on Av Borges de Medeiros, good rate, cash only. **Cultural centres** Sociedade Brasileira da Cultura Inglesa, Praça Mauricio Cardoso 49, Moinhos de Vento. Instituto Goethe, 24 de Outbro 122, (Mon-Fri 0930-1230, 1430-2100), occasional concerts, bar recommended for German

Apfelkuchen. See also Casa de Cultura Mário Quintana and Usina do Gasômetro, see page 390. **Embassies and consulates Argentina**, R Coronel Bordini 1033, Moinhos de Vento, T/F051-3321 1360 (0900-1600). **Germany**, R Prof Annes Dias 112, 11th floor, T051-3224 9255 (0830-1130). **Italy**, Praça Marechal Deodoro 134, T051-3228 2055 (0900-1200). **Japan**, Av João Obino 467, Alto Petrópolis, T051-3334 1299, (0900-1230, 1500-1700). **Portugal**, R Prof Annes Dias 112, 10th floor, T/F051-3224 5767 (0900-1500). **Spain**, R Eng Ildefonso Simões Lopez 85, Três Figueiras, T051-3338 1300, (0830-1330). **UK**, R Itapeva 110, Sala 505, Edif Montreal, Bairro Passo D'Areia, T/F051-3341 0720, (0900-1200, 1430-1800). **USA**, R Riachuelo 1257, 2nd floor, T051-3226 3344, (1400-1700). **Uruguay**, Av Cristóvão Colombo 2999, Higienópolis, T051-3325 6200, (0900-1500). **Internet** Ciber Café, Câncio Gomes e C Colombo 778, T051-3346 3098, (0900-2300). Dot.Com Cyber Café, R da Praia Shopping, S17, R dos Andradas 1001, T051-3286 4244, www.com-cybercafe.co.br. US$3 per hr. Livraria Saraiva Megastore, Shopping Praia de Belas, T051-3231 6868, www.livraria saraiva.com.br, (Mon-Sat 1000-2200). PC2 Publicidad Café, Duque de Caxias 1464, T051-3227 6853, pc2.com@terra.com.br. US$2 per hr. Portonet, R Maracheal Floriano 185, T051-3227 4696, (0900-2100), US$2.50 per hr. **Language courses** Portuguese and Spanish, **Matilde Dias**, R Pedro Chaves Barcelos 37, Apdo 104, T051-3331 8235, malilde@estadao.com.br. US$9 per hr. **Laundry** Several along Av Andre da Rocha including **Lavandería Lav-Dem**, No 225. US$1.50 per kg wash and dry. **Post office** R Siqueria Campos 1100, Centro, (Mon-Fri 0800-1700, Sat 0800-1200).

UPS, T051-3343 4972 (Alvaro).
Telephone R Siqueira de Campos 1245 and upstairs at the *rodoviária*.

Beaches around Porto Alegre
p378, map p378
Banks Banco do Brasil, 15 de Novembro 236, Torres and at the Torres *rodoviária*.

Gramado *p379*
Banks Banco do Brasil, R Garibáldi corner Madre Verónica. **Internet** Cyber, Av Borges de Medeiros 2016, T054-3286 9559, (1300-2300), US$2.80 per hr.

Canela *p380*
Banks Banco do Brasil, Av Julio de Castilhos 465. **Internet** Posto Telefónico, Av Júlio de Castilhos 349, Sala 5, T054-3282 3305, (0800-2100, Sat 0900-2000, Sun 1000-1200, 1400-1800).

Pelotas *p380*
Banks Banco do Brasil, corner R Gen Osório and R Lobo da Costa. Also at R Anchieta 2122. Will change TCs. It is difficult to change money at weekends.

Rio Grande *p381*
Embassies and consulates Denmark, R Mcal Floriano 122, T053-233 7600, (0800-1200, 1330-1800). **UK**, R Riachuelo 201, T053-3233 7700, (0800-1200, 1330-1730). **Telephone** R Gen Neto 227.

Santo Ângelo and the Jesuit Missions *p383*
Banks Banco do Brasil charges a commission of US$15 for TCs. Good rates for cash at the garage with red doors opposite Hotel Maerkli on Av Brasil.

At a glance

⊖ **Getting around** Buses and internal flights. Car hire a possibility for the coast.

◉ **Time required** 2-3 days for Salvador; 5 days for Salvador and beaches; 7-10 days for Salvador, the Chapada Diamantina and beaches.

☀ **Weather** Varies greatly over such a large a region. Hot summer (Oct-Mar), warm winter (Apr-Sep). Hot and dry in the *sertão* all year round except Dec-Feb.

✖ **When not to go** Apr-May and Nov-Dec are wettest on the coast. Dec-Feb are wet in the *chapada*.

White-sand beaches backed by coconut palms, steep winding streets lined with pastel-coloured houses, ornate baroque churches, Afro-Brazilian ceremonies, gymnastic martial art ballet, the rhythm of the *berimbau*, the aroma of spices ... Bahia conjures up as many exotic images, sounds and smells as Rio de Janeiro and has as an equally strong claim to be the heart of Brazil. The state capital, Salvador, was the country's first city for far longer than any other, and is considered by many to be the country's cultural centre.

Brazil's most famous novelist, Jorge Amado, was a Bahian, as were many of its greatest musicians; it was Bahia that gave the world samba, capoeira, Carnaval and *candomblé*. The state has some of the best cuisine in the country, along with many of its best beaches. Bahia's beautiful coast stretches far to the north and south of Salvador and is dotted with resorts along its length: laid-back little places like Itacaré, Morro de São Paulo and Trancoso, and larger more hedonistic party-towns like Porto Seguro and Arraial de Ajuda. Inland, in the wild semi-desert of the *sertão*, is one of Brazil's best hiking destinations, the Chapada Diamantina, whose towering escarpments are cut by clear-water rivers and dotted with plunging waterfalls.

Salvador and the Recôncavo

→ *Colour map 4, A6. Phone code: 071. Population: 3.2 million.*

Salvador is the capital not just of Bahia but of African Brazil. The country's African heritage is at its strongest here – in the ubiquitous Orixá spirit gods and goddesses, the carnival rhythms of the drum troupe orchestras of Ilê Aiyê and Olodum, the rich spicy cooking, the rituals of candomblé (Brazil's equivalent of santeria) and in the martial art ballet of capoeira. You will see the latter being played on Salvador's beaches and in the squares and cobbled streets of the city's historical centre, the Pelourinho. The Pelourinho is also home to one of the most impressive collections of colonial architecture in South America. There are myriad baroque churches here. Some, like the Convento do São Francisco, have interiors covered with tons of gold plate. Others, like Nossa Senhora do Rosário, are decorated with statues of black saints and art that celebrates African Brazilian culture. The city is famous for its frenetic carnival which, unlike Rio's, takes place in the streets to the pounding rhythms of axé music. The crowds are overwhelming.

The Recôncavo is Brazil's largest bay and is dotted with islands; many of them are privately owned by the northeast's wealthy, others serve as weekend resorts for people from Salvador. The best known is Itaparica, a long thin island lined with palms, with a pretty colonial capital and some reasonable beaches. Many buses run from here and taking the ferry across from Salvador and then road transport from Itaparica is the quickest way of getting to southern Bahia. ➤➤ *For listings, see pages 416-432.*

Ins and outs

Getting there

Air Domestic and international flights arrive at the new **Luís Eduardo Magalhães airport** ① *32 km east of the centre, Praça Gago Coutinho, São Cristóvão, T071-3204 1010, www.luis eduardomagalhaes.ba.gov.br,* previously known as Dois de Julho. ATM machines are tucked away round the corner on the ground floor to the right as you arrive. The tourist information booth (open 24 hours, English spoken), has a list of hotels and a useful map. An air-conditioned *executivo* bus service runs from the airport to the historic centre (every 30 minutes, Monday to Friday 0500-2200, weekends 0600-2200, US$3). This service stops at all the hotels along the coast road en route – a long way round if you are going to the centre. *Ônibus coletivo* (city buses), US$0.80, are more direct but more crowded. Fixed-rate taxis go both to Barra and the centre; tickets can be bought from the desk next to the tourist information booth) for around US$35. Ordinary taxis leave from outside the airport, US$30.

Bus Interstate buses arrive at the **rodoviária** ① *5 km east of the centre, near Iguatemi Shopping Centre.* There are regular bus services to the centre, Campo Grande, Barra and Rio Vermelho. An executive bus leaves from outside the shopping centre (reached from the bus station by a walkway; be careful at night) and runs to Praça da Sé or the lower city (Comércio) via the coast road. Taxi to the centre, US$15. ➤➤ *See Transport, page 430.*

Ferries and catamarans The main ferry dock, principally for car ferries although also for catamarans and passenger boats, is the **Marítimo de São Joaquim** ① *Av Oscar Pontes 1051, T071-3254 1020, www.twbmar.com.br.* It is known colloquially as 'ferry-boat' (pronounced 'fairhee bort)'. The terminal has a bank, cafés and some small shops. Ten car ferries per day arrive here from the little town of Bom Despacho on Itaparica as well as catamarans from Morro de São Paulo (two hours).

Salvador's other boat terminal is smaller and serves only passengers. It lies opposite the Mercado Modelo, five minutes' walk from the historic centre, and is known as the **Terminal Marítimo de Mercado Modelo** or Terminal Marítimo Turistico. Ferries and catamarans run between here and the Baía de Todos os Santos, including the village of Mar Grande on Itaparica (every 30 minutes) and there are catamarans from Morro de São Paulo (five a day in high season; three in low season; the last leaves at 1400).

Getting around
The city is built on a broad peninsula and is at the mouth of the Baía de Todos os Santos. On the opposite side of the bay's entrance is the Ilha de Itaparica (see page 413). The commercial district of the city and its port are on the sheltered, western side of the peninsula; residential districts and beaches are on the open, Atlantic side. Barra lies at the point of the peninsula.

1 Salvador orientation

To Peripeni
BR 093 to Alagoinhas & Recife
BR 324 to Aratu, Feira de Santana,
Rio de Janeiro & Brasília

PLATAFORMA

Baía de Todos os Santos

Praia do Bogari
NS da Penha
RIBEIRA
Enseada dos Tainheiros

BR 324

BA 337

Península de Itapagipe
Rio São Francisco
NS do Bonfim
ALAGADOS
LOBATO

Forte Monte Serrat
Boa Viagem
Caminho de Areia
Eng Austriciliano
CALABETÃO

L Tarquínio
Av Bonfim
Cabral Beira Mar

Marítimo de São Joaquim
LIBERDADE
Pau Miúdo
Av San Martin
Cento Administrativo da Bahia

To Itaparica & Morro de São Paulo

CENTRO HISTÓRICO
CIDADE NOVA
Barros Reis
Acesso Norte
Av Luiz Viana Filho
Parque Pituaçu
Jorge Amado
To Airport

Carmo
MATATU
Av Barros Reis
CABULA

Djalma Dutra
Seabra
Estádio Otávio Mangabeira
Leal Ferreira
BROTAS
Rodoviária

VITÓRIA

Av de contorno
Costa e Silva
Dique de Tororó
Graça Lessa
Horto Florestal
Shopping Iguatemi
Antônio C Magalhães
Estr Jaqer Clube
Paulo VI
ARMAÇÃO

Av 7 de Setembro

CAMPO GRANDE
Vasco de Gama da Silva
Jardim dos Namorados
To Jaguaripe, Piatã & Itapoã

GRAÇA
Miguel Calmon
Av Garibaldi
Av Juracy Magalhães
SANTA CRUZ
Parque da Cidade
PITUBA

Marquês de Leão
Av Centenário
Av de Barros
Pres Vargas
Rua O Cruz
Av Amaralina

ONDINA
BARRA
Av Oceânica
RIO VERMELHO
AMARALINA

Atlantic Ocean

N
1 km
1 mile

Sleeping
Blue Tree Towers 1
Catharina Paraguaçu 2
Ibis 3
Pestana Bahia 4

➡ Salvador maps
1 Salvador orientation, page 399
2 Salvador centre, page 403
3 Pelourinho, page 408
4 Salvador south to Barra, page 411

The centre of the city is divided into two levels, the **Cidade Alta** (Upper City) where the historic centre lies, and the **Cidade Baixa** (Lower City), which is the commercial and docks district. The two levels are connected by a series of steep hills called *ladeiras*. The easiest way to go from one level to the other is by the *Lacerda* lift, which connects Praça Municipal (Tomé de Sousa) in the Upper City with Praça Cairu and the famous Mercado Modelo. There is also the *Plano Inclinado Gonçalves*, a funicular railway that leaves from behind the cathedral going down to Comércio, the commercial district.

Most visitors limit themselves to the centre, Barra, the Atlantic suburbs and the Itapagipe peninsula, which is north of the centre. The roads and avenues between these areas are straightforward to follow and are well served by public transport. Other parts of the city are not as easy to get around, but are of less interest to most visitors. If going to these areas, a taxi may be advisable until you know your way around. → See Transport, page 430.

Best time to visit
It can rain at any time of year, but the main rainy season is between May and September. The climate is usually pleasant and the sun is never far away. Temperatures range from 25°C to 32°C, never falling below 19°C in winter.

Tourist information
The main office of **Bahiatursa** ① *Av Simon Bolivar, 650, T071-3117 3000, www.bahia tursa.ba.gov.br, Mon-Fri 0830-1800*, has lists of hotels and accommodation in private homes, can advise on travel throughout the state of Bahia, and has noticeboards for messages. There are also branches at the following locations: **airport** ① *T071-3204 1244, daily 0730-2300*; **Mercado Modelo** ① *Praça Visconde de Cayru 250, T071-3241 0242, Mon-Sat 0900-1800, Sun 0900-1330*; **Pelourinho** ① *R das Laranjeiras 12, Pelourinho, T071-3321 2133/2463, daily 0830-2100*; **Rodoviária** ① *T071-3450 3871, daily 0730-2100*; **Instituto Mauá** ① *Praça Azevedo Fernandes 1, Porto da Barra, T071-3264 4671, Mon-Fri 0900-1800, Sat 1000-1500*, **Shopping Barra** ① *Av Centenário, 2992, Chame-Chame, T071-3264 4566, Mon-Fri 0900-1900, Sat 0900-1400*, **Shopping Iguatemi** ① *Av Tancredo Neves 148, Pituba, T071-3480 5511, Mon-Fri 0900-2130, Sat 0900-1330*. The website www.bahia-online.net lists cultural events and news.

Maps Available from **Fundação Instituto Brasileiro de Geografia e Estatística** ① *Av Estados Unidos 476, 4th floor, opposite Banco do Brasil, Cidade Baixa*. Illustrated maps of the Pelourinho are available from newsagents and general stores in the historic centre.

Safety
There is a lot of paranoia about safety in Salvador but as long as visitors follow common sense and a few rules they should be fine. The civil police are helpful and resources have been put into policing Barra, the Pelourinho and the old part of the city. All are well lit at night, however, police are little in evidence after 2300. The Pelourinho area is generally safe, although there's plenty of begging/touting and pick-pocketing and even occasional muggings do occur. Avoid going to the toilet on the Praça do Reggae and other large communal washrooms on show nights as we have had reports of intimidation by groups of thieves; choose a restaurant loo instead. Be vigilant and wary at all times after dark and avoid carrying credit cards or wads of cash. Buses and the area around the Lacerda lift are unsafe at night. Never venture into the *favelas* unless on a tour or with a trustworthy local friend. Foreign women often receive unwelcome amounts of attention, especially during Carnaval when levels of physical contact in crowds can be very unpleasant.

Background

On 1 November 1501, All Saints' Day, the navigator Amérigo Vespucci discovered the bay and named it after the day of his arrival – Baía de Todos os Santos. The bay was one of the finest anchorages on the coast, and became a favourite port of call for French, Spanish and Portuguese ships. However, when the Portuguese crown sent Martim Afonso to set up a permanent colony in Brazil, he favoured São Vicente in São Paulo.

It was not until nearly 50 years later that the bay's strategic importance was recognized. When the first governor general, Tomé de Sousa, arrived on 23 March 1549 to build a fortified city to protect Portugal's interest from constant threats of Dutch and French invasion, the bay was chosen as the place from which the new colony of Brazil was to be governed. Salvador was formally founded on 1 November 1549 and, despite a short-lived Dutch invasion in 1624, remained the capital of Brazil until 1763.

The city grew wealthy through the export of sugar and the import of African slaves to work on the plantations. By the 18th century, it was the most important city in the Portuguese empire after Lisbon and ideally situated on the main trade routes of the 'New World'. Its fortunes were further boosted by the discovery of diamonds in the interior. However, as the sugar industry declined, the local economy could not rival the gold and coffee booms of the southeast and this led to the loss of capital status and the rise of Rio de Janeiro as Brazil's principal city. Nevertheless, the city continued to play an influential part in the political and cultural life of the country.

African presence

For three centuries, Salvador was the site of a thriving slave trade, with much of the workforce for the sugar cane and tobacco plantations coming from the west coast of Africa. Even today, Salvador is described as the most African city in the Western hemisphere, and the University of Bahia boasts the only choir in the Americas to sing in the Yoruba language. The influence permeates the city: food sold on the street is the same as in Senegal and Nigeria, the music is fused with pulsating African polyrhythms, men and women nonchalantly carry enormous loads on their heads, fishermen paddle dug-out canoes in the bay, and the pace of life is more relaxed than in other parts of the country.

Modern Salvador

Salvador today is a fascinating mixture of old and modern, rich and poor, African and European, religious and profane. The city has 15 forts, 166 Catholic churches and 1000 *candomblé* temples. It remains a major port, exporting tropical fruit, cocoa, sisal, soya beans and petrochemical products. However, its most important industry is tourism, and it is the second largest tourist attraction in the country, after Rio.

Local government has done much to improve the fortunes of this once run-down, poor and dirty city. Major investments are being made in its infrastructure and public health areas. A new comprehensive sewage system has been installed throughout the city, with a view to improving living conditions and dealing with pollution.

The once-forgotten Lower City, Ribeira and the Itapagipe Peninsula districts have received major facelifts. Bahia has become more industrialized, with major investments being made by multinational firms in the automotive and petrochemical industries, principally in the Camaçari complex, 40 km from the city. The Bahian economy is currently the fastest growing in the country.

Centro Histórico

Most of the interesting sights are concentrated in the Cidade Alta (Upper City). From Praça Municipal to the Carmo area, 2 km north along the cliff, the Centro Histórico is a national monument and protected by UNESCO. It was in this area that the Portuguese built their fortified city, and it is here that some of the most important examples of colonial architecture in the Americas can be found today. The historic centre has undergone a massive restoration programme. The colonial houses have been painted in pastel colours. Many of the bars have live music, which spills out onto the street on every corner. Patios have been created in the areas behind the houses, with open-air cafés and bars. Artist ateliers, and antique or handicraft stores have brought new creative blood to what was once the bohemian part of the city. Many popular traditional restaurants and bars from other parts of Salvador have opened new branches in the area.

Praça Municipal (Tomé de Souza) and the Praça da Sé

These adjacent squares, connected by the Rua da Misericórdia, link with neighbouring Terreiro de Jesus (Praça 15 de Novembro) to form an almost entirely pedestrianized area. A decade ago this area was tawdry but it has been tidied up in recent years. It's a good place to see impromptu capoeira shows (but beware of taking pictures and getting aggressively pressured into parting with cash) and there's good shopping at the many street-side stores and stalls.

The **Praça Municipal** is the oldest part of Salvador. From here the city grew in a bewildering panoply of architectural styles, many of which can be seen around the square. Dominating the view are the neoclassical columns of the former council chamber (1660), now the **Paço Municipal**, and the imposing **Palácio Rio Branco** ① *Tue-Sat 0930-1700, free*. Like many of Brazil's opulent eclectic buildings, this was built in homage to the French for the state-governor, in 1918. The palace now houses municipal offices. On the western side of the square is the star of many postcards: the huge, art deco **Elevador Lacerda** ① *US$0.05*, which whisks people from the Cidade Alta to the Cidade Baixa, 70 m below, in a manner of seconds. It was built in the late 1920s to replace an old steam lift, which in turn replaced the original rope and pulley system first installed by the Jesuits. There are wonderful views over the bay from here.

Heading north from the *praça*, Rua da Misericórdia runs past the church of **Santa Casa Misericórdia** ① *T071-3322 7666, open by arrangement 0800-1700*, (1695), with its high altar and beautiful painted *azulejo* tiles, to **Praça da Sé**. This is one of central Salvador's most attractive squares, decorated with modernist fountains, shaded by mimosa and flamboyant trees and lined with stately buildings, many of which house smart shops or European-style cafés. The square preserves a statue of Salvador's founder, Thomé da Souza, and affords good views of the bay. Look out for the Fallen Cross (Cruz Caída) a sculpture sitting on a plinth by one of Latin America's foremost sculptors, Mário Cravo Junior (www.cravo.art.br). It is dedicated to the old Igreja da Sé (cathedral), which was pulled down in 1930, together with an entire street of 18th and early 19th century townhouses, to make way for the now defunct tramline. The cathedral's contents has been uncovered and are now displayed in a sad looking viewing pit, another of which showcases the remains of slaves and mariners who were buried in the church's grounds in the 16th century.

Salvador centre

➡ **Salvador maps**
1 Salvador orientation, page 399
2 Salvador centre, page 403
3 Pelourinho, page 408
4 Salvador south to Barra, page 411

Sleeping 🛏
O Convento do Carmo **7**
Portas Velhas **8**
Pousada das Flores **2**
Pousada do Boqueirão **3**
Pousada do Pilar **5**
Pousada Redfish **1**
Pousada Villa Carmo **4**
Villa Santo Antônio **6**

Eating 🍴
Al Carmo **1**
Amado **2**
Olivier **3**
SoHo **4**
Trapiche Adelaide **5**

Terreiro de Jesus (Praça 15 de Novembro)

Less than 100 m northeast of Praça da Sé, the Terreiro de Jesus is a large *praça* surrounded by handsome colonial townhouses and some of the city's most impressive churches. The square is the centre of tourist activity and bustles with bars, cafés and myriad souvenir stalls proffering everything from *acarajé* to *berimbaus*. It's particularly lively on Tuesday and weekend nights when there are shows or concerts (see Bars and clubs, page 423), and there are regular displays of capoeira – presented without joy and for the tourist dollar; if you stop to watch, you'll be expected to pay. Beware, too, of the persistent *Baianos* offering *fitas* (brightly coloured ribbons given as a good luck present), who swoop down like hawks on new arrivals. The streets that run off the south side of the Terreiro are frequented by drug dealers and beggars – best avoided, especially after dark.

The Terreiro de Jesus takes its name from the 'Church of the Society of Jesus' that dominates it. It is now **Catedral Basílica** ① *daily 0900-1100, 1400-1700*, devolving its ownership to the main body of the Catholic church in 1759, after the Jesuits were expelled from all Portuguese territories. The cathedral, whose construction dates from between 1657 and 1672, is one of the earliest examples of baroque in Brazil – a style that came to dominate in the 18th century and reached its full glory in Minas Gerais. The interior is magnificent: the vast vaulted ceiling and 12 side altars, in baroque and rococo, frame the main altar and are completely leafed in gold. This lavish display is offset by a series of Portuguese *azulejos* on in blue, white and yellow, which swirl together in a tapestry pattern.

The church is built on the site of the original Jesuit chapel built by Padre Manuel da Nóbrega in the 16th century. Nóbrega was part of the crew on that came from Portugal with Brazil's first governor-general, Tomé de Sousa, arriving in Bahia on 29 March 1549. Together with Padre José de Anchieta, he founded many of the Jesuit seminaries and churches that later became the cities of modern Brazil, including Rio, Recife and São Paulo. Antônio Vieira, one of the greatest orators in Portuguese history and a campaigner for the protection of the *indígenas* in the Amazon, preached some of his most famous sermons in the church. Inside is the **tomb of Mem de Sá**, the great Portuguese *conquistador* general who more than perhaps anyone was responsible for the establishment of the Brazilian territories: after liberating Rio from the French, he quelled an insurrection that threatened to overthrow the colony. Note the interesting sculptures, particularly those on the altar of Saint Ursula in a huge chest carved from the now almost extinct *jacarandá* tree, encrusted with ivory, bone and turtle shell.

Across the square is the church of **São Pedro dos Clérigos** ① *Sun 0800-0930*, which is beautifully renovated. Alongside is the church of the early 19th-century **Ordem Terceira de São Domingos** ① *Mon-Fri 0800-1200, 1400-1700, US$0.25*, which has a beautiful painted wooden ceiling.

There are a number of interesting museums on the square. The **Museu Afro-Brasileiro** ① *Mon-Fri 0900-1800, Sat and Sun 1000-1700, US$3*, charts the history of the Portuguese slave trade. Between 1440-1640, Portugal monopolized the export of slaves from Africa and they were the last European country to abolish it. Over the course of 450 years, they were responsible for transporting more than 4.5 million Africans – some 40% of the total. There are also panels comparing West African and Bahian *orixás* (deities) and some beautiful murals and carvings by the artist Carybé (Hector Julio Páride Bernabó) who lived most of his life in Bahia. Carybé became famous with the *antropofagismo* movement, illustrating Mario de Andrade's *Macunaíma*, and won the prize as the best draughtsman in Brazil in 1955. He was later celebrated for his depictions of *candomblé* rituals and *orixás*. In the basement of the same building, the **Museu Arqueológico e**

Candomblé

Candomblé is a spiritual tradition that developed from religions brought over by Yoruba slaves from West Africa. It is focused on relationships with primordial spirits or *orixás* who are linked with natural phenomena and the calendar. The *orixas* are invoked in *terreiros* (temples). These can be elaborate, decorated halls, or simply someone's front room with tiny altars. Ceremonies are divided into two distinct parts. The first is when the *orixás* are invoked through different rhythms, songs and dances. Once the dancers have been possessed by the *orixá*, they are led off in a trance-like state to be changed into sacred, often very elaborate costumes, and come back to the ceremonial area in a triumphant procession in which each one dances separately for their deity. Overseeing the proceedings are *mães* or *pães de santo*, priestesses or priests.

Candomblé ceremonies may be seen by tourists, usually on Sundays and religious holidays – although many are just for show and not the real thing. The ceremonies can be very repetitive and usually last several hours, although you are not under pressure to remain for the duration. Appropriate and modest attire should be worn; visitors should not wear shorts, sleeveless vests or T-shirts. White clothing is preferred, black should not be worn especially if it is combined with red. Men and women are separated during the ceremonies, women always on the left, men on the right. No photography or sound recording is allowed. Most temples are closed during Lent, although each one has its own calendar. **Bahiatursa** (see page 400) has information about forthcoming ceremonies, but accurate information on authentic festivals is not always easy to come by.

Etnográfico ⓘ *Mon-Fri 0900-1700, US$1*, houses archaeological discoveries from Bahia, such as stone tools, clay urns, an exhibition on the people of the *Rio Xingu* of the Alto area. The **Memorial de Medicina** (museum of medicine) is in the same complex.

Facing Terreiro de Jesus is the Largo Cruzeiro de São Francisco, crowded with souvenir stalls and dominated by a large wooden cross and the church and convent of **São Francisco** ⓘ *Praça Anchieta s/n, T071-3322 6430, 0800-1730, cloisters US$2*. This is the jewel in the crown of Salvador's colonial centre and one of the finest baroque churches in Latin America. The simple façade belies the treasure inside and the 64 years it took to complete the church after it was recovered from the invading Dutch who had sacked the city in 1686. The entrance leads to a sanctuary with a spectacular trompe l'oeil painting by local artist **José Joaquim da Rocha** (1777). From here, a set of cloisters decorated with minutely detailed and hand-painted *azulejos*; many are by the celebrated Portuguese artist **Bartolomeu Antunes de Jesus** and depict scenes from the life of St Francis. A beautiful sculpture of St Peter of Alcântara, venerated for his mystical visions attained in a state of painful ecstasy, is agonisingly captured by the Bahian artist **Manoel Inácio da Costa**, who carved the sculpture from a single hunk of rainforest wood. Some say that the saint's pale complexion and drawn features are an allusion to da Costa's tuberculosis. The main body of the church is the most opulent in Brazil – a vast, ornate exuberance of woodcarving in *jacarandá* depicting a riot of angels, animals, floral designs and saints, covered with some 800 kg of solid gold and dedicated to the patron saint of the poor. Many believe that the distorted features of the carvings are a silent protest against the Portuguese on the part of the indigenous and African slaves who decorated the church (in a similar vein to the protest made by artists like Aleijadinho in Minas Gerais, see page 274).

The beat of the doldrums in Salvador

Bahia is famous worldwide for its music. But ironically and sadly, the state's music scene has never been in a worse state. Long gone is the richness and diversity that brought Brazil samba and the rhythms of capoeira and subsequently **Tom Zé**, **Caetano Veloso** and **Gilberto Gil's** *tropicália* and the rock of **Raul Seixas**. Even the great *batucada* drum orchestras like **Olodum**, the **Filhos de Gandhi** and **Ilê Aiyê** haven't done anything but rest on their laurels for years.

The reason for this is the dominance and ubiquity of the highly commercial *axê* music, which initially became popular during Salvador's carnival in the 1990s, and is sweeping all other styles aside in a tide of frenetic, flippant pop. There simply isn't support for other musical forms and for a sense of the vibrancy and creativity of Brazilian music you will have to go further north to Recife, São Luís or Belém, or south to Rio or São Paulo.

But all is not doom and gloom. **Carlinhos Brown** (see page 425) continues to produce wonderful music from his community project in the Candeia *favela* and has been instrumental both literally and figuratively in bring a great new act, **Candombless**, to the fore. And in 2007 a wonderful new samba singer from Lençóis won the prestigious TIM newcomer award, **Mariene de Castro** (see box, page 425). You can see her play live on and around the Pelourinho solo and with the **Ganhadeiras de Itapoan** community group which includes some of Bahia's finest old samba musicians.

Next door is the church of the **Ordem Terceira de São Francisco** ⓘ *0800-1200 and 1300-1700, US$1*, (1703), with its intricately carved sandstone façade being the only example in Brazil of the Spanish plateresque style – a late Gothic form that takes its name from its mimicry in stone of the elaborate filigree work undertaken by silversmiths. There's a huge and intricately decorated altar piece inside and a chapterhouse covered in striking images of the Order's most celebrated saints and a series of *azulejos* many depicting scenes of Lisbon before the devastating earthquake in 1755.

The Pelourinho

The streets north of the Terreiro de Jesus, which run over a series of steep hills to the neighbourhood of Santo Antônio, are referred to as the Pelourinho. The area takes its name from the whipping post where the African slaves were auctioned off or punished by their Brazilian-Portuguese masters. Its steep cobbled streets, lined with brightly painted colonial houses and churches, form the centre of one of the largest conglomerations of colonial architecture in the Americas. It is one of Salvador's most popular areas for nightlife, particularly popular on Tuesdays and at weekends.

Until 1993 the area was very run down; subsequent refurbishment has greatly improved the area but there is still some way to go before it becomes as salubrious as the centre of São Luís or Ouro Preto. The city's African Brazilian communities suffered decades of neglect under Bahia's long-serving governor Antônio Carlos Magalhaes and, despite the current, more progressive executive, the city's wealthy business and social elite remain notoriously uninterested in Salvador's African heritage and oblivious to the world's interest in African Brazilian culture.

The Pelourinho's main thoroughfares run north off the Terreiro de Jesus. Rua Alfredo Brito and Rua João de Deus and the side streets that run off them are lined with three- or four-storey townhouses occupied by shops, restaurants and boutique hotels. Both descend in steep cobbles to the **Largo de Pelourinho**, a large sunny square watched over by one of Salvador's most important African-Brazilian monuments, the church of **Nosso Senhora Do Rosário Dos Pretos** ① *US$1.50*, built by former slaves over a period of 100 years, with what little financial resources they had. In colonial times, black Bahians were not even allowed to walk in front of the churches reserved for the white elite, let alone go inside them, and had to worship in their own building.The side altars honour black saints such as São Benedito and the painted ceiling and panels by Jose Joaquim da Rocha are very impressive. The overall effect is of tranquillity, in contrast to the complexity of the cathedral and the São Francisco church. The church remains a locus for black Bahian culture and has strong connections with *candomblé*. On Tuesdays, following a show by Olodum on the Pelourinho, there is an African-Brazilian mass with singing accompanied by percussion from repiques, tambors and tamborins. There is a haunting **slave cemetery** at the back of the building.

At the corner of Alfredo Brito and Largo do Pelourinho is a small museum dedicated to the work of Bahia's most famous author Jorge Amado, **Fundação Casa de Jorge Amado** ① *Largo do Pelourinho s/n, T071-3321 0070, Mon-Sat 0900-1800, free.* Amado was born and brought up around Ilhéus but spent much of his life in this house. The people of this part of Salvador provided the inspiration for the larger-than-life characters that populate some of his most famous novels including *Dona Flor e seus dois Maridos* (*Dona Flor and Her Two Husbands*, 1966). Information is in Portuguese only, but the walls of the museum café are covered with colourful copies of his book jackets and all of his work is on sale.

The **Museu Abelardo Rodrigues** ① *Solar do Ferrão, R Gregório de Matos 45, Pelourinho, Tue-Sat 1300-1800, US$1*, preserves one of the most important and impressive collections of religious art outside the São Paulo's Museu de Arte Sacra (see page 203). It is housed in one of the Pelourinho's best-preserved and most stately 18th-century town houses – once a Jesuit college – and showcases some impressive statuary, engravings, paintings and lavish monstrances from Brazil, all over Latin America and the Far East. All were collected by the Pernambucan who gave the museum its name.

The **Museu da Cidade** ① *Praça Jose de Alencar 3, Largo do Pelourinho, T071-3321 1967, Tue-Fri 0900-1800, free*, is in two adjacent 18th-century houses and has exhibitions of arts and crafts, old photographs of the city, many fascinating objects from *candomblé* rituals and effigies of the *orixás*. From the higher floors there is a good but seldom photographed view of the Pelourinho.

Below Nossa Senhora do Rosario dos Pretos is the **Conjunto do Benin** ① *R Padre Agostinho Gomes 17, Pelourinho, T071-3241 5679, casadobenin@yahoo.com.br, Mon-Fri 1200-1800*, which has displays of African-Brazilian crafts, photos and a video on Benin and Angola. It hosts exhibitions, dance shows and other artistic events. The **Casa da Nigéria** ① *R Alfredo de Brito 26, Pelourinho, T071-3328 3782*, offers a similar programme orientated more to Yoruba culture and has showcases of African and African Brazilian arts and crafts, photographs and an important library. Yoruba language classes are available here and both cultural centres are important nexuses of African-Brazilian culture and society in Bahia. The **Quilombo do Pelô** hotel (see page 417), also serves as a cultural centre for Jamaican culture. There are occasional shows in the restaurant – where Jamaican food is served – and the hotel receives many Jamaican celebrity guests. There's also Jamaican music played in the **Bar do Reggae** (see page 424).

3 Pelourinho

➡ **Salvador maps**
1 Salvador orientation, page 399
2 Salvador centre, page 403
3 **Pelourinho, page 408**
4 Salvador south to Barra, page 411

O Pagador de
  Promessas **7** *A3*
Pelourinho **8** *B3*
Pousada Gloria **2** *D3*
Quilombo do Pelô
  & Restaurant **11** *B2*
Solara **9** *A3*
Solar dos Romanos **10** *B2*
Villa Bahia **12** *D2*

Jardim das Delícias **8** *C2*
Mama Bahia **11** *B2*
Maria Mata Mouro **7** *D3*
O Nilo **13** *D3*
Pomerô **16** *B2*
Senac **4** *A3*
Sorriso de Dadá **1** *C3*
Uauá **6** *B3*

N

50 metres
50 yards

Sleeping 😴
Albergue das Laranjeiras,
  Café & Creperie **4** *D3*
Albergue do Passo **1** *A3*
Albergue do Peló **5** *A3*
Albergue São Jorge **6** *B2*
Lucas Guesthouse **3** *A3*

Eating 🍴
Axego **3** *C2*
Bahiacafe.com **5** *C1*
Coffee Shop **10** *C1*
Encontro dos Artistas **14** *D3*
Gramado **15** *C1*

Bars & clubs 🍸
Cantina da Lua **18** *C2*
Casa do Olodum **17** *C3*
Do Reggae **20** *A3*
O Cravinho **19** *C1*
Quereres **2** *C3*

Towards Morro do Carmo

The Ladeira do Carmo climbs up the steep **Morro do Carmo** hill running north from the Largo do Pelourinho, past the **Igreja do Santissimo Sacramento do Passo** and the steps that lead up to it (which were the setting for the city scenes in Anselmo Duarte's award winning socio-political tragedy, *O Pagador de Promessas*, 'keeper of the promises'), to the **Largo do Carmo**. This little *praça*, at the junction of the Ladeira do Carmo and Rua Ribeiro dos Santos, is watched over by a series of Carmelite buildings. The most impressive is the **Igreja da Ordem Terceira do Carmo** ① *Mon-Sat 0800-1130, 1400-1730, Sun 1000-1200, US$0.30*, once a piece of striking baroque dating from 1709 but completely gutted in a fire 67 years later and restored in the 19th century. It is in a poor state of repair but houses one of the sacred art treasures of the city, a sculpture of Christ made in 1730 by **Francisco Xavier 'O Cabra' Chagas** ('the Goat'), a slave who had no formal training but who is celebrated by many locals as the Bahian Aleijadinho, who carved *O Cabra*. Two thousand tiny rubies embedded in a mixture of whale oil, ox blood and banana resin give Christ's blood a ghostly, almost transparent appearance and the statue itself is so lifelike it appears almost to move. There is a small museum with a collection of ornate icons and period furniture. The adjacent **Igreja do Carmo** ① *Mon-Sat 0800-1200, 1400-1800, Sun 0800-1200, US$1*, has a pretty interior with some beautiful wood carving, while the **Convento do Carmo**, which served as a barracks for Dutch troops during the 1624 invasion, has been tastefully converted into Salvador's most luxurious hotel (see Sleeping, page 416).

Cidade Baixa and Mercado Modelo

Salvador's lower city, which sits at the base of the cliff that runs from Santo Antônio in the north to Praça Municipal and Lacerda lift in the south, was once as delightful and buzzing with life as the Pelourinho. Today, its handsome imperial and early republican 19th-century buildings, many of them covered in *azulejos*, are crumbled and cracked. Others have been pulled down and replaced with ugly concrete warehouses. There are numerous gorgeous baroque churches in a similar state of disrepair. With the exception of the ferry docks, the whole area is dangerous and down at heel – especially at night. However, there are plans for restoration and a large US hotel group has bought one of the 19th-century mansion houses.

There are few sights of interest. Even if you are glutted with religious architecture after wandering the Pelourinho it's hard not to be impressed by the striking, octaganol **Igreja de Nossa Senhora da Conceição da Praia** ① *R Conceição da Praia at Av Contorno*. The church, which dates from 1736, was built in *lioz* marble in Portugal by Manuel Cardoso de Saldanha, disassembled bit by bit with the stones given numbers, then transported to Salvador and reconstructed. It has an unusual octagonal nave and diagonally set towers, modelled on churches in Portugal such as the Guarda cathedral. Inside it is magnificent, with a stunning ceiling painting of an Italianate panoply of saints gathered around the Madonna in glorious Renaissance perspective – the masterpiece of Mestre Athayde (José Joaquim da Rocha).

Bahia's best souvenir shopping is in the **Mercado Modelo** ① *Praça Visconde Cayru, Cidade Baixa, Wed-Mon 0900-1900, Sun 0900-1300, closed Tue*. This former customs house is thick with stalls selling everything from musical instruments to life-size sculptures hacked out of hunks of wood. Look out for the colourful handbags, made out of hundreds of can ring-pulls sewn together with fishing twine, and the *orixá* effigies and postcards. There are frequent capoeira shows between 1100 and 1300 on weekdays (you will have to pay to take pictures), occasional live music and numerous cafés and stalls selling Bahian cooking.

South of the centre

The modern city, which is dotted with skyscraper apartment blocks, sits to the south of the old centre towards the mouth of the bay. Rua Chile leads to **Praça Castro Alves**, with its monument to the man who started the campaign that finally led to the abolition of slavery in 1888. Two streets lead out of this square: Avenida 7 de Setembro, busy with shops and street vendors selling everything imaginable; and, parallel to it, Rua Carlos Gomes. **São Bento monastery** ① *Av 7 de Setembro, Mon-Sat 0630-1200, 1300-1600, closed Wed, www.saobento.org*, another of Bahia's oldest religious buildings, dating from 1582 but with much later construction. The cool, colonial spaces and cloistered garden are a welcome quiet space within the bustle of the city. The monastery was used as an arsenal by the Dutch during their occupation in 1624 and narrowly avoided going the way of much of colonial Rio and São Paulo in the 20th century, razed to the ground to make way for ugly modern skyscrapers.

Museu de Arte Sacra da Bahia ① *R do Sodré 276 off R Carlos Gomes, T071-3243 6511, Mon-Fri 1130-1730, US$1.50*, is in the 17th-century monastery and church of Santa Teresa d'Avila, at the bottom of the steep Ladeira de Santa Tereza. Many of the 400 carvings are from Europe, but there are some beautiful pieces by the artists who worked on the city's finest churches, such as Frei Agostinho de Piedade and José Joaquim da Rocha. Look out for the hauntingly life-like statue of Christ by the latter, carved from a piece of ivory and crucified on a *jacarandá* cross. Among the reliquaries of silver and gold is one made from gilded wood by Aleijadinho (see page 274). The views from the patio, out over the Baía de Todos os Santos, are breathtaking and very little photographed. Opposite is **Temporal** ① *R do Sodré 276, Tue-Fri 0900-1830, Sat and Sun 0900-1800*, a private museum of postcards. Just inland near Campo Belo is the **Dique do Tororo** ① *Av Vasco de Gama*, a lake and leisure area decorated with 3-m-high *orixá* statues by the Bahian sculptor Tati Moreno. There are large *candomblé* celebrations here at dawn on 2 February before the **Festa da Yemanjá** when priestesses offer presents to Oxum (the spirit of the waters).

The **Mosteiro São Bento** ① *Largo de São Bento 1, Centro T071-2106 5200, Mon-Fri 0900-1130 and 1300-1630, Mass Mon-Fri 0700 and 1820, Sat 0700, Sun 1000 (Gregorian chant)*, is one of the oldest Benedictine buildings in Latin America, founded in 1582 and altered through the centuries. It is a peaceful retreat from the bustle of Salvador and houses a religious art museum with some 2000 priceless antiquities.

Further south, the **Museu de Arte Moderna** ① *off Av Contorno, T071-3329 0660, Tue-Fri 1300-2100, Sat 1500-2100, Sun 1400-1900*, converted from an old estate house, is only open for special exhibitions. The buildings themselves are worth seeing. Slaves from Africa arrived here and were crammed together in the building's dungeon-like rooms. The museum is close to a *favela* and there are occasional muggings particularly after dark; it's best to take a taxi.

Heading towards Porta da Barra, the **Museu de Arte da Bahia** ① *Av 7 de Setembro 2340, Vitória, Tue-Fri 1400-1900, Sat and Sun 1430-1900, US$2*, has interesting paintings by Bahian and Brazilian artists from the 18th to the early 20th century.

Museu Carlos Costa Pinto ① *Av 7 de Setembro 2490, Vitória, www.guasar.com.br/ mccp/mccp.htm, Mon and Wed-Fri 1430-1900, Sat and Sun 1500-1800, US$2*, is a modern house with collections of crystal, porcelain, silver and furniture. It ostensibly has the world's only collection of *balangandãs* (slave charms and jewellery) and is highly recommended.

200 metres
200 yards

Sleeping
Albergue do
 Porto 11
Bahia do Sol 2
Bahia Flat 3
Bella Barra 1
Da Barra 9
Farrol Barra Flat 10
La Habana 12
Marazul 4
Monte Pascoal
 Praia 5
Pousada Azul 6
Pousada Hotel
 Ambar 7
Pousada Malu 8
Pousada Marcos 13
Tropical 14
Villa Romana 15
Village Novo
 Beach Suites 16

Eating
Barravento 2
Cantina Panzone 3
Caranguejo do
 Farol 4
Oceánica 5
Quattro Amicci 1

➡ **Salvador maps**
1 Salvador orientation, page 399
2 Salvador centre, page 403
3 Pelourinho, page 408
4 **Salvador south to Barra, page 411**

Porto da Barra and the Atlantic beach suburbs

Barra is one of the most popular places to stay in Salvador and the best inner-city beaches are in this area. The strip from Porto da Barra as far as the Cristo at the end of the Farol da Barra beach has some of the city's liveliest cafés, restaurants, bars and clubs. A night out here, in nearby Campo Belo and in the exclusive restaurants and bars of the city's most upmarket venue, **Praça dos Tupinambas**, give an idea of how polarized Salvador society is. The clientele is much more middle class than the Pelourhino; the music, food and conversation are more European and American and, in Brazil's African heart, there's hardly a black face in sight.

There are a few sights of moderate interest around Barra. The **Forte de Santo Antônio** and its famous lighthouse are right at the mouth of the bay where Baía de Todos os Santos and the South Atlantic Ocean meet. On the upper floors, the **Museu Hidrográfico** ① *Tue-Sat 1300-1800, US$2*, has fine views of the coast. A promenade leads away from the fort, following the coast to the beach suburbs of **Ondina**, **Amaralina** and **Pituba**. Confusingly, the road is known as both Avenida Oceânica and Avenida Presidente Vargas, but with different numbering. Beyond Pituba are the best ocean beaches at **Jaguaripe**, **Piatã** and **Itapoã** (take any bus from Praça da Sé marked Aeroporto or Itapoã, about one hour). En route the bus passes small fishing colonies at **Amaralina** and **Pituba**, where *jangadas* (small rafts peculiar to the northeast) can be seen. Near Itapoã is the **Lagoa do Abaeté**, a deep freshwater lake surrounded by brilliant, white sands. This is where local women come to wash their clothes and then lay them out to dry in the sun. The road leading up from the lake offers a panoramic view of the city in the distance with white sands and freshwater less than 1 km from the sea.

Near the lighthouse at **Itapoã** are two campsites on the beach. A little beyond them are the magnificent ocean beaches of **Stella Maris** and **Flamengo**, both quiet during the week but very busy at the weekends. Beware of strong undercurrents in the sea.

Rio Vermelho

This modern coastal suburb, between Ondina and Pituba, has long been the home of many of Salvador's well-to-do artists and musicians and is rapidly becoming the most exciting nightlife centre outside the Pelourinho. Unlike the beachfront neighbourhoods around Barra, the clientele is a healthy mix of middle class and African-Brazilian. There's a lively market with many little spit and sawdust bars, a handful of decent restaurants and small eateries serving some of the city's best *acarajé*. The area is busy at night, especially at weekends, and there are a number of venues playing traditional Bahian music. On 2 February the beach at Rio Vermelho is packed with *candomblé* pilgrims for the **Festa de Yemanjá**. To get here from the city centre, it is a 10-minute taxi ride (US$8-10) or a 20-minute bus journey. There are some good hotels nearby.

North of the centre

Bonfim and Itapagipe

The most famous sight in the northern suburbs is the church of **Nosso Senhor do Bonfim** ① *Mon 0630-0800, Tue-Sun 0600-1200, 1400-2000*, (1745), on the Itapagipe peninsula. It draws extraordinary numbers of suppliants (particularly on Friday and Sunday), making ex-voto offerings to the image of the Crucified Lord set over the high altar. The processions over the water to the church on the third Sunday in January are particularly interesting. Also on the Itapagipe peninsula is a colonial fort on Monte Serrat point, and at Ribeira, the church of **Nossa Senhora da Penha** (1743). The beach here has many restaurants, but the sea is polluted. To get here, take a bus from Praça da Sé or Avenida França.

Excursions from Salvador ⊜❷▲⊜ ▶▶ pp416-432.

From the Cidade Baixa, the *Trem do Leste* (train) leaves Calçada for a 40-minute journey through the following bay-side suburbs: **Lobato**; **Plataforma**, which has canoes and motor boats for Ribeira on the Itapagipe peninsula; **Escada**, with its 17th-century church; **Praia Grande**; **Periperi**; and **Paripe** (take a bus for the 17th-century church at São Tomé de Paripe). The train runs Monday to Friday only; the same trip can be made by bus – a more comfortable journey but less picturesque.

About 36 km south of the city is the **Museu do Recôncavo** (**Museu do Vanderlei do Pinho**) ⓘ *near the town of São Francisco do Conde, 7 km from the main highway, Tue, Thu and Sun 0900-1700*. The museum is based in the old Freguesia Mill (1552) and houses artefacts and pictures of the economic and social life of this region, going back three centuries. The *Casa Grande e Senzala* (the home of the landowner and the combined dwelling and working area of the slaves) is still intact. It is a peaceful way to spend an afternoon, but difficult to get to by public transport.

Ilha de Itaparica → *Phone code: 071. Colour map 4, A6.*

Across the bay from Salvador lies the island of Itaparica, 29 km long and 12 km wide. The town of **Itaparica** is very picturesque and well worth a visit, with a decent beach and many fine residential buildings from the 19th century. The church of **São Lourenço** is one of the oldest in Brazil, and a stroll through the old town is delightful. In summer the streets are ablaze with the blossoms of the beautiful flamboyant trees. From Itaparica town, take a bus or *combi* along the coast road (Beira Mar), which passes through the villages of **Manguinhos**, **Amoureiras** and **Ponta de Areia**. The beach at Ponta de Areia is one of the best on the island and is always very popular. There are many *barracas* on the beach, the most lively is **Barraca Pai Xango**. There are many *pousadas* in **Mar Grande** and at the nearby beaches of **Ilhota** and **Gamboa** (both to the left as you disembark from the ferry). The beaches at Mar Grande are fair but can be dirty at times.

Ilha de Itaparica

Ins and outs The island is connected to the mainland by bridge or boat. The main passenger ferry runs from the São Joaquim terminal in Salvador (see page 398) to **Bom Despacho**, every 45 minutes 0540-2230. A one-way ticket for foot passengers during the week costs US$1, US$1.20 at weekends. A catamaran service for Bom Despacho departs twice daily, US$3. **Mar Grande** can be reached by a small ferry (*lancha*) from the Terminal Marítimo, in front of the Mercado Modelo in Salvador. The ferries leave every 45 minutes and takes 50 minutes, US$3 return. There is a bridge on the southwest side of the island. Buses from mainland towns such as Nazaré das Farinhas, Valença and Jaguaribe (a small, picturesque colonial port), arrive at Bom Despacho.

From Bom Despacho there are many buses, *combis* and taxis to all parts of the island. The best beaches are at Ponta de Areia, Mar Grande (US$1 by *combi*), Berlinque, Aratuba and Cacha Pregos. *Combis* and taxis can be rented for trips around the island but be prepared to bargain, US$30 for a half-day tour. ➨ *See Transport, page 431.*

Nazaré das Farinhas → *Phone code: 075 Population: 25,000*

On the mainland, 60 km inland from Itaparica, Nazaré das Farinhas is reached across a bridge by bus from Bom Despacho. This 18th-century town is celebrated for its market, which specializes in the local ceramic figures, or *caxixis*. There is a large market in Holy Week, particularly on Holy Thursday and Good Friday. From here buses run to southern Bahia. About 12 km from Nazaré (taxi from Salvador US$4.25, bus at 1530) is the village of **Maragojipinha**, which specializes in making the ceramic figures.

Recôncavo Baiano 🏠🚗🏍️⊛🅾️🔺🅰️🅰️ ➨ *pp416-432.*

The area around the bay and immediately south of Salvador is known as the Recôncavo Baiano. This was one of the chief centres of sugar and tobacco cultivation in the 16th century and there is some fine colonial architecture here. Places of interest include the sleepy colonial towns of Cachoeira and São Felix, on the banks of the muddy Rio Paraguaçu, which are famous for their festivals and strong connection to *candomblé*. There are also small fishing villages on the bay that are worth exploring, and dotted throughout the countryside are the decaying ruins of once-productive *engenhos* (sugar refineries), some of which can be visited.

Leaving Salvador on the Feira road, fork left at Km 33 on the BR-324 to visit the **Museu do Recôncavo Vanderlei de Pinho**. Further west, round the bay, is **São Francisco do Conde**, 54 km from Salvador, with a church and convent of 1636 and the ruins of Don Pedro II's agricultural school, said to be the first in Latin America.

Santo Amaro da Purificação and around → *Colour map 4, A6. Phone code: 075.*

Some 73 km from Salvador, Santo Amaro da Purificação is an old and sadly decaying sugar centre. It is noted for its churches (which are often closed because of robberies), the most famous of which is the **Igreja Matriz Santo Amaro da Purificação** ① *Praça da Purificação, T075-3241 1172, Mon-Fri 0800-1200 and 1400-1700, Sat 0800-1200*, which has a superb painted ceiling by José Joaquim da Rocha. There is also a municipal palace (1769), a fine *praça* and ruined sugar baron mansions including **Araújo Pinto**, the former residence of the Barão de Cotegipe. It is also the birthplace of Caetano Veloso and his sister Maria Bethânia. Other attractions include the splendid beaches of the bay, the falls of Vitória and the grotto of Bom Jesus dos Pobres. There are a number of interesting festivals (see page 427) and craftwork is sold on the town's main bridge. There are no good hotels or restaurants. There are at least 20 buses a day from Salvador to Santo Amaro and onward buses to Cachoeira.

About 3 km beyond Santo Amaro on the BR-420, turn right onto the BA-878 for **Bom Jesus dos Pobres**, a small, traditional fishing village with a 300-year history. There is one good hotel (see Sleeping, page 420). To get there, take a bus from Salvador's *rodoviária* (four a day, **Camurjipe**, US$3).

Cachoeira and São Felix → *Colour map 4, A6. Phone code: 075.*

Set deep in the heart of some of the oldest farmland in Brazil, **Cachoeira** and its twin town, São Felix, were once thriving river ports that provided a vital supply link with the farming hinterland and Salvador to the east. The region was the centre of the sugar and tobacco booms, which played such an important role in the early wealth of the colony. The majestic *saveiro* (a gaff-rigged boat) traditionally transported this produce down the Rio Paraguaçu to Salvador across the bay. These boats can still occasionally be seen on the river. The town was twice capital of Bahia: once in 1624-1625 during the Dutch invasion, and once in 1822-1823 while Salvador was still held by the Portuguese.

With the introduction of roads and the decline of river transport and steam, the town stopped in its tracks in the early 20th century and thus maintains its special charm. As in Salvador, *candomblé* plays a very important part in town life (see box, page 405). Easy access by river from Salvador allowed the more traditional *candomblé* temples to move in times of religious repression. Cachoeira was the birthplace of Ana Néri, known as 'Mother of the Brazilians', who organized nursing services during the Paraguayan War (1865-1870).

There are a few interesting sights in Cachoeira. The **Casa da Câmara e Cadeia** ⓘ *Praça de Aclimação, T075-3425 1018, daily 0800-1200 and 1400-1800*, (1698-1712) was, for a brief period when Cachoeira was the state capital in 1822, the seat of the governance of Bahia. Upstairs is the town hall (with stern notices saying no shorts or Havaianas allowed). Downstairs there is a **slavery museum**, housed in the heavy walled dungeon where slaves were imprisoned behind two sets of strong bars. The dungeon has a sad and oppressive atmosphere. The **Museu Regional de Cachoeira** ⓘ *Praça da Aclamação 4, Centro, T075-3425 1123, Mon-Fri 0800-1200 and 1400-1700, Sat 0800-1230, book ahead*, has a collection of period furniture, sacred images and ecclesiastical items, paintings and documents relating to the history of the town. The dark mark on the walls near the staircase at the entrance show where the river reached during the 1989 flood.

The **Santa Casa de Misericórdia** (1734) was the colonial hospital and has a fine church attached. Other churches include: the 16th-century **Ajuda** chapel (now containing a fine collection of vestments) and the convent of the **Ordem Terceira do Carmo**, whose church has a heavily gilded interior; the **Igreja Matriz**, with 5-m high *azulejos*; and **Nossa Senhora da Conceição do Monte**. All churches are either restored or in the process of restoration.

The **Fundação Hansen Bahia** ⓘ *R 13 de Maio, T075-3425 1453, Tue-Fri 0900-1700, Sat and Sun 0900-1400*, has fine engravings by the German artist Karl Meinz Hansen, who was born in Hamburg and lived on the Pelourinho in Salvador during the 1950s. In a series of xylographs he documented the miserable lives of the downtrodden women who prostituted themselves for pennies. The museum itself is the former house of Ana Néri's, Brazil's Florence Nightingale who nursed the injured during the Paraguayan War.

There is a great woodcarving tradition in Cachoeira and many of its artists can be seen at work in their studios. ▸▸ *See Shopping, page 429.*

A 300-m railway bridge built by the British in the 19th century spans the Rio Paraguaçu to **São Felix**, where the **Danneman cigar factory** ⓘ *Av Salvador Pinto 30, 0830-1200 and 1300-1630*, can be visited to see hand-rolling in progress. A trail starting near the **Pousada do Convento** leads to some freshwater bathing pools above Cachoeira. There are beautiful views from above São Félix.

Ins and outs Cachoeira/São Felix are 116 km from Salvador, and 4 km from the BR-420. There are more than 20 daily buses from Salvador to Cachoeira (2½ hours). The quickest way to get back to Salvador is to take a motorbike taxi from Cachoeira to the BR-420 and wait at the bus stop there; buses pass every 15 minutes and are up to an hour quicker because they have fewer stops than buses that leave from Cachoeira's town centre.

Cachoeira has a **tourist office** ⓘ *R Ana Néri 4, T075-3425 1123*. It is hard to get lost as there are only a handful of streets, all spreading out from the river. The centre of the city and best point for orientation is the Praça da Aclamação and the Igreja da Ordem Terceira do Carmo.

Excursions from Cachoeira

About 6 km from Cachoeira, on the higher ground of the Planalto Baiano, is the small town of **Belém** (the turning is at Km 2.5 on the road to Santo Amaro), which has a healthy climate and is a popular place for summer homes. **Maragojipe**, a tobacco exporting port with a population of 39,000, is 22 km southeast of Cachoeira along a dirt road (BA-123); it can also be reached by boat from Salvador. If you visit, look out for the old houses and the church of São Bartolomeu, with its museum. The main festival is **São Bartolomeu**, in August. Good ceramic craftwork is sold in the town. The tobacco centre of **Cruz das Almas** can also be visited, although transport is poor.

◉ Salvador and the Recôncavo listings

For Sleeping and Eating price codes and other relevant information, see pages 42-47.

● Sleeping

Salvador *p398, maps p399, p403, p408 and p411*

The Centro Histórico is the ideal place to stay. The **Pelourinho** is best if you're on a tight budget. Santo Antônio has reasonably priced hotels with charm and character. **Barra** also has some reasonable options; especially for apartments with kitchens, and it lies on the seafront. Business visitors will find good services and hotels in **Rio Vermelho**, overlooking the ocean and a 10-min taxi ride from the centre or airport.

Accommodation in the city tends to get very full over Carnaval and New Year, when prices go up. During Carnaval it is a good idea to rent a flat or stay in a shared room in a *pensionato* (private house), as hotels and hostels will be heaving. *Pensionatos* usually charge anything from US$5 to US$35 per person. Be careful with your belongings as not all householders are honest. The tourist office has a list of estate agents for flat rental (eg José Mendez, T071-3237 1394/6) or you can find flats through Bahia Online, www.bahia-online.net or Bahia Land, T071-8133 1441, williamwisden@gmail.com.

Houses or rooms can be rented from **Pierre Marbacher**, R Carlos Coqueijo 68A, Itapoã, T071-3249 5754 (Caixa Postal 7458, 41600 Salvador), who is Swiss, owns a beach bar at Rua K and speaks English.

There are various campsites in the area; but be careful of swimming in the sea nearby. **Camping Clube do Brasil**, R Visconde do Rosario 409, Rosario, T071-3242 0482. **Camping de Pituaçu**, Av Prof Pinto de Aguiar, Jardim Pituaçu, T071-3231 7143. **Ecológica**, R Alameida da Praia, near the lighthouse at Itapoã, T071-3374 3506. Bar, restaurant, hot showers. Highly recommended. To get there, take a bus from Praça da Sé direct to Itapoã, or to Campo Grande or Barra, change there for Itapoã (1 hr), then 30 mins' walk. **Igloo Inn**, Terminal Turistico de Buraquinho, Praia Lauro de Freitas, T071-3379 2854.

The Pelourinho

LL O Convento do Carmo, R do Carmo 1, T071-3327 8400, www.pousadas.pt. Far and away the best in the city and the best historical hotel in the whole of Brazil, with a range of suites in a beautifully converted baroque convent. Facilities include an excellent restaurant and spa, a small swimming pool and business services. **LL-L Hotel Villa Bahia**, Largo do Cruzeiro de São Francisco 16-18, T071-3322 4271, www.villabahia.com. This boutique hotel, part of the French **Voyeur** group, is housed in a renovated 18th-century town house right next to the the Convento de São Francisco. It has a series of themed rooms, the airiest and brightest of which is the Goa room, with a huge hardwood bed, 2-m-high shuttered windows and polished wood floors. The public set the mood with classical music. There's a little mosaic pool out back and a hot tub on the roof.

LL-L Portas Velhas, Largo da Palma 6, Santana, T071-3324 8400, www.casadas portasvelhas.com.br. A little themed boutique hotel in the square made famous by Jorge Amado's *Dona Flor and Her Two Husbands*. Small but tastefully decorated a/c rooms, 1 larger suite and a good restaurant. The streets running from here to the centre are unsafe at any time of day so take a taxi.

B Hotel Pelourinho, R Alfredo Brito 20, T071-3243 2324, www.hotelpelourinho.com. A newly refurbished 1960s hotel with bright tiled and white-walled a/c en suites. The bathrooms have marble basins and glass shower cubicles and a few offer great views out over the Baía de Todos os Santos.

B-D Hotel Quilombo do Pelô, R Alfredo Brito 13, T071-3322 4371. A range of rooms from simple dorms and doubles to the top floor 'Rei Zumbi' suite with its own jacuzzi and views out over the city. All are themed and the restaurant serves Jamaican food.

C Hotel Solar dos Romanos, R Alfredo Brito 14a, T071-3322 6158. A range of basic cavernous rooms in a colonial house; some of which are gloomy and without windows and the best of which are a/c with sea views.

C Lucas Guesthouse, R do Passo 7, T071-3327 5746. A spacious upper suite with a little terrace and space for up to 4 people. Also 4 very simple fan-cooled rooms partitioned with chipboard.

C Solara, Praça José de Alencar 25, T071-3326 4583. A cavernous building with very basic rooms, all en suite, with lino floors and mattresses covered in uncomfortable plastic. Some have TVs and fridges. The best have good views out over the Pelourinho. Recently painted but still in need of refurbishment.

C-E Albergue das Laranjeiras, R Inácio Acciolli 13, T/F071-3321 1366, www.laranjeiras hostel.com.br. IYHA hostel with a range of dorms, doubles and family rooms in a colonial building in the heart of the historic centre. Café and crêperie downstairs, English spoken and a full range of hostel services. Can be noisy but good for meeting other travellers.

C-E Albergue do Passo, R Ladeira do Passo 3, T071-3326 1951. Clean, safe and friendly, with breakfast and standard hostel services.

C-E Albergue do Peló, R Ribeiro dos Santos 5, T071-3242 8061, www.alberguedopelo.com.br. A bright reception area leads to simple but freshly painted and slate-floored dorms for 4-12. All are single sex. Breakfast included.

C-E Albergue São Jorge, R Alfredo de Brito, T071-3266 7092. Brightly painted but cramped single-sex dorms, and a few doubles. Internet access and breakfast.

C-E Pousada Gloria, R das Laranjeiras 34, T071-3321 8249. Clean and well-kept rooms some of which have en suites and views out over the historical centre. No breakfast.

D-E O Pagador de Promessas, Ladeira do Carmo 19, T071-3243 5716, www.opagador depromessas.com.br. Much the best option for backpackers in the Pelourinho, with a series of fan-cooled dorms and doubles in a converted colonial house, all immaculately clean, with hardwood floors and in cool, high-ceilinged rooms. Tours organized. No breakfast.

Santo Antônio

Santo Antônio is a quiet district just 5 mins' walk northeast of Pelourinho, beginning immediately after the Largo do Carmo. In recent years it has been a popular place for Europeans to open up carefully designed *pousadas* in beautifully restored buildings. A number have magnificent views of the bay. Most are mid-range, but there are a handful of cheaper options too.

A-AL Pousada das Flores, R Direita de Santo Antônio 442, T071-3243 1836, www.pflores. com.br. A beautiful, tranquil old house decorated in colonial style and owned by a Brazilian/French couple. Great breakfast. Full of character.

AL-A Pousada do Boqueirão, R Direita do Santo Antônio 48, T071-3241 2262, www.pousadaboqueirao.com.br. The most stylish of all the *pousadas* in Salvador. Lovingly renovated by the Italian interior-designer owner and her brother – a former merchant seaman. There are a variety of themed rooms; the best at the top of the building, with wonderful views out over the Baía de Todos os Santos. Service and breakfast are excellent and the *pousada* sells some fine Brazilian arts and crafts from important artists like Zé Caboclo, for an excellent price. Several languages spoken.

AL-A Pousada Redfish, Ladeira do Boqueirão 1, T071-3243 8473, www.hotel redfish.com. English-owned stylish little boutique with plain, large rooms, some with terraces and open-air showers.

AL-A Villa Santo Antônio, R Direita de Santo Antônio 130, T071-3326 1270, www.hotel-santoantonio.com. Very stylish, bright and comfortable converted colonial town house, the best rooms have magnificent views out over the bay from your bed. All the a/c rooms have en suites and little balconies; all are different. Good service and breakfast.

A-B Pousada do Pilar, R Direita do Santo Antônio 24 , T071-3241 6278, www.pousada dopilar.com. The a/c rooms are large, modern, very well kept and functional and have cable TV. They are decked out in raw wood and light plaster and have verandas with those excellent Baía de Todos os Santos views. Good breakfast, friendly service. Wi-Fi in reception and a pleasant roof terrace bar.

B Pousada Villa Carmo, R do Carmo 58, T/F071-3241 3924, www.pousadavilla carmo.com.br. Very comfortable, rooms with fan or a/c in an Italian/Brazilian-owned colonial house. Several languages spoken.

South of the centre

Campo Grande/Vitória is a quiet, upmarket residential area, between Barra and the city centre, convenient for museums.

L Tropical, Av Sete de Setembro 1537, Campo Grande, T071-2105 2000, www.tropicalhotel.com.br. A recently renovated 1950s business hotel. Good service, pool, sauna, business facilities and a discount for **Varig** customers. Convenient central location.

A Bahia do Sol, Av 7 de Setembro 2009, T071-3338 8800, www.bahiadosol.com.br. Comfortable and safe family-run hotel in a 1970s tower. Good breakfast and restaurant, bureau de change, but no pool. Rooms have a/c, fridges, safes and en suites. The best are on the upper floors and have recently been refurbished. Ask to see at least a couple.

Porto da Barra and the Atlantic beach suburbs

Barra is the best beach neighbourhood in the historic centre. The sea is none too clean but the neighbourhood has plenty of restaurants, beach bars and nightlife.

A Bahia Flat, Av Oceânica 235, T071-3339 4140, www.bahiaflat.com.br. A range of flats. The best are tastefully decorated and newly refurbished with Miró prints on the walls, patent leather sofas, glass coffee tables, large fridges, sound system and expansive mirror-fronted wardrobes. The best have sea views. The hotel has a pool and sauna.

A Marazul, Av 7 de Setembro 3937, T071-3264 8151, www.marazulhotel.com.br. Blocky 1970s tower on the seafront with standard 3-star rooms with anonymous catalogue furniture. The best are at the top of the building and have magnificent views. The restaurant has a pool, conference facilities and business services.

A Monte Pascoal Praia, Av Oceânica 176, Farol beach, T071-3203 4000, www.monte pascoal.com.br. Newly renovated 1970s hotel decorated in garish colours but well-kept and well-run. With pool, sauna, gym, restaurant and decent service.

B Farol Barra Flat, Av Oceanica 409, T071-3339 0000, www.farolbarraflat.com.br. Over 100 faded, simple yet well-kept apartments with kitchenettes; all with microwaves, TVs and the best with sweeping ocean views.

B Pousada Azul, R Praguer Fróis. A quiet *pousada* in a semi-residential street. Spartan rooms furnished with solid hardwood beds and commodes.

B La Habana, Av Oceânica 84, T071-3237 5105, www.hospederiadelahabana.com.br. Newly renovated brilliant yellow seafront hotel with 13 a/c rooms; all with polished brick floors and en suites. Quiet during the week but popular at the weekends. With a lively bar and restaurant.

B Village Novo Beach suites, Av 7 de Setembro 3659, T071-3267 4362, www.villagenovo.com. A 125-year-old converted town house with a range of tastefully decorated mock-boutique hotel rooms with terraces, a large roof patio and a pleasant little café restaurant.

B-C Villa Romana, R Lemos Brito 14, T071-3264 6522, www.villaromana.com.br. Simple a/c rooms with wooden floors, desks, wardrobes and en suites.

C Pousada Hotel Ambar, R Afonso Celso 485, T071-3264 3791, www.ambar pousada.com.br. A French-owned *pousada* with very simple, small fan-cooled rooms gathered around a colourful little courtyard. Internet and decent breakfast.

C-D Pousada Malu, 7 de Setembro 3801, T071-3264 4461. Small, somewhat boxy rooms along an external corridor in a hotel overlooking the sea. Some rooms are musty. With breakfast, cooking and laundry facilities.

D Bella Barra, R Afonso Celso 439, T071-3264 3260, www.hotelbellabarra.com.br. Very simple a/c whitewash and brown-tiled rooms with foamy mattresses and en suites. In need of a lick of paint.

D Hotel da Barra, Av Almirante Marques de Leão 138, T071-3264 2481. Clean, bright but very simple fan-cooled or a/c rooms all with en suites (with no shower curtains). The best are on the upper floors.

E-F Albergue do Porto, R Barão de Sergy 197, T071-3264 6600, www.albergue doporto.com.br. IYHA hostel in a turn-of-the-20th-century house. Spacious, high ceilinged fan-cooled rooms with wooden floors; a comfortable communal area and good breakfast, English spoken and double a/c rooms with baths available alongside dorms. Other facilities include, kitchen, laundry, safe, TV lounge, games room and internet. Very popular.

E-F Pousada Marcos, Av Oceânica 281, T071-3264 5117, www.pousadamarcos.com.br. A very simple hostel-style guesthouse. In a good location near the lighthouse. Always busy.

Rio Vermelho

LL Pestana Bahia, R Fonte de Boi 216, T071-3453 8000, www.pestanahotels.com.br. Newly revamped tower with wonderful views out over the ocean but no access to the beach. Pool, gym, restaurant, sauna and very good business facilities. Online discounts available. With restaurant and bar.

LL-L Blue Tree Towers, R Monte Conselho 505, T071-3330 2233, www.bluetree.com.br. Smart new business hotel in this excellent Brazilian chain. Very good service and decent facilities including pool, tennis courts and a respectable restaurant.

A-B Catharina Paraguaçu, R João Gomes 128, Rio Vermelho, T071-3247 1488, www.hotelcatharinaparaguacu.com.br. Small colonial-style hotel with attractive courtyards and a range of decent rooms, some of which are distinctly better than others. Very good service. Recommended.

C Ibis, R Fonte do Boi 215, T071-3330 8300, www.accorhotels.com.br. Blocky new hotel in this budget business chain. Safe, a/c and great seaviews from the upper floors. Very good value.

Ilha de Itaparica *p413, map p413*

A Pousada Arco Iris, Estrada da Gamboa 102, Mar Grande beach, T071-3833 1130. Magnificent though dishevelled 19th-century building romantically set in a garden of mango trees. Decent restaurant with slow service, a pool and unkempt but shady camping facilities available in the owners' adjacent property.

B Quinta Pitanga, Itaparica town, T071-3831 1554. Beautifully decorated beachfront property lovingly run by owner, Jim Valkus. 3 suites, 2 singles and an excellent restaurant open to non-guests.

B-C Galeria Hotel, Praia do Sol, Barra Grande, T071-3636 8441, www.galeria-hotel.com. German/Brazilian-owned *pousada* with simple tile-floored a/c en suites around a large pool. Good restaurant.

C Pousada Canto do Mar, Av Beira Mar s/n, Praia de Aratuba, T071-3638 2244, www.pousadaumcantodomar.com.br. Brightly coloured, simple *cabañas* overlooking what is a lively beach in summer and a quiet beach the rest of the year. Friendly staff, decent breakfast.

D Pousada Casarão da Ilha, near the church in the main *praça*, Mar Grande beach, T071-3833 1106. Spacious a/c rooms, pool and a great view of Salvador across the bay.

D Pousada Estrela do Mar, Av NS das Candeias 170, Mar Grande beach, T071-3833 1108. Modest but well-kept a/c or fan-cooled rooms.

D Pousada Scórpio, R Aquárius, Mar Grande beach, T071-3823 1036. Simple rooms set around a little swimming pool. Reasonable breakfast and a weekend restaurant.

D Pousada Sonho do Verão, R São Bento 2, Mar Grande beach. Chalets and apartments with cooking facilities, French and English spoken. Bike and horse rental (US$3/5 per hr).

D Pousada Zimbo Tropical, Aratuba beach, Estrada de Cacha Pregos, Km 3, R Yemanjá, T/F071-3838 1148. Pretty little bungalows in a tropical garden. Good breakfast, optional evening meals.

E Hotel Village Sonho Nosso, Estrada Praia Cacha Pregos, Km 9 Cacha Pregos, T071-3837 1040. Very clean huts on one of the island's cleanest beaches. The good service includes pick-up from anywhere on the island. Bom Despacho *combis* stop a 5-min walk from the front door.

Santo Amaro da Purificação *p414*

A Água Viva, T075-699 1178, reservations T071-3359 1132. On one of the region's oldest farms and the beachfront. Chalets or apartments, a/c or fan, good breakfast and restaurant. Good beach. Recommended.

Cachoeira *p414*

C Pousada do Convento de Cachoeira, R Praça da Aclamação s/n, T075-3425 1716, www.pousadadoconvento.com.br. Newly refurbished rooms in an historic building in the centre of the town. The best are on the upper floor overlooking a grassy courtyard and have high wooden ceilings and chunky, handsome furniture. Those on the ground floor are simpler in white-wash and tile and some are only fan-cooled.

D-E Pousada La Barca, R Inocência Boaventura 37, 200m downstream of the Praça Aclamação, T075-3425 10170, www.labarca.zip.net. Little rooms in a bright orange annexe and public areas decorated with the paintings by the artist-owner Cristina. No a/c.

D-F Pousada d'Ajuda, R Largo d'Ajuda s/n, T075-3425 5278. Spacious and clean doubles with little corners cordoned off for showers (ask to see a few rooms, some have saggy mattresses) and dorms for up to 4. Right next to the Igreja da Boa Morte.

E-F Pousada Tia Rosa, R Ana Neri 12, near Casa Ana Neri, T075-3725 1692. Very basic and simple but with a reasonable breakfast. The best are on the upper storeys and have views. The friendly owner is very well-connected in the city.

⊘ Eating

Salvador *p398, maps p399, p403, p408 and p411*

The Pelourinho and Santo Antônio

₸₸₸ Mama Bahia, R Alfredo Brito 21, T071-3322 4397, www.mamabahia.com.br. Steaks and northeastern meat dishes like *carne do sol* accompanied by a respectable, if modest, list of Argentinian, Brazilian and Chilean wines.

₸₸₸ Maria Mata Mouro, R da Ordem Terceira 8, T071-3321 3929. International menu, excellent service, relaxing atmosphere in a quiet corner in the bustling Pelourinho.

₸₸₸ O Nilo, R das Laranjeiras 44, T071-9159 0937. Superior Lebanese food in an intimate little restaurant decorated with black-and-white prints. Great tagines and a vegetarian degustation menu.

₸₸₸ Sorriso de Dadá, R Frei Vicente 5, T071-3321 9642, www.dada.com.br. Bahia's most famous chef has cooked for, amongst others,

Jorge Amado, Gilberto Gil and Hillary Clinton. Her *moqueca de camarão* and her *vatapas* are signature dishes. But all has sadly, fallen somewhat from grace and the food is now very patchy. Lets hope she wakes up from resting on her laurels.

₸₸₸ Uauá, R Gregorio de Matos, 36, T071-3321 3089. Elegant, colonial restaurant and bar serving northeastern cooking and seafood, including some Bahian specialities. The restaurant's name means 'firefly' in Tupi.

₸₸₸-₸₸ Al Carmo, R Rua do Carmo 66, Santo Antônio, T071-3242 0283. A favourite spot to watch the sun sink over the Baía de Todos os Santos, caipirinha or chilled wine in hand. The Italian food is rather stodgy and heavy with cheese. Opt for a starter only. The music (usually a guitarist and singer) has an optional cover charge.

₸₸₸-₸₸ Axego, R João de Deus 1, T071-3242 7481. An established restaurant celebrated for its seafood. The *moquecas* are among the best in the Centro Histórico and there is excellent *feijoada* on Sun lunchtime.

₸₸₸-₸₸ Encontro dos Artistas, R das Laranjeiras 15, T071-3321 1721. Excellent seafood and *moquecas* served in a little streetside restaurant decorated with a mock-Da Vinci *Last Supper*, set in Salvador.

₸₸₸-₸₸ Jardim das Delícias, R João de Deus, 12, T071-3321 1449. An award-winning, elegant restaurant and antiques shop set in a pretty tropical garden serving Bahian and international food accompanied by live classical or acoustic music. Very good value for its quality.

₸₸₸-₸₸ Olivier, R Direita de Santo Antônio 61, T071-3241 3829, olivierestaurante@ hotmail.com. A cosy little French restaurant with live light jazz and MPB out back on most weekend nights in season, decent *caipirinhas* and a Franco-Brazilian menu strong on fish. 30-something crowd.

₸₸ Quilombo do Pelô, R Alfredo Brito 13, T071-3322 4371. Daily 1100-2400. Rustic Jamaican restaurant, good food with relaxed, if erratic service. One of the few places offering vegetarian options.

Senac, Praça José Alencar 13-15, Largo do Pelourinho, T071-3324 4557. A catering school with 2 restaurants. Upstairs is typical Bahian cooking; downstairs is per kilo and open for lunch; both are a/c. Dishes are better upstairs but there is plenty of choice in the buffet and options for vegetarians.

Pomerô, R Alfredo Brito 33, T071-3321 5556, www.pomero.com.br. Closed Mon. Good value, simple and barely garnished grilled meats, fish steaks, bar snacks and lightly spiced *moquecas* in a popular restaurant housed in a colonial house.

Bahiacafe.com, Praça da Sé, 20, T071-3322 1266. Smart, Belgian-run internet café with good coffee, a European-style breakfast menu and decent snacks.

Coffee Shop, Praça da Sé 5, T071-3322 7817. Cuban-style café serving sandwiches. Excellent coffee and tea served in china cups. Doubles as cigar shop.

Gramado, Praça da Sé 16, T071-3322 1727. Lunch only. The best of the few per kilo restaurants in the area. Scrupulously clean and with a reasonable choice.

Porto da Barra and Atlantic beach suburbs

There are many a/c restaurants from cheap to medium-priced in **Shopping Barra** and the **Barra Center Shopping**.

Amado, Av Lafayete Coutinho 660, Comércio, T071-3322 3520, www.amado bahia.com.br. The best of Salvador's top-end restaurants on the Baía de Todos os Santos waterfront. The space is beautiful, set on a deck overlooking the lapping aquamarine of the Baía de Todos os Santos. But the real winner here is the food from Edinho Engel, who had an award-winning restaurant in São Paulo. The emphasis on seafood with dishes such as squid stuffed with crab and garlic in provencale sauce with a white carrot mousseline. The haute cuisine *moquecas* are excellent.

Barravento, Av Oceanica 814, T071-3247 2577. Very popular beach bar restaurant and hang-out with a marquee roof. Decent cocktails, *chope* and a menu of seafood, *moquecas* and steaks.

SoHo, Av Contorno 1010, Bahia Marina, Salvador, T071-3322 4554. The restaurant's long bar is where Salvador's 'A-list' drink their *caipirinhas*. Great sushi and sashimi combinations from Paulistano chef Marcio Fushimi are served in the chic glass-walled dining room and at the open-air veranda tables overlooking the ocean. Come for a late dinner 2130-2200, dress smart casual.

Trapiche Adelaide, Praça Tupinmabas 2, Av Contorno, T071-3326 2211, www.trapicheadelaide.com.br. Salvador's most self-consciously chic restaurant in a mood-lit glass-walled rectangle built out over the water and with stunning views of the bay. The seafood is excellent but people really come here to be seen in the cavernous modernist open-air dining room or the neighbouring cozy-chic **Bar da Ponta**. Dress well and take a taxi to get here.

Cantina Panzone, Av Oceánica 114, T071-3264 3644. Reasonable wood-fired pizza and pasta and a lively crowd in high season.

Oceánica, Presidente Vargas 1, T071-3264 3561. A long-established popular Bahian seafood restaurant. Open until late, especially on weekends.

Quatro Amicci, R Dom Marcos Teixeira 35. Excellent wood-fired oven pizzas served in a bright modern space in a converted 19th-century house. Lively weekend crowd.

Caranguejo do Farol, Av Oceánica 235, T071-3264 7061. A buzzing bar and seafood restaurant serving great Bahian food in *refeição* portions large enough for 2. Cheap bottled beer. Strong *caipirinhas*.

Rio Vermelho

Casa da Dinha, R João Gomes 25, just west of the **Catharina Paraguaçu Hotel** and a few yards from the Largo de Santana, T071-3333 0525. One of the best mid-range Bahian restaurants in the city with a varied menu peppered with Bahian specialities, steaks, fish and standard international options like pasta.

Bahian cuisine

Bahian cooking is spiced and peppery. The main dish is *moqueca* – seafood cooked in a sauce made from coconut milk, tomatoes, red and green peppers, fresh coriander and *dendê* (palm oil). It is traditionally cooked in a wok-like earthenware dish and served piping hot at the table. *Moqueca* is often accompanied by *farofa* (manioc flour) and a hot pepper sauce which you add at your discretion – it's usually extremely hot so try a few drops before venturing further. The *dendê* is somewhat heavy and those with delicate stomachs are advised to try the *ensopado*, a sauce with the same ingredients as the *moqueca*, but without the palm oil.

Nearly every street corner has a *Bahiana* selling a wide variety of local snacks, the most famous of which is the *acarajé*, a kidney bean dumpling fried in palm oil, which has its origins in West Africa. To this the *Bahiana* adds *vatapá*, a dried shrimp and coconut milk paté (also delicious on its own), *pimenta* (hot sauce) and fresh salad. For those who prefer not to eat the palm oil, the *abará* is a good substitute. *Abará* is steamed and wrapped in banana leaves.

Bahians usually eat *acarajé* or *abará* with a chilled beer on the way home from work or the beach at sunset. Another popular dish with African origins is *xin-xin de galinha*, chicken on the bone cooked in *dendê*, with dried shrimp, garlic and squash.

Recommended *Bahianas* are; **Chica**, at Ondina beach (in the street behind the Bahia Praia Hotel); **Dinha**, in Rio Vermelho (serves *acarajé* until midnight, extremely popular); **Regina** at Largo da Santana (very lively in the late afternoon); and **Cira** in Largo da Mariquita. Seek local advice on which are the most hygienic stalls to eat from.

Ilha de Itaparica *p413, map p413*

There are many Bahianas selling *acarajé* in the late afternoon and early evening, in the main *praça* and by the pier at Mar Grande.
♥♥♥ **Philippe's Bar and Restaurant**, Largo de São Bento, Mar Grande. The best restaurant on the island with delicious fish dishes cooked by the French owner.
♥ **Rafael**, in the main *praça*, Mar Grande. Basic with pizzas and snacks.

Cachoeira *p414*

♥ **Café com Arte Sebo Ana Néri**, R 13 de Maio 16, T061-9161 1581. *Petiscos*, good coffee, beer and art from a mixture of local and international artists. Lovely space in a colonial house and a friendly eastern European and fully Bahian owner.
♥ **Casa Comercial NS Rosário o Recanto do Misticismo**, Praça da Aclamação s/n. Nowhere could be more 'Cachoeira' than this pizza café and restaurant with 2 *candomblé*-inspired shrines – one to the 5 African nations and one to the 5 elements. As well as pizza, there's great *carne do sol* and fried chicken with chips, rice and beans and occasional live music.
♥ **Pouso da Palavra**, Praça da Aclamação s/n Arty little café opposite the Casa da Camara museum. Great cappuccinos in a cosy period house, owned by poet Damário Da Cruz. Local artists' work decorate the walls and the café sells some great CDs, souvenirs and beautiful mandala candle shades by Graca Mascarehenses.

🎵 Bars, clubs and live music

Salvador *p398, maps p399, p403, p408 and p411*

Centro Histórico

Nightlife is concentrated on and around the Pelourinho and the Terreiro de Jesus, where there is always a free live street band on Tue and at weekends. The Pelourinho area is also a good place to browse the bars, but be wary after 2300. There are many bars on the **Largo de Quincas Berro d'Água**, and along **R Alfredo do Brito**. **R João de Deus** and its environs are dotted with simple pavement bars with plastic tables.

The most famous music from Salvador is the *batucada* of drum orchestras like **Olodum** and **Ilê Aiyê**, whose impressive sound can be heard frequently around the Pelourinho (Olodum played on Paul Simon's *Rhythm of the Saints* album). Both groups have their own venues and play in the individual parades or *blocos* at Carnaval. See box, page 426, for times and venues of the *bloco* rehearsals.

Bar do Reggae and Praça do Reggae, Ladeiro do Pelourinho, by the Nossa Senhora dos Rosarios dos Pretos church. Live reggae bands every Tue and more frequently closer to Carnaval. Be wary of pick-pockets.

Cantina da Lua, Praça Quinze de Novembro 2, Terreiro De Jesus, T071-3322 4041. Open daily. Popular spot on the square with outdoor seating, but gets crowded and the food isn't great.

Casa do Ilê Aiyê, R das Laranjeiras 16, T071-3321 4193, www.ileaiye.org.br. Ilê Aiyê's headquarters and shop, where you can find information about their shows and Carnaval events.

Casa do Olodum, R das Laranjeiras, T071-3321 5010, www2.uol.com.br/olodum. Olodum's headquarters where they perform live every Tue and Sun at 1900 to packed crowds.

O Cravinho, Praça 15 de Novembro 3, T071-3322 6759. Dark little bar with occasional live music. Always busy. Greasy bar food is served at tree-trunk tables, usually accompanied by plentiful *cachaça*, which is made here and stored in barrels behind the bar. Be careful in this area after 2300.

Quereres, R Frei Vicente 7, T071-3321 1616. Lively little club in a colonial house playing Brazilian samba funk, hip hop and *axê*. Busy on Tue and Fri.

Porto da Barra and Atlantic beach suburbs

Barra nightlife is concentrated around the **Farol da Barra** (lighthouse) and **R Marquês de Leão**, which is busy with pavement bars. Like the Pelourinho the whole area is good for a browse, but be wary of pickpockets.

Concha Acústica, Teatro Castro Alves, Praça 2 de Julho, Campo Grande, T071-3339 8000, www.tca.ba.gov.br. The city's premier small concert venue with quality national and international acts such as Tom Zé and Naná Vasconcelos.

Fashion Club, Av Octávio Mangabeira 2471, Jd dos Namorados, T071-3346 0012. Not very fashionable at all – despite the name – but busy (especially on Thu) with a predominantly 20-something crowd.

Habeas Copos, R Marquês de Leão 172. A popular and traditional street-side bar – something of a Salvador institution.

Korunn, R Ceará 1240, Pituba, T071-3248 4208. Lively dance club with a bohemian crowd. Very popular Thu-Sat.

Lotus, Av Almirante Marques de Leão, T071-3264 6787. Salvador's branch of the famous New York and São Paulo club. A little frayed on the inside and populated with a fashionable upper-middle class crowd dancing to old-hat European and US club sounds.

Rio Vermelho and the north

The district of **Rio Vermelho** was once the bohemian section of town and it still has good live music and exciting bar nightlife. There are a number of lively bars around the **Largo de Santana**, a block west of Hotel Catharina Paraguaçu.

Café Calypso, Travessa Prudente Moraes 59, T071-3334 6446. Live Brazilian rock music on Tue and Fri.

Casa da Mãe R Guedes Cabral 81, T071-3334 3041 or T071-9601 6616 (mob). Live *samba de roda* several times a week and roots Bahian music. Ring ahead for schedule.

Havana Music Bar, R Cardeal da Silva 117, T071-3237 5107. Live bands (mostly rock) Wed-Sat. Best after 2230.

Bahia's musicians recommend

Mariene de Castro is one of Brazil's most exciting new samba acts. Her debut CD *Abre Caminho* won several of Brazil's top music awards in 2007. She told *Footprint* where to go out in Salvador: "The best and most exciting music in Bahia has its roots firmly in the samba tradition. Some of the best artists are members of the Santo de Casa cultural movement who play in the Praça Pedro Arcanjo near the Pelourinho on Saturday evenings."

Carlinhos Brown is one of Brazil's greatest percussionists and the founder of the Timbalada drum troupe. He is one of the icons of Bahian music and a star of Carnaval. We asked him where to go to hear live music in Salvador: "At our community centre here in Candeal you can hear my band Timbalada as well as great new acts like Candombless and Beat Gabot." To get there, take a taxi to Candeal for 1800 on a Sunday and ask for 'A Casa de Carlinhos Brown'.

Pimentinha, Boca do Rio. One of the few clubs to be lively on a Mon.

Rock In Rio Café, Aeroclube Plaza Show, Boca do Rio, T071-3461 0300. Dance club with a young crowd and an emphasis on rock and MPB. Busiest at the weekends.

Teatro Sesi Rio Vermelho, R Borges dos Reis 9, T071-3334 0668. One of the best venues in the city for contemporary Bahian bands.

Cachoeira *p414*

Casa do Licor, R 13 Maio 25. Interesting bohemian bar with a range of bizarre drinks. Try the banana-flavoured spirit. Live music at the weeekend.

⊕ Entertainment

Salvador *p398, maps p399, p403, p408 and p411*

The **Fundação Cultural do Estado da Bahia** edits *Bahia Cultural*, a monthly brochure listing the main cultural events for the month. These can be found in most hotels and **Bahiatursa** information centres. Local newspapers *A Tarde* and *Correio da Bahia* have good listing for cultural events in the city.

Cinema

The impressive Casa do Comércio building near Iguatemi houses the **Teatro do SESC** which has a mixed programme of theatre, cinema and music Wed-Sun.

The main shopping malls at Barra, Iguatemi, Itaigara and Brotas, and **Cineart** in Politeama (Centro), showcase more mainstream movies.

Theatre and classical music

Associação Cultural Brasil Estados Unidos (**ACBEU**), Corredor de Vitória. US cultural shows and cinema.

Teatro Gregorio de Matos, Praça Castro Alves, T071-3322 2646. Programmes dedicated to showcasing new productions and writers.

Teatro Vila Velha, Passeio Publico, T071-3336 1384. Márcio Meirelles, the theatre's director, works extensively with **Grupo Teatro Olodum**; although performed in Portuguese, productions here are very visual and well worth investigating.

Teatro XVIII, R Frei Vicente, T071-3332 0018. Experimental theatre in Portuguese.

Theatro Castro Alves, Largo 2 de Julho, Campo Grande, T071-3339 8000. The city's most distinguished performance space and the home of the Bahian Symphony Orchestra and the Castro Alves Ballet Company. The theatre also hosts occasional performances by more cerebral MPB artists and contemporary performers like Hermeto Pascoal or Egberto Gismonti.

Carnaval in Bahia

Carnival in Bahia is the largest in the world and encourages active participation. It is said that there are 1.5 million people dancing on the streets at any one time.

The **pre-carnival festive season** begins with São Nicodemo de Cachimbo (penultimate Sunday of November), followed by Santa Bárbara (4 December), then the Festa da Conceição da Praia, centred on the church of that name (open 0700-1130) at the base of the Lacerda lift. The last night is 8 December (not for those who don't like crowds!). The Festa da Boa Viagem takes place in the last week of December, in the lower city; the beach will be packed all night on 31 December. The new year kicks off on 1 January with a beautiful boat procession of Nosso Senhor dos Navegantes from Conceição da Praia to the church of Boa Viagem, on the beach of that name in the lower city. The leading boat, which carries the image of Christ and the archbishop, was built in 1892. You can follow in a sailing boat for about US$1; go early (0900) to the dock by the Mercado Modelo. A later festival is São Lázaro on the last Sunday in January.

Carnaval itself officially starts on Thursday night at 2000 when the keys of the city are given to the Carnaval King 'Rei Momo'. The unofficial opening though is on Wednesday with the Lavagem do Porto da Barra, when throngs of people dance on the beach. Later on in the evening is the Baile dos Atrizes,

starting at around 2300 and going on until dawn, very bohemian, good fun. Check with **Bahiatursa** for details on venue and time (also see under Rio for Carnaval dates).

There are two distinct musical formats. The **afro blocos** are large drum-based troupes (some with up to 200 drummers) who play on the streets, accompanied by singers atop mobile sound trucks. The first of these groups was the Filhos de Gandhi (founded in 1949), whose participation is one of the highlights of Carnaval. Their 6000 members dance through the streets on the Sunday and Tuesday of Carnaval dressed in their traditional costumes, a river of white and blue in an ocean of multi-coloured carnival revellers. The best known of the recent *afro blocos* are Ilê Aiye, Olodum, Muzenza and Malê Debalê. They all operate throughout the year in cultural, social and political areas. Not all of them are receptive to foreigners among their numbers for Carnaval. The basis of the rhythm is the enormous *surdo* (deaf) drum with its *bumbum bumbum bum* anchorbeat, while the smaller *repique*, played with light twigs, provides a crack-like overlay. Ilê Aiye take to the streets around 2100 on Saturday night and their departure from their headquarters at Ladeira do Curuzu in the Liberdade district is not to be missed. The best way to get there is to take a taxi to Curuzu via Largo do Tanque, thereby avoiding traffic jams. The ride is a little longer but much quicker. A

⊛ Festivals and events

6 Jan Epiphany. Public holiday with many free concerts and events. Beautiful masses in many of the historic churches.
Jan Festa do Nosso Senhor do Bonfim. Held on the 2nd Sun after Epiphany.

On the preceding Thu there is a colourful parade at the church with many penitents and a ceremonial washing of the church itself. Great for photographs.
Feb Carnaval, see box page 426.
2 Feb Pescadores do Rio Vermelho. Boat processions with gifts for Yemanjá, Goddess of the Sea, accompanied by African Brazilian music.

good landmark is the Paes Mendonça supermarket on the corner of the street, from where the *bloco* leaves. From there it's a short walk to the departure point.

The enormous **trios eléctricos**, 12-m sound trucks with powerful sound systems that defy most decibel counters, are the second format. These trucks, each with its town band of up to 10 musicians, play songs influenced by the *afro blocos* and move at a snail's pace through the streets, drawing huge crowds. Each *afro bloco* and *bloco de trio* has its own costume and its own security personnel, who cordon off the area around the sound truck. The *bloco* members can thus dance in comfort and safety.

The traditional Carnaval route is from Campo Grande (by the Tropical Hotel da Bahia) to Praça Castro Alves near the old town. The *blocos* go along Avenida 7 de Setembro and return to Campo Grande via the parallel Rua Carlos Gomes. Many of the *trios* no longer go through the Praça Castro Alves, once the epicentre of Carnaval. The best night at Praça Castro Alves is Tuesday (the last night of Carnaval), when the famous '*Encontro dos Trios*' (Meeting of the Trios) takes place. *Trios* jostle for position in the square and play in rotation until the dawn on Ash Wednesday. It is not uncommon for major stars from the Bahian (and Brazilian) music world to make surprise appearances.

There are grandstand seats at Campo Grande throughout the event. Day tickets for these are available the week leading up to Carnaval. Check with Bahiatursa for information on where the tickets are sold. Tickets are US$10 (or up to US$30 on the black market on the day). The *blocos* are judged as they pass the grandstand and are at their most frenetic at this point. There is little or no shade from the sun so bring a hat and lots of water. Best days are Sunday to Tuesday. For those wishing to go it alone, just find a friendly *barraca* in the shade and watch the *blocos* go by. Avoid the Largo da Piedade and Relógio de São Pedro on Avenida 7 de Setembro: the street narrows here, creating human traffic jams.

The other major centre for Carnaval is Barra to Ondina. The **blocos alternativos** ply this route. These are nearly always *trios eléctricos*, connected with the more traditional *blocos* who have expanded to this now very popular district. Not to be missed here is Timbalada, the drumming group formed by the internationally renowned percussionist Carlinhos Brown.

Ticket prices range from US$180 to US$450. The quality of the *bloco* often depends on the act that plays on the *trio*. For more information see the official Carnaval site, www.carnaval. salvador.ba.gov.br.

Mar/Apr Holy Week. The week before Easter sees many colourful processions around the old churches in the upper city.

Santo Amaro da Purificação *p414*
24 Jan-2 Feb Festival of Santo Amaro.
2 Feb Nossa Senhora da Purificação.
13 May Bembé do Mercado.

Cachoeira *p414*
24 Jun São João, 'Carnival of the Interior'. Celebrations include dangerous games with fireworks, well attended by tourists.
Mid-Aug Nossa Sehora da Boa Morte.
4 Dec A famous *candomblé* ceremony at the Fonte de Santa Bárbara.

O Shopping

Salvador p398, maps p399, p403, p408 and p411

Arts, crafts and cigars

Artesanato Santa Bárbara, R Alfredo Brito 7, Pelourinho. Excellent handmade lace.

Atelier Totonho and Raimundo, Ladeira do Carmo, Pelourinho. 2 adjacent galleries run by a co-operative of some 28 naïve art artists, including Totonho, Calixto, Raimundo Santos and Jô. Good prices.

FIEB-SESI, Av Tiradentes 299, Bonfim; Av Borges dos Reis 9, Rio Vermelho; and Av 7 de Setembro 261, Mercês. Some of the best artisan products in the city ranging from textiles and ceramics to musical instruments.

Goya Lopes. R Gregorio de Mattos, Pelourinho, T071-3321 9428, www.goyalopes.com.br. African Brazilian designer clothing on Goya's Didara label, which features very simple, rustic cotton clothing and beach shawls stamped with intricate motifs in very bright colours from Afro-Brazilian cultural life.

Instituto Mauá, R Gregorio de Matos 27, Pelourinho. Tue-Sat 0900-1800, Sun 1000-1600. Good-quality items, better value and quality than the Mercado Modelo.

Loja de Artesanato do SESC, Largo Pelourinho, T071-3321 5502. Mon-Fri 0900-1800 (closed for lunch), Sat 0900-1300.

Oficina de Investigação Musical, Alfredo Brito 24, Pelourinho, T071-3322 2386. Mon-Fri 0800-1200 and 1300-1600. Handmade traditional percussion instruments (and percussion lessons for US$15 per hr).

Rosa do Prado, R Inacio Aciolly 5, Pelourinho. Cigar shop packed with every kind of Brazilian *charuto* imaginable.

Bookshops

Graúna, Av 7 de Setembro 1448, and R Barão de Itapoã 175, Porto da Barra. English titles.

Livraria Brandão, R Ruy Barbosa 104, Centre, T071-3243 5383. Second-hand English, French, Spanish and German books.

Livraria Planeta, Carlos Gomes 42, loja 1. Sells used English books.

Jewellery

Casa Moreira, Ladeira da Praça, just south of Praça da Sé. Exquisite jewellery and antiques. Most are expensive, but there are some affordable charms.

Scala, Praça da Sé, T/F071-3321 8891. Handmade jewellery using locally mined gems (eg aquamarine, amethyst and emerald), workshop at back.

Markets

Feira de Artesanjato, Santa Maria Fort, Wed 1700-2100. Arts and crafts in the fort at the far end of Porto da Barra beach.

Feira de São Joaquim, 5 km from Mercado Modelo along the seafront, daily 0800-1900, Sun 0800-1200. The largest and least touristy market in the city selling mainly foodstuffs and a few artisan products. Very smelly.

Mercado Modelo, Praça Cairu, Cidade Baixa, Sat 0800-1900, Sun 0800-1200. Live music and dancing, especially Sat. Expect to be asked for money if you take photos. Many tourist items such as woodcarvings, silver-plated fruit, leather goods, local musical instruments. Lace items for sale are often not handmade (despite labels), are heavily marked up, and are much better bought at their place of origin (eg Ilha de Maré, Pontal da Barra and Marechal Deodoro).

Music and carnival souvenirs

Boutique Olodum, Praça José Alencar, Pelourinho. Olodum CDs, music, T-shirts and musical instruments.

Cana Brava records, R João de Deus 22, T071-3321 0536, www.bahia-online.net. Great little CD shop with a friendly and knowledgeable American owner. Stocks a whole range of classy Brazilian artists, less internationally famous names and back catalogue artists.

Flashpoint, Shopping Iguatemi. One of the best general music and CD shops in the city.

Ilê Aiyê, R das Laranjeiras 16, T071-3321 4193, www.ileaiye.org.br. Bags, clothes, books, music and other such items from this famous Carnaval drum orchestra and *bloco*.

Shopping centres

These are the most comfortable places to shop in Salvador – havens of a/c cool in the heat of the Bahian summer offering a chance to rest over an ice-cold beer, to lunch and to shop for essentials like Havaianas, bikinis, CDs and beach wraps along with comestibles like batteries, supermarket food and suntan cream. **Barra** and **Iguatemi** are the largest and best stocked.

Cachoeira *p414*
Woodcarving studios

Worth stopping by to look or to buy are: **Davi Gonçalves**, JJ Seabra 68, Centro T075-3425 2686; **Doidão**, R Ana Nery 42, T075-3425 2764; **Fory**, R Treze de Maio 31, Centro, T075-3425 1142; and **Louco Filho**, R Treze de Maio 18, Centro, T075-3425 4310.

▲ Activities and tours

Salvador *p398, maps p399, p403, p408 and p411*
Football

Otávio Mangabeira Stadium, Trav Joaquim Maurício, Nazaré, T/F071-3242 3322. 90,000-seat stadium which is home to the **Esporte Clube Bahia** and **Vitória** football clubs. 10 mins away from the Pelourinho, and the Barroquinha terminal.

Tour operators

Bus tours are available from several companies, including: **Alameda Turismo**, T071-3248 2977, US$15 per person; **Itaparica Turismo**, T071-3248 3433; **LR Turismo**, T071-3264 0999, which also offers boat trips; and **Tours Bahia**, T071-3322 3676.

Cultour, R João Gomes, 88 Sala 8 Sobrado da Praça, Rio Vermelho, T071-3335 1062, www.cultour.it. Offer some of the best cultural tours in the city. Less 'touristy' than operators in the Pelourinho area.

Tatur Turismo, Av Tancredo Neves 274, Centro Empresarial Iguatemi, Salas 222-224, T071-3114 7900, www.tatur.com.br. Excellent private tours of the city and the state as well as general travel agency services including flight booking and accommodation. Can organize entire packages prior to arrival for the whole of Brazil. Good English, reliable. Owned by Conor O'Sullivan from Cork.

Ilha de Itaparica *p413, map p413*
Tour operators

Small boats for trips around the bay can be hired privately at the small port by the Mercado Modelo in Salvador. A pleasant trip out to the mouth of the bay should take 1½ hrs as you sail along the bottom of the cliff. When arranging to hire any boat check that the boat is licensed by the port authority (Capitânia dos Portos) and that there are lifejackets on board.

Companhia de Navegação Bahiana,
T071-3321 7100. Sails 5 times a week to
Maragojipe on the Rio Paraguaçu to the west
(see page 416). The trip across the bay and
up the valley of the river takes 3 hrs. There are
some very beautiful views along the way with
2 stops. A good trip would be to continue to
Cachoeira by bus from Maragojipe and return
to Salvador the following day. Departures
from Salvador from the Terminal Turístico in
front of the Mercado Modelo, Mon-Thu 1430
(1530 in summer). Fri departure is at 1130.
Departures from Maragojipe Mon-Thu
0500 and Fri 0830, US$4.50.
Steve Lafferty, R do Sodré 45, apt 301,
T071-3241 0994. A US yachtsman, highly
recommended for enjoyable sailing trips
around Salvador, for up to 4 people.

Recôncavo Baiano *p414*
Guides Claudio, T075-3982 6080, a local
tour guide, doesn't speak much English,
but is friendly and knowledgeable.

⊖ Transport

Salvador *p398, maps p399, p403,
p408 and p411*
Air
To get to the airport: a/c *combis* leave from
Praça da Sé bus stop via the coast road and
Barra 0630-2100, US$4, 1-1½ hrs (1 hr from
Barra). Ordinary buses 'Aeroporto' from the
same stop cost US$1.50. A taxi to the airport
costs around US$30 or US$35-40 after 2200
and on weekends and public holidays.
Travel agencies and some hotels can
also organize transfers.

There are domestic flights to all of Brazil's
major cities, some with connections through
Recife, **Belo Horizonte** or **São Paulo**; the
best prices are usually to **Rio de Janeiro** and
São Paulo. There are international flights to
Europe and flights to the USA are set to
begin in 2009/2010.

Airlines flying from Salvador include:
Abaete, www.abaete.com.br; **Addey**,

www.addey.com.br; **Aero Star**, www.aero
star.com.br; **Passaredo**, www.voe
passaredo.com.br; **Webjet**, portal.web
jet.com.br; and **Varig**, portal.varig.com.br.
International flights are with: **Air Europa**,
www.aireuropa.com; **Airtours/Thomas
Cook**, www.thomas cook.com; **Condor**,
www10.condor.com; **TAP**, www.flytap.com.

Bus
Local US$1.50, a/c *executivos* US$2, or US$3
depending on the route. On buses and at the
ticket sellers' booths, watch your change and
beware pickpockets (one scam used by thieves
is to descend from bus while you are climbing
aboard). Take a 'Barra' bus from Praça da Sé for
the nearest ocean beaches. The 'Aeroporto'
frescão (last 2130) leaves from R Chile, passing
Barra, **Ondina**, **Rio Vermelho**, **Amaralina**,
Pituba, **Costa Azul**, **Armação**, **Boca do Rio**,
Jaguaripe, **Patamares**, **Piatã** and **Itapoã**,
before turning in to the airport. The glass-sided
'Jardineira' bus goes to **Flamengo** beach
(30 km from the city), following the coastal
route. It passes all the best beaches and leaves
from Praça da Sé daily 0730-1930, every
40 mins, US$1.50; sit on the right-hand side
for best views. For beaches beyond Itapoã,
take the *frescão* to **Stella Maris** and **Flamengo**
beaches. These follow the same route as
the Jardineira.

Long distance To get to the *rodoviária*
take bus RI or RII, 'Centro-Rodoviária-Circular',
(US$1) from the lower city at the foot of the
Lacerda Lift; the journey can take up to 1 hr
especially at peak periods. On weekdays, a
quicker executive bus (US$2) runs from Praça
da Sé or Praça da Inglaterra (by McDonalds),
Comércio, to **Iguatemi Shopping Centre**
from where there is a walkway to the
rodoviária (take care in the dark). Alternatively
take a from the centre, US$15.

There are frequent services to the majority
of destinations; a large panel in the main
hall of the bus terminal lists destinations and
the relevant ticket office. For bus information
contact the *rodoviária*, Av Antônio Carlos
Magalhães 4362, T071-3460 8300, daily 0600-

2200, and see www.itapemerim.com.br, www.aguiabranca.com.br, www.real expresso.com.br and www.gontijo.com.br.

To **Aracaju**, 3 daily (first 0630, last 2200, 4½ hrs, US$29, leito US$35 with **Bomfim**). To **Belém**, US$55 *comercial* with **Itapemirim**. To **Ilhéus**, 8 daily, 7 hrs, US$36, *executivo* US$46, *leito* US$80 with **Bomfim**. To **Maceio**, 4 daily, first at 0630, last 2200, 4½ hrs, US$42, *leito* US$67 with **Bomfim**. To **Porto Seguro**, 1 daily at 2000, 10 hrs, US$77 with **Aguia Branca**. To **Recife**, US$90, 13 hrs, 1 daily and 1 *leito*, with **Itapemerim**, T071-3358 0037. To **Rio de Janeiro**, leaves at 0700 Mon-Sat, 26 hrs, US$125, *leito* US$145, with **Itapemirim** and **Aguia Branca**, good stops, clean toilets, recommended. To **São Paulo,** 30 hrs, US$120, US$155, with **São Geraldo** (Mon, Wed and Fri at 0830 and 1930, Sun, Mon and Sat at 2000), daily *leito* at 2200. To **Fortaleza**, 20 hrs, US$105 at 0900 with **Itapemirim**. To **Lençóis** at 2200, 6-8 hrs, US$30 with **Real Expresso**, via **Feira de Santana**, T071-3358 1591. To **Belo Horizonte**, **Gontijo**, T071-3358 7448, at 1700, US$120. There are also bus services to **Brasília** along the fully paved BR-242, via Barreiras, 3 daily, 23 hrs; **Palmas**, **Natal**, **João Pessoa**, **Penedo** (via **Maceio**), **Vitória** and **Teresina**. For the shortest route to **Valença**, take the ferry from São Joaquim to Bom Despacho on Itaparica island, from where it is 130 km to Valença via Nazaré das Farinhas (see page 414).

Car hire

There are various car hire booths in the airport: **Hertz**, www.hertz.com.br, **Interlocadora**, www.interlocadora.com.br, and **Localiza**, www.localiza.com.

Taxi

Meters start at US$1.50 and then US$0.70 per 100 m. They charge US$25 per hr within city limits, and 'agreed' rates outside. **Taxi Barra-Centro**, US$10 daytime; US$12 at night. Watch the meter; the night-time charge should be 30% higher than daytime charges. **Teletaxi** (24-hr service), T071-3321 9988.

Ferry and boat

See also Ins and outs, page 398, and Ilha de Itaparica, page 413. Boats and catamarans to **Ilha de Itaparica**, other islands in the Baía de Todos os Santos and to **Morro de São Paulo** leave from one of 2 ferry docks in Salvador's Cidade Baixa. From the main ferry dock, **Marítimo de São Joaquim**, Av Oscar Pontes 1051, T071-3254 1020, www.twbmar.com.br, there are 10 car ferries per day to **Itaparica** as well as catamarans to **Morro de São Paulo** (2 hrs). From Salvador's other boat terminal, the **Terminal Marítimo de Mercado Modelo** (or Terminal Marítimo Turístico), ferries and catamarans run to the **Baía de Todos os Santos**, including **Itaparica** around every 30 mins. Catamarans also run to **Morro de São Paulo**, 5 a day. See www.morrodesaopaulo.com.br for the latest ferry timetable.

Ilha de Itaparica *p413, map p413*
Ferry

There are regular ferry services to **Salvador**. The main passenger ferry leaves from Bom Despacho and runs to the **Marítimo de São Joaquim** ferry dock. The first ferry to Salvador is at 0515 and the last one at 2300, running at intervals of 45 mins, During the summer months the ferries are much more frequent. (Buses for Calçada, Ribeira stop across the road from the ferry terminal; the 'Sabino Silva–Ribeira' bus passes in front of the Shopping Barra). Enquiries at the **Companhia de Navegação Bahiana** (CNB), T071-3321 7100, open 0800-1700. A one-way ticket for foot passengers Mon-Fri is US$1, Sat-Sun US$1.20. There is also a catamaran service which departs from Bom Despacho twice daily, US$3.

From Mar Grande a smaller ferry (*lancha*) runs to the **Terminal Marítimo**, in front of the Mercado Modelo in **Salvador**. The ferries leave every 45 mins and the crossing takes 50 mins, US$3 return.

Recôncavo Baiano *p414*
Bus To **Salvador** (Camurjipe) every hour from 0530. To **Feira Santana**, 2 hrs, US$3.

○ Directory

Salvador *p398, maps p399, p403, p408 and p411*

Banks Selected branches of major banks have ATMs (which accept Visa and Cirrus cards) and exchange facilities. All shopping centres, the bus station and the airport have branches of **Bradesco**, and there is a branch at R Chile 23, T071-3321 3154. Changing money at banks (open 1000-1600) can be bureaucratic and time-consuming. **Citibank**, R Miguel Calmon 555, Comércio, centre, changes TCs. Branch at R Almte Marquês de Leão 71, Barra, has an ATM. **Banco do Brasil**, Av Estados Unidos 561, Comércio, in the shopping centre opposite the rodoviária (also a *câmbio* here), very high commission on TCs, at the airport on the 1st floor (Mon-Fri 0830-1530, 1600-2100 and Sat, Sun and holidays 0900-1600); branches in Barra, R Miguel Bournier 4, in Shopping Barra and in Ondina. **Cultural centres** Associação Cultural Brasil-Estados Unidos, Av 7 de Setembro 1883, has a library and reading room with recent US magazines, open to all, free use of internet for 30 mins. **Cultura Inglesa**, R Plínio Moscoso 357, Jardim Apipema. **German Goethe Institut**, Av 7 de Setembro 1809, also with a library and reading room. **Embassies and consulates** France, R Francisco Gonçalves 1, sala 805, Comércio, T071-3241 0168 (Mon, Tue, Thu 1430-1700). Germany, R Lucaia 281, 2nd floor, Rio Vermelho, T071-3334 7106 (Mon-Fri 0900-1200). Holland, Av Santa Luzia, 1136 Edif, Porto Empresarial Sala 302, T071-3341 0410 (Mon-Fri 0800-1200). Italy, Av 7 de Setembro 1238, Centro, T071-3329 5338 (Mon, Wed, Fri 1500-1800). Portugal, Largo Carmo, 4, Sto Antonio, T071-3241 1633.

Spain, R Mcal Floriano 21, Canela, T071-3336 1937 (Mon-Fri 0900-1400). Switzerland, Av Tancredo Neves 3343, 5th floor, sala 506b, T071-3341 5827. UK, Av Estados Unidos 4, 18B, Comércio, T071-3243 7399 (Mon-Thu, 0900-1100, 1400-1600, Fri 0900-1100). USA, R Pernambuco, 51 Pituba, T071-3345 1545 (Mon-Fri), 0900-1130, 1430-1630.
Immigration Polícia Federal, Av O Pontes 339, Aterro de Água de Meninos, Lower City, T071-3319 6082. Open 1000-1600. For extensions of entry permits show an outward ticket or sufficient funds for your stay, visa extension US$15. **Internet** There are numerous internet cafés throughout the touristy parts of the city. **Language courses** Casa do Brasil, R Milton de Oliveira 231, Barra, T071-3264 5866, www.casadobrazil.com.br. Portuguese for foreigners. Diálogo, R Dr João Pondé 240, Barra, T071-3264 0007, www.dialogo-brazilstudy.com, with optional dance, *capoeira* and cooking classes and accommodation arranged with host families. Superlearning Idiomas, Av 7 de Setembro 3402, Ladeira da Barra, T071-3337 2824, www.allways.com.br/spl. **Laundry** Kit Lavaderia, Av Amaralina 829, Amaralina. Laundromat, R Oswaldo Cruz, Rio Vermelho. Lav e Lev, Av Manoel Dantas da Silva 2364, loja 7. Unilave, Av Magalhães Neto 18, Pituba. **Medical services** Clinic, Barão de Loreto 21, Graça. Delegação Federal de Saúde, R Padre Feijó, Canela. Free yellow fever vaccinations.

Cachoeira *p414*
Banks Bradesco, in the main square, ATM accepts Visa credit but not debit cards, Mon-Fri 0830-1700. **Post office** In the main square, Mon-Fri 0900-1700.

The Cocoa and Dendê Coast

South of Salvador and the Reconcavo, Bahia descends in a series of glorious beaches, offshore islands and jungly peninsulas, many of them fringed with coral and mangrove or backed by endless kilometres of coconut palms. Sluggish tropical rivers undulate their way across lowland Bahia from the Chapada Diamantina ('diamond mountains') of the interior and interrupt the coastline, while potholed roads connect crumbling colonial towns like Ilhéus and Olivença, which grew fat on the cocoa and dendê oil trade but have since been slowly withering under the tropical sun.

The glorious coast is within easy reach of Salvador and every year an increasing number of tourists are discovering its forgotten fishing villages. The surf mecca of Itacaré is gradually turning chic. The expat community of Morro de São Paulo, on the island of Tinharé, is finding its beach haven is getting crowded; the nightlife here is notoriously lively. Those seeking seclusion should head for the Peninsula de Maraú, a little further south, or to the little-explored wild beaches beyond Una. ▶▶ *For listings, see pages 440-446.*

Valença ●●● ▶▶ *pp440-446. Colour map 4, A5.*

→ *Phone code: 075.*

Although Valença has a few colonial buildings and two moderately interesting churches, it is essentially an ugly town. The best reason to come here is to take a boat to/from Tinharé, taking an hour or two perhaps to stroll around the dirty market and visit the church of **Nossa Senhora do Amparo**, from where there are good views out over the town, the estuary and the surrounding mangroves. Valença is in the middle of an area that produces black pepper, cloves and *piaçava* (used in making brushes and mats) but it markets itself as the prawn capital of Brazil, and smells the part. Other industries include the building and maintenance of *saveiros* (fishing boats).

Ins and outs

Long-distance buses arrive at the **new rodoviária** ⓘ *Av Maçônica, T075-3741 1280*, while the **old rodoviária** is for local buses. There are frequent buses between Valença and Salvador. The fastest go via the island of Itaparica (two to three hours including the ferry). Avoid touts at the *rodoviária*; it's better to visit the friendly **tourist office** ⓘ *at the port, T075-3641 3311, http://valenca.ba.gov.br*, which has maps and transport information. Boats arrive from Tinharé at least once a day.

Tinharé and Morro de São Paulo ●●●●▲●● ▶▶ *pp440-446.*

→ *Colour map 4, A5. Phone code: 075.*

Depending on whom you ask, Tinharé is either a single large island separated from the mainland by the estuary of the Rio Una and mangrove swamps, or a mini archipelago divided by estuaries, mangroves and an impossibly turquoise sea. Either way it is stunning: a semi-wild of bird-filled *Mata Atlântica* forest fringed with swaying coconut palms and white-sand beaches that until recently were known only to fishermen and a few intrepid Brazilian beach travellers. Before the 1990s the main town here, **Morro de São Paulo**, on the northern tip of the island, was one of the world's great secret tropical island getaways, together with Ko Phi Phi in Thailand and Zanzibar. Now it is rapidly going the same way as these two former Shangri-Las. It began with the Italians who built a string of small-scale but largely tasteful resorts. By the turn of the millennium, Spanish developers with gold Rolexes and nowhere left to turn into concrete on their own crowded coast, were rubbing their hands in glee. Fishermen's houses and environmental concerns are easily bulldozed out of the way by the power of the euro. Indeed many of the original fishermen who lived on the gorgeous beaches that line Tinharé have already been relocated to ugly makeshift villages in the interior. Every beach for 20 km south of town is now backed by hotels and Morro has become a veritable tourist hotspot.

Morro Town itself is dominated by a lighthouse and the ruins of an early 17th-century colonial fort, built as a defence against European raiders. However, this did not stop the Dutch and French using the waters around the island as hiding places for attacks on the Portuguese and even establishing bases here for brief periods of time.

Morro de São Paulo

Situated at the northern tip of the island, boats to Morro from Salvador enter through the stone arch that once marked the gateway to the fortress. The battlements are now largely in ruin, perched on top of the craggy hill in front of a series of little streets that branch off a small colonial *praça*. The main thoroughfare runs south to the town's beaches. Another path runs north to the lighthouse and a ruined lookout post complete with cannon (dolphins can be seen in August) and inland to the village of **Gamboa**. From Gamboa it's possible to visit the **Fonte de Ceu** waterfall; make sure you check the tide times, or ask around for a guide. It's possible to take a boat from Gamboa back to Morro (US$10-15).

The five beaches are all idyllic but are quieter the further from town you go. There is swimming in the sea or in the saltwater coral pools that appear at low tide. The beaches are named prosaically: **Primeira** (first), **Segunda** (second), **Terceira** (third), **Quarta** (fourth) and **Quinta** (fifth). There are boardwalks and a heavy build-up of shacks, beach bars, restaurants and hotels all the way to Terceira. Primeira is barely a beach at all and has the bulk of the hotels. Segunda is a party beach and is very popular with 20-somethings. Quinta is the furthest from town and is the quietest with little noise but the gentle lap of the sea. Before deciding to walk all the way to Quinta (1½ to two hours) check the tide times as the beach gets cut off at high tide. On 7 September there is a big festival at Morro with live music on the beach.

Ins and outs

Getting there There are direct 20-minute flights from Salvador's airport to the third beach at Morro de São Paulo with **Addey Taxi Aereo** ① *T075-3652 1242, www.addey.com.br*, and **Aerostar Taxi Aereo** ① *T075-3652 1312*. Both fly three times daily and cost around US$90 return. Catamarans run from both of Salvador's ferry terminals (see page 398), taking around two hours US$27. Times vary according to the weather but there are usually several a day 0800-1400; check with the tourist office or **Catamarã Gamboa do Morro** ① *T075-9975 6395*. Part of the trip is on the open sea, which can be rough. There are also numerous water taxis. Modified fishing and speed boats also run from Salvador via Valença (which is connected to southern Bahia) and Itaparica. The website www.morrodesaopaulo.com.br is a useful website with the latest boat times and general information in English, Spanish and Italian. There is a port tax of US$4 payable at the *prefeitura* on arrival to Morro and US$0.80 on leaving the island. It is resented by many. ▶▶ *See Transport, page 445.*

Getting around Morro is tiny and the first four beaches are easily negotiable on foot. A walk from town to Quarta Praia takes around 40 minutes. Until 2008 all roads were sand or dirt tracks but there is now a partially paved section between the town and the beaches, and this is plied by regular VW buses, motorbikes and beach buggies. These leave from the **Receptivo**, a little café that marks the beginning of the road just behind the second and third beaches; it's not hard to find but if in doubt ask for '*Receptivo*' or '*a estrada*'. There are daily transfers to Boipeba by Toyota at 0930, bookable through hotels or the myriad agencies on the island.

Boat trips around Tinharé island can be organized through hotels or agencies in the village; a full day costs US$20-30. Most of these go in a clockwise direction around Tinharé, visiting Boipeba and the villages to the south (including Moreré), the offshore reef pools for snorkelling, followed by the tiny colonial town of Cairu on the mainland and the shores of the Mangrove-line Rio Cairu, before returning.

Best time to visit Morro is expensive between December and March and gets very crowded during public holidays and prices can more than double. Beware of drug dealers and robbery at the busiest times.

Tourist Information There is a tourist booth, **Centro de Informações ao Turista (CIT)** ⓘ *Praça Aureliano Lima s/n, T075-3652 1083, www.morrosp.com.br*. However, the website www.morrodesaopaulo.com.br is more useful and provides lists of agencies, hotels and other information in several languages.

Ilha de Boipeba 〇🔵🔵〇 ▶▶ *pp440-446. Colour map 4, A5.*

Ilha de Boipeba, a few hours south of Morro, is a similar but far quieter island and with less infrastructure. Accommodation is grouped in three places: the little town on the banks of the Rio do Inferno where the ferry arrives; the adjacent beach, **Boca da Barra**, which is more idyllic; and the fishing village of **Moreré**, a 30-minute boat ride to the south (only possible at high tide). With just a few simple restaurants and a football field on the beach overlooking a beautiful turquoise bay, life here is tranquil even by Bahian standards. Expect to pay at least US$30 for a boat to Moreré. Walking along the beaches will take about two hours. Have your camera at the ready, bring sunscreen and go at low tide as there is a river to ford.

Ins and outs Boat trips leave daily from Morro de São Paulo at 0900; book through a travel agent or your hotel. The return journey costs around US$30, and you have to pay this even if you are intending to stay on the island. Tractors and 4WDs leave from Morro's second beach every morning at around 0800 (one hour, US$15), and return at midday; contact **Zé Balacha**, T075-9148 0343, or ask at your hotel.

South to Itacaré 〇🔵🔵〇🔵 ▶▶ *pp440-446. Colour map 4, A5.*

Ituberá and Camamu → *Phone code: 073.*
These two towns, which have yet to be overrun by seasonal visitors, are the first stops south on the bus route from Valença. Neither have good beaches but both have access to decent ones by boat. **Ituberá** is a tiny town sitting on a deep inlet; the most beautiful

beach in the area, **Barra do Carvalho**, is two hours away by boat. Some 30 km further south, **Camamu** is tucked away in a maze of mangroves. It is the jumping-off point for the peninsula of Maraú; the next stretch of the Bahian coast in line for beach resort development. The town has a handful of pretty colonial buildings, including the 17th-century church of **Nossa Senhora da Assunção**.

Barra Grande and the Peninsula de Maraú → *Phone code: 073.*

This long thin peninsula stretches north from the town of **Maraú**, near Itacaré, towards the southern extremity of the island of Tinharé and is fringed with beautiful beaches along its entire length both on the ocean side and along the beautiful Baía de Camamu. The bay is lined with thick mangrove at its far southern end and sealed at **Tremembé**, with a plunging waterfall that cascades directly into the sea. The main centre of population is the little fishing village of **Barra Grande** at the tip of the peninsula, fronted by a glorious beach and yachts bobbing at the end of a pier. The sandy streets are lined with a handful of *pousadas* and shaded by *casuaring* and palms. Few non-Brazilian tourists make it here.

Ins and outs   The peninsula is 200 km south of Salvador, 150 km north of Ilhéus. There is a small airport at Barra Grande, served by scheduled air taxis from Morro de São Paulo and Salvador. Boats run from Camamu to Barra Grande several times a day between October and March and once a day in the morning all year round (boats: one hour, US$3; *lancha*: 20 minutes, US$15). It's also possible to reach the peninsula by road from Itacaré.

Access is difficult to many of the Maraú beaches if you don't have a car (and only possible with a 4WD in wet weather), but some can be reached on foot or by taxi/*combi* from Barra Grande. Tractors run from the village to the more remote beaches further south. There are excellent two- to five-day tours with **Orbitá** (see page 445), leaving from Ilhéus or Itacaré. There are plenty of *pousadas* in Barra (see Sleeping, page 446); the website www.barragrande.net has lots of useful information.

Itacaré → *Phone code: 073.*

Itacaré is a pretty little surfer town at the far end of the Peninsula de Maraú surrounded by glorious forest-fringed beaches. Paulistanos decided it was cool at the turn of the millennium and a handful of beaches are now backed by some of Bahia's most exclusive (and increasingly over-sized) resorts, such as **Txai**. Those close to the town itself are more hippy, with an informal surfer-dude feel and a mix of cheaper restaurants and places to stay and more fashionable spots for those swooping in for the evening. Much of the old town remains a simple fishing village whose houses in thick *gouache* shades huddle together under a golden sun around a broad harbour on the banks of the Rio de Contas.

Ins and outs   The *rodoviária* is a few minutes walk from town. There are at least four buses a day from Ilhéus (one hour). Porters are on hand with barrows to help with luggage. For information contact the **Secretaria de Turismo de Itacaré** ⓘ *T073-3251 2134, www.itacare.com.br. Pousadas* are concentrated on and around **Praia da Concha**, the first beach south of the town centre and the river. More deserted beaches lie along dirt roads to the south and north. To explore the area to the full you will need a car. If you speak some Portuguese, its worth taking the time to find your way to one of the smaller places. Itacaré is very busy with Brazilian tourists in high season but receives relatively few international visitors.

Itacaré beaches from north to south

Do Pontal Immediately across the Rio de Contas from town and reached by passenger ferry. Long, deserted and stretching all the way to Barra Grande some 40 km away – if you're prepared to swim across rivers and camp out.

Coroinha At the harbour, urban and none too clean but with pretty views of the town and the 18th-century church of São Miguel, especially at sunset.

Da Concha Urban and with the bulk of the *pousadas*.

Do Resende A little bay with powdery white sand, swaying coconut palms and a handful of *pousadas*. 10 minutes' walk from Da Concha.

Tiririca The best surf beach in Itacaré, *pousadas* with a beatnik surfer crowd. 10 minutes' walk from Resende.

Do Costa A little bay with strong waves and reasonable surf. 10 minutes' walk from Tiririca.

Do Ribeira The end of the road from town. Very pretty with calm water and rainforest rising at each end. Beach *barracas* sell fish and snacks and there's a little stream for kids. 10 minutes' walk from Do Costa.

Prainha More private and accessible by trail from Ribeira. Good surf. In a protected area (US$1.50 entry fee). 20-30 minutes' walk from Do Ribeira.

Ilhéus and around ⊖🖬🟦▲⊖🟢 ⇥ *pp440-446. Colour map 4, A5.*

→ *Phone code: 073. Population: 242,500.*

Everyone is happy to point out that Ilhéus is the birthplace of Jorge Amado (1912) and the setting of one of his most famous novels, *Gabriela, Cravo e Canela* (Gabriela, Clove and Cinnamon, 1958). Amado also chronicled life on the region's cocoa plantations in two novels, *Cacau*, (1933) and the much better-known *Terras do Sem Fim* (The Violent Lands, 1942). A later novel, *São Jorge dos Ilhéus* (1944), continues the story.

Ilhéus's history stretches back to the earliest days of Portuguese colonization, when it was one of the captaincies created by King João III in 1534. Today the port serves a district that produces 65% of all Brazilian cocoa. Shipping lines call regularly. There are good views of the city from the **Convento de Nossa Senhora da Piedade**. Most tourists stay a day or so before heading north towards Itacaré or south towards Porto Seguro.

The town has a number of sights. The church of **São Jorge** ① *Praça Rui Barbosa*, (1556), is the city's oldest and has a small museum. The cathedral of **São Sebastião** ① *Praça Dom Eduardo*, is a huge, early 20th-century building. In Alto da Vitória is the 17th-century **Nossa Senhora da Vitória**, built to celebrate a victory over the Dutch. The house where Jorge Amado grew up and wrote his first novel is now a small **museum** ① *R Jorge Amado 21, 0900-1600, US$1*. Immortalized by Amado in *Gabriela, Cravo e Canela*, the **Bataclã** ① *Av 2 de Julho 75, T073-3634 7835*, was once a famous bordello and poker palace. It was used by the region's powerful cacão *coroneis* and linked to other parts of the town by a series of secret tunnels, through which (presumably) the macho men would flee in fear of their wives.

Ins and outs The **airport** ① *3 km from the centre, in Pontal on the south bank of the river, is linked to Ilhéus by bridge; taxi into town US$4*, receives flights from Salvador, Belo Horizonte, São Paulo, Brasília, Curitiba, Porto Seguro and Rio de Janeiro. The **rodoviária** ① *R Itabuna, 4 km from the centre*, has regular bus connections with Salvador. However, the

Itabuna–Olivença bus runs through the centre of Ilhéus. The **tourist office** ① *on the beach opposite Praça Castro Alves*, is a few minutes' walk from the cathedral. Staff are friendly and can provide maps (US$2, recommended).

Around Ilhéus

The city beach itself is polluted but the beaches around the town are splendid and increasingly deserted the further you go. North of Ilhéus, two good beaches are **Marciano**, with reefs offshore and good surfing, and **Barra**, 1 km further north at the mouth of the Rio Almada. South of the river, the beaches at **Pontal** can be reached by 'Barreira' bus; alight just after the **Hotel Jardim Atlântico**. Between Ilhéus and **Olivença** are a number of fine beaches, including **Cururupe**, **Batuba** and **Cai n'Água** (in Olivença itself), both popular surf spots. The **Balneário de Tororomba** ① *on the Rio Batuba, 19 km from Ilhéus, bus from São Jorge, Canavieiras or Olivença*, has ferruginous mineral baths.

From Ilhéus, buses run every 30 minutes to **Itabuna** (32 km), the trading centre of the rich cocoa zone; there are also many lumber mills. **Ceplac installations** ① *Km 8, on the Itabuna– Ilhéus road, T073-214 3000, Mon-Fri 0830-1230*, demonstrates the processing of cocoa. Tours of cocoa plantations can be arranged through the **Ilhéus Praia** hotel (see Sleeping, page 443).

Also at Km 8, the Projeto Mico-Leão Baiano at the **Reserva Biológica de Una** ① *www.ecoparque.org.br, book through Orbitá, see page 445*, was founded to protect the golden-faced tamarin. This is the wettest part of Bahia, most notably in October. Jeeps leave from the *rodoviária*. The reserve lies along a dirt road and most easily reached on a tour or by public jeep which leave when full from the *rodoviária*.

Ilhéus

Sleeping 🛌
Barravento **4**
Britânia **1**
Ilhéus Praia **2**
Jardim Atlântico **5**

Pier do Pontal **6**

Eating 🍴
Acarajé de Irene **1**
Cabana Gabriela **2**

Marostica **3**
Vesúvio **4**

N
Not to scale

Jorge Amado

Amado is by far the most popular Brazilian writer of the 20th century. Born in 1912 on a cocoa plantation near Ilhéus, he had a very adventurous youth, and had direct experience of the endemic violence surrounding land claims, which he later dramatized in novels such as *Terras do sem-fim* (The Violent Land, 1943). His political commitment was always to the Left, though his position has softened in later years, accompanying changes in his fiction. In his early works (1931-1952), his views were manifested in an interest in the rural and urban poor. In novels such as *Jubiabá* (1935), about the self-education of a black man, and *Capitães da Areia* (1937), one of his best, centred on a gang of street children, he began to show interest in the power of *candomblé* (Afro-Brazilian religion) as a way of raising political consciousness.

In 1946 he became a federal deputy for the communist party. However, two years later the party was banned and he went into exile in Europe wehre he was something of a propagandist for Soviet Communism, receiving the Stalin Peace Prize in 1951. The fiction he wrote at this time, including *Seara vermelha* (Red Harvest), is considered to be his worst.

In 1953 he returned to Brazil and abandoned politics for comedy and myth. His career was given a new lease of life in 1958, with the publication of *Gabriela, cravo e canela* (Gabriela, Clove and Cinnamon). The novel, set in Ilhéus in the 1920s when the harbour is about to open, is presented to us through a colourful array of characters, at the centre of whom are Nacib, an Arab immigrant and shopkeeper, and spicy Gabriela, a girl from the interior whose cooking and sexual prowess keep him in her thrall. It is a modern, optimistic version of Alencar's *Iracema*: immigrant meets native girl, and has to adjust to her culture, while in the background, the economy (exporting cocoa) is opening up. *Gabriela* was a phenomenal success, selling 100,000 copies in just over a year. In part, Amado had tuned into the optimism created in the years of the Kubitschek presidency, which led to the foundation of Brasília.

Sex, comedy and cookery proved a potent combination. Other novels since *Gabriela* have been equally successful, including *Dona Flor e seus dois maridos* (Dona Flor and her Two Husbands, 1966), about a cookery teacher whose respectable second marriage is haunted by the ghost of her bohemian first husband (it actually provides the reader with recipes); and *Tenda dos milagres* (The Tent of Miracles,1969) about racial discrimination. Many of them are set in the city of Salvador (Bahia).

Amado has been attacked by critics as being unconsciously anti-feminist and even racist (his black characters tend to be stereotypically good-hearted, with a perpetual smile on their face). However, perhaps this is missing the point, for Amado is essentially a popular novelist in the tradition of Scott, Dumas and others, who were, in effect, predecessors of television soap operas. His work has often been successfully adapted to that medium.

Beyond Ilhéus, the paved coastal road continues south through **Olivença** and **Una**, ending at **Canavieiras**, a picturesque town which benefited from the cocoa boom. It has several fine beaches worth exploring. A rough road continues from there to Porto Seguro.

⊚ The Cocoa and Dendê Coast listings

For Sleeping and Eating price codes and other relevant information, see pages 42-47.

⊜ Sleeping

Valença *p433*

A Portal Rio Una, R Maestro Barrinha, T/F075-3741 5050, www.portalhoteis.tur.br. Resort hotel by the riverside. Facilities include a pool, tennis courts and organized activities.
B Do Porto, Av Maçônica 50, T075-3741 3066. Clean, helpful, safe, good breakfast and a reasonable restaurant.
B Guabim, Praça da Independência, T075-3741 3408. Modest but well looked after with singles, doubles and triples.
D Valença, R Dr H Guedes Melo 15, T075-3741 1807. Simple hotel with plain but well-kept rooms and a good breakfast. Recommended.

Tinharé and Morro de São Paulo *p433*

In Morro de São Paulo, there are many cheap *pousadas* and rooms to rent near the Fonte Grande (fountain), but this part of town does not get a breeze at night.

There are 4 beaches next to Morro town, which are quieter the further from town you go. The 1st and 2nd beaches are designated party areas, with throbbing bars and shacks selling food and drinks well into the night. There are only *pousadas* and a few restaurants on the final 2 beaches. To reach the beaches turn right at the end of the main street; there is only one trail out of town. You'll have to walk as there are no cars on the island; porters can be hired to transport your luggage to the hotel in a wheelbarrow.
LL-A Hotel Vila dos Orixás, Praia do Encanto, T075-3652 2055, www.hotelvilados orixas.com. A Spanish-run *pousada* on one of Morros loneliest beaches with a series of spacious chalets set in a coconut garden, next to a pool and overlooking the beach. Very

peaceful and romantic but a 30-min car ride from town. The hotel runs regular shuttles.
LL-A Pousada da Torre, 2nd beach, T075-3652 1038, www.pousadadatorre.com.br. A very tasteful little boutique hotel on the beach front which looks particularly enticing at night when both the building and the turquoise pool are mood lit under the palms. The plushest rooms are on the upper floor, are decked out in jaqueira wood and raw stone and have balconies with sea views behind big French windows. Rooms in the back annexe are a good deal cheaper, plainer but are large with king-sized beds and rich wood walls.
L-A Pousada Catavento, 4th beach, T/F075-3652 1052, www.cataventopraiahotel.com.br. One of the most luxurious and secluded of the hotels on the island, with well-appointed mock-colonial rooms arranged around a beautiful sculpted swimming pool, a decent restaurant and good service.
A Pousada Vistabella, 1st beach, T075-3652 1001, www.vistabelapousada.com. Good rooms, all with fans and hammocks. Rooms at the front have lovely views and are cooler. The owner Petruska is very welcoming. Recommended.
A-C Agua Viva, 3rd beach, T075-3652 1217, www.pousadaaguavivamorro.com.br. The best rooms in this simple *pousada* are at the front and have little balconies overlooking the beach. They have a/c, fridges and TVs, polished concrete floors and are decorated with art painted by the Morro owners.
A-C Fazenda Vila Guaiamú, 3rd beach, T075-3652 1035, www.vilaguaiamu.com.br. 7 tastefully decorated chalets of various sizes and styles set in their own tropical gardens and visited by marmosets, tanagers and rare cotingas. The hotel has a spa service with wonderful massage. The Italian photographer owner runs an ecotourism project protecting a rare species of crab, which live in the river

that runs through the *fazenda*. Guided rainforest walks available. Excellent food. The best option for nature lovers.

B Pousada Colibri, R do Porto de Cima s/n, Centro, near the fountain. In Morro de São Paulo. One of the few that stays cool in this part of town. 6 apartments with pleasant sea views. The owner, speaks English and German.

B Pousada Farol do Morro, 1st beach, T075-3652 1036, www.faroldomorro.com.br. Little huts running up a steep slope. All are a little small but have a sea view and are reached by a private funicular railway. The pool sits perched on the edge of the hill. Brazilian-owned.

C Pousada Ilha da Saudade, 1st beach, T075-3652 1015, www.ilhada saudade.com.br. Elegant hillside *pousada* with a beautiful pool with a view, a small gym and deluxe suites with jacuzzis. Restaurant, bar and good breakfast.

C-D Pousada Grauça, 3rd beach, T075-3652 1099, www.pousadagrauca.com.br. Simple but well-kept a/c and fan-cooled rooms with en suites in concrete *cabañas* away from the beach. Formerly called the 'Aradhia'. Recommended.

D Pousada Ilha do Sol, 1st beach, T075-8871 1295, www.pousadailhadosol.com. A big, blocky hotel with modest but well-kept rooms on long balcony corridors. The best have sea views. Generous breakfast.

D Tia Lila, 3rd beach, T075-3652 1532, www.pousadatialila.com.br. Very simple a/c rooms with television. Attentive, friendly service. Check a few rooms as some beds are spongy. Very good restaurant with delicious *moqueca de camarão*. Local-owned.

Ilha de Boipeba *p435*

Accommodation is split between the little town where the riverboat ferry arrives; the adjacent beach, **Boca da Barra**, which is more idyllic; and the fishing village of **Moreré** ½-hr boat ride to the south (high tide only).

A Pousada Tassimirim, R Com Madureira 40, Valença, Tassimirim Beach, T075-9981 2378,

30-min walk south of town. A coconut grove shading bungalows, bar, restaurant and pool. The price includes breakfast and dinner. Secluded and very tranquil.

A-B Vila Sereia, Boca da Barra beach, T075-3635 6045. Elegantly simple duplex wooden chalets overlooking the beach. Breakfast on your own private veranda. Very romantic.

A-C Santa Clara, Boca da Barra beach, T075-3653 6085, www.santaclaraboipeba.com. Californian-owned *pousada* with the island's best restaurant and large, tastefully decorated duplex *cabañas*. Very good-value room for 4 (**D** per person). Superlative therapeutic massages available.

B-D Horizonte Azul, Boca da Barra beach, T075-3653 6080, ww.amabo.org.br/ horizonteazul.html. Pretty little *pousada* next door to **Santa Clara**, with a range of chalets from very comfortable to fairly simple. The hillside garden is visited by hundreds of rare birds from the nearby Atlantic coast rainforest. Very friendly owners who speak English and French. Lunch available.

D Cheiro do Mar, Moreré town. Hillside cabins, the best of which has a breathtaking view. Ask for Fatima or João.

D Mar e Coco, Moreré, T075-3653 6013. A couple of very simple rooms with a Bahian family and a wonderful seafood restaurant. 5 mins north of town. The restaurant **Paraiso** next door is as good and also rents a room (**D**). Ask for Gentil or Angelica.

D Pousada Luar das Águas, T075-9981 1012. Simple and good value.

D Pousada Moreré, Moreré town, T075-9987 1513. Simple fan-cooled rooms, some of which are a little musty. Good restaurant which doubles up as the town's only bar. The owner is the island's *prefeito* (mayor).

Ituberá and Camamu *p435*

C Rio Acaraí, Praça Dr Francisco Xavier, T073-3255 2315, www.hotelrioacarai.com.br. Ugly modern *pousada* with a pool and restaurant.

D Tropical, Av Hildebrando Araújo Góes 270, Ituberá, T073-3256 2233. Standard, simple, small town *pousada* with a/c rooms, a restaurant, bar and pool.

E Green House, next to the *rodoviária*, T073-255 2178. Very basic and friendly with breakfast and a simple restaurant.

Barra Grande and the Peninsula de Maraú *p436*

LL Kiaroa, Praia Taipus de Fora, T073-3258 6215, www.kiaroa.com.br. The best of the peninsula's resorts, on a glorious beach, with a range of well-appointed rooms and an excellent restaurant, pampering and various organized activities.

AL-A Lagoa do Cassange, Praia do Cassange, T073-3258 2166, www.maris.com.br. Family resort with a pool, restaurant and 14 individual chalets overlooking the beach.

AL-A Taipú de Fora, Praia Taipus de Fora, T073-3225 2276, www.taipudefora.com.br. Small upscale mini-resort with a good range of activities including diving and kayaking. The beach is glorious, little-known but one of Bahia's very best, and buried here in text so that only discerning readers will discover it!

C El Capitan, Av Vasco Neto s/n, T073-3258 6078, www.elcapitan.com.br. Cabins in a garden decorated with rusting anchors and nautical bric-a-brac. All are basic in tile and concrete, have terracotta-tile roofs and hammock-slung terraces gathered around a pool a block from the beach at the mainland end of the town, 200 m from the pier.

D Meu Sossego, R Dr Chiquinho 17, Barra town, T073-3258 6012, www.meu sossego.com. 19 plain a/c rooms with fridges a stroll from the beach.

D Porto da Barra, R Beira Mar, T073-3258 6349, www.pousadaportodabarra.com. Family-run *pousada* right on the beach with simple concrete and tile a/c rooms in long annexes. The best are on the upper floor. Decent breakfast. Friendly owner.

Itacaré *p436*

The area is becoming very popular and prices are going up all the time. Book well ahead in high season.

LL Txai Resort, Praia de Itacarezinho, T073-3634 6956, www.txai.com.br. The most comfortable hotel around Itacaré, set on a deserted beach with very spacious and tastefully appointed bungalows overlooking a long, deep-blue pool shaded by its own stand of palms. Excellent spa and a full range of activities including diving and horse riding.

AL-A Art Jungle, T073-9996 2167, www.artjungle.org. A modern sculpture garden with 6 treehouses in the middle of the forest. All have views out to the sea and to the Rio de Contas. A favourite with celebrities such as Sean Penn, Jade Jagger and Gisele Bündchen.

AL-A Sage Point, Praia de Tiririca, T073-3251 2030, www.pousadasagepoint.com.br. Ocean-front *pousada* with smart wooden chalets in a tropical garden overlooking the sea, each with their own hammock-strewn terraces. Some are a little small but all have wonderful views. The Cuban owner, Ana, speaks English and can organize trips to nearby beaches.

AL-A Vila de Ocaporan, T073-3251 2470, www.viladeocaporan.com.br. Brightly coloured spacious chalets gathered around a charming little pool in a hammock-filled garden. Between the town and Praia da Concha. Good Bahian restaurant.

A-C Maria Farinha, T073-3251 3515, www.mariafarinhapousada.com.br. Simple family-run *pousada* with plain rooms in a concrete annexe overlooking a little pool. Pleasant *maloca*-shaped communal breakfast area, quiet and good for families. Disabled access.

B-C Pousada da Lua, Praia da Concha, T073-3251 2209, www.itacare.com.br/ pousadadalua. A handful of little chalets in a forest filled with marmosets and parakeets. Great breakfast.

C-D Estrela, R Pedro Longo 34, Centro, T073-3251 2006, pousadaestrela@backpacker.com.br. A range of well-maintained, simple rooms and an excellent home-made breakfast with a huge choice. Very friendly.

D-E Pedra Bonita, R Lodonio Almeida 120, T073-9141 4372, www.itacarehostel.com.br. Pleasant little IYHA hostel with small doubles and dorms (**E** per person) in an annexe, a small pool, internet and TV area. Friendly staff.

Ilhéus and around *p437, map p438*
There are plenty of cheap hotels in Ilhéus near the municipal *rodoviária* in centre; not all are desirable (check for hot-pillow establishments that rent rooms by the hour).

LL Fazenda da Lagoa, Rodovia BA-001, Una, T073-3236 6046, www.fazendada lagoa.com.br. Carioca Lia Siqueira and Mucki Skowronski's super-chic beach bungalows offer privacy and intimate designer luxury that lures celebrities. However, the real star here is the wilderness landscape: the vast, empty beach and pounding ocean; the adjacent rainforest and mangrove wetlands; and the beautiful river and lake. This area, as well as the nearby primate sanctuary at Una (see page 438) offers some of the best wildlife and birdwatching in coastal Brazil. Unfortunately the owners have little knowledge of natural history, so nature-lovers are advised to organize their own guides (with prior notice) through **Orbitá** in Ilhéus (see page 445).

A Hotel Barravento, on Malhado beach, R Nossa Senhora das Graças 276, Ilhéus, T/F073-3634 3223, www.barravento.com.br. The smartest hotel in the city. Ask for the penthouse (there is usually no extra charge), which includes breakfast and a fridge.

A Jardim Atlântico, Rodovia Ilheus-Olivenca Km 2, Jardim Atlântico, Ilhéus, T073-3632 4711, www.hoteljardimatlantico.com.br. One of Bahia's few luxurious beach hotels that not only welcomes children but provides kids' clubs, activities and a little water park. There

are tennis courts, sauna, gym and activities for the adults. Rooms have their own little garden and hammock terraces and, thankfully, as the restaurant is a long way away, food is decent.

B-C Ilhéus Praia, Praça Dom Eduardo, on the beach, Ilhéus, T073-3634 2533, www.ilheus praiacom.br. A concrete block on the beach offering a/c tile floor rooms with low beds and sea views. Pool, helpful staff.

B-C Pier do Pontal, Av Lomanto Jr, Pontal 3.5 km, T073-3632 4000, www.pierdopontal. com.br. A small-scale beach hotel 20 mins' drive from town with a cluster of rooms in a 3-storey building overlooking a pool. Modern, decent service and a good option if you need to be in the city and have a car (or take a taxi).

C-D Britânia, R Jorge Amado s/n, Ilhéus, T073-3634 1722, www.brasilheus.com.br/britania_ por.htm. The best value in the town centre with large rooms in an early 20th-century wooden hotel just west of the cathedral square. Safe area with lots of restaurants.

🍴 Eating

Tinharé and Morro de São Paulo *p433*
There are plenty of restaurants in Morro de São Paulo town and on the 2nd and 3rd beaches. Most of them are okay though somewhat overpriced. For cheap eats stay in a *pousada* that includes breakfast, stock up at the supermarket and buy seafood snacks at the *barracas* on the 2nd beach.

🍴 **Tia Dadai**, Praça Aureliano Oliveira Lima, T075-3652 1621. Very tasty *casquinha de siri* (baked crab in its shell), and *filé de badejo a Portuguesa* (fillet of bream in tomato and onion sauce). In a great space on the main *praça*. Lively in the evening.

🍴 **Tinharé**, down a little set off steps off R Caminha de Praia, The food here bursts with flavour, especially the delicious *peixe escabeche* (fresh fish cooked in coconut milk and served in a sizzling cast iron pot). The portions are so generous they serve for 2 or even 3.

♈-♈ Sabor da Terra, R Caminho da Praia, T075-3652 1156. A very popular lunchtime per kilo and à la carte evening restaurant serving great *moquecas* and sea food.
♈ Pulcinella, 2nd beach. A tiny beach *barraca* run by Luciana from Valença, who serves great *beiju de tapioca*, juices, coffee and snacks, and is eternally cheerful.

Ilha de Boipeba *p435*
Boipeba has cheap eats in the town and surprisingly good food at the **Pousada Santa Clara** and the rustic restaurants in Moreré.
♈♈ Santa Clara (see page 441), Boipeba. San Francisco panache in rustic but elegantly decorated tropical surrounds. Come for dinner. Highly recommended.
♈ Mar e Coco (see page 441), Boipeba. Very fresh seafood in idyllic surroundings, shaded by coconuts and next to a gently lapping bath-warm sea.

Itacaré *p436*
There are plenty of restaurants in Itacaré, most of them on **R Lodônio Almeida**. Menus here are increasingly chic and often include a respectable wine list.
♈♈♈ Casa Sapucaia, R Lodônio Almeida, T073-3251 3091. Sophisticated Bahian food with an international twist from 2 ex-round-the-world sailors. Try the delicious king prawn caramelized with ginger.
♈♈♈ Dedo de Moça, R Plinio Soares 26 (next to the São Miguel church), T073-3251 3391. One of Bahia's best restaurants. The chef was trained by Vagner Aguiar, who worked at São Paulo's award-winning **Laurent** restaurant, and her menu of dishes that combine Brazilian ingredients with French and Oriental techniques has been expanded by local chef Carol. Offerings include ultra-fresh fish encrusted with Brazilian nuts. Good cocktails at the little garden bar and a romantic atmosphere.
♈♈♈ O Casarão Amarelo, Praia da Coroinha, T073-9996 0599. Swiss-owned restaurant in one of the most beautiful colonial buildings in the town. International menu which is good in parts. The fish is always a reliable choice.

♈♈ Beco das Flores, R Lodônio Almeida 134, T073-3251 3121. The busiest restaurant in Itacaré, serving good wood-fired pizzas in tastefully decorated surroundings to a well-dressed post-beach crowd.
♈♈ La In, R Lodônio Almeida 116, Centro, T073-3251 3054. Great little Bahian and seafood restaurant decorated with colourful art painted by the owner, Marcio, and serving very good value lunches and dinners. Be sure to try the house speciality: fish in prawn sauce baked in a banana leaf. Right next to the IYHA.
♈ O Restaurante, R Pedro Longo 150, T073-3251 2012. One of the few restaurants with a *prato feto*, alongside a mixed seafood menu.

Ilhéus and around *p437, map p438*
Specialities include the local drink, *coquinho*, coconut filled with *cachaça*, which is only for the strongest heads. There are cheap eats from the various seafood stalls on the *praça* and near the cathedral.
♈♈♈ Vesúvio, Praça Dom Eduardo, T073-3634 4724. Next to the cathedral, made famous by Amado's novel (see box, page 439), now Swiss-owned. Very good but pricey.
♈♈ Marostica, Av 2 de Julho 966, T073-3634 5691. Superior pizzas and pastas, the best in town and very popular on weekend evenings.
♈ Acarajé de Irene, Praça Castro Alves. Great traditional *acarajé* and other Bahian snacks. Long a local favourite; people come from all over the city just to eat here.
♈ Cabana Gabriela, R Rui Penalva 109, T073-3632 1836. Good *moquecas* and seafood dishes. Well-known to locals as a great place for Bahian food.

🔊 Bars and clubs

Tinharé and Morro de São Paulo *p433*
There is always plenty going on in Morro. The liveliest bars are on the 2nd beach where you'll also find the throbbing **Pulsa** nightclub. These tend to get going after 2300 when the restaurants in town empty.

Ilha de Boipeba *p435*
Nightlife on Boipeba is limited to star-gazing or having a beer in town.

Itacaré *p436*
The liveliest bars of the moment are Toca do Calango, Praça dos Cachorros and Mar e Mel on the Praia das Conchas. The Casarão Amarelo restaurant becomes a dance club after 2300 on weekends. There is frequent extemporaneous *forró* and other live music all over the city and most restaurants and bars have some kind of music Oct-Apr.

🎭 Festivals and events

Ilhéus and around *p437, map p438*
17-20 Jan Festa de São Sebastião.
Feb Shrove Tue, Carnaval.
23 Apr Festa de São Jorge.
28 Jun Foundation day.
Oct Festa do Cacau.

⛰ Activities and tours

Tinharé and Morro de São Paulo *p433*
Tour operators
Morro Paraíso, 2nd beach, morroparaiso@hotmail.com. One of many little agencies offering boat trip bookings, flights and transfers to Boipeba. There's an internet café here too.

Ilhéus *p437, map p438*
Tour operators
Orbitá, R Marquês de Paranaguá 270, T073-3634 7700, www.orbitaexpedicoes.com.br. Organizes adventure trips, visits to Maraú and general tours. The guides are excellent and knowledgeable. The company also operates out of both Itacaré and Una on a pre-arranged pick-up scheme. Transfers can be arranged to Fazenda da Lagoa and throughout Bahia as far as the Chapada Diamantina.

🚍 Transport

Valença *p433*
Bus Long-distance buses run from the new *rodoviária* on Av Maçônica. Many buses a day to **Salvador**, 5 hrs, US$6, several companies, including **Aguia Branca**, T075-3450 4400. **São Jorge** to **Itabuna**, 5 hrs, US$5, very slow. For the shortest route to **Salvador**, take a bus via Nazaré das Farinhas to Bom Despacho (130 km), and take a ferry from there to the São Joaquim ferry terminal. To **Bom Despacho** on Itaparica, Camarujipe and Águia Branca companies, 16 a day, 1 hr 45 mins, US$3.60.

Ferry There are boats to **Gamboa** (1½ hrs) and **Morro de São Paulo** (1½ hrs) from the main bridge in Valença, 5 times a day (signalled by a loud whistle). The fare is US$2.50. The *lancha rápida* takes 25 mins and costs US$8. Only Salvador–Valença buses leaving 0530-1100 connect with ferries. If not stopping in Valença, get out of the bus by the main bridge in town, don't wait until you get to the *rodoviária*, which is a long way from the ferry. Private boat hire can be arranged if you miss the ferry schedule. A responsible local boatman is **Jario**, T075-3741 1681; he can be contacted to meet travellers arriving at the *rodoviária* for transfer to Morro. He also offers excursions to other islands, especially Boipeba. There is a regular boat from Valença to **Boipeba** on weekdays 1000-1230 depending on tide, return 1500-1700, 3-4 hrs.

Tinharé and Morro de São Paulo *p433*
Air There are several daily direct flights from the 3rd beach at Morro de São Paulo to **Salvador**. These cost US$90 one way. Times vary seasonally and from year to year but are usually as follows: Salvador–Morro (0815, 1430, 1500), Morro–Salvador (0900, 1015, 1315, 1715). For further details ask your hotel to contact **Addey** T071-3377 1993, www.addey.com.br, or drop into the airport office next to the landing strip on Morro.

Ferry Several companies run catamarans from Morro de São Paulo to the Terminal Marítimo in front of the Mercado Modelo in **Salvador** (1½-2 hrs). Times vary according to the season and weather but there are usually several a day 0800-1400; check with the tourist office or **Catamarã Gamboa do Morro**, T071-9975 6395. There are also water taxis.

Boats from Morro de São Paulo and **Gamboa** run to the main bridge in **Valença** (1½ hrs) 5 times a day, US$2.50 (see under Valença, above). There is also a *lancha rápida* which takes 25 mins and costs US$8. Private boat hire can also be arranged, contact Jario, T075-3741 1681 or book through your *pousada*.

Ilha de Boipeba *p435*
Boat Day-trips to the island run from Morro de São Paulo (see page 434). There is a regular boat from Boipeba to **Valença** on weekdays 1500-1700, 3-4 hrs. Overnight excursions to the village are possible. Contact Zé Balacha, T075-9148 0343, or book through your *pousada* in Morro or Boipeba.

Barra Grande and the Peninsula de Maraú *p436*
Air There are scheduled air taxis from the airport at Barra Grande to **Morro de São Paulo** and **Salvador**.

Boat Boats run from Barra Grande to **Camamu** several times a day Oct-Mar and once daily year round (boats: 1 hr, US$3; *lancha*: 20 mins, US$15).

Itacaré *p436*
Bus Frequent buses to **Ilhéus** (the nearest town with an airport), 45 mins, US$7 along the newly paved road. To **Salvador**, change at Ubaitaba (3 hrs, US$3), Ubaitaba–Salvador, 6 hrs, US$12, several daily.

Ilhéus and around *p437, map p438*
Air A taxi from town to the airport costs US$4. There are flights to **Salvador**, **Belo Horizonte**, **São Paulo**, **Brasília**, **Curitiba**, **Porto Seguro** and **Rio de Janeiro** with GOL, www.voegol.com.br, TAM, www.tam.com.br, and Webjet, www.webjet.com.br. Services are often cut back in low season.

Bus and boat Most long-distance buses leave from the *rodoviária*, 4 km from town. However, the **Itabuna–Olivença** bus goes through the centre of Ilhéus. Several buses run daily to **Salvador**, 7 hrs, US$14.40 (*leito* US$29, Expresso São Jorge), the 0620 bus goes via **Itaparica**, leaving passengers at Bom Despacho ferry station on the island (from where it is a 50-min ferry to **Salvador**). To **Itacaré**, 4 hrs, US$5. To **Eunápolis**, 5 hrs, US$5.40, this bus also leaves from the central bus terminal. Local buses leave from Praça Cairu.

Taxi Insist that taxi drivers have meters and price charts.

⊙ Directory

Valença *p433*
Banks There is a Bradesco and Banco do Brasil in town, which have ATMs and *câmbios*.

Tinharé and Morro de São Paulo *p433*
Banks There are no banks on the island, but cash dollars can be exchanged in *casas de câmbio* in the village. **Internet** There is access in the town in several cafés.

Itacaré *p436*
Banks and internet Theres a Bradesco and Banco do Brasil in town and the usual plethora of internet cafés.

Ilhéus and around *p437, map p438*
Banks Empresa de Cambio e Turismo, T073-3634 3900, will change money.

The Discovery and Whale Coast

The beaches of the far south of Bahia are among the finest in Brazil – long strands of fine white sand washed by bath-warm sea, or pounded by bottle-green surf and backed by swaying rows of coconut palms. Some are remote and completely deserted, others are watched over by busy resorts and party towns like Porto Seguro and Arraial d'Ajuda, or forgotten little villages like Caraíva, Corumbau and Curumuxatiba with only a handful of simple pousadas. Pretty Trancoso is perhaps the chicest beach destination north of Punta del Este in Uruguay, with a ream of gorgeous beach boutiques of the kind that grace the pages of Departures magazine or Taschen coffee-table books. Offshore, in the far south, are the Abrolhos: an archipelago of rocky coral islands fringed with reef. The islands form part of one of Brazil's most carefully protected marine reserves and are one of the best places in South America for seeing humpback whales. Back on the mainland, Bahia's far south is dotted with indigenous Pataxó villages and has extensive areas of Mata Atlântica rainforest This area, around the pyramidal mountain at Monte Paschoal, is under threat from eucalyptus plantations used to produce toilet paper.

The Discovery Coast takes its name from the first landing by the Portuguese. In AD 1500, Pedro Álvares Cabral became the first European to see Brazil, sighting land at Monte Pascoal south of Porto Seguro. The sea here was too open to offer a safe harbour, so Cabral sailed his fleet north, entering the mouth of the Rio Burnahém to find the harbour he later called 'Porto Seguro' (safe port).
▶▶ For listings, see pages 457-464.

Porto Seguro ●❼❶❻ ▶▶ pp457-464. Colour map 4, B5.

→ Phone code: 073. Population: 96,000.

Modern Porto Seguro is rapidly developing into southern Bahia's largest and most cosmopolitan coastal city, with residents from all over the world. Located on the Rio Buranhém, which separates the city from Arraial across the water, the attractive dockland area retains a handful of pretty colonial houses. While high up on the hill above is the higgledy-piggledy old centre, a peaceful place with lovely gardens and panoramic views. Here you will find three churches: **Nossa Senhora da Misericórdia** (1530), **Nossa Senhora do Rosário** (1534) and **Nossa Senhora da Pena** (1718). The former jail is also here, with a stone monument marking the landfall of Gonçalo Coelho, the first Portuguese to explore and subsequently map the coast of northeastern Brazil.

Ins and outs

Getting there **Aeroporto de Porto Seguro** ① *Estrada do Aeroporto s/n, 2 km north of town, T073-3288 1880*, has connections with Rio de Janeiro, São Paulo, Belo Horizonte, Ilhéus, Salvador, Porto Alegre, Brasília, Curitiba and Vitória. There are banks and a car rental booth in the terminal. A taxi to the centre costs US$8. The **rodoviária** ① *2 km west of the centre, on the road to Eunápolis*, receives direct buses from Ilhéus, Salvador, São Paulo and Rio de Janeiro (direct bus at 1600). Other buses go via via Eunápolis, which has connections with Porto Seguro every 30 minutes (US$5, one hour). The *rodoviária* has cafés and snack bars. Taxis charge US$6 to the town or ferry (negotiate at quiet times).
▶▶ See Transport, page 463.

Porto Seguro

CIDADE HISTÓRICA

To ⑨ & Santa Cruz de Cabrália

☐ Farol

NS da Pena

NS da Misericórdia

Praça Pero Campos Tourinho

Gonçalo Coelho Monument

NS do Rosário

Praia do Cruzeiro

To ⑩ & Airport

Av Beira-Mar BR-367

Av dos Navegantes

R 15 de Novembro

R Mal Deodoro da Fonseca

R Cova da Moça

R da Faca

R do Cajueiro

R do Golfo

AV 22 de Abril

Banco do Brasil

Praça Inaiá

Praça Visconde de Porto Seguro

R Pero Vaz de Caminha

R Antônio Osório

M Batista

NS do Brasil

R 7 de Julho

Av Getúlio Vargas

R São Pedro

R 7A Cabral

Bradesco

R Assis Chateaubriand

Rio Buranhém

Praça da Bandeira

Praça dos Pataxós

To Arraial da Ajuda (5 minutes)

N

100 metres
100 yards

Sleeping
Albergue Porto Seguro 7
Camping Mundaí Praia 9
Estalagem Porto Seguro 1
Navegantes 2
Pousada Casa Azul 3

Pousada dos Raizes 6
Solar da Praça 4
Solar do Imperador 10
Tabapiri Country 8
Vela Branca 5

Eating
Da Japonêsa 2
Portinha 3
Sambuca 1

The festival of Nossa Senhora da Pena

The cult of Nossa Senhora da Pena began in Leiria, Portugal, a century after the reconquest of the country from the Moors. The tradition began in Porto Seguro in 1535 when a Portuguese noble, Donatário Pero do Campo Tourinho (a recipient of one of Brazil's 16th-century *capitanias*), brought with him a small image of Nossa Senhora da Pena (Our Lady of Suffering). He named his captaincy 'Villa de Nossa Senhora da Pena de Porto Seguro' and built a small church to house his favourite saint. The church was rebuilt in the 18th century.

Nossa Senhora da Pena is the patron saint of art and literature. She is celebrated on 8 September in the historic city on the cliff, overlooking the beach hotels of the modern resort of Porto Seguro. Devotees of the cult, called *romeiros,* travel great distances to her shrine and the surrounding area becomes a huge campsite of tents, caravans and tour buses.

The festival resembles a cross between a Brazilian street party and a market, with cheap clothes, household goods, ice-cold beer and barbecued meat on sale. Throughout the weekend there are displays of capoeira and nightly dances of *pagôde* and *forró*. After prayers on the afternoon of the 8th, the festival is officially closed with a religious procession through the streets of this beautiful colonial town.

Getting around Buses run throughout the city from the waterfront to the to the old *rodoviária* near the port every 30 minutes, US$0.50. Regular buses run along the seafront from Praça dos Pataxós to the northern beaches, or take a bus to Porto Belo or Santa Cruz Cabrália from the port. For beaches south of the Rio Buranhém, see Arraial d'Ajuda (below) and points further south.

Tourist Information The tourist office, **Secretária de Turismo de Porto Seguro** ① *R Pero Vaz de Caminha 475, Centro, T073-3288 3708, www.portosegurotur.com.br,* has information on tours. Alternatively, contact **Portomondo**, www.portomondo.com. ⟩⟩ *See Arraial de Ajuda Activities and tours, page 462.*

North of Porto Seguro ◉ ⟩⟩ *pp457-464*.

Heading north of town, on the BR-367 to Santa Cruz Cabrália (known as Avenida Beira Mar), is Bahia's second most popular tourist area, with a series of hotels and beaches. The best beaches are **Itacimirim**, **Curuípe**, **Mundaí** and **Taperapuã**, which have some lively *barracas*. The biggest (and busiest) are **Barra Point**, **Toá Toa**, **Axé Moi**, **Vira Sol** and **Barramares**. The latter are mainly Brazilian package-tour destinations and offer jet-ski hire and other watersports facilities.

A few kilometres before Cabrália, a tourist village, **Coroa Vermelha**, has sprouted at the site of Cabral's first landfall and a cross marks the spot where the first Mass was celebrated. It has a rather uncoordinated array of beach bars, hotels, rental houses and souvenir shops selling indigenous Pataxó items. Buses from Porto Seguro take about 20 minutes.

Santa Cruz Cabrália → *Phone code: 073. Colour map 4, B5.*

About 10 minutes north of Coroa Vermelha (25 km north of Porto Seguro), Santa Cruz Cabrália is a delightful small town at the mouth of the Rio João de Tiba. It has a lovely beach, river port, and a 450-year-old church with a fine view. It is believed to be the site of the first landing in Brazil by the Portuguese explorer Pedro Álvares Cabral in 1500. A good trip from here is to **Coroa Alta**, a reef 50 minutes away by boat. It passes along the tranquil river to the reef with crystal waters and good snorkelling. There is a daily departure at 1000. A recommended boatman is Zezé (T/F073-3282 1152), who can usually be found on the square by the river's edge; he is helpful and knowledgeable. The trip costs around US$25 without lunch.

A 15-minute river crossing by ferry to a new road on the opposite bank gives easy access to the deserted beaches of **Santo André** and **Santo Antônio**. As yet, few tourists make it to here, but the new road is certain to change this. Hourly buses run between Santa Cruz and Porto Seguro (23 km).

Jaqueira Pataxó village

Some 8 km north of Porto Seguro, the beautiful and inspiring *Pataxó* indigenous reserve of Jaqueira is well worth a visit. Its traditional houses lie in the heart of a stand of native-owned rainforest. All the food is either grown or hunted using traditional techniques. And a small craft shop selling beautiful ceramics, sacred incense and art provides extra revenue. The project was conceived by two impressive *Pataxó* sisters who despaired at the loss of *Pataxó* culture in the villages of southern Bahia. Their eco-tourism and cultural recuperation model has completely rejuvenated *Pataxó* culture. Young people are speaking their own language again and rediscovering their identity. It is possible to visit or even stay in the village. Trips can be organized with **Portomondo**, www.portomondo.com, who work closely with the *Pataxó*. For further information visit www.rabarsa.com/pataxo.

South of Porto Seguro ⬛🚻👤🛶🏔🅿🅸
▸▸ pp457-464. Colour map 4, B5.

Arraial da Ajuda → Phone code: 073.
A five-minute float across the Rio Buranhém from the docks at Porto Seguro brings you to Arraial da Ajuda, a pretty little colonial village turned beach-party town and a more popular base for travellers than Porto. Arraial is an ideal place to get stuck, with a string of gorgeous beaches that begin at the mouth of the river at **Araçaipe** and continue south indefinitely. The little hotels behind the sand are on a far smaller scale than

Around Porto Seguro

To Itabuna & Salvador
Guaiú
Santo Antônio
Santo André
Ponta do Mutá
Santa Cruz Cabrália
Eunápolis
Coroa Vermelha
Recife de Fora
BR 367
Taperapua
Mundaí
Jaqueira Pataxó
Curuípe
Porto Seguro
Rio Buranhém
Araçaipe
Arraial da Ajuda
Mucugé
Parracho
Itabela
Pitinga
Rio da Barra
Lagoa Azul
Rio dos Frades
Taipé
Monte Pascoal
Trancoso
Nativos
Coqueiros
Itapororoca
Caraíva
Espelho
Parque Nacional de Monte Pascoal
Corumbau
Itamaraju
Barra do Caí
BR 101
Curumuxatiba
Praia das Ostras
Atlantic Ocean
Prado
Guaratiba
Rio Itanhém
Alcobaça
To Teixeira de Freitas, Linhares & Vitória
To Teixeira de Freitas
Barra de Caravelas
Caravelas
To Parque Nacional Marinho dos Abrolhos
N
20 km
20 miles

The Pataxó

"This is our land. You have to respect the land you are walking on because it is ours. When you arrived here this land was already ours. And what did you do to us? You stopped our progress with riot squads, gunfire and tear gas. With our blood we commemorate once more the Discovery of Brazil". (Pataxó indigenous leader during the response to the celebration of Brazil's discovery in 2000.)

The first indigenous people to meet the Portuguese were the Pataxó, a Bahian warrior tribe who lived (and live) around Porto Seguro. Since contact was made the tribe have suffered greatly. The greatest destruction was in 1951 when one of the most important villages was, ostensibly, caught in a gun battle between bandits and police. Hundreds of Pataxó, including women and children, were murdered. The Pataxó had long been campaigning to have their tribal lands in the Monte Pascoal national park returned to them. After the massacre, the Pataxó communities in southern Bahia seemed to have lost their spirit, lapsing into poverty and alcoholism, until two remarkable Pataxó sisters began a cultural renovation project in their village of Jaqueira. They re-introduced the Pataxó language, traditional agricultural methods and implemented an ecotourism project to provide income for the community. Young Pataxó people have found new pride in their culture rather than leaving the community. And the tribe are utilizing the tools of the outside world to strengthen their voice. They were instrumental in a change in the Brazilian law in 2008 which declared that "the study of the history and culture of African-Brazilian and Indigenous Brazilian culture … would be mandatory". The journalist Aricema Pataxó of the University of Bahia publishes a blog on the Pataxó (http://aricemaindiosdabahia. blogspot.com). A visit to Jaqueira is one of the highlights of a journey through southern Bahia (see opposite page).

Porto's package-tourist towers and cater to shallow as well as deep pockets. The town itself has a string of pleasant little bars and restaurants; all of which are easily manageable on foot. Arraial is also one of the best places in Brazil to learn capoeira. At Brazilian holiday times (especially New Year and Carnaval) it is very crowded, almost to bursting point

The town centre is clustered around the pretty 16th-century church of **Nossa Senhora da Ajuda** (1549), which sits high on a cliff, affording great views of the palm-covered coast. The principal streets extend off the square in front of the church. The largest, which is lined with shops, bars, restaurants and *pousadas*, is called *Broadway*. There's a party here or on one of the beaches almost every night in high season.

Arraial's beaches are splendid: some pounded by surf, others are little bays gently lapped by an Atlantic tamed by offshore reef. Most have *barracas* selling good simple seafood and chilled drinks, and playing music. From north to south they are as follows. **Araçaípe** is popular with families and day-visitors from Porto, and has several pretty beach hotels and *pousadas*. **D'Ajuda** is in front of the town and has a small protected area. **Mucugê** just to the south of town, has good surf, plenty of beach *barracas* for *forró* and lambada parties in the summer. To reach these, take Rua da Praia out of town.

South beyond Mucugê is **Parracho**, which is popular for windsurfing and kayaking (rental available); followed by **Pitinga**, with strong waves breaking on the offshore reef creating some decent surf. The penultimate beach is **Lagoa Azul**, backed by cliffs, with gorgeous sand and strong surf. Few make it to the beach farthest south, **Taipé**, an hour's walk from Arraial. It is backed by sandstone cliffs and has glassy water and a handful of *barracas*. At low tide it is possible to walk to from Taipé to Trancoso (see below) along the beach via the village of **Rio da Barra**; allow two hours. A dirt road behind the beach follows the same route and is plied by taxis and cars; it is easy to hitch a lift.

Ins and outs Ferries from Porto Seguro run across the Rio Buranhém to the south bank, every 30 minutes day and night (three minutes, US$0.60 for foot passengers, US$5 for cars). From there, it is a further 5 km to Arraial da Ajuda town centre (US$1 by bus, *combis* charge US$1.50 per person, taxis US$5), although the first *pousadas* are literally on the Arraial river bank. It is not necessary to return to Porto Seguro to venture into the rest of Bahia. Arraial is connected by bus to Eunápolis and Caraíva, and Trancoso to the south. Various agencies in town offer transfers by buggy or Land Rover to Corumbau and beyond all the way to Abrolhos. **Portomondo** (see Activities and tours, page 462) is by far the best and most reliable.

Trancoso → *Colour map 4, B5. Phone code: 073.*
In the last five years this once-sleepy little village, 15 km south of Arraial, has become Bahia's chicest beach destination, beloved of the Brazilian and international jet-set for its combination of low-key atmosphere and high-fashion labels. The coolest São Paulo names

Arraial da Ajuda

To ③ ④ ⑪ & Ferry to Porto Seguro

To *Praia Araçaipe*

Sleeping		**Eating**
Arraial Hostel 1	Pousada Flamboyant 7	Don Fabrizio 1
O Cantinho 2	Pousada Mar Aberto 8	Manguti 2
Pousada Canto d'Alvorada 3	Pousada Pitinga 9	Nipo 3
Pousada do Roballo 5	Pousada Tubarão 10	Paulinho Pescador 4
Pousada Erva Doce 6	Quinta do Porto 4	Pizzaria do Arraial 5
	Sole Mio 11	

To ⑨, Praia Parracho, Praia Pitinga, Lagoa Azul & Taipé

100 metres
100 yards

Drastic plastic

There are few places on the planet where the ravages of plastic waste are more apparent than in the windswept far north-east of Brazil. It is everywhere: snagged and billowing in trees on the edges of the Lençóis Maranhenses, floating like jellyfish in the wild waters of the Delta do Parnaíba, piled up as drift on the beaches of Ceará and strewn along roadside verges between towns and cities throughout the region. The UN Environment Programme estimates that there are now 46,000 pieces of plastic litter floating in every square mile of ocean on earth.

In 1993 the Brazilian Newton Diniz invented a type of plastic that bio-degrades in 18-48 months and invested money in a biodegradable plastics factory. His company, Polibag, www.polibag.com.br, now provides the whole of the city of Porto Seguro, including all the supermarkets and hotels, with biodegradable plastic as well as myriad clients in the USA, Europe and Japan. This is despite forceful resistance from the petro-chemical industry who set up an NGO campaigning against Polibag's work.

fill the tiny shopping centre and the town and beaches are dotted with smart designer boutiques and haute-rural restaurants offering the best food outside Rio de Janeiro and São Paulo. Celebrities come here to be recognized only by those they wish to be recognized by, especially the Mario Testino set. Despite its status, Trancoso remains a simple little town at heart, and herein lies its charm. It is glossy but intimate, with life focussing on the **Quadrado**, a long grassy square where locals play football in the evening. The square is crowned with the little whitewashed 17th-century church of **São João Batista**, and lined with colourful little *casas*, each housing a bikini boutique, crafts shop, fashionable restaurant, bar or guesthouse. The houses are particularly enchanting at night, when they contrast with the dark indigo canvas of the rainforest, under a dome of stars.

Below the Quadrado are a stretch of beaches extending away to the north and south. The most famous and the closest to town are **Praia do Trancoso** and **Praia dos Nativos**, both washed by gentle waves, with coral far off shore and a cluster of chic-shack *barracas* that host parties for the designer-label brigade during the summer months. **Coqueiros** across the little river to the north is quieter, with one simple restaurant and a view. To the south beyond Trancoso beach are **Rio Verde**, with a little river, and beyond it **Itapororoca** a deserted beach with just a few very expensive houses and good clear-water snorkelling.

Ins and outs In high season, *combis* ply the dirt road along the coast between Arraial and Trancoso, leaving when full. Buses run along the newly paved road between Porto Seguro, Arraial de Ajuda and Trancoso at least once an hour in high season (US$3 from Porto Seguro, US$2 from Arraial). There are two daily buses from Caraíva; with an extra bus in high season. Taxis from Arraial cost around US$30; from Porto airport US$40-50. Like any of the Bahian resorts, It is also possible to organize air taxis from Rio or São Paulo or helicopter transfers from Arraial, Caraíva and Corumbau. See **Portomondo**, page 462, for details. Trancoso can be packed out in high season. Be sure to book ahead. There are no really cheap rooms. Various tour operators around the main square sell *combi*, bus and air tickets for destinations throughout Bahia and organize day trips to Espelho and beyond. The easiest way to get around town is by bike, on foot or motorbike taxi.

Espelho

A 50-minute drive along the dirt road to Caraíva, Espelho is one of the state's most beautiful beaches: a glassy bay fringed with white sand and rocks with a handful of very plush beach hotels and a delightful restaurant. The Caraíva bus will drop you at the turn off to the beach, from where it is a 5-km walk; or visit as part of a tour.

Caraíva → Colour map 4, B5. Phone code: 073.

This incredibly peaceful, atmospheric fishing town, 65 km south of Porto Seguro, is on the banks of the Rio Caraíva. Electricity (during the daytime only) and hot water were only installed in 2008 and the streets are sand so there are no cars. The marvellous beaches here make a real escape from Trancoso, Arraial and Porto Seguro. Despite difficult access, Caraíva is becoming increasingly popular.

There is a good walk north to **Praia do Satu** (where Señor Satu provides an endless supply of coconut milk), or 6 km south to a rather sad Pataxó indigenous village; watch the tides as you may get cut off. Horses can be hired through any of the *pousadas* and buggy rides to Corumbau (from where buses connect to Cumuruxatiba) can be organized from the town square with the Pataxó (US$40). Or you can walk the 12 km along the beach to the river that separates Caraíva's last beach with Corumbau village; there is a boatman here for crossings (US$2, 10 minutes). Boats can be hired (US$50 per day) at the river port in Caraíva for excursions to Caruípe beach, Espelho, snorkelling at Pedra de Tatuaçu reef or Corombau (take your own mask and fins), or for trips up the beautiful river Rio Caraíva which gets into wild, pristine rainforest some 10 km inland. **Prainha** river beach, about 30 minutes away, and mangrove swamps can also be visited by canoe or launch.

Ins and outs   Caraíva is connected to Trancoso by two daily (three in high season), along a very poor dirt road. The journey involves a river crossing and can take as long as three hours in the wet season (April to June). If arriving by bus from the south, change buses in Itabela (departs at 1500), or take a taxi; about 50 km. The high season is December to February and July. There are plenty of cheap *pousadas* and restaurants along the rustic sandy streets. Most bars have live *forró* in the summer. Flip-flops are best for walking along the sand streets, and take a torch as it is very dark at night.

Parque Nacional de Monte Pascoal

ⓘ *16 km north of Itamaraju, Caixa Postal 076, CEP 45830-000, Itamaraju, T073-3281 2419.*
The national park was set up in 1961 to preserve the flora, fauna and birdlife of the coast where Europeans first landed in Brazil. There is a bus from Itamaraju at 0600 (Monday to Friday); taxis run from Itamaraju cost around US$50 for the round trip including waiting time. Or the park can be visited with a tour group such as **Portomondo**, see page 462.

Corumbau

This tiny fishing village sits on a little promontory of land that sticks out into the deep blue of the Bahian Atlantic. It's a one-beach buggy town, with a tiny church and a handful of very cheap *pousadas* and restaurants; but it is fringed with beaches every bit as gorgeous as any of those around Caraíva or Trancoso. There is great snorkelling from the beach to the south of town. Foreigners are few and far between, except for a handful who come to stay at the exclusive and beautifully designed resorts to the south of the town. Set on a a private reserve on Tauá beach, **Tauana** (see Sleeping, page 460) is the finest and most romantic small beach hotel in Brazil.

Capoeira

Capoeira is the most visually spectacular and gymnastic of all martial arts and the only one to have originated in the Americas. Salvador is the capoeira centre of Brazil and seeing a fight between good Bahian capoeristas is an unforgettable experience. Fighters spin around each other in mock combat, never touching but performing a series of lunges, kicks and punches with dizzying speed and precision. Some wear razor blades on their feet. A ring or *roda* of other capoeristas watches, clapping, singing and beating time on a *berimbau* and hand-held drum. Every now and then they exchange places with the fighters in the centre of the ring.

Although many claim that capoeira derives from an Angolan foot-fighting ritual, this is incorrect. Capoeira originated in Brazil and there is strong evidence to suggest that it was invented by indigenous Brazilians. Padre José de Anchieta a 16th-century ethnologist makes an aside in his 1595 book *The Tupi Guarani Language* that the 'Indians amuse themselves by playing capoiera' and other Portuguese explorers like Martim de Souza recall the same. The word capoeira itself comes from Tupi-Guarani and means 'cleared forest' and the postures, including many of the kicks, spins and the crouching position taken by those in the circle are all Brazilian-Indian. It was in indigenous capoeiras that the fight was passed on to African plantation slaves who modified them, added African chants and rhythms and the *berimbau*; an instrument probably brought to Brazil from West Africa. The art was used as a weapon against the soldiers of the enslaved African king Zumbi who established the Americas' only free slave state just north of Bahia in the 1700s.

Ins and outs Corumbau is not easy to reach. The best way is to organize a transfer with an agency like **Portomondo** (see page 462). However, it is possible to get here by catching the bus to Caraíva and then either sharing a buggy ride from the main square (US$40) or walking the 12 km to the river and catching the ferry boat (see above). There is one daily bus from Itamaraju.

Cumuruxatiba → *Colour map 4, B5. Phone code: 073.*

The road from Itamaraju leads to Cumuruxatiba (www.cumuru.com.br), which is also connected to Corumbau (and across the river to Caraíva) via a dirt road. In low season, Cumuruxatiba is a sleepy local beach resort; in high season it is a lively, young party town, popular with families and 20-something groups from the south of Brazil. There are plenty of little *pousadas* and restaurants. As yet the region is unspoilt and there are some almost completely deserted beaches both to the north and south, great for hours of wandering.

Ins and outs Cumuruxatiba is 29 km south of Corumbau and 21 km north of Prado and is served by daily buses from both, with more frequent services in high season. Buses from Salvador, Porto Seguro and elsewhere in the state run via Itamaraju, 60 km inland on the BR-101, from where there is a daily bus to Cumuruxatiba.

Prado → *Colour map 4, B5. Phone code: 073.*

Prado is a scruffy town sandwiched between a long sand spit and the sluggish Rio Tucuruçú, lined with mangroves. There are two species of mangrove: stately, tall red mangroves near the sea, and white mangroves in the fresher water. The river and trees are a haven for birdlife with at least three kingfisher species, ospreys and numerous herons and waders. There are southern otters and, further upstream, spectacled caiman. The beaches around town, especially near the **Barra do Prado** about 3 km downstream, are some of the best in southern Bahia: vast, lonely stretches of powder-soft sand that disappear into the distant horizon. It is possible to walk to the beaches from the town centre (about 45 minutes), or boats run from the quay. Bring plenty of sun shade, water and snacks, as there are no facilities except in the highest season.

Ins and outs Prado is well connected to the rest of Bahia, with direct buses to Caravelas (for Abrolhos), numerous daily connections to Itamaraju (for the rest of the state) and three daily buses to Cumuruxatiba. Day-trips to the beaches cost around US$40 for a boat.

Caravelas → *Colour map 4, B5. Phone code: 073.*
Continuing south, Caravelas is a charming little town on the banks of the Caravelas estuary, surrounded by mangroves. There are eight fine white-sand beaches nearby. The town is well known for its Catholic festivals, which attract thousands of pilgrims. Caravelas was a major trading port in the 17th and 18th centuries and the town's name was taken from the Portuguese sailing boats whose technology opened up the world to Lisbon. It is now slowly developing as a resort for Brazilian tourism. The best beaches are about 10 km away at the fishing village of **Barra de Caravelas** (hourly buses). There is a helpful tourist information, **Ibama Centro de Visitantes** ① *Barão do Rio Branco 281*.

Ins and outs Caravelas is 36 km south of Prado on the BA-001, on the banks of the Rio Caravelas and is served by frequent buses from Eunápolis and Itamaraju from where there are connections to the rest of the state. There are two weekly buses from Porto Seguro and daily connections to Prado to the north. The town is the departure point for the Abrolhos islands.

Parque Nacional Marinho dos Abrolhos
Abrolhos is an abbreviation of *Abre os olhos*, 'Open your eyes', from Amérigo Vespucci's exclamation when he first sighted the reef in 1503. Established in 1983, the park consists of five small islands: **Redonda**, **Siriba**, **Guarita**, **Sueste** and **Santa Bárbara**, which are volcanic in origin. There are also abundant coral reefs and good diving. Darwin visited the archipelago in 1830 and Jacques Cousteau studied the marine environment here.

The archipelago national park protects the most extensive coral reefs in the south Atlantic with four times as many endemic species than the reefs and atolls in the Caribbean. There are numerous endemic species, including giant brain corals, crustaceans and molluscs, as well as marine turtles and mammals threatened by extinction and huge colonies of nesting seabirds. In addition, the seas around the islands are one of the most important south Atlantic nurseries for humpback whales – which can always be seen in season.

In 2002, the Abrolhos region was declared an area of Extreme Biological Importance by the Brazilian Ministry of Environment, based on the Brazilian commitment to the international Convention on Biodiversity. For more information see **Conservation International**, www.conservation.org. The archipelago is administered by **Ibama** and a navy detachment mans a lighthouse on Santa Bárbara, which is the only island that may be visited. Visitors are not allowed to spend the night on the islands, but may stay overnight on schooners.

Ins and outs The Parque Nacional Marinho dos Abrolhos is 70 km east of Caravelas. The journey to the islands takes three to four hours depending on the sea conditions. Between July and early December, humpback whale sightings are almost guaranteed. Boats leave at 0700 from the Marina Porto Abrolhos some 5 km north of Caravelas town centre (around US$50 depending on numbers) and they return at dusk. It is possible to dive or snorkel at Abrolhos. If you are coming from Porto Seguro everything including transfers and accommodation in Caravelas can be arranged by **Portomondo**, T073-3575 3686, www.porto mondo.com. In Caravelas, book with **Abrolhos Turismo**, or **Catamarã Veleiro Sanuk**, or through any of the hotels listed above; or directly at the Marina Porto Abrolhos.

◉ The Discovery and Whale Coast listings

For Sleeping and Eating price codes and other relevant information, see pages 42-47.

● Sleeping

Porto Seguro *p447, map p448*
Prices rise steeply Dec-Feb and Jul. Off-season rates can drop by 50%, negotiate the rate for stays of more than 3 nights. Room capacity is greater than that of Salvador. Outside Dec-Feb, rooms with bath and hot water can be rented for about US$150 per month.
A Pousada Casa Azul, 15 de Novembro 11, T/F073-3268 1032. TV, a/c, good pool and garden and in a quiet part of town.
B Estalagem Porto Seguro, R Mcal Deodoro 66, T073-3288 2095, www.hotelestalagem. com.br. Terraced rooms in a deep blue colonial house in the town centre. Great atmosphere and a stroll from nearby restaurants. The hotel help with tours and transfers.
B Solar do Imperador, Estr do Aeroporto, T073-3288 8450, www.solardoimperador. com.br. Well-appointed, spacious and modern a/c rooms with en suites and balconies in a medium-sized resort hotel on the road to the airport. Large pool and wonderful views from the upper deck in the public area.
B-C Vela Branca, R Dr Antonio Ricaldi, Cidade Alta, T073-3288 2318, www.vela branca.com.br. Enormous family resort with 2 pools, 4 tennis court and anonymous package hotels rooms catering to groups from Brazil and Europe. Cheapest rates online or with groups. Some way out of town on the beach.

C Solar da Praça, R Assis Chateaubriand 75, Passarela do Álcool, Centro, T073-3288 2585, www.pousadasolardapraca.com. Pretty little renovated colonial town house with a range of basic but well-kept rooms dominated by a bed. Some with a/c and en suites in an adjacent annexe. Opt for those on the upper floors as they are less musty. The staff can organize excursions.
C-D Hotel Navegantes, Av 22 de Abril 212, T073-3288 2390, www.portonet.com.br/ navegantes. Simple, plain white wall and tile floor a/c rooms, with en suites and TVs, crowding over a little pool and concrete deck in the centre of town.
C-D Pousada dos Raizes, Praça dos Pataxós 196, T/F073-3288 4717, pousadaraizes@ hotmail.com.br. Well-kept unpretentious city hotel with helpful staff. Cheaper without breakfast. Recommended.
C-F Albergue Porto Seguro, R Cova da Moça 720, T073-3288 1742, www.porto segurohostel.com.br. IYHA hostel. Cheaper prices per person in dorms. Smart little hostel in the centre of town with internet, excursions and discount rates at their sister beach hotel on Praia Taberapuan north of town.

Camping
Camping Mundaí Praia, 5 km north of the town centre, T073-3679 2287, www.camping mundai.com.br. Great-value beachside camping sites with power, restaurant/ snack bars. There are plans to construct chalets; phone ahead to check.

Tabapiri Country, BR-367, Km 61.5, next to the *rodoviária* on the road leading to the Cidade Histórica, T073-3288 2269.

Santa Cruz Cabrália *p449*
L Toca do Marlin, Estr BA-001, Km 40.5, Santo André, T073-3671 5009, ww.tocadomarlin.com.br. One of the most luxurious beach resorts in South America, with spacious a/c *cabañas* next to a ranch overlooking a quiet, beautiful beach some 50 km north of Porto Seguro. Excellent food and excursions.
A-B Baía Cabrália, R Sidrack de Carvalho 141, centro, T/F073-3282 1111, www.baiaca bralia.com.br. Medium-size family resort with a large pool, sauna and gym.
B-C Victor Hugo, Villa de Santo André, Km 3, Santa Cruz Cabrália, T073-3671 4064, www.portonet.com.br/victorhugo. Smart, tastefully decorated little *pousada* right on the beach. Rooms are plain and scrupulously clean, with whitewashed walls and dark wood floors.
C Pousada do Mineiro, T073-3282 1042. A/c rooms around a pool and with a sauna, friendly staff and a *churrascaria* barbecue. Recommended.
C Tribo da Praia, Av Beira de Santo André, T073-3282 1620. *Pousada* with a helpful American owner.

Arraial da Ajuda *p450, map p452*
At busy times such as New Year's Eve and Carnaval, don't expect to find anything under US$15 per person in a shared room, with a minimum stay of 5-7 days.
A Pousada Pitinga, Praia Pitinga, T073-3575 1067, www.pousadapitinga.com.br. Wooden chalets in a coconut-filled rainforest garden on a hill overlooking the sea. Tranquil atmosphere, great food and a pool. A member of the **Roteiros de Charme** group, see page 43. Recommended.
A-C Pousada Canto d'Alvorada, on the road to the Arraial d'Ajuda ferry, T073-3575 1218, www.cantodalvorada.com.br. Cheaper out of season. Pretty, Swiss-run *pousada* facing the beach on the edge of town

with 21 cabins, a restaurant, pool, sauna and laundry facilities.
A-C Quinta do Porto, Ponta do Apaga Fogo 1, T073-3575 1022, www.quintadoporto.com.br. Rooms in long corridors above a smart pool set in tropical gardens right on the river opposite Porto Seguro. Convenient for both Arraial and Porto towns (*combis* from Porto every 10 mins, ferries from Porto every 15 mins), and with an excellent travel agencies for onward excursions. The beach is 10-15 mins' walk.
C O Cantinho, Praça São Bras, T073-3575 1131, www.pousadacantinho.com.br. Terraces of smart a/c and fan-cooled rooms around a fruit tree garden courtyard. Excellent breakfast, pleasant public areas and off-season discounts.
C Pousada do Roballo, Estr do Mucugê, T073-3575 1053, www.pousadado roballo.com.br. Welcoming *pousada* with a set of small rooms, each with a tiny hammock-hung veranda. Set in pleasant garden surroundings and with a pool.
C Pousada Erva Doce, Estr do Mucugê 200, T073-3575 1113, www.ervadoce.com.br. Well-appointed chalets and a decent restaurant, set in a lawned garden and with a pool.
C Pousada Mar Aberto, Estr do Mucugê 554, T/F073-3575 1153, Pretty little *pousada* with brick chalets set on the crest of a hill and set in lush gardens close to Mucugê beach and the centre. With a pool. At the lower end of the price category.
C Pousada Tubarão, R Bela Vista, beyond the church on the right, T073-3575 1086, www.tubarao.arraialdajuda.com. With sweeping views of the sea, a cool sea breeze and a reasonable restaurant.
C Sole Mio, T073-3575 1115, just off the beach road leading from the ferry to Arraial. French owners, English spoken, laid-back with 4 chalets and an excellent pizzeria.
D Pousada do Mel, Praça São Bras. Simple but clean and with a good breakfast. Recommended.
D Pousada Flamboyant, Estr do Mucugê, T089-3875 1025. Rooms arranged around a little courtyard. Good breakfast and a pool.

E-F Arraial Hostel, R do Campo 94, T073-3575 1192/1998, www.arraial dajudahostel.com.br. Price per person. Smart well equipped modern backpacker hostel with IYHA discount in a large and colourful little house on the edge of town. Good facilities include a pool, bar, internet and book exchange.

Trancoso *p452*

LL Villas de Trancoso, Estr Arraial D'Ajuda, T073-3668 1151, www.mybrazilianbeach.com. A series of luxurious cabins gathered on a lawn next to a pool and a relaxed bar and rustic wood-weight gym area on the adjacent beach. The duplex suite is perhaps the most luxurious in the town. American-run and owned and with a Californian feel. Can be hot as there isn't much shade.

L Etnia, R Principal, T073-3668 1137, www.etniabrasil.com.br. This captivating eco-chic *pousada* a stroll from the Quadrado is a glossy magazine favourite, with a series of elegant and individually style bungalows gathered around a lush designer pool and set in a tropical forest garden filled with brilliantly coloured birds and butterflies. Run with *gaúcho* and Italian style, panache and efficiency.

L-AL Mata N'ativa Pousada, Estr Velha do Arraial s/n (next to the river on the way to the beach), T073-3668 1830, www.matanativa pousada.com.br. The best in town for nature

lovers and those seeking a quiet, relaxed retreat. A series of elegant and romantic cabins are set in a lovingly maintained orchid and heliconia garden by the riverside, which is a good few degrees cooler than anywhere else in Trancoso in the heat of the day. Nothing is too much trouble for the warm-hearted owners Daniel and Daniela. Both are knowledgeable about flora and fauna in the *Mata Atlântica* rainforest and can organize wildlife or birdwatching excursions. Good English, Spanish and Italian. Great breakfast. See also page 14 of the colour section.

A Capim Santo, to the left of the main square, T073-3668 1122, www.capim santo.com.br. Friendly, beautifully designed little *pousada* right on the edge of Quadrado and with a series of well-appointed rustic chic rooms and cabins. The restaurant is one of the best and most romantic in town. Superb breakfasts and dinners.

B Pousada Calypso, Parque Municipal, T073-3668 1113, www.pousadacalypso.com.br. Comfortable, spacious rooms, jacuzzis, a library and sitting area and helpful staff who speak German and English. Just off the Quadrado.

C Pousada Quarto Crescente, R Principal, T073-3668 1014, www.quartocrescente.net. About 500 m inland, away from main square, on the main road to the beach. With cooking facilities, laundry and helpful owners who speak English, German, Dutch and Spanish. Map, bus times and directions on the website.

Caraíva p454

AL-A Vila do Mar, R 12 de Outubro s/n, T073-3668 5111, www.pousadavila domar.com.br. The plushest hotel in town, with spacious, stylish airy, wooden *cabañas* overlooking the beach set on a lawn around an adult and children's pool.

B-C Bar Pousada Varandão, on the ridge above the hill on the northern bank of the river, T073-9199 4563, varandaocaraiva@ yahoo.com.br. Rooms in a big house for up to 10 people (**E** per person) and a suite for a couple. Superb views. With breakfast.

C Pousada Flor do Mar, R 12 de Outubro s/n, Caraiva, on the beach, T073-9985 1608, www.caraiva.tur.br/flordomar. Charming beachfront *pousada* with airy rooms with a view – the best right at the beachfront.

Corumbau p454

LL Fazenda São Francisco, T011-3078 4411, www.corumbau.com.br. Spacious, well-appointed hard wood and cream cabins gathered around a pool in a palm-shaded garden 5 mins' walk from the beach.

LL Tauana, T073-3668 5172, www.tauana.com. Currently the finest small luxury beach hotel in Brazil, with a series of huge and beautifully appointed mock indigenous cabins overlooking a secluded beach. Perfect for a honeymoon or intimate break.

LL Vila Naia, T011-3061 1872, www.vilanaia.com.br. Tastefully appointed, luxurious bungalows set in a little garden back from the beach. Very popular with fashionable Paulistanos. Intimate and romantic but not of the same standard as Tauana.

D Pousada Corumbau, Corumbau s/n, no phone. Very simple and right on the beach front. Corumbau is only a collection of houses so it is easy to find. Rooms are fan-cooled.

Cumuruxatiba p455

B-C Vereda Tropical, Av Beira Mar s/n, T073-3573 1070, www.pousadavere datropical.com.br. A series of terracotta-roofed apartments in a little garden right in front of the beach. The lime green rooms

have tiled floors, pretty palm-frond lamps and a small veranda with wooden chairs. Rooms have queen-sized beds, mosquito nets and a/c. Book ahead for chalets close to the sea.

C Pousada Axé, Av Beira Mar 1030, T073-3573 1030, www.pousadaaxe.com.br. 20 beachside chalets gathered around a pool. Generous breakfast and friendly service.

C-D Pousada Urupê, Estrada rural s/n, Cumuruxatiba, T073-3573 1444. Plain white-wall and tile rooms with bathrooms in a mock colonial building next to the Rio do Peixe Pequeno at the Corumbau end of town.

E Aleksandro, Av 13 Maio s/n, T073-3573 1050, www.portonet.com.br/aleksandro. A very simple space a block from the beach with fan-cooled rooms in a wind next to a garden. Cool even in the heat of the day.

Prado p455

A-B Ilha da Alegria, Prado, T073-3021 1111, www.ilhadaalegria.com.br. A large family-orientated resort on an island 10 mins' downstream from Prado town centre, and reached via the river docks. Functional, plain rooms are in a series of annexes gathered around an artificial lake and there is a big pool and water park area (with slides) for children. Excursions include trips on the river and to local beaches and tours to the Abrolhos islands.

C Casa de Maria, R Seis, Novo Prado, Prado, T073-3298 1425, www.casademaria.com.br. Annexes of rooms in a 2-storey building built around a pool near the beach. Abrolhos excursions organized. Claims to serve the best breakfast in southern Bahia.

C Novo Prado, Praia Novo Prado, Prado, T073-3298 1455, www.novoprado.com.br. Pleasant beachside *pousada* near the town centre, with colourful rooms, airy public areas, a little library, sauna and pool and a range of a/c and fan-cooled rooms.

C-D Abaetê, R IV, lote 35, Novo Prado, T073-3298 1611, www.portonet.com.br/ abaete. Modest tiled, a/c en suites dominated by a double bed and with a little fridge and a/c. All overlook a concrete deck and pool and the hotel is a block from the town beach at the north end of the city. There are many other options nearby, including the slightly cheaper **D Vivenda da Praia**, next door.

Caravelas *p456*

B Marina Porto Abrolhos, R da Baleia, 5 km outside of the town at the port from where boats leave for the Abrolhos islands, T073-3674 1060, www.marinaportoabrolhos.com.br. One of the most comfortable hotels in town with a range of individual and family suites housed in faux-Polynesian chalets and gathered in a palm-tree garden around a large pool. Activities include trips to the Abrolhos.

C Pousada Liberdade, Av Ministro Adalicio Nogueira 1551, Caravelas, T073-3297 2076, www.pousadaliberdade.com.br. Spacious but simple chalets in a large, lawned garden area next to a lake and just outside the town centre. Excursion organized to the Abrolhos islands.

C-D Pousada dos Navegantes, R das Palmeiras 45, Centre, T073-3297 1830, www.pousadanavegantes.com.br. Simple *pousada* with a pool near the beach organizing tours to the Abrolohos, dive excursions and dive certification. Friendly and helpful.

🍴 Eating

Porto Seguro *p447, map p448*

🍴 **Sambuca**, Praça Pataxós 216, T073-3288 2366. Right next to the ferry port to Arraial. Varied à la carte menu and decent wood-oven cooked pizzas.

🍴-🍴 **Portinha**, R Saldanha Marinho 33, T073-3288 2743. The most popular buffet in Porto with a huge choice of hot and cold dishes and juices for lunch and dinner and great deserts. A very popular meeting point, Always busy and buzzing with people.

🍴 **Da Japonêsa**, Praça Pataxós 38. Open 0800-2300. Excellent value with a varied Brazilian and Japanese menu. Recommended.

Arraial da Ajuda *p450, map p452*

Food in Arraial is pricey and restaurants tend to look better than the dishes they serve. There are numerous *barracas* selling simple seafood, juices and beer on Mucugê beach, as well as the popular **Barraca de Pitinga** and **Barraca do Genésio** on Pitinga beach.

🍴🍴🍴 **Don Fabrizio**, Estrada do Mucugê 402, T073-3575 1123. The best Italian in town, in an upmarket open air-restaurant with live music and reasonable wine.

🍴🍴🍴 **Manguti**, Estrada do Mucugê, T073-3575 2270, www.manguti.com.br. Reputedly the best in town, though the food looks like mutton dressed as lamb. Meat, pasta, fish served as comfort food alongside other Brazilian dishes. Very popular and informal.

🍴🍴 **Nipo**, Estrada do Mucugê 250, T073-3575 3033. Reasonably priced but decent Japanese with hotel delivery.

🍴🍴 **Pizzaria do Arraial**, Praça São Bras 28. Basic pizzeria and and popular pay-by-weight restaurant.

🍴 **Paulinho Pescador**, R São Bras 116. Open 1200-2200. Excellent seafood, also chicken and meat, one price (US$6), English spoken, good service. *Bobó de camarão* highly recommended. Very popular, there are often queues for tables.

Trancoso *p452*

Food in Trancoso is expensive. Those on a tight budget should shop at the supermarket between the main square and the new part of town. There are many fish restaurants in the *barracas* on the beach. Elba Ramalho, when in town, gigs at her restaurant, **Para Raio**.

🍴🍴🍴 **Cacão**, Quadrado 96, T073-3668 1296. The restaurant of choice for those who want to eat Bahian in Trancoso. The menu is strong on flavour and spices which includes starters like mini *acarajé* balls with *vatapá* or *caruru* and mains like *camarão nativo* (local prawns), served twitchingly fresh.

🍴🍴🍴 **Capim Santo**, R de Beco 55, Quadrado, T073-3668 4112, www.capimsanto.com.br. Paulistana ex-pat Sandra Marques' cooking is quintessentially Trancoso. Seafood dishes with a Bahian twist like prawn in manioc flour balls or tuna carpaccio are served under the stars by candlelight in a little tropical garden just off the Quadrado. Be sure to begin the evening with a *caipisake com abacaxi e gengibre* (sake with crushed ice, fresh crushed pineapple and root ginger).

¶¶¶ Japaiano, Quadrado 1, in the **Hotel da Praça**. A Brazilian-Asian fusion menu created by Rio's hot young kitchen maverick Felipe Bronze who learnt his trade at **Le Bernardin** and **Nobu** in New York and his name at **Zuka** and **Z Contemporâneo** in Rio. Dishes include *moqueca de camarões e lulas com curry verde tailandês* (prawn and squid *moqueca* with a green Thai curry sauce).

¶¶¶ Maritaca, Quadrado, T073-3668 1258. A Marrakech theme may seem odd in hippy-chic Trancoso. But the sumptuous back deck at this new restaurant – with its open sky and beautiful drop-off view out to the sea – attracts a faithful cocktail crowd. The Italian food is adequate but lacks sparkle; slow service.

¶¶ Barraca Do Andrea, Coqueiros beach. The most fashionable place to sip and sun. Run by a Sardinian who serves great Italian wood-fired pizza, super-fresh ceviche and a gamut of fruity *caipirinhas* and tropical juices.

¶¶ Laila, in the new shopping area just before the main square. Elegant little restaurant serving good Moroccan and Lebanese food.

¶ Dona Maria. This joyful old lady and and her 9-year-old grandson sell delicious home-baked bread, tiny prawn, chicken *empadas* (meat pies) and steaming hot treacle-sweet black coffee to fishermen (or visiting surfers) who rise with the sun. You can find them before 0900 on a tiny little tile stall on the Quadrado in front of the Ainarí boutique.

¶ Portinha, Quadrado. Good-value pay-by-weight options and a wealth of juices.

🍷 Bars and clubs

Arraial da Ajuda *p450, map p452*
Porto Seguro does not have much in the way of nightlife; most visitors stay in Arraial across the water. In Arraial, the *lambada* is danced at the **Jatobar** bar (in summer), by the church on the main square (opens 2300, *pensão* at the back is cheap, clean and friendly). **Limelight** has raves all year round. Many top Brazilian bands play at the beach clubs at **Praia do Parracho** in summer, entry is about US$20. Entry to other beach parties is about US$10.

🥾 Activities and tours

Arraial da Ajuda *p450, map p452*
Portomondo, Ponta do Apaga Fogo 1, Marina Quinta do Porto Hotel, T073-3575 3686, www.portomondo.com. The best operator in southern Bahia with tours from around Trancoso, Caraíva and Corumbau to Monte Pascoal and Abrolhos. Excellent diving and ecotourism itineraries and car or helicopter transfers to hotels in Trancoso and further south.

Trancoso *p452*
Joácio, T073-3668 1270, or ask at Bouganvillea restaurant on the main square. Good day trips to Espelho Beach, Caraíva and other beaches and forested areas in the area. Expect to pay US$10-15 per person depending on group size and distance.

Parque Nacional Marinho dos Abrolhos *p456*
See also Ins and outs, page 457. All-inclusive trips from Porto Seguro can be arranged with **Portomondo** (see above). From Caravelas, book with **Abrolhos Turismo**, Praça Dr Emílio Imbassay 8, T073-3297 1149, www.abrolhosturismo.com.br or **Catamarã Veleiro Sanuk**, T073-3297 1344, www.catamarasanuk.cjb.net.

⊙ Transport

Porto Seguro *p447, map p448*
Air Taxi to airport (T073-3288 1880), US$15. Flights to **Belo Horizonte**, **Rio de Janeiro**, **Salvador**, **São Paulo** and **Ilhéus** in high season with **GOL**, www.voegol.com.br, **Tam**, www.tam.com.br, and **Webjet**, www.webjet.com.br.

Boat Boats cross the river to **Arraial da Ajuda** on the south bank, 5 mins, US$1 for foot passengers, US$5 for cars, every 15-30 mins day and night.

Bus At Brazilian holiday times, all transport should be booked well in advance. **Expresso Brasileiro** buses run from Praça dos Pataxós along the BR-367 stopping at the beaches north of town. Buses for **Caraíva** go via Eunápolis and Itabela (leaving Eunápolis at 1330, 2 hrs), or from Arraial D'Ajuda, via Trancoso daily at 0700 and 1600, extra bus at 1100 in high season (**Viação Águia**

Azul, T073-3875 1170). To **Eunápolis**, 1 hr, US$5, very frequent. To **Curumuxatiba**, **Prado** and destinations further south, take a bus to Eunápolis, Texeira de Freitas or Itamaraju and an onward bus from there. For **Caraíva** bus leaves at 0700, 1330 (high season) and 1500 (via Trancoso). To **Trancoso**, 2 daily buses, but easier to take the ferry to Arraial and catch one of the more frequent buses or *combis* from there. Other services via Eunápolis (those going north avoid Salvador) or Itabuna (5 hrs, US$25).

To **Rio de Janeiro**, daily, direct, 1745, US$80, *leito* US$70 (São Geraldo), 18 hrs (very cold a/c, take warm clothes); or take the 1800 to Ilhéus and change at Eunápolis. To **Belo Horizonte**, daily, direct, US$80 (São Geraldo). To **São Paulo** direct, 1045, 25 hrs, not advisable, very slow; much better to go to Rio then take the Rio–São Paulo express. To **Salvador** (Águia Branca), daily, 12 hrs, US$80. To **Vitória**, daily, 11 hrs, US$60. To **Ilhéus**, daily 0730, 4½ hrs, US$45.

Car hire Several companies at the airport, including **Localiza**, T073-3288 1488 (and R Cova da Moça 620, T073-3288 1488) and **Nacional**, T073-3288 4291.

Cycle hire Oficina de Bicicleta, Av Getúlio Vargas e R São Pedro, US$15 for 24 hrs; also at Praça de Bandeira and at 2 de Julho 242.

Arraial da Ajuda *p450, map p452*
Ferry Take a bus or *combi* to Rio Buranhém, from where boats cross the river to **Porto Seguro**, on the north bank, 5 mins, US$1 for foot passengers, US$5 for cars, every 15-30 mins day and night.

Trancoso *p452*
Bus Buses run regularly on the newly paved road between **Porto Seguro**, **Arraial d'Ajuda** and **Trancoso**, at least every hour from Arraial in high season. To Porto Seguro

US\$4, to Ajuda US\$2.40. Arriving from the south, change buses at Eunápolis from where the newly paved Linha Verde road runs to Trancoso. Buses for **Caraíva** leave twice daily at 0800 and 1700, with an extra bus at 1200 in high season.

Caraíva *p454*

Access roads are poor and almost impossible after heavy rain. **Aguia Azul** buses run to **Porto Seguro** twice daily (3 times in high season), along a very poor dirt road involving a river crossing. If heading south, take a bus to **Itabela** or **Eunápolis** (0600, 3 hrs).

Parque Nacional de Monte Pascoal *p454*

To **Caraíva** there is a river crossing by boats which are always on hand. There is one bus a day Mo-Fri to **Itamaraju**, 16 km to the south.

Corumbau *p454*

Beach buggy taxis take you to the river crossing (US\$40) to **Caraiva**, or it's about a 10-km walk. The punt ferry across the river costs around \$10. Buses run to **Itmaraju** and beyond to **Curumuxatiba**.

Cumuruxatiba *p455*

There are 3 daily buses to **Prado** and **Itamaraju** and a bus every other day direct to **Porto Seguro**. One bus a day to **Corumbau** via Itamaraju.

Prado *p455*

Frequent buses to **Itamaraju**, 3 daily to **Curumuxatiba** and **Caravleas** (via Alcobaça).

Caravelas *p456*

Air There are flights to **Belo Horizonte**, **São Paulo** and **Salvador**. Another option is to fly via **Porto Seguro**.

Bus Caravelas is well connected, with buses to **Texeira de Freitas** (4 a day), **Salvador**, **Nanuque**, **Itamaraju** and **Prado**.

ⓘ Directory

Porto Seguro *p447, map p448*
Banks Agência do Descobrimento, Av Getúlio Vargas, also arranges flight tickets and house rental. Banco do Brasil, Av Beira Mar, 1000-1500, changes TCs and US\$ cash, also Visa ATMs. Also at airport. Bradesco, Av Getulio Vargas, Visa ATMs. Deltur, in the new shopping centre, near Banco do Brasil. **Internet** Dotted throughout town. **Laundry** New Porto, Shopping Av, daily 0900-2230, priced per item. **Post office** In the mini-shopping centre on the corner of R das Jandaias and Av dos Navegantes. **Telephone** Shopping Av, daily 0700-2300, corner of Av dos Navegantes and Av Beira Mar, also at Praça dos Pataxós, beside ferry terminal. Daily 0700-2200, cheap rates after 2000, receives and holds faxes, F073-3288 3915.

Arraial da Ajuda *p450, map p452*
Banks There is a Banco do Brasil with a *câmbio* and ATM in the small shopping centre on Estrada do Mucugê. Several bars on Broadway change US\$ cash, but rates are poor. **Internet** Dotted throughout town. **Post office** Praça São Bras. **Telephone** Telemar on the main square. Daily 0800-2200, number for receiving faxes is F073-875 1309, US\$1.

Trancoso *p452*
Banks Banco do Brasil ATM which only sometimes works with international Visa cards. Best to bring cash from Arraial. Most places accept TCs. **Internet** Several on the main square.

Prado *p455*
Banks There is a Bradesco with ATM in the town centre.

Caravelas *p456*
Banks The Banco do Brasil, Praça Dr Imbassahi, does not change money but has an ATM. There is also a Bradesco.

Linha Verde and the northern coast

Heading north from Salvador airport, the BA-099 coast road, or Estrada de Coco (Coconut Highway), passes many coconut plantations and 50 km of beautiful beaches. From south to north the best known are Ipitanga (famous for its reefs), Buraquinho, Jauá, Arembepe, Guarajuba, Itacimirim, Castelo Garcia D'Ávila (where there is a 16th-century fort) and Forte. North of the smart mini-resort town of Praia do Forte, the road is called the 'Linha Verde' (Green Line), which runs for 142 km to the Sergipe state border. The road is more scenic than the BR-101, especially near Conde.

Linha Verde

There are very few hotels or pousadas in the more remote villages. Among the most picturesque are Subaúma and Baixio; the latter, where the Rio Inhambupe meets the sea, is very beautiful. Buses serve most of these destinations. ➤➤ *For listings, see pages 466-468.*

Arembepe → *Colour map 4, A6. Phone code: 071.*
Some 45 km north of Salvador, this former fishing village is now a quiet resort. There is an 'alternative' village of palm huts, 30 minutes' walk along the beach, behind the sand dunes, with a café and swimming. The best beaches are 2 km north of town. A music festival is held on the following Carnaval celebrations.

Praia do Forte → *Colour map 4, A6. Phone code: 071.*
Some 80 km north of Salvador, is this pleasant mini resort town much beloved of wealthy people from Salvador. Praia may no longer be a fishing village but it still feels low key. Aside from the town's main street, Alameda do Sol, most of the streets aresand. Much of the area around the town is protected, with turtle-nesting beaches, remnant coastal *restinga* forest, and a small area of marshland, which is home to a large number of birds, caymans and other animals. Birdwatching trips on the Pantanal wetlands, which is home to many species of wading birds, spectacled caiman and capbybara, are rewarding and can be organized through the town's large-scale 'eco' resort.

The **Projeto Tamar** ⓘ *Caixa Postal 2219, Rio Vermelho, Salvador, Bahia, T071-3876 1045, www.tamar.org.br,* is a national project that studies and preserves the sea turtles that lay their eggs in the area. Praia do Forte is the headquarters of the **national turtle preservation programme** and is funded by the Worldwide Fund for Nature. There is a visitor centre at the project (US$1.50 for turtle sanctuary). The coast here is ideal for windsurfing and sailing, owing to constant fresh Atlantic breezes.

Praia do Forte takes its name from the castle built by a Portuguese settler, Garcia D'Avila, in 1556, to warn the city to the south of enemy invasion. He was given a huge area of land, from Praia do Forte to Maranhão, on which he made the first farm in Brazil. He brought the first herd of cattle to the country, cleared the virgin Atlantic forest and brought the first coconut and mango trees to Brazil.

Imbassaí → Colour map 4, A6. Phone code: 071.

About 14 km from Praia do Forte is the simple village of Imbassaí, which has a beach at the mouth of the Rio Barroso. Other nearby beaches are **Praia de Santo Antônio**, 4 km away, with sand dunes and a small fishing village, and **Porto Sauípe**, 22 km north, which has recently been transformed into an ugly and old-fashioned mega-resort modelled on those which infected southern Spain in the 1980s. It caters almost exclusively to the worst kind of national and international package tourism.

Sítio do Conde → Colour map 2, C5. Phone code: 075.

Situated on the coast, 6 km from Conde, Sítio do Conde is a site for **Projeto Tamar** (see Praia do Forte, page 465). The beaches are not very good but its an ideal base to explore other beaches at **Barra do Itariri**, 12 km south, at the mouth of a river, and has fine sunsets. The road passes unspoilt beaches; the best are **Corre Nu** and **Jacaré**. You can also go to **Seribinha**, 13 km north of Sítio do Conde. The road goes along the beach through coconut groves and mangroves; at Seribinha are beach huts serving cool drinks or food.

Mangue Seco → Colour map 2, C5. Phone code: 075.

The last stop on the Linha Verde is Mangue Seco. The town was immortalized in Jorge Amado's book *Tieta*. A steep hill rises behind the village to white-sand dunes that offer superb views of the coast. The encroaching dunes have caused the mangrove to dry up.

The peninsula is connected to Pontal in the state of Sergipe by boat or canoe on the Rio Real (10-minute crossing). Buses run between Pontal and Estancia twice a day. The ferry across the river usually leaves before 1000 in the morning. A private launch will cost US$10, but it is usually possible to find someone to share the ride and cost.

◉ Linha Verde and the northern coast listings

For Sleeping and Eating price codes and other relevant information, see pages 42-47.

● Sleeping

Arembepe p465

B-C Arembepe Refúgio Ecológico, Estr Aldeia Hippie, T071-3624 1031, www.aldeia arembepe.com.br. 11 well-appointed a/c chalets around a pool in a protected area by the **Tamar** turtle project. Very peaceful.
C-D Gipsy, R Eduardo Pinto, Km 3, T071-3624 3266, www.gipsy.com.br. 40-room hotel with a/c rooms and a pool.

Praia do Forte p465

The town's main street had its name changed from Alameda do Sol to **Av ACM**. This street doesn't have numbers marked, so you just have to walk along to find your hotel.

Prices rise steeply in the summer season. It may be difficult to find very cheap places to stay.

LL-AL Praia do Forte Eco-Resort, Av do Farol, T071-3676 4000, www.praiado forte.com. Large-scale family resort set in tropical gardens on the beach and with programmes to visit the nearby protected areas. Room are spacious, well appointed and comfortable. Service, which includes a spa and entertainment, is excellent. Beautiful pool.

L-AL Aloha Brasil Pousada, R da Aurora, T071-3676 0279, www.pousadaaloha brasil.com.br. Relaxing tropical garden and pool. Rooms are not big but are charming with king-sized beds and verandas.

L-AL Porto Zarpa Hotel, R da Aurora, T071-3676 1414, www.portozarpa.com.br. Large 2-storey building surrounded by garden, close to the beach, cable TV, parking, pool, good for families.

AL-A Sobrado da Vila, Av ACM, T/F071-3676 1088, www.sobradoda vila.com.br. The best in the village itself with a range of individually decorated rooms with balconies and a good-value restaurant, convenient for the town.

A Ogum Marinho, Av ACM, T071-3676 1165, www.ogummarinho.com.br. A/c, cheaper with fan, nice little courtyard garden, good restaurant and service. It has an art gallery with work by Brazilian artists.

A-B Pousada Casa de Praia, Praça dos Artistas 08-09, T071-3676 1362, www.casadepraia.tur.br. Good value and location, rooms with and without a/c, popular.

B-C Pousada João Sol, R da Corvina, T071-3676 1054, www.pousadajoaosol.com.br. 6 well-appointed and newly refurbished chalets. The owner speaks English, Spanish and German. Great breakfast.

C Pousada Tatuapara, Praça dos Artistas 1, T071-3676 1466, www.tatuapara.com.br. Spacious and well-maintained, fan, fridge. Good breakfast. Recently refurbished. Pool.

D Pousada Tia Helena, just east of Praça dos Artistas, at Alameda das Estrelas, T071-3676 1198, T071-9901 2894 (mob), www.tiahelenapraiadoforte.com.br. Helena, the motherly proprietor provides an enormous breakfast, simple rooms. Recently refurbished reductions for 3-day stays.

E Albergue da Juventude, Praia do Forte, R da Aurora 3, T071-3676 1094, www.albergue.com.br. Price per person. Smart youth hostel with decent shared rooms and rooms with en suites (**B-C**), a large breakfast, fan, kitchen and shop, cheaper for HI members.

Imbassaí p466

B Pousada Caminho do Mar, T/F071-3832 2499. Bungalows with a/c, restaurant, German-run.

B Pousada Imbassaí, T/F071-3876 1313. A/c chalets and apartments.

C Pousada Lagoa da Pedra, T071-3248 5914. Chalets set in large grounds, some English spoken, friendly.

D Pousada Anzol de Ouro, T071-3322 4422. Modest fan-cooled chalets around a simple pool.

Sítio do Conde p466

A Hotel Praia do Conde, T075-3429 1129 (in Salvador T071-3321 2542). Smart a/c chalets with en suites around a pool.

C Pousada Oasis, T075-3421 2397. Very simple, plain accommodation either fan-cooled or a/c rooms. With breakfast.

Mangue Seco p466

There are plenty of small cheap places along the seafront from the jetty, none with addresses or phone numbers (the village is tiny). There are simple restaurants around the main square next to the church. The beach has a handful of *barracas* serving cheap fish.

B-C Asa Branca, T075-3445 9054, www.infonet.com.br/asabranca. The plushest in town with a range of simple a/c rooms in terraces overlooking a rectangular pool. Good restaurant.

🍴 Eating

Arembepe p465
🍴 **Mar Aberto**, Largo de São Francisco 43, T071-3824 1257. Good seafood with a French twist.

Praia do Forte p465
🍴 **Bar Do Souza**, Av do Sol, on the right as you enter the village. Best seafood in town, open daily, live music at weekends. Recommended.
🍴 **O Europeu**, Av ACM, T071-3676 0232. Anglo-Brazilian owned, with the most adventurous menu in town with well-prepared homely dishes. The owners, William and Vera, are very friendly and knowledgeable about the area. Recommended.
🍴 **Restaurante Casa da Nati**, Av ACM, T071-3676 1239. Per kilo and Bahian food from a Praia do Forte native.
🍴 **Restaurante Point do Ivan**, Av ACM, T071-9997 1711. Bahian food, good *moqueca*, *bobo de camarco* and cheap *prato feito*.
🍴 **Café Tango**, Av ACM, T071-3676 1637. Pleasant open-air tea and coffee bar with great pastries and cakes.

🛍 Shopping

Praia do Forte p465
Galeria de Arte Claudia Ferraris, Alameda das Estrelas, T071-9125 1191 or T071-9165 8325, www.claudiaferraris.com. Incredible European-born artist who paints small capoeira pictures that beautifully capture the movement and colour of the martial art dance.
Joia Rara, Av ACM, T071-3676 1503. Tailor-made jewellery using Brazilian precious stones set in white gold, gold or silver. The client chooses the stone which is then polished. These include Bahian emeralds, aquamarines, tourmalines and amethysts, The shop doubles up as the artists studio. Authentic and good value.
Nativa, Av ACM, T071-3676 0437. Artisan clothing from Brazils northeast region. Beautiful hand work embroidered shirts, skirts, and bags. Quite chic and unusual.

▲ Activities and tours

Praia do Forte p465
Tour operators
Praia do Forte is ideal for windsurfing and sailing owing to constant fresh Atlantic breezes.
Odara Turismo, in the EcoResort Hotel, T071-3676 1080. Imaginative tours to surrounding areas and outlying villages and beaches using 4WD vehicles. They are very friendly and informative. Recommended. The owners, Norbert and Papy, speak English and German.

🚍 Transport

Arembepe p465
Bus To the Terminal Francês in **Salvador**, every 2 hrs, 1 hr, US$5, last bus at 1800. Buses also run to **Itapoã**.

Praia do Forte p465
Bus It is easy to flag down buses from the crossroads on the main highway out of town. To get there take a *combi* (every 15 mins, US$0.25) from town. Taxis are a rip-off. To **Salvador** buses run 5 times daily, 1 hr, US$2 (**Santa Maria/Catuense**). To **Estancia** in Sergipe, 4-5 daily, US$5.

Sítio do Conde p466
Bus To **Salvador** with **São Luís**, T071-3358 4582, 3 a day, 4 on Fri, US$7.25.

Chapada Diamantina and the sertão

The beautiful Chapada Diamantina national park comprises a series of escarpments covered in cerrado, caatinga and moist tropical forest, dripping with waterfalls and studded with caves. It is one of the highlights of inland Bahia. Although little of the forest is original, there is still plenty of wildlife including jaguar and maned wolf, and the area is good for birdwatching. Various trails cut through the park offering walks from a few hours to a few days, and many leave from the little colonial mining town of Lençóis, the ideal base for visiting the region.

The road from Salvador to Lençóis and the chapada passes through Feira de Santana, famous for its Micareta, an extremely popular out-of-season carnival. The harsh beauty of the sertão and its hospitable people are the reward for those wanting to get off the beaten track. The region has been scarred by droughts and a violent history of bandits, rebellions and religious leaders. Euclides da Cunha and Canudos are good places to start exploring this history. The Raso da Catarina, once a hiding place for Lampião, and the impressive Paulo Afonso waterfalls, can both be visited from the town of Paulo Afonso located on the banks of the São Francisco. This important river runs through the sertão, linking agricultural settlements such as Juazeiro, Ibotirama and Bom Jesus da Lapa and has its headwaters in northern Minas Gerais. ➤➤ For listings, see pages 476-478.

Lençóis and around ⊜⊘⊘⊙⚠⊙⊙ ➤➤ pp476-478. Colour map 4, A5.

➔ *Phone code: 075. Population: 9000.*

Lençóis is the best place from which to explore the *chapada*. It's a pretty little colonial village set on the banks of the fast-flowing Rio Lençóis, in the middle of the park. Many of the sights can be visited on foot from town. Lençóis was established as a mining town in 1844 and takes its name from the tents assembled by the prospectors who first arrived here (*lençóis* means 'white sheets' in Portuguese) set on the brown and green of the hillside. While there are still some *garimpeiros* (gold and diamond prospectors) left, tourism is now the main economic mainstay. Rather than precious metals, visitors are attracted by the cool climate, the relaxed atmosphere and the wonderful trekking in the Diamantina hills. The streets of Lençóis are lined with rustic houses, many of which are now *pousadas*, restaurants or shops selling quirky handicrafts and semi-precious stones.

Ins and outs   The **airport** ⓘ *20 km from town, Km 209, BR-242, T075-3625 8100*, receives air taxis but no scheduled flights, although TAM ostensibly has plans to begin services in 2009/2010. There are direct buses from Salvador and other cities in Bahia via Feira de Santana. Buses from Recife and the northeast come via Seabra, west of Lençóis. There is a tourist office, **Sectur**, inside the market next to the river.

Excursions from Lençóis

On walking trips from Lençóis it is possible to visit the *serrano* (in the hills above town), which has wonderful natural pools in the river bed, which give a great spring-water massage when you sit under them; or the **Salão de Areia**, where the coloured sands for the bottle paintings come from. **Ribeirão do Meio** is a 45-minute walk from town; here locals slide down a long natural water chute into a big pool (it is best to watch someone else first and take something to slide in). Also near Lençóis are two very pretty waterfalls: the **Cachoeira da Primavera**; and the **Cachoeira Sossego**, a calendar photo cascade plunging into a deep blue pool.

Other towns in the chapada

There is simple accommodation and a handful of tour operators in **Palmeiras**, some 55 km west of Lençóis. The town makes a far quieter alternative base for exploring the *chapada*. *Combis* run sporadically between Palmeiras and Lençóis. **Mucugê** town in the far south, 134 km from Lençóis is sleepier still, and has a fascinating white-wash cemetery filled with elaborate mausoleums and set against the dark granite of the hillside. There are bus connections with Lençóis and Feira de Santana. The adjacent **Parque Municipal de Mucugê** was set-up to protect the *sempre viva* or *chuveirinho* plant – a beautiful globe of white flowers whose popularity with flower arrangers in Brazil almost led to their extinction in the late 20th century. **Igatu** has a population of approximately 350 people, some of them live in the largely abandoned stone houses built into or around Cyclopean

Lençóis

Sleeping
Camping &
  Pousada Lumiar **1**
Canto das Aguas **2**
Casa da Geleia **3**
Casa de Hélia **4**
Estalagem de Alcino **5**

Lençóis **6**
Pousada dos Duendes **7**
Pousada Vila Serrano **8**
Pousada Violeiro **9**

Eating
Artistas de Massa **1**

Cozinha Aberta **2**
Gaya **3**
Neco's **4**

Bars & clubs
Fazedinha e Tal **5**

N

Not to scale

boulders that dot the landscape. Wandering around the village and the ruins is a haunting experience. There are two *pousadas* in the village.

Feira de Santana → *Colour map 2, C4. Phone code: 075. Population: 450,500.*

Located 112 km northwest of Salvador, Feira de Santana is the centre of a great cattle breeding and trading area. Its Monday market, known as **Feira do Couro** (leather fair), is said to be the largest in Brazil and attracts great crowds to its colourful display of local products. The **artesanato market** in the centre, however, has a bigger selection. The *rodoviária* has an interesting wall of painted tiles (made by **Udo-Ceramista**, whose workshop is in Brotas, Avenida Dom João VI 411, Salvador). The **Micareta**, held in late April, is the biggest out-of-season carnival in Bahia and attracts many popular *axé* music groups from Salvador. Buses run to Salvador every 20 minutes, 1½ hours and there are connections to other towns throughout the state.

Parque Nacional da Chapada Diamantina

The Chapada Diamantina national park was founded in 1985 and comprises 1500 sq km of escarpment broken by extensive tracts of *caatinga* scrub forest, *cerrado*, patches of moist Atlantic coast forest and pântano (wetlands with permanent plant growth). The diversity of ecosystems have an associated diversity of flora and fauna. There is very little primary forest left, but the area is nonetheless home to rare large mammals such as maned wolf, jaguar and ocelot and birds endemic to all of the ecosystems. Spectaculars include the king vulture, crowned eagle, red-legged seriema and blue-winged macaw. There are birding guides available in Lençóis (see page 478).

Ins and outs

The **park headquarters** ① *R Barão do Rio Branco 25, T075-3332 2420,* is at Palmeiras, 50 km from Lençóis. However, Lençóis is a much more practical source of information and the numerous agencies make it easy to find out what's what. See also www.infochapada.com.

Roy Funch, an American who used to manage the park and who now offers guided walks (see page 478), has written an excellent book on the *chapada*: *A Visitor's Guide to the Chapada Diamantina Mountains* (Collection Apoio 45), in English and Portuguese. The book includes history and geology of the region, an itinerary of all the principal sights, with instructions on how to reach them, and a thorough, though not comprehensive checklist of birds and mammals. It is widely available in Lençóis.

Background

The *chapada* forms part of the Brazilian shield, one of the oldest geological formations on earth, dating from the when the world was only one land mass. It extends north into the Serra da Capivara and Jalapão, and south into the Serra do Espinhaço and Serra da Canastra in Minas and the mountains of Mato Grosso and northern Bolivia.

Cave paintings and petroglyphs suggest that people have been living in and around the *chapada* for millennia. However, there were no permanent settlers in the hills in recorded history until the arrival of Portuguese prospectors in the 1700s, who discovered gold and diamonds in the extreme south of the *chapada* near Livramento de Nossa Senhora and in the north near Jacobina. The Portuguese kept the findings secret for fear of driving down world gem prices, and ceding the *chapada* to other European powers, notably the Dutch and Spanish, who were invading and occupying Brazilian territory repeatedly during this period.

The *chapada* didn't open up fully to mining until 1844, when Mucugê, Rio de Contas and subsequently Lençóis were founded and settled by miners from neighbouring Minas Gerais and western Bahia, followed by Portuguese noblemen from the Bahian coast. The latter evolved into *coroneis*: robber barons who set-up ruthless local fiefdoms run by gun-toting

Chapada Diamantina

Trails
.... Morro do Pai Inácio–Capão
.... Lençóis–Capão
.... Lençóis–Cachoeira da Fumaça
.... Igatu– Andaraí
.... Vale do Paty
.... Travessia Diamantina

jangada henchmen. The most famous was Horácio de Mattos, a prototype for many modern-day rural Brazilian politicians. De Mattos sucked all the money out of the *chapada* with his personal campaigns. He carried out famous vendettas against two other *coroneis*, Manuel Fabrício de Oliveira and Militão Rodrigues Coelho, to establish patriarchal dominance, overthrew the state government, routed the federal army and chased the infamous communist Prestes column all the way across Brazil and into Bolivia. He was in the back in Salvador in 1930.

Visiting the park

The *chapada* is cut by dirt roads, trails and rivers, which lead to waterfalls, viewpoints on table-top mountains, caves and natural swimming holes. There are many different hikes, and many of the routes have been used for centuries by the local farmers and miners, but finding your own way is difficult and it is best to visit on a guided trip.

There are more than 24 tour operators in Lençóis and organizing a trip to even the most distant sights is straightforward. Most tours tend to be car-based and rather sedentary as these are more profitable. But there are plenty of great hikes and sights around Lençóis, so consider all the options before signing up. Brazilian tourists are often more interested in chatting loudly among themselves than in hearing the quiet music of nature, so it can be difficult to see wildlife. ▶▶ *See Activities and tours, page 478.*

The most impressive sights in the *chapada* are included in the standard packages. Most have an entrance fee. These include: the extensive **Gruta do Lapa Doce** (US$5) and **Pratinha** caves (US$5); the latter of which are cut through by glassy blue water. The table-top mountains at the **Morro de Pai Inácio**, US$2, 30 km from Lençóis, offer the best view of the *chapada*, especially at sunset. The 384 m high **Cachoeira da Fumaça** (Smoke or Glass Waterfall) is the second highest in Brazil and lies deeper within the park 2½ hours hike from the village of **Capão**. The view is astonishing; the updraft of the air currents often makes the water flow back up creating the 'smoke' effect. The **Rio Marimbus** flows through and area of semi-swamp reminiscent of the Pantanal and very rich in birdlife whilst the **Rio Mucugezinho** plunges over the blood-red **Cachoeira do Diabo** in an extensive area of *cerrado* just below the craggy **Roncador** ('snorer') waterfall.

Hiking in the chapada

It is essential to use a guide for treks as it is easy to get lost. Trail-walking in the park can involve clambering over rocks and stepping stones so bring strong shoes. A reasonable level of physical fitness is advisable. There are a lot of mosquitos in campsites so carry repellent. For overnight trips it is highly advisable to bring a fleece and sleeping bag as nights in the 'winter' months can be cold. Sometimes, guides can arrange these. A tent is useful but optional; although many camps are beside reasonably hospitable caves. Torches (flashlights) and a water bottle are essentials.

The **Morro do Pai Inacio to Capão** trail is a 25-km day-hike that leads from the summit of the Pai Inácio escarpment around other table-top mountains, passing through *cerrado*, *caatinga* and arable areas to the Capão valley. Another day hike is from **Lençóis to Capão**, along a series of rivers (great for swimming) and around the base of the mountains, with a car ride back at the end of the walk.

The **Cachoeira da Fumaça** trail leaves direct from Lençóis and takes two to three days to reach the base of the falls, from where there is a steep hike to the top. If you only have one day, it's possible to drive the 70 km to the **Vale do Capão** and hike the steep 6-km trail to the top of the falls. Both trails are very popular in high season.

A trail runs from **Igatu to Andaraí**, leaving from the central square of the former town past the cemetery and following the Xique-Xique river. The walk takes four hours and offers wonderful views of the mountain landscape. There are plenty of river bank stops for a cooling swim. There are longer treks too.

The **Vale do Paty** hike is a four- to six-day walk running through the heart of the Serra along a valley surrounded by imposing *meseta* table-top mountains. There are many good stopping places with viewpoints, caves, swimming holes and waterfalls. The route usually departs from Capão in the north or from the village of Guiné just west of Andaraí town.

For a full cross-section of the park, hike the 112-km **Travessia Diamantina**, which runs from the Vale do Capão in the north right across the park via the Vale do Paty, to the Cachoeira do Buracão in the far south. Accommodation is in tents and rustic *pousadas* and there are side-trips off to the Cachoeira da Fumaça (near Capão), Igatu, Poço Encatado, and the Marimbus pantanal area and Roncador falls. Establish which of the sights you would like to visit with the tour company before setting off.

The sertão 😑😊 ▸▸ pp476-478. Colour map 2, C4.

Most of Bahia is arid: a rock and scrub semi-desert covered in leafless *caatinga* forest, cut by the blue vein of the majestic Rio São Francisco and dotted with little settlements where local people scratch a meagre living from the sun-baked earth. This is the *sertão* – a backland that has produced some of Brazil's most enduring mythical figures. **Antônio Conselheiro**, a purple-robed desert prophet whose rag-tag band of marauders and bandits converted to Christianity in the late 19th-century and built Canudos, crushed two armies and almost broke the Brazilian state. **Lampião** – the *sertão*'s brutal Robin Hood – who pillaged the rich *coroneis*, distributed wealth and brutal justice to the desert villages in the early 20th century and died in a gun battle in a town famous for its troubadours and poets. Their legacy, the iron hand of *coroneis* who impose rough justice to this day and countless forgotten, timeless festivals and rites still characterize the dust and dirt towns of this vast interior. Tourists are seldom seen and are always a curiosity.

Euclides da Cunha and Monte Santo → Phone code: 075.

North of Feira de Santana, at Km 225 on the BR-116 road to Fortaleza, **Euclides da Cunha**, is a good base for exploring the Canudos area with a couple of standard hotels. The bus station is on the BR-116, T075-3271 1365.

About 38 km west is the famous hill shrine of **Monte Santo** in the *sertão*, reached by 3.5 km of steps cut into the rocks of the **Serra do Picaraça**. It's a 45-minute walk each way, so set out early. This is the scene of pilgrimages and great religious devotion during Holy Week. The shrine was built by an Italian who had a vision of the cross on the mountain in 1765. One block north of the bottom of the stairs is the **Museu do Sertão**, with pictures from the 1897 Canudos rebellion.

Canudos → Phone code: 075.

Canudos itself is 100 km away. Religious rebels, led by Antônio Conselheiro, defeated three expeditions sent against them in 1897 before being overwhelmed. The Rio Vaza Barris, which runs through Canudos, has been dammed, and the town has been moved to **Nova Canudos** by the dam. Part of the old town is still located 10 km west in the **Parque Estadual de Canudos**, created in 1997. For tourist information see www.canudosnet.com.br. There are direct buses to Canudos from Salvador.

Paulo Afonso and Parque Nacional de Paulo Afonso → *Colour map 2, C5. Phone code: 075.*
Part of the northern border of Bahia is formed by the Rio São Francisco. From Salvador, the paved BR-110 runs 471 km north to the river at **Paulo Afonso**. The town was founded in 1913 when a large dam was constructed. Handicrafts (embroidery, fabrics) are available from **Núcleo de Produção Artesanal** ① *Av Apolônio Sales 1059*. Nearby is the **Raso da Catarina** ① *T075-3281 3347*, a series of trails in the *caatinga* that was used as a hideout by the bandit Lampião. A guide and a 4WD vehicle are recommended for exploring the trails, due to the heat and lack of shade.

About 25 km northwest of the town is the **Parque Nacional de Paulo Afonso**, an oasis of trees amid a desert of brown scrub and cactus. The **Cachoeira de Paulo Afonso** ① *in a security area, admission 0800-1100 only, by car or taxi, accompanied by a guide from the tourist information office, T075-3282 1717, 2 hrs, US$6 per car*, was once one of the great waterfalls of the world but is now exploited for hydroelectric power. The falls are 270 km from the mouth of the São Francisco river, which drains a valley three times the size of Great Britain. The source of the river is 2575 km upstream in Minas Gerais. The 19th-century British linguist and explorer, Sir Richard Burton, took an expedition down the river and negotiated some of its treacherous rapids. Below the falls is a deep, rocky gorge through which the water rushes. The best time to visit the falls is in the rainy season (January-February); only then does much water pass over them, as almost all the flow now goes through the power plant. The best view is from the northern (Alagoas) bank.

The Rio São Francisco is navigable above the falls from above the thriving twin towns (linked by a bridge) of Juazeiro, in Bahia, and Petrolina, in Pernambuco. Navigation is possible as far as **Pirapora** in Minas Gerais, linked by road to the Belo Horizonte–Brasília highway (see page 294).

Ins and outs The **airport** ① *4 km from town*, receives flights from Recife and Salvador. The **rodoviária** ① *Av Apolônio Sales*, has connections to Maceió, Recife and Salvador. For information and tours, contact **InfoTur** ① *Av Apolonio Sales s/n, T075-2812 7757*.

Juazeiro and around → *Colour map 2, C4. Phone code: 074. Population: 172,500.*
Juazeiro is located at an important crossroads where the BR-407 meets the Rio São Francisco. For information on river transport call T075-3811 2465. On the opposite bank in Pernambuco is **Petrolina** (see page 509). The local economy revolves around agriculture and its exportation. There is a market on Friday and Saturday and simple hotels in town, see www.juazeiro.ba.gov.br. The bus from Canudos (five hours) gets crowded; buy tickets early to ensure a seat. The second half of the route is unpaved.

Xique-Xique and Ibotirama → *Colour map 2, C2. Phone code: 074.*
The next major town upriver is Xique-Xique, an agricultural town 587 km from Salvador. The remains of what may be a pre-Neanderthal man have been found in the nearby caves, whose paintings suggest that it could well have been used as an observatory. The next town upriver, **Ibotirama**, 650 km from Salvador on the BR-242, is famous for its fishing, especially for *surubim* and *pocomã*. There are a few moderately priced hotels with restaurants.

Bom Jesus de Lapa → *Colour map 4, A4. Phone code: 077.*
An important stop on the Rio São Francisco, 148 km from Ibotirama on the BR-242, is Bom Jesus de Lapa. The **Igreja Nossa Senhora da Soledad** is situated within a grotto near to Praça da Bandeira. This sanctuary, discovered by a monk in the 17th century, is the centre

of a *romaria* (pilgrimage) between July and September, which attracts thousands of visitors to the town. There are a few places to stay and a bank in town. **Bom Jesus airport** ⓘ *Av Manuel Novais, T077-3481 4519*, receives flights from Salvador. There are also several daily buses from Salvador.

◉ Chapada Diamantina and the sertão listings

For Sleeping and Eating price codes and other relevant information, see pages 42-47.

● Sleeping

Lençóis *p469, map p470*

L Canto das Águas, Av Senhor dos Passos, T/F075-3334 1154, www.lencois.com.br. Medium-size riverside hotel with modest a/c or fan-cooled rooms, a pool and efficient service. The best rooms are in the new wing; others can be musty.

AL Hotel de Lençóis, R Altinha Alves 747, T075-3334 1102, www.hoteldelencois.com.br. Plain, dark wood and white-tiled rooms with terracotta roofs set in a handsome colonial house in a grassy garden on the edge of the park. Good breakfast, pool and a restaurant.

A Pousada Vila Serrano, R Alto do Bonfim 8, 3334 1486, www.vilaserrano.com.br. Warm and welcoming mock-colonial *pousada* over-looking a patio and little garden 5 mins from town. Excellent service, breakfast, trips organized. Very friendly and knowledgeable.

C-D Estalagem de Alcino, R Gen Viveiros de Morais 139, T075-3334 1171. An enchanting and beautifully restored period house with a range of rooms furnished with 19th-century antiques. Most have shared bathrooms. The superb breakfast is served in the little garden with hummingbirds, near the owner's pottery workshop. Great library and book exchange.

D Casa da Geleia, R Gen Viveiros 187, T075-3334 1151, www.casadageleia.com.br/. A handful of smart chalets set in a huge garden at the entrance to the town. English spoken, good breakfast, including sumptuous jams and honeys made or collected by the owner. Zé Carlos is a keen birdwatcher and an authority on the region.

D Casa de Hélia, R da Muritiba, T075-3334 1143, www.casadehelia.com.br. Attractive and welcoming little guesthouse. English spoken. Good facilities, legendary breakfast.

D Pousada dos Duendes, R do Pires, T/F075-3334 1229, www.pousadadosduendes.com. Run by English Olivia Taylor and often crowded with backpackers. Rooms are basic with shared showers, modest breakfast and dinner (with veggie options). Their tour agency, **H2O Expeditions**, arranges tours and treks from 1 to 11 days. Check with other agencies in town before committing.

D Pousada Violeiro, R Prof Assis 70, T075-3534 1259, www.pousadavioleiro.com.br. Very simple rooms with room for up to 4 (**E**) just behind the bus stop near the river. Quiet and conservative.

D-E IYHA Lençóis, R Boa Vista 121, T075-3334 1497, www.hostelchapada.com.br. A large, friendly and well-run hostel with an adventure sports agency in one of the town's grand old colonial houses. The building has been completely restored and has singles, en suite doubles and single-sex 4-6 room dorms; shared kitchen and a large, airy garden with hammocks and littered with outdoor chairs.

House rental

There are mostly very simple houses to rent throughout Lençóis, bookable through **Destino Chapada**, Praça Horácio de Matos 3, Centro, T075-33341395, www.destinochapada.com.br.

Camping

Camping and Pousada Lumiar, near the Rosário church in the town centre, T075-3334 1241. A large grassy area for pitching tents and a series of very simple rooms (**D**) and bungalows (**C**). Popular restaurant. Friendly.

Feira de Santana *p471*
There are several cheap hotels in Praça da Matriz and near the *rodoviária* (fairly central).
A Feira Palace, Av Maria Quitéria 1572, T075-3221 5011, www.feirapalacehotel.com.br. Blocky 1970s hotel in need of renovation, but the best in town; with a restaurant and pool.
B-C Acalanto, R Torres 77, T075-3625 3612, www.hotelacalanto.com.br. Modern, standard, small-town hotel with around 50 modest rooms with en suites.
D Paládio, Av Getúlio Vargas 294, T075-3623 8899. Far less grand than its name but well kept.

Euclides da Cunha and Monte Santo *p474*
B Do Conselheiro, Av Mcal Juarez Tavora 187, Euclides, T075-3275 1814. Standard town hotel with breakfast in the price.
C Grapiuna, Praça Monsenhor Berenguer 401, Euclides, T075-3275 1157. Basic rooms with a/c and cheaper options without bath. Recommended.

Canudos *p474*
E Brasil, Nova Canudos. Very simple rooms with en suites and fans. Cheaper without breakfast.

Paulo Afonso and Parque Nacional de Paulo Afonso *p475*
B Belvedere, Av Apolônio Sales 457, Paulo Afonso, T075-3281 3314. Plain rooms with a/c and pool.
B Grande Hotel de Paulo Afonso, Parque Nacional Paulo Afonso, at the falls. T075-3281 1914. A/c rooms and a pool. There are simple rooms in the adjacent guesthouse (reservations recommended).
B Palace, Av Apolônio Sales (next door to Belvedere), Paulo Afonso, T075-3281 4521. The best in town with a/c rooms and a pool.

Xique-Xique and Ibotirama *p475*
B Carranca Grande, Xique-Xique, Km 1, T/F074-3661 1674. Standard blocky hotel with a pool and restaurant.

Eating

Lençóis *p469, map p470*
††† Cozinha Aberta, Rui Barbosa 42, T075-3334 1309, www.cozinhaaberta.com.br. The best in town with organic and slow food from Paulistana chef Deborah Doitschinoff. Just east of the main *praça*.
†† Artistas da Massa, R Miguel Calmon. Italian dishes, mainly pasta and pizza.
†† Neco's, Praça Maestro Clarindo Pachêco 15, T075-3334 1179. Set meal of local dishes of the kind once eaten by the *garimpeiro* miners, such as saffron-stewed mutton accompanied by prickly pear cactus, crisp, tart *batata da terra* and fried green banana.
† Gaya, Praça Horácio Matos s/n, T075-3334 1167. Organic and wholefood with large salads generous juices and sandwiches. The owners organize trips into the *chapada*.

Bars and clubs

Lençóis *p469, map p470*
Clube Sete, R das Pedras. Little dance club open Fri and Sat nights.
Doce Barbaros, R das Pedras, 21. Lively little bar almost any night of the week.
Fazendinha e Tal, R das Pedras 125. Very popular bar with rustic *garimpeiro* decoration serving hundreds of different *cachacas* and with occasional live music.

Shopping

Lençóis *p469, map p470*
There is a little market in the main square selling arts and crafts.
Instrumentos, R das Pedras 78, T075-3334 1334. Unusual faux-Brazilian and African musical instruments by quirky ex-pat Argentinian Jorge Fernando.
Zambumbeira, R das Pedras at Tamandare, T075-3334 1207. Beautiful ceramics by reknowned artisans like Zé Caboclo, jewellery, walking sticks and arty bric-a-brac.

▲ Activities and tours

Lençóis *p469, map p470*
Guides
Guides offer their services at most *pousadas* (about US$20-30 per trip); most of them are very young. The following are recommended:
Chapada Adventure, Av 7 de Setembro 7, T075-3334 2037, www.chapada adventure.com.br. A small operator offering good value car-based tours and light hiking throughout the *chapada*.
Edmilson (known as Mil), R Domingos B Souza 70, T075-3334 1319. Knows the region extremely well, knowledgeable and reliable.
For a da Trilha, R das Pedras 202, www.foradatrilha.com.br. Longer hikes and light adventures, from canyoning to rapelling.
Gaya, Praça Horácio Matos s/n, T075-3334 1167, T075-9992 2820 (mob), rafa.gaya@ yahoo.com.br, see Eating, page 477. Rafa organizes budget backpacker trips in and around the *chapada* in an old Toyota Bandeirante. Tours cost around US$200 for 300-km round-trips for up to 10 people, and include unusual locations such as the Cachoeira do Mosquito. Book ahead if possible.
Luiz Krug, contact via Vila Serrano, T075-3334 1102. An independent, English-speaking guide specializing in geology and caving.
Roy Funch, T/F075-3334 1305, www.fcd.org.br. The ex-director of the Chapada Diamantina National Park is an excellent guide and has written a visitors' guide to the park in English. It is recommended as the best for information on history, geography and trails of the *chapada*. Highly recommended. He can be booked through www.elabrasil.com.
Trajano, contact via **Vila Serrano** or **Casa da Hélia**, T075-3334 1143. Speaks English and Hebrew and is a good-humoured guide for treks to the bottom of the Cachoeira da Fumaça.
Venturas e Aventuras, Praça Horácio de Matos 20, T075-3334 1304. Excellent trekking expeditions, up to 6 days.
Zé Carlos, T075-3334 1151, contact through Casa da Geleia or Vila Serrano. The best guide for birdwatching.

Body and soul
The *chapada* is a centre for alternative treatments. All the practitioners listed come highly recommended.
Anita Marti, T075-9989 8328. Healing and therapeutic massage and treatments.
Dieter Herzberg, T075-9984 2720, dieterherzberg@yahoo.com.br. All manner of therapeutic and healing massage.
Jaques Gagnon, T075-3334 1281, www.janeladaalma.com. Neuro-structural therapy and healing massage.

☉ Transport

Lençóis *p469, map p470*
Air Airport, Km 209, BR-242, 20 km from town T075-3625 8100. Air taxi only. No scheduled flights; although **TAM** reportedly have plans.

Bus Real Expresso to **Salvador** 3 a day, US$24, *comercial* via **Feira de Santana**. Book in advance, especially at weekends and holidays. For the rest of Bahia state change at Feira de Santana; it is not necessary to go via Salvador. Buses also to **Recife**, **Ibotirama**, **Barreiras** or **Palmas** (for Jalapão), **Chapada dos Veadeiros** and **Brasília**, 16 hrs, US$60 (all with transfer in Seabra, several buses daily).

Bom Jesus de Lapa *p475*
The airport in Bom Jesus has flights to **Salvador** with **Abaete**, www.abaete.com.br, and buses.

⊙ Directory

Lençóis *p469, map p470*
Banks and post office There is a Bradesco with an ATM, and a post office (Mon-Fri 0900-1700) on the main square.

Feira de Santana *p471*
Banks Banco 24 Horas, Av Senhor dos Passos 1332. Banco do Brasil, Av Getúlio Vargas 897. There is also a Bradesco in town.

Contents

Footprint features

At a glance

⊖ **Getting around** Mostly by bus. Car hire recommended for the coast but not for the interior as roads can be poor.

◉ **Time required** 2 days for Recife and Olinda, 3-5 days for the coast, 2-3 days for Fernando de Noronha.

☼ **Weather** Hot and wet summers (Mar-Jul), hot and drier winters (Sep-Feb).

✖ **When not to go** Apr and May are wet. Jun and Jul are wetter but are the best months for festivals.

★ Don't miss ...

★ Penedo, page 489.

1 Olinda, page 505.

2 Carnaval in Recife and Olinda, page 516.

3 Fernando de Noronha, page 521.

4 Carirí, page 530.

5 Souza, page 531.

6 São João celebrations in Campina Grande, page 534.

The four states that comprise this region – Sergipe, Alagoas, Pernambuco and Paraíba – are often overlooked by visitors. Most travellers whizz through, perhaps stopping for a beach break at Porto de Galinhas or Fernando de Noronha, and a few days in colourful, colonial Olinda. But those who spend time in the region, exploring its buildings, sampling the music and arts scene in Recife or getting lost in the crowds at the great festivals in the *sertão* find it one of the most interesting, diverse and least spoilt parts of Brazil.

In the first centuries of its colonial history, the region grew rich through sugar and became the commercial and intellectual centre of Brazil. Pernambuco, in particular, retains many magnificent buildings from that period, while the convents in Olinda and Igarassu are fine examples of Iberian baroque. In the late 19th century, the sugar boom subsided and poverty began to spread across the state. Yet the proud intellectual tradition continued, with notables such as Marechal Deodoro, the founder of the Brazilian republic, Gilberto Freyre, who helped forge Brazil's identity and Francisco Brennand, the surreal artist, all from the area.

The region has never been more culturally exciting than today. In the 1980s Recife saw the explosion of an artistic movement called *mangue beat*, which sought to fuse the rich heritage of Pernambuco folk art and music with social activism and post-modernism. The resulting cultural fluorescence has helped to make Pernambuco Brazil's most vibrant cultural state. Artists have ateliers on every other corner in Olinda, while numerous festivals showcase the country's most innovative film-making and resurrect popular culture. Carnaval in Recife or Olinda is considered by many to be the best and most traditional in the country.

Sergipe and Alagoas

Few tourists stop off in these two tiny states between Bahia and Pernambuco, but herein lies their charm. Both have fine beaches, easily accessible from the state capitals: Aracaju and Maceió. And both have a series of very pretty Portuguese towns where visitors are still a novelty. The most impressive are Penedo (on the banks of Brazil's 'other' great river, the São Francisco, which forms the border between the two states), Marechal Deodoro (the birthplace of the founder of the Brazilian Republic) and São Cristóvão (the Portuguese capital of Sergipe and Brazil's fourth oldest town). Of the capitals, Maceió is by far the more salubrious, with some excellent beaches and lively nightlife.
▶▶ *For listings, see pages 491-496.*

Aracaju ⬤⬤⬤⬤⬤⬤⬤⬤ ▶▶ *pp491-496. Colour map 2, C5.*

→ *Phone code: 079. Population: 462,600.*

Founded in 1855, this state capital stands on the south bank of the Rio Sergipe, about 10 km from its mouth and 327 km north of Salvador. The river itself is pleasant enough and lined with handsome buildings, but the city centre is tawdry and unpleasant, especially at night, and there is very little to see. Most visitors stay at **Praia Atalaia** (see below), a 10-minute taxi (US$12) or 20-minute bus ride south of town.

Overlooked by most international visitors, Aracaju has a lively off-season carnival immediately prior to the one in Salvador, with the same music and floats. The commercial area is on Rua Itabaianinha and Rua João Pessoa, leading up to Rua Divina Pastora and Praça General Valadão.

Ins and outs

Getting there **Santa Maria airport** ⓘ *12 km from the centre, Av Senador Júlio César Leite, Atalaia, T079-3243 1388*, receives flights from Maceió, Rio de Janeiro, São Paulo, Recife, Salvador, and other towns. Interstate buses arrive at the **rodoviária** ⓘ *4 km west of the centre*, which is linked to the local bus system from the adjacent terminal (buy a ticket before going on to the platform). Bus 004 'T Rod/L Batista' goes to the centre, US$0.50. Buses from Laranjeiras and São Cristóvão (45 minutes) arrive at the **old bus station** at Praça João XXIII. Look for routes written on the side of buses and at bus stations in town.
▶▶ *See Transport, page 495.*

Tourist information The principal tourist office, **Bureau de Informações Turísticas de Sergipe** ⓘ *Centro de Turismo, Praça Olímpio Campos s/n, Centro T079-3179 1947, daily 0800-2000*, has town maps and staff speak some English. **Emsetur** ⓘ *Trav Baltazar Goís 86, Edif Estado de Sergipe, 11th-13th floors, T079-3179 7553, www.emsetur.se.gov.br, Mon-Fri 0700-1300*, also has information. There is a tourist booth on the seafront on **Praia Atalaia** ⓘ *Arcos da Orla de Atalaia 243, between R Maynard and Rotary, daily 1000-2100, www.visitearacaju.com.br*, but staff do not speak English and information is limited. There are other branches at the airport (0600-2400) and the *rodoviária* (0800-2230).

Private tour operators offer trips around the city, including rafting on the Rio São Francisco and the river delta. The best is **Brisamar Tur** ⓘ *on the beach, Av Rotary s/n, Hotel Beira Mar, Praia de Atalaia, T079-3223 1781, www.brisamartur.com.br*, English spoken.

Aracaju beaches

Praia Atalaia is the nearest beach to Aracju and a much better place to stay. Although it can't compete with Bahia or Alagoas, there is a long beach of fine white sand, lined with *forró* clubs, restaurants and bars. The beach is lively with families and smooching couples who wander along the esplanade at sunset and the entire area feels as safe and old fashioned as a British Butlins seaside resort. There's even an artificial lake in a tiny theme park where you can hire pedal boats.

Continuing south along the Rodovia Presidente José Sarney, is a long stretch of sand between the mouths of the Rio Sergipe and Rio Vaza Barris; the further you go from the Sergipe, the clearer the water. One of the best beaches is the 30-km-long **Nova Atalaia**, on Ilha de Santa Luzia across the river. It is is easily reached by ferry from the **Terminal Hidroviária** ① *Av Rio Branco, near Praça General Valadão*. Boats cross the river to **Barra dos Coqueiros** every 15 minutes (US$1). Services are more frequent at weekends, when it is very lively with with fishing and pleasure craft.

Excursions from Aracaju

By far the most interesting excursion is to the canyons and beaches of the **Rio São Francisco**. The blue waters course their way through the hills of Minas Gerais and the desert backlands of Bahia before cutting through a series of dramatic gorges near the **Xingó** dam, and subsequently through fields of windswept dunes before washing out into the deep green Atlantic in northern Sergipe. **Brisamar Tur** (see above) runs day-trips down the river stopping at deserted beaches along the way; US$20-40 per person, depending on numbers.

About 23 km northwest from Aracaju is **Laranjeiras**, a tiny and sleepy colonial town with a ruined church on a hill. It is reached by taking the São Pedro bus from the old *rodoviária* in the centre of Aracaju (45 minutes). The town was originally founded in 1605 and has several churches dating back to the imperial period, when it was an important producer of sugar. The 19th-century **Capela de Sant'Aninha** has a wooden altar inlaid with gold.

South of Aracaju ⬤🕖 ⟫ *pp491-496. Colour map 2, C5.*

São Cristóvão

The old Sergipe capital lies 17 km southwest of Aracaju on the road to Salvador, sitting pretty on a little hill and on the shores of a briny lake. Founded by Cristóvão de Barros in 1590, it is Brazil's fourth oldest town, and one of myriad pretty, crumbling towns that dot this part of the country. The colonial centre is unspoilt, with whitewashed mansions, townhouses and churches offset by the oil-paint yellows and blues, green slat-shutters and woodwork. Strings of gorgeous Portuguese buildings make it a good quieter option for a day trip to a colonial town than visiting Cachoiera from Salvador. Alternatively, it's a pleasant spot for a quiet few days in the back of beyond. The town is lively during both the Sergipe pre-Carnaval celebrations and Carnaval itself.

The town attracts very few international tourists yet there are a few interesting sights to explore. The **Museu de Arte Sacra e Histórico de Sergipe** ① *Tue-Fri 1000-1700, Sat and Sun 1300-1700*, in the **Convento de São Francisco** contains ornate religious objects and heavy furniture from the 17th to 19th centuries. Also worth visiting is the **Museu de Sergipe** (same opening hours) in the former **Palácio do Governo**; both are on Praça de São Francisco. On the same square are the churches of **Misericórdia** (1627) and the **Orfanato Imaculada Conceição** (1646, permission to visit required from the sisters).

Palmares and Zumbi

From the first days of slavery in Brazil, *fujões* (runaways) would disappear into the interior and set up villages or *mocambos*. Between the 1630s and the end of 17th century these *mocambos* prospered (especially during times of crisis such as the Dutch invasion in 1630) and together formed *quilombos*, free territories which accepted not only runaway slaves but freed ones and whites who had fallen out with the re-established Portuguese colony. The most famous of these *quilombos*, established in what is now the state of Alagoas, was called Palmares after the large number of palm trees in the area. It consisted of 30,000 people living in several *mocambos* in an area of 17,000 square miles (44,000 sq km). According to reports from Bartholomeus Lintz, the leader of a Dutch expedition in 1640, the largest settlement in Palmares had 220 buildings, a church, four smithies and a meeting house.

The political and social structures were very similar to those found in West Africa, and although Catholicism was practised, so was polyandry, mainly due to the lack of women in the republic. The leader of Palmares was Ganga-Zumba who was revered like a king, but it appears he was

killed by his followers in 1680 after making some concessions to the Portuguese two years earlier. He was succeeded by the republic's brave military commander, Zumbi, who is said to have been an African king.

The existence of Palmares was a constant thorn in the side of Portuguese domination of Brazil and dozens of attempts were made to destroy it. However, Zumbi managed to defend the republic until it was finally smashed in 1695 by the Portuguese with *bandeirante* help. Zumbi was killed and his decapitated head was put on display in Recife to discourage other potential runaways and prove that he was not immortal as his followers believed. He is still remembered every year on 20 November, Brazil's Black Consciousness Day. He has also become a popular icon at Carnaval time. There are still small *quilombo* communities throughout Brazil.

The site of the Palmares Republic is situated on the Serra da Barriga, close to modern União do Palmares in Alagoas state, reached by driving north out of Maceió on the BR-101, turning left after Messias and driving for 40 km along a paved road.

On Praça Senhor dos Passos are the churches of **Senhor dos Passos** and **Terceira Ordem do Carmo** (both built 1739), while on the Praça Getúlio Vargas (formerly Praça Matriz) is the 17th-century **Igreja Matriz Nossa Senhora da Vitória** ① *all are open Tue-Fri 1000-1700, Sat and Sun 1500-1700*. Also worth seeing is the old **Assembléia Legislativa** ① *R Coronel Erundino Prado*.

Estância → *Phone code: 079. Population: 57,000.*

Estância is 247 km north of Salvador, on the BR-101, almost midway between the Sergipe-Bahia border and Aracaju. It is one of the oldest towns in Brazil. Its colonial buildings are decorated with Portuguese tiles (none are open to the public). The town's heyday was at the turn of the 20th century and it was one of the earliest places in Brazil to get electricity and a telephone system. Estância is also called 'Cidade Jardim' because of its parks. The month-long festival of **São João** in June is a major event.

→ *Phone code: 082. Population: 780,000.*

The capital of Alagoas is one of coastal Brazil's most attractive and safest cities, with a string of beautiful white-sand beaches, a pretty little colonial centre and a low-key feel. There are a handful of low-key beach resorts a short bus ride away; the best is at **Praia do Frances**, near the old Portuguese capital of Marechal Deodoro. The city has a lively street carnival and traditional **Festas Juninhas**.

Ins and outs

Getting there Flights arrive at **Zumbi dos Palmares airport** ① *Rodovia BR-104, Km 91, T082-3214 4000, 25 km from the city centre and beaches,* from Aracaju, Brasília, Rio de Janeiro, Florianópolis, Salvador, São Paulo, Recife, Belo Horizonte and Porto Alegre. A bus runs from the airport to most popular city beach, Ponta Verde/Pajuçara, every 30 minutes 0630-2100 (allow 45 minutes); look for name of the beach on the front of the bus. Taxis charge a flat rate of around US$23. Interstate buses arrive at the **rodoviária** ① *5 km from the centre,* situated on a hill, with good views. Luggage store is available. Take bus Nos 711 or 715 to Ponta Verde/Pajuçara or buses marked 'Ouro Preto p/centro'; these run every few minutes. A from the bus station to Pajuçara costs around US$13. ▸▸ *See Transport, page 495.*

Getting around and orientation Ponta Verde, Pajuçara and adjacent Praia de Jaticúa are easy to walk around as is the commercial centre. You will need to take public transport between them. Local buses connect Ponta Verde and Pajuçara with the tiny historic city centre every few minutes, leaving from the the beachside road Avenida Robert Kennedy/ Alvaro Otacilio and stopping at various points including the cathedral. Bus stops are little blue elongated concrete stands. *Combi*s for the nearby beaches like Praia do Frances and Marechal Deodoro leave from in front of the Hospital Santa Casa.

Tourist information **Semptur** ① *Av da Paz 1422, Centro, T082-3336 4409, www.maceio tour.com.br,* offers information on the city and environs, including maps. The state tourism authority **Setur** ① *R Boa Vista 453, Centro, T082-3315 5700, www.turismo.al.gov.br,* also has branches at the airport and *rodoviária.* The website has a comprehensive list of public services, hotels, restaurants, bars and other contacts. Far more convenient is the **tourist information post** on Pajuçara beach, next to the Sete Coqueiros artisan centre. For very entertaining city tours or trips to Marechal Deodoro, Praia do Francês and beyond contact **Del** (see Activities and tours, page 495), who speaks several languages including English.

Maceió beaches

The sea in Maceió is an impossibly brilliant shade of misty greens and blues and it washes onto some of the finest white-sand beaches in urban Brazil. **Trapiche**, **Sobral** and **Avenida**, immediately in front of the city, look appetizing and are pounded by an impressive surf but they are far too filthy for anything but brown trout. The best beaches for bathing (and the best places to stay in Maceió) are **Pajuçara**, **Ponta Verde** and **Jatiúca**, becoming increasingly plush the further they are from the centre.

   Pajuçara has the bulk of the budget accommodation and a nightly crafts market. At weekends there are wandering musicians and entertainers here, and patrols by the cavalry on magnificent *Manga Larga Marchador* horses. Periodically, especially on *candomblé* anniversaries, there are rituals to the *orixá* of the sea, *Yemanjá*. There is a natural swimming pool 2 km off the beach, **Piscina Natural de Pajuçara**, and low tide leaves lots of natural pools to explore in the exposed reef. Check the tides; there is no point going at high tide. *Jangadas* (simple platforms with sails) cost US$10 per person per day (or about US$40 to have a *jangada* to yourself). On Sunday or local holidays in the high season it is overcrowded. At weekends lots of *jangadas* anchor at the reef, selling food and drink.

The next beach is **Ponta Verde**, which is quieter and forms the cape separating Pajuçara from the best of the urban beaches, **Jatiúca**. The better hotels are here and the beach is fronted by a pretty esplanade, lined with cafés and smart restaurants. It is tastefully lit at night. The principal restaurant area in Maceió lies just inland of northern Jatiúca.

After Jatiúca the beaches are: **Cruz das Almas**, **Jacarecica** (9 km from the centre), **Guaxuma** (12 km), **Garça Torta** (14 km), **Riacho Doce** (16 km), **Pratagi** (17 km) and **Ipioca** (23 km). Cruz das Almas and Jacarecica have good surf. Bathing is best three days before and after a full or new moon because tides are higher and the water is more spectacular.

Maceió

Sleeping 🛏	Ponta Verde Praia 6	Divina Gula 2
Casa Grande da Praia 1	Pousada Estalagem 7	
Coqueiros Express 2	Ritz Praia 8	**Bars & clubs** 🍸
Corais 3		Lampião 3
Gogó da Ema 4	**Eating** 🍴	Maikai 4
IYHA Alagamar Hostel 5	Barrica's 1	

N
500 metres
500 yards

Sights

The centre of Maceió can easily be wandered around in less than an hour. It is pretty, with a handful of handsome Portuguese buildings and some half-decent art deco. On Praça dos Martírios (Floriano Peixoto) is the **Palácio do Governo**, which also houses the **Fundação Pierre Chalita** (Alagoan painting and religious art) and the church of **Bom Jesus dos Mártires** (built 1870 and covered in handsome *azulejo* tiles). These are two of the oldest buildings in the city and well worth visiting. The **cathedral**, Nossa Senhora dos Prazeres (1840) is on Praça Dom Pedro II. The **Instituto Histórico e Geográfico** ① *R João Pessoa 382, T082-3223 7797*, has a small but good collection of indigenous and Afro- Brazilian artefacts.

Lagoa do Mundaú, a lagoon, whose entrance is 2 km south at **Pontal da Barra**, limits the city to the south and west. Excellent shrimp and fish are sold at its small restaurants and handicraft stalls and it's a pleasant place for a drink at sundown. Boats make excursions in the lagoon's channels (T082-3231 7334).

Buses 🚌
Rodoviária 1
To Marechal Deodoro
   & Praia do Francês 2
To Riacho Doce 3
To Praia Francês 4

Excursions from Maceió
🚌 ▸▸ *pp491-496*.

Marechal Deodoro and around

The former capital of Alagoas is 22 km south of Maceió across the impressive brackish lakes that give the state its name, and just behind one of the best resort beaches in the northeast, **Praia do Francês**. The town is well worth a visit, not only for its delightful crumbling buildings and expansive lake, but because of it has a wonderful, laid-back feel and is unspoilt by tourism. It's built on a hill, overlooking **Lake Manguaba**. Boat trips can be organized through tour guides such as **Del** (see Activities and tours, page 495).

The town is named after Marechal Deodoro da Fonseca, the charismatic general who founded the Brazilian republic after the deposition of Emperor Dom Pedro II. The modest townhouse where he grew up is now the **Museo Marechal Deodoro** ① *R Marechal Deodoro, daily 0800-1700, free*. It offers an interesting insight into the simplicity of life in Brazil at the end of the 19th century, even for those in the upper middle classes. Marechal Deodoro's large family lived in a few simple rooms; it is easy to imagine them dining together by oil lamp around the plain hard-wood table, watched over by the family patriarch. Typical northeastern *macramé* lace can be bought outside the museum in the adjacent houses.

Nelson da Rabeca

There are more orchestras in Marechal than in any town of this size in Brazil and the town has produced some famous musicians, such as like **Nelson da Rabeca**, whose statue stands at the gateway to the town. Nelson's is a very Brazilian story: in the 1960s, he was an illiterate 54-year-old sugar-cane cutter who had barely left Alagoas. When television first came to the town he went to a local bar to watch and saw an orchestra perform. He'd never seen a violin before and became obsessed with the instrument; its shape and its sound. So he decided to make a violin of his own, heading into the forest and cutting a sapling.

He carving the instrument from the raw wood, together with a bow, which he fitted with horsehair. It was a failure. So he built another, and then another. Until he had a working fiddle – or *rabeca* (as they are called in Portuguese). He learnt to play and began to perform with his wife. Today he is one of the most famous folk violinists in Brazil and his *rabecas* are owned and played by the finest musicians in South America including fellow Alagoan, Hermeto Pascoal. It's possible to visit Nelson's home and see his workshop as part of a guided tour, see page 495.

The town is very pleasant to wander around, which takes all of 20 minutes. The cobbled streets are lined with attractive colonial houses, some of which have been converted into modest restaurants and *pousadas*. These lead to a series of squares watched over by impressive if decrepit Portuguese churches. Some are almost beyond repair, but the most impressive, the **Igreja Matriz de Nossa Senhora da Conceição** built in 1783 has undergone full restoration, returning to its full baroque glory in late 2008. Be sure to have a peek inside. The 17th-century **Convento de São Francisco** on Praça João XXIII, has another fine baroque church, **Santa Maria Magdalena**, with a superb wooden altarpiece that has been badly damaged by termites. You can climb the church tower for views of the town. Adjoining it is the **Museu de Arte Sacra** ⓘ *Mon-Fri, 0900-1300, US$0.50, guided tours available, payment at your discretion.*

It is easy to visit Marechal on a day trip from Maceió and still have time left over to enjoy the sun and surf on **Praia do Francês**. It is one of the state's most beautiful beaches, pounded by glass-green surf at one end, protected by a fringing reef at the other and shaded by towering coconut palms along its entire length. There are plenty of *barracas*, restaurants and bars selling drinks and seafood.

There are more beaches beyond Francês, including **Barra de São Miguel**, entirely protected by the reef. It gets crowded at weekends. Several good, cheap *barracas* serve food and drink and there are some decent places to stay. Carnaval is very lively here.

Ins and outs

Minivans run to Marechal Deodoro and Praia do Francês from in front of Hospital Santa Casa next to the Texaco station on Avenida Rio Branco in the city centre. They run 0430-2200 and leave when full (every 20 minutes or so) in high season and at weekends. The journey takes 20 minutes and costs around US$1. Taxis cost around US$30. Tour operators in Maceió offer day trips and can organize air-conditioned private transport (see page 495).

Praia do Francês and Marechal Deodoro have accommodation. For more information see www.praiadofrances.net and www.turismo.al.gov.br.

→ *Phone code: 082. Population: 57,000.*

A more interesting crossing into Alagoas than the usual arrival, along the coast from north or south, can be made by frequent ferry crossings from **Neópolis** in Sergipe, to Penedo some 35 km from the mouth of the Rio São Francisco.

Penedo is a delight – a kind of forgotten Ouro Preto sweltering in the tropical heat on the banks of the sluggish Rio São Francisco, just across the water from Sergipe. Its colonial streets clamber up a series of hills from the banks of the river and are lined with wonderful old buildings. There's a stunning baroque church at every other turn, and barely a tourist in sight. The town was founded in 1565; it was overthrown by the Dutch (who built a fort here) in 1637, and then re-taken by the Portuguese shortly after. It developed as a trading port in the 17th and 18th centuries and grew rich from the gold and diamonds transported down the Rio São Francisco from the interior of Bahia and Minas. Very few of the long two-masted sailing vessels that used to cruise on the river can be seen now, although there are plenty of smaller craft. Boats travel down the river to a series of beautiful white-sand beaches in both Sergipe and Alagoas; these include **Arambipe** and **Peba**. The latter (in Alagoas) is also reachable by road. Either side of the river mouth are turtle nesting grounds, which are protected.

Ins and outs

The *rodoviária* is on the river front on Avenida Beira Rio, near the service station. There is one daily bus from Salvador (via Aracaju). Four buses a day run from Maceió, as well as *combis* 0500-1620. ↠ *See Transport, page 496.*

The very friendly and helpful **tourist office** ① *T082-3551 3907, Praça Barão de Penedo 2, www.penedo.al.gov.br, Mon-Fri 0730-1330,* has useful maps of the city marked with all the principal sights, hotels and restaurants and can organize guided tours of the baroque buildings, sometimes in English.

Sights

The most impressive building in the city is the church of **Nossa Senhora da Corrente** (1784) ① *Praça 12 de Abril s/n, Centro, Tue-Sun 0800-1700,* named 'Our Lady of the Current' presumably in homage to the river, which ran swiftly and powerfully past the town until the construction of the Rio São Francisco dam in the late 20th century. It is one of the finest pieces of Portuguese baroque in northeastern Brazil, built on an intimate scale such as those in Ouro Preto, rather than being grand like the churches of Olinda or Salvador. The simple façade hides a rich interior covered in gold leaf and centred on a splendid painted and gilt altarpiece replete with blue and rose marble. The nave is lined with masterful *azulejo* panels, and paintings by the Pernambucan Portuguese artist Libório Lázaro Lial, who was also responsible for much of the ecclesiastical decoration in the city. According to legend, fugitive slaves were hidden inside the church by a trap door behind one of the side altars.

On Praça Barão de Penedo is the neoclassical **Igreja Matriz** (closed to visitors) and the 18th-century **Casa da Aposentadoria** (1782). East and a little below this square is the Praça Rui Barbosa, where you'll find the **Convento de São Francisco** (1783) and the church of **Nossa Senhora dos Anjos** ① *Praça Rui Barbosa s/n, Centro, Tue-Fri 0800-1100 and 1400-1700, Sat and Sun 0800-1100,* whose façade is topped with typically Portuguese-baroque filigree flourishes. As you enter the church, the altar on the right depicts God's eyes on the world, surrounded by the three races (indigenous, black and white). The church a fine trompe l'oeil ceiling (1784), also by Libório Lázaro Lial, which recalls Mestre Atahyde's ceiling in the Igreja São Francisco de Assis in Ouro Preto (see page 265). The convent is still in use.

The church of **Rosário dos Pretos** ⓘ *Praça Marechal Deodoro*, (1775-1816), is open to visitors, as are **Nossa Senhora da Corrente** ⓘ *Praça 12 de Abril* (1764), and **São Gonçalo Garcia** ⓘ *Av Floriano Peixoto, Mon-Fri 0800-1200, 1400-1700*, (1758-1770). The latter has a particularly fine baroque interior and several market are held outside on weekdays. A wander around them feels like a trip back in time to an older Alagoas. Fishermen sell estuary bream straight out of the wheelbarrow, hacked up bits of cow hang unrefrigerated from meat-hooks in the heat next to stalls offering everything from baskets of home-made soap to pocket calculators. Vast sacks of grain, rice, flour and beans sit next to little hand-drawn carts in front of algae-covered walls of 400-year-old buildings and above the flurry and fluster megaphones blare out special offers and political slogans, broken by the occasional peel of a baroque church bell.

On the same street is the pink **Teatro 7 de Setembro** ⓘ *Av Floriano Peixoto 81, Mon-Fri 0800-1200, 1400-1730, Sat morning only*, with a lovely little conch-shaped auditorium dating from 1884. There are river views from the **Rocheira** just behind **Pousada Estylos**. Before the construction of the São Francisco dam, the river used to wash against the stones immediately below the parapet; you can still see the tide mark, some 4 m higher than it is today.

There are two museums. The most interesting is the **Paço Imperial** ⓘ *Praça 12 de Abril 9, Centro, T082-3551 2498, Tue-Sat 1100-1700, Sun 0800-1200*. Emperor Dom Pedro II stayed in this handsome mansion in 1859 and the building has been trading on the glory ever since. It now preserves a wonderful ceiling painting by Francisco Lopes Ruis, as well as furniture and artefacts that once belonged to the Portuguese high society families and church art. There are great views out over the river from the second floor. The **Casa de Penedo** ⓘ *R João Pessoa 126, signs point the way up the hill from Floriano Peixoto, T082-551 2516, Tue-Sun 0800-1200 and 1400-1800*, displays photographs and books on, or by, local figures.

North of Maceió ⬤◐❶ ›› *pp491-496*.

There are many interesting stopping points along the coast between Maceió and Recife. At **Paripueira**, a 40-minute bus ride from the *rodoviária* in Maceió, the beach is busy only during high season; low tide leaves lots of natural swimming pools.

Barra de Santo Antônio → *Colour map 2, C6*.
Some 45 km north of Maceió is this busy fishing village, with a palm-fringed beach on a narrow peninsula, a canoe ride away. The beaches nearby are beautiful: to the south, near the village of Santa Luzia, are **Tabuba** and **Sonho Verde**. To the north is **Carro Quebrado**, from where you can take a beach buggy to **Pedra do Cebola**, or further to **Praia do Morro**, just before the mouth of the Rio Camaragibe.

Maragogi → *Colour map 2, C6*.
Unlike many of the resorts just to the north (such as Porto de Galinhas), this little beach town has preserved its local character. Outside the high season, when the Maragogi gets crowded, life goes on pretty much as it has done before tourists began to arrive in the 1980s. And yet the beach is glorious: a seemingly infinite stretch of broad, fine sand washed by a turquoise sea. Some 6 km offshore, a fringing reef reveals a series of deep swimming pools at low tide. The current is full of sergeant majors and wrasse and with the occasional visiting turtle. Trips out there are easy to organize (expect to pay around US$10).

Ins and outs From Maceió there are two buses a day and frequent *combis* and shared taxis to Maragogi. *Combis* leave from the Maxi service station (Maxi *posto*) at Cruz de Almas on the BR-101 highway in Maraju on the northern outskirts of Maceió city (taxi from the *rodoviária* US$5). There are also two buses daily from Recife; or take a bus to São José da Coroa Grande, and take a *combi* from there.

Beyond Maragogi, a coastal road, unpaved in parts, runs to the Pernambuco border and **São José da Coroa Grande**. The main highway, BR-101, heads inland from Maceió before crossing the state border to Palmares.

◉ Sergipe and Alagoas listings

For Sleeping and Eating price codes and other relevant information, see pages 42-47.

◉ Sleeping

Aracaju *p482*
The city centre is unpleasant and seedy at night and pretty much all the hotels are scruffy and home to more than just humans. Staying here is not recommended. The beach is only 10-20 mins away.
D Amado, R Laranjeiras 532, T079-3211 9937, www.infonet.com.br/hotelamado. The best of a poor selection, with a range of a/c and fan-cooled rooms, a decent breakfast and laundry facilities. Look at several rooms before deciding.
D Brasília, R Laranjeiras 580, T079-3214 2964. It's hard to believe that these corridors of gloomy and often windowless rooms with damp, old air offer the second best sleeping option in the city centre … but they do.

Aracaju beaches *p483*
Hotels are invariably blocky affairs but there are plenty of them, along the main thoroughfare, **Av Santos Dumont**, next to the beach.
L-A Celi Praia, Av Oceânica 500, T079-2107 8000, www.celihotel.com.br. This big beige block looks like a set of offices – which is appropriate as it caters principally to business clientele. Rooms are plain but large, modern and comfortable, All have balconies, internet and there is a gym, 24-hr business centre, pool, sauna and one of the best restaurants on the beach. Good online rates.

B San Manuel, R Niceu Dantas 75, Atalaia, T079-3218 5203, www.sanmiguelpraia hotel.com.br. Pleasant, modern, well-appointed rooms decorated in tile and cream walls with Wi-Fi, international TV and business facilities (including conference rooms). The best views have sea views and terraces.
C-D Oceânica, Av Santos Dumont 413, Atalaia, T079-3243 5950, www.pousadaoceanica-se.com.br. A lemon yellow block facing the beach with scrupulously clean simple rooms tiled, painted light blue and furnished with little wooden tables and commodes.
D Relicário, Av Santos Dumont 622, Atalaia, T079-3243 1584. A mock-Chinese hotel with simple plain a/c and fan-cooled rooms right next to one of the main beach nightlife areas.

Excursions from Aracaju *p483*
D-E Pousada Vale dos Outeiros, Av José do Prado Franco 124, Laranjeiras, T079-3281 1027. A handful of a/c and fan-cooled rooms and a restaurant. Look at several – the best are on the upper floors and have views.

São Cristóvão *p483*
There are no hotels, but families rent out rooms near the *rodoviária* at the bottom of the hill.

Estância *p484*
There are a number of cheap, very simple hotels around the Praça Barão do Rio Branco.
C-D Jardim, R Joaquim Calazans 202, Estância, T079-3522 1656, www.hoteljardim-se.com.br. A modern home in a what looks like a converted town house. A range of tile and whitewash a/c rooms and a a huge buffet breakfast.

D Turismo Estanciano, Praça Barão do Rio Branco 176, T079-3522 1404, www.hotel estanciano.com. Very simple en suites with little more than a bed, fridge and a table.

Maceió p485, map p486

There are many hotels on **Pajuçara** mostly along Av Dr Antônio Gouveia and R Jangadeiros Alagoanos but many of the cheapest are not to be trusted with your belongings. The best rooms are on the beaches **Ponta Verde** and **Jatiúca**. It can be hard to find a room during the Dec-Mar holiday season, when prices go up.

L Ponta Verde Praia, Av Álvaro Otacílio 2933, Ponta Verde, T082-2121 0040, www.hotel pontaverde.com.br. The best option on the beach in an enviable location with easy walking access to the *forró* clubs and restaurants to the north and Praia Pajuçara to the west. The range of a/c rooms are all well-appointed and comfortable and with international TV and Wi-Fi. The best on the upper floors have wonderful sweeping views out over the sea. Generous buffet breakfast.

B Pousada Estalagem, R Engenheiro Demócrito Sarmento Barroca 70, T082-3327 6088, www.pousadaestalagem.com.br. Flats with little cookers in a quiet back street above a photo shop. Some have space for up to 6 in one room, making this in the **D** category for groups.

B Ritz Praia, R Eng Mário de Gusmão 1300 Laranjeiras, Ponta Verde, T082-2121 4600. This is a hotel of 2 halves the refurbished rooms on the upper 4 floors are bright and airy and have views. Those yet to be refurbished are rather gloomy but well-maintained have frowsty en suites with marble fittings. The hotel is only a block from the beach and there is a sun deck on the top floor with a pool the size of a small car.

B-C Coqueiros Express, R Desportista Humberto Guimarães 830, Ponta Verde, T082-3327 5510, www.coqueirosexpress.com.br. The best rooms in this spruce, well-run hotel are on the upper floors and have partial sea views. All are well-appointed (refurbished in

2006) and decorated in tile and light green and hanging with faux-modernist minimalist *jangada* prints. There's a garden-pond sized pool next to reception and breakfast is hearty.

D Casa Grande da Praia, R Jangadeiros Alagoanas 1528, Pajuçara, T082-3231 3332, Check the rooms here as some have spongy beds and are rather musty. The best by far are on the upper floor annexe overlooking a small garden. Staff are friendly and offer a decent service which includes a good breakfast. Very close to the beach.

D Gogó da Ema, R Laranjeiras 97, T082-3327 0329. Very simple tile and lime green rooms dominated by large double beds with decent mattresses. En suites come with little marble sinks. The hotel lies in a quiet back street a hop from the sand and offers a generous breakfast.

D-E Corais, R Desportista Humberto Guimarães 80, Pajuçara, T082-3231 9096. Very basic, musty rooms in corridors around a little garden courtyard. All are frayed, fan-cooled and en suites. Perfect if you plan to spend as little time as possible asleep and as much time as possible on the beach, which is only a few hundred metres away.

D-E IYHA Alagamar Hostel, R Pref Abdon Arroxelas 327, T082-3231 2246, alag@ superig.com.br. It can be hard to get a room here; you'll need to book 2 months in advance in high season and about a week in advance in low season. In either case the hostel requires a 50% up front deposit into their bank account – a bureaucratic ritual in Brazil. The rooms aren't that great either: all need a lick of paint and the mattresses are covered with plastic. Dorms are single-sex. Avoid the lower floors which are musty.

Camping

Camping Clube do Brasil site on Jacarecica beach, T082-3235 3600. A 15-min taxi ride from the town centre.

Camping Pajuçara, Largo da Vitória 211, T082-32121 7561. Clean, safe, food for sale. Recommended.

Marechal Deodoro and around *p488*

A Village Barra Hotel, R Sen Arnon de Mello, Barra de São Miguel, T082-3272 1000, www.villagebarrahotel.com.br. Facilities include a pool and restaurant. Excursions.

B Pousada Bougainville e Restaurant Chez Patrick, R Sargaço 3, T082-3260 1251. A pretty little *pousada* near the beach with a/c, rooms with TVs, a pool, seafood and a good French and seafood restaurant cooking.

C Pousada da Barra, Av Oceanica 249, Praia Sta Irene, Barra de São Miguel, T022-2771 3109, www.pousadadabarra-rj.com.br. Good.

C Pousada Le Soleil, R Carapeba 11, Praia do Francês, T082-3260 1240, www.pousadalesoleil.kit.net. An anonymous concrete block of a hotel with balconies close to the beach. Decent breakfast. Wi-Fi.

C-D Capitães de Areia, R Vermelha 13, Praia do Francês, 100 m from the beach, T082-3260 1477, www.capitaesdeareia.com.br. A terracotta-coloured block with terraces of rooms near the beach, a pool and a restaurant. Good low season discounts.

Penedo *p489*

C São Francisco, Av Floriano Peixoto, T082-3551 2273, www.hotelsaofrancisco.tur.br. A big, ugly 1970s block with boxy little balconied rooms all with a/c, TV and fridge. Showing its age far more than the colonial hotels.

C-D Pousada Colonial, Praça 12 de Abril 21, 5 mins' walk from the bus station, T082-3551 2355. A converted colonial building with creaky wooden floors and huge rooms – the best with views out over the river. All are fan-cooled but for the suites. Friendly, efficient reception staff.

D-E Pousada Estylos I, Praça Jácome Calheiros 79, T082-3551 2465; with another branch, **Pousada Estylos II** at R Damaso do Monte 86, T082-3551 2429. A modest modern hotel near the river with a range of a/c and fan-cooled rooms. Open sporadically, but always in high season.

D-F Imperial, Praça Coronel Peixoto 43, T082-3551 4749. Simple a/c and fan-cooled rooms with a bath, fan and hot water. The best are on the upper floors and have river views **F** for single rooms and doubles with shared bathrooms.

Barra de Santo Antônio *p490*

This is a tiny place with no visible addresses. Locals will point you to *pousadas* but it is a struggle to get lost.

D São Geraldo. Very simple but very clean, and with a restaurant.

D-E Pousada Buongiorno, T082-2121 7577 (Maceió). 6 modest rooms in a farmhouse, bathrooms but no electricity, many fruit trees.

Maragogi *p490*

C Jangadeiros, Beira Mar s/n, T082-3296 2167, www.pousadadosjangadeiros.com.br. Plain but modern tile-floor and whitewash rooms in a concrete hotel a block from the beach 5 mins north of the town centre. A little pool and good breakfast. Friendly staff.

C-D Agua de Fuego, Rodovia AL 101 Norte, T082-3296 1326, www.aguadefuego.com. The best small hotel in Maragogi with a range of spacious tile floor rooms right overlooking the beach. Friendly Argentinian owner, great breakfast and a pool. In a quiet area 15 mins' walk south of town along the beach.

D-E O Tempo e o Vento, Travessia Lourenco Wanderley 22, T082-3296 1720. Tiny little rooms right near the beach. The best are closest to the seafront. Those overlooking the town *praça* can be noisy. **F** for single.

🍴 Eating

Aracaju *p482*

🍴🍴🍴 **Cantina d'Italia**, Av Santos Dumont s/n, T079-3243 3184. The chicest option on the beachfront serving pizza and pasta to the city's middle classes. The best tables are on the upper deck.

🍴🍴 **O Dragão**, Av Santos Dumont, Atalaia, T079-3243 0664. Japanese and Chinese food, including a bottomless sushi and sashimi buffet. Served in a large mock-oriental pavilion right on the beach next to the lake.

Cariri, Av Santos Dumont 243, T079-3243 1379, www.cariri-se.com.br. Northeastern cooking including *frango caipira* (chicken cooked in a tomato and onion sauce) and *carne do sol* (beef jerky). Live *forró* music Tue-Sat. One of several similar lively clubs on this part of the beach.

São Cristóvão *p483*
Senzala do Preto Velho, R Messias Prado 84. Recommended northeastern specialities.

Maceió *p485, map p486*
The best restaurants, bars and clubs are on and around R Engenheiro Paulo B Nogueira on **Jatiúca** beach. There are many other bars and restaurants in **Pajuçara** and along Av Antônio Gouveia.

For 5 km from the beginning of Pajuçara, through Ponta Verde and Jatiuca in the north, the beaches are lined with *barracas* (thatched bars) with music, snacks and meals until 2400 (later at weekends). Vendors on the beach sell beer and food during the day; clean and safe.

There are many other bars and *barracas* at Ponto da Barra, on the lagoon side of the city and a string of cheap but high-quality stalls next to the **Lampião club** in Jatiúca in front of the **Maceió Atlantic** suites hotel. Local specialities include oysters, *pitu*, a crayfish (now scarce), and *sururu*, a type of cockle. The local ice cream, 'Shups', is recommended.
Divina Gula, R Engenheiro Paulo B Nogueira 85, T082-3235 1016, www.divin agula.com.br. Closed Mon. The best restaurant in the city, with a lively atmosphere and busy crowd. The large menu includes many overly-cheesed Italian options, pizzas, seafood and northeastern meat dishes. Portions are large enough for 2.
Barrica's, Av Álvaro Calheiros 354, Ponta Verde, www.barricaspizzaria.com.br. One of the liveliest of the waterfront bars in Maceió with live music every night, a buzzing crowd and a range of dishes from pasta to grilled or fried meat or fish, the inevitable pizzas and a handful of veggie options.

Bars and clubs

Maceió *p485, map p486*
The bars here are relaxed and varied and there are nightclubs to suit most tastes.
Lampião, Praia de Jatiúca s/n, diagonally opposite the **Maceió Atlantic** suites hotel. A very lively beachside *forró* bar with live bands every night playing live music to an eager crowd. The house band dress up as Lampião himself – in straw hats and with yokely shirts and leather jerkins and they are fronted by a bottle-blonde in a sparkly cap who has everyone up and dancing. Packed on Fri and Sat. Food available.
Maikai, R Engenheiro Paulo B Nogueira quadra 14, T082-3305 4400, www.maikai maceio.com.br. Restaurant and adjacent club with space for thousands and a range of northeastern acts, playing music from *forró* to *axé*. Currently the busiest and most popular club in town.

Entertainment

Maceió *p485, map p 486*
Cinema Arte 1 and 2, Pajuçara and Iguatemi shopping centres. **Cinema São Luiz**, R do Comércio, in the centre. All show foreign films dubbed except the cinema in **Shopping Farol**.

Festivals and events

Aracaju *p482*
1 Jan Bom de Jesus dos Navegantes, procession on the river.
1st weekend in Jan Santos Reis (Three Kings/Wise Men).
Feb/Mar Pre-carnival Carnaval.
Jun Festas Juninas.
8 Dec Both Catholic (Nossa Senhora da Conceição) and *umbanda* (*Iemenjá*) festivals.

Excursions from Aracaju *p483*
Jan The main festival in Laranjeiras is São Benedito in the first week of the month.

São Cristóvão *p483*
Mar Senhor dos Passos, held 15 days after Carnaval.
8 Sep Nossa Senhora de Vitória, the patron saint's day.
Oct/Nov Festival de Arte (moveable).

Estância *p484*
Jun The month-long festival of São João is a major event.

Maceió *p485, map p486*
27 Aug Nossa Senhora dos Prazeres.
16 Sep Freedom of Alagoas.
8 Dec Nossa Senhora da Conceição.
15 Dec Maceiofest, a great street party with *trios eléctricos*.
24 Dec Christmas Eve.
31 Dec New Year's Eve, half-day.

O Shopping

Aracaju *p482*
The *artesanato* is interesting, with pottery figures and lace a speciality. A fair is held in Praça Tobias Barreto every Sun afternoon. The municipal market is a block north of the *hidroviária* (ferry terminal).

Penedo *p489*
There is a daily market on the streets off Av Floriano Peixoto, with good hammocks. Ceramics are on sale outside Bompreço supermarket, on Av Duque de Caxias.

▲ Activities and tours

Maceió *p485, map p486*
Jose dos Santos Filho (Del),
T082-3241-4966, Mb082-8859 3407, jalbino.filho@hotmail.com. Bespoke tourist guide offering trips along the coast and in the city – including visits to Nelson da Rabeca's house in Marechal Deodoro. Very friendly, knowledgeable and with a comfortable a/c car and reasonable command of English.

⊖ Transport

Aracaju *p482*
Air The airport is 12 km from the centre. Flights to **Brasília**, **Maceió**, **Rio de Janeiro**, **Salvador**, **São Paulo** and **Recife**, with GOL, www.voegol.com.br, Oceanair, www.oceanair.com.br, and TAM, www.tam.com.br.

Bus Buses run from the old bus station at Praça João XXIII to **Laranjeiras** and **São Cristóvão** (45 mins, US$3).
Long-distance buses run from the *rodoviária*, 4 km from the centre. Buses to the *rodoviária* run from Praça João XXIII, the terminal near the *hidroviária* and from Capela at the top of Praça Olímpio Campos. To **Salvador**, 6-7 hrs, at least 11 a day with Bonfim, US$25, executive service at 1245, US$35 (1 hr quicker). To **Maceió**, US$25 with Bonfim. To **Recife** at 2330, US$35, 10 hrs. To **Rio**, US$20, 30 hrs. To **São Paulo**, US$120, 35 hrs **Belo Horizonte** US$85, 20 hrs, **Foz de Iguaçu**, US$200, 22 hrs. To **Estância**, US$5, 1½ hrs. To **Penedo**, 3 hrs, US$7, 2 a day.

São Cristóvão *p483*
Bus São Pedro buses run to the old *rodoviária* in the centre of **Aracaju** (45 mins, US$1.25).

Estância *p484*
Bus Many buses stop at the *rodoviária*, on the main road. To **Salvador** 4 hrs, US$12-14.

Maceió *p485, map p486*
Air Buses marked 'aeorporto' run to the airport from Ponta Verde/Pajuçara, every 30 mins 0630-2100; allow 45 mins. Taxis charge a flat rate of around US$23. There are flights to **Aracaju**, **Brasília**, **Florianópolis**, **Rio de Janeiro**, **Salvador**, **São Paulo**, **Recife**, **Belo Horizonte** and **Porto Alegre** with GOL, www.voegol.com.br, TAM, www.tam.com.br, and Webjet Linhas Aéreas, www.webjet.com.br.

Bus Taxis from town go to all the northern beaches (for example 30 mins to Riacho Doce), but buses run as far as Ipioca. The Jangadeiras bus marked 'Jacarecica-Center, via Praias' runs past all the beaches as far as **Jacarecica**. From there you can change to 'Riacho Doce-Trapiche', 'Ipioca' or 'Mirante' buses for **Riacho Doce** and **Ipioca**. These last 3 can also be caught in the centre on the seafront avenue below the Praça Sinimbu (US$1 to Riacho Doce). To return take any of these options, or take a bus marked 'Shopping Center' and change there for 'Jardim Vaticana' bus, which goes through Pajuçara. *Combis* to **Marechal Deodoro**, **Praia do Francês** and **Barra de São Miguel** leave from opposite the Hospital Santa Casa in front of the Texaco service station. *Combi* US$2 to Marechal Deodoro, 30 mins, calling at Praia do Francês in each direction. Last bus back from Praia do Francês to Maceió at 1800.

Long distance The 'Ponte Verde/Jacintinho' bus runs via Pajuçara from the centre to the *rodoviária*, also take 'Circular' bus (25 mins Pajuçara to *rodoviária*). Bus to **Recife**, 10 a day, 3½ hrs express (more scenic coastal route, 5 hrs), US$15. To **Aracaju**, US$18, 5 hrs (potholed road). To **Salvador**, 10 hrs, 4 a day, US$50 (*rápido* costs more). To **Penedo**, 4 buses a day and *combis* from outside the *rodoviária*. **Car hire** Localiza, and others in the airport and through hotels.

Penedo *p489*

Bus Daily bus to **Salvador** via **Aracaju**, 6 hrs, at 0600, US$25, book in advance. Also a bus direct to Aracaju, 3 hrs, US$7. Buses south are more frequent from **Neópolis**, 6 a day 0630-1800, change here for **Aracaju**, 2 hrs, US$7. To **Maceió**, 115 km, 4 buses a day in either direction, US$12, 3-4 hrs and *combis*. **Ferry** Frequent launches for foot passengers and bicycles across the river to **Neópolis**, 10 mins, US$0.50, for connections by bus to **Aracaju**. The dock in Penedo is on Av Duque de Caxias, below Bompreço. The ferry makes

3 stops in Neópolis, the second is closest to the *rodoviária* (which is near the **Clube Vila Nova**, opposite the Texaco station). There is also a car ferry (every 30 mins, US$3, take care when driving on and off).

ⓘ Directory

Aracaju *p482*

Banks Visa ATMs at shopping centres, **Banco do Brasil**, Praça Gen Valadão and **Bradesco** in the city centre. MasterCard ATMs at Banco 24 hrs, Av Francisco Porto and Av Geraldo Sobral, in the city centre close to the Shell gas station.

Maceió *p485, map p486*

Banks Open 1000-1500. Good rates at Banespa. Plenty of branches of **Bradesco** for ATMs. Cash against MasterCard at Banorte, R de Comércio, 306, Centro. **Internet** There are myriad internet cafés throughout the city. **Laundry** Lave-Sim, R Jangadas Alagoanas 962, Pajuçara. Washouse, R Jangadas Alagoanas 698, Pajuçara. **Medical services** Unimed, Av Antonio Brandao 395, Farol, T082-221 1177, used to be São Sebastião hospital. Pediatria 24 horas, R Durval Guimaraes 519, Ponta Verde, T082-3231 7742/7702. **Dentist**: Pronto Socorro Odontologico de Maceio, Av Pio XV11, Jatiuca, T082-3325 7534. **Post office** R João Pessoa 57, Centro, 0700-2200.

Penedo *p489*

Banks Bradesco, on Av Duque de Caxias, opposite Bompreço supermarket, with Visa ATM. Open 0830-1300. **Restaurant e Bar Lulu**, Praça 12 de Abril, will change cash if conditions suit the owner, fair rates. **Post office** Av Floriano Peixoto, opposite Hotel Imperial. **Telephone** On Barão de Penedo.

Maragogi *p490*

Banks Bradesco in the town centre.

Pernambuco

Once the main producer of the world's sugar, today the state of Pernambuco offers a variety of attractions from beaches to traditional culture, colonial cities and museums. Recife, the state capital, is the main industrial and commercial centre with a very lively cultural scene and extensive urban beaches, while Olinda offers colonial elegance and a number of magnificent churches. Towns such as Caruarú and Nova Jerusalém, in the sertão, host very lively festivals and have some of the country's strongest artisan traditions working with clay, straw and leather handicrafts.

Pernambuco is saturated with music. In the 1970s, musician Naná Vasconcelos took the traditional beats of forró, ciranda and maracatú to New York, Miles Davis and beyond. In the 1980s and 1990s the mangue beat movement fused them with rock, electronica and trance. Many of Brazil's most famous contemporary avant-garde musicians are from Pernambuco, and Recife is considered Brazil's musical capital. Carnaval in the city of Recife and nearby Olinda is one of the best in the country. Nana Vasconcelos opens the festival leading a drum orchestra that dwarfs those in Bahia, and the maracatu prepares the way for three days of African-Brazilian cultural processions and relentless partying. ▶▶ *For listings, see pages 510-520.*

Recife and around ⊜⊘⊕⊗⊙▲⊙⊙ ▶▶ pp510-520. Colour map 2, B6.

→ *Phone code: 081. Population: 1.2 million.*

Recife is one of the most attractive large cities in Brazil. From afar it looks as blighted by skyscrapers as Rio de Janiero or Belo Horizonte, but in the shadows are many fine colonial buildings from the sugar boom, watching over little shady squares or sitting on the edge of the filigree of canals and waterways that divide up the city. The colonial heart is **Recife Antigo**; a no-go area like Rio's Lapa until a decade ago, but now the centre of the city's booming music and alternative culture scene. To the south of the centre are a string of urban beach suburbs – **Pina**, **Boa Viagem** and **Piedade** – which although frequented by bull sharks are among the cleanest urban beaches in the country. The city prides itself on good food and unique fashion and has many fine restaurants and boutiques. Although they retain separate names, Recife and Olinda have long ceased to be two cities. Olinda is now Recife's colonial suburb.

Ins and outs

Getting there International and domestic flights arrive at **Gilberto Freyre airport** ① *Guararapes, 12 km from the city centre, near the hotel district of Boa Viagem*. The airport is modern and spacious, with a tourist office, banks, shops, post office and car rental and tour agencies. Airport taxis cost US$5 to the seafront; bus No 52 runs to the centre, US$0.40.

Long-distance buses arrive at the **Terminal Integrado dos Passageiros (TIP)** ① *12 km outside the city near the Oficina Brenn and cultural museum at São Lourenço da Mata, T081-3452 1999*, pronounced 'chippy'. To get to the centre from the *rodoviária*, take the metrô to Central station, 30 minutes. If going to Boa Viagem, get off the metrô at Central station (Joanna Bezerra station is unsafe) and take a bus or taxi (US$8) from there. ▶▶ *See Transport, page 519.*

Getting around **City buses** cost US$0.30-0.60; they are clearly marked and run frequently until about 2230. Many central bus stops have boards showing routes. On buses, especially at night, look out for landmarks as street names are hard to see. Commuter services, known

1 Recife orientation

➡ **Recife maps**
1 **Recife orientation, page 498**
2 Recife centre, page 501
3 Boa Viagem, page 504

OLINDA

Alto da Sé

To Northern Beaches

J Nabuco

Av Presidente Kennedy

Rio Beberibe

Santa Teresa

ENCRUZILHADA

Convention Centre & Empetur

Av Olinda

Estrada de Belém

Gov A Magalhães

Av Cruz Cabugá

Rio Beberibe

RECIFE

Av Norte

Estrada Arraial

Casa Amarela, Sítio Trindade & Casa Forte complex

Av Rosa e Silva

Cemitério Santo Amaro

P de Limoeiro

A Lisboa

Estr do Encanamento

Museu do Homem do Nordeste

POÇO

J Bonifácio

Museu do Estado

Av João de Barros

Praça 13 de Maio

To Dois Irmãos Zoo & Botanical Gardens

Rio Capibaribe

Av Rui Barbosa

Av Caatauna

BOA VISTA

MADALENA

Gov A Magalhães

Dom Bosco

Central Metrô Station

To Várzea

Av Caxanga

Atlantic Ocean

Joaquei Clube

M Gonçalves da Luz

Estr dos Remédios

Joana Bezerra

Dantas Barreto

Bacia do Pina

A de Góis

To the North & João Pessoa

Av Abdias de Carvalho

Afogados Ipiranga

R São Miguel

R Imperial

H Bandeira

3

Mangueira

Rio Jiquiá

PINA

Rio Pina

Av Domingos Ferreira

Av Boa Viagem

Santa Luzia

Av Central

Rio Tejipió

Edgar Werneck

Barro

Dr J Rufino

IMBIRIBEIRA

Av Sul

Av Marechal Mascarenhas Morais

To Rodoviária (5 stops)

BR 101

Gen MacArthur

Shopping Center Recife

Canal Jordão

BOA VIAGEM

Praça Boa Viagem

N

1 km
1 miles

IBURA

To the South & Maceió

Gilberto Freyre

To Monte Guararapes & NS das Prazeres

To Piedade

Rock in Recife

Forget Rio. Ignore São Paulo. Recife is the capital of modern Brazilian music. You'll find no re-sampled old-hat bossa nova or cheesy funk here, and no identikit Salvador carnival bands fronted by a woman in a tiny skirt. Instead, bursting from the city's various grungy streetside bars and pouring in from the rocky desert of the state's interior, is a seemingly endless diversity of bands and artists fusing the old with the new: octogenarian mouth organists playing psychedelic *forró*, agonized students thrashing out *maracatu* fired-glum rock, hip hopsters fusing dub with *embolada* desert poetry …

Every day there is a new name on everyone's lips and a new band tipped for stardom on the Brazilian or international stage. Some have already made it there,

including Naná Vasconcelos (see page 500), Otto and DJ Dolores. But it wasn't always this way. Recife's musical revolution began in the 1980s with Chico Science and his band Nação Zumbi who invented a movement called mangue beat – a kind of Bauhaus of rock that embraced all styles in an angry shout against the conservatism and conformity that had dominated music here until then. Nação Zumbi still play regularly in Recife, sadly without Chico who died in a car accident in the 1990s.

Be sure to catch some live music while you're in Recife and check out www.manguebeat.com.br for a podcast of the latest offerings, or www.reciferock.com.br for the latest gigs. For venues, see page 514.

as the **metrô** but not underground, leave from the Central station; they have been extended to serve the *rodoviária* (frequent trains, 0500-2300, US$0.40 single). Integrated bus-metrô routes and tickets (US$1) are explained in a leaflet issued by **CBTU Metrorec**, T081-3251 5256. Trolleybuses run in the city centre. Taxis are plentiful; fares double on Sunday, after 2100 and during holidays.

Orientation The city centre consists of three sections: Recife proper, Santo Antônio and São José, and Boa Vista and Santo Amaro. The first two are on islands formed by the rivers Capibaribe, Beberibe and Pina, while the third is made into an island by the Canal Tacaruna, which separates it from the mainland. The centre is always very busy by day; the crowds and narrow streets, especially in the Santo Antônio district, can make it a confusing city to walk around. But this adds to its charm. This is one of the few cities in Brazil where it is possible to get lost and chance upon a shady little square or imposing colonial church or mansion. Recife has the main dock area, with the commercial buildings associated with it. South of the centre is the residential and beach district of **Boa Viagem**, reached by bridge across the Bacia do Pina. **Olinda**, the old capital, is only 7 km to the north (see page 505). Although the streets are generally too full to present danger it is wise to be vigilant where the streets are quiet. Always take a taxi after dark if you are walking alone or in a pair.

Tourist information The main office for **Empetur** ⓘ *Centro de Convenções, Complexo Rodoviário de Salgadinho, T081-3427 8000, www.empetur.com.br*, is between Recife and Olinda. There are other branches in Boa Viagem (T081-3463 3621), and at the airport (T081-3224 2361, open 24 hours); they cannot book hotels, but the helpful staff speak English and can offer leaflets and decent maps.

Naná Vasconcelos

Brazilian music without Recife's master percussionist Naná Vasconcelos would be like jazz without Charles Mingus. Bossa nova had been introduced into the USA by Stan Getz. But it was Naná and Paranense Airto Moreira who placed Brazilian percussion in the upper echelons of the serious jazz world. Naná was introduced to the US jazz scene by Miles Davis who went to one of the percussionist's concerts in the 1970s. And during a 25-year sojourn in New York he added his trademark *berimbau* and percussion to scores of records by artists like the CODONA trio

(which he led with Don Cherry and Colin Walcott), Jan Garbarek, Pat Metheny, Gato Barbieri and numerous others. His most remarkable work, though, is purely Brazilian. Together with Egberto Gismonti and on albums like *Dança das Cabecas* (ECM), he created a new musical genre which fused jazz, classical and Brazilian styles. And his *Fragmentos* (Nucleo Contemporaneo/Tzadik) and *Storytelling* (EMI) albums are complex, mesmerizing tapestries of percussion and vocals that beautifully evoke Brazilian landscapes and local people.

Safety Opportunistic theft is unfortunately common in the streets of Recife and Olinda (especially on the streets up to Alto da Sé). Keep a good hold on bags and cameras, and do not wear a watch. Prostitution is reportedly common in Boa Viagem, so choose nightclubs with care. Should you have any trouble contact the **tourist police** ① *T081-3326 9603/ T081-3464 4088*.

Sights

Recife's architecture is far less celebrated than its pretty neighbour, Olinda, but it retains some very attractive buildings. Rua da Aurora, which watches over the Capibaribe river, is lined with stately palladian and neoclassical buildings. The islands to the south, over the filigree of bridges, are dotted with imposing churches and surprisingly lavish civic structures, especially around the Praça da República. The city began with the Dutch and the twin forts on the island today known as **Recife Antigo** (Old Recife). The **Forte do Brum** ① *Tue-Fri 0900-1600, Sat and Sun 1400-1600, donation optional*, is now an army museum. The **Forte das Cinco Pontas**, was built by the Dutch in 1630, seven years before Maurice of Nassau sacked and burned Olinda. The two forts controlled access to the port at the northern and southern entrances respectively. Within Forte das Cinco Pontas is the **Museu da Cidade do Recife** ① *Mon-Fri 0900-1800, Sat and Sun 1300-1700, US$0.50 donation*, which houses a cartographic history of the settlement of Recife.

   Recife is replete with churches. The most famous is the **Concatedral de São Pedro dos Clérigos** ① *Pátio de São Pedro, R Barão da Vitória at Av Dantas Barreto, Mon-Fri 0800-1200 and 1400-1600, T081-3224 2954*, a towering baroque building with a beautiful painted interior, overlooking one of the city's best-preserved colonial squares. The area has been renovated and is filled with little shops, restaurants and bars, and nominated as a national historical monument. There are sporadic music and poetry shows evenings from Wednesday to Sunday. Also worth visiting is the 18th-century **Basílica e Convento de Nossa Senhora do Carmo** ① *Av Dantas Barreto, Santo Antônio, T081-3224 3341, Mon-Fri 0800-1200 and 1400-1900, Sat 0700-1200, Sun 0700-1000*, named after the city's patron saint, which has a magnificent painted ceiling and high altar. The **Capela da Ordem Terceira do São Francisco** ① *R do Imperador, Santo Antônio, T081-3224 0994, Mon-Fri*

2 Recife

➡ **Recife maps**
1 Recife orientation, page 498
2 **Recife centre, page 501**
3 Boa Viagem, page 504

Sleeping
América **2**
Central **3**
Pousada Villa Boa Vista **5**
Recife Plaza **4**
São Domingos **2**

Eating
Gelattos **2**
Leite **3**

Churches
Basílica de Nossa Senhora de Penha **14**
Capela da Ordem Terceira do São Francisco **13**
Capela Dourada **1**
Espírito Santo **2**
Madre de Deus **3**
Matriz de Boa Vista **4**

Nossa Senhora da Conceição dos Militares **5**
Nossa Senhora do Carmo **6**
Nossa Senhora do Livramento **7**
Nossa Senhora do Rosário dos Pretos **8**
Pilar **9**
Santo Antônio **10**
São José do Ribamar **11**

São Pedro dos Clérigos **12**

Buses
To Itamaracá & Igarassu **1**
To Porto da Galinhas **2**
To Boa Viagem **3**

0800-1130 and 1400-1700, Sat 0800-1130, (1695-1710 and 19th century), is one of the finest baroque buildings in northeast Brazil and is another national monument. The lavish façade conceals a gorgeous gilt-painted interior with ceiling panels by Manuel de Jesus Pinto. The **Basílica de Nossa Senhora de Penha** ① *Praça Dom Vital, São José, T081-3424 8500, Tue-Thu 0800-1200 and 1500-1700, Fri 0600-1800, Sat 1500-1700, Sun 0700-0900*, is an Italianate church that holds a traditional 'blessing of São Felix' on Fridays, attended by hundreds of sick Pernambucans in search of miracles.

West of the centre

About a kilometre to the west of the fort around the **Praça Treze de Maio** is a lively bar area with many live music venues thronging with a bohemian crowd. This area is to Recife what Lapa is to Rio and remains at the centre of the city's musical boom, which begun with mangue beat (see box page 499). This style of music was named in homage to the mangroves that fill Recife's rivers and canals, and has spawned artists like Otto, Siba and DJ Dolores. Be sure to take a taxi there and back for safety.

Following Avenida Rui Barbosa west of the centre, the **Museu do Estado** ① *Av Rui Barbosa 960, Graças, Tue-Fri 0900-1700, Sat and Sun 1400-1700*, has excellent paintings by the 19th-century landscape painter, Teles Júnior.

About 7 km west of the centre, the **Museu do Homem do Nordeste** ① *Av 17 de Agosto 2223, Casa Forte*, is a museum complex comprising the following: **Museu de Arte Popular**, containing ceramic figurines (including some by Mestre Alino and Zé Caboclo); the **Museu do Açúcar**, on the history and technology of sugar production, with models of colonial mills and collections of antique sugar bowls; the **Museu de Antropologia**; the **Fundação Joaquim Nabuco** ① *Av 17 de Agosto 2187, T081-3073 6363, www.fundaj.gov.br*; and the modern museum of popular remedies, **Farmacopéia Popular** ① *T081-3441 5500, Tue, Wed, Fri-Sun 1300-1600, Thu 0900-1600, US$2*. To get to the museum complex, take the 'Dois Irmãos' bus (check that it's the correct one, with 'Rui Barbosa' posted in window, as there are two) from outside the Banorte building near the post office on Guararapes, but it is much easier to take a taxi (around US$15).

South of the centre

The **Oficina Brennand** ① *Propriedade Santos Cosme e Damião s/n, Várzea, T081-3271 2466, www.brennand.com.br, Mon-Fri 0800-1700, US$3*, is a Dali-esque fantasy garden and museum preserving hundreds of monumental ceramic sculptures by Latin America's most celebrated ceramic artist, Francisco Brennand. Enormous snake penises in hob-nailed boots are set in verdant lawns; surrealist egret heads look out over a Burle Marx garden from 10-m-high tiled walls; haunting chess-piece figures in top hats gaze at tinkling fountains. The museum has a very good air-conditioned restaurant and gift shop. There is no public transport here so take a taxi from Recife (around US$15 including waiting time; alternatively take a local bus to the *rodoviária* or to Varzea suburb and do a round trip from there, US$10).

The Brennands are one of the wealthiest old-money families in Brazil and Ricardo Brennand – as if not to be outdone by his brother – has his own museum 10 minutes' taxi ride away. The **Instituto Ricardo Brennand** ① *Alameda Antônio Brennand, Várzea, T081-2121 0352, www.institutoricardo brennand.org.br, Tue-Sun 1300-1700 (last entry 1630), US$3*, is a priceless collection of European and Brazilian art (including the largest conglomeration of Dutch-Brazilian landscapes in the world), books, manuscripts and medieval weapons housed in a fake Norman castle with its own moat and giant swimming pool.

Brazilian dance

Dance is one of the world's great expanding art forms and pastimes, with salsa (which originated in Hispanic America and is little known in Brazil), probably being the most popular Latin dance worldwide. Brazil has numerous dance styles which are perhaps even more beautiful and infectious than salsa and involve similar steps over music, also in 2/4 time. The most famous and probably the most difficult is samba, which comes in varying forms and can be danced either individually or as a couple. As a rhythm, samba finds its origins in a Bahian two-time drum beat called *batucada*. In its current form it was born in the slums of Rio, where hand claps, whistles, tambourines, guitars, *cavaquinhos* and the squeaky *cuíca* drum were added to produce a fevered syncopated soup. The basic steps, particularly of the solo samba danced at Carnaval are notoriously difficult to master and tiring to dance. But they are an astoundingly beautiful combination of grace and energy, unrivalled by any other Latin American dance: head and body perfectly poised and floating over the perpetual, sensual motion of the hips.

Forró, which is the most popular beach dance for young Brazilians, especially in the northeast, is a good deal easier than samba and was especially invented for Anglo Saxons who dance like they have two left feet. The name is thought to be a corruption of 'for all', after 'For alls', which were end-of-the-week parties held by British railway workers in Pernambuco during their construction of the Brazilian Great Western Railway at the turn of the 19th century. The rhythm was brought to national popularity by Luiz Gonzaga in the 1950s and 1960s and has now become the party and carnival music of choice north of Bahia. *Forró* is also in 2/4 time but is far choppier than samba, with the driving rhythm coming from the accordion rather than from drums. It is danced in pairs.

Pernambuco has produced numerous others dances, including *frevo*, which is danced at Carnaval, *coco* and *ciranda*, all of whose rhythms can be heard underneath many *mangue beat* songs.

Most other Brazilian styles are variations of samba or *forró*; such as *pagode* which comes from the former, and lambada, from the latter. Tango is also popular, mainly in Rio where it is danced every Saturday at the antiques market on Rua do Lavradio in Lapa.

Boa Viagem → *See map page 504.*
This is the main residential and hotel quarter, currently being developed at the northern end of town. The 8-km promenade lined with high-rise buildings commands a striking view of the Atlantic, but the beach is backed by a busy road, crowded at weekends and not very clean. During the January breeding season, sharks come close to the shore. You can go fishing on *jangadas* at Boa Viagem at low tide. The main *praça* has a good market at weekends.

Ins and outs   To get there from the centre, take any bus marked 'Boa Viagem'; from Nossa Senhora do Carmo, take buses marked 'Piedade', 'Candeias' or 'Aeroporto', which run along Avenida Domingos Ferreira, two blocks parallel to the beach, all the way to Praça Boa Viagem (at Avenida Boa Viagem 500). To get to the centre, take a bus marked 'CDU' or 'Setubal' from Avenida Domingos Ferreira.

3 Boa Viagem

R José Paes de Barros
R José Rodrigues
R do Aeroclube
R Vita Teimosa
R Domingo Ferreira
R Atlântico
R Tomé
R Gibson
R Joaquim
R Silva
Praça das Casuarinas
Av Domingos Ferreira
Av Boa Viagem
Praia de Boa Viagem
R Raul
R Artur Muniz
R Zeferino Galvão
R Francisco da Cunha
R Henrique Capitulino
R Prof Eduardo Wanderley Filho
Av Conselheiro Aguiar
R Prof José Brandão
R Ten João Cícero
R Pe Bernardino Pessoa
R Maria Carolina
R Antônio Falcão
Av Domingos Ferreira
R Mamanguape
R Félix de Brito
R Faustino Porto
R Pe Carapuceiro
Shopping Center Recife
R Prof José Medeiros
R Fernando Simões Barbosa
R Bruno Veloso
Av Domingos Ferreira
R dos Navegantes
Av Boa Viagem
Praia de Boa Viagem
R Gen Edson Amancio
R Visc de Jequitinhonha
R Dom José Lopes
R Mq de Valença
R Barão de Souza Leão
NS de Boa Viagem
Praça Boa Viagem
To Airport

To 10 & Recife Centre

Atlantic Ocean

Boa Viagem detail

Av Conselheiro Aguiar
R dos Navegantes
R Petrolina
Av Boa Viagem
R SH Cardim
Praça Boa Viagem
NS de Boa Viagem
R Barão de Souza Leão

➡ Recife maps
1 Recife orientation, page 498
2 Recife centre, page 501
3 **Boa Viagem, page 504**

200 metres
200 yards

Sleeping ⬤
Albergue do Mar **9**
Aconchego **1**
Coqueiral **2**
Do Sol **4**
Maracatú do Recife **3**
Pousada da Julieta **5**
Pousada da Praia **6**
Praia **10**
Recife Monte **7**
Uzi Praia **8**

Eating ⬤
Bargaço **1**
Chica Pitanga **2**
Churrascaria Porcão **3**
Ilha da Kosta **5**
La Capannina **6**
La Maison **7**
Parraxaxa **8**
Peng **9**
Real Eza **10**
Romana **11**
Tempero Verde **12**
Tio Dadá **13**

→ *Colour map 2, B6. Phone code: 081. Population: 350,000.*

About 7 km north of Recife is the old capital, a UNESCO World Heritage Site, founded in 1537. The compact network of cobbled streets is steeped in history and very inviting for a wander. Olinda is a charming spot to spend a few relaxing days, and a much more appealing base than Recife. A programme of restoration, partly financed by the Dutch government, was initiated in order to comply with the recently conferred title of 'national monument', but much is still in desperate need of repair.

Ins and outs

Getting there and around From Recife, take any bus marked 'Rio Doce', No 981, which has a circular route around the city and beaches; or No 33 from Avenida Nossa Senhora do Carmo, US$1; or 'Jardim Atlântico' from the central post office at Siqueira Campos (US$1, 30 minutes). From the airport, take the 'Aeroporto' bus to Avenida Domingos Ferreira in Boa Viagem and change to one of the buses mentioned above. From the Recife *rodoviária*, take the metrô to Central station (Joana Bezerra is unsafe) and then change. In all cases, alight in Olinda at Praça do Carmo. Taxi drivers between Olinda and Recife often try to put their meters on rate 2 (only meant for Sundays, holidays and after 2100), but should change it to rate 1 when queried. A taxi from Boa Viagem should cost around US$8, US$12 at night. From Olinda to the centre of Recife, take a bus marked 'Piedade/Rio Doce' or 'Barra de Jangada/Casa Caiada'

Tourist information The **Secretaria de Turismo** ⓘ *Praça do Carmo, T081-3429 9279, daily 0900-2100*, provides a complete list of all historic sites and a useful map, *Sítio Histórico*. Guides with identification cards wait in Praça do Carmo. They are former street children and half the fee for a full tour of the city (about US$12) goes to a home for street children. If you take a guide you will be safe from mugging, which does unfortunately occur.

Sights

The city boasts an ornate church on almost every corner, but its 16th-century monastery and convent are particularly worth seeking out. **Basilica e Mosteiro de São Bento** ⓘ *R São Bento, Mon-Fri 0830-1130, 1430-1700, Mass Sat 0630 and 1800; Sun 1000, with Gregorian chant; monastery closed except with written permission*, was founded 1582 by the Benedictine monks, burnt by the Dutch in 1631 and restored in 1761. It is the site of Brazil's first law school and where slavery in Brazil was first abolished. The magnificent gold altar was on loan to New York's Guggenheim Museum at the time of writing. Despite its weathered exterior, the **Convento de São Francisco** ⓘ *Ladeira de São Francisco, (1585)*, has splendid woodcarving and paintings, superb gilded stucco. The **Capela de São Roque**, within the church of **Nossa Senhora das Neves** ⓘ *in the same building, Tue-Fri 0700-1130, 1400-1700, Sat 0700-1200, US$0.40, Mass Tue at 1900, Sat at 1700 and Sun at 0800*, is adorned with *azulejos*.

It's worth making the short, but very steep, climb up the **Alto da Sé** to the cathedral for views out over Olinda, the palm tree-fringed beaches and the distant skyscrapers of Recife. The plain and simple **Igreja da Sé** ⓘ *Mon-Fri 0800-1200, 1400-1700, (1537)*, has been a cathedral since 1677 and was the first church to be built in the city. The **Igreja da Misericórdia** ⓘ *R Bispo Coutinho, daily 1145-1230, 1800-1830, (1540)*, a short stroll downhill from the cathedral, has some beautiful *azulejo* tiling and gold work but seemingly random opening hours. The **Igreja do Carmo** (1581), on a small hill overlooking Praça do Carmo, is similarly impressive, but has been closed for years despite assurances that it would be refurbished. Olinda has many handsome civic buildings too, including streets of 17th-century houses with latticed balconies, heavy doors and brightly painted stucco walls. Some, like the mansion housing the **Mourisco** restaurant (Praça João Alfredo 7), are in the Portuguese Manueline style, their façades replete with Moorish architectural motifs.

There's a thriving arts and crafts community in Olinda and this is a good place to stock up on regional souvenirs. Look out for terracotta figurines and woodcarvings. The figurines are often by named artisans (look for their autograph imprinted in the clay on the base) and are becoming collectors' items. You'll find shops selling arts and crafts near the cathedral and in the handicraft shops at the **Mercado da Ribeira** ① *R Bernardo Vieira de Melo*, and the **Mercado Eufrásio Barbosa** ① *Av Segismundo Gonçalves at Santos Dumont, Varadouro*.

Sleeping 🛏	Pousada dos Quatro	Maison do Bonfim 2
7 Colinas 1	Cantos 7	Mourisco 4
Albergue do Fortim 2	Pousada Peter 8	Oficina do Sabor 5
Olinda Hostel 3	Pousada São Francisco 9	
Pousada do Amparo 6	São Pedro 10	Bars & clubs 🍸
Pousada d'Olinda 4		Bodega do Veio 7
Pousada d'Olinda	Eating 🍽	Farandola 6
no Varadouro 5	Goya 1	Marola 3

The beaches close to Olinda are polluted, but those further north, beyond Casa Caiada, at **Janga**, and **Pau Amarelo**, are beautiful, palm-fringed and usually deserted (although the latter can be dirty at low tide). There are many simple cafés where you can eat *sururu* (clam stew in coconut sauce), *agulha frita* (fried needle-fish), *miúdo de galinha* (chicken giblets in gravy), *casquinha de carangueijo* (seasoned crabmeat) and *farinha de dendê* (served in crab shells). Visit the Dutch fort on Pau Amarelo beach where there is a small craft fair on Saturday nights. To get to the beaches, take either a 'Janga' or 'Pau Amarela' bus; to return to Recife, take a bus marked 'Varodouro'.

Southern coast ⊜▲ ▶▶ *pp510-520.*

Gaibú and around

Heading south from Recife are some of the best beaches in the state. The first stop is the beautiful and quiet beach at **Gaibú**, 30 km south, where there are *pousadas* and cheap restaurants. The scenic **Cabo de Santo Agostinho**, with a ruined fort, is 5 km to the east. About 1 km on foot from Gaibú is the beautiful **Praia Calhetas**. The beach at **Itapuama** is even emptier. Buses to Gaibú and the beaches run frequently from **Cabo**, Pernambuco's main industrial city, which has a few interesting churches and forts and a **Museu da Abolição**, which has dusty displays about the history and abolition of the slave trade. To get to Cabo take a bus signed 'Centro do Cabo' from the airport in Recife.

Nearby, **Suape** has many 17th-century buildings, while the **Reserva Biológica de Saltinho** preserves some of the last vestiges of Atlantic forest in the northeast.

Porto de Galinhas → *Phone code: 081.*

Sixty kilometres south of Recife, Porto de Galinhas – whose name means 'port of chickens' because slaves were smuggled here in chicken crates – was one of the first of a string of low-key beach resorts discovered in the 1990s. Back then it was little more than a beach and two sandy streets; the myth of its tranquil charm endures – but it is only a myth. Today Porto de Galinhas is well on its way to becoming a full-scale resort comparable those near Porto Seguro in Bahia. The sandy streets are asphalted and lined with shops and restaurants, while the beaches are backed with *pousadas* and resort hotels for several kilometres north and south. There is a reef close to the shore, so swimming is only possible at high tide.

Buses and minivans run from Avenida Dantas Barreto and Rua do Peixoto in Recife, at least hourly. Taxis cost around US$50. The **Centro de Informacões Turisticas** ① *R da Esperança s/n, T081-3552 1728, www.bureaudeinformacoes.tur.br*, has maps, information on transport, hotels and tour operators and a few English-speaking staff.

South of Porto de Galinhas

Eighty kilometres south of Recife are the beaches of **Barra do Sirinhaém**, with some tourist development and three hotels, including **Dos Caraventos** (**D**). Fishermen make trips to offshore islands (good views). Beyond these are the little towns of **Tamandare** and **São José da Coroa Grande**, which are quieter than Porto de Galinhas, and have a few simple places to stay.

Northern coast ●●●●● ▸▸ pp510-520.

Igarassu → *Colour map 2, B6. Phone code: 081. Population: 77,500.*
Some 39 km north of Recife on the road to João Pessoa, Igarassu has the first church built in Brazil, **SS Cosme e Damião** (1535) and the convent of **Santo Antônio**, a beautiful baroque building with some very fine gilt work and *azulejos*.

Itamaracá → *Phone code: 081. Population: 14,000.*
North of Igarassu the road passes through coconut plantations to **Itapissuma**, where there is a bridge to **Itamaracá** island. According to the locals, this is where Adam and Eve spent their holidays (so does everyone else on Sunday now). It has the old Dutch **Forte Orange**, built in 1631; an interesting penal settlement with gift shops, built round the 1747 sugar estate buildings of Engenho São João, which still have much of the old machinery, charming villages and colonial churches, as well as some fine, wide beaches. At one of them, **Praia do Forte Orange**, Ibama has a centre for the study and preservation of manatees, **Centro Nacional de Conservação e Manejo de Sirênios** or **Peixe-boi** ① *Tue-Sun 1000-1600*.

There are pleasant trips by *jangada* from Praia do Forte Orange to **Ilha Coroa do Avião**, a recently formed sandy island, which has rustic beach bars and a research station for the development of wildlife and migratory birds. The beaches of **Sossego** and **Enseada** also have some bars but are quiet and relatively undiscovered. The crossing is 3 km north of Itamaracá town; recommended for sun worshippers.

Further north again, two hours from Recife by bus, is **Pontas de Pedra**, an old fishing village with a nice beach, lots of bars and opportunities for fishing and diving.

At the Pernambuco–Paraíba border, a 27-km dirt road goes to the fishing village of **Pitimbu**, with *jangadas*, surf fishing, lobster fishing and lobster-pot making. There are no tourist facilities but camping is possible and food is available from **Bar do Jangadeiro**. To get here, take a bus from Goiana, US$1.

West of Recife ●●●●● ▸▸ pp510-520.

Bezerros → *Colour map 2, B6. Phone code: 081. Population: 52,000.*
The town of Bezerros, 15 km west of Recife on the BR-232, is set next to the Rio Ipojuca. It has some old houses, fine *praças* and churches. Some, like the **Igreja de Nossa Senhora dos Homens Pretos**, **São José** and the **Capela de Nossa Senhora**, date from the 19th century. The former railway station has been converted into the **Estação da Cultura**, with shows and other cultural performances. The best known artist and poet is José Borges (born 1935), whose work has been exhibited internationally. The city's main attraction is handicrafts, which are found in the district of **Encruzilhada de São João**. Most typical are the Papangu masks, made of painted papier mâché, and used at Carnaval as interior decoration. Wooden toys are also popular, as well as items made from leather and clay. About 10 km from the centre of Bezerros, near the village of Serra Negra, a small eco-tourism park, **Serra Negra ecological tourism trail**, has been set up. Trails lead to caves and springs; the flora is typical of the *agreste*.

Carnaval here is famed throughout Brazil and is known as **Folia do Papangu**, see Festivals, page 517. For tourist information contact the **Departamento de Turismo** ① *Praça Duque de Caxias 88, Centro, T081-3328 1286*. The artisans association, **Associação dos Artesãos de Bezerros**, is at the same address.

Caruaru → *Colour map 2, B6. Phone code: 081. Population: 254,000. Altitude: 554 m.*

Situated 134 km west of Recife, this small town in the *sertão* is famous for its huge **Festas Juninhas**, held throughout June (see Festivals and events, page 517), and its little clay figures (*figurinhas* or *bonecas de barro*) originated by Mestre Vitalino (1909-1963), and very typical of northeast Brazil. Most of the potters live at **Alto da Moura**, 6 km away, where you can visit the **Casa Museu Mestre Vitalino** ① *buses from Caruaru, a bumpy 30-min ride, US$0.50*, once owned by Vitalino and containing personal objects and photographs, but no examples of his work. UNESCO has recognized the area as the largest centre of figurative art in the Americas.

Ins and outs The *rodoviária* is 4 km west of town; buses from Recife stop in the town centre. Alight here and look for the **Livraria Estudantil**, on the corner of Vigário Freire and Rua Anna de Albuquerque Galvão; this is a useful landmark. Follow Galvão down hill from the bookshop, turn right on Rua 15 de Novembro to the first junction, 13 de Maio; turn left, and finally cross the river to the Feira do Artesanato (arts and crafts market).

During the **Festas Juninhas**, there is a tourist train, **Train do Forró**, from Recife, which is a very spirited affair with bars, and bands playing in the carriages. See www.tremdo forro.com.br for information.

Fazenda Nova and Nova Jerusalém

During Easter Week each year, various agencies run package tours to the little country town of **Fazenda Nova**, 23 km from Caruaru. Just outside the town is **Nova Jerusalém**. Every day from the day before Palm Sunday up to Easter Saturday, an annual Passion play is enacted here, on an open-air site about one third the size of the historic quarter of Jerusalem. Nine stages are used to depict scenes from the Passion of Christ, which is presented using 50 actors and 500 extras to re-enact the story with the audience following in their footsteps. *TV Globo* stars often play the starring roles and the sound and lighting effects are state of the art. Performances begin at 1800 and last for about three hours.

There is little accommodation in Nova Jerusalém/Fazenda Nova and it is usually full during the Passion. **Empetur** in Recife/Olinda has details of agencies that offer trips. During the Easter period there are direct bus services from Recife (and from Caruaru at other times).

Petrolina and the sertão

Beyond Serra Talhada the BR-232 continues to **Salgueiro**, where it meets the BR-116 heading north to Fortaleza. The BR-232 becomes the BR-316 and heads northwest to **Araripina** before entering **Piauí**. This part of Pernambuco was the haunt of the bandit Lampião until his death in 1938. Even today the area is still quite lawless and buses are often escorted by armed police. Cultivation of marijuana in the area between Salgueiro and Floresta means that visitors are not generally welcome.

Petrolina, on the banks of the Rio São Francisco, is best visited from Juazeiro in Bahia. The city is famous for the production of *carrancas* (boat figureheads, mostly grotesque) of wood or ceramic, and for having the closest vineyards to the equator in the world. The city has its own airport. Near the runway is the small **Museu do Sertão**, with relics of rural life in the northeast and the age of the *coronéis* and the bandit Lampião.

Reserva Biológica de Serra Negra, in the centre of the state, has some of the last remaining forest at higher altitude in the interior. For information contact **Ibama** ① *Av 17 de Agosto 1057, Casa Forte, CEP 52060-590, Recife, T081-3441 5033.*

⊕ Pernambuco listings

For Sleeping and Eating price codes and other relevant information, see pages 42-47.

⊜ Sleeping

Recife *p497, maps p498 and p501*
For the city centre, the best pace to stay is **Boa Vista**. Be careful walking back to hotels after dark. During **Carnaval** and for longer stays, individuals rent private rooms and houses in Recife and Olinda; listings can be found in the classified ads of *Diário de Pernambuco*. This accommodation is generally cheaper, safer and quieter than hotels.
A Pousada Villa Boa Vista, R Miguel Couto 81, Boa Vista, T081-3223 0666, www.pousada villaboavista.com.br. The only modern hotel in town, with plain, comfortable a/c rooms (all en suites have modern bathrooms and powerful showers), around a courtyard. Quiet, safe and a 5-min taxi ride from the centre.
A Recife Plaza, R da Aurora 225, Boa Vista, T081-3231 1200, www.recifeplazahotel.com.br. Overlooking the Rio Capibaribe. Comfortable old-fashioned business hotel with a reasonable restaurant, which is very popular at lunchtime.
D América, Praça Maciel Pinheiro 48, Boa Vista, T081-3221 1300. Frayed, very simple rooms with low, foamy beds, lino floors and tiny en suites. The best rooms are on the upper floors with views out over the city.
D Central, Av Manoel Borba 209, Boa Vista, T081-3222 4001. A splendid 1920s building with its original French open lifts and plain, but freshly painted rooms with parquet flooring and flat-pack furniture. The bathrooms have enormous iron tubs (without plugs). The upper floors have wonderful views of the city.
D São Domingos, Praça Maciel Pinheiro 66, Boa Vista, T081-3223 0060. An old grand dame from the 1960s now fallen on hard times. The parquet-floored rooms are scuffed and come with huge 1960s commodes. The upper rooms have good views.

Boa Viagem *p503, map p504*
Boa Viagem is the main tourist district and although it has plenty of hotels it is a long way from the centre of Recife. The beach is notorious for shark attacks. The main beachfront road is **Av Boa Viagem**; hotels here are mostly tower blocks and tend to be more expensive.
A Recife Monte, on the corner of R Petrolina and R dos Navegantes 363, T081-3465 7422. Very smart and good value for the category, caters to business travellers.
B Aconchego, Félix de Brito 382, T081-3326 2989, aconchego@novaera.com.br. Motel-style rooms around a pleasant pool area, a/c, sitting room. English-speaking owner, will collect you from the airport.
B Do Sol, Av Boa Viagem 978, T081-3465 6722, reservas@hsol.com.br. Decent, if rather bland, with business facilities.
B Setúbal, R Setúbal 932, T081-3341 4116. Helpful standard town hotel with good breakfast and fairly comfortable rooms.
C Casa da Praia, Av Beira Mar 1168, Praia de Piedade, T081-3461 1414. On a quiet street, with garden, good breakfast, owner speaks French. Recommended.
C Coqueiral, R Petrolina, 43, T081-3326 5881. Dutch-owned (English and French spoken). Small, homely rooms with a/c and a pretty breakfast room. Recommended.
C Praia Mar, Av Boa Viagem 1660, T081-3465 3759. Intimate and safe. Recommended.
C Uzi Praia, Av Conselheiro Aguiar 942, T/F081-3466 9662. Plain rooms with a/c and a cosy, sister hotel across the road.
D Pousada da Julieta, R Prof José Brandao 135, T081-3326 7860, hjulieta@elogica.com.br. Friendly and clean. One block from beach, very good value. Recommended.
D Pousada da Praia, Alcides Carneiro Leal 66, T081-3326 7085. TV, safe, a/c, rooms vary (some tiny), very helpful. Roof-top breakfast room.
E Albergue do Mar, R dos Navegantes 81, T081-3326 2196. Youth hostel with good breakfast and atmosphere.

E Maracatú do Recife, R Maria Carolina 185, T081-3326 1221, www.geocities.com/albergue maracatu. IYHA hostel. Large, well-kept dorms, simple, safe, cooking facilities and a decent breakfast.

Camping
Paraíso Camping Clube, Av Dantas Barreto 512, loja 503, T081-3224 3094. Can provide information on camping throughout the state. There is no camping within the city.

Olinda *p505, map p506*
Prices at least triple during Carnaval when 5-night packages are sold. Rooms at regular prices can often be found in Boa Viagem during this time. In the historic centre, accommodation is mostly in converted mansions, which are full of character. If you can afford it, staying in one of these *pousadas* is the ideal way to absorb Olinda's colonial charm. All *pousadas*, and most of the cheaper hotels outside the old city, have a pool.
AL 7 Colinas, Ladeira de Sao Francisco 307, T/F081-3439 6055, www.hotel7colinas. com.br. Spacious, new hotel with all mod cons, set in private, gated gardens and with a large swimming pool.
AL Pousada do Amparo, R do Amparo 199, T081-3439 1749, www.pousadoamparo. com.br. Olinda's best hotel is a gorgeous, 18th-century house, full of antiques and atmosphere in the **Roteiros do Charme** group (see page 43). Rooms have 4-poster beds and each is decorated differently. The public areas include a spacious foyer with a high ceiling decorated with art, a pool and sauna area surrounded by a little flower-filled garden and an excellent, delightfully romantic restaurant.
B-C Pousada dos Quatro Cantos, R Prudente de Morais 441, T081-3429 0220, www.pousada4 cantos.com.br. A large converted townhouse with a little walled garden and terraces. The maze of bright rooms and suites are decorated with Pernambuco arts and crafts and furnished mostly with antiques. Warm, welcoming and full of character.

C Pousada São Francisco, R do Sol 127, T081-3483 2109, www.pousadasao francisco.com.br. Well-kept and airy a/c rooms with little terraces, slate floors and pokey bathrooms. The pool and bar area are set in pleasant gardens visited by humming birds in the early morning and there is a small restaurant and parking. Outside the historic centre but within walking distance.
C-D Pousada Peter, R do Amparo 215, T081-3439 2171, www.pousadapeter.com.br. The rather pokey white-tiled a/c rooms in this converted town house contrast with the spacious lobby lounge decorated with Pernambuco crafts and colourful artwork. Breakfast is served on the terrace overlooking distant Recife and the modest pool.
C-E Olinda Hostel, R do Sol 233, T081-3429 1592, www.alberguedeolinda.com.br. IYHA youth hostel with fan-cooled 8-bed dorms with shared en suites, and doubles. The hostel has a tropical garden, TV room, and a shady area with hammocks next to a pool.
C-E Pousada d'Olinda, P João Alfredo 178, T/F081-3494 2559, www.pousadado linda.com.br. Basic but well-kept dorms and doubles around a pool, garden and communal breakfast area and lunchtime restaurant. Discount of 10% for owners of *Footprint* guides. English, French, German Arabic and Spanish spoken.
C-E Pousada d'Olinda no Varadouro, R 15 de Novembro 98, T081-3439 1163, www.pousadadolindavaradouro.com.br. Little suites in a converted townhouse and cheaper communal rooms. The best are on the upper floors. Spacious open-air dining area/restaurant and a small pool.
D São Pedro, R 27 Janeiro 95, T081-3439 9546, www.pousadapedro.com. Quiet little *pousada* with a walled garden, a small pool shaded by frangipani and bamboo. Has a delightful breakfast area and lobby decorated with art and antiques. The rustic rooms are tiny but tastefully decorated and all a/c. The best are on the upper floor.
D-E Albergue do Fortim, R do Sol 151, T081-3429 1939, www.pousadadofortim.com.br.

Very simple but clean boxy rooms with a/c at the cheapest rates in Olinda. Some are big enough for 4. Breakfast is US$2 extra.

Camping
Olinda Camping, R Bom Sucesso 262, Amparo, T081-3429 1365. US$5 per person, space for 30 tents, 5 trailers, small huts for rent, quiet, well-shaded, town buses pass outside. Recommended.

Gaibu p507
L-E Casa dos Golfinhos, Gaibu beach, T081-8861 4707, www.gaibu-bedandbreakfast.com. Bed and breakfast accommodation close to the beach, under German management.

Porto de Galinhas p507
There are plenty of cheap *pousadas* and hotels in town along **R da Esperança** and its continuation **R Manoel Uchôa**; also along **R Beijapurá**, which runs off R da Esperança.
L Village Porto de Galinhas, T081-3552 2945, www.villageportodegalinhas.com.br. All-inclusive family beach resort right on the ocean and with a large pool, restaurant, a/c rooms. Some 7 km from town.
C-E IYHA Pousada A Casa Branca, Praça 18, T081-3552 1808, www.pousadaacasabranca.com.br. Very clean, well-kept, newly opened hostel with some a/c rooms and several dorms. To get there take the right turn (away from the sea) off R Beijupira opposite R Carauna and walk inland for 400 m. The *pousada* is in a little square 150 m before the Estrada Maracaipe.

C-E La Vila delle Rose, R Manoel Uchôa 11, T081-3552 1489, www.laviladellerose.com.br. Simple, bright and well-kept doubles and shared rooms in a large house very close to the beach. Good breakfast and friendly service. All en suites.

Igarassu p508
Camping
Engenho Monjope, 5 km before Igarassu coming from Recife, T081-3543 0528, US$5. A Camping Clube do Brasil site on an old sugar estate, now a historical monument (bus US$1, alight at the 'Camping' sign and walk 5-10 mins).

Itamaracá p508
B Casa da Praia, Av da Forte Orange, T081-3544 1255. With pool, minibar, breakfast and optional dinner.
C Pousada Itamaracá, R Fernando Lopes 205/210, T081-3544 1152. Away from the beach, but has a pool.
C Pousada Jaguaribe, R Rios 355 (close to bus terminal) near the beach. Fans and mosquito nets in all rooms, kitchen, laundry facilities, swimming pool.

Caruaru p509
A large number of cheap *hospedarias* can be found around the central square, Praça Getúlio Vargas.
A Grande Hotel São Vicente de Paulo, Av Rio Branco 365, T081-3721 5011. A good, centrally located hotel with a/c,

laundry, garage, bar, restaurant, pool, TV. It also houses the local cinema.

C Centenário, 7 de Setembro 84, T081-3722 4011. Also has more expensive suites and a pool. The breakfast is good. As the hotel is in the town centre it can be noisy, but otherwise recommended.

C Central, R Vigario Freire 71, T081-3721 5880. Suites or rooms, all with a/c, TV, good breakfast, in the centre. Recommended.

Petrolina *p509*

Choices here are poor; avoid the Central Hotel at all costs.

C Hotel Neuman, Av Souza Filho 444, T081-3961 0595. Overpriced with pokey little a/c rooms all with en suites.

D Pousada da Carranca, BR-122, Km 4, T081-3961 3421. Pleasant and fairly well looked after but a little inconvenient for the town.

🍴 Eating

Recife *p497, maps p498 and p501*

There is a good variety of restaurants in the city and along the beach at **Boa Viagem** (see below). Be careful of eating the local small crabs, known as *guaiamum*; they live in the mangrove swamps which take the drainage from Recife's *mocambos* (shanty towns).

There are many cheap *lanchonetes* catering to office workers, they tend to close in evening.

ᵗᵗᵗ Leite, Praça Joaquim Nabuco 147/53 near the Casa de Cultura, Santo Antônio. Frequently voted the best in the city, and an institution for 130 years, with a live pianist and a varied menu of around 100 dishes.

ᵗ Gelattos, Av Dantas Barreto, 230. Great *sucos* (try the delicious *guarana do amazonas* with nuts), hamburgers and sandwiches. Recommended.

Boa Viagem *p503, map p504*

Restaurants on the main beach road of **Av Boa Viagem** are pricier than in the centre. Venture a block or 2 inland for cheaper deals.

There are many a/c cheapies in the Shopping Center Recife, T081-3464 6000.

ᵗᵗᵗ Bargaço, Av Boa Viagem 670. Typical northeastern menu specializing in seafood dishes. Sophisticated with small bar.

ᵗᵗᵗ La Maison, Av Boa Viagem, 618, T081-3325 1158. Fondue restaurant in low-lit basement with an illicit feel. Appropriately cheesy and good fun, with rosé wine and peach melba on menu.

ᵗᵗ Chica Pitanga, R Petrolina, 19, T081-3465 2224. Upmarket, excellent food by weight. Be prepared to queue. Recommended.

ᵗᵗ Churrascaria Porcão, Av Eng Domingos Ferreira 4215. Good for meat- and salad-eaters alike, very popular.

ᵗᵗ Ilha da Kosta, R Pe Bernardino Pessoa, 50, T081-3466 2222. Open from 1100 until the last client leaves. Self-service seafood, sushi, pizza and Brazilian cuisine.

ᵗᵗ La Capannina, Av Cons Aguiar 538, T081-3465 9420. Italian pizzas, salad, pasta and sweet and savoury crêpes. Recommended.

ᵗᵗ Parraxaxa, R Baltazar Pereira, 32, T081-9108 0242. Rustic-style, award-winning buffet of northeastern cuisine, including breakfast. Recommended.

ᵗ Gibi, Av Cons Aguiar, 542. Basic but popular hamburger joint.

ᵗ Peng, Av Domingos Ferreira, 1957. Self-service, some Chinese dishes. Bargain, rather than gourmet food.

ᵗ Real Eza, Av Boa Viagem, on corner with Av Atlântico. Beachfront location, hamburgers, snacks and pizza.

ᵗ Romana, R Setubal, 225. Deli/bakery with a few tables and chairs. Pastries, coffee, yoghurt for breakfast and snacks.

ᵗ Tempero Verde, R SH, Cardim, opposite Chica Pitanga. Where the locals go for a bargain meal of beans, meat and salad, US1.50. Simple, self-service, street tables.

ᵗ TioDadá, R Baltazar Pereira, 100. Loud, TV screens, good-value portions of beef.

Cafés

Café Cordel, R Domingos José Martins. Northeastern dishes, Cordel literature,

regional books (some in English), good CD collection with requests accepted.
Savoy, Av Guararapes, open since 1944 and a haunt of Pernambucan intellectuals. Simone de Beauvoir and Jean Paul Sartre once ate here according to a book written about the bar. Poetry all over the walls.

Olinda *p505, map p506*

Try *tapioca*, a local dish made of manioc with coconut or cheese. The traditional Olinda drinks, *pau do índio* (with 32 herbs) and *retetel* are manufactured on R do Amparo.

There are a number of *lanchonetes* and fast-food options along the seafront, including **Mama Luise** and **Gibi**, Av Min Marcos Freire, and **Leque Moleque**, Av Sigismundo Gonçalves 537.

₸₸₸ **Goya**, R do Amparo 157, T081-3439 4875. Regional food, particularly seafood, beautifully presented.

₸₸₸ **Oficina do Sabor**, R do Amparo 355, T081-3429 3331. Probably the city's best restaurant, consistently wins awards. Pleasant terrace overlooking city, food served in hollowed-out pumpkins and lots of vegetarian options.

₸₸ **Maison do Bonfim**, R do Bonfim 115, T081-3429 1674. Serene, fan-cooled, rustic-style restaurant. French cuisine, such as chicken chasseur and escargots, as well as Brazilian and Italian food.

₸₸ **Samburá**, Av Min Marcos Freire 1551. With terrace, try *caldeirada* and *pitu* (crayfish), also lobster in coconut sauce or daily fish dishes, very good.

₸ **Grande Pequim**, Av Min Marcos Freire 1463, Bairro Novo. Good Chinese food.

₸ **Mourisco**, Praça João Alfredo. Excellent, good-value food by weight in lovely, part-covered garden. Delicious deserts. A real find. Warmly recommended.

Itamaracá *p508*

₸₸₸ **Vila Velha**, T081-3971 2962. For a splurge take lunch and a swim at this charming villa on the hill. It's easy to find – the island is tiny. And it was once the mansion house for the Captain who governed this part of

Pernambuco. Ask for Newton Bezerra, dealer for the artist Luís Jasmim. Any art purchase comes with a free lunch, allow all afternoon for a visit.

Caruaru *p509*

Alto da Moura is a real tourist spot and gets very busy.

₸₸ **Catracho's**, close to São Sebastião hospital. Has a Caribbean feel and the Honduran owner mixes great cocktails.

₸₸ **Costela do Baiano**, close to Igreja do Rosário. Very good value northeastern cooking with good seafood.

₸ **A Massa**, R Vidal de Negreiros. The best of a number of cheap lunch restaurants in the centre near Banco do Brasil. With respectable pizzas and pasta.

ⓞ Bars and clubs

Recife *p497, maps p498 and p501*

Recife Antigo is the best place in the city for weekend nightlife. Many exciting bands post mangue beat fusion bands and DJs play in the bars and clubs around **R Tomazino** (R do Burburinho); and there is always a lively crowd. The area is not safe to walk to so take a taxi. The best listings site is www.reciferock.com.br and has information on live post-mangue beat music.

Armazém 14, Av Alfredo Lisboa s/n, Cais do Porto, Recife Antigo. One of the top live music venues for the alternative scene. Big names like Mundo Livre and Mombojo play here.

Boratcho, Galeria Joana Darc, Pina, T081-3327 1168. Tex Mex restaurant and live music venue for alternative *mangue beat* bands. Alternative and gay crowd.

Burburinho R Tomazino s/n, T081-3224 5854. The best of the live music spots in Recife Antigo. Grungy, arty crowd and a range of sounds from psychedelic *forró* funk to *frevo* rock and all things mixed. Other bars lie near by – start here and wander.

Central, R Mamede Simões 144, Boa Vista, T081-3222 7622, www.centralrecife.com.br.

Fred Zeroquatro recommends

Mundo Livre S/A, www.mundolivresa.com, are one of the most exciting Recife bands. Together with **Chico Science** they invented *mangue beat* in the 1990s. Their iconic lead singer, Fred Zeroquatro gave us his tips for what to do when in Recife and Olinda.

→ All the great alternative Recife bands play at carnival usually at the *Marco Zero* event. Contacting Marco Zero productions (T081-3222 2720) for information. And be sure not to miss carnaval's *A Noite dos Tambores Silenciosos* (the night of the silent drums), in the Pátio do Terço (held by the church of Nossa Senhora do Terço next to Rua Direita). It's one of the best percussion events in the northeast; very African and with a strong sacred and ritualistic feel.

→ For roots and alternative Pernambuco music head for the **Casa da Rabeca** (Rua Curupira 125, Cidade Tabajara, Olinda; bus from PE-15 bus terminal) This little showhouse was founded by Mestre Salustiano, who sadly died in 2008, and showcases traditional and emerging artists. Come after 2100 on a weekend night.

→ Every Tuesday and Saturday there are *Terça Negra* and *Sabado Mangue* shows. These are free concerts given by the best new musicians at the **Pátio de São Pedro** (in front of São Pedro church, Recife Antigo).

The drinking hole of choice for the city's musical and artistic middle-class community. Decent bar food, lunches and breakfast.
Depois Dancing Bar, Av Rio Branco 66, T081-3424 7451. Well-established alternative dance club with live bands.
Estação Pirata, R do Apolo, Recife Antigo. Good live bands – look out for Eddie and Tine who play here.
Garagem, R Amélia at Av Ruy Barbosa, no lado da Torre. A tyre shop by day and grungy bar packed with Recife underground figures by night. Live music and electronica.

Olinda *p505, map p506*
Beginning at dusk, but best after 2100, the **Alto da Sé** becomes the scene of a small street fair, with arts, crafts, makeshift bars, barbecue stands, and impromptu traditional music. Every Fri night band musicians walk the streets serenading passers-by. Each Sun from 1 Jan to Carnaval there is a mini carnival in the streets of the city, with live music and dancing.
Bodega do Veio, R do Amparo, T081-3429 0185. An Olinda institution with live music Thu-Sun. Sat nights are hosted by a famous local fiddle player, Mestre Saluciano,

and his band, who play traditional *pe na serra forró*. Great *petiscos* (especially the *prato frio*) and *caipirinhas*.
Cantinho da Sé, Ladeira da Sé 305, T081-3439 8815. Lively, good view of Recife, food served.
Farandola, R Dom Pedro Roeser, 190, tucked away behind Igreja do Carmo church. Mellow bar with festival theme and big top-style roof. Live music nightly, plans for a circus next door. Drinks are cheap; try *bate bate de maracuja* (smooth blend of *cachaça*, passionfruit juice and honey) or *raspa raspa* fruit syrup. Warmly recommended.
Marola, Tr Av Dantas Barreto 66, T081-3429 2499. Funky wooden *barraca* on rocky shoreline specializing in seafood. Great *caiprifrutas* (frozen fruit drink with vodka – try the cashew). Can get crowded. Recommended.
Pernambucanamente, Av Min Marcos Freire 734, Bairro Novo, T081-3429 1977. Live, local music every night.

Itamaracá *p508*
Bar da Lia, R do Jaguaribe, close to the Forte Orange, weekends feature *cirandas* danced at the bar, led by the well-known singer, Dona Lia, and her band. Also serves food.

Carnaval in Olinda and Recife

Carnaval in Olinda and Recife vies with Rio and Salvador as the best in Brazil. While Rio Carnaval moves along the dedicated arena of the Sambódromo to the sound of samba, and Salvador is a riotous two million strong street party energized by pounding *axé* music, Recife and Olinda are more traditional street celebrations powered by Pernambuco's myriad rhythms such as *frevo*, *coco* and *maracatu*. *Maracatu* is also the name given to the schools and *blocos* in Pernambuco, each of whom were originally enslaved denizens of particular African nations who used proto-Carnaval celebrations to articulate their individual identities in a foreign land – leading to intense rivalries that persist to this day. Here are the essential facts for planning your Recife Carnaval:

→ Times and *blocos* are announced in the local press and in tourist offices (who are very helpful with all Carnaval related information; such as details of the Carnaval press offices and of where tourists can learn Carnaval dance steps).

→ Avenida Guararapes in Recife, Pina near Boa Viagem, Largo do Amparão and Mercado Eufrásio Barbosa (Varadouro) in Olinda are the main centres for the festivities. The best place to see the groups is from the balconies of **Hotel do Parque** or **Recife Palace Hotel** in Recife and the various hotels that line the streets of Olinda. Seats in the stands and boxes can be booked up to a fortnight in advance at the central post office in Avenida Guararapes, Recife.

→ There is a *pre-carnavalesca* week which starts with the *Bloco da Parceria* in Boa

Viagem (with many top Recife acts) and the *Virgens de Bairro Novo* in Olinda led by drag queens. These are followed by carnival balls such as *Baile dos Artistas* (popular with the gay community) and the *Baile Masque* held at the Portuguese club, Rua Governador Agamemnon Magalhães.

→ Carnaval is officially opened on the first Saturday by the *bloco* Galo da Madrugada – a giant cockerel float – and the great Recife percussionist Naná Vasconcelos usually leads the drum troupes. Crowds reach over one million. This is followed by other events between Sunday and Tuesday.

→ The *maracatu blocos* dance at the doors of all the churches they pass; they usually go to the church of Nossa Senhora do Rosário dos Pretos, patron saint of the slaves (Rua Estreita do Rosário, Santo Antônio), before proceeding into the downtown areas. A small car at the head bears the figure of an animal and is followed by the king and queen under a large, showy umbrella. Next comes the *dama do passo* carrying a small doll, or *calunga*. After the *dama* comes the *tirador de loas* who chants to the group which replies in chorus, and last comes a band of local percussion instruments.

→ Look out for the *caboclinhos* in indigenous costume with bright feathers round their waists and ankles, colourful cockades, bead and animal teeth necklaces and a dazzle of medals on their red tunics. The dancers beat out the rhythm with bows and arrows; others play indigenous and African musical instruments. The dance is spectacular: spinning, leaping, and stooping with almost mathematical precision.

❁ Festivals and events

Recife *p497, maps p498 and p501*
For Carnaval, see box, above.
1 Jan Universal Brotherhood.

12-15 Mar Parades to mark the city's foundation.
Mid-Apr Pro-Rock Festival, a week-long celebration of rock, hip-hop and *mangue beat* SP at Centro de Convenções, Complexo de

Salgadinho and other venues. Check *Diário de Pernambuco* or *Jornal de Comércio* for details.
Jun Festas Juninhas, see box, page 535.
11-16 Jul Nossa Senhora do Carmo, patron saint of the city.
Aug Mes do Folclore.
Oct Recifolia, a repetition of the Carnaval over a whole weekend; dates vary.
1-8 Dec Festival of Lemanjá, with typical foods and drinks, celebrations and offerings to the goddess.
8 Dec Nossa Senhora da Conceição.

Olinda *p505, map p506*

Feb Carnaval. Thousands of people dance through the narrow streets of the old city to the sound of the *frevo*, the brash energetic music that normally accompanies a lively dance performed with umbrellas. The local people decorate them with streamers and straw dolls, and form themselves into costumed groups (*blocos*), which you can join as they pass (take only essentials). Among the best-known *blocos*, which carry life-size dolls, are O homem da meianoite (Midnight Man), A Corda (a pun on 'the rope' and 'acorda' – wake up!), which parades in the early hours, Pitombeira and Elefantes. Olinda's carnival continues on Ash Wed, but is much more low-key, *a quarta-feira do batata* (Potato Wednesday), named after a waiter who claimed his right to celebrate Carnaval after being on duty during the official celebrations). The streets are very crowded with people dancing and drinking non-stop. The local cocktail, *capeta* (guaraná powder, sweet skimmed milk and vodka) is designed to keep you going.
12-15 Mar Foundation Day, 3 days of music and dancing, night-time only.

Bezerros *p508*

Feb Carnaval celebrations are famous throughout Brazil and known as Folia do Papangu. Papangu characters wear masks that resemble a cross between a bear and a devil and are covered from head to foot in a costume like a bear skin (or an all-covering white tunic).
Jun São João.

Caruaru *p509*

Mar/Apr Semana Santa, Holy Week, with lots of folklore and handicraft events.
18-22 May The city anniversary.
13 Jun Santo Antônio.
24 Jun São João, a particularly huge *forró* festival, part of Caruaru's Festas Juninhas. The whole town lights up with dancing, traditional foods, parties like the Sapadrilha, when the women dress as men, and the Gaydrilha, where the men dress as women, and there is even a *Trem do Forró*, which runs from Recife to Caruaru, rocking the whole way to the rhythms.
Sep Micaru, a street carnival. Also in Sep is Vaquejada, a Brazilian cross between rodeo and bullfighting; biggest in the northeast.

O Shopping

Recife *p497, maps p498 and p501*
Markets

The permanent craft market is in the Casa da Cultura; prices for ceramic figurines are lower than Caruaru.
Cais de Alfândega, Recife Barrio. With local artisans work, first weekend of the month.
Domingo na Rua, Sun market in Recife Barrio, stalls of local *artesanato* and performances.
Hippy fair, Praça Boa Viagem, seafront. Sat-Sun only. Life-sized wooden statues of saints.
Mercado São José (1875), for local products and handicrafts.
Sítio Trindade, Casa Amarela. Sat craft fair during the feast days of 12-29 Jun, fireworks, music, dancing, local food. On 23 Apr, here and in the Pátio de São Pedro, one can see the *xangô* dance. Herbal remedies, barks and spices at Afogados market.

Shopping malls

Shopping Center Recife, between Boa Viagem and the airport, www.shopping-recife.com.br. One of the largest in the country, with clothes, CDs, bookshops and lots more.

Shopping Tacaruna, Santo Amaro. Buses to/from Olinda pass.

Bezerros *p508*
The city's main attraction is handicrafts, which are found in the district of **Encruzilhada de São João**; items in leather, clay, wood, papier mâché and much more.

Caruaru *p509*
Caruaru is most famous for its markets which, combined, are responsible for about 70% of the city's income. The **Feira da Sulanca** is basically a clothes market supplied mostly by local manufacture, but also on sale are jewellery, souvenirs, food, flowers and anything else that can go for a good price. The most important day is Mon. There is also the **Feira Livre** or **do Troca-Troca** (free, or barter market). On the same site, Parque 18 de Maio, is the **Feira do Artesanato**, leather goods, ceramics, hammocks and basketware, all the popular crafts of the region; it is tourist orientated but it is on a grand scale and is open daily 0800-1800.

▲ Activities and tours

Recife *p497, maps p498 and p501*
Diving
Offshore are some 20 wrecks, including the remains of Portuguese galleons; the fauna is very rich.
Mergulhe Coma, T081-3552 2355, T081-9102 6809 (mob), atlanticdivingasr@hotmail.com. English-speaking instructors for PADI courses.
Seagate, T081-3426 1657, www.seagate recife.com.br. Daily departures and night dives.

Football
Recife's 3 clubs are Sport, Santa Cruz and Náutico. **Sport** play at Ilha do Retiro, T081-3227 1213, take Torrões bus from the central post office on Av Guararapes. **Santa**

Cruz play at Arruda, T081-3441 6811, take Casa Amarela bus from the central post office. **Náutico** play at Aflitos, T081-3423 8900, take Água Fria or Aflitos bus. Local derbies are sometimes full beyond safe capacities. Avoid *arquibancada* tickets for Santa Cruz-Sport games. For games at Arruda, dress down.

Tour operators
Jacaré e Cobra de Água Eco-Group, T081-3447 3452, T081-3968 7360 (mob), www.truenet.com.br. Regular excursions in Pernambuco.
Souto Costa Viagens e Turismo Ltda, R Felix de Brito Melo 666, T081-3465 5000, and Aeroporto de Guararapes (American Express representative).
Student Travel Bureau (STB), R Padre Bernardino Pessoa 266, T081-3465 4522, stbmaster@stb.com.br. ISIC accepted, discounts on international flights but not domestic Brazilian flights.
Trilhas, T081-3222 6864, recommended for ecologically oriented excursions.

Olinda *p505, map p506*
Tour operators
Viagens Sob O Sol, Prudente de Moraes 424, T/F081-429 3303, T081-971 8102 (mob), English spoken, transport, car hire.
Victor Turismo, Av Santos Domont 20, loja 06, T081-3494 1467. Day and night trips to Recife.
Victor Turismo, Felitur, R Getulio Vargas 1411, Bairro Novo, T/F081-439 1477.

Porto de Galinhas *p507*
Diving
AICA Diving, Nossa Senhora do Ó, T/F081-552 1290 or T081-968 4876 (mob), run by Mida and Miguel. For diving and canoeing trips, as well as excursions to Santo Aleixo island.
Porto Point Diving, Praça Principal de Porto de Galinhas, T081-552 1111. Diving and canoeing trips, as well as excursions to Santo Aleixo island.

⊖ Transport

Recife *p497, maps p498 and p501*
Air
Bus No 52 runs to the airport, US$0.40.
International flights to **Lisbon** and **Milan**.
Domestic flights to **Brasília**, **Campina
Grande**, **Fernando de Noronha**, **Fortaleza**,
João Pessoa, **Juazeiro do Norte**, **Maceió**,
Natal, **Paulo Afonso**, **Petrolina**, **Rio de
Janeiro**, **Salvador** and **São Paulo**.

Airline offices Gol, T081-3464
4793, www.voegol.com.br and the airport.
Nordeste/RioSul, Av Domingos Ferreira
801, loja 103-5, T081-465 6799 (RioSul,
T081-3465 6799), at airport, T081-3341
3187. Oceanair, www.oceanair.com.br.
TAM, T081-342 5011, at airport T081-3462
4466. TAP/Air Portugal, Av Conselheiro
de Aguiar 1472, Boa Viagem T081-3465
8800, at airport T081-3341 0654. TRIP,
T081-3464 4610 (for flights to Noronha)
www.voetrip.com.br and the airport. United,
R Progresso 465/802, T081-3423 2444. Varig,
R Conselheiro de Aguiar 456, Boa Viagem,
T081-3464 4440, R J E Favre 719, T081-
3339 2998, at airport T081-3341 4411.

Bus
To get to the *rodoviária*, take the metrô from
the central railway station, entrance through
Museu do Trem, opposite the Casa da Cultura,
2 lines leave the city, take train marked
'Rodoviária', 30 mins. From Boa Viagem a taxi
all the way costs US$20, or go to central metrô
station and change there. Bus from the centre
(1 hr) or from Boa Viagem. Bus tickets are sold
at Cais de Santa Rita (opposite EMTU).

Buses to the nearby destinations of
Igarassu (every 15 mins) and **Itamaracá**
(every 30 mins) leave from Av Martins de
Barros, in front of Grande Hotel. To **Olinda**
take any bus marked 'Rio Doce', No 981,
which has a circular route around the city
and beaches, or No 33 from Av Nossa
Senhora do Carmo, US$1, or 'Jardim
Atlântico' from the central post
office at Siqueira Campos.

To **Cabo** (every 20 mins) and beaches
south of Recife from Cais de Santa Rita. To
Salvador, daily 1930, 12 hrs, US$18-25, 4 a
day (all at night) (1 *leito*, 70). To **Fortaleza**,
12 hrs, US$20 *convencional*, US$30 *executivo*.
To **Natal**, 4 hrs, US$9. To **Rio**, daily 2100,
44 hrs, US$58-65. To **São Paulo**, daily 1630,
50 hrs, US$60-70. To **Santos**, daily 1430,
52 hrs, US$60. To **Foz do Iguaçu**, Fri and
Sun 1030, 55 hrs, US$90. To **Curitiba**, Fri and
Sun, 52 hrs, US$76. To **Brasília**, daily 2130,
39 hrs, US$49-60. To **Belo Horizonte**, daily
2115, 34 hrs, US$41. To **São Luís**, 28 hrs,
Progresso at 1430 and 1945, US$75.
To **Belém**, 34 hrs (Boa Esperança bus
recommended). To **João Pessoa**, every
30 mins, US$2.50. To **Caruaru**, every hour,
3 hrs, US$3. To **Maceió**, US$9, 3½ hrs
(express), 6 hrs (slow), either by the main
road or by the coast road daily via 'Litoral'.

Car hire
Budget, T081-3341 2505. 24 hrs, just outside
Guararapes airport. Hertz, T081-462 3552.
Localiza, Av Visconde de Jequitinhonha 1145,
T081-3341 0287, and at Guararapes airport,
T081-3341 2082, freephone, T0800-992000.

Olinda *p505, map p506*
Bus To **Recife**, the No 981 bus has a circular
route around the city and beaches. The No 33
runs to Av Nossa Senhora do Carmo, US$1.
Or take the metrô from Praça do Carmo to
Central station.

Taxi To **Boa Viagem** US$8, US$12 at night.
Make sure the meter is set to rate 1, except
on Sun, holidays or after 2100, when rate
2 applies.

Igarassu *p508*
Bus Buses run to Cais de Santa Rita,
Recife, 45 mins, US$1.

Itamaracá *p508*
Bus Buses run to **Recife** (Av Martins de
Barros opposite the Grande Hotel), US$1.10,
very crowded) and **Igarassu**.

Caruaru *p509*

Bus Buses from the centre, at the same place the Recife buses stop, to *rodoviária*, US$0.40. Many buses run to **TIP** in **Recife**, 2 hrs express, US$3. Bus to **Maceió**, 0700, 5 hrs, US$9. Bus to **Fazenda Nova** 1030, 1 hr, US$2, returns to Caruaru 1330.

🅾 Directory

Recife *p497, maps p498 and p501*
Banks Open 1000-1600, hours for exchange vary between 1000 and 1400, sometimes later. Banco do Brasil, R Barão da Souza Leão 440, Boa Viagem; Av Dantas Barreto, 541, Santo Antonio, exchange and credit/debit cards, TCs. **Bradesco**, Av Cons Aguiar 3236, Boa Viagem, T081-3465 3033; Av Conde de Boa Vista, Boa Vista; R da Concordia 148, Santo Antônio, 24-hr VISA ATMs, but no exchange. **Citibank**, Av Marquês de Olinda 126, T081-3216 1144, takes MasterCard. Av Cons Aguiar, 2024, ATM. Lloyds Bank, R AL Monte 96/1002. MasterCard, Av Conselheiro Aguiar 3924, Boa Viagem, cash against card. There are money changers at **Anacor**, Shopping Center Recife, loja 52, also at Shopping Tacaruna, loja 173. **Monaco**, Praça Joaquim Nabuco, *câmbio*, TCs and cash, all major currencies, no commission but poor rates. **Norte Cambio Turismo**, Av Boa Viagem 5000, also at Shopping Guararapes, Av Barreto de Menezes. **Cultural centres** British Council, Av Domingos Ferreira 4150, Boa Viagem, T081-3465 7744, www.britcoun.org/br. 0800-1500, reading room with current British newspapers, very helpful. Alliance Française, R Amaro Bezerra 466, Derby, T081-3222 0918.
Embassies and consulates Denmark, Av Marques de Olinda 85, Edif Alberto Fonseca 2nd floor, T081-3224 0311 (0800-1200, 1400-1800). France, Av Conselheiro Aguiar 2333, 6th floor, T081-3465 3290. **Germany**, Av Dantas Barreto 191, Edif Santo Antônio, 4th floor, T081-3425 3288. **Japan**, R Pe Carapuceiro, 733, 14th floor, T081-3327 7264. **Netherlands**, Av Conselheiro Aguiar 1313/3, Boa Viagem, T081-3326 8096. **Spain**,

R Sirinhaem, 105, 2nd floor, T081-3465 0607. **Switzerland**, Av Conselheiro Aguiar 4880, loja 32, Boa Viagem, T081-3326 3144. **UK**, Av Eng Domingos Ferreira 4150, Boa Viagem, T081-3465 7744 (0800-1130). **USA**, R Gonçalves Maia 163, Boa Vista, T081-3421 2441. **Internet** Shopping Centre Recife, Boa Viagem. Also, **Lidernet**, Shopping Boa Vista, city centre. **Popul@r.net**, R Barao de Souza Leao, near junction with Av Boa Viagem, daily 0900-2100. **Laundry** AcquaClean, Domingos Ferreira, 4023, Boa Viagem, T081-3466 0858, Mon-Fri 0630-1900, Sat 0800-1600. **Medical services** Dengue fever has been resurgent in Recife. Previous sufferers should have good insurance as a 2nd infection can lead to the haemorrhagic form, requiring hospitalization. Hospital Santa Joana, R Joaquim Nabuco 200, Graças, T081-3421 3666. **Unicordis**, Av Conselheiro Aguiar 1980, Boa Viagem, T081-3326 5237 and Av Conselheiro Rosa de Silva 258, Aflitos, T081-3421 1000, equipped for cardiac emergencies. **Post office** Poste Restante at Central Correios, Av Guararapes 250, next to Rio Capibaribe. 0900-1700, outgoing mail leaves at 1500 each day. Also has a philately centre. Another on R 24 de Maio 59. Poste Restante also with American Express representative **Souto Costa**, R Félix Brito de Melo 666, T081-3465 5000, and at Av Conselheiro Aguiar, Boa Viagem.

Olinda *p505, map p506*
Banks There are no facilities to change TCs, or ATMs, is the old city. Banco do Brasil, R Getulio Vargas 1470. Bandepe, Av Getulio Vargas, MasterCard ATMs. **Bradesco**, R Getulio Vargas 729, Visa ATMs. **Internet** Studyo Web, Praça do Carmo, US$1.20, 30 mins, a/c. **Olind@.com**, Av Beira Mar 15, US$1.50, 30 mins. **Laundry** Cooplav, Estr dos Bultrins, cost per weight of laundry, easily visible from main road, take Bultrins bus from Olinda. **Medical services** Prontolinda, R José Augusto Moreira 1191, T081-3432 1700, general, but equipped for cardiac emergencies. **Post office** Praça do Carmo, 0900-1700.

Fernando de Noronha

This small volcanic island rising from the deep, on the eastern edge of the mid-Atlantic ridge 350 km off the coast, is the St Barts of Brazil and one of the world's great romantic destinations. It is blessed with exceptional natural beauty; rugged like the west of Ireland, covered in maquis like Corsica and fringed by some of the cleanest and most beautiful beaches in the Atlantic. Many of the beaches are exposed to the full force of the ocean and pummelled by a powerful bottle-green surf that has earned the island the nickname 'the Hawaii of the Atlantic'. Surf championships are held on Cacimba do Padre beach. However, there are numerous coves where the sea is kinder and the broad beaches are dotted with deep clear-water rock pools busy with juvenile reef fish. The water changes through shades of aquamarine to deep indigo and is as limpid as any on earth. Diving here rivals Mexico's Cozumel and the Turks and Caicos.

Despite the fact that two-thirds of the island is settled, it is an important nesting ground for turtles and marine birds, both the island itself and the seas around it are a marine park, protected by Ibama. All that is needed to make it a sanctuary of international standing is to remove the non-native feral monitor lizards (brought here in the 20th century to kill rats), goats and the island's abundant cats and dogs. Tourism, however, is controlled and only limited numbers can visit the island at any time. Book well in advance. ▶▶ *For listings, see page 523.*

Ins and outs

Getting there and around Flights to the island from Recife and Natal are run by **TRIP**, www.voetrip.com.br, and **Varig**, www.varig.com. **CVC**, www.cruisevacationcenter.com, operates a small cruise liner, which sails from Recife to Noronha and then back to Recife via Fortaleza and Natal. Buggy hire, motorbike hire and jeep tours are available in town.

Fernando de Noronha

Best time to visit The rains are April to July. The vegetation turns brown in the dry season (August to March), but the sun shines all year round. Noronha is one hour later than Brazilian Standard Time. There are far fewer mosquitos here than on the coast but bring repellent.

Tourist information Ibama has imposed rigorous rules to prevent damage to the nature reserve and everything, from development to cultivation of food crops to fishing, is strictly administered. Many locals are now dependent on tourism and most food is brought from the mainland. Entry to the island is limited and there is a tax of US$30 per day for the first week of your stay. In the second week the tax increases each day. Take sufficient *reais* as it's difficult to change money. For information see www.fernandonoronha.com.br.

Sights

The island was discovered in 1503 by Amerigo Vespucci and was for a time a pirate lair. In 1738 the Portuguese built a charming little baroque church, **Nossa Senhora dos Remedios**, some attractive administrative buildings and a fort, **O Forte dos Remédios**, which was used as a prison for political dissidents by the military dictatorship in the late 20th century. The most famous was the communist leader Luis Carlos Prestes, who led the famous long march, the Prestes Column, in 1925-1927. Many people were tortured and murdered here. The islands were occupied by the USA during the Second World War and used as a naval base. US guns sit outside the *prefeitura* in the centre of the main town, **Vila dos Remédios**, which overlooks the coast on the eastern shore.

Some of the best beaches lie immediately south of the town, clustered around an imposing granite pinnacle, the **Morro do Pico**. The most beautiful are **Conceição**, **Boldró**, **Americano**, **Baía do Sancho**, **Cacimba do Padre** and the turquoise cove at **Baía dos Porcos**, which sits on the edge of the beginning of the marine park. Beyond is the **Baía dos Golfinhos**, with a lookout point for watching the spinner dolphins in the bay. On the south, or windward side, there are fewer beaches, higher cliffs and the whole coastline and offshore islands are part of the marine park. As with dive sites, **Ibama** restricts bathing in low-tide pools and other sensitive areas to protect the environment.

There are good possibilities for hiking, horse riding and mountain biking. A guide will take you to the marine park and to beaches such as **Atalaia**, which has the best snorkelling.

Wildlife and conservation

The island is a UNESCO World Heritage Site. It may look like an ecological paradise but it has been the victim of much degradation. Almost all of the native vegetation was chopped down in the 19th century, when the island was used as a prison, to prevent prisoners from hiding or making rafts. A giant native rodent, recorded by Amerigo Vespucci was wiped out and linseed, feral cats, dogs, goats, rats, mice, tegu lizards and cavies were introduced in the 16th century. These continue to damage bird and turtle nesting sites and native vegetation. Nonetheless, the island remains an important sanctuary for sea bird species. Ruddy turnstone, black and brown noddy, sooty tern, fairy tern, masked booby, brown booby and white-tailed tropicbird all nest here. Some endemic bird species still survive: the Noronha vireo (*Vireo gracilirostris*); a tyrant flycatcher, the Noronha elaenia or cucuruta (*Elaenia spectabilis reidleyana*); and the Noronha eared dove or arribaçã (*Zenaida auriculata noronha*). There is an endemic lizard (*Mabuya maculate*) and at least 5% of the fish species are unique to the archipelago. The most spectacular animals are the nesting hawksbill and green turtles, and the spinner dolphins. Good terrestrial wildlife guides are non-existent on Noronha and even Ibama spell the species names incorrectly on their information sheets. There are a number of reasonable dive shops; though biological knowledge is minimal.

Fernando de Noronha listings

For Sleeping and Eating price codes and other relevant information, see pages 42-47.

Sleeping

Fernando de Noronha *p521, map p521*
Some of the most luxurious hotels on the island are built on illegally occupied land.
L Zé Maria, R Nice Cordeirol, Floresta Velha, T081-3619 1258, www.pousadazemaria. com.br. Spacious bungalows with cream tile floors, hardwood ceilings and generous beds. Verandas and hammocks have views out to the Morro do Pico. The highlight is the delicious, but small deep-blue half-moon pool.
L-AL Solar dos Ventos, T081-3619 1347, www.pousadasolardosventos.com.br. Next door to the **Maravilha** and sharing the same spectacular view; although not in the same league. The wood, brick and tile bungalows are well-appointed, though small. No pool.
AL Pousada do Vale, T081-3619 1293, www.pousadadovale.com. Friendly, well-run *pousada* with comfortable en suite rooms decorated with mosaics. The best are the duplex wooden bungalows. 300 m from Vila dos Remedios town centre.
A-B Pousada dos Corais, Conj Residencial Floresta Nova, T081-3619 1147, www.pousada corais.com.br. 8 simple a/c rooms, small pool.

Eating

Fernando de Noronha *p521, map p521*
††† Ecologiku's, Estr Velha do Sueste, T081-3619 1807. Bahian cooking served in an open-sided, mood-lit restaurant with a little garden.
††† Porto Marlin, Porto de Santo Antônio, T081-3619 1452. Good Japanese, with all-you-can-eat buffet on Thu and Sat from 1800.
† Açai e Raizes, BR-363, Floresta Velha. Roadside sandwich bar with snacks, puddings and delicious cream of Cupuaçu and Açai.
† Cia da Lua, Bosque dos Flamboyantes. Coffee, snacks, internet, car and buggy rental.

† Jacaré, Praça Presidente Eurico Dutra. The best-value on the island, with seafood buffet.

Bars and clubs

Fernando de Noronha *p521, map p521*
Vila dos Remédios town, which is the size of a postage stamp, has several bars with lively weekend *forró* from 2200 on weekends, and a bar with live reggae nightly in high season.

Activities and tours

Fernando de Noronha *p521, map p521*
Tour and dive operators
It is possible to see hatching turtles in season. For details, contact **Fundação Pró-Tamar**, Caixa Postal 50, CEP 53990-000, Fernando de Noronha, T081-3619 1269.
Atlantis Divers, T081-3619 1371, www.atlantisdivers.com.br. **Águas Claras** and **Noronha Divers** all offer the same dive locations around Noronha and the offshore islands, as well as dive 'baptism' for complete beginners. Diving costs US$50-75 for 2 tanks and is by far the best in Brazil aside from Atol das Rocas, 2 days off Bahia.
Barco Naonda, Vila do Porto, T081-3619 1307, www.barconaonda.com.br. One of many companies offering boat trips around the island. The best leave at lunchtime, catching the late afternoon light on their return.
Locadora Ilha do Sol, T081-3619 1132, www.pousada dovale.com. Offers buggy rental and guided tours of the island.

Transport

Fernando de Noronha *p521, map p521*
Air Daily flights to **Recife** with Varig and TRIP (1 hr 20 mins, US$400 return). To **Natal** with TRIP (1 hr, US$300 return).

Paraíba

Travellers used to bypass Paraíba, but they are beginning to discover that there are many reasons to stop. The beaches are some of Brazil's best and least spoilt. Some of the most important archaeological sites in the Americas are tucked away in the haunting, rugged landscapes of its interior and the state capital, João Pessoa, is an attractive colonial city with a lively nightlife. Each year in June, Campina Grande, on the edge of the sertão, hosts one of the country's biggest festivals, the Festa do São João, with live music and up to a million people dancing forró into the small hours.

The dense tropical forest that once covered the entire coastal strip now only survives in patches, one of which is within the city of João Pessoa; forming one of the largest areas of wilderness within any city in the world. The seaboard is marked for much of its length by offshore reefs. Inland from the coastal plain the Zona da Mata is an abrupt line of hills and plateaux, a transitional region between the humid coast and the much drier interior. Most people live in this zone, especially in and around the state capital and a couple of other industrial centres. ▶▶ *For listings, see pages 531-536.*

João Pessoa and around ●❼❶❸❽⊙▲❺❻ ▸▸ pp531-536. Colour map 2, B6.

→ *Phone code: 083. Population: 598,000.*

João Pessoa is the state capital yet retains a small town atmosphere. It has some attractive colonial architecture and is set on the Rio Paraíba amid tropical forest. The atmosphere is restful and laid-back, yet there are plenty of bars and restaurants along the beachfront, particularly popular at weekends. The main beach, **Tambaú**, is pleasant but rather built up.

Ins and outs

Getting there and around It is a two-hour bus ride through sugar plantations on a good road from Recife (126 km) to João Pessoa. **Presidente Castro Pinto airport** ⓘ *11 km south of the centre, T083-3232 1200*, receives flights from São Paulo, Brasília, Recife and Rio de Janeiro. A taxi from the airport to centre costs US$8, to Tambaú US$12. Alternatively, the airlines **GOL** flies from São Paulo or Rio to Recife, then provides free bus transport to João Pessoa. The **rodoviária** ⓘ *R Francisco Londres, Varadouro, 10 mins west of the centre, T083-3221 9611*, has a luggage store and helpful **PBTUR** information booth. A taxi to the centre costs US$1.50, to Tambaú US$5. All city buses stop at the *rodoviária* and most go via the Lagoa (Parque Solon de Lucena). From the centre, take No 510 for Tambaú, No 507 for Cabo Branco. The **ferroviária** ⓘ *Av Sanhauá, Varadouro, T083-3221 4257*, has train connections to Bayeux and Santa Rita in the west, and Cabedelo to the north.

Tourist information **PBTUR** ⓘ *Centro Turístico Almte Tamandaré 100, Tambaú, T083-3214 8279 or T0800-3281 9229, 0800-1900*, and others at the *rodoviária*, and airport, provide useful information, pamphlets and maps. Some staff speak good English, and some French.

Background

The Portuguese did not gain a foothold on this part of the coast until the end of the 16th century. Their fort became the city of Filipéia, which grew to become the third largest in Brazil. This was later re-named Parahyba and then João Pessoa, in honour of the once state governor who refused to form alliances with other powerful politicians during the 1930s run for the vice-presidency. This led to his assassination, an event that swept his running mate, the fascist, Getúlio Vargas to power. Pessoa's '*nego*' ('I refuse') is written on the state's flag.

① Joâo Pessoa orientation

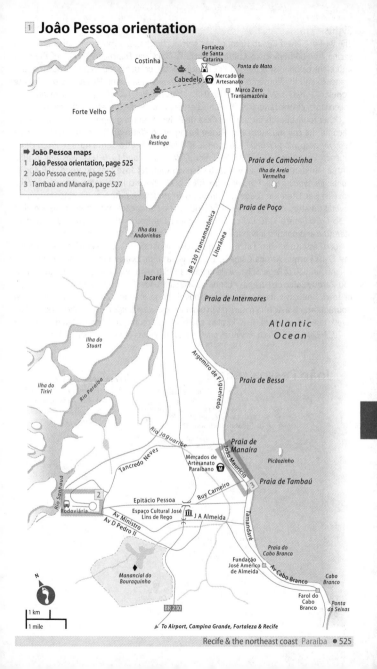

Joâo Pessoa maps
1 Joâo Pessoa orientation, page 525
2 Joâo Pessoa centre, page 526
3 Tambaú and Manaíra, page 527

Costinha

Fortaleza de Santa Catarina

Ponta do Mato

Cabedelo

Mercado de Artesanato

Marco Zero Transamazônica

Forte Velho

Ilha da Restinga

Praia de Camboinha

Ilha de Areia Vermelha

Praia de Poço

Ilha das Andorinhas

BR 230 Transamazônica

Litorânea

Jacaré

Praia de Intermares

Ilha do Stuart

Atlantic Ocean

Ilha do Tiriri

Rio Paraíba

Argemiro de Figueiredo

Praia de Bessa

Rio Jaguaribe

Praia de Manaíra

João Maurício

Picãozinho

Tancredo Neves

Mercados de Artesanato Paraibano

Praia de Tambaú

Rio Sanhauá

Ruy Carneiro

Rodoviária

Epitácio Pessoa

Espaço Cultural José Lins de Rego

J A Almeida

Tamandaré

Av Ministro

Av D Pedro II

Praia do Cabo Branco

Manancial do Bouraquinho

Fundação José Américo de Almeida

Av Cabo Branco

Cabo Branco

N

1 km
1 mile

Farol do Cabo Branco

Ponta do Seixas

BR 230

To Airport, Campina Grande, Fortaleza & Recife

Sights

The well-preserved Centro Histórico has several churches and monasteries that are worth seeing. The **São Francisco Cultural Centre** ① *Praça São Francisco 221*, one of the most important baroque structures in Brazil, includes the beautiful 16th-century church of São Francisco and the Convento de Santo Antônio, which houses the **Museu Sacro e de Arte Popular** ① *T083-3221 2840, Tue-Sat 0800-1100, Tue-Sun 1400-1700*, with a magnificent collection of colonial artefacts. This is the best point to see the sunset over the forest.

Other tourist points include the **Casa da Pólvora**, an old gunpowder store which has become the city museum, and **Museu Fotográfico Walfredo Rodríguez** ① *Ladeira de São Francisco, Mon-Fri 0800-1200 and 1330-1700*. The **Teatro Santa Rosa** ① *Praça Pedro Américo, Varadouro, T083-3218 4382, Mon-Fri 0800-1200 and 1330-1800*, was built in 1886 with a wooden ceiling and walls. The **Espaço Cultural José Lins de Rego** ① *R Abdias Gomes de Almeida 800, Tambauzinho, T083-3211 6222*, a cultural centre named after the novelist (see Literature, page 791), includes an art gallery, history and science museums, several theatres, cinema and a planetarium. The **Fundação José Américo de Almeida** ① *Av Cabo Branco 3336, Cabo Branco*, should be visited by those interested in modern literature and politics; it is in the former house of the novelist and sociologist.

João Pessoa prides itself in being a green city and is called 'Cidade Verde'. Its parks include the 17-ha **Parque Arruda Câmara**, also known as Bica, located north of the centre in the neighbourhood of Roger; it has walking trails, an 18th-century fountain, an aviary and a small zoo. **Parque Solon de Lucena** or **Lagoa** is a lake surrounded by impressive palms in the centre of town, the city's main avenues and bus lines go around it. **Mata** or **Manancial do Bouraquinho** is a 471-ha nature reserve of native *Mata Atlântica*, one of the largest urban forest reserves in Brazil. It is located south of the centre and administered by **Ibama** ① *T083-3244 2725*, which organizes guided walks; access is otherwise restricted.

② João Pessoa centre

➡ João Pessoa maps
1 João Pessoa orientation, page 525
2 João Pessoa centre, page 526
3 Tambaú and Manaíra, page 527

Sleeping 🛌
Aurora 1
Guarany 2
JR 3

N — Not to scale

③ Tambaú & Manaíra

To Cabedelo

Av Flávio
R Coutinho
Av Edson Ramalho
Av Gov Argemiro de Figueiredo

Mega Shopping

*Atlantic
Ocean*

MANAÍRA

Av S Gonçalo
Av João Maurício
Av Euguiano Barreto
Maj Ciraulo
Av Maurício Calixtelas
Av Umbuzeiro
Av Guaralba
Av Radalho
Av Esperança
Av Bananeiras
Av França
Av Geraldo Costa

*Praía de
Manaíra*

TAMBAÚ

Av Sen Rui Carneiro
Av Silvino Lopes
Av Targino Marques
Av Olinda
Av Monteiro Lobato
Av Nego
Av Helder
Meira Lima
Antônio Lira
Av Alm Tamandaré
R Carlos Alverga
R João Maurício

**To ④, Praia de Tambaú
& Cabo Branco**

N

200 metres
200 yards

➡ **João Pessoa maps**
1 João Pessoa orientation, page 525
2 João Pessoa centre, page 526
3 **Tambaú and Manaíra, page 527**

Sleeping
Caiçara 2
Littoral 1
Pousada Mar Azul 10
Royal Praia 5
Solar Filipéia 9
Tambía Praia 7
Tropical Tambaú 3
Victory Business Flat 6
Villa Mare Apt Hotel 8
Xênius 4

Eating
Adega do Alfredo 1
Cheiro Verde 4
Gulliver 2
Mangaí 3

Bars & clubs
Fashion Club 5
Incognito 6
Mr Caipira 8
Zodiaco 7

Urban beaches

The beachfront stretches for some 30 km from Ponta do Seixas (south) to Cabedelo (north); the ocean is turquoise green and there is a backdrop of lush coastal vegetation. By the more populated urban areas the water is polluted, but away from town the beaches are reasonably clean; some spots are calm and suitable for swimming while others are best for surfing. About 7 km from the city centre, following Avenida Presidente Epitáceo Pessoa, is the beach of **Tambaú**, which has many hotels, restaurants and the state tourism centre and is, for all intents and purposes, the centre of the city. The pier by **Hotel Tambaú** affords nice views (bus No 510 'Tambaú' from outside the *rodoviária* or the city centre, alight at **Hotel Tropical Tambaú**). South of Tambaú are **Praia de Cabo Branco** and **Praia do Seixas** and to the north are the beaches of **Manaíra**, **Bessa**, **Intermares**, **Poço** and **Camboinha**, before reaching the port of Cabedelo (see below).

Excursions from João Pessoa

About 14 km south of the centre, down the coast, is the **Cabo Branco** lighthouse at Ponta do Seixas, the most easterly point of continental Brazil and South America (34° 46' 36" W) and thus the first place in the Americas where the sun rises; there is a panoramic view from the clifftop. **Cabo Branco** is much better for swimming than Tambaú. Take bus No 507 'Cabo Branco' from outside the *rodoviária* to the end of the line and hike up to the lighthouse from there. At low tide you can walk from Tambaú to Ponta do Seixas in about two hours.

The port of **Cabedelo**, on a peninsula between the Rio Paraíba and the Atlantic Ocean, is 18 km north by road or rail. Here, Km 0 marks the beginning of the **Trans-amazônica highway**. At the tip of the peninsula are the impressive but run-down walls of the 17th-century fortress of **Santa Catarina**, in the middle of the commercial port. The **Mercado de Artesanato** is at Praça Getúlio Vergas in the centre.

The estuary of the Rio Paraíba has several islands; there is a regular boat service between Cabedelo and the fishing villages of **Costinha** and **Forte Velho** on the north bank; Costinha had a whaling station until the early 1980s.

The beaches between João Pessoa and Cabedelo have many bars and restaurants and are very popular with the locals on summer weekends (**Bar do Sumé**, Rua Beira Mar 171, Praia Ponta do Mato, Cabedelo, has good fish and seafood). Take a bus marked Cabedelo-Poço for the beach as most Cabedelo buses go inland along the Transamazônica. A taxi from Tambaú to Cabedelo costs US$24.

At Km 3 of the Transamazônica, about 12 km from João Pessoa, is the access to **Jacaré**, a pleasant beach on the Rio Paraíba (take the 'Cabedelo' bus and walk 1.5 km or take the train and walk 1 km, taxi from Tambaú US$10). There are several bars along the riverfront where people congregate to watch the lovely sunset to the sounds of Ravel's *Bolero*. Here you can hire a boat along the river to visit the mangroves or ride in an ultralight aircraft. ➤➤ *See Activities and tours, page 535.*

From Tambaú tour boats leave for **Picãozinho**, a group of coral reefs about 700 m from the coast which at low tide turn into pools of crystalline water, suitable for snorkelling (US$20 per person). Further north, boats leave from Praia de Camboinha to **Areia Vermelha**, a large sandbank surrounded by corals. This becomes exposed at low tide, around the full and new moon, and is a popular bathing spot (US$20 per person tour, US$5 per person transport in a *jangada*). Floating bars are set up at both locations, travel agencies arrange trips.

Paraíba coast ○○ ➤➤ *pp531-536.*

The Paraíba coastline has 117 km of beautiful beaches and coves, surrounded by cliffs and coconut groves. These are among the least developed of the northeast.

Tambaba → *Colour map 2, B6.*

The best-known beach of the state is Tambaba, the only official nudist beach of the northeast and one of only two in Brazil. It is located 49 km south of João Pessoa in a lovely setting: the green ocean, warm water, natural pools for swimming formed by the rocks, cliffs up to 20 m high full of caves, palms and lush vegetation. Two coves make up this famous beach: in the first bathing-suits are optional, while the second one is only for nudists. Strict rules of conduct are enforced, unaccompanied men are not allowed in this area and any inappropriate behaviour is reason enough to be asked to leave. The only infrastructure is one bar, where meals are available.

Access is from **Jacumã**, via the BR-101, 20 km south from João Pessoa to where the PB-018 goes 3 km east to Conde and continues 11 km to the beach of Jacumã; from here a dirt road goes 12 km south to Tambaba. Buses run hourly to Jacumã from the João Pessoa *rodoviária*. In summer, dune buggies can be hired at Jacumã to go to Tambaba. Buggy from João Pessoa to Tambaba US$25 per person return (leaves 0930, returns 1730). A day-trip by taxi costs US$95.

Between Jacumã and Tambaba are several good beaches such as **Tabatinga**, which has many summer homes built on the cliffs, and **Coqueirinho**, which is surrounded by pleasant vegetation, and is good for bathing, surfing and exploring caves. There are plenty of cheap and mid-range *pousadas* at both and a very good seafood restaurant at Coqueirinho, **Canyon de Coqueirinho**, on the beach. Near the border with Pernambuco is the 10-km long beach of **Pitimbu**.

Campina and around

The best beaches of northern Paraíba are in the vicinity of the fishing village of **Campina**; although there is little infrastructure in this area, the shore is worth a visit. Access is via a turnoff to the east at Km 73.5 of the BR-101, 42 km north of João Pessoa. It is 28 km along a dirt road (PB-025) to Praia Campina, with a wide beach of fine sand, palms and hills in the background. Nearly 3 km south is **Praia do Oiteiro**, in which the white sand stands out in contrast with the multicoloured cliffs and calm blue ocean. About 2 km north of Campina is **Barra do Mamanguape**, where Ibama runs a preservation centre for marine manatee.

Some 85 km from João Pessoa is **Baia da Traição**, a fishing village and access point for a number of beaches. Its name means 'Bay of Betrayal' and refers to the massacre of 500 residents of a sugar plantation in the 16th century. There is a reserve near town where wood and string crafts are made by the local indigenous people; an annual festival, **Festa do Toré**, takes place on 19 April. Fisherman offer boat tours to the area's less accessible beaches (US$15 per person). **Barra de Camaratuba**, 17 km north of Baia da Traição, is a popular surfing beach.

The sertão ⬤⬤⬤⬤⬤ ➤➤ *pp531-536.*

The semi-arid region of thorn and bush that makes up the hinterland of the northeast is known as the *sertão*. The Transamazônica runs right through the heart of the region, due west of João Pessoa as the BR-230, and along the axis of the state of Paraíba.

Campina Grande → *Colour map 2, B6. Phone code: 083. Population: 340,500.*

Set in the Serra da Borborema, 551 m above sea level and 130 km west of João Pessoa, the second city in Paraíba has a very pleasant climate. Known as the *'porta do sertão'* (door of the sertão), it is an important centre for light industry and an outlet for goods from most of northeast Brazil. In the 1920s it was one of the most important cotton producing areas in the world; a decline in this industry brought a decrease in prosperity in the 1940s and 1950s and the diversification of industry to areas such as sisal and leather. The city's two universities have been instrumental in technological development and reactivation of the local economy.

Ins and outs The **João Suassuna airport** ⓘ *7 km south of centre on the road to Caruaru, T083-3331 1149*, receives daily flights from Recife. A taxi from the airport to the centre costs US$7. A city bus runs to Praça Clementino Procópio, behind Cine Capitólio. The **rodoviária** ⓘ *Av Argemiro de Figueiredo, T083-3321 5780*, is a 20-minute bus ride from the centre. Tourist information is available from **PBTUR** ⓘ *T156*, or **DEMTUR** ⓘ *T083-3341 3993*.

Sights Avenida Floriano Peixoto is the main street running east–west through the entire city, with Praça da Bandeira at its centre. The **Museu de Arte Assis Chateaubriand** ⓘ *Parque do Açude Novo, T083-3341 3300, Mon-Fri 0900-1200, daily 1400-2200*, has a collection of paintings and etchings by Brazilian artists and temporary exhibits. **Museu Histórico de Campina Grande** ⓘ *Av Floriano Peixoto 825, Centro, daily 0800-1130, 1300-1645*, is the city museum housed in a 19th-century building, with a photo and artefact collection reflecting the cycles of prosperity and poverty in the region. **Museu da História e Tecnologia do Algodão** ⓘ *Centro Nacional de Produção do Algodão, Oswaldo Cruz 1143, Centenário, T083-3341 3608, Mon-Fri 0730-1130, 1330-1730, Sat and Sun 0800-1200*, has machines and related equipment used in the cotton industry in the 16th and 17th centuries. **Museu Regional de São João** ⓘ *Largo da Estação Velha, Centro, T083-3341 2000, daily 0800-1300*, houses an interesting collection of objects and photographs pertaining to the June celebrations.

The **Teatro Municipal Severino Cabral** ① *Av Floreano Peixoto*, is a modern theatre where there are regular performances. The main parks in town are: the **Parque do Açude Novo** (Evaldo Cruz), a green area with playgrounds, fountains and restaurants; the nearby **Parque do Povo** with its *forródromo* where the main festivities of the city take place; and the **Açude Velho**, a park around a dam south of the centre. The **Mercado Central**, where a large roof has been built over several blocks of old buildings, has regional crafts and produce, is worth a visit.

Excursions from Campina Grande

About 10 km north from Campina Grande is **Lagoa Seca**, where figures in wood and sacking are made, and there is a **Museu do Índio**.

Some 35 km east of Campina Grande, off the road to João Pessoa, is **Ingá**, site of the **Pedra de Itacoatiara** archaeological centre, where inscriptions dated as 10,000 years old were found on a boulder 25 m long and 3 m high. A small museum at the site contains fossils of a giant sloth and a Tyrannosaurus rex. During the June festivities there is a train service to Itacoatiara.

The **Boqueirão** dam on the Rio Paraíba, 70 km southeast of town, is where locals flock on holidays for watersports; there is a hotel-*fazenda* (T081-3391 1233).

Cariri

The *sertão* proper begins near São João do Cariri an hour or so from Campina Grande. This is an area of fascinating rock formations, with giant weather-worn boulders sitting on top of gently curved expanses of rock that look out over a plain of low bushes and stunted trees. Although the vegetation is quite different to the landscape itself; the arid conditions and the size of the trees recalls the Australian outback (the rocks themselves have been compared to the Devil's Marbles). The most spectacular of all the formations sit in the private grounds of **Fazenda Pai Mateus** (see Sleeping, page 533). Like various other sites in Paraíba and Rio Grande do Norte, boulders here are covered in important pre-Columbian rock art, some of which has been controversially dated as pre-Clovis (making it older than the accepted datings for the first waves of American population coming from over the Bering Strait). A famous local holy man lived inside one of the giant hollowed-out stones and the views from his former home at sunset are particularly spellbinding. The *fazenda* itself is a very pleasant place to stay and there is rich, though depleted wildlife in the area and good birdwatching. Tours can be organized with **Manary Ecotours** (see Essentials, page 66), who provide fascinating information about the archaeological sites but have little knowledge of the fauna in the region. The *fazenda*'s guides are informative about life in the *sertão* and the use of medicinal plants, but again as ever in Brazil, knowledge of birds and animals is poor.

North of Cariri, 46 km from Campina Grande, is **Areial**, the main town of the Brejo Paraibano, a scenic region of green hills and valleys, with a pleasant climate, where colonial sugar *fazendas* have been transformed into hotels.

Patos → *Colour map 2, B5. Population: 84,500.*

West of Campina Grande the landscape turns to vast, flat expanses, flanked by rolling hills and interesting rock formations; very scenic when green, but a sad sight during the prolonged *sertão* droughts. Situated 174 km from Campina Grande is Patos, the centre of a cattle-ranching and cotton-growing area. It's also an access point for the **Serra do Teixeira**, 28 km away, which includes **Pico do Jabre**, the highest point in the state, at 1130 m above sea level. There are various hotels and restaurants in Patos.

Souza → *Colour map 2, B5. Phone code: 081. Population: 59,000.*

About 130 km northwest of Patos, the pleasant *sertão* town of Souza, has high temperatures year-round and is gaining fame for the nearby dinosaur tracks and prehistoric rock carvings. The *rodoviária* is 1 km from the centre, there are no city buses, walk (hot), take a moto-taxi (US$1) or a taxi (US$5). The **Igreja do Rosário** at the Praça Matriz has paintings dating to the Dutch occupation of the area. It currently functions as a school. About 3 km from the centre, atop a hill, is a **statue of Frei Damião**, an important religious leader of the northeast who died in 1997. Frei Damião was an Italian friar who came to Brazil in the 1930s and stayed to become an inspiration for the faith of its most recent generation of dispossessed. He is seen as belonging to the same tradition as O Conselheiro and Padre Cícero.

Fossilized dinosaur prints of up to 90 different species, which inhabited the area between 110 and 80 million years ago, are found in a number of sites in the Souza region. These were extensively studied by the Italian palaeontologist Giussepe Leonardi in the 1970s and 1980s. The **Vale dos Dinossauros**, on the sedimentary river bed of the Rio do Peixe, is one of the closest sites to Souza; it has some impressive Iguanodontus prints. Access is 4 km from town along the road north to Uiraúna; the best time to visit is the dry season, July to October. The area has no infrastructure and is best visited with a guide. Try to contact Robson Marques of the **Movisaurio Association** ① *R João Rocha 7, Souza, PB 58800-610, T083-3522 1065*, who is very knowledgeable; otherwise contact the Prefeitura Municipal. Tours can be organized through **Manary Ecotours** in Natal (see Essentials, page 66), these can be combined with visits to Cariri.

Cajazeiras → *Colour map 2, B5. Population: 51,000.*

Some 37 km west of Souza, the Transamazônica (BR-230) reaches Cajazeiras, the centre of a cotton-growing area, with an impressive tower on the main church and various hotels. This is an access point for the **Brejo das Freiras** thermal mineral baths 32 km to the north, an oasis with natural springs in the middle of the *sertão*.

From Cajazeiras it is 17 km to the Ceará border; the Transamazônica continues west across the *sertãos* of Ceará and Piauí and on to Maranhão, Tocantins and Pará. Southwest of Cajazeiras it is 118 km to Juazeiro do Norte, an important pilgrimage centre, see page 570.

◉ Paraíba listings

For Sleeping and Eating price codes and other relevant information, see pages 42-47.

● Sleeping

João Pessoa centre *p524, map p526*
The town's main attractions are its beaches, where most tourists stay. Hotels in the centre are poorer and tend to cater for business clients. The centre is very quiet after dark and it is difficult to find a restaurant. Cheaper hotels can be found near the *rodoviária*; look carefully as some are sleazy. The most convenient beach and the focus of nightlife and restaurants is **Tambaú**. There are good

restaurants and a few hotels in **Manaíra**, north of Tambaú. There are also a few in the southern beach suburb of **Cabo Branco**, but this is quieter and has fewer eating options.

B-C Hotel JR, R João Ramalho de Andrade, T083-3241 6262, www.bomguia.com.br/jr. 1990s business hotel with basic facilities and a restaurant. The largest and most comfortable in the centre.

C-D Guarany, R Almeida Barreto 181 and 13 de Maio, T/F083-3241 5005, guarany@ bomguia.com.br/guarany. Cheaper in low season, or without a/c and TV. A pleasant, safe, extremely good-value establishment with a self-service restaurant. Recommended.

D Aurora, Praça João Pessoa 51, T083-3241 3238. A/c or cheaper fan-cooled rooms, on an attractive square.

D Ouro Preto, Idaleto 162, T083-221 5882, Varadouro near *rodoviária*. Very simple rooms with baths and a fan.

Urban beaches *p527, map p527*

Accommodation can also be found in the outer beaches such as **Camboinha** and **Seixas**, and in **Cabedelo**.

L Littoral, Av Cabo Branco 2172, T083-3247 1100. A full luxury service. Low-season discounts.

AL Caiçara, Av Olinda 235, T/F083-3247 2040, www.hotcaicarara.com.br. A slick, business-orientated place with a pleasant restaurant.

AL Tropical Tambaú, Av Alm Tamandaré 229, T083-3247 3660, www.tropical hotel.com.br. An enormous round building on the seafront which looks like a rocket-launching station and has comfortable motel-style rooms around its perimeter. Good service. Recommended.

AL Xênius, Av Cabo Branco 1262, T083-3226 3535, www.xeniushotel.com.br. Popular standard 4-star hotel with a pool, good restaurant. Well-kept but standard a/c rooms, low-season reductions.

A-B Royal Praia, Coração de Jesus, T083-2106 3000, www.royalhotel.com.br. Comfortable a/c rooms with fridges, pool.

A-B Victory Business Flat, Av Tamandaré 310, T083-3247 3011, www.victoryflat.com.br. Furnished apartments with a pool and sauna. Cheaper in low season.

B Pouso das Águas, Av Cabo Branco 2348, Cabo Branco. A homely atmosphere with landscaped areas and a pool.

B Tambía Praia, R Carlos Alverga 36, T083-3247 4101, www.tambiahotel.hpg.com.br. Centrally located and 1 block from the beach. Intimate, with balconies and sea view. Recommended.

B Villa Mare Apartment Hotel, Av Négo 707, T083-3226 2142, www.pbnet.com.br/openline/george. Comfortable apartments for 2 or 3 people with full amenities per

night or from US$400-500 per month. Helpful staff. Recommended.

B-C Pousada Casa Rosada, Av Cabo Branco 1710, Cabo Branco. T083-3247 2470. Well-kept rooms with bath and fans run by a friendly family. Cheaper with shared bath.

C Pousada Casa Grande, R Infante Dom Henrique 750, Manaíra, T083-3226 2071, www.holandahhoteisezdir.net. Well-kept, simple rooms with en suites and friendly staff in a discreet small family hotel, 2 blocks from the beach.

C-D Solar Filipéia, Av Incognito Coração de Jesus 153, www.solarfilipeia.com.br. Brand-new, very smart hotel with large, bright rooms with bathrooms in tile and black marble and excellent service. Good value.

E Pousada Mar Azul, Av João Maurício 315, T083-3226 2660. Very clean large rooms, the best are on the upper level, on the oceanfront road. Some have a/c and private bath, others have fans. Well kept, safe and a real bargain.

E-F Hostel Manaíra, R Major Ciraulo 380, Manaíra, T083-3247 1962, www.manaira hostel.br2.net. Friendly new hostel close to the beach, with a pool, internet, barbecue, cable TV and breakfast. A real bargain.

Camping

Camping Clube do Brasil, Praia de Seixas, 13 km from the centre, T083-3247 2181.

Tambaba *p528*

B Chalé Suiço, R Chalé Suiço 120, Tabatinga, T083-3981 2046. Small, shared bath, restaurant, upstairs rooms have ocean-view balconies.

B Pousada Corais de Carapebus, Av Beira Mar, Carapebus, T083-3290 1179, a few kilometres south of Jacumã. With bath, pool, restaurant and a nice breeze since it is located on a cliff across from the ocean.

B Vivenda Ocean, R Sidine C Dore 254, Carapebus, T083-3226 6017. Chalets for 5, with restaurant.

C Vallhalla, R Niterói, Jacumã, T083-3290 1015. Away from the beach with good views. Rooms are simple with a fan as the only extra. Swedish run and the restaurant has a varied menu.

Camping

Camping is possible in **Tambaba** with permission from the guards, also in **Coqueirinho**; no infrastructure in either.

Campina *p529*

C Pousada Ponto do Sol, Dom Pedro II 537, Baia da Traição, T083-3296 1050. Rooms with baths and fridges, restaurant. On the same street are the simpler *pousadas* Alvorada and 2001, T083-3296 1043. Several others in town.
C Pousada Porto das Ondas, Barra de Camaratuba, T083-3247 2054. Bath, restaurant.

Campina Grande *p529*

Many hotels around Praça da Bandeira.
A Ouro Branco, João Lourenço Porto 20, T083-3341 2929. Cheaper if you pay with cash.
A Serrano, Tavares Cavalcante 27, T083-3341 3131. Luxury standard with pool and restaurant. You can get discounts for cash.
B Mahatma Gandhi, Floriano Peixoto 338, T/F083-3321 5275. With bath, a/c, fridge.
B Souto Maior, Floriano Peixoto 289, T083-3321 8043. Rooms include bath a/c and fridge.
C Regente, Barão do Abiaí 80, T083-3321 3843. With bath, a/c or fan, fridge.
C-D Pérola, Floriano Peixoto 258, T083-3341 5319. With bath and a/c, cheaper with fan, parking and a very good breakfast.
D Avenida, Floriano Peixoto 378, T083-3341 1249. With fan, good value, cheaper with shared bath.
D Verona, 13 de Maio 232, T083-3341 1926. With bath, fan, good value, friendly service.
D-E Eliu's, Maciel Pinheiro 31B, 1st floor, T083-3321 4115. Clean, friendly, a/c and bath (cheaper with fan/without bath), good value.
E Aurora, 7 de Setembro 120, T083-3321 4874. Shared bath, very basic and run down.

Cariri *p530*

A visit to **Fazenda Pai Mateus**, www.pai mateus.com.br, can be organized through **Manary Ecotours**, see Essentials, page 66.
B Gadelha Palace, Trav Luciana Rocha 2, Cariri, T081-3521 1416. With bath, a/c, fridge, pool and restaurant.

C Dormitório Sertanejo I, R Col Zé Vicente, Cariri. Rooms nice and clean with bath and fan. No breakfast, but good value. Recommended.
E Dormitório Aguiar, R João Gualberto, Cariri. Very basic.

Cajazeiras *p531*

A Estância Termal Brejo das Freiras, São João do Rio do Peixe, T081-3522 1515. Rooms or chalets with bath, a/c, fridge. Pool, restaurant.
C Regente, 15 mins' walk from *rodoviária*, in the centre, a/c (cheaper without), TV, bath.
E Cacique, near *rodoviária*, cheaper with fan.

🍴 Eating

João Pessoa *p524, maps p525 and p526*

There are few eating options in the city centre. Locals eat at the stalls in **Parque Solon de Lucena** next to the lake, where there are a couple of simple restaurants.

Urban beaches *p527, map p527*

Every evening on the beachfront, stalls sell all kinds of snacks and barbecued meats. At **Cabo Branco** there are many straw huts on the beach serving cheap eats and seafood.
♦♦♦ Adega do Alfredo, Coração de Jesus. Very popular traditional Portuguese restaurant in the heart of the club and bar area.
♦♦♦ Gulliver, Av Olinda 590, Tambaú. Trendy French/Brazilian restaurant frequented by João Pessoa's middle classes.
♦♦ Cheiro Verde, R Carlos Alverga 43. Self-service, well established, regional food.
♦♦ Mangaí, Av General Édson Ramalho 696, Manaíra, T083-3226 1615. This is one of the best restaurants in the northeast to sample the region's cooking. There are almost 100 different hot dishes to chose from, sitting in copper tureens over a traditional wood-fired stove some 20 m long. The open-sided dining area is very welcoming and spacious. Very good Italian too with a charming atmosphere.
♦♦ Sapore d'Italia, Av Cabo Branco 1584, Standard Italian fare including pizza.

Campina Grande *p529*
R 13 de Maio by Rui Barbosa in the centre has several good restaurants. There are many bars near **Parque do Povo**, busy at weekends.
� **A Cabana do Possidônio**, 13 de Maio 207 T083-3341 3384. A varied menu of regional and international dishes.
� **La Nostra Casa**, R 13 de Maio 175, T083-3322 5196. Modest but friendly pasta and pizza restaurant.
♥ **Carne & Massa**, R 13 de Maio 214, T083-3322 8677. Regional cooking including *carne de sol*, pasta and a range of desserts.
♥ **La Suissa**, Dep João Tavares 663. Good savoury and sweet snacks.
♥ **Lanchonette Casa das Frutas**, Marquês de Herval 54. Good-value meals, fruit juices and snacks.
♥ **Manoel da Carne de Sol**, Félix de Araújo 263. T083-3321 2877. One of the city's best-value regional restaurants including an excellent *carne de sol* lunch with runner beans, *farofa* manioc flour and vegetables.
♥ **Vila Antiga**, R 13 de Maio 164, T083-3341 4718. A popular pay by weight restaurant with a broad range of regional dishes, pastas, salads and desserts.

Souza *p531*
Several restaurants are on R Col Zé Vicente.
♥ **Diagonal**, Getúlio Vargas 2. Ordinary but reasonable pizzeria.

❶ Bars and clubs

João Pessoa *p524, maps p525, p526 and p527*
There are many open bars on and across from the beach in Tambaú and Cabo Branco; the area known as **Feirinha de Tambaú**, on Av Tamandaré by the Tambaú Hotel and nearby streets, sees much movement even on weekend nights, with **R Coração do Jesus** being the epicentre. There are numerous little bars and *forró* places here and this is the place for a night-time browse. Other beachfront neighbourhoods also have popular bars.

Fashion Club, Mega Shopping, Manaíra. The most popular nightclub in the city, with a 20-something crowd and mostly techno and MPB. Large beachfront *baracca* restaurant with live music at weekends.
Incognito, R Coração do Jesus. A very popular and lively bar and dance club. There are many others here including KS.
Mr Caipira, Av João Maurício 1533, Manaíra, T083-246 7597. Live acoustic music, Brazilian barbecued food, *feijoada* and a smart 30-something crowd. On the seafront road.
Zodiaco, Incognito Coração do Jesus 144. One of several nightclubs in the area attracting a lively young crowd especially at the weekends.

❀ Festivals and events

João Pessoa *p524, maps p525, p526 and p527*
Feb Pre-carnival celebrations in João Pessoa are renowned: the *bloco* Acorde Miramar opens the celebrations the Tue before Carnaval. On Wed, known as **Quarta Feira de Fogo**, thousands join the **Muriçocas de Miramar**, forming a *bloco* second only to Recife's **Galo da Madrugada** with as many as 300,000 people taking part.
5 Aug The street celebrations for the patroness of the city, **Nossa Senhora das Neves**, last for 10 days to the rhythm of *frevo*.

Campina Grande *p529*
Apr **Micarande**, the out-of-season Salvador-style carnival.
Jun-Jul Campina Grande boasts the largest São João celebrations in Brazil; from the beginning of Jun into the 1st week of Jul the city attracts many visitors; there are bonfires and *quadrilhas* (square dance groups) in every neighbourhood; *forró* and invited artists at the Parque do Povo; *quentão*, *pomonha* and *canjica* are consumed everywhere.
Aug The annual **Congresso de Violeiros**, which gathers singers and guitarists from all across the northeast.

The world's greatest barn dance – the Festas Juninhas

Carnaval is essentially an urban, black Brazilian celebration. The Festas Juninhas, which take place throughout Brazil during June, are a rural celebration. While carnival pounds to samba, the Juninhas pulsate to the triangle and accordion of *forró*. Rather than wearing feathers and sequins, Juninhas revellers dress up as *caipiras* (yokels) in tartan shirts and reed hats; and they eat *canjica* (maize porridge) and drink *quentão* (a Brazilian version of mulled wine).

And they do it in enormous numbers. During the most important weekend of the festivals – the eve of St John's Day on 23 June – over one million mock-*caipiras* descend on the little backland towns of Campina Grande in Paraíba and Caruaru in Pernambuco. Both towns are entirely taken over by *forró* bands, cowboys, stalls selling *doce de leite* and other country produce, and the percussion of fireworks and bangers. Foreign visitors are still a rare curiosity.

○ Shopping

João Pessoa *p524, maps p525, p526 and p527, map p526*
Cheaper arts and crafts can be bought at **Mercado de Artesanato**, Centro de Turismo, Almte Tamandaré 100, Tambaú, daily 0800-1800; **Mercados de Artesanato Paraibano**, Av Rui Carneiro, Tambaú, daily 0900-1700; **Bosque dos Sonhos**, by the Cabo Branco lighthouse. Weekends only.
Terra do Sol, R Coração do Jesus 145, T083-3226 1940, www.terradosol.art.br. The best place to buy regional crafts, including lace, embroidery and ceramics. Very elegant, high-quality bedspreads, bath robes, hammocks and tablecloths made from natural cotton. Also sells work by Paraíba artists and artisans.

▲ Activities and tours

João Pessoa *p524, maps p525, p526 and p527*
Cliotur, Av Alm Tamandaré 310, Sala 2, T083-3247 4460. Trips to the *sertão*. Also offers light adventure activities.
Roger Turismo, Av Tamandaré 229, T083-3247 1856. Half-day city tours (US$6), day trips to Tambaba (US$8) and Recife/Oldina (US$12). A large agency with some English-speaking guides and a range of other tours.

Excursions from João Pessoa *p527*
Flaviano Gouveia, Jacaré, T083-3982 1604. Ultralight aircraft rides, US$19 for 8-min ride or US$115 for 1 hr.
Sea Tech, PO Box 42, João Pessoa, 56001-970, T083-3245 1476. Run by Brian Ingram, originally from England. Boatyard and frequent port of call for international yachtspeople plying the Brazilian coast.

○ Transport

João Pessoa *p524, maps p525, p526 and p527*
Air A taxi to the airport costs US$8 from the centre or US$12 from Tambaú. Flights to **São Paulo**, **Brasília**, **Recife** and **Rio de Janeiro**. Gol flies to **São Paulo** or **Rio** from Recife, and provides free bus transport from João Pessoa.

Airline offices GOL, www.voegol.com.br, and at the airport. Oceanair, www.ocean air.com.br, **TAM**, T083-3247 2400, Av Senador Rui Carneiro 512, T083-3247 2400. **Varig**, Av Getúlio Vargas 183, Centro, T083-3247 8383.

Bus From the *rodoviária* or Lagoa (Parque Solon de Lucena), take bus No 510 for **Tambaú**, No 507 for **Cabo Branco**.

Buses to **Recife** with Boa Vista or Bonfim, every 30 mins, US$2.50, 2 hrs. To **Natal** with Nordeste, every 2 hrs, US$8 *convencional*,

US$7.50 *executivo*, 3 hrs. To **Fortaleza** with Nordeste, 2 daily, 10 hrs, US$18. To **Campina Grande** with Real, every 30 mins, US$4, 2 hrs. To **Juazeiro do Norte** with Transparaíba, 2 daily, US$14, 10 hrs. To **Salvador** with Progresso, 4 weekly, US$30, 14 hrs. To **Brasília** via Campina Grande, with Planalto, 2 weekly, US$57, 48 hrs. To **Rio de Janeiro** with São Geraldo, daily, US$67 *convencional*, US$80 *executivo*, 42 hrs. To **São Paulo** with Itapemirim, daily, US$73 *convencional*, US$76 *executivo*, 47 hrs. To **Belém** with Guanabara, daily, US$46, 36 hrs.

Car hire Avis, Av Nossa Senhora dos Navegantes, 402, T083-3247 3050. Localiza, Av Epitácio Pessoa 4910, T083-3247 4030, and at the airport, T0800-992000. Tempo, Almte Tamandaré 100, at the Centro de Turismo, T083-3247 0002.

Train Regional services west to **Bayeux** and **Santa Rita**, and **Cabedelo** in the north.

Tambaba *p528*
Bus From Tambaba a dirt road leads 12 km north to the beach of **Jacumã**, from where the PB-018 goes 11 km west to **Conde** and continues 3 km to the BR-101, which runs 20 km north to **João Pessoa**. There are hourly buses from Jacumã to **João Pessoa** 0530-1900.

Campina Grande *p529*
Air Daily flights to **Recife** with Nordeste. Taxi to airport US$7. City bus Distrito Industrial from Praça Clementino Procópio, behind Cine Capitólio.

Bus To **João Pessoa**, with Real, every 30 mins, US$3, 2 hrs. To **Souza** with Transparaíba, 6 daily, US$7, 6 hrs. To **Juazeiro do Norte** with Transparaíba, 2 daily, US$10, 9 hrs. To **Natal** with Nordeste, 0800 daily, US$6, 18 hrs. To **Rio** with Itapemirim, 1600 daily, US$65, 42 hrs. To **Brasília** with Planalto, 2 weekly, US$55, 46 hrs.

Car hire On R Tavares Cavalcante are Intermezzo, No 27, T083-321 4790; Kelly's,

No 301, T/F083-3322 4539. Also **Localiza**, R Dr Severino Cruz 625, T083-3341 4034, and at the airport, T083-3331 4594.

Souza *p531*
Bus To **Campina Grande** with Transparaíba, 6 daily, US$7, 6 hrs. To **João Pessoa** with Transparaíba, 6 daily, US$10, 8 hrs. To **Juazeiro do Norte** with Transparaíba or Boa Esperança, 4 daily, US$4, 3½ hrs. To **Mossoró**, RN, with Jardinense, 4 daily, US$6, 4½ hrs.

ⓘ Directory

João Pessoa *p524, maps p525, p526 and p527*
Banks Banco 24 horas, Av Almirante Tamandaré 100, Tambaú, ATM for Cirrus, Visa and MasterCard. Banco do Brasil, Praça 1817, 3rd floor, Centro, Isidro Gomes 14, Tambaú, behind Centro de Turismo. HSBC, R Peregrino de Carvalho, 162, Centre, ATM for cirrus and visa. Mondeo Tour, Av Négo 46, Tambaú, T083-3226 3100. 0900- 1730, cash and Tcs. PB Câmbio Turismo, Visconde de Pelotas 54C, Centro, Mon-Fri 1030-1630, cash and TCs. **Internet** Cyberpointy Café, Av Almirante Tamandaré, 100, in Centro Turístico Tambaú, daily 0800-2100, US1.60 per hr. **Post office** Main office is at Praça Pedro Américo, Varadouro; central office is at Parque Solon de Lucena 375; also by the beach at Av Rui Carneiro, behind the Centro de Turismo. **Telephone** Calling stations at: Visconde de Pelotas and Miguel Couto, Centro; Centro de Turismo, Tambaú; Av Epitácio Pessoa 1487, Bairro dos Estados; *rodoviária* and airport.

Campina Grande *p529*
Banks Banco do Brasil, 7 de Setembro 52, cash and TCs at poor rates. Mondeo Tour, R Índios Cariris 308, cash at good rates and TCs, Mon-Fri 1000-1600. **Post office** R Marquês do Herval, Praça da Bandeira. **Telephone** Floriano Peixoto 410 by Praça da Bandeira in the industrial district and at the *rodoviária*.

Contents

Footprint features

At a glance

☺ **Getting around** Bus and internal flights. Car hire is not recommended as roads can be poor and badly signposted, especially in the interior.

☺ **Time required** 1 day for Fortaleza; 2-3 days for São Luís and Alcântara; 2-3 days for the Lençóis Maranhenses; 10 days for the whole region.

☼ **Weather** Hot and wet Jan-Jun, hot and dry Jul-Dec.

✕ **When not to go** Mar and Apr have the most rain and least sunshine.

★ **Don't miss ...**

1 Pipa, page 545.
2 Areia Branca, page 545.
3 Parque Nacional de Sete Cidades and Parque Nacional Serra da Capivara, pages 587 and 590.
4 Delta do Parnaíba, page 588.
5 São Luís, page 595.
6 Alcântara, page 599.
7 Parque Nacional Lençóis Maranhenses, page 600.

Bahia may have the prettiest stretches of coastline in Brazil but the northeast has some of the most dramatic. In Rio Grande do Norte, broken, striated cliffs and imposing dunes tower above the wild and deserted beaches of Natal, Genipabu, Pipa and Areia Branca. In neighbouring Ceará the coast becomes touristy again, especially around the state capital, Fortaleza, a sunny, planned city whose charm is somewhat sullied by a plethora of cheap package tours. Just to the north is the Western hemisphere's kitesurfing capital, Cumbuco, where the only Brazilians you'll see are working in the hotels and restaurants.

Beyond the state border at Jericoacoara, the cliffs and dunes give way to the wilderness of the Delta do Parnaíba, the largest delta in the Western hemisphere. The wetlands of the Rio Parnaíba spread like an outstretched palm to divide the land into myriad islands and a maze of narrow channels, which hide some of Brazil's least visited and least spoilt beaches. Most visitors head for Maranhão state and the coastal desert of the Lençóis Maranhenses: a huge sea of coastal dunes, pocked with freshwater lakes and fringed by deserted beaches and forgotten wind-blown fishing villages. Further north, and almost inaccessible, the swamps and inlets of the Reentrâncias Maranhenses preserve the largest bank of coral in Atlantic South America, the Parque Estadual Marinho do Parcel Manoel Luís, which is just beginning to open up to diving.

Maranhão's capital, São Luís, is famous for its Bumba-Meu-Boi festival in June and its historic centre, whose colonial buildings are covered in blue and white Portuguese *azulejos* and filled with decaying baroque churches. The city is one of two World Heritage Sites in the region, the other being the Parque Nacional da Serra da Capivara, whose bizarre honeycomb domes tower over canyons covered in what may be the oldest rock painting in the Americas.

Rio Grande do Norte

This state is famous for its beaches and dunes, especially around Natal. The coastline begins to change here, becoming gradually drier and less green, as it shifts from running north–south to east–west. The vast sugar cane plantations and few remaining stands of Mata Atlântica (coastal forest) are replaced by the dry caatinga vegetation and caju orchards. The people are known as 'Potiguares', after an indigenous tribe that once resided in the state. ⏵ *For listings, see pages 547-554.*

Natal ⬤🏠🔆⬤▲⬤⬤ ⏵ *pp547-554. Colour map 2, B6.*

→ *Phone code: 084. Population: 713,000.*

The state capital, located on a peninsula between the Rio Potengi and the Atlantic Ocean, is pleasant enough but has few sights of interest. Most visitors head for the beaches to the north and south. During the Second World War, the city was, somewhat bizarrely, the second largest US base outside the United States and housed 8000 American pilots.

Ins and outs

Getting there Flights arrive at **Augusto Severo International Airport** ① *Parnamirim, 18 km south of centre, 10 km from Ponta Negra, T084-3644 1070*, from Belém, Brasília, Fernando de Noronha, Fortaleza, Recife, Rio de Janeiro, Salvador and São Paulo. A taxi to the centre costs US$25; US$20 to Ponta Negra. Buses run every 30 minutes to the old *rodoviária* near the centre, US$1 from where there are connections to Ponta Negra on route 54 or 56 amongst others, or take the 'Aeroporto' bus to the city centre and then bus Nos 54 or 46 south to Ponta Negra.

Interstate buses arrive at the new **Rodoviária Cidade do Sol** ① *Av Capitão Mor Gouveia 1237, Cidade da Esperança, 6 km southwest of the centre, T084-3205 4377*. A taxi to Ponta Negra costs around US$18; to the Via Costeira around US$25. Alternatively, take bus No 66 to Ponta Negra. This passes close to the hotel strip whilst not taking Avenida Erivan Franca (the street that runs along the seafront). For Praia do Meio beach and the Via Costeira take bus No 40 and alight at Praia do Meio for an easy walk to any of the hotels on that beach or Praia dos Artistas. Or take any of the Via Costeira buses.

Buses from the south pass Ponta Negra first, where you can ask to alight. The city buses 'Cidade de Esperança Avenida 9', 'Areia Preta via Petrópolis' or 'Via Tirol' run from the new *rodoviária* to the centre. It is also possible to travel between Natal and Fortaleza by beach buggy: an exciting trip but not a very environmentally responsible one as buggies have seriously eroded the coast. ⏵ *See Transport, page 553.*

Getting around Unlike most Brazilian buses, in Natal you get on the bus at the front and get off at the back. The **old rodoviária** ① *Av Junqueira Aires, by Praça Augusto Severo, Ribeira*, is a central point where many bus lines converge. Buses to some of the nearby beaches also leave from here. Taxis are expensive compared to other cities (eg four times the price of Recife); a typical 10-minute journey costs US$15. Buses are the best option. Route 54 and 46 connect Ponta Negra with the city, the former via Via Costeira and the old *rodoviária*.

Natal

Natal orientation

Sleeping 🛏
Bruma **4**
Casa Grande **1**
Imirá Plaza **2**
Maine **3**
Porto Mirim **5**

Eating 🍴
A Macrobiótica **1**
Raro Sabor **2**

Tourist information The state tourist office, **SETUR** ① *Centro de Turismo R Aderbal de Figueiredo 980, Petrópolis, T084-3211 5013 www.setur.rn.gov.br www.rosaleao.com.br/clientes/ setur*, covers the whole of Rio Grande do Norte state, although their information and English is very limited, and the office is not conveniently located. However, there are **tourist information booths** at the airport, the bus station, on Avenida Presidente Café Filho on Praia das Artistas beach and Erivan Franca on Ponta Negra, all open daily 0800-2100. See www.nataltrip.com, www.natal.com.br and www.rn.gov.br for more information.

Sights

No-one comes to Natal for sightseeing, but the city is not without culture. The oldest part is the **Ribeira** along the riverfront, where a programme of renovation has been started. This can be seen on Rua Chile and in public buildings restored in vivid art deco fashion, such as the **Teatro Alberto Maranhão** ① *Praça Agusto Severo, T/F084-3222 9935*, built 1898-1904, and the **Prefeitura** ① *R Quintino Bocaiuva, Cidade Alta*. The **Cidade Alta**, or Centro, is the main commercial centre and Avenida Rio Branco its principal artery. The main square is made up by the adjoining *praças*, **João Maria**, **André de Albuquerque**, **João Tibúrcio** and **7 de Setembro**. At Praça André de Albuquerque is the old **cathedral** (inaugurated 1599, restored 1996). The modern cathedral is on Avenida Deodoro. The church of **Santo Antônio** ① *R Santo Antônio 683, Cidade Alta, Tue-Fri 0800-1700, Sat 0800-1400*, dates from 1766, and has a fine, carved wooden altar and a sacred art museum.

The **Museu Câmara Cascudo** ① *Av Hermes de Fonseca 1440, Tirol, T084-3212 2795, www.mcc.ufrn.br, Tue-Fri 0800-1130, 1400-1730, Sat, Sun 1300-1700, US$2.50*, has exhibits on *umbanda* rituals, archaeological digs, the sugar, leather and petroleum industries; there is also a dead whale.

The 16th-century **Forte dos Reis Magos** ① *T084-3202 9006, daily 0800-1630, US$1.50*, is at Praia do Forte, the tip of Natal's peninsula. Between the fort and the city is a military installation. Walk along the beach to the fort for good views (or go on a tour, or by taxi).

At Mãe Luiza is a **lighthouse** with beautiful views of Natal and surrounding beaches (take a city bus marked 'Mãe Luiza' and get the key from the house next door).

Ponta Negra

Sleeping 🛏
Albergue da Costa 15
Bella Napoli 8
Caminho do Mar 5
Ingá Praia 6
IYHA Lua Cheia 12

Manary Praia 1
Miramar 7
Ocean Paláce 14
O Tempo e o Vento 4
Pousada América do Sol 10

Pousada Maravista 11
Pousada Porta do Sol 9
Praia Azul Mar 2
Verdes Mares 13

South to Ponta Negra

The urban beaches of **Praia do Meio**, **Praia dos Artistas** and **Praia de Areia Preta** have recently been cleaned up. The first two are sheltered by reefs and good for windsurfing. The beachside promenade, **Via Costeira**, runs south beneath the towering sand dunes of **Parque das Dunas** (access restricted to protect the dunes), joining the city to the neighbourhood of Ponta Negra. A cycle path parallels this road and provides great views of the coastline.

The vibrant and pretty **Ponta Negra**, 12 km south of the centre (20 minutes by bus), is justifiably the most popular beach and has many hotels. The northern end is good for surfing, while the southern end is calmer and suitable for swimming. **Morro do Careca**, a 120-m-high sand dune, surrounded by vegetation, sits at its far end. It is crowded on weekends and holidays. The poorly lit northern reaches can be unsafe after dark.

Excursions from Natal

The beautiful beaches around Natal – some of which are developed, others are deserted and accessible only by trails – are good all year round for day trips or longer stays. Those north of the city are known as the **Litoral Norte**, where there are extensive cashew plantations; those to the south form the **Litoral Sul**. The areas closest to the city are built-up and get busy during the summer holidays (December to Carnaval), when dune-buggy traffic can become excessive.

Popular tours from Natal include boat trips on the **Rio Potengi**, along the nearby beaches of the Litoral Sul, and to **Barra do Cunhaú**, 86 km south of Natal. The latter goes through mangroves and visits an island and a salt mine, Passeio Ecológico Cunhaú ① T084-9934 0017, www.barradocunhau.com.br. Other popular pastimes include buggy tours, marlin fishing (11 km from shore, said by some to be the best in Brazil) and microlight flights over the Rio Potengi and sand dunes north of Natal. ➤ See Activities and tours, page 553.

The **Centro de Lançamento da Barreira do Inferno** ① 11 km south of Natal on the road to Pirangi, T084-3216 1400, www.clbi.cta.br, visits by appointment on Wed from 1400, is the launching centre for Brazil's space programme.

Southern coast ☺❼❶❶▲❺ ➤ pp547-554.

South of Natal, the Rota do Sol/Litoral Sul (RN-063) follows the coastline for some 55 km and provides access to beaches south of Ponta Negra. From here the coast becomes more remote and long curves of white sand backed by multicoloured sandstone cliffs and sweeping dunes, fragments of Atlantic forest alive with rare birds, black tea lagoons and bays filled with dolphins, make this one of the most popular stretches in the northeast. Thankfully development is small scale and it still feels relaxed (outside high season). Several species of turtles, including giant leatherbacks, still nest here, although numbers are declining as the popularity of beach buggy tourism grows. The best place to stay along this stretch of coast is **Pipa**, a lively little town with good *pousadas* and restaurants.

Ins and outs

Buses run along Litoral Sul from both Natal's bus stations, every 30 minutes in summer, stopping at **Pirangi** (US$4, one hour), and **Tabatinga** (US$5, 1¼ hours); there are six daily buses to **Tibau** and **Pipa** (two to three hours).

From João Pessoa in Paraíba you will have to change at Goaianinha on the main road to Natal. This route is also run by *combis*, which leave when full up and cost about 20% more than the buses. *Combis* connect Pipa and Tibau until around 2300.

Lampião – Brazil's bloodthirsty Robin Hood

Cangaceiros: were they subversives, common criminals or heroes? The debate rages on about the armed band led by Virgulino Ferreira da Silva, better known as Lampião. He is regarded by some as a Robin Hood of the northeast, stealing from the *coroneis* (wealthy landowners) and urban gentry, to give to the ubiquitous poor of the *sertão*. Others look on Lampião and his followers as nothing more than common criminals; looting, raping and killing as they terrorized towns in the northeast during the 1920s and 1930s. This was the *Cangaço*, the reign of banditry, which inspired so much fear and fascination throughout Brazil and attracted worldwide attention.

The controversial religious leaders of the *sertão* were also involved. Lampião claimed the spiritual protection of Padre Cícero, and the legacy of the Cangaço retains an unusual religious dimension. For example, the tomb of Jararaca (one of Lampião's lieutenants who was captured during the band's unsuccessful 1927 siege of Mossoró and supposedly buried alive), is attributed miraculous powers and has become a site of pilgrimage. Yet Jararaca is reputed to have been a ruthless killer.

Several early cinematographers from the US, Germany and France tried to film Lampião and his band, but only Lebanese-born Benjamin Abrahão was sufficiently taken into his confidence to do so. Abrahão spent almost seven months recording the day-to-day life of the *cangaceiros*. His footage was considered so subversive that he was subsequently murdered under mysterious circumstances and his film confiscated by the government of Getúlio Vargas. It languished in an official vault for 20 years, much of it destroyed by time and the elements.

Today the Sociedade Brasileira de Estudos do Cangaço is one of the organizations which collects data, anecdotes and artefacts from this important episode in the region's and the nation's history. It also carries on the unresolved debate as to whether the *cangaceiros* were really heroes or villains.

Rota do Sol

Praia do Cotovelo, 21 km from Natal, offers a view of the Barreira do Inferno rocket-launching centre to the north. At its southern end it has some cliffs and coconut palms where camping is possible.

Pirangi do Norte, 25 km from Natal (30 minutes by bus) has calm waters and is popular for watersports and offshore bathing (500 m out) when natural pools form between the reefs. Nearby is the world's largest *cajueiro* (cashew tree); branches springing from a single trunk cover 7300 sq m. The snack bar by the tree has schedules of buses back to Natal. Lacemakers offer bargains for clothing and tableware. Pirangi has a lively **Carnaval**.

Búzios, 35 km from Natal, has a pleasant setting with vegetation-covered dunes and coconut palms. The water is mostly calm and clear, making it good for bathing.

Barra de Tabatinga, 45 km from Natal, is surrounded by cliffs used for parasailing. Waves are strong here, making it a popular surfing beach. A new 'shark park' complete with resident biologist is its latest attraction.

Camurupim and **Barreta**, 46 km and 55 km from Natal respectively, have reefs near the shore, where bathing pools form at low tide; this area has many restaurants specializing in shrimp. Beyond Barreta is the long, pristine beach of **Malenbar** or **Guaraíra**, accessible on foot or on a 10-minute boat ride across the Rio Tibau. Buggy tours from Natal cost US$100.

Tibau do Sul and Pipa → *Colour map 2, B6. Population 6124.*

The little fishing town of **Tibau do Sul** has cobbled streets and sits high on a cliff between surf beaches and the manatee-filled Lago de Guaraíra. Boat trips can be arranged from here to the *lago* or to see dolphins in the calm waters offshore. Although most tourists head straight for Pipa, which is more developed, the beach *barracas* in Tibau are lively at night with *forró* and MPB. Natal's finest restaurants are also here (see Eating, page 550) and there are a handful of decent *pousadas* in town.

From Tibau, a series of white-sand crescents, separated by rocky headlands and backed by high cliffs crowned with coconut groves and remnant coastal forest, stretches south to **Pipa**. This is one of Natal's most enchanting little tourist towns, whose mix of local fishermen and settlers from all over Brazil has formed an eclectic alternative community. There are excellent *pousadas* and restaurants in all price ranges and the nightlife is animated. The town is becoming increasingly popular and the number of people can feel overwhelming during Carnaval and New Year.

The town beach is somewhat developed, but there are plenty of others nearby. **Praia dos Golfinhos** to the south and **Madeiro** beyond it have only a few hotels and **Praia do Amor** to the north is surrounded by cliffs and has reasonable surf. Access to the shore is down the steps built by the few clifftop hotels or by walking along the beach from Pipa at low tide. There are tours to see dolphins from US$10 per person and also around the mangrove-lined **Lagoa Guaraíra** at Tibau, particularly beautiful at sunset.

Just north of town, on a 70-m-high dune, is the **Santuário Ecológico de Pipa** ① *T084-3211 6070, www.pipa.com.br/santuarioecologico, 0800-1600, US$3*, a 60-ha park created in 1986 to conserve the *Mata Atlântica* forest. There are several trails and lookouts over the cliffs, which afford an excellent view of the ocean and dolphins. Although larger animals like cats and howler monkeys are long gone, this is one of the few areas in the state where important indicator bird species, such as guans, can be found.

Genipabu and the northern coast ⊜▲⊕ ⤖ *pp547-554.*

The coast north of Natal is known for its many impressive, light-coloured sand dunes, some reaching a staggering 50 m in height. **Genipabu**, a weekend resort for the Natal middle classes, is the most famous of these and is only a very short bus ride from the city. The country beyond the resort is well off the tourist trail, with vast long beaches backed by multicoloured cliffs, dunes and salt lakes. It is dramatic terrain, so much so that it has been used as the backdrop to numerous biblical films. Three crosses stand over the cliffs at **Areia Branca**, left there by one of the most recent productions, *Maria, A Mãe do Filho de Deus*. The best way to experience the majesty of the coastal landscape is to walk and listen to the wind on the sand. Buggy tourism has led to the degradation of many of the northeast's dunes. Fixed dunes are protected and should not be disturbed, but shifting dunes can be visited by buggy, camel or horse. Ask locally for advice.

Ins and outs

Areia Branca and the other small towns along the northern coast are reachable from Mossoró, the second largest town in the state but with little in the way of tourist attractions. Galinhos, in the far north, sits on a long broad sandspit and is connected to the mainland by ferry from the little village of Guamaré. From here, there are buses to both Mossoró and Natal via the small town of Jandaíra.

Redinha → *Colour map 2, B6.*

A 25-minute ferry crossing on the Rio Potengi or a 16-km drive from Natal up the Rota do Sol/Litoral Norte, takes you to Redinha, an urban beach with ocean and river bathing and buggies for hire. The local delicacy is fried fish with tapioca, served at the market. About 5 km north of Redinha, on a point, is **Santa Rita**. From its high dunes there is a great view of the surrounding coastline.

Genipabu and around

The best-known beach in the state, Genipabu, is 30 km north of Natal. Its major attractions are some very scenic dunes and the **Lagoa de Genipabu**, a lake surrounded by cashew trees where tables are set up on a shoal in the water and drinks are served. There are also many bars and restaurants on the seashore. Buggy rental and microlight flights can be arranged. ▶▶ *See Activities and tours, page 553.*

North of Genipabu, across the Rio Ceará Mirim, are several beaches with coconut groves and dunes, lined with fishing villages and summer homes of people from Natal; access is via the town of Extremoz. One of these beaches, **Pitangui**, 35 km from Natal, is 6 km long and has a crystalline lake where colourful schools of fish can be seen. **Jacumã**, 49 km from Natal, has a small waterfall and the inland Lagoa de Jacumã, a lake surrounded by dunes where sand-skiing is popular.

Muriú, 44 km from Natal, is known for its lovely green ocean where numerous small boats and *jangadas* anchor; the beach has attractive palms (buggy tour from Natal, including shifting dunes US$100). About 5 km to the north is **Prainha** or **Coqueiro**, a beautiful cove with many coconut palms and strong waves.

Lovely beaches continue along the state's coastline; as you get further away from Natal the beaches are more distant from the main highways and access is more difficult. Around 83 km north of Natal, in the centre of a region known for its coconuts and lobsters, is the ugly resort town of **Touros**. From here the coastline veers east–west.

Far north → *Phone code: 084.*

As the coast turns to the west, the terrain becomes more dramatic and bleak. Sheltered coves are replaced by vast beaches stretching in seemingly interminable broad curves. Behind them are pink, brown and red cliffs, or large expanses of dunes. Highlights are the sleepy little village of **Galinhos**, with its sand streets and beautiful, gentle beach washed by a calm sea, and the **Costa Branca** near the little fishing towns of **Areia Branca**, **Ponta do Mel** and **Rosadao**, where huge pink and white dunes converge behind magnificent long beaches.

The sertão → *Population: 11,000.*

The interior of Rio Grande do Norte, like that of its neighbours, is a combination of semi-desert *sertão*, with hilly areas covered in green vegetation, and pleasant temperatures of between 16°C and 25°C. The state is rich in archaeological sites, and numerous caves with primitive paintings have been found.

In the mountainous south-central region of the state is **Acari**, with the 18th-century church of Nossa Senhora da Guia. Acari is the access point for the Serra do Bico de Arara and is 221 km from Natal. South of town, in the **Seridó** area, are multicoloured cave paintings where human remains dating back 11,000 years have been discovered.

In the centre of the state, on the east shore of the Armando Rua Gonçalves dam, is **São Rafael**. The town is surrounded by granite mountains on top of which are natural waterholes of up to 3 m deep that contain many fossils of giant fauna of the Pleistocene period. There are also rock paintings and engravings on boulders in this area.

Some 76 km southwest of Mossoró is **Apodi**, a town with colonial mansions, where people make their living from agriculture, ceramics and lime extraction. About 10 km from town is **Lajedo de Soledade**, a limestone shelf, 1 km wide and 2 km long, which has been weathered into canyons, grottoes and interesting formations. Paintings of animals and geometric figures, dating from 3000 to 5000 years ago, have been found in the caves.

◉ Rio Grande do Norte listings

For Sleeping and Eating price codes and other relevant information, see pages 42-47.

◉ Sleeping

Natal and south to Ponta Negra
p540, map p541

Economical hotels are easier to find in Natal than at the outlying beaches or Ponta Negra, but very few people stay here and what they save by doing so is often spent on public transport to and from the beaches.

The distinction between **Praia do Meio** and **Praia dos Artistas** is often blurred. Most hotels are on the beachfront **Av Pres Café Filho**, the numbering of which is illogical.

The **Via Costeira** is a strip of enormous, upmarket beachfront hotels, which are very isolated, with no restaurants or shops within easy walking distance.

L Maine, Av Salgado Filho 1741, Lagoa Nova, T084-4005 5774, www.hotelmaine.com.br. A business-orientated 4-star in a concrete tower in Natal town, with reasonable service and a restaurant.

AL-A Imirá Plaza, Via Costeira 4077, Praia Barreira d'Agua, T084-3211 4104, www.imiraplaza.com.br. A vast, sprawling package resort on the beach and with a pool and tennis court. Popular with families. Cheaper in low season.

AL-C Porto Mirim, Av Café Filho 682, Praia dos Artistas, T084-3220 1600, www.porto mirim.com.br. A smart, modern seafront hotel with spacious public areas but small tiled rooms and little rooftop pool and deck with nice views. Cheaper off season.

A-B Bruma, Av Pres Café Filho 1176, T/F084-3202 4303, www.hotelbruma.com.br. A small, family-run beachfront hotel with 25 balconied rooms around a little pool. Popular with Brazilian families.

B Casa Grande, R Princesa Isabel 529, Centro, T084-3211 4895. Built around a family home, popular with business visitors. A/c, cheaper without bathroom. Pleasant, good breakfast, excellent value with off-season discounts. Recommended.

Ponta Negra *p543, map p542*

Ponta Negra is the ideal place to stay, with its attractive beach and concentration of restaurants. The most popular hotels are those right on the beach, on **Av Erivan França** facing the sea, and on **R Francisco Gurgel** behind that street. The latter is quieter.

LL Ocean Palace, Km 11, near Ponta Negra, T084-3220 4144, www.oceanpalace.com.br. A 5-star with large, comfortable suites, smaller, pokier family rooms and a string of bungalows in a regimented line near the beach. Public areas include a lovely ocean-front pool and terrace. Relaxed and friendly.

LL-L Manary Praia, R Francisco Gurgel 9067, T/F084-3204 2900, www.manary.com.br. The best and most tranquil hotel facing the beach and the only one with a trace of style. The rooms, which are decorated in hardwood and pastel colours, have ample bathrooms and secluded private terraces. Good food. A **Roteiros de Charme** hotel, see page 43.

AL Praia Azul Mar, R Franscisco Gurgel 92, T084-4005 3555, www.praiaazulmar

hotel.com.br. Pleasant and well-run package holiday hotel, with a/c rooms and a pool overlooking the beach.

A-B Hotel e Pousada O Tempo e o Vento, R Elias Barros 66, T/F084-3219 2526, www.otempoeovento.com.br. Small terracotta and whitewash hotel a block back from the beach with a range of a/c rooms gathered around a pool. The *luxo* rooms are by far the best, others have a fan and there are low season discounts.

B Caminho do Mar, R Dr Ernani Hugo Gomes 365, T084-3219 3761. Simple plain rooms and breakfast, a short walk from the beach.

B Ingá Praia, Av Erivan França 17, T084-3219 3436, www.ingapraiahotel.com.br. A pink cube on the beach with comfortable well-kept rooms and a rooftop terrace. Recommended.

B Miramar, Av da Praia 3398, T084-3219 3131. Well-maintained, family-run *pousada*. English spoken.

C Pousada América do Sol, R Erivan França 35, T084-3219 2245, www.pousada americadosol.com.br. Very simple a/c rooms with pokey bathrooms and TVs. Good breakfast in a terrace overlooking the beach and substantial off-season reductions.

C Pousada Porta do Sol, R Erivan França 9057, T084-3236 2555, www.pousadaporta dosol.com.br. Basic rooms with TV, fridge, fan and an excellent breakfast, pool, beachfront, good value.

C-D Bella Napoli, Av Erivan França 3188, T084-3219 2666, www.pousadabella napoli.com.br. Pokey little a/c rooms with fridge, in a hotel above the restaurant of the same name. In need of renovation but it's right on the beach. Cheaper in low season.

D Pousada Maravista, R da Praia 223, T084-3236 4677, marilymar@hotmail.com. Plain and simple but with a good breakfast, English spoken, TV, fridge.

D-F IYHA Lua Cheia, R Dr Manoel Augusto Bezerra de Araújo 500, T084-3236 3696, www.luacheia.com.br. One of the best youth hostels in Brazil; in a 'castle' with a 'medieval' **Taverna Pub** in the basement. IYHA, low prices per person, includes breakfast.

D-F Albergue da Costa, Av Praia de Ponta Negra 8932, T084-3219 0095, www.albergue dacosta.com.br. A simple hostel in a great location, with public areas strewn with hammocks and with rather scruffy little rooms and dorms. The low prices are per person.

D-F Verdes Mares, R das Algas 2166, Conj Algamar, T084-3236 2872. IYHA youth hostel, price per person, includes breakfast, discount in low season.

Camping

Vale das Cascatas, Via Costeira Km 8.5, Ponta Negra beach. Little shade, swimming pool, leisure facilities.

Rota do Sol *p544*

A-B Chalés de Pirangi, R Sebastião 56, Pirangi do Norte, T084-3238 2260. Standard apartment hotel with a/c rooms and en suites.

B Pousada Vista do Atlântico, R do Cajueiro 88, Pirangi do Norte, T084-3238 2316. In the town itself but within walking distance of the beach. The upstairs rooms are better ventilated and have good views.

B-C Varandas de Búzios, Av Beira Mar s/n, Búzios, T084-3239 2121, www.rcentrium.com/cl/varandasbuzios. Regimented rows of cabins and a large central restaurant and public area with a pool right on the beach. Reasonable restaurant.

C Pousada Esquina do Sol, Av Deputado Márcio Marinho 2210, Pirangi do Norte, T084-3238 2078, www.esquinadosol.com.br. Small hotel a stroll form the beach with a range of fan-cooled and a/c rooms and kitchenettes in a low-rise concrete block with verandas. Small pool and generous breakfast.

Camping

Camping Clube do Brasil, R Abel Cabral 142, Parnamirim. Reached off via a lane off the BR-101 at Km 98, T084-3208 4824.

Tibau do Sul and Pipa *p545*

In Pipa more than 30 *pousadas* and many private homes offer accommodation.

LL-A Sombra e Água Fresca, Praia do Amor, T084-3246 2258, www.sombraeagua fresca.com.br. Cheaper in low season. Tastefully decorated but small chalet rooms and vast luxury suites with separate sitting and dining areas. All with magnificent views.

LL-A Toca da Coruja, Praia da Pipa, T084-3246 2226, www.tocadacoruja.com.br. One of the best small luxury hotels in Brazil with a range of chalets set in forested gardens and decorated with northeast Brazilian antiques and art. Beautiful pool and an excellent restaurant. A member of the **Roteiros de Charme** group, see page 43.

L Ponta do Madeiro, R da Praia, Estr para Pipa Km 3, T/F084-3246 4220, www.pontado madeiro.com.br. Very comfortable spacious a/c chalets, beautiful pool with bar and spectacular views over the Praia do Madeiro. Excellent service and a good restaurant. Highly recommended.

L Village Natureza, Canto do Madeiro, Pipa, T/F084-3246 4200, www.village natureza.com.br. Beautifully appointed a/c chalets nestled in tropical wooded gardens overlooking the sea and Madeiro beach. Gorgeous circular pool, pleasant grounds, lovely views and a long series of steep steps leading to the beach.

AL-A Marinas Tibau Sul, Tibau do Sul, T/F084-3246 4111, www.hotelmarinas.com.br. Cabins for 4, pool, restaurant, watersports, horse riding and a boat dock.

A-B Mirante de Pipa, R do Mirante 1, Praia da Pipa, T084-3246 2055, www.mirante depipa.com.br. A/c and fan-cooled chalets with a veranda set in a forested garden. Wonderful views.

C-D A Conchego, R do Ceu s/n, Praia da Pipa, T084-3246 2439, www.pipa.com.br/ aconchego. Family-run *pousada* with simple chalets with red-tiled roofs and terraces, in a garden filled with cashew and palm trees. Tranquil and central. Good breakfast.

D Pousada da Pipa, Praia da Pipa, T084-3246 2271, www.pipa.com.br/pousadadapipa. Small rooms decorated with a personal touch. The best are upstairs and have a large shared

terrace with glazed terracotta tiles, sitting areas and hammocks. Large breakfast.

D Vera-My house, Praia da Pipa, T084-3246 2295, www.pipa.com.br/veramyhouse. Good value, friendly and well maintained though simple rooms with bath, **E-F** per person in dormitory, use of kitchen, no breakfast. Recommended.

Camping

Eco-Camping da Pipa, Av Baía dos Golfinhos 10a, Praia da Pipa, T084-3222 0432/9413 5337, www2.uol.com.br/mochilabrasil/ ecocamping.shtml. Great full-powered campsite with cooking facilities, showers and cabins (**D**) for those who don't want to use a tent. Right near Golfinhos beach.

Genipabu and around *p546*

AL-A Pousada Sinos do Vento, Praia das Garças, Touros, 6 km from town, T084-3263 2353, www.sinosdovento.com.br. Attractive seaside *pousada* with accommodation in 14 spacious chalets on a deserted stretch of beach and surrounded by forested gardens. Offers a range of activities including horse riding, bike rental and buggy tours.

A Genipabu, Estr de Genipabu s/n, 2 km from beach, T084-3225 2063, www.genipabu.com.br/portugues. A very relaxing spa hotel on a hillside outside of town with wonderful views out over the beaches and sea. Smart and very well-kept a/c rooms with en suites. Treatments include Ayurvedic massage, reiki, yoga, body wraps and facials, see www.spanaturalis.com.br. Attractive pool and a sauna. Sister hotel on the beach, **Peixe Galo**, www.pousada peixegalo.com.br.

B do Gostoso, Praia Ponta de Santo Cristo, 27 km west of town, T084-3263 4087, www.pousadadogostoso.com.br. Rustic chalets on a lonely stretch of beach and in the style of *sertão* houses. Simple restaurant.

B Pousada Villa do Sol, Enseada do Genipabu, Km 4, T084-3225 2132, www.villa dosol.com.br. 20 attractive a/c chalets, the best of which are the 5 newest, with views over the river. Small pool and restaurant with good service.

C Bangalôs Muriú, Muriú, T/F084-3213 0248, www.residencialespana.com. Modest furnished chalets on a beautiful, lonely stretch of sand. With breakfast.

C Tabuão, R Principal, Genipabu, T084-4005 2134. Modest furnished bungalows in the main town. No breakfast.

D Aldeia, R Principal, Estr de Genipabu, T/F084-3225 2011. Five comfortable and nicely decorated bungalows for up to 4 people, a pool and a decent restaurant.

Far north *p546*

There are plenty of *pousadas* in **Tibau** and many restaurants and bars along the beach. Although there are some *pousadas* in **Areia Branca**, it isn't a good base for the beaches. **Ponta do Mel**, which is flanked by 2 magnificent beaches, is better and has a couple of very basic *pousadas* in the town.

Galinhos town is very sleepy and *pousadas* often close up for a few days whilst their owners go away. There are at least 7 in town so it is always possible to find a room, either on the ocean or the coastal side.

A Pousada Costa Branca, Ponta do Mel, Costa Branca, T084-3332 7062, www.costa branca.com.br. The best hotel between Genipabu and Ceará with a range of cabins on a bluff with magnificent views over an endless stretch of beach. Organized tours to the dunes to the south, which are among the most spectacular in the state. Good restaurant, service and pool, and Lord Byron tribute bar with live music.

B Dunas Praia, Praia das Manoelas, Tibau, T084-3326 2304. Friendly staff, a restaurant and a series of chalets, all with fridge.

D Panorama, Tibau, T084-3236 2208. Very basic rooms with a bath and more expensive options with fans.

D Pousada e Restaurante Brasil Aventura, Galinhos, T084-3552 0085. One of several very simple beachfront *pousadas* with a fish restaurant. Plain but well kept and popular with backpackers.

The sertão *p546*

D Conceição Palace Hotel, R Otávio Lamartine 432, Jardim do Seridó, some 27 km south of Acari, T084-3472 2249. A simple option.

E Pousada do Gargalheiras, Açude Marechal Dutra, about 5 km from Acari, T084-3504 4151. With a pool, restaurant and good views.

● Eating

Natal and south to Ponta Negra
p540, map p541

Prawns feature heavily on menus as Natal is the largest exporter of prawns in Brazil. Check out the beach *barracas* for snacks and fast food.

♥♥♥ Chaplin, Av Pres Café Filho 27, Praia dos Artistas. Traditional seafood restaurant with sea views. Part of a leisure complex with a bar, English pub and a nightclub.

♥♥♥ Doux France, R Otávio Lamartine, Petrópolis. Authentic French cuisine, outdoor seating.

♥♥♥ Estação Trem de Minas, Av Pres Café Filho 197, Praia dos Artistas, T084-3202 2099. Charming rustic style, distinctly upmarket. 40 brands of *cachaça*, live music nightly, terrace and cocktails. Self-service lunch and dinner.

♥♥♥ Raro Sabor, R Seridó 722, Petrópolis, T084-3202 1857. Exclusive bistro with Russian caviar on the menu.

♥♥ A Macrobiótica, Princesa Isabel 524, Centro. Vegetarian restaurant and shop. Lunch only.

♥♥ Bob's, Av Sen Salgado Filho. Daily 1000-2200. Hamburger chain.

♥♥ Camarões Express, Av Sen Salgado Filho, Centro. Open for lunch only at weekends. Express prawns in 15 styles.

♥♥ Carne de Sol Benigna Lira, R Dr José Augusto Bezerra de Medeiros 09, Praia do Meio. Traditional setting, regional cuisine.

♥♥ Fiorentina, Augusto Bezerra de Medeiros 529, delivery T084-3202 0020. An Italian pizzeria with a huge range of seafood, try the lobster with spaghetti. Friendly service, 10% tax. Warmly recommended.

Ψ Peixada da Comadre, R Dr José Augusto Bezerra de Medeiros 4, Praia dos Artistas. Lively seafood restaurant with popular prawn dishes.
Ψ Saint Antoine, R Santo Antônio 651, Cidade Alta, Centro. Mediocre self-service pay by weight establishment.
Ψ-Ψ Farol Bar, Av Sílvio Pedrosa 105 (at the end of Via Costeira on Praia Areia Preta). Famous dried meat dishes – a local speciality.

Ponta Negra *p543, map p542*
ΨΨΨ Manary, Manary Praia Hotel, R Francisco Gurgel (see page 547). The best seafood in the city in a poolside restaurant overlooking Ponta Negra beach.
ΨΨΨ Roschti, Av Erivan França, T084-3219 4406. International cuisine in a relaxed beachfront bistro and more formal upstairs dining room.
ΨΨΨ Sobre Ondas, Av Erivan França 14, T084-3219 4222. Average seafood and international dishes in an intimate beachfront setting with an underwater theme.
ΨΨ Atlântico, Av Erivan França 27, T084-3219 2762. Relaxed, warm service, semi open air, beachfront. Portuguese-owned, Italian and Portugese dishes, fish and *carne do sol*. Recommended.
ΨΨ Barraca do Caranguejo, Av Erivan França 1180, T084-3219 5069. Eight prawn dishes for US$8 and live music nightly from 2100.
ΨΨ Camarões, Av Eng Roberto Freire 2610. Also at Natal shopping centre. Touristy, but very good seafood.
ΨΨ Cipó Brasil, Av Erivan 3, T0800-3284051. Funky little Playa del Carmen-style bar with a jungle theme, 4 levels, sand floors, lantern-lit, very atmospheric. Average food (pizzas, crêpes), good cocktails, live music from 2100.
ΨΨ Ponta Negra Grill, Av Erivan 20, T084-3219 3714. A large, popular restaurant with live music and several terraces overlooking the beach. Steaks, seafood and cocktails.
Ψ Ponta Negra Mall. Stalls sell sandwiches and snacks.

Tibau do Sul and Pipa *p545*
There are many restaurants and bars along Pipa's main street, Av Baía dos Golfinhos.

ΨΨΨ Al Buchetto, Av Baía dos Golfinhos 837, Pipa, T084-3246 2318. Decent, Italian-made pasta and a lively atmosphere.
ΨΨΨ Camamo Beijupirá, Tibau do Sul, T084-3246 4195. One of the best restaurants in Brazil with a eclectic mix of fusion dishes like prawns and slices of leek in a spicy cashew sauce with raisins and ginger, served with fervent enthusiasm by owner Tadeu Lubambo. Excellent wine list.
ΨΨΨ Toca da Coruja, Praia da Pipa (see page 549). Superlative and beautifully presented regional food in a tropical garden setting. Intimate and romantic. Highly recommended.
ΨΨΨ Vivendo, Av Baía dos Golfinhos, Pipa. One of the town's best seafood restaurants and a good place to watch the passers-by.
Ψ Casa de Taipe and Shirley-My House, Av Baía dos Golfinhos 1126 and 1213, Praia da Pipa. Very cheap but decent self-service restaurants, the latter owned by the sister of Vera of **Vera-My House** (see page 549).
Ψ São Sebastião, R do Ceu, Pipa. Vegetarian and wholefood. Good value. Good juices.
Ψ Sopa de Patrick/Chez Lisa, Av Baía dos Golfinhos s/n, Praia da Pipa. Generous portions of various delicious soups, in a little shack beyond the main square.
Ψ Tatoo Batata, R do Ceu, Pipa, T084-9419 7181. Enormous baked potatoes with fillings like cheese and sweet corn. Salads and juices too. Friendly owner. Next to **A Conchego** *pousada* (see Sleeping).

◐ Bars and clubs

Natal *p540, map p541*
Dance is an important pastime in Natal. In an area in the centre known as **Ribeira**, there are a few popular bars/nightclubs in restored historic buildings in R Chile.
Amiça, Av Engenheiro Roberto Freire s/n. New club with techno and house, popular with locals and tourists.
Blackout B52, R Chile 25, T084-3221 1282. Lively venue with a 1940s theme. The best night is 'Black Monday'. There is live

rock, blues and MPB on other nights. The crowd is 20s and early 30s.

Budda Pub, Av Engenheiro Roberto Freire (an annexe of the Tiberius). A little bar with good bar food and a laid-back atmosphere.

Centro de Turismo (see Shopping, below) has *Forró com Turista*, a chance for visitors to learn this fun dance, Thu at 2200. There are many other enjoyable venues where visitors are encouraged to join in.

Chaplin, Av Presidente Café Filho 27, Praia dos Artistas, T084-3202 1188. Different zones with everything from MPB and *forró* to techno and progressive house.

Novakapital, Av Presidente Café Filho 872, Praia dos Artistas, T084-3202 7111. With *forró*, live music, especially rock and foam parties, US$4, from 2400.

Ponta Negra *p543, map p542*
Although there is a handful of respectable clubs, Ponta Negra beach is now somewhat seedy. The municipal authorities are coming down very hard on the sex industry and its clients, and are installing video cameras all along the beach. Alto Ponta Negra is very lively and has live music and a range of bars and clubs open until dawn.

Baraonda, Av Erivan França 44, T084-9481 3748. Live music nightly except Tue, including *forró* and MPB from 2300 until late.

Taverna Pub, R Dr Manoel, Araújo 500, Alta Ponta Negra, T084-3236 3696. Medieval-style pub in youth hostel basement. Eclectic (rock, Brazilian pop, jazz, etc) live music Tue-Sun from 2200, best night Wed. Recommended.

In front of the Taverna is a cluster of small venues including **Tapiocaria Salsa Bar** and the **Calderão da Bruxa**.

Tibau do Sul and around *p545*
Tibau do Sul has various beach *barracas*. There is always something going on in Pipa, whatever the night and whatever the month.

Aruman, Av Baía dos Golfinhos, Pipa. Good cocktails and a trendy crowd.

Blue Bar, Av Baía dos Golfinhos, Pipa. Live *pagodé* and samba on Wed.

Calangos, Baía dos Golfinhos s/n (at the southern end of Pipa). A club with famous DJs like Patife. Techno and MPB Thu-Sun.

Carvalho do Fogo, Tibau do Sul. *Forró* until dawn every Wed.

Reggae Bar, just off Av Baía dos Golfinhos, Pipa centre. Live reggae bands, usually on Tue.

☺ Festivals and events

Natal *p540, map p541*
Jan Festa de Nossa Senhora dos Navegantes, when numerous vessels go to sea from Praia da Redinha, north of town.
Mid-Oct Country show, **Festa do Boi** (bus marked Parnamirim to the exhibition centre), gives a good insight into rural life.
Mid-Dec Carnaval, the Salvador-style out-of-season carnival, a lively 4-day music festival with dancing in the streets.

○ Shopping

Natal *p540, map p541*
Centro de Turismo, R Aderbal de Figueiredo, 980, off R Gen Cordeiro, Petrópolis, T084-3212 2267. Sun-Wed 0900-1900, Thu 2200. A converted prison with a wide variety of handicraft and antiques shops, art gallery and tourist information booth. Good view of the Rio Potengi and the sea,
Centro Municipal de Artesanato, Av Pres Café Filho, Praia dos Artistas. Daily 1000-2200. Sand-in-bottle pictures are very common in Natal and there are plenty here alongside other touristy items.
Natal Shopping, Av Senador Salgado Filho, 2234, between Via Costeira and Ponta Negra. Large mall with restaurants, cinemas and 140 shops. Free shuttle service to major hotels.

Tibau do Sul and around *p545*
Pipa is a good place for raw cotton and costume jewellery made from tropical seeds.
The Bookshop (next to the **Reggae Bar**, see Bars and clubs, above). Run by the

wonderfully knowledgeable and eccentric Cyntia, who rents out books of all genres from Oscar Wilde to Dostoyevsky.

▲ Activities and tours

Natal *p540, map p541*
Boat trips
Boat trips on the Rio Potengi and along the nearby beaches of the Litoral Sul. A 2-hr tour includes hotel pickup, a snack, and allows time for a swim, US$25 per person. Boat trips to Barra do Cunhaú, 86 km south of Natal, go through mangroves, visit an island and a salt mine (Passeio Ecológico Cunhaú).

Buggy tours
Buggy tours are by far the most popular, US$40-90 and can be organized through the hotels. Be sure to check that only shifting dunes are visited. Fixed dunes are protected by Brazilian environmental law. It is possible to hire a buggy, or take a tour, all the way to Fortaleza (US$800 for 4 people) with companies like Buggy e Compania, www.buggy ecia.com.br. Avoid the huge operators like Brésil-Aventure who journey in huge convoys. Manary Ecotours, below, can recommend environmentally sensitive operators.

Ecotourism
Manary Ecotours, R Francisco Gurgel 9067, T/F084-3219 2900, www.caririecotours.com.br. Excellent tours to some of the most interesting sights in the northeastern interior, such as Souza, Cariri and the Serra da Capivara. Short on information about local fauna but good on history and geology.

Tibau do Sul and Pipa *p545*
Buggy tours to Barra de Cunhaú US$50, from Pipa to Natal US$115.

Genipabu *p546*
Associação dos Bugueiros, T084-3225 2077. US$25 for dune buggy tour. Microlight flights are also available.

⊖ Transport

Natal *p540, map p541*
Air Buses to the airport run every 30 mins from the old *rodoviária* and are marked 'Aeroporto'. A taxi to the airport costs US$25; US$20 from Ponta Negra. There are flights to **Brasília**, **Fortaleza**, **Recife**, **Rio de Janeiro**, **Salvador**, **São Paulo**; **Belo Horizonte**, **Goiânia**, **São Luís**, **Fernando de Noronha**, **Vitória**, **Porto Alegre**. There are international flights to **Lisbon** with TAP.

Airline offices GOL, www.voe gol.com.br, at airport. Oceanair, www.ocean air.com.br. TAM, Av Campos Sales 500, Tirol, T084-3201 2020, at airport, T084-3643 1624, freephone T0800-123100, www.tam.com.br. TAP, www.flytap.com, has connections with Portugal. TRIP, T084-3234 1717, freephone T0800-2747, www.voetrip.com.br. Varig, R Mossoro 598, Centro, T084-3201 9339, at airport, T084-3743 1100, freephone T0800-997000, www.varig.com.br. Webjet, www.webjet.com.br.

Bus
Local Regional tickets are sold on street level of the new *rodoviária* in Cidade da Esperança; interstate tickets are available on the 2nd floor. A taxi to the bus station costs around US$25 from town, or US$18 from Ponta Negra, or there are regular local buses (see Ins and outs, page 540).

From the old *rodoviária* Viação Campos runs to **Pirangi**, US$0.60, 5 times a day 0630-1815, 3 on Sun 0730, 0930, 1645. In summer, buses run from both *rodoviárias*, every 30 mins to **Pirangi**, US$2, 1 hr; to **Tabatinga** US$3, 1¼ hrs.

Long-distance From the new *rodoviária*, there are 6 buses a day to **Tibau do Sul**, US$5, 2 hrs, starting at 0600, and going on from Tibau to **Pipa**, US$7, 15 mins more. To **Recife** with Napoles, 5 daily, US$15 *convencional*, US$12 *executivo*, 4 hrs. With Nordeste to **Mossoró**, US$10 *convencional*, US$15 *executivo*, 4 hrs. To **Aracati**, US$14, 5½ hrs. To **Fortaleza**, US$15 *convencional*,

US$210 *executivo*, US$35 *leito*, 8 hrs. To **João Pessoa**, every 2 hrs, US$4 *convencional*, US$8 *executivo*, 3 hrs. With **São Geraldo** to **Maceió**, buses both direct and via Recife, US$21 *convencional*, US$30 *executivo*, 10 hrs. To **Salvador**, US$50 *executivo*, 20 hrs. To **Rio de Janeiro**, US$90. To **São Paulo**, US$90 *convencional*, US$100*executivo*, 46-49 hrs. With **Boa Esperança** to **Teresina**, US$40 *convencional*, US$45 *executivo*, 17-20 hrs. To **Belém**, US$70, 32 hrs.

Car hire Car hire offices can be found at the airport and through mid- to top-range hotels. **Avis**, at airport, www.avis.com. **Hertz**, airport, www.hertz.com. **Localiza**, Av Nascimento de Castro 1792, www.localiza.com.

Tibau do Sul and Pipa *p545*
Bicycle hire From Blue Planet, Pipa. US$5 for a half day, US$10 full day.

Buggy It is possible to travel all the way to **Fortaleza** by buggy with **Top Buggy**, www.topbuggy.com.br, via the stunning Rio Grande do Norte dunes and beaches.

Bus *Combis* connect Pipa and Tibau until around 2300. 6 buses a day to **Natal**'s new *rodoviária*, US$5, 2 hrs, from Pipa via Tibau do Sul, leaving Pipa 0500-1600. Minivans also do this run and are easiest to catch from the beach.
    Buses to **Paraíba** pass through Goianinha on the interstate road. Frequent *combis* connect **Goianinha** with Pipa (30 mins, US$1.50).

Taxi Carlos, T084-9977 0006, after-hours taxi, speaks basic English.

Redinha *p546*
Bus Regular bus service from the old *rodoviária* to **Genipabu**.

Ferry There is a frequent ferry service to Cais Tavares de Lira, **Ribeira**, weekdays 0530-1900, weekend and holidays 0800-1830, US$1 per person, US$5 for car.

ⓘ Directory

Natal and south to Ponta Negra
p540, map p541
Banks There are Bradesco and HSBC banks for international ATMs at the *rodoviária*, airport and throughout the city: Banco 24 horas, Natal Shopping, Cirrus, Visa, MasterCard and Plus. Also, Av Rio Branco 510, Cidade Alta, US$ cash and TCs at poor rates, cash advances against Visa, Mon-Fri 1000-1600. **Banespa**, Av Rio Branco 704, Cidade Alta, US$ cash and TCs at dolar turismo rate, Mon-Fri 1000-1430. **Sunset Câmbio**, Av Hermes da Fonseca 628, Tirol, T084-3212 2552, cash and TCs, 0900-1700. **Dunas Câmbio**, Av Roberto Freire 1776, Loja B-11, Capim Macio (east of Parque das Dunas), T084-3219 3840, cash and TCs, 0900-1700. **Embassies and consulates** Germany, R Gov Sílvio Pedrosa 308, Areia Preta, T084-3222 3596. Italy, R Auta de Souza 275, Centro, T084-3222 6674. **Spain**, R Amintas Barros 4200, Lagoa Nova, T084-206 5610. **Internet** Internet cafés on Ponta Negra and around the main beach areas. **Post office** R Princesa Isabel 711, Centro; Av Rio Branco 538, Centro; Av Engenheiro Hildegrando de Góis 22, Ribeira. Poste restante is in Ribeira, near the old *rodoviária*, at Av Rio Branco and Av General Gustavo Cordeiro de Farias, hard to find. **Police** Tourist police (Delegacia do Turista): T084-3236 3288, 24 hrs. **Telephone** R Princesa Isabel 687 and R João Pessoa, Centro, also a the *rodoviária*.

Ponta Negra *p543, map p542*
Banks Banco do Brasil, Seafront ATM for Cirrus, Visa, MasterCard and Plus. **Embassies and consulates** Canada, Av Roberto Freire 2951, bloco 01, loja 09-CCAB Sul, T084-3219 2197. **Internet** Sobre Ondas, (also bar and restaurant, see Eating), 0900-2400, 10 centavos 1 min. **Post office** Av Praia de Ponta Negra 8920. **Telephone** Av Roberto Freire 3100, Shopping Cidade Jardim, Av Roberto Freire.

Ceará

Ceará calls itself the 'Terra da Luz' (Land of Light) and much of its 573-km coastline and bone-dry interior is baked under permanent sunshine. It could just as well be called the land of wind: kitesurfers and windsurfers are quickly discovering that there is nowhere better in the world for their sports. Locations such as Cumbuco and Jericoacoara are blown by strong winds almost 365 days a year, and the Atlantic Ocean offers varied conditions from glassy flat through to rolling surf. Ceará boasts some beautiful beaches, too – though poor when compared to the rest of Brazil perhaps – with long, broad stretches of sand backed by ochre cliffs or towering dunes. Sadly they are increasingly populated by ex-pat and profiteering Europeans. Many of the little fishing villages that lay undiscovered for decades are losing their character to ugly condos and concrete hotels. In places like Canoa Quebrada, Jericoacoara and Cumbuco, Italian and German are spoken as much as Portuguese. Even the state capital Fortaleza has been affected. Plane-loads of foreign tourists have turned its once-lively nightlife increasingly tawdry; and while the state authorities are cracking down hard on the exploitation it can be hard to meet locals who aren't cynical about foreigners or soliciting work. ▸▸ *For listings, see pages 572-584.*

Fortaleza ●●●●●●▲●● ▸▸ *pp572-584. Colour map 2, A5.*

→ *Phone code: 085. Population: 2.1 million.*

Brazil's fifth largest city is a stretch of concrete towers along a series of white-sand beaches behind a gloriously misty green and blue Atlantic dotted with rusting wrecks. The water temperature is permanently in the high 20s and there's a constant sea breeze. The sea is surprisingly clean, even in Iracema near the centre, but the best beaches for swimming are further east and west.

Fortaleza has a long history and a number if sights of historic interest. However, most tourists are drawn here by the city's reputation for lively nightlife. The sound of *forró* still reverberates in the streets behind Iracema beach, but nowadays it's hard to find anywhere that isn't over-run with groups of Italian men and professional local women. Many locals are angry about their city's poor reputation and have become sour towards tourists; police and local hotel owners are increasingly suspicious of guests. If you don't want to be disappointed, remember that Fortaleza's golden days are gone.

Ins and outs

Getting there International and domestic flights arrive at **Aeroporto Pinto Martins** ⓘ *Praça Eduardo Gomes, 6 km south of the centre, T085-3392 1200.* There are connections with São Luís and Belém, as well as the Guianas, various destinations in Portugal and Italy. The airport has a 24-hour tourist office, T085-3477 1667, car hire, a food hall, internet facilities, bookstore, **Banco do Brasil** for exchange and **Bradesco** and **HSBC** for international ATMs. Bus No 404 runs from the airport to Praça José de Alencar in the centre, US$1. **Expresso Guanabara** minibuses run to the *rodoviária* and Beira Mar (US$2). Bus No 066 runs from Papicu to Parangaba; bus No 027 runs from Papicu to Siqueira. Taxis to the centre, Avenida Beira Mar or Praia do Futuro charge a fixed fee of US$20, or US$25 at night (30 minutes, allowing for traffic).

Interstate buses arrive at the **Rodoviária São Tomé** ⓘ *Av Borges de Melo 1630, Fátima, 6 km south of the centre, T085-3256 2100*. Information is available from *Disque Turismo* booth, open 0600-1800, which also has lockers for storing luggage.

Opposite the *rodoviária* is **Hotel Amuarama**, which has a bar and restaurant; there's also a *lanchonete*. Many city buses run to the centre (US$1) including No 78, which goes to Iracema via the Centro Dragão do Mar. If in doubt, the tourist information booth will point you in the right direction. A taxi to Praia de Iracema, or Avenida Abolição costs around US$15. Minivans to Jericoacoara leave from in front of the **Hotel Casa Blanca** (see Sleeping, page 572). ▸▸ *See Transport, page 581.*

Getting around The city is spread out, with its main attractions in the centre and along the seashore; transport from one to the other can take a long time. The city bus system is efficient if a little rough; buses and vans cost US$1 per journey. The cheapest way to orientate yourself within the city is to take the 'Circular 1' (anti-clockwise) or 'Circular 2'

Fortaleza

N
200 metres
200 yards

Sleeping ⬤		
Abrolhos Praia 1 *B6*	Casa de Praia 3 *A4*	IYHA Albergue Atalaia
Backpackers 21 *B3*	Colonial Praia 5 *B4*	Anexo 11 *A3*
Beira Mar 19 *B6*	Ibis 15 *B4*	IYHA Pousada Atalaia 4 *A4*
Big 16 *B1*	Ideal Praia 10 *B5*	Luzeiro Beira Mar 13 *B6*
Casa Blanca 2 *B4*	Imperial Othon Palace 7 *B6*	Ondas Verdes 9 *A4*
		Panorâmica 14 *B4*

(clockwise) buses which pass Avenida Beira Mar, the Aldeota district, the university (UFC) and cathedral via Meireles, Iracema, Centro Dragão do Mar and the Centre, US$1.50. Alternatively, take the new *Top Bus* run by **Expresso Guanabara** ① *T0800-991992, US$2.50*, an air-conditioned minibus starting at Avenida Abolição.

When driving outside the city, have a good map and be prepared to ask directions frequently as road signs are non-existent or are placed after junctions.

Tourist information The main office of the state tourism agency, **Setur** ① *Centro Administrativo Virgílio Távora, Cambeba, T085-3101 4639, www.setur.ce.gov.br*, has maps and brochures and can help with hotels and tours. There are also information booths at the airport and *rodoviária*, and at the Farol de Mucuripe (old lighthouse), open 0700-1730. The **Posta Telefônica Beira Mar** ① *Av Beira Mar, almost opposite Praiano Palace Hotel*, provides information, sells *combi* tickets to Jericoacoara, and has postcards, clothes and magazines. If you have problems, contact the **tourist police** ① *R Silva Paulet 505, Aldeota, T085-3433 8171*.

Ponta Mar **6** *B6*
Pousada do Suíço **12** *A4*
Pousada Salinas **22** *B6*
Praia de Iracema **17** *A4*
Seara Praia **20** *B6*
Villamaris **1** *B6*

Eating 🍴
Amici's **1** *A2*
Brazão **2** *A4*
Colher do Pau **5** *A3*
Estoril **4** *A3*
Habanera **10** *A3*

Ideal **9** *B5*
La Fiorentina **8** *A3*
Romagna Mia **7** *A4*
Santa Clara Café
  Orgânico **1** *A2*
Sobre O Mar **3** *A3*

Bars & clubs 🍸
Pirata **6** *A3*

Safety The city is generally safe for visitors. However, tourists should avoid the following areas: Serviluz *favela* between the old lighthouse (Avenida Vicente de Castro), Mucuripe and Praia do Futuro; the *favela* behind the railway station; the Passeio Público at night; and Avenida Abolição at its eastern (Nossa Senhora da Saúde church) and western ends.

Sights

Walking through the centre of Fortaleza, it is hard to ignore the city's history, which dates back to the 17th century. Pedestrian walkways radiate from the **Praça do Ferreira**, the heart of the commercial centre, and the whole area is dotted with shady green squares. The **Fortaleza Nossa Senhora da Assumpção** ① *Av Alberto Nepomuceno, T085-3255 1600, telephone in advance for permission to visit, daily 0800-1100, 1400-1700*, originally built in 1649 by the Dutch, gave the city its name. Near the fort, on Rua Dr João Moreira, is the 19th-century **Praça Passeio Público** (or Praça dos Mártires), a park with old trees and statues of Greek deities. West of here a neoclassical former prison (1866) houses a fine tourist centre, the **Centro de Turismo do Estado (Emcetur)** ① *Av Senador Pompeu 350, near the waterfront, T0800-991516, closed Sun*, with museums, theatre and craft shops. It houses the renovated **Museu de Arte e Cultura Populares** and the **Museu de Minerais** ① *T085-3212 3566*. Further west along Rua Dr João Moreira, at **Praça Castro Carreira**, (commonly known as Praça da Estação), is the nicely refurbished train station, **Estação João Felipe** (1880), which runs commuter services.

The **Teatro José de Alencar** ① *Praça José de Alencar, T085-3229 1989, Mon-Fri 0800-1700, hourly tours, some English-speaking guides, US$1, Wed free*, was inaugurated in 1910 and is worth a visit. It is a magnificent iron structure imported from Scotland and decorated in neoclassical and art nouveau styles. It also houses a library and art gallery. The **Praça dos Leões** or Praça General Tibúrcio on Rua Conde D'Eu has bronze lions imported from France. Around it stand the 18th-century **Palácio da Luz** ① *T085-3231 5699*, former seat of the state government, and the **Igreja Nossa Senhora do Rosário**, built by slaves in the 18th century. Also here is the former provincial legislature, dating from 1871, which houses the **Museu do Ceará** ① *R São Paulo, next to Praça dos Leões, T085-3251 1502, Tue-Fri 0830-1730, Sat 0830- 1400, US$0.80*. The museum has displays on history and anthropology. To get there, take bus marked 'Dom Luís'.

The new **cathedral** ① *Praça da Sé*, completed in 1978, in Gothic style but constructed out of concrete with beautiful stained-glass windows, stands beside the new semi-circular **Mercado Central**.

There are several worthwhile museums to visit in and around Fortaleza. The **Museu do Maracatu** ① *Rufino de Alencar 231*, at Teatro São José, has costumes of this ritual dance of African origin. The new and exciting **Centro Dragão do Mar de Arte e Cultura** ① *R Dragão do Mar 81, Praia de Iracema, T085-3488 8600, www.dragaodomar.org.br, Tue-Thu 1000- 1730, Fri-Sun 1400-2130, US$0.75 for entry to each museum/gallery, free on Sun*, hosts concerts, dance performances and exhibitions of art and photography. It has various entrances, from Rua Almirante Barroso, Rua Boris, and from the junction of Monsenhor Tabosa, Dom Manuel and Castelo Branco. The latter leads directly to three museums: on street level, the **Memorial da Cultura Cearense**, with changing exhibitions; on the next floor down is an art and cultural exhibition; in the basement is an excellent audio-visual museum of **El Vaqueiro**. Also at street level is the **Livraria Livro Técnico**. There is a **planetarium** with a whispering gallery underneath. The centre also houses the **Museu de Arte Contemporânea do Ceará**. This area is very lively at night.

Some 15 km south of the centre, the **Museu Artur Ramos** ① *in the Casa de José de Alencar, Av Perimetral, Messejana, T085-3229 1898, Mon 1400-1730, Tue-Sun 0800-1200, 1400-1700*, displays artefacts of African and indigenous origin collected by the anthropologist Artur Ramos, as well as documents from the writer José de Alencar.

Beaches

The urban beaches between Barra do Ceará (west) and Ponta do Mucuripe (east) are polluted and not suitable for swimming. There are a number of minibus day tours to other beaches from US$6 and to Jericoacoara, US$15; minibuses gather along the seafront. The agency **CPVTUR** ① *Av Monsenhor Tabosa 1001, T085-3219 2511*, also runs trips.

Heading east from the centre, **Praia de Iracema** is one of the older beach suburbs, with some original early 20th-century houses. It is not much of a sunbathing beach as it has little shade or facilities and swimming is unsafe, but at night it is very lively. Of its many bars and restaurants, the **Estoril**, housed in one of the earliest buildings, has become a landmark. The Ponte Metálica and the Ponte dos Ingleses, built in homage to and as an imitation of English seaside piers, are very popular beauty spots at sunset. It is often possible to see dolphins.

East of Iracema, the **Avenida Beira Mar** (Avenida Presidente Kennedy) connects Praia do Meireles (divided into **Praia do Ideal**, **Praia dos Diários** and **Praia do Meireles**) with Volta da Jurema and Praia do Mucuripe; it is lined with high-rise buildings and most luxury hotels are located here. A *calçado* (walkway), following the palm-lined shore, becomes a night-time playground as locals promenade on foot, roller skates, skateboards and bicycles. Children ride mini-motorbikes, scooters or the 'happiness' train with its Disney characters. Take in the spectacle while sipping an *agua de coco* or *caiprinha* on the beachfront, where there are volleyball courts, bars, open-air shows and a crafts fair in front of the **Imperial Othon Palace Hotel**.

Praia do Mucuripe, 5 km east of the centre, is Fortaleza's main fishing centre, where *jangadas* (traditional rafts with triangular sails) bring in the catch; there are many restaurants serving *peixada* and other fish specialities. The symbol of this beach is the statue of Iracema, the main character of the romance by José de Alencar (see Background, page 792). From the monument there is a good view of Mucuripe's port and bay. At Mucuripe Point is a **lighthouse** built by slaves in 1846, which houses the **Museu de Fortaleza** (now sadly run down and not a safe area, according to the tourist office). There is a lookout at the new lighthouse, good for viewing the *jangadas*, which return in the late afternoon, and the sunset.

Praia do Futuro, 8 km southeast of the centre, is the most popular bathing beach. It is 8 km long with strong waves, sand dunes and freshwater showers, but no natural shade. Vendors in straw shacks serve local dishes such as crab. On Thursday nights it becomes the centre for the city's nightlife, with people enjoying live music and *forró*. The south end of the beach is known as **Caça e Pesca**; water here is polluted because of the outflow of the Rio Cocó. Praia do Futuro has few hotels or buildings because the salt-spray corrosion is among the strongest in the world.

At **Praia de Sabiaguaba**, 20 km southeast of the centre, is a small fishing village known for its seafood; the area has mangroves and is good for fishing.

Some 29 km southeast of the centre is **Praia Porto das Dunas**, a pleasant beach that is popular for watersports, such as surfing. Buggies and microlight tours can be arranged. The main attraction is **Beach Park** ① *US$20*, the largest water park in South America, with pools, water toboggans, sports fields and restaurants.

The coast east of Fortaleza ⊖⊛▲⊕① ▸▸ pp572-584.

The most prominent feature of the eastern coast is the impressive coloured sand cliffs. There are also freshwater springs near the shore, along with palm groves and mangroves. Lobster fishing is one of the main activities. It is possible to hike along much of the eastern coast: from Prainha to Águas Belas takes seven hours (bring plenty of water and sun protection). Where there are rivers to cross, there is usually a boatmen. Fishing villages have accommodation or hammock space.

Aquiraz and around → Colour map 2, A5. Phone code: 085. Population: 61,000.

Some 31 km east of Fortaleza, Aquiraz was the original capital of Ceará. It retains several colonial buildings and has a religious art museum. It is also the access point for a number of beaches.

Six kilometres east of Aquiraz, **Prainha** is a fishing village and weekend resort with a 10-km beach and dunes. The beach is clean and largely empty and the waves are good for surfing. You can see *jangadas* coming in daily in the late afternoon. The village is known for its lacework; the women using the *bilro* and *labirinto* techniques at the **Centro de Rendeiras**. In some of the small restaurants it is possible to see displays of the *carimbó*, one of the north Brazilian dances. Just south of Prainha is **Praia do Presídio**, with gentle surf, dunes, palms and *cajueiros* (cashew trees).

About 18 km southeast of Aquiraz is **Praia Iguape**, another fishing village known for its lacework. The beach is a large, elbow-shaped sandbank, very scenic especially at Ponta do Iguape. Nearby are high sand dunes where sand-skiing is popular. There is a lookout at Morro do Enxerga Tudo; one-hour *jangada* trips cost US$8.50. Lacework is sold at the **Centro de Rendeiras**. Locals are descendants of Dutch, Portuguese and indigenous peoples; some traditions such as the *coco-de-praia* folk dance are still practised. Some 3 km south of Iguape is **Praia Barro Preto**, a wide tranquil beach, with dunes, palms and lagoons.

Ins and outs There are regular buses to the beaches and to the city of Aquiraz from the *rodoviária* in Fortaleza. For further information on the area, including accommodation and restaurants, visit www.aquiraz.ce.gov.br.

Cascavel → Phone code: 085.

Cascavel, 62 km southeast of Fortaleza, has a Saturday crafts fair by the market. It is the access point for the beaches of Caponga and Águas Belas, where traditional fishing villages coexist with fancy weekend homes and hotels. **Caponga**, 15 km northeast of Cascavel, has a wide, 2-km-long beach lined with palms. *Jangadas* set sail in the early morning; arrangements can be made to accompany fishermen on overnight trips, a 90-minute ride costs US$14 for up to five people. There is a fish market and crafts sales (ceramics, embroidery and lacework) on the beach. A 30-minute walk south along the white-sand beach leads to **Águas Belas**, at the mouth of the Rio Mal Cozinhado, offering a combination of fresh and saltwater bathing (access also by road, 15 km from Cascavel, 4 km from Caponga). The scenery here, and 5 km further east at Barra Nova, changes with the tide. A walk north along the beach for 6 km takes you to the undeveloped **Praia do Batoque**, which is surrounded by cliffs and dunes.

Morro Branco and Praia das Fontes → *Phone code: 085.*

Beberibe, 78 km from Fortaleza, is the access point for Morro Branco and Praia das Fontes, some of the better-known beaches of the east coast.

About 4 km from Beberibe, **Morro Branco** has a spectacular beach, coloured craggy cliffs and beautiful views. *Jangadas* leave the beach at 0500, returning at 1400-1500. Lobster is the main catch in this area. The coloured sands of the dunes are bottled into beautiful designs and sold along with other crafts such as lacework, embroidery and straw goods. *Jangadas* may be hired for sailing (one hour for up to six people US$30). Beach buggies cost US$100 for a full day; taxis are also available for hire. The beach is lined with summer homes and can get very crowded during peak season.

South of Morro Branco and 6 km from Beberibe is **Praia das Fontes**, which also has coloured cliffs with freshwater springs. There is a fishing village and, at the south end, a lagoon. Near the shore is a cave, known as **Mãe de Água**, visible at low tide. Buggies and microlights can be hired on the beach. A luxury resort complex has been built here, making the area expensive.

South of Praia das Fontes are several less developed beaches including **Praia Uruaú** or **Marambaia**, about 6 km from Praia das Fontes along the beach or 21 km by road from Beberibe, via Sucatinga on a sand road. The beach is at the base of coloured dunes; there is a fishing village with some accommodation. Just inland is **Lagoa do Uruaú**, the largest in the state and a popular place for watersports. A buggy from Morro Branco costs US$45 for four people.

About 50 km southeast of Beberibe is **Fortim**. From here, boats run to **Pontal de Maceió**, a reddish sand point at the mouth of the Rio Jaguaribe, from where there is a good view of the eastern coast. In the winter the river is high and there is fishing for shrimp; in the summer it dries up, forming islands and freshwater beaches. There's a fishing village about 1 km from the ocean with bars, restaurants and small *pousadas*.

Prainha do Canto Verde → *Phone code: 085.*

Some 120 km east of Fortaleza, in the district of Beberibe, is Prainha do Canto Verde, a small fishing village on a vast beach, which has an award-winning community tourism project. There are guesthouses or houses for rent (see Sleeping, page 574), restaurants (good food at **Sol e Mar**) and a handicraft cooperative. Each November there is a **Regata Ecológica**, with *jangadas* from up and down the coast competing. *Jangada* and catamaran cruises are offered, as well as fishing and a number of walking trails. This a simple place, where people make their living through artesanal fishing, without the use of big boats or industrial techniques. The village has built up its tourism infrastructure without any help from outside investors, and has been fighting the foreign speculators since 1979. The people are friendly and visitors are welcome to learn about the traditional way of life, although knowledge of Portuguese is essential.

Ins and outs To get to Prainha do Canto Verde, take a São Benedito bus to Aracati or Canoa Quebrada, buy a ticket to Quatro Bocas and ask to be let off at Lagoa da Poeira, two hours from Fortaleza. If you haven't booked a transfer in advance, Márcio at the **Pantanal** restaurant at the bus stop may be able to take you, US$2.75. The website www.fortal net.com.br/~fishnet, is a good source of information.

Aracati → *Phone code: 088. Population: 62,000.*

Situated on the shores of the Rio Jaguaribe, Aracati is the access point to the Ceará's most southeasterly beaches. The city is best known for its **Carnaval** (the liveliest in the state) and for its colonial architecture, including several 18th-century churches and mansions with Portuguese tile façades. There is a **religious art museum** (closed lunchtime and Sunday afternoon), a Saturday morning crafts fair on Avenida Coronel Alexandrino, and a number of simple *pousadas* (**B-E**) on the same street.

Canoa Quebrada → *Colour map 2, A5. Phone code: 088.*

Canoa Quebrada stands on a sand dune 10 km from Aracati backed by crumbling, multi-coloured sandstone cliffs. It remained an isolated fishing village until 1982, when a road was built. It is now a very popular resort, with many package hotels, busy bars and restaurants. But the village is almost entirely devoid of its once legendary laid-back, weed smoking hippy beach feel. The nightlife is good in season (especially over Christmas, New Year and Carnaval, when it can be very difficult to find a room). Canoa is famous for its *labirinto* lacework, coloured sand sculpture and beaches. Sand skiing is popular on the dunes and there is good windsurfing and kitesurfing on the Jaguaribe estuary, just outside town, with plenty of options for lessons and equipment rental (see page 581).

Local fishermen have their homes in **Esteves**, a separate village also on top of the cliff; they still live off the sea and rides on *jangadas*, buggy tours and light adventure on zip lines and sandboards can easily be organized in town or on the beach.

Ins and outs Canoa is served by at least four daily buses from Fortaleza; *expresso* or *leito* are fastest. Very frequent *combi* vans connect to Arati from where there are connections into Rio Grande do Norte. Note that the nearest place to change money or find an international ATM is in Aracati. To avoid biting insects and *bicho do pé* (burrowing fleas that frequent dirty beaches), it is best to wear shoes or sandals. For more information, including extensive accommodation listings, visit www.portalcanoaquebrada.com.br.

South of Canoa Quebrada

Heading south from Canoa Quebrada, **Porto Canoa** is a resort town that opened in 1996, fashioned after the Greek islands. It includes beach homes and apartments, shopping areas, restaurants and hotels, and there are facilities for watersports, horse riding, microlight flights, buggy and *jangada* outings.

South of here, **Majorlândia** is a very pleasant village with multi-coloured sand dunes, used in bottle pictures and cord crafts, and a wide beach with strong waves that are good for surfing. The arrival of the fishing fleet in the evening is an important daily event; lobster is the main catch. It is a popular weekend destination with beach homes for rent and plenty of *pousadas*. Unlike many beach locations in Ceará, the area is predominantly Brazilian. **Carnaval** here is quite lively, but you will have no trouble finding a room outside the peak season. The town is easy to find your way around.

About 5 km south along the beach from Majorlândia is the village of **Quixaba**, on a beach surrounded by coloured cliffs, with reefs offshore and good fishing. At low tide you can reach the popular destination of **Lagoa do Mato**, some 4 km south. The *lagoa* can also be reached by buggy from Canoa Quebrada beach (US$30 for four people). There's a hotel, restaurant and pristine beach surrounded by dunes, cliffs and palms.

Ponta Grossa → *Phone code: 088.*

Ponta Grossa, 30 km southeast of Aracati near Icapuí, is the last municipality before Rio Grande do Norte (access from Mossoró) and is reached via a sand road just before Redonda. It's a very pretty place, nestled at the foot of the cliffs, with a beautiful beach.

Ponta Grossa has its own tourism development initiative. The fishing community has many members of Dutch origin, following a shipwreck in the 19th century, and many people have fair hair. It is also one of the few places where *peixe boi marinho* (manatees) can be spotted. There's a good lookout from the cliffs (four-hour buggy ride, US$75 for four).

Beach trips go from Canoa Quebrada (see above) to Ponta Grossa for lunch, but it is possible to stay here (it helps if you can speak Portuguese). A number of cabins are being built and there are several restaurants/bars. The tourism coordinator is Eliabe, T088-3432 5001/9964 5846. For information on community tourism and the preservation of traditional ways of life in Ceará, contact **Instituto Terramar** ① *R Pinho Pessoa 86, Joaquim Távora, Fortaleza, T085-3226 4154/8804 0999, ask for Esther Neuhaus, www.terramar.org.br.*

To the south are the beaches of **Redonda**, another very pretty place, and **Barreiras**, which is good for surfing and has a handful of hotels.

The coast west of Fortaleza 😊🕐🏕️🖂 ⟫ *pp572-584.*

The coast northwest of Fortaleza has many wide beaches backed by fixed or shifting dunes, and surrounded by swathes of coconut groves. The main roads are some distance from the shore, making access to the beaches more difficult than on the eastern coast. This means the fishing villages have retained a more traditional lifestyle and a responsible attitude towards travel is especially important.

Praia Barra do Ceará

This long beach lies 8 km Northwest of the centre of Fortaleza, where the Rio Ceará flows into the sea (take a 'Grande Circular 1' bus). Here are the ruins of the 1603 **Forte de Nossa Senhora dos Prazeres**, the first Portuguese settlement in the area, partially covered by dunes, from which you can watch the beautiful sunsets. The palm-fringed beaches west of the Rio Ceará are cleaner but have strong waves. An iron bridge has been built across this river, making the area more accessible and open to development, as at **Praia de Icaraí**, 22 km to the northwest, and **Tabuba**, 5 km further north.

Cumbuco

Cumbuco is a long, white-sand beach backed by foreign-owned hotels and condominiums, a few palms and a handful of little beach shacks; and has a problem with rubbish. The beach itself is nothing special, unless you're a kitesurfer in which case you'll be amazed. There is no better place in Brazil and perhaps the world to learn how to kitesurf; ideal conditions can be guaranteed almost every day of the year. Sadly, as Cumbuco is largely European-owned and locals can no longer afford to buy property here, the town has entirely lost its Brazilian personality. Portuguese is rarely heard and the only locals that remain work in the hotels or restaurants. As well as kitesurfing and windsurfing, there are buggies, horse riding and *jangadas*, as well as dunes (known locally as *skibunda*), which you can slide down into the freshwater **Lagoa de Parnamirim**. A buggy tour costs around US$15 per person.

Cumbuco is served by regular buses from Fortaleza. Allow one to two hours for the journey. For more information visit www.kite-surf-brazil.com.

Pecém and Taíba → *Phone code: 085. Population: 5500 (Pecém).*

Some 58 km northwest of Fortaleza, **Pecém** is a village set in a cove with a wide beach, dunes and inland lagoons. There is strong surf and surfing and fishing championships are held here. From Pecém it is 19 km by road to **Taíba**, a 14-km-long beach with a long palm-covered point extending into the sea. Nearby is **Siupé**, a village that maintains colonial characteristics, where embroidered hammocks, a trademark of Ceará, are made.

Pecém and Taíba are serviced by regular buses from Fortaleza; both have a few simple *pousadas*. The town's central telephone exchange can be reached on T085-344 1064 and T085-3340 1328; any three-digit numbers listed are extensions on these central lines.

Paracuru and Lagoinha → *Phone code: 085. Population: 28,000 (Paracuru).*

Some 106 km northwest of Fortaleza, **Paracuru** is a fishing port which hosts the most important **Carnaval** on the northwest coast, including street dancing and parades, decorated boats, sports championships and a beauty contest. It has some lovely deserted white-sand beaches with good bathing and surfing, and the people are very friendly. There are several *pousadas* in the centre. Restaurant **Ronco do Mar** has good fish dishes. **Boca do Poço** bar has *forró* at weekends. Buses from Fortaleza run at least every hour during the day to the central *rodoviária*, US$5.

West of Paracuru and 12 km from the town of Paraipaba is **Lagoinha**, a very scenic beach with hills, dunes and palms by the shore. There's a fishing village on one of the hills and nearby are some small but pleasant waterfalls. About 3 km west of town is **Lagoa da Barra**, a lake surrounded by dunes. Local legend says that one of the hills, Morro do Cascudo, has hidden treasure left by French pirates. There are six daily buses from Fortaleza to Paracuru and frequent transfers from there to Lagoinha (**Brasileiro**, three hours, US$6); there are plenty of cheap seafood restaurants and *pousadas*.

Fleixeiras and around → *Colour map 2, A4. Phone code: 085.*

Further northwest, some 135 km from Fortaleza, is **Trairi**, access point to a series of beaches that have kept their natural beauty and, until the mid-1990s, were untouched by tourism. North of Trairi, 15 km by road, is **Fleixeiras**, where pools that are good for snorkelling form near the beach at low tide. There are three daily buses from Fortaleza to Fleixeiras (US$7, information T085-3272 4128).

About 5 km west is **Imboaca**, a scenic beach with interesting rock formations and shifting dunes. Further west, at the mouth of the Rio Mundaú, is **Mundaú**, another beautiful area, with a beach, palms, dunes and an old working lighthouse. Take a raft across the spit and walk for hours on deserted sands, see wind-eroded dunes or take a boat from the quay up the river to see the mangroves. Access roads from Imboaca and Cana to the south are often impassable because of shifting dunes; at low tide it is possible to reach it along the beach from Fleixeiras. There is a fishing village near the beach with some *pousadas* and restaurants.

Jericoacoara ●🏠🏃⛺🏭🌊🕐 » *pp572-584. Colour map 2, A4.*

→ *Phone code: 088.*

Jericoacoara is another of the northeast's paradise beaches that is getting spoilt. Up until the 1980s it was a magical place: a collection of little fishermen's shacks lost under towering dunes and surrounded by wonderful long, sweeping beaches. São Paulo middle-class hippies used to live here for months, surfing, dancing *forró* and smoking copious amounts of weed. Slowly Jeri began to grow. Then buggies began to race up and down the dunes –

Environmental concerns in Jericoacoara

Jericoacoara is ostensibly part of an environmental protection area that includes a large coconut grove, lakes, dunes, mangroves and hills covered in *caatinga* vegetation. Degradation, over-building and the marginalization of the local community led Jericoacoarans to write a letter to the World Bank at the turn of the millennium, expressing their concerns about the exploitation within the area and corruption in the federal environmental body, Ibama. The issues persist and there is a growing rubbish problem, but Jeri's beautiful landscape has not been destroyed beyond recuperation. Whether it remains beautiful and wild depends largely on visitors' spending choices. Here are some tips – gleaned from talking to local people.

→ Avoid staying in large hotels, especially the European-run hotels on the beach. One of the largest has cut down protected mangroves to build its facilities.

→ Avoid buying property in Jeri or anywhere along the Ceará coastline. This increases property prices and forces locals off their own land.

→ Where possible we have tried to recommend local, or at least Brazilian businesses or hotels in Jeri. Choosing them will ensure that local families have enough income to continue living in their home town.

→ Buggy tourism has disturbed the dunes and their flora and fauna and has been responsible for a proliferation of plastic litter and cans. Choose to walk on the dunes instead and if you decide to take a buggy tour choose a local small operator and take responsibility for the disposal of your rubbish.

→ Make an effort to speak Portuguese. Generally only non-local Brazilians will speak English. By insisting on speaking English you help create tourist demand that most local fishermen cannot fulfil.

including the most delicate, those with fixed vegetation – and local villages started to become tourist attractions. In the 1980s, the Italians discovered Jeri and building began, much of it with little or no environmental considerations; buggies whizzed up and down from dawn to dusk like a plague of motorized flies. Today, few properties or tourism businesses are locally owned and the fishermen and their families are being sidelined and priced out of town.

That said, Jeri remains beautiful and it has a long way to go before it becomes as spoilt as Morro de São Paulo or even Cumbuco. If careful choices are made by tourists (such as supporting local businesses, trying to speak Portuguese, participating in Brazilian culture and avoiding buggy tours and large European-run beachfront resorts), it could turn itself into an inspiring sustainable, small-scale resort (see box, above). The nearby beaches offer superb conditions for kitesurfing and windsurfing – both practices that do little to damage the environment – and there is excellent walking and cycling along the long flat beaches to beauty spots like the crumbling chocolate-coloured rock arch at **Pedra Furada**. Sandboarding is popular and watching the sunset from the top of the large dune just west of town, followed by a display of *capoeira* on the beach, is a tradition among visitors.

Ins and outs

There are two direct buses a day from Fortaleza to Jijoca from where *jardineiras* (Toyota pick-ups) do the 45-minute transfer to Jeri. Be sure to take a *VIP* or *executivo* as the journey takes five to six hours (seven to eight hours on other buses). It is far more comfortable to take an air-conditioned mini-van; these can be organized through *pousadas* in Jeri. Hotels and tour operators run two- to three-day tours from from Fortaleza. If not on a tour, 'guides' will besiege new arrivals in Jijoca with offers of buggies, or guiding cars through the tracks and dunes to Jeri for US$5.55. If you don't want to do this, ask if a pickup is going or contact **Francisco Nascimento** ⓘ *O Chicão, at Posta do Dê, or T088-3669 1356*, who charges US$3.70 per person for the 22-km journey (30 minutes). There are connections with the rest of the state through Sobral. Arrivals from Maranhão and Piauí come via Parnaíba (see page 588) and Camocim. There are no banks in town; most *pousadas* and restaurants accept Visa but it is wise to bring plenty of cash in reais. ⇥ *See Transport, page 583.*

Around Jericoacoara

Going west along the beach takes you through a succession of sand dunes and coconut groves; the views are beautiful. After 2 km is the beach of **Mangue Seco**, and 2 km beyond this is an arm of the ocean that separates it from **Guriú** (across the bridge), where there is a village on top of a fixed dune. There is good birdwatching here and if you wish to stay hammock space can be found. The village musician sings his own songs in the bar. It's a four-hour walk from Jericoacoara, or take a boat across the bay.

The best surfing, kitesurfing and windsurfing is 10 minutes from town on the pebbly **Praia de Malhada**, reachable either by walking east along the beach or by cutting through town. Top-quality equipment can be rented in Jeri. A 3- to 4-km walk to the east takes you to the **Pedra Furada**, a stone arch sculpted by the sea, one of the landmarks of Jeri, only accessible at low tide (check the tide tables at the **Casa do Turismo**). Swimming is dangerous here as waves and currents are strong. In the same direction but just inland is **Serrote**, a large hill with a lighthouse on top; it is well worth walking up for the magnificent views.

The best kitesurfing and windsurfing beaches are beyond Jeri, some 15 km east of town (43 km by road via Jijoca and Caiçara), at **Praia do Preá** and **Praia de Guriú**. Both beaches are reachable on day tours for around US$50 if you have your own kitesurf. Tours including equipment (US$60) can be arranged in Jeri through www.kiteclubprea.com. There is accommodation on both beaches. At low tide on Preá, you can visit the **Pedra da Seréia**, a rock pocked with natural swimming pools.

Some of the best scenery in the area is around **Nova Tatajuba**, about 35 km west of Jeri. One Toyota a day passes through the town on the way to the ferry point at Camocim and almost all buggy tours visit. There are simple *pousadas* and restaurants and the village is far smaller and less touristy than Jeri. ⇥ *See Sleeping, page 575.*

Some 10 km beyond Praia do Preá (62 km by road) is the beach of **Barrinha**, with access to the picturesque **Lagoa Azul**. From here it's 10 km inland through the dunes (20 km along the road) to **Lagoa Paraíso** or **Jijoca**, a turquoise, freshwater lake, great for bathing (buggy US$10 per person).

Cruz

Some 40 km east of Jijoca is Cruz, an obligatory stop if travelling by bus from Sobral to Jericoacoara. It is a small pleasant town, surrounded by a *carnauba* palm forest (used in making brooms). At the south end is a large wooden cross dating from 1825, nearby is a statue to São Francisco. There is a lively market on Sunday when, at dawn, *pau d'arara* trucks, mule carts and bicycles converge on the town. There are two very basic hotels.

Sobral → *Colour map 2, A4. Phone code: 088. Population: 145,000.*

Sobral, 238 km west of Fortaleza (four hours by bus, US$5), is the principal town in western Ceará and the access point to beaches in the west of the state. The city has a handful of well-preserved colonial buildings including the **Catedral da Sé**, **Teatro São João** and a mansion on the Praça da Sé. There is a **Museu Diocesano** ⓘ *Praça São João*, a Cristo Redentor statue and a monument to the 1919 solar eclipse. Near town is the **Parque Ecológico Lagoa da Fazenda**.

Chapada de Ibiapaba

In the Chapada de Ibiapaba, an area of tablelands, caves, rock formations, rivers and waterfalls, is **Tianguá**. The town is surrounded by waterfalls; 3 km to the north is Cachoeira de São Gonçalo, a good place for bathing; 5 km from town are natural pools at the meeting place of seven waterfalls. About 16 km from town on the edge of the BR-222 is Cana Verde, a 30-m-high waterfall surrounded by monoliths and thick vegetation.

Some 30 km north of Tianguá is **Viçosa do Ceará**, a colonial town also within the *chapada*, known for its ceramics, hang-gliding, food and drink. The Igreja de Nossa Senhora das Vitórias, a stone church on top of the 820-m-high **Morro do Céu**, is reached by walking up 360 steps. There is an excellent view of the town, the surrounding highlands and the *sertão* beyond. Near the town are interesting rock formations such as the 100-m-wide **Pedra de Itagurussu** with a natural spring. There is good walking in the area. Basic walking maps are available at the **Secretaria de Turismo**, near the old theatre to the right of the *praça* on which the church stands. Ask about visiting the community that makes sun-baked earthenware pots. To get there take an **Expresso Serrana** bus from Fortaleza, six hours, US$8.40, five a day via Sobral.

Parque Nacional Ubajara → *Colour map 2, A4.*

Eighteen kilometres south of Tianguá, at an altitude of 840 m, is the town of **Ubajara** (tourist information, T085-3634 1300 ext 231), with an interesting Sunday morning market selling produce of the *sertão*. Some 3 km from the town is the **Parque Nacional Ubajara**, with 563 ha of native highland and *caatinga* brush. It is the smallest of Brazil's national parks and its main attraction is the **Ubajara cave** on the side of an escarpment. Fifteen chambers extending for a total of 1120 m have been mapped, of which 360 m are open to visitors. Access is along a 6-km footpath and steps (two to three hours, take water) or by a **cable car** ⓘ *T088-3634 1219, 0900-1430, last up at 1500, US$1.50*, which descends the cliff to the cave entrance. Lighting has been installed in nine caverns of the complex.

Ins and outs An **Ibama** guide leads visitors through the cave, which is completely dry and home to 14 types of bat. Several rock formations look like animals, including a horse's head, jacaré and snake. At the park entrance is an **Ibama office** ⓘ *5 km from the caves, T085-3634 1388, www.ibama.gov.br,* and a bar by the entrance serving juices, snacks and drinks. In the park there is a new easy walkway through the woods with stunning views at the end. Start either to the left of the park entrance or opposite the snack bar near the cable car platform. There is a good 8-km trail to the park from Araticum (7 km by bus from Ubajara). This route is used by locals and passes through *caatinga* forest. For more information, including accommodation, see http://portalubajara.com.br and www.ubajara.ce.gov.br.

South from Ubajara

The Chapada de Ibiapaba continues south from Ubajara for some 70 km. Other towns in the highlands are: **Ibiapina**, with the nearby Cachoeira da Ladeira, reached by a steep trail, a good place for bathing; **São Benedito**, known for its straw and ceramic crafts and a working *engenho* sugar mill; and **Carnaubal**, with waterfalls and a bathing resort.

Ipu, 80 km south of Ubajara, is a town at the foot of the Serra de Ibiapaba, on the edge of the *sertão*. It's an interesting transition as you descend from the green serra, with its sugar cane, tall *babaçu* palms and cattle, down the escarpment to the *sertão*. Ipu's main claim to fame is the **Bica do Ipu**, a 180-m waterfall plunging off the sheer edge of the *serra* into a pool; it is said to be the site of the legendary love affair between Iracema, a local *indígena*, and the founder of Fortaleza. You can cool off under the falls and there are basic facilities and a few places to stay around town.

If driving, you can cross the *sertão* on good roads via **Varjota** on the large lake of the **Açude de Araras** (33 km), **Santa Quitéria** (a further 41 km) to **Canindé** (111 km on the CE-257).

Monsenhor Tabosa, in the centre of the state, has the highest peak in Ceará. The area around the mountain, called **Cabeço Branco**, has been made into an environmental protection area, with *caatinga* and patches of *Mata Atlântica*. This remote town is very friendly, with four hotels (see Sleeping, page 576). It can get very wet in the rainy season (around March). The easiest way to get there is by car or **Horizonte** bus on the CE032 from Canindé, but there are roads from Nova Russas, south of Ipu, and the BR-020 from Boa Viagem (which is very rough).

Continuing south, the greenery of the Chapada de Ibiapaba eventually gives way to the dry **Sertão dos Inhamuns**. One of the main towns in this area is **Crateús**, about 210 km south of Sobral, a remote settlement with rich folkloric traditions seen during the festivals of **Mergulho Folclórico** in August, and the **Festival de Repentistas**, in September. Nearby are archaeological sites with rock inscriptions. There is a regular bus service on the paved road to Fortaleza (347 km). The bus service from Crateús runs along the very bad road to Teresina, every other day.

South of Fortaleza ⬤❀▲ ›› pp572-584.

Serra de Baturité → *Colour map 2, A5. Phone code: 085. Population: 32,000. Altitude: 171 m.*
The town of **Baturité**, the largest in the area, is surrounded by the hills and waterfalls of the **Maciço de Baturité**, an irregular massif with beautiful scenery. Baturité is more in the foothills than in the *serra* proper. It has some colonial buildings and a historical museum and is home to the **Pingo de Ouro** distillery, which can be visited. There are several hotels and restaurants, or you can also stay in the **Jesuit Seminary** ① *T085-3347 0362 in advance*, where a few monks still work in the local community and tend the cloister garden (**E** per person, full board US$11.10 per day including morning and afternoon coffee with local fruits, ask for 'Jesuitas' if taking a taxi, or walk up). The *rodoviária* is beyond town on the way out to Guaramiranga.

Sixteen kilometres northwest of Baturité, is **Guaramiranga**, the centre of a fruit and flower growing area. At 365 m above sea level, it is reached by a very twisty road through lush vegetation and fruit trees full of birds. There are several *pousadas* along the way. The town is packed with visitors at weekends; if you want to stay overnight you must book in advance. During **Carnaval** (February) there is a **Festival of Jazz and Blues**. To ensure a bed during this time you must book in November. The town also holds a **Festival Nordestino de Teatro** in September in the **Teatro Municipal Rachel de Queiroz**. This is in the centre of town and around it are a number of restaurants including **Café com Flores**, **Taberna Portuguesa**, **O Alemão**, **Confrari** (for pasta and fondue). For information contact secultguaramiranga@hotmail.com.

About 7 km further north is **Pacoti**, with large botanical gardens (*horto forestal*). There are trails for viewing the highland flora, and several waterfalls that are good for a dip. On the main road to Pacoti, turn left at Forquilha to climb **Pico Alto** (1115 m above sea level), previously thought to be the highest peak in Ceará, which offers special views and sunsets. You can go up by car, or if you leave early in the morning you may be able to catch a lift with the school bus.

Canindé → *Colour map 2, A4.*

The pilgrimage centre of Canindé, 108 km southwest of Fortaleza, is located in the **Sertão Central** of Ceará. A large modern church stands on a hill and has carved baptistry doors and many ex-votos. It receives hundreds of thousands of pilgrims from all over the northeast between 26 September and 4 October, devotees of São Francisco das Chagas, 'O pobrezinho de Asis', many of them dressed like Franciscan priests. The pilgrims flock to town on foot, by bus and mostly on *pau de arara* trucks. It is reputed to be second in the world, after Assisi, as a pilgrimage centre for Saint Francis. There is a regional **museum** with artefacts representative of northeast culture, and several restaurants.

There is a daily bus service from Fortaleza *rodoviária* with **Viação Nova Esperança** (three hours), and interesting dry-land vegetation along the route. From Canindé south to the Sertão Central (Quixadá), CE-456 is under repair. The majority of the road is not too bad, but there are some rough bits (95 km).

Quixadá → *Phone code: 088. Population: 64,500.*

Quixadá is on the **Serra do Estevão**, with its rocky outcrops and dry hills representative of the central *sertão*. It is one of the top hang-gliding sites in the world and is also good for climbing and trekking. The town has a dam, **Açude de Cedro**, built by ex-slaves during the empire of Dom Pedro II, following the terrible drought of 1877-1879. You can walk across the dam to view the surrounding scenery, and reach the restaurants and bars. Activities include a two-hour trail (take an **ATEC** guide) to interesting rock formations such as the **Galhina Choca** ('broody hen'), as well as climbing and abseiling on the rocks by the dam. There is a historical museum in the town.

Nossa Senhora Inmaculada Rainha do Sertão is a pilgrimage centre 10 km from town, halfway up the highest peak in the region, **Pico do Urucum**, or Serra Preta, at 600 m. The views are tremendous. It's a modern sanctuary (inaugurated 1995) accommodating over 800 worshippers, and is decorated with the flags and images of the patron saints of every Latin American country and Italy. The main festival is 11 February, so the whole month is packed with visitors. The main launch ramp for hang-gliding ramp is just below the church.

About 21 km from Quixadá is **Gruta do Pajé**, a complex of religious buildings dating from the early 1900s. ▶▶ *See Sleeping, page 577.*

Quixeramobim is an important regional hub and the geographical centre of Ceará, 20 minutes from Quixadá. The town centre is pleasant with a lovely old market building, and is being completely refurbished. There is a **Memorial de Antônio Conselheiro** (of Canudos), who was born here in 1830 and lived in the town until, shamed by his first wife's adultery, he left for a wandering life before becoming the religious figure famous in history and novels. The memorial has some sculptures, high-relief pictures and a tiny remnant of railway. Nearby is an old iron railway bridge, another 'postcard' view of the town and **archaeological sites** ① *contact Sr Simão, R Mons Salviano Pinio 233, T088-638 0000*, with ancient inscriptions on boulders. The regional dam has been used for irrigation with good results. In August, an important musical event, the **Festival de Violas e Violeiros**, is held. ►► *See Festivals and events, page 580.*

Juazeiro do Norte ●●●● ►► pp572-584. Colour map 2, B4.

→ *Phone code: 088. Population: 200,000.*

The south of the state is known as the **Cariri region**, the name of an indigenous group that lived in the interior and resisted Portuguese colonization for a long time. The main centre in this area is Juazeiro do Norte, the second largest city in Ceará. Along with its two satellites, **Crato** and **Barbalha**, 10 km to the west and south respectively, they form an oasis of green in the dry *sertão*.

Juazeiro was home to one of Brazil's most venerated Catholic figures: the miracle working priest, Padre Cícero Romão Batista, a controversial and very popular figure who championed the rights of Ceara's poor from the 1870s to the 1930s. Even before his death, Padre Cícero had become a legend after a consecrated communion wafer he passed to a woman at Mass reportedly bled in her mouth, and Juazeiro do Norte an important pilgrimage site, drawing the faithful from throughout the northeast and, increasingly, from the whole nation. Today it is the most important pilgrimage centre of the region and visiting during a pilgrimage is an incredible experience. The town is dominated by the imposing Italiante **Sanctuário do Sagrado Coração de Jesus** basilica and a huge

Juazeiro do Norte

Sleeping ●
Aristocrata **3**

Panorama **2**
Plaza **4**

San Felipe **5**

Not to scale

sombre **statue of Padre Cicero**, gazing at a distant horizon from the top of the **Colina do Horto** hill, 8 km from the town centre. To get there, either take the pilgrim trail up the hill (one hour, start early because of the heat) or take the **Horto** city bus to the summit. There are also two museums devoted to the priest. The **Memorial Padre Cicero** ① *R São José 242, T088-3512 2240, Mon-Sat 0800-1100 and 1300-1600, Sun 0900-1100 and 1400-1700, free*, is based in the house where he lived and preserves some of his personal belongings and myriad messages from pilgrims including lottery tickets and football coupons that provided winnings after Cicero answered pilgrims prayers. There are even more covering the walls of the **Museu Vivo do Padre Cicero** ① *Colina do Horto, daily 0800-1200 and 1400-1700, free*, together with numerous effigies and devotional books. The priest is buried in the simple church of **chapel of Nossa Senhora do Perpétuo Socorro** ① *Praça do Cinqüentenário, daily 0800-1800, free*, which is completely packed with pilgrims during religious celebrations. Also worth seeing is the **church of Nossa Senhora das Dores** with the adjacent pilgrimage grounds, roughly fashioned after St Peter's Square in Rome.

The town receives six main annual pilgrimages (see Festivals and events, page 580), but visitors arrive all year round and religious tourism is the principal source of income. Another cultural manifestation seen throughout the Cariri region is the *bandas cabaçais ou de pífaros*, musical groups that participate in all celebrations. As well as playing instruments, they dance, imitating animals, and perform games or fights

Ins and outs
Cariri airport ① *Av Virgílio Távora 4000, T088-3572 0700*, is 6 km from the city and receives flights from Brasília, Fortaleza, Recife, Rio de Janeiro and São Paulo (Guarulhos). A taxi to the centre costs US$5.75 (motorcycle taxi US$3); a taxi to the bus station costs US$8.40. The **rodoviária** ① *Av Delmiro Gouveia s/n, T088-3571 2309*, is on the road to Crato. A taxi to the centre costs US$3 (motorcycle taxi US$0.60). ▶ *See Transport, page 584.*

Excursions from Juazeiro do Norte
The **Chapada do Araripe**, a tableland about 850 m high, is south of Juazeiro do Norte and extends from east to west for 220 km. The area is believed to have been forced upwards and numerous fossilized plants and animals including giant sloths have been found. It has one of the most important native forest reserves in the state, the **Floresta Nacional do Araripe** ① *20 km from Crato*, with grottoes, palaeontological sites, springs and cloudforest with ferns and orchids. Some 22 km south of Juazeiro do Norte, within the *chapada*, is the **Balneário do Caldas**, a pool fed with natural spring water (0700-1700); access is via Barbalha.

In the area of **Jardim**, 34 km south of Barbalha, there are several natural springs, while by **Missão Velha**, 22 km east of Barbalha, there are rapids on the Rio Salgado and an attractive waterfall. Another point pf access to the *chapada* is through **Santana do Cariri**, 60 km west of Juazeiro do Norte. The main attraction here is the **Nascente dos Azedos**, a natural spring good for bathing. There is also a palaeontology museum and one basic hotel. Transport is with **Pernambucana**, daily at 1430, returning 0600, US$2.50, two hours.

Crato is an older city which lost its significance in the region, owing to the increased importance of Juazeiro do Norte. It has several pleasing *praças* and a small **Museu de Fósseis** ① *Praça da Sé 105, Mon-Fri 0800-1200, 1400-1800, free*, housing an impressive collection of fossils from the Cretaceous period gathered in the Chapada do Araripe.

For Sleeping and Eating price codes and other relevant information, see pages 42-47.

● Sleeping

Fortaleza *p555, map p556*

Almost all hotels offer reduced prices in the low season. There are many *pousadas* in the Iracema/Meireles area, but they change frequently. Most hotels in Fortaleza have a strict policy of not accepting overnight visitors except with prior reservations.

C Caxambu, Gen Bezerril 22, opposite the cathedral, T085-3231 0339, caxambu@ accvia.com.br. Discounts in low season. Rooms have a/c, TV and fridge. Room service available, breakfast included. Probably best bet in centre, good value.

D-F Backpackers, R Dom Manuel 89, T085-3091 8997, www.backpackers.ce.cjb.net. Central, basic, shared bathrooms, no breakfast, helpful owner. Price per person in lower bracket.

E Big, Gen Sampaio 485, Praça da Estação, Centro, T085-3212 2066,. All rooms have fan, old lino and clean sheets. Cheaper without TV, even cheaper without bath, simple breakfast, OK, but caution needed at night as it's right in thick of the central scrum.

Beaches

LL-L Beira Mar, Av Beira Mar 3130, T085-4009 2000, Meireles, www.hotelbeiramar.com.br. Newly reformed beachfront hotel with some seafront rooms, others have a side view. Comfortable and safe, with a pool, 24-hr business centre with internet and parking. Good value, especially in low season.

LL-L Imperial Othon Palace, Av Beira Mar 2500, Meireles, T085-3466 5500, www.othon.com.br. Large hotel on the beachfront with all the usual facilities, business and tourists catered for, pool, sauna, massage (recommended *feijoada* on Sat).

LL-L Luzeiro Beira Mar, Av Beira Mar 2600, Meireles, T085-4006 8585, www.hotel luzeiros.com.br. A tall tower built at the turn of the millennium and with functional, business-like rooms, a large pool, sauna and Wi-Fi in public areas and rooms.

LL-L Seara Praia, Av Beira Mar 3080, Meireles, T085-4011 2200, www.hotelseara.com.br. 30% cheaper in low season, smart, comfortable luxury hotel with pool, gym, cyber café, French cuisine.

L Ponta Mar, Av Beira Mar 2200, Meireles, T085-4006 2200, www.ponta mar.com.br. Aimed more at the business market, but still a good location and similar facilities.

AL Colonial Praia, R Barão de Aracati 145, Iracema, T085-4005 4644, www.colonialpraia hotel.com.br. 4 stars, **B** in low season, pleasant grounds and big pool, low-rise, which is unusual, popular with families, laundry service.

A Ibis, Atualpa Barbosa de Lima 660, Iracema, T085-3219 2121, www.accor hotels.com.br. In *Accor* style, with all the usual facilities, pool. Breakfast extra.

A-B Casa Blanca, R Joaquim Alves 194, T085-3219 0909, www.casablancahoteis.com.br. The best rooms on the upper floors of this tall tower have wonderful sweeping ocean views. All are a/c, well-appointed (if anonymous) and have international TV. Breakfasts are a feast and there's a tiny rooftop pool, a little gym and massage service. Minivans leave from in front of the hotel to Jericoacoara; if waiting for a minivan, an a/c room costs US$50 for 4 hrs.

B Abrolhos Praia, Av Abolição 2030, 1 block from the beach, Meireles, T/F085-3248 1217, www.abrolhospraia hotel.com.br. Pleasant, TV, fridge, hot shower, a/c, rooms look a bit sparse but no different from others in this category, soft beds, discount in low season, internet.

B Praia de Iracema, Raimundo Girão 430, Iracema, T085-3219 2299, www.hotelpraia deiracema.com. 20% discount in low season, a/c, TV, fridge, safe in room, coffee shop, pool, brightly coloured bedcovers, on corner so traffic outside, but OK for value and comfort.

B Villamaris, Av Abolição 2026, Meireles, T085-3248 0112, www.hotelvillamaris.com.br. **C** Plain, simple a/c rooms with cream painted, crinkle concrete walls a tiny work table and international TV. Good location.

B Casa de Praia, R Joaquim Alves 169, T085-3219 1022, www.hotelcasadepraia.com.br. Well-kept, modest a/c rooms in warm colours and with international TV, Wi-Fi. The best are above the 4th floor and have partial ocean views. There's a little rooftop pool. Minivans leave from in front of the hotel of Jeri.

B-C Ideal Praia, R Antonele Bezerra 281, T085-3248 7504, www.hotelideal.com.br. A mock-colonial hotel in a quiet little back street offering 2 kinds of rooms. Those on the ground floor are decorated with mock-marble tiles and have little windows. Those on the upper floors have ocean views and little terraces. All are well-kept, homey and have international TV and a/c. There's a mouse-size pool on the roof.

B-C Pousada do Suíço, R Antônia Augusto 141, Iracema, T085-3219 3873, www.pension-vom-schweizer.com.br. Must reserve mid-Oct-Feb. Very private, quiet street, variety of rooms, some with kitchens, small pool, a/c, TV, fridge, Swiss run, changes cash and TCs. Recommended.

C IYHA Pousada Atalaia, Av Beira Mar 814, Iracema, T/F085-3219 0755, www.atalaia hostel.com.br. Hostel, **E-F** in dorms, a/c, fan, TV, good breakfast, prices fall in low season.

C Pousada Salinas, Av Zezé Diogo 3300, Praia do Futuro, T085-3234 3626, www.pousadasalinas.com.br. **D** in low season, popular, a/c, TV, fridge, parking, just across from sea, some English spoken.

C-D Ondas Verdes, Av Beira Mar 934, Iracema, T085-3219 0871, www.hotel ondasverdes.com.br. Scruffy hotel beloved of backpackers even though there are better options nearby. Rooms are musty; be sure to look at several.

C-D Panorâmica, R Idelfonso Albano 464, T085-3219 8347, www.portalde hospedagem.com.br. Very simple peach and grey tile boxes. The best by far are on the upper floors, have partial ocean views and little terraces. In a quiet location.

D-F IYHA Albergue Atalaia Anexo, Av Almte Barroso 1006, T085-3219 9509. A well-kept, spruce hostel that opened in late 2007, with clean and bright rooms and public areas, internet and decent service.

Camping
Fortaleza Camping Club (do Professor), R Vereador Pedro Paulo Moreira 505, Águas Frias, T085-3273 2544. Around 10 km east of the airport. Lots of shade, US$7 per person.

Pousada dos Pinheiros, R Paulo Mendes 333, Praia do Futuro, T085-3234 5590, marcosacleite@ig.com.br. On the beach.

Aquiraz and around *p560*
In Águas Belas, there are simpler rooms available in private houses.

B Kalamari, Av Beira Mar, Porto das Dunas beach.

B Pousada Villa Francesa, Av Beira Mar, Prainha, 1.5 km from the beach, T085-3361 5007, www.villafrancesa.com. Tiny 8 room, French-run beach hotel that opened in 2005. Rooms are gathered around a smart pool and the hotel offers tours and internet.

B-C Pousada Mama Rosália Via Local 19, Porto das Dunas beach T085-3361 7491, www.pousadamamarosalia.com.br. Family-run beach hotel with simple tile-floor and whitewash rooms with en suites, a restaurant and a pool.

Morro Branco and Praia das Fontes *p561*
L Praia das Fontes, Av A Teixeira 1, Praia das Fontes, T085-3338 1179, www.oasisatlantico.com. Luxurious resort, watersports, horse hire, tennis courts and a simple spa. Recommended.

B Das Falésias, Av Assis Moreira 314, Praia das Fontes, T085-3327 3052, www.hotel falesias.com.br. Pleasant German-owned cliff-side *pousada* with a pool and tidy rooms.

B Recanto Praiano, Morro Branco, T085-3338 7229, www.recantopraianopousada.com.br. Peaceful little *pousada* with a good breakfast. Recommended.

C Pousada Sereia, on the beach, Morro Branco, T085-3330 1144. Lovely simple *pousada* with an excellent breakfast and friendly staff. Highly recommended.

D Rosalias, Morro Branco, T085-3330 1131. Very simple and somewhat run down but only 50 m from the bus stop, and with a shared kitchen.

Prainha do Canto Verde p561

There are also houses for rent (eg **Casa Cangulo** or **Vila Marésia**). Note that prices rise by 30% for the regatta and over Christmas and Semana Santa.
E Dona Mirtes. Price includes breakfast, will negotiate other meals.

Canoa Quebrada p562

Villagers will let you sling your hammock or will put you up cheaply. **Verónica** is recommended, European books exchanged. **Sr Miguel** rents good clean houses for US$10 a day.
AL Tranqüilândia, R Camino do Mar, T088-3421 7012, www.tranquilandia.it. A range of thatched roofed, a/c chalets around a smart pool in a lawned tropical garden. Decent restaurant. Italian-owned and with facilities for kitesurfers.
B Pousada Latitude, R Dragão do Mar (Broadway), T088-3241 7041, www.pousada latitude.com.br. Large a/c 2-storey bungalows in a large complex off the main street. Not intimate but with decent service.
B-C Pousada Lua Estrela, R Nascer do Sol 106, T088-3421 7040, www. Luaestrela.com. A smart hostel/*pousada* with with fan-cooled rooms with great sea views, fridges and hot showers and a/c rooms without views in the garden. 20 m off R Dragão do Mar.
C Pousada Alternativa, R Francisco Caraço. Rooms with or without bath. Centrally located and recommended.
C Pousada Oásis do Rei, R Nascer do Sol 112, T088-3421 7081, www.oasisdorei.com.br

Simple rooms around a pool in a little garden, with polished concrete or tiled floors; some with sea views and some with bed space for 3 or 4.
C Pousada Via Láctea, just off R Dragão do Mar (Broadway), www.pousadavialactea.com. This chunky brick building may not be beautiful, but the views are and the beach is only some 50 m away. English spoken and tours organized. Highly recommended.
C-E Pousada Azul, R Dragão do Mar (Broadway) s/n, T088-9932 9568 (mob). Very simple, small concrete and blue tile a/c or fan-cooled boxes, a sunny upper deck, miniature pool and warm service from the owner Saméa.
E-F Albergue Ibiza, R Dragão do Mar (Broadway) s/n, T088-8804 7603 (mob), www.portalcanoaquebrada.com.br/canoa_q uebrada_albergue_ibiza.htm. Tiny, boxy but astonishingly cheap and fairly spruce doubles and dorms 200 m from the beach.

Paracuru and Lagoinha p564

There are a number of cheaper hotels on both beaches; it's worth shopping around.
C Dunas, Paracuru, T085-3344 1965, http://hoteldunas.com.br. Family-orientated hotel with a small water park next door and range of very simple rooms gathered around a pool.
C-D Mar e Vista, Av Francisco Azevedo 170, Lagoinha, T085-3363 5038, www.pousada-maravista.com. The are great views from this clifftop hotel more than make up for the very simple rooms; ask for one at the front with a shared terrace and hammock area.

Jericoacoara p564

There are crowds at weekends mid-Dec to mid-Feb, in Jul and during Brazilian holidays. Many places full in low season too. For New Year's Eve, 4- to 5-day packages are available. Prices rise by as much as 40% in peak season (New Year and Carnaval).
L Vila Kalango, R do Ibama s/n, T088-3669 2289, www.vilakalango.com.br. The smartest option in town with well-appointed rooms in stilt house cabins in a tree-filled garden just

set-back from the beach. Lovely pool and bar area, a decent restaurant and excellent facilities for kitesurfers and windsurfers. There's a sister hotel, **Rancho do Peixe**, on Praia da Preá. Shuttle buses to/from Fortaleza.

A-B Espaço Nova Era, R do Forró s/n, T088-3669 2056, www.novaerapousada.com.br. A mock-Mediterranean main lobby house leads to a set of large circular a/c or fan-cooled cabins in terracotta brick and polished concrete. These sit in an Italianate garden shaded by numerous trees and coloured with tropical flowers. Room for 5 in the larger cabins making this an economical option. Italian-owned.

B Barão, R do Forró 433, T088-3669 2136 www.recantodobarao.com. Duplex rooms in two corridors strung with hammocks. All overlook the corridors and *pousada* gardens and the brightest and best-kept rooms are on the upper floors. The *pousada* has a small pool and attractive sitting areas furnished with sun beds. There is a popular *churrascaria* next door. São Paulo owned.

C Papagaio, R Travessa do Forró s/n, T088-3669 2142, pousadapapagaio@hotmail.com, Attractive, stone-floored a/c rooms with pretty pebble-dash bathrooms and hammock-strung verandas overlooking a courtyard garden shaded by prickly pears and with a tiny pool. Brazilian owned.

C Pousada Tirol, R São Francisco 202, T088-3669 2006, www.jericoacoarahostel.com.br IYHA-affiliated hostel with dorms (**E** per person) with hot water showers and scrupulously cleaned doubles (**C-D** in low season) with barely room for a double and a single bed. Very friendly and popular with party-loving travellers. Very busy cyber café, US$3 per hr; 10 mins free use for all guests.

C Pousada Zé Patinha, R São Francisco s/n, T088-3669 2081, www.sandjeri.com.br, Simple, a/c or fan-cooled tiled rooms and plain white rooms in 2 parallel corridors. No outside windows, just overlooking the corridor. Cool in the heat of the day, quiet, with decent mattresses and locally owned.

D Pousada Zé Bento, R São Francisco s/n, T088-3669 2006, Small, tiled rooms with

white walls and little en suites off a small, palm shaded and sandy garden annex. Friendly, tours organized, locally owned.

Around Jericoacoara *p566*

D Rancho do Peixe, Praia do Preá, T088-9966 2111, www.ranchodopeixe.com.br. Chic bungalows set right on the beach next to a long pool. All have hammock verandas and are fan-cooled. Special rates and excellent facilities for kitesurfers and windsurfers.

Tatajuba

There are a handful of very simple *pousadas* in this village between Camocim and Jericoacoara. These include:

E Pousada Brisa do Mar, T088-9961 5439 with Spartan and very basic rooms some with en suites. There are plenty of simple seafood restaurants in town, the most famous of which is the **Barraca de Dona Delmira**.

Cruz *p566*

F Hospedaria, R 6 de Abril 314. Very basic, simple little *pousada* with tiny rooms.

F Hotel Magalhães, R Teixeira Pinto 390. Very basic, shared bath, friendly, meals available.

Western Ceará *p567*

D Pousada Doce Lar, R Felipe Sampaio 181, Centro, Itapajé, T085-3346 1432. Clean and comfortable; ask for a room with a mountain view. No restaurant on site but some close by.

Sobral *p567*

A Beira Rio, R Conselheiro Rodrigues 400 across from the *rodoviária*, T088-3613 1040. A/c (cheaper with fan), fridge.

A Visconde, Av Lúcia Saboia 473, 10 mins from the *rodoviária*, T088-3611 4222. Friendly, a/c (cheaper with fan), good breakfast.

B Cisne, Trav do Xerez 215, T/F088-3611 0171. A/c, cheaper with fan, friendly.

B Vitória, Praça Gen Tibúrcio 120, T088-3613 1566. Bath, a/c (cheaper with fan), some rooms without bath (**C**), restaurant.

D Francinet's, R Col Joaquim Ribeiro 294. With fan, bath (cheaper with shared bath).

Chapada de Ibiapaba *p567*

A Serra Grande, about 2 km from town, BR-222, Km 311, T088-3671 1818. All the usual amenities, good.

C Complexo de Lazer Rio's, Viçosa do Ceará, Km 4.5 on the road from Tianguá, T088-3632 1510/1099. Swiss-style chalets, water park, good local food in the restaurant.

Parque Nacional Ubajara *p567*

B-C Pousada da Neblina, Estrada do Teleférico, near the park, 2 km from town, T/F085-3634 1270, www.pousada neblina.com.br. In beautiful cloudforest, swimming pool, with breakfast (cheaper without) and private shower, restaurant open 1100-2000. Meals recommended. Campsite (US$15 per tent).

C Le Village, on Ibiapina road 4 km south from Ubajara town, T085-3634 1364. Restaurant, pool, sauna, good value.

C Pousada Gruta da Ubajara, T088-3634 1375, portalubajara.com.br/pousada gruta.htm almost opposite, close to park entrance, rustic, restaurant.

D Paraíso, in the centre, Ubajara, T085-3634 1728. Reckoned to be the best in town.

D Pousada da Neuza, R Juvêncio Luís Pereira 370, Ubajara, T085-3634 1261. Small restaurant.

D Sítio do Alemão, take Estrada do Teleférico 2 km from town, after the Pousada da Neblina turn right, signposted, 1 km to Sítio Santana, in the coffee plantation of **Herbert Klein** (Caixa Postal 33, Ubajara, CEP 62350-000, T088-9961 4645). Down a path are 3 small chalets with full facilities, and 2 older ones with shared bath (**E**) and views from the breakfast/hammock area to the *sertão*. If the chalets are full Klein may accommodate visitors at the house. No meals other than breakfast but **Casa das Delícias** in Ubajara will send lasagne if necessary (it's owned by Klein's partner). Excursions organized and bicycle hire. Warmly recommended.

South from Ubajara *p568*

B Pousada de Inhuçu, R Gonçalo de Freitas 454, São Benedito, T088-3626 1173. With pool and restaurant.

D Crateús Palace Hotel, Crateús. Very reasonable and clean, with breakfast, good restaurant. **Churrascaria Pequena Cabana** is at the back of the hotel.

E Bar e Churrascaria Pousada da Bica, Ipu, T088-3683 2236. Serves very good, cheap *comida caseira* lunch and has rooms, with breakfast included.

E Hotel Ipu, upper town, Ipu. Basic, friendly. A *pousada* is being built at the SAT *posta* on the exit to Varjota and Sobral; it also has a *churrascaria*.

Cabeço Branco

There are 3 basic *pousadas*: **dos Viajantes** and **São Sebastião**, both contactable through the phone exchange (T088-3826 1150), and **Pousada Gaia**, just behind the cemetery on the road out to Santa Quitéria (T088-3696 1904); ask for Márcia or Honório Júnior. Honório will draw rough walking maps and, if asked, can arrange for the *forró* band to play.

Serra de Baturité *p568*

A Estância Vale das Flores, Sítio São Francisco, Pacoti, T085-3325 1233. Chalets and rooms by the lake, fridge, restaurant, pool, sauna, horse riding. Price includes lunch.

B Remanso Hotel da Serra, 5 km north of Guaramiranga, T088-3325 1222. Bath, restaurant, pool, lake, sports fields.

B Senac Hotel Escola de Guaramiranga, Guaramiranga, T/F088-3321 1106, escola_hotelaria@ce.senac.br. 500 m outside town up a road from the main street, past Parque das Trilhas. Bath, fridge, hot water, restaurant, pool, on top of a hill in an 8-hut estate which includes forest, orchards and an old convent, it doubles as a tourism school. Lots of events held here, so it is often full.

B-C Hofbräuhaus, Estrada de Aratuba, Chapada de Lameirão, Mulungu, T085-3221 6170, www.hofbrauhaus-brasil.com. Run by Wolfgang Helmut Rühle, who has restaurants in Guaramiranga (O Alemão), Pacoti and 2 in Fortaleza; he speaks German, English and Portuguese. Rooms are homely and each one is designed in a different style (Spanish, Arabic, Japanese, etc) with all comforts, very clean and smart. Rooms with veranda cost a little more. Prices are cheaper Mon-Thu (a bargain). The restaurant is German and Cearense. All vegetables and herbs (for all the restaurants) are grown on the property, also has a snail farm for the house speciality. Lots of flowers and grapes, far-reaching views over the *sertão*, mini-disco, small business centre, completely safe. Exceptional.

Quixadá *p569*

C Casa de Reposo São José, Gruta do Pajé, 21 km from Quixadá, T088-3412 0927. A popular hotel run by nuns, with bath.
C Hotel Fazenda Parelhas, Km 133 Rodovia do Algodão, a short distance out of Quixeramobim, just off the Quixadá road, T088-3402 2847/9946 7640, aceterbr @yahoo.com.br. Ricardo Porto is the owner and set this up in 1998 as the first *turismo rural* place in Ceará. Price includes breakfast, full board is US$7.50 extra. Chalets with a/c, TV, fridge and cold water. It's a working sheep and goat farm in the *caatinga*, offering horse rides of 1½-3 hrs, or 30 km to Serra do Caboclo, also pony and trap rides and river bathing.
C Pedra dos Ventos, Near Juatama between Quixadá and Quixeramobim, T088-3451 2028, www.pedradosventos.com.br. Cheaper with fan, all rooms with TV, hot water, fridge. Great views (even at night) as it is built high up on a rock. Good breakfast, pool, 3 trails of 30 mins each, can help with adventure sports. You need a car to get there although the **Redenção** bus passes the turn-off.
D Hotel Fazenda Magé, Km 3 Antiga Estrada de Baturité, T088-3412 0467, nemesio@ quixadanet.com.br. With breakfast in the *fazenda*, all facilities, cold water, cheaper singles with fan. Down a track is the

restaurant which has tables under an overhanging rock, open Sat, Sun and once a month at full moon, has hammocks. The rock has a viewpoint, climbing and abseiling routes, equipment hire US$5.55, plus US$7.40 for instructor.

Juazeiro do Norte *p570, map p570*

Expect prices to be higher during pilgrimages. There are many basic hotels and *hospedarias* for pilgrims on R São José and around Nossa Senhora das Dores basilica.
AL Verde Vales Lazer, Av Plácido Alderado Castelo s.n, Lagoa Seca, 3 km from town on the road to Barbalha, T/F088-3566 2544, www.hotelverdesvales.com.br. A resort housed in a large modern mansion house next to a water park on the edge of the city. The 97 rooms are in the annexe – spread along long corridors. All are modern, spruce and orientated to both families and business travellers. Facilties include a games room, pool, internet access, tennis courts, sauna and restaurant.
B-C Panorama, Santo Agostinho 58, T088-3566 3150, www.panoramhotel.com.br. An 8-storey tower conveniently located in the centre of the city with great views from the upper floors. Rooms are simple but fairly well- appointed and with decent beds. The best are the 5 suites. There's a tiny, unappealing pool, restaurant and internet access.
C-D Plaza, Padre Cícero 148, T088-3511 0493. With bath, a/c, cheaper with fan and cheaper still with shared bath.
D Hotel Aristocrata, R São Francisco 402, T088-3511 1889. A very simple family-run 2-star option in the city centre, with a/c rooms, the cheapest without fridges and a small restaurant.
D San Felipe, Av Dr Floro Bartolomeu 285, T088-3511 7904, www.sanfelipehotel.com.br. A range of plain but recently refurbished a/c rooms in a little concrete block in the town centre. Those on the upper floors have with a good view of Padre Cicero's statue.

Excursions from Juazeiro do Norte *p571*
A Hotel das Fontes, Balneário do Caldas, T088-3532 9066, with bath, fridge, restaurant.
B-D Crato, R Bárbara de Alencar 668, near Praça Cristo Rei, Crato, T088-3521 2824. A friendly hotel with bath, a/c, cheaper with fan, restaurant.

Eating

Fortaleza *p555, map p556*
Iracema and Dragão do Mar
Two good areas for restaurants, with plenty of variety. There are many eateries of various styles at the junction of **Tabajaras** and **Tremembés**, mostly smart.
¶ **Amici's**, R Dragão do Mar 80. Pasta, pizza and lively atmosphere in music-filled street, evenings only. Some say it's the best at the cultural centre.
¶ **Colher do Pau**, R Tabajaras 412, Iracema. Daily from 1830. *Sertaneja* food, seafood, indoor and outdoor seating, live music. Recommended.
¶ **Estoril**, R dos Tabajaras 397, Iracema. Varied food in this landmark restaurant, which is also a catering school.
¶ **Romagna Mia**, R Joaquim Alves 160. Very good fresh seafood, pasta and genuine thin crust Italian pizza made by an Italian ex-pat resident of at least 20 years and served in a little garden shaded by vines tiled with mock-Copacabana dragon's tooth paving.
¶ **Sobre O Mar**, R Rua dos Tremembés 2, T085-3219 6999, www.sobreomardiracema.com.br. The perfect vantage point for watching the sky fade from deep red through to lilac over the pier and the green sea at the end of the day. Sit with an icy batida in hand (the *vodka com abacaxi* is excellent) or a petit gateau with chocolate sauce under your spoon. But eat your main course elsewhere.
¶ **Brazão**, R João Cordeiro corner of Av R Girão, Iracema. The only place open 24 hrs, but the food is not that special.
¶ **Habanera**, R Tabajaras at Ararius, T088-3219 2259. Cuban cigars, great

coffee and pastries or, as they are known in Portuguese, *salgados*. Try the *empadas*.
¶ **Santa Clara Café Orgânico**, R Dragão do Mar 81, at end of red girder walkway (or upstairs depending which way you go), www.santaclara.com.br. Café, delicious organic coffees, juices, cold drinks, plus sandwiches and desserts.

Beaches
Several good fish restaurants at **Praia de Mucuripe**, where the boats come ashore 1300-1500. **R J Ibiapina**, at the Mucuripe end of Meireles, 1 block behind the beach, has pizzerias, fast food restaurants and sushi bars.
¶¶-¶ **La Fiorentina**, Osvaldo Cruz 8, corner of Av Beira Mar, Meireles. Some seafood expensive, but there's also fish, meats and pasta. Unpretentious, attentive waiters, good food, frequented by tourists and locals alike.
¶¶-¶ **Ideal**, Av Abolição e José Vilar, Meireles. Open 0530-2030. Bakery serving lunches, small supermarket and deli, good, handy.

Cumbuco *p563*
Accommodation can be organized through **Hi Life** (see Activities and tours, page 581).

Jericoacoara *p564*
There are several restaurants serving vegetarian and fish dishes.
¶ **Bistrogonoff**, Beco do Guaxelo 60, T088-3669 2220. Fish and meat combinations, stroganoffs and a healthy selection of pastas. Convivial atmosphere, very popular in the evenings. Owners from São Paulo.
¶ **Na Casa Dela**, R Principal, T088-3669 2024. Northeastern Brazilian and Bahian cooking from owners from São Paulo and Rio Grande do Norte, including delicious sun-dried meat with onions, manioc flour, rice and pureed squash. The dining is intimate with tables mood-lit and sitting in the sand under their own private *palapa*. Waitresses are dressed in colourful regional dresses.
¶ **Sky**, R Principal on the beach. A popular sunset bar and evening chill-out space with tables under the stars, mood-music

and decent though somewhat over-priced cocktail standards.

¶ **Do Sapão**, R São Francisco s/n, T088-9905 8010. Good-value *prato feito*, set meals including a delicious vegetarian pizzas and pastas. Live music. Named in homage to the giant toads that appear everywhere in Jeri after dark.

¶ **Kaze Sushi**, R Principal. Decent, fresh sushi and sashimi, miso soups and fruit juices.

Bars and clubs

Fortaleza *p555, map p556*
Fortaleza is renowned for its nightlife and prides itself on having the liveliest Mon night in the country. Some of the best areas for entertainment, with many bars and restaurants are: **Av Beira Mar**, **Praia de Iracema**, the hill above **Praia de Mucuripe** and **Av Dom Luís**. *Forró* is the most popular dance and there is a tradition to visit certain establishments on specific nights. The most popular entertainment areas are the large **Dragão do Mar** complex and the bars just east of the Ponte dos Ingleses and around O Pirata.

Mon *Forró* is danced at the **Pirata Bar**, Iracema, US$5, open-air theme bar, from 2300, and other establishments along R dos Tabajaras and its surroundings.
Tue Live golden oldies at **Boate Oásis**, Av Santos Dumont 6061, Aldeota.
Wed Regional music and samba-reggae at **Clube do Vaqueiro**, city bypass, Km 14, by BR-116 south and E-020, at 2230.
Thu Live music, shows at Pirata and in the adjacent bars.
Fri Singers and bands play regional music at **Parque do Vaqueiro**, BR-020, Km 10, past city bypass.
Sat *Forró* at **Parque Valeu Boi**, R Trezópolis, Cajueiro Torto, **Forró Três Amores**, Estrado Tapuio, Eusêbio and **Cantinho do Céu**, CE-04, Km 8.
Sun *Forró* and *música sertaneja* at **Cajueiro Drinks**, BR-116, Km 20, Eusêbio.

The streets around Centro Cultural Dragão do Mar on R Dragão do Mar are lively every night of the week. Brightly painted, historic buildings house restaurants, where musicians play to customers and the pavements are dotted with cocktail carts.
Caros Amigos, R Dragão do Mar 22. Live music at 2030: Tue, Brazilian instrumental; Wed, jazz; Thu, samba; Sun, Beatles covers, US$1 (also shows music on the big screen).
Restaurant e Crêperie Café Crème, R Dragão do Mar 92. Live music on Tue.

Jericoacoara *p564*
There are frequent parties to which visitors are welcome. About once a week in high season there is a folk dance show that includes *capoeira*. There is nightly *forró* in high season at the **Casa do Forró**, R do Forró, a couple of blocks inland from the beach (low season on Wed and Sat only); starts about 2200. This is the centre of Jeri nightlife, aside from the bars near or along the beach like the European-orientated **Planeta Jeri** on R Principal.

Entertainment

Fortaleza *p555, map p556*
Cinema For information about cinema programming, T139.

Theatre In the centre are **Teatro José de Alencar**, Praça José de Alencar (see page 558), and **Teatro São José**, R Rufino de Alencar 363, T085-3231 5447, both with shows all year.

Festivals and events

Fortaleza *p555, map p556*
6 Jan Epiphany.
Feb Ash Wed.
19 Mar São José.
Jul Last Sun in Jul is the **Regata Dragão do Mar**, Praia de Mucuripe, with traditional

jangada (raft) races. During the last week of Jul, the out-of-season Salvador-style carnival, **Fortal**, takes place along Av Almte Barroso, Av Raimundo Giro and Av Beira Mar. In Caucaia, 12 km to the southeast, a **vaquejada**, traditional rodeo and country fair, takes place during the last weekend of Jul.

15 Aug, the local *umbanda terreiros* (churches) celebrate the **Festival of Iemanjá** on Praia do Futuro, taking over the entire beach from noon till dusk, when offerings are cast into the surf. Well worth attending (members of the public may *'pegar um passo'* – enter into an inspired religious trance – at the hands of a *pai-de-santo*). Beware of pickpockets and purse-snatchers.
Mid-Oct Ceará Music, a 4-day festival of Brazilian music, rock and pop, is held in Marina Park.

Canoa Quebrada *p562*
Jul In the second half of the month is the **Canoarte** festival, which includes a *jangada* regatta and music festival.

Quixada *p569*
12-15 Jun Festa de Santo Antônio.
Aug Festival de Violas e Violeiros is an important music festival drawing participants from near and far.
Sep Grande Vaquejada de Quixeramobim, a typical *sertão* rodeo.

Juazeiro do Norte *p570, map p570*
6 Jan Reis Magos (Epiphany).
2 Feb Candeias (Candelmas), Nossa Senhora da Luz.
24 Mar Padre Cícero's birth and one of the biggest pilgrimages and celebrations of the year.
20 Jul Padre Cícero's death. With up to 300,000 pilgrims from all over the northeast.
10-15 Sep Nossa Senhora das Dores, the city's patron saint.
1-2 Nov Finados, the city receives 600,000 visitors for the All Saints Day pilgrimages.

O Shopping

Fortaleza *p555, map p556*
Bookshops
Livraria Livro Técnico, see Dragão do Mar, page 558. Several branches including on Dom Luís, Praça Ferreira, **Shopping Norte** and at UFC university.
Livraria Nobel bookstore and coffee shop in **Del Paseo** shopping centre in Aldeota.
Siciliano, bookstore and coffee shop in new part of **Iguatemi** shopping mall, with just a bookstore in the old part.

Handicrafts
Fortaleza has an excellent selection of locally manufactured textiles, which are among the cheapest in Brazil, and a wide selection of regional handicrafts. The local craft specialities are lace and embroidered textile goods; hammocks (US$15-100); fine alto-relievo woodcarvings of northeast scenes; basket ware; leatherwork; and clay figures (*bonecas de barro*). Bargaining is okay at the **Mercado Central**, Av Alberto Nepomuceno (closed Sun), and the **Emcetur Centro de Turismo** in the old prison. Crafts also available in shops near the market, while shops on R Dr João Moreira 400 block sell clothes. Every night (1800-2300) there are stalls along the beach at Praia Meireiles. Crafts also available in the commercial area along Av Monsenhor Tabosa.

Shopping centres
The biggest is **Iguatemi**, south of Meireles on way to Centro de Convenções; it also has modern cinemas. Others are **Aldeota** and **Del Paseo** in Aldeota, near Praça Portugal.

▲ Activities and tours

Fortaleza *p555, map p556*
Diving
Projeto Netuno/Manta Diving Center, R Oswaldo Cruz 2453, Dionísio Torres, T085-3264 4114, www.pnetuno.com.br.

Kitesurfing, windsurfing and surfing

Ceará is one of the best palces in the world for kitesurfing and windsurfing. The major centres are **Cumbuco** and **Jericoacoara**. The sport is also popular in **Canoa Quebrada**. Rental equipment can be found at all 3 (see the relevant section, below). In Fortaleza, equipment for kitesurfing and windsurfing can be rented at some of the popular beaches, such as **Porto das Dunas**. Surfing is popular on a number of Ceará beaches. **Bio Board**, Av Beira Mar 914, T085-3242 1642, www.bioboard.com.br. A windsurfing and kitesurfing school Looks after equipment for you.

Hi Life, Av Beira Mar 2120, Praia dos Diários, T085-9982 5449, www.kite-surf-brazil.com. The best kitesurf school in the area (see Cumbuco, below, for further details).

Tour operators

Many operators offer city and beach tours. Others offer adventure trips further afield, most common being off-road trips along the beaches from Natal in the east to the Lençois Maranhenses in the west.
Ceará Saveiro, Av Beira Mar 4293, T085-3263 1085. *Saveiro* and yacht trips, daily 1000-1200 and 1600-1800 from Praia de Mucuripe.
Dunnas Expedições, R Silva Paulet 1100, Aldeota, T085-3264 2514, www.dun nas.com.br. Off-road tours with a fleet of white Land Rovers. Experienced, environmentally and culturally aware, very helpful and professional staff.
Martur, Av Beira Mar 4260, T085-3263 1203. Sailing trips, from Mucuripe, same schedule as Ceará Saveiro.
Sunny Tour, Av Prof A Nunes Freire 4097, Dionísio Torres, T085-3258 2337, also has a stand on Av Beira Mar near the craft fair. Beach tours and trips to Jericoacoara.

Canoa Quebrada *p562*

Kite Flat Water, R Dragão do Mar, T085-9604 4953, www.brasilkiteflatwater.com. Kitesurfing rental and excursions at Canoa Quebrada.

Cumbuco *p563*

Hi Life, Av Dos Coqueiros s/n, Cumbuco, Caucaia, T085-3318 7195, www.kite-surf-brazil.com. One of the leading kitesurf schools in Ceará. Can arrange full tours from Europe and organize hotels in Cumbuco and transfers.

Jericoacoara *p564*

Buggy tours cost US$44.45 for a buggy to all the sites; contact the **Associação de Bugueiros (ABJ)**, R Principal, *barraca* near Ibama. If seeking a *bugueiro* who speaks English, Spanish, Italian and French, ask for Alvaro, the school teacher, who is Uruguayan. **Vila Kalango** and **Peixe Galo**, are orientated to kitesurfers and organize some of the best kitesurf excursions in Jeri.
Clube dos Ventos, R das Dunas, T088-621 0211, www.clubventos.com. Windsurfing and kitesurfing at Preá and Lagoa Jijoca. Equipment hire, courses and transfers.

Quixadá *p569*

Assossiação de Montanhismo e Escalada de Quixadá, Secretário, Henrique Cavalcante, T088-9956 4722. Climbing up to grade VII. Henrique can help with every type of adventure sport, trekking, orienteering and historical information.
Assossiação de Turismo Ecológico (ATEC) Guides US$11 for a day, city tour prices depend on group size.
Sertão and Pedras, R Basílio Pinto 365, Centro, Quixadá, T088-3412 5995, www.sertaoepedras.com.br. A wide range of light adventure activities around Quixada and Fortaleza, including kayaking, canopy walkways, rapelling, rock climbing and treks. The company also offers city tours.

⊘ Transport

Fortaleza *p555, map p556*
Air

To get to the airport, bus No 404 runs from Praça José de Alencar in the centre, US$1. **Expresso Guanabara** minibuses run from the *rodoviária* and Beira Mar (US$2). Taxis to the centre cost US$20, US$25 at night (30 mins, allowing for traffic). **Cooperativa Taxi Comum** or **Taxi Especial Credenciado** are recommended. There are domestic flights to most major cities, as well as **Juazeiro do Norte**. There are regular international flights to **Portugal** (Lisbon), **Italy** (Milan, Rome and Verona) and the **Guianas**.

Airline offices Air Italy, www.airitaly.it. GOL, Av Santos Dumont 2727, Aldeota, T085-3266 8000, freephone T0800-997000, www.voegol.com.br. Oceanair, www.ocean air.com.br. TAF, www.voetaf.com.br. TAM, www.tam.com.br. TAP Air Portugal, www.fly tap.com. Webjet, www.webjet.com.br.

Bus
Local Many city buses run to the *rodoviária* (US$1), including 'Aguanambi' 1 or 2 which go from Av Gen Sampaio, 'Barra de Fátima-Rodoviária' from Praça Coração de Jesus, 'Circular' for Av Beira Mar and the beaches, and 'Siqueira Mucuripe' from Av Abolição. A taxi from Praia de Iracema or Av Abolição costs about US$15.

For the eastern beaches near Fortaleza (**Prainha**, **Iguape**, **Barro Preto**, **Batoque**) and towns such as **Aquiraz**, **Eusêbio** or **Pacajus**, you must take São Benedito buses, T085-3272 2544, from the *rodoviária*. To **Beberibe**, 10 a day US$2. To **Cascavel** US$1.10. To **Morro Branco** at 0745, 1000, 1515, 1750, US$2.25. To **Canoa Quebrada** at 0830, 1100, 1340, 1540 (plus 1730 on Sun) US$4.25. To **Aracati** at 0630, 0830, 1100, 1340, 1540, 1900 last back at 1800, US$3.90.

Long-distance Redenção buses from Fortaleza to **Jericoacoara** from the *rodoviária* 0900, 1700 and the Av Beira Mar at the Posta Telefônica opposite **Praiano Palace Hotel** 30 mins later. The day bus goes via **Jijoca** and the night bus via **Preá**. The journey takes 6 hrs and costs US$15 one way. Always check times of the **Redençao** buses from Fortaleza as they change with the season. The night bus requires an overnight stop in Preá; make your own way

to Jeri next day. A *jardineira* (open-sided 4WD truck) meets the **Redenção** bus from Fortaleza at Jijoca (included in the Redenção price). Several a/c *combis* a day leave from outside the **Casa Blanca hotel** for to **Jeri** via **Jijoca** (US$50, 4 hrs).

Nordeste to **Mossoró**, 10 a day, US$12; to **Natal**, 8 daily, US$25 *semi- leito*, US$30 *executivo*, US$50 *leito*, 7½ hrs; to **João Pessoa**, 2 daily, US$40 *semi-leito*, US$45 *leito*, 10 hrs. **Boa Esperança** stops at Fortaleza on its **Belém–Natal** route. Itapemirim to **Salvador**, US$85, 1900, 23 hrs. Guanabara to **Recife**, 5 daily, US$45 *executivo*, US$60 *leito*, 12 hrs, book early for weekend travel; to **Teresina**, several daily, US$40, *leito* US$50, 10 hrs; to **Parnaíba** US$40; to **Belém**, 2 daily, US$65 *executivo*, 23 hrs; to **São Luís**, 3 daily, US$65, 18 hrs; **Sobral** US$10; **Ubajara** 0800, 1800, return 0800, 1600, 6 hrs, US$12; to **Piripiri** for **Parque Nacional de Sete Cidades**, US$30, 9 hrs, a good stop en route to Belém. Ipu Brasília to **Sobral**, US$14, and to **Camocim**, 1120, 1530; to **Majorlândia**, US$7, **Campina Grande**, US$40, 13 hrs; to **Juazeiro do Norte**, Rio Grande/Rápido Juazeiro, 5 a day from 1230-2145, 8-9 hrs, US$50, *leito* US$90. Redenção to **Quixadá**, many daily, US$7; to **Redentora**, 0600,1200 via Baturité. Redenção to **Almofala** 0700, 1730, US$10; to **Cruz** 0900, 1030, 1630, 1830, US$10. Redenção from *rodoviária* to **Gijoca**, US$12, 1030, 1830 and **Jeri**, 0900, 1830, US$10. Tickets are also sold at the **Posta Telefônica** Beira Mar, on Beira Mar almost opposite **Praiano Palace**.

Bus companies Açailândia, T085-3256 8525; Boa Esperança, T085-3256 5006; Eucatur/União Cascavel, T085-3256 4889, run Pantanal–Palmas, Gontijo–São Paulo, São Gonçalo–Belo Horizonte; Guanabara, T085-3256 0214; Nordeste, T085-3256 2342; Rio Grande/ Rápido Juazeiro, T085-3254 3600; Transbrasiliana, T085-3256 1306.

Car hire
Many car hire places on Av Monsenhor Tabosa: **Amazônia**, No 1055, T085-3219 0800;

Reta, No 1171, T085-3219 5555; **Shop**, No 1181, T085-3219 7788, and many more at the junction with Ildefonso Albano. **Brasil Rent a Car**, Av Abolição 2300, T085-3242 0868, www.brasillocadora.com.br. **Localiza**, Av Abolição 2236, T0800-992020. There are also many buggy rental shops.

The coast east of Fortaleza *p560*
Bus Daily bus service from Fortaleza *rodoviária* to **Prainha**, 11 daily, US$3; to **Iguape**, hourly 0600-1900, US$3. To **Caponga**: direct bus from Fortaleza *rodoviária* (4 a day, US$3) or take a bus from Fortaleza to **Cascavel** (80 mins) then a bus from Cascavel (20 mins); bus information in Caponga T088-3334 1485. For bus information in Fortaleza, **São Benedito**, T088-3272 2544, at *rodoviária*: to **Beberibe**, 10 a day, US$4; to **Cascavel**, US$3; to **Morro Branco**, 0745, 1000, 1515, 1750, US$4; to **Canoa Quebrada**, 0830, 1100, 1340, 1540 (plus 1730 Sun), US$7; to **Aracati**, more than 10 per day first at 0500, last at 1900, last back at 1800, US$7; onward connections from Arati to **Natal** (at least 10 per day), **Recife** (2 per day), **Salvador** (1 per day). **Natal–Aracati** bus via **Mossoró**, 6 hrs, US$7.50; from Mossoró (90 km) US$2.50, 2 hrs; **Fortaleza–Aracati** (142 km), besides São Benedito, Guanabara or Nordeste many daily, US$7, 2 hrs; Aracati to **Canoa Quebrada** from Gen Pompeu e João Paulo, US$3; taxi US$15.

Pecém and Taíba *p564*
Bus There are 11 daily buses to **Fortaleza** and 4 daily buses to **Siupé**.

Paracuru and Lagoinha *p564*
Bus There are 8 daily buses to **Fortaleza** *rodoviária*, US$3 to **Paracuru**. For information contact T085-272 4483 (in Fortaleza).

Jericoacoara *p564*
Bus Redenção buses to **Fortaleza**, twice daily at 1400 (via **Preá**) and 2230 (via **Jijoca**). The journey takes 6 hrs and costs US$15 one way. Always check times of the Redençao

buses as they change with the season. A *jardineira* (4WD truck) meets the bus and transfers to **Jijoca** (included in the price). *Combis* also run to **Fortaleza** via Jijoca, US$50, 4 hrs.

If heading to **Belém** (US$28.25, 20 hrs) or other points north and west, take the *jardineira* to **Jijoca**, from where buses run to **Cruz**. In Cruz, you can change for **Sobral**; there is only one bus a day Cruz–Sobral, US$7.25, 3-4 hrs, but Redenção runs from Cruz to **Fortaleza** several times daily, US$6.40.

To get to **Parnaíba**, take a Toyota to **Camocim** (US$10) from leaving at around 0900; book through your hotel or ask around for buggy or *jardineira* (US$25 per person).

Motorcycle If on a motorcycle, it is not possible to ride from Jericoacoara to **Jijoca** (unless you have an excellent scrambler). Safe parking for bikes in Jijoca is not a problem.

Cruz *p566*
Bus The bus to **Jijoca** goes through town at about 1400, US$4 or US$7 to **Jericoacoara**, wait for the bus by 1330. To **Jijoca** daily at about 1400, US$1.25; the bus meets *jardineira* for Jericoacoara (US$2.20). Alternatively, take an *horário* pick-up from Cruz to **Jijoca**.

Chapada de Ibiapaba *p567*
Bus To **Fortaleza** US$8; to **Belém** US$30.

Serra de Baturité *p568*
Bus From **Baturité**, there are 4 Redentora buses a day to **Fortaleza** *rodoviária*, 3 hrs. To **Guaramiranga** Mon-Fri 0830, daily 1030, 1700, also to **Aratuba**. Pinheiro, T085-3256 3729, also runs to **Guaramiranga** and **Aratuba**.

Quixadá *p569*
Bus Redenção bus to **Fortaleza** *rodoviária*, many daily, 3 hrs, US$7. Redentora, to **Fortaleza** 0600, 1200 via **Baturité**. Redenção to **Quixeramobim**, 4 hrs, US$9.

Juazeiro do Norte *p570, map p570*

Air A taxi to the airport from the centre costs US$5.75; US$2 by motorcycle taxi. There are flights to **Brasília**, **Fortaleza**, **Recife**, **Rio de Janeiro** and **São Paulo** (Guarulhos), with Gol, www.voegoel.com.br and Oceanair, www.oceanair.com.br.

Bus To **Fortaleza** with Rio Negro, 2 daily, US$17 *convencional*, US$35 *executivo*, 8 hrs. To **Picos** with Boa Esperança, 2 daily, US$5.75, 5 hrs. To **Teresina** with Boa Esperança, Progresso or Aparecida, 3 daily, US$16, 11 hrs. To **São Luís** with Progresso, US$20, 16 hrs. To **Belém** with Boa Esperança, 1 daily (often full), US$70, 25 hrs. To **Campina Grande** with Transparaiba, 2 daily, US$25, 9 hrs. To **João Pessoa** with Braga, 1 daily, US$50, 10 hrs. To **Recife** with Braga, 1 daily, US$35, 11 hrs. To **Salvador** with Itapermirim, 2 weekly, US$17.50, 14 hrs. To **São Paulo** with Itapemirim, 1 daily, US$90, 40 hrs.

Car hire IBM, Santo Agostinho 58, T088-3511 0542. **Localiza**, at the airport and at Av Padre Cícero Km 3, No 3375, T088-3571 2668. **Unidas**, Av Padre Cícero, Km 2 on road to Crato, T088-3571 1226.

🛈 Directory

Fortaleza *p555, map p556*
Banks Bradesco, Av Pontes Vieira 357, and Av Santos Dumont 2110, for international ATM. Banco do Brasil, R Barão do Rio Branco 1500, also on Av Abolição (high commission on TCs). Banco Mercantil do Brasil, R Mayor Facundo 484, Centro, Praça do Ferreira, cash against MasterCard. Exchange at **Tropical Viagens**, R Barão do Rio Branco 1233, T085-3221 3344, English spoken. Libratur, Av Abolição 2194, T085-3248 3355, Mon-Fri 0900-1800, Sat 0800-1200 Recommended. More *câmbios* on Av Mons Tabosa: eg TourStar, No 1587, **Sdoc**, No 1073, T085-3219 7993. **Embassies and consulates** France, R Bóris 90, Centro, T085-3254 2822. Germany, R Dr Lourenço

2244, Meireles, T085-3246 2833, gja435@ sec.secrel.com.br. **Italy**, R E 80, Parque Wáshington Soares, T085-3273 2606. Netherlands, Av Pe Antônio Tomás 386, T085-3461 2331. UK, c/o Grupo Edson Queiroz, Praça da Imprensa s/n, Aldeota, T085-3466 8888. US, Nogueira Acioli 891, Centro, T085-3252 1539. **Internet** Many internet cafés around the city. Beira Mar Internet Café, Av Beira Mar 2120A, Meireles, US$2.60 per hr also international phones. Cyber Net, Av Beira Mar 3120 in small mall, smart, US$2.20 per hr. Internet Express, R Barão de Aracati opposite Colonial Praia, opens 0800. **Laundry** Laundromat, Av Abolição 3038, Meireles. **Medical services** Instituto Dr José Frota (IJF), R Barão do Rio Branco 1866, T085-3255 5000, recommended public hospital. **Post office** Main branch at R Senador Alencar 38, Centro; Av Monsenhor Tabosa 1109 and 1581, Iracema; at train station; opposite the *rodoviária*. Parcels must be taken to Receita Federal office at Barão de Aracati 909, Aldeota (take 'Dom Luís' bus). **Telephone** International calls from Emcetur hut on Iracema beach and from **Telemar** offices: R Floriano Peixoto 99, corner of R João Moreira, Centro; also at *rodoviária* and airport.

Coast east of Fortaleza *p560*
Banks Canoa Quebrada has a Banco do Brasil ATM but these do not usually accept international cards. **Aracati** has money changers, banks and international ATMs.

Jericoacoara *p564*
Internet There are plenty of internet cafés in town but no banks.

Juazeiro do Norte *p570, map p570*
Banks Banco do Brasil, R São Francisco, near Praça Pradre Cícero, poor rates, Mon-Fri 1100-1600, **Bradesco**, R Conceição 503, Centro T088-3512 2830 and at R Sta Luzia 321, T088-3512 2966. No *câmbios* in town. **Post office** R Conceição 354 and at *rodoviária*. **Telephone** R São Pedro 204, half a block from Praça Padre Cícero and at *rodoviária*.

Piauí

But for a sliver of coast Piauí is dry sertão, pocked with jagged hills cut by canyons and dotted with weather-worn ancient mounds of rock. Few tourists stop here, but those that do seldom regret it. Torrid Teresina is a friendly and well-planned capital where foreigners are a curiosity, Parnaíba is a pretty colonial river port, and the dry interior is broken by a number of stunning and intriguing state and national parks. These include the enigmatic Serra da Capivara, Sete Cidades and the almost inaccessible Serra dos Confusões, beehive mounds sticking up out of the desert whose canyon walls are daubed with some of the oldest rock art in the Americas. And while Piauí's coast is tiny it includes the magnificent Delta do Parnaíba: one of the largest river deltas in the world, replete with mangrove swamps and tiny islands fringed with golden beaches and home to traditional communities who seldom see tourists. After neighbouring Maranhão, Piauí is the poorest state in Brazil. Its population is about 2.7 million, but many leave to seek work elsewhere. The economy is almost completely dependent upon agriculture and livestock, both of which in turn depend on how much rain, if any, falls. *For listings, see pages 591-594.*

Background

The state's long, thin, wineskin shape derives from its history and the course of the Parnaíba river, which winds 1480 km through the arid *sertão* to the Piauí coast. Piauí is the only state to have been founded from the interior rather than as a coastal port. It was initially explored from the Bahia and Pernambuco through the sertão by 18th-century ranchers looking for fresh pasture land. Long forgotten colonial towns such as Oerias date from this period. Other towns sprung up along the Parnaíba river, like Floriano, Amarante and, in 1852, Teresina. The latter remains the only northeastern capital to lie inland. The river's delta eventually became the coastal frontier of the state.

Until the early 19th century Piauí was under the control of neighbouring Maranhão. At Independence, there was bitter, bloodthirsty fighting between supporters of the Portuguese colony and the Brazilians who sought their freedom. And well into the 20th century Piauí maintained a strong tradition of Portuguese-inspired *Coronelismo*, see box page 544, whose vestiges persist to this day.

Teresina ⬤🅿️❄️⬤⬤⬤ » *pp591-594. Colour map 2, A3.*

→ *Phone code: 086. Population: 716,000.*

Piauí's capital is a pleasant friendly city with abundant woodland, some attractive colonial buildings and the usual gamut of Brazilian concrete apartment blocks. It lies about 350 km from the coast, at the confluence of the Rio Poti and the Rio Parnaíba. It is flat with a grid of streets, some of which are lined with handsome terracotta roofed 19th-century buildings. There are more than 30 urban parks. The city was founded in the 18th century as the Vila do Poti and was renamed in honour of the empress of Brazil and wife of Dom Pedro II, Teresa Cristina, who had supported the idea of moving the capital from Oreias. Teresina has a lively cultural scene and a famously vibrant nightlife. The city itself is reputed to be the hottest after Cuiabá, with temperatures up to 42°C and an annual mean of around 30°C.

Ins and outs

The **Senador Petrônio Portela airport** ⓘ *5 km from the centre, Av Centenário s/n, T086-3133 6270*, receives flights from Fortaleza, Brasília, Rio de Janeiro, São Paulo, Goiâna and São Luís. Outside the airport, buses run straight into town and to the *rodoviária*. The **rodoviária** is 4 km the centre. There are buses running into the town every few minutes. There are direct bus connections with Fortaleza (a scenic nine-hour journey), Belém, Recife and São Luís. ▶▶ *See Transport, page 594.*

For tourist information, there are several offices of **Piemtur** ⓘ *R Álvaro Mendes 2003, Caixa Postal 36; R Magalhães Filho, next to 55 N; and R Acre, Convention Centre, T086-3221 7100*. There are also kiosks at the *rodoviária* and the airport. The **Sindicato dos Guiás de Turismo de Piauí (Singtur)** ⓘ *R Paissandu 1276, T086-3221 2175*, has information booths at the Centro de Artesanato, Praça Dom Pedro II (helpful, friendly), the Encontro das Águas, Poty Velho and on the shores of the Rio Poty. Another office is **Ana Turismo** ⓘ *R Álvaro Mendes 1961, Centro, T/F086-3221 2272. The website www.teresina.pi.gov.br* is also a useful source of information.

Sights

Praça Pedro II lies at the heart of the city and is the hub of Teresina life. There are many bars and restaurants in the surrounding streets, where diners are frequently serenaded by *violeiros* (Brazil's equivalent of *mariachis*). Many *violeiros* also congregate at the **Casa do Cantador** ⓘ *R Lucia 1419, Vermelha, T086-3211 6833, 1400-2000, Wed is the best night*, a little *boteco* outside the city centre surrounded by mangroves. There is live poetry, a gallery of art and shows at the **Oficina da Palavra** ⓘ *R Benjamin Constant 1400, Centro, T086-3223 4441, www.oficinadapalavra-pi.com.br, Mon-Fri 0800-1200 and 1400-2000, Sat and Sun 0800-1200*. The centre has some attractive buildings including the **Teatro 4 Setembro** and the old art deco cinema, the **Rex**. There's a decent crafts market at the **Central do Artenasato**, which is well-known for its opals, carved wood and hammocks. The **Museu do Piauí** ⓘ *Praça Marechal Deodoro s/n, Tue-Fri 0730-1730, Sat and Sun 0800-*

Teresina

Sleeping		
Formula Flat Europa 5	Luxor Piauí 6	Rio Poty 7
	Real Palace 1	Sambaíba 3

Cabeça-de-Cuia

Crispim was a fisherman who lived in Teresina, at the confluence of the rivers Poti and Parnaíba. One day, returning home after a hard day's fishing with no catch whatsoever, he discovered that there was no food in the house. Infuriated, he grabbed a large bone which was lying nearby and beat his mother to death. Her dying curse was that Crispim should live out his days as a hideous monster with an enormous head.

A young and single man, Crispim was driven to despair by his now terrifying appearance. He drowned himself in the Parnaíba. Legend has it that Crispim's life and good looks will be restored when he has managed to eat seven virgins named Maria. Young laundresses, when they go to the river, are still afraid of him.

Cabeça-de-Cuia means 'head of a gourd'. Carvings of this strange figure are a common sight in Teresina.

1200, US$1.50, is in a mansion house dating from 1859 and has been completely refurbished. It preserves a collection of sacred art by local artists from the 19th century, as well as impressive woodcarvings by Mestre Dezinho Nonato de Oliveira and an extensive collection of frowsty fossils. The **Palácio de Karnak** ① *just west of Praça Frei Serafim, T086-3221 9820, Mon-Sat 0800-1800 (visits to the inside of the palace by appointment only)*, is a grand neoclassical edifice set in pretty gardens landscaped by Roberto Burle Marx, and has been the governor's palace since 1926. Inside is a collection of period furniture and artefacts and a rare set of lithographs of the Middle East in 1839 by the Scottish artist David Roberts, famous for his depictions of unexcavated temples throughout the Middle East and most notably in Egypt. The **Casa da Cultura** ① *R Rui Barbosa 348, Centro, T086-3215 7849, Mon-Fri 0800-1900, Sat 0900-1300, Sun 1300-1600*, is devoted to the history of the city and to the lives of famous ex-residents such as the journalist Carlos Castelo Branco and the photographer Jose de Medeiros. The reception desk has a programme of cultural events taking place in Teresina.

Every morning along the picturesque river, with washing laid out to dry on its banks, is the *troca-troca* (market), where people buy, sell and swap. Most of the year the rivers are low, leaving sandbanks known as *coroas* (crowns). The confluence of the two rivers is at the **Parque Encontro dos Rios** ① *Av Boa Esperanca s/n, Poti Velho, T086-3217 5020, daily 0800-1800*, where there is a statue of the Cabeça de Cuia river demon, Crispim, see box above). Canoes are available for hire on the river.

Around Teresina ●▲▸ *pp591-594*.

Parque Nacional de Sete Cidades → *Colour map 2, A3.*
Some 190 km northeast of Teresina, this interesting 6221 ha park has strange eroded rock formations which, from the ground, look like a medley of weird monuments. They are grouped into *cidades* (cities), each of which holds a different view. The best is from Segunda Cidade, especially in the late afternoon when the golden light brings out the panoply of colours on the rocks and casts haunting shadows. Inscriptions on some of the rocks have never been deciphered and are thought to be from between 5000 and 10,000 years old. One theory suggests links with the Phoenicians, and the Argentine Professor Jacques de Mahieu considers them to be Nordic runes left by the Vikings.

With 22 springs, the park is an oasis in the dry surroundings and forms a transition zone between *caatinga* vegetation and *cerrado*. There is abundant wildlife including white-tailed deer, paca, various armadillos, tamandua anteaters and well over 100 bird species, some of them rare *sertão* endemics. Large iguanas descend from the trees in the afternoon.

The park spans 12 km and can be walked across in a long day, beginning at the Portaria Sul (south gate) and finishing at the Portaria Norte (north gate). Trails are well signposted, but beware of rattlesnakes when hiking.

Ins and outs The park is 26 km northeast of the little town of Piripiri on the BR-343. There are buses to Piripiri from Parnaíba and Teresina as well as Fortaleza, Ubajara and São Luís (though these buses have many stops). From Piripiri there is an **Ibama** bus direct to the park at 0700 daily, from by the Telemar office in front of the Praça da Bandeira (it is ostensibly for employees, but usually possible to hitch a ride). The bus passes in front of the **Hotel Fazenda Sete Cidades** at 0800, reaching the park 10 minutes later; it returns at 1630. *Moto-táxis* in Piripiri charge (US$10) to the park, or a standard taxi costs US$20.

If coming from Parnaíba, Barreirinhas (in the Lençóis Maranhenses) or Jericoacoara, agencies such as **Eco Dunas**, offer trips often as part of an interstate transfer.▸▸ *See Activities and tours, page 608.*

The park is open daily 0800-1700. There is accommodation in Piripiri and right next to the park. Information and maps are available from **Ibama** ① *Av Homero Castelo Branco 2240, Teresina, T086-3343 1342, www.ibama.com.br*. Another useful website is www2.uol.com.br/mochilabrasil/setecidades.shtml.

Parnaíba and around ●●●●● ▸▸ *pp591-594. Colour map 2, A3.*

→ *Phone code: 086. Population: 133,000.*

Parnaíba makes a good break in the journey north or south. It's a relaxed, friendly place, with a pretty colonial centre overlooking the Parnaíba river. If crossing the delta, buy all provisions here. There are beaches at **Luís Correia**, 14 km from Parnaíba, with radioactive sands. About 18 km from Parnaíba is **Pedra do Sal**, with dark blue lagoons and palm trees. At **Lagoa de Portinho**, 12 km from Parnaíba, there are bungalows, a bar, restaurant and canoes for hire; it is possible to camp. **Praia do Coqueiro** is a small fishing village with natural pools formed at low tide. Seafood is good at **Alô Brasil** and **Bar da Cota**.

Ins and outs The **rodoviária** ① *5 km south of centre on BR-343, T086-3323 7300*, has bus connections with São Luís, Tutóia (for the Lençóis Maranhenses), Piripiri (for Parque Nacional da Sete Cidades) and Camocim (for Jericoacoara). Buses marked Praça João Luíz run to the centre; taxi US$6. About 14 km from the town centre, on the Parnaíba river, is the Porto dos Tatus, where boats leave for the delta.▸▸ *See Transport, page 594.*

For tourist information contact **Piemtur** ① *R Dr Oscar Clark 575, T086-3321 1532*; there is another branch at **Porto da Barca**, a pleasant shopping and entertainment complex in the colonial centre, with several good restaurants and an open-air bar on the riverside.

Delta do Parnaíba

The Delta do Parnaíba, which separates Piauí from Tutóia (see page 602) and the spectacular Lençóis Maranhenses (see page 600) in neighbouring Maranhão, is one of the largest river deltas in the world. It's a watery labyrinth of mangroves, broad rivers and narrow creeks, with unspoilt tropical islands fringed by gorgeous deserted beaches. The interiors of these islands are home to largely unstudied wildlife, including many rare birds, and traditional Caiçara fishing communities, who seldom see tourists. Renting hammock space with them is straightforward and simple make-shift *pousada* accommodation can be arranged. Many people in this region live as they have done for generations, in adobe houses, on a diet of fresh fish cooked in baked-earth ovens. Illiteracy is the norm. There is no mains electricity and the nearest shopping is at Parnaíba or Tutóia.

Ins and outs Crossing the delta is no longer possible by public ferry, but it's possible to charter a launch (up to 12 people, US$175) in Tutóia or at Porto dos Tatus (also called Porto da Barca), 10 km north of Parnaíba. Recommended boatmen include **Capitão Báu** ⓘ *T086-3323 0145, T086-8831 9581 (mob)*. Alternatively, take a boat from Parnaíba to the crab-fishing village of Morro do Meio on Ilha das Canarias (Monday at high tide, usually in the small hours). It is sometimes possible to hitch a lift from Ilha das Canarias to Tutóia with a crab fisherman. It's more interesting and better value to cross the delta rather than returning to the same place, but allow plenty of time. ▶▶ *See Transport, page 594.*

Tours can be arranged from Parnaíba for US$30-50 per person (minimum four people) with **Clipe Turismo** ⓘ *Av Presidente Vargas 274, Loja 01, Centro, Parnaíba, T086-3322 3129, www.clipecoturismo.com.br.* Day trips also run from Porto dos Tatus, either on a huge boat full of noisy people or a smaller launch. The former include food and drink and cost around US$15 per person. The latter are by charter only (US$250-300 for up to six).

Ilha do Caju → *Population: 70. Www.ilhadocaju.com.br.*
ⓘ *Trips are arranged through Pousada Ecológica Ilha do Caju, see Sleeping, page 592.*
This beautiful island, named after the extensive stands of cashew tree that fringe its shores, has an astonishing variety of terrain, with lakes, forest, marshes and an expanse of white dunes to the northwest. It has remained virtually unchanged for four centuries, thanks in part to the conservation efforts of the Englishman James Frederick Clark, who stumbled here in 1847. The whole island is environmentally protected and no chemical pesticides are used.

Much of the water, including the sea, is *salobre* (a mixture of fresh and salt). Swimming from the vast, shimmering beach through the currents of alternating sea and river water is a recommended experience. There are lakes on the island, caused by flooding, in which trees that have been killed by the brine content stand bleached and knotted – an unnerving image of lifelessness surrounded by vigorous vegetation. Walking through the forest surrounding the lake is magical: nesting herons, ospreys and kingfishers take off in clouds of flashing green; tiny, long-legged jacanas and gallinules hop from leaf to leaf on the water lilies; and myriad butterflies hover around your head.

Southern Piauí ⬤⊗▲◉ ▶▶ *pp591-594.*

Oeiras
The old capital of Piauí, 320 km from Teresina, is a pretty colonial treasure almost completely unknown to most Brazilians – let alone international tourists. The state government is restoring some of the colonial buildings, such as the bishop's palace and the church of Nossa Senhora da Vitória. There are some impressive celebrations during holy week, including a huge fireworks display and costumed parade on Maundy Thursday, serenaded by local mandolin players.

Parque Nacional Serra da Capivara → *Colour map 2, B3.*

ⓘ *35 km from São Raimundo Nonato. The agency Trilhas da Capivara, T089-3582 1294, trilhascapivara@uol.com.br, runs excursions from US$40. For the most up-to-date information on transport and logistics, contact Fundham, below.*

About 500 km south of Teresina is this 130,000-ha park, on the UNESCO World Heritage list. Some 30,000 prehistoric rock paintings on limestone have been found, dating from between 6000 and 12,000 years ago. The paintings are of daily life, festivities and celebrations, as well as hunting and sex scenes. Excavations by Brazilian and French archaeologists have uncovered fossilized remains of extinct animals such as the sabre-toothed tiger, giant sloths larger than elephants and armadillos the size of a car.

Nearly 400 archaeological sites have been identified in the park since research began in 1970. About 22 of them have been set up to receive tourists. Roads and all-weather paths allow visitors to view the sites with ease. Specially trained guides are available. The area is good for hiking in the *caatinga*, with its canyons and mesas. It is also possible to see much of the *caatinga* wildlife, in particular the birds.

Much investment has gone into the park, not just for visitors' facilities, but also to educate the local population about protecting the paintings and to establish a bee-keeping project to provide income in times of drought.

São Raimundo Nonato

São Raimundo Nonato is best known as the administration centre and access point for the Parque Nacional Serra Da Capivara. The **Fundação Museu do Homem Americano** (**Fundham**) ⓘ *Centro Cultural Sérgio Motta, Bairro Campestre, T089-3582 1612, www.fumd ham.org.br,* has a fascinating collection of artefacts found in the *serra*. These are well displayed, though the information in English is poor. In September, the city hosts the **Festival Internacional Serra da Capivara** with music, theatre and parades.

There are bus connections with Teresina (a bumpy 540-km journey) and Petrolina in Pernambuco (300 km away).

Parque Nacional Serra dos Confusões

The largest and most remote national park in northeastern Brazil covers over 5000 sq km of rugged weather-beaten sandstone escarpments and towering crags surrounded by *cerrado* and *caatinga* forests. Like the Serra da Capivara to the north, its canyons and caves are covered in rock art. The park is replete with rare and endangered wildlife – particularly birds. Species include puma, jaguar, pampas deer, red-handed howler monkey yellow-legged tinamou and black-fronted piping-guan,

The park is 640 km south of Teresina. There is currently no administration or infrastructure. Although it is not officially open to tourism, visits are possible. Guides can be organized in the nearby *sertão* town of Caracol.

Parque Nacional das Nascentes do Parnaíba and hyacinth site

This huge 733,162-ha park in the far south of Piauí, straddling the border with Tocantins, Maranhão and Bahia, preserves pristine areas of *cerrado* and *caatinga* forest. Ochre table-top mountains covered in waterfalls form part of the ancient rocks of the Brazilian shield. The wildlife is exuberant, including more than 60 mammal species and 211 birds – many of them endemic or endangered.

In the far southwest of the park, 20 km from **São Gonçalo do Piauí**, is the best place in the world for seeing the very rare **hyacinth macaw**. The hyacinth site is on private land in a region of *cerrado* with red sandstone cliffs where the macaws nest. An illegal bird trade used to flourish in the area, but local people now guard the site, which is supported by the **Kaytee Avian Foundation** and others. Many other *cerrado* birds may be seen, together with black-and-gold howlers and, less commonly, maned wolves and giant anteaters.

Accommodation is in very simple huts with mosquito nets, sand floors and shared bathrooms. Meals are served at the site. Access is via the airport at **Barreiras** (see page 563) in western Bahia, 340 km south, and a five- to six-hour drive. Currently tours are only possible through **Focus Tours**, www.focustours.com.

◎ Piauí listings

For Sleeping and Eating price codes and other relevant information, see pages 42-47.

● Sleeping

Teresina *p585, map p586*
There are many cheap places on R São Pedro and R Alvaro Mendes. The cleanest and best is **Glória**, No 823, blocks 800 and 900. There are other cheap hotels and *dormitórios* around Praça Saraiva.
AL-A Rio Poty, Av Mcal Castelo Branco 555, Ilhota, T086-4009 4009, www.riopoty.com. 5 stars. One of the better options in town with rooms in a large concrete Benidorm-style block overlooking a big swimming pool.
B Real Palace, R Areolino de Abreu 1217, T086-2107 2700, www.realpalacehotel.com.br. Business orientated hotel with a range of old-fashioned rooms and suites and a small business centre.
B-C Luxor Piauí, Praça Mal Deodoro 310, Centro, T086-3221 3306, www.luxor.com.br. Business hotel with small, simply appointed rooms with a bed, desk and armchair squeezed in. The hotel has a business centre with broadband and a small pool.
B-C Sambaíba, R Gabriel Ferreira 230-N, T086-3222 3460. A functional 2-star with very simple a/c rooms.
C Formula Flat Europa, R José Olímpio de Melo 3330, Ilhotas, T086-3223 7100,

www.formulaflateuropa.com.br. Bright, modern and well appointed flats with microwaves, kitchenettes and living areas. Space for up to 3 people making this an **E-F** option per person.
D Santa Teresinha, Av Getúlio Vargas 2885, opposite the *rodoviária*, T086-3211 0919. With a/c or fan, clean, friendly.

Parque Nacional de Sete Cidades *p587*
Piripiri, 26 km from the park, is a cheap place to break the Belém–Fortaleza journey. As well as those listed, there are other options near bus offices and behind the church.
C-D Fazenda Sete Cidades, 8 km from the park entrance, T086-3276 2222. A converted farmhouse with large though simple fan-cooled and a/c rooms, horse riding, river water swimming pools and a play area for kids.
C-D Parque Hotel Sete Cidades, Km 63 on BR-222, 6 km from the park entrance, T086-9424 0024, www.hotelsetecidades.com.br. Tile-floor chalets with private bath and room for 3-4 (in double beds). Natural river-water swimming pool, good restaurant and bicycle or horse transport; also has a free pickup to the park (and a most unpleasant zoo). At the bottom end of this price range.
D-E Hotel Rodoviário I and **Hotel Rodoviário II**, in front of the terminal *rodoviária* Luiz Menezes, Piripiri, T086-8819 3299. Pink concrete blocks hiding a series

of very simple fan-cooled or a/c rooms with shared baths or en suites. Convenient for transit passengers.

E Hotel California, R Dr Antenor de Araujo Freitas 546, Piripiri, T086-3276 1645. There's plenty of room in the Hotel California, with 32 rooms all with a/c and en suites. 24-hr reception so you can check out any time you want. Convenient for the 0700 bus to the park from nearby Praça da Bandeira.
E Ibama hostel, in the park, T086-3343 1342. Price per person. Rooms with bath, pleasant, good restaurant, natural pool nearby, camping. Recommended. Not open all year round, so book ahead or check with Ibama, www.ibama.com.br, in Teresina.

Parnaíba and around p588
AL-A Pousada dos Ventos, Av São Sebastião 2586, Universidade, T086-3322 2555, www.pousadadosventos.com.br. The best business hotel in town, a 10-min taxi ride from the centre, with spacious, simple rooms and an attractive breakfast area next to the pool.
C Pousada Chalé Suiço, Av Padre R J Vieira 448, Fátima, T086-3321 3026, www.chale suico.com.br. Cheaper without a/c or breakfast, bar, laundry, pool, tours arranged, windsurfing, sandboarding, buggies and bikes.
C Pousada das Barcas, R do Comércio 100, T086-3321 2718, www.pousadaportodas barcas.com.br. The best in town, with rooms arranged in a charming 17th-century building in the old colonial centre right next to the river. Lots of arty little shots and cafés here. The best area to stay in.
D-E Igaraçu, R Almirante Gervasio Sampaio 390, T086-3322 3342. Right next to **Bradesco** bank, 5 mins walk from the centre. Very plain rooms, some with no windows, and with only a chair and table for furniture gathered around a scruffy courtyard. The best are the a/c doubles with bunks (these have firmer mattresses).
D-E Residencial, R Almirante Gervásio Sampaio 375, T086-3322 2931, www.residencial

pousada.com.br. Very plain, simple doubles, dorms and plusher en suites with cold water showers gathered around a plant-filled courtyard. There are many other basic hotels nearby in the centre.

Delta do Parnaíba p588
F Ilha das Canarias, Morro do Meio Caiçara Comunidade. Bring a hammock and ask at the **Raimundo Aires** restaurant (US$15 per person per night) great fish in the restaurant and idyllic beaches nearby. Very simple, no showers – just the river.

Ilha do Caju p589
A Pousada Ecológica Ilha do Caju, contact: Av Presidente Vargas 235, Centro, Parnaíba, T086-3321 1179, www.ilhadocaju.com.br. Comfortable rustic cabins, each has its own hammock outside, but inside there is a huge bed, handmade by the same craftsmen who made much of the *pousada*'s highly individual furniture. The owner, Ingrid, and senior staff speak English and are helpful and welcoming. Children must be aged 14 or over. The *pousada* will organize all transfers.

Oeiras p589
D-E Pousada do Cônego, Praça das Vitórias 18, Centro, T089-3462 1219. Very simple hotel housed in a large and somewhat decrepit town house and a small pizza restaurant with tables on the sunny veranda under the shade of tropical trees.

Parque Nacional Serra da Capivara p590
D Serra da Capivara, Estrada PI-140 exit for Teresina, Km 2, T089-3582 1389. Intimate country hotel near the park, with a pool and 18 a/c cabins and a restaurant.

São Raimundo Nonato p590
D Pousada Lelinha, R Dr Barroso 249, Aldeia, T089-3582 2993, www.lelinha pousada.com.br. One of the better

options in the town with large, airy rooms the biggest of which have room for up to 5. Breakfasts are generous and the staff can give advice on visiting the *serra*.
D Pousada Zabelê, Praça Major Toinho 280, Centro, T089-3582 2726. Simple standard town hotel with a range of fan-cooled and a/c rooms. Helpful staff.

Parque Nacional Serra dos Confusões *p590*
D-E Hotel Pousada Caracol, Praça Aristídes Dias, s/n, Centro, T089-3589 1132. Very simple hotel with plain rooms and fan-cooled and a/c rooms.

🍴 Eating

Teresina *p585, map p586*
There are many places for all budgets around Praça Dom Pedro II.
🍴🍴🍴 **Camarão do Elias**, Av Pedro Almeida 457, T086-3232 5025. Best restaurant in the city, with fish and prawn dishes. Try the fish of the day in caper and lemon sauce.
🍴🍴 **Pesqueirinho**, R Domingos Jorge Velho 6889, Poty Velho district, T086-3225 2268. Excellent fish restaurant on the riverbank.
🍴 **Sabores Rotisserie**, R Simplício Mendes 78, Centro. Per kilo food, good quality and variety.

🎉 Festivals and events

Teresina *p585, map p586*
Feb/Mar Teresina is proud of its **Carnaval**, which is then followed by **Micarina**, a local carnival in Mar.
Jul/Aug There is much music and dancing at the **Bumba-Meu-Boi**, which takes place in Teresina on a smaller scale to São Luís **Festidanças**, and a convention of itinerant guitarists.

Oeiras *p589*
Feb/Mar Procissão do Fogaréu aka O Procissão de Bom Jesus dos Passos on Maundy Thursday. Also Easter parades.

🛍 Shopping

Teresina *p585, map p586*
Crafts Teresina is an excellent and cheap place to buy *artesanato*, for which Piauí is renowned throughout Brazil. Panels of carved and painted hardwood, either representing stylized country scenes or images of religious significance, are a good buy, as are clay or wooden models of traditional rural characters. Many of these eccentric figures come from the region's rich fund of myths and legends. Hammocks, straw and basket ware are also made here, as well as leather and clothes.

Parnaíba *p588*
Crafts Artesanato de Parnaíba, R Dom Pedro II 1140, and **Cooperativa Artesanal Mista de Parnaíba**, R Alcenor Candeira, both sell local handicrafts.

⛰ Activities and tours

Parque Nacional de Sete Cidades *p587*
Tours can be arranged with **Eco Dunas** (see page 608) and **Clipe** (see page 589) as well as most agencies in Jericoacoara (see page 581).

Parque Nacional Serra da Capivara *p590*
Trips can be organized via **Trilhas da Capivara**, T089-3582 1294, and **Manary** (see page 553) in Natal. See **Fundham**, www.fundham.org.br, for information.

⊖ Transport

Teresina *p585, map p586*
Air Flights to **Fortaleza**, **Brasília**, **Rio de Janeiro**, **São Paulo**, **Goiânia** and **São Luís**.
Bus The bus journey to **Fortaleza** is scenic and takes 9 hrs (US$13.50). There are direct buses to **Belém** (13 hrs, US$23.40), **Recife** (16 hrs, US$27) and **São Luís** (7 hrs, US$12).

Parnaíba *p588*
Bus If travelling west up the coast from Parnaíba, there are 3 buses a day to **Tutóia** (2½ hrs, US$8) with **Nazaré** at 0700, 1200 and 1400. From Tutóia, Toyotas leave when full from the dock area for **Paulinho Neves** (1 hr, US$6), further Toyotas leave from here to **Barreirinhas** (2 hrs, US$10) near the **Parque Nacional Lençóis Maranhenses**.

It's also possible to take a bus inland to **São Luís** (4-6 hrs, US$12, US$48 – a very bad road, better to go via Tutóia) and from there to **Barreirinhas** (Cisne Branco, 3-3½ hrs on a new road, US$20, 4 per day). See São Luís transport, page 609.

If travelling east down the coast to **Jericoacoara** take a bus to **Camocim** (2 daily with **Guanabara**, 1½-2 hrs, US$12). To avoid getting stuck in Camocim, take the early bus at around 0700. This connects with the 1100 Toyota to **Jericoacoara** (2 hrs, US$10) via the ferry (US$1 per foot passenger) across the river separating Piauí and Ceará, and the village of Tatajuba.

Parnaíba is also connected to **Fortaleza** (10 hrs, US$50) and **Teresina** (6 hrs, US$50). Buses for the **Porto da Barca** (Tatuís) leave from the *rodoviária* every hour and take 10 mins. Taxis cost around US$10.

Delta do Parnaíba *p588*
Boat Boats can be chartered from **Tutóia** (connected to Barreirinhas and Caburé in the Lençóis Marnahenses, via Paulino Neves, and direct to São Luís) or at **Porto dos Tatus** (also called Porto da Barca), 10 km north of Parnaíba. A boat for 12 people costs for around US$175 with **Capitão Báu**, T086-3323 0145, T086-8831 9581 (mob) or contact **Clipe Turismo**, www.clipecoturismo.com.br.

Oerias *p589*
Bus The *rodoviária* is on Av Transamazônica s/n, T089-3462 2006. Buses to **Teresina** (310 km), **São Raimundo Nonato** (280 km) and connections to **Tocantins**.

Parque Nacional Serra da Capivara *p590*
Bus The *rodoviária* is at R Cândido Ferraz, T089-3582 1266. There are buses to **Teresina** (530 km) and connections to **Pernambuco**.

⊙ Directory

Teresina *p585, map p586*
Banks Banks with ATMs include: Banco do Brasil and Bradesco, R Alvaro Mendes 991, Centro, T086-3221 5050 and in the airport. Itaú, in same avenue at P Center Shopping.

Parnaíba *p588*
Banks There is a Bradesco and an HSBC in the town centre for international ATMs and numerous branches around town including: Banco do Brasil, Praça da Graça 340, and Bradesco, Av Pres Getúlio Vargas 403, T086-3321 3032. **Medical services** Pró- Médica, Av Pres Vargas 799, T086-322 3645, 24-hr emergency ward. **Post office** Praça da Graça. **Telephone** Av Pres Getúlio Vargas 390.

Maranhão

Although far less visited than neighbouring Ceará, Maranhão is one of Brazil's most fascinating states with spectacular natural sights and a rich traditional culture with a strong African heritage. The capital, São Luís, was founded by the French but built by the Portuguese, whose azulejos and ornate baroque flourishes grace the elegant buildings of its colonial centre. Every Friday and Saturday night its little praças erupt to the riotous rhythms of cacuria, and in June the city becomes the backdrop for one of the most colourful spectacles in the northeast: the Bumba-Meu-Boi pageant.

The city is enclosed on both sides by natural beauty. To the southeast are the Lençóis Maranhenses, a 155,000-ha coastal desert of vast shifting dunes and isolated communities, cut by broad rivers and in the rainy season (between June and September), pocked with lakes, whose clear reflective waters are a vivid sky blue against brilliant white sand. To the northwest are the little-explored deltas of the Reentrâncias Maranhenses, which preserve the largest concentration of mangrove forest in Brazil, and which are fringed by the south Atlantic's longest coral reef.

Inland, Maranhão is remote and desperately poor but filled with fascinating forgotten villages and wilderness areas such as the Chapada das Mesas in Carolina: a forest-shrouded escarpment dripping with waterfalls that forms the transition zone between the hot, dry northeast and the wet and warm Amazon. ▸▸ *For listings see pages 604-610.*

São Luís ●●●●●●●▲●● ▸▸ *pp604-610. Colour map 2, A2.*

→ *Phone code: 098. Population: 870,000.*

The capital and port of Maranhão state, founded in 1612 by the French and named after St Louis of France, stands upon São Luís island between the bays of São Marcos and São José. It's a beautiful city that rivals Recife and Salvador for colonial charm, and following extensive refurbishment it is in better condition than both. Like both cities, São Luís was a slaving port, initially for indigenous Amazonians who were brought in here in huge numbers to grow sugar cane, and subsequently for Africans. São Luís retains an African identity almost as strong as Salvador and Recife. The city is as Amazonian as it is northeastern and is subject to heavy tropical rains. However, a large proportion of the surrounding deep forest has been cut down to be replaced by *babaçu* palms, the nuts and oils of which are the state's most important products.

Ins and outs

Getting there **Marechal Cunha Machado airport** ⓘ *13 km from centre, Av Santos Dumont, T098-3217 6100*, receives flights from most Brazilian capitals via Fortaleza or Belém, as well as direct flights from Parnaíba and Teresina and international flights from the Guianas and Portugal. **Gol** and **Tam** have offices in the terminal, there is car rental, a tourist office (daily 0800-2200), cyber-café, a **Banco do Brasil** and an office for the Lençóis Maranhenses tour company **Eco Dunas**. *Colectivo* mini-vans run from outside the terminal to Praça Deodoro in the city centre (every 40 minutes until 2200, US$1, one hour). A taxi to the centre costs US$20 but it is cheaper to call a radio taxi, T098-3232 3232, US$12.

From the **rodoviária** ⓘ *12 km from the centre on the airport road*, the bus marked 'Rodoviária via Alemanha' runs to Praça João Lisboa in the centre (US$1).

Ferries cross the bay from Alcântara to the São Luís docks, **Terminal Hidroviário** ⓘ *Rampa Campos Mello, Cais da Praia Grande, US$4 foot passenger, US$25 car*, usually in the afternoon. To check ferry times call T098-3222 8431. ▸▸ *See Transport, page 609.*

Tourist information **Central de Servicos Turísticos** ⓘ *Praça Benedito Leite, T098-3212 6211, www.turismo.ma.gov.br*, and **São Luís Turismo** ⓘ *www.saoluisturismo.com.br*, have useful websites. Also see http://saoluis-ma.com.br. Look out for Corbis photographer Barnabás Bosshart's masterfully photographed map-guides to São Luís and Alcântara.

São Luís

Sleeping 🛏
Cantaria 4

Grand São Luís 7
Internacional 5
Lord 3
Portas da Amazônia 1
Pousada Colonial 2
Solar das Pedras 6

Eating 🍴
Antigamente 1
Armazen Estrela 2
Padaria Frances Valery 4
Papagaio Amarelo 3
Scorpions 5

Bars & clubs 🍸
Reggae (Roots) 6
Reggae do Porto 7

Sights

The old part of the city, on very hilly ground with many steep streets, has been beautifully restored and is replete with colonial art nouveau and art deco buildings. The damp climate encouraged the use of ceramic *azulejo* tiles for exterior walls. *Azulejos* are a common sight in Portugal but their civic use is relatively rare in Brazil; São Luís displays a greater quantity and variety than anywhere else in the country. Most of the tiles are Portuguese (particularly from Porto), with a handful of print designs from Holland and France.

A good place to start a tour of the centre is **Avenida Dom Pedro II**. This was the heart of the original Tupinambá island village of Upaon Açu. When the French arrived in 1612, captained by Daniel de la Touche, they planted a huge wooden cross in the ground and, with a solemn Mass, decreed the land for France. La Touche renamed the village after Louis XIII, the emperor of France, and declared it the capital of the new land of 'France Equinoxiale' (Equinoctial France). There is a bust of La Touche in the 17th-century **Palácio de la Ravardière** ① *Av Dom Pedro II s/n, T089-3212-0800, Mon-Fri 0800-1800*.

Part of the original wall of the French fort still remains in the bulwarks of the **Palácio dos Leões** ① *Av Dom Pedro II, T089-3214 8638, Mon, Wed and Fri 1500-1800, US$3*, which was extensively embellished by the Portuguese after they re-conquered the city in 1615. When Maranhão became part of the newly independent Brazil in the 19th century, the palace was taken over by the governor. The rooms are furnished with period antiques from Portugal, France and the UK, with a series of paintings by artists including Vitor Meirelles, who was responsible for Imperial Brazil's most famous painting: *A Batalha de Guararapes*. The building is replete with stunning tropcial dark *jacarandá* wood and light *cerejeira* polished floors; visitors are required to use carpet slippers. There are marvellous views from the terrace.

Together with neighbouring Belém, Portuguese São Luís was the centre of a voracious slave trade. *Banderiante* expeditions roamed far into the interior capturing indigenous men, murdering their wives and children and bringing the prisoners to Maranhão to work on the cane fields. Entire Amazon civilizations, including the *Omagua*, were wiped-out this way. The Jesuits were appalled by the cruelty and their most famous politician-priest, Antônio Vieira (see box, page 272), came to São Luís as a missionary to protest against the slave trade in 1653: "At what a different price the devil buys souls today compared with what he used to offer for them! There is no market in the world where the devil can get them more cheaply than in our own land … In Maranhão … what a cheap market! An Indian for a soul! That Indian will be your slave for the few days that he lives; but your soul will be enslaved for eternity… Break the chains of injustice and free those whom you hold captive and oppressed! … It is better to live from your own sweat than from the blood of others". The naves of São Luís's churches once echoed with his hell fire sermons, including the simple **Catedral da Sé** ① *Praça Dom Pedro II, s/n, T089-3222 7380, daily 0800-1900, free*, (1629), with its beautiful 19th-century baroque altarpiece, **Nossa Senhora do Carmo** ① *Praça João Lisboa 350, T098-3222 6104, daily 0700-1115 and 1430-1800, free*, (1627), which has an extraordinary, elaborate façade, and the **Igreja do Desterro** ① *Largo do Desterro s/n, daily 0800-1130 and 1500-1830, free*, which was perhaps the first church built in the city. Vieira was eventually driven out of the city and went to Pará where he met with similar failure.

Before he left, Vieira inaugurated the **Convento das Mercês** ① *R da Palma 506, T098-3211 0062, Mon-Fri 0800-1800, Sat 0800-1400*, which houses copies of his 17th-century sermons, along with numerous rare Portuguese and French books (available on request). The main body of the convent is given over to exhibits devoted to Brazilian presidency of Jose Sarney, a former Maranhão senator of dubious repute, whose dynasty continues to rule over Brazil's poorest state with an iron hand, and reap the benefits.

Miraculously some indigenous groups managed to avoid the ravages of the slave trade and still survive in Maranhão. Their cultures are touched upon, from an old-fashioned anthropological perspective, in the **Casa de Nhozinho** ① *R dos Portugueses s/n, T098-3218 9951, 0900-1900, free*. There are also exhibitions devoted to Maranhão *caboclo* life. Nhozinho, who came from Curupuru and gives the house its name, was a famous local wooden toy maker in the mid-20th century.

When the *indígenas* died from exhaustion and the slave trade ran dry, Maranhão and the rest of Brazil turned to Africa for their slaves, thus beginning the world's largest skin trade. Like Salvador and Recife, the strong African heritage is celebrated most powerfully in the city's exuberant music and festivals. São Luís is famous for reggae, but this is just the commercial tip of a huge musical iceberg. The exuberance and variety of music can be sampled on any weekend night throughout the year with *cacuriá* dancing and live shows, but becomes most obvious in May and June during the local festivals of **Bumba-Me-Boi** in São Luís, and the syncretistic **Festo do Divino** in Alcântara.

The **Centro de Cultura Popular Domingos Vieira Filho (Casa da Festa)** ① *R do Giz 225, T098-3218 9924, Tue-Sun 0900-1900*, has exhibitions on the **Festa do Divino**, together with the African-Brazilian *Tambor-de-Mina* spirit religion (similar to *candomblé*), and Christmas festivities. The old customs building, **Casa do Maranhão** ① *R do Trapiche s/n, Praia Grande, on the waterfront at the far end of R Portugal*, houses a museum devoted to the **Bumba-Meu-Boi** festival (see box, page 607) and Maranhão music. Downstairs is an exhibition hall with artefacts, costumes and video shows of previous Bumba festivals. Upstairs is a series of rooms devoted to a different Bumba-Meu-Boi African-Brazilian rhythm and instruments associated with the festival.

The centre of the African slave trade in the city was the **Cafua das Mercês** ① *R Jacinto Maia 54, Praia Grande, Mon-Fri 0900-1800*. It is now a museum of African-Brazilian culture with an extensive collection of musical and religious instruments, clothing and cultural artefacts. The **Casa das Minas** ① *R do Sol 302, T098-3221 4537, Tue-Sun 0900-1800*, is one of the oldest sacred spaces in Brazil for African-Brazilian religions and is an important centre of black culture in São Luís.

There are numerous other buildings of interest. Although the prettiest and liveliest colonial streets are **Rua Portugal** and **Rua do Giz** (28 de Julho), it is Caixa Econômica Federal in the 19th-century **Edifício São Luís** ① *R da Nazare at R do Egíto*, that preserves what is probably the largest *azulejo*-fronted building in the Americas. It now houses a bank. The **Teatro Arthur de Azevedo** ① *R do Sol 180, T089-3232 0299, daily 1500-2000 or when there are shows*, is a very handsome 19th-century theatre restored to its original spendour in the 1990s. Some of the city's best performances are held here. The **Centro Histórico Solar dos Vasconcelos** ① *R da Estrela 462, Praia Grande, T098-3231 9075, Mon-Fri 0800-1900, Sat and Sun 0900-1900, free*, is a fine colonial town house devoted to the history of the city with many interesting paintings, photographs and exhibits. The first floor of the **Museu de Artes Visuais** ① *R Portugal 293, Praia Grande, T098-3231 6766, Tue-Fri 0900-1900, Sat and Sun 0900-1800,* has a collection of some of the city's most precious and intricate European *azulejos*, mostly from Portugal but with some pieces from England, Holland and Belgium. Upstairs is a collection of important Brazilian art including pieces by Tarsila do Amaral, Cícero Dias and Alfredo Volpi.

Excursions from São Luís

Calhau is a huge beach, 10 km away. **Ponta D'Areia** is nearer to São Luís but more crowded. **Raposa**, a fishing village built on stilts, is a good place to buy handicrafts; there are a few places to stay on Avenida Principal. To get there, take a bus from the Mercado Central in São Luís (one hour with **Viação Santa Maria**, every 30 minutes). Another fishing village, **São José de Ribamar**, has a church dedicated to the patron saint and is a centre for *romeiros* in September. Many bars on the seafront serve local specialities such as fried stonefish. It is a 30-minute bus ride with **Maranhense** from the market in São Luís.

Alcântara → *Colour map 2, A2. Phone code: 098. Population: 22,000.*

The former state capital, Alcântara, is on the mainland bay of São Marcos, 22 km by boat from São Luís. Construction of the city started at the beginning of the 17th century and it is now a historical monument. There are many old churches, such as the ruined **Matriz de São Matias** (1648), and colonial mansions, including the **Casa** and **Segunda Casa do Imperador**, and the old cotton barons' mansions with their blue, Portuguese-tiled façades. In the Praça da Matriz is the **Pelourinho** ① *0900-1330, US$0.75*, (1648), the traditional pillory, and a small museum. You can also see the **Forte de São Sebastião** (1663), now in ruins, and the **Fonte de Miritituia** (1747).

Canoe trips go to **Ilha do Livramento**, where there are good beaches and walks around the coast. It can be muddy after rain, and watch out for mosquitoes after dark. A rocket-launching site has been built nearby.

Alcântara

Sleeping
Pousada Bela Vista **2**
Pousada da Josefa **4**
Pousada dos Guarás **1**
Sítio Tijupá **3**

Eating
Bar do Lobato **1**

Ins and outs Launches run to Alcântara from the **Terminal Hidroviário** ① *Rampa Campos Mello, Cais da Praia Grande, São Luís*, at around 0700 and 0930 (US$20), returning to São Luís at about 1630, depending on the tide. The journey takes about an hour. The sea can be very rough between September and December. Catamaran tours can be booked through in São Luís. ▸ *See Activities and tours, page 608.*

Parque Nacional Lençóis Maranhenses ⊜🐦🏛🏖 ▸ *pp604-610. Colour map 2, A3.*

→ *Phone code: 098. www.parquelencois.com.br.*

Northeastern Brazil's windswept coast is broken by extensive dunes all the way from Natal to the Amazon. In eastern Maranhão they become so vast that they form a coastal desert stretching for some 140 km between Tutóia on the Delta do Parnaíba and Primeira Cruz, east of São Luís. The Parque Nacional Lençóis Maranhenses, which encloses only a part of the *lençóis*, covers an area of 1550 sq km. The sand extends up to 50 km inland and is advancing by as much as 200 m a year. Dumped by the sea and blown by the wind, it forms ridges 50 m high in long flowing patterns that change constantly. From the air the undulating, talcum powder-white dunes look like giant wrinkled bed sheets ('lençóis' in Portugese). Between December and June the dunes are pocked with freshwater lakes that shine a brilliant blue under the tropical sky and provide a startling contrast with the brilliant white sand.

The coast of the Lençóis Maranhenses provides a refuge for severely endangered species including manatee. Leatherback and green turtles come here to lay their eggs in late summer; while in the forests and scrubland around the Rio Preguiças there are resident puma, jaguar and spectacled caiman. The Lençóis are home to numerous rare species of fish including the South American lungfish, which cocoon themselves in moist mud under the seasonally flooded lake beds in the dry, and shoals of huge game fish like *camurupim* (tarpon) live in the estuaries and rivers. The dunes are a breeding ground for migratory birds such as the lesser yellowlegs, which come all the way from the Arctic to feed here. Recent studies have shown the sparse vegetation to include grasses that are unknown elsewhere.

Excavations begun in 1995 on the supposed site of a Jesuit settlement which, according to local rumour, was buried intact by a sandstorm.

The *lençóis* are not difficult to visit. Travellers who have a few days to spare are rewarded by an amazing panorama of

Barreirinhas

Sleeping 🛏
Belo Horizonte 4
Buriti 1
Pousada Igarapé 2
Tia Cota 3

Eating 🍴
Barlavento Carlão 1
Bona Mesa Pizzaría 3
Maré Mansa Mineiro 4
Paladar 5

200 metres
200 yards

Murder and slavery in modern Brazil

Much of the interior of northeastern and northern Brazil is still plagued by the spectre of *coronelismo*. This is a brutal, medieval system of peonage whereby a landowner or *coronel* and his army of hired hands rule over a swathe of villages with an iron hand. Villagers are required to work as virtual slaves in exchange for a meagre livelihood and they have no land rights. The situation is handed down through the generations. It is still relatively common place for dissenting villagers to be brutally intimidated or even murdered with impunity and the situation is at its most acute in Piauí, Maranhão and Pará where *coronelismo* is often connected to conservation and logging or agri-business. The oppression rarely makes it into the international or even the national press. But it did in February 2005 when the 74-year-old Catholic nun Dorothy Stang was gunned down for defending the rights of villagers in Pará whose subsistence smallholdings were threatened by *coroneis* working in the soya, logging and ranching businesses. She had received repeated death threats since she began her work in 1972. A report subsequently published by Brazilian NGOs CPT (the Pastoral Land Commission), Global Justice and Terra de Direitos reported that since her work began there had been 772 murders related to land disputes; only eight have gone to trial. Three of these were rancher Vitalmiro de Moura and his two gunmen, convicted perhaps only because of the attention Dorothy Stang's murder received. For more information see www.green peace.org.uk/blog/forests/amazon-communities-threatened-following-nuns-murder.

dunes reaching from horizon to horizon, deserted beaches washed by a powerful surf, boat rides on the aptly named **Rio Preguiça** (Lazy River), and tiny, quiet towns and hamlets where strangers are still a relative novelty.

Visiting the park

The *lençóis* are divided into two areas. To the west of Rio Preguiça is the park proper and the **Grandes Lençóis**, which stretch between Ponta Verde in the far west and the town of **Barreirinhas** on the banks of the Preguiça. Barreirinhas is the tourist capital for the region and has plenty of *pousadas* and restaurants and tour operators, such as **Eco Dunas**, offering trips into the park. From here it is easy to arrange tours and transfers along the Rio Preguiça both up and downstream and onwards through the Delta do Parnaíba to Jericoacoara.

The dunes east of the Rio Preguiça form the **Pequenos Lençóis**, which extend to **Tutóia**. These are easier to travel through than the Grandes Lençóis but less easy to visit on an organized tour. **Paulino Neves**, a town rather than a hamlet on the Rio Cangata, is just south of a series of large dunes at the eastern end of the *lençóis*.

There are several small, friendly settlements in the Pequenos Lençóis. Most lie on the Rio Preguiça. The two-shack town of **Vassouras** is literally at the feet of the *lençóis*; its make-shift huts are watched over by a spectacular, looming dune whose crest affords wonderful views. Further downstream at **Mandacaru** there is a lighthouse with great views out over the coast and some craft shops selling Buriti palm-weave work and carvings. **Atins** and **Caburé** are miniature beach resorts sandwiched between a rough and windy Atlantic and the lazy blue waters of the Preguiça. Both are surrounded by a bleak sea of sand.

You can walk into parts of the Grandes Lençóis from Atins and into the Pequenos Lençóis from Caburé (see below). Many of the overland tours from Jericoacoara finish in Caburé. Be careful of broken glass – especially in Caburé where rubbish is buried rather than collected.

Ins and outs

There are four buses a day to Barreirinhas from São Luís (four hours, US$7) and numerous transit combis and Toyotas bookable through São Luís hotels. There is Toyota transport east between Barreirinhas and Paulino Neves and further connections from here to the scruffy port town of Tutóia and the Delta do Parnaíba, or onward buses to Parnaíba town for the rest of Piauí and Jericoacoara and Fortaleza in Ceará. Many of the towns along the route have a bad wind-blown rubbish problem and their streets are littered with billowing plastic bags and the corpses of discarded bottles.

Traversing the Pequenos Lençóis

It is possible to walk or cycle along the coast in front of the Pequenos Lençóis between **Caburé** and **Tutóia** in either direction; allow about three days. Camping is permitted, but you must take all supplies with you including water, since some dune lakes are salty. The area is very remote and you may not see another person for the duration of the walk. Because of the hot and sandy conditions, this is a punitive trek, only for the very hardy. Do not try the treacherous hike inland across the dunes or a hike into the Grandes Lençóis without a guide. The dunes are disorientating and there have been a number of cases of hikers becoming lost and dying of heat exposure or starvation.

Northern Maranhão and the Reentrâncias Maranhenses ◉▲▶ *pp604-610.*

Northern Maranhão is separated from neighbouring Para by the Reentrâncias Maranhenses, the wildest, most remote and least visited stretch of coast in Brazil's northeast. It is made up of deep inlets thick with mangroves and brackish swamps, jewel-like forested islands and vast dunes of shifting sand. The *reentrâncias* are home to a scattered handful of fishing communities and millions of rare and endangered endemic and migratory waterbirds, making them one of the world's most important wetland areas,

Barreirinhas to Jericoacoara

protected by **Ramsar**, www.ramsar.org (see also www.wetlands.org). This is pioneer territory for tourists of any kind, including birders.

Offshore, in the **Parcel Manoel Luís State Marine Park**, are the most extensive reef systems in South America dotted with the broken remains of some 200 ships, from Portuguese Caravels to modern tankers and with very rich marine life, with many endemics and abundant potato cod and large sharks. Visibility is around 35m, with an average depth of 30 m and water temperature a balmy 32°C. The reef is almost completely unexplored by divers as it is almost 70 km offshore and some 200 km from São Luís. There are few operators and tides and currents are very strong.

Ins and outs

The *reentrâncias* span the coast between Alcântara and Carutapera on the Para border. Access is difficult as there are few roads, little infrastructure and scant accommodation. The main centre for the little tourism that exists are the coastal fishing villages of **Apicum-Açu** and **Cururupu**, both connected by daily, bumpy bus to Alcântara. Only part of the road is paved to the former and access is tough in the wet and there a very simple *pousadas* in both villages.

Boats leave Apicum-Açu for the **Ilha dos Lençóis**, a small fishing community lost in time, huge dunes and mangroves near Parcel Manoel Luís State Marine Park. At present diving in that park can be organized (with plenty of notice) only through larger dive shops in São Paulo.

Southern Maranhão ⬤🅐🅝🅝⬤🅞 ➤➤ *pp604-610.*

Imperatriz ➔ *Colour map 2, A1. Phone code: 098. Population: 232,000.*

Maranhão's second largest city sits on the eastern bank of the broad and beautiful Rio Tocantins, some 630 km southwest of São Luís, in the centre of a large and rapacious cattle and agri-bisiness region. The city is situated on the main BR-010 highway between Palmas in Tocantins, and is a junction on the long bus journey north or south between Belém and São Luís and Tocantins, Brasília and Goiás. It is also the transfer point for buses to Carolina. The city is closer to Belém than it is to São Luís and the vegetation and hot, humid climate feel more Amazonian than northeastern Brazilian. River beaches appear between July and October when the water is low. Book hotels in advance.

Ins and outs **Prefeito Renato Moreira Airport** ① *4 km from the centre, Acesso Aeroporto, s/n T099-3524-4666,* receives flights from Altamira, Araguaína, Belém, Brasília and São Luís. The **rodoviária** ① *R Lias Barros, Nova Carolina, T098- 3542 1276,* has bus connections with Belém, Palmas, Brasília, São Luís, Carolina and Teresina. It is often quicker to reach Carolina through Imperatriz than to go direct from São Luís or Teresina; check when buying a ticket. For more information see www.imperatriz.ma.gov.br.

Carolina → *Phone code: 099. Population: 23,000.*

Carolina is a pretty colonial town of whitewashed houses and terracotta roofs on the banks of the Tocantins river. The climate is hot and damp, the sunsets over the river spectacular and the town is set in the midst of the **Chapada das Mesas**, an area of waterfalls and escarpments covered in a mix of *cerrado* and tropical forest and replete with wildlife.

The **Cachoeira da Pedra Caída**, on the Rio Farinha just off the BR-010, 35 km outside town is one of the northeast's most beautiful: a three-tiered waterfall that plunges into a rocky gorge. The **Cachoeiras do Itapecuru** off the BR-230, 33 km from Carolina are two conjoined falls that fall into a huge swimming hole surrounded by pretty white-sand beaches. The Rio Farinha, a tributary of the Tocantins, has a further series of spectacular falls including the **Cachoeira São Romão** a thundering curtain of water more than 100m and Farinha itself which falls into wide, deep and clear plunge pool. You'll need a guide with a 4WD to visit them. But come soon as they are threatened by a hydroelectric project.

The **Cachoeira da Prata** 40 km from town falls next to the **Morro das Figuras**, hill which is covered with rock inscriptions thought to have been carved by the ancestors of the Tupi people. Access is by unsealed road from the BR-230, requiring a 4WD. The Chapada das Mesas has a series of other table top mountains, including the **Morro do Portal**, which affords wonderful views and is easy to reach from Carolina.

Between June and August the Tocantins river is low and lined with beaches, the best of which are on the opposite side of the river in the little town of **Filadélfia**, in Tocantins. The city's goes out at night on the **Ilha dos Botes**, a river island 5 km from town filled with simple bars and restaurants.

Ins and outs   Carolina lies 221 km south of Imperatriz on a road which joins the BR-010. There are frequent buses. The **rodoviária** ① *T099-3531 2076*, is in the centre. A ferry connects the town with Filadelfia in Tocantins on the opposite bank of the river (10 minutes). For information contact **Secretaria de Turismo** ① *R Duque de Caxias 522, T098- 3731 1613, Mon-Fri 0800-1300.* Guides and transport cost US$20-30 per half day and can be organized through *pousadas*.

◉ Maranão listings

For Sleeping and Eating price codes and other relevant information, see pages 42-47.

● Sleeping

São Luís *p595, map p596*

Although many Brazilians opt to stay on the beach the sand is not as clean as it is in Piauí and Ceará, while the city centre is charming and full of life. Cheap hotels can be found in R das Palmas, very central, and R Formosa.
AL Pestana São Luís, Av Avicência, Praia do Calhau, T098-2106 0505, www.pestanasao luis.com.br A fully renovated resort hotel housed in a former 1970s grand hotel. This is much the best option for families or business. Rooms are well-appointed with work stations

and good desks, there's a full business centre and the various leisure options include a large pool, games area and tennis courts.
A Grand São Luís Hotel, Praça Dom Pedro II 299, T098-2109 3500, www.grandsaoluis. com.br. A newly refurbished 1960s grand dame with plain rooms, the best of which have sea views. Business facilities, pool and gym.
B Portas da Amazônia, R do Giz 129, T098-3222 9937, www.portasdaamazonia.com.br. Tastefully converted wood-floor rooms in a colonial building in the the heart of the centre. Smart and well run. Internet.
B-C Pousada Colonial, R Afonso Pena 112, T098-3232 2834, www.clickcolonial.com.br. Clean, well-kept rooms set in a beautiful restored, tiled house, a/c, comfortable, quiet.

C-D Lord, R de Nazaré 258, facing Praça Benedito Leite, T/F098-3221 4655. The carpets and scruffy walls in the lobby and on the stairs don't look as if they've been changed since the hotel opened in the 1970s, but the long, plain tiled rooms are spacious and clean, and they offer views out over the colonial centre from tiny terraces. Noisy a/c, cheapest with shared bathroom. Check for spongy mattresses.

D Hotel Cantaria, R da Estrela 115, T098-3221 3390. Spartan but bright single, double, a/c or fan-cooled triple rooms with good views out over R da Estrela.

D-E Internacional, R da Estrela 175, T098-3231 5154. Very scruffy, tiny fan-cooled boxes with button-sized windows in a dilapidated house reached by rickety stairs. Bizarrely very popular with backpackers but definitely only for the desperate. Other options nearby.

D-E Solar das Pedras, R da Palma 127, T098-3232 6694, www.ajsolardaspedras.com.br. By far the best backpacker option in town. Well-run, with tidy 4-6 person dorms (**E** pp) and doubles, internet, lockers and a little garden.

Excursions from São Luís *p599*

In Raposa there are hotels on Av Principal.
C Hotel Sol e Mar, Av Gonçalves Dias 320, São José de Ribamar. With a restaurant.

Alcântara *p599, map p599*

B Pousada dos Guarás, Praia da Baronesa, T098-3337 1339. A beach front *pousada* with a series of bungalows with en suites, a good restaurant, canoe hire and advice on excursions around the town.

D Pousada Bela Vista, Vila Jerico s/n, Cema, T098-3337 1569, email: danniloalcantara@ig.com.br. Cabins and pretty suites with great views out over the bay and a restaurant with delicious Maranhense food.

D-E Sítio Tijupá, R de Baixo s/n at the Post Office, T098-3337 1291. Tiny simple *pousada* with 4 small but well-kept fan-cooled rooms.

E Pousada da Josefa, R Direita, T098-3337 1109. A friendly, family-run restaurant and pousada right in the centre with a range of very simple, plain rooms. Look at several.

Parque Nacional Lençóis Maranhenses *p600, map p600*

Barreirinhas

Most hotels can organize tours. Bring a hammock for flexibility; in the smaller hamlets it is always possible to rent space in a beach bar or restaurant for a few dollars.

A Buriti, R Inácio Lins s/n, T098-3349 1800, www.pousadadoburiti.com.br. Corridors of large, plain rooms with concrete terraces near a pool and breakfast area. Simple but the best in the centre of town.

C Belo Horizonte, R Joaquim Soeiro de Carvalho 245, T098-3499 0054, www.bh mirante.com.br. Well-kept tiled and white-washed rooms near the central square. The quietest are at the front. Good service from the welcoming owner, Albino and a pleasant rooftop breakfast area. Sister *pousada* in Caburé.

C-D Pousada Igarapé, R Coronel Godinho 320, T098-9111 0461. Small, boxy fan-cooled or a/c doubles set in corridors opposite the Assembleia de Deus church, which has noisy hellfire sermons at weekends.

D Tia Cota, R Coronel Godinho 204, T098-3349 1237. Simple fan or a/c whitewashed rooms, with decent beds and mattresses, ranging from phone box-sized with shared baths to more spacious en suite doubles.

Caburé, Vassouras, Mandacaru and Atins

It is possible to rent hammock space in the restaurant shacks in Vassouras or Mandacaru for around US$20/day with food included.

C-D Rancho Pousada, R Principal, Praia do Atins, Atins, T098-9616 9646, www.rancho pousada.com. Comfortable, though simple beach chalets cooled by the constant sea breeze. The best are close to the waterfront. The *pousada* has a simple restaurant and a pool. There are a couple of other, simpler options in the village.

D-E Pousada do Paulo, Praia do Caburé, T098-9143 4668. Rooms for up to 4. Well-kept. The owner was the first to settle here and named the town after a local bird. Best food in the village. Watch out for glass on the vast, sweeping Atlantic beach. There are other options in town and rooms are always available outside peak season.

Paulino Neves and Tutóia
Tutóia is an ugly, scruffy town surrounded by wastelands of billowing plastic bage. It's a good idea to try and arrive early and leave quickly.
C Tutóia Palace Hotel, Av Paulino Neves 1100, Tutóia, T098-3479 1247. Crumbling mock colonial hotel in garish pink with 12 fading rooms, 5 of which have a/c.
D-E Oasis dos Lençóis, Av Rio Novo, Centro, Paulino Neves T098-9966 1351. A very friendly river bank *pousada* run by Dona Mazé and her family. Public areas are decorated with old photos of the Lençóis, the breakfasts generous, but the fan-cooled rooms are very simple and in need of refurbishment.
E-F Tremembés, Praça Tremembés, Tutóia, T098-3479 1354. Very, very simple, with fan-cooled plain boxes and shared bathrooms. Look at several.

Reentrâncias Maranhenses *p602*
Cururupu
D-E Hotel Kelma, R Cesario Coimbra, Centro, T098-3391 1252. Twenty very simple rooms with shared baths and fans.
D-E Hotel Natalia, Av Liberalino Miranda 53, Jacaré, T098-3391 2359. A friendly family-run guesthouse with 8 plain little rooms with shared bathrooms and a large breakfast,

Imperatriz *p603*
There are many cheap hotels near the *rodoviária* should you get stuck in town.
A-B Posseidon, R Paraíba 740, T086-3529 8500, www.posseidonhotel.com.br). The best in the city, oriented to business and with internet access and a pool.

Carolina *p604*
There are a handful of very simple *pousadas* near the bus station.
B-C Chalés da Pedra Caída, Praça do Estudante 460, T099-3531 2318.

Chalets with fan, restaurant, natural pool and 3 neighbouring waterfalls.
C-D Pousada do Lajes, Estr por Riachão (BR-230), Km 2, T099-3531 2452, www.pousadadolajes.com.br. Chalets with a/c gathered around a little pool outside town with a restaurant and a small play area for kids.

🍴 Eating

São Luís *p595, map p596*
Bases provide simple home cooking, although most are found away from the centre and beaches. Typical dishes are *arroz de cuxá* and *torta de camarão* and desserts or liqueurs made from local fruits. Try the local soft drink *Jesús* or *Jenève*. **R da Estrela** has many eating places with outdoor terraces. **R dos Afogados** has good places for lunch. There is further choice in the **São Francisco** district, just across bridge. The centre is very lively on Fri and Sat but on Sun most people go to **Praia Calhau**.
₸₸₸-₸₸ Antigamente, R da Estrela 210. Portuguese and Brazilian standards, decent fish and pizza in this restaurant decorated with local art, colourful bottles and bric-a-brac. Lively on weekends and Mon-Fri after 0800.
₸₸₸-₸₸ Armazen Estrela, R da Estrela 401, T098-3254 1274. A fine dining restaurant upstairs, offering French-Brazilian dishes like partridge in *cajá* sauce and standards like steak diane. Downstairs there's a great little *botequin* in a long, stone-walled cool room with Romanesque brick arches, offering good *petisco* snacks and live music on weekends.
₸₸₸-₸₸ Papagaio Amarelo, R da Estrela 210. Varied menu with excellent fish and regional standards and tables that spill out into the plaza. Both this restaurant and neighbouring **Antigamente** are the liveliest spots in this busy streets and have good live music at weekends.
₸ Padaria Frances Valery, R do Giz (28 de Julho) 164. Delicious cakes, faux-French eclairs, quiches, tropical fruit juices and coffee, friendly.
₸ Scorpions, R da Palma 83. Great value per kilo with a good choice of stews, salads and *pratos feitos*. Near the IYHA.

Bumba-Meu-Boi

Throughout the month of June the streets of São Luís are alive to the sound of *tambores* and dancers recreating the legend of Catirina, Pai Francisco and his master's bull. Although this mixture of African, indigenous and Portuguese traditions exists throughout the north, it is in Maranhão that it is most developed, with around 100 groups in São Luís alone. Here there are various styles called *sotaques*, which have different costumes, dances, instruments and *toadas*. These are Boi de Matraca da Ilha and Boi de Pindaré, both accompanied by small percussion instruments called *matracas*, Boi de Zabumba marked by the use of a type of drum, and Boi de Orquestra accompanied by string and wind instruments. Although there are presentations throughout June the highlights are the 24th (São João) and the 29th (São Pedro) with the closing

ceremony lasting throughout the 30th (São Marçal), particularly in the bairro João Paulo. The shows take place in an *arraial*, which are found all over the city, with the ones at Projeto Reviver and Ceprama being more geared towards tourists (however be aware that a livelier more authentic atmosphere is to be found elsewhere in other *bairros*, such as Madre Deus). The Centro de Cultura Popular Domingos Vieira Filho at Rua do Giz 221, Praia Grande is the place to learn more about these variations as well as many other local festivals and traditions such as Tambor de Crioula or Cacuriá, both sensual dances derived from Africa. A good location to see these dances and capoeira practised is Labouarte, Rua Jansen Muller, Centro (Cacuriá de Dona Tetê is particularly recommended, with participation encouraged).

Parque Nacional Lençóis Maranhenses *p600, map p600*
Barreirinhas
†¶-¶ **Barlavento Carlão**, Av Beira Rio s/n, T098-3349 0627. Fillet of fish in Passion fruit sauce, açaí pulp with guarana and various simple meat and poultry dishes and fresh juices.
¶ **Bona Mesa Pizzaria**, R Inacio Lins s/n. Wide choice of pizzas cooked in a traditional wood-fired oven and delicious *doce de buriti* dessert.
¶ **Maré Mansa Mineiro**, Rio Preguicas at Joaquim Diniz. A floating restaurant, bar and dance club with live reggae every Wed and Sat. Very busy after 2300 with a crowd ranging from 18 years old to 80.
¶ **Paladar**, Coronel Godinho 176. Very cheap but hearty *prato feitos* with meat, chicken or fish options, rice, beans, vegetables and salad.

Alcântara *p599, map p599*
¶ **Bar do Lobato**, Praça da Matriz. Pleasant with good simple food, fried shrimps highly recommended.

Imperatriz *p603*
¶¶ **Rafaello Grill**, in Imperatriz Shopping, Av Dorgival Pinheiro Sousa 1400. Self-service. Modest *churrascaria* with a reasonable choice of side dishes.
¶ **Fogão Mineiro**, Av Getúlio Vargas 2234. Minas Gerais wood-oven cooking with a range of heavy, meaty dishes and side vegetables like squash.

🍸 Bars and clubs

São Luís *p595, map p596*
There is *cacuriá* dancing, drum parades and buzzing nightlife every Fri and Sat along the north end of **R do Giz** and along **R João Gualberto**.
Antigamente, Praia Grande. Live music Thu-Sat.
Reggae Bar do Porto, R do Portugal 49, T098-3232 1115. One of the best reggae bars in the city with a broad range of live acts and DJs and a vibrant crowd at weekends.

Reggae (Roots) Bar, R da Palma 86, T098- 3221 7580. Live reggae and Maranhão roots music most nights. Especially lively at weekends.

Imperatriz p603
Fly Back Disco Club, Beira Rio, north of the ferry crossing. 2 dance floors, 1 fast, 1 slow (for couples only), good.

🎭 Entertainment

São Luís p595, map p596
Cinema Colossal, Av Mcal Castelo Branco 92, São Francisco. **Passeio**, R Oswaldo Cruz 806.
Theatre Teatro Artur de Azevedo, see page 598. Teatro Viriato Correa, Av Getúlio Vargas, Monte Castelo, T098-3218 9019.

🎉 Festivals and events

São Luís p595, map p596
24 Jun Bumba-Meu-Boi, see box, page 607. For several days before the festival, street bands parade, particularly in front of São João and São Benedito churches. There are dances somewhere in the city almost every night in Jun and a whole string of smaller Boi-related festivals and very lively *cacuriá* and reggae at weekends all year round, especially on R Giz.
Aug São Benedito, at the Rosário church.
Oct Festival with dancing, at **Vila Palmeira** suburb (take bus of same name).

Alcântara p599, map p599
Jun Festa do Divino, at Pentecost (Whitsun). On 29 Jun is **São Pedro** saint day.
Aug São Benedito.

🛍 Shopping

São Luís p595, map p596
Arts and crafts
IDAM, **Coisa da Terra** and **Mil Cores Rua Portugal**, on R Portugal sell wicker and weave work, pottery and figurines from Maranhão.

Arte Indígena Maranhense, R do Giz at João Gualberto, T098-3221 2940. Sells Maranhão art made by indigenous peoples.

Music and books
Rodrigo CDs Maranhenses, R João Vital s/n between Estrela and Giz, T098-3232 4799, sells a huge selection of Maranhão and north-eastern roots, traditional and contemporary music. This is one of the best music shops in northeastern Brazil.
Poeme-Sé, R João Gualberto 52, Praia Grande, T098-3232 4968. Cosy little bookshop and cybercafé with a selection of Maranhão music.

Parque Nacional Lençóis Maranhenses p600, map p600
Barreirinhas
There is an arts and crafts market next to the river selling *buriti* palm waevework bags, mats and homeware. Light and excellent value.

🥾 Activities and tours

São Luís p595, map p596
Eco Dunas, with an office in São Luís airport T098-3349 0545, also at R Inácio Lins 164, Bareirinhas, www.ecodunas.com.br. The best option for tours of Lençóis Maranhenses, the delta and tours all the way from São Luís to Jericoacoara or vice versa. Excellent guides, infrastructure and organization. English spoken and flights organized. Can arrange wonderful scenic flights over the Lençóis with pilot Amirton for around US$100.
Francinaldo dos Santos, T098-8839 0578, fran-live@hotmail.com. Freelance guide in Barreirinhas. Good for groups only. Excellent rates and adventure trips. A local who grew up in the area. Portuguese only.
Phylipi, T098-8118 1710, phylipi@ hotmail.com. Very good guide for São Luís and Alcântara. Fluent English and French. US$25 for a 2- to 3-hr city centre tour. Around US$80/day for groups of up to 10. Trips run to the Lençóis Maranhenses; also offers transfers to the Delta do Parnaíba and Jericoacoara.

Footprint Mini Atlas
Brazil

Map 2

Map 5

PARAGUAY

ARGENTINA

URUGUAY

PARANA

RIO GRANDE DO SUL

Amambaí
Eldorado
Mundo Novo
Guaíra
Palotina
Represa de Itaipu
Foz do Iguaçu
Ciudade del Este
Iguaçu Falls
Parque Nacional Foz do Iguaçu
Rio Iguaçu
Medaneira
Catanduvas
Cascavel
Toledo
Campo Eré
Pato Branco
São Lourenço d'Oeste
São Miguel d'Oeste
Bom Jesus
Horizont
Xanxerê
Chapecó
Treze Tília
Concórdia
Joaçaba
Campos Novos
Tupitanga
Erexim
Barragem Passo Fundo
Itapiranga
Iraí
Federico Westphalen
Salto do Yucumã
Santa Rosa
Porto Xavier
Porto Alegre

Paranavaí
San Iñac
Maring
Cianorte
Umuarama
Campo Mourão
Termas d Juréma
Campina
Iretama
Pitanga
Laranjeiras do Sul
Guarapua
Represa de Salto Santiago

São Luís Gonzaga
Santo Ângelo
São Miguel das Missões
Santo Tomé
São Borja
Encruzilhada
Itaquí
Santiago
Ijuí
Cruz Alta
Carazinho
Passo Fundo
Lagoa Vermelha
Soledade
Caxi do Sul
Bento Gonçalves
Farroupilha
Garibaldi
Lajeado
Novo Petrópo
Novo Hambur
Sapucaia do Su
São Leopoldo
Estêio
Canoas
Guaíba
Paso de los Libres
Uruguaiana
Manuel Viana
Alegrete
Santa Maria
Candelária
Santa Cruz do Sul
Rio Jacuí
Barra do Quaraí
Bella Unión
Quaraí
Rosário do Sul
São Gabriel
Caçapava do Sul
Encruzilhada do Sul
Barra do Ribeiro
Santana do Livramento
Rivera
Aguas Brancas
Camaquã
Tape
Lagoa d Patos
Santa Rita
Arambaré
Bagé
Canguçu
São Lourenço do Sul
Mostard
Tavares
Parque Nacion Lagoa do Peix
Aceguá
Pelotas
Dunas
Bojuru
Estreito
São José do Norte
Rio Grande
Cassino
Jaguarão
Rio Branco
Lagoa Mirim
Estação Ecológica do Taim
Curral Alto
Laguna Mangabeira
Santa Vitória do Palmar
Chuí

Index

Reentrâncias Maranhenses *p602*
For those interested in diving in the Parcel
Manoel Luís State Marine Park contact **SCAFO**,
Universitário SENAC, Av Eng Eusébio Stevaux
823, Santo Amaro, São Paulo, T011-5682
7766, www.scafo.com.br. Can organize
dive operators and boats in São Luís.
Give plenty of notice.

⊙ Transport

São Luís *p595, map p596*
Air Minivans run to the airport from Praça
Deodoro in the centre, every 40 mins until
2200, US$1, 1 hr. As well as local flights, there
are connections through **Belém**, **Teresina** or
Fortaleza to the rest of Brazil and international
flights to the **Guianas** and **Portugal**.
  Airline offices GOL, www.voe
gol.com.br and TAM, www.tam.com.br have
offices at the airport. Other airlines include:
Litoranea, www.voelitoranea.com.br;
Oceanair, www.oceanair.com.br; **TAF**,
www.voetaf.com.br; and **TAP Air
Portugal**, www.flytap.com.

Boat Boats to **Alcântara** leave from the
Terminal Hidroviario da Praia Grande Rampa
Campos Melo s/n, Cais da Praia Grande, São
Luís, T098-3232 0692. There are departures in
the morning usually at 0700 and 0930 but
times vary according to the tide. The trip
takes 1 hr, US$4.

Bus To **Fortaleza**, US$270, 4 a day, 18 hrs.
To **Belém**, 13 hrs, US$30, **Transbrasiliana**
at 1900 and 2000 (no *leito*). Also to **Recife**,
US$50, 25 hrs, all other major cities and local
towns. To **Barreirinhas**, 3 hrs on a newly
paved road US$10. More comfortable
on a private bus, US$30 – organize
through **Eco Dunas** (see page 608)
or your hotel.

**Parque Nacional Lençóis
Maranhenses** *p600, map p600*
Hotels in São Luís can book minivan trips for
the same price as the bus. See Ins and outs
page 602. A regular boat service plies the
river between **Barreirinhas** and **Caburé**
and/or **Atins** stopping at **Vassouras** and
Mandaracu on the way. Boats leave daily at
1000-1100 from the end of the **Orla** next to
the town dune (US$4, 3-4 hrs to Caburé or
Atins; both 4 hrs, US$10); the boat returns
with the tide. Speedboats can be organized
at Barreirinhas through **Eco Dunas** (see
page 608), and it is possible to reach both
Paulino Neves or even **Tutóia** by boat.
  Marcelo T098-3349 1964, organizes
freelance boat trips for a good price to
anywhere in the region. **Mão**, T098-9608
0624, has 4WD transfers to Tutóia from
Barreirinhas via the other towns and villages.

Alcântara *p599, map p599*
Boat Boats from Alcântara to **São Luís**
leave daily at 0830 and 1600.

Imperatriz *p603*

Air There are flights to **Altamira**, **Araguaína**, **Belém**, **Brasília** and **São Luís**. Air taxi: **Heringer**, at airport, T098-3722 3009.

Airline offices Penta, R Luís Domingues 1420, T098-3723 1073. **TAM**, R Ceará 678, T098-3722 3148. **Varig/RioSul**, R Luís Domingues 1471, T098-3723 2155.

Bus There are regular bus connections with **Belém** and **Brasília** along the BR-010, there are also connections on this route for **Jalapão** via **Palmas** and the **Chapada dos Veadeiros** in northern Goiás. There is a slow, crowded bus service to **Teresina**. Local buses run frequently to **Carolina** to the south. To get to **Marabá** on the Transamazônica, you can either take a **Transbrasiliana** bus direct, 7-10 hrs (starting on the Belém highway, the bus then turns west along a poorer road, passing finally through destroyed forest, new *fazendas* and unplanned cities), or a faster route, involving taking a ferry across the river in the early morning (0600-0700) to catch a pickup on the other side, takes about 5 hrs, but is more expensive. To get to the ferry across the river, go along R Luís Domingues, which runs parallel to Av Getúlio Vargas.

Car hire Interlocadora, Av Dorgival Pinheiro de Souza 990, T098-3722 3050. **Localiza**, BR-010, Setor *rodoviária*, T098-3721 4507, and at airport, T098-3721 8611.

Train Trains to **Pará** and **Maranhão**.

● Directory

São Luís *p595, map p596*
Banks There are branches of all the major Brazilian banks. **Bradesco** Av Magalhães Almeida 300, T098-3212 2359 and at the airport. **Banco do Brasil**, Praça Deodoro, for TCs and Visa ATMs and at the airport. **HSBC**, off Praça João Lisboa, accepts MasterCard/Cirrus/ Maestro at ATMs. **Agetur**, R do Sol 33A. **Embassies and consulates** France, R Santo Antônio 259, T098-3231 4459. **Germany**, Praça Gonçalves Dias 301, T098-3232 7766. **Italy**, R do Genipapeiro, Jardim São Francisco, T098-3227 0270. **Spain**, Praça Duque de Caxias 3, João Paulo, T098-3223 2846. **USA**, Av Daniel de La Touche, Jardim Buriti, T098-3248 1769. **Internet** Plenty of internet cafés in the centre of town. HCG, R Paparaúbas 11, São Francisco. **Language courses** Senhora Amin Castro, T098-3227 1527, for Portuguese lessons. Recommended. **Laundry** Nova China, R da Paz 518. **Libraries** Arquivo Público, R de Nazaré 218, rare documents on local history. **Medical services** Clínica São Marcelo, R do Passeio 546, English-speaking doctor. **Hospital Monte Sinai**, R Rio Branco 156, T098-3232 3260, 24 hrs. **Post office** Praça João Lisboa 292. **Telephone** Embratel, Av Dom Pedro II 190.

Alcântara *p599, map p599*
Banks There are no longer any **Bradesco** banks in Alcântara – bring cash from São Luís. Banco do Estado do Maranhão, R Grande 76, changes US$ and TCs. **Post office** R Direita off Praça da Matriz. **Telephone** Telemar, R Grande, 0700-2200.

Imperatriz *p603*
Banks Banco do Brasil, Av Getúlio Vargas 1935. **Medical services** Santa Mônica, R Piauí, T098-3722 3415, 24-hr emergency ward. **Telephone** R Rio Grande do Norte 740, a side street off Av Getúlio Vargas, near Hotel Posseidon, 0630-2400.

Carolina *p604*
Banks Banco do Brasil, A Mascarenhas 159. **Medical services** FNS, R Benedito Leite 57, T098-3731 1271. **Telephone** Av E Barros, 0730-2230.

Contents

Border crossings

The Amazon

At a glance

⊙ **Getting around** Internal flights, boat and some buses, but very few passable roads. This area is as large as Western Europe.

◉ **Time required** 3 days for Manaus or Belém. 2-3 days for Cristalino Jungle Lodge or Mamirauá. 10 days to travel between Manaus and Belém. 2-4 weeks to get off the beaten track.

☀ **Weather** Hot and wet year round. Belém wettest Dec-Apr, Manaus Mar-May; Sep-Nov is the wettest in the southern Amazon.

✖ **When not to go** Good to visit year round but least comfortable in the wetter months.

The Amazon is a region of great geographical diversity. In the north, along the border with Venezuela, are the forests and savannahs of the Guiana Shield: the ancient heart of the South American continent, covered in a forest that grows like a giant filigree over white sand and recycles 99.9% of its water and nutrients. Giant boulders the size of mountains break intermittently through the canopy.

In the east lie the expansive Amazon savannahs, which stretch across Roraima and southern Venezuela into the Rupununi of Guyana. The world's largest table-top mountains tower over them, their brows heavy with perpetual thunder cloud. South of here, the Amazon pours out into the ocean leaving an island of silt the size of Denmark in its wake and turning the Atlantic fresh for 100 miles offshore. The forest gets thicker and more vibrant and the mud on which it grows is as red and sticky as blood.

In the far west, the forest is gentler and more fertile; filled with life around the magical Rio Javarí, where the trees seem permanently full of parrots, macaws and monkeys and where grey and pink dolphins surface from the deep, languid brown river. To the south, the trees are broken by the squares of giant fields, which cut into the green with greedy geometric order, and the Amazon exists as mere segments.

The Amazon

Many people imagine the Amazon as a single river but, in reality, it is a huge network of rivers extending into nine countries. Before the Andes were formed, some 15 million years ago, the Amazon flowed west into the Pacific. But as the crash of continental plates pushed up the mountains, the river was cut off from its ocean and became a vast inland sea, hemmed in by the Guiana Shield to the east. Over millions of years this sea eroded the ancient sandstone shield, until it eventually burst through into the Atlantic. It left behind a vast filigree of veins that today make up the Amazon river system, populated by prehistoric air-breathing fish and unique freshwater species such as the Amazon stingray, whose closest relatives still live in the Pacific.

The Amazon contains a third of the world's fresh running water, whose colours range from vodka clear and tea black to coffee with milk and opaque aquamarines sprinkled with pink blind dolphins. Even its tributaries dwarf the world's other rivers: the Madeira, Tapajos, Rio Negro and Tocantins all have flows far greater than that of the Mississippi. At Santarém, 800 miles inland, the river spans a distance greater than London to Paris, while the river mouth itself contains an island the size of Denmark.

Many who come here expect to see animals, and common sightings include caiman, monkeys and dolphins. However, the forest offers plenty of cover for lowland animals, and most birds and primates live high in the canopy. Even in the small rainforest lodges on the tiniest tributaries, animals are hard to spot. Far more can be seen in Goiás or the Pantanal, yet the Amazon is unforgettable. There are few places in the world where the power of nature can be felt more potently or where a way of life in tune with that power survives more successfully. ➤➤ *For history and environmental issues see Background page 815.*

Ins and outs

The Brazilian Amazon is a vast region of vastly different landscapes, larger than Western Europe and it shares borders with eight other countries. While most visitors spend only a few days here either in and around Manaus or Belém it is possible to spend months in here without ever tiring of its wonders or scratching the surface of what there is to see.

Getting to the Amazon

The Amazon belongs to six Brazilian states: Amazonas, Pará, Roraima, Amapá, Rondônia and Acre, with further areas extending into northern Mato Grosso and Tocantins. Its terrain varies greatly and, while much of what is most interesting lies well off the tourist trail, requiring properly funded expeditions, visiting the rainforest is easy.

There are two major entrance points to the Amazon: **Manaus**, a city of 1½ million people in the middle of the Amazon Basin, is the best place to organize safari cruises and lodges. It also offers the best access (by boat or air) to smaller towns further into the forest, such as Tefé. This is where one of the two best Amazon rainforest lodges lies: **Mamirauá Ecological Reserve** (see page 659). The other truly excellent Amazon rainforest lodge is **Cristalino Jungle Lodge** in Mato Grosso (see the Pantanal, page 766). Manaus is also the the point of departure for Parintins and the **Boi Bumba** festival.

Belém, at the mouth of the Amazon, began as a colonial slaving port and grew into a city with one of the best alternative cultural scenes in the north of Brazil. There are no forest lodges near Belém but it is possible to visit the rainforest on a cruise, with a small operator or whilst staying on one of the river islands like Marajó. It is also possible to visit the forest from Santarém, a small city at the meeting of the Tapajós river and the Amazon.

The Amazon and the theory of evolution

While the Spanish and Portuguese came to the Amazon to plunder, pillage and enslave, the Europeans who followed them in the 18th and 19th centuries were more interested in beetles and botany than gold. Among the first was the Frenchman Charles Marie de la Condamine, who came to the Andes in the mid-1700s to ascertain whether the earth was a perfect sphere. He narrowly escaped being stoned by a superstitious mob in Cuenca, Ecuador, and fled to Cayenne. In doing so he was obliged to cross the Amazon, producing the first accurate map of the basin along the way and bringing rubber back to Europe. De la Condamine inspired other Enlightenment scientists to follow him. The greatest was Alexander von Humboldt, today known for the Humboldt Current (which he did not discover) and the Humboldt River (which he never saw), but who, in his time, was considered the pre-eminent scientist in Europe. During his stay on the upper Rio Negro, this great German collected some 12,000 specimens and survived shocks by electric eels, *curaré* poison and bathing with piranhas. He captured and dissected a 7-m caiman and established the region as the best in the world for the study of natural sciences. The English followed him: Henry Bates, Richard Spruce and, in 1848, Alfred Russel Wallace, who wrote: "I'd be an Indian here, and live content, to fish and hunt, and paddle my canoe, and see my children grow, like wild young fawns, In health of body and peace of mind, rich without wealth, and happy without gold! "

The seemingly infinite variety of plants and animals in the Amazon caused Wallace to reflect on how all this variety had come about: "so alike in design yet so changeable in detail? "Places not more than fifty or a hundred miles apart have species of insects and birds at the one which are not found at the other. There must be some boundary which determines the range of each species, some external peculiarity to mark the line which each one does not pass."

Charles Darwin had the same thought two years earlier after his return from Brazil and while reading an essay by Thomas Malthus on population. In his essay the economist argued that the realization of a happy society will always be hindered by its tendencies to expand more quickly than its means of subsistence. If this is true of animals, thought Darwin, then they must compete to survive and Nature must act as a selective force, killing off the weak, and species must evolve each from another through this process. Darwin was terrified by the implications of his thought and did not commit it to paper for six years, then sealing it and handing it to his wife with instructions to publish it after his death.

Alfred Russel Wallace was younger and less timid. While in a high fever on a field trip in Indonesia he was pondering over the thoughts that had haunted him since his days on the Amazon, and he too recalled the same essays by Malthus. The same thought which had struck Darwin, flashed into his own mind: "I saw at once that the ever-present variability of all living things would furnish the material from which, by the mere weeding out of those less adapted to the actual conditions, the fittest alone would survive the race." Wallace wrote to Darwin who was, at that time, the most famous natural scientist in Britain, explaining his theory and asking for his advice. Darwin's hand was forced and, after papers written by both scientists were presented at the Linnean Society on the same day, the theory of evolution was born.

International flights into the Amazon

Flights from the USA or Europe tend to come via Fortaleza, Rio de Janeiro, São Paulo or Salvador, with airlines such as **TAP**, www.flytap.com.

However, the region also has direct international connections. There are flights to **Manaus** from Miami with **TAM**, www.tam.com.br; from Panama, Santa Cruz (Bolivia), Havana and cities in Central America and the USA (including Miami) with **Copa**, www.copaair.com; from Guayquil and Quito in Ecuador with **TAME**, www.tame.com.ec. To **Belém** from Miami with **TAM**; from Haiti, Martinique and Cayenne (Guyane) with **Air Caribes**, www.aircaraibes.com, with connections from Paris; from Georgetown (Guyana) and Paramaribo (Suriname) with **META**, www.voemeta.com; and from Cayenne (Guyane) with **TAF**, www.voetaf.com.br. To **Boa Vista** from Georgetown and Paramaribo with **META**. To **Macapá** from Cayenne with **TAF**. Destinations in Colombia can be reached through **Leticia**, which is conjoined with Tabatinga on the far western Amazonian border.

International borders

The Brazilian Amazon has a number of borders permitting overland or river crossings.

Venezuela can be reached from Boa Vista (Roraima) via Santa Elena, from where there are buses to Caracas; or with far more difficulty from São Gabriel da Cachoeira (Amazonas) via Cucuí (Amazonas) and San Carlos de Río Negro in Venezuela for Puerto Ayacucho, which also has buses to Caracas and the rest of the country. See page 678.

Peru can be reached easily from Tabatinga or Benjamin Constant (Amazonas), from where there are boats running to Iquitos in Peru and onward boats to Pucallpa or flights to Lima. Peru can also be reached through Brasiléia (Acre) from where there are *combis* to Iñapari and from there on to Puerto Maldonado and Cuzco. See page 660 and page 661.

Bolivia is reached from Guajará-Mirim (Rondônia), from where launches cross the river to Guayará Merin in Bolivia for buses to Rurrenabaque and La Paz. See pages 686 and 688.

Colombia is easily reached from Tabatinga (Amazonas) which is twinned and contiguous with the Colombian city of Leticia, from where there are flights to Bogotá. See page 661.

Guyane (French Guiana) can be reached from Macapá (Amapá) by bus to Oiapoque, from where there are onward *combis* to St Georges Oyapock (Guyane), onward to Cayenne and all the way through Suriname to Guyana. See page 622.

Guyana is easily reached by bus from Boa Vista via Bonfim (Roraima) to Lethem (Guyana), from where there are buses to Georgetown. See page 678.

Getting around the Amazon

By road Aside from routes to Belém from the Atlantic Coast and from Tocantins, bus routes are limited to the following: **Amazonas/Roraima**: Manaus–Boa Vista (via Presidente Figueiredo), paved. **Roraima**: Boa Vista–Venezuela, paved. Boa Vista– Guyana, paved. **Amazonas**: São Gabriel da Cachoeira–Cucuí, paved and dirt. **Amapá**: Macapá–Oiapoque (from where there is boat and road access to French Guiana), dirt. **Pará**: Santarém–Cuiabá (in the Pantanal) is being improved and buses now run intermittently along the route through Pará into Mato Grosso with changes at Itauba for Alta Floresta and the Rio Cristalino; enquire at the *rodoviára* in Cuiabá or Santarém for the latest details. **Amazonas/Rondônia**: Humaitá–Porto Velho. **Rondônia/Acre**: Porto Velho–Rio Branco with onward buses to Cruzeiro do Sul and Peru, weather permitting. There are services to Guajará-Mirim along a small branch road, paved and dirt. **Rodônia/Mato Grosso**: Porto Velho–Cuiabá and onwards to the rest of Brazil, paved. There are dirt roads Manaus–Porto Velho, and Santarém–Porto Velho, but these are currently overgrown and impassable.

The legend of the rubber tree

Once upon a time, an Amazonian *indígena* called Maitá was unfairly accused of theft. As a punishment, the chief of his tribe cruelly condemned him to a very peculiar task: to empty a small lake by using a wicker basket. The work was of course extremely unproductive, as the water always flowed through the holes of the basket. Maitá soon realized that he would have to work for the rest of his life and still never empty the lake.

Knowing that Maitá was innocent, a forest fairy approached the poor *indígena* and asked him to follow her. They walked in the jungle until they reached a very large tree. There, she showed Maitá how to make some cuts in the tree and, as he did, he noticed that a milk-like liquid started to flow.

The tree was a rubber tree and the liquid was natural latex. Then the fairy told him to spread the sticky liquid over the basket and wait for a while. As the liquid started to dry, he realized that a thin layer of a water resistant material (rubber) was covering all the holes. On returning to the lake, he was very pleased to see that he had no problem in scooping out large amounts of the lake's water. He gratefully thanked the fairy and finished his task in a few days.

As in all good fairy tales, there was a happy ending. The chief discovered he had made a mistake and apologized to Maitá on his return to the tribe. A big party was held to celebrate Maitá's return and, most of all, an important secret had been revealed: the secret of the rubber tree.

By plane Flight networks within the Amazon are extensive. **Rico**, www.voerico.com.br, flies Manaus–Belém with stops at Santarém and Parintins and to a number of smaller towns. **Trip**, www.voetrip.com.br, flies Manaus–São Gabriel da Cachoeira via Barcelos, and Manaus–Tabatinga via Tefé; it also links Manaus with Brasília, Cuiabá and Campo Grande and Alta Floresta with Brasília, Cuiabá and the rest of Brazil. **META**, www.voemeta.com, flies Belém–Boa Vista, Belém–Georgetown (Guyana) via Paramaribo (Suriname), Belém–Santarém, Boa Vista–Georgetown and Boa Vista–Paramaribo. **TAM**, www.tam.com.br, links Alta Floresta, Altamira, Santarém and all the Amazon state capitals with the rest of Brazil and with Cuzco (Peru). **GOL**, www.voegol.com.br, connects all of the state capitals with the rest of Brazil. **Oceanair**, www.oceanair.com.br, flies to Manaus, Porto Velho and Alta Floresta.

Flight schedules are constantly changing and routes frequently close and re-open. Check the airline websites for the latest details and for prices.

By boat River boats are the buses of the Amazon and serve an extensive network, connecting both major and minor settlements. You won't see a great deal from the deck, especially if travelling downstream, as the boats stay in the middle of the river to catch the current. Going upstream, you will see an endless line of trees broken by the occasional village. However, the atmosphere on board is lively. Food is served, usually consisting of meat, beans and rice (which is brown as it is cooked in river water) and there is often a bar serving drinks and snacks. The size and quality of the boats varies greatly. The best boats ply the busiest routes: Manaus–Santarém–Belém and Manaus–Tabatinga. Overcrowding can be a problem.

The cheapest way to travel is **hammock class**, out in the open on the deck. Be sure to take water, a cable and padlock for your bags, a jumper (nights on the water can be cool) a good book and, most importantly, a *rede* (hammock) with two pieces of rope (each about 1 m long) to string it up across the beams. The boats that travel on the Amazon itself are largely mosquito free – except when they moor; it's a good idea to bring a *mosquiteiro* *para rede* (mosquito net) for your hammock. Hammocks and nets can be bought easily in any of the larger Amazon towns, usually in the downtown area near the river. Arrive early to get a good spot. Some boats also have air-conditioned berths and **cabins** and, for a higher price, **suites** with attached bathroom.

Many boats ply the following routes: Manaus–Belém via Parintins, Óbidos and Santarém (four days); Manaus–São Gabriel da Cachoeira via Barcelos and Santa Isabel (six days); Manaus– Porto Velho via Manicoré and Humaitá (four days); Manaus–Tefé (36 hours); Manaus– Parintins (20 hours); Manaus–Tabatinga (six days); Belém–Santarém (two to three days); Belém–Macapá (36 hours); Macapá–Manaus (seven to 10 days).
▸▸ *See Transport, page 670.*

Health
There is a danger of **malaria** in Amazônia, especially on the brown-water rivers. Mosquito larvae do not breed well in the black-water rivers as they are too acidic. Mosquito nets are not required when in motion as boats travel away from the banks and are too fast for mosquitos to settle. However, nets and repellent can be useful for night stops. Wear long, loose trousers (tight ones are easy to bite through) and a baggy shirt at night and put repellent around shirt collars, cuffs and the tops of socks. **Johnsons Off** is an effective brand and is available in pharmacies throughout Brazil.

A **yellow fever** inoculation is strongly advised. It is compulsory to have a certificate when crossing borders and those without one will have to get inoculated and wait 10 days before travelling. Other common infections in the Amazon are **cutaneous larva migrans** (a spot that appears to move), which is easily treated with **Thiabendazole**, and **tropical ulcers**, caught by scratching mosquito bites, which then get dirty and become infected. ▸▸ *See Health, page 53.*

Amazon food
The Amazon has a distinctive range of dishes that make use of the thousands of fruits and vegetables and the abundant unique fish. Must-tries include *tacacá*, a soup made with jambo leaves, which numbs the tongue and stimulates energy. The best fish are pacu and tambaqui, both types of vegetarian piranha; the carnivorous ones can be eaten too. Pirarucu, one of the world's largest freshwater fish, is delicious, however, due to overfishing it is in danger of becoming extinct. Specialities of Pará state include duck, often served as *pato no tucupi*, in a yellow soup made from the juice of the root of the *tucupi* (manioc) and served with *jambo*. *Maniçoba* is made with the poisonous leaves of the *cassava* (bitter manioc), simmered for eight days to get rid of the cyanide. *Caldeirada* is a fish and vegetable soup, served with *pirão* (manioc puree), and is a speciality of Amazonas. There is also an enormous variety of tropical and jungle fruits, many unique to the region. Try them fresh, or in ice creams or juices. The best include *tapereba*, *cupuaçu*, *cajú* (the fruit of the cashew nut), *cacão* (the fruit of the cocoa bean) and *camu camu*, which has the highest vitamin C content of any fruit in the world. Avoid food from street vendors, except those selling *tacacá* at the Boi bumba.

Banks
There are plenty of ATM facilities in all the Amazon's main towns and whenever there is a **Bradesco** or **Banco 24 horas**. Small amounts of US dollars cash can usually be exchanged away from banks at a poor rate, but are not accepted as local currency. The rate of exchange for exchange traveller's cheques is appalling.

Amapá and Pará

Sometimes called Brazilian Guyana, the isolated border state of Amapá was once exploited for its natural resources and suffered from heavy deforestation. However, efforts are now being made towards sustainable development. Located near the French territory of Guyane, with its cheap air links to Paris, it is another good port of entry into northern Brazil. Tourist infrastructure outside the provincial riverside capital of Macapá is negligible. The state is a quarter of the size of France and has a population of just under half a million.

Pará is just across the river from Amapá – a distance that would span Switzerland. In the 1990s, the state capital, Belém, was dangerous and down at heel, but extensive refurbishment in the last decade has transformed it into an attractive colonial city. The state itself is barely aware of the existence of tourists. Although there are many beautiful natural sights, such as the vast river island of Marajó in the Amazon delta and the Amazônia National Park on the River Tapajós, infrastructure is poor, with no jungle lodges at all in the extensive rainforests. While areas north of the Amazon have been afforded at least nominal protection since 2006, in the south of the state rapid deforestation is making space for vast soya plantations.

Santarém, a quiet little town at the junction of the Tapajós and Amazon rivers, is the world's largest soya-export port. Thankfully ecotourism is gradually catching on here: a few tour companies offer trips to the river beaches at Alter do Chao and the failed rubber plantation towns of Belterra and Fordlândia – set up by Henry Ford in the early 20th century. Monte Alegre, whose caves have revealed evidence of a significant pre-Columbian Amazon culture, are a day's boat ride away upstream. Travel in Pará takes time (as it does anywhere in the Amazon) and the more isolated parts of the state are often linked only by boat and air. Even when there are roads, rain and forest encroachment makes even asphalted areas impassable. ▶▶ *For listings, see pages 636-648.*

Macapá ⬤🅟🅘🅕🅧🅢🅞⚠🅐🅒 ▶▶ *pp636-648. Colour map 1, A5.*

→ *Phone code: 096. Population: 284,000.*

The capital of Amapá is a pleasant city on the banks of the northern channel of the Amazon delta. It has an impressive fortress as well as a monument to the equator, which divides the city. There is a museum detailing the research being carried out in the rainforest and at nearby Curiaú, a village originally formed by escaped slaves.

The town was founded around the first Forte de São José do Macapá, built in 1688. In 1751 more settlers from the Azores arrived to defend the region from Dutch, English and French invasions and the *aldea* became a *vila* in 1758. Many slaves were later brought from Africa for the construction of the fort.

Ins and outs

Getting there The **airport** ① *R Hildemar Maia, 3 km from the centre, T096-3223 4087*, receives flights from Belém, Brasília, Foz do Iguaçu, Rio de Janeiro, São Paulo, São Luís, Fortaleza, Marabá and Cayenne (Guyane). Taxis to the centre cost around US$7.

Buses arrive at the new **rodoviária** ① *on the BR-156, 3 km north of Macapá*. Buses from Oiapoque pass through the city centre after a long and uncomfortable journey over mainly unsurfaced roads. This journey can take even longer during the rainy season (January to May). Boats from Belém and Santarém arrive at nearby Porto Santana, which is linked to Macapá by bus or taxi. ▶▶ *See Transport, page 644.*

Getting around There is an air-taxi service to some towns, however, most are linked by the trucks, buses and community minibuses, which leave from the new *rodoviária*. Buses to other parts of the city leave from a bus station near the fort. The centre and the waterfront are easily explored on foot.

Tourist information SETUR ① *Av Binga Uchôa 29, T096-3212 5335, www.setur.ap.gov.br, Mon-Fri 1000-1800*, also has a branch at the airport. For information on national parks, contact **Ibama** ① *R Hamilton Silva 1570, Santa Rita, CEP 68906-440, Macapá, T/F096-3214 1100, www.ibama.co.br*. The website www.macapaturismo.com.br is also useful.

Sights
Each brick of the **Fortaleza de São José do Macapá**, built between 1764 and 1782, was brought from Portugal as ballast. Fifty iron cannon still remain and there is a museum. The *fortaleza* is used for concerts, exhibitions and colourful festivities on the anniversary of the city's founding on 4 February. **São José cathedral**, inaugurated by the Jesuits in 1761, is the city's oldest landmark. The **Centro de Cultura Negra** ① *R General Rondon*, has a museum and holds frequent events. The **Museu do Desenvolvimento Sustentável** ① *Av Feliciano Coelho 1509, Tue-Fri 0830-1200, 1500-1800, Mon and Sat 1500-1800*, exhibits research on sustainable development and traditional community life in Amazônia. The museum shop sells arts and crafts.

Macapá

Sleeping
Atalanta 1
Ceta Ecotel 8
Frota Palace 3
Gloria 4
Holliday 9
Macapá 5
Mercúrio 6
Pousada Ekinox 2
Santo Antônio 7
Vista Amazônica 10

Eating
Bom Paladar Kilo's 3
Cantinho Baiano 2
Chalé 1
Divina Arte 5
Divina Gula 6
Flora 7
Sarney 8

The riverfront has been landscaped with trees, lawns and paths and is a very pleasant place for an evening stroll. The **Complexo Beira Rio** has food and drink kiosks and a lively atmosphere. The recently rebuilt *trapiche* (pier) is a lovely spot for savouring the cool of the evening breeze, or watching the sun rise over the Amazon.

There is a monument to the equator, **Marco Zero** (take Fazendinha bus from Avenida Mendonça Furtado). The equator also divides the enormous football stadium nearby, aptly named O Zerão. The Sambódromo stadium is located nearby. South of here are the **botanical gardens** ① *Rodovia Juscelino Kubitschek, Km 12, Tue-Sun 0900-1700.*

Excursions from Macapá

Some 16 km from the centre, **Fazendinha** is a popular local beach, which is very busy on Sunday and has many seafood restaurants. **Curiaú**, 8 km from Macapá, is inhabited by the descendants of African slaves, who have maintained many of the customs of their ancestors. They are analogous to the Bush Negroes of Suriname, making the village the only one of its kind in Brazil. It is popular at weekends for dancing and swimming. The surrounding area is an environmental reserve with many water buffalo.

North of Macapá ●●●● ➤➤ *pp636-648.*

North of Macapá the road divides at **Porto Grande**, and a branch heads northwest to **Serra do Navio** where manganese extraction has now ended (**Hotel Serra do Navio** and several bars and restaurants). The BR-156 continues north, passing the turnings for two jungle hotels. The paved road goes as far as **Ferreira Gomes** on the shores of the Rio Araguari. Further on is **Amapá**, formerly the territorial capital and location of a Second World War American airbase. There are a few hotels. Beyond Amapá is **Calçoene**, with a government-owned hotel that serves expensive food in an adjoining canteen; very cheap sleeping space is also advertised in a café on the Oiapoque road. North of Calçoene a road branches west to **Lourenço**, whose goldfields still produce even after decades of prospecting. The main road continues north across the Rio Caciporé and on to the border with French Guyane at **Oiapoque**, on the river of the same name.

Oiapoque → *Colour map 1, A5. Population: 13,000.*

This is a ramshackle little gold-mining town with dirt streets lined with little guesthouses, spit-and-sawdust bars and shops buying the precious metal by the gram. It lies 90 km inland from **Cabo Orange**, Brazil's northernmost point on the Atlantic Coast and the site of one of its wildest and remotest national parks. Access to the park is very difficult although guides can sometimes be arranged through the boatmen on the river docks in Oiapoque.

Oiapoque town has its share of contraband, illegal migration and drug trafficking and can be a little rough; visitors should be cautious, especially late at night. With the building of the road between St-Georges Oyapock and Cayenne, the town has become a popular spot for French Guianan weekenders, most of them single men and in search of more than a drink. The **Cachoeira Grande Roche** rapids can be visited, upstream along the Oiapoque river, where it is possible to swim, US$30 by motor boat. The **Associação dos Povos Indígenas de Oiapoque**, in front of the Banco do Brasil, provides information about the indigenous peoples that live in the area, and the indigenous Uaçá reserve.

The road construction has led to significant environmental damage with much deforestation along the Brazilian side of the road in Amapá, and Brazilian *garimpeiros* and hunters illegally flooding into Guyane have been causing havoc in pristine forests.

Border essentials: Brazil–Guyane

Oiapoque (Brazil)–St-Georges Oyapock (Guyane)

From Macapá, only the first section of the road north to the Guyane border (BR-156) is paved. It is precarious in places but open year-round with buses and pickups operating even in the wet season. Take food and water for the journey as services are scarce. Petrol and diesel are available along the road, but drivers should take extra fuel at Macapá. There are at at least two buses a day to from Macapá to Oiapoque. From Oiapoque there are frequent launches to Guyane across the river (US$5, 10 minutes). A bridge is being built and should be complete in 2010. *Combis* to Cayenne leave from St-Georges Oyapock before lunch so be ready by 1000.

Belém ⬤🅿️🚗⊛⊙🔺⬤🅒 ▶▶ *pp636-648. Colour map 1, A6.*

→ *Phone code: 091. Population: 1.3 million.*

Belém do Pará is the great port of the Amazon. The city has much of cultural interest, a fascinating market, and is the starting point for trips along the river. With mean temperatures of 26°C, it is hot, but frequent showers freshen the streets. The city has its share of crime and is prone to gang violence. Take sensible precautions, especially at night. The river in front of Belém rises by many metres during the seasonal floods.

Ins and outs

Getting there **Val-de-Cans international airport** ① *Av Júlio César s/n, 12 km from the city, T091-3210 6000*, receives flights from the USA, Caribbean, the Guianas and the major Brazilian capitals. The airport bus 'Perpétuo Socorro-Telégrafo' or 'Icoaraci' runs every 15 minutes to the Prefeitura on Praça Felipe Patroni (US$1.50, allow 40 minutes). A taxi from the airport into town costs US$15. Ordinary taxis are cheaper than co-operatives, buy ticket in advance in departures side of airport. There are ATMs in the terminal, tourist information, cafés and car rental.

There are road connections from São Luís and the northeastern coast as well as a three-day bus link from São Paulo via Brasília. Interstate buses arrive at the **rodoviária** ① *end of Av Gov José Malcher, 3 km from the centre*. There are showers (US$0.10), a good snack bar, and agencies with information and tickets for riverboats. Buses to the centre cost US$0.50; taxis charge US$5-7. At the *rodoviária* you are given a ticket with the taxi's number on it; threaten to go to the authorities if the driver tries to overcharge.

Boats arrive at the port from Macapá, Manaus and Santarém as well as other parts of the Amazon region and delta. ▶▶ *See Transport, page 645.*

Getting around The city centre is easily explored on foot. City buses and taxis run to all the sites of interest and to transport hubs away from the centre.

Tourist information **Paratur** ① *Praça Waldemar Henrique, Reduto, on the waterfront, T091-3242 1118, www.paraturismo.pa.gov.br*, has information on the state and city. Some staff speak English and can book hotels and tours to Marajó island. For information on national parks contact **Ibama** ① *Av Conselheiro Furtado 1303, Batista Campos, CEP 66035-350, T091-3241 2621, www.ibama.com.br*. The website www.belemonline.com.br is also useful.

Background

Established in 1616 because of its strategic position, Belém soon became the centre for slaving expeditions into the Amazon Basin. The Portuguese of Pará, together with those of Maranhão, treated the *indígenas* abominably. Their isolation from the longer- established colonies allowed both places to become relatively lawless. In 1655, the Jesuits, under Antônio Vieira, attempted to lessen the abuses, while enticing the *indígenas* to descend to the *aldeias* around Belém. This unfortunately led to further misery when smallpox spread from the south, striking the Pará *aldeias* in the 1660s.

Soon after Brazil's Independence, the Revolta da Cabanagem, a rebellion by the poor blacks, *indígenas* and mixed-race *cabanos*, was led against the Portuguese-born class that dominated the economy. The movement came to an end in 1840 when the *cabanos* finally surrendered, but the worst years of violence were 1835-1836. Some estimates say 30,000 were killed. The state's strategic location once again became important during the Second World War, when Belém was used as an airbase by the Americans to hunt German submarines in the Atlantic.

Sights

Belém used to be called the 'city of mango trees' and there are still many such trees remaining. There are some fine squares and restored historic buildings set along broad

1 Belém orientation

➡ Belém maps
1 Belém orientation, page 623
2 Belém centre, page 624

avenues. The largest square is the **Praça da República**, where there are free afternoon concerts; the main business and shopping area is along the wide Avenida Presidente Vargas, leading to the river, and the narrow streets which parallel it.

The recently restored neoclassical **Teatro da Paz** ⓘ *Tue-Fri 0900-1800, tours US$1.50,* (1874), is one of the largest theatres in the country and worth a visit. It stages performances by national and international stars, and offers free concerts and shows.

West of here, at the **Estação das Docas**, the abandoned warehouses of the port have been restored into a complex with an air-conditioned interior and restaurants outside. The Terminal Marítimo has an office of **Valverde Tours**, which offers sunset and night

2 Belém

➡ **Belém maps**
1 Belém orientation, page 623
2 Belém centre, page 624

Baía do Guajará

Sleeping
Fortaleza 13
Grão Pará 1
Itaoca Belém 2
Le Massilia & Restaurant 3
Machado's Plaza 8
Novo Avenida 4
Palácio 5
Regente 6
Unidos 10

Eating
Açaí (Hilton Hotel) 6
Boteco das Onze 4
Cantina Italiana 1
Churrascaria Rodeio 8
Churrascaria Tucuruvi 9
Doces Bárbaros 2
Govinda 10
Lá em Casa 5
Mãe Natureza 11
Manjar das Garças 7
Portinha 12
Sabor Paraense 3

Bars & clubs
A Pororó 13
Café Com Arte 15
Carousel 14
do Gilson 16
Mormoço 17
São Mateus 18

200 metres
200 yards

cruises. The Boulevard das Artes contains the **Cervejaria Amazon** (brewery), with good beer and simple meals, an archaeological museum and arts and crafts shops. The Boulevard de Gastronomia has smart restaurants and the five-star **Cairu** ice cream parlour (try açaí or the *pavê de capuaçu*). In the Boulevard das Feiras there are trade fairs. Live music is transported between the pavilions on a moving stage. Also in the complex are ATMs, internet café, phones and good toilets.

Heading south, the 17th-century **Mercês church** (1640) is the oldest in Belém. It forms part of an architectural group known as the Mercedário, the rest of which was heavily damaged by fire in 1978 and has now been restored.

Near the church, the Belém market, known as **Ver-o-Peso**, was the Portuguese Posto Fiscal, where goods were weighed to gauge taxes due, hence the name: 'see the weight'. It now has lots of gift shops selling charms for the local African-derived religion, *umbanda*, and interesting medicinal herb and natural perfume stalls. You can see giant river fish being unloaded around 0530, with frenzied wholesale buying for the next hour. A new dock for the fishing boats has been built just upriver from the market. The whole area swarms with people, including many armed thieves and pickpockets.

Around Praça Dom Pedro II is a cluster of interesting buildings. The **Palácio Lauro Sodré** and **Museu do Estado do Pará** ⓘ *Praça Dom Pedro II, T091-3225 3853, Mon-Fri 0900-1800, Sat 1000-1800*, is a gracious 18th-century Italianate building. It contains Brazil's largest framed painting, *The Conquest of Amazônia*, by Domenico de Angelis. The building was the work of the Italian architect Antônio Landi, who also designed the cathedral, and was the administrative seat of the colonial government. During the rubber boom many new decorative features were added. Also on Praça Dom Pedro II is the **Palácio Antônio Lemos**, which houses the **Museu de Arte de Belém** as well as the **Prefeitura** ⓘ *Tue-Fri 0900-1200, 1400-1800, Sat and Sun 0900-1300*. It was originally built as the Palácio Municipal between 1868 and 1883, and is a fine example of the Imperial neoclassical style. In the downstairs rooms there are old views of Belém; upstairs, the historic rooms, beautifully renovated, contain furniture and paintings, which are all well explained.

The **cathedral** ⓘ *Praça Frei Caetano Brandão, Mon 1500-1800, Tue-Fri 0800-1100, 1530-1800*, (1748), is also neoclassical, and contains several remarkable paintings. Directly opposite is the restored 18th-century **Santo Aleixandre church**, which is noted for its woodcarving.

Also in the old town is the **Forte do Castelo** ⓘ *Praça Frei Caetano Brandão 117, T091-3223 0041, daily 0800-2300*, which was rebuilt in 1878. The fort overlooks the confluence of the Rio Guamá and the Baía do Guajará and was where the Portuguese first set up their defences. There is a good restaurant, the **Boteco Onze**, where you can watch the sunset (entry US$1, drinks and *salgadinhos* served on the ramparts from 1800). At the square on the waterfront below the fort, the açaí berries are landed nightly at 2300, after being picked in the jungle. Açaí berries, ground up with sugar and mixed with manioc, are a staple food in the region.

East of the centre, the **Basílica de Nossa Senhora de Nazaré** ⓘ *Praça Justo Chermont, Av Magalhães Barata, Mon-Sat 0500-1130, 1400-2000, Sun 0545-1130, 1430-2000*, was built in 1909 from rubber wealth. It is romanesque in style and has beautiful marble and stained-glass windows. The *basílica* feels very tranquil and sacred, especially when empty. A museum here showcases one of the largest and most colourful festivals in the North of Brazil, the **Círio de Nazaré** (see page 642). The botanic gardens, **Bosque Rodrigues Alves** ⓘ *Av Almirante Barroso 2305, T091-3226 2308, Tue-Sun 0800-1700*, is a 16-ha public garden (really a preserved area of original flora), with a small animal collection. To get there, take the yellow bus marked 'Souza' or 'Cidade Nova' (any

The Jesuits and the slave trade

Cristobal de Acuna, a Jesuit who visited the Amazon in the 1620s, describes an incredible density of villages along the lower Amazon. He writes of the happy and abundant life of the Omagua people, the largest of the tribal nations, who lived in large towns with handsome houses, fired pottery as fine as any in Europe, baked bread, wove cotton and farmed turtles. Within 100 years of his visit they and all the *indígenas* of the lower Amazon nations were killed and their cultures and achievements lost for ever.

The were lost to 'Red Gold', the little-known Amazon slave trade. The *indígenas* were rounded up in droves and brought to São Luís and Belém to farm the burgeoning sugar plantations where they were forced to live in appalling conditions and work until they died. Only the Jesuits sought to abate this human traffic. They had long defended the Guaraní in southern Brazil by persuading them to move into settlements organized along European lines, which were known as reductions or *aldeias*. They were determined to do the same in the Amazon. Their leader, Antônio Viera, berated the people of São Luís and Belém with hellfire sermons: "What is a human soul worth to Satan?" he asked; "There is no market on earth where the devil can get them more cheaply than right here in our own land … What a cheap market! An Indian for a soul! Christians, nobles," he begged "break the chains of injustice and free those whom you hold captive and oppressed!"

Viera was successful... for a while. The captive *indígenas* would be sent to Jesuit reductions from where they would be on loan to plantation owners for six months each year. The *indígenas* were certainly treated with less cruelty by the Jesuits. However, the Order were, in effect, equally responsible for the loss of indigenous life and culture. The reductions were breeding grounds for European disease and the *indígenas* were forced to completely abandon their religious and social practices. And when the Order was forced to leave Iberian America after a campaign against them by Portugal's Marquis de Pombal, the *indígenas* who had been under their charge were enslaved and treated with renewed viciousness.

A typical Jesuit reduction was rectangular and built around a large *praça de armas*. To the rear of the plaza stood the church. On one side of the church was the cemetery and on the other the claustro, where the Jesuits themselves lived and studied. Near this were the workshops in which the works of art were produced. Behind the church were the gardens. Around the other sides of the plaza were the houses in which the *indígenas* lived. The streets between the buildings were at right angles to each other and the settlement could easily be expanded along this plan. Chapels were built on the sides of the plaza. Other buildings included the *cabildo* (the municipal building of the *indígenas*), the *cotiguazu* (a house for widows), a prison, a hospital and an inn for visitors.

number), 30 minutes from Ver-o- Peso market, or from the cathedral. The **Museu Emílio Goeldi** ① *Av Magalhães Barata 376, Tue-Thu 0900- 1200, 1400-1700, Fri 0900-1200, Sat and Sun 0900-1700, US$1*, takes up an entire city block and consists of the museum proper (with a fine collection of indigenous Marajó pottery and an excellent exhibition of Mebengokre tribal lifestyle), a rather sad zoo and botanical exhibits including Victoria Régia lilies. Buses run from the cathedral.

The **Murucutu** ruins, an old Jesuit foundation, are reached by the Ceará bus from Praça da República; entry is via an unmarked door on the right of the Ceará bus station.

A *foca* (passenger ferry) to the small town of **Barcarena** ⓘ *daily departures from Ver-o-Peso, but best Tue-Fri, US$1,* makes an interesting half-day trip. A return trip on the ferry from Ver-o-Peso to Icaoraci provides a good view of the river. Several restaurants here serve excellent seafood; you can eat shrimp and drink coconut water and appreciate the breeze coming off the river. **Icaoraci** is 20 km east of the city and is well known as a centre of ceramic production. The pottery is in Marajóara and Tapajonica style. Artisans are friendly and helpful, will accept commissions and send purchases overseas. A bus from Avenida Presidente Vargas in Belém runs to Icoaraci.

The nearest beach to Belém is at **Outeiro** (35 km), on an island near Icoaraci. It takes about an hour by bus and ferry (the bus may be caught near the **Maloca**, an indigenous-style hut near the docks that serves as a nightclub). A bus from Icoaraci to Outeiro takes 30 minutes.

Further north is the island of **Mosqueiro** (86 km), accessible by bridge and an excellent highway, with many beautiful sandy beaches and jungle inland. It is popular in July and at weekends, when traffic can be heavy and the beaches get crowded and polluted. Buses from Belém to Mosqueiro run every hour from the *rodoviária* (US$1.50, 80 minutes). There is also a ferry from Porto do Sal, on the street between Forte do Castelo and the cathedral. It takes about two hours. There are many hotels and weekend villas in the villages of Mosqueiro and Vila, which are recommended, but these may be full during peak times.

Islands around Belém

The mouth of the Amazon, formed by the confluence of that river in the north and the Tocantins in front of Belém, is dotted with myriad islands and mangrove lined backwaters. There are 27 islands around Belém; the largest of which, **Marajó** (see below), is as big as Switzerland. Many of the islands can be visited on a day trip from the capital, others are a longer haul. Most are lined with long beaches of fine sand broken by strands of clay and dark stones heavy with iron ores. The water that washes them looks as expansive as an ocean, stretching to a vast horizon, but even out in what is geographically the Atlantic, it is fresh water and brown.

Ilha do Cotijuba, www.cotijuba.com, and the more built-up **Ilha do Mosqueiro**, www.mosqueiro.com.br, are reachable from Belém in a couple of hours. Both have a number of *pousadas* and small restaurants, stretches of forest and, on Cotijuba, gorgeous beaches. The islands get very crowded at Christmas and during Carnaval. The **Ilha da Mexiana** in the Marajó archipelago is more remote and less visited.

Ilha de Maiandeua is more commonly known by the name of its principal town, **Vila** do Algodoal, which is a small-scale traveller resort very popular with French backpackers. It's a three-hour bus and boat journey from Belém, off the Atlantic coast. The island is a semi-protected area at the junction of the sea, the Amazon and the Rio Maracanã. It is very tranquil and has sand dunes, small lakes and a number of isolated beaches lapped by an Atlantic heavy with the silt of the Amazon. The main town is tiny with a cluster of sandy streets lined with little houses, many of them *pousadas*. Donkey carts connect it with the island's other beaches, notably Farol (with its flat tidal sands) and Princesa (with its dunes and many of the cheap beach *pousadas*). All accommodation is low-key and simple.

Roads to nowhere

In the early 1970s, Brazil's military rulers became increasingly unnerved by what they saw as foreign designs upon the resources of the Amazon basin. This real or imaginary fear of invasion was directed against not only the rich, developed countries, but also Brazil's neighbours, who the Brazilians felt were slowly encroaching upon the country's borders. In the early 1960s, Peru's president, Fernando Belaunde Terry, had proposed the construction of the Carretera Marginal in order to link Peru's jungle with the rest of the country. Under the slogan '*Integrar para não entregar*' (takeover not handover), the Brazilian military announced the construction of the **Transamazônica Highway**. The road was originally designed to link João Pessoa, Paraíba, with Acre, thence to link up with the Peruvian road system to complete a road route across South America to the Pacific and open up Brazilian products to Asian markets. The Transamazônica itself would be 5400 km

and would unify Amazônia from east to west and integrate it with the rest of the nation. In addition, it would give opportunities for people from the northeast to resettle in areas not affected by drought and to become economically active in small agricultural schemes. In the often-quoted words of President Emílio Garrastazu Médici, it would move "*Homens sem terra para terras sem homens*"' (people without land to land without people). All along the highway, purpose-built *agrovilas* would offer Brazil's poor a new life. The project was proposed in 1970; huge financial investment failed to make it work. Not only did fewer than anticipated northeasterners take up the offer, but those that did found that the Amazonian soils did not permit the type of rewards that they had been led to expect. The colonizers also found that the social infrastructure did not meet their needs and both the road and the project began to deteriorate. By the late 1980s, a

Ins and outs Boats run to Cotijuba from the docks in Belém (especially at the weekends), however, the quickest way to reach all the islands is from the port in **Icoaraci**, 20 km north of Belém (30 minutes bus ride from the *rodoviária* or from near the Ver o Peso market; taxi US$25). There are at least four boats a day from here to **Cotijuba**; the first at 0900. Others only leave when full. The fastest take 20 minutes, the slowest one hour.

Mosqueiro is connected to the mainland by road. At least four buses a day leave from the *rodoviária* taking around 90 minutes to get to the main towns (Praia do Paraíso, Carandaduba and Vila Mosqueiro).

Algodoal is reached by taking a bus from Belém to Marudá town, from where you catch a ferry. It is easy to find a room on arrival, except for weekends and holidays.

There are no banks on any of these islands, so bring cash from Belém.

Ilha de Marajó → *Colour map 1, A5.*

The largest island near Belém is also the largest riverine island in the world (although some claim that as it abuts the Atlantic the title belongs to Bananal, see page 725). Like the rest of the Amazon, Marajó is partly flooded in the rainy season between January and June. The island is home to feral water buffalo, which can be seen in large numbers; they are said to have swum ashore after a shipwreck. Many are now farmed and Marajó is famous throughout Brazil for its *mozarela* cheese. The island's police force use the buaffalo instead

'Movement for Survival' along the Transamazônica had been set up by the farmers.

Another road which was intended to promote development in the Amazon region was the **BR-364**, from Cuiabá to Acre state. In the mid-1970s, the government hoped that the road would reinvigorate settlement in the Amazon, in a way that the Transamazônica had failed to do. Like the latter, the BR-364 was supposed to encourage small landholders to follow the building of the main highway and its feeder roads, but in Rondônia the main colonizers were cattle ranchers and land speculators who speeded up the process of deforestation and caused land conflicts with the traditional cultivators, forest farmers and indigenous people.

A third road in the Amazon which has come to grief, even more so than the other two, is the **BR-319** from Manaus to Humaitá on the Transamazônica. Planned in 1960 and opened to traffic in 1975, the road has become a route from nothing to nowhere. The people living along it have been deserted, the only maintenance being the occasional team from Embratel who come to look at the telephone lines which follow the road. Initially there were farms, hotels, petrol stations and restaurants along the BR-319. Most have now gone. Access to health clinics and schools is all but impossible and the only public transport on the southern part of the road is a once-weekly truck. The only people to benefit are the shipping owners who take the traffic, which would have used the road, on barges along the Rio Madeira. The journalist Giuliano Cedroni tried to drive the BR-319 in the late 1990s. He and his companions made it through, but not without a tow from the weekly truck after their jeep broke down. One inhabitant of the region pleaded with him: "Tell the people down there [in the south] what is happening in the north. This here is not a life."

of horses to get around the beaches. The island is also home to numerous bird species, including thousands of roseate spoonbills, and black caiman, river turtles and other wildlife. The island was the site of the pre-Columbian Marajóaras culture, celebrated for its ceramics. It gets very busy in the July holiday season.

The capital of Marajó is **Soure** (good restaurants and services), with the other principal town being **Salvaterra** (better beaches and accommodation); both are on the eastern side of the island, which has the only readily accessible shore. There are many fine beaches around both towns: **Araruna** (2 km from Soure; take supplies and supplement with coconuts and crabs), from where it's a beautiful walk along the shore to **Praia do Pesqueiro** (13 km from Soure; bus from Praça da Matriz at 1030, returns 1600, food available at Maloca), a deserted beach; and **Caju-Una** 15 km from Soure. **Praia de Joanes** between the point of arrival on Marajó (Porto de Camará) is a popular place to stay with a laid-back feel, some impressive Jesuit ruins and cliffs overlooking the beach. In the far south of the Marajó archipelago is the little town of **Ponta de Pedras**, which has a few colonial buildings and a fine beach. Fishing boats make the eight-hour trip to **Cachoeira do Arari** (one hotel, D), where there is a fascinating **Marajó museum**. A 10-hour boat trip from Ponta de Pedras goes to the **Arari lake** where there are two villages: **Jenipapo** and **Santa Cruz**. The latter is less primitive and less interesting; a hammock and a mosquito net are essential. Bicycles can be hired on Marajó for around US$1 per hour to explore beaches and the interior of the island.

Ins and outs A ferry from **Belém** sails twice daily (once daily at weekends), from the Armazem 10 dock in town (US$5). Boats also run from **Porto de Icoaraci**, 20 km north of Belém (30 minutes bus ride from the *rodoviária* or from near the Ver-o-Peso market; taxi US$25). Boats take three hours for the 30 km crossing to the island's main arrival point, **Porto de Camará**, (20 km south of Salvaterra). From here, small craft await to transfer passengers to Salvaterra village (US$12, 10 minutes), or take a bus/ferry to Soure. There is also a taxi-plane service direct to Soure from Belém. The capital has a **Banco do Brasil** ATM, but this is unreliable. Changing money is only possible at very poor rates. Take plenty of insect repellent.

Salinópolis → *Colour map 1, A6. Population: 33,500.*

Some 223 km from Belém, at the extreme eastern end of the Amazon delta, this seaside resort has many small places where you can eat and drink at night by the waterfront. There is a fine sandy beach nearby (buses and cars drive onto the beach) but the water is murky. It is a peaceful place mid-week but very busy at weekends and in high season and is at its peak during the holiday month of July.

Atalaia, an island opposite Salinópolis, is pleasant and can be reached by taxi (US$6) or by boat. Salinópolis is four hours from Belém by bus on a good road, US$6.

The little riverside village of **Tomé-Açu**, south of Belém on the Rio Acará-Mirim, affords a view of life on a smaller river than the Amazon. Three buses a day run from Belém, US$8. The **Hotel Las Vegas** has a friendly owner, Fernando. The boat back to Belém on Sunday leaves at 1100, arriving 1800, US$5.

South of Belém ⊖🖋⊖⊙ ⇒ *pp636-648.*

Marabá and around → *Colour map 1, B5. Phone code: 094. Population: 170,000. Altitude: 84 m.*
Near Marabá are beaches on the Tocantins and Itacaiúnas rivers, which are best visited from June to October. There is a bridge across the Tocantins at Marabá. The town was moved as a result of the Tucuruí dam, but it still suffers from flooding. There are essentially three parts of the town: **Marabá Velha** (also called Marabá Pioneira), **Marabá Nova** and **Cidade Nova**. The distance between Marabá Nova and Velha is about 2.5 km. A good travel agent is **IBR Travel** on the main street of Marabá Velha. **Banco do Brasil** will not cash traveller's cheques; the parallel market operates in larger stores, such as **Supermercado Bato Logo**.

The **Serra Pelada** gold mines, made famous by Sebastião Salgado, whose images made them look like the circles of Hell, are now worked by heavy machinery. This huge excavation was the scene of much human misery and also some fabulous fortunes. To get there, take a bus to Km 6 and change for the Serra Pelada bus, US$6, three hours, last bus back 1400. About 11 km before the town is a police post where searches are carried out for weapons and alcohol (forbidden). There is a second search point at the airport, 2 km from the mine.

Ins and outs The **Aeroporto de Marabá** ⓘ *4.5 km from the centre, Transamazônica Km 1, Marabá, T094-3324 1271,* receives flights from Belém, São Luís, Imperatriz and other towns. The **rodoviária** ⓘ *Nova Marabá, 4 km on PA-150, T094-3321 1892,* has bus connections with the main regional cities as well as Rio de Janeiro and São Paulo. There are river services from Belém (24 hours) and Santarém (18 hours). ⇒ *See Transport, page 646.*

Monte Alegre

Monte Alegre is the site of archaeological discoveries that have threatened to radically alter current views of the spread of civilization in South America. In the 1990s, Dr Anna C Roosevelt, of the Field Museum of Natural History, Chicago, found pottery fragments in a cave which, according to radiocarbon dating, appear to be from 7000-8000 BC. This pre-dates by some 3000 years what was thought to be the earliest ceramic ware in South America (from Colombia and Ecuador). Subsequent artefacts discovered here, however, have radiocarbon dates of 15,000 BC, which calls for a significant rethink of the original idea that people moved from the Andes into the Amazon Basin. These finds suggest that the story of the people of the Americas is more diverse than hitherto understood. The cave that Dr Roosevelt excavated is called Caverna da Pedra Pintada. Also in the area are pictographs, with designs of human and animal figures and geometric shapes. Trips can be arranged; many thanks to Philip W Hummer, who sent us a description of a tour led by Dr Anna Roosevelt.

Carajás

The main attraction here is an impressive iron ore mine, operated by the **Companhia Vale Rio Doce** (**CVRD**) ① *T091-3327 5300, or enquire at Av Graça Aranha 26, 16th floor, Centro, Rio de Janeiro*. The mine is a giant red hole in a green jungle and the ore is almost pure iron oxide and therefore extremely profitable. It is ground, washed and shipped to São Luís by trains up to 2 km long, without further treatment or chemical processing. Apart from iron ore, other metals such as manganese are also mined by the CVRD in the area. As a result of the mining, a city has built up around Carajás, but most of it is within CVRD bounds. To get into Carajás (the Núcleo and to visit the mine) and to pass the checkpoint 35 km from the project, you must have a permit, available from CVRD. You need to apply in advance and have a good reason for visiting. There is accommodation in **Parauapebas**, built as a temporary settlement for the Carajás construction workers, and now a town in its own right.

Ins and outs The **Aeroporto De Carajás** ① *Estr Raimundo Mascarenhas Km 150, Parauapebas, T094-3327 1103, 18 km from the town centre*, receives flights from Belém, Marabá, Belo Horizonte, Brasília, Manaus and Tucuruí. The *rodoviária* is in the town centre and has bus connections with cities as far away as Rio de Janeiro and São Paulo. There are also trains from Marabá (1930, two hours, US$4) and São Luís. ▸▸ *See Transport, page 646.*

West of Belém

Along the Transamazônica

The Transamazônica, an almost impassable dirt road riddled with potholes and infringing forest throughout its 5000 km, connects Brazil's eastern and western extremities. And for no good reason. Millions of dollars were spent on constructing this road, while others of real economic importance in the east of the country were left to crumble. Together with grandiose and unnecessary schemes such as the Amazon dams, the Transamazônica was a major contributor to the country's national debt and to deforestation (see box, above).

The Transamazônica crosses the Rio Xingu at **Favânia**, 41 km east of Altamira, a busy, booming Amazonian town with many gold dealers. A road is being paved 46 km north to the fishing village of **Vitória** on the lower Xingu, from where boats go to Belém. The dock is a good place to watch *garimpeiros* (gold prospectors), who have been responsible for destroying huge areas of the forest, working below the last rapids. There are no organized trips but a boat can be hired, US$25 per day, for a trip up the Xingu, which is highly recommended (buy food in Altamira). The area is an indigenous Assurine reserve and it is forbidden to enter villages without permission. Many animals can be seen.

Ins and outs It is possible to make your way along sections of the road using public transport, but there is no predicting whether the route will be open. Some sections are impassable throughout the rainy season. Others have sporadic scheduled bus services. Conditions change constantly so detailed local enquiry is essential before heading out. Driving the road is sometimes possible in a 4WD, but it is challenging and can be dangerous. Do not leave without spare tyres, 20 litres of water, food for a day and plenty of reais. It is essential to speak some Portuguese as you will need to enquire about road conditions along the way.

Towards Amazonas state ☺❶❷❸❹❺▲❻❼ ›› *pp636-648.*

Santarém → *Colour map 1, B4. Phone code: 093. Population: 262,500.*
The third largest city on the Brazilian Amazon is small enough to walk around in a morning. It was founded in 1661 as the Jesuit mission of Tapajós; the name was changed to Santarém in 1758. There was once a fort here, and attractive colonial squares overlooking the waterfront still remain. Standing at the confluence of the Rio Tapajós with the Amazon, on the southern bank, Santarém is halfway (three days by boat) between Belém and Manaus. Most visitors breeze in and out of town on a stopover.

In front of the market square, the yellow Amazon water swirls alongside the green blue Tapajós river at the meeting of the waters, which is nearly as impressive as that of the Negro and Solimões near Manaus (see page 657). A small Museu dos Tapajós, Centro Cultural João Fora, on the waterfront, downriver from where the boats dock, has a collection of ancient Tapajós ceramics, as well as various 19th-century artefacts. The unloading of the fish catch between 0500 and 0700 on the waterfront is interesting.

There are good beaches nearby on the Rio Tapajós. Prainha, a small beach, is between town and the port, by a park with many mango trees (Floresta–Prainha bus from centre). On the outskirts of town is Maracanã, with sandy bays (when the Tapajós is low) and some trees for shade (Maracanã bus from the centre, 20 minutes). Santarém has been at the centre of rapid deforestation in the last decade – fuelled by soya (see box, page 635).

Ins and outs Aeroporto Maestro Wilson Fonseca ① *15 km from town, Praça Eduardo Gomes, s/n, T093-3523 4328*, receives flights from Fortaleza, Belém, Salvador, Brasília, Manaus and other towns in the Amazon. From the **rodoviária** ① *outskirts of town, T093-3522 3392*, buses run to the waterfront near the market, US$0.55. Boats from Belém and Manaus dock at the **Cais do Porto**, 1 km west of town (take 'Floresta-Prainha', 'Circular' or 'Circular Externo' bus; taxi US$4); boats from other destinations, including Macapá, dock by the waterfront near the centre of town. The tourist office, **Comtur**① *R Floriano Peixoto 434, T/F093-3523 2434*, has good information available in English. ›› *See Transport, page 646.*

Alter do Chão → *Colour map 1, B4.*

Alter do Chão is a friendly village on the Rio Tapajós, at the outlet of Lago Verde, 34 km west. There is good swimming in the Tapajós from the beautiful clean beach. Close to Alter do Chão (30 minutes by boat), the joining of the Rio Tapajós with the Aruã and the Arapiuns creates an island surrounded by clean rivers of differing colours, each teeming with life. The forested island is being developed as an ecopark, **Parque Ecoturístico Arapiuns**, with accommodation for visitors; it is already becoming popular. Monkeys and birds inhabit the woodlands, protected more for commercial reasons than any other. For information, contact **Paratur** ⓘ *T091-3223 2130, Belém.*

Floresta Nacional do Tapajós → *Colour map 1, B4.*
ⓘ *Information from Paratur in Belém, www.paraturismo.pa.gov.br.*

At Km 123, south of Santarém on BR-163, there is a section of the Floresta Nacional do with a vehicle track running due west through it. The other parts of the park are on the other bank of the river. It is beautiful rainforest which can be entered with permission from **Ibama** if accompanied by one of their guides. It is well worth a visit if only to see the butterflies. Trips can be organized with tour operators in Santarém, see page 644.

Santarém

N
Not to scale

Sleeping	Mirante 4	Eating
Brasil 1	New City 5	Mascote 2
Brasil Grande 2	Santarém Palace 7	Mascotinho 3
Grão Rios 6		Piracaia 4
Horizonte 3		Sabor Caseiro 5

Belterra and Fordlândia → *Colour map 1, B4. Phone code 093.*

Fordlândia, 300 km south of Santarém, was Henry Ford's first rubber plantation. He founded it in 1926 in an attempt to provide a cheaper source of rubber for his Ford Motor Company than the British and Dutch controlled plantations in Malaya. There is **Hotel Zebu**, in old Vila Americana (turn right from the dock, then left up the hill), one restaurant, two bars and three shops on the town square. There is a little pebble beach north of town.

Closer to Santarém, 37 km south on a dirt road, is **Belterra**, where Henry Ford established his second rubber plantation. In the highlands overlooking the Rio Tapajós. It is nearer to the town than his first project, which was turned into a research station. At Belterra, Ford built a well laid-out town, where the houses resemble the cottages of Michigan summer resorts, many with white paint and green trim. The town centre has a large central plaza that includes a bandstand, the church of Santo Antônio (circa 1951), a Baptist church and a large educational and sports complex. A major hospital, which at one time was staffed by physicians from North America, is now closed.

Ford's project, the first modern attempt to invest in the Amazon, was unsuccessful. It was difficult to grow the rubber tree in plantation conditions, where it was unprotected from the heavy rains and harsh sun, and indigenous parasites were attracted by the concentrations of trees. Boats could only come this far upriver in the rainy season and there was a series of disputes between the American bosses and the local employees. Ford sold up in 1945 and the rubber plantation is now deserted.

Around Santarém

Blood crop

Ten years ago Santarém was surrounded by trees. Since then, the ranchers have arrived and the trees are disappearing, just as they are further south in Mato Grosso and the Goiás *cerrado* forests, in order to make way for lucrative soya plantations. In 2003 the huge multinational company Cargill built a soya grain terminal in Santarém so that the crop could be transferred to ocean going vessels in the north of the country and not the south. The decision had a far reaching impact. The road cutting up to Santarém from the centre west was renovated and agriculture began to expand into the Amazon. With such an easy means of export on the city's doorstep, developers moved in to Santarém itself, claiming they would bring food and jobs to the poor. The area occupied by farms around the city rose rapidly to over 750 sq km and was planted on land that had been cleared from secondary forest, as well as some 10% on newly felled rainforest Indigenous *caboclo* communities who had made their homes on the land coveted by the farmers were displaced. The ranchers came armed with a ream of false title deeds – just as they did with the *caiçairas* on the Costa Verde (see page 177). Some *caboclos* sold up. Others were forced off through threats of violence. A few stubbornly stayed. They were intimidated, then beaten. Some were killed. Very few found work on the plantations where the machinery is high tech and the manpower required minimal. And the soya plantations continued to expand. In 2006 Brazil became the world's biggest soya exporter. After a long Greenpeace campaign, in June 2008 the Brazilian environmental minister Carlos Minc called for a deal to curb appropriation of land for soya farms. But Brazil has a powerful elite and a long history of lip service. The country's current strict environmental legislation is rarely enforced. So for now the vegetarian option is as complicit in death and deforestation as hardwood tables or beef.

Óbidos → *Colour map 1, A4. Phone code: 093. Population: 46,500.*

Óbidos is the last major town between Santarém and the border with Amazonas state. It is located at the narrowest and deepest point on the river where, millions of years ago, the Amazon (which at that stage was a giant lake in the middle of Brazil) squeezed through the gap in the Guyana and Brazilian highlands to meet the Atlantic. The town was strategically important in the Portuguese expansion of the Amazon. The **Forte Pauxi** (Praça Coracy Nunes, 1697) is a reminder of this fact. Today, Óbidos is a picturesque and clean city with many beautiful tiled buildings and some pleasant parks. Worth seeing are the **Prefeitura Municipal** ① *T093-3547 1194*, the *cuartel* and the **Museu Integrado de Óbidus** ① *R Justo Chermont 607, Mon-Fri 0700-1100 and 1330-1730*. There is also a **Museu Contextual**, which consists of a system of plaques with detailed explanations of historic buildings throughout town. Boating and fishing trips can be arranged and there is a popular beach at **Igarapé de Curuçambá** (with bus connections).

Ins and outs The small airport has flights to Manaus, Santarém and Parintins. Óbidos is five hours upriver from Santarém by boat (110 km). A poor road runs east to Alenquer, Monte Alegre and Prainha and west to Oriximiná, impassable in the wet season.

For Sleeping and Eating price codes and other relevant information, see pages 42-47.

Sleeping

Macapá *p619, map p620*
AL Ceta Ecotel, R do Matodouro 640, Fazendinha, T096-3277 3396, www.ecotel.com.br. A rainforest-themed hotel with sloths and monkeys in the trees and a series of trails. All the furniture is made on site. 20 mins from the town by taxi.
AL-A Atalanta, Av Coracy Nunes 1148, T096-3223 1612. By far the best hotel in town with a rooftop pool and comfortable modern a/c rooms with bathrooms. Includes a generous breakfast. 10 mins' walk from the river.
A Macapá, Av Francisco Azarias Neto 17, on the waterfront, T096-3217 1350. The city's grandest hotel, overlooking the river, with a pool, tennis courts and children's play area. Rooms are past their best. Popular with families from Guyane.
A-B Pousada Ekinox, R Jovino Dinoá 1693, T096-3223 0086, www.ekinox.com.br. One of the best in town, with chalets set in a little tropical garden and with a library. Helpful, French-speaking staff and a good restaurant.
B Frota Palace, R Tiradentes 1104, T096-3223 3999, www.hotelfrota.com.br. Plain, faded rooms with en suites. Airport pickup service for US$3.
C Gloria, Leopoldo Machado 2085, T096-3222 0984. A clean, well-kept, simple hotel with a/c rooms all with en suite, TV and hot water. Breakfast included in the price.
D Mercúrio, R Cândido Mendes 1300, 2nd floor, T096-3224 2766. Very basic, but close to Praça São José (where the bus from Porto Santana stops).
D-E Holliday, Av Henrique Gallúcio 1623, T096-3223 3122. Very simple, though recently repainted, little boxy a/c rooms 20 mins' walk from the river. Breakfast included.
D-E Vista Amazônica, Av Beira Rio 1298 (about 1.5 km beyond the Cantino Baiano

restaurant away from town), T096-3222 6851. A simple *pousada* and restaurant sitting right opposite the Amazon, with simple but well-maintained tiled rooms with en suites.
E-F Santo Antônio, Av Coriolano Jucá 485, T096-3222 0226. Very simple and slightly musty downstairs rooms and brighter a/c rooms upstairs.

Oiapoque *p621*
There are plenty of cheap hotels in Oiapoque, but they are not well maintained. The noisiest and least reputable are closest to the river; the best a few blocks behind.

Belém *p622, map p624*
A series of new openings and renovations has seen Belém's hotels improve greatly, although they are still not up to much. All are fully booked during **Círio** (see Festivals, page 642). There are many cheap hotels close to the waterfront (none too safe) and several others near the *rodoviária* (generally okay).
A Itaoca Belém, Av Pres Vargas 132, T091-4009 2400, www.pousadadosguaras.com.br. Well-kept, bright, no-nonsense a/c rooms with writing desks and en suites. The best are on the upper floors away from the street noise, and with river views. Decent breakfast.
A Machado's Plaza, R Henrique Gurjão 200, T091-4008 9800. Bright, brand-new boutique hotel with smart and tastefully decorated a/c rooms, a small business centre, plunge pool and a pleasant a/c breakfast area. Good value.
A Regente, Av Gov José Malcher 485, T091-3181 5000, www.hotelregente.com.br. Small, newly refurbished a/c rooms decorated in cream and white tile and with standard 3-star fittings, above a noisy street. Popular with US tour groups.
B Le Massilia, R Henrique Gurjão 236, T091-3224 2834, www.massilia.com.br. An intimate, French-owned boutique hotel with chic little duplexes and more ordinary doubles. Excellent French restaurant and a tasty French breakfast.

B-C Brisa, R Senador Lameira Bittencourt 5, Centro (in front of the Orla), T093-3522 1018, brisahotel@hotmail.com. Plain but airy and well-maintained rooms, friendly staff and a decent breakfast.

C-D Grão Pará, Av Pres Vargas 718, T091-3224 9600, www.hotelgraopara.com.br. Well-kept, new a/c rooms with contemporary fittings and smart en suites in black marble, and a boiler for hot water. The best have superb river views. Excellent breakfast. Great value.

D Hotel Beira Rio, R Adriano Pimentel 90A, T093-3522 2519. The best cheap rooms in the city. Small and simple but clean and fresh. The hotel has friendly staff and offers a good breakfast.

D Novo Avenida, Av Pres Vargas 404, T091-3223 8893, www.hotelnovoavenida.com.br. Slightly frayed but spruce en suite rooms. Decent breakfast. Groups can sleep in large rooms for **E-F** per person. Good value.

D Unidos, Ó de Almeida 545, T091-3229 0600. Simple but spruce, spacious a/c rooms with cable TV and clean en suites.

E-F Fortaleza, Trav Frutuoso Guimarães 276, T091-3212 1055. Unkempt hotel with a range of very simple wood-floor rooms and dorms around a communal sitting area. Popular with backpackers. Be careful in this area after dark.

E-F Palácio, Trav Frutuoso Guimarães, T091-3212 8422. Opposite and almost identical to the Fortaleza, though with scruffier communal areas and slightly cleaner rooms, and a snack bar/restaurant. Be careful in this area after dark.

Islands around Belém *p627*
Cotijuba
C-D Pousada Farol, T091-3259 7144, T091-9943 0237 (mob). Chalets and rooms in annexes set in a little garden right in front of the beach. Good rates during the week. Friendly owners. On the opposite side of the island from the port.

Mosqueiro
There are plenty of opportunities for camping on Mosqueiro and a wealth of *pousadas* in all price brackets.

B Farol, Praia Farol, Olha do Mosqueiro, T091-3771 1219. With 1920s architecture but in good repair, small restaurant, rooms face the beach, good views.

Vila do Algodoal
B-C Jardim do Éden, http://onlinehotel.com.br/ para/ilha-do-algodoal/ jardim-do-eden-pousada/index.htm. A series of bizarre neo-Gothic brick *cabañas* with kitchenettes overlooking the beach on Praia do Farol. Well kept and well run and with more personality than most on the island. Tours available and camping in the grounds (on the beach). Discounts available online.

B-C Pousada Bela-Mar, Av Beira Mar, Vila do Algodoal beach, T091-3854 1128, www.bela mar.hpgvip.com.br. A very simple beachside hotel with tiny rooms, set in a garden. Close to the boat jetty.

B-C Pousada Chalés do Atlântico, Vila do Algodoal, T091-3854 1114. Recently renovated. 11 simple little *cabañas* with mosquito screening, en suites and cold showers.

Ilha de Marajó *p628*
A Pousada dos Guarás, Av Beira Mar, Salvaterra, T/F091-3765 1133, www.pousadadosguaras.com.br. Well-equipped little resort hotel on the beach with an extensive tour programme.

C Paracuary, T091-3225 5915, www.paracauary.com.br. A/c rooms with en suites in mock colonial chalets around a pool 3 km from Soure and on the banks of the Rio Paracuary.

C Ventania, www.pousadaventania.com. Pretty little cliff-top *pousada* in a lawned garden a stroll from the beach. Each apartment has room for 2 couples **D**. Bike rental, French, Dutch, English and Spanish spoken.

Salinópolis *p630*
A Atalaia, Ilha Atalaia, 15 km from Salinópolis, T/F091-3464 1122. A simple *pousada* in a pleasant setting. Reserve in advance for the weekend, take a taxi.

A Joana d'Arc, Av João Pessoa 555, T/F091-3823 1422. Modest but well looked after and with a generous breakfast.
A Solar, Av Beira Mar, T091-3823 1823. The best in town with smart en suite rooms and a good restaurant.
B Diolindina, Av Pres Médici 424, Capanema, T091-821 1667. Small clean a/c rooms with fridge and bath. The price includes breakfast and safe parking. Recommended. There are good restaurants and a supermarket opposite.

Marabá and around *p630*
There are seedy cheap hotels by the *rodoviária*.
A Del Príncipe, Av Marechal Rondon 95, Cidade Nova, T094-3324 1175. A/c rooms with TV and fridge in modest hotel with a restaurant and games room.
A Vale do Tocantins, Folha 29, Cidade Nova, 7 km, T094-3322 2321. Modern and characterless, with a restaurant and travel agency.
B Dallas, Nova Marabá. Well run and convenient for the *rodoviária* (immediately next door). Recommended.
B Plaza, Folha 32, quadra 10, lote 06, T094-3322 3543. Fan-cooled rooms in a quiet and friendly hostel serving a very good breakfast. Some English spoken. Recommended.

Santarém *p632, map p633*
All hotels, except **Amazon Park**, are in the compact grid of streets in the heart of the city near the waterfront.
A Amazon Park, Av Mendonça Furtado 4120, T091-3523 2800, amazon@ stm.interconect.com.br. Large 1970s hotel, 4 km from the centre, with a swimming pool and friendly, competent staff.
C Brasil Grande Hotel, Trav 15 de Agosto 213, T091-522 5660. Family-run. Restaurant.
C New City, Trav Francisco Corrêa 200, T091-523 3149. Standard town hotel with plain a/c rooms and an airport pickup service. River trips can be organized from here.
C-D Santarém Palace, Rui Barbosa 726, T091-3523 2820. A 1980s hotel with 44 comfortable but simple a/c rooms with TV and fridge.

D Brasil, Trav dos Mártires 30, T091-3523 5177. Pleasant, family-run, with fan-cooled rooms with shared bathrooms, breakfast and a small restaurant.
D Mirante, Trav Francisco Correa 115, T091-3523 3054, freephone T0800-707 3054, www.mirantehotel.com. One of the new and cleaner cheapies. A/c rooms with fridges, TVs, and some with a balcony and individual safes. Internet facilities available. Recommended.
D-F Horizonte, Trav Senador Lemos, 737, T091-3522 5437, horizontehotel@bol.com.br. Plain, simple, well-kept rooms with a/c or fan.
E Grão Rios, in a little alley off Av Tapajós between Trav dos Mártires and 15 de Agosto. Well-kept a/c rooms, some with a river view.

Alter do Chão *p633*
B Belas Praias Pousada, R da Praia s/n at the praca, T093-3527 1365. Belaspraias@ gmail.com. Located on the river front of the beaches, and offering the best rooms – a/c and well appointed with river views.
B-C Agualinda Hotel, R Dr Macedo Costa s/n, T093-3527 1314. A comfortable, clean modern hotel with friendly staff who can help organize forest and river tours.
D-E Albergue Pousada da Floresta, T093-3527 1172, www.alberguedafloresta.com. A simple backpacker hostel with basic cabanas and a very cheap open-space for slinging hammocks. Facilities include tour organizing, canoe and bike rental, kitchen and in a great location next to the forest just south of the village. Prices include breakfast. Ask for Angelo.

Belterra *p634*
E Hotel Seringueira. 8 simple fan-cooled rooms and a pleasant restaurant.

Óbidos *p635*
C Braz Bello, R Corrêia Pinto, on top of the hill. Clean rooms with shared bathrooms. Optional full board.
C-D Pousada Brasil, R Corrêia Pinto. Basic with fan-cooled rooms with en suites or shared bathrooms.

🍴 Eating

Macapá p619, map p620
The waterfront *praça* has many open-air restaurants and bars, concentrated at the *trapiche* (pier). These are lively after 1800, especially at weekends.

₩₩₩ **Chalé**, Av Pres Vargas 499, T096-3222 1970. The best restaurant in the city with good fish, Brazilian dishes and a pleasant atmosphere.

₩₩ **Cantinho Baiano**, Av Beira-Rio 1, T096-3223 4153. Overlooking the river 10 mins' walk south of the fort and with some of the best river fish in town. There are many other restaurants along this stretch about 1.5 km beyond the Cantinho Baiano.

₩₩ **Flora**, Rodovia Salvador de Diniz 1370-A, Km 15, T096-3283 2858. A lively little restaurant on the riverside next to a little marina 15 km from the fort (travelling away from town). Good fish and local dishes; try the fish infused with energetic Amazon fruits.

₩ **Bom Paladar Kilo's**, Av Pres Vargas 456, T096-223 0555. Pay-by-weight buffet with excellent ice cream made from local fruits; make sure you try the *cupuaçu*.

₩ **Divina Arte**, Av Pres Vargas 969, T096-3222 1877. A decent lunchtime menu restaurant and per kilo buffet. Plenty of choice.

₩ **Divina Gula**, Av Pres Vargas 993, T096-3083 2091. Pleasant little café serving coffee, cakes and snacks.

₩ **Sarney**, R Gal Rondon 1501. Simple but very cheap and filling per kilo restaurant. Good value. Lunchtime only.

Oiapoque p621
Gourmets will find themselves in a desert but there are many cheap places serving fish, beans and rice, and several spit-and-sawdust bars in the blocks around the river.

Belém p622, map p624
All the major hotels have upmarket restaurants. There are numerous outdoor snack bars serving far cheaper meals. Good snack bars serving *vatapá* (Bahian dish) and

tapioca rolls are concentrated on **Assis de Vasconcelos** on the eastern side of the Praça da República. There are many decent a/c restaurant, bar and café options in the smart and newly renovated **Estação das Docas** on the riverfront where the boats dock.

₩₩₩ **Açaí, Hilton Hotel**, Av Pres Vargas 882, T091-3242 6500. Come for lunch or dinner daily, or Sun brunch. Regional dishes such as roasted duck with *tucupi* sauce and jambo leaves.

₩₩₩ **Boteco das Onze**, Praça FC Brandão s/n, T091-3224 8599. Just about the best regional cooking in Belém with live music every night and a view out over the river. Packed at weekends. Try the *filetena brasa* or the excellent *tambaqui*.

₩₩₩ **Churrascaria Rodeio**, Rodovia Augusto Montenegro, Km 4, T091-3248 2004. A choice of 20 cuts of meat and 30 buffet dishes for a set price. Well worth the short taxi ride to eat all you can.

₩₩₩ **Churrascaria Tucuruvi**, Trav Benjamin Constant 1843, Nazaré, T091-3235 0341. Enormous slabs of pork, beef, lamb and a range of sausages; all in vast portions and served with salads and accompaniments.

₩₩ **Cantina Italiana** Trav Benjamin Constant 1401, T091-225 2033. Excellent Italian, with hotel delivery.

₩₩ **Lá em Casa**, Estação das Docas. Very good local cooking, especially the buffet and the à la carte *menu paraense*. Try the excellent *tacacá no tucupi* (an acrid soup with prawns cooked with jambo leaves that make the mouth go numb).

₩₩ **Le Massilia**, see Sleeping. French-owned and run with dishes including frogs' legs, *sole meunière* and *magret de canard*. Excellent cocktails.

₩₩ **Manjar das Garças**, Praça Carniero da Rocha s/n, Arsenal da Marinha, Mangal das Garças, T091-3242 1056. Huge lunch and evening buffet. The restaurant sits next to the river in a small park filled with scarlet ibis on the edge of town. Taxis US$5. Well worth it for an all you can eat meal at weekends.

Natural energy drinks

There is nowhere better for fruit juices than Brazil: the choice is staggering. Some juice bars in the Amazon and in Rio's beach suburbs have over 30 different flavours to choose from – many from fruits that are unknown and unavailable outside of South America. Must-tries include *cupuaçu*, a fragrant, pungent juice extracted from a relative of the *cacao* bean; *cajú* made from the fruit of the cashew nut tree; and *tapereba* – tangy, deliciously refreshing and made from an Amazon fruit related to the Brazil nut. If you are looking to top up your energy levels opt for an *açai an acerola* or a *camu camu*. *Açai* is a meal in itself, served thick, sweet, icy cold and dark maroon, and packed with electrolytes and vitamins. *Acerola*, which comes originally from the Yucatán, is a tropical cherry with a sharp, refreshing flavour and what was thought until recently to be the highest of all naturally occurring levels of vitamin C.

This accolade is now accorded to *camu camu*, a light-orange fruit from the Amazon which on average contains about 2g of vitamin C per 100g – 30 times as much as an average orange. *Camu camu* is also a significant source of vitamin B, phosphorus, potassium and iron, together with the full complement of other minerals and amino acids which aid the absorption of vitamin C.

Many of these juices are available as constituents of various non-alcoholic cocktails or *vitaminas*; made up with either water or milk, sugar and often *guaraná* powder – a naturally occurring stimulant made from a pounded Amazon nut. Some are used in *batidas* – vodka and fruit juice infusions. More standard fruits such as limes (*limao*), passion fruit (*maracuja*) and strawberries (*morango*) are used to flavour *caipirinhas* and their vodka and sake counterparts, the *caipiroska* and *caipisake/sakirinha*.

♈ **Sabor Paraense**, R Sen Manoel Barata 897, T091-3241 4391. A variety of fish and meat dishes such as crab in coconut milk served in a bright, light dining room.

♈-♐ **Mãe Natureza**, R Manoel Barata 889, T091-3212 8032. Lunch only. Vegetarian and wholefood dishes in a bright clean dining room.

♐ **Doces Bárbaros**, R Benjamin Constant 1658, T091-3224 0576. Lunch only. Cakes, snacks, sandwiches and decent coffee in a/c surrounds.

♐ **Govinda**, R Ó de Almeida 198. Lunch only. Basic but tasty vegetarian food.

♐ **Portinha**, R Dr Malcher 434, T091-3223 0922. Thu-Sun evenings only. Wonderful pastries, *takaka*, *carnes* and juices.

Islands around Belém *p627*

♈ **Hotel Ilha Bela**, Av 16 de Novembro 409, Mosqueiro. No evening meals. Recommended for fish.

♈ **Marésia**, Praia Chapeu Virado, Mosqueiro. Highly recommended.

♐ **Sorveteria Delícia**, Av 16 de Novembro, Mosqueiro. Serves good local fruit ice creams and the owner buys dollars.

Ilha de Marajó *p628*

There are a number of cheap places to eat in Soure but few restaurants of any distinction.

♐ **Canecão**, Praça da Matriz, Soure. Sandwiches and standard beans, rice and cheap meals. Recommended.

Salinópolis *p630*

♐ **Bife de Ouro**, Av Dr Miguel Santa Brígida, opposite petrol station. Simple, but excellent for fish and shrimp. Always busy at lunchtime.

♐ **Gringo Louco**, 15 km (take taxi or hitch), at Cuiarana beach (follow signs). The US owner serves good, unusual dishes, and some 'wild' drinks known as 'bombs'. Popular.

Marabá and around *p630*

There are a few good *churrascarias* around the central *praça*.

♯♯ **Bambu**, Pedro Carneiro 111, Cidade Nova, 3 km. Open 1100-1500, 1800-2300. Mainly fish, clean, good value.

♯♯ **Lanchonete Domino**, opposite the *rodoviária*. Recommended.

Santarém *p632, map p633*

As with other small towns in the interior of Brazil, most restaurants in Santarém serve basic café-style food, lunch (consisting of rice, beans, chips and a choice of beef, chicken or fish) and juices. The best choice is to be found along the waterfront in the centre.

♯♯ **Mascote**, Praça do Pescador 10, T091-3523 2844. Open 1000-2330. Fish-orientated restaurant with a bar and ice cream parlour. Avoid *piraracu*.

♯♯ **Mascotinho**, Praça Manoel de Jesus Moraes, on the riverfront. Bar and pizzeria attracting a lively crowd at sunset. Great river view.

♯♯ **Santo Antônio**, Av Tapajós 2061, T091-3523 2356. Barbecued meat and fish.

♯ **Piracaia**, R Floriano Peixoto 557, Centro, T091-3522 2881. The best value quality per kilo restaurant in town with a great choice of meat, fish and a few veggie options. General Brazilian cuisine.

♯ **Sabor Caseiro**, R Floriano Peixoto 521, Centro, T091-3522 5111. Northern cooking with Takaka soups, river fish and prawn dishes alongside the usual chicken/meat and rice, beans and chips.

Alter do Chão *p633*

♯ **Lago Verde**, Praça 7 de Setembro. Good fresh fish, try *calderada de tucunaré*.

Óbidos *p635*

There are plenty of cheap fish restaurants near the waterfront and in the upper town.

🎵 Bars and clubs

Macapá *p619, map p620*

The food and drink kiosks in **Complexo Beira Rio** have live music most evenings. **ETNA** is the current dance club of choice, vibrating to the frenetic local rhythm *brega*, which sounds like *forró* on speed.

Belém *p622, map p624*

Belém has some of the best and most distinctive live music and nightlife in northern Brazil. It's well worth heading out on the town at weekends.

A Pororó. Vast warehouse jam packed with techno *brega* acts playing a kind of up tempo disco driven 2/4 dance to thousands of people every Fri and Sat.

Bar do Gilson, Travessa Padre Eutíquio 3172, T091-3272 1306. A covered courtyard space decorated with arty black and white photography and with live samba and *choro* on weekends. The bar owner, Gilson, often plays mandolin in the band.

Café com Arte, Av Rui Barbosa 1436. Good after 2300. A colonial house with 3 floors devoted to live rock and DJs, attracting an alternative studenty crowd at weekends.

Carousel, Av Amirante Barroso at Antônio Baena. Live *aparelhagem* – a kind of up-tempo techno with twanging guitars played by DJs on a sound stage that looks like the flight control gallery for a 1970s starship. Has to be seen to be believed. Every Fri.

Mormoço, Praça do Arsenal s/n, Mangal das Garças. A warehouse-sized building on the waterfront which showcases some of the best live bands in Belém at weekends, playing local rhythms like *carimbó* and Brazilianized reggae and rock.

São Mateus, Travessa Padre Eutíquio 606. A mock Carioca *boteco* street bar with space for some 300 people who gather to listen to Belém rock and Brazilian soul most nights.

Albery Albuquerque recommends

There is no one quite like Albery Albuquerque, www.myspace.com/alberyalbuquerque. He makes music from the rainforest by spending months recording birds and wild animals in the heart of the Amazon and precisely reproducing their calls with keyboard, voice and stringed instruments within his complex instrumental music. Here are his recommendations for what to do in Belém.

→ Take a taxi to Ver-o-Rio (Pedro Alvares Cabras near to Moinho Santa Rosa) for sunset. The views out over the river and the colours in the sky are magical.
→ If you have only a little time in Belém be sure to visit Cotijuba island for a taste of the forest and a sense of the size and magnificence of Amazonian nature.

🌐 Entertainment

Macapá *p619, map p620*
Art galleries Cândido Portinari, corner of R Cândido Mendes and Av Raimundo Álvares da Costa. Exhibitions of local art.

Cinemas In Macapá Shopping, R Leopoldo Machado 2334.

Theatre Teatro das Bacabeiras, R Cândido Mendes. Concerts, poetry and plays.

Belém *p622, map p624*
Art galleries Debret, R Arcipreste Manoel Theodoro 630, Batista Campos, T091-222 4046. Contemporary painting and sculpture, also has library specializing in art and philosophy.
Casa das 11 Janelas (1768), Praça Frei Caetano Brandão, T091-3219 1105. Cultural performances and art exhibitions, panoramic view.

Cinema Olímpia, Av Pres Vargas 918, T091-3223 1882. The first cinema in Belém, opened over 80 years ago, but now shows films for lonely men. But **Nazaré** a few doors down is respectable and there are plenty of multiplexes in the city's shopping malls.

Theatre Margarida Schiwwazappa, Av Gentil Bittencourt 650, T091-3222 2923.

🌐 Festivals and events

Macapá *p619, map p620*
Apr/May Marabaixo is the traditional music and dance festival held for 40 days after Easter.
Jun The Sambódromo has parades of Escolas de Samba at **Carnaval** and Quadrilhas during São João.
14 Aug Festa de São Joaquim held in Curiaú.

Belém *p622, map p624*
Apr Maundy Thu, half-day; Good Fri, all shops closed, all churches open and there are processions.
9 Jun Corpus Christi.
15 Aug Accession of Pará to Independent Brazil.
7 Sep Independence Day, commemorated on the day with a military parade, and with a student parade on the preceding Sun.
30 Oct Círio. The festival of candles, based on the legend of Nossa Senhora de Nazaré whose image was found on the site of her Basílica around 1700. On the 2nd Sun in Oct a procession carries the Virgin's image from the Basílica to the cathedral; it is returned 2 weeks later. The festival attracts many artists and musicians and has become a massive national celebration with carnival performers and rock groups. Highly recommended.

Coletivo Radio Cipo recommend

Coletivo Radio Cipo, www.myspace.com/coletivoradiocipo, play a vibrant mix of reggae, *carimbó*, roots and rock. They are one of the most exciting bands on the vibrant Belém music scene and often play life in the city. Their singer Carlinhos recommends the following: 'For me the **Bar do Gilson** (see page 641) is a great spot to listen to music, eat and chat. In the 1970s when a group of friends who loved *chorinho* and other such music found there was nowhere to play it in Belém they began to gather here. Some great names have played at the venue over the years, when they pass through Belém, such as Paulino da Viola, Beth Carvalho, Cristina Buarque and Sivuca, together with musicians from Japan, Cuba and other countries. It's a great place and there's always a good show.'

2 Nov All Souls' Day.
8 Dec Immaculate Conception.
24 Dec Christmas Eve, half-day.

Santarém *p632, map p633*
22 Jun Foundation of the city.
29 Jun São Pedro, with processions of boats on the river and Boi-Bumba dance dramas.
8 Dec Nossa Senhora da Conceição, the city's patron saint.

Alter do Chão *p633*
2nd week in Sep Festa do Çairé, religious processions and folkloric events. Recommended.

O Shopping

Macapá *p619, map p620*
Macapá and Porto Santana were declared a customs-free zone in 1992. There are now many cheap imported goods available from shops in the centre. In the handicraft complex **Casa do Artesão**, Av Azárias Neto, Mon-Sat 0800-1900, craftsmen produce their wares on site. A feature is pottery decorated with local manganese ore, also woodcarvings and leatherwork.

Belém *p622, map p624*
There is an arts and crafts market in the **Praça da República** every weekend selling attractive seed and bead jewellery, wicker, hammocks and raw cotton weave work, toys and other knick-knacks. Belém is a good place to buy hammocks: look in the street parallel to the river, 1 block inland from Ver-o-Peso. There is a bookshop with English titles in the arcade on **Av Pres Vargas**.
Complexo São Brás, Praça Lauro Sodré. Has a handicraft market and folkloric shows in a building dating from 1911.
Parfumaria Orion, Trav Frutuoso Guimarães 268. Has a wide variety of perfumes and essences from Amazonian plants, much cheaper than tourist shops.
Ná Figueredo, Av Gentil Binttencourt 449, Nazaré and Estação das Docas, T091-3224 8948, www.nafiguredo.com.br. One of the best music shops in the north of Brazil selling a wealth of local sounds from the very best bands and unusual music from throughout Brazil. Funky T-shirts and casualwear.
Shopping Iguatemi, Trav Padre Eutique 1078. Belém's shopping mall.

Santarém *p632, map p633*
Muiraquitã, R Lameira Bittencourt 131. Good for ceramics, woodcarvings and baskets.

▲ Activities and tours

Macapá *p619, map p620*
Tour operators
Amapá Turismo, Hotel Macapá, T096-3223 2667. **Fénix**, R Cândido Mendes 374, T/F096-3223 8200, and R Jovino Dinoá 1489, T096-3223 5353.

Belém *p622, map p624*
Tour operators
Amazon Star, R Henrique Gurjão 236, T091-3241 8624, T091-3982 7911 (mob), www.amazonstar.com.br. Offers 3-hr city tours and river tours. The company also books airline tickets and hotel on Marajó.

Santarém *p632, map p633*
Tour operators
Amazon Tours, Trav Turiano Meira 1084, T091-3522 1928, T091-3975 1981 (mob), www.amazonriver.com. Owner Steve Alexander is very friendly and helpful and has lots of tips on what to do, he also organizes excursions for groups to Bosque Santa Lúcia with ecological trails. Recommended.
Gil Serique, 80 R Adriano Pimentel, T093-9973 8951, gilserique@gmail.com. Enthusiastic, larger than life English speaking tour guide who visits the creeks, flooded forest, primary forests and savannahs around Santarém, including the Tapajos National Park. Good on conservation.
Milly Turismo, R Siqueira Campos 277-A, Centro, T091- 3523 5938. Email: millyturismo@bol.com.br. Flights, bus tickets tours and very efficient friendly service.
Santarém Tur, R Adriano Pimental 44, T091-3522 4847, www.santaremtur.com.br. Branch in **Amazon Park Hotel** (see Sleeping). Friendly, helpful foreign-owned company offering individual and group tours (US$50 per person per day for a group of 5), to Tapajós National Forest, Maiça Lake and Fordlândia. Recommended.

☻ Transport

Macapá *p619, map p620*
Air Taxis to the airport cost around US$7. There are flights **Belém**, **Brasília**, **Foz do Iguaçu**, **Rio de Janeiro**, **São Paulo**, **São Luís**, **Fortaleza**, **Marabá** and **Cayenne** (Guyane), amongst others.

Airline offices Gol, www.voe gol.com.br. META, airport, T0300-789 5503 www.voemeta.com. **Puma**, T096-3039 3939, www.pumaair.com.br. TAM, airport, T096-4002 5700, www.tam.com.br. **Varig**, R Cândido Mendes 1039, T096-3223 4612, www.varig.com.br.

Boat Boats leave from Porto Santana, which is linked to Macapá by bus or taxi. To **Belém**, *Atlântica*, fast catamaran 8 hrs, 3 times a week, US$30, reservations at **Martinica**, Jovino Dinoá 2010, T096-2235 777. Slower but slightly cheaper boats are *Bom Jesus*, *Comandante Solon*, *São Francisco de Paulo*, *Silja e Souza* of **Souzamar**, Cláudio Lúcio Monteiro 1375, Porto Santana, T096-3281 1946, car ferry with **Silnave**, T096-3223 4011. Purchase tickets from offices 2 days in advance (**Agencia Sonave**, R São José 2145, T096-3223 9090, sells tickets for all boats). Also smaller boats to **Breves** as well as a regular direct service to **Santarém**).

Bus Estrela de Ouro, office on the main square in front of the cathedral, leaves daily at 2000; and **Cattani**, office on Nunes between São José and Cándido Mendes, leaves daily at 0630 to **Amapá** (US$20), **Calçoene** (US$25, 7 hrs) and **Oiapoque** (12 hrs in the dry season with several rest stops, 14-24 hrs in rainy season, US$35). The Oiapoque bus does not go into Amapá or Calçoene and it is therefore inconvenient to break the trip at these places.

Pickup trucks run daily to various locations throughout Amapá: crowded on narrow benches in the back, or pay more to ride in the cab. Despite posted schedules, they leave when full. To **Oiapoque** at 0800, 10-12 hrs, US$35 cab, US$15 in back, to **Lourenço** at 0900.

Car hire Localiza, R Independência 30, T096-3223 2799, and airport T096-3224 2336. **Sila Rent a Car**, Av Procópio Rola 1346, T096-3224 1443.

Train Limited services between **Porto Santana** and **Serra do Navio**.

Oiapoque *p621*
Air Flights to **Macapá** 3 times a week.

Boat Frequent launches across the river to **Guyane** (US$5, 10 mins). Occasional cargo vessels to **Belém** or **Macapá** (Porto Santana).

Bus Estrela de Ouro leaves for **Macapá** from the waterfront, twice daily at 1000 and after lunch, 10-12 hrs (dry season), 14-24 hrs (wet season), US$35, also **Cattani**. Pickup trucks depart from the same area when full, US$35 in cab, US$15 in the back. *Combis* to **Cayenne** leave from St-Georges Oyapock in the morning.

Belém *p622, map p624*
Air To get to the airport, take bus 'Perpétuo Socorro-Telégrafo' or 'Icaraci', every 15 mins, from the prefeitura, Praça Felipe Patroni (US$1.50, 40 mins). A taxi to the airport costs US$15. There are flights to most state capitals and many others. Internationally, there are flights to **Cayenne** (Guyane), **Fort-de-France** (Martinique), **Port au Prince** (Haiti), **Paramaribo** (Suriname) and **Miami** (USA).
Airlines Air Caribe, www.caribbean-airlines.com; GOL, www.voegol.com.br; META, www.voemeta.come; SETE, www.voe sete.com.br; TAF, www.voetaf.com.br; TAM, www.tam.com.br **TOTAL**, www.total.com.br.

Boat Boats leave from the Companhia das Docas at the Armazém 10 dock in town to Porto de Camará near Salvaterra on **Ilha de Marajó**, Mon-Sat 0630 and 1430, Sun 1000. Boats to Marajó also run from the port at Icoaraci (20 km north of Belém, 30 mins by bus from the *rodoviária* or from the Ver o Peso market, taxi US$25), Mon-Fri 0630, 0730, Sat 1600, 1700, Sun 1600, 1700 and 1800.

There are river services to **Santarém**, **Manaus** (see Routes in Amazônia, page 670) and intermediate ports. The larger ships berth at **Portobrás/Docas do Pará** (the main commercial port), either at Armazém (warehouse) No 3 at the foot of Av Pres Vargas, or at Armazém No 10, a few blocks further north (entrance on Av Marechal Hermes, corner of Av Visconde de Souza Franco). The guards will sometimes ask to see your ticket before letting you into the port area, but tell them you are going to speak with a ship's captain. Ignore the touts who approach you. Smaller vessels (sometimes cheaper, usually not as clean, comfortable or safe) sail from small docks along the **Estrada Nova** (not a safe part of town). Take a *Cremação* bus from Ver-o-Peso.

There is a daily service to **Macapá** (Porto Santana) with *Silja e Souza* of **Souzamar**, Trav Dom Romualdo Seixas, corner of R Jerônimo Pimentel, T091-222 0719, and Comandante Solon of **Sanave** (**Serviço Amapaense de Navegação**, Av Castilho Franca 234, opposite Ver-o-Peso, T091-3222 7810). To **Breves**, ENAL, T091-3224 5210. There are 2 desks selling tickets for private boats in the *rodoviária*; some hotels (eg **Fortaleza**) recommend agents for tickets. Purchase tickets from offices 2 days in advance. Smaller boats to Macapá also sail from Estrada Nova.

Bus To get to the *rodoviária* take Aeroclube, Cidade Novo, No 20 bus, or **Arsenal** or **Canudos** buses, US$0.50, or taxi, US$5 (day), US$7 (night).

Regular bus services to all major cities: Transbrasiliana go direct to **Marabá**, US$20 (16 hrs). To **Santarém**, via Marabá once a week (US$45, more expensive than by boat and can take longer, goes only in dry season). To **São Luís**, 2 a day, US$20, 13 hrs, interesting journey through marshlands. To **Fortaleza**, US$35-40 (24 hrs), several companies. To **Salvador**, US$50.

Car hire Avis, R Antônio Barreto 1653, T091-3230 2000, www.avis.com, also at airport, T0800- 558 066. **Localiza**, Av Pedro Álvares Cabral 200, T091-3212 2700, www.localiza.com.br, and at airport, T091-3257 1541.

Ilha do Marajó *p628*
Air
There is a taxi-plane service between Soure **Belém**. There are regular flights at weekends and its is worth ringing ahead to see if there is any space on a plane.

Airline offices **Aeroval Táxi Aéreo**, Av Senador Lemos (Aeroclube do Pará), T091-3233 3528; **Táxi Aéreo Soure**, Av Senador Lemos, Pass São Luiz s/n (Aeroclube do Pará), T091-3233 4986; **Táxi Aéreo Cândido**, Av Senador Lemos, Pass São Luiz s/n (Aeroclube do Pará), T091-9608 9019.

Boat
Boats run from Porto de Camará near Salvaterra to **Porto de Icoaraci** (Mon-Fri 1600 and 1700, Sat 1600 and 1700, Sun 1600, 1700 and 1800. **Henvil** sell tickets through their booth at the *rodoviária* (T091-3246 7472). Boats also run from Camará do Porto to the Armazém 10 dock in **Belém**, Mon-Sat 0630, 1500, Sun 1500 (3 hrs, US$5). Timetables regularly change so check beforehand.

Boat companies Arapari Navegação, R Siqueira Mendes 120, Cidade Velha, Belém, T091-3242 1870 and **Companhia Docas do Pará**, portão 15, T091-3242 1570. **Henvil Navegação**, Av Bernardo Sayão 4440, Praça Princesa Isabel, Jurunas, Belém, T091-3249 3400/3246 7472 and **Porto de Icoaraci**, R Siqueira Mendes s/n.

Marabá and around *p630*
Air Flights to **Belém**, **Brasília**, Balsas, Carajás, **Conceição do Araguaia**, **Imperatriz**, **Ourilândia do Norte**, **Redenção**, Santana do Araguaia, **São Félix do Xingu**, Macapá, and **São Paulo**.

Airline offices GOL, www.voe gol.com.br; META, www.voemete.com.br, Rico, www.rico.co.br, Sete, www.voe sete.com.br; TAM, T091-3324 3644, www.tam.com.br; TRIP, www.trip.com.br, Varig, T091-3322 1965, www.varig.com.br.

Bus Buses to the *rodoviária* run from the waterfront near the market, US$0.50. Buses leave daily for **Belém** (654 km, paved, US$20), for **Santarém** (34 hrs) and many daily for **Imperatriz** (7-10 hrs, US$10). There is also a pickup to the bank of the Tocantins river opposite Imperatriz (5 hrs, but more expensive). Buses can be caught going south at Tocantinópolis, opposite Porto Franco on the Belém–Brasília road. Also a bus can be taken to **Araguaína** (12½ hrs, US$20); to **Goiânia** (change at Araguaína); to **Santa Inês**, Maranhão, on the Belém–Teresina road (19 hrs, US$55). **Transbrasiliana** bus to **Altamira** daily, 1300, if road is passable, (15 hrs, US$30). There are direct buses to **Rio** and **São Paulo**; take plenty of food and drink as local supplies are expensive.

Carajas *p631*
Air Flights to **Belém**, **Marabá**, **Ourilândia do Norte**, **São Félix do Xingu** Altamira, **Araguaína**, **Belo Horizonte**, **Brasília**, **Itaituba**, **Manaus**, **Parintins**, **Santarém**, **Trombetas**, **Tucuruí**, **Uberaba** and **Uberlândia** with Sete, www.voe sete.com.br and TRIP, www.voetrip.com.br.

Santarém *p632, map p633*
Air
The bus to the airport from the centre leaves from Rui Barbosa every 80 mins, 0550-1910; taxis US$8. The hotels **Amazon Park**, **New City** and **Rio Dourado** have free buses for guests; you may be able to take these. There are flights

to **Belém**, **Fortaleza**, **Manaus**, **Recife**, **Salvador**, **São Luís**; **Altamira**, **Itaituba**, **Monte Dourado**, **Oriximiná**, **Manaus**; **Araguaína**, **Belo Horizonte**, **Brasília**, **Carajás**, **Parintins**, **Trombetas**, **Tucuruí**, **Uberaba** and **Uberlândia**.

Airline offices GOL, www.voegol.com.br, META, R Siqueira Campos 162, T091-3522 6222, www.voemeta.com.br. **Penta**, Trav 15 de Novembro 183, T091-3523 2532. **Rico**, www.rico.com.br. **TRIP**, www.voe trip.com.br. **TAM**, www.tam.com.br.

Bus

To get to the *rodoviária* take the 'Rodagem' bus from the waterfront near the market, US$0.50. To **Itaituba**, US$11, 11 hrs, 2 a day. To **Marabá** on the Rio Tocantins (via **Rurópolis** US$7.50, 6 hrs, and **Altamira** US$23, 28 hrs), 36 hrs (can be up to 6 days), US$41, with **Transbrasiliana**. Also to **Imperatriz**, via Marabá; office on Av Getúlio Vargas and at the *rodoviária*. Enquire at the *rodoviária* for other destinations. Beware of vehicles that offer a lift, which frequently turn out to be taxis. Road travel during the rainy season is always difficult, often impossible.

Buses to **Belterra** leave from Trav Silvino Pinto between Rui Barbosa and São Sebastião, Mon-Sat 1000 and 1230, US$4, about 2 hrs. There is a 1-hr time difference between Santarém and Belterra, so if you take the 1230 bus you'll miss the 1530 return.

Boats

There are local services to **Óbidos** (US$10, 4 hrs), **Oriximiná** (US$12.50), **Alenquer**, and **Monte Alegre** (US$10, 5-8 hrs). Boats for **Belém** and **Manaus** leave from the Cais do Porto, 1 km west of town (take 'Floresta-Prainha', 'Circular' or 'Circular Externo' bus; taxi US$4); boats for other destinations, including **Macapá**, leave from the waterfront near the centre of town. For further information on services to Manaus, Belém, Macapá, Itaituba and intermediate ports, see Routes in Amazônia for details, page 670.

Alter do Chão *p633*
Bus Tickets and information from the bus company kiosk opposite **Pousada Tupaiulândia**. Buses to **Santarém** leave from the bus stop on Av São Sebastião, in front of Colégio Santa Clara, US$1, about 1 hr.

Belterra and Fordlândia *p634*
Bus Bus from Belterra to **Santarém** to Belterra Mon-Sat 1300 and 1530, US$4, about 2 hrs. There is a 1-hr time difference between Santarém and Belterra.

Boat Boats that run **Santarém–Itaituba** stop at Fordlândia if you ask (leave Santarém 1800, arrive 0500-0600, US$12 for 1st-class hammock space); ask the captain to stop for you on return journey, about 2300. The alternative is to take a tour with a Santarém travel agent.

◉ Directory

Macapá *p619, map p620*
Banks Banco do Brasil, R Independência 250, and **Bradesco**, R Cândido Mendes 1316, have Plus ATMs for VISA withdrawals. For *câmbios* (cash only), **Casa Francesa**, R Independência 232. **Monopólio**, Av Isaac Alcoubre 80. Both US$ and euros can be exchanged here. Best to buy euros in Belém if heading for Guyane as *câmbios* in Macapá are reluctant to sell them and they are more expensive and hard to obtain at the border. **Embassies and consulates** France, at Pousada Ekinox (see Sleeping, page 636). Visas are not issued for non-Brazilians. **Internet** @llnet in Macapá Shopping and numerous others. **Medical services** Hospital Geral, Av FAB, T096-3212 6127. Hospital São Camila & São Luiz, R Marcelo Candia 742, T096-3223 1514. **Post office** Av Corialano Jucá. **Telephone** R São José 2050, open 0730-2200.

Oiapoque *p621*
Banks It is possible to exchange US$ and reais to euros, but dollar rates are low and TCs

are not accepted anywhere. **Banco do Brasil**, Av Barão do Rio Branco, 1000-1500, reais to euros and Visa facilities. Visa users can also withdraw reais at **Bradesco**, exchanging these to euros. Gold merchants, such as **Casa Francesa** on the riverfront and a *câmbio* in the market, will sell reais for US$ or euros. Rates are even worse in St-Georges. Best to buy euros in Belém, or abroad.
Immigration Polícia Federal for Brazilian exit stamp is on the road to Calçoene, about 500 m from the river. **Post office** Av Barão do Rio Branco, open 0900-1200, 1400-1700.

Belém *p622, map p624*
Banks Banks open 0900-1630, but foreign exchange only until 1300. **Banco do Brasil**, Av Pres Vargas, near Hotel Itaoca, good rates, ATMs; **Bradesco** throughout the city for ATMs. HSBC, Av Pres Vargas near Praça da República has MasterCard Cirrus and Amex ATMs. **Embassies and consulates** Suriname, Rua Gaspar Viana 488, T091-3212 7144. For visas allow 4 days. **Colombia**, Av Almirante Barroso, 71, apt 601, bloco B, Ed. Narciso Braga, T091-3246 5662. **Venezuela**, R Presidente Pernambuco 270, T091-3222 6396, convenbelem@canal13.com.br. Allow at least 1 day for visas. **UK**, Av Governador José Malcher, 815 - SL 410, T091-3222 0762; **USA**, www.embaixada.americana.org.br. **Internet** Throughout the city including: **Amazon**, 2nd floor of Estação das Docas; **Convert**, Shopping Iguatemi, 3rd floor, US$1.40 per hr; **InterBelém**, Av Jose Malcher 189, US$1 per hr, helpful South African owner, English spoken. **Language schools** Unipop, Av Sen Lemos 557, T091-3224 9074, Portuguese course for foreigners. **Laundry** Lav e Lev, R Dr Moraes 576. **Lavanderia Paraense**, Trav Dom Pedro 1104, T091-3222 0057, dry and steam cleaning. **Libraries** UFPA, Av Augusto Correa 1, T091-3211 1140, university library with many titles on Amazônia. **Medical services** A yellow fever certificate of inoculation is mandatory (see

Health, page 53) It is best to get one at home (always have your certificate handy). Medications for malaria prophylaxis are not sold in Belém pharmacies. You can theoretically get them through the public health service, but this is hopelessly complicated. Such drugs are sometimes available at pharmacies in smaller centres, eg Santarém and Macapá. Bring an adequate supply from home. **Clínica de Medicina Preventativa**, Av Bras de Aguiar 410 (T091-3222 1434), will give injections, English spoken, open 0730-1200, 1430-1900 (Sat 0800-1100). **Hospital da Ordem Terceira**, Trav Frei Gil de Vila Nova 59, T091-3212 2777, doctors speak some English, free consultation. Surgery Mon 1300-1900, Tue-Thu 0700-1100, 24 hrs for emergencies. The British consul has a list of English-speaking doctors. **Police** For reporting crimes, R Santo Antônio and Trav Frei Gil de Vila Nova. **Post office** Av Pres Vargas 498. Also handles telegrams and fax. **Telephone** Telemar, Av Pres Vargas.

Marabá and around *p630*
Banks Banco do Brasil, Praça Duque de Caxias 966. **Hospitals** Celina Gonçalves, T091-3322 1031.

Santarém *p632, map p633*
Banks There are Bradescos in town with Visa ATMs. **Internet** Amazon's Star Cyber, Av Tapajos, 418 em frente a Orla, T093-3522 3648. Fast connection. English speaking. Tips and information available. Global Cyber, R Siqueira Campos 175 B, Centro. Hip grunge/graffiti décor, fast connection, good a/c, drinks, friendly staff. **Laundry** Storil, Trav Turiano Meira 167, 1st floor. **Post office** Praça da Bandeira 81. **Medical services** Hospital São Raimundo Nonato, Av Mendonça Furtado 1993, T091-3523 1176. **Telephone** Posto Trin, R Siqueira Campos 511. Mon-Sat 0700-1900, Sun 0700-2100.

Amazonas and the Amazon River

Amazonas is the largest state in Brazil (1.6 million sq km), bigger than any country in South America except Argentina, but with a population of just 2.8 million. Half of the inhabitants live in the capital, Manaus, with the rest spread out in remote communities often linked only by air and river.

The scenery in Amazonas is magnificent. Nothing can prepare you for the vast skies, the pure air, the endless shades of green, and rivers that stretch to the horizon. Nowhere does the Amazon feel more like the inland sea it once was than here. Rivers merge in vast swirls of myriad shades, from the translucent black of strong iced tea to café-au-lait brown, through vast forest-fringed lakes covered with giant water lilies or through eerie strands of flooded igapó or varzea forest. And in the rivers' depths swim 4-m-long horny-tongued fish, bull sharks, dolphins, stingrays and catfish big enough to swallow a man whole.

Amazonas state preserves Brazil's most extensive and unspoilt areas of lowland tropical forest, and the tourist industry here is developing fast. Most tours and trips to jungle lodges begin in Manaus, a sprawling rubber-boom town with good national and international connections. Beyond Manaus are the giant boulder mountains of the upper Rio Negro, which rise to Brazil's highest peak, the flooded wilds of Mamirauá Ecological Reserve near Tefé, and the Javari near Tabatinga, which are among the best places in the Amazon for spotting wildlife.

But the vast forests of Amazonas are not uninhabited. Civilizations have been living here from anywhere between 11,000 and 5000 BC and these people and their caboclo descendants maintain a rich cultural life. Although indigenous villages are very difficult to visit, their heritage can be experienced at the festivals in São Gabriel and the Boi Bumba in Parintins. The latter is the largest and most spectacular in the country after Carnaval and takes place on an island in the middle of the Amazon river at the end of June. ▸▸ *For listings, see pages 663-674.*

Visiting the forest

What to visit

A visit to the Amazon is about experiencing the spectacular scenery and vastness of the landscapes. Animals are very difficult to see in the rainforest, far more so than on the African savannah or in the Pantanal. The scenery is at its best on the **Rio Negro**, especially around the Anavilhanas, and further upstream where the mountains of the Guiana Shield punctuate the forest like giant worn crocodile teeth. However, the Rio Negro is an acidic, black-water river and consequently has a lower level of biodiversity than the more PH-neutral brown-water rivers like the Solimões (Amazon). So if you are intent on seeing wildlife, you will see far more in the regions south of Manaus, on the smaller river tributaries, creeks (*igarapés*) and flooded forest areas (*varzea* and *igapós*), especially those that are farthest from people. One of the best and most readily accessible places is **Mamirauá Ecological Reserve** near Tefé, a flight away from Manaus. Some of the lodges around Manaus have their own reserves, which have been populated with rescued primates and birds. The best of these is **Amazon Ecopark** (see page 665). Others, such as those around Lago Piranha or Lago Mamori, are in semi-protected areas where species levels are recovering.

When to visit

There is no best time to visit the forest; it depends what you want to see. The Amazon around Manaus is far more than a big river; think of it rather as an inland sea. Water is everywhere, especially during the **wet season**, which lasts from November to May. During the floods, the water rises by 5-10 m and the forests around the main rivers form areas known as *varzea* (on brown-water rivers) and *igapó* (on black-water rivers). Trees are submerged almost to their canopies and it is possible to canoe between their trunks in search of wildlife. In the morning you can often hear the booming call of huge black caiman and the snort of dolphins. And as the boats pass through the trees, startled hatchet fish jump into the bows. It is possible to canoe for tens of kilometres away from the main river flow, as *varzea* and *igapós* often connect one river to another, often via oxbow lakes covered in giant lilies. The lakes are formed when a meandering river changes course and leaves part of its previous flow cut off from the stream. In the **dry season** the rivers retreat into their main flow, exposing broad mudflats (on the brown-water rivers) or long beaches of fine white sand. Caiman and giant river turtles can often be seen basking on these in the evening sun, and wildlife spotting is generally a little easier at this time of year. Trees in the Amazon bear fruit at different times throughout the year; whenever a particular tree is in fruit it attracts large parrots, macaws and primates.

Choosing a tour or lodge

Once you have decided on when and where to go, the next decision is to choose a lodge or an operator. Those used to the quality of wildlife information supplied by rainforest tour operators in Costa Rica, Peru, Ecuador or Bolivia will be disappointed by the lack of professional wildlife knowledge and ecotourism services offered by many of the operators in Manaus. If you are interested first and foremost in wildlife and want accurate information, be sure to request a specialist wildlife guide (see page 670) and question your tour company carefully to test their knowledge. A good way of doing this is to ask whether they can supply a species list for the area around their lodge or for the forests they visit during their tours. Few can. Serious wildlife enthusiasts and birders looking to visit the Brazilian Amazon should think about heading for **Mamirauá Ecological Reserve** near Tefé (see page 659) or **Cristalino Jungle Lodge** (see page 766) in Mato Grosso.

Standard tours from Manaus or the rainforest lodges involve a walk through the forest looking at plants and their usage, caiman spotting at night (many guides drag caiman out of the water, which has negative long-term effects and should be discouraged), piranha fishing and boat trips through the *igapós* (flooded forests) or the *igarapés* (creeks). They may also visit a *caboclo* (river village) or one of the newly established indigenous villages around the city. Other trips involve light adventure such as rainforest survival, which involves learning how to find water and food in the forest, and how to make a shelter and string up a hammock for a secure night's sleep.

Trips vary in length. A half-day or a day trip will usually involve a visit to the 'meeting of the waters' and the Lago de Janauri nature reserve, where you are likely to see plenty of birds, some primates and river dolphins. The reserve was set up to receive large numbers of tourists so there are captive parrots on display and numerous tourist shops. Yet ecologists agree that the reserve helps relieve pressure on other parts of the river. Boats for day trippers leave the harbour in Manaus constantly throughout the day, but are best booked at one of the larger operators. Those with more time can take the longer cruises with a company like **Amazon Clipper** (see page 669) or stay in one of the rainforest lodges. To see virgin rainforest, a five-day trip by boat is needed.

Prices vary but usually include lodging, guide, transport, meals (but not drinks) and activities. The recommended companies charge US$60-95 per person for a day trip, or US$195-285 for three days.

Beware of the touts

There are many hustlers at the airport in Manaus and on the street (particularly around the hotels and bars on Joaquim Nabuco and Miranda Leão), and even at hotel receptions. It is not wise to go on a tour with the first friendly face you meet. All go-betweens earn a commission so recommendations cannot be taken at face value and employing a freelance guide not attached to a company is potentially dangerous as they may not be qualified; check out their credentials. Tourist offices are not allowed by law to recommend guides, but can provide you with a list of legally registered companies. Unfortunately, disreputable companies are rarely dealt with in any satisfactory manner, and most continue to operate. Book direct with the company itself and ask for a detailed, written contract if you have any doubts.

What to take

Leave luggage with your tour operator or hotel in Manaus and only take what is necessary for your trip. Long-sleeved shirts, long trousers, walking boots and insect repellent are advisable for treks in the jungle, where insects can be voracious. A hat offers protection from the sun on boat trips. Powerful binoculars are essential for spotting wildlife (at least 7x magnification is recommended, with the ability to focus at between 2.5 m and infinity). Buying bottled water at the local villages is a sure way to help the local economy, but it can be expensive in the lodges and it produces a great deal of waste plastic that is usually just chucked into the river directly or indirectly. Bring iodine, purification tablets or a modern water filter like PUR Scout or Aquapure (best with iodine for Amazon river water).

Lodges → *See page 665 for a list of recommended lodges.*

Most of the lodges around Manaus do not adhere to proper ecotourism practices; this guide lists the exceptions. Good practice includes integration and employment for the local community, education support, recycling and proper rubbish disposal, and trained guides with good wildlife lodges. Ecotourism in Brazil is often a badge for adventure tourism in a natural setting and few operators conform to the best practices of the **International Ecotourism Society**, www.ecotourism.org. Neither the environment nor the local communities receive much from Brazilian 'ecotourism'. In Manaus, a relatively small number of communities have benefited from a boom which has seen the total number of beds rise from just six in 1979 to more than 1000 today. Only 27% of labour derives from local communities and very few of the lodges are locally owned.

Manaus ⬤🚹🚻🏧❄⬤▲⬤🚍 » *pp663-674. Colour map 1, B3.*

→ *Phone code: 092. Population: 1.4 million.*

Manaus, the state capital, sits at 32 m above sea level some 1600 km from the Atlantic. The city sprawls over a series of eroded and gently sloping hills divided by numerous creeks, and stands at the junction of the liquorice-black Rio Negro and the toffee-coloured Solimões, whose waters flow side by side in two distinct streams within the same river. The city is the commercial hub for a vast area including parts of Peru, Bolivia and Colombia, and ocean-going container vessels often dock here.

New-found wealth has turned Manaus from tawdry to tourist-friendly in the last five years. The historic centre, which huddles around the green and gold mock-Byzantine dome of the opera house, has been tastefully refurbished and now verges on elegant. The area is a pleasant place to stroll around and sip a cool juice or a strong coffee, and many of the best hotels and guesthouses are found here. There are plenty of restaurants, bars and clubs, which support a lively, colourful nightlife.

Despite the city's size, the forest is ever present on the horizon and always feels just a short boat trip away. Beaches fringe its western extremities at Ponta Negra, whose sands are backed by towering blocks of flats, making it feel like a kind of Amazonian Ipanema.

There are plenty of sights near Manaus. The most vaunted are generally the least interesting. However, the Anavilhanas – the largest river archipelago in the world, comprising a beautiful labyrinth of forested islands fringed with white-sand beaches lapped by the jet-black waters of the Rio Negro – should not be missed. Try to be there for sunset when thousands of swifts descend to roost and the light is a deep, rich gold.

Manaus

Sleeping		
Ana Cássia Palace	Itália	6
Best Western Lord	Krystal	12
Manaus	2	Lider	11
Brasil	3	Manaós	8
Central	10	Mônaco	9
Dez de Julho		Taj Mahal	5
& Iguana Tours	4	Tropical	16
		Tropical Business	7

Eating	
Alemã	1
Búfalo	3
Canto da Peixada	14
Fiorentina	4
Himawari	6
La Barca	2
O Naturalista	10

Pizzeria Scarola 7
Senac 8
Skina dos Sucos 9
Sorveteria Glacial 5

Manaus is also the main departure point for rainforest tours. There are many lodges around the city, from 20 minutes to four hours away. And although animals here are not as easy to see as in Tefé or on the **Rio Javari**, the scenery is breathtaking.

Ins and outs

Getting there The modern **Eduardo Gomes airport** ① *10 km north of the city centre, T092-3652 1120*, receives flights from all of Brazil's principal cities and there are international connections with Ecuador, Bolivia, Mexico and the USA. The restaurant serves good à la carte and buffet food during the day. Airport buses run to Praça Adalberto Vale, near the cathedral in the centre of town (every 30 minutes 0500-2300, US$1). A taxi to the centre costs around US$17.50 on the meter. Taxi drivers often tell arrivals that no bus to town is available, be warned.

The only usable road runs north to Boa Vista, Guyana and Venezuela. Visitors almost invariably arrive by plane or boat. The only long-distance buses arriving in Manaus **rodoviária** ① *5 km out of town at the intersection of Av Constantino Nery and R Recife*, are from Boa Vista, Presidente Figueiredo and Itacoatiara. To get to the centre, take a bus marked 'Cidade Nova', taxi US$5.

Boat passengers arrive at the newly renovated **floating docks** ① *in the centre, a couple of blocks south of Praça da Matriz*, with direct access to the main artery of Avenida Eduardo Ribeiro, and 10 minutes' walk from the opera house and main hotel area. Those arriving by boat (eg from Leticia) who have not already had their passports stamped, must go to the immigration office on the first of the floating docks next to the tourist office. To get there, take the dock entrance opposite the cathedral, bear right, after 50 m left, pass through a warehouse to a group of buildings on a T-section. ▶▶ *See Transport, page 671.*

Getting around The city centre is easily explored on foot. All city bus routes start on Marques da Santa Cruz next to the Praça da Matriz. Information on local buses can be found on www.embarque.com.br. Taxis can be found near the opera house, at the *rodoviária*, airport and in Ponta Negra. Many of the upmarket hotels are in Ponta Negra, which is 13 km from the city centre and can feel somewhat isolated.

Tourist information There are several **Centros de Atendimento ao Turista (CAT)** ① *main office: 50 m south of the opera house, Av Eduardo Ribeiro 666, T092-3622 0767, Mon-Fri 0800-1700, Sat 0800-1200*, throughout the city. There are also offices in **Amazonas Shopping** ① *Av Djalma Batist 482, Chapada, T096-3236 5154, Mon-Sat 0900-2200, Sun 1500-2100*; at the **airport** ① *T096-3652 1120 or T0800-280 8820, daily 0700-2300*; at the **port** ① *regional terminal, R Marquês de Santa Cruz, armazém 07, Mon-Fri 0800-1700*, and ① *international terminal, R Marquês de Santa Cruz, armazém 10*, which opens only when cruise liners dock. There is a **CAT** trailer in the **rodoviária** ① *R Recife s/n, Flores, Mon-Sat 0800-1200*.

The website for tourism in the Amazon, www.amazonastur.am.gov.br, has extensive information on accommodation throughout the state in Portuguese and English. *A Crítica* newspaper lists local events.

Centro histórico

The colonial streets that spread out from Praça São Sebastião are a reminder of Manaus's brief dalliance with wealth and luxury. Eduardo Ribeiro, the state governor who presided over these golden years, was determined to make 19th-century Manaus the envy of the world: a fine European city in which the nouveau riche could parade their linen and lace. He spared no expense. Trams were running in Manaus before they were in Manchester or Boston and its roads were lit by the first electric street lights in the world. The city's confidence grew with its majesty. Champagne flowed under the crystal chandeliers and prices rose to four times those of contemporaneous New York. Extravagance begot extravagance and rubber barons eager to compete in statements of affluent vulgarity fed their horses vintage wine or bought lions as guard cats.

In the 1890s, Ribeiro decided to put the icing on his cake, commissioning Portuguese architect Domenico de Angelis to build an Italianate opera house, the **Teatro Amazonas** ① *Praça São Sebastião, T096-622 1880, Mon-Sat 0900-1600, 20-min tour US$7, students US$2.50,* and to surround it with stone-cobbled streets lined with elegant houses, plazas, and gardens replete with ornate fountains and gilded cherubs. Masks adorning the theatre walls were made in homage to four great European artists: Shakespeare, Mozart, Verdi and Molière. The stage curtain depicted the meeting of the waters and *Iara*, the spirit of the river Amazon, and the driveway was paved in rubber to prevent the sound of carriage wheels spoiling performances. After the theatre doors were opened in 1896, Caruso sang here and Pavlova danced. But for all its beauty and expense the theatre was used for little more than a decade. In the early 20th century the rubber economy collapsed. Seeds smuggled by

Around Manaus

N

Not to scale

Sleeping 🛏
Acajatuba Jungle Lodge **1**
Aldeia dos Lagos Lodge **10**
Amazon Ecopark Lodge **2**

Amazon Lodge **3**
Ariaú Amazon Towers **5**
Boa Vida Jungle Resort **4**
Juma **12**

Othon Jungle Palace **9**
Pousada dos
Guanavenas **8**
Tiwa Amazone Resort **6**

Englishman Henry Wickham, to the Imperial Gardens at Kew and thence to Malaysia, were producing a higher yield. The wild-rubber economy dwindled and the doors to the opera house closed. Over the decades, the French tiles on the dome began to crack, the Italian marble darkened and the fine French furniture and English china slowly began to decay. What you see today is the product of careful restoration, which has returned the *teatro* to its original glory. There are regular performances, which sell out very quickly, and an arts festival every April. Until less than 10 years ago the streets around the opera house were down at heel and seedy, but they have now been refurbished. The colonial houses have all been freshly painted; several are now little cafés and souvenir shops and the area is a safe and pleasant place to while away an hour or two.

The city's other sights are huddled around the waterfront. The **Mercado Adolfo Lisboa** ① *R dos Barés 46*, was built in 1882 as a miniature copy of the now-demolished Parisian Les Halles. The wrought ironwork, which forms much of the structure, was imported from Europe and is said to have been designed by Eiffel. It's worth coming here if only to see the astonishing array of bizarre fish from tiger-striped catfish to enormous *piraíba* (said to be able to eat a man) and *pacu*, a large vegetarian piranha with molars powerful enough to crack a Brazil nut.

The remarkable harbour installations, completed in 1902, were designed and built by a Scottish engineer to cope with the Rio Negro's annual rise and fall of up to 14 m. The large **floating dock** is connected to street level by a 150-m-long floating ramp, at the end of which, on the harbour wall, can be seen the high-water mark for each year since it was built. When the river is high, the roadway floats on a series of large iron tanks measuring 2.5 m in diameter. The large beige **Alfândega** (**Customs House**) ① *R Marquês de Santa Cruz, Mon-Fri 0800-1300*, stands at the entrance to the city when arriving by boat. Said to be have been modelled on the one in Delhi, it was entirely prefabricated in England, and the tower once acted as a lighthouse.

Dominating the streets between the opera house and the waterfront; and right next to the local bus station, is the **Catedral Municipal**, on Praça Osvaldo Cruz, built in simple Jesuit style and very plain inside and out. Originally constructed in 1695 in wood and straw, it was burnt down in 1850 and rebuilt in neoclassical style. Nearby is the main shopping and business area, the tree-lined **Avenida Eduardo Ribeiro**, crossed by Avenida 7 de Setembro and bordered by ficus trees. There are a few other interesting buildings worth visiting if you have time to spare.

Tropical **7**
Tropical Business **7**
Wild Cabanas **11**

The **Biblioteca Pública (Public Library)** ① *R Barroso 57, T096-3234 0588, Mon-Fri 0730-1730*, inaugurated in 1871, is part of the city's architectural heritage. Featuring an ornate European cast-iron staircase, it is well stocked with 19th-century newspapers, rare books and old photographs, and is worth a visit.

The **Museu do Homem do Norte** ① *Av 7 de Setembro 1385, near Av Joaquim Nabuco, T096-3232 5373, Mon-Thu 0900-1200, 1300-1700, Fri 1300-1700, US$1*, is an interesting review of the way of life of the Amazonian population, or 'men of the north', although it has deteriorated in recent years. Social, cultural and economic aspects are displayed with photographs, models and other exhibits.

The **Centro Cultural Palácio RioNegro (Museu de Imagem e Son)** ① *Av 7 de Setembro 1546, T096-233 2850, Tue-Fri 1000-1700, Sat and Sun 1600-2100*, was the residence of a German rubber merchant until 1917 and later because the state government palace. It now holds various cultural events, including exhibitions, shows and films. There is also a café.

The **Museu do Índio** ① *R Duque de Caxias 296, near Av 7 de Setembro, T096-234 1422, Mon-Fri 0830-1200 and 1400-1700, Sat 0800-1130, US$3*, is managed by the Salesian missionaries who have been responsible for the ravaging of much of the indigenous culture of the upper Rio Negro. It is rather run down and betrays a Victorian view of indigenous culture. The displays are dusty but there are plenty of artefacts, including handicrafts, ceramics, clothing, utensils and ritual objects from the various indigenous tribes of the upper Rio Negro. There is also a small craft shop.

North of the centre

The **Parque Municipal do Mindú** ① *R Perimetral s/n, Parque Dez suburb, T096-236 7702, Tue-Sun 0900-1700; take bus No 423 or 433 from Praça da Matriz*, is a 33-ha ecological reserve and education centre with a system of trails, elevated walkways, a little amphitheatre and orchid gardens. If you are very lucky you may catch a glimpse of one of the world's rarest monkeys, the pied bare-face tamarin (*Saguinus bicolor bicolor*), a subspecies of bare-faced tamarin thought to live only near Manaus and threatened with extinction.

The **Jardim Botânico Chico Mendes** (Horto Municipal) ① *Av André Araujo s/n, daily 0800-1200 and 1400-1700; take bus for 'Aleixo' or 'Coroado'*, contains a collection of plants from the Amazon region.

West of the centre

The **Instituto Geográfico e Histórico do Amazonas** ① *R Bernardo Ramos 117, near the Prefeitura, T096-232 7077, Mon-Fri 0900-1200 and 1300-1600, US$0.20*, is located in a fascinating older district of central Manaus. It houses a museum and library of over 10,000 books, which thoroughly document Amazonian life through the ages.

The **zoo** ① *Estrada Ponta Negra 750, T096-625 2044, Tue-Sun 0900-1630, US$3, free on Sun, take bus No 12o from R Tamandaré by the cathedral, US$0.70, every 30 mins, get off 400 m past the first infantry barracks, a big white building*, is run by **CIGS**, the Brazilian Army Unit specializing in jungle survival. It has recently been expanded and improved. About 300 Amazonian animals are kept in the gardens, including anacondas in a huge pit.

Just north of the centre, the **Hotel Tropical** has a small zoo and many kinds of birds can be seen in and around the grounds, including flycatchers (kingbirds and kiskadees), swallows, yellow-browed sparrows, aracaris (a member of the toucan family), woodpeckers, woodcreepers, thrushes, anis, three species of tanager and two types of parrot (dusky and blue-headed). Sloths and monkeys may also be seen. For further information, contact Moacir Fortes or Andrew Whittaker, birding@internext.com.br.

East of the centre

There is a curious little church, **Igreja do Pobre Diabo**, at the corner of Avenida Borba and Avenida Ipixuna, in the suburb of Cachoeirinha. It is only 4 m wide by 5 m long, and was built by a local trader, the 'poor devil' of the name. To get there, take the 'Circular 7 de Setembro Cachoeirinha' bus from the cathedral to Hospital Militar.

The **botanic gardens** are maintained by the **Instituto Nacional de Pesquisas da Amazônia (INPA)** ① *Estrada do Aleixo, Km 3, near the natural science museum, see below, T096-643 3377, Mon-Fri 0900-1100, 1400-1630, Sat and Sun 0900-1600, US$2; take bus No 519 from the local bus depot by the cathedral,* which conducts research into all aspects of the Amazon. There is a small park that is good for a taste of rainforest flora and fauna before you head out to the forest. The animals here are kept in less distressing conditions than in the city zoo. Paca (*Agouti paca*), agouti (*Myoprocta exilis*), squirrel monkeys (*Saimiri scicureus*) and tamarins (*Saguinus sp*) roam free, and among the other animals on display are Amazonian manatee (*Trichechus inunguis*) and giant otter (*Pternura brasiliensis*).

The **Museu de Ciências Naturais da Amazônia (Natural Science Museum)** ① *Al Cosme Ferreira, Cachoeira Grande suburb, 15 km from centre, T096-644 2799, Mon-Sat 0900-1700, US$4, best to combine with a visit to INPA, and take a taxi from there (see above),* is one of the city's little-known treasures. The remote museum is run by Japanese, with characteristic efficiency, and the exhibits are beautifully displayed and clearly labelled in Japanese, Portuguese and English. The main building houses hundreds of preserved Amazon insects and butterflies, together with stuffed specimens of a selection of the river's bizarre fish. You can also see live versions, including the endangered pirarucu (*Arapaima gigas*), which can grow up to 3.5 m, and a primitive osteoglottid fish that breathes air.

Beaches

Manaus has two sandy beaches on the outskirts of the city. The **Praia da Ponta Negra**, which lies upstream of the city's pollution, is the most popular and the most heavily developed. It is backed by high-rise flats and lined with open-air restaurants, bars and areas for beach volleyball and football. Nightlife here is lively, especially at weekends. However, on most nights at least one of the bars (such as **O Laranjinha**, see page 667) will have Boi Bumba dance shows. Many of the better hotels, including the **Tropical**, are situated here. To get here take any bus marked 'Ponta Negra' (eg No 120) from the local bus station next to the cathedral. The beach can also be reached on the Tropical's shuttle bus (see Sleeping, page 663).

The city's other beach, **Praia Amarelinho**, in the Educandos neighbourhood, is a little too close to the centre to avoid pollution and is not recommended.

The meeting of the waters

About 15 km from Manaus is the confluence of the coffee-coloured **Rio Solimões** (Amazon) and the black-tea coloured **Rio Negro**, which is itself some 8 km wide. The two rivers run side by side for about 6 km without their waters mingling. This phenomenon is caused by differences in the temperature, density and velocity of the two rivers. Tourist agencies run boat trips to this spot (US$60-160). The simplest route is to take a taxi or bus No 713 'Vila Buriti' to the Careiro dock, and take the car ferry across. The boat is very basic with no shelter on deck and departs at 0700 returning 1000, and 1500 returning 1800. There are also small private launches, which take 40 minutes and cost about US$10-15 per seat; ask for the engine to be shut off at the confluence. You should see dolphins, especially in the early morning. Alternatively, hire a motorized canoe from near the market (about US$15; allow three to four hours to experience the meeting properly). A 2-km walk along the Porto Velho road from the Careiro ferry terminal leads to some ponds, some way from the road, in which huge Victoria Regia water lilies can be seen from April to September.

Excursions from Manaus

Manacapuru → *Colour map 1, B3*.
This typical Amazon market town is situated on the Solimões river, 110 km west of Manaus. It has three basic hotels and **Il Maccarone** pizzeria (Avenida Eduardo Ribeiro 1000). It is 84 km by road (four buses daily, US$5, two hours including ferry crossing) on the AM-070. Around 25 km from Manaus is the **Piranha Lake Sustainable Development Reserve**, comprising a series of lakes and protecting large areas of *varzea* forest, dotted with gigantic trees such as sumaumeira. The area is a refuge for migratory birds and a breeding ground for many endemic herons, storks, egrets and ducks. There is excellent sport fishing.

Mamori
This village on the Rio Mamori has plenty of wildlife close at hand, and canoes can be hired to spot animals from the river. Many of the jungle lodges lie a little upstream on the Rio Mamori, around Lago Mamori. There is malaria in this area (see Health, page 54). To get here, take bus No 11 from the Manaus *rodoviária* in the direction of Castanho. The journey takes three hours, including the ferry at the confluence of the Negro and Solimões, and costs US$1.50. Buses leave Manaus at 0600 and 1100.

Arquipélago de Anavilhanas
This filigree of more than 350 brilliant-green islands in the jet-black Rio Negro – some fringed with white-sand beaches, others anchored only by their roots – is one of the area's must-see sights. The scene is particularly beautiful at the end of the day when the sky looks vast and warm and the light on the trunks of the partially submerged trees is a thick orange-yellow. Birds fly into the Anavilhanas to roost and millions of bats leave for their night hunt. The air is silent but for bird calls, the lapping of the river and the bluster of river dolphins surfacing for air. The islands are 80 km upstream of Manaus. Several companies arrange visits to the archipelago (US$195-285, one day) as can most of the Rio Negro lodges. Rio Negro safari cruises almost all visit the Anavilhanas.

Downstream from Manaus ☺☻ ▶▶ *pp663-674*.

Parintins → *Colour map 1, B4. Phone code: 092. Population: 90,000*.
Parintins is situated between Manaus and Santarém, just before the Amazonas-Pará border, on the Ilha Tupinambana. In the dry season, boat trips run to the river beaches and to nearby lakes. In colonial times, this was the resting point of a group of coastal indigenous Brazilians who made an astonishing trek through thousands of miles of dense forest to escape the ravages of the Portuguese slave trade. However, they didn't evade it for long. Within a generation they had been found by slavers from Belém who took all the women and children and murdered all the men. Ironically the island is now the site of one of the country's most important and spectacular festivals, Boi Bumba, which celebrates the triumph of the indigenous and *caboclo* poor over a *coronel* (tyrannical landowner).

Festa do Boi Bumba

The Boi Bumba festival in Parintins is a competition between two rival groups, similar to the samba schools in Rio, called Caprichoso (whose colour is blue) and Garantido (red). The two teams present a pageant, which originates from Braga in Portugal, but has been heavily syncretized with indigenous and Afro-Brazilian themes. It was brought to Parintins in the early 20th century by settlers from São Luís in Maranhão. The pageant tells the story of Pai Francisco and his wife Mãe Catirina who steal the prize bull from the landowner that they work for, and kill it. The landowner discovers this and threatens to kill them if they fail to resurrect his bull by midnight. The couple employ the talents of a shaman, a priest and an African *pai santo*, and these characters invoke the female spirit of rainforest fertility, the Cunhã-poranga, played by a beautiful young dancer. The story is told to the backdrop of vast four-storey floats with moving parts and troupes of hundreds of dancers. It is performed in the purpose-built *bumbódromo* stadium which holds almost 40,000 spectators. Previews of the festival in miniature are held in the **Hotel Tropical** in Manaus throughout the year and there are always Boi Bumba dancers on weekend evenings in the Ponta Negra bars in Manaus.

The **Festa do Boi Bumba** (see box, above) is the most vibrant in Brazil after Carnaval and draws tens of thousands of visitors to Parintins on the last three days of June each year. But since the town has only two small hotels, finding a room can be a challenge. Everyone sleeps in hammocks on the boats that bring them to the festival from Manaus and Santarém (a large vessel will charge about US$130 per person, including breakfast, for the duration).

Ins and outs The **airport** ⓘ *Estrada Odovaldo Novo s/n, Parintins, T092-3533 2700*, receives flights from Manaus, Óbidos and Santarém and others. Boats stop here on the Belém-Manaus route. there are also sailings from Óbidos and Santarém. ▸▸ *See Transport, page 673.*

Upstream from Manaus 🏨🍴🏕️💰🎭 ▸▸ *pp663-674.*

Tefé → *Colour map 1, B2. Phone code: 097. Population: 65,000.*

Tefé is a scruffy town roughly halfway between Manaus and the Colombian border. The local airport authorities confiscated all of the city's rubbish lorries in a dispute over the municipal dump, and now it is piled up willy-nilly. But few come here for the town itself, for this is the access point to one of the world's most important primate and waterfowl reserves, the **Mamirauá Ecological Reserve** ⓘ *T097-3343 4160, www.mamiraua.org.br*. This is a **Ramsar**, www.ramsar.org, site set up with British support to protect huge areas of terra firme, gallery, *varzea* and *igapó* forest at the confluence of the Solimões and Japurá rivers, and to manage them sustainably with the local riverine people. There are abundant birds including numerous rare trogons, cotingas, currasows, hoatzin, harpy eagle and five species of macaw. There are black caiman (one of which lives under the floating lodge), both species of Amazon dolphin, and numerous rare primates – the most spectacular of which are the endemic black-headed squirrel monkey and the endangered white uakari, known locally as the 'macaco Ingles' because of its red complexion and its genitalia. A visit is unforgettable.

The reserve has a small floating lodge, the **Pousada Uacari** (see Sleeping, page 666) on the Mamirauá river and visitors stay here in simple but elegant wooden rooms. Trips include walks in terra firme forest, boat and canoe trips to *igarpe* creeks, *varzea* and *igapó* forest and the vast Mamirauá lake. Visits must be booked in advance.

Ins and outs Tefé is connected to Manaus by air three times a week on Rico, with onward flights to Tabatinga. There are regular boats (at least one a day) from Manaus or from Tabatinga. The town is small enough to negotiate on foot.

Border with Colombia and Peru

Benjamin Constant → *Colour map 1, B1. Phone code: 097. Population: 23,000.*
This tiny town, with a big sawmill and a series of little tiled houses set in bougainvillea gardens, sits on the frontier with Peru, just opposite Leticia in Colombia. There is an interesting **Ticuna indigenous cultural centre and museum** ① *Av Castelo Branco 396, T096-415 5624*, with artefacts, information panels and a gift shop. The music is haunting but sadly not for sale. Ticuna people run the museum.

Ins and outs There are boat services from Manaus (seven days or more), to Manaus (four days or more) and from Iquitos in Peru. There are no facilities in Benjamin Constant, but it is possible to buy supplies for boat journeys. Benjamin Constant is two hours from Tabatinga and Leticia (ferry/*recreio* US\$2; 25 minutes by speedboat, US\$4 per person, cheaper if more passengers). ►► *For boats to/from Manaus, see Routes in Amazônia, page 670.*

Tabatinga → *Colour map 1, B1. Phone code: 097. Population: 38,000.*
Tabatinga is theoretically 4 km from Leticia (in Colombia) but, in reality, it is the scruffy half of the same town: a long street buzzing with mopeds, a port and some untidy houses in between. There is an important Ticuna centre here, and the town is the headquarters of one of the country's most important indigenous NGOs, **FIUPAM**, fiupam@yahoo.com.br. However, there is little of interest for tourists, who are better off staying in Leticia. Flights arrive in Leticia (see below) from where a minibus to Tabatinga costs US\$1.

The port area in Tabatinga is called Marco and the port captain is very helpful and speaks good English. There are regular boats from Manaus and from Benjamin Constant, across the water, and from Iquitos in Peru. A mosquito net for a hammock is essential if sailing upstream from Tabatinga, much less so downstream. A good hammock will cost US\$15 in Tabatinga (try **Esplanada Teocides**).

Ins and outs Travel between Tabatinga and Leticia (Colombia) is very informal. Taxis between the towns charge US\$5 (more if you want to stop at immigration offices or change money), or US\$0.80 in a *colectivo* (more after 1800). Beware of taxi drivers who want to rush you expensively over the border before it 'closes'. It is not advisable to walk the muddy path between Tabatinga and Leticia as robberies occur here. Boats from Manaus normally start from Tabatinga and spend a day or two here before returning; you can stay on board. ►► *For boats to/from Manaus, see Routes in Amazônia, page 670.*

Leticia (Colombia) → *Colour map 1, B1. International phone code +57. Phone code: 9859.*
This riverside city is clean and modern, though run down, and is rapidly merging into one town with neighbouring Marco in Brazil. Leticia is a good place to buy indigenous

Border essentials: Brazil–Colombia–Peru

It is advisable to check requirements and procedures before arriving at this multiple border. No foreign boats are allowed to dock at the Brazilian, Colombian and Peruvian ports, so travellers should enquire carefully about embarkation/disembarkation points and where to go through immigration formalities. If waiting for transport, the best place for accommodation, exchange and other facilities is Leticia in Colombia.

Brazilian immigration Entry and exit stamps are given at the **Polícia Federal**, 2 km from the Tabatinga docks (Monday to Friday 0800-1200, 1400-1800); through the docks to the end of the road, turn right at this T-junction for one block to a white building opposite Café dos Navegantes; also at the airport (Wednesday and Saturday only). Proof of sufficient funds (US$500) or an onward ticket may be asked for. One week's transit in Tabatinga is permitted. In this area, carry your passport at all times. The **Colombian consulate** (0800-1400) is near the border on the road from Tabatinga to Leticia, opposite Restaurant El Canto de las Peixadas. Tourist cards are issued on presentation of two passport photos. **Note** If coming from Peru, you must have a Peruvian exit stamp and a yellow fever certificate.

Colombian immigration Exit stamps to leave Colombia by air or overland are given by **DAS**, Calle 9, No 8-32, Leticia, no more than one day before you leave. If flying into Leticia prior to leaving for Brazil or Peru, get an exit stamp while at the airport. Check both offices for entry stamps before flying into Colombia. To enter Colombia you must have a tourist card to obtain an entry stamp, even if you are passing through Leticia en route between Brazil and Peru (the Colombian consul in Manaus may tell you otherwise; try to get a tourist card elsewhere). The Colombian consulate in Tabatinga (see above) issues tourist cards; 24-hour transit stamps can be obtained from DAS. If visiting Leticia without intending to go anywhere else in Colombia, you may be allowed to enter without immigration or customs formalities (but traveller's cheques cannot be changed without an entry stamp). The **Brazilian consulate** in Leticia is at Calle 11, No 10-70 (Monday to Friday 1000-1600); onward ticket and two black-and- white photos needed for visa (photographer nearby); allow 36 hours. The **Peruvian consulate** is at Cra 11, No 6-80 (0830-1430); no entry or exit permits are given here.

Peruvian immigration Peruvian entry/exit formalities take place at Santa Rosa; reais and dollars can be exchanged here. Every boat leaving and entering Peru stops here. Entry formalities into Brazil takes place at Tabatinga; for Colombia, In Leticia. There is an immigration office in Iquitos (Mcal Cáceres 18th block), where procedures for leaving can be checked. Also in Iquitos are the **Brazilian consulate** (Calle Sargento Lores 363, T005194-232081), and **Colombian consulate** (Calle Putumayo 247).

products typical of the Amazon, and tourist services are better than in Tabatinga or Benjamin Constant. The best time to visit the area is in July or August, the early months of the dry season. At weekends, accommodation may be difficult to find.

The **museum** ① *Cra 11 y Calle 9*, set up by **Banco de la República**, covers local ethnography and archaeology and is set in a beautiful building with a library and a terrace overlooking the Amazon. There is a small **Amazonian zoo** ① *US$1*, and botanical garden on the road to the airport, within walking distance of town (20 minutes).

Ins and outs The **airport** ① *1.5 km from town*, receives flights from Manaus (three times a week with **Rico**) via Tefé. It is a small terminal with few facilities. A taxi to the centre costs US$1.60. There is a **tourist office** ① *C 10, No 9-86, Ministerio del Medio Ambiente, Cra 11, No 12-05*, for general information on national parks.

Up the Rio Negro

It is possible to get a public passenger boat from Sao Raimundo port on the outskirts of Manaus up the Rio Negro (see Routes in Amazônia, page 670). There are hardly any villages of more than a few houses, but these places are important in terms of communications and food resources. It is vital to be self-sufficient in terms of food and cash and to be able to speak Portuguese or have a Brazilian guide. **Nova Airão**, on the west bank of the Negro, is an overnight, eight-hour boat trip upstream. It has a large boat-building centre at the south end, and a fish and vegetable market at the north end. Ice and bread can also be purchased here. It has a telephone, from which international calls can usually be made. There is road access and a bus service from Manaus.

It's two days from Nova Airão to the **Parque Nacional Jaú**. The only way to get here is with a tour; there is no transport or facilities. Permits are necessary; contact **Ibama** ① *R Ministro João Gonçalves de Souza, BR-319, Km 1, Distrito Industrial, Caixa Postal 185, Manaus, CEP 69900, T096-3237 3718/3710, www.ibama.com.br.*

Moura is about five days upstream from Manaus. It has basic medical facilities and the military base has an airstrip (only usable September to December) and tele-communications. About a day further upstream is **Carvoeira**, almost opposite the mouth of the Rio Branco. There is a vibrant festival in the first week of August. A couple of days beyond is **Barcelos**, with a daily air service, except Sundays, the centre for bass fishing on the Amazon. There are a couple of places to stay here.

São Gabriel da Cachoeira and on towards Venezuela → *Colour map 1, A2.*

A great distance further upstream is São Gabriel da Cachoeira, some 900 km and 10 days from Manaus by boat. The city is tiny and sits under a hulking boulder mountain in front of a series of dramatic rapids. There are fine white-sand beaches on the Negro during the dry season. São Gabriel is near the **Pico da Neblina National Park**, named after the highest mountain in Brazil (3014 m). Contact the **Ibama** office in Manaus for more information and details of guides and trips to indigenous villages (not very traditional any more).

Ins and outs There are flights four times a week with **Trip**, www.airtrip.com.br. You can continue from São Gabriel to Venezuela or to Colombia; be sure to get an exit stamp for Brazil here and an entry stamp for Colombia. Visas for Venezuela must be obtained in Manaus. There is a Colombian consulate in São Gabriel near the **FOIRN** indigenous headquarters. In São Gabriel there are two banks but no exchange facilities and the **Vaupes** hotel (**E**). Cargo boats go to **Cucuí** at the border between Brazil, Colombia and Venezuela. There is also a twice-weekly bus, US$5 (one hotel, ask for Elias, no restaurants). From Cucuí there are daily boats to Guadalupe (Colombia) and infrequent boats to Santa Lucía (Venezuela).

South on the Rio Madeira

Humaitá → *Phone code: 097. Colour map 1, B3. Population: 33,000.*

Humaitá is situated at the crossroads of the Rio Madeira with the Transamazônica highway and the BR-319 north to Manaus. Cattle ranching has begun in the area around the town. There are several basic hotels on the eastern edge of town and the *rodoviária* in the centre.

Ins and outs There is very little traffic on the Transamazônica from Humaitá east to Itaituba (1025 km); local drivers may give lifts. A ferry crosses the Rio Aripuanã at Vila do Carmo. The road is good for about 350 km from Humaitá, then it deteriorates badly. It is hilly, narrow, and the jungle usually grows over the side of the road. Buses run to **Apuí** (**Hotel Goaino**, basic), 458 km, about 12 hours, US$36; and to **Jacareacanga**, erratic service, another 222 km (the town is 8 km off the highway). You need to stay overnight and catch the Transbrasiliana bus to Itaituba (24 hours, schedule erratic, the bus is replaced occasionally by a truck). **Hotel São Cristóvão** (**D**) has a good restaurant, or try the filling station, on the Transamazônica near the Jacareacanga turning, for hammock space. Travel times depend on the weather conditions, the condition of the bus, and whether the driver decides to stop somewhere for the night. There are flights from Jacareacanga to Itaituba.

It is also possible to travel to Itaituba by boat; not daily, ticket from fuel station, US$25, 1½ days, very basic, hammock space only. About 70 km before Itaituba there are rapids; the rest of the journey is done by pickup, US$10.

⦿ Amazonas and the Amazon River listings

For Sleeping and Eating price codes and other relevant information, see pages 42-47.

⦿ Sleeping

Manaus *p651, map p652*

Although the area around Av Joaquim Nabuco and R dos Andradas has lots of cheap hotels, this is a low-key red-light district and not particularly safe at night. A better alternative is the nearby **Zona Franca**, which is convenient for shops, banks, restaurants and the port area. However, Zona Franca is very quiet at night and not too safe. The best area to stay now is around the **Teatro Amazonas**, where the Italianate colonial houses and cobbled squares have been newly refurbished.

L Tropical, Av Coronel Teixeira 1320, Ponta Negra, T092-3659 5000, www.tropical hotel.com.br. A lavish 5-star hotel 20 km outside the city in a semi-forested parkland setting next to the river. The hotel has a private beach, tennis court and a large pool with wave machine. There are several restaurants

including a decent *churrascaria*. The river dock is a departure point for many river cruises. To get here take a minibus from R José Paranaguá in front of the Petrobras building at the corner of Dr Moreira, US$5 return, 0830, 0930, 1130 to hotel, 1200, 1400, 1500, 1800 to town, or take a Ponta Negra bus, US$0.70, then walk. A taxi to the centre costs around US$20. The hotel charges a 12% service tax and offers substantial discounts for those arriving on **Varig** flights. Service can be slow. The hotel tour agency organizes excursions.

L Tropical Business, Av Coronel Teixeira 1320, Ponta Negra, T092-2123 3000, www.tropicalhotel.com.br. The business companion to the **Tropical** and just a few doors away. Rooms and suites are modern and well appointed, housed in a large tower block with great views out over the river from the upper floors. The hotel has the best business facilities in the city.

AL Taj Mahal Hotel, Av Getúlio Vargas 741, Centre, T092-3627 3737. A large, well-run business hotel near the opera house in the centre. Facilities include a tour agency, revolving restaurant and a spa.

A Ana Cássia Palace, R dos Andradas 14, Centre, T092-3622 3637, hacassia@internext.com.br. Gloriously faded large rooms, some with great views of the port. The hotel has a decent restaurant and pool.

A Best Western Lord Manaus, R Marcílio Dias 217, T092-3622 2844, www.bestwestern.com. Pleasant, spacious lobby and standard well-kept a/c rooms. Conveniently located for boats and shops, in the heart of the Zona Franca.

A Manaós, Av Eduardo Ribeiro 881, T092-3633 5744, www.hotelmanaos.com.br. Recently renovated and right next to the Teatro Amazonas. Spruce a/c rooms with marble floors and smart bathrooms. Decent breakfast.

A-B Mônaco, R Silva Ramos 20, T092-2121 0004, www.hotelmonaco.tur.br. Clunky 1970s mock art deco old hotel decked out with ugly furniture and plastic pot plants but with wonderful views from the top-floor rooms, restaurant and little rooftop pool.

B-C Central, R Dr Moreira 202, T092-3622 2600, www.hotelcentralmanaus.com.br. A business hotel in the heart of the Zona Franca with a range of rooms, many very scruffy although some well kept; look at a few. Excellent large breakfast.

B-C Krystal, R Barroso 54, T092-3233 7535, www.krystalhotel.com.br. A range of small though business-like, well-maintained modern a/c rooms.

B-C Lider, Av 7 de Setembro 827, T092-3621 9700, www.liderhotelmanaus.com.br. Small modern a/c rooms with marble floors, little breakfast tables and en suite bathrooms. The best are at the front of the hotel on the upper floors. Very well kept.

C-D Brasil, Av Getúlio Vargas 657, T092-2123 6575, hotel-brasil@internext.com.br. Faded cavernous a/c rooms decorated with tacky art and with tiny en suite bathrooms and even tinier balconies. Small pool.

D Dez de Julho, R 10 de Julho 679, T092-3232 6280, www.hoteldezdejulho.com. By far the best cheap option, very clean though simple rooms (some with a/c and hot water), with laundry, tour operator and efficient, English-speaking staff. There have been complaints about security recently.

D Itália, R Guilherme Moreira 325, T092-3234 7934. Very simple but well-kept rooms in the heart of the Zona Franca. The best are on the upper floors. Generous breakfast.

E Hostel Manaus, R Lauro Cavalcante 231, Centro, T092-3233 4545, www.hostel manaus.com. **F** for HI members. HI hostel in one of the city's original houses. Good-value dorms and private rooms. Reasonably central with views of the city from the rooftop patio and quiet. Australian-run. Great place to join a jungle tour. Not to be confused with a non-HI hostel in the city using a similar name.

Lodges accessible from Manaus

LL-L Othon Jungle Palace, office at R Saldanha Marinho 700, Manaus, T092-3633 6051, www.junglepalace.com.br or book through **Iguana Tours** or **Gero's Tours** in Manaus. A floating lodge with very comfortable a/c 4-star rooms and a pool, on a black-water tributary of the Rio Negro some 5 km from the Anavilhanas. Excellent guides and service but, as ever with lodges close to Manaus, somewhat depleted forest.

L Acajatuba Jungle Lodge, Lago Acajatuba, 4 hrs up the Rio Negro from Manaus. Office at Conjunto Vila Municipal, R 07 No 87, Adrianópolis, Manaus, T092-3642 0358, www.acajatuba.com.br. 40 apartments, a bar and a restaurant. About as comfortable as a damp forest can get but with pet wild animals, so not best practice ecologically.

L Ariaú Amazon Towers, 60 km and 2 hrs by boat from Manaus, on the Rio Ariaú, 2 km from Archipélago de Anavilhanas; office at R Leonardo Malcher 699, Manaus, T092-2121 5000, www.ariautowers.com.br. With 271 rooms in complex of towers connected by walkways, a pool, meditation centre, large restaurant and gift shop, this is a jungle hotel

more than a jungle lodge. If you are after intimacy with the forest you won't find it here. But the hotel is a good option for older people or those with small children. The guided tours are generally well run, although specialist wildlife guides are not available and tame wildlife hangs around the lodge.

L Pousada dos Guanavenas, Ilha de Silves, 300 km from Manaus on the road to Itacoatiara, then by boat along the Rio Urubu. T092-3656 1500, www.guana venas.com.br, book through **Iguana Tours** or **Gero's Tours**. A large lodge in cleared grounds overlooking the black-water Lago Canacari, some 4-5 hrs from Manaus. The hotel has a pool, excellent restaurant and very comfortable a/c rooms with hot water. The hotel's tours run like clockwork – sometimes too much so.

L-AL Amazon Ecopark Lodge, Igarapé do Tarumã, 20 km from Manaus, 15 mins by boat, T092-2547 7742 or T092-9146 0594 www.amazonecopark.com.br. Book through **Gero's Tours** in Manaus. The best lodge close to Manaus, in a private reserve that would otherwise have been destroyed. The lodge makes a real effort at conservation and good practice. The apartment cabins are very comfortable (hot showers) and set in the forest. The lodge has a lovely white-sand beach and is close to the **Amazon Monkey Jungle**, an ecological park where primate species (including white uakari) are treated and rehabilitated in natural surroundings. The **Living Rainforest Foundation**, which administers the ecopark, also offers educational jungle trips and overnight camps (bring your own food), entrance US$15.

A Amazon Lodge, T092-656 3878, Lago do Juma, 80 km from Manaus, 30 mins by Careiro ferry, then 1½ hrs by bus, then 2 hrs by boat. A floating lodge with 12 basic apartments (cold showers), restaurant, good excursions. Highly recommended.

A Boa Vida Jungle Resort, Rodovia AM-010; 53 km from Manaus on the AM-010 highway towards Itacoatiara, T092-3231 1661, www.boavidahotel.com.br or through **Iguana Tours** or **Gero's Tours** in Manaus. A very small, intimate lodge with just 7 apartments and 6 chalets all with showers and fridges and a communal bar and restaurant. In an area with good wildlife and few tourists.

A Juma, Lago da Juma, T092-3232 2707, www.jumalodge.com or through **Gero's Tours** in Manaus. Newly refurbished lodge in a beautiful location, with a burgeoning interest in birdwatching and proper wildlife tours.

A Tiwa Amazone Resort, Lago Salvador, 10 mins across the Rio Negro from Ponta Negra, T092-3088 4676, T092-9995 7892, www.tiwaamazone.com or through **Iguana Tours** or **Gero's Tours** in Manaus. A medium-sized resort lodge with very comfortable spacious cabanas with en suites and a/c, built out over a small caiman-filled lake. The resort itself has a large pool and bar. Too close to Manaus for much wildlife, but an option as an alternative city hotel, especially for a business trip. Good tours.

A Wild Cabanas, 80 km from Manaus, book through **Brazilian Safaris**. Comfortable rooms and hammock space in a large *maloca*-style building on a caiman-filled lake close to the Rio Mamori. Popular with backpackers.

A-B Aldeia dos Lagos Lodge, near Silves, run by the **Silves Project**, T092-3248 9988, www.viverde.com.br/aldeia. A community-based eco-project with WWF support. Set in a system of lakes with high environmental diversity. Good for birds and caiman.

Tefé *p659*

L Pousada Uacari, T097-3343 4672 or T097-3343 4160, www.uakarilodge.com.br. Together with **Cristalino Jungle Lodge** (see page 766), this is the best lodge for wildlife, guiding and ecotouristic practice in the Brazilian Amazon. The lodge is in a magical location in the Mamirauá reserve, floating on a river, with 10 suites of 25 sq m each linked by floating bridges. Tours are excellent. Look out for the friendly black caiman which lives in the water under the restaurant. The lodge and the trips in the reserve can be booked in Manaus through **Iguana Tours**, at either their shop or their office in Manaus airport. Book well in advance.

D Anilce, Praça Santa Teresa 294. Clean, a/c, very helpful. Don't leave valuables in your room.
E Hotel Panorama, R Floriano Peixoto 90. Recommended, with a good restaurant.

Benjamin Constant *p660*

There are a number of very cheap and very simple *pousadas* in town.
B Benjamin Constant, R Getúlio Vargas 36, beside the ferry, T092-3415 5638; postal address Apdo Aéreo 219, Leticia, Colombia. All rooms have a/c, some with hot water and TV. Good restaurant, arranges tours.

Tabatinga *p660*

C Pousada do Sol, General Sampaio, T092-3412 3355. Simple rooms but in a hotel with a sauna and a pool. Friendly owners.
D-E Travellers Jungle Home, R Marechal Rondon 86. A little hostel and tour operator with Brazilian/French owners and a pet snake.

Leticia (Colombia) *p660*

The international phone code for Colombia is +57. The code for Leticia is 9819.
AL Anaconda, Cra 11 No 7-34, T9819-27119. The plushest in town with large a/c rooms, hot water, a restaurant, good terrace and swimming pool.
B Colonial, Cra 10 No 7-08, T9819-27164. A/c or fans, swimming pool, cafeteria, noisy.
C-D Residencias Fernando, Cra 9, No 8-80, T9819-27362. Simple but well appointed and clean. Recommended.
D Residencias La Manigua, C 8 No 9-22, T9819-27121. Friendly staff and modest but well-maintained rooms.
D Residencias Marina, Cra 9 No 9-29, T9819-26014. Standard cheap hotel rooms, TV, some with a/c, cold water, good breakfast and meals at attached restaurant.
E Residencia Internacional, Av Internacional, between the centre and the Brazilian border. Basic rooms with attached bathrooms and fans. Hard beds.
F Residencias Colombia, C 10 at C 8. Very basic rooms with a shared bathroom. Good value.

🍴 Eating

Manaus *p651, map p652*
Many restaurants close Sun night and Mon.
🍴🍴🍴 **Himawari**, R 10 de Julho 618, opposite Teatro Amazonas, T092-3233 2208. Swish restaurant serving sushi and Japanese food. Attentive service, open Sun night when many restaurants close. Recommended.
🍴🍴🍴 **La Barca**, R Recife 684, T092-3642 3040. Very swanky and popular, with a wide variety of fish dishes. Often has live music.
🍴🍴🍴 **Restaurant Tarumã** in Hotel Tropical (see page 663). The best restaurant in town, formal and open for dinner only.
🍴🍴 **Búfalo**, Av Joaquim Nabuco 628, T092-3633 3733, www.churrascariabufalo.com.br. The best *churrascaria* in Manaus, with a US$8 all-you-can-eat Brazilian barbecue and a vast choice of meat. Come with an empty stomach.
🍴🍴 **Canto da Peixada**, R Emílio Moreira 1677 (Praça 14 de Janeiro), T092-3234 3021. Superb fish dishes, lively atmosphere, unpretentious, a short taxi ride from the centre.
🍴🍴 **Fiorentina**, R José Paranaguá 44, Praça da Polícia, T092-3232 1295. Fan-cooled traditional Italian with cheesy vegetarian dishes and even cheesier piped music. Great *feijoada* on Sat, half-price on Sun. Dishes are served with mugs of wine.
🍴🍴 **Pizzeria Scarola**, R 10 de Julho 739, corner with Av Getúlio Vargas, T092-3232 6503. Standard menu and pizza delivery, popular.
🍴 **Alemã**, R José Paranaguá, Praça da Polícia. Food by weight with great pastries, hamburgers, juices, sandwiches.
🍴 **O Naturalista**, R 7 de Setembro 752, 2nd floor. Open for lunch only. The best pay-by-weight vegetarian in the city.
🍴 **Senac**, R Saldanha Marinho 644, T092-3633 2277. Lunch only. Cookery school with a self-service restaurant. Highly recommended.
🍴 **Skina dos Sucos**, Eduardo Ribeiro and 24 de Maio. A large choice of Amazonian fruit juices and bar snacks.
🍴 **Sorveteria Glacial**, Av Getúlio Vargas 161, and other locations. Recommended for unusual ice creams such as *açaí* and *cupuaçu*.

Tefé *p659*
🍴🍴-🍴 **Au Bec d'Or** by the port. With simple but very tasty French cuisine using Amazon ingredients.

Leticia (Colombia) *p660*
There are plenty of lunchtime *almuerzo* restaurants serving cheap dishes of the day in the centre of town. Fried banana and meat, fish and fruit is sold at the market near the harbour and there are many cheap café/bars overlooking the market on the river bank. Take your own drinking water or beer.
🍴 **Sancho Panza**, Cra 10 No 8-72. Good-value meat dishes, big portions, Brazilian beer.

🍸 Bars and clubs

Manaus *p651, map p652*
Manaus has lively nightlife with something going on every night. **O Laranjinha** in Ponta Negra is popular any week night and has a live *Boi Bumba* dance show on Wed. Be wary of piranhas of the female, human kind after 2400.

DJ (Djalma) Oliveira, T092-9112 3942 (or book through **Gero's Tours**), will take visitors out to sample Manaus club life. He is cheaper than a taxi and speaks a little English.
Mon Coração Blue, Estr Ponta Negra. Live *forró* and general dance in a large club. US$2 entrance.
Tue Hollywood Rock, Estr Ponta Negra. Live *pagodé*. US$2 entrance.
Wed Antares, Estr Dom Pedro, Kisia. Live *brega* (a frenetic northern Brazilian form of *forró*), US$2.
Thu Clube do Forró, Estr do Aleixo. Live *forró*, US$2.
Fri Simbola, Estr Ponta Negra, Big club with 3 floors playing a mix of club music, *forró* and *pagodé*, US$3.50.
Sat Numerous clubs especially **Simbola** and **Talismã Forró Club** in Cachoeirinha. There are a number of other bars in Cachoeirinha offering music and dancing.
Sun Hollywood Rock and Simbola.

⊙ Entertainment

Manaus *p651, map p652*
Cinema
In R 10 de Julho and 8 screens at the **Amazonas Shopping Centre**, bus 'Cidade Nova 5', or Nos 204, 207, 208, 307. Most foreign films are shown with original soundtrack and Portuguese subtitles. Afternoon performances are recommended as long queues often form in the evenings.

Performing arts
For **Teatro Amazonas** and **Centro Cultural Pálacio Rio Negro**, see pages 654 and 656. In Praça da Saudade, R Ramos Ferreira, there is a Sun **funfair** from 1700; try prawns and *calaloo* dipped in *tacaca* sauce. A 'train' circling the old town with loud music and cartoon characters is good fun for children.
Teatro da Instalação, R Frei José dos Inocentes, T/F092-234 4096. Performance space in restored historic buildings with free music and dance (everything from ballet to jazz), May-Dec Mon-Fri at 1800. Charge for performances at weekends. Recommended.

⊛ Festivals and events

Manaus *p651, map p652*
6 Jan Epiphany.
Feb Carnaval in Manaus has spectacular parades in a *sambódromo* modelled on Rio's, but with 3 times the capacity. Tourists may purchase grandstand seats, but admission at ground level is free (don't take valuables). Carnaval lasts for 5 days, culminating in the parade of the samba schools.
3rd week in Apr Week of the Indígena, indigenous handicrafts.
Jun Festival do Amazonas, a celebration of all the cultural aspects of Amazonas life, indigenous, Portuguese and from the northeast, especially dancing. Also in Jun is the **Festival Marquesiano**, with typical dances from those regions of the world which have sent immigrants to

Amazonas, performed by the students of the Colégio Marquês de Santa Cruz.
29 Jun São Pedro, boat processions on the Rio Negro.
Sep Festival de Verão do Parque Dez, 2nd fortnight, festival with music, fashion shows, beauty contests and local foods at the Centro Social Urbano do Parque Dez. In the last week of Sep is the **Festival da Bondade**, with stalls from neighbouring states and countries offering food, handicrafts, music and dancing at SESI, Estr do Aleixo, Km 5.
Oct Festival Universitário de Música (FUM), the most traditional festival of music in Amazonas, organized by the university students, on the university campus.
8 Dec Procesão de Nossa Senhora da Conceição, from the Igreja Matriz through the city centre and returning to Igreja Matriz for a solemn mass.

Parintins *p658*
Jun Festa do Boi Bumba. Huge 3-day festival attracting 40,000 people (see box, page 659).
24 Dec-6 Jan Parintins' other main festival is the **Pastorinhas**.

São Gabriel de Cachoeira *p662*
Oct Festribal is a very lively indigenous festival in the city.

⊙ Shopping

Manaus *p651, map p652*
All shops close at 1400 on Sat and all day Sun. Since Manaus is a free port, the whole area a few blocks off the riverfront is full of electronics shops. This area, known as the Zona Franca, is the commercial centre, where the shops, banks and hotels are concentrated.

Bookshops
Livraria Nacional, R 24 de Maio 415. Stocks some French books.
Usados CDs e Livros, Av Getúlio Vargas 766. Selection of used books, English, German, French and Spanish.

Valer, R Ramos Ferreira 1195. A few English classics stocked. The best in the city.

Markets and souvenirs

To buy a hammock head to the **Casa das Redes** and other shops on R dos Andradas. There are now many handicrafts shops in the area around the theatre. The souvenir shop at the **INPA** (see page 657) has some interesting Amazonian products on sale. The markets near the docks are best in the early morning. There is a very good Sun market in the **Praça do Congresso**, Av E Ribeiro. **Ponta Negra** beach boasts a small 'hippy' market, very lively at weekends. There is a good supermarket at the corner of Av Joaquim Nabuco and R Sete de Setembro.

Artesanato da Amazônia, R José Clemente, 500, loja A, opposite Teatro Amazonas, has a good, reasonably priced selection of regional products.

Central Artesanato, R Recife, near Detran. Local craftwork.

Ecoshop, 10 de Julho 509a, near the theatre, www.ecoshop.com.br. Good little a/c café.

Mamirauá Shop, R 10 de Julho 495, near the theatre. Range of indigenous crafts and books and information on the Mamirauá Reserve.

Mercado Adolfo Lisboa (see page 655), Mon-Sat 0500-1800, Sun and holidays 0500-1200. Go early in the morning when it is full of good-quality regional produce, food and handicrafts. Look out for *guaraná* powder or sticks, scales of *pirarucu* fish (used for manicure), and its tongue (used for rasping *guaraná*).

Selva Amazônica, Mercado Municipal. For woodcarvings and bark fabric.

▲ Activities and tours

Manaus *p651, map p652*
Swimming

Swimming is possible at **Ponta Negra** beach, 13 km from the centre (Soltur bus, US$0.70), although the beach virtually disappears beneath the water Apr-Aug.

There is good swimming at waterfalls on the Rio Tarumã, where lunch is available, shade, crowded at weekends. Take the Tarumã bus from R Tamandaré or R Frei J dos Inocentes, 30 mins, US$0.70 (very few on weekdays), getting off at the police checkpoint on the road to Itacoatiara. There is also superb swimming in the natural pools and under falls of clear water in the little streams which rush through the woods, but take locals' advice on swimming in the river; electric eels and various other kinds of unpleasant fish, apart from the notorious piranhas, abound, and industrial pollution of the river is growing.

Every Sun, boats depart from the port in front of the market for beaches along **Rio Negro**, US$2, leaving when full and returning at the end of the day. This is a real locals' day out, with loud music and foodstalls on the sand.

Amazon tours

Amazon Clipper, T092-3656 1246, www.amazonclipper.com.br. The leading small boat cruise operator. Excellent trips along the Rio Negro with knowledgeable wildlife guides.

Amazon Explorers, R Nhamundá 21, Praça NS Auxiliadora, T092-633 3319, www.amazonexplorers.com.br. Day tours including the 'meeting of the waters', Lago do Janauari, rubber collecting and lunch, (US$60). Highly recommended. The *Amazon Explorer* boat is available for hire at about US$230 per day.

Amazonas Indian Turismo, R dos Andradas 311, T/F092-633 5578. Offers a different, authentic experience, staying with local river people, for around US$60 per day.

Amazonatours, T092-323 28271 or in Spain T+34-61-521 9070, www.amazonatours.com. Spanish/Brazilian-run agency offering trips further afield and to their small lodge in the Tupana Natural Reserve.

Brazilian Safaris, R 10 de Julho 632, T092-3232 6830, braziliansafaris@hotmail.com. Ground operator for many of the smaller

agencies and with their own lodge off the Rio Mamori and a range of good budget trips.
Gero's Tours, R10 de Julho 679, T092-3232 4755 or T092-9983 6273, www.amazon gerotours.com. Backpacker-orientated tours south of the Solimões and bookings made for lodges everywhere. Gero, the owner is very friendly and dedicated.
Heliconia, R Col Salgado 63, Aparecida, T092-3234 5915, www.heliconia-amazon.com. Run by French researcher Thérèse Aubreton.
Iguana Tour, R 10 de Julho 679, T092-3663 6507, www.amazonbrasil.com.br. Offers an extensive range of trips of various lengths. Good facilities including riverboat and campsite in the forest. Also has an office at the airport in Manaus.

Guides

Guides sometimes work individually as well as for tour agencies, and the best ones will normally be booked up in advance. Some will only accompany longer expeditions and often subcontract shorter trips. The easiest way to find a guide, however, is through an agency. Advance notice and a minimum of 3 people for all trips is required by the following guides, who are among the best in the city.
Matthias Raymond, T092-8115 5716, raymathias@hotmail.com. A Waipixana indigenous guide offering trips to further reaches of the forest including the Pico da Neblina (book in advance). Many languages.
Moreno Ortelli, T092-9605 0519, morenojivaro@hotmail.com. One of the few guides in Manaus who knows his birds. Excellent knowledge of indigenous culture and fascinating trips. Many languages.
Samuel Basilio, T092-3635 7740 or T092-9616 3124 (mob), samuelbasilio@hotmail.com. A guide from the upper Rio Negro specializing in long expeditions; has worked on many BBC documentaries as a location finder.

Leticia (Colombia) *p660*
Amazon Jungle trips, Av Internacional, 6-25, T9819-27377. Lodge-based tours offering a variety of adventure options.

Anaconda Tours, Hotel Anaconda, T9819-27119. Tours to Amacayacu, Isla de los Micos and **Sacambu Lodge**.
Elvis Cuevas, Av Internacional, 6-06, T0819-27780. An independent guide offering trips to Amacayacu and indigenous communities nearby.

🚌 Transport

Routes in Amazônia
Belém–Manaus Via **Breves**, **Almeirim**, **Prainha**, **Monte Alegre**, **Curua-Uná**, **Santarém**, **Alenquer**, **Óbidos**, **Juruti** and **Parintins** on the lower Amazon. 5 days upriver, 4 days downriver, including an 18-hr stop in Santarém, suite US$350 upriver, US$250 down, double berth US$180 upriver, US$150 down, hammock space US$75 upriver, US$65 down. Vehicles: small car US$250, *combi* US$320 usually including driver, other passengers extra, 4WD US$450 with 2 passengers, motorcycle US$80. *Nélio Correa* is best on this route. *Defard Vieira*, very good and clean, US$75. *São Francisco* is largest, new and modern, but toilets smelly. *Cisne Branco* of similar quality. *Cidade de Bairreirinha* is the newest on the route, a/c berths. *Lider II* has good food and pleasant atmosphere. *Santarém* is clean, well organized and recommended. *João Pessoa Lopes* is also recommended. The Belém–Manaus route is very busy. Try to get a cabin if you can.

Belém–Santarém Same intermediate stops as above. 2½ days upriver, 1½ days downriver, suite US$150, berth US$135, hammock US$45 upriver, US$38 down. All vessels sailing Belém–Manaus will call at Santarém.

Santarém–Manaus Same intermediate stops as above. 2 days upriver, 1½ days downriver, fares berth US$85, hammock US$30. All vessels sailing Belém–Manaus will call in Santarém and there are others operating only the Santarém–Manaus route, including: *Cidade de Terezinha III* and *IV*, good. *Miranda Dias*, family-run and friendly. Speedboats (*lanchas*) are sometimes available on this route, 16 hrs sitting, no hammock space, US$35.

Belém–Macapá (Porto Santana)
Non-stop, 8 hrs on fast catamaran, *Atlântica*, US$30, 3 days a week, or 24 hrs on large ships, double berth US$110, hammock space US$30 per person, meals not included but can be purchased onboard (expensive), vehicle US$90, driver not included. *Silja e Souza* (Wed) is best. *Comandante Solon* (Sat) is state run, slightly cheaper, crowded and not as nice. Same voyage via Breves, 36-48 hrs on smaller riverboats, hammock space US$25 per person including meals. *ENAL* (Sat); *Macamazônia* (every day except Thu), slower and more basic; *Bartolomeu I* of Enavi, food and sanitary conditions OK, 30 hrs; *Rodrigues Alves* has been recommended. *Golfinho do Mar* is said to be the fastest.

Macapá (Porto Santana)–Santarém
Via **Vida Nova**, **Boca do Jari**, **Almeirim**, **Prainha**, and **Monte Alegre** on the lower Amazon (does not call at Belém). 2 days upriver, 1½ days downriver, berth US$130, hammock US$40. Boats include *Viageiro V* (nice) and *São Francisco de Paula*.

Santarém–Itaituba
Along the Rio Tapajós, 24 hrs (bus service on this route is making the river trip less common).

Manaus–Porto Velho
Via **Borba**, **Manicoré** and **Humaitá** on the Rio Madeira. 4 days upriver, 3½ days downriver (up to 7 days when the river is low), double berth US$180, hammock space US$65 per person. Recommended boats are *Almirante Moreira II*, friendly owner, clean; *Lord Scania*, friendly; *Ana Maria VIII*, modern. The *Eclipse II* is a very nice boat which sails Manaus–Manicoré (2 days, US$80 double berth, US$20 hammock). Many passengers go only as

far as Humaitá and take a bus from there to Porto Velho, much faster.

Manaus–Tefé
Via **Codajás** and **Coari**, 24-36 hrs, double berth US$70, 1st-class hammock space US$20 per person. *Capitão Nunes* is good. *Jean Filho* also okay. Note that it is difficult to continue west from Tefé to Tabatinga without first returning to Manaus.

Manaus–Tabatinga
Via **Fonte Boa**, **Foz do Mamaria**, **Tonantins**, **Santo Antônio do Iça**, **Amataura**, **Monte Cristo**, **São Paulo de Olivença** and **Benjamin Constant** along the Rio Solimões. Up to 8 days upriver (depending on cargo), 3 days downriver, double berth US$220, hammock space US$65 per person (can be cheaper downriver). When going from Peru into Brazil, there is a thorough police check some 5 hrs into Brazil. *Voyagers*, *Voyagers II* and *III* recommended; *Almirante Monteiro*, *Avelino Leal* and *Capitão Nunes VIII* all acceptable; *Dom Manoel*, cheaper, acceptable but overcrowded.

Manaus–Caracaraí (for Boa Vista)
Along the Rio Branco, 4 days upriver, 2 days downriver, many sandbars, impassable during the dry season. Now that the BR-174 (Manaus-Boa Vista) has been paved, it is almost impossible to get a passage on a boat. The only tourist boat is erratic.

Manaus–São Gabriel da Cachoeira
Via **Novo Airão**, **Moura**, **Carvoeiro**, **Barcelos** and **Santa Isabel do Rio Negro** along the Rio Negro. Berth US$180, hammock US$60, most locals prefer to travel by road. Boats on this route: *Almirante Martins I* and *II*, *Capricho de Deus*, *Manoel Rodrigues*, *Tanaka Netto* departing from São Raimundo dock, north of main port.

Manaus *p651, map p652*
Air
Taxi fare to airport US$17.50, fixed rate, or take bus marked 'Aeroporto Internacional' from Marquês de Santa Cruz at Praça

Adalberto Vale, near the cathedral, US$1, or from Ed Garagem on Av Getúlio Vargas every 30 mins. No buses 2200-0700. It is sometimes possible to use the more regular, faster service run by the **Hotel Tropical**; many tour agencies offer free transfers without obligation. Check all connections on arrival. Allow plenty of time at Manaus airport, formalities are very slow especially if you have purchased duty-free goods.

Many flights depart in the middle of the night and while there are many snack bars there is nowhere to rest. Local flights leave from Terminal 2. Check in advance which terminal you leave from.

There are international flights to **Guayaquil** and **Quito** (Ecuador), **La Paz** (Bolivia), **Mexico City**, **Miami**, **Orlando** and **Santa Cruz**. For the **Guianas**, a connection must be made in Boa Vista. Domestic flights to **Belém**, **Boa Vista**, **Brasília**, **Cruzeiro do Sul**, **Macapá**, **Parantins**, **Porto Velho**, **Rio Branco**, **Rio de Janeiro**, **Santarém**, **São Paulo**, **Tabatinga**, **Tefé** and **Trombetas**.

Make reservations as early as possible; flights get booked up quickly. Do not rely on travel agency waiting lists; go to the airport 15 hrs early and get on the airport waiting list. Domestic airport tax US$7.

Airline offices GOL, T0800-701 2131, www.voegol.com.br. **TAM** T0800-123100, www.tam.com.br. **Varig**, T0800-997000, www.varig.com.br. Regional airlines include: META, T0300-789 5503, www.voemeta.com; Rico, T092-3633 5155, www.voerico.com.br; Trip, T0300-789 8747, www.airtrip.com.br; Total, T092-4004 1464, www.total.com.br.

Boat
See also Routes in Amazônia, page 670. Boats run to **Santarém**, **Belém**, **Porto Velho**, **Tefé**, **Tabatinga** (for Colombia and Peru), **São Gabriel da Cachoeira**, and intermediate ports. Almost all vessels now berth at the first (downstream) of the floating docks, which is open to the public 24 hrs a day. Bookings can be made up to 2 weeks in advance at the ticket sales area by the port's pedestrian entrance (bear left on entry). The names and itineraries of departing vessels are displayed here as well as on the docked boats themselves. Touts will engulf you when you arrive at the pedestrian entry; be calm, patient and friendly. Travellers still recommend buying tickets from the captain on the boat itself. The port is relatively clean, well organized, and has a pleasant atmosphere.

ENASA (the state shipping company) sells tickets for private boats at its office in town (prices tend to be high here), T092-633 3280. Local boats and some cargo barges still berth by the concrete retaining wall between the market and Montecristi. Boats for **São Gabriel da Cachoeira**, **Novo Airão**, and **Caracaraí** go from São Raimundo, upriver from the main port. Take bus No 101 'São Raimundo', No 112 'Santo Antônio' or No 110, 40 mins; there are 2 docking areas separated by a hill, the São Raimundo *balsa*, where the ferry to Novo Airão, on the Rio Negro, leaves every afternoon (US$10); and the Porto Beira Mar de São Raimundo, where the São Gabriel da Cachoeira boats dock (most departures Fri).

Manaus–São Paulo it is cheaper to go by boat from Manaus to Porto Velho, then bus to São Paulo, than to fly direct or go by boat to Belém then bus. Departures to the less important destinations are not always known at the **Capitânia do Porto**, Av Santa Cruz 265, Manaus. Be careful of people who wander around boats after they've arrived at a port; they are almost certainly looking for something to steal.

Bus
To get to the *rodoviária* take a local bus from the centre, US$0.70, marked 'Aeroporto Internacional' or 'Cidade Nova' (or taxi, US$5). There are many daily services to **Boa Vista** on Eucatur; the best are at night leaving at 2030 and 2100 (10 hrs, US$28). Most go via **Presidente Figueiredo** (3 hrs, US$10). There are also 8 daily buses to **Itacoatiara** (4 hrs, US$15).

Other towns in the state are best visited by air or boat, especially during the November to May wet season when road travel is next to impossible.

Car

The road north from Manaus to **Boa Vista** (770 km) is described on page 676. The Catire Highway (BR-319), from Manaus to **Porto Velho** (868 km), has been officially closed since 1990. Several bridges are out and there is no repair in sight. The alternative for drivers is to ship a car down river on a barge, others have to travel by boat (see above). To **Itacoatiara**, 285 km east on the Amazon; now paved route AM-010, 266 km, through Rio Preto da Eva.

Car hire Localiza, R Major Gabriel 1558, T092-233 4141, and airport, T092-652 1176.

Parintins *p658*

Air A taxi or motortaxi to the airport costs US$3. Flights to **Manaus** (1¼ hrs), **Altamira**, **Araguaína**, **Belém**, **Belo Horizonte**, **Brasília**, **Carajás**, **Itaituba**, **Santarém** (1 hr 20 mins), **Trombetas**, **Tucuruí**, **Uberaba** and **Uberlândia** with Rico, www.rico.com.br and TRIP, www.trip.com.br.

Boat Boats call on the Belém-Manaus route: 60 hrs to **Belém** (depending on boat and if going up or down river), 10-26 passengers. There are irregular sailings to **Óbidos** (ask at the port), 12-15 hrs. A boat to **Santarém** takes 20 hrs.

Tefé *p659*

Air The airport has a connection to **Manaus** with Varig, 3 times a week.

Boat If travelling on to **Tabatinga**, note that Manaus–Tabatinga boats do not usually stop at Tefé. You must hire a canoe to take you out to the main channel and try to flag down the approaching ship.

Benjamin Constant *p660*

Boat Boats to **Iquitos** leave from a mudbank called **Islandia**, on the Peruvian side of a narrow creek, a few metres from Benjamin Constant. The journey takes a minimum of 2 days upstream, 8-36 hrs downstream, depending on the speed

of the boat. On ordinary boats, fares range from US$30-40 per person, depending on standard of accommodation, food extra. Speedboats charge US$75 per person, three a week are run by **Amazon Tours and Cruises**. All boats call at Santa Rosa (2-3 days upstream to Iquitos were immigration formalities are carried out).

Tabatinga *p660*

Boat Amazon Tours and Cruises operates a luxury service between **Iquitos** and Tabatinga leaving Sun, returning from Tabatinga on Wed, US$695 per person in the Río Amazonas. Also *Arca* US$495 per person, return journey Wed-Sat.

Leticia (Colombia) *p660*

Air Expect to be searched before leaving Leticia airport, and on arrival in Bogotá from Leticia. Trip fly to **Manaus** (sporadically via **Tefé**). There are onward flights from Leticia to **Bogota**. For the border crossing, see box, page 661.

⊕ Directory

Manaus *p651, map p652*

Banks Banco do Brasil, Guia Moreira, and airport changes US$ cash, 8% commission, both with ATMs for Visa, Cirrus, MasterCard and Plus. Most offices shut at 1500; foreign exchange operations 0900-1200 only, or even as early as 1100. **Bradesco**, Av 7 de Setembro 895/293, for Visa ATM. **Credicard**, Av Getúlio Vargas 222 for **Diner**'s cash advances. Cash at main hotels; **Câmbio Cortez**, 7 de Setembro 1199, converts TCs into US$ cash, good rates, no commission. **HSBC**, R Dr Moreira 226, ATM for Visa, Cirrus, MasterCard and Plus. Do not change money on the streets. **Embassies and consulates** Most open in the morning only. **Bolivia**, Av Efigênio Sales 2226, Qd B No 20, T092-3236 9988. **Colombia**, R 24 de Maio 220, Rio Negro Centre, T092-3234 6777, check whether a Colombian tourist card can be obtained at the border. **France**, Av Joaquim

Nabuco 1846, T092-3234 2947. **Germany**, R 24 Maio 220, Rio Negro Centre, sala 812, T092-3234 9045, 1000-1200. **Italy**, R Belo Horizonte 240, Adrianópolis, T092-3611 4877. **Japan**, R Fortaleza 460, T092-3232 2000. **Netherlands**, R Miranda Leão 41, T092-3622 1366. **Peru**, R A, casa 1, Conj Aristocrático, Chapada, T092-3236 3012. **Portugal**, R Terezina 193, T092-3234 5777. **Spain**, Al Cosme Ferreira 1225, Aleixo, T092-3644 3800. **UK**, R Paraquê 240, T092-3237 7869. **USA**, R Recife 1010, Adrianópolis, T092-3633 4907, will supply letters of introduction for US citizens. **Venezuela**, R Ferreira Pena 179, T092-3233 6004, (0800-1200), everyone entering Venezuela overland needs a visa. The requirements are 1 passport photo, an onward ticket and the fee, usually US$30 (check in advance for changes to these regulations – it is reported that a yellow fever certificate is not needed). Takes 24 hrs. **Immigration** To extend or replace a Brazilian visa, take bus from Praça Adalberto Vale to Kissia Dom Pedro for Polícia Federal post; people in shorts not admitted. **Internet** Many around the Teatro, including **Loginet**, R 10 de Julho 625. **Amazon Cyber Cafe**, Av Getúlio Vargas, 626, corner with R 10 de Julho, US$1.50 per hr. **Discover Internet**, R Marcílio Dias 304, next to Praça da Polícia, cabins in back of shop with internet phones and scanners, US$1.50 per hr. Free internet access is available from all public libraries in city, eg **Biblioteca Arthur Reis**, Av 7 de Setembro 444, open 0800-1200 and 1400-1700, with virtual Amazon library and English books. **Laundry** Lavanderia Amazonas, Costa Azevedo 63, near Teatro Amazonas, US$0.40 per item, closed Sat afternoon and Sun. **Lavanderia Central**, R Quintino Bocaiúva 602. **Lavalux**, R Mundurucus 77, fast service washes. **Lavlev**, Av Sen A Maia 1108. One of few self-service laundries is opposite

the cemetery, open Sun, a taxi ride away. **Medical services** Clínica Sao Lucas, R Alexandre Amorin 470, T092-3622 3678, reasonably priced, some English spoken, good service, take a taxi. **Hospital Tropical**, Av Pedro Teixeira (D Pedro I) 25, T092-3656 1441. Centre for tropical medicine, not for general complaints, treatment free, some doctors speak a little English. Take bus Nos 201 or 214 from Av 7 de Setembro in the city centre. **Pronto Soccoro 28 de Agosto**, R Recife, free for emergencies. **Post office** Main office including poste restante on Mcal Deodoro. On the 1st floor is the philatelic counter where stamps are sold, avoiding the long queues downstairs. Staff don't speak English but are used to dealing with tourists. For airfreight and shipping, **Alfândega**, Av Marquês Santa Cruz (corner of Marechal Deodoro), sala 106. For airfreight and sea mail, **Correio Internacional**, R Monsenhor Coutinho and Av Eduardo Ribeiro (bring your own packaging). **UPS**, T092-3232 9849 (Custódio). **Telephone** International calls can be made from call boxes with a phone card. Also at **Telemar**, Av Getúlio Vargas 950.

Tabatinga *p660*
Banks There is a Banco do Brasil, Av da Amizade, which changes TCs at a poor rate and has a Visa ATM. It is easier to get Peruvian money for reais in Leticia. **Internet** Infocenter, Av Amizade 1581.

Leticia (Colombia) *p660*
Banks Banco de Bogotá, will cash Tcs, has ATM on Cirrus network, good rates for Brazilian reais. Banco Ganadero, Cra 11, has a Visa ATM. There are street money changers, plenty of *câmbios*, and banks for exchange. Shop around. **Post office** Avianca office, Cra 11 No 7-58. **Telephone** Cra 11/C 9, near Parque Santander.

Roraima

This extreme northern state is one of the country's newest and is only just beginning to exploit its strategic position on the border with Gran Sabana in Venezuela and the stunning Parakaima mountains in Guyana. The state capital is Boa Vista, a safe, tidy modern city with a very lively out-of-season carnival. Beyond the city, the rainforest gives way to extensive grasslands overlooked by precipitous table-top mountains. The most famous of these is Conan Doyle's lost world, Roraima, which can be visited from Boa Vista. Others, such as Tepequen and those on the upper Rio Branco, are more remote and less visited, their wildernesses replete with wildlife. Guyana and Venezuela are a couple of hours from Boa Vista and all visa formalities can be sorted out in that city. Contrary to popular belief, crossing into both countries is easy and painless and there are excellent onward transport services to Caracas or Georgetown. ▸▸ *For listings, see pages 679-680.*

Background

Roraima covers an area nearly twice the size of England but supports a population of just 325,000. Land grants in the 1970s to encourage agricultural development resulted in a rapid increase in population (from only 25,000 in 1960). Then, in the late 1980s a gold rush in the northwest of Roraima drew prospectors from all over the country. The mining took place on the indigenous Yanomami reserve, devastating their traditional way of life. Further tragedy came in January 1998 when forest fires spread across the state, causing massive destruction. The forest cover gives way to grasslands in the northeast and there is a pronounced dry season. The *várzea* (flood plain) along the main rivers irrigates the southeast of the state. Cattle ranching is important as is rice cultivation on the flood plain of the Rio Branco. Other crops are maize, beans, manioc and banana. Some mining continues but at a reduced level.

Around Boa Vista

Towards Boa Vista

The road that connects Manaus and Boa Vista (a ferry crosses the Rio Branco at Caracaraí) is fully paved and regularly maintained. There are service stations with toilets and camping sites every 150-180 km; all petrol is low octane. At Km 100 is **Presidente Figueiredo**, with many waterfalls and a famous cave with bats. There are also shops and a restaurant. About 100 km further on is a service station at the entrance to the **Uaimiri Atroari Indian Reserve**, which straddles the road for about 120 km. Private cars and trucks are not allowed to enter the reserve between sunset and sunrise, but buses are exempt from this regulation. Nobody is allowed to stop within the reserve at any time. At the northern entrance to the reserve there are toilets and a place to hang your hammock (usually crowded with truckers overnight). At Km 327 is the village of **Vila Colina** where **Restaurante Paulista** is clean with good food, and you can use the shower and hang your hammock. At Km 359 there is a monument to mark the **equator**. At Km 434 is the clean and pleasant **Restaurant Goaio**. Just south of Km 500 is **Bar Restaurante D'Jonas**, a good place to eat; you can also camp or sling a hammock. Beyond here, large tracts of forest have been destroyed for settlement, but already many homes have been abandoned.

Boa Vista ⬛🚻👤▲🛏🅿 ▸▸ pp679-680.
Colour map 1, A3.

→ **Phone code: 095. Population: 200,000.**

The capital of the extreme northern state of Roraima, 759 km north of Manaus, is a very pleasant, clean, laid-back little town on the Rio Branco. Tourism is beginning here and there are a number of interesting new destinations offering a chance to explore far wilder country than that around Manaus, with correspondingly richer wildlife. The landscape is more diverse, too, with tropical forest, savannah and highlands dotted with waterfalls. However, the area immediately around the city has been heavily deforested.

Boa Vista lies within easy access of both Venezuela and Guyana and crossing the border to either is straightforward. When the river is low, it is possible to swim in the Rio Branco, 15 minutes by bus from the town centre (too polluted in Boa Vista). As a result of heavy international pressure, the Brazilian government expelled some 40,000 gold prospectors from the Yanomami Reserve in the west of the state in the early 1990s. The economic consequences were very severe for Boa Vista, which went from boom to bust. An increase in cattle ranching in the area has not taken up the slack.

Boa Vista

Euzébio's & Restaurant **2**
Ideal **4**
Uiramutam Palace **3**

Eating 👤
1000 Sabores **1**
Frangão **2**
Peixada Tropical **3**

Sleeping 🛏
Aipana Plaza **1**
Barrudada Palace **5**

The river of doubt

In 1913, Colonel Rondon invited the former US president Theodore Roosevelt to accompany him on one of his surveys. Together they explored the Rio da Dúvida – the River of Doubt – in 1914, following it to the Rio Aripuanã, thence to the Madeira. On the expedition they suffered great difficulties on the river itself, and Roosevelt contracted a fever which incapacitated him on the voyage and from which he never fully recovered. Rondon rechristened the Rio da Dúvida the Rio Roosevelt. The former president's account is told in *Through the Brazilian Wilderness* (London:

John Murray, 1914), which contains photographs of the expedition. Further insights into the project are found in the *Mato Grosso ao Amazonas* telegraph by Coronel Cândido Mariano da Silva Rondon, 1907-1915, which has photos and includes details of the Roosevelt-Rondon expedition.

Written in 1993, Sam Moses' *Down the River of Doubt* (*Travelers' Tales Brazil*) gives an account of an expedition following in Roosevelt's footsteps, which highlighted the effects of the late 20th-century mahogany trade on the Cinta Larga tribe who live on the Rio Roosevelt.

Ins and outs

The **airport** ① *4 km from the centre*, receives national and international flights. There are no exchange or left luggage facilities. A taxi to the centre costs US$12; to the *rodoviária*, US$10. There is a bus to the centre, US$0.40, or a 45-minute walk.

The **rodoviária** ① *Av das Guianas, 3 km out of town at the end of Av Ville Roy, T095- 3224 0606*, receives several daily buses from Manaus, Bonfim (from the Guyanese border) and Santa Elena in Venezuela. A taxi to the centre costs US$5, or the 10-minute bus ride costs US$0.45. The local bus terminal is on Avenida Amazonas, by Rua Cecília Brasil, near the central *praça*.

The city has a modern functional plan, which often means long hot treks from one place to another. There's a very ineffectual **tourist office** ① *R Brigadeiro Eduardo Gomes, Centro, T095-3623 1230*, with booths at the *rodoviária*, T095-3623 1238 and the airport. ▸ See Transport, page 680.

To Venezuela and Guyana 😊🅿🚌🚗🚐 ▸▸ *pp679-680*.

Boa Vista has road connections with the Venezuelan frontier at **Santa Elena de Uairén**, 237 km away. The road is paved, but the only petrol available is 110 km south of Santa Elena. Boa Vista is also linked to Bonfim for the Guyanese border at **Lethem**. Both roads are open all year.

Santa Elena de Uairén (Venezuela) → *International phone code +58*.

Santa Elena de Uairén is the gateway to the Venezuelan Highlands for those entering the country from Brazil. It is a pleasant frontier town, 10-12 hours by bus from Ciudad Bolívar, which is nine hours from Caracas. The road is paved all the way and there are also flights. The landscape is beautiful, an ancient land of flat- topped mountains and waterfalls. The road skirts the **Parque Nacional Canaima**, which boasts the highest waterfall in the world, the **Angel Falls** (Salto Angel). Not far north of Santa Elena is the route to Mount Roraima.

Border essentials: Brazil–Venezuela–Guyana

Pacaraima (Brazil)–Santa Elena de Uairén (Venezuela)

Searches are thorough and frequent at this border crossing; it is essential to have a yellow fever vaccination. Officials may give only two months' stay and car drivers may be asked to purchase an unnecessary permit; ask to see the legal documentation. Everyone who crosses the border must have a visa for Venezuela. The current procedure is to take a filled-out visa form, onward ticket, passport photo and deposit slip from the Banco do Brasil (US$30) to the **Venezuelan consulate** in Boa Vista; be prepared to wait an hour. It may be possible to get a visa at the border; check requirements in advance. There is also a Venezuelan consulate in Manaus which issues one-year, multiple entry visas (see page 674). The **Brazilian consulate** in Uairén is near the bus terminal opposite the Corpoven petrol station (open 0800-1200, 1400-1800). Buses leave Boa Vista *rodoviária* at 0730, 1000 and 1400 for Santa Elena de Uirén, stopping at all checkpoints, US$7.50, 3½ to six hours; take water for the journey.

Bonfim (Brazil)–Lethem (Guyana)

The main border crossing between Brazil and Guyana is from Bonfim, 125 km (all paved) northeast of Boa Vista, to Lethem. The towns are separated by the Rio Tacutu, which is crossed by small boats for foot passengers (five minutes, US$2). Vehicles cross by ferry on demand, US$4, or drive across in the dry season. The river crossing is 2.5 km from Bonfim, about 1.5 km north of Lethem. A bridge is under construction. It is essential to have a yellow fever vaccination both to leave Brazil and to enter Guyana. The bus passes through **Brazilian immigration** where you receive your exit stamp before crossing the river. On the other side, there are taxis to take you to **Guayanese immigration** office (US$3). You are given a visa for the exact amount of time you stipulate. The border is open 24 hours but officials tend to leave immigration after 1800.

Santa Elena has plenty of hotels and places to eat, as well as money-changing facilities, a phone office with international connections, and tour companies for trips into the Gran Sabana – as the region is known.

Ins and outs The **rodoviária** ① *C Mcal Sucre*, receives arrivals from Ciudad Bolívar (Venezuela) several times daily; the journey takes 10-12 hours and buses are run by a number of companies. There are plenty of accommodation options in Santa Elena de Uairén, but just one basic hotel on the Brazilian side of the border. ►► *See Transport, page 680.*

Lethem (Guyana)

A small but scattered town on the Brazilian border (see below), this is the service centre for the Rupununi and for trade with Brazil. There are many small stores, a small hospital (T772 2006), a police station (T772 2011) and government offices. A big event at Easter is the rodeo, visited by cowboys from all over the Rupununi. Prices are about twice as high as in Georgetown. About 2½ km south of town at St Ignatius there is a Jesuit mission dating from 1911. In the nearby mountains there is good birdwatching and there are waterfalls to visit.

There is another border crossing at **Laramonta** from where it is a hard but rewarding walk to the Guyanese town of Orinduik.

Roraima listings

For Sleeping and Eating price codes and other relevant information, see pages 42-47.

Sleeping

Boa Vista *p676, map p676*

B Aipana Plaza, Joaquim Nabuco 53, Praça do Centro Cívico, T095-3224 4116. The best in town with plain rooms decorated in cream and dark tiles, and photos of Roraima. Hot water, a/c, marble bathrooms and cable TV. Attractive pool area with a shady little bar.
B Uiramutam Palace, Av Capt Ene Garcez 427, T095-3624 4700, uiramutam@technet.com.br. A business hotel with modest a/c rooms with writing desk and armchair, cable TV and large bathrooms. Decent pool.
C Barrudada Palace Hotel, R Araújo Filho 228, T095-3623 9335. Simple a/c rooms in a modern tower block very close to the centre. Rooms on the upper floors have views of the river. Breakfast and lunch included.
D Euzébio's, R Cecília Brasil 1107, T095-3623 0300. Spruce, modest rooms with a/c and en suites with cold showers. The best are airy and on the upper floors. Pleasant pool and a laundry service.
F Hotel Ideal, R Araújo Filho 481, T095-3224 6342. Very simple but well-kept rooms with en suites. Some have a/c. Friendly staff and generous breakfast. Convenient for the centre.

Camping

Rio Caaumé, 3 km north of town. Pleasant unofficial site with small bar and clean river.

Eating

Boa Vista *p676, map p676*

Most restaurants close at night, except for pizzerias. There are a number of restaurants serving snacks and juices on the riverside along **R Floriano Peixoto** and several open-air restaurants and cafés on the **Orla Taumanan**, a complex of little bars and eating places overlooking the river. Nightlife and bars are concentrated here; it is quiet during the week but livelier at weekends. There are many little juice stands around **Praça do Centro Cívico**.
♈ Churrascaria La Carreta, R Pedro Rodrigues 185, 500 m from **Euzébio's**. Good. US$3 buffet, nice atmosphere. Recommended.
♈ Euzébio's (see Sleeping). Decent fish, *feijoada* and meat dishes. Generous breakfast.
♈ Peixada Tropical, R Pedro Rodrigues at Ajuricaba, T095-224 6040. River fish dishes in a variety of styles from Bahian sauces to *milanesa* accompanied by beans, rice and salads.
♈ 1000 Sabores, R Araújo Filho at Benjamin Constant. Opens early and closes late. Pizzas, snacks and juices.
♈ Frangão, R Homem de Melo at Cecília Brasil. Chicken and river fish with salads, rice, beans.

Bars and clubs

Boa Vista *p676, map p676*

R Floriano Peixoto is lively after dark at weekends when there is live music in and around the Orla Taumanan.
Toca Boat, Orla Taumanan, T095-9971 5454. River cruises with live music and dancing

Activities and tours

Boa Vista *p676, map p676*

Aguia Tours, R Benjamin Constant 1683, T095-3624 1516. Can book buses and flights and the owner speaks some English.
Roraima Adventures, R Sebastião Diniz 787, T095-3624 9611, T095-9115 4171 (mob), www.roraima-brasil.com.br. Interesting trips to little-known and little-visited parts of Roraima state including the spectacular Tepequem and Serra Grande mountains and the Rio Uraricoera, which is replete with wildlife. Groups get the best prices, which are competitive with those in Manaus. Helpful with visas for Venezuela.

● Transport

Boa Vista *p676, map p676*
Air
A taxi to the airport costs US$12. Flights and buses can be booked through **Aguia Tours** (see Activities and tours, above).

The airport has flights to the **Guianas**, **Belém**, **Brasília**, **Macapá**, **Manaus**, **Santarém** and **São Paulo**. Confirm flights before reaching Boa Vista as they are often fully booked. Air taxis can be booked with **Rondônia**, Praça Santos Dumond, T095-3224 5068.

Airline offices GOL, www.voe gol.com.br. META, Praça Santos Dumond 100, T095-3224 7677, www.voe meta.com.br. TAM, www.tam.com.br.

Bus
Note that it is difficult to get a taxi or bus to the *rodoviária* in time for early morning departures; as it's a 25-min walk, book a taxi the previous evening. To **Manaus**, with **Eucatur**, US$28, 10-12 hrs, 4 daily each way, can be crowded, advisable to book at least a few hours in advance. To **Caracaraí** US$9, 3 hrs. **Amatur** to **Bonfim**, daily 0730, 1430, 1700, 2 hrs, US$3.70.

Car hire
Localiza, Av Benjamin Constant 291E, T/F095-3224 5222. **Yes**, Av Maj Williams 538, T/F095-3224 3723.

Hitchhiking
Hitching to **Santa Elena** (Venezuela) can be difficult; either wait at the bridge and police checkpoint on the road to the border, or try to find a Venezuelan driver on the square. Hitching from Boa Vista to **Manaus** is fairly easy on the many trucks travelling south; try from the service station near the *rodoviária*. You may have to change trucks at Caracaraí. At the ferry crossing over the Rio Branco there is usually a long queue of waiting hikers; try to arrange a lift on the ferry. Truck drivers ask for approximately half the bus fare to take passengers in the cab, which is a

bargain; it's even cheaper or free in the back. The view from the truck is usually better than from the bus and you can see the virgin forest of the indigenous reserve in daylight. Take some food and water.

Taxis
For radio taxis contact **Tupã**, R Monte Castelo 318, T095-3224 9150.

Border with Venezuela *p678*
Bus Buses from Santa Elena to **Boa Vista** leave at 0830, 1200, 1500 and 1600, stopping at all checkpoints, US$7.50, 3½-6 hrs, take water. It is possible to share a taxi.

Border with Guyana *p678*
Bus Bonfim–Boa Vista at least 3 a day, US$3.70. Weekly jeep **Laramonta–Boa Vista** US$30.

Boat To cross the river, take a canoe, US$0.25. No boats at night.

● Directory

Boa Vista *p676, map p676*
Banks US$ and Guyanese notes can be changed in Boa Vista. TCs and cash in **Banco do Brasil**, Av Galycon de Paiva 56, 1000-1300 (minimum US$200), will not change *bolívares*. There is no official exchange agency and the local rates for bolivares are low. **Bradesco**, Jaime Brasil e Getúlio Vargas, Visa ATM. Best rate for dollars, **Casa Pedro José**, R Araújo Filho 287, T095-3224 4277, also changes TCs and bolivares. **Timbo's** (gold and jewellery shop), on the corner of R Cecília Brasil e Av Getúlio Vargas, will change money.
Embassies and consulates Venezuela, Av Benjamin Constant 1675, open mornings only. Visas available. Laid-back service. Allow 24-48 hrs. **Guyana**, R Benjamin Constant 1171, T095- 9112 7017, open mornings only.
Medical services Geral, Av Brig Eduardo Gomes, T095-3623 2068. Free yellow fever inoculations at a clinic near the hospital.

Rondônia and Acre

The state of Rondônia is largely populated by migrants from other parts of Brazil. Foreigners are welcomed without question or curiosity and there is no regional accent. A local academic described the state as 'a land where nobody has a name and everyone can have a dream'. Most visitors tend to arrive via the BR-364 from Cuiabá or the Rio Madeira from Manaus.

The intriguing state of Acre, rich in natural beauty, history and the seringueiro culture, is still very much off the beaten track. The area is beginning to develop its considerable potential for adventure, as links are opening up with neighbouring Peru and Bolivia. ▸▸ *For listings, see pages 689-692.*

Background

Rondônia

When the Portuguese first arrived in Rondônia, they thought the land they had found was an enormous island. The Madeira, Guaporé and Amazon rivers do almost form a circle, but the Guaporé was thought, erroneously, to link with the Rio Paraguai on the southwestern side. A group of indigenous Tupinambá, who fled from the Portuguese colonists on the Atlantic Coast, migrated up the Rio São Francisco to the Madeira, settling eventually on the Ilha de Tupinambaranas near the river's mouth. It was probably their accounts of the rivers in this region which encouraged the idea that the Amazon and Río de la Plata systems were linked, making Brazil an island.

Slave and gold hunters in the 18th century used the Guaporé and Madeira rivers for their expeditions. As a frontier area between Portuguese and Spanish colonization, the rivers were scenes of tension between the opposing powers, as well as of conflicts between indigenous tribes and slave-traders, and *bandeirantes* and Jesuits.

Rondônia became a state in 1981 after the central government's push to open up the unpopulated, undeveloped far west brought roads and settlers to the region. The destructive effects of this are well documented (see box, page 628). One of those roads, the BR-364 highway, which was prompted by plans for exaggerated growth, led to widespread deforestation and the erosion of the way of life of many indigenous groups.

The state was named after Colonel Cândido Mariano da Silva Rondon, who founded the **Indian Protection Service (SPI)** in 1910. Rondon was of partly indigenous origin and the policies that he incorporated into the SPI included respect for native institutions, guarantee of permanent ownership by the *indígenas* of their land, the right to exclusive use of natural resources on their land, and protection against rapid change once contact between indigenous and 'civilized' worlds had been made. The pressures of contact between the *indígenas* and the people who subsequently encroached on their world (ranchers, gold prospectors, rubber tappers, Brazil nut gatherers and so on) made the SPI's task very difficult.

Rondônia falls within the same climatic zone as the rest of western Amazônia, with average temperatures of 24-26°C and 2-3 m of rain a year. The wettest months are November to April, the driest June and August. Rondônia can be subject to the phenomenon known as the *friagem*, a sudden drop in temperature to about 6°C, as a result of low pressure over the Amazon Basin attracting polar air from the south Atlantic. The cold weather can last for a week or more and occurs in the winter months. It is said to be an effect of El Niño, the changing patterns in ocean currents in the Pacific at Christmas time.

A voice from the Amazon

"Humanity finds itself at a critical point. Can science solve the mounting problems which confront us in every corner of the globe? Soon after human beings lost themselves to the blind, unconscious forces of systematic self-interest and greed, we, the Indians, found ourselves robbed both of what lay buried beneath our lands and of our lands themselves.

Thankfully, through the power of memory our history has been preserved, continues, and is passed on from generation to generation. Thankfully, the memory of Indians cannot be blotted out so easily.

We Indians have the power to see the truth behind history. Just as we have cures for those abounding problems which then, as now, are the consequence of systematic self-interest and greed.

The United Nations have not succeeded in bringing peace to our world. This is because wars do not begin with nations. They begin inside each and every one of us. What we must do, and with urgency, is to reintegrate humankind with its spiritual leaders and with them bring about a cure in the interior life and the repayment of our interior debts.

In much of the world tourism continues a destructive path without thinking of the consequences of its actions for future generations. But whilst this is happening there are many individual tourists who after speaking with true spiritual masters and shamans find truth and a solution to eternal problems."

Manoel Fernandes Moura, head of FIUPAM, an organization seeking to unite indigenous spiritual leaders from around the world and based in Tabatinga in the Amazon, is one of the leading indigenous rights campaigners of his generation. He was instrumental in helping to halt the Calha Norte northern perimeter road project in Roraima and Amazonas states. Moura is the seventh son of seven generations of shamans. FIUPAM, fiupam@yahoo.com.br.

Acre

In the mid-19th century, what is now Acre was disputed land between Brazil and Bolivia. The Treaty of Ayacucho, 1866, gave the territory to Bolivia. However, the onset of the rubber boom in the 1880s upset this arrangement because many of the landowners who were exporting rubber from Acre and down the Rio Madeira were Brazilian. They resented the fact that the Bolivian government had nominal control, exacting duties, but had signed economic rights over to North American interests. Many *Nordestinos* also migrated to this western frontier at the time in search of fortune. In 1899 the Brazilians rebelled. Four years later the Bolivian government yielded the territory to Brazil under the Treaty of Petrópolis and the American company received US$2 million compensation. In 1913, Rio Branco became capital of the new Território Federal do Acre, which attained statehood in 1962.

Acre has a population of only 500,000 but, as its land is much more productive than that of Rondônia. In the 1990s there was a flood of migration from Acre's landless south into the its neighbouring state, and conditions have yet to be improved. Acre is slightly drier than Rondônia, with 1.5-2 m of rain a year.

Porto Velho » pp689-692. Colour map 1, B2.

→ *Phone code: 069. Population: 330,000.*

Porto Velho stands on a high bluff overlooking a curve of the Rio Madeira, one of the Amazon's main tributaries. The city has seen the rubber, gold and timber booms come and go. Service and IT industries are now the major employers. The city is a large sprawl of streets, laid out in blocks stretching 8 km into the interior. The lack of town planning means that many of the best shops, hotels and banks are now a fair distance from the old centre near the river.

Ins and outs

Getting there Domestic flights arrive at the **airport** ① *8 km west of town, T069-3225 1755*. A taxi to downtown costs US$15. Interstate buses from Rio Branco and Cuiabá arrive at the **rodoviária** ① *east of the centre, Jorge Teixeira, between Carlos Gomes and Dom Pedro II*. There are buses to downtown. » *See Transport, page 691.*

Getting around Urban bus services are good. Consider hiring a car if you're going to stay for some time. Be patient as even local residents get confused with directions. Taxis in town are cheap and plentiful. Find your favourite driver and stick with him; all have mobile phones and work with partners to give prompt 24-hour service.

Tourist offices **Funcetur** ① *Av 7 de Setembro, above Museu Estadual, T069-3221 1881, seplan@ronet.com.br*, is very helpful and publishes a free annual events list, *Calendario do Porto Velho*. Also useful is the **Departamento de Turismo** ① *R Padre Chiquinho 670, Esplanada das Secretarias, CEP 78904-060, T069-3221 1499*. The **Fundação Cultural do Estado de Rondônia (Funcer)** is at the same address. Street maps are hard to find. For a free map go to the **Teleron office** ① *Av Pres Dutra 3023, 0600-2300*, and ask for the *Guia de Porto Velho*, which includes a map and city services listings.

Safety The city is relatively safe for tourists despite rising crime and unemployment. Caution is advised in the evenings and at all times near the railway station and port.

Porto Velho

Mirante I

Mirante II

Railway Station, Museu Ferroviário & Museu Geológico

Rio Madeira

Port

N

Av Farquhar · Santos Dumont · Rogério Weber · Av Pres Dutra · José de Alencar · José Bonifácio · Gonçalves Dias · Júlio de Castilhos · Av Campos Sales · Tenreiro Aranha · Mal Deodoro

Av Pinheiro Machado

Duque de Caxias

Carlos Gomes

Palácio do Governo · José do Patricínio · Prefeitura · **Cathedral** · Dom Pedro II

Fruit & Veg · Praça Getúlio Vargas · Br Rio Branco

Praça Henrique Dias · Afonso Pena

Praça Madeira-Mamoré

Praça Mcal Rondon · City Bus Terminal · da Cunha · Osorio

Av 7 de Setembro

Paulo Leal

Almirante Barroso

Joaquim Nabuco · Av Brasília

To BR 364, Rio Branco & Cuiabá · Av Nações Unidas

To ❹ & Rodoviária

300 metres
300 yards

Sleeping 🛏
Central 1

Líder 2
Vila Rica 3

Chico Mendes – the first eco-martyr

The most famous *seringueiro* (rubber tapper) was Francisco (Chico) Alves Mendes, born in 1944. Chico's father had come to Acre from northeast Brazil as a *soldado da borracha*, engaged in providing rubber for the Allies during the Second World War. Chico learnt the trade of his father, became a leader of the Xapuri Rural Workers' Union and was a founder member of the CNS. He was instrumental in setting up a number of extractive reserves, parcels of land preserved for sustainable exploitation by those that lived there. He was shot dead on 22 December 1988 by cattle ranchers, to whose land-grabbing Mendes was in open opposition. He was by no means the only *seringueiro* who had been killed in such circumstances (he was the 90th rubber tapper to be killed in 1988 alone), but his murder was the culmination of a decade of *fazendeiro-seringueiro* confrontation. Over 4000 people attended his funeral; the world's media latched onto the story and Chico Mendes became the first

globally-recognized eco-martyr. He was honoured by the United Nations for his efforts to stop the destruction of the rainforest. The universal outcry at his assassination led to the arrest, trial and imprisonment of his killers, members of the family of Darly Alves da Silva; a rare event in the history of Amazon land disputes. His death inspired changes in government policy on environmental protection, greater involvement of rubber tappers and other forest workers in local organizations, and the development of extractive reserves, first promoted in 1985 as protected areas for the *seringueiros*. Father Andre Ficarelli, assistant to the Bishop of Acre, said that Mendes' murder was like "the lancing of a tumour, exposing all the corruption and problems which the government [chose] to ignore". To others it was an opportunity to portray the whole affair in Hollywood-style melodrama; there was fierce competition for the film rights to Mendes' life story.

Sights

At the top of the hill on Praça João Nicoletti is the **cathedral**, built in 1930, with beautiful stained-glass windows. The **prefeitura** (town hall) is across the street. The principal commercial street is Avenida 7 de Setembro, which runs from the railway station to the upper level of the city, near the *rodoviária*. The centre is hot and noisy, but not without its charm, and the port and old railway installations are interesting. As well as the **Museu Ferroviário**, there is a **Museu Geológico** ① *both open 0800-1800*, at the old railway yards, known as Praça Madeira-Mamoré. Also here is the **Casa do Artesão** (see Shopping, page 690) and a promenade with riverside bars; a good place to watch the sunset.

The neoclassical **Palácio do Governo** faces Praça Getúlio Vargas, while Praça Marechal Rondon is spacious and modern. There are several popular viewpoints overlooking the river and railway yards. **Mirante I** (with restaurant) is at the end of Rua Carlos Gomes; **Mirante II** (with a bar and ice cream parlour) is at the end of Rua Dom Pedro II and **Mirante III** (with restaurant) is at the end of Benjamin Constant.

It is possible to visit the **cemetery**, where many of the people who died during the construction of the railway are buried. It's about 3 km from the railway station and best to go with a local guide, as it is located in a poorer part of town and difficult to find. It is an eerie place, with many of the tombstones overgrown, some of which have been tampered with by practitioners of *macumba*, and there are rumoured to be ghosts.

Parque Nacional Municipal de Porto Velho ① *Av Rio Madeira s/n, 10 km, T069-221 2769, Thu-Sun, volunteer guides*, is a small zoo with 12 km of marked trails.

Excursions from Porto Velho

The **Cachoeira de Santo Antônio**, a series of rapids on the Rio Madeira, 7 km upriver from Porto Velho, is a popular destination for a swim during the dry season. In the rainy season the rapids may be underwater and swimming is dangerous. Access is by boat from Porto Cai N'Água (one hour); or by city bus No 102, 'Triângulo' (every 50 minutes from the city bus terminus or from the bus stop on Rua Rogério Weber, across from Praça Marechal Rondon). Gold dredges may be seen working near Porto Velho.

The **Banho do Souza** is a bar, restaurant and swimming area, 36 km out of town on the BR-364. A coolbox of beers and soft drinks is left by your table and you pay for what you've drunk at the end of the afternoon, swimming is free.

Along the BR-364 😊😊 ➤ *pp689-692.*

The **Marechal Rondon Highway**, BR-364, runs 1550 km from Porto Velho to Cuiabá in Mato Grosso. The paving of this road has led to the development of farms and towns. Cattle ranches can be seen all along the road, with the lowest population density in the south between Pimenta Bueno and Vilhena.

Pousada Ecológica Rancho Grande ① *contact Caixa Postal 361, Ariquemes, Rondônia 78914, T/F069-535 4301, pousada@ariquemes.com.br*, is a working *fazenda* about 250 km south of Porto Velho. It contains millions of rare butterflies, about 450 bird species and numerous mammals, all of which can be seen on the 20 km of trails. Owner, Harald Schmitz, speaks English, German and Spanish. Highly recommended, especially for butterfly lovers. Reservations and tours can be arranged through **Focus Tours**, see Tours operators, page 65. The **Bradesco** changes money and has an ATM.

Ji Paraná → *Colour map 1, B3. Phone code: 069. Population: 95,500.*

On the shores of the Rio Machado, 376 km from Porto Velho and halfway to Cuiabá is this pleasant town with a small riverside promenade and several bars, which are lively at night. There is swimming in the river, beware of the current, and a **telegraph museum** on Avenida Marechal Rondon.

Parque Nacional dos Pacaás Novos → *Colour map 1, B2.*

Pacaás Novos protects some 765,800 ha of *cerrado*, rainforest and tropical savannah and lies west of the BR-364. The fauna includes all the spectacular mammals such as jaguar, brocket deer, puma, tapir, peccary and maned wolf. The average annual temperature is 23°C, but this can fall as low as 5°C when the cold front known as the *friagem* blows up from the south pole. Information is available from **Ibama** ① *Av Jorge Teixeira 3477, CEP 78904-320, T069-223 2599/3597, Porto Velho, or R João Batista Rios, CEP 78958-000 Pacaás Novas-RO*. Also enquire here about the **Jaru Biological Reserve** in the east of the state.

Reserva Biológica do Guaporé → *Colour map 1, C3.*

① *Av Limoeira, CEP 78971, Guaporé, T069-3651 2239.*

On the Rio Guaporé, the Guaporé Biological Reserve contains the **Forte Príncipe da Beira**. The fort was constructed in 1777 to defend the border with Bolivia and is currently being restored. It can be reached from Costa Marques (20 km by road), which is some 345 km by

Border essentials: Brazil–Bolivia

Gujurá-Mirim (Brazil)–Guayaramerín (Bolivia)
Immigration Brazilian exit/entry stamps can be obtained from the Polícia Federal, Avenida Pres Dutra 70, corner of Avenida Quintino Bocaiúva, T069-3541 4021.
Transport Speedboats take five minutes to cross the Rio Mamoré (border), US$1.65, and run all day. There is also a 20-minute ferry crossing for vehicles, T069-3541 3811, Monday to Saturday 0800-1200, Monday to Friday 1400-1600.

unpaved road west of **Rolim de Moura**. This unplanned town, 40 km west of Pimenta Bueno, relies on agriculture, livestock and a small furniture industry. There are a few basic hotels and guesthouses, which are easy to find and do not require reservations.

Guajará-Mirim ◉▲◉◐ ›› pp689-692. Colour map 1, C2.

→ Phone code: 069. Population: 39,000.

From Porto Velho, the paved BR-364 continues 220 km southwest to **Abunã** (with a few cheap hotels), where the BR-425 branches south to Guajará-Mirim. About 9 km east of Abunã is a ferry crossing over the Rio Madeira, where it receives the waters of the Rio Abunã. The BR-425 is a fair road, partly paved, which uses the former rail bridges. It is sometimes closed from March to May. Across the Mamoré from Guajará-Mirim is the Bolivian town of **Guayaramerín**, which is connected by road to Riberalta, from where there are air services to other Bolivian cities.

Guajará-Mirim is a charming town. The **Museu Municipal** ⓘ T069-3541 3362, 0500-1200, 1400-1800, at the old Guajará-Mirim railway station beside the ferry landing, is interesting, diverse, and recommended. An ancient stern wheeler plies the Guaporé. Return trips of 1250 km, taking 26 days, can be made from Guajará-Mirim to Vila Bela in Mato Grosso; the fare includes food.

Guayaramerín (Bolivia) → International phone code +591.

The Bolivian town of Guayaramerín is a cheerful, prosperous little place, on the bank of the Río Mamoré. It has an important **Zona Libre**. There are flights to Trinidad, La Paz, Cobija, Cochabamba and Santa Cruz, as well as buses to La Paz, Santa Cruz, Trinidad, Cobija and other destinations, but the roads are in poor shape and appalling in the wet season. Boats sail to Trinidad.

Rio Branco ◉◉◉▲◉◐ ›› pp689-692. Colour map 1, B2.

→ Phone code: 068. Population: 253,000.

The Rio Acre is navigable upstream as far as the borders with Peru and Bolivia. It divides Rio Branco, the state capital, into two districts called Primeiro (west) and Segundo (east), on either side of the river, linked by two bridges. The central Primeiro district contains most of the sights including the shady main square, **Praça Plácido de Castro**. Nearby, along Avenida Brasil, is the **cathedral**, Nossa Senhora de Nazaré. On the same street, the **Casa do Seringueiro** ⓘ Av Brasil 216, corner of Avenida Getúlio Vargas, Mon-Fri 0700-1200, 1400-1700, has a good exhibition on rubber tappers and on Chico Mendes in particular; the Hélio Melo room has a display of Melo's paintings, mainly on the theme of the forest. Just around the corner, the neoclassical **Palácio Rio Branco** is on Rua Benjamin Constant, across from Praça Eurico Gaspar Dutra. North of Praça Plácido de Castro, the **Museu da Borracha** (rubber museum) ① *Av Ceará 1177, Mon-Fri 0900-1700*, is housed in a lovely old building with a tiled façade. It has information about the rubber boom, a section about indigenous Acreano, documents and memorabilia from the annexation and a display about the Santo Daime doctrine (see Excursions from Rio Branco, page 688), recommended.

In the Segundo district is the **Calçadão da Gameleira**, a pleasant promenade along the shore, with plaques and an old tree marking the location of the original settlement.

There are several large parks in the city. The **Horto Forestal**, in Vila Ivonete (Primeiro), 3 km north of the centre, is popular with joggers and has native Amazonian trees, a small lake, walking paths and picnic areas (take a city bus to 'Conjunto Procon' or 'Vila Ivonete'). The **Parque Zoo-Botânico**, on the UFAC campus is 5 km from the centre, along the BR-364.

Ins and outs

The **airport** ① *on the AC-40, Km 1.2, in the Segundo distrito, T068-3224 6833*, receives flights from several Brazilian cities. A taxi from the airport to the centre costs a flat rate of US\$20, or take a bus marked 'Norte–Sul' or 'Vila Acre'. Buses arrive at the **rodoviária** ① *Av Uirapuru, Cidade Nova, Segundo distrito, T069-3224 1182*. To get to the centre, take a city bus marked 'Norte–Sul'. For tourist information, contact the **Secretaria de Indústria e Comércio** ① *Av Getúlio Vargas 659, Centro*, or the **Departamento de Turismo** ① *BR-364, Km 05, Distrito Industrial, T068-3224 3997*.

Rio Branco

To Cruzeiro do Sul

Stadium

Museu da Borracha

Prefeitura

Praça Plácido de Castro

PRIMEIRO DISTRITO

Casa do Seringueiro

Cathedral

Palácio Rio Branco

Rio Acre

To Segundo Distrito, Rodoviária, Airport & Porto Velho

N

100 metres
100 yards

Sleeping
Albemar 1
Inácio Palace 2
Nacional 6

Pinheiro Palace 3
Rio Branco 4
Rodoviária 5

Eating
Anexos 1
Pizzeria Tutti Frutti 2

Border essentials: Brazil–Bolivia

Brasiléira (Brazil)–Cobija (Bolivia)
There are two official crossings between Cobija and Brasiléria: one is by ferry to Cobija's boat wharf, just off Calle Bolívar, at the west end of town. The other is via the international bridge, east of the ferry. The former is often quicker, and certainly cheaper (US$0.35), as taxis are expensive (US$12). All visitors must carry a yellow fever certificate. The *polícia federal* in Brasiléria gives entry/exit stamps.

Safety Despite improved air and road links, Rio Branco remains at the 'end of the line', a frontier outpost whose depressed economy, high unemployment and prevalent drug-running make the city unsafe at night, and some caution is advised at all hours.

Excursions from Rio Branco
About 8 km southeast of town, upriver on the Rio Acre, is **Lago do Amapá**, a U-shaped lake good for boating and water sports; access is by river or by land via route AC-40. About 2 km beyond along the AC-40 is **Praia do Amapá**, a bathing beach on the Rio Acre; an annual arts festival is held here in September. Excursions can be made to **rubber plantations** and rubber extraction areas in native forest (*seringais nativos*).

Some 13 km from Rio Branco is **Colônia Cinco Mill** (access along AC-10), a religious centre of the followers of the Santo Daime doctrine. Its members, many originally from outside Acre and Brazil, live a communal life, working in agriculture and producing crafts made of latex. The religion centres around the use of *ayahuasca*, a hallucinogenic potion adopted from local *indígenas*. Visitors are usually welcome, but enquire beforehand.

Cruzeiro do Sul → *Colour map 1, B1. Population: 65,000.*
From Rio Branco, the BR-364 continues west (in principle) to Cruzeiro do Sul and Japim, with a view to reaching the Peruvian frontier when completed. It is very difficult to get from Rio Branco to Cruzeiro do Sul by road because there is no bus service, but the occasional truck travels through, mainly in the dry season. The road is frequently impassable and open, on average, around 20 days a year.

Cruzeiro do Sul is an isolated Amazonian town on the Rio Juruá in western Acre. Cheap excursions can be made on the river, for example to the village of **Rodrigues Alves**, two to three hours' return by boat or 15 km by road. In the jungle it's possible to see rubber tapping and the collecting of latex in *borrachas*. It's very difficult to change money in Cruzeiro do Sul.

Ins and outs Flights connect the town with Rio Branco (**Varig**) and Pucallpa in Peru. In the wet season there are sporadic boats to Manaus. There are a few basic boxy hotels in town (near the cathedral and facing the river), many offer full board.

Border with Bolivia and Peru
The BR-317 from Rio Branco heads south and later southwest, parallel to the Rio Acre; it is paved as far as **Xapuri**. Here is the **Fundação Chico Mendes**, with very basic lodging and two restaurants. The road continues to **Brasiléia**, opposite the Bolivian town of Cobija, on the Rio Acre. In Brasiléia is a handful of hotels and restaurants. There are three buses daily

to and from Rio Branco, five hours in the wet season, US$10. It is possible to stay in **Epitaciolândia** (Hotel Kanda, **D**, five minutes' walk from the police post) and cross the border into Bolivia early in the morning.

The road ends at **Assis Brasil**, where the Peruvian, Bolivian and Brazilian frontiers meet. Across the Rio Acre are **Iñapari** (Peru), where the border crossing is difficult, even out of the wet season, and **Bolpebra** (Bolivia). A bus service operates only in the dry season beyond Brasiléia to Assis Brasil; access in the wet season is by river. In Assis Brasil there is a basic but clean hotel. It is sometimes possible to wade across the river between Iñapari and Assis Brasil. There is no *polícia federal* in the village, get entry/exit stamps in Brasiléia. Take small denomination bills or Peruvian soles as there is nowhere to change money on the Peruvian side.

Cobija (Bolivia) is roughly 500 km northwest of La Paz and there are air and road connections. The town is popular with Brazilians and Peruvians for duty-free shopping.

◉ Rondônia and Acre listings

For Sleeping and Eating price codes and other relevant information, see pages 42-47.

◉ Sleeping

Porto Velho *p683, map p683*
AL Vila Rica, Av Carlos Gomes 1616, T/F069-3224 3433, www.hotelvilarica.com.br. Tower block hotel with a restaurant, pool and sauna.
A Rondon Palace, Av Gov Jorge Teixeira 491, corner R Jacy Paraná, away from the centre, T/F069-3224 2718. Business-orientated hotel with a restaurant, pool and travel agency.
B Central, R Tenreiro Aranha 2472, T069-3224 2099, www.enter-net.com.br/hcentral. Clean and friendly hotel with a/c rooms with TVs and fridges. Good breakfast. Highly recommended.
C Vitória Palace, R Duque de Caxias 745. A/c and cheaper fan-cooled rooms. Basic, clean and friendly.
D Líder, Av Carlos Gomes near the *rodoviária*. Honest and welcoming but only reasonably clean. Rooms are fan cooled.
E Tía Carmen, Av Campos Sales 2995, T069-3221 7910. Very friendly and with simple well-kept rooms. The snack bar in front of the hotel serves good cakes. Highly recommended.

Ji Paraná *p685*
There are a number of hotels in the town, which is tiny and easy to negotiate. Reservations are not necessary.

Guajará-Mirim *p686*
A Pakaas Palafitas Lodge, Km 18, Estrada do Palheta, T/F069-3541 3058, www.pakaas.com.br. 28 smart bungalows in a beautiful natural setting out of town.
C Jamaica, Av Leopoldo de Matos 755, T/F069-3541 3721. Simple but the best hotel in town. Rooms have a/c and fridges. Parking.
C Lima Palace, Av 15 de Novembro 1613, T069-3541 3421. Similar to the Jamaica but with slightly scruffier rooms.
D Chile, Av Q Bocaiúva. Basic but well run. Includes breakfast, good value.
D Mamoré, R Mascarenhas de Moraes 1105, T069-3541 3753. Clean, friendly and popular with backpackers.

Rio Branco *p686, map p687*
There are few economical hotels in the centre, but a reasonable selection by the *rodoviária*.
A Pinheiro Palace, R Rui Barbosa 91, 1st district (west bank), T068-3224 7191, pinheiro@mdnet.com.br. Business-orientated hotel with a pool. Recommended.
B Rio Branco, R Rui Barbosa 193, by Praça Plácido de Castro, 1st district (west bank), T068-3224 1785. Simple but well-looked-after hotel with a/c rooms all with fridges and TVs.
B-D Rodoviária, R Palmeiral 268, Cidade Nova by the *rodoviária*, T068-3224 4434. Convenient and with a range of plain a/c rooms with fridge and TV, and cheaper options with shared baths and fans. Good value.

C Inácio Palace, R Rui Barbosa 72, 1st district (west bank), T068-224 6397. The budget sister hotel to the Pinheiro Palace (same email) with a/c rooms and a modest restaurant.
C Triângulo, R Floriano Peixoto 727, 1st district (west bank), T068-224 9265. Simple a/c rooms with TV and fridge.
C-D Albemar, R Franco Ribeiro 99, 1st district (west bank), T068-224 1938. Well-kept a/c rooms with a fridge and TV and a good breakfast. Recommended.
D-F Nacional, R Palmeiral 496, 2nd district, Cidade Nova, T068-224 4822. Fan-cooled rooms and options with a shared bath.

🍴 Eating

Porto Velho *p683, map p683*
Avoid eating too much fish because of mercury contamination. There are good restaurants around the intersection of Dom Pedro II and Av Joaquim Nabuco, and plenty of snack bars and *padarias*.
🍴🍴🍴 Carovela do Madeira, R José Camacho 104. The city's business lunch venue, with a/c. Reasonable international menu.
🍴🍴 Almanara, R José de Alencar 2624. Good authentic Lebanese food, popular but not cheap. Recommended.
🍴🍴 Bella Italia, Av Joaquim Nabuco 2205. Pasta, pizza and other basic Italian fare alongside Brazilian home cooking.
🍴 Bar do Dico, Av Joaquim Nabuco 955. The best fish in town and lively in the evenings.
🍴 Natal, Av Carlos Gomes 2783. Standard *churrascaria* with decent side dishes.
🍴 Ponto Certo, Av Rio Madeira 45. Excellent view of river and the best *churrascaria* cuts in town, closed Mon.

Rio Branco *p686, map p687*
There are boats on the river serving cheap but good food. The local delicacy is *tacacá*: a soup served piping hot in a gourd, made from *goma* (manioc starch), cooked *jambu* leaves which numb the mouth and tongue, shrimp, spices and hot pepper sauce.

🍴🍴 Kaxinawa, Av Brasil at the corner of Praça Plácido de Castro. The best in town for Acreano regional food.
🍴🍴 Pizzeria Tutti Frutti, Av Ceará 1132, across from the Museu da Borracha. Expensive pizzas and exotic ice cream.
🍴 Anexos, R Franco Ribeiro 99, next door to Albemar Hotel. Popular with young people and families for meals and drinks.
🍴 Churrascaria Triângulo, R Floriano Peixoto 727. As much charcoal-grilled meat as you can eat. Recommended.
🍴 Remanso do Tucunaré, R José de Melo 481, Bairro Bosque. Excellent river fish – though avoid the *pirarucu*.
🍴 Sorveteria Arte Sabor, Trav Santa Inés 28, corner Aviario, 1st district (west bank), 15 mins' walk from the centre. Excellent home-made ice cream, many jungle-fruit flavours. Highly recommended.

🍸 Bars and clubs

Porto Velho *p683, map p683*
Maria Fumaça collective, T069-224 4385. Organizes regular raves, concerts and *festas* around town. Check radio and newspapers for details.
Tom Brasil, club at Peixe Noturnos, near airport (taxi US$15, essential to book return fare). Every Sun night from 2200, US$3 entry for men.

🛍 Shopping

Porto Velho *p683, map p683*
Indigenous handicrafts
Hammocks are pricier than in Manaus.
Casa do Artesão, Praça Madeira-Mamoré, behind the railway station, Thu-Sun 0800-1800.
Casa do Índio, R Rui Barbosa 1407.

Markets
There is a clean fruit and vegetable market at the corner of R Henrique Dias and

Av Farquhar and a dry goods market 3 blocks to the south, near the port. On Sun there is a general market off Av Rogério Weber near port, excellent bargains but no souvenirs. Watch out for pickpockets.

Rio Branco *p686, map p687*
Arts and crafts
Fair in Praça do Seringueiro on Sun evenings. Market in 1st district (west bank), off R Epaminondas Jácome.

▲ Activities and tours

Porto Velho *p683, map p683*
Ecoporé, R Rafael Vaz e Silva 3335, Bairro Liberdade, T069-3221 5021, carol@ronet.com.br. For ecotourism projects in rubber tappers' communities on the Brazil/Bolivia border, US$50 per person per day, full details from Carol Doria, who speaks English.

Guajará-Mirim *p686*
Alfatur, Av 15 de Novembro 106, T/F069-3541 2853. Tour operator.

Rio Branco *p686, map p687*
Inácio's Tur, R Rui Barbosa 91, at **Hotel Pinheiro Palace**, T068-3224 9626.
Nilce's Tour, R Quintino Bocaiúva 20, T/F068-3223 2611, for airline tickets, helpful, 15 mins' walk from the centre.
Serra's Tur, R Silvestre Coelho 372, T068-3224 4629.

☉ Transport

Porto Velho *p683, map p683*
Air
To get to the airport take bus 'Aeroporto' (last one between 2400 and 0100). Flights to **Brasília**, **Manaus** and **Rio Branco**.
 Airline offices TAM, R J Castilho 530, T069-3224 2180. **Varig**, Av Campos Sales 2666, T069-3224 2262, English spoken.

Boat
See Routes in Amazônia, page 670. There is a passenger service to **Porto Cai N'Água** (which means 'fall in the water'). For the best price buy directly on the boat, avoid touts on the shore. The Rio Madeira is fairly narrow, so the banks can be seen and there are several 'meetings of waters'.
 Shipping a car São Matheus Ltda, Av Terminal dos Milagros 400, Balsa, takes vehicles on pontoons, meals, showers, toilets, cooking and sleeping in your car is permitted. 6 days a week a boat leaves at 1800 for **Manaus** from Manicoré, at the confluence of the Rio Madeira and Rio Manicoré, 2 nights and 1 day's journey, food included. There are boats from Porto Velho to **Manicoré** on Mon, Wed and Sat (1800, arrives 0200, but you can sleep on board), connecting with Manicoré–Manaus boats (a recommended boat is *Orlandina*).

Bus
To get to the *rodoviária* from town take 'Presidente Roosevelt' bus No 301 (if on Av 7 de Setembro, the bus turns at Av Mcal Deodoro); 'Aeroporto' and 'Hospital Base' (No 400) also go to *rodoviária*. Health and other controls at the Rondônia–Mato Grosso border are strict. To break up a long trip is much more expensive than doing it all in one stretch.
 Buses run to **Humaitá**, US$5, 3 hrs. To **São Paulo**, 60-plus hrs, US$75. To **Cuiabá**, 23 hrs, US$45, expensive food and drink is available en route. To **Guajará-Mirim**, see below. To **Rio Branco**, Viação Rondônia, 5 daily, 8 hrs, US$12.50. Daily bus with **Eucatur** from **Cascavel** (Paraná, connections for Foz do Iguaçu) via **Maringá**, **Presidente Prudente**, **Campo Grande** and **Cuiabá** to Porto Velho (Porto Velho-**Campo Grande** 36 hrs, US$60). To **Cáceres** for the Pantanal, 18 hrs, US$30.

Car
To **Cuiabá** is 1550 km on the BR-364 (Marechal Rondon highway), fully paved. To **Rio Branco**, 554 km, BR-364, poorly

paved; north to **Humaitá** (205 km) on the Madeira river or the BR-319, paved, connecting with the Trans- amazônica, BR-230 (frequently closed, ascertain conditions before travelling). The BR-319 north from Humaitá to **Manaus** is closed indefinitely. Road journeys are best done in the dry season, the 2nd half of the year.

Car hire LeMans, Av Nações Unidas 1200, T069-3224 2012. **Silva Car**, R Almte Barroso 1528, T069-3221 1423/6040. **Ximenes**, Av Carlos Gomes 1055, T069-3224 5766.

Taxi
Radio Taxi: **Marmoré**, T069-3224 7070.

Ji Paraná *p685*
Bus The bus station, R dos Mineiros, T069-3422 2233, has services to **Porto Velho**, US$16.25, 16 hrs. To **Cuiabá**, 15 hrs.

Guajará-Mirim *p686*
Bus To **Porto Velho**, 5½ hrs or more depending on season, 8 a day with **Viação Rondônia**, US$18. A taxi to the Porto Velho *rodoviária* costs US$25 per person for 4-5 people, 3 hrs, and leaves when full.

Rio Branco *p686, map p687*
Air Taxis to the airport use the meter and usually cost around US$15. There are flights to **Porto Velho**, **Manaus**, **Brasília**, **São Paulo**, **Cuiabá** and **Campo Grande**; once a week to **Cruzeiro do Sul**.
Airline offices Varig, T068-3211 1000.

Bus To **Porto Velho**, Viação Rondônia, 5 daily, 8 hrs, US$12.50. To **Guajará-Mirim**, daily with **Rondônia** at 1130 and 2200, 5-6 hrs, US$10; or take **Inácio's Tur** shopping trip, 3 per week.

Car hire Car rentals with nationwide agencies are more expensive in Acre than other states. **Locabem**, Rodovia AC-40, Km 0, 2nd district, T069-3223 3000. **Localiza**, R Rio Grande do Sul 310, T069-3224 7746, airport T069-3224 8478. **Unidas**, T069-3224 5044.

❶ Directory

Porto Velho *p683, map p683*
Banks Open in the morning only. Banco do Brasil, Dom Pedro II 607 and Av José de Alencar, cash and TCs with 2% commission, minimum commission US$10, minimum amount exchanged US$200. **Marco Aurélio Câmbio**, R José de Alencar 3353, T069-3223 2551, very quick, efficient, good rates for US$ cash, Mon-Fri 0900-1500. **Parmetal** (gold merchants), R Joaquim Nabuco 2265, T069-221 1566, cash only, good rates, open Mon-Fri 0730-1800, Sat 0730-1300. Local radio and newspapers publish exchange rates. Exchange is difficult elsewhere in Rondônia. **Laundry** Lavanderia Marmoré, Pinheiro Machado 1455B. **Medical services** Hospital Central, R Júlio de Castilho 149, T/F069-3224 4389, 24-hr emergencies. Dentist at Carlos Gomes 2577; 24-hr clinic opposite. **Post office** Av Pres Dutra 2701, corner of Av 7 de Setembro. **Telephone** Av Pres Dutra 3023 and Dom Pedro II, daily 0600-2300.

Guajará-Mirim *p686*
Banks Banco do Brasil, foreign exchange in the morning only. Loja Nogueira, Av Pres Dutra, corner Leopoldo de Matos, cash only. There is no market in Brazil for bolivianos. **Embassies and consulates** Bolivia, Av C Marquês 495, T069-3541 2862, visas are given here. **Medical services** Regional, Av Mcal Deodoro, T069-3541 2651. **Post office** Av Pres Dutra. **Telephone** Av B Ménzies 751.

Rio Branco *p686, map p687*
Banks There are no banks but the hotel owner may be persuaded to oblige. **Hospitals** Santa Casa, R Alvorada 178, T068-224 6297. **Post office** On the corner of R Epaminondas Jácome and Av Getúlio Vargas. **Telephone** Av Brasil between Mcal Deodoro and Av Getúlio Vargas, long delays for international calls.

Contents

Footprint features

At a glance

⊖ **Getting around** Internal flights and buses. Car hire is a possibility when using one location as a base but is not good over the whole region, which is vast.

● **Time required** 1 day for Brasília; 7 days for Brasília and Goiás; 5-7 days for Jalapão.

☼ **Weather** Varies across the region. The north of Tocantins is similar to the northern Amazon – hot and wet Dec-Apr. Brasília and Goiás are hot and dry Apr-Sep and warm and wet Oct-Mar.

✖ **When not to go** Brasília, Goiás and southern Tocantins in Dec and Jan.

★ Don't miss ...
1 Brasília, page 696.
2 Cidade de Goiás, page 711.
3 Pirenópolis, page 713.
4 Chapada dos Veadeiros, page 714.
5 Jalapão, page 724.
6 Ilha do Bananal, page 725.

The country's capital, Brasília, is the symbol of the nation's commitment to its empty centre. Although not generally viewed as a tourist attraction, it is interesting as a city of pure invention similar to Australia's Canberra or Washington in the United States. Its central position makes it a natural crossroads for visiting the north and interior of Brazil and, when passing through, it is well worth undertaking a city tour to view its innovative modern design.

Like Brasília, Goiás is rarely on the itinerary for first-time visitors to Brazil. But those who know the country well often consider it their favourite state. There is so much of interest here: colonial cities as beautiful as any in Minas and far less visited; colourful and bizarre festivals; national parks as wild as the Pantanal; and trekking, wildlife- and birdwatching that is second only to the Pantanal and the Amazon. Its people are among the country's most welcoming. They are quietly spoken, poetic and obsessed with dreadful *sertanejo* music, which laments lost love through videos of girls in little shorts intercut with prize bulls. The state is easily visited from Brasília or on the way to or from the Pantanal and the coast.

Further north is the state of Tocantins, dominated by vast rivers, *cerrado* forests and, increasingly, soya plantations. The deserts of Jalapão lie here: landscapes that at first sight seem a strange fusion of North Africa and outback Australia but which, unlike both, are broken by myriad lakes and waterfalls. Further to the west on the frontier of Mato Grosso is the Bananal – one of the largest river islands in the world and home to large groups of indigenous Brazilians.

Brasília

→ *Colour map 4, A2. Phone code: 061. Population: 2.1 million.*
This planned and impersonal capital city, sitting like a monument to the space age in a vast plain surrounded by ever-expanding favelas and chaos, may seem very un-Brazilian to those who are new to the country. This is, after all, a nation famous for its laissez-faire attitude. But it also has 'Order and Progress' written proudly on its flag, in homage to the ideas of Comte. And the grandiose schemes of many of its 20th-century leaders have long been influenced by a desire to propel the country into a Positivist vision of the future. Brazil's capital was intended by its conceivers, Lúcio Costa and Oscar Niemeyer, and then president Juscelino Kubitschek, as a statement of that future in concrete; an attempt perhaps to make real the cliché repeated by every other Brazilian leader that this is 'the country of the future'. Although many of the remarkable buildings, such as the dome and saucer of the Congresso Nacional, would in themselves make a trip here worthwhile, Brasília is every bit as Brazilian as Rio Carnaval and Pelé and a visit here is a must for those interested in the psychology of the country. ▸▸ *For listings, see pages 702-708.*

Ins and outs

Getting there
Air Flights arrive at the **international airport** ① *12 km south of the centre, T061-3364 9000, www.aeroportodebrasilia.gov.br.* Tourist information is available from **Adetur** ① *T061-3325 5730, daily 0730-2230.* **Infraero** ① *2nd floor, open 24 hrs,* has information on airport buses. A taxi to the centre costs around US$15, meter rate two is used. Alternatively, take bus Nos 102 or 118 (US$1, 30 minutes) from outside the terminal building. There are left-luggage facilities at the airport (locker tokens US$1.50), banks, car rental agencies, a post office and various restaurants and shops.

Bus and train Interstate buses arrive at the combined bus and train station, the **rodoferroviária** ① *west of town, T061-3363 2281; information from Adetur daily 0800-2000.* From here bus No 131, US$1.25, runs to the **municipal rodoviária** ① *T061-3327 4631, www.guiadebrasilia.com.br/cidade/turistas/rodoferroviaria.htm,* in the city centre. Both bus stations have large luggage lockers. The *rodoviária* has a post office, telephone facilities and showers (US$1.50). A taxi to the northern hotel zone (Setor Hoteleiro Norte) costs US$12.

Getting around
A good and cheap way of seeing Brasília is by taking bus rides from the municipal *rodoviária* at the centre: the destinations are clearly marked. The circular bus routes Nos 106, 108 and 131 go round the city's perimeter. If you go around the lake by bus, you must change at the Paranoá Dam; to or from Paranoá Norte take bus No 101, 'Rodoviária'; and to and from Sul, take bus No 100, bypassing the airport. If staying in a hotel outside the centre, it's worth contacting them in advance to ask how to get there. A new urban railway, the metrô, runs to the southwest suburbs but is very limited. ▸▸ *See Transport, page 707.*

Orientation
A competition for the best general plan was won by Professor Lúcio Costa, who laid out the city in the shape of a bent bow and arrow. It is also described as a bird or aeroplane in flight. The official name for central Brasília is the **Plano Piloto**.

The **Eixo Monumental** divides the city into **Asa Norte** and **Asa Sul** (north and south wings) and the **Eixo Rodoviário** divides it east and west. Buildings are numbered according to their relation to them. For example, 116 Sul and 116 Norte are at the extreme opposite ends of the city. The 100s and 300s lie west of the Eixo and the 200s and 400s to the east; *quadras* 302, 102, 202 and 402 are nearest the centre, and 316, 116, 216 and 416 mark the end of the Plano Piloto.

Residential areas are made up of large six-storey apartment blocks called 'Super-Quadras'. Each Super-Quadra houses 3000 people and has a primary school and playgroup. Each group of four Super-Quadras should have a library, police station, club, supermarket and secondary school. All *quadras* are separated by feeder roads, along which are the local shops. There are also a number of schools, parks and cinemas in the spaces between the *quadras* (especially in Asa Sul), though not as systematically as was originally envisaged. On the outer side of the 300s and extending the length of the city is **Avenida W3**, and on the outer side of the 400s is **Avenida L2**, both of these being similarly divided into north and south according to the part of the city they are in.

Asa Norte is growing very fast, with standards of architecture and urbanization that promise to make it more attractive than Asa Sul in the near future. The main shopping areas, which have more cinemas, restaurants and other facilities, are situated on either side of the municipal bus station (*rodoviária*). There are now several parks and green areas. The private residential areas are west of the Super-Quadras, and on the other side of the lake.

At right angles to these residential areas is the 'arrow', the 8-km-long, 250-m wide **Eixo Monumental**. The **Eixo Rodoviário** (the main north–south road), in which fast-moving traffic is segregated, follows the curve of the bow, the radial road is along the line of the arrow; intersections are avoided by means of underpasses and cloverleaves. Motor and pedestrian traffic is segregated in the residential areas.

Best time to visit

The climate is mild and the humidity refreshingly low, but overpowering in the dry season (May to mid-October). The noonday sun beats hard, but summer (October to April) brings heavy rains and the air is usually cool by night. It's best to visit in the dry season when the stark modernist buildings stand out against the deep blue sky.

Tourist information

The tourist office, **Adetur** ① *Centro de Convenções (convention centre), 3rd floor, T061-3325 5700, 0800-1200 and 1300-1800,* has helpful English-speaking staff, and can provide a good map of Brasília. There are branches at the *rodoferroviária* and at the airport (see above), which have more limited information but will book hotels and provide city maps. **Embratur** ① *Setor Comercial Norte, quadra 2, bloco G, T061-224 9100, www.braziltour.com,* also has a branch at the airport. The **tourist office** in the centre of Praça dos Tres Poderes has a colourful map and lots of information. The staff are friendly and have interesting information about Brasília and other places in Goiás, but only Portuguese is spoken. Other useful information is available from www.infobrasilia.com.br, www.dicasde brasilia.com.br, www.guiade brasilia.com.br and www.aboutbrasilia.com

Maps Maps of Brasília showing individual streets are almost impossible to find. But city maps with each *quadra* marked are available from larger newsagents and at the airport. Slightly less detailed maps are available from **Adetur**.

Background

Brasília was a project powered by the indefatigable will of one man. Plans to build a new capital in the centre of the country had been drawn up as early as 1822. But it took Juscelino Kubitschek, Brazil's self-proclaimed great modernizer, whose famous election winning catchphrase was "50 years in five", to realize the dream. His capital was rushed through from start to finish within one term of presidential office. The blueprint was cleared by Congress in 1956. Work began the following year and by the time Eisenhower laid the cornerstone of the US embassy in February 1960, accompanied by a great media fanfare, the new capital was largely complete.

Sights

Most of the interesting sights are concentrated on or around the **Eixo Monumental**, an inner-city highway forming the 'arrow' of Brasília's bow. They can be visited by car, taxi or tour over the course of a morning. The **television tower** ① *Mon 1400-2000, Tue-Sun 0800-2000, closed Mon morning*, between the Setor Hoteleiro Norte and the Setor Hoteleiro Sul is a good place to begin a tour and to orientate oneself. It offers excellent panoramic views from the observation platform 75 m up, as do many of the tall hotels nearby.

Praça dos Três Poderes and around

The most important buildings are clustered together at the western end of the Eixo Monumental around the Praça dos Três Poderes; named after the three powers of the

1 **Brasília: Plano Piloto**

federal state that flank it. To the north is the seat of presidential power, the **Palácio do Planalto** ⓘ *Praça dos Três Poderes, 30-min tours available on Sun 0930-1330*. A wall of glass between twin white concrete platforms, it is reached by a long low ramp flanked by guards in red-and-white uniforms. The flag flies when the president is in attendance. Opposite, the **Supremo Tribunal Federal** is smaller and more perfectly formed, with Niemeyer's trademark fluted columns hiding patrolling secret service guards in sharp suits. The famous modernist statue of blind justice sitting in front of the building is by the Mineiro sculptor Alfredo Ceschiatti. To the west, the seat of the Senate and Congress, **Congresso Nacional** ⓘ *Praça dos Três Poderes, Mon-Fri 0930-1200, 1430-1630, take your passport, free guided tour in English 1400-1600*, is the most famous and stately group of buildings in Brasília – a tour de force of simple lines and curves. The concave and convex domes of the Chamber of Deputies and the Senate are juxtaposed and balanced by the twin towers of the executive: a geometric tension and harmony in which Niemeyer intended to symbolise that of government. These monumental buildings are offset beautifully by the vast expanse of the square, the artificial ponds and the lawns.

There are a handful of other interesting buildings in the plaza: the **Espaço Lucio Costa** ⓘ *Tue-Sun 0900-1800, free*, with a scale model of the city; a monument to Juscelino Kubitschek; the **Panteão da Liberdade e Democracia** built in homage to Democracy and Liberty; and, most notably, Bruno Giorgio's **Candangos** – twin bronze figures sculpted in homage to the Candango workers who built the city from nothing in the middle of what was a vast plain, and who received the satellite *favelas* that ring the city as their reward.

Beyond the *praça* to the east and on the shores of Lago Paranoá is the **Palácio Alvorada**, residence of the president and not open to the public.

Less than a kilometre west of the *praça* are two further Niemeyer buildings of note. The **Palácio de Itamarati** is one the finest pieces of modernist architecture in Brazil; its elegant columns rising from a lily pond, which acts like a huge mirror for the entire building. Inside there is a series of rooms each decorated with fine sculpture and paintings including Pedro Américo's *O Grito de Ipiranga*, showing the moment when Dom Pedro shouted his declaration of Brazilian Independence, and Jean-Baptiste Debret's painting of the emperor's subsequent coronation. There are also works by Brazilian modernists Alfredo Volpi, Candido Portinari and Pedro Correia de Araújo. The building is named after the Conde de Itamaraty. Opposite Itamarati is the **Palácio da Justiça** ⓘ *Mon-Fri 0900-1200, 1500-1700*, its walls broken by a series of broad fountains that climb up the façade of the building and drop water into the pond that sits at the building's feet.

➡ **Brasília maps**
1 Brasília: Plano Piloto, page 698
2 Brasília hotel zone, page 703

Lago Do Paranoá

Palácio da Alvorada
Palácio do Jabaru

Palácio do Planalto
Praça dos Três Poderes
Panteão Tancredo Neves

Avenida das Nações

N

200 metres
200 yards

Oscar Niemeyer and Brasília

Oscar Niemeyer Soares Filho (born 1907 in Rio de Janeiro) was educated at the Escola Nacional de Belas Artes and in 1936 joined the group of architects charged with developing Le Corbusier's project for the Ministry of Education and Health building in Rio de Janeiro. His first international project was the Brazilian pavilion at the New York International Fair in 1939 in partnership with Lúcio Costa. In the 1940s he was one of the main designers of Pampulha and in 1947 he worked on the United Nations headquarters in New York. This was the period in which he affirmed his style, integrating architecture with painting and sculpture. He transformed utilitarian constructions with the lightness of his designs, his freedom of invention and the use of complex, curved surfaces. Throughout the 1950s he was commissioned to design a wide variety of national and international projects, but it was the years 1956-1959 that stamped his signature on the architectural world. This was when he worked on Brasília, specifically the Palácio da Alvorada, the ministries, the Praça dos Três Poderes, the cathedral, university and, in 1967, the Palácio dos Arcos e da Justiça. After Brasília Niemeyer continued to work at home and abroad; among his more famous later projects were the Sambódromo in Rio (1984) and the Memorial da América Latina in São Paulo (1989). The Royal Institute of British Architects awarded him the prestigious Royal Gold Medal for Architecture in 1998.

Many of Brazil's most famous architects, sculptors and designers were involved in Brasília. The city was built during Juscelino Kubitschek's term as president (1955-1960) and was unparalleled in scale and architectural importance in Latin America at that time. A description of the city, and its effect on the economy at the time of its construction are dealt with elsewhere in the book. Niemeyer was appointed chief architecture and technical adviser to Novacap, the government authority which oversaw the new capital. But while it is common knowledge who the famous names were, it is also worth noting that 30,000 workers were involved in bringing the plan to reality. Most of them came from the northeast. The city has been honoured not just for its architecture, but also for being the first purpose-built capital of the 20th century. In 1987 it was named a Unesco World Cultural Heritage Site, the first contemporary city to gain such protection from the United Nations.

Niemeyer himself has said "The modern city lacks harmony and a sense of occasion. Brasília will never lack these". And it is true that the principal buildings, and the overall plan itself, are strikingly powerful. The whole enterprise is deeply rooted in the 20th century, not just in its design, but also in the idea that it is a city you jet into and out of. If you arrive by road (which most people do not), the experience is even more fantastic. After hours and hours in the bus, travelling across the unpopulated central plateau, you come to this collection of remarkable buildings and sculptures in the middle of nowhere. The vastness of the landscape demands a grand city and yet, for all its harmony, it is almost as if not even Brasília can compete with the sky and the horizon.

Niemeyer is still working in his late 90s. In 2002, a museum about Niemeyer, designed by the architect himself opened in Curitiba. It is spectacular, sitting like a giant black eye on a pedestal in one of the city's parks, fully living up to Niemeyer's proclamation that 'the most important element in any work of art is to surprise, to startle'. His mostly recently opened grand buildings are the Biblioteca Nacional and the dome-shaped and Oca-like Museum of Brasília, which opened in the capital in 2006.

West along the Eixo Monumental

The Eixo stretches for some 8 km west of Praça dos Três Poderes eventually reaching the *rodoferroviária*. Almost all of the city's other important monuments lie on either side of the road. We follow them here from east to west.

The government ministry buildings line the Eixo east of the *praça* like dominos, or a series of commissars standing to attention. Eventually they reach Niemeyer's striking **Catedral Metropolitana Nossa Senhora Aparecida** ① *Esplanada dos Ministérios, Eixo Monumental, T061-3224 4073, 0800-1930*; a crown of thorns in concrete and glass sitting in a toroidal lake and watched over by Alfredo Ceschiatti's four evangelists, standing sentinel-like in concrete. The entrance to the cathedral is via a subterranean tunnel, emerging from relative darkness into an arena bright with stained glass and light marble.

Next to the cathedral are two of the most recently built Niemeyer buildings; which opened to the public in 2008: the **Museu Nacional de Brasília**, a striking dome-shaped building with an entrance halfway up its side reached by a snaking ramp; and the cuboid **Biblioteca Nacional** next door. Less than a kilometre west, a few blocks south, is the **Santuário Dom Bosco** ① *Av W3 Sul, quadra 702, T061-3223 6542, 0800-1800,* a modernist cube with tall Gothic arches filled with stained glass, which projects shades from light blue to indigo as it ascends. It is particularly beautiful in the late afternoon when shafts of light penetrate the building. The church is named after the 19th-century saint and founder of the Salesian order, who proclaimed that a new civilization would arise in the third millennium between the 15th and 16th parallels and on the edge of an artificial lake. The trunk of the enormous cross hanging over the altar was carved from a single piece of tropical cedar.

Beyond the TV tower, which lies at the intersection of the Eixo and the hotel zones, are two other interesting groups of buildings. The **Memorial Juscelino Kubitschek (JK)** ① *Tue-Sun 0900-1800, US$1.50, toilets and café,* stands high above a marble plinth waving towards the Praça dos Três Poderes. The former president's tomb lies beneath the marble together with a collection of memorabilia. In front of the memorial is the **Memorial dos Povos Indígenas** ① *Tue-Sun 0900-1800, US$2*; a round concrete building shaped like a *Bororo* communal house or *maloca* and reached by a tongue-like ramp. Inside is a small but fascinating collection of indigenous art and cultural artefacts. On the other side of the Memorial JK, east of Praça do Cruzeiro, is the city's second Niemeyer cathedral, the **Catedral Militar de Nossa Senhora da Paz** ① *Tue-Sun 0900-1800*. This is a brilliant white wedge of concrete cut with jagged windows, whose design echoes Notre Dame du Haut, designed by Niemeyer's mentor, Le Corbusier. The church marks the entrance to the **Quartel General do Exército**; an enormous and imposing complex of military buildings centred on an elliptical auditorium made of a single wave of concrete and added to Brasília during the military dictatorship, as if to compensate for the lack of army presence on the Praça dos Três Poderes. All are by Niemeyer. There is a small **military museum** ① *Tue-Sun 0900-1800,* on the site.

The **Templo da Boa Vontade** ① *Setor Garagem Sul 915, lotes 75/76, T061-3245 1070, www.tbv.com.br, open 24 hrs,* is a seven-faced pyramid dedicated to all philosophies and religions topped by one of the world's largest rock crystals. To get there, take bus No 151 from outside the Centro do Convenções or on Eixo Sul to Centro Médico.

The **Panteão Tancredo Neves** is a 'temple of freedom and democracy', built 1985-1986 by Niemeyer. It includes an impressive homage to Tiradentes (see box, page 272).

The **Monumental Parade Stand** has unique and mysterious acoustics (the complex is north of the Eixo Monumental, between the 'Memorial JK' and the *rodoferroviária*). There are remarkable stained-glass panels, each representing a state of the Federation, on the ground floor of the Caixa Econômica Federal.

Around Brasília

About 15 km along the Belo Horizonte road is the small wooden house, designed by Niemeyer, erected in only 10 days and known as **O Catetinho**. President Kubitschek stayed here in the late 1950s during his visits to the city when it was under construction; it is open to visitors and houses memorabilia and some of JK's furniture and personal items.

Some 40 km northeast of the Plano Piloto via Saída Norte is **Planaltina**, originally a settlement on the colonial pack route from the mines of Goiás and Cuiabá to the coast. The old part still contains many colonial buildings. There are two good *churrascarias* on the main street and it is a good place for a rural Sunday lunch. About 5 km outside Planaltina is the **Pedra Fundamental**, the foundation stone laid by President Epitácio Pessoa in 1922 to mark the site that was originally chosen for the new capital.

Also outside Planaltina, at Km 30 on the BR-020, lies **Águas Emendadas**. From the same point spring two streams that flow in opposite directions to form part of the two great river systems: the Amazon and the Plate. Permission from the biological institute in Brasília is required to visit. At Km 70 is the town of **Formosa**. Some 20 km north of the town is the **Itiquira waterfall** (158 m high). From the top are spectacular views and the pools at the bottom offer good bathing, but it gets crowded at weekends. There are four smaller falls in the area and camping is possible. To get there from the centre of Formosa, follow the signs or ask. The only bus from Formosa to Itiquira leaves at 0730 and returns at 1700.

Parque Nacional de Brasília → *Colour map 3, A6.*
ⓘ *10 km northwest of the rodoferroviária, around 15 mins by car. Contact Ibama, Via L Quatro Norte, www.ibama.gov.br, or at the park's office, Via Epia SMU, T061-3233 3251.*
This park was founded in 1961 to preserve a remnant of the original *cerrado* flora and fauna that Brasília replaced. The park covers some 28,000 ha, but only a small portion is open to the public without a permit. There is a swimming pool fed by clear river water, a snack bar and a series of trails through gallery forest, which is popular with joggers in the early morning and at weekends. The rest of the park is rolling grassland, gallery forest and *cerrado* vegetation. Large mammals include tapir, maned wolf and pampas deer; birdwatching is good, especially for Brasília tapaculo, horned sungem, yellow-faced parrot and nighthawk.

◉ Brasilia listings

For Sleeping and Eating price codes and other relevant information, see pages 42-47.

● Sleeping

Brasília *p696, maps p698 and p703*
The best area to base yourself is in the northern hotel zone, which has lots of shops and restaurants nearby. Prices usually include breakfast. Weekend discounts of 30% are often available if you ask. The best area for cheap accommodation is around W3 703 and 704 in the Asa Sul where many residential houses have been turned into hostels. The quietest areas are northwest of the main Av W3 Sul. Beware of bus station touts. The tourist office has a list of *pensões*.

Southern hotel zone
L Nacional, quadra 1, bloco A, T061-3321 7575, www.hotelnacional.com.br. This huge old-fashioned city landmark was *the* place to stay in the 1970s and 1980s. Now rooms look rather old-fashioned, but on the upper floors they offer sweeping views. Several restaurants.

A Alvorada, quadra 4, bloco A, T061-2195 1122, www.alvoradahotel.com.br. Another relic with simple, well-kept small rooms and good views from the roof terrace. Avoid the noisy streetside rooms on the lower floors.

C-E Pousada Dom Bosco, Av W-3 Sul, quadra 704, bloco M, casa 09, T061-3223 1133, www.pousadadombosco.com.br. The best of the cheapies, with simple but neat rooms, some spacious and airy, some small and windowless. Owner Getúlio Valente will pick up from the airport or bus station if you phone ahead. There are a range of other rooms around the city as well as cheap city tours (in Portuguese only).

D Pousada da Nilza, W3 Sul 703, bloco A, T061-3226 5786. Pokey and slightly musty dorms and doubles but popular with travellers. There are various similar options next door.

D-E Pousada 47, 703 Sul, bloco A, casa 97, T061-3323 5718, www.pousada47.hpg.com.br. Very simple fan-cooled dorms and doubles, the best of which are at the front. Internet.

D-E Pousada do Sol, 703 Sul, bloco K, casa 3, T061-3224 9703 or T061-9969 6636. A range of simple dorms and doubles for up to 5 people, some without windows.

Northern hotel zone

LL-L Kubitschek Plaza, quadra 2, bloco E, T061-3319 3543, www.plazabrasilia.com.br. Popular business hotel with modern rooms and excellent facilities. Broadband access in each room, pool, sauna and gym. The **Manhattan Plaza**, next door is similar and also run by the **Plaza** group (same website).

AL-A Aristus, quadra 2, bloco O, T061-3328 8675, www.aristushotel.com.br. Newly painted and delightfully dated 1970s block with simple a/c rooms and breakfast.

A Casablanca, quadra 3, bloco A, T061-3328 8586, www.casablancabrasilia.com.br. A mock-Niemeyer block complete with modernist Gothic arches echoing the Palácio do Itamarati. Room are newly refurbished 1970s shells with standard catalogue furniture. The best are on the upper floors.

B El Pilar, quadra 3, bloco F, T061-3328 5915, www.elpilar.com.br. Plain, well-kept fan-cooled and a/c rooms with tiled floors and en suites. Avoid those below street level as they collect car fumes.

C Mirage, quadra 2, bloco N, T/F061-3328 7150. Simple rooms with a fan but good value for the area.

Other areas

LL-L Blue Tree Park, Trecho 1, lt 1-B, Bl C (Lago Norte), T062-3424 7000, www.blue tree.com.br. The city's newest, most luxurious business hotel, with rooms in a giant red horseshoe overlooking the lake, an enormous pool and excellent business facilities.

2 Brasília hotel zone

➡ **Brasília maps**
1 Brasília: Plano Piloto, page 698
2 Brasília hotel zone, page 703

N

100 metres
100 yards

Sleeping 😴		Pousada 47 **6**
Alvorada **1**		Pousada da
Aristus **2**		Nilza **7**
Casablanca **3**		Pousada Dom
El Pilar **5**		Bosco **8**
Nacional **4**		Pousada do Sol **9**

🍴 Eating

Brasília *p696, maps p698 and p703*
The Southern Hotel Sector has more
restaurants than the north. At weekends, few
restaurants in central Brasília are open. There
is plenty of choice in all price brackets in the
Pier 21 entertainment mall on the lakeshore.
Other cheaper options are along R 405/406.

Snack bars serving *prato feito* or *comercial*
(cheap set meals) can be found all over the
city, especially on **Av W3** and in the **Setor
Comercial Sul**. Other good bets are the
Conjunto Nacional and the **Conjunto
Venâncio**, 2 shopping/office complexes
on either side of the municipal *rodoviária*.
Tropical fruit flavour ice cream can be
found in various parlours, eg **Av W3
Norte 302**. Freshly made fruit juices
are available in all bars.

Asa Sul
There are good mid-range options on and
around Av Anhanguera between Tocantins and
Goiás; but by far the best choice is on and
around **Praça Tamandaré** and **Av República
Líbano**. For cheap bars/restaurants, try around
Praça Tamandaré and on **R 68** in the centre.
There are many cheap places on **Av W3 Sul**,
eg at **Blocos 502** and **506**.

¶¶¶ Kosui, SCES, Trecho 4, lote 1B, Academia
de Tênis, T061-3316 6900. The best of the
city's Japanese food, from Tokyo-born chef
Ryozo Koniya. Great Japanese banquet.
¶¶¶ La Chaumière, Av W3 Sul, quadra 408,
bloco A, loja 13, T061-3244 3875, lunch only
on Sun. The city's favourite French cuisine
in classical surroundings.
¶¶¶ Le Français, Av W3 Sul, quadra 404,
bloco B, loja 27, T061-3225 4583. French
food served in bistro atmosphere, classic
and modern dishes, 40-bottle wine list.
¶¶¶ O Convento, SHIS, QI 9, conjunto 9, casa 4,
T061-3248 1211, www.oconvento.com.br.
The best for regional and Brazilian cuisine
in a mock-farmhouse dining room decorated
with antiques and arts and crafts.

¶¶¶ Piantella, SCLS 202, bloco A, loja 34, T061-
3224 9408, www.piantella.com.br. A favourite
of senior politicians for decades and is a good
place to watch power lunches in action. The
vast menu combines *feijoada*, Italian food,
steaks and seafood. The wine list is excellent.
¶¶¶ Porcão, Sector de Clubes Sul, Trecho 2, cj 35,
rest 3, T061-3223 2002, www.porcao.com.br.
Upmarket chain restaurant specializing in
churrasco, piano bar, large veranda.
¶¶ O Espanhol, Av W3 Sul, quadra 404,
bloco C, loja 07, T061-3224 2002. Open
daily. Host to the city's annual Spanish
festival and serving respectable seafood.
¶¶ Oca da Tribo, SCES Trecho 2, opposite
Agepol, T061-3226 9880, www.ocada
tribo.com.br. A wholefood restaurant
in a mock-indigenous communal house
decorated with artefacts from the Xingu.
Plenty of vegetarian options and others by
Dutch Cordon Bleu chef Gabriel Fleijsman
and a good lunch buffet.
¶¶ Vercelli, SCLS 410, bloco D, loja 34, T061-
3443 0100, www.vercelli.com.br. Lunch only.
Pizzas, pastas and lots more on a huge menu.
¶ Naturama, SCLS 102, bloco B, loja 9,
T061-3225 5125. Vegetarian and
wholefood dishes. Lunchtime only.

Asa Norte
All of the large hotels in this area
have upmarket restaurants.
¶¶¶ Alice, SHIN, Qi 11, conjunto 9, casa 17,
Lago Norte, T061-3368 1099, www.restau
rantealice.com.br. Voted the best restaurant
in the by *Veja* magazine innumerable times
with a menu of French and Brazilian-French
fusion cooking. Excellent wine list.
¶¶¶ Trattoria da Rosario, SHIS QI 17, bloco H,
Loja 215, Lago Sul, Fashion Park, T061-3248
1672. Closed Mon, lunch only on Sun.
Northern Italian food from chef Rosario
Tessier. Excellent Uruguayan lamb.
¶¶¶ Universal Diner, SCLS 210, bloco B, loja 30,
T061-3443 2089, www.universaldiner.com.br.
Lunch only on Sun. One of the city's best
contemporary restaurants with strong

Bingo!

Visitors to Brazil may be surprised to see bingo halls all over the major cities. But these are not mere temples to blue-rinse gambling. Brazil's bingo halls are the stuff of scandal. People have suspected for a long time that many of the bingo halls were rackets for drug and car theft money laundering. In 2004 their influence was seen to extend to the highest level, shaking the (until then) squeaky clean reputation of the country's president Luís Inácio Lula da Silva. *Epoca* magazine revealed that one of his senior aides, Waldomiro Diniz, had accepted bribes from a notorious Rio bingo mogul, known as 'Carlinhos the Waterfall' shortly after the 2002 election. 'The Waterfall' has long been regarded as a kingpin in the Rio numbers game; a Brazilian form of street bingo based on animal names which is hugely lucrative for those who run it. Within a week, Brazil's stock market crashed 10% and the *real* fell almost 2% against the dollar, prompting Lula to fire Diniz and promise a full enquiry. There were further pledges to ban the bingo halls. But as usual in Brazil it was all sound and fury … The report was a whitewash declaring the bingo halls models of propriety. They remain open and Brazil awaits the discovery of yet further scandal.

Asian influences from New York-trained chef Mara Alcamim.

Boa Saúde, Av W3 Norte, quadra 702, edif Brasília Rádio Center. Sun-Fri 0800-2000. Respectable vegetarian with a range of salads, quiches and pies.

Bom Demais, Av W3 Norte, quadra 706. Comfortable, serving fish, beef and rice, live music at weekends (cover charge US$0.50).

Conjunto Nacional, SDN, Cj A. Enormous mall and food court with 50 restaurants.

Bars and clubs

Brasília *p696, maps p698 and p703*

Arena Café, CA 7, bloco F1, loja 33, T061-3468 1141, www.cafearena.hpg.com.br. Popular gay bar with DJs from Thu to Sat.

Bar Brasília, SHC/S CR, quadra 506, bloco A, loja 15, parte A, T061-3443 4323. Little *boteco* with 1950s decor, draught beer and wooden tables. Lively after 1900, especially on Fri.

Bier Fass, SHIS, quadra 5, bloco E, loja 52/53, T061-3248 1519, www.bierfass.com.br. Cavernous bar/restaurant with live music

Tue- Sun and 20/30s crowd. Happy hour from 1800.

Café Cancún, Shopping Liberty Mall, SCN, Quadra 3, bloco D, loja 52, T061-3327 1566, www.cafecancun.com.br. Tacky Mexican restaurant by day, 20-something beautiful people club after dark.

Clube de Choro, SDC, quadra 3, bloco G, T061-3327 0494, www.clubedechoro.com.br. (Wed-Sat). One of the best clubs in the country devoted to the music that gave rise to samba. Top names from the city and all over Brazil. Great atmosphere. Tickets sold 9 days in advance.

Frei Caneca, Brasília Shopping, SCN, quadra 5, bloco A, lojas 82s/94s, T061-3327 0202. Similar to **Café Cancún**. Dreadful 'flashback' night on Thu. Most interesting at weekends.

Gates Pub, Av W3 Sul 403, T061-3225 4576, www.gatespub.com.br. Great for *forró* dancing and live music with a young middle-class crowd.

UK Brasil Pub, SCLS 411, bloco B, loja 28, T061-3346 5214. Some of the best live bands in the city play here to a crowd of all ages. Guinness, sandwiches.

🎭 Entertainment

Brasília *p696, maps p698 and p703*
Entertainment listings are available in
2 daily papers, *Jornal de Brasília* and *Correio
Brasiliense*. Any student card (provided it
has a photograph) will get you a 50%
discount at the cinema/theatre/concert
hall. Ask for '*uma meia*' at the box office.

Cinema
There are 15 cinemas in the Plano Piloto.
For programme details call T139.
Tickets are half price on Wed.
Pier 21, SCSS, Trecho 2, Cj 32/33.
An enormous complex with 13 cinema
screens, nightclubs, restaurants, video
bars and children's theme park.

Live music
Concerts are given at the **Escola Parque**,
quadras 507-508 Sul; the **Ginásio Presidente
Médici**, Eixo Monumental, near TV tower;
the **Escola de Música**, Av L2 Sul, quadra 602;
and the outdoor **Concha Acústica**, at
the edge of the lake in the northern
hotel zone.

Other
Planetarium, Setor de Divulgação Cultural,
T061-325 6245, next to the TV tower.
Re-opened in early 2008.

Theatre
Teatro Nacional, Setor Cultural Norte, Via
N 2, next to the bus station, T061-3325 6109,
foyer open 0900-2000, box office opens at
1400. There are 3 auditoria: the **Sala Villa-
Lobos** (1300 seats), the **Sala Martins
Pena** (450), and the **Sala Padre José
Maurício** (120). The building is in the
shape of an Aztec pyramid.
　　The Federal District authorities have
2 theatres, the **Galpão** and **Galpãozinho**,
between Quadra 308 Sul and Av W3 Sul.

✪ Festivals and events

Brasília *p696, maps p698 and p703*
Feb Ash Wednesday.
Apr Maundy Thursday (half-day).
8 Dec Immaculate Conception.
24 Dec Christmas Eve.

🛍 Shopping

Brasília *p696, maps p698 and p703*
Books
Good selection of English books at **Livraria
Sodiler** in Conjunto Nacional and at the airport.

Handicrafts
For handicrafts from all the Brazilian states try
Galeria dos Estados (which runs underneath
the *eixo* from Setor Comercial Sul to Setor
Bancário Sul, 10 mins' walk from the
municipal *rodoviária*, south along Eixo
Rodoviário Sul). For Amerindian handicrafts,
Artíndia SRTVS, quadra 702, also in the
rodoviária and at the airport. There is a
feira hippy at the base of the TV tower at
weekends and holidays selling leather goods,
woodcarvings, jewellery and bronzes.

Jewellery
H Stern, branches in the **Nacional** and
Carlton hotels and at the **Conjunto Nacional**
and **Parkshopping**. Fine jewellery.

Shopping centres
The best shopping centres are **Shopping
Brasília** below the southern hotel zone and
Patio Brasília below the northern hotel zone.
Both have a wide range of boutiques and fast
food restaurants. Others include the vast
Conjunto Nacional on the north side of the
rodoviária; the **Conjunto Venâncio** on the
south side; the **Centro Venâncio 2000** at the
beginning of Av W3 Sul; the **Centro Venâncio
3000** in the Setor Comercial Norte; **Parkshopping** and the **Carrefour** hypermarket just
off the exit to Guará, 12 km from the centre.

▲ Activities and tours

Brasília *p696, maps p698 and p703*
Tour operators
Many tour operators have their offices in the shopping arcade of the **Hotel Nacional**. 3- to 4-hr city tours with English commentary can be booked on arrival at the airport – a convenient way of getting to your hotel if you have heavy baggage.

However, we have received criticism that some tours are too short or that the guides speak poor English. For night-time tours, the floodlighting is inadequate on many buildings.

3 Turismo, SCLS 402, bloco A, lojas 27/33, Asa Sul, T061-225 2686, www.buriti turismo.com.br. Tours around the city and Goiás and American Express representative.
Presmic Turismo, SHS Q 1, bloco A, loja, 35, T061-3233 0115, www.presmic.com.br. Full-day, half-day and night-time city tours (at 0845, 1400 and 1930 respectively).

◉ Transport

Brasília *p696, maps p698 and p703*
Air
To get the airport take bus Nos 102 or 102 from the municipal bus station, 30 mins US$1.50. Brasília airport has connections with most major cities in Brazil and a number of international destinations. TAP, www.flytap.com, has flights to **Lisbon**.

Airline offices BRA, SHS quadra 1, bloco A, loja 71/72, in front of Hotel Nacional, and in Shopping Flamingo and Shopping Sia, T061- 2105 0909, www.voebra.com.br. GOL, airport, T061-3364 9370, premium rate number, T0300-789 2121, www.voegol.com.br. Oceanair, T0300-789 8160, www.oceanair.com.br. Passaredo, www.voepassaredo.com.br. Sete, www.voesete.com.br. TAM/Brasil Central, SHN Hotel Nacional, Gallery Store, 36/37, T061-3325 1300; airport, T061-3365 1000, www.tam.com.br. TOTAL, www.total.com.br. Varig, SCN quadra 4, bloco B, T061-3329 1240; airport, T061-3364 9219, www.varig.com.br. Webjet, www.webjet.com.br.

Bus
Local bus No 131 goes from the municipal bus station to the *rodoferroviária*. All major destinations served. Bus tickets for major companies are sold in a subsidiary office in Taguatinga, Centro Oeste, C8, lotes 1 and 2, loja 1; and at the city *rodoviária*.

To **Rio**, 17 hrs, 6 *comuns* daily (US$60) and 3 *leitos* (about US$100). To **São Paulo**, 16 hrs, 7 *comuns* (about US$60) and 2 *leitos* (about US$90) daily (**Rápido Federal** recommended). To **Goiânia**, numerous daily. Change in Goiânia for **Cidade de Goiás**. To **Pirenópolis**, 2 daily; the quickest in the morning. To **Palmas**, 2 daily, best in the afternoon; via **Alto Paraíso** in the Chapada dos Veadeiros. To **Belo Horizonte**, 12 hrs, 9 *comuns* (US$60) and 2 *leitos* (US$90) daily. To **Belém**, 36 hrs, 4 daily (US$85, **Trans Brasília**, T061-3233 7589), buses are poorly maintained, but no alternative. To **Recife**, 40 hrs (US$100). To **Salvador**, 24 hrs, 3 daily (US$100). To **Campo Grande**, **São Luís**, 15 hrs, 1915, US$120, or **Viação Motta** via São Paulo 0930, 1930, or 1820 direct. To **Corumbá**, US$90. To **Cuiabá**, 17½ hrs (US$80) daily at 1200 with São Luís. **Mato Grosso**, generally Goiânia seems to be the better place for Mato Grosso destinations. **Barra do Garças**, 0830 and 2000, takes 9 hrs with **Araguarina**, T061-3233 7598, US$60 return.

Car hire
All large companies are represented at the airport. **Avis**, T/F061-3365 2780. **Interlocadora**, T061-3365 2511 and **Localiza**, Setor Locadoras, T0800-992000. **Unidas**, T061-3365 1412.

❶ Directory

Brasília *maps p698 and p703*

Banks Foreign currency can be exchanged at branches of **Banco Regional de Brasília** and **Banco do Brasil**, Setor Bancário Sul, latter also at airport, US$20 commission for TCs. **American Express**, Buriti Turismo, CLS 402 bloco A, lojas 27/33, T061-3225 2686. **Diners Club**, Av W3 Norte 502. **MasterCard**, for cash against a card, SCRN 502, bloco B, lojas 30 e 31, Asa Norte. Good exchange rates at **Hotel Nacional** and from hotels with 'exchange-turismo' sign. **HSBC**, SCRS 502, bloco A, lojas 7/12, ATM. **Cultural centres** Aliança Francesa, Sul Entrequadra 707-907, bloco A, T061-3242 7500. **American Library**, Casa Thomas Jefferson, Av W4 Sul, quadra 706, T061-3243 6588. **British Council**, Setor C Sul, quadra 01, bloco H, 8th floor, Morro Vermelho building, T061-3323 6080. **Cultura Inglesa**, SEPS 709/908 Conj B, T061-3243 3065. **Instituto Cultural Goethe**, Edif Dom Bosco, Setor Garagem Sul 902, lote 73, bloco C, T061-3224 6773. Mon-Fri, 0800-1200, also Mon, Wed, Thu 1600-2000. **Embassies and consulates** Australia, Caixa Postal 11-1256, SHIS QI-09, Conj 16, Casa 1, T061-3248 5569.

Austria, SES, Av das Nações 40, T061-3243 3111. **Canada**, SES, Av das Nações 16, T061-3321 2171. **Denmark**, Av das Nações 26, T061-34438 188 (0900-1200, 1400-1700). **Germany**, SES, Av das Nações 25, T061-3443 7330. **Guyana**, SDS, Edif Venâncio III, 4th floor, sala 410/404, T061-3224 9229. **Netherlands**, SES, Av das Nações 5, T061-3321 4769. **South Africa**, SES, Av das Nações, lote 06, T061-3312 9503. **Sweden**, Av das Nações 29, Caixa Postal 07-0419, T061-3243 1444. **Switzerland**, SES, Av das Nações 41, T061-3443 5500. **UK**, SES, quadra 801, Conjunto K, or Av das Nações, Caixa Postal 070586, T061-3225 2710. **USA**, SES, Av das Nações 3, T061-3321 7272. **Venezuela**, SES, Av das Nações 13, T061-223 9325. **Internet** Café.Com.Tato, CLS 505, bloco C, loja 17, Asa Sul, open daily. **Liverpool Coffee Shop**, CLS 108, R da Igreijinha. **Laundry** Lavanderia Laundromat, CLN 104, bloco C, loja 106, Asa Norte. Self-service. **Post office** Poste restante, Central Correio, 70001; SBN-Cj 03, BL-A, Edif Sede da ECT, the central office is in the Setor Hoteleiro Sul, between hotels Nacional and St Paul. Also at Ed Brasília Rádio, Av 3 Norte.

Goiás

With an area of 364,714 sq km and some four million inhabitants, Goiás is one of Brazil's most rapidly developing frontier agricultural areas. The land is used for producing coffee, soya and rice, most of Brazil's tin and tungsten, and for raising beef on some of the country's largest cattle ranches.
▶▶ *For listings, see pages 716-722.*

Goiânia ☺️🚹🚻🛏️🏕️♿🏧 ▶▶ *pp716-722. Colour map 3, B5.*

→ *Phone code: 062. Population: 1.1 million.*

Just off the BR-060, 209 km southwest of Brasília, is the second of Brazil's planned state capitals, after Belo Horizonte. Goiânia was founded in 1933 and replaced Goiás Velho as capital four years later. The city is famous for its street cafés and is a good place to stop between Brasília and the rest of the interior. Tourism is not as developed here as in other parts of the country, but the city is pleasant and there are some interesting sights within easy reach. Goiânia is spacious with more parks and gardens than any other of Brazil's large cities and many are filled with interesting forest and *cerrado* plants, as well as marmosets and remarkably large numbers of birds.

Ins and outs

Getting there Santa Genoveva airport ① *R Capitão Frazão s/n, T062-3265 1500, 8 km from the centre off R 57*, receives flights from several of Brazil's main cities. There are several car hire firms at the airport. A taxi to the centre costs US$10. Buses arrive at the **rodoviária** ① *R 44, No 399 in the Norte Ferroviário sector, T062-3224 8466*. Buses to the centre 'Rodoviária-Centro' (No 404) and 'Vila União-Centro' (No 163) leave from the stop on the city side of the terminal, US$1.50; No 163 goes on to the Praça Tamandaré.

Tourist information AGETUR ① *R 30 at R 4, Centro de Convenções, 2ª Andar, T062-3201 8122, www.goiasbrasil.com.br*. Useful websites include www.goias.gov.br.

Sights

The centre of the city is **Praça Cívica**, with well-lit main avenues radiating out in all directions. On the *praça* stand the government palace, the main post office and the **Museu Zoroastro Artiaga** ① *Praça Cívica 13, T062-3201 4676*. The museum has a small but interesting collection of historical objects, fossils and religious items as well as cases depicting indigenous and early settler life in Goiás. The museum was twice the size before it was cherry-picked by local politicians for their private collections.

From the *praça*, Avenida Araguaia runs northeast to the shady **Parque Mutirama**, with recreational facilities and a **planetarium** ① *Sun 1530 and 1630*.

More tranquil is the **Bosque dos Buritis** ① *1 km west of Praça Cívica along R 10*, which has shaded walks in *buriti*-filled tropical gardens and a turtle-filled pond. In the gardens of the Bosque dos Buritis is the **Museu de Arte de Goiânia** ① *R 1 605, T062-524 1190, Mon-Fri 0800-1700, Sat 0800-1300, free*, which showcases the work of a number of local artists including Siron Franco, who is nationally renowned. The **Parque Zoólogico** ① *Av Anhangüera, Tue-Sun 0700-1800*, 1 km west of the **Castro's Park** hotel is set in large gardens and is a good place to while away an afternoon.

A kilometre east of Praça Cívica, the **Museu Antropológico do UFG** ① *Praça Universitária, Mon-Fri 0900-1700*, houses wide-ranging ethnographic displays on the *indígenas* of the Centre West.

The **Casa do Indio** ① *Av Jamel Cecílio 2000, Pedro ludovico*, is a centre for indigenous arts and craft production and an important meeting place for indigenous peoples such as the Xavantes. The shop there sells a variety of handicrafts.

Goiânia

Sleeping	Oeste Plaza **6**	**Eating**	Giraffa **8**
Address **10**	Paissandú **9**	Bella Luna **1**	Mineiro **9**
Antoninho's **8**	Papillon **5**	Buffalo's Grill **11**	Primo Patio **10**
Augustus **1**	Rio Vermelho **7**	Celson & Cia **3**	Tribo do Açai **4**
Castro's Park **2**		Chão Nativo **2**	Walmor **6**
Goiânia Palace **3**		Floresta **7**	

200 metres
200 yards

The **Memorial do Cerrado Museum** ① *Av Bela Vista, Km 2, Jd Olímpico, T062- 562 4141, Mon-Sat 0800-2200, Sun 0800-1800, US$2*, just outside the city towards Cidade de Goiás, provides an interesting introduction to *cerrado* life, with reconstructions of indigenous villages, *quilombos* and colonial streets as well as planted *cerrado* vegetation.

Excursions from Goîania

The thermal springs at **Cachoeira Dourada**, 240 km south on the Rio Paranaíba, are worth a visit, as are the fantastic rock formations of the Serra das Galés at **Paraúna**, 160 km south-southwest off BR-060. There are a host of delightful, colonial mining villages within two hours' drive on good (often paved) roads. Travel agents in Goîania can arrange day tours. ▶▶ *See Activities and tours, page 721.*

Caldas Novas → *Colour map 3, B5. Phone code: 062. Population: 40,000.*

Goiás's most beloved resort is a hot-water theme park for families and weekenders. Hundreds of hotels line the hot river and are dotted around the various thermal springs at **Fontes de Pirapetinga** (7 km from town) and **Rio Quente** (29 km from the town, bus from Caldas Novas). There are many buses from Goîania; best reached from Morrinhos on BR-153 (Goîania-São Paulo). The bus from Morrinhos costs US$1, 30 minutes.

Anápolis and Cristalina → *Colour map 3, B5/6. Phone code: 062.*

Anápolis, a busy but uninteresting trading centre, is 57 km closer to Brasília than Goîania. The **Centro de Gemologia de Goiás** ① *quadra 2, módulo 13, Daia, Mon-Fri 0730-1630*, about 10 km out on the Brasília highway (near the Embratel tower), has a fine collection of gemstones. Lapidary courses are offered, and staff will show visitors how real and synthetic gemstones are distinguished. There is a library and shop.

The scruffy, unpleasant town of **Cristalina** is also famous for its semi-precious stones, which can be bought cheaply in local shops. An interesting excursion is to the panning and mining sites amid magnificent **rock formations**, about 6 km away. Take the BR-040 (Brasília–Belo Horizonte road) and at Km 104 turn left along a dirt road, just after the highway police post, to the **Cristalina waterfall** (11 km along this road).

Cidade de Goiás (Goiás Velho) ●❻❽❾🅐🅛🅔 ▶▶ *pp716-722. Colour map 3, A5.*

→ *Phone code: 062. Population: 30,000.*

This delightful town, nestled in the midst of *cerrado*-covered ridges, is one of central Brazil's hidden beauties. Cobbled streets lined with colourful yellow and blue Portuguese buildings gather around a little river watched over by a collection of elegantly simple baroque churches. Horses and old VWs clatter along the heavy stone flags and the local residents go about their day-to-day business as they always have done, treating visitors like guests or curiosities rather than tourists.

The town was founded in 1727 as Vila Boa and, like its Minas counterparts, became rich on gold, before becoming the capital of Goiás state, which it remained until just before the Second World War. But while towns like Ouro Preto and Tiradentes lavished their churches in gilt, Goiás chose modesty, erecting simple façades whose more classical lines stand strong against the intense blue of the sky. Interiors, too, were plain with simple panelling that beautifully offset both the richly painted wooden ceilings and the virtuoso sculpture of the *Goiás Aleijadinho* by Veiga Valle.

Ins and outs

Cidade de Goiás is well connected by bus with Goiânia, 130 km away, but there are few services from anywhere else. The **rodoviária** ① *Av Dario da Paiva, Bairro João Francisco*, is 2 km out of town. All buses also stop at the *rodoviária velha* (old bus station) next to the Mercado Municipal, 500 m west of the central Praça do Coreto. The **tourist office** ① *Praça Brasil Caiado (Largo do Chafariz), T062-3371 4564, daily 0900-1700*, is housed in the Quartel do Vinte, a former barracks where many of the German soldiers who fought in the Paraguayan war were housed. The Museu Casa de Cora Coralina is a better source of information.

Sights

The most interesting streets in the colonial part of town spread out from the two principal *praças*: **Praça Brasil Caiado** and immediately below it towards the river **Praça do Coreto**. The former is dominated by the Chafariz de Cauda, a lavish baroque fountain, which once supplied all the town's water. The best of the churches and museums are in the small cobbled town centre that radiates out from the two central plazas and spreads a little way along the riverbank. It is easily navigable on foot. The oldest church, **São Francisco de Paula** ① *Praça Zacheu Alves de Castro*, built in 1763, sits on a platform overlooking the market and the Rio Vermelho. It has a beautiful 19th-century painted ceiling by André Antônio da Conceição, depicting the life of St Francis de Paula. **Nossa Senhora da Abadia** ① *R Abadia s/n*, has a similarly understated but impressive painted ceiling, while the other 18th-century churches like **Nossa Senhora do Carmo** ① *R do Carmo*, on the riverside, and **Santa Bárbara** ① *R Passo da Pátria*, are almost Protestant in their simplicity. The latter sits on a hill a kilometre or so east of the town from where there are wonderful sunset views.

Cidade de Goiás has a handful of interesting museums. The **Museu das Bandeiras** ① *Praça Brasil Caiado/Largo do Chafariz, T062-3371 1087, Tue-Fri 0900-1700, Sat 1200-1700, Sun 0900-1300, US$1*, was once the centre of local government. The museum tells the story of the Goiás Bandeira exhibitions, which sit over a small but forbidding dungeon. The former governor's palace, the **Palácio Conde dos Arcos** ① *Praça do Coreto, T062-3371 1200, Tue-Sat 0800-1700, Sun 0900-1300, US$1*, sits in the square below Praça Brasil Caiado and was the governor's palace before the state capital moved to Goiânia. It has a display of 19th-century furniture, portraits of all the governors, and a pretty little walled garden. Across the way the **Museu de Artes Sacras** ① *Praça do Coreto, T062-3371 1207, Tue-Sat 0800-1700, Sun 0900-1300, US$1*, houses some clunky 18th-century church silverware and a series of painted wooden statues by one of Brazil's most important religious sculptors, José Joaquim da Veiga Valle. Veiga Valle was entirely self taught and had little knowledge or access to the Latin American baroque style that he was later seen to represent. Look out for the double 'V' signatures in the patterns of the fingers and the uncannily realistic stained-glass eyes.

From Praça do Coreto, a stroll downhill and across the river, will bring you to the **Museu Casa de Cora Coralina** ① *R do Candido 20, T062-3371 1990, Tue-Sun 0900-1700, US$1*, the former home of Goiás's most respected writer, with a collection of her belongings and a beautifully kept riverside garden at the back. Staff here are extremely helpful and knowledgeable about the city, though they speak no English. The 18th-century **Mercado Municipal**, next to the old *rodoviária*, is a wonderful spot for a snack and photography. All manner of interesting characters gather here and the small stall shops sell everything from shanks of beef to Catholic kitsch. **Espaço Cultural Goiandira do Couto** ① *R Joaquim Bonifacio 19, T062-3371 1303, Tue-Sun 0900-1700, US$1*, has chocolate box-style paintings of the city made entirely from different coloured sands from the surrounding *serra*. The artist, now in her 90s, has exhibited all over the world.

Pirenópolis ◉❶❷❸◉▲⊙ ↦ pp716-722. Colour map 3, A/B5.

→ Phone code: 062. Population: 23,000. Altitude: 770 m.

This lovely colonial silver mining town, 165 km due west of Brasília, sits in the midst of rugged hills dripping with waterfalls and covered in rapidly disappearing but still pristine *cerrado*. Like Cidade de Goiás it was founded by *bandeirantes* in search of gold and then by small-scale cattle ranchers. Its centre remains well preserved and only a little less pretty than Cidade de Goiás, leading it to be declared a National Heritage Site in 1989. Pirenópolis's proximity to Brasília has made it a favourite weekend playground for the capital's middle classes who congregate in the lively restaurants and bars, which line the northern end of Rua do Rosario. But the town's home-grown culture still thrives; one of Central Brazil's most unusual and vibrant festival takes place here every May/June (see Festivals and events, page 720) and on weekends the Praça Central fills to the brim with *peões* in stetsons and spurs blasting out *sertanejo* music from their souped-up cars. Pirenópolis is a great place to pass a few days or even weeks. The surrounding countryside offers good walking and light adventure activities and there are plenty of tour operators, though as elsewhere in Brazil, little English is spoken.

Ins and outs

The bus station is in the centre of town. Pirenópolis is served by two buses a day from Brasília. Tourist information is available at the **Centro de Atendimento ao Turista** ① *R do Bonfim, Centro Histórico, T062- 3331 2729*, but they don't speak much English.

Sights

The **Igreja Matriz Nossa Senhora do Rosário** has undergone restoration after being gutted by a fire in 2002. It is the oldest church in the state, dating from 1728, and before the fire had one of the most magnificent painted interiors in Goiás; sadly unrestored. **Nosso Senhor do Bonfim** (1750-1754), which houses an impressive life-size crucifix from Bahia, was transported here on the backs of 260 slaves. The more subtly beautiful image of Our Lady is Portuguese. The church of **Nossa Senhora do Carmo** ① *daily 1300-1700*, serves as a museum of religious art. Another, the **Museu Família Pompeu** ① *R Nova 33, Tue-Fri 1300-1700, Sat 1300-1500, Sun 0900-1200*, displays regional historical items and documents. The tiny, privately owned **Museu das Cavalhadas** ① *R Direita 37, Fri and Sat 0800-1700, US$1*, has a collection of masks, photographs and costumes from the Festa do Divino. **Fazenda Babilônia** ① *25 km southwest, no public transport, Sat and Sun 0800-1700, US$2*, is a fine example of an 18th-century sugar *fazenda*. It's now a small museum with the original mill and a lovely little chapel.

Around Pirenópolis

The *cerrado* and hills around the town have so far managed to resist the onslaught of soya and there are still opportunities to get out into the midst of some genuine wild country. There are plenty of walks and adventure activities on offer, birdwatching is good and there is a reasonably healthy population of maned wolf and various South American cats, including jaguar. The landscape is rugged, with many waterfalls and canyons. Guides are essential as many of the attractions are well off the beaten track.

Santuário de Vida Silvestre Vagafogo ① *T062-3335 8490, visits through Drena (see Activities and tours, page 721)*, is the labour of love of Evandro Engel Ayer who bought an area of the *cerrado* intending to start a farm. After falling in love with the plants and animals living here he instead decided to create a wildlife reserve. There is good birdwatching, with various rare species, a species list and a library. Mammals seen here include ocelot, brown capuchin and a rare subspecies of tufted-eared marmoset. Evandro is helpful and knowledgeable, speaks good English and serves one of the best lunches in Goiás.

The **Mosteiro Buddhisto** ① *information through Drena, see Activities and tours, page 721*, is a simple Zen monastery near a series of beautiful waterfalls in the heart of pristine *cerrado* forest. Day visits can be arranged that involve light walks or longer term retreats. This is particularly magical at sunset.

Chapada dos Veadeiros ⊜⊙⊿⊜ ➤➤ *pp716-722. Colour map 3, A6.*

① *Entry only with a guide. The park is reached by paved state highway BR-118. Tours can be arranged from Alto Paraíso de Goiás or São Jorge, see below.*

These table-top mountains, drained by countless fast-flowing rivers that rush through deep gorges and plummet over spectacular waterfalls, are less famous than Diamantina or Guimarães, but are less spoilt and more subtly beautiful. The national park, which protects only a fraction of their area, is almost twice the size of Diamantina and eight times the size of Guimarães. And unlike both those areas, its forests have never been felled. It was designated as a UNESCO World Heritage Site in 2001. At present trips within the park itself are limited to day visits only; but there are plans to change this. Walks of up to nine days can be easily organized at a good price within the wilderness areas in the park's environs, together with a range of adventure activities from canyoning to rappelling. There is plenty of accommodation in Alto Paraíso and São Jorge and transport to and from Brasília is straightforward.

Like most of wild Goiás, the Chapada is covered in *cerrado* forest – a habitat of such floral diversity that it has recently been declared a biological hot-spot by **Conservation International**. Rare mammals including jaguar, maned wolf, puma, tapir, ocelot and giant anteater are abundant and, although no one has yet compiled a serious bird list, spectaculars and rarities include red-shouldered macaw, coal-crested finch, helmeted manakin and various key indicator species like rusty-margined guan and bare-face currasow; king vultures are abundant.

Alto Paraíso and São Jorge → *Colour map 3, A6.*

The ramshackle town of **Alto Paraíso de Goiás** is filled with crystal shops and has become famous over the years as a centre for alternative therapies. Judging only by appearance many of these seem superficial. But there are some serious practitioners here doing excellent work, and at a fraction of the price of those in other parts of the world. The town is connected to Brasília and the rest of Goiás state by the paved state highway BR-118. There are bus connections to Brasília and to Palmas in Tocantins. Alto Paraíso is the best point to stock up on provisions before a trek in the Chapada dos Veadeiros and has the best of the tour operators and hotels. Access to the eastern attractions like the Vale de Lua are only really possible from Alto Paraíso. There is a small **tourist booth** on the main street (no English).

The tiny village of **São Jorge** is 40 km from Alto Paraíso on a partly paved road. With its three dirt streets, it is smaller and prettier than Alto Paraíso but has fewer restaurants and tour services. Several buses run daily between Alto Paraíso and São Jorge. The town lies only 1 km from the park entrance itself but the guides are less professional.

Serranópolis → Colour map 3, B4.

This little town is close to some remnant *cerrado* forest that clings to a series of small table-top mountains in the flat sea of soya, which is gradually taking over Goiás. Important cave paintings have been found here; these are now carefully protected and can be reached via a series of well-maintained trails. There are a few simple hotels in town and two excellent forest *pousadas*, which are carefully designed, wonderfully peaceful and great for birdwatching or just relaxing.

Parque Nacional das Emas → Colour map 3, B4.

This 133,000-ha park, protecting low *campo sujo cerrado* forests, black water rivers and savannah is Goiás's third UNESCO World Heritage Site – the others being Chapada dos Veadeiros and Cidade de Goiás. The park protects large populations of maned wolf, puma and jaguar as well as many rare *cerrado* bird species. These include red-shouldered and blue-winged macaw, greater rhea, bare-face currasow and diverse tyrant flycatchers and woodpeckers, as well as several species of macaw. It is a favourite destination for wildlife documentary film crews.

Ins and outs The most convenient base for visiting the park is **Chapadão do Céu**, www.chapadaodoceu.go.gov.br, about 30 minutes to the east. This newly created soya town has some decent hotels and tour operators to take visitors to the park. Four-day, three-night visits to the park can be arranged through agencies and tour operators such as **Drena** in Pirenópolis, www.drena.tur.br (see page 721), the **Pantanal Bird Club** in Cuiabá (see page 768), or **Focus Tours** (see page 65).

Aruanã and the Rio Araguaia ▲▲ ‣ pp716-722. Colour map 3, A5.

Any Brazilian will tell you that the 2630-km-long Rio Araguaia is richer in fish than any other in the world, and a visit to the 220-km stretch between Aruanã and the Ilha do Bananal during the fishing season is quite an experience. As the receding waters in May reveal sparkling white beaches, thousands of Brazilian and international enthusiasts pour into the area, intent on getting the best camping spots. As many as 400 tent cities spring up, and vast quantities of fish are hauled in before the phenomenon winds down in September, when the rivers begin to rise again and flood the surrounding plains. Without Brazilian contacts, the best way of experiencing this annual event is with one of the specialist tour operators.

The Araguaia is most readily accessible from the port town of **Aruanã**, 180 km northwest of Goiás Velho by paved highway, which sees little excitement outside the winter fishing season when its comfortable hotels are booked up for months. Boats can be rented to visit some of the beautiful lakes and beaches nearby. Brazilian canoeing championships are also held along the river. The *rodoviária* has bus connections with Araguapaz, Britânia and Goiânia.

For Sleeping and Eating price codes and other relevant information, see pages 42-47.

⦿ Sleeping

Goiânia *p709, map p710*

The best hotels are 1 km from the centre in the Setor Oeste with restaurants and bars. Hotels in the centre are frayed 1970s blocks.

L Castro's Park, Av República do Líbano 1520, Setor Oeste, T062-3212 4428, www.castrospark.com.br. A 5-star hotel in a tower a few blocks from the centre, with gym and swimming pool.

L-A Address Hotel, Av República do Líbano, 2526, Setor Oeste T062-3257 1000, www.addresshotel.com.br. The best hotel in the city with good promotional rates. Modern suites with comfortable beds; the best with separate living areas and good views. Excellent business facilities. Plenty of restaurants and bars nearby.

AL-A Papillon, Av República do Líbano 1824, T062-3219 1500, www.papillonhotel.com.br. A tower in the new centre with modern tiled rooms and suites, a pool, gym, sauna, business facilities and 24-hr room service. Very popular, book ahead.

B Oeste Plaza, R 2 No 389 Setor Oeste, T062-3224 5012, www.oesteplaza.com.br. Well-maintained modern tower with small a/c rooms with tiled floors and en suites. Those on the higher floors have good views. Small pool and gym.

C Augustus, Praça Antônio Lisita 702, T062-3224 1022, www.augustushotel.com.br. Blocky B-grade 1970s business hotel with rather gloomy apartment rooms, a pool, sauna and gym. Conveniently located for the centre. Official rates higher but these are not adhered to.

D Rio Vermelho, R 4 No 26, T062-3213 2555, www.hotelriovermelho.com.br. Simple hotel in a quiet street with lots of cheap restaurants. The cheapest rooms are fan cooled. With breakfast. Close to the centre.

D-F Goiânia Palace, Av Anhangüera 5195, T062-3224 4874, goiâniapalace@terra.com.br. Art-deco building with a range of rooms from simple fan-cooled doubles to suites. Good breakfast. Friendly and well located.

F Antoninho's, R 68 No 41, T062-3223 1815. Very basic but clean and well looked after. Only a few rooms have windows. Friendly, safe and with good breakfasts.

F Paissandú, Av Goiás 1290 at R 55, T062-3224 4925. Very simple fan-cooled or a/c rooms 8 blocks north of the centre. Breakfast.

Camping

Itanhangá municipal site, Av Princesa Carolina, Km 13, T062-292 1145. Attractive wooded location, reasonable facilities.

Caldas Novas *p711*

L-AL Pousada do Rio Quente, T062-3452 1122, www.caldasnovas.com.br. 4-star complex at Rio Quente. Breakfast and lunch, transport to main pools and recreation facilities included in price. Good accommodation in main buildings or chalets, the **Turismo** has a private airstrip.

Camping

At **Esplanada**, and **Camping Clube do Brasil** site on the Ipameri Rd, 5 km from the centre.

Anápolis and Cristalina *p711*

AL Estância Park, in a parkland setting 6 km northeast of Anápolis, T062-3318 1200. Pool, tennis court and an unpleasant mini-zoo, but the best in town.

C Hotel Goyás, R da Saudade 41, Cristalina. With fan and fridge.

D Serra Dourada, Av Brasil 375, Anápolis, T062-3324 0051. One of many cheap hotels around the *rodoviária* (Av Brasil-Norte). Restaurant, parking, fans, good value.

Cidade de Goiás p711

AL Fazenda Manduzanzan, on the road to Cachoeira das Andorinhas, 8 km, T062-9982 3373, www.manduzanzan.com.br. 10 apartments set in the *cerrado* near the region's prettiest waterfalls. Sauna, horse riding, spring-water swimming pools. Lunch included in the price.

AL-B Vila Boa, Av Dr Deusdete Ferreira de Moura, 1 km southeast on the Morro do Chapéu do Padre, T062-3371 1000. The best option, but out of town and inconvenient for the centre. Pool, bar, restaurant and good views. The best rooms are the 4 suites.

B Casa da Ponte, R Moretti Foggia s/n, T062-3371 4467. An art deco building next to the bridge across the Rio Vermelho with small well-maintained a/c rooms with en suites and parquet flooring. The best overlook the river.

C-D Pousada do Ipê, R Cel Guedes de Amorim 22, T062-3371 2065. Cloisters of rooms gathered around a courtyard dominated by a huge mango tree. The annexe has a swimming pool and bar area. Breakfast is included.

C-D Pousada do Vovô Jura, R Sta Barbara 38, T062-3371 1746. A colonial house set in a little garden with views out over the river and *serra*.

D-E Pousada do Sol, R Americano do Brasil, T062-3371 1717. Well-maintained, plain, fan-cooled rooms with lino or wood floors.

E Pousada do Sonho, R 15 Novembro 22, T062-3372 1224. A simple, well-kept residential house with plain rooms with shared bathrooms. Good breakfast.

E Pousada Reis, R 15 Novembro 41, T062-3371 1565. A simple cheapie next to the *Sonho* offering similar rooms to Pousada do Sonho but shoddier service.

Camping

Attractive, well-run **Cachoeira Grande** campground, 7 km along the BR-070 to Jussara (near the tiny airport), with bathing place and snack bar. More basic site (**Chafariz da Carioca**) in town by the river.

Pirenópolis p713

There are plenty of rooms in town, but they fill up during Festa do Divino so book ahead or visit from Brasília (about a 90-min drive).

A Casa Grande, R Aurora 41, T062-3331 1758, www.casagrandepousada.com.br. A big old house near the centre decorated with colonial furniture and with chalet rooms in a small garden visited by many birds.

A O Casarão, R Direita 79, T062-3331 2662, www.ocasarao.pirenopolis.tur.br. A colonial home decorated with period furniture, there's a little pool set in heliconia-filled gardens. Rooms have 4-poster beds and mosquito nets.

B-C Do Arvoredo, R Direita s/n, T062-3331 3479, www.arvoredo.tur.br. Peaceful little *pousada* set in a little wood. Clean, modest fan-cooled rooms are set around a small pool and there are good rates on weekdays.

C Pouso do Sô Vigario, R Nova 25, T062-3331 1206, www.pousadaspirenopolis.com.br. Small rooms but pleasant public spaces with objets d'art and posters from European painting exhibitions. Good location. Decent breakfast in a little garden next to the pool.

E Rex, Praça da Matriz 15, T062-3331 1121. 5 rooms, all with fridge and TV, around a courtyard. Good breakfast and location.

Camping

Camping Roots, R dos Pireneus 96, T062-3331 2105, camproots@yahoo.com. Sites with electricity, hot showers and English-speaking staff. 10-min walk from the centre.

Alto Paraíso and São Jorge p714

Prices in São Jorge often go up at weekends.

AL Casa das Flores, T061-9976 0603, São Jorge, www.pousadacasadasflores.com.br. Elegant little *pousada* with tasteful rooms (lit only by candlelight), sauna, pool and great breakfast in the decent attached restaurant. The best in town, but overpriced.

A-B Camelot, on the main road just north of Alto Paraíso, T061-3446 1581, www.pousada camelot.com.br. Delightfully kitsch mock-

Arthurian castle with proper hot showers and comfortable a/c rooms with satellite TV.

A-B Portal da Chapada, 9 km along the road from Alto Paraíso to São Jorge, T061-3446 1820, www.portaldachapada.com.br. The best choice for birdwatchers, with comfortable a/c wooden cabins in the midst of the *cerrado*.

B Casa Rosa, R Gumersindo 233, Alto Paraíso, T061-3446 1319, www.pousadacasarosa.com.br. The best in town with a range of well-kept a/c rooms, the best are in chalets near the pool. Also known as 'As Cerejeiras'.

B Trilha Violeta, São Jorge, T061-3455 1088, www.trilhavioleta.com.br. Fan-cooled violet rooms with private bathrooms around a bougainvillea-filled garden. Reasonable restaurant. Friendly.

B-C Aquas de Março, São Jorge, T061-3347 2082, www.chapadadosveadeiros.com.br. Simple duplex rooms decorated with paintings by local artist, Moacir. Pleasant garden, saunas, *oforo* baths and decent breakfast.

D-E Pousada do Sol, R Gumersindo 2911, Alto Paraíso, T061-446 1201. Small and simple, with a range of rooms, the best with balconies and fridges.

E Casa Grande, São Jorge, T061-9623 5515, www.pousadacasagrande.com.br. Simple but well-kept rooms and a good breakfast.

Camping

Tattoo, at the top of São Jorge, tattoo@travessia.tur.br. Powered sites from only US$3. Decent wood-fired pizzas and a small bar. English spoken. Very friendly and helpful.

Serranópolis *p715*

A-B Aldeia Ecológica Guardiões do Cerrado, about 15 km south of Serranópolis at Km 70 off the BR-184, take a taxi from the town (about US$20). A magical forest *pousada* with a ring of beautifully appointed chalets all decorated individually, many with Xavantes indigenous art and tasteful photographs. Great food and walks and much wildlife. Currasows and maned wolf visit the camp for breakfast each morning.

A-B Araras, T064-3668 1054, www.pousada dasararas.com. Tasteful little chalets in an armadillo-filled garden next to a clear-water river with a natural swimming area. Trails lead to the various archaeological sites.

Parque Nacional das Emas *p715*

A Fazenda Santa Amélia, Estrada Serranópolis, Chapadão do Céu, T064-3634 1380. A working *fazenda* with a range of wildlife tours in the property's remnant *cerrado* forest (none in Emas except with special arrangement). Comfortable chalets, a pool and full board in the price.

D Paraná, Av Indiaiá, Chapadão do Céu, T064-3634 1227. Simple, clean and well run with fan-cooled rooms.

E Rafael, Av Indiaiá, Chapadão do Céu, T064-3634 1247. Very simple and clean with fan-cooled rooms and shared bathrooms.

🍴 Eating

Goiânia *p709, map p710*

Goiânian cooking is like that of Minas – lots of meat with huge portions of vegetable dishes and, of course, beans and rice. Local specialities include *arroz com piqui*, rice with a cruel *cerrado* fruit, a practical joke of evolution whose outer flesh is soft and sweet but if bitten leaves the mouth full of sharp spines that have to be surgically removed. Beware!

The city has a good range of restaurants and bars, especially around **Praça Tamandaré** and **Av República Líbano** in the Setor Oeste where there are options in all price brackets.

Pamonharías (street stands) sell *pamonha* snacks, tasty pastries made with green corn, sweet, savoury, or *picante* (spicy); all are served hot and have cheese in the middle, some include sausage.

🍴🍴🍴 **Bella Luna**, R 10 704, Praça Tamandaré, T062-3214 3562. Some of the best Italian food in Goiânia, including excellent pizza, pasta and northern Italian seafood dishes.

🍴🍴🍴 **Celson & Cia**, R 15 539 at C 22, T062-3215 3043, www.celsonecia.com.br. Very popular meat restaurant with a good cold buffet. Evenings only except at weekends.

₮₮₮ Chão Nativo, Av República Líbano 1809 (opposite hotel **Papillon**), T062-3223 5396. The city's most famous Goiânian restaurant also serving local and Mineira food. Lively after 2000 and lunchtime on weekends.

₮₮ Tribo do Açaí, R 36 590, T062-3281 6971. Buzzing little fruit juice bar with excellent buffet salads and health food. Just round the corner from **Shopping Bougainville**.

₮₮ Walmor, R 3 1062 at R 25-B, T062-3215 5555, www.churrascariadowalmor.com.br. Large portions of excellent steaks served in an attractive open-air dining area.

₮₮-₮ Floresta, R 2 at R 9, T062-3224 9560. Lively corner bar with grilled steaks, standard rice and beans dishes, and snacks. Open until late. Good draft lager.

₮ Buffalo's Grill, Praça Tamandaré, T062-3215 3935. Pizzas, grilled meat and chicken, sandwiches and crêpes. Open 24 hrs.

₮ Giraffa, Av República Líbano 1592, T062-3225 1969. Fast food joint with some sumptuous set plates including steak/chicken with rice, beans and chips.

₮ Mineiro, R 4 53 (opposite **Rio Vermelho**, see Sleeping), T062-3224 9113. Cheap, good per kilo buffet with lots of choice and some veggie options. One of several on this block.

₮ Primo Patio, Av República Líbano (opposite Castro's Plaza), T062-3213 3366, Pizza, pasta and grilled steak and chicken (with the inevitable rice, beans and chips).

Cidade de Goiás *p711*

For the best very cheap options head for the **Mercado Municipal** between the São Francisco church and the river.

₮₮ Dali, R 13 de Maio 26, T062-3372 1640. Riverside restaurant with a little patio offering a wide range of international and local dishes.

₮₮ Flor do Ipê, Praça da Boa Vista 32, at the end of the road leading from the centre across the bridge, T062-3372 1133. The best in town for Goiânian food, with an enormous variety on offer, a lovely garden setting with views of the river and *serra*. Highly recommended.

₮ Degus't Fun Pizzeria, R Quinta Bocaiuva, next to Praça do Coreto, T062-3371 2800. Pizza, casseroles, soups and very friendly service from a mother-and-daughter team.

Pirenópolis *p713*

There are plenty of options along **R do Rosário**, serving a surprising range of international food including some vegetarian and Asian options. Many have live music at night (and an undisclosed cover charge – be sure to ask). There are cheaper options near the Igreja Bonfim in the upper part of town.

₮₮ Caffe Tarsia, R do Rosário 34, T062-3331 1274, www.caffetarsia.com.br. Much the best in town with a menu of Mediterranean dishes, Goiás food and steaks. Live music and weekends. Good *caipirinhas*.

₮₮ Chiquinha, R do Rosário 19, T062-3331 3052. Local cuisine with an emphasis on meat.

₮₮ Emporio do Cerrado, R do Rosário 21, T062-3331 3874. Great Goiás food like Pequi risotto with chicken in orange sauce served in a dining room decorated with black and white photos. Live music at weekends.

₮ Alma Vegetariana, R dos Pireneus at Praça do Correto, T062-3331 2938. Vegetarian pies, pastas, sandwiches and good juices.

₮ O Cafeteria, R do Rosário 38, T062-9972 7953. Light food and about the cheapest option in town.

Alto Paraíso *p714*

The best of the restaurants are in Alto Paraíso. São Jorge has a few basic options.

₮₮-₮ Oca Lila, Av João Bernades Rabelo 449, T061-3446 1773. Decent pizza and sandwiches, live music at the weekend, good atmosphere and a decent veggie buffet at lunch.

₮ Jatô, R Coleto Paulino 522, T061-3446 1339. Open Thu-Sun. Self-service; veggie options.

₮ Pizza 2000, Av Ari Valadão 659, T061-3446 1814. The centre of the town's early evening social life. Respectable pizzas.

⊙ Bars and clubs

Goiânia *p709, map p710*

Goiânia is surprisingly lively, with some of the best nightlife in central Brazil. This is especially true during the various festivals and Carnaval. There is an active gay scene and plenty of choices of clubs and bars. Most locals tend to drink in the restaurants (many of which double up as bars) before heading to a club at around 2300.

Café Cancún, Shopping Flamboyant and Av Jamel Cecilio 3, T062-3546 2035, www.cafe cancun.com.br. With a lively *forró* night on Wed and a mix of club music on others.

It's, Av 136, 960, Edifício Executive Tower, Térreo, Setor Marista, T062-3241 8477, www.its.art.br. The city's current favourite with a range of different music on different nights – from techno and hip hop to MPB.

Pulse, R9 1087, T062-215 6133, www.pulse.com.br. Crowded little club with a small sound system and rather tired decoration. Sweaty and packed on Sat.

Pirenópolis *p713*

Bars along **R do Rosário** cater for those from Brasília and the children of the hippies who migrated here in the 1970s. Locals hang out near the **Igreja Bonfim** where there are 2 spit-and-sawdust bars and booming car stereos.

⊛ Festivals and events

Cidade de Goiás *p711*

Feb **Carnaval** is joyous and still little known to outsiders. There are plans to make it into a traditional 19th-century masked parade with formal balls.

Apr The streets of Cidade de Goiás blaze with torches during the solemn **Fogaréu processions of Holy Week**, when hooded figures re-enact Christ's descent from the cross and burial.

Apr-May **Festa Divino Espírito Santo** processions, serenades and the formal distribution of food to the poor.

May **Encontro Afro Brasileiro**, a celebration of black Brazilian culture with live music, Afro-Brazilian food. Attended by people come from all over Brazil.

Jun **International Film Festival**, live music by acts like Gilberto Gil and Titãs and films from almost 100 different countries and especially from Latin America.

24-26 Jul **Birthday of the City**, the city becomes once more the capital of the state and there are processions in homage to the patron saint, Santa Ana, and various shows.

Pirenópolis *p713*

May/Jun **Festa do Divino Espírito Santo**, held 45 days after Easter (Pentecost), is one of Brazil's most famous and extraordinary folkloric/religious celebrations. It lasts 3 days, with medieval costumes, tournaments, dances and mock battles between Moors and Christians, a tradition held annually since 1819. The city throbs with life over this period and there are numerous and frequent extemporaneous *forró* and *sertanejo* parties.

⊙ Shopping

Goiânia *p709, map p710*

Ceramic, sisal and wooden handicrafts from **Centro Estadual do Artesanato**, Praça do Trabalhador (0800-1800); **Sun handicrafts markets** at the Praça Cívica (morning) and Praça do Sol (afternoon). The latter starts after 1530, until 2100, known as the **Honey Fair** as all types of honey are sold; also good for a Sun snack, with many sweets and tarts sold along the street. See also **Casa do Indio**, page 710.

Cidade de Goiás *p711*

There are little artisan shops springing up all over the town.

Frutos da Terra, R Dom Cândido Penso 30, next to Cora Coralina Museum. Wide range of items from bags and belts to leather sandals and ceramics. Most is made in the town.

Pirenópolis *p713*
There are many jewellery and arts and crafts shops in the streets in the historic centre.

▲▲ Activities and tours

Goiânia *p709, map p710*
There are many sporting facilities throughout Goiânia and visitors are welcome. For sunbathing, swimming and waterskiing try the **Jaó Club**, T062-261 2122, on a reservoir near the city.
Turisplan Turismo, R 8 Q 7, 388 lt 50 s 1 - Setor Central, T062-3224 7076. Arranges tours to Paraúna and the mining villages. Also sells bus tickets.

Cidade de Goiás *p711*
Massage and treatments
Cleonice Albino, T062-3372 1119/062-9902 7344. Very good-value Ayurvedic massage and colour therapy. Either at the therapist's clinic, or can come to your hotel.

Wildlife and adventure tours
Frans and Susana Leeuweenberg, contact through **Serra Dourada**, below. A husband-and-wife team of biologists who have been working hard to protect the *cerrado* for many years. English, French and Dutch spoken.
Serra Dourada Aventura, T062-3371 4277/T062-9238 5195, www.vilaboadegoias.com.br. Hikes in the surrounding forest and within the state park, visits to waterfalls, kayaking and canyoning and longer distance trips to the Rio Araguaia. Very good value.

Pirenópolis *p713*
Drena, R do Carmo 11, across the bridge and up the hill, on the left, T062-3331 3336, www.drena.tur.br. Walks, adventure activities and visits to the Vagafogo private reserve and the Mosteiro Buddhisto and trips further afield to destinations like Emás and the Rio Araguaia. Good value, well organized and excellent English spoken.

Chapada dos Veadeiros *p714*
Alpatour, R dos Nascentes, T062-3446 1820, www.altoparaiso.com. Van-based tours to the principal sights. Suitable for all ages.
Alternativas, T062-3446 1000, www.alternativas.tur.br. Very well-organized tours, walks and adventure trips including canyoning, rapelling and abseiling, throughout the region. Enthusiastic guides, some of whom speak English and the only tour operator in the region owned and run by locals.
Chapada Ecotours, T062-3446 1345, www.transchapada.com.br. Light adventure and visits to the major sights.
Travessia, T062-3446 1595, www.travessia.tur.br. Treks from a few days to over a week with rappelling and canyoning from one of the most respected instructors, Ion David.

Alto Paraíso and São Jorge *p714*
Massage and treatments
Atash, R do Segredo 37, Alto Paraíso, T061-3446 1028. Ayurvedic and classical Thai massage and breathing meditation from a long-experienced practitioner.
Sílvia Luz, R 12 Dezembro 217, Alto Paraíso, T061-3446 1585, T061-9956 9685, silviapraxis@hotmail.com. One of the best Ayurvedic and Reiki practitioners in the country. Also works with Tuiná and Shiatsu. Highly recommended

Parque Nacional das Emas *p715*
Tours are available through **Drena** (see above), www.drena.tur.br. Alternatively, contact the tourist office in the **Prefeitura Municipal**, Chapadão do Céu, www.chapadaodoceu.go.gov.br, for a list of authorized tour operators. Interest is growing but visits to Emas are still in the early stages.

Aruanã and the Rio Araguaia *p715*
Boats trips
US$25 per hr. Wildlife guides can be hired in Aruanã, Britânia, Barra do Garças or Porto Luís Alves. Interesting walks in surrounding jungle.

Tour operators
KR International Travel, R Mexico 8th floor,
S 801, Rio de Janeiro, T021-3210 1238.
Ex-Peace Corps manager, good for
information on the centre-west region.
Serra Dourada Aventura, T062-3371 4277,
www.vilaboadegoias.com.br. Boat and
walking trips along the Rio Araguaia. Very
good value. Book at least 10 days in advance.
Transworld, R 3 No 546, Goiânia, T062-224
4340, F212 1047. One-week group trips in
a 'botel' out of Aruanã to Bananal.

● Transport

Goiânia *p709, map p710*
Air Flights to **Brasília**, **Palmas**, **Rio de
Janeiro**, **São Paulo**, **Belo Horizonte**
(Pampulha), **Cuiabá**, **Ribeirão Preto**, **Rio de
Janeiro** (Santos Dumont), **São José do Rio
Preto**, **São Paulo** (Guarulhos), **Uberlândia**,
Campo Grande and **São Félix do Araguaia**.
   Airline offices Varig, Av Goiás 285,
T062-3224 5059, www.varig,com.br. and
at the airport. Also at the airport are
GOL, www.voegol.com.br, and TAM,
www.tam.com.br. Also at the airport.

Bus To **Brasília**, 207 km, at least 15
departures a day, 2½ hrs, US$5, and **São
Paulo**, 900 km via Barretos, US$25, 14½ hrs,
leito services at night. To **Goiás Velho**,
136 km, hourly from 0500, 2½ hrs, US$5.
Pirenópolis, 0700 and 1700, 2 hrs, US$5.
Campo Grande, 935 km, 4 services daily,
18 hrs, US$30. To **Cuiabá** (Mato Grosso),
916 km on BR-158/070 via Barra do Garças, or
928 km on BR-060/364 via Jataí (both routes
paved, most buses use the latter route),
4 buses a day, US$25, 15-16 hrs, continuing
to Porto Velho (**Rondônia**) and Rio Branco
(**Acre**), a very trying journey.

Car hire Millenium, T062-9612 7842
(24 hrs); **Siga**, T062-207 8388.

Cidade de Goiás *p711*
Bus Hourly bus services to **Goiânia** (2½ hrs)
0530-2000, change here for other places.

Pirenópolis *p713*
Bus 2 buses a day to **Brasília** (2½-4 hrs).

Chapada dos Veadeiros *p714*
Bus **Brasília–Alto Paraíso–São Jorge**
leaves at 1100 (3-4hrs), returning 0900.
There is a night bus **Palmas–Brasília**,
arriving from Brasília 2200.

Parque Nacional das Emas *p715*
Bus One daily bus from **Serranópolis** to
Chapadão do Céu, leaving at 0800. To get
to Chapadão do Céu from Campo Grande,
go via Costa Rica or Chapada do Sul.

● Directory

Goiânia *p709, map p710*
Banks There are several branches of
Bradesco, HSBC and Banco do Brasil.
In the centre and along Av Rep Líbano.
Travel agents will exchange cash, poor rates
for TCs. **Immigration** Immigration office,
R 235, Setor Universitário. **Internet** There
are numerous internet cafes throughout
the city.

Parque Nacional das Emas *p715*
Banks There is a Banco do Brasil with
a Visa ATM in Chapadão do Céu.

Tocantins

Tocantins is not on the tourist track but it offers some of the most exciting opportunities for adventure tourism in Brazil's interior. Jalapão – an enormous wilderness of cerrado forest, table-top mountains, dune deserts, waterfalls and whitewater rivers – lies on the borders of Tocantins and Piauí. It is as spectacularly beautiful as the Chapada dos Veadeiros or the Chapada Diamantina but far less visited. The world's largest river island, Ilha do Bananal, lies at the southern end of the state. Its northern extremes are almost as rich in wildlife as the Pantanal and the interior of the island is home to numerous indigenous groups (who cannot be visited without authorization from FUNAI). The serra around the planned modern capital, Palmas, is covered with rainforest dotted with beautiful waterfalls. The northwestern corner of the state sees the end of the cerrado and the beginnings of the Amazon rainforest. ▸▸ *For listings, see pages 725-726.*

Palmas ⊜😊🞊🕭🞊🕓 ▸▸ *pp725-726. Colour map 1, B5.*

→ *Phone code: 063. Population: 130,000.*

Palmas is the newest capital city in the country's newest state (Tocantins was carved out of Goiás in the late 1980s). It sits on the banks of the flooded Tocantins river at the foot of low forested mountains, which are bathed in a rich tropical light at dusk. It is a city built for mathematicians and cars, with an arcane street numbering system and wide, long avenues broken by roundabouts. Rather fascistic monuments to the autocrat who founded the state (and whose family still largely run Tocantins like a private fiefdom) can be seen around town, especially on Praça dos Girassóis in the centre. Palmas is an essential jumping-off point for trips to Bananal and Jalapão and there are many waterfalls and forest trails in the surrounding hills.

Palmas

Sleeping 😴
Alfredo's 1
Arataú 2
Carvalho's 3

Pousada das Artes 4
Pousada dos Girassois 6
Roma 5

Eating 🍴
Cabana do Lago 1
Dom Virgílio 2
Paço do Pão 3

Ins and outs

Palmas airport ⓘ *20 km from town, Av NS 5, T063-3321 61237*, receives flights from Brasília, São Paulo and Belém. A taxi into town costs around US$20 and there is an irregular shuttle bus. The **rodoviária** ⓘ *ACSUSO 40, T061-3216 1603*, is 10 km from the centre; city buses are plentiful and cheap. The city is divided into four sectors: **Noroeste (NO)**, **Nordeste (NE)**, **Sudoeste (SO)** and **Sudeste (SE)**. Like Brasília, the different blocks are named by use and location. Some address abbreviations are **Área Central (AC)**, **Área de Comércio** and **Serviço Urbano (ACSU)** and **Área Administrativa (AA)**. For tourist information contact **ADETUR** ⓘ *Praça dos Girassóis, T061-3218 2015*, on the *praça*.

Sights

It is worth spending a few hours wandering across the central **Praça dos Girassóis**, an enormous grassy square dotted with monuments and imposing public buildings. The most impressive is the **Palácio Araguaia**, a massive government palace topped with a golden globe that looks like it has been dragged here from North Korea. It is surrounded by other monuments; most whiff of totalitarianism. The state's founding *caboclo* pioneers hold their arms up in adulation as if they had discovered the promised land. Carlos Prestes – the communist leader who was, bizarrely, much admired by the fascist governor and state founder, José Wilson Siqueira Campos – stands with his troops around a tattered flag. And Siqueira Campos is everywhere, immortalized by himself out of love for the people of Tocantins, on plaques and public buildings. There's a forgotten Niemeyer building too: a long low rectangle next to the Prestes sculpture, also built in homage to the leader.

Excursions from Palmas ● ›› *725-726*.

There are numerous waterfalls in the nearby **Serra do Lajeado**, most of them reached via light trails through primary rainforest rich with birdlife. These include the **Cachoeira de Taquaruçu** near the town of the same name, **Macaco** and **Brejo do Chiqueiro**. The first trail to the falls is at Km 18 on the Estrada do Rio Negro. At Km 36 there are trails along the river to the **Brejo da Lagoa** waterfall and eventually to the 60-m-high **Cachoeira do Roncador**. Most of the falls have deep pools good for swimming. About 8 km away at Canelas is the **Praia da Graciosa**, a beach on the River Tocantins, with floating bars, sports courts, shows, and a campsite. It is particularly busy at weekends.

Jalapão → *Colour map 1, B5. Phone code 062.*

Jalapão is one of the highlights of a visit to the Brazilian interior: table-top mountains tower over seemingly endless plains covered in *caatinga* and *cerrado* forest, fast-flowing blackwater rivers lead to plunging waterfalls, sweeping sand dunes, bubbling clear-water springs and sleepy *caboclo* villages. The air so clear you can see for over 100 km and, other than the Serra dos Confusões in Piauí, there is probably nowhere in Brazil where *sertão* and *cerrado* is more pristine. It is still possible to see the world's rarest large parrot, spix's macaw, in the stands of *buriti* palms and one of the world's rarest water birds, the Brazilian merganser duck, on the smaller rivers. There's plenty of other wildlife too, best seen at dawn and in silence (avoid trips with Brazilian groups if possible). Maned wolf, giant anteater and white-tailed deer are numerous and there is a healthy population of all the larger cat species.

Jalapão is a six-hour drive from Palmas on the border of Tocantins, Piauí, Maranhão and Bahia. At present only **Korubo**, www.korubo.com.br, offers trips here, staying at their very comfortable safari camp next to one of the larger rivers (see page 726 for details). It's possible to visit on a self-drive trip, though only with a 4WD; prepare as if for the Australian outback, with plenty of spare fuel, two ropes and at least 20 litres of water. There is simple accommodation in the scattered small towns.

Ilha do Bananal → *Colour map 1, B5. Phone code 062.*

① *Permission to visit the park should be obtained in advance from Ibama, R 219, No 95, Setor Universitário, 74605-800, Goiânia. Access is through the small but pleasant town of Santa Teresinha. It is far easier, however to visit on an organized trip with Bananal Ecotour in Palmas, www.bananalecotour.com.br.*

Bananal is the world's largest river island and is located on the northeastern border of Mato Grosso. The island is formed by a division in the south of the Rio Araguaia and is approximately 320 km long. The entire island was originally a national park (called Parque Nacional Araguaia), which was then cut in half and later further reduced to its current size of 562,312 ha. But there are still plenty of wild areas that are rich in fauna, several permanent lakes, marshland areas and seasonally flooded habitats similar to those in the Pantanal. The vegetation is a transition zone between the *cerrado* (woody savannah), *varzea*, *igapó*, Amazon *terra firme* forest and gallery forest.

The fauna is also transitional. More than 300 bird species are found here, including the hoatzin, hyacinth macaw, harpy eagle and black-fronted piping guan. The giant anteater, maned wolf, bush dog, giant otter, jaguar, puma, marsh deer, pampas deer, Brazilian tapir, yellow anaconda and South American river turtle can also be spotted. The island is flooded most of the year, with the prime visiting time being the dry season from June to early October, when the beaches are exposed.

◉ Tocantins listings

For Sleeping and Eating price codes and other relevant information, see pages 42-47.

● Sleeping

Palmas *p723, map p723*

AL Pousada das Artes, 103 Sul, Av, LO1 78, T063-3219 1500, www.arteshotel.com.br. Very comfortable, well-kept a/c rooms with marble and mosaic bathrooms, restaurant, sauna and swimming pool. Only the master suite has external windows.

A Hotel Arataú, Av JK 104 Norte 123, T063-3215 5323, hotelaratau@bol.com.br. Spacious tiled rooms; the best are on the upper floors.

A Pousada dos Girassois, Av NS 1, 103 Sul, conj 03, lote 44, T063-3219 4500, www.pousadadosgirassois.com.br. Overlooking the main grassy square. Rooms are small and modern with a/c and cable TV but tiny windows. Very good restaurant. The departure point for **Korubo's** Jalapão tours.

B Hotel Roma, Av LO2-104 Norte, lote 23, T063-3215 3033, www.hotelroma-to.com.br. Pleasant, intimate little hotel with bright and airy tiled rooms in terracotta and cream. Internet access.

C Carvalho's, Av 103 Sul, SOO1, lote 11, T063-3215 5758. Modest, well-kept a/c en suites some with no external windows.

D-E Alfredo's, Av JK, 103 Sul, Quadra 101, lotes 23/24, T063-3215 3036. Simple fan-cooled and a/c rooms gathered around a little garden courtyard visited by hummingbirds. Trips to the Ilha do Bananal and Jalapão. Cheapest with 4 or more people.

Ilha do Bananal *p725*

A Bananal, Praça Tarcila Braga 106, CEP 78395 (Mato Grosso). Full board. There is only room for 10 people so reserve well ahead, allowing several months for the mail to get through.

There is some simple accommodation for scientists at the park, which can sometimes be reserved at the address above or from the national parks department in Brasília. Bring your own food and bedding. The severely underpaid but dedicated staff appreciate any extra food or financial help, although it will not be solicited. A boat to the park can be arranged at **Hotel Bananal**, above.

🍴 Eating

Palmas *p723, map p723*
🍴 **Cabana do Lago**, Praia da Graciosa, T063-3215 6055. Local fish grills and sauce dishes like *tucunaré* (peacock bass) and Goiás meat dishes like *carne do sol* beef and guinea fowl in coconut milk. Overlooking the river.
🍴 **Dom Virgilio**, Av JK 103, Norte 159, T063-3212 1400. Great buffet lunch with generous salads and pizzas in the evening.
🍴 **Paço do Pão**, Av JK 154, 103 Sul, T063-3215 5665. Very good, large wood-fired pizzas.

🛍 Shopping

Palmas *p723, map p723*
Na Natureza, Av JK 103 Sul, Conj 01, lote 150, Sala 04, T063-3215 2391. Beautiful baskets and earrings in Capim Dourado, indigenous ceramics and bead necklaces and bracelets made with Amazonian and *cerrado* seeds.
Palm Blue Shopping, ACSUSO 10, Conj 2.

🏔 Activities and tours

Palmas *p723, map p723*
Also see *pousada* Carvalho's, Sleeping, above.
Bananal Ecotour, quadra 103 Sul Conjunto 02, lote 02, sala 03, T063-3219 4200, www.bananal ecotour.com.br. Trips to Bananal and the waterfalls and trails around Palmas.
Korubo Expeditions, São Paulo, T011-3667 5053, www.korubo.com.br. Excellent but expensive tours to Jalapão. Guides are very good (specialist wildlife guides should be booked in advance) and accommodation is in

very comfortable African-style safari tents with beds. Activities included in the price are whitewater rafting, treks, 4WD tours, wildlife spotting and visits to typical Jalapão villages. Avoid going with a large group of Brazilians as noise means wildlife spotting is difficult.

Ilha do Bananal *p725*
See also **Bananal Ecotour** in Palmas, above. Bananal can be visited from São Félix do Araguaia (with permission from Funai in the town) by crossing the river to the Carajá village of Santa Isabela de Morra and asking to see the chief, who can tell you the history of the tribe. The island can be crossed from São Félix to São Miguel de Araguaia by taking an 8-hr trip. From São Miguel, a 5-hr bus trip brings you to Porangatu (**D Hotel Mauriti**, restaurant) on the Belém-Brasília highway.

🚍 Transport

Palmas *p723, map p723*
Air Daily flights to **Brasília**, **São Paulo**, **Curitiba Florianópolis** and **Goiânia** with GOL, www.voe gol.com.br, and TAM, www.tam.com.br. Offices at the airport.
Boat The port is 9 km from the city. Ferries to **Miracema do Tocantins** and **Paraíso do Tocantins**.
Bus Buses to Brasília often run via the Chapada dos Veadeiros. To **Brasília** (12 hrs), **Belém** (10 hrs), **Goiânia** (14 hrs), **Salvador** (20 hrs), **São Luís** (14 hrs) and **Teresina** (12 hrs).
Car hire Hertz, Av Nossa Senhora, T063-3978 1900, and Localiza, ACSO 11-CL02, lote 41, T063-3216 1104, and at the airport.
Taxi Rádio Táxi Palmas, T063-3213 2001.

🏢 Directory

Palmas *p723, map p723*
Medical services Hospital Regional and Proctology, Praça ARSE, quadra 51, setor serrano, T063-3214 1424. **Post office** Av Joaquim Teotônio Segurado.

Contents

Footprint features

Border crossings

At a glance

Getting around Plane, bus, jeep, boat and horseback.

Time required 3-4 days for one of the cities and a *fazenda* or Pantanal tour. 1-2 days for Bonito.

Weather Hot and wet Oct-Feb, hot and drier Mar-Apr, dry May-Sep.

When not to go Dec-Feb is very wet, the Pantanal is flooded and there are many mosquitos.

★ **Don't miss ...**
1 Fazendas around Miranda, page 748.
2 Camping in Nhecolândia, page 753.
3 The Transpantaneira, page 762.
4 Alta Floresta and the Rio Cristalino, page 763.

AMAZONAS

Rio Madeira

Manicoré

Jacarèacanga

Rodovia Transamazônica

Rio Juruena

São Manuel

Cristalino

Aripuanã

Bandeirantes

Paranaíta

Alta Floresta ④

Guarantã do Norte

Santa Terezinha

Juruena

Peixoto Azevedo

Confresa

Caçoal

Pimento Bueno

Juará

Porto dos Gaúchos

São Félix do Araguaia

Ilha do Bananal

RONDONIA

MATO GROSSO

Sinop

Parque Indígena do Xingu

Sandolândia

Vilhena

BR163

Piúva

São Miguel do Araguaia

Comodoro

Arenópolis

Mozorlândia

Ananá

Crixás

Vila Bela da Sma Trindade

Tangará da Serra

Nobres

Parque Nacional da Chapada dos Guimarães

Planalto do Mato Grosso

GOIÁS

Pontes e Lacerda

Água Fria

Rio Paraguai

Cuiabá

Cnl Ponce

Barra do Garças

Bala Grande

Cáceres

São Vicente

Primavera do Leste

Guaíra

Goiás

San Matías

Poconé

Rondonópolis

Guaratinga

Iporá

BOLIVIA

Pixaim ③

Porto Jofre

Itiquira

Alto Garças

Diamantino

Serra das Divisões

Paraúna

Indi

L Gaíba

B de Castelo

Pantanal Matogrossense

Sonorá

Coxim

Plaça de Mineiros

Parque Nacional das Emas

Mineiros

Jataí

Rio Verde

São Domingos

Edéia

Parque Nacional do Pantanal Matogrossense

MATO GROSSO DO SUL

Serranópolis

Caçu

Aporé

Barragem de São Simão

Corumbá

Puerto Suárez

Estr Par

Paraíso

Morrinho ②

Guaicurus ①

Rochedo

Camapuã

Raimundo

Porto Esperança

Miranda

Capim Verde

Parapaíba

Rio Grande

Fernandópolis

Bodoquena

Aquidauana

Bonfim

Campo Grande

Aparecida do Taboado

Nhandeará

Parque Nacional Serra da Bodoquena

Bonito

Sidrolândia

Santa Rita do Pardo

Água Clara

Três Lagoas

Major Prado

Tietê

Araçatuba

Porto Murtinho

Jardim

Maracaju

Novo Alvorada

Bataguassu

Panorama

Presidente Prudente

Penápolis

Bela Vista

Itaum

Itapora

Ivinhema

Santo Inácio

Rancharia

Tupã

PARAGUAY

Antônio João

Dourados

Ponta Porã

Caarapó

Paranavaí

Marília

Assis

Pedro Juan Caballero

Amambaí

Rio Paraná

Londrina

Ourinhos

Eldorado

Umuarama

Maringá

Arapongas

Jacarezinho

N

100 km

100 miles

The Pantanal, which is an enormous seasonally flooded wetland on the borders of Brazil, Paraguay and Bolivia, is the best place in the Americas for spotting wild animals, and one of the best places in the world to see birds. Capybara, anaconda, peccary, giant otter, metre-long macaws and ocelots are common sights and it is even possible to see that most elusive of South American mammals, the jaguar. At the end of the dry season, between June and August, the number of water birds, raptors and parrots has to be seen to be believed. Visiting the wetlands is easy with a large choice of camping tours from Campo Grande, Cuiabá, Corumbá or Miranda; or there's the more comfortable option of staying at one of the *fazenda* ranch houses that are increasingly opening their doors to tourists. Families with children will enjoy the little resort town of Bonito, which is famous for its clear-water rivers and caves, and makes a good base for visiting the Pantanal.

The Pantanal lies within two Brazilian states: Mato Grosso do Sul and Mato Grosso. Until the second half of the 20th century these were little-explored wildernesses of table-top mountains, *cerrado*, savannah and dense rainforest. The famous British explorer, Colonel Percy Fawcett, was lost, and perhaps murdered, in the forests of the Xingu, and Theodore Roosevelt contracted a fatal disease on an expedition here in previously uncharted territory. These days, even the Pantanal is grazed by cattle, and the great Amazonian forests of northern Mato Grosso state are steadily giving way to soya beans, planted for the vegetarians of the USA and Europe and the kitchens of China. However, substantial pockets of forest still remain for now, particularly around the Rio Cristalino near the town of Alta Floresta, where one of the best jungle lodges in the Americas can be found.

The Pantanal

The Pantanal UNESCO Biosphere Reserve is the world's largest freshwater wetland and one of the best places on earth for seeing wildlife, particularly birds. Within Brazil it comprises a plain of around 21,000 sq km but the Pantanal extends beyond Brazil into Bolivia, Paraguay and Argentina to form an area totalling 100,000 sq km. The plain slopes 1 cm in every kilometre north to south and west to east to the basin of the Rio Paraguai and is rimmed by low mountains. From these, 175 rivers flow into the Pantanal and after the heavy summer rains they burst their banks, as does the Paraguai itself, to create vast shallow lakes broken by patches of high ground and stands of cerrado forest. Plankton then swarm on the water to form a biological soup that contains as many as 500 million micro algae per litre. Millions of amphibians and fish spawn or migrate to consume them. And these in turn are preyed upon by waterbirds and reptiles. Herbivorous mammals graze on the stands of water hyacinth, sedge and savannah grass and at the top of the food chain lie South America's great predators – the jaguar, ocelot, maned wolf and yellow anaconda. In June, at the end of the wet season, when the sheets of water have reduced, wildlife concentrates around the small lakes or canals and then there is nowhere else on earth that you will see such vast quantities of birds or such enormous numbers of crocodilians. Only the plains of Africa can compete for mammals and your chances of seeing a jaguar or one of Brazil's seven other species of wild cat are greater here than anywhere on the continent.

Background

To the indigenous groups who arrived in the area tens of thousands of years before the Europeans, the Pantanal was a sea, which they called 'Xaraes'. Myths about this sea quickly reached the ears of the Spanish and Portuguese *conquistadores*, who set out to explore it. As if to presage the future, the first to arrive, in 1543, was a Spaniard called Cabeza de Vaca (Cow Head) who complained about the swarms of mosquitoes and vampire bats and promptly turned westward into the Paraguayan *chaco*. The fate of the Pantanal and its myriad indigenous residents was left to the ruthless Portuguese and their *bandeirantes*. Apart from a few skirmishes they left the Pantanal alone for 200 years, but then gold was discovered glittering in a stream they called the River of Stars (or 'Cuiabá' by the local people). A settlement was established and soon the Portuguese were scouring the area for native slave labour for their mines. The *indígenas* were understandably aggrieved by this and two of the fiercest tribes, the Guaicurú and the Paiaguá, combined forces to attack the Portuguese. Their tactics were highly effective: they worked in small guerrilla bands, laying ambushes when the Europeans least expected it. The Guaicurú were horsemen, charging into battle naked but for jaguar skins, clubs, lances and machetes; crouched low on their stolen Andalusian horses, or riding on the horse's sides rather than their backs and thus invisible to the Portuguese. They used no saddles or stirrups and had just two chords for reins. The Paiaguá attacked by water and were excellent swimmers, advancing in their canoes and then leaping into the water and using the sides of the boats as shields. They would then suddenly right their boats and fire several volleys of arrows during the time it took the *bandeirantes* to fire one. They soon defeated the Europeans, regaining control of the Pantanal for almost 100 years. The Portuguese were furious and accused the Guaicurú in particular of dishonourable tactics. "They fight only to win," the Portuguese claimed, "attacking only when the enemy seemed weaker". The Guaicurú responded by exposing the hypocrisy of the Portuguese: "Since the Portuguese and Spaniards claim to go to heaven when they die, they do well to die quickly. But, since they also claim that the

The plight of the Guaraní

"On my land, cattle is worth more than Indians. The cattle stomp on their gardens and tractors knock down their houses. The rivers are dirty with the waste from large farms in the region: pesticides, mercury. They finished with our forests, they are finishing with what is left of our savannahs. For this reason young Guaraní are killing themselves, they are searching for the end, hanging themselves." (Marta Silva Vito Guaraní, President of the Kaguateca Association for Displaced Indians in an address to the US House of Representatives, 10 May 1994.)

The Guaraní in Brazil, one of the country's largest indigenous groups, are suffering terribly from the theft of almost all their land. Nowhere is their plight more urgent than in the Pantanal, where thousands of Guaraní-Kaiowá live crowded onto tiny plots hemmed in by ranches and plantations. The surrounding ranch land has long been hunted and farmed by the tribe but has been forcibly taken from them by gunmen hired by ranch owners. One community, which has a federal act recognizing its right to 1240 ha of land, is crammed into an area of barely 60 ha, hemmed in by electric fences and patrolled by armed guards. They are forced by these men to work as cheap labour on the land that has been stolen from them. The situation has proved intolerable for many young Guaraní. More than 300 have committed suicide since 1986, drinking a mixture of rum and pesticide. The youngest was nine years old.

In desperation, the tribe began to campaign internationally in the 1990s, and one group was granted land rights by the Brazilian government in 2002. But the law has not been upheld. Many Guaraní groups were forced from the little land they had, their homes were burnt and, in early 2003, Marcos Veron, a 70-year-old shaman, leader of the Guaraní-Kaiowá and land rights campaigner, was beaten to death by thugs employed by the ranchers who had taken over his homeland, Takuára.

In January 2004 a group of several thousand *indígenas*, enraged by lack of activity from the government, invaded several farms close to Brazil's border with Paraguay. The ranch owners fled in fear. The invasions were widely reported in the international press, forcing the Brazilian government to promise to review the tribe's land rights in Matto Grosso do Sul. What will happen remains to be seen.

Guiacurú go to hell after death, in that case the Guiacurú want to die as late as possible." (John Hemming, *Red Gold*). But through subterfuge the pact was broken and in 1734 the Portuguese regained control by means of a devastating ambush that decimated the Paiaguá. The tribes then retreated into the depths of the Pantanal where their numbers slowly diminished as a result of punitive *bandeirantes* expeditions, inter-tribal conflict and European diseases.

Today Pantaneiros boast of their proud traditions, which are barely three generations old. Nearly 25 million of their cattle roam the Pantanal and the true indigenous Pantaneiros have largely disappeared. Of the 25,000 Guiacurú present in 1500, some 200 survive in their Kadiweu and Mbayá subgroups. The Paiaguá have been reduced to a sad remnant living on an island reservation near Asunción in Paraguay. Other tribes, such as the Parecis, who were enslaved in the mines, fared even worse and, of the great indigenous groups of the Pantanal, only the Bororo, who allied with the Portuguese, retain any significant numbers. Even their traditions have been greatly damaged by the aggressive missionary tactics of the Salesians in the 20th century.

Wildlife and vegetation

Wildlife → *See Ecology and conservation, page 734.*

Mammals Outside Africa there is nowhere better for seeing wild mammals than the Pantanal, especially between July and late September. During this time, there are groups of capybara – the world's largest rodent – at just about every turn. Critically endangered marsh deer (who have webbed feet to help them run through the swamp), or their more timid cousins, the red brocket, and the pampas deer wander in every other stretch of savannah alongside giant anteaters. Few visitors leave without having seen both species of wild pig (the solitary collared and herd-living white-lipped peccaries), giant otters and at least one species of cat. Lucky visitors may even see a jaguar or tapir. There are at least 102 mammal species here and, although most of them are bats (including vampires), the list includes eight of South America's 10 wild cats, four dog species and numerous primates ranging from the tiny palm-sized pygmy marmoset to South America's second largest primate, the red howler monkey.

The cats are usually top of everyone's 'most wanted' list. The largest is the jaguar (most easily seen here at **Fazenda San Francisco**, in the south or on the Transpantaneira), followed by the more elusive puma, which has the widest distribution of any feline in the world. Even more common is the retriever-sized ocelot and the tawny or black jaguarundi, which is about twice the size of a domestic cat, though more slender. The most elusive creature is the pampas cat, which has a fawn body and striped legs, but scientists are yet to agree on its species. The other cats are all spotted and are, in size order, the margay, Geoffroy's cat (the most hunted in the America's) and, the most beautiful of all, the oncilla or tiger cat.

Other carnivores include crab-eating foxes, coatis and racoons (who often hang around the *fazendas* at night), the maned wolf, and short-eared and bush dogs (found in the drier semi-deciduous forests). Monkeys are not as varied here as they are in the Amazon, but visitors will hear or see red or black howlers, the smaller brown capuchin and possibly the pygmy or silvery marmoset. Other species present include various titi monkeys and night monkeys, which are most easily seen around **Fazenda Bela Vista** on the Estrada Parque in the south. Woolly monkeys can be found in the dry forests.

Reptiles After birds, the easiest animals to see in the Pantanal are caimans, of which the dominant species is the jacaré caiman, a smaller sub-species of the spectacled caiman found in the Amazon. Jacaré caimans reach a maximum length of about 1.5 m. Yellow anaconda, the world's heaviest snake, are abundant but difficult to see; your best chance is on the Estrada Parque in the south, which they frequently cross during the day. Other snakes, the majority of which are not venomous, are also abundant but hard to spot. The venomous species, which include pit vipers, such as the fer de lance or jararaca, are nocturnal.

Birds There are more than 700 resident and migratory bird species in the Pantanal. Birding on the Transpantaneira road in the north or at one of the *fazendas* in the south can yield as many as 100 species a day. From late June to early October the vast numbers of birds have to be seen to be believed. Try to visit as many habitat types as possible and, as well as trail-walking, jeep rides and horseback excursions, be sure to include river trips in your itinerary. Night safaris will maximize sightings of more unusual herons, such as the boat-billed, agami and zigzag, and the numerous nightjars and potoos. Specialities in the Pantanal include the metre-long hyacinth macaw (the world's largest parrot), the golden-collared macaw, blue-fronted parrot, blue-crowned nanday, blaze-winged and green-cheeked parakeets, the giant flightless rhea, chestnut-bellied and spix's guan, crowned eagle, bare faced currasow and helmeted manakin. Remember to bring good binoculars and a field guide. A book such as Nigel Wheatley's *Where to watch birds in South America* can give far greater detail than this book has space for. ▸▸ *For recommended birding guides, see Books, page 819.*

Vegetation

Although the Pantanal is often described as an ecosystem in its own right, it is actually made up of many habitats, which have their own, often distinct, biological communities. The Pantanal is of recent geological origin and has very few endemic plant species. Botanically it is a mosaic: a mixture of elements from the Amazon region including *varzea* and gallery forests and tropical savannah, the *cerrado* of central Brazil and the dry *chaco* region of Paraguay.

Pantanal cerrado forest The *cerrado* is found both in the upland areas, which are not prone to flooding, and in some areas that may be inundated for a short period. It is dominated by the *cerrado* pequi tree (*Caryocar brasiliense*) whose fruits have a famous spiny interior, the legume *Bowdichia virgiloides* and the sandpaper tree (*Curatella americana*). But the most conspicuous trees in the *cerrado* are tabebuia (*ipê* or trumpet trees); these are characterized by their brilliant colours (indigo in *Tabebuia impetignosa* and yellow in *Tabebuia aurea*) and no leaves in the dry season. Sometimes these trees stand as the dominant species in vast areas of semi-agrarian parkland. Within the dry *cerrado* are numerous stands of bocaiúva palm (*Acrocomia aculeate*) characterized by its very spiny trunk and leaves. Its fruit is an important food source for macaws and larger parrots. In the wetter *cerrado* are numerous islands of dense savannah forest or *cerradão*, often thick with acuri palm (*Attalea phalerata*), whose woody fruit is the principal food for the hyacinth macaw and, when fallen, for peccaries (bush pigs; *javalo*i n Portuguese) and agouti (rabbit-sized, tailless rodents; *cutia* in Portuguese). *Cerrado* habitats are also important refuges for the larger sheltering mammals, such as jaguar and tapir, who will flee into the densest wet *cerrado* to escape predators.

Semi-deciduous tropical forest This taller, denser forest occurs on higher ground such as the Serra do Bodoquena south of Miranda, and comprises a mix of species from the Paraguayan *chaco* and the Amazon. For instance jutai (*Hymenaea courbaril*), from which the sacred copal resin is extracted, comes from the Amazon; while the monkey-ear plant (*Enterolobium contortisquam*), recognized by its curved seed pods, is a common *chaco* species. More primate species can be found here than elsewhere in the Pantanal, along with smaller toucans, such as the chestnut eared aracari, and rare mammals like bush dog (*Cachorro vinaigre*) and tayra (*Iara*).

Swamp and seasonally flooded land This varies greatly, from Amazonian habitats characterized by riverine forests such as *varzea* (seasonally flooded riverbank forest) to seasonally flooded grassland and palm savannah dominated by carunda palm trees. Alongside these are permanently marshy areas and open lakes and oxbows thick with floating plants. This diversity of habitats means a great diversity of species and nowhere is better than these areas for seeing large concentrations of birds and mammals. *Varzea*, which is best seen by canoe or paddle boat, is good for mammals such as tapir and giant otter, and for riverine birds like the southern screamer (*tachã*), the five species of Brazilian kingfisher (*Martim pescador*), black-collared hawks (*Gaviao belo*) and the myriad species of heron and stork, including the giant 1.2-m-tall jabiru (*tuiuiu*). Apart from *varzea*, much swampland is dominated by the papyrus-like sedge (*Cyperus giganteus*) or reed mace (*Typha dominguensis*) or by floating plants like water hyacinth (*Eichhornia crassipes*), which caiman and capybara use as cover.

Xeric vegetation This permanently dry scrub forest found in elevated areas is dominated by *chaco* species such as various types of cacti (such as *Cereus peruvianus* and *Opuntia stenarthra*) together with the swollen-trunked, baobab-like pot-bellied chorisia (*Bombacaceae*). Many distinct species occur here, including one of the world's rarest cats, the pampas cat, and rare birds, such as black-legged seriemas and *chaco* earthcreepers.

Ecology and conservation

Only one area of the Pantanal is officially a national park, the 135,000-ha **Parque Nacional do Pantanal Matogrossense** in the municipality of Poconé, only accessible by air or river. You can obtain permission to visit from **Ibama** ① *R Rubens de Mendonça, Cuiabá, T065-3644 1511/ 1581*. Hunting is strictly forbidden throughout the Pantanal and is punishable by four years' imprisonment. However, most *fazendeiros* regularly shoot and kill jaguar, many locals still offer their services as jaguar hunters and some landowners even allow illegal private hunts. Fishing is allowed with a licence, US$25, according to strict quotas. It is not permitted in the spawning season or *piracema* (1 October to 1 February in Mato Grosso do Sul; 1 November to 1 March in Mato Grosso). There are also restrictions on the size of fish that may be caught, but poaching is rife and there are plans to halt all fishing for four years due to severe stock depletion. Application forms are available from **Banco do Brasil** or **Ibama Campo** ① *T067-3782 2966, www.sema.ms.gov.br*, or ask travel agents. Catch and release is the only kind of fishing allowed on rivers Abobral, Negro, Perdido and Vermelho. Like other wilderness areas, the Pantanal faces significant threats to its integrity. Agrochemicals and *garimpo* mercury, washed down from the neighbouring *planalto*, are a hazard to wildlife.

The **International Union for the Conservation of Nature** (IUCN), www.iucn.org, is concerned at the amount of poaching, particularly of *jacaré* skins, birds and capybara. The forestry police have built control points on all major access roads to the Pantanal. Biologists interested in research projects should contact the **Coordenador de Estudos do Pantanal** ① *Departamento de Biologia, Universidade Federal do Mato Grosso do Sul, Campo Grande, T067-3787 3311 ext 2113*, or the IUCN about their **Fazenda Rio Negro programme** ① *T067-3326 0002, www.fazendarionegro.com.br*, or **Projeto Gadonça** ① *Fazenda San Francisco, www.fazendasanfrancisco.tur.br*. See also **Fazenda San Francisco**, page 749.

Visitors can make an important contribution to protecting the Pantanal by acting responsibly and choosing guides accordingly. Take your rubbish away with you, don't fish out of season, don't let guides kill or disturb fauna, don't buy products made from endangered species, don't buy live birds or monkeys, and report any violation to the authorities. The practice of catching caiman, even though they are then released, is traumatic for the animals and has potentially disruptive long-term effects.

Ins and outs

Getting there and around

The Pantanal can be reached from both Mato Grosso and Mato Grosso do Sul states. In Mato Grosso access is from the capital city, Cuiabá, which has an airport. In Mato Grosso do Sul, access is from the state capital, Campo Grande, or from Corumbá on the border with Bolivia (both cities have airports); or from the little cattle ranching town of Miranda (connected to the rest of Brazil by bus and train), which lies between them.

There are three ways to visit the Pantanal. The cheapest (and most popular with backpackers) is to take an **organized tour**. These involve camping, perhaps with a night in a *fazenda* (ranch house), and a range of activities, including hiking, canoeing and wildlife and birdwatching. Guides tend to emphasize light adventure and have reasonable general knowledge of the Pantanal but poor knowledge of specific plants or animals.

Another option is to organize a tour through a **fazenda**. Although some are very modest, *fazendas* are generally comfortable with air-conditioned rooms and good home cooking. Many (if requested in advance) can organize decent wildlife guides who know English and scientific names for birds and animals. *Fazendas* can also be booked through tour operators, such as **Impacto** in Campo Grande (see page 753), **Aguas do Pantanal Turismo** in Miranda (see page 753) or **Natureco** in Cuiabá (see page 768).

It is also possible to visit the Pantanal on a **self-drive tour**, by hiring a 4WD in Cuiabá or Campo Grande. Those considering this option should speak good Portuguese and stick to the two principal dirt roads that enter the Pantanal: the Transpantaneira in Mato Grosso and the Estrada Parque in Mato Grosso do Sul.

For further information on the Pantanal, consult www.braziltour.com, www.brazil tourism.org, www.turismo.ms.gov.br and www.sedtur.mt.gov.br.

Visiting the Southern Pantanal → *For details see Mato Grosso do Sul, page 738.*
Access to the southern Pantanal is from Campo Grande (see page 738), Miranda (see page 743) and Corumbá (see page 745), all in Mato Grosso do Sul.

Campo Grande offers most of the tours, both upmarket (through agencies such as **Impacto**) and the myriad budget operators like **Ecological Expeditions**, whose touts are ready and waiting for buses arriving from destinations in eastern Brazil like Foz do Iguaçu.

Corumbá, near the Bolivian border, was once the capital of backpacker tourism in the Pantanal but, although many of the budget operators maintain offices here and cheap tours can be readily organized, the town is now used more as a departure point for boat trips. ▸ *See Choosing a budget tour, page 736.*

Miranda lies half way between Campo Grande and Corumbá at the turn off to Bonito. It is still a Pantanal ranching town free of touts, and the best of the *fazendas* (ranch house safari hotels) are situated close by. There are two excellent operators and the town is friendly and

Choosing a budget tour

Most tours include accommodation in lodges and activities such as 'safari' jeep trips, riverboat trips, piranha fishing and horse riding. A two-day trip, with a full day taken up with travel, allows you to experience most of what is on offer. Extended tours tend to have the same activities spread out over a longer period of time. The best way to enjoy a tour is not to have fixed expectations about what you will see, but to take in the whole experience that is the Pantanal.

Budget travellers are often approached in the streets or at the cheaper hotels by salesmen who speak their language and promise tours at low prices; they then hand their clients over to agencies, who often speak only Portuguese, and may deliver something quite different. Some travellers have reported unpleasant experiences, so it is important to select a guide with great care. Although we list a few of the most reputable guides, there are other good ones and most travellers enjoy a pleasant experience.

→ Ask travellers who have just returned from a tour for recommendations. Most guides also have a book containing comments from their former clients.
→ Ask who will lead the party and how big it will be. Less than four is not economical; there will be cuts in boats or guides.
→ Do not rush to sign up when first approached; compare several alternatives.
→ Do not pay everything in advance and try to deal directly with agencies or guides, not salesmen (it can be difficult to tell).
→ Discuss the itinerary carefully and try to get it in writing (this is seldom possible); threaten to go to someone else if necessary.
→ Always get an itemized receipt.
→ Act responsibly and don't expect to get something for nothing.

What to take Most tours arrange for you to leave your baggage in town, so you need only bring what is necessary for the tour. In winter (June-August), temperatures fall to 10°C; warm clothing and sleeping bag are needed at night. It's very hot and humid during summer and a hat and high-factor sun protection is vital. This is available cheaply in the larger towns. Wear long sleeves and long trousers and spray clothes as well as skin with insect repellent. Insects are less of a problem in July and August. Take insect repellent from home as mosquitoes, especially in the northern Pantanal, are becoming immune to local brands. Drinks are not included in the price of packages and tend to be overpriced, so if you are on a tight budget bring your own. Most importantly, make sure you take a pair of binoculars. See also Tour operators, pages 753 and 767.

relaxed. Although there are excellent *fazendas* off the Estrada Parque road, there are also an increasing number opening up to tourism around Miranda. These include the stylish, upmarket **Refúgio Ecológico Caiman**, the closest thing central Brazil has to a Mexican hacienda (and similarly beloved of the chic) and **Fazenda San Francisco**, which is probably the best spot in the entire Pantanal for big cats, especially ocelot, which you can almost be guaranteed to see. ▶▶ *See Sleeping, page 749, and Activities and tours, page 753.*

Many of the tours and some of the *fazendas* lie off a dirt road running off the BR-262 Campo Grande to Corumbá highway. This road, which is known as the **Estrada Parque**, begins halfway between Miranda and Corumbá at a turn-off called Buraco da Piranha (the Piranha hole), heads north into the Pantanal and then, after 51 km, turns west to Corumbá at a point called the Curva do Leque. This is the overland access point to

Nhecolândia – a region particularly rich in wildlife. Four-wheel drives run by the tour operators or the *fazendeiros* wait at the Buraco da Piranha to meet tour buses arriving from Campo Grande. They then take visitors either to *fazendas* or to campsites in Nhecolândia. *Fazendas* in this area include **Fazenda Rio Negro**, a project run in conjunction with Conservation International and now closed to tourism, **Fazenda Barra Mansa, Fazenda Barranco Alto** and **Fazenda Santa Sophia, Fazenda Bela Vista**, which has a wealth of primates; and **Fazenda Rio Vermelho**, which is famous for sightings of the larger carnivores. ►► See Sleeping, page 748.

Visiting the Northern Pantanal → For details see Mato Grosso, page 738.
There are two main access points to the northern Pantanal: the **Transpantaneira road** (see page 762), which cuts through the wetland and is lined with *fazendas*; and the town of **Barão de Melgaço** (see page 762), which is surrounded by large lakes and rivers and is not as good for wildlife. Both are reached from Cuiabá in Mato Grosso.

The Transpantaneira was built in 1976 and was originally planned to connect Cuiabá with Corumbá, but it currently goes only as far as the border at Porto Jofre on the Rio Cuiabá. Work has been suspended indefinitely – ostensibly because of the division of the two Mato Grosso states – and is a superb spot for wildlife watching. Hundreds of thousands of birds congregate here, particularly between June and September, to wade through the shallow wetlands to either side of the road. And at any time of year there seems to be a raptor on every other fence post. Mammals and reptiles can often be spotted crossing the road or even sitting on it, particularly at dawn and dusk. Most of the northern Pantanal's tourist-orientated *fazendas* are here. The road is unpaved, potholed and punctuated by numerous rickety wooden bridges and, although it can be driven in a standard hire car, progress is slow. It is probably better to see the Transpantaneira as part of a tour as most of the guides have access to the *fazendas* along the way. If you choose to go alone, be sure to book in advance; private individuals who turn up unannounced may or may not be welcome at some *fazendas*.

The easiest access is in the dry season (July to September). In the wet, especially January and February, there is no guarantee that you will get all the way to Porto Jofre. Bring plenty of water and some extra fuel as petrol stations often run out. If you choose not to take a tour or hire a car you can hitch a ride along the Transpantaneira from Poconé. Do not travel alone and be prepared for a bumpy ride in the back of a truck. ►► For further information, see Sleeping, page 763, Activities and tours, page 767, and Transport, page 769.

When to go
The Pantanal is worth visiting at any time of year. However, the dry season from June to October is the ideal time to see wildlife as animals and birds congregate at the few remaining areas of water. This is also the breeding season, when birds form vast nesting areas, with thousands crowding the trees, creating an almost deafening cacophony of sounds. The white-sand river beaches are exposed, *jacarés* bask in the sun, and capybara frolic in the grass. It is during these months you are most likely to see jaguars, however, July sees lots of Brazilian visitors and the increased activity decreases the chances of sightings. From the end of November to the end of March (wettest in February), most of the area, which is crossed by many rivers, is subject to flooding. At this time mosquitoes abound and cattle crowd onto the few islands remaining above water. In the southern part of the Pantanal, many wild animals leave the area, but in the northern Pantanal, which is slightly higher, the animals remain.

Mato Grosso do Sul

Mato Grosso do Sul is dominated by the Pantanal wetlands in the north and by the low Serra da Bodoquena mountains in the south, which surround the family-orientated ecotourism town of Bonito. The mountains are honeycombed by caves and cut by numerous glassy clear streams. There are only a few towns of any size and the state is a centre of soya plantations and cattle ranching. Many of the designated backpacker tours of the Pantanal leave from the state capital, Campo Grande, which is a prosperous, modern city with lively nightlife. However, they take half a day to reach the Pantanal itself, which begins in earnest east of Campo Grande, near the cattle-ranching town of Miranda. Many of the best fazenda ranch houses are in the area surrounding Miranda, as well as a handful of small, upmarket tour operators. The town also has one of the Pantanal's liveliest festivals, O Festa do Homen Pantaneiro, in November. Corumbá, on the banks of the Rio Paraguai, is another popular departure point for the Pantanal, and lies close to the Estrada Parque dirt road (which runs through the wetlands) and to Nhecolândia, a wilderness area visited by most of the Campo Grande backpacker tours. ▶▶ *For listings, see pages 747-756.*

Campo Grande ⊖⊙⊕⊖⊙▲⊖⊙ ▶▶ *pp747-756. Colour map 3, C3.*

→ *Phone code: 067. Population: 665,000.*

A major gateway to the Pantanal, Campo Grande is a pleasant, modern city on a grid system, with wide avenues. It was founded in 1899 and became the state capital in 1979. Because of the *terra roxa* (red earth), it is known as the 'Cidade Morena'.

In the centre is a shady park, the **Praça República**, commonly called the Praça do Rádio after the Rádio Clube on one of its corners. Three blocks west is **Praça Ari Coelho**. Linking the two squares, and running east–west through the city, is the broad Avenida Afonso Pena; much of its central reservation is planted with yellow *ypé* trees. In spring, their blossom covers the avenue, and much of the city besides. The avenue's eastern reaches are the centre of a burgeoning restaurant and nightlife scene. City tours are on offer everywhere but they are generally expensive and there are few obvious sights.

Ins and outs

Getting there The **airport** ① *Av Duque de Caxias, 7 km, T067-3368 6000,* receives flights from Cuiabá, Londrina, São Paulo and Santa Cruz (Bolivia). A bus leaves every 10 minutes from outside the airport terminal for the city centre and bus station. A taxi costs US$6 (10 minutes). It is safe to spend the night at the airport if you arrive late. Banco do Brasil at the airport exchanges dollars; the Bradesco just outside has a Visa ATM. The airport also has a tourist information booth (little English, many pamphlets), a post office, car rental and airline offices.

Campo Grande is well connected by bus to cities in the southern Pantanal and onwards to Bolivia and Paraguay, and to São Paulo, Cuiabá and Brasília/Goiânia. The **rodoviária** ① *in the block bounded by R Barão do Rio Branco, R Vasconcelos Fernandes, R Dom Aquino and R Joaquim Nabuco, T067-3383 1678,* has shops, *lanchonetes* and a cinema, together with a number of budget tour operators for the Pantanal. Town buses leave from the Rua Vasconcelos Fernandes end of the bus station; state and interstate buses leave from the Rua Joaquim Nabuco end. A taxi to Praça República costs US$4, or it's a 1-km walk.

The BR-262 is paved most of the way from Campo Grande to Corumbá and the Bolivian border; a rail service along this route is due to recommence in early 2009 and is likely to be expensive. It is best to make this journey during the day to take advantage of the marvellous scenery. ▸▸ *See Transport, page 754.*

Tourist information The municipal **Centro de Informação Turística e Cultural** ① *Av Noroeste 5140, corner of Afonso Pena, T067-3324 5830, www.campograndeturismo.com.br, Tue-Sat 0800-1900, Sun 0900-1200*, is housed in Pensão Pimentel, a beautiful mansion built in 1913. It sells maps and books and has a database of city services and cultural information.

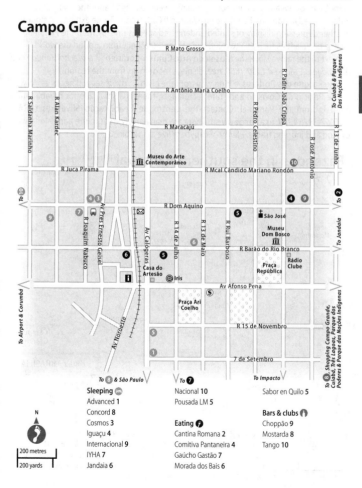

Campo Grande

Sleeping 🛏
Advanced **1**
Concord **8**
Cosmos **3**
Iguaçu **4**
Internacional **9**
IYHA **7**
Jandaia **6**

Nacional **10**
Pousada LM **5**

Eating 🍴
Cantina Romana **2**
Comitiva Pantaneira **4**
Gaúcho Gastão **7**
Morada dos Bais **6**

Sabor en Quilo **5**

Bars & clubs 🍸
Choppão **9**
Mostarda **8**
Tango **10**

N
200 metres
200 yards

Sights

Just north of the Praça República, is the **Museu Dom Bosco** ⓘ *Av Alfonso Pena, Parque Naçoes Indígenas, T067-3312 6491, www.museu.ucdb.br, usually Tue-Sat 0800-1800, Sun 0800-1200 and 1400-1700, US$1.50, but with a temporary restriction on visits in early 2009, contact Professor Dirceu or Señor Juliano on T067-3326 9788*, which contains relics of the tribes who suffered at the hands of aggressive Salesian missionaries in the early and mid-20th century. The largest collections are from the Tukano and Bororo people from the upper Rio Negro and Mato Grosso respectively, both of whose cultures the Salesians were responsible for almost completely wiping out. Traditional practices such as sleeping in *malocas* or wearing indigenous clothing were banned, and the *indígenas* were indoctrinated in rigorous, literalistic pre-Vatican II Catholicism. These exhibits sit alongside a rather depressing display of stuffed endangered species (mostly from the Pantanal), as well as peculiarities such as a two-headed calf, and seashells from around the world.

Next to the railway line, the **Museu do Arte Contemporâneo** ⓘ *Marechal Rondón and Av Calógeras, Mon-Fri 1300-1800, free*, displays modern art from the region.

The **Parque dos Poderes**, a long way from the centre, covers several hectares. As well as the Palácio do Governo and state secretariats, there is a small zoo for rehabilitating animals from the Pantanal. Contact the **Centro de Reabilitação Silvestres (CRAS)** ⓘ *T067-3326 1370*, to arrange a visit. There are many lovely trees in the park, along with cycling and jogging tracks. Plenty of capybara live in the lakes.

Fazendas in the southern Pantanal

Sleeping ⓘ

Cacimba de Pedra **4**
Fazenda 23 de Março **1**
Fazenda Baia Grande **2**
Fazenda Barra Mansa **3**

Fazenda Barranco Alto **9**
Fazenda Campo Lourdes **5**
Fazenda Meia Lua **7**
Fazenda San Francisco **6**
Fazenda Santa Ines **11**

Fazenda Santa Sophia **13**
Fazenda Xaraés **12**
Pousada Rio Vermelho **10**
Refúgio Ecológico Caiman **8**

Border essentials: Brazil–Paraguay

Ponta Porã (Brazil)–Pedro Juan Caballero (Paraguay)

Immigration There are no border posts between the two towns and people pass freely for local visits. For entry/exit visas, go to the **Brazilian Federal Police office**, Rua Marechal Floriano 1483 (second floor of the white engineering supply company building), T067-3431 1428, Monday to Friday 0730-1130, 1400-1700. The two nations' consulates face each other on Rua Internacional (border street), a block west of Ponta Porã's local bus terminal; some nationalities require a visa from the **Paraguayan consul**, Rua Internacional, next to Hotel Internacional, Monday to Friday 0800-1200. Check requirements carefully, and ensure your documents are in order; without the proper stamps you will inevitably be sent back somewhere later on in your travels. Taking a taxi between offices can speed things up if pressed for time; drivers know about border crossing requirements, US$7.

Transport From the border, there are frequent buses (around six hours) to Asunción, and flights there from Pedro Juan Caballero. A road also runs to Concepción on the Rio Paraguai, where boat connections can be made.

Coxim → *Phone code: 067. Population: 28,500.*

Coxim, 242 km north of Campo Grande on the BR-163 and halfway between Campo Grande and Rondonópolis, also provides access to the Pantanal. It sits in a green bowl, on the shores of the Rio Taquari. The area has great potential for tourism, with waterfalls nearby at Palmeiras, and the Pantanal in close proximity. But as yet there are no official tours other than a few small charter boat operators at the town port. There are a few hotels including some cheap options around the bus station.

Ponta Porã to the border ●●● ↦ *pp747-756. Colour map 3, C2.*

→ *Phone code: 067. Population: 54,000.*

Right on the border, Ponta Porã is separated from the town of **Pedro Juan Caballero** in Paraguay by only a broad avenue. With paved streets, good public transport and smart shops, Ponta Porã is decidedly more prosperous than its neighbour, although Brazilian visitors flock across the border to play the casino and buy cheaper foreign goods. An animal show is held each October at the **Parque das Exposições**, by the *rodoviária*.

The town can be reached by bus or plane from Campo Grande. The *rodoviária* is 3 km out on the Dourados road, from where the 'São Domingos' bus runs to the centre, taxi US$3.

Bonito and around ●●●▲●● ↦ *pp747-756. Colour map 3, C2.*

→ *See also map page 742. Phone code: 067. Population: 17,000.*

The designated tourist town of Bonito lies just south of the Pantanal in the **Serra da Bodoquena** hills. It is surrounded by beautiful *cerrado* forest cut by clear-water rivers rich with fish and dotted with plunging waterfalls and deep caves. The town was 'discovered' by *Globo* television in the 1980s and has since grown to become Brazil's foremost ecotourism destination. There are plenty of opportunities for gentle adventure activities such as caving, rafting and snorkelling, all with proper safety measures and great even for very small children. Those looking to see animals and contemplate nature should opt for the forest walks of the Sucuri river. Despite the heavy influx of visitors, plenty of wildlife appear on and around the trails when it is quiet. Paca and agouti (large, tailless foraging rodents), brown capuchin monkeys and toco toucans are abundant, as are endangered species like the tiny and aggressive bush dog and cats such as ocelot and jaguarundi. Bare-faced currasows (magnificent turkey-sized forest floor birds) can often be seen strutting around the pathways. Rarely seen small toucans such as the chestnut-eared aracari are relatively easy to spot here, flitting in and out of the trees.

Ins and outs

Getting there and around The *rodoviária* is on the edge of town. Several buses daily run to/from Campo Grande (five hours), Miranda (two to three hours) and Corumbá (five hours). Bonito town is a grid layout based around one principal street, Rua Coronel Pilad Rebuá, which extends for about 2 km. The town is easily negotiated on foot.▸ See Transport, page 754.

Tourist information The **tourist office** ⓘ *Praça Rachid Jauli, www.bonito-ms.com.br or www.guiabonitopantanal.com.br*, has limited information and staff do not speak English. Prices in Bonito have risen sharply over the years, making the area prohibitively expensive for those on a budget. Local attractions can only be visited with prior booking through one of the town's numerous travel agents. With the exception of specialist activities like cave diving, all agents offer exactly the same products at exactly the same price, but only a few offer transport. Taxis to the sights are exorbitantly expensive; an alternative would be to hire a car. ▸ See Activities and tours, page 753, and Car hire, page 755.

Bonito

Sleeping
Albergue do Bonito 3
Canaã 2
Pira Miuna 6
Pousada Muito Bonito 1
Pousada Olho d'Água 4
São Jorge Hostel 5
Tapera 7

Eating
Cantinho do Peixe 3
Da Vovó 2
Mercado da Praça 5
Santa Esmeralda 1
Tapera 4

Bars & clubs
Bollicho 7
O Taboa 8

Best time to visit The number of visitors to Bonito is limited so pre-booking is essential during December and January, Carnaval, Easter and July; prices during these times are also very high. The wet season is in January and February; December to February are the hottest months; July and August coolest.

Sights

Lagoa Azul ① *26 km from Bonito, US$10 municipal tax*, is a cave with a lake 50 m long and 110 m wide, 75 m below ground level. The water's temperature is 20°C, and it is a jewel-like blue, as light from the opening is refracted through limestone and magnesium. Prehistoric animal bones have been found in the lake. The light is at its best in January and February, from 0700 to 0900, but is fine at other times. A 25-ha park surrounds the cave. **Nossa Senhora Aparecida cave** has superb stalactites and stalagmites and can be visited, although there is no tourism infrastructure.

On the banks of the Rio Formoso, the **Balneário Municipal** ① *7 km on road to Jardim, US$4*, has changing rooms, toilets, camping, swimming in clear water and plenty of colourful fish to see. Strenuous efforts are made to keep the water and shore clean. The **Horminio waterfalls** ① *US$1*, consist of eight falls, which are suitable for swimming. There's a bar and camping is possible. **Rafting** is also a popular activity. The 2½-hour trip combines floating peacefully downriver, swimming and shooting down the four waterfalls. ▸▸ *See Activities and tours, page 753.*

The **Aquário Natural** ① *US$25*, is one of the springs of the Rio Formoso. Here you can swim and snorkel with five types of fish (remove suntan oil before swimming). A peaceful tour (US$10) involves birding and swimming or snorkelling in crystal-clear water from the springs of the **Rio Sucuri** to its meeting with the Formoso. Other tours include **Aquidaban**, a series of waterfalls in dense forest, and **Rio da Prata** (US$24), a beautiful spring with underground snorkelling for 2 km. Parrots and animals can be seen on the trip. There are also plenty of chances for walking along ecological trails, horse riding and fishing trips. The **fishing** season is from 1 March to 31 October. In late October and early November is the *piracema* (fish run). The fish return to the spawning grounds and hundreds can be seen jumping the falls.

Jardim

Jardim, reached by paved road (60 km from Bonito) could be an alternative base to Bonito for trips on clear-water rivers and visits to caves. There is far less infrastructure and consequently far fewer tourists and cheaper accommodation, restaurant and taxi prices. The town itself has a wide, tree-lined main street, a handful of hotels and basic café-restaurants. The official town website, www.jardim.ms.gov.br, has information and photos of what to see and do. The *rodoviária* has regular bus connections with Campo Grande and other towns (see Transport, page 755). From Bonito a road leads to **Porto Murtinho**, where a boat crosses to Isla Margarita in Paraguay (entry stamp available on the island).

Miranda ⊜🌐🏫🛖🏞🎓 ▸▸ *pp747-756. Colour map 3, B2.*

→ *See also map page 744.* Population: 23,000.

This little farming town built around a now disused mill and a railway station lies some 200 km west of Campo Grande at the turn-off to Bonito. It has long been overlooked as a gateway to the Pantanal and Bonito, but is actually far closer to both than either Corumbá or Campo Grande. Many of the best of the southern Pantanal *fazendas* are found here:

San Francisco has an impressive big cat project and almost guaranteed ocelot or jaguar sightings, while **Refúgio Ecológico Caiman** would sit comfortably within the pages of *Condé Nast Traveller*. Miranda is also a real town, preoccupied more with its own local economy and culture than with tourism. It lies in the heart of indigenous Terena land and the communities have a large **cultural and arts centre** ① *at the entrance to town, Mon-Fri 0700-2200, Sat and Sun 0800-2200, free*, with panels on Terena history and arts and crafts for sale. Every October Miranda throws the spectacular **Festa do Homem Pantaneiro**: four days of rodeos, lassoing and general revelry that combine well with the water festival in Corumbá. For dates ask tour operators (see page 753). The crystal-clear river Salobrinho just outside town has great birdlife and a community of giant otters. There is a wonderful British girder bridge just west of town given as a gift to Brazil by King George V.

Ins and outs The Campo Grande–Corumbá road crosses the Rio Miranda bridge (two service stations before it), then continues paved all the way to cross the Rio Paraguai. Miranda is served by numerous daily buses from Corumbá, Campo Grande and Bonito. There is a tourist booth just outside the *rodoviária*, opposite the **Zero Hora** bakery and supermarket. Rail services to Corumbá, onwards to Bolivia and eventually to Campo Grande are due to recommence in 2009. There is no tourist office but Aguas do Pantanal can provide information in English, see also www.mirandaemfoco.com. The town is tiny and can be walked from end to end in less than 10 minutes.

Miranda

N

Not to scale

Sleeping 🛏
Aguas do Pantanal 1
Chalé 2
Diogo 3

Pantanal 4

Eating 🍴
Cantina dell'Amore 1

Zero Hora 2

→ *Phone code: 067. Population: 95,000.*

Situated on the south bank of the Rio Paraguai, by a broad bend, 15 minutes from the Bolivian border, Corumbá has long been considered the best starting point for visiting the southern part of the Pantanal. While many tour operators have moved to Campo Grande, Corumbá offers trips by boat or jeep and access to the major hotel and farm accommodation. Almost all of the Campo Grande agencies have offices here and there are still a number of upmarket cruise companies along the waterfront.

Corumbá was one of South America's most important river ports in the 19th century and has beautiful views along the river, especially at sunset, and some remnant colonial architecture. The compact streets include the spacious **Praça da Independência** and **Avenida General Rondon** (between Frei Mariano and 7 de Septembro), which has a

Corumbá

N

100 metres
100 yards

Sleeping 🛏
Aguas do Pantanal **2**
Angola **5**
Corumbá IYHA **7**
Nacional Palace & Pérola
do Pantanal Tours **1**

Premier **4**
Salette **6**
Santa Rita **3**

Eating 🍴
Almanara **3**

Avalom **6**
Laço de Ouro **5**
Panela Velha **4**
Peixeria de Lulú **2**
Verde Frutti **1**

Border essentials: Brazil–Bolivia

Corumbá (Brazil)–Puerto Suárez (Bolivia)

You will need to present a yellow fever vaccination certificate to enter Bolivia. If you arrive in Brazil without a yellow fever vaccination certificate, you may have to go to Rua 7 de Setembro, Corumbá, for an inoculation. There are money changers only at the border and in Quijarro (Bolivia).

Immigration Formalities are constantly changing, so check procedures in advance at the tourist office or *polícia federal*. At present passports are stamped at the *rodoviária* Monday to Friday 0800-1130 and 1330-1700, and at the **Brazilian Polícia Federal** (Praça da República 37, Corumbá) at weekends 0800-1130 and 1330-1700. The visa must be obtained on the day of departure. If exiting Brazil in order to get a new visa, remember that exit and entry must not be on the same day.

Transport Leaving Brazil, take Canarinho city bus marked 'Fronteira' from the port end of Rua Antônio Maria Coelho to the Bolivian border (15 minutes, US$0.35), walk over the bridge to Bolivian immigration (blue building), then take a *colectivo* to Quijarro or Puerto Suárez. Taxis to the border cost US$6-8.

When entering Brazil from Quijarro, take a taxi or walk to the Bolivian border to go through formalities. Just past the bridge, on a small side street to the right, is the bus stop for Corumbá. Take a bus marked 'Fronteira' or 'Tamengo' to Praça da República (US$0.80, every 45 minutes 0630-1915); don't believe taxi drivers who say there is no bus. Taxi to the centre US$6. Brazilian immigration formalities are carried out at the *polícia federal*.

Into Bolivia Over the border from Corumbá are Arroyo Concepción, Puerto Quijarro and Puerto Suárez. From Puerto Quijarro a 650-km railway runs to Santa Cruz de la Sierra. There is a road of sorts. A better road route is from Cáceres to San Matías, then to San Ignacio (see page 761). There are internal flights from Puerto Suárez.

---

palm-lined promenade that comes to life in the evenings. The **Forte Junqueira**, the city's most historic building, which may be visited only through a tour agency, was built in 1772. In the Serra do Urucum hills to the south is the world's greatest reserve of manganese, now being worked.

Ins and outs

The **airport** ① *4 km west of town*, receives flights from Campo Grande, Cuiabá, Londrina and São Paulo (via Campo Grande). There is no public transport from the airport to town; you have to take a taxi (US$6). The **rodoviária** ① *R Porto Carreiro at the south end of R Tiradentes*, is next to the railway station. A city bus to Praça da República costs US$0.80. Taxis are extortionate, but moto-taxis charge only US$0.65. Corumbá is well connected by bus to Campo Grande and Bolivia.

The municipal tourist office, **Sematur** ① *R América 969, T067-231 7336*, provides general information and city maps. The combination of economic hard times and drug running make the city unsafe late at night.

There is a lively festival every October. Corumbá is hot (particularly between September and January), with 70% humidity; June and July are cooler. Mosquitoes can be a real problem from December to February.

Mato Groso do Sul listings

For Sleeping and Eating price codes and other relevant information, see pages 42-47.

Sleeping

Campo Grande *p738, map p739*
The better hotels lie near the city centre. There are lots of cheaper hotels in the streets around the *rodoviária* so it is easy to leave bags in the *guarda volumes* and shop around. This area is not safe at night.
L Jandaia, R Barão do Rio Branco 1271, T067-3316 7700, www.jandaia.com.br. The city's best hotel, aimed at a business market. Modern well-appointed rooms (with Wi-Fi) in a tower. The best are above the 10th floor. Pool, gym and some English spoken.
A-B Advanced, Av Calógeras 1909, T067-3321 5000, www.hoteladvanced.com.br. Clean, spacious, spartan rooms with en suites and boiler-heated showers, in a 1980s block with a very small pool. Cheaper with fan.
A-B Internacional, R Alan Kardec 223, T067-3384 4677, www.hotelinternacional.com.br. Small but comfortable rooms with a/c or fans and flatpack furniture, or newly renovated suites with smart bathrooms in slate and tile and cable TV. Pool and restaurant. Quiet street near the *rodoviária*.
C Concord, Av Calógeras 1624, T067-3384 3081, www.hotelconcordinn.com.br. A standard town hotel with a small pool and renovated a/c rooms with modern fittings.
D-E Iguaçu, R Dom Aquino 761, T067-3384 4621, www.hoteliguacu.com.br. Very popular well-kept hotel next to the *rodoviária* with smart, simple a/c rooms with cable TV. Good breakfast.
D-E Nacional, R Dom Aquino 610, T067-3383 2461, hotelnacional@ig.com.br. Quiet, well-kept hotel with simple rooms with fans and proper mattresses. Some

en suites. TV room and internet. Better value than the nearby IYHA.
E IYHA, R Joaquim Nabuco 185, opposite *rodoviária*, T067-3321 0505, ajcampo grande@hotmail.com. Simple, musty little rooms with saggy foam mattress beds and frayed en suites. Laundry, kitchen, internet, reception open 24 hrs. **Ecological Expeditions** (see Activities and tours, page 753) offers Pantanal trips from their office next door. The other IYHA in the **Rocha Hotel** at R Barão Rio Branco 343, T067-3325 6874, has marginally better rooms for 10% more, but the mattresses are still hot and foamy.
E-F Cosmos, R Dom Aquino 771, near the *rodoviária*, T067-3384 4270. Very simple but bright and well-kept 1980s rooms with decent mattresses and en suites.
E-F Pousada LM, R 15 de Novembro 201, by Praça Ari Coelho, T067-3321 5207, www.lmhotel.com.br. Tiny, basic en suites set around a courtyard, all with TV and fridge, some with terraces. Cheaper with fan.

Ponta Porã *p741*
Brazilian hotels include breakfast in tariff; Paraguayan ones do not.
A-B Barcelona, R Guia Lopes 45, T067-3431 3061. Simple but well kept, with a/c or fan-cooled rooms. Bar and sauna.
C Alvorada, Av Brasil 2977, T067-3431 5866. With a good café, close to post office, good value but often full.
C-D Internacional, R Internacional 1267, T067-3431 1243. Cheaper without a/c. Hot water, good breakfast. Recommended.
E Dos Viajantes, R Albino Torraca 591, T067-3421 8817, across park opposite the railway station. Very basic and only for those on the tightest budget.

Bonito *p741, map p742*

AL Pira Miuna, R Luís da Costa Leite 1792, T067-3255 1058, www.piramiunahotel. com.br. Huge, ugly brick building with the most comfortable a/c rooms in the centre and a large pool area with jacuzzis and a bar.

AL Pousada Olho d'Água, Rod Três Morros, Km 1, T067-3255 1430, www.pousadaolhod agua.com.br. Comfortable accommodation in fan-cooled cabins set in an orchard next to a small lake. Horse riding, bike rental, solar-powered hot water and great food from the vegetable garden. Recommended.

A Tapera, Estrada Ilha do Padre, Km 10, on the hill above the Shell station on the road to Jardim, T/F067-3255 1700, www.tapera hotel.com.br. Peaceful location with fine views and cool breezes. Very comfortable, but own transport an advantage.

C Canaã, R Col Pilad Rebuá 1376, T067-3255 1282, www.hotelcanaabonitoms.com.br. A scruffy lobby leads to gloomy though reasonably well-maintained 1980s motel-style rooms with a/c and en suites. Also has a tour agency.

C-E Albergue do Bonito, R Lúcio Borralho 716, Vila Donária, T/F067-3255 1462, www.aj bonito.com.br. IYHA youth hostel. A well-run hostel with a travel agency, pool, kitchen and laundry facilities. English spoken, very friendly. Price per person for dorms.

C-E São Jorge Hostel, R Col Pilad Rebuá 1605, T067-3255 4046, www.pousadasao jorge.com.br. Clean dorms with bunks and en suites (the best with 2 bathrooms) and a pleasant public dining area with snack bar. Price per person for dorms.

D Pousada Muito Bonito, R Col Pilad Rebuá 1448, T/F067-3255 1645, www.muito bonito.com.br. Price per person in en suites or dorm-style rooms with bunk beds, all with a nice shared patio. Clean, excellent and with helpful owners and a tour operator (Mario Doblack at the tour office speaks English, French and Spanish). The price includes breakfast.

Camping

Camping Rio Formoso, Rodovia Bonito/ Guia Lopes da Laguna km 06, T067-9284 5994. With space for 60 tents.

Ilha do Padre, 12 km north of Bonito, US$10 by taxi, T/F067-9986 4598. On an island with natural pools, very pleasant, no regular transport. 4 rustic cabins with either 4 bunk beds or 2 bunks and a double, US$10 per person. Youth hostel with dorms, US$5 per person, same price for camping. Toilets, showers, clothes washing, meals available, bar, electricity, lots of trees. You can swim anywhere. To enter the island for a day US$3.

Miranda *p743, map p744*

A-D Aguas do Pantanal, Av Afonso Pena 367, T067-242 1242, www.aguasdopantanal. com.br. Much the best in town with a good range of very comfortable a/c rooms and cheaper backpacker accommodation, an attractive pool surrounded by tropical flowers and a very helpful travel agency (see page 753). They usually have a rep waiting at the *rodoviária*.

C Hotel Chalé, Av Barão do Rio Branco 685, T067-242 1216, hotelchale@star5.com.br. Plain a/c motel-like rooms with tiled floors and en suites, and a pool.

C Pantanal Hotel, Av Barão do Rio Branco 609, T067-3242 1068. Standard town hotel with pool and well-maintained a/c rooms with en suite, set along a gloomy corridor.

D-E Diogo, Av Barão do Rio Branco s/n, T067-242 1468. Very simple but well-kept doubles, triples and quadruples, some with a/c.

Fazendas around Miranda

Prices below include accommodation, all food and at least 2 guided trips per day. Standard packages include jeep trips, trail walks, horse riding, boat trips (where the *fazenda* has a river) and night safaris. They do not always include transfer from Miranda or the Buraco da Onca and this should be checked when booking. Unless otherwise indicated the standard of wildlife guiding will be poor, with common familial or generic names known only for animals and little awareness of species diversity or numbers. Keen birdwatchers should request a specialist birding guide through their tour operator or *fazenda*. Also take a good pair of binoculars and some field guides (see Books, page 821). The following *fazendas* can be booked through **Impacto** in Campo Grande, page 753, or **Águas do Pantanal Turismo** in Miranda, page 753. Tours are the same price even if you are on your own, but there are almost always other guests.

LL Refúgio Ecológico Caiman, 36 km from Miranda, T011-3706 1800, www.caiman.com.br. The most comfortable, stylish accommodation in the Pantanal in a hotel reminiscent of a Mexican hacienda. Tours and guiding are excellent. Part of the **Roteiros de Charme** group (see page 43).

AL Cacimba de Pedra, Estr Agachi, T067-9982 4655, www.cacimbadepedra.com.br. A Jacaré caiman farm and *pousada* in beautiful dry deciduous forest cut by trails and dotted with lakes. A/c rooms are simple but spruce and sit in front of an inviting pool. The forest is abundant with wildlife. There is a hyacinth macaw nest on the farm and tapir sightings are common.

AL Fazenda Campo Lourdes, T067-3026 5786, www.campolourdes.com.br. One of the most remote *fazendas* in the heart of wild country. Rustic but comfortable accommodation.

AL Fazenda San Francisco, turn off BR-262 30 km west of Miranda, T067-3242 3333, www.fazendasanfrancisco.tur.br. One of the best places in the Pantanal to see wild cats, which are preserved through Roberto Coelho's imaginative **Gadonça** project, www.procarnivoros.org.br, a pioneering initiative that encourages the preservation of natural big cat prey to reduce losses from jaguar kills on cattle. The scheme has been a great success. Birding is also excellent. Accommodation is simple but very well kept in rustic a/c cabins around a pool in a garden filled with rheas. There are plans to build chic new cabins. Food and guides are excellent. Birdwatchers should request Alyson (see Activities and tours, page 753) at least a week in advance.

AL Fazenda Santa Ines, Estr La Lima, Km 19, www.fazendasantaines.com.br. A very comfortable family-orientated *fazenda* overlooking an artificial lake. Tours are aimed firmly at the Campo Grande weekend market and although there is little wildlife here, food is excellent and there is a range of light adventure activities for kids.

AL-A Fazenda Baia Grande, Estr La Lima, Km 19, T067-3382 4223, www.fazendabaia grande.com.br. Very comfortable a/c rooms set around a pool in a bougainvillea and *ipê*-filled garden. The *fazenda* is surrounded by savannah and stands of *cerrado* broken by large lakes. The owner, Alex, is very friendly, eager to please and enthusiastic.

AL-A Fazenda Meia Lua, BR-262 Km 551, T067-8118 9757/3341 8143, www.brasil adentro.com.br/112432. Charming *fazenda* with a pool, lovely garden filled with hummingbirds and accommodation in chic a/c cabins or simple a/c rooms. The owners are very friendly and attentive. Only 10 mins from Miranda, a good option for those attending the Festa do Homem Pantaneiro.

A Fazenda 23 de Março, T067-3321 4737, www.fazenda23demarco.com.br. Simple rustic *fazenda* with only 4 rooms near Miranda in Aquidauna. There are programmes orientated to budget travellers, and **Centrapan**, a centre for the preservation of Pantanal culture, where visitors can learn to lasso, ride a bronco and turn their hand to other Pantanal cowboy activities.

Fazendas on the Estrada Parque

The Estrada Parque is a dirt road that cuts through the Pantanal near Miranda – running in a right angle through the wetlands and eventually arriving in Corumbá town. See map page 740.

LL-L Fazenda Xaraés, www.xaraes.com.br. One of the most luxurious *fazendas*, with a pool, tennis court, sauna, airstrip and modest but well-appointed a/c rooms in cream and terracotta. The immediate environs have been extensively cleared, but there are some wild areas of savannah and *cerrado* nearby and there are giant otters in the neighbouring Rio Abodrai.

L-AL Fazenda Barra Mansa, www.hotel barramansa.com.br. One of the better lodges in the region in a wild area right on the banks of the Rio Negro and between 2 large tracts of wetland. Like all the Rio Negro *fazendas* it is famous for its jaguars. Specialist guiding is available on request; be sure to stipulate this in advance. The farm also offers sport fishing, horseback riding and canoe trips on the river. Accommodation for up to 16 is in rustic a/c rooms with hammocks. There is a small library of field guides at the *fazenda*.

L-AL Fazenda Barranco Alto, Caixa postal 109, Aquidauana, Mato Grosso do Sul, T067-3241 4047, www.fazendabarrancoalto.com.br. A beautiful, remote large ranch on the banks of the Rio Negro and owned and run by and agronomist and his biologist wife. Along with the neighbouring **Fazenda Rio Negro**, it is one of the oldest *fazendas* in the Pantanal with farm buildings dating from the first half of the 20th century. The surrounding area has stands of *cerrado* set in seasonally flooded savannah cut by the river. Guiding is good but stipulate your interest in wildlife in advance, especially if you are a birder.

L-AL Fazenda Bela Vista, www.pousada belavista.com.br. 12 comfortable rooms in a *fazenda* on the banks of the Rio Papagaio in the foothills of the Serra do Urucum hills. This is a transition zone between Pantanal and higher ground and the range of habitats is one of the best in the southern Pantanal, with oxbows, savannah, *cerrado*, dry deciduous forest and xeric (grass and scrub) vegetation. Bird and primate life is very rich. Guiding is good if visitors stipulate their interest in wildlife in advance.

L-AL Fazenda Santa Sophia, T067-9648 9352, www.fazendasantasophia.com.br. A beautiful old wood and plaster *fazenda* on the Rio Negro near Barranco Alto. There are

no specialist nature guides (organize your own) but the scenery is wonderful and rich in wildlife and the accommodation simple but comfortable. All excursions are on horseback.

AL Pousada Rio Vermelho, T067-3321 4737, www.pousadariovermelho.com.br. A rustic *fazenda* in a wild area on the banks of a river famous for its population of jaguars. Simple but well-kept a/c rooms, with fridge. Organize your trip well in advance as the *fazenda* lies a long way off the Parque Estrada road.

Corumbá *p745, map p745*

There are hostels around the bus station, however this is a 10-min walk from the centre of town where most of the hotels, restaurants and tour agencies are found.

A-B Aguas do Pantanal, R Dom Aquino Corrêa 1457, T067-3231 6582, www.aguasdo pantanalhotel.com.br. The smartest in town together with the **Nacional Palace**, with a/c rooms in a 1980s tower, a pool and sauna.

A-B Nacional Palace, R América 936, T067-3234 6000, www.hnacional.com.br. Smart, modern a/c rooms, a decent pool and parking.

C-D Angola, R Antônio Maria Coelho 124, T067-3231 7727. Huge, scruffy a/c and fan-cooled rooms with en suites. Internet access. Safe as it lies in front of the *polícia federal*.

C-E Salette, R Delamaré 893, T067-3231 6246. Cheap and cheerful with a range of rooms, the cheapest with fans and shared bathrooms. Recommended.

D Premier, R Antônio Maria Coelho 389, T067-3231 4937. Basic *pousada* with small a/c rooms without windows. Prices negotiable.

D Santa Rita, R Dom Aquino 860, T067-3231 5453. Modern, well-kept hotel with a/c rooms, all with TVs and en suites.

D-E Corumbá IYHA, R Colombo 1419, T067-3231 1005, www.corumbahostel.com.br. A newly opened, well-equipped modern hostel with helpful staff and a pool. A/c or fan-cooled rooms and dorms.

O Eating

Campo Grande *p738, map p739*
Local specialities include *caldo de piranha* (soup), *chipa* (Paraguayan cheese bread, sold on the streets, delicious when hot) and the local liqueur, *pequi com caju*, which contains *cachaça* (sugar-cane rum). There are many cheap restaurants around the *rodoviária* and many others in the **Shopping Campo Grande** mall.

¶¶¶ Comitiva Pantaneira, R Dom Aquino 2221, T067-3383 8799. Hearty, tasty and very meaty regional dishes served by waiters in cowboy gear or as a buffet. Lunchtime only.

¶¶¶ Gaúcho Gastão, R 14 de Julho 775, T067-3384 4326. The best *churrascaria* in town, famous for its beef. Comfortable. Lunch only.

¶¶ Cantina Romana, R da Paz, 237, T067-3324 9777. Established for more than 20 years, Italian dishes, salads and a lunchtime buffet, good atmosphere.

¶¶-¶ Sabor en Quilo, R Barão do Rio Branco 1118 and R Dom Aquino 1786, T067-3383 3911. Lunchtime only. Self-service per kilo restaurants with plenty of choice including sushi on Sat.

¶ Morada dos Bais, Av Noroeste, 5140, corner with Afonso Pena, behind tourist office. Brazilian and Italian dishes, snacks and coffee served in a pretty courtyard, Lunchtime only.

Bonito *p741, map p742*

¶¶¶-¶¶ Santa Esmeralda, R Col Pilad Rebuá 1831. Respectable Italian food in one of the few a/c dining rooms.

¶¶ Cantinho do Peixe, R 31 de Março 1918, T067-3255 3381. À la carte Pantanal fish dishes including good *pintado na telha* (grilled surubim).

¶¶ Tapera, R Col Pilad Rebuá 480, T067-3255 1110. Good, home-grown vegetables, breakfast, lunch, pizzas, meat and fish dishes, opens 1900 for the evening meal.

¶ Da Vovó, R Sen F Muller 570, T067-3255 2723. A great per kilo restaurant serving Minas and local food all cooked in a traditional wood-burning aga. Plenty of veg and salads.

¶ Mercado da Praça, R 15 Novembro 376, T067-3255 2317. The cheapest in town. A snack bar housed in the local supermarket, offering sandwiches and juices 0600-2400.

Miranda *p743, map p744*

¶¶ Cantina Dell'Amore, Av Barão do Rio Branco 515, T067-3242 2826. The best in town with fish, pasta and *jacaré* steak.

¶ Zero Hora, Av Barão do Rio Branco at the *rodoviária*, T067-3242 1330. 24-hr snack bar, provision shop and, at the back, there's an average but good-value per kilo restaurant, with its own private waterfall.

Corumbá *p745, map p745*
Local specialities include *peixadas corumbaenses*, a variety of fish dishes prepared with the catch of the day; as well as ice cream, liquor and sweets made of *bocaiúva*, a small yellow palm fruit, in season Sep-Feb. There is a range of decent restaurants in R Frei Mariano including a number of *churrascarias* and pasta restaurants. You'll find plenty of good simple fish restaurant bars on the waterfront.

¶¶¶-¶¶ Avalom, R Frei Mariano 499, T067-3231 4430. Chic little restaurant bar with streetside tables and decent pasta, pizza and fish. Buzzing with a young middle-class crowd, especially after 2100 on Fri.

¶¶ Almanara, R América 961. Arabic and Turkish food from felafel to *baba ganoush*.

¶¶ Laço de Ouro, R Frei Mariano 556, T067-3231 7371. Very popular fish restaurant with a lively atmosphere and tables spilling out onto the street. Similar crowd to **Avalom**.

¶¶-¶ Peixeria de Lulú, R Dom Aquino 700, T067-3232 2142. A local institution that has been selling good river fish for many years.

¶ Panela Velha, R 15 de Novembro 156, T067-3232 5650. Popular lunchtime restaurant with a decent, cheap all-you-can-eat buffet.

¶ Verde Frutti, R Delamaré 1164, T067-3231 3032. A snack bar with a wide variety of juices and great, ice-cold *acai na tigela*.

🕤 Bars and clubs

Campo Grande *p738, map p739*
The best of the chic bars are on R Afonso Pena, beyond the monument, and along the streets to the north of Afonso Pena.
Choppão, R Dom Aquino 2331, T067-3383 9471. Lively open-sided bar with live music from Thu to Sat.
Morada dos Bais, see Eating, above. Restaurant and *choperia*, live music in the courtyard, daily from 2030, free.
Mostarda, Av Afonso Pena 3952, T067-3026 8469. Popular 20- and 30-something bar which is always lively after 2200 and hosts live music at weekends.

Clubs
There are a number of clubs open Thu-Sat, including **Tango**, R Cândido Mariano 2181, www.tangobar.com.br, and for something a little more alternative try **Bazar** or **Garagem**, R Doutor Temístocles 94.

Bonito *p741, map p742*
Bollicho Bar, R Col Pilad Rebuá 1996, T067- 3255 3299. Always thronging with young people any night of the week and serving hot chocolate, *caipirinhas*, snacks and *chopp* to the sound of live music at weekends.
O Taboa, R Col Pilad Rebuá 1837, T067-3255 1862. The liveliest in town with occasional bands and good *caipirinhas* and *chopp*.

🎪 Festivals and events

Miranda *p743, map p744*
Mid-Oct/early Nov Festa do Homem Pantaneiro, rodeos, lasso competitions, live *sertanejo* bands, barn dances and 4 days of cowboy revelry. Can be combined with Corumbá's water festival. For dates contact **Aguas do Pantanal** in Miranda (see page 753).

Corumbá *p745, map p745*
2 Feb Festa de Nossa Senhora da Candelária, Corumbá's patron saint, all offices and shops are closed.
24 Jun Festa do Arraial do Banho de São João, fireworks, parades, traditional food, processions and the main event – the bathing of the image of the saint in the Rio Paraguai.
21 Sep Corumbá's anniversary, includes a Pantanal fishing festival held on the eve.
Mid-Oct Festival Pantanal das Águas, with street parades featuring giant puppets, street dancing and occasional water fights.

🛍 Shopping

Campo Grande *p738, map p739*
Local native crafts, including ceramics, tapestry and jewellery, are of good quality. A local speciality is *os bugres da conceição* (squat wooden statues covered in moulded wax). Very good selections are found at **Casa do Artesão**, Av Calógeras 2050, on the corner with Av Afonso Pena. Mon-Fri 0800-2000, Sat 0800-1200. Also try: **Barroarte**, Av Afonso Pena 4329, and **Arte do Pantanal**, Av Afonso Pena 1743. There is a market (*Feira Livre*) on Wed and Sat. **Shopping Campo Grande**, Av Afonso Pena 4909, www.shoppingcampo grande.com.br, is the largest shopping mall in town, on its eastern edge.

Corumbá *p745, map p745*
Shops tend to open early and close by 1700.
Casa do Artesão, R Dom Aquino 405, in a converted prison. Mon-Fri 0800-1200, 1400-1800, Sat 0800-1200, good selection of handicrafts and a small bookshop.
CorumbArte, Av Gen Rondon 1011. Good silk-screen T-shirts with Pantanal motifs.
Frutal, R 13 de Junho 538. Open 0800-2000. Supermarket.
Livraria Corumbaense, R Delamaré 1080. Useful for state maps.
Ohara, Dom Aquino 621, corner Antônio João. Supermarket.

▲ Activities and tours

Wildlife guides for the Pantanal
See also tour operators and guides for the northern Pantanal, page 767 and box page 736.
Alyson is a Londrina-based birding guide who works with **Neblina Forest Tours** (www.neblinaforest.com); available through **Fazenda San Francisco**.
Juan Mazar Barnett, T+54 (0)11-4312 6345, www.seriemanaturetours.com. Very experienced Buenos Aires-based birding guide and editor of *Cotinga* magazine. Expert on *chaco* and Pantanal birds. Book well ahead; expensive.

Campo Grande *p738, map p739*
City Tour, T067-3321 0800, or through the Campo Grande Pantanal visitor centre and most larger hotels. Half-day tours of the city's sights including the Museu Dom Bosco and the Parque das Nações Indígenas.

Tours to the southern Pantanal
Ecological Expeditions, R Joaquim Nabuco 185, T067-321 0505, www.pantanal trekking.com; with another office in Corumbá, see below. Attached to the youth hostel at the bus station. Offers budget camping trips and lodge-based trips in **Nhecolândia** (sleeping bag needed) for 3, 4 or 5 days ending in Corumbá. The first day, which involves travel to the Buraco da Piranha, is free.
Impacto, R Padre João Crippa 686, T067-3325 1333, www.impactotour.com.br. Very helpful Pantanal and Bonito tour operator established over 10 years. Prices vary according to standard of accommodation; a wide range is offered. 2-day packages for 2 people US$190-600. Transfers and insurance included. English spoken.
Open Door Tour, R Allan Kardec 87, Galeria Maria Auxiliadora, sala 4, T067-3321 8303, www.opendoortur.com.br. Specialists in the Pantanal and Amazon. Booking agents for flights and buses.

Bonito and around *p741, map p742*
There is very little to choose between agencies in Bonito. English speakers are hard to come by. We list only those who also offer transport or a specialist service such as cave diving. Rafting trips cost US$15 per person, minimum 4 people for a 2½-hr trip.
Impacto, R Col Pilad Rebuá 1515, T067-3255 1414. English-speaking staff. Can be pre-booked through their efficient head office in Campo Grande or through **Aguas do Pantanal Turismo** in Miranda (see below).
Ygarapé, R Col Pilad Rebuá 1956, T067-3255 1733, www.ygarape.com.br. English spoken. PDSE accredited cave diving.

Miranda *p743, map p744*
Tours to the southern Pantanal
Both of the operators below can organize accommodation during the **Festa do Homem Pantaneiro** (see Festivals and events, above).
Aguas do Pantanal Turismo, Aguas do Pantanal hotel, Av Afonso Pena 367, T067-3242 1242, www.aguasdopantanal.com.br. Very well-organized tours to the *fazendas* around Miranda, to those on the Estrada Parque, and to the sights around Bonito. Also offers exclusive 1- or 2-day trips on the Rio Salobrinha to the Sanctuario Baía Negra. This is a little-visited clear water river that's great for snorkelling and teeming with life – particularly birds. Expect to see 4 species of kingfisher, screamers, bare-faced currasow and cocoi, boat-billed heron and numerous other varieties, storks and ibises. Bring insect repellent. Can also organize scenic flights.
Explore Pantanal, R Dr Alexandre 305, T067-3242 4310, T067-9638 3520, www.explore pantanal.com. Run by a Kadiweu indigenous guide and his Swiss partner, with many years of experience. Very good English, German, French, Spanish and Italian and decent Hebrew. Great for small groups who want to get off the beaten track. Trips to Bonito (including pre-arranged transport), camping tours and day tours. Prices are competitive with budget operators in Campo Grande and Corumbá. For best rates book ahead.

Corumbá *p745, map p745*

Tours to the southern Pantanal
Ecological Expeditions, R Antônio Maria
Coelho 78. Main office in Campo Grande.
Mutum Turismo, R Frei Mariano 17, T067-
3231 1818, www.mutumturismo.com.br.
Cruises and upmarket tours (mostly aimed
at the Brazilian market) and help with
airline, train and bus reservations.
Pantur, R América 969, T067-3231 2000,
www.pantur.com.br. Packages to Bonito
and the *fazendas* on the Estrada Parque,
including some of the less visited, such
as **Bela Vista** (the best for primates) and
the luxurious **Xaraes**. Flights and bus
tickets can be booked here too.
Confusing website; click on the
flags for tour details.

Pantanal fishing and river cruises
Pérola do Pantanal, Nacional Palace
(see Sleeping), T067-3231 1470,
www.peroladopantanal.com.br. Fishing
and 'eco' tours on their large river boat,
Kalypso, with options of added jeep
trips on the Estrada Parque.

☉ Transport

Campo Grande *p738, map p739*
Air The airport is 7km from the city centre;
to get there take city bus No 158, which
stops outside the airport; taxi US$6.

As ever, the cheapest flights are
available on line. Agencies in the city
(many offices in front of the *rodoviária*)
will book online and charge to credit cards.
Campo Grande has flights to **Brasília**,
Cuiabá, **Manaus**, **Porto Alegre**, **Santa
Cruz** (Bolivia), **São Paulo**, **Ji-Paraná**,
Porto Velho, **Corumbá**, **Goiânia**,
Londrina, **Belo Horizonte**, **Dourados**,
Campinas, **Corumbá**, **Cuiabá**,
Curitiba, **Salvador** and many others.

Airlines include: **GOL**, www.voe
gol.com.br, **Oceanair**, www.oceanair.com.br,
TAM, www.tam.com.br; **TRIP**, www.voetrip.
com.br; and **Webjet**, www.webjet.com.br.

Bus Town buses leave from the
R Vasconcelos Fernandes end of the
rodoviária, while state and interstate buses
leave from the R Joaquim Nabuco end.

To **São Paulo**, US$80, 14 hrs, 9 buses
daily, first at 0800, last at 2400, 3 *leito* buses
US$105. To **Cuiabá**, US$45, 10 hrs, 12 buses
daily, *leito* at 2100 and 2200, US$55. To
Brasília, US$80, 23 hrs at 1000 and 2000.
To **Goiânia**, with São Luís at 1100, 2000,
15 hrs on 1900 service, US$65, others 24 hrs,
but only US$5 cheaper. **Rio de Janeiro**,
US$80, 21 hrs, 4 buses daily, *leito* at 1540,
US$100. To **Belo Horizonte**, 22 hrs, US$80.
To **Corumbá**, with **Andorinha**, 8 daily
from 0600, 6 hrs, US$35. Campo Grande–
Corumbá buses connect with those from
Rio and São Paulo, similarly those from
Corumbá through to Rio and São Paulo.
To **Ponta Porã**, 5 hrs, 9 buses daily, US$15.
To **Dourados**, 4 hrs, 14 daily (Queiroz),
US$14. Beyond Dourados is **Mundo Novo**,
from where buses go to **Ponta Porã** (0530)
and to **Porto Frajelli** (very frequent). From
Mundo Novo, ferries for cars and passengers
go to **Guaíra** for US$3. Twice daily direct
service to **Foz do Iguaçu** (17 hrs) with
Integração, 1600, US$45; same company
goes to **Cascavel**, US$40. To **Pedro Juan
Caballero** (Paraguay), del Amambay
company, 0600, US$21. **Amambay** goes
every Sun morning to **Asunción** (Paraguay).

Car hire Hertz, Av Afonso Pena 2620
and airport, T067-3383 5331. **Locagrande**,
Av Afonso Pena 466, T067-3721 3282.
Localiza, Av Afonso Pena 318, T067-3382
8786, and at the airport, along with various
others T0800- 992000. **Unidas**, Av Afonso
Pena 829, T067-3384 5626, at airport,
T067-3363 2145.

Ponta Porã p741
Bus To **Campo Grande**, 9 a day 0100-2130, 4 hrs, US$15.

Bonito p741, map p742
Bus To **Campo Grande**, 0530, US$15, 5½-6 hrs. Buses use the MS-345, with a stop at **Autoposto Santa Cruz**, Km 60 (all types of fuel, food and drinks available). Several daily buses to **Miranda**. Some buses to Corumbá and Campo Grande buses call in here; check at the *rodoviária*. There is a bus that runs Corumbá– Miranda–Bonito–Jardim–Ponta Porã, Mon-Sat, leaves either end at 0600, arriving Bonito at 1230 for **Ponta Porã** or 1300 for **Miranda**; for **Campo Grande** it's also possible to change in Jardim (1400 for 1700 bus) or Miranda, which have better connections. The fare to **Corumbá** is US$15. There are also connections on the 1230 route to **Bela Vista** at 2000 or **Asunción** (Paraguay) and **Col Oviedo** (Paraguay). Ticket office opens at 1200.

Car hire Unidas, R das Flores s/n, T067-255 1066. **Yes Rent a Car**, R Senador Filinto Muller 656, T067-255 1702.

Jardim p743
Bus To **Campo Grande**, 0530, 1200, 1600 and 2 at night, US$25, 5 hrs. To **Bonito** (US$6.50), **Miranda** and **Corumbá** at 1130. To **Dourados**, 0600. To **Bela Vista** (Paraguayan border) 0200, 1030, 1500, 1930. To **Porto Murtinho**, 0010 and 1530 (bus from Bonito connects). To **Ponta Porã**, 0600, 1500; Sun only at 1400 to **São Paulo**.

Miranda p743, map p744
Bus To **Campo Grande**, 12 a day (2- 3 hrs), US$15. To **Corumbá**; 10 daily (3-4 hrs), US$15. To **Bonito**, 1 daily (2-3 hrs), US$9 at 1630.

Car hire Mavel, Av Afonso Pena 31, T067-3242 1734 or through **Aguas do**

Pantanal hotel. Also bookable through **Explore Pantanal** (with a surcharge).

Corumbá p745, map p745
Air The airport is 3 km from the city centre; taxi US$6 or there is an infrequent bus. Flights to **Brasília** and **Campo Grande** with Tam, www.tam.com.br, and **Trip**, www.voetrip.com.br.

Boat The *Acurí*, a luxury vessel, sails between Corumbá and **Cáceres** once a week, US$600 including return by air. For further details, see Cáceres transport, page 769.

Bus Andorinha services to all points east. To **Campo Grande**, 7 hrs, US$25, 13 buses daily 0630-2400, interesting journey ('an excursion in itself'); take an early bus for a chance of seeing wildlife, connections from Campo Grande to all parts of Brazil. To **São Paulo** direct, 22 hrs, US$90, 1100 and 1500, confirm bus times in advance as these change (T067-3231 2033). To **Rio de Janeiro** direct, 30 hrs, US$105, daily 1100. Cruzeiro do Sul operates the route south to the **Paraguayan border**. To **Ponta Porã**, 12 hrs, US$40, Bonito (6 hrs, US$20) and Jardim (9 hrs, US$25). At least 4 daily to **Miranda**. Mon-Sat at 0600; ticket office open 0500-0600 only, at other times call T067-3231 2383.

Car hire Localiza, airport and R Cabral 2064, T067-231 6000. **Unidas**, R Frei Mariano 633, T/F067-231 3124.

ⓘ Directory

Campo Grande p738, map p739
Banks Banco do Brasil, 13 de Maio and Av Afonso Pena, open 1100-1600, charges commission US$10 for cash, US$20 for TCs, regardless of amount exchanged. Visa ATMs at **Bradesco**, 13 de Maio and Av Afonso Pena;

at HSBC, R 13 de Maio 2837; and at **Banco 24 horas**, R Maracaju, on corner with 13 de Junho. Also at R Dom Aquino and Joaquim Nabuco. **Overcash Câmbio**, R Rui Barbosa 2750, Mon-Fri 1000-1600. **Embassies and consulates** Bolivia, R João Pedro de Souza 798, T067-382 2190. Paraguay, R 26 Agosto 384, T067-324 4934. **Internet** Cyber Café Iris, Av Afonso Pena 1975, and **Cyber Café**, R Alan Kardec 374, T067-3384 5963 near the Hotel Turis. Also in the IYHA. **Medical services** Yellow and dengue fevers are both present in Mato Grosso do Sul; the former only in very remote areas. There is a clinic at the railway station, but it's not very hygienic, best to get your immunizations at home. **Post office** On corner of R Dom Aquino and Av Calógeras 2309, and Barão do Rio Branco on corner of Ernesto Geisel, both locations offer fax service, US$2.10 per page within Brazil. **Telephone** Telems, R 13 de Maio and R 15 de Novembro, daily 0600-2200.

Ponta Porã *p741*
Banks Banco do Brasil changes TCs. Many in the centre of town (but on Sun change money in hotels). Bradesco has a Visa ATM.

Bonito *p741, map p742*
Banks The town has a Bradesco bank for Visa ATM on Av Coronel Pilão Rebuá, 535. Banco do Brasil, R Luís da Costa Leite 2279 for Visa. Some hoteliers and taxi drivers may change money. **Post office** R Col Pilad Rebuá. **Telephone** Santana do Paraíso.

Jardim *p743*
Banks Elia, a taxi driver, will change money; ask around.

Miranda *p743, map p744*
Banks The town has both a Bradesco and a Banco do Brasil. **Internet** Star Informatica, R Francisco Rebúa 149, T067-3242 2100.

Corumbá *p745, map p745*
Banks Banco do Brasil, R 13 de Junho 914, ATM. HSBC, R Delamaré 1068, ATM. HSBC, R Delamaré 1068, ATM. Câmbio Mattos, R 15 de Novembro 140, Mon-Fri 0800-1700, good rates for US$ cash, US$5 commission on TCs. Câmbio Rau, R 15 de Novembro 212, Mon-Fri 0800-1700, Sat 0900-1200, cash only, good rates. **Embassies and consulates** Bolivia, R Antônio Maria Coelho 881, T067-231 5605, Mon-Fri 0700-1100, 1500-1730. A fee is charged to citizens of those countries that require a visa. A yellow fever vaccination certificate is also required. **Internet** Pantanalnet, R América 430, US$2.50 per hr. **Laundry** Apae, R 13 de Junho 1377, same day service. **Post office** Main office at R Delamaré 708, fax service. Branch at R 15 de Novembro 229. **Telephone** R Dom Aquino 951, near Praça da Independência, daily 0700-2200. To phone Quijarro/Puerto Suárez, Bolivia, costs slightly more than a local call; dial 214 + the Bolivian number.

Mato Grosso

Mato Grosso, immediately to the north of Mato Grosso do Sul, shares the Pantanal with that state and has equally well-developed tourism facilities. Although there are just as many opportunities for seeing wildlife, trips to the Pantanal near the state capital, Cuiabá, tend to be more upmarket than those leaving from Corumbá in Mato Grosso do Sul. The state also has abundant though rapidly depleting areas of Amazon forest; Alta Floresta, in the north, has an excellent birdwatching and wildlife lodge. The much-vaunted Chapada dos Guimarães hills near Cuiabá afford reasonable walking and birdwatching, although the natural landscape has been greatly damaged by farming and development. ▶ *For listings, see pages 763-770.*

Background

The area that is now Mato Grosso and Mato Grosso do Sul was first demarcated as Spanish territory, but it was the Portuguese Aleixo Garcia who was the first to explore it in 1525. Jesuits and then bandeirantes entered the Mato Grosso for their different ends during the 17th and early 18th centuries, and, when gold was discovered near Cuiabá, a new influx of explorers began. Mato Grosso became a captaincy in 1748 and the borders between Portuguese and Spanish territories were decided in the following years. Throughout the 19th century, after the decline in gold extraction, the province's economy stagnated and its population dwindled. This trend was reversed when the rubber boom brought immigrants in the early 20th century to the north of the region. Getúlio Vargas's 'March to the West' in the 1940s brought added development, accompanied first by the splitting off of Rondônia and by the formation of Mato Grosso do Sul in 1977.

Cuiabá ⊜🌐🎧🕙⚠️🏧🍴☕ ▶ *pp763-770. Colour map 3, A2.*

→ *Phone code: 065. Population: 470,000.*

An important starting point for trips into the Pantanal, Cuiabá is the state capital and a visibly wealthy city. It has a number of leafy *praças* and is known as the 'Cidade Verde' (green city). Situated on the Rio Cuiabá, an upper tributary of the Rio Paraguai, it is in fact two cities: **Cuiabá** on the east bank of the river, and **Várzea Grande** on the west. It is very hot; the coolest months for a visit are June, July and August in the dry season.

Ins and outs

Getting there Flights arrive at **Marechal Rondon airport** ① *R Gov Ponce de Arruda, s/n, Várzea Grande, T065-3614 2500, 10 km from the centre*, from Campo Grande, São Paulo, Rio and Salvador, amongst others. There are ATMs outside the airport, as well as a post office and **Sedtur** office. To get to the centre, take any white **Tuiuiú** bus (the name will be written on the side), from in front of the airport to Avenida Tenente Coronel Duarte. Taxis cost US$15. Interstate buses arrive at the **rodoviária** ① *north of the centre at R Jules Rimet, Bairro Alvorada*. Town buses stop at the entrance of the *rodoviária*. ▶ *See Transport, page 769.*

Getting around Many bus routes have stops in the vicinity of Praça Ipiranga. Bus Nos 501 or 505 ('Universidade') to the university museums and zoo (ask for 'Teatro') leave from Avenida Tenente Coronel Duarte by Praça Bispo Dom José, a triangular park just east of Praça Ipiranga.

Tourist information **Sedtur** ⓘ *Praça da República 131, next to the post office building, T/F065-3613 9300, Mon-Fri 0700-1800*, provides maps and general information on hotels and car hire. Staff are friendly and speak English and Spanish. They are very helpful in settling disputes with local tour companies. **Ramis Bucair** ⓘ *R Pedro Celestino 280*, is good for detailed maps of the region.

Sights

The most pleasant public space in Cuiabá is the lush **Praça da República** which is surrounded by a cluster of imposing buildings and dotted with sculptures and shady trees. Other pedestrian shopping streets and further squares lead off the *praça*. The brutalist façade of the **cathedral**, flanked by two functionalist clock towers, dominates the square. Until the late 1960s a beautiful 18th-century baroque church stood here but this was demolished to make way for the current building in a sweep of modernization that saw almost all the city's colonial charm destroyed.

On **Praça Ipiranga**, at the junction of avenidas Isaac Póvoas and Tenente Coronel Duarte, a few blocks southwest of the central squares, there are market stalls and an iron bandstand from Huddersfield in the UK, or Hamburg in Germany, depending on which story you believe.

On a hill beyond the square is the extraordinary church of **Bom Despacho**, built in the style of Notre Dame. It is best viewed from afar as it is sadly run down and not open to

Around Cuiabá

Sleeping 🏠
Araras Lodge **1**
Fazenda Piuval **2**
Fazenda Santa Teresa **6**

Pousada Rio Clarinho **3**
Pousada Rio Claro **4**
Pouso Alegre **5**

visitors. In front of the Assembléia Legislativa on Praça Moreira Cabral, is a point marking the **Geodesic Centre of South America** (see also under Chapada dos Guimarães, below).

The rather dusty **Museus de Antropologia, História Natural e Cultura Popular** ⓘ *Fundação Cultural de Mato Grosso, Praça da República 151, Mon-Fri 0800-1730, US$0.50,* are worth a look. There are interesting historical photos, a contemporary art gallery, indigenous weapons, archaeological finds and pottery. The section of stuffed wildlife from the Pantanal is disturbingly compelling.

At the entrance to the Universidade de Mato Grosso by the swimming pool, 10 minutes by bus from the centre, is the small **Museu do Índio/Museu Rondon** ⓘ *T065-3615 8489, www.ufmt.br/ichs/museu_rondon/museu_rondon.html, Tue-Sun 0800-1100, 1330-1700, US$1,* with artefacts from tribes mostly from the state of Mato Grosso. Particularly beautiful are the **Bororo** and **Rikbaktsa** headdresses made from macaw and currasow feathers, and the **Kadiwéu** pottery (from Mato Grosso do Sul). Continuing along the road through the campus, signed on the left before a right turn in the road, is the **Zoológico**

Cuiabá

To ❸ ❹

To ❽ ❾, Rodoviária & Chapada dos Guimarães   To Av CPA

Fauna Tour ❺
Ramis Bucair

❶ Cândido Mariano

Banco do Brasil ❺
❷
Bradesco ❸
Praça Alencastro   Buses to Rodoviária

Cathedral ✝

❹ Museus do Antropologia, História Natural e Cultura Popular   Praça da República ⓘ ✉

To University, Museu do Índio & Zoo

Praça Bispo Dom José

Praça Ipiranga Ⓜ

To Airport

Praça Moreira Cabral & Centro Geodésico da América do Sul

To Natureco

Bom Despacho

To Airport

To ❿ & Casa de Artesão

To University, Museu do Índio/Museu Rondon, Zoo & BR 364 to Campo Grande & Goiána

N
Not to scale

Sleeping 🛏
Amazon Plaza **2**
Best Western Mato Grosso Palace **1**
Ipanema **9**
Las Velas **10**
Mato Grosso **3**

Nacional **8**
Panorama **7**
Portal do Pantanal **6**
Pousada Eco do Pantanal **5**
Samara **4**

Eating 🍴
Choppão **4**
Getúlio **3**
Lanchonete da Marilda **2**
Miranda's **5**
Panela de Barro **1**

① *Tue-Sun 0800-1100, 1330-1700, free*. The jacaré, capybara, tortoise and tapir pen can be seen at any time, but are best in the early morning or late afternoon. It also has coatis, otters, rhea, various monkeys and peccaries and a few, birds.

The **Águas Quentes** hot springs are 86 km away (9 km south of the BR-163, 77 km east of Cuiabá) and can be visited as a day trip.

Chapada dos Guimarães ⊜🄑🄞🄐🄜🄑🄒 ➤ *pp763-770. Colour map 3, A2.*

➔ *Phone code: 065. Population: 13,500. www.chapadadosguimaraes.amm.org.br*

Although greatly damaged by agriculture and careless tourism development, the Chapada dos Guimarães is one of the oldest plateaux on earth and one of the most scenic areas in Mato Grosso. It begins to rise from the hot plains around Cuiabá some 50 km from that city, reaching over 700 m, and its sweeping savannahs are broken by patches of *cerrado* forest, curiously eroded rocks and many lovely grottoes, peaks and waterfalls.

Once the centre of an important diamond-prospecting region, today the area is a popular place for Cuiabanos to escape the heat of the city. It can be very busy on weekends and holidays. The Chapada lays claim to being the geodesic heart of the South American continent and about 8 km east of Chapada dos Guimarães town, at the **Mirante do Ponto Geodésico**, there is a monument officially marking this. It overlooks a great canyon with views of the surrounding plains, the Pantanal and Cuiabá's skyline on the horizon.

The region is shrouded in lore. Crystals abound, as do UFO spotters, and the rocks are said to have peculiar energizing properties. This is not as far fetched as it may at first seem: a local magnetic force that reduces the speed of cars has been documented here. Birdwatching here is fruitful, particularly as enthusiasts will find that the plateau, grassland and *cerrado* species complement those found in Alta Floresta and the Pantanal. Guides listed under the northern Pantanal (see page 768) can organize one- or two-day trips here and many are even based in the little town of Chapada dos Guimarães. Mammals, such as puma, jaguarundi, giant river otter and black-tailed marmoset can also be seen.

Chapada dos Guimarães town

The pleasant town of Chapada dos Guimarães, 68 km northeast of Cuiabá, is the most convenient and comfortable base for excursions. It has the oldest church in the Mato Grosso, **Nossa Senhora de Santana** (1779), a bizarre blending of Portuguese and French baroque styles, and a huge spring-water public **swimming pool** ① *R Dr Pem Gomes*, behind the town.

Ins and outs Frequent, regular buses run between Cuiabá and Chapada dos Guimarães town (about 1½ hours). The *chapada* can be visited in a long day trip either by self-drive (although access is via rough dirt roads that may deteriorate in the rainy season), bus or most easily through agencies such as **Fauna Tour** and **Natureco** (see page 768). The **tourist office** ① *R Quinco Caldas 100, near the praça*, provides a useful map of the region and can help organize tours. The **Festival de Inverno** is held in the last week of July; during this time, and around **Carnaval**, the town is very busy and accommodation is scarce and expensive.

Parque Nacional da Chapada dos Guimarães

This begins just west of Chapada dos Guimarães town, near where the Salgadeira tourist centre offers bathing, camping and an unsightly restaurant right beneath the **Salgadeira**

Border essentials: Brazil–Bolivia

Cáceres (Brazil)–San Matías (Bolivia)

An unpaved road runs from Cáceres to the Bolivian border at San Matías. Exit and entry formalities are carried out at **Brazilian immigration**, Rua Col Farías, Cáceres, closed Sunday. When closed, go to the **Polícia Federal**, Avenida Rubens de Medarca 909. **Bolivian immigration** in San Matías is open 1000-1200, 1500-1700. If crossing from Bolivia into Brazil, there are three luggage checks for drugs before the border.

San Matías is a busy little town with hotels, restaurants and a bank. The next major town in Bolivia is San Ignacio de Velasco, which is on the road route to Santa Cruz de la Sierra. Buses run from San Matías to San Ignacio and San Ignacio to Santa Cruz; there are also flights. See Transport, page 769.

waterfall. The beautiful 85-m **Véu da Noiva waterfall** (Bridal Veil), 12 km from the town, near Buriti (well signposted; take a bus to Cuiabá and ask to be dropped you off), is less blighted and can be reached by either a short route or a longer one through forest. Other sights include: the **Mutuca** beauty spot, named after a vicious horsefly that preys on tourists there; **Rio Claro**, a viewpoint over the breathtaking 80-m-deep **Portão do Inferno gorge**; and the **Cachoeirinha falls**, where there is another small restaurant.

An excursion can be made to the **Cidade de Pedra** rock formations, 25 km from town along the road to the diamond prospecting town of Água Fria. Nearby is a 300-m wall formed by the Rio Claro. About 60 km from town are the archaeological sites at **Pingador** and **Bom Jardim**, which include caverns with petroglyphs dating back some 4000 years.

Cáceres ⊜❶❷❸⊙▲❶❻ ↠ pp763-770. Colour map 3, A1.

→ Phone code: 065. Population: 86,000.

Cáceres is a very hot but hospitable town on the banks of the Rio Paraguai, 200 km west of Cuiabá. It has a number of well-preserved 19th-century buildings painted in pastel colours and is known for its many bicycles. Until 1960, Cáceres used to have regular boat traffic; today it is limited to a few tour boats and pleasure craft. River trips from Cuiabá to Corumbá are very difficult since boats on the Cuiabá river are few and irregular, but you can sometimes get to Corumbá by river from here; be prepared to wait around for a few days and travel in a pair or group if possible.

The **Museu de Cáceres** ⓘ R Antônio Maria by Praça Major João Carlos, is a small local history museum. Exhibits include indigenous funerary urns. The main square, **Praça Barão de Rio Branco**, has one of the original border markers from the Treaty of Tordesillas, which divided South America between Spain and Portugal. The praça is pleasant and shady during the day and, in the evenings between November and March, the trees are packed with thousands of chirping swallows (andorinhas); beware of droppings. The square is full of bars, restaurants and ice-cream parlours and comes to life at night.

The beautiful **Serra da Mangabeira** is about 15 km east, crossed by the road from Cuiabá; the town is also at the edge of the Pantanal. Vitória Regia lilies can be seen north of town, just across the bridge over the Rio Paraguai along the BR-174. There are archaeological sites on the river's edge north of the city.

Ins and outs

The **rodoviária** ① *Terminal da Japonesa, T065-3224 1261*, has bus connections with Cuiabá and Porto Velho. It is also possible to arrive on the *Acuri*, a luxury boat that travels between Corumbá and Cuiabá. At the waterfront you can hire a boat for a day trip, US$5 per person per hour, minimum three people; on holidays and some weekends there are organized day trips on the river. ▸▸ *See Transport, page 769.*

Along the Transpantaneira 😊😊 ▸▸ *pp763-770.*

Poconé to Porto Jofre → *Colour map 3, A2. Phone code: 065.*
A paved road turns south off the main Cuiabá to Cáceres road to **Poconé**, a scruffy town founded in 1781 and known as the 'Cidade Rosa' (pink city). Until 1995 there was much *garimpo* (illicit gold mining) activity north of town and many slag heaps can be seen from the road. There are numerous cheap hotels in town but there is no real advantage in staying here and most travellers pass through after organizing their tours direct with *fazendas* or through agents in Cuiabá (see page 767).

From Poconé it is 63-km south to Pixaim, a journey of two hours in the dry season and up to five in the wet. This is the only easily accessible settlement in the northern Pantanal with any tourist infrastructure – amounting to two hotels, a fuel station and a tyre-repair shop.

Barão de Melgaço and around → *Colour map 3, A2.*
Barão de Melgaço, 130 km from Cuiabá on the banks of the Rio Cuiabá, is far less visited than the Transpantaneira. Standing on the edge of extensive areas of lakeland and seasonally flooded *cerrado*, it is reachable by two roads. The shorter, via Santo Antônio do Leverger, is unpaved from Santo Antônio to Barão (closed in the wet season). The route via São Vicente is longer but is more extensively paved.

The best way to see the Pantanal from here is by boat down the Rio Cuiabá. Near the town, the riverbanks are lined with farms and small residences but become increasingly forested with lovely combinations of flowering trees (best seen September to October). After a while, a small river to the left leads to the Chacororé and Sia Mariana lakes, which join up via an artificial canal. The canal has resulted in the larger of the two lakes draining into the smaller one, and it has begun to dry out. Boats can continue beyond the lakes to the Rio Mutum, but a guide is essential because there are many dead ends. The area is rich in birdlife and the waterscapes are beautiful.

Boat hire costs up to US$85 for a full day and is available from **Restaurant Peixe Vivo** on the waterfront, or enquire with travel agencies in Cuiabá. The best time for a boat trip is sunset, but this will involve a return trip in the dark.

North of Cuiabá 😊😊 ▸▸ *pp763-770.*

Some 145 km north of Cuiabá is the little town of **Nobres**, which, like Bonito in Mato Grosso do Sul (see page 741), is surrounded by clear water rivers full of dourado fish, and many beautiful caves. Unlike Bonito, there are few tourists and the attractions are accordingly cheaper and less spoilt. The most spectacular cave is the **Gruta do Lagoa Azul**, which is open according to the whims of **Ibama**, Brazil's environmental protection agency; consult www.ibama.com. The town is served by regular buses from Cuiabá and Sinop/Alta Floresta, and **Natureco** (see Cuibá, page 768) offers trips here.

Alta Floresta → *Phone code: 065. Colour map 1, B4. Population: 71,500.*

The road that runs due north from Cuiabá to Santarém (1777 km) is passable in all weather conditions as far as **Sinop**, and has recently been asphalted as far as **Santarém**. This will enable soya from Mato Grosso to be shipped via the Amazon to the Atlantic. **Cargill** have already built an enormous plant in Santarém in anticipation. The areas around the road are among the principal victims of active deforestation, with land being cleared for cattle and soya farms. Soya is spreading beyond Mato Grosso into southern Pará.

There are, however, still extensive tracts of forest intact, especially near the **Rio Cristalino**, above which there is an extensive park and a vast military area. The rivers here are tributaries of the Tapajós and are mostly clear or black water, fairly mosquito free and overflowing with wildlife. Harpy eagles nest in the grounds of the **Floresta Amazônica** hotel in Alta Floresta town and can also be seen, along with other spectacular species, around the **Cristalino Jungle Lodge**, one of the best wildlife and birding lodges in the Brazilian Amazon. ▸▸ *See Sleeping, page 766.*

Ins and outs **Aeroporto Deputado Benedito Santiago** ⓘ *4 km from the city centre, Av Ariosto da Rivas s/n, T066-3521 2159*, has connections with both Cuiabá and Brasília with two of Brazil's larger airlines. There are also daily overnight buses from Cuiabá, 12 hours. The town was built in the late 1970s and laid out on a grid pattern. Finding your way around in straightforward. **Cristalino Jungle Lodge** representatives will meet you at the airport or bus station and transfer you to their hotels by 4WD.

East of Cuiabá ⊜⊘▲⊜ ▸▸ *pp763-770.*

São Félix do Araguaia → *Colour map 1, C5, Population: 14,500.*

This town has a high population of indigenous Carajás, whose handicrafts can be found between the pizzeria and **Mini Hotel** on Avenida Araguaia. There is some infrastructure for fishing. Indigenous *fazenda* owners may invite you as their guest. If you accept, remember to take a gift: pencils, radio batteries, a few sacks of beans or rice, or a live cockerel will be much appreciated. Many river trips are available for fishing or wildlife spotting. ▸▸ *See Activities and tours, page 769.*

Ins and outs Access to São Félix and Santa Teresinha is by bus from Cuiabá. The *rodoviária* is 3 km from the centre and waterfront, taxi US$5.

⊛ Mato Grosso listings

For Sleeping and Eating price codes and other relevant information, see pages 42-47.

⊜ Sleeping

Cuiabá *p757, map p759*
L Amazon Plaza, Av Getúlio Vargas 600, T065-2121 2000, www.hotelamazon.com.br. By far the best in the centre with very smart

modern rooms in a tower with good views. The chairs and decking in the relaxing, shady pool area are painted with pictures of Amazon wildlife. Excellent service. Broadband internet in all rooms.
L Hotel Águas Quentes, Águas Quentes spring, 86 km from Cuiabá, see page 760, whose pools of thermal waters are 36-42°C.

AL Best Western Mato Grosso Palace, Joaquim Murtinho 170, T065-3624 7747, www.hotelmt.com.br. Conveniently located behind Praça República. Practical, clean, standard 3-star rooms with cable TVs, fridges and excellent boiler-heated showers.

A Las Velas, Av Filinto Müller 62, T065-3682 3840, resvelas@terra.com.br. Less than 100 m from the airport. Clean, spacious a/c rooms (the executive ones are best and only a little more expensive) with newly renovated bathrooms, cable TV and boiler-heated showers. Free airport transfer for luggage.

B Nacional, Av Jules Rimet 22, T065-3621 3277. Opposite the front of the bus station and convenient for those who are just passing through. Plain a/c rooms with newly renovated en suites.

B-C Mato Grosso, R Comandante Costa 643, T065-3614 7777, www.hotelmt.com.br. The best-value mid-range option in the centre with newly renovated a/c or fan-cooled rooms with tiled floors and chintzy beds, the brightest of which are on the 2nd floor or above.

B-C Panorama, Praça Moreira Cabral 286, T065-3322 0072. A frayed 1980s tower with very simple, plain a/c or fan-cooled rooms with en suites; some have good views.

C Ipanema, Av Jules Rimet 12, T065-3621 3069. Opposite the front of the bus station. Very well-kept a/c or fan-cooled rooms, some with armchairs, cable TVs and smart en suites. Internet access and a huge lobby TV for films or football. Many other options between here and the **Nacional**.

C Portal do Pantanal, Av Isaac Póvoas 655, T/F065-3624 8999, www.portaldo pantanal.com.br. Youth hostel. Price per person, breakfast included, internet access (US$2.50 per hr), laundry, kitchen.

C Pousada Eco do Pantanal, R Campo Grande 487, T065-3624 1966, http://ecodo pantanal.com. The best-value economy option with well-kept, clean rooms with spacious en suites in a converted town house. Facilities include excellent tour agency, **Faunatour**, laundry service,

internet and free airport/bus station pickup (with 12 hrs' notice).

C Samara, R Joaquim Murtinho 270, T065-3322 6001. Very simple, scruffy rooms with en suite cold showers. No breakfast. Only come here if the other options are full.

Chapada dos Guimarães p760

See www.chapadadosguimaraes.com.br for further details.

L Pousada Penhasco, 2.5 km on Av Penhasco, Bom Clima, T065-3301 1555. Good views out over the plain from the *chapada*. 40 a/c rooms, tennis courts, swimming pool and a games area for children.

AL Solar do Inglês, R Cipriano Curvo 142, Centro, T065-3301 1389, www.chapada dosguimaraes.com.br. In an old converted house near town centre with 7 rooms, each with private bathroom, TV and frigobar. Garden, swimming pool and sauna. Breakfast and afternoon tea included.

A Estância San Francisco, at the entrance to town from Cuiabá (MT-251, Km 61), T065-3791 1102. On a 42-ha farm with 2 lakes, said to have the best breakfast in town fresh from the farm. Good for birding.

B Turismo, R Fernando Corrêa 1065, a block from the *rodoviária*, T065-3791 1176. A/c rooms with a fridge, cheaper with fan, restaurant, breakfast and lunch excellent, very popular, German-run. Ralf Goebel, the owner, is very helpful in arranging excursions.

B-C Rio's Hotel, R Tiradentes 333, T065-3791 1126. A/c rooms with a fridge, cheaper with fan, cheaper with shared bath, good breakfast.

C Pousada Bom Jardim, Praça Bispo Dom Wunibaldo, T065-3791 1244. Comfortable fan-cooled rooms with parking and good breakfast.

D São José, R Vereador José de Souza 50, T065-3791 1152. Fan-cooled rooms. Cheaper with a shared bath and no fan, hot showers, basic, good, owner Mário sometimes runs excursions.

Camping

Aldeia Velha, in the Aldeia Velha neighbourhood at the entrance to town from Cuiabá, T065-322 7178. Fenced area with bath, hot shower, some shade, guard.
Salgadeira, camping is possible 16 km from town at the tourist centre, watch out for your belongings.

Cáceres *p761*

A Caiçaras, R dos Operários 745 corner R Gen Osório, T065-3223 3187. Modern town hotel with a/c rooms and cheaper options without a fridge.
B Ipanema, R Gen Osório 540, T065-3223 1177, www.ipanemahotelmt.com.br. Simple town hotel with a/c rooms, a pool and a restaurant.
B-D Rio, Praça Major João Carlos 61, T065-3223 3387. A range of rooms, the cheapest can have shared bathrooms and no a/c.
C-D Charm, Col José Dulce 405, T/F065-3223 4949. A/c and fan-cooled rooms, with or without a shared bath.
D-E União, R 7 de Setembro 340. Fan-cooled rooms, cheaper with shared bath, basic but good value.

Along the Transpantaneira *p762*
Fazendas

See also page 748. Distances are given in kilometres from Poconé town. For tour operators, see Activities and tours, page 767.
L Fazenda Santa Teresa, Km 75, www.santaterezahotel.hpg.ig.com.br. A working *fazenda* with rustic a/c or fan-cooled accommodation, a pool and hearty food. There are giant otters in the river adjacent to the farm which are fed daily for show, making sightings almost guaranteed.
L Pousada Rio Clarinho, Km 42, book through Eco do Pantal (see page 763). Charming option on the Rio Clarinho. What it lacks in infrastructure, it makes up for in wildlife. The river has rare waterbirds such as agami heron and nesting hyacinth macaw, as well as river and giant otters and, occasionally, tapir. The boatman, Wander, has very sharp eyes be sure

to ask for him. Not to be confused with the nearby Pousada Rio Claro.
L Pousada Rio Claro, Km 42, www.pousadarioclaro.com.br, book through Eco do Pantanal or Natureco. Comfortable *fazenda* with a pool and simple a/c rooms on the banks of the Rio Claro, which has a resident colony of giant otters.
L Pouso Alegre, Km 36, T065-3626 1545, www.pousalegre.com.br. Rustic *pousada* with simple a/c or fan-cooled accommodation on one of the Pantanal's largest *fazendas*. It's overflowing with wildlife and particularly good for birds (especially on the morning horseback trail). Many new species have been catalogued here. The remote oxbow lake is particularly good for waterbirds (including agami and zigzag herons). The lodge is used by Ornitholidays and Neblina tours. Proper birding guides can be provided with advance notice. Best at weekends when the very knowledgeable owner Luís Vicente is there.
AL Araras Lodge, Km 32, T065-3682 2800, www.araraslodge.com.br. Book direct or through Eco do Pantanal or Natureco. One of the most comfortable places to stay with 14 a/c rooms. Excellent tours and food, home-made *cachaça*, a pool and a walkway over a private patch of wetland filled with capybara and caiman. Very popular with small tour groups from Europe. Book ahead.
A Fazenda Piuval, Km 10, T065-3345 1338, www.pousadapiuval.com.br. The first *fazenda* on the Transpantaneira and one of the most touristy, with scores of day visitors at weekends. Rustic farmhouse accommodation, a pool, excellent horseback and walking trails as well as boat trips on their vast lake. Very good for spotting hyacinth macaw.

Barão de Melgaço *p762*

There is a handful of cheaper options near the waterfront.
L Pousada Passárgada, www.pousadapassargada.com, reservations through Nature Safaris, or through agencies in Cuiabá, São Paulo (T011-3284 5434) or Rio

(T021-3287 3390). Much cheaper if booked direct with the owner, Maré Sigaud, Mato Grosso, CEP 786807, Pousada Passárgada, Barão de Melgaço. Programmes are for a minimum of 3 days and include full board, boat, 4WD and trekking expeditions. Transport from Barão de Melgaço either by boat or 4WD can be arranged with the owner who speaks English, French and German. Closed Dec-Feb.

C Barão Tour Hotel, Barão de Melgaço town. Apartments with a/c, restaurant, boat trips and excursions (contact the owner in Cuiabá T065-3322 1568).

Alta Floresta p763

L Cristalino Jungle Lodge, reservations Av Perimetral Oeste 2001, T065-3512 7100, www.cristalinolodge.com.br. A beautifully situated and well-run lodge. Trips from the lodge include canoeing and snorkelling in clear-water rivers, as well as the usual caiman spotting and piranha fishing. Also more adventurous options such as rapelling and canyoning. Birding is superb and the lodge has a lookout with a view over the canopy.
B Floresta Amazônica, Av Perimetral Oeste 2001, T065-3521 3601. In the park with lovely views, pool, sports, all facilities.
C Italian Palace, Av das Figueiras 493, Sinop, T065-3531 2109. With a restaurant, bar, sauna.
C Pirâmide Palace, Av do Aeroporto 445, T065-3521 2400. A/c rooms with fridges, restaurant.
D Grande Hotel Coroados, R F1 No118, T065-3521 3022. Not very well kept but has a/c, pool and bar.

São Félix do Araguaia p763

C Xavante, Av Severiano Neves 391, T062-3522 1305. A/c, frigobar, excellent breakfast, delicious *cajá* juice, the owners are very hospitable. Recommended.
E Pizzeria Cantinho da Peixada, Av Araguaia, next to the Texaco station, overlooking the river, T062-3522 1320. Rooms to let by the owner of the restaurant, better than hotels. He also arranges fishing trips.

⊘ Eating

Cuiabá p757, map p759

Many of the restaurants in the centre are only open weekdays for lunch. On **Av CPA** there are many good restaurants and small snack bars. **R Jules Rimet**, across from the *rodoviária*, has several cheap restaurants and *lanchonetes*.

₸₸₸ Getúlio, Av Getúlio Vargas 1147, at São Sebastião, T065-3264 9992. An a/c haven to escape from the heat. Black-tie waiters, excellent food with meat specialities and pizza, and a good buffet lunch on Sun. Live music upstairs on Fri and Sat from significant Brazilian acts.
₸₸₸-₸₸ Choppão, Praça 8 de Abril, T065-3623 9101. Established 30 years ago, this local institution is buzzing at any time of day or night. Huge portions of delicious food or *chopp*. The house speciality chicken soup promises to give diners drinking strength in the early hours and is a meal in itself. Warmly recommended.
₸₸ Panela de Barro, R Cmte Costa 543. Self-service, a/c lunchtime restaurant with a choice of tasty regional dishes.
₸₸-₸ Miranda's, R Cmte Costa 716. Decent self-service per kg lunchtime restaurant with good value specials.
₸ Lanchonete da Marilda, R Cmte Costa 675. Simple lunchtime snack bar with generous *prato feito*.

Chapada dos Guimarães p760

Pequi is a regional palm fruit with a deadly spiky interior used to season many foods; *arroz com pequi* is a popular local rice and chicken dish.

₸₸ Nivios, Praça Dom Wunibaldo 631. The best place for good regional food.
₸₸ O Mestrinho, R Quinco Caldas 119. Meat, regional dishes, *rodízio* at weekends.
₸₸ Trapiche, R Cipriano Curvo 580. Pizza, drinks, regional dishes.
₸ Choppada (O Chopp da Chapada), R Cipriano Curvo near the *praça*.

Drinks and meals, regional dishes, live music at weekends.
Fogão da Roça, Praça Dom Wunibaldo 488. Good *comida mineira* in generous portions. Recommended.

Cáceres *p761*
Corimbá, R 15 de Novembro s/n, on the riverfront. Fish and general Brazilian food.
Gulla's, R Col José Dulce 250. Per kg buffet, good quality and variety. Recommended.
Panela de Barro, R Frei Ambrósio 34, near the *rodoviária*. Brazilian *comida caseira* (home cooking) with the usual range of meat dishes with squash, rice, black beans and salads.

São Félix do Araguaia *p763*
Pizzeria Cantinho da Peixada, Av Araguaia, next to the Texaco station, over-looking the river. As well as serving pizza, the owner, Klaus, also rents rooms.

Bars and clubs

Cuiabá *p757, map p759*
Cuiabá is quite lively at night, bars with live music and dance on Av CPA.
Café Cancun, R Candido Mariano at São Sebastião. One of a chain of popular Brazilian club-bars attracting a mid-20s to 40s crowd.
Choppão, see Eating above.
Rush, Isaac Póvoas at Presidente Marquês. Teen and 20-something techno bar.
Tucano, Av CPA, bar-restaurant specializing in pizza, with beautiful view, open daily 1800-2300.

Entertainment

Cáceres *p761*
Traditional folkloric dance groups:
Chalana, T065-3223 3317, and **Tradição**, T065-223 4505, perform shows at different locations.

Festivals and events

Cáceres *p761*
Mid-Mar Piranha Festival.
Mid-Sep International Fishing Festival.
There's also an annual cattle fair.

Shopping

Cuiabá *p757, map p759*
Local handicrafts in wood, straw, netting, leather, skins, Pequi liquor, crystallized caju fruit, compressed guaraná fruit and indigenous crafts are on sale at the airport, *rodoviária*, craft shops in the centre and at the daily market in the Praça da República, interesting. There's a picturesque fish and vegetable market at the riverside.
Casa de Artesão, Praça do Expedicionário 315, T065-3321 0603. All types of local crafts in a restored building.

Chapada dos Guimarães *p760*
João Eloy de Souza Neves is a local artist; his paintings, music and history of the chapada: *Chapada dos Guimarães da descoberta aos dias atuais*, are on sale at **Pousada Bom Jardim**.
Casa de Artes e Artesanato Mato Grossense, Praça Dom Wunibaldo. Crafts, indigenous artefacts, sweets and locally made honey.
Doceria Olho de Sogra, Praça Dom Wunibaldo 21. Regional sweets.

Cáceres *p761*
Náutica Turismo, R Bom Jardim 119A, by the waterfront. For fishing/camping supplies and boat repairs.

Activities and tours

Cuiabá *p757, map p759*
Travel agencies in Cuiabá also offer trips to the *chapada*.

Tours to the northern Pantanal

You should expect to pay US$60-90 per person per day for tours in the Pantanal. Budget trips are marginally more expensive (around US$10 per day) than those in the southern Pantanal, but accommodation in the *fazendas* is more comfortable. For longer tours or special programmes, book in advance.

Fauna Tour, R Campo Grande 487, T065- 3624 1996, T065-9958 1966 (mob), http://ecodopantanal.com. One of several budget operators in town, but much the best option. 2- to 5-day tours to the Pantanal *fazendas* and safaris, *chapada* and Rio Xingu with excellent wildlife guides; ask for Alex Gomes Ramos (T065-9204 5827). Camping trips available Jun-Oct with advance notice.

Natureco, R Benedito Leite 570, Cuiabá, T065-3321 1001, www.natureco.com.br. A range of *fazenda*-based Pantanal tours, trips to the Chapada dos Guimarães and to the caves at Nobres. Specialist wildlife guides available with advance notice. Some English spoken.

Pantanal wildlife and birding guides

All guides work freelance; companies employ extra guides for trips when busy. Most guides wait at the airport for incoming flights; compare prices and services in town if you don't want to commit yourself. The tourist office recommends guides, however, their advice is not always impartial. Those recommended below can be booked with advance notice through **Eco do Pantanal** or **Natureco**.

Boute Expeditions, R Getúlio Vargas 64, Várzea Grande, near airport, T065-3686 2231, www.boute-expeditions.com. Paulo Boute is one of the most respected birding guides in the Pantanal; works from home and speaks good English and French.

Fabricio Dorileo, fabriciodorileo18@ yahoo.com.br or through Eduardo Falcão – rejaguar@bol.com.br. Excellent birding guide with good equipment, good English and

many years experience in the Pantanal and Chapada dos Guimarães. Trained in the USA. Book him through any of the Cuiabá operators.

Giuliano Bernardon, T065-8115 6189, T065-9982 1294, giubernardon@gmail.com. Young birding guide and photographer from the Chapada dos Guimarães, with a good depth of knowledge and experience in the Chapada, Pantanal, Mato Grosso, Amazon and Atlantic coastal forest.

Pantanal Bird Club, T065-3624 1930, www.pantanalbirdclub.org. Recommended for even the most exacting clients, PBC are the most illustrious birders in Brazil with many years of experience. Braulio Carlos, the owner, has worked with Robert Ridgely and Guy Tudor and his chief guide, Juan Mazar Barnett, is one of the editors of *Cotinga* magazine. Tours throughout the area and to various parts of Brazil.

Chapada dos Guimarães *p760*

AC Tour, R Tiradentes 28, T065-3791 1122. Cássio Martins often waits at the *rodoviária*. 4-hr tours are from US$20 per person; 7-8 hrs, US$25; a horse-riding day tour, costs around US$25 per person. Guided hikes, 8-10 km, US$20 per person. Bicycle tour with guide, US$20 per person.

Ecoturismo Cultural, Praça Dom Wunibaldo 464, T/F065-3791 1393. Recommended tours with Jorge Belfort Mattos who speaks English and knows the area well; several itineraries, 4-6 hrs, US$20-50 per person.

José Paulino dos Santos is a guide working with the tourist office, Mon-Fri 0800-1100, 1300-1800, T065-3791 1245.

Cáceres *p761*

Cáceres, Av Getúlio Vargas 408, T065-223 1428. Fishing and photo tours to Pantanal, also boat hire. Cláudio Duarte is a helpful guide.

Pantanal Tour, R Col Fária 180, T065-223 1200. Boat hire, fishing trips, tickets.

Vereda Turismo, R Padre Cassemiro 1121, T065-223 4360. Tours, boat hire, fishing.

São Félix do Araguaia p763
Boat trips
Icuryala, Goiânia, T062-223 9518. Excellent food and service, US$100 per day, independent visitors welcome. Recommended.
Juracy Lopes, contact through **Hotel Xavante** (see Sleeping, page 766). A very experienced guide with many friends, including the chief and council in Santa Isabela. Trips to the village or to see wildlife cost US$15 for 2; longer trips can be made to the meeting of the waters with the Rio das Mortes, or for a night in the jungle sleeping in hammocks.

⊕ Transport

Cuiabá p757, map p759
Air Marechal Rondon international airport is 10 km from the city; taxi US$15, or take the 'Aeroporto' bus from Praça Ipiranga, US$0.50 or the terminal. Flights can be booked in the airline offices at the airport or through **Eco do Pantanal**, see page 764, which also handle bus tickets. Cuiábá has connections with **Brasília**, **Campo Grande**, **Curitiba**, **Manaus**, **Porto Alegre**, **Porto Velho**, **Salvador**, **São Paulo**, **Alta Floresta**, **Belo Horizonte**, **Goiânia**, **Rio de Janeiro** and several others, with **GOL**, www.voegol.com.br, **Oceanair**, www.oceanair.com.br, **Passaredo**, www.voepassaredo.com.br, **TAM**, www.tam.com.br, **TRIP**, www.voetrip.com.br, **Webjet**, www.webjet.com.br.

Bus Bus No 202 runs to the *rodoviária* from R Joaquim Murtinho by the cathedral, 20 mins.
Comfortable buses (with toilets) to **Campo Grande**, 10 hrs, US$25, 12 buses daily, *leito* at 2000 and 2100, US$50. To **Goiânia**, 14 hrs, US$40. Direct to **Brasília**, 24 hrs, US$40, *leito* US$60. To **Porto Velho**, 6 União Cascavel buses a day, US$75, 21 hrs. **Andorinha** 1700 bus **São Paulo** connects with **Porto Velho** service. Several to **São Paulo**, eg Motta, US$80.

To **Rio de Janeiro**, US$90. To **Barra do Garças**, Xavante 0800, 1300 and 2030, US$45, also **Barattur**. Connections to all major cities.

Car hire **Atlântida**, Av Isaac Póvoas, T065-3623 0700. **Localiza**, Av Dom Bosco 965, T065-3624 7979, and at airport, T065-3682 7900. **Unidas**, airport, T065-3682 4062. **Vitória**, R Comandante Costa 1350, T065-3322 7122.

Chapada dos Guimarães p760
Bus 7 departures daily to **Cuiabá** (Rubi, 0700-1900, last return 1800), 1½ hrs, US$5.

Cáceres p761
Bus Colibrí/União Cascavel buses to **Cuiabá**, US$15, many daily 0630-2400 from the *rodoviária*, (book in advance, very crowded), 3½ hrs. To **Porto Velho**, US$50.

Boat The *Acurí*, a luxury tourist vessel, sails to **Corumbá**, 1-week cruise including return by air from Corumbá to Cuiabá, US$600 per person. For information on other boat sailings, ask at the **Capitânia dos Portos**, on the corner of the main square at the waterfront. Try to phone in advance to Cáceres, Posto Arrunda, T065-3221 1707, to find out if any boats are going. Also **Portobrás** on the outskirts at the waterfront (T065-3221 1728). In the dry season there are practically no boats to Corumbá.

Car hire **Localiza**, R Padre Cassimiro 630, T065-3223 1330, and at airport. **Locavel**, Av São Luís 300, T065-3223 1212.

Border with Bolivia p761
Bus From Cáceres to **San Matías**, US$20 with **Transical-Velásquez**, Mon-Sat at 0630 and 1500, Sun 1500 only (return at same times). Trans Bolivia to **San Matías**, Sun, Mon, Fri at 1500, Tue, Wed, Thu and Sat at 0700. For details of crossing the border, see box, page 761.

Along the Transpantaneira *p762*
Bus From Poconé to **Cuiabá**, US$10 with
TUT, T065-3322 4985, 6 a day 0600-1900.

Car Poconé has a 24-hr petrol station with
all types of fuel, but closed on Sun.

Alta Floresta *p763*
Air Cristalino Jungle Lodge offers a free
pick-up and drop-off for guests. There's little
reason to come if you're not going to the
lodge. There are flights to **Brasília**, **Cuiabá**,
Curitiba, **Porto Alegre**, **Campinas**,
Cascaval, **Ji-Paraná**, **Londrina**, **Maringá**,
Rondonópolis, **Sinop** and **Vilhena**,
with Oceanair, www.oceanair.com.br,
or Trip, www.voetrip.com.br.

Bus To **Cuiabá** daily, several (12 hrs, US$35).
The *leito* night bus is the best option.

São Félix do Araguaia *p763*
Bus To **Barra do Garças** at 0500, arrive
2300; or 1730, arrive 1100 next day. Also
to **Tucumã**, 6-8 hrs, and to **São José do
Xingu**, 10 hrs. No buses to Marabá.

⊕ Directory

Cuiabá *p757, map p759*
Banks Banco do Brasil, Av Getúlio Vargas
and R Barão de Melgaço, commission US$10
for cash, US$20 per transaction for TCs (there
are several branches of **Bradesco** for ATMs.
Embassies and consulates Bolivia,
Av Isaac Póvoas 117, T065-3623 5094,
Mon-Fri. **Internet** Copy Grafic, Praça
Alencastro 32, fax and email, English
spoken, friendly. **Post office** Main
branch at Praça da República, fax service.

Chapada dos Guimarães *p760*
Banks Bradesco in town. **Post office**
R Fernando Corrêa 848.

Cáceres *p761*
Banks Banco do Brasil, R Col Jose Dulcé
234. HSBC, R Col Jose Dulcé 145. **Casa de
Câmbio Mattos**, Comte Bauduino 180,
next to main *praça*, changes cash and
TCs at good rates.

Contents

Footprint features

Background

History

Indigenous peoples

Origins
Some 50,000 years ago the very first peoples crossed the temporary land bridge spanning Asia and America at the Bering Straits, and began a long migration southwards. They were hunters and foragers, following in the path of huge herds of now extinct animals, such as mammoth, giant ground sloth and antecedents of the camel and horse. The first signs that these people had reached South America date from around 10,000 BC, if not earlier.

Archaeological evidence
The major handicap to archaeological study of tropical cultures is that most material remains deteriorate rapidly in the warm, humid climate. Since the majority of cultural output from Brazil was in perishable materials such as feathers, wood, baskets, and woven textiles, little has survived for modern analysis. Nevertheless various artefacts have been discovered from all around the country, showing considerable artistic and technical skill. The pottery produced by the early peoples was of a high standard. Early ceramics have been found on Marajó island at the mouth of the Amazon. The Annatuba culture lived here in small villages by the river. Most of their ceramics found are round bowls and jars, including huge funeral urns, which have been dated with increasing antiquity; the earliest from around 980 BC. Textile production was done mainly with hand-twisted fibres, using both cotton and bast. Objects found in Rio Grande do Sul, dating from AD 550 or earlier, included twined bags, nets and ropes. Most of the textiles found throughout Brazil were simple everyday items, such as hammocks and straps, with little decoration.

It was assumed that the first humans in Brazil came down to the lowlands from the Andean chain, following the east-facing river valleys. Some very early human remains have been found in central and northeastern Brazil. In Pedra Furada, in northeast Brazil, a rock-shelter named Toca do Boqueirão yielded evidence of human presence from as early as 47,000 years ago. The cave, in a region well-known for its prehistoric rock paintings, had previously been explored and was known to have been occupied by hunters about 8000 years ago. However, a team of Brazilians, co-ordinated by Paulista archaeologist Niède Guidón, probed more deeply into the ground and claims to have found evidence of much earlier human presence. Guidón's claims sparked hot debate among other experts, many of whom argued that what she described as ash from fireplaces was in fact the remains of naturally caused forest fires. This claim has led to some accusations of racism by Brazilians who argue that if Guidón were American she would have been taken more seriously. This appears not to be the case, for similar controversy was sparked by the findings of a scion of one of the most famous American families, Anna Roosevelt. She claimed that findings in a cave in Monte Alegre, opposite Santarém on the Rio Solimões, suggested that the Amazon had been peopled since at least 11,000 BC and that it had supported large civilizations, also pre-dating previous estimates. These, and other controversial claims have caused a bitter rift in the world of archaeology and led some experts to raise the theory of original human migration from across the Pacific Ocean and others to accuse the newcomers of undertaking amateurish, unprofessional research. For a full account see Charles Mann's excellent *1491* (Vintage 2006).

Amazon lifestyles

Roosevelt's research, together with that being undertaken by ethno-biologists like Wade Davis, anthropologists like Gerardo Reichel-Dolmatoff and Mesoamerica archaeologists and epigraphers like Linda Schele, began to change radically once widely-accepted ideas of the pre-Columbian Americans. Gone is a notion based on an analysis of their technology and concluding that they were prehistoric, primitive peoples, instead is an analysis based on their rich societal structure, speculative philosophy and the mythology which sustained it. We now see the first Americans as a divergent range of peoples who arrived in the Americas at varying times and probably from various locations. Between them they shared a common philosophical world-map – an idea of being – which was radically different from our own Greco-Roman idea and which was rooted in shamanism. In philosophical terms shamanism assumes that being is as vital a component of reality as energy and matter; and like those two it is shared. In other words the basic stuff of the Universe is threefold – matter (energy), space and time (position) and the perception of those two (being); on which they both depend for their existence. The essence of being can be directly apprehended behind the mind by seers or shaman (Portuguese *pajé*). In most first American societies it was shaman – together with powerful civic leaders (Portuguese *cacique*) who guided tribal societies; be they Mayan or Ticuna.

Little is known of these people largely because of the colonial ideas that were handed down to Western archaeologists by the Spanish and Portuguese, who burned and plundered many of the artefacts and books of the first Americans. The Amazonian peoples were decimated by the Portuguese slave trade long before their knowledge could be shared; and as most of their treasures were made from perishable materials like feather, bark and reed, the products of their labour and their knowledge rotted into the forest floor. What we know is scant and trivial. The earliest people lived mainly on the flood plains of the great rivers and caught fish and manatee using spears thrown from the shore, or from dugout canoes. Besides fishing, these people also cultivated manioc and other plants found on the forest floor. They kept turtles in corrals at the river's edge, for eating and also for making tools and other artefacts from their shells.

Their nomadic lifestyle was carefully planned, and they followed planting and harvesting seasons in accordance with the periodic rising and falling river levels. At first, as hunters and gatherers, they built simple, temporary houses out of tree trunks and palm leaves, and slept in hammocks made from plant fibres. Where clothing was used it was simple; a large, ankle-length tunic called a *kushma* was the main garment worn. Although this may sound impractical wear for people living in a warm, humid climate, the *kushma* provided much-needed protection against biting insects. Compensating for their plain clothing, the people painted their bodies and wore colourful jewellery, such as feather head-dresses; the designs for which were often rich and elaborate and drawn from an extensive mythology. Little has remained of the perishable adornments, but cylindrical and flat ceramic stamps have been found throughout Amazônia, which may have been used to apply ink designs onto the face and other parts of the body, still common today among Brazilian ethnic groups.

Migration to the coast

Around 7000-4000 BC a climatic change increased the temperature throughout the south of Brazil, drawing people down from the inland *planalto* region to the coasts, and leading to an upsurge in population here. These coastal inhabitants lived on shellfish collected from the water's edge, as evidenced by *sambaquis* (huge shell mounds), discovered on the coast. In rare cases they also fed on whales that had probably been beached, but they did not go far out to sea to fish. Some of the *sambaquis* found measure up to 25 m high; many of them also served as dwellings, with floors and fireplaces, and as burial sites, with graves often underneath the houses. The dead were buried with personal adornments and some domestic artefacts.

Settlement and political structure

By about 100-200 BC, people throughout Brazil were settled in structured, fixed communities by the coasts and rivers, living increasingly by farming instead of nomadic hunting and gathering. The subsequent population growth spread communities further along river courses and into seasonally flooded savannah lands.

Until Anna Roosevelt's research it had been thought that unlike the great empires of the Andes, the lowland peoples did not form political groupings much larger than a few villages. However it is now suggested that much of Brazil was settled by chiefdoms, some of which were substantial and the seat of sophisticated civilizations. The most notable of these was probably Marajó which Roosevelt has called 'one of the outstanding indigenous achievements of the New World.' The Marajó people occupied thousands of square kilometres in the lower portion of the Amazon basin in a civilization which perhaps numbered around 100 000 people and which endured for some 1000 years. They had an advanced tropical rainforest agriculture in which fruit-bearing and utilitarian trees were planted within the forest (as opposed to in cleared areas); in much the same way as the Lacandon Maya today. The Marajó people were either influential on Brazilian indigenous people as a whole or they were part of a widespread practice, for by about 2000 BC peoples throughout the lower Amazon were planting at least 138 species of crop plant; including manioc which remains a staple in Brazilian diet to this day.

Linguistic groups

The most widespread linguistic grouping in Brazil at the time of the European conquest was the Tupi-Guarani. These people originated from the Atlantic coast around AD 500-700. By the 1500s the Tupi-Guarani, who often moved from place to place could be found from north of the Amazon south to Rio de la Plata, and west into Paraguay and Bolivia; they were probably the first Americans the Portuguese encountered

Another large, organized group of people were the Tupinambá. They lived on the coast, from the mouth of the Amazon south to São Paulo state. The Tupinambá lived by cultivating crops, such as manioc, sweet potato, yams, as well as cotton, gourds and tobacco. They lived in villages of four to eight large, rectangular, thatched houses, each containing up to 30 families. They usually built their villages on an elevation to catch the breeze, and moved to new sites every five years or so.

Cannibalism was also an important custom for the Tupinambá, as it had been for many other peoples throughout South America for thousands of years. The practice was a highly ritualized military practise, using prisoners of war. The victims were kept as slaves, often for long periods, being well fed and looked after; in some cases even marrying the owner's daughter or sister, who had their children. But all such slaves were eventually eaten, after an elaborate ceremony with much singing and dancing. An appointed executioner would kill them with a club and they were then cooked and different parts of the body divided up among various participants in the ritual. There have been many theories as to why people practised cannibalism; since they tended to eat victims of war it was thought that it gave them power over the spirits of their dead enemies. It is most commonly argued that human flesh supplemented the diet for large populations who had scarce resources. But this was not the case for the Tupinambá, who had ample food supplies. When the Tupinambá themselves were asked why they ate human meat they simply said they liked the taste of it.

European colonization

Arrival of the Portuguese
Pedro Álvares Cabral is believed to be the first Portuguese explorer to land on the Brazilian coast, having been blown off his course to India and making landfall on 22 April 1500. He claimed the territory for Portugal as a result of agreements with Spain under the papal bull of 1493 and the Treaty of Tordesillas (1494), but it was some years before the Portuguese realized that this was not just another island as the Spanish had found in the Caribbean – in reality they had stumbled across a huge new continent. Further expeditions were sent out in 1501 and 1503-1504 and a few trading stations were set up to export the only commodity they felt was of commercial interest: a species of dyewood known as 'pau do brasil'. Little attention was paid to the new colony, as the Portuguese concentrated on the more lucrative trade with Africa, India and the Far East. Some settlers, often banished criminals as well as merchants, gained acceptance with the local indigenous tribes and intermarried, fathering the first hybrid cultural Brazilians.

Colonization
The coastal trading stations at Salvador da Bahia, Pernambuco, São Vicente and Cabo Frio soon attracted the attention of French and British traders, who seized Portuguese ships and started to trade directly with the indigenous tribes. The French even proclaimed the right to trade in any part of Brazil not occupied by the Portuguese. This forced the Portuguese Crown to set up a colony and in 1530, Martim Afonso de Sousa was sent out with about 400 men. Faced with the impossibly huge task of colonizing the Brazilian coastline, the Crown turned to private enterprise to stake its claim. In 1534 the coast was divided into 15 captaincies, each of which was donated to an individual captain and governor to develop on behalf of the Crown. Although successful settlements were established in Pernambuco in the north and São Vicente in the south, the problems faced in most captaincies, indigenous resistance, lack of capital and the difficulty of attracting settlers, led to the reassertion of Crown control in 1549. The *indígenas* had been happy to barter brazil wood with the Portuguese and had helped in the logging and transporting of timber, but the introduction of sugar plantations was a different matter and the hunter-gatherers had no experience of such exhausting work. When they refused to co-operate in this profitable enterprise, the Portuguese took the *indígenas* as slaves on a massive scale, which destroyed the good relations previously enjoyed and led to attacks on Portuguese settlements.

The Jesuits
Tomé de Sousa was sent out as governor-general to the vacant captaincy of Bahia in 1549. He established his seat at Salvador, which became the first capital of Brazil. With him

travelled six Jesuit priests, the first of what was to become a hugely powerful missionary and educational order in Brazil. Their role was to smooth the path between the indigenous tribes and Europeans, converting and educating them in Christian ways and organizing them into special villages, or *aldeias*. This last move brought them into conflict with the settlers, however, for their control over the labour market, and with the clergy, who regarded the *indígenas* as savages who could be enslaved. As a result of disagreements with the first Bishop of Brazil, Fernandes Sardanha, the Jesuits moved in 1554 from Bahia to the captaincy of São Vicente, where they set up an *aldeia* at Piratininga, which later became the city of São Paulo. In 1557 a new governor was appointed, Mem de Sá, who was more sympathetic to the Jesuits and their aims, and the *aldeias* began to spread.

French and Dutch incursions

The Crown still had difficulties in consolidating its hold on Brazil and other European powers continued to encroach on its territory. A Protestant French expedition found an area which had not been settled by the Portuguese and stayed there from the mid-1550s until they were finally ousted in 1567. Their colony was replaced by a new royal captaincy and a town was founded: Rio de Janeiro. São Luís was also occupied by the French in 1612-1615, but it was the Dutch who posed the greatest threat on both sides of the Atlantic. They seized Pernambuco in 1630, Portuguese Angola in 1641 and dominated the Atlantic trading routes until the Portuguese managed to regain Angola in 1648-1649 and Pernambuco in 1654.

Sugar and slaves

Throughout the colonial period Brazil produced raw materials for Portugal. The colonial economy experienced a succession of booms and recessions, the first of these was based on sugar, as during the 17th century the northeastern provinces of Pernambuco, Bahia and Paraíba were the world's main producers of sugar. As European settlement had led to the death of much of the native population (over a third of the *indígenas* in coastal areas died in epidemics in 1562-1563 alone) and slavery was unsuccessful, the Portuguese imported African slaves to meet the demand for labour on the sugar plantations (*engenhos*). "The most solid properties in Brazil are slaves", wrote the Governor in 1729, "for there are lands enough, but only he who has slaves can be master of them." As many as 10 million African slaves may have survived the dreadful conditions of the Atlantic crossing before the trade was abolished in 1854.

The gold rush

As the sugar industry declined in the late 17th century in the face of competition from British, French and Dutch Caribbean colonies, gold was discovered inland in 1695 in Minas Gerais, Mato Grosso and other areas. Despite the lack of communications, prospectors rushed in from all over Europe. Shortly afterwards, diamonds were found in the Serra do Frio. The economy was largely driven by gold until the 1760s and a revival of world demand for sugar in the second half of the 18th century. Thereafter, there was diversification into other crops such as cacao, rice, cotton and coffee, all of which were produced for export by large numbers of slaves.

The gold rush shifted the power centre of Brazil from the northeast to the centre, in recognition of which new captaincies were created in Minas Gerais in 1720, Goiás in 1744 and Mato Grosso in 1748, and the capital was moved from Salvador to Rio de

Janeiro in 1763. Legacies of the period can be seen today in the colonial towns of Mariana, Congonhas, São João del Rei, Diamantina and, above all, in the exceptionally beautiful city of Ouro Preto, a national monument full of glorious buildings, paintings and sculpture.

Marquês de Pombal

The decline of gold in the mid-18th century made economic reform necessary and the Marquês de Pombal was the minister responsible for a new programme for Portugal and her empire. Imbalances had arisen particularly in trade with Britain. Portugal imported manufactured goods and wheat but her exports of oil and wine left her in deficit, which for a while was covered by Brazilian gold. Pombal was a despotic ruler from 1750 to 1777, modernizing and reforming society, education, politics and the economy. In order to revive Portugal he concentrated on expanding the economy of Brazil, increasing and diversifying exports to cover the deficit with Britain. Cacao, cotton and rice were introduced by the new monopoly company of Grão Pará e Maranhão in the north and a similar company for Paraíba and Pernambuco revitalized the sugar industry in the northeast. The monopoly companies led to high prices and were not entirely successful so were closed in 1778-1779, but the effects of Pombal's reforms were felt in the latter part of the 18th century and Portugal's trade with Britain turned into a surplus. From 1776 when the American colonies revolted, Britain was constantly at war and Portugal was able to supply rising British demand.

Rebellion

Pombal's influence on society enabled the Portuguese Empire to last much longer than the Spanish Empire. He deliberately offered posts in the militia and the bureaucracy to Brazilians and was careful not to alienate the Brazilian elites. White Brazilians were on the same standing as the Portuguese and identified strongly with the mother country. Although rebellion was rare, it still occurred, influenced partly by the turmoil that was going on in Europe with the French Revolution. In 1788-1789 a famous plot was uncovered in Minas Gerais called the *inconfidência mineira* (see box, page 272), which aimed to establish an independent republic in protest at the decline of the gold industry and high taxes. The rebels, who included many people from the upper echelons of society, were punished and the most prominent leader, Tiradentes (the tooth-puller), was hanged. Other plots were discovered in Rio de Janeiro in 1794, Pernambuco in 1801 and Bahia in 1807, but they were all repressed.

The Brazilian empire

At the beginning of the 19th century, Napoleon Bonaparte caused a major upheaval in the monarchies of Europe. His expansion into the Iberian peninsula caused panic in both Spain and Portugal. In August 1807 he demanded that Portugal close its ports to British ships but the British sent a fleet to Lisbon and threatened to attack Brazil if that happened. In November of the same year the French invaded and occupied Portugal. The Prince Regent decided to evacuate the court to Brazil and under British escort sailed to Rio de Janeiro, which became the capital of the empire in 1808. The court stayed there even after 1814 when Napoleon was defeated and Portugal was ruled by the regency council, but King João VI was forced to return to Portugal in 1820 after a series of liberal revolts in the mother country, leaving his son Dom Pedro as prince regent in Brazil.

Independence from Portugal

Dom Pedro oversaw a growing rift between Portugal and Brazil as the liberals in Lisbon tried to return Brazil to its former colonial status, cancelling political equality and the freedom of trade granted when the King left Portugal in the hands of the French. In October 1821 the government in Lisbon recalled the prince regent but Brazilians urged him not to go. Encouraged by his chief minister, José Bonifácio de Andrada e Silva, a conservative monarchist, Dom Pedro announced on 9 January 1822 that he would stay in Brazil, thereby asserting his autonomy. After another attempt to recall the prince regent, Dom Pedro made the final break with Portugal, proclaiming Brazil's independence on 7 September 1822. He was crowned emperor and Brazil became a constitutional monarchy in its own right. There was resistance in the north and northeast, particularly from the militia, but by 1824 violence had subsided. In 1825, under pressure from Britain, Portugal recognized the independent state of Brazil.

The first years of independence were unsettled, partly because of the emperor's perceived favouritism for the Portuguese faction at court and lack of attendance to the needs of the local oligarchy. De Andrada e Silva resigned as opposition grew. In 1823 Dom Pedro dissolved the constituent assembly amidst fears that he had absolutist designs. However, he set up a royal commission to draft a new constitution which lasted from 1824 until the fall of the monarchy in 1889. This gave the emperor the right to appoint and dismiss cabinet ministers, veto legislation and dissolve parliament and call for elections. The parliamentary government consisted of two houses, a senate appointed by the monarch and a legislature indirectly elected by a limited male suffrage. A council of state advised the monarch and ensured the separation of the executive, the legislature and the judiciary. Catholicism remained the official religion and the monarchy was supported by the church.

Abdication

Dom Pedro still failed to gain the trust of all his people. A republican rebellion broke out in Pernambuco in 1824, where the elite were suffering from the declining sugar industry, and there was further resentment from all the planter oligarchy as a result of the Anglo-Brazilian Treaty of 1826. This treaty granted British recognition of the independent Brazil in return for certain trading privileges, but, almost more importantly, stipulated that the Atlantic slave trade should come to an end in three years. There was also a territorial dispute in 1825 with the Argentine provinces over the left bank of the Río de la Plata, called the *Banda Oriental*, which flared up into war and was only settled in 1828 with the creation of Uruguay as a buffer state. The mistrust between the Portuguese and the Brazilians became even more pronounced. Portuguese merchants were blamed for the rising cost of living and in 1831 rioting broke out in Rio de Janeiro. Dom Pedro shuffled and reshuffled his cabinet to appease different factions but nothing worked and on 7 April he abdicated in favour of his five-year-old son, Dom Pedro II, choosing to leave Brazil a week later on a British warship.

Regency and rebellion

During the 10 years of the young prince's boyhood, there were many separatist movements and uprisings by the oppressed lower classes. In 1832-1835 there was the War of the Cabanos, in Pernambuco, a guerrilla war against the slave-owning plantocracy of the northeast; in 1835 the Cabanagem rebellion of free indigenous tribes and *mestizos* took place in Pará after a white secessionist revolt and sporadic fighting continued until

Estimated slavery statistics

Country	Voyages	Slaves transported
Denmark	250	50,000
British North America and USA	1500	300,000
Holland	2000	500,000
France (including French Caribbean)	4200	1,250,000
Spain (including Cuba)	4000	1,600,000
Britain	12,000	2,600,000
Portugal (including Brazil)	30,000	4,650,000

Cited from *The Slave Trade Hugh Thomas Phoenix Press*

1840 (see page 623); in 1837-1838 in Bahia there was a federalist rebellion; in 1835 Rio Grande do Sul proclaimed itself a republic, remaining independent for nearly 10 years, with the movement spreading into Santa Catarina, which also declared itself a republic. By 1840 there was a general consensus that although he had not come of age, it was imperative that the 14 year old, Pedro, should ascend the throne. He was duly crowned. Administration of the country was centralized again, the powers of provincial assemblies were curtailed, a national police force set up and the council of state restored.

The second empire
It took a couple of years for the balance of power to be worked out between the conservative elites of Rio de Janeiro and the liberal elites of São Paulo and Minas Gerais, but once the interests of different groups had been catered for, the constitutional monarchy worked smoothly for 20 years. Coffee was now the major crop in São Paulo and Minas Gerais and it was important that the wealthy oligarchy who produced it shared in the power structure of the nation in order to prevent secessionist movements.

Abolition of slavery
Despite the Anglo-Brazilian Treaty of 1826, the slave trade continued until the British Royal Navy put pressure on Brazilian ships carrying slaves in 1850 and the trade was halted soon afterwards. As slaves in Brazil did not reproduce at a natural rate because of the appalling conditions in which they lived and worked, it was clear that an alternative source of labour would eventually have to be found. Anti-slavery movements gathered strength and in 1871 the first steps towards abolition were taken. A new law gave freedom to all children born to slaves from that date and compensation was offered to masters who freed their slaves. During the 1870s large numbers of European immigrants, mostly from Italy and Portugal, came to work on the coffee plantations, and as technology and transport improved, so the benefits of slavery declined. During the 1880s the abolition movement became unstoppable and, after attempts to introduce compensation for slave owners failed, a law abolishing slavery was finally passed on 13 May 1888. Some plantation owners went bankrupt, but the large majority survived by paying immigrant workers and newly freed slaves a pittance. Those freed slaves who left the plantations to find employment in the cities were equally exploited and lived in poverty.

Proclamation of the Republic

The first Republic: 1889-1930

The monarchy did not long survive the end of slavery. The São Paulo coffee producers resented abolition and resented their under-representation in the structures of power nationwide, while being called upon to provide the lion's share of the treasury's revenues. The republican movement started in the early 1870s in cities all over Brazil, but grew strongest in São Paulo. It gradually attracted the support of the military, who also felt under-represented in government, and on 15 November 1889 a bloodless military coup d'état deposed the monarchy and instituted a federal system. The constitution of the new republic established 20 states with wide powers of self-government, a directly elected president of a national government with a senate and a chamber of deputies. Suffrage was introduced for literate adult males (about 3% of the population) and the church and state were separated. Although the birth of the republic was bloodless, there were pockets of resistance in rural areas such as the northeast, where the sugar estates were in recession. In the 1890s O Conselheiro led tens of thousands of followers against the secular republic at Canudos, nearly all of whom were eventually killed by government troops. In 1911 there was another rebellion in the southern states of Paraná and Santa Catarina, led by a Catholic visionary in defence of the monarchy. The Contestado movement lasted until 1915, when it too was destroyed by the military.

Brazilian politics were now dominated by an alliance known as café con leite (coffee with milk), of the coffee growers of São Paulo and the cattle ranchers of Minas Gerais, occasionally challenged by Rio Grande do Sul, with periodic involvement of the military. The first two presidents of the republic were military: Marshal Deodoro da Fonseca (1889-1891) and Marshal Floriano Peixoto (1891-1894). In some ways the military took the place of the Crown in mediating between the states' oligarchies, but its interventions were always unconstitutional and therefore gave rise to political instability. By the 1920s tensions between São Paulo and Minas Gerais had come out into the open with the cattle ranchers resenting the way in which the coffee growers used their position to keep the price of coffee artificially high at a time when there was an oversupply. Other social groups also became restive and unsuccessful coup attempts were launched by junior army officers in 1922, 1924 and 1926.

The end of the First World War saw the rise of the USA as an industrial power and the decline of Britain's traditional supremacy in trade with Latin America. Although Brazil was still exporting its raw materials to Europe at ever lower prices, it now imported its manufactured goods from the USA, leading to difficulties with finance and fluctuating exchange rates. Brazil's terms of trade had therefore deteriorated and the profitability of its export-led economy was declining before the crash of Wall Street in 1929. The cost of stockpiling excess coffee had led to a rise in debt and by 1930 the government was spending a third of its budget on debt servicing. The growth of nationalism was a key feature of this period as well as the emergence of new political factions and parties such as fascists and communists.

Vargas and the Estado Nôvo: 1930-1945

The Wall Street crash led to a sudden decline in demand for coffee and the São Paulo elite saw its hegemony wiped out. The elections of 1930 saw another win for the São Paulo candidate, but the results were disputed by a coalition of opposition forces. After several months of tension and violence, the army intervened, deposed the outgoing president and installed the alternative candidate of Rio Grande do Sul, Getúlio Vargas, a wealthy rancher, as provisional president. Vargas in fact held office until 1954, with only one break in 1945-1950. His main aim, when he took office, was to redress the balance of power away from São Paulo and in favour of his own state. However, the effects of his reforms were more far-reaching. He governed by decree, replacing all state governors with 'interventors' who reduced the state militias, and reorganized the system of patronage within the states in favour of his own. São Paulo naturally resisted and there was a rebellion in 1932, but it was soon put down by federal troops, effectively wiping out the threat to Vargas' authority. In 1934 a constituent assembly drew up a new constitution that reduced the power of the states and gave more power to the president. The assembly then elected Vargas as president for a four-year term.

With the decline of traditional oligarchic blocs came the rise of political parties. The first to fill the vacuum were the fascists and the communists, who frequently took to street violence against each other. The fascists, called Integralists, were founded by Plínio Salgado in 1932. The Aliança Libertadora Nacional (ALN), a popular front including socialists and radical liberals, was founded by the Brazilian Communist Party in 1935. The ALN attempted to gain power by infiltrating the junior ranks of the army and encouraging rebellions, but Vargas clamped down on the movement, imprisoning its leaders. The fascists aimed to take power in 1938, the year elections were due, at which Vargas was not eligible to stand. However, in October 1937, Vargas declared a state of siege against an alleged communist plot and suspended the constitution which had prevented him being re-elected. Instead, he proclaimed a new constitution and a new state, *Estado Nôvo*. The fascists tried to oust him but failed, leaving Vargas with no effective opposition whatsoever.

The *Estado Nôvo* was also a response to an economic crisis, brought on by a fall in coffee prices, rising imports, a resulting deficit in the balance of payments, a high level of debt and soaring inflation. Vargas assumed dictatorial powers to deal with the economic crisis, censoring the press, banning political parties, emasculating trade unions and allowing the police unfettered powers. There followed a transition from export-led growth to import substitution and industrialization with heavy state intervention. Agricultural resources were channelled into industry and the government became involved in mining, oil, steel, electricity, chemicals, motor vehicles and light aircraft. The military were allowed free rein to develop their own armaments industry. As war approached in Europe, Vargas hedged his bets with both Nazi Germany and the USA, to see who would provide the greatest assistance for Brazil's industrialization. It turned out to be the USA, and in return for allowing US military bases to be built in northern Brazil he secured loans, technical assistance and other investments for a massive steel mill at Volta Redonda and infrastructure projects. Brazil did not declare war on Germany until 1944, but it was the only Latin American country to send troops to join the allies, with a force of 25,000 men going to Italy.

The elections of 1943 had been postponed during the War, but Vargas scheduled a vote for December 1945 in an attempt to dispel his fascist image. He allowed the formation of political parties, which included two formed by himself: the Social Democratic Party (PSD), supported by industrialists and large farmers, and a Labour Party (PTB), supported by pro-Vargas trade unions. There was also the National Democratic Union (UDN), opposed to Vargas, and the newly legalized Communist Party. However, there were growing fears that Vargas would not relinquish power, and when he appointed his brother as chief of police in Rio de Janeiro, the military intervened. Faced with the prospect of being deposed, Vargas chose to resign in October 1945, allowing the elections to take place as planned in the December. They were won by the PSD, led by General Eurico Dutra, a former supporter of the *Estado Nôvo*, who had encouraged Vargas to resign.

The second Republic: 1946-1964

Yet another constitution was drafted by a constituent assembly in 1946, this one based on the liberal principles of the 1891 constitution but including the labour code and the social legislation of the *Estado Nôvo*. Industrialization through state planning was retained, the foreign-owned railways were nationalized, hydroelectric power was developed, but deflation was necessary to bring down spiralling prices. The Communist Party was banned again in 1947. Meanwhile Vargas was elected Senator for Rio Grande do Sul, his home state, and kept active in politics, eventually being elected as candidate for the PSD and PTB alliance in the 1950 presidential elections. Although it was his third presidency, it was only his first by direct elections.

The third Vargas presidency was beset by the problems of fulfilling populist election promises while grappling with debt and inflation. Rapid industrialization required levels of investment which could only be raised abroad, but the nationalists were opposed to foreign investment. He failed to reconcile the demands of the USA and the nationalists, particularly with regards to oil and energy, and he failed to control inflation and stabilize the economy. There were rumours of corruption, and after the president's bodyguard was implicated in a plot to kill a journalist, which went wrong and another man was shot, the army issued him with another ultimatum to resign or be ousted. Instead, on 24 August 1954, Vargas shot himself, leaving a suicide note denouncing traitors at home and capitalists abroad.

The next president was Juscelino Kubitschek, who took office in January 1956 with the aim of achieving economic growth at any cost, regardless of inflation and debt. He is best known for building the new capital of Brazil, Brasília, nearly 1000 km northwest of Rio de Janeiro in the state of Goiás. This massive modernist project served in the short term to expand the debt and in 1961, the next president, Jânio Quadros, inherited huge economic problems which brought his government down after only seven months and Congress unexpectedly accepted his resignation. Power passed to his vice-president, João Goulart, a populist and former labour minister under Vargas, who was mistrusted by the armed forces and the right wing. His powers were curtailed with the appointment of a prime minister and cabinet who would be jointly answerable to Congress. The 1960s were a turbulent time in Brazil as elsewhere, with the universities a hotbed of revolutionary socialism after the Cuban Revolution, Trotskyist and Communist agitators encouraging land occupations, strikes in industry and a move to secure trade union rights for the armed forces. A nationalist Congress passed legislation cutting foreign companies' annual profit remittances to 10% of profits, which sparked a massive outflow in foreign capital and a halving of US aid. Goulart was forced to print money to keep the economy going, which naturally put further pressure on an already soaring inflation rate. When Goulart clashed with Congress over approval of an economic adjustment programme and tried to strengthen his position by appealing for popular support outside Congress, he alarmed the middle classes, who unexpectedly supported a military coup in March 1964. Goulart took refuge in Uruguay.

Military rule: 1964-1985

The 1964 coup was a turning point in Brazilian political history. This time the armed forces did not return to barracks as they had before. Opposition leaders were arrested, the press censored, labour unions purged of anyone seen as left wing, and the secret police were given wide powers. The political parties were outlawed and replaced by two officially approved parties: the government Aliança Renovadora Nacional (ARENA) and the opposition Movimento Democrático Brasileiro (MDB). Congress, consisting only of members of these two parties, approved a succession of military presidents nominated by the armed forces. A new constitution, introduced in 1967, gave the president broad powers over the states and over Congress. The worst period of repression occurred between 1968 and 1973 with a wave of urban guerrilla warfare. Around this time, the military government's economic adjustment programme paid dividends and the economy began to grow, making life easier for the middle classes and reducing any potential support for guerrilla groups. In 1968-1974 the economy grew at over 10% a year, which became known as the Brazilian 'economic miracle'. This spectacular growth, achieved because of the authoritarian nature of the regime, masked a widening gulf between the rich and poor, with the blacks and mulattos, always at the bottom in Brazilian society, suffering the most. Edwin Williamson (*The Penguin History of Latin America*) quotes statistics showing that in 1960 the richest 10% of the population received 40% of the national income; by 1980 they received 51%, while the poorest 50% received only 13%. In the shanty towns, or *favelas*, which had mushroomed around all the large cities, but especially São Paulo, disease, malnutrition and high mortality rates were prevalent and their citizens battled constantly in appalling housing lacking sewerage, running water and electricity.

By 1973 some military officers and their civilian advisors had become alarmed at the rising level of opposition. Arguing that repression alone would merely lead to further opposition and even to attempted revolution, they pressed for 'decompression': policies to relax the repression while remaining in power. The attempt to carry out this policy by legalizing political parties, permitting freer trade unions and strikes and reducing censorship, gave greater space for the opposition to demand an end to military rule. Attempts to introduce elections to Congress which were less controlled faced the same obstacle: they tended to result in victories for candidates who favoured civilian rule.

One of the main reasons for the military deciding to return to their barracks was the dire state of the economy. The armed forces had taken over in 1964 when the economy had hit rock bottom, their authoritarian regime had allowed rapid expansion and change which brought about the 'economic miracle', yet by 1980 the economy had gone full circle. Inflation was running at 100% a year and was set to go through the roof, foreign debt was the highest in Latin America, estimated at over US$87 billion, and unemployment was soaring. When international interest rates rose sharply in 1982, Brazil was no longer able to service its debt and it suspended interest payments. Unwilling to go through another round of authoritarianism and repression, the military decided to let the civilians have a go. Elections in 1982 produced a majority for the pro-government Social Democratic Party (PDS) in the electoral college which was to elect the next president, but splits in the PDS led to the election in January 1985 of the opposition candidate, (see under São João del Rei, page 279).

The return to democracy

Corruption and impeachment

In 1985 Tancredo Neves was elected as the first civilian president for 21 years. Before he could take office he fell ill and died. His vice-president José Sarney became president at a time of economic crisis, with inflation at 300%. Sarney introduced the Cruzado Plan in 1986, freezing prices and wages, but inflation exploded when the freeze was lifted.

A new constitution brought direct presidential elections in November 1989. After two rounds of voting Fernando Collor de Melo, of the small Partido da Reconstrução Nacional, won 53% of the vote to narrowly defeat his left-wing rival, Luís Inácio da Silva (popularly known as Lula). Collor launched controversial economic reforms, including opening the economy to imports, privatisation and a freeze on savings and bank accounts. The policies failed and by 1991 inflation reached 1500% and foreign debt payments were suspended.

Just over half way through his term, Collor was suspended from office after Congress voted overwhelmingly to impeach him for corruption. He avoided this by resigning on 29 December 1992. Vice-president Itamar Franco took over, but had scant success in tackling poverty and inflation until the introduction of an anti-inflation package that introduced the *real* as the new currency.

The plano real

The architect of the *real* plan was finance minister Fernando Henrique Cardoso. Three decades earlier he had been a high-profile leftist and opponent of military rule, forced into exile after the 1964 military coup. The success of the *real* plan led to his election as president in October 1994. After trailing Lula of the Workers Party (PT), Cardoso gained such popularity that he won the election in the first round of voting. However, his alliance of the Brazilian Social Democrat Party (PSDB), the Liberal Front (PFL) and the Labour Party (PTB) failed to gain a majority in either house of Congress. This severely hampered plans to reform the tax and social security systems and the civil service. The government was also criticized for its slowness in addressing social problems. Such problems ranged from the need for land reform and violence associated with landlessness, to the slave-like working conditions in agricultural areas and the human rights of the *indígenas* and of street children in large cities.

Towards the end of 1997 the financial crisis in Asia sapped investor confidence throughout the world, and threatened Brazil's currency and economic stability. The failure to cut public spending had swollen the budget deficit and the *real* was exposed to speculation. Cardoso was obliged to take actions to prevent an upsurge in inflation and devaluation of the currency, but at the cost of slowing down economic growth. Crisis was avoided and inflation remained in single figures, in contrast to the hyperinflation of earlier periods.

The government still faced the serious social imbalances that it had failed to redress. However, Cardoso managed to beat Lula again in October 1998 without the need for a second poll. In doing so he became the first Brazilian president to be elected for a second term.

Cardoso's second term

Cardoso and his PSDB party emerged victorious from the 1998 elections with 99 Deputies, but they needed allies both in the 513-seat Chamber of Deputies and in the Senate. Political opponents had also won many powerful state governorships. The PSDB's relations with its major ally, the PFL, came under increasing strain. Unlike the PSDB, the PFL is a conservative group dominated by old-style politicians, typified by its leader Antônio Carlos Magalhães, who increasingly controlled Congress. There were rumours of corruption in Cardoso's government, with not even the president himself above implication. Another financial crisis threatened, which was averted by an IMF loan of US$18 billion at the end of 1998, but the delayed social security reforms had still not been passed. Finally when ex-president Itamar Franco, governor of Minas Gerais, refused to pay his state's debts to the Federal Government in January 1999, foreign investors lost confidence. The pressures on the *real* became too great and the central bank had to let it float freely against the dollar. It lost 50% of its value in the process. Two more stable years followed, but with its economic credibility eroded and shifting alliances in Congress the Cardoso government made little progress with its policies.

The 2002 elections

As in the USA, Brazilian presidents cannot run for a third term. Four front-runners emerged in the 2002 elections. Taking an early commanding lead in the opinion polls was Luiz Inácio Lula da Silva, best known as Lula, who was making his fourth bid for the presidency. With a refurbished image, a new suit, moderated policies and a millionaire running mate, the veteran firebrand, gained support from all classes.

Against a backdrop of global crises, the *real* again lost some 50% of its value in less than a year. Foreign investors were concerned about repeated budget deficits, and the prospect that a more left-wing government might default on debts. In August 2002, the IMF again came to the rescue, this time with a record US$30-billion loan, subject to tough conditions. On 27 October 2002 Lula won a convincing victory against government-backed José Serra. The new president – once shoe-shine boy, ex-leader of the Metal Workers' Union and head of the Workers' Party – set out to lead the first left-wing government in Brazil for 40 years.

For foreigners, what was perhaps most remarkable about Lula's first term of office was how little changed. Whilst Chávez in Venezuela and Ivo Morales in Bolivia forged policies allying their countries with Cuba and Cuban ideology, which included preaching a gospel of hatred and mistrust against the United States, Lula forged a middle way. In one of the first meetings with George Bush, the new president made it clear that Brazil was open for business and that he expected the USA to be open to Brazilian exports, particularly agricultural products that had long been denied access to US markets. Lula also wanted to acknowledge Brazil as a regional power. Nor did Brazil plummet into economic crisis as was predicted by the likes of George Soros. Its economy continued to grow steadily, albeit at a slower rate than its counterparts in Asia. And publicly Lula distanced himself from firebrand left wing Latin Americans like Chávez; preferring to foster closer trade relations with China and India. Lula also attempted to introduce reforms that ran against the grain of Brazilian society and political practice, by filtering money from the elite and the public service establishment to the less privileged. Brazil's public services are among the most cumbersome, financially draining, bureaucratic and corrupt in the world. And none are more so than the pension system. Many public sector professionals collect several pensions and many retire on pensions higher than their final salary. Judges for example receive an average of US$2500 per month. Army officers do even better and pass on their pensions to the second generation after their death. In contrast state pensions to the private sector average US$120 per month. In 2002 the state pension ran a deficit worth 4.3% of GDP or US$18 billion. One of Lula's early achievements was to get the Senate to pass a bill on pensions reform, capping public pensions at US$750 per month (still two times higher than the average middle class salary), raising the retirement age and introducing new pension taxes. This resulted in strikes by half of the country's federal workers and the blocking of the bill by judges; a process which can take years to unravel in Brazil's equally bureaucratic courts.

2004-2009

In mid-2004 Lula published an impressive proposed bill on Agrarian Reform which promised far more than any Brazilian government ever has: 400,000 families are to be settled via expropriation, 200,000 to be settled on land purchased by a Credito Fundiário small loans bank, designed to sell to small farmers at subsidized interest rates. He also launched a *Fome Zero*, or 'no hunger' programme, designed to give all poor Brazilians enough to eat.

But the second half of Lula's first term saw his good intentions frustrated by a combination of incompetence and corruption. Municipal governments, principally individual mayors, tried to control the disbursement of funds both for the Credito Fundiário and the Fome Zero programme; raking off public money has long been a way of life in Brazil. As so often in Brazil's history, money dedicated for the poor was ending up in private bank accounts. And in 2005 a corruption scandal called the Mensalão rocked Lula's federal government. Public funds had been used to bribe smaller parties to vote for Lula's government in the two federal chambers. Lula's deputy resigned, together with several senior PT members. Lula denied involvement but was severely compromised and was branded either oblivious and therefore incompetent or corrupt himself. A savage press campaign against him boded ill for the federal elections of 2006. But Lula won again; buoyed by popular support from the poor urban majority. Well into his second term it still remains to be seen whether his reforms will prove more far-reaching. Lula seems more intent on consolidating Brazil's ever strengthening position in a post credit-crunch world – as a repository of great mineral (and following a major discovery), oil and water wealth and one of the largest food producers on the planet.

Culture

People

Indigenous peoples

There were probably between three and five million indigenous people in Brazil when the Portuguese arrived. Today there are between 200,000 and 300,000. The effects of European colonization were devastating – whole tribes were wiped out under the Portuguese Amazon slave trade and others set to fight against each other for Portuguese advantage. Present-day tribal groups number about 220; each has a unique dialect, but most languages belong to four main linguistic families, Tupi-Guarani, Gê, Carib and Arawak. A few tribes remain uncontacted, others are exclusively nomadic, others are semi-nomadic hunter-gatherers and farmers, while some are settled groups in close contact with non-indigenous society. There is no agreement on precisely how many tribes are extant, but the Centro Ecumênico da Documentação e Informação (CEDI) of São Paulo said that of the 200 or so groups it documented, 40% have populations of less than 200 people and 77% have populations of less than 1000. Hemming underlines this depressing statistic when he reports that tribes contacted in recent decades have, as have others in previous centuries, suffered catastrophic reductions in numbers as soon as they encounter diseases which are common to non-indigenous people, but to which their bodies have no immunity.

Most of Brazil's indigenous people live in the Amazon region; they are affected by deforestation, encroachment from colonizers, small- and large-scale mining, and the construction of hydroelectric dams. Besides the Yanomami, other groups include the Xavante, Ticuna, Tukano, Kreen-Akrore, Kaiapó, Bororo and Arara. The struggle of groups such as the Yanomami to have their land demarcated in order to secure title is well-documented. The goal of the Statute of the Indian (Law 6.001/73), for demarcation of all Indian land by 1978, is largely unmet. It was feared that a new law introduced in January 1996 would slow the process even more. However all is not bleak. The populations of many indigenous groups have grown over the last decade and a number have their land rights, which have been protected under Brazilian Law, by Fernando Henrique Cardoso and by Lula (although the latter is alleged to have reneged on a

Indigenous people of Brazil

As a percentage of population Brazil has few indigenous people. But total numbers are large, with estimates varying between 450,000 and almost a million; in some 227 tribal nations. These are scattered throughout the country from the far south to the Amazon; with the greatest numbers in that region. In addition some 30% of Brazilians are part indigenous, many being *caboclo* (a word in the interior or north and northeast) or *caiçara* (used on the south and southeast coast) peoples leading traditional semi-indigenous largely self-sufficient lives. There are also traditional communities founded by African fugitives from slavery – or *quilombos*. It is possible to visit all of these communities. This should always be organized beforehand. Visitors who arrive unannounced will not be welcome and in some areas may be putting themselves at considerable risk. Details of how to visit are given in the relevant section of the text.

promise to enshrine an important area territory in Roraima into law at the 11th hour in exchange for support by powerful members of the state elite). On occasion indigenous land rights are enforced. A flight out over the Xingu in northern Mato Grosso shows this starkly, with the indigenous territory as a huge green island in a sea of soya and cattle plantations. Funai, the National Foundation for the Support of the Indian, a part of the Interior Ministry, is charged with representing the Indians' interests, but lacks resources and support. There is no nationwide, representative body for indigenous people, although the Amazon indigenous lobbying group, COIAB, is increasingly powerful and Manoel Moura's FIUPAM (fiupam@yahoo.com.br) is growing daily.

Mestiços

At first the Portuguese colony grew slowly. From 1580 to 1640 the population was only about 50,000 apart from the million or so *indígenas*. In 1700 there were some 750,000 non-indigenous people in Brazil. Early in the 19th century Humboldt computed there were about 920,000 whites, 1.96 million Africans, and 1.12 million *indígenas* and people of mixed Portuguese and indigenous origin (*mestiços*): after three centuries of occupation a total of only four million, and over twice as many Africans as there were whites.

The arid wastes of the *sertão* remain largely uncultivated. Its inhabitants are *mestiço*; most live off a primitive but effective method of cultivation known as 'slash and burn'. This involves cutting down and burning the brushwood for a small patch of ground, which is cultivated for a few years and then allowed to grow back.

Afro-Brazilians

Racism is culturally rife in Brazil and often openly expressed in all-white company. Though there is no legal discrimination against black people, the economic and educational disparity – by default rather than intent of the Government – is such that successful Afro-Brazilians are active almost exclusively in the worlds of sport, entertainment and the arts.

Brazilian culture, however would be nothing without its African influences. Those interested in the development of Afro-Brazilian music, dance, religion, arts and cuisine will find the cities of Rio de Janeiro, Bahia and São Luís, which retain the greatest African influences, particularly fascinating. Black Pride movements are particularly strong in Bahia.

After the rigours of transatlantic shipment in tiny rat-infested spaces, the Africans suffered further trauma on arrival at the Brazilian ports. They were often sold in groups that were segregated to avoid slaves from the same family or speaking the same language being together. By breaking all cultural and sentimental ties, the Portuguese hoped to eradicate ethnic pride and rebellions on the estates. As a result African spiritual cults became mixed and syncretistic even before they mixed with Portuguese Catholicism and indigenous spirituality. In what is now modern day Nigeria, for instance, there were different groups of people, each with its own divinity or *orixá* (pronounced 'orisha'). These *orixás* were normally the spirit of a distinguished ancestor or a legendary hero and were worshipped only in a particular region. As the slaves went to Brazilian estates in groups made up of people from different African regions, they soon started to worship all the *orixás*, instead of just one. As a result uniquely Afro-Brazilian religions were born out of the template of African spirituality, notably *candomblé*, *umbanda*, and *macumba*.

Europeans

Modern immigration did not begin effectively until after 1850. Of the 4.6 million immigrants from Europe between 1884 and 1954, 32% were Italians, 30% Portuguese, 14% Spanish, 4% German, and the rest of various nationalities. Since 1954 immigrants have averaged 50,000 a year. Most of the German immigrants settled in Santa Catarina, Rio Grande do Sul, and Paraná. The Germans (and the Italians, Poles and other Slavs who followed them) did not, in the main, go as wage earners on the big estates, but as cultivators of their own small farms. Here there is a settled agricultural population cultivating the soil intensively.

Asians

There are some one million Japanese-descended Brazilians; they grow a fifth of the coffee, 30% of the cotton, all the tea, and are very active in market gardening. Today the whites and near-whites make up about 53% of the population, people of mixed race about 34%, and Afro Brazilians 11%; the rest are either indigenous or Asian. There are large regional variations in the distribution of the races: the whites predominate greatly in the south, which received the largest flood of European immigrants.

Arts and crafts

Woodcarving

Woodworking has two principal origins, the African and the Jesuit. In northeastern Brazil, many woodcarving and sculpting techniques are inherited from the African slaves who were brought across the Atlantic to work the sugar plantations. One of the most prominent examples is the *carranca*, the grotesque figurehead that was placed on a boat's prow to ward off evil spirits. *Carrancas* are an adaptation of the African mask-making tradition and other carved and sculpted masks can be found in the northeast. The Jesuits passed on skills in the carving and painting of religious figures in wood. Originally they encouraged their indigenous converts in the techniques, but today others practice the art. Woodcarving is widespread in Pernambuco and Bahia in the northeast. In Rio de Janeiro many contemporary artists work in wood and Embu, near São Paulo (see page 210), is a centre for wooden sculptures and furniture making.

Ceramics

In northeastern Brazil, religious figures are also made in clay, for instance the unglazed, life-sized saints made from red clay in Tracunhaém, near Recife. Another centre for similar work is Goiana, also in Pernambuco. A third place from which the ceramics are even more famous is Alto da Moura, near Caruaru (Pernambuco – see page 509). Here, Mestre Vitalino began modelling scraps of clay into little figures depicting everyday life (work, festivals, dancing, political events). He died in 1963, but the tradition that he started has continued and is known throughout Brazil.

The pots that are made in the Amazon region come in various styles, some of them quite strange. Bahian and other northeastern pottery shows African influence.

Textiles, clothing and leather

Ceará, in the north, is famous for its lace-making, and beautiful pieces are sold all over Brazil. In other parts of the north, hammocks and other woven items are found. The hammock is, of course, an essential household item and you may well need to buy one if you are travelling up the Amazon on a boat. Other utilitarian articles which have become craft items are the rugs and capes made in the highlands further south, such as Minas Gerais, to keep out the night-time cold.

In the northeast, traditional costumes have their roots in the rituals of the African religions that came to Brazil with the slave trade. In southern areas where European immigration was heaviest, many traditional costumes can be seen, usually at the festivals and dances that have survived. Another type of clothing from the south is that associated with the *gaúchos*, the Brazilian cowboys of Rio Grande do Sul. As well as the clothes, which normally use hide in their manufacture, you may also buy saddlery, stirrups, silverware and the gourds used for drinking *maté*.

Leatherwork is not confined to the south, but can be found in any region where cattle are raised.

Musical instruments

The most popular instruments that tourists like to buy are those connected with African music, especially the hand and friction drums like the *zabumba*, cuica and *reco reco*, shakers and the *berimbau* (the one-stringed bow that is twanged in accompaniment to capoeira). Here again, the best place to look is in the northeast where the African heritage is strongest. You can also purchase guitars and other stringed instruments. For a glossary of instruments see Music and dance section, page XV.

Basketware

In Amazônia, a huge variety of raw materials are available for making baskets, nets, hammocks, slings for carrying babies, masks and body adornments. In the northeast, too, baskets come in all shapes and sizes, especially in Bahia, Pernambuco and Paraíba. Another northeastern craft, which does not fit into the above categories, is pictures made in bottles with coloured sands (Lençóis, Bahia, and Natal, Rio Grande do Norte, are good places to buy them). In Minas Gerais, two very common things to see and buy are soapstone carvings (for instance birds and animals) and the cooking pots used in *mineira* kitchens.

Gemstones

Even before the discover of rich mineral deposits in the interior of the country, legends told of mountains full of precious stones. Prospectors looked for diamonds and emeralds as well as gold and silver to make them wealthy. The existence of gems was known about almost from the earliest days of the Portuguese colony, from the reports given to the new arrivals by the *indígenas* and from scattered discoveries of different stones. But there was nothing to bring riches on the scale of the silver and gold found in the Spanish colonies. Gold was found in Minas Gerais in the 17th century and diamonds in 1725 at Diamantina (Minas Gerais) and thus Brazil's mineral wealth began to appreciate. The search for new deposits has never flagged.

Commercially mined stones include: **diamonds**, found in Minas Gerais, Roraima, Bahia, Tocantins, Mato Grosso and Mato Grosso do Sul. Brazil was the world's largest producer of diamonds until South Africa entered the market in the 19th century. **Emeralds**, not discovered in Brazil until 1963 (many green beryls had been mined before then, but were known not to be true emeralds), are now mined in Bahia, Minas Gerais and Goiás. **Aquamarine** is a clear blue beryl from Rio Grande do Norte, Paraíba, Bahia, Minas Gerais and Espírito Santo. **Ruby** and **sapphire** are two shades of the same mineral, corundum, the former rich red, the latter a deep blue. Rubies are found in Santa Catarina, sapphires in Minas Gerais. The two most valued forms of **topaz** found are the rare Imperial Topaz from Ouro Preto (Minas Gerais), which comes in a range of colours from honey-coloured through shades of red to pink, and Blue Topaz from Minas Gerais and Rondônia.

Tourmalines are also found and come from Minas Gerais, Ceará and Goiás; they have the widest range of colours of any gemstone, from colourless (white) to red, yellow, greens, blues, lilac and black. They even come in bi- and tri-coloured varieties. **Opals**, unique for their rainbow flecks, are mined in Piauí and Rio Grande do Sul. **Amethyst**, a quartz which ranges in colour from pale lilac to deep purple, is mined in Tocantins, Pará, Bahia, Mato Grosso do Sul and Rio Grande do Sul. From the last three states, plus Minas Gerais, comes **citrine**, another quartz which is predominantly yellow. Less well-known, but equally beautiful are **kunzite**, a rare pinkish-violet stone, and **chrysoberyl**, both found in Minas Gerais. Chrysoberyl is found in a variety of forms, a golden-yellow-brown, 'cat's eye' chrysoberyl, which has an luminous thread running through it, and the very rare **alexandrite**, which changes colour according to the light. Its most spectacular form changes from green in daylight to red in artificial light.

Festivals

Brazilians love a party and the mixing of different ethnic groups has resulted in some particularly colourful and varied celebrations. The difficulties of daily life are often relieved by the fantasy and release of Carnaval as well as the many other popular festivals held throughout the year. Wherever you go you will find street vendors selling ice-cold beer and the smell of *churrasco* coming from improvised barbecues accompanied by loud vibrant music and dancing in the streets. ▶▶ *For festival dates, see Essentials page 48, and relevant chapters throughout the book.*

Carnaval

Almost all Brazilian towns have some form of Carnaval festivities. Although the most famous is Rio de Janeiro, there are equally spectacular and different traditions in Bahia and Pernambuco, as well as a number of other good locations for those who wish only to party. The colonial mining towns of Diamantina and Ouro Preto in the interior of Minas Gerais are good locations to spend Carnaval in atmospheric surroundings. Florianópolis and Laguna on the coast of Santa Catarina have less traditional but still very popular and lively carnivals.

Out of season carnivals
Street carnivals with *trios eléctricos* in the style of Bahia are held throughout Brazil at various times of the year. Some of the most popular are **Micareta** in Feira de Santana (April), **Fortal** in Fortaleza (July) and **Carnatal** in Natal (December). Although by no means traditional they are nonetheless exuberant and enjoyable.

Other popular festivities
There are several other festivals which are almost as important to Brazilians as Carnaval. **Reveillon** (New Year's Eve) is a significant event and is generally celebrated on beaches. This can be either a hedonistic party as at Copacabana and Arraial D'Ajuda with the revellers dressed in white for luck, or as a respectful *candomblé* ceremony in which flowers are launched into the sea at midnight as an offering to Yemanjá.

The **Fiestas Juninhas** (São João) are extremely popular especially in the northeast and are held around 24 June (St John's day). Fires are built and *forró* is the music of choice with the festivities lasting for over a week at times. Fireworks and the co-ordinated dancing of groups called *quadrilhas* are also part of the celebrations.

In the north, the African and Indian cultures have mixed to form the Boi-Bumba tradition. In Amazonas, the **Festa do Boi** has become more commercialized but is still very impressive and popular. In Maranhão, where it is known as **Bumba-Meu-Boi**, the festivities are more traditional but equally as popular.

There are many Catholic saints' days that are sometimes celebrated in conjunction with African deities (especially in Bahia). Every town has a patron saint and his or her day will be an excuse for civic festivities, in addition to those of the foundation day of the town.

Immigrants from Europe to the south of Brazil and elsewhere have brought festivals from their own cultures such as the **Oktoberfest** held in Blumenau, believed to be second only to Munich.

Literature

The colonial period
Some of the major differences between Brazil and Spanish America spring from the history of colonization in the two areas. There were no great empires with large cities like those of the Incas or the Aztecs, and Portuguese exploitation concentrated first on extractive, then on cultivated export products (brazil-wood, then sugar). Although cities like Recife, Bahia and Rio de Janeiro did finally develop, there was, incredible as it may seem, no printing press in Brazil until the flight of the Regent, King João VI to Rio in 1808. This is not to say that there was no colonial literature, though scholars can still quarrel about how 'Brazilian' it was. When the Portuguese set foot in Brazil in 1500, the letter sent back to King Manuel by Pero Vaz de Caminha, already wondering at the tropical magnificence of the country and the nakedness of the inhabitants, set themes that would recur in many later works. The first plays to be put on in Brazil were religious dramas, staged in three languages – Portuguese, Spanish, and Tupi – by the Jesuit **José de Anchieta** (1543-1597). The most notable 17th-century poet is **Gregório de Matos** (1636-

1696), famous for his sharp satires on the corrupt life of the city of Salvador, and its tempting black and mulatta women. In the late 18th century, a group of poets from the gold-mining area of Minas, foremost among them **Tomás Antônio Gonzaga** (1744-1810), were at the centre of the early, abortive move for independence, the *Inconfidência* (1789; see page 272). Although best known as a lyric poet, Gonzaga has been proved to be the author of the anonymous satirical poem *Cartas chilenas*, which gives a vivid portrait of colonial society.

The 19th century

It is helpful to understand Brazilian literature, even long after political independence, as a gradual and, to some extent, contradictory process of emancipation from foreign models. Every European literary movement – Romanticism, Realism, Symbolism, etc – had its Brazilian followers, but in each there was an attempt to adjust the model to local reality. A good example is the first of these, Indianism, which flourished in the mid-19th century, and produced two central figures: the poet **Antônio Gonçalves Dias** (1823-1864), himself partly of indigenous descent, and the novelist **José de Alencar** (1829-1877). It is a form of Romanticism, idealizing the noble savage, and with plots adapted from Walter Scott, and it happily ignored what was happening to real indigenous tribes at the time. However, it does express national aspirations and feelings, if in nothing else, in the nostalgia for a kind of tropical Eden expressed in perhaps the most famous Brazilian poem, Gonçalves Dias *Canção do exílio*: "My land has palm-trees/ where the sabiá sings. /The birds that sing here/ don't sing like those back home." Alencar's novels, not all of them about Indians, are a systematic attempt to portray Brazil in its various settings, including the city. *O guarani* (1857), turned into a famous opera by Carlos Gomes, and *Iracema* (1865), are his most popular. The latter is perhaps the most complete mythical version of the Portuguese conquest, allegorized as a love affair between a native woman and an early colonist, Martim Soares. Iracema, "the virgin with the honeyed lips" dies in childbirth at the end, but the future lies with their mixed-blood son, Moacir.

After his death, Alencar was succeeded as the chief figure in Brazilian letters by **Joaquim Maria Machado de Assis** (1839-1908). Perhaps Brazil's best writer, and certainly the greatest to appear in Latin America until well into the 20th century, he had to fight against formidable obstacles: he was of relatively poor origins, was mulatto, he had a stammer and, in later life, was subject to epileptic fits. He wrote nine novels and more than 200 short stories as well as poetry and journalism. He ended his life as an establishment figure and founder of the Brazilian Academy of Letters. But his novels, especially those written after 1880, when he published *Memórias póstumas de Brás Cubas*, and the best of his stories are surprisingly subversive, covert attacks on slavery and on male power, for instance. He avoided detection by not using his own voice, hiding behind quirky, digressive narrators who are not always trustworthy. All the novels and most of the stories are set in Rio, which he hardly left, and give a remarkably varied account of the city and its different social levels. His most famous novel, *Dom Casmurro* (1900) is one of the best-disguised cases of an unreliable narrator in the history of the novel, and still arouses critical polemics.

Machado's atmosphere is predominantly that of the empire, which fell in 1889, a year after the abolition of slavery. In the Republic, a younger generation, more overtly rebellious in their aims, and affected by new scientific ideas from Europe, came to the fore. If Machado is the most famous Brazilian author, perhaps *Os sertões*, by **Euclides da Cunha** (1866-1909) is the most famous book. It is an account of the Canudos campaign in the interior of the state of Bahia in 1896-1897. The campaign was a horrific failure, victory being won only at a huge cost in casualties, and Euclides da Cunha, sent to cover it as a journalist, turned this failure into an indictment of a social system, which excluded huge groups of people. Written in a dramatic, somewhat self-indulgent style, with extensive use of scientific words, it has been excellently translated as *Rebellion in the Backlands*.

The other important prose writer of this period, the novelist **Afonso Lima Barreto** (1881-1922), was mulatto like Machado, but there resemblances end. Much more openly rebellious and less of a conscious artist than Machado, his novels, the most notable of which is *Triste fim de Policarpo Quaresma*, are overt attacks on intellectual mediocrity, and the corruption and despotism into which the Republic soon fell. A passing mention ought to be made, too, of one of the 'unclassifiable' books in which Brazilian literature abounds: **Helena Morley**'s *Minha vida de menina* (translated by Elizabeth Bishop as *The Diary of Helena Morley*), and only published in 1942. It is the precocious, funny, and remarkably perceptive teenager's diary, written in Diamantina, Minas Gerais, at the end of the 19th century.

The 20th century

In general, the poetry of the turn of the century was imitative and stuffy. Renewal did not come until the early 1920s, when a group of intellectuals from São Paulo, led by the unrelated **Mário de Andrade** (1893-1945) and **Oswald de Andrade** (1890-1954) began the movement known as modernism. This is conveniently supposed to have begun in 1922, the centenary of political independence, with a Week of Modern Art in São Paulo; in fact it began earlier, and took until the mid-1920s to spread to the provinces. In great part, modernism's ideology was nationalist, and though the word spanned the political spectrum, at its best it simply meant the discovery of a real Brazil behind stereotypes. Mário travelled throughout the country, attempting to understand its variety, which he embodied in his major prose-work, the comic 'rhapsody' *Macunaíma* (1928), which in its plot and language attempts to construct a unity out of a complex racial and regional mix. Also in 1928, Oswald launched the 'anthropophagist', or cannibalist programme, which proclaimed that Brazilian writers should imitate their native predecessors, and fully digest European culture: a new kind of Indianism, perhaps.

The most enduring artistic works to have emerged from modernism, however, are poetic – two of Brazil's major modern poets, **Manuel Bandeira** (1886-1968) and **Carlos Drummond de Andrade** (1902-1987) were early enthusiasts of modernism, and corresponded at length with Mário. Bandeira, the older man, made a slow transition to the new, freer style; his poems, often short and based on everyday events or images, nevertheless have a power and rhythmic accuracy that are deceptively simple. Drummond's poetry is more self-conscious, and went through a complex intellectual development, including a period of political enthusiasm during the Second World War, followed by disillusionment with the beginning of the Cold War. His themes, including some remarkable love-poetry addressed by a 50-year-old to a younger woman, and a lifelong attachment to Itabira, the small town in Minas Gerais where he was born, are very varied. Readers without Portuguese can best approach Drummond, widely regarded as Brazil's greatest poet, through an excellent anthology, *Traveling in the Family*.

The 1930s were a crucial decade. With increasing political mobilization, the growth of cities, and of an aspiring middle class, literature began to look to a wider audience; however, at first, it still reflected the dominance of rural life. The realism of this period, which often had a strong regionalist bias, had its raison d'être in a society still divided by huge social and/or geographical differences, and indeed played its part in diminishing those differences. Many of the first group came from the economically and socially backward northeast. **José Lins do Rego** (1901-1957) is perhaps the most characteristic figure. He was highly influenced by the ideas of **Gilberto Freyre** (1900-1987), whose *Casa grande e sensually* (*The Masters and the Slaves*), published in 1933, was one of the most important and readable of Brazilian books. It is a study of the slave-based, sugar-plantation society, and one of the first works to appreciate the contribution made by Blacks to Brazil's culture. It remains, however, very paternalist, and Lins do Rego's fiction, beginning with the semi-autobiographical *Menino de engenho*, reflects that, commenting on the poverty and filth of the (ex-)slave-quarters as if they were totally natural. His 'sugar-cane cycle' sold in large editions, in part because of its unaffected, simple style.

A greater novelist belonging to the same group is **Graciliano Ramos** (1892-1953). His fiction is much more aggressive, and in later life he became a communist. His masterpiece, turned into an excellent film in the 1960s, is *Vedas secas*, which returns to the impoverished interior of *Os sertões*, but concentrates on an illiterate cowhand and his family, forced from place to place by drought and social injustice; it is a courageous attempt to enter the mental world of such people. *Memórias do cárcere*, published after Ramos's death, is his unflinching account of his imprisonment for a year during the Vargas regime.

The essential novelist to read for anyone visiting the south of Brazil is **Érico Veríssimo** (1905-1975), especially his epic trilogy collectively entitled *O tempo e o vento* (*O continente* [1949], *O retrato* [1951], and *O arquipélago* [1961]) spread over two centuries of the turbulent history of Rio Grande do Sul.

Gradually, in the 1940s and 1950s, a subtler and more adventurous fiction began to be published alongside the regionalist realism that was the major heritage of the 1930s. Three writers stand out: João Guimarães Rosa, Clarice Lispector and João Cabral de Melo Neto. **João Guimarães Rosa** (1908-1967) published his major novel, *Grande sertão: veredas* in 1956. Almost Joycean in its aspirations and linguistic innovations, it is a kind of mixture of a cowboy story and a modern version of Faustian pact with the devil. For those without stamina (and excellent Portuguese), the translation (*The Devil to Pay in the Backlands*) is unfortunately not an adequate alternative. Rosa is best approached through his stories, those of Sagarana (particularly *A hora e vez de Augusto Matraga*) being perhaps the best.

The stories and novels of **Clarice Lispector** (1920-1977) now have a considerable audience outside Brazil, as well as a huge one inside it. Her stories, especially those of *Laços de família* (1960), are in general set in middle-class Rio, and usually have women as their central characters. The turbulence, family hatreds, and near-madness hidden beneath routine lives are conveyed in unforgettable ways, with a language and symbolism that is poetic and adventurous without being exactly difficult (she said she fought with the Portuguese language daily). Some of her novels have over-ambitious metaphysical superstructures, and may not be to some readers' tastes – *A paixão segundo G H*, for instance, concerns a housewife's confrontation with a dead cockroach in her maid's room, and her final decision to eat it, seen as a kind of "communion". When at her best, in some of her journalism, in her late, deliberately semi-pornographic stories, and above all in the posthumous novel, *A hora da estrela*, which approaches the poor in an utterly unsentimental way, Lispector can stimulate and move like no one else.

The greatest poet of this generation is **João Cabral de Melo Neto** (1920-1999), whose best poetry concerns his home state, Pernambuco. The drought-ridden interior, the lush but oppressive landscape of the sugar-plantations, and the city slums are all present in the verse-play *Morte e vida severina* (1956), and his tight, sparse poetry often returns to the same places, or analogous ones in the several countries (most importantly, in Spain) in which he has resided as a diplomat.

The 1964 military coup, and the increasing use of torture and censorship in the late 1960s and early 1970s, had profound effects on literature, especially as they were accompanied by vast economic changes (industrialization, a building boom, huge internal migration, the opening up of the Amazon). At first, censorship was haphazard, and the 1960s liberation movements had their – increasingly desperate – Brazilian equivalents. Protest theatre had a brief boom, with *Arena conta Zumbi*, about a 17th-century rebel slave leader, produced by **Augusto Boal** (born 1931), being one of the most important. The best fictional account of those years can be found in two novels by **Antônio Callado** (born 1917), *Quarup* (1967), set in the northeast and centred on a left-wing priest, and *Bar Don Juan* (1971), whose focus is on the contradictions of a group of middle-class guerrillas; and in **Ivan Ângelo**'s *A festa* (1976), set in Belo Horizonte, a funny and hard-hitting account of a varied set of people, which chronicles the impact of the 'sex and drugs' revolution alongside its political concerns. A remarkable documentary account of the period is ex- guerrilla (subsequently leader of the Green Party) **Fernando Gabeira**'s *O que é isso companheiro?* (1982), which chronicles his involvement in the kidnapping of the American ambassador in 1969. Poetry at this time went through a crisis of self-confidence, and it was widely thought that it had emigrated into the (marvellous) lyrics of such popular composers as **Chico Buarque de Holanda** and **Caetano Veloso**, who were also the foremost standard-bearers of political protest in the 1970s.

It is impossible in the space available to give more than a few suggestions of some of the best work published in recent decades, concentrating on books which have been translated. A brilliant satirical novel by **Paulo Emílio Salles Gomes** (1916-1977) about the São Paulo upper middle class is *Três mulheres e três Pppês* (1977); **Darcy Ribeiro** (born 1922), an anthropologist and politician, took time off to write *Maíra* (1978), an updating of Indianism, but with real *indígenas* and a threatened Amazon environment; **Rubem Fonseca** (born 1925), whose story *Feliz ano novo* (1973) created a scandal because of its brutal treatment of class differences, has dedicated himself to the writing of hard-nosed thrillers like *A grande arte* (1983); **Caio Fernando Abreu** (1948-96) is a short-story writer of considerable talent, dealing with the alienated urban young in such books as *Morangos mofados* and *Os dragões não conhecem o paraíso*; finally, **Milton Hatoum**'s *Relato de um certo oriente* (1989) is a vivid novel set in Manaus, amongst the Lebanese immigrant community. He followed it with the highly acclaimed *The Brothers*. Patricia Melo has devoted her writing to exploring social problems in her native Rio. Several of her books have been filmed; most notably *O Matador* (*O Homen do Ano* or *Man of the Year*), the story of a man who accidentally becomes a ruthless hired gun. The country's leading literary export is without a doubt the popular mystical novelist, Paulo Coelho, most famous for his whimsical novel, *The Alchemist*.

Recommended reading

Essays and books that can be wholeheartedly recommended for those who want more information are: Ray Keenoy, David Treece and Paul Hyland, *The Babel Guide to the Fiction of Portugal, Brazil and Africa in English Translation* (London: Boulevard Books, 1995). Irwin Stern (ed) *Dictionary of Brazilian Literature* (New York: Greenwood Press, 1988). Mike

González and David Treece, *The Gathering of Voices* (Verso, 1992) (on 20th-century poetry). Elizabeth Bishop and Emanuel Brasil (eds) *An Anthology of Twentieth-Century Brazilian Poetry* (Wesleyan University Press, 1972); John Gledson, *Brazilian Fiction: Machado de Assis to the Present*, in John King (ed), *Modern Latin American Fiction: A Survey* (Faber, 1987). Many of the essays in Roberto Schwarz, *Misplaced Ideas: Essays on Brazilian Culture* (Verso, 1992), especially those on *Machado de Assis*, and *Culture and Politics in Brazil, 1964-1969* are very stimulating. ▸▸ *See also Books, page 819.*

Fine art and sculpture

The colonial era: 16th and 17th centuries

No visitor to Brazil should miss visiting a colonial church. During the colonial period in Brazil the Church dominated artistic patronage, with the religious orders vying with each other to produce ever more lavish interiors. In the 17th century the Benedictines included several notable sculptors among their ranks. Much of the magnificent gilded interior of the monastery of São Bento in Rio de Janeiro is by **Frei Domingos da Conceição** (circa 1643-1718), who worked there during the 1660s. His *Crucifixion* of 1688 in the monastery of São Bento in Olinda sets up a deliberately shocking contrast between the sinuous elegance of Christ's body and the terrible lacerations of his flesh. **Frei Agostinho de Piedade** (died 1661) of the Benedictine community in Salvador produced some old-fashioned terracotta reliquary busts during the 1630s and 1640s (Museu de Arte Sacra, Salvador) but the powerful *Penitent Peter* in Salvador's Nossa Senhora do Monte (circa 1636), also attributed to him, prefigures the emotional intensity of subsequent generations.

A distinctive feature of colonial interiors is the incorporation of decorative scenes in blue and white painted tiles, *azulejos*, around the walls. These were imported from Portugal from the earlier 17th century onwards, with subject matter as often secular as religious. Good examples include the Franciscan foundations in Olinda, Salvador and Recife, and the church of Nossa Senhora da Glória in Rio de Janeiro, which has hunting scenes in the sacristy, Old Testament figures in the choir, and in the nave, astonishingly, scenes of pastoral love loosely based on the *Song of Songs*.

The 18th century

Although 17th-century church decoration is often lavish there is little warning of the extraordinary theatricality which characterizes the work of the 18th century. Behind their sober façades churches open out like theatres, with the equivalent of balconies and boxes for the privileged, and a stage for the high altar with a proscenium arch and wings of carved and gilded wood. Cherubs whisper to each other or gesticulate from their perches amongst the architectural scrolls; angels, older and more decorous, recline along a cornice or flutter in two dimensions across an illusionist ceiling. The object of devotion is usually placed high above the altar on a tiered dais, surrounded by a Bernini-esque sunburst of gilded rays. A skilled exponent of this type of design was the Portuguese-born sculptor **Francisco Xavier de Brito** (died 1751), as in Nossa Senhora do Pilar, Ouro Preto and São Francisco de Penitência, Rio.

Xavier de Brito was largely responsible for bringing the Baroque style to Brazil and this style reaches its most ornate and theatrical in the work of Xavier de Brito's pupil, **Aleijadinho**, the 'Little Cripple' (1738-1814) a mulatto artist who worked in the province of Minas Gerais. As by far the most famous artist in the colonial period in the whole of Latin America it is perhaps not surprising to find his name attached to an impossible number of projects, but a consideration even of the securely documented reveals a man of extraordinary passion and energy who worked as a painter, architect and, above all, sculptor. The church at Congonhas do Campo offers the most dramatic example of Aleijadinho's art. Pilgrims paying homage to the miracle-working Bom Jesus do Matozinhos approach the church along a penitential road winding up the hill between six small chapels, each housing scenes from Christ's Passion represented by life-size expressive statues of polychrome wood. The final ascent is up an imposing double staircase under the stony gaze of 12 judgmental prophets who variously lament, threaten or cajole, addressing the heavens, the distant horizon, each other, or the faithful on the stone steps below them. In a building beside the church a fascinating display of drawings and photographs of the many accidents and emergencies from which the Good Jesus has saved people, testifies to the continuing popularity of this shrine.

The paint equivalent to Aleijadinho's sculptures can be found in the work of his contemporary, **Manuel da Costa Ataíde** (1762-1830) from Mariana, whose vividly colourful narrative scenes decorate numerous churches in Minas Gerais. Ataíde's rococo settings are populated with solidly-built saints and angels whose rolling eyes and exaggerated gestures give them an earthy vigour sometimes at odds with the spirituality of the subject matter, as in the illusionist ceiling of São Francisco de Assis, Ouro Preto, a church whose design is traditionally attributed to Aleijadinho. Both Aleijadinho and Athayde were probably friends of the insurrectionist Tiradentes and criticisms of the Portuguese and the appalling treatment of non-European Brazilians is implicit in their work (for more details see box, page 268)

In Bahia, **José Joaquim da Rocha** (1737-1807), see page 405, was one of the most successful artists of his day and his slightly Italianate ceiling paintings survive in many churches in Salvador. The best sculptor of the late colonial period in Bahia was **Manuel Inácio da Costa** (1763-1857) whose figures, often dramatically gaunt with protruding veins and large eyes, are reminiscent of Aleijadinho's work (see, for example, his *Christ at the Column* in the Museu de Arte Sacra in Salvador). It is in Rio that sculpture first begins to sober up again, as for example in the work of the sculptor Valentim de Fonseca e Silva, known as **Mestre Valentim** (circa 1750-1813), which can be seen in several churches including São Francisco de Paula and Nossa Senhora da Glória. Valentim also designed the first public gardens in Rio: the *Passeio Público* was inaugurated in 1783 and included walks, seats decorated with *azulejos* and pavilions. A unique series of six painted views of Rio and Guanabara Bay by **Leandro Joaquim** (1738-1798), originally made for one of the pavilions, are now in the Museu Histórico Nacional in Rio.

French influence in Imperial Brazil

After the transfer of the Imperial court to Rio in 1808, João VI made a determined effort to renovate Brazilian culture, and in 1816 the French Artistic Mission – a boatload of painters, sculptors, architects, musicians and craftsmen – arrived from France to found what was to become the Imperial Academy. Two artists were particularly influential: **Nicolas-Antoine Taunay** (1755-1830) and **Jean-Baptiste Debret** (1768-1848). Taunay's luminous landscapes of the area around Rio and Debret's lively street scenes helped to open up new areas of secular Brazilian subject matter, and inspired artists throughout the 19th century. The Academy provided scholarships to send promising young artists to Paris, so reinforcing the French influence, and there are echoes of Delacroix in the work of **Vítor Meireles** (1832-1903) as for example, in his *Battle of the Guararapes* of 1879 in the Museu Nacional de Belas Artes, Rio, and of Ingres in *La Carioca* (1882) of **Pedro Américo**

50 of the best Brazilian musicians

1 Albery Albuquerque, www.myspace.com/alberyalbuquerque. Jungle jazz with real forest animals.

2 Acid-X, www.acidx.com.br. Carioca Acid Jazz. *Na Estrada* is a classic.

3 Adriana Calcanhotto, www.adriana calcanhotto.com. Smoochy, clever, smooth.

4 Afro Reggae, www.myspace.com/afroreggae. *Capa de Revista* is the real sound of the *favela* funk outrage.

5 Airto Moreira, www.airto.com. Along with Naná Vasconcelos, perhaps the world's greatest ever percussionist. *Identity* is the album.

6 Ana Cascardo, www.ana cascardo.com.br. Classic contemporary MPB à la Milton Nascimento.

7 Andreia Dias, www.andreiadias.com.br. Sultry, smoky and the modern São Paulo sound; her first CD *Vol 1* is sumptuous.

8 Antônio Carlos Jobim, one of the inventors of bossa nova and great innovators of Brazilian music. *Garota da Ipanema* is the most famous, but *Matita Pere* is also recommended.

9 Arkestra One, www.cosmicsounds-london.com. Nina Miranda of *Smoke City's* greatest Brasil-trip hop moment.

10 Axial, www.axialvirtual.com. Wonderful percussion, seductive singing. *Papaloko* is gorgeous.

11 Baden Powell, not the scout master but Brazil's greatest ever samba guitarist.

12 Banda Black Rio, www.banda blackrio.com. Rio funk soul maestros, go for *Gafieira Universal*.

13 Bezerra da Silva, the father of political samba and an all round joyfully cynical genius.

14 Cabruera, www.myspace.com/cabrueramusic. Mangue beat samba rock from Paraíba.

15 Caetano Veloso, www.caetano veloso.com.br. Brazil's Bowie and the co-founder of *tropicália*.

16 Carlinhos Brown, www.carlinhos brown.com.br. Salvador's great musical iconoclast and a thorn in the side of the white elite. Is there anything funkier than *Pandeiro-Deiro*? See box, page 425.

17 Cassia Eller, if Kurt Cobain had been a lesbian from Brasília he'd have sounded like this. She even did a version of *Smells like Teen Spirit*.

18 CéU, www.myspace.com/ceuambulante, Where samba, *electronica* and intelligence meet. *Malemolencia* is as good enough as melted chocolate.

19 Chico Science, this genius invented mangue beat, died young, and went to rock Olympus. *Macô* is a track that should be listened to loud and in an altered state.

20 Clara Moreno, www.myspace.com/claramoreno. *Forget Tanto Tempo Electromblé* is what Brazilian *electronica* should always sound like.

21 Clepsidra, www.myspace.com/clepsidrarelogiodeagua. Clever art electronica-samba-bossa nova-indie rock-jazz fusion from Belém. With violins.

22 Coletivo Radio Cipo, www.my space.com/coletivoradiocipo. See our opener and download *Cowboy Sem Lei*.

23 Curimbó de Bolso, it's hard to find but *Cantação Amazônica* is a sonic sliver of pure trance-inducing tropical jungle joy. Get it from Ná Figueredo in Belém.

24 DJ Dolores, www.myspace.com/djdoloresaparelhagem. Where mangue beat goes club.

25 DJ Patife, www.djpatife.com.br. The father of the drum 'n bass with DJ Marky, djmarky.uol.com.br.

26 Djavan, www.djavan.com.br. Brazil's Stevie Wonder. We like *Bicho Solto O XIII*.

27 Dori Caymmi, www.doricaymmi.com. Carefully crafted, beautiful jazz-tinged music from Bahia. We love his fusion work with Larry Coryell and Billy Cobham on *Live from Bahia*.

28 Dorival Caymmi, Brazil mourned when he died in 2008. The father of Bahian music.

29 Ed Motta, one of the most important musicians in Rio soul and jazz. *Aystelum* is a classic.

30 Elis Regina, to many she's Brazil's greatest ever singer. *Elis e Tom* is a landmark album.

31 Érika Machado, www.erika machado.com.br. Quirky Mineira, see box, page 260.

32 Hermeto Pascoal, www.hermeto pascoal.com.br. If Stockhausen were genetically fused with Mingus and raised in Alagoas perhaps he'd play something like this extraordinary *Música Universal*.

33 Gilberto Gil, www.gilbertogil.com.br. Funky, smart ex-minister of culture and co-founder of *tropicália*. His albums are patchy. Cherry pick.

34 Itamar Assumpção. Difficult, odd, witty, intensely rewarding and impossible to play. Try *Navalha Na Liga*.

35 João Bosco, www.joaobosco.com.br. The pinnacle of erudite sung samba. *Casa de Marimbundo* is like a bolt of pure rhythmic energy.

36 Jorge Ben, www.jorgeben.com.br. One of Rio's great funkster tunesmiths – including *Mas que Nada*.

37 Karnak, www.andreabujamra.com. São Paulo art rock samba.

38 Madame Sataan, www.myspace.com/madamesaatan, Superb power metal from the Amazon. Singer Sammliz sings like a female Eddie Vedder and is as beautiful as bossa.

39 Marcel D2, www.marcelod2.com.br. Irresistibly funky samba-rap. Try *Loadeando*.

40 Mariene de Castro, www.mariene decastro.com.br. Great modern Bahian samba. See box, page 425.

41 Marlui Miranda, her *Tudos os Sons* brought the music of the indigenous Amazonians to the world. A masterpiece.

42 Max de Castro. Vanguard experimentalism from São Paulo. *Silêncio No Brooklyn* twists and turns with endless inventiveness. Wonderful. See box, page 215.

43 Milton Nascimento. *Clube da Esquina* is simply one of the greatest records of all time.

44 Naná Vasconcelos, www.nana vasconcelos.com.br. Vies with Airto for the title of world's greatest ever percussionist. Endlessly inventive. *Fragmentos* is the album. Or *Storytelling*. See box, page 500.

45 Orchestra Imperial, www.myspace.com/orquestraimperial. Joyful, masterful, delicious tongue-in-cheek big band samba from master producer Kassin and his pals.

46 Rappin Hood, www.trama.uol.com.br/ rappinhood. Infectious samba funk rapper whose *Sou Negao* (with Possumente Zulu) bursts with danceability.

47 Relogios de Frederico, www.relogiosdefrederico.mus.br. Inventive funk rockers from Porto Alegre.

48 Seu Jorge, www.seujorge.com. The current Brazilian ambassador to the musical world plays Jorge Ben samba funk with a political theme, We love all of *America Brasil*, especially *Mina do Condomínio*.

49 Zeca Baleiro, www2.uol.com.br /zecabaleiro. *Meu Tribo Sou Eu* should be a national anthem for the post-racial world. He also wrote a very funny song about Stephen Fry.

50 Zé Ramalho, www.zeramalho. com.br. A kind of desert troubadour whose gravel voiced post-psychedelia would be great in David Lynch film. His most famous track is called *Brave New Cow* and is a work of genius.

(1843-1905) in the same museum. The influence of Courbet can be seen in the so-called belle époque of the first republican years (1889-1922), in particular in the work of Meireles' pupil, **José Ferraz de Almeida Júnior** (1850-1899).

The 20th century, towards a Brazilian vision

Brazil moved from this essentially academic tradition straight into the radicalism of the early 20th century, and movements such as Cubism, Futurism, Fauvism and Constructivism were quickly translated into distinctively Brazilian idioms. **Lasar Segall** (1891-1957), **Anita Malfatti** (1896-1964) and the sculptor **Vitor Brecheret** (1894-1955) were pioneers of modernism, working in relative isolation before the 1922 Semana da Arte Moderna (Modern Art Week) in São Paulo drew together a group of artists and intellectuals whose influence on Brazilian culture can still be felt today. They sought to challenge established bourgeois attitudes, to shake off the traditional cultural subservience to Europe, and to draw attention to the cultural diversity and social inequality of contemporary Brazil. **Emilio di Cavalcanti** (1897-1976) mocked the artificiality of white middle-class socialites and championed Blac Brazilian beauty (examples in the Museu de Arte Contemporânea, São Paulo). **Tarsila do Amaral** (1886-1973) borrowed her loud colours from popular art while her imagery includes ironic reworkings of European myths about the savage cannibalistic *indígenas* supposed to inhabit the Brazilian jungle. **Cândido Portinari** (1903-1962) used murals to expose the exploitation and injustice suffered by workers and peasants, while **Osvaldo Goeldi** (1895-1961) explored similar themes in his powerful wood engravings. Portinari, in an interesting revival of the colonial use of *azulejos*, created murals in blue and white painted tiles for modern architecture such as the MES building by Costa and Niemeyer of Rio, begun in 1937, and Niemeyer's church of São Francisco in Pampulha, Belo Horizonte (1943).

The economic strength of the middle years of the century encouraged state patronage of the arts. President Getúlio Vargas recognized that art and architecture could be used to present an image of Brazil as a modern industrialized nation, with Brasília being the culmination of this vision. Museums of Modern Art were founded in São Paulo and Rio, and in 1951 São Paulo hosted its first **Bienal Internacional**, which attracted abstract artists from Europe and the US and confirmed Abstraction – symbol of progress and technological modernization – as the dominant mode in Brazil during the 1950s. Rivalry between the artistic communities of Rio and São Paulo helped to produce some outstanding avant-garde art. In the 1950s **Waldemar Cordeiro** (1925-1973), leader of the São Paulo Grupo Ruptura, painted what at first sight appear to be rather simple geometric patterns in bright, contrasting colours, but on closer attention the flat surface seems to break up, suggesting recession, space and restless movement, in some ways prefiguring the British Op Art movement of the 1960s. The Neo-Concrete group of artists of Rio argued for the integration of art into daily life, and experimented with art that made sensory and emotional demands on the 'spectator' whose participation leads in turn to creation. During the early 1960s, **Lygia Clark** (1920-1988) made *bichos* (*animals*) out of hinged pieces of metal which, as the name implies, are like creatures with a life of their own: they can be rearranged indefinitely but because of their complexity it is impossible to predetermine what shape will result from moving a particular section. Nowadays, unfortunately, they are displayed in museums where touching is not encouraged (as in the Pinacoteca do Estado, São Paulo). **Hélio Oiticica** (1937-1980) took the idea further, working with people (poor and often black) from the samba schools in the Rio *favelas* to create artistic 'happenings' involving dance, music and flamboyant costumes called *parangolés* (capes). The notion that a key function of art should be to shock the bourgeoisie was first voiced in the 1922 Week of Modern Art. Oiticica often succeeded, and he and other artists of the 1960s also realized another of the aims of the first modernists: to create Brazilian modern art that was not the poor relation of developments in Europe or the US. A museum of his work is now open in Rio. Other important figures of this generation include the neo-concretist painter **Ivan Serpa** (1923-1973), **Sérgio Camargo** (1930-1990), who produced textured rhythmic constructions of white on white but because they are made with off-cuts of wood they suggest the tensions between form and material, geometry and nature; and **Amílcar de Castro** (born 1920) whose deceptively simple sculptures are often cut from one large panel of cast iron.

The military coup of 1964 marked the beginning of a period of political repression and of renewed artistic energy, with figurative tendencies re-emerging. In 1970 **Antônio Enrique Amaral** (born 1935) took as his theme the banana, so often used in dismissive references to Latin America, and in an extended series of paintings monumentalized it into an extraordinary symbol of power and productivity. In an ironic neo-colonial altarpiece (circa 1966) installed in the Museu de Arte de São Paulo, **Nelson Leirner** (born 1932) makes the object of devotion the neon-lit head of pop star Robert Carlos. Conceptual art offers different ways of confronting the dominant ideology. Both **Cildo Meireles** (born 1948) and **Jac Lierner** (born 1961) have used, misused or forged banknotes, for example, and both they and **Waltercio Caldas** (born 1946) and **Tunga** (born 1952) have created installations which draw attention, directly and indirectly to environmental issues. The painter **Siron Franco** (born 1947) also often addresses the issue of the destruction of the Amazon rainforest, but his disturbing surreal images explore many other areas – industrial pollution, sexual fantasy, political corruption, national identity – making him one of the most exciting artists in Brazil today.

Architecture

Brazilian colonial style: houses and civic buildings

The earliest Portuguese colonizers to arrive in Brazil in the 16th century faced many problems in building their houses, forts, churches and other necessary structures. First of all there was a lack of building materials, such as bricks, roof tiles and mortar. Second, there were few trained craftsmen, such as carpenters and bricklayers, in the colony. They therefore had to improvise by developing unusual building techniques and trying different materials. In the hinterland, in places like São Paulo, Goiás and Minas Gerais the majority of the houses were built with *taipa de pilão*. This technique consisted in using a wooden form to build thick walls. These forms were filled with a mixture of clay, vegetable fibres, horsehair, ox blood and dung. This paste was then compacted with a pestle and allowed to dry for two to three days before the next layer was added. The roof tiles were often moulded on a female slave's thigh and dried in the sun.

It is quite easy to identify a house in Brazilian colonial style. Their shapes, colours and building techniques remained virtually unchanged for almost three centuries. Firstly, they always had large, visible roofs, made with red clay tiles, finishing in eaves extending beyond the walls. All the buildings were painted in a white wash, with bright colours used only on window and door frames. These were made of wood and had, mostly, elegant arches at the top. In the 19th century, sash windows with squared 10 sq cm pieces of glass were added in many houses, as can be seen in cities like Paraty, Ouro Preto and Salvador.

Urban colonial houses had doors and windows opening directly onto the street. Courtyards were never placed in front of the house, but internally, forming airy patios which protected the privacy of the family. The furniture was extremely simple and rough. Often, the only pieces of furniture in a bedroom would be the bed itself and a leather box to store clothes and personal belongings. In the colonial period, the highest status symbol was to live in a *sobrado* (a house with more than one floor, usually two). The ground floor was normally a commercial business and above it the residence of the owner's family.

Churches, convents and religious buildings: the baroque in Brazil

Houses, public buildings and other colonial civic edifices were generally unelaborate. All the refinement, style and sophistication in art, architecture and decoration was lavished on churches, convents and monasteries. The great religious orders, such as the Jesuits, Franciscans, Carmelites and Benedictines brought to Brazil the latest artistic trends from Europe, mainly the Baroque and Rococo.

Two separate strands in Brazilian religious architecture evolved. In the most important cities, close to the seaboard and more influenced by European culture, the churches and convents were built according to designs brought from Portugal, Italy and Spain. Some were merely copies of Jesuit or Benedictine temples in Europe. Examples of this can be found in Salvador (the main cathedral, the São Francisco church), Rio de Janeiro (the Mosteiro de São Bento, the Convento de Santo Antônio) and Olinda (church and convent of Nossa Senhora das Neves).

Brazilian baroque

At the end of the 17th century gold was found in the region of Minas Gerais. One of the first administrative acts of the Portuguese crown in response to this discovery was to banish the traditional European orders from the mining region. The royal administration wanted to control the mining itself, taxation and traffic in gold and, as the friars were regarded as among the most shameless of smugglers of the metal, the orders in this instance were denied the support they were given elsewhere in the Portuguese colonies. Therefore the majority of the churches in cities like Ouro Preto, Mariana, Congonhas and Sabará were built by local associations, the so-called 'third orders'. These lay orders had the gold and the will to build magnificent temples but, although they wanted their projects to be as European as possible, the original designs were hard to obtain in such out-of-the-way places. So the local artists had to find their own way. Inspired by descriptions and second-hand information, they created their own interpretation of the Baroque, thoroughly infused with regional influences and culture. This is the reason why the 'Barroco Mineiro' is so original.

Curved churches and the decline of the Gold Era

At the beginning of the 18th century, when gold was easily found in Minas Gerais, the main attraction was the inside of the church; richly and heavily decorated in carved wood and gold. Many of the churches built in this period will be a total surprise for the visitor. Their façades and exteriors are so simple and yet the naves and altars are so highly and artistically decorated. As the mines started to decline, the outside of the buildings became more sophisticated, with curves, round towers and sinuous walls, such as the churches of São Francisco de Assis and Rosário, in Ouro Preto. As the gold for covering walls ran out, it was replaced by paintings and murals.

The 19th century and the neoclassic style

The beginning of 19th century brought a major change in the history of Brazilian architecture. When Napoleon invaded Portugal in 1808, the Portuguese royal family and some 15,000 nobles and wealthy families fled to Rio de Janeiro, bringing with them their own view of what was sophisticated in the arts. In 1816 the king, Dom João VI, invited a group of French artists (The French Artistic Mission) to Brazil to introduce the most recent European trends in painting, sculpture, decoration and architecture. This was the beginning of the neoclassic style in Brazil. An Imperial Academy of Fine Arts was created and all the new government buildings were built in neoclassic style. The great name of this period was the French architect Grandjean de Montigny, who planned and built many houses and public buildings throughout the city of Rio de Janeiro.

The rich and famous also wanted their houses in this newly fashionable style, which revolutionized the Brazilian way of building. The large roofs were now hidden by a small wall, the plat band. Windows and doors acquired round arches and walls were painted in ochres and light tones of pink. Public buildings and churches started to look like ancient Greek temples, with triangular pediments and columns. This new style was not best suited to Brazil's climate. The earlier, large colonial roofs were much more efficient in dealing with heavy tropical rains and, in consequence, the neoclassic style never became popular in the countryside.

Even when the coffee planters, in the second half of 19th century, started to become extremely rich and fond of imported fashions, they would build their urban mansions in the neoclassic style, but still keep their farm houses with large roofs, sometimes adding small neoclassic details in windows, doors and internal decoration. Good examples of this 19th-century rural architecture can be found very close to Rio de Janeiro, in cities like Vassouras, Valença, Barra do Piraí and Bananal, where some of the old farm houses are open to visitors.

There are many examples of urban neoclassic building in Rio de Janeiro, such as the Museu Nacional, the Santa Casa da Misericórdia, the Casa de Rui Barbosa and the Instituto Benjamin Constant. Also very close to Rio, in Petrópolis, the Museu Imperial (formerly the emperor's summer palace) is also a perfect example of the style. This neoclassic style remained popular in Brazil until the end of the 19th century, being also the 'official' style of the first and the second Brazilian empires.

The early 20th century and the eclectic style

After the republic, in 1889, the neoclassic style lost favour since it had been serving the king and the emperors for such a long time. A new style, or better, a new harmony of different styles started to gain popularity, also under the influence of Paris and the belle époque. There were elements of neoclassic architecture, but also an excess of decoration and adornment on the façades. A broad 'boulevard' was constructed in Rio de Janeiro in 1906, the Avenida Central (today Avenida Rio Branco), with the idea of creating a 'Paris in the Tropics'. There are many examples of buildings in the eclectic style on this avenue: the Biblioteca Nacional, the Teatro Municipal (opera house) and the Museu Nacional de Belas Artes, all of them built within the first decade of 20th century. Also in Manaus, during the rubber boom, many buildings adopted this style, such as the Teatro Amazonas (opera house). During the first two decades of this century, the eclectic style remained very popular.

The 'Modern Art Week' of 1922 and national pride

In 1922 a group of artists, painters, poets and architects organized in São Paulo 'A Semana da Arte Moderna' or the Modern Art Week, during which they exhibited their distaste at the influence of foreign standards in Brazilian art. They considered their role to be a quest for a genuine Brazilian form of expression. This resulted in the rejection of all imported standards and, as far as architecture was concerned, two main currents emerged: neocolonial and modernism.

The Neocolonial

The first movement sought its true Brazilian style in the past, in the colonial period. Architects like Lúcio Costa, studied the techniques, materials and designs of the 16th, 17th and 18th centuries, soon producing houses with a colonial look, but also combining elements which were only previously found in baroque churches. These included pediments and decorated door frames. The style was called neocolonial and remained popular until the 1940s, especially in Rio de Janeiro and São Paulo.

In search of greater authenticity, architects employed original materials brought from demolished old houses. A good example of this can be found in Rio de Janeiro, in the Largo do Boticário (very close to the train station for Corcovado, in Cosme Velho), a small square surrounded by neocolonial houses painted in fancy, bright colours.

Modernism

The other current generated by the Semana da Arte Moderna looked to the future for its inspiration for Brazilian-ness. Architects such as Oscar Niemeyer, Lúcio Costa, Affonso Eduardo Reidy, the landscape designer Roberto Burle Marx and many others started to design functional and spacious buildings, with large open areas and *pilotis* (pillars carrying a building, leaving the ground floor open). The use of concrete and glass was intense and the masterpiece of the Brazilian architectural modernism is Brasília, the capital, planned from scratch in the 1950 by Lúcio Costa and Oscar Niemeyer.

Many examples of modernist building can be found all over Brazil: in Brasília, the cathedral, the National Congress, the Palácio do Planalto (the presidential palace), in fact the whole city, with its broad freeways and spacious urban blocks, called *quadras*; in Belo Horizonte, the church of São Francisco de Assis, in Pampulha; in São Paulo, the MASP (Museum of Art of São Paulo), the Memorial da América Latina, and many commercial buildings along the Avenida Paulista; in Rio de Janeiro, the Ministério da Educação e Saúde, the Museu de Arte Moderna, the Catedral Metropolitana, the Petrobrás building (Brazilian State Petrol Company), the BNDES building (National Bank of Social and Economic Development), all in the central area of the city.

Brazilian contemporary architecture

The most recent trend is the postmodern. Many business centres, shopping malls and residential buildings are being designed in a style which uses coloured mirror glass, granite and stylized structures reminiscent of classical temples.

Brazilian architects are also famous worldwide for their techniques in designing houses for construction on steeply-inclined hills. In Rio de Janeiro, if you are driving along the coastal road in the neighbourhoods of Barra and São Conrado you can see many of these astonishing projects, which are homes of the very wealthy.

Land and environment

Geography

Brazil is the largest country in South America and the fifth largest in the world. It is almost as large as the USA and over covers 4300 km from north to south and the same from east to west, with land borders of 15,700 km and an Atlantic coastline of 7400 km. It borders all the other mainland South American countries except Chile and Ecuador and occupies almost half the total area of the continent. Its population of 162 million is the fifth largest in the world, and over half that of South America.

Geology

Although Brazil is dominated by the vast river basins of the Amazon and the Paraná which account for about three-fifths of the country, not much of it is 'lowlands'. Ancient rock structures, some of the oldest in the world, underlie much of the area creating resistant plateaux and a rounded hilly landscape. These ancient Pre-Cambrian rocks culminate in the Guiana highlands to the north and the crystalline ranges which run close to the coastline all the way from near the Amazon to the Uruguayan frontier.

It is believed that South America and Africa were joined in the geologic past, and there is a tolerable fit between the easterly bulge of Brazil and the Gulf of Guinea. Persuasive evidence has been found of identical ostracod fossils (freshwater fish) in corresponding Cretaceous rocks in both Brazil and Gabon, overlain by salt deposits that could have been the first appearance of the South Atlantic Ocean. This suggests that the split began some 125 million years ago. What is now accepted is that the South American Plate continues to move westwards with the consequent elevation of the Andes on the other side of the continent where it meets the Pacific Plates.

Amazon basin

The Amazon river is the greatest in the world in area of drainage, about 7,000,000 sq km, and in volume of discharge into the sea averaging 180,000 cu m per second (or 170 billion gallons per hour), 10 times that of the Mississippi, and more than all the rivers of Europe put together. Such is the flow that the salinity of the Atlantic Ocean is affected for 250 km out from the river delta. It is 6400 km long (marginally shorter than the Nile) from its sources in the Andes of Peru, and still has over 3000 km to go through Brazil when it leaves Leticia on the Colombia/Brazil border, yet with only a fall of 80 m to sea level. Unlike most major world rivers, the basin is reduced in width near its mouth, indeed hills come down to the river near Monte Alegre only 200 km from the delta. Some 200 km above this at Óbidos, the river is over 75 m deep, that is the bottom is well below sea level. This reflects the more recent geological history of the basin which until the latter part of the Tertiary Period (say 25 million years ago) was connected to the Pacific and drained through what is now Ecuador. With the uplift of the Andes, this route was closed off, and a huge inland sea was formed, helped by a downward folding of the older rocks (some geologists believe there was also significant rifting of the strata) to create a huge geosyncline. Eventually the water broke through the crystalline rocks to the east and made the new connection to the Atlantic. Deep layers of sediment were laid down and have been added to ever since, with today's heavy tropical rains continuing to erode the surrounding mountains. This gives the largest, more or less, level area in Brazil, but it is so heavily forested and the soils so continually leached by the climate, with vast expanses frequently under floodwaters, that the potential for agriculture is strictly limited.

A characteristic of virtually all the tributaries which join the Amazon from the south is that upstream navigation ends where the rivers tumble off the plateaux of central Brazil creating dramatic waterfalls and in many cases now providing hydroelectric power.

Centre West

South of the Amazon basin is a large area of undulating highlands, a dry plateau mostly between 200 m and 800 m. These are ancient rocks, back as far as Pre-Cambrian crystallines. They produce poor soils but sufficient to provide the grasslands or *cerrado* of the Mato Grosso, Goiás, western Paraná and adjacent areas, widely used for ranching, though now increasingly found suitable for soya bean production, one of Brazil's foremost exports.

From Minas Gerais southwards, the rivers drain into the second largest basin of Brazil, the Paraná, which eventually reaches the Atlantic by way of the River Plate of Argentina/Uruguay. This is another large river system, 4000 km long, of which about half is in Brazil. A principal tributary of the Paraná is the Rio Paraguai which, in its early stages, flows into a wide depression now filled with many thousands of metres of sediments and known in Brazil as the Pantanal. Further south, the swamps continue into the Chaco of Paraguay and Argentina. To the east of this, again the rivers fall off the old highland strata to form rapids and waterfalls, the largest of which was the former Sete Quedas Falls (Salto de Guaíra) on the Paraná, sadly drowned by the Itaipu Dam lake in 1982. Nearby however are the Iguaçu Falls, the most impressive of South America, created by very resistant layers of basalt.

The coast and escarpment

Highlands follow the coastline, only a short distance inland, for 3000 km. The ancient crystalline/granite ridges, known as *serras*, stretch from Porto Alegre in the south to near Belém in the north, just short of the Amazon estuary. Long stretches are in the form of a single or stepped escarpment, abrupt in the east and sloping more gently inland to the west. They are not high in South American terms – the highest point, Pico da Bandeira is only 2890 m – but it is no more than 120 km from the ocean near Vitória. The narrowness of the coastal strip has had a profound effect on the history of settlement. Until comparatively recent times, the lack of natural access to the hinterland confined virtually all economic activity to this area, and today most of the major cities of Brazil and 80% of the population are on or near the coast.

Because of varying erosion over many millions of years, there are a number of interesting natural features in these highlands. The many granite 'peaks' in and around Rio de Janeiro are the resistant remnants of very hard rocks providing spectacular viewpoints, Pico da Tijuca (the highest, 1012 m), Corcovado (710 m) and Pão de Açúcar (396 m) the best known. There are others in the neighbouring state of Espírito Santo. Near Curitiba are the eroded sandstones of Vila Velha and the wild scenery through the Serra do Mar towards the coast. In the state of Bahia, there are remarkable caves and waterfalls in the Chapada da Diamantina National Park. In many places, what rivers there are flowing eastwards necessarily have to lose height quickly so that gorges and waterfalls abound. There are also many kilometres of spectacular coastline and fine beaches. South of Porto Alegre, eroded material moved down the coast by the southerly ocean currents added to alluvials brought north from the River Plate by subsidiary currents, have created long sand bars to form several large freshwater lagoons. The longest, Lagoa dos Patos, is over 250 km long.

Rio São Francisco

The escarpment forces most of the rain run-off to flow west into the interior to feed the Amazon and Paraná river systems. However, one major river breaks through the barrier to flow into the Atlantic. The São Francisco rises south of Belo Horizonte – one important tributary starts only 250 km from the sea – but flows, north then east, for 2900 km before it gets there. Almost 500 km of rapids through the escarpment culminate in the 75 m Paulo Afonso falls, before completing the final 240 km to the sea. Where it turns east is one of the driest areas of the country, known as the *sertão*. The river is therefore of great significance particularly as the rains here are so unreliable. Together with the link it provides to so much of the interior and its course wholly within the country (unlike the Amazon and the Paraná), the São Francisco is revered by the Brazilians as the 'river of national unity'. Its value for irrigation, hydroelectric power, fish and navigation above the rapids is inestimable, but because of sand bars at its mouth and close proximity to the fall line, the river has not proved useful for shipping or access generally to the ocean in spite of being the third largest river system on the continent.

Northern highlands

After sinking below the Amazon estuary, the Brazilian highlands reappear to the north and sweep round to the west to form the border with the Guianas and Venezuela. The highest tabular uplands are near where Guyana, Venezuela and Brazil meet at Monte Roraima (2810 m) and further west along the border where a national park has been set up focussed on Pico de Neblina, 3014 m, the highest point in Brazil.

Climate

The climate of Brazil is a function of latitude and altitude. The average annual temperature exceeds 26°C along the northeast coast and in the central Amazon with little variation throughout the year. The highlands are cooler and further south there are seasonal variations: Brazil extends to 34° south, which is equivalent to the latitude of North Carolina. High summer temperatures can occur almost anywhere here, yet frosts are not uncommon in July and August as coffee producers know only too well. Rainfall is more complicated. The northeast trade winds bring moist air to the coast north of the Amazon, where there is heavy precipitation all year round. The same winds push saturated air into the Amazon basin where rainfall is progressively greater from east to west throughout the year and virtually on a daily basis. The abrupt rise of the Andes beyond the borders of Brazil increases the precipitation and feeds the many tributaries.

During the period December-May, the northeast trade winds move north and Brazil between Belém and Recife receives less rain-bearing winds. From Salvador, the southeast trade winds bring moisture from the South Atlantic and it is the gap between these two systems, known as the 'doldrums', that explains the dry areas of northeast Brazil. On average there is significant rainfall here, but sometimes it fails to arrive causing prolonged periods of drought. Precipitation in the southern states of Brazil is concentrated in the escarpment thus feeding the Paraná system and is well distributed throughout the year.

Although there are occasional storms causing local damage, for example in the *favelas* (shanty towns) of Rio, Brazil is not subject to hurricanes or indeed to other natural disasters common elsewhere in Latin America such as earthquakes, volcanic eruptions or unexpected widespread and catastrophic floods.

Ecosystems, flora and fauna

The neotropical region is a land of superlatives, it contains the most extensive tropical rainforest in the world, and is drained by the Amazon, which has by far the largest volume of any river system. The fauna and flora are abundant. There are more birds, primates, reptiles, amphibians, freshwater fish and plant species here than in any other region in the world. Ecosystems are to a large extent determined by the influence of the great rivers and mountains: the Amazon river system and the Andes (which, although not part of Brazil, dramatically affect the climate and river drainage) and the far older iron and sandstone hills and depleted soils of the Guiana and Brazilian shields that lie at the heart of the continent in the north along the border with Venezuela and in the heart of Brazil in Goiás, Tocantins and large parts of the Mato Grossos around the world's largest wetland, the Pantanal.

South America's isolation from the rest of the world, until the joining of the continent with North America some four million years ago years ago, has been another crucial contributing factor to its biodiversity. Unique families of birds called the sub-oscine passerines (which are unable to sing in the same way as other songbirds because of a physical peculiarity in their larynx) developed because of this isolation. And prior to the invasion from the north by more aggressive and competitive mammals (like the coatimundi and the puma) South America was home to large numbers of marsupials; a few of which cling on in the numerous opossum families.

Brazil can be divided into biogeographical zones: two huge **river basins** comprising the River Amazon and the River Plate; **mountains**, comprising the Guiana highlands to the north and the Brazilian highlands to the south where the *cerrado* forests lie; and a **coastal strip** of Atlantic rainforest.

Mata Atlântica (Atlantic rainforest)

The Atlantic rainforest used to cover 2,600,000 sq km in a coastal strip 160 km wide and 4200 km long but now covers less than 5% of that. As the forest ranges from sea level to over 2000 m and has been isolated biologically from the Amazon and Andes, it is one of the most biodiverse regions in the world; so much so; that it is one of Conservation International's designated world biodiversity hotspots: see www.hotspots.com, for further details. There are 21 different primate species found here (compared to, for example Costa Rica's four). Seventeen of these are endemic to the *Mata Atlântica*, and of these, 13 species including the golden lion tamarin, are endangered. South America's largest primate, the woolly spider monkey, known locally as *muriqui*, was hunted close to extinction by European colonists who first settled along this coastal zone and subsequently by Brazilian peasant farmers. But the monkey still clings on in private reserves like **REGUA** in Rio de Janeiro state (see page 168) and the Parque Nacional Caparaó in Minas Gerais.

Drift net and long line fishing in the 1960s decimated one of the healthiest populations of fish in the tropical Atlantic and the once abundant dolphin fish and tunny are now rarely seen and small fishing villages cannot survive on their catch. This loss in fish stocks has been exacerbated by the destruction of coastal mangroves throughout Brazil. Mangroves provide a breeding ground for numerous species including many that are commercially important and the shallow lagoons near the swamps are important for one of Brazil's two species of manatees. Now extensive areas of mangroves are limited to the Delta da Parnaíba in Piauí and stretches around Boipeba in Bahia and Cananéia in São

Wild animals in Brazil – where to see what

Mammals
Jaguar Refugio Ecológico Caiman, Miranda, Mato Gross do Sul (see page 749).
Fazenda San Francisco, Pantanal, Mato Grosso do Sul (see page 749).
Pousada Rio Vermelho, Pantanal, Mato Grosso do Sul (see page 750).
Pouso Alegre, Pantanal, Mato Grosso (see page 765). Cristalino Jungle
Lodge, Amazon, Mato Grosso (see page 766). Mamirauá Reserve,
Amazonas (see page 659).
Puma Parque Nacional das Emas, Goiás (see page 715).
Ocelot Fazenda San Francisco, Pantanal, Mato Grosso do Sul (see page 749).
Parque Nacional Superagüi, Paraná (see page 326).
Jaguarundi Parque Nacional das Emas, Goiás (see page 715).
Transpantaneira, Mato Grosso (see page 762).
Maned wolf Serra do Cipó, Minas Gerais (see page 290). Parque Natural de Caraça,
Minas Gerais (see page 257). Parque Nacional das Emas, Goiás (see page 715).
Bush dog Rio Sucuri, Bonito, Mato Grosso do Sul (see page 743).
Giant otter Fazenda Barra Mansa, Pantanal, Mato Grosso do Sul (see page 750).
Pousada Rio Vermelho, Pantanal, Mato Grosso do Sul (see page 750).
Tapir Refugio Ecológico Caiman, Mato Grosso do Sul (see page 749).
Uakari monkeys and spider monkeys Amazon Ecopark, Amazonas
(see page 665). Mamirauá Reserve, Amazonas (see page 659).
Saki monkeys Cristalino Jungle Lodge, Amazon, Mato Grosso (see page 766).
Titi monkeys Fazenda Bela Vista, Pantanal, Mato Grosso do Sul (see page 750).
Woolly spider monkey Parque Nacional Caparaó, Minas Gerais (see page 299).

Reptiles
Black and spectacled caiman Rio Javari (page 653). Rio Negro (see page 662).
Pantanal caiman Any locations near Miranda or the Estrada Parque,
Mato Grosso do Sul (see page 736) or the Transpantaneira,
Pantanal, Mato Grosso (see page 762).
Anaconda Transpantaneira, Pantanal, Mato Grosso (see page 762).
Estrada Parque, Pantanal, Mato Grosso do Sul (see page 736).

Birds
Greater rhea Anywhere in the Pantanal (see page 727).
Hyacinth macaw Fazenda San Francisco, Pantanal, Mato Grosso do Sul
(see page 749). Fazenda Xaraés, Pantanal, Mato Grosso do Sul (see page 749).
Other macaws Cristalino Jungle Lodge, Amazon, Mato Grosso (see page 766).
Mamirauá Reserve, Amazonas (see page 659).
Harpy eagle Floresta Amazônica Hotel at Cristalino Jungle Lodge,
Alta Floresta, Mato Grosso (see page 766).

Paulo. The once abundant *restinga* that lies behind the mangrove forests has also been
greatly depleted. *Restinga* consists of shrub forest, coastal sand dunes, ponds and

wetlands; there are remnants in areas like **REGUA** (see page 168) and in the Delta do Parnaíba (see page 588). The lush coastal rainforest itself extends to 800 m in elevation and grades into cloud forest between 800 m and 1700 m and although greatly depleted is still abundant in parts of Bahia, São Paulo, Paraná and Rio de Janeiro. In the cloud forests (which can be seen in Itatiaia), drenching by mist, fog and rain leads to a profusion of plant growth, trees and shrubs that are covered with a great variety of epiphytes, orchids (including the famous Cattleya which comes from Rio state), mosses, lichens and bromeliads. At the highest elevations, the forest gives way to mountain grasslands or *campos de altitude*. In the southern zone of the Atlantic forest, in Rio Grande do Sul and Santa Catarina, there are large stands of *araucária*, a relative of the monkey puzzle tree. The best places to see the *Mata Atlântica* are Itatiaia national park in Rio, the mountains behind Paraty and Ubatuba, and the coastal zone between Cananéia in São Paulo and Paranaguá in Paraná. The forest is immensely rich in bird life, with over 930 bird species, 144 of which are endemic species. The Serra dos Tucanos in Rio is perhaps the best place in Brazil for *Mata Atlântica* birding – with excellent guiding and facilities, followed closely by **REGUA** (see page 168). Self-guided birding is immensely rewarding – from the hills above Paraty, in the Serra dos Órgãos, in Itatiaia or the forests on the Ilha do Cardoso near Cananéia. The latter island is one of the few places where caiman still bask on coastal beaches. The best places to see the *Mata Atlântica* itself are Itatiaia national park, in Rio, the mountains behind Paraty and Ubatuba and the coastal zone between Cananéia in São Paulo and Paranaguá in Paraná.

Amazon rivers

The Amazon basin, which is made-up of myriad different rivers; more than four of which are by water volume the largest rivers in the world, contains the greatest area of tropical rainforest in the world, 6,000,000 sq km, 60% of which is located in Brazil. It is home to 20% of the world's plant and bird species; perhaps 10% of mammal species; an inestimable number of insects and perhaps some 2000 species of fish inhabiting the 1000 tributaries of the Amazon. When in flood the great river inundates the forest for a short period in its upper reaches to create a unique habitat called *várzea*; in the lower reaches this flooding may last for four to seven months forming *igapó* swamp forest.

The rivers of the Amazon are either classified as blackwater or whitewater rivers. The former are black-tea coloured due to the brown humic acids derived from the decomposing materials on the forest floor but contain little suspended material. The white waters owe their colour to the suspended soil particles which originate in the run-off from the Andes. Each has its characteristic fish. Within a 30-km radius of Manaus, there are estimated to be over 700 species of fish. Many are biologically curious. The pirarucu or *arapaima*, which can reach over 3 m and weigh in at over 150 kg has a primitive lung that enables it to live in oxygen-depleted water. Its habit of surfacing for air makes it easy prey for fishermen. Despite being served on tables throughout the Amazon it is a threatened species, protected by Ibama; the state environmental body. The piraiba is one of the world's largest catfish; aggressive and big enough to swallow a human. The candiru is one of the world's smaller catfish. It is parasitic, swimming into the gill spaces of other fish and lodging there to gorge blood. It is said to be attracted to urea and to swim up the urethra of swimmers who pee in the water, with unpleasant or even fatal consequences. The various species of piranha, are much maligned. The largest and most fearsome are the red piranhas and the grey piranhas, but although these fish can be dangerous when trapped in small pools in the dry season Amazonians quite happily swim in oxbow lakes filled with the fish in the wet. The pacu is

Destruction of the rainforest

Brazilian deforestation figures are huge. But the country has very progressive environmental legislation. In forested areas like the *Mata Atlântica* and the Amazon farmers are allowed to use only 20% of their land for crops. 80% must be left intact. A drive through the Goiás *cerrado* or the Amazon belies the law. Only about one in 10 farmers respects the law. And the law is strong only on paper.

one of the various species of vegetarian piranha, which feeds on fruit falling from trees in the flooded forest. More dangerous than piranhas are electric eels and sting rays; both of which are relatively common; as are bull sharks. An electrical shock of 650 volts has been recorded from a captive electric eel and the German naturalist and explorer Alexander Von Humboldt talked of them being able to knock out a fully grown horse.

Amazon forests

There are various forest types associated with and largely unique to the Amazon rivers. All the Amazonian forests are highly species rich. It has been estimated that 4 sq km of forest can harbour some 1200 vascular plants, 600 species of tree, and 120 woody plants. Gallery forests are those which are found along the banks of rivers; and which are subject to rapid erosion when the river changes course. These forests tend to grow on nutritionally rich soil and are often high in fruiting plants. *Várzea* is a biodiverse seasonally flooded forest found along the banks of the whitewater rivers; it is very nutritionally rich as a consequence of the huge amount of silt and nutrients washed out of the mountains and trapped by the massive buttress-rooted trees. It can be flooded for as much as seven months of the year and is found throughout the Amazon system. One of the most common *várzea* trees, the Pará rubber tree (*Hevea brasiliensis*), is the source of latex. The Brazilian rubber industry foundered in the 19th century when seeds of this tree were smuggled to Asia by the British and grown in vast rubber plantations, which flourished in the absence of Amazonian pest species. Another *varzea* tree is camu-camu, whose juice has by far the highest vitamin C content of any fruit in the world; despite claims made for various Australian berries. *Varzea* forests are good places to spot waterbirds such as the Amazon's many heron, egret, ibis, duck, cormorant and stork species, at least five kingfisher species, numerous raptors like black-collared hawks and endemic birds like hoatzin. These are generally found along waterways where it feeds on leaves and fruit. The newly hatched chicks of this primitive bird have claws at the tip of each wing which enable them to crawl around in the foliage. *Varzea* is frequently visited by parrots and macaws and by primates, who are all after seasonal fruit and nuts.

Igapó forests are seasonally inundated forests found on blackwater rivers. They grow in sandy soil, which lies as beautiful exposed beaches in the dry. The largest areas of *igapó* are found in the Rio Negro system, which joins the Amazon in Manaus. Despite being flooded for up to seven months of the year to a possible depth of 15 m, palms dominate the *igapó*, interspersed with large hardwood trees like kapok. During the wet season, these flooded forests are inhabited by turtles and small fish, and the predators that feed upon them – like giant otters and various species of caiman, which can be heard calling to each other at dawn. Bird and primate life is rich with similar families to *várzea*, though with less diversity as *igapó* has fewer fruiting trees.

Flooded meadows are frequently found in the still-flowing reaches of the *várzea*. These vast carpets of floating waterlilies (including the metre-wide *Vitória regia*), water lettuce and water hyacinth are home to the Amazonian manatee, a large herbivorous aquatic mammal, only a little smaller than the manatee associated with Florida and the Caribbean and the dugong of Australia. It is very difficult to see. Two species of dolphin hunt for fish in the *várzea* and *igapó*, as well as in the larger rivers, using sonar to catch their prey. The Amazonian dolphin, or *boto* is unique to the river system, and is bubble-gum pink. There are also enormous numbers of spectacled caiman that populate the forest and feed on the highly productive fish community. The most common species are the spectacled caiman (with a yellow eyelid) and the far larger black caiman.

Várzea and *Igapó*, together with terra firme forest, are the best places to spot wildlife in the wet. In the dry the best locations are the river corridors. Caiman and turtles are commonly seen basking on the riverbanks, and if you are really lucky you may see a jaguar or ocelot draped over a branch or a tapir, the largest South American mammal, taking a bathe or a drink. Birdlife is only a little less rich in the dry than the wet, with fewer migratory species but greater concentrations of water birds hunting for the dwindling supplies of fish. **Giant otters** are found in *várzea* and *igapó* as well as in oxbow lakes and on smaller Amazonian tributaries. They can grow to up to 2 m in length and are active by day when they hunt for food, often in small groups.

In the terra firme forests, which grow on permanently dry soil, the soaring canopy some 45 m overhead is home to the greatest numbers of animals. It is a habitat thick with strangling vines and numerous epiphytic plant species amongst which troupes of squirrel monkeys, in various species, and **capuchins** forage, alongside **uakari**, **saki** and **titi** monkeys. In the high canopy groups of **spider monkeys** perform their lazy aerial acrobatics, whilst lower down, clinging to epiphyte-clad trunks and branches, groups of tiny **tamarins** and **marmosets** forage for gums, blossom, fruit and the occasional insect prey. Small arboreal cats such as **margay** and large weasels, and racoons like **tayra** and **coatimundi**, prey on them. Families of **howler monkeys** noisily roar out their territorial boundaries at dawn and dusk. Birdlife is very rich, with high numbers of uniquely neotropical species such as turkey-sized **currasows** and **guans**, spectacularly coloured **cotingas**, **trogons** and **motmots**, myriad **tyrant flycatchers** and as many **woodpeckers**, **woodcreepers** and **foliage gleaners**; many associated with particular tree families. Brilliant **tanagers** and **hummingbirds** flit through the canopy flowers and all are watched over by a succession of **raptors**; the largest of which is the elusive metre-tall **harpy eagle**, with ankles as thick as a woman's wrist. These are big and powerful enough to pluck the larger monkeys and the various species of sloth out of the tops of trees. **Antbirds** and **manakins** flutter silently through the forest below; the former in various species each of which follow troupes of specific army ant families through the forest eating the insects they startle as they pass. The best places to see the Amazon wildlife are Cristalino Jungle Lodge (see page 766), Mamirauá Reserve (see page 659), the Anavilhanas Islands (see page 658), preferably on a cruise, and from the best of the jungle lodges around Manaus (see page 665).

The Pantanal

This ecologically diverse zone includes the largest area of wetlands in the world and is the best place in South America for seeing wild animals. Alongside the wetlands are dry savannahs, *cerrado*, chaco scrublands as well as gallery forest. The area is very flat and flooded by the rising rivers leaving isolated islands or cordilheiras between vast lakes or *baías*, which become saline as the waters evaporate. This mixed ecosystem supports a highly diverse fauna characteristic of the constituent habitat types which includes 200 species of mammal. **Capybara** (a large aquatic rodent that looks like a giant guinea pig), **tapir** and South America bush pigs or **peccaries** are common along the waters edge as are the **web-footed marsh deer**. **Jaguar**, the largest cat in the Americas weighing up to 150 kg, and **puma**, which are only a little smaller are more commonly associated with the forest and savannahs and prey on these herbivores and the cattle and feral pigs which graze here. **Giant anteater**, **armadillos** and **rhea** (South American ostrich(are seen in the grassland areas. Spectacular assemblages of **wading birds** such as egrets, jabiru storks, ibises, spoonbills and herons prey on the abundant invertebrate and fish. **Anacondas** and **Pantanal caiman** (a sub-species of spectacled caiman) are still common, although the large black caiman has been hunted out. The best places to see animals in the Pantanal are the Transpantaneira (see page 762) in Mato Grosso and the *fazendas* around Miranda (see page 748).

The cerrado

The *cerrado* is Brazil's outback and makes up most of the interior of the country between the coast and the Amazon basin, much of Mato Grosso and Mato Grosso do Sul including parts of the Pantanal, almost all of Goiás, Tocantins, Minas Gerais and the far west of the northeastern states are *cerrado*. It is the most extensive woodland-savannah region in South America. Like the Australian outback, the *cerrado* comprises forest, grassland and scrub broken by rivers and underground streams. Also like the outback it grows on ancient, eroded rock and it bursts into bright bloom in the wet. Within the *cerrado*, there is a tapestry of different vegetation types, including tree and scrub savanna, grassland with scattered trees, and occasional patches of a dry, closed canopy forest called the *cerradão*. Gallery forests are found throughout the region, although they are technically not considered part of the typical *cerrado* formations. Unlike the outback the *cerrado* gets plenty of rain (around 1500 m per year), usually between October and April. For the rest of the year the *cerrado* is dry – so much so that many of the plants have adapted to drought conditions – with leathery or waxy leaves and some deciduous tendencies. Much of the vegetation is also adapted to fire. The *cerrado* is Brazil's most critically threatened biome. It is also one of the world's greatest botanical repositories with an estimated 10,000 plant species, of which about 4400 are endemic. Herbaceous species, which include herbs rather than woody plants, are almost entirely endemic. Some of the most remarkable plants in the *cerrado* include the conspicuous *Mauritia flexuosa* palms (known locally as *buritis*) that grow along the swampy headwaters of streams and rivers, and the spectacular *ipê* trumpet flower trees (*tabebuia*), which are leafless when in bloom and have brilliant purple, pink, yellow or white flowers. There are some 600 bird species, nearly 20 of which are endemic and all of Brazil's spectacular mammals can be seen here. The best places to see the *cerrado* are Chapada dos Veadeiros (see page 714), Jalapão (see page 724), the Parque Estadual São Gonçalo do Rio Preto near Diamantina (see page 291), the Serra da Canastra, the Serra do Cipó and Parque Nacional das Emás (see page 715).

The sertão and caatinga

The sertão is a region which lies in the dry hinterlands of northeastern Brazil; ecologically it is made up principally of *caatinga*. This is South America's least scientifically studied biome and is completely unique to Brazil. The *caatinga* is made up of xeric desert-adapted plants – small, thorny deciduous trees, cacti, succulent plants, and fire-adapted grassland savannahs. There are many unique flowering plants that burst into brilliant bloom in the wet. The biome has two seasons: winter (May-November) when it is very hot and dry, and the summer (January-April) when it is very hot and wet. During the dry winter periods trees are bare and their roots begin to protrude through the surface of the stony soil which can reach temperatures of up to 60°C. When the rains begin in January, the bleak, desert-like landscape of the *caatinga* is transformed in an exuberance of green and bright flowers; the rivers start to fill up and birds begin to sing in the trees.

Caatinga makes up some 11% of Brazilian territory, yet only 1% of its habitats are protected – a reflection on the respect given to the sertão by both federal and state governments. And there are no tour operators offering wildlife trips to the region (although companies like **Manary Ecotours**, see page 66, do operate here). Animal life in the *caatinga* has been adversely affected by hunting and human occupation. Many species have become extinct locally, while others, such as the **three-banded armadillo**, **collared anteater**, **jaguar** and **tufted capuchin**, survive in reduced numbers. Bird species include some of the world's rarest parrots – Lear's and Spix's **macaws** live in tiny numbers on the fringes of Jalapão (see page 724) and near the Serra da Capivara (see page 590) and **cactus parakeets**, **long-billed wrens**, **scarlet-throated tanagers** and **yellow-faced siskins** occur throughout the biome. Beyond hearsay, little is known about the *caatinga* except that it is critically vulnerable. There are no statistics available for flora or fauna species or numbers. The best places to see *caatinga* are anywhere in the sertão, especially the Serra da Capivara and the remote Serra dos Confusões in southern Piauí.

National parks

On paper Brazil has stringent environmental legislation and a large system of very well-protected national parks. However, hunting is rife as none of the parks have rangers. Until recently, unscrupulous and influential businessmen and politicians logged and abused the parks with impunity; a situation which began to change only with the exposure of a logging scandal involving the state governments and **Ibama** (Instituto Brasileiro do Meio Ambiente e dos Recursos Naturais Renováveis – the Brazilian Institute for the Environment and Renewable Natural Resources) in Brazil's southern Amazon and Central West in the new millennium. This still compares favourably with Britain though where agriculture, logging and road construction is permitted within national parks even when they are world heritage sites. Ibama has in its care 57 national parks (Parques Nacionais, or PARNA). They are by no means the whole picture, though. They form part of a system of protected areas which go under different titles and which have varying degrees of public access. The network comprises, in addition to the national parks: *estações ecológicas* (ecological stations), *reservas biológicas* (biological reserves), *reservas ecológicas* (ecological reserves), *áreas de relevante interesse ecológico* (areas of relevant ecological interest), *reservas particulares do patrimônio nacional* (private national heritage reserves) and *áreas sob proteção especial* (areas of special protection). In all these entities, the exploitation of natural resources is completely forbidden. They are for research, education and recreation only. Three other types of entity are designed to allow the sustainable use of natural resources, while still preserving their biodiversity: *florestas nacionais* (national forests), *áreas de proteção ambiental* (areas of environmental protection) and *reservas extrativas* (extractive reserves, such as the rubber-tapping zones in Acre state). A new initiative is the **Projeto Corredores Ecológicos** (Ecological Corridors Project), which aims to create avenues of forest between isolated protected areas so that fauna may move over a greater area to breed, thus strengthening the stock of endangered animals, which might otherwise suffer the ills of inbreeding. An example of this is a project to link the *Mata Atlântica* of Poço das Antas with other pockets of coastal forest to help the survival of the golden lion tamarin.

Ibama was created in 1989 by uniting four separate bodies: the environmental secretariat (SEMA), the Brazilian Institute of Forest Development (IBDF), and the superintendencies for the development of fishing and rubber (SUDEPE and SUDHEVEA). Brazil has a long history of passing laws to protect natural resources, such as that of 1808 that excluded from international trade the export of *pau-brasil* and other woods. At the same time though, enforcement of such laws has not been easy. Today, the achievement of Ibama's goals is determined by resources, but funds are insufficient to commit either enough money or staff to the job of protecting the areas that have been designated for preservation. Sad though this is, there are still a large number of parks open to visitors that can give a good idea of the variety of Brazil's natural resources and the value that they hold for the country.

This book does not describe all of Brazil's national parks or other conservation entities, but only those which have easy access. Nor does it list all the offices of Ibama or its related departments throughout the country, but those nearest to the parks described are given and it is to these that you should apply to if a permit is needed to visit a specific park.

For more information, contact **Ibama** ① *national headquarters, SAIN, Av L-4, bloco B, Térreo, Edifiço Sede do Ibama, CEP 70 800-200, Brasília DF, T061-3226 8221/9014, www.ibama.gov.br*, or at a local branch listed throughout the text.

Information can also be obtained from the environment ministry, **Ministério do Meio Ambiente (MMA)** ① *Esplanada dos Ministérios, bloco B, 5-9 andar, CEP 70068-900, Brasília DF, www.mma.gov.br*. See also the book *Nacionais Brasil, Guias Philips* (1999), which has a good map, beautiful photographs, sections on history, flora and fauna and tourist services, US$15.

An environmental history of the Amazon

The first white man to cross the Amazon was the conquistador Francisco de Orellana, who ended up here by accident in 1541. The river and its environs were called the 'Land of the Amazons' after accounts by local indigenous people of a tribe of warrior women who dominated the lowland region, documented by the expedition's chronicler, Gaspar de Carvajal. This led to the myth that the Amazon area was a land of great wealth; an idea that has endured to this day and which powers the numerous attempts to exploit the forest.

Since the arrival of the Europeans, successive colonial and Brazilian governments have been hell-bent on developing Amazonia. First it was the gold of the Amazons. Then it was the sugar cane around São Luís and Belém; an industry which saw the introduction of slavery and the genocide of entire indigenous nations, including the magnificent Omagua people – an important pre-Columbian civilization. Then it was rubber, whose harvesting from wild *hevea brasiliensis* trees turned Manaus from a collection of mud huts to being a full-blown belle époque city with an opera house and some of the first street lights and trams in the Americas. Thousands of river people and indigenous tribes lost their liberty and their lives while the rubber barons became rich (see the film *A Selva* for a visual account). But the Amazon forest survived relatively untouched until the building of Brasília. This began to change in 1954 under President Juscelino Kubitschek, who believed in Brazil's destiny as a great country, and whose slogan was 'fifty years in five'.

Kubitschek built a new capital in the middle of what was then nowhere, which he called, Brasilia, and he linked it to Belém with the first Amazon road. This marked the beginnings of expansion into the vast Brazilian interior, and the US installed military dictatorship that came to power via a coup in 1964 continued the process.

The military planned massive relocations of the population, mostly the rural poor, to secure what they referred to as empty areas, and to ease the mounting pressure for land reform. The politic rhetoric was one of progress and the protection of Brazil's national security and borders, even from countries as small and impoverished as Guyana, whose entire national population was less than the number of soldiers serving in Brazil's armed forces. Inspired by the slogan 'Integra par no entregar' (integrate to avoid annexation) landless peasants were encouraged to relocate to the new states of Roraima and Rondônia and carve out their own property from the forests. 'The people without land', would be transferred to 'the land without people'. The disputed territories they left behind them could then be incorporated into the vast ranches owned by the powerful political oligarchy of landowners (many of whom were descended from the original Portuguese settlers) who were the political allies of the military, and the Amazon would become a profitable and productive area of export agriculture.

Money for these and other schemes were borrowed from and approved by the World Bank and IMF. A communication network would be crucial. In 1972, the military decided that they should link the Pacific and Atlantic oceans with a trans-Amazon highway, and build a network of filter roads off it, linking the interior with Sao Paulo and Minas Gerais. *Agrovilas*, purpose-built settlements were strung out along these new roads and families were airlifted in from the northeast and south of the country. A network of over a hundred hydroelectric dams was planned to provide energy at places like Presidente Figueiredo and on the Tocantins. They are appallingly inefficient. Another ambitious project, Greater Carajás, followed in 1980, when an 18-billion-ton iron ore mountain was discovered in the eastern Amazon, and in the early 1990s further plans were announced by the military to build 'Calha Norte', a road cutting across the northern Amazon, through the heart of the largest untouched section of virgin rainforest in South America. Its building was thwarted only by the courageous campaigns by the indigenous people of upper Rio Negro.

The 'opening of the Amazon' was a disaster for Brazil's indigenous tribes, as well as the forest and the economic prosperity of the country as a whole. Neither the new settlers in Roraima and Rondônia, nor the government had been aware that the Amazon soils they had planned to farm were so nutrient-poor that they would sustain crops or cattle for only a year or two at most, before turning to desert. Farmers and ranchers ate into the forest near the new roads at a terrifying rate. Soon they had encroached on indigenous territories, inciting conflict in which the *indígenas* invariably came off worse, or spreading western disease to which the tribes had no immunity. Not since the days of the Portuguese had the Amazon's *indígenas* suffered so badly.

In 1990, after the discovery of gold in Yanomami territories in western Roraima, *garimpeiro* (gold miners) from throughout Brazil flooded into the territory of the largest remaining isolated tribe in the Americas, the Yanomami. Many were supplied and supported by local businessmen, who saw them as the vanguard of a new colonization and were eager for a slice of the gold-rich territory. Indigenous 'hunts' were common. In 1990s Boa Vista, it is said that even taxi drivers offered safaris of the *indígenas* to visitors: bring a gun and shoot a wild native. Since then, at least 2000 Yanomami have died. Many more have been deprived of their land, either through annexation by gold miners or the pollution of their rivers with mercury and soil. Other tribes fared equally badly. The Parakanâ were deliberately infected with smallpox, influenza, tuberculosis and measles by FUNAI, the government's indigenous peoples' agency, ostensibly set up to protect them. Hundreds died. Then they were forcibly moved to make way for the Transamazon highway, and then again for the Tucuruí dam. The Xavantes lost their territory to the Italian company Liquigas; the Waimiri Atroari saw part of their reserve flooded by the Balbina dam; the Nambiquara were displaced first by a dam and then the Santarém to Cuiabá road, and the uru-Weu-Wau-Wau and the Zorro were in the way of the World Bank funded Polonoroeste road and development project. Ticuna, Guarani and many others were murdered by loggers, gold prospectors or settlers.

The forest's *caboclo* people suffered too. Although the forests were no longer producing rubber in the quantities they once had, rubber tappers still lived and worked in the forests of Acre, Amapá, Rondônia and Roraima, and when the cattle ranchers and their vanguard of displaced (mostly northeastern) peasants began to invade their territories and destroy their livelihood, they set up a resistance movement, organized by unions. A series of *empates*, or passive stand-offs, in the tradition of Gandhi and Martin Luther King, lead by charismatic locals like Francisco 'Chico' Alves Mendes, brought the plight of the rubber tappers to the attention of the world. It did little to assuage the ranchers, who killed and murdered rubber tappers aided and abetted by the local police. As he had predicted, Chico Mendes himself was shot dead in 1988.

Opening up the Amazon did little to help Brazil's economy, although a number of landowners and politicians managed to save enough to bank in the Cayman Islands and buy mansions in Miami. The new roads cost billions and many are now impassable. Many of the dams were built in valleys that were insufficiently deep and narrow for the rapid water flow required to produce cheap electricity. The Balbina dam north of Manaus, which was the personal project of President Figueiredo, the last of the military rulers of Brazil, produces electricity four times more expensive than that available on the world market. There are so many rotting logs in its flooded valley that the acidity of the water requires the turbines to be replaced every few years. The Greater Carajás project, which the then finance minister Delfim Neto claimed would provide enough iron ore to pay off the foreign debt in fact it doubled it, and the surrounding forest was cleared for his cattle-ranching friends. Brazil's economy and the Amazon suffered deeply through the 'Integrar para no Entregar' project. Together with the rising cost of oil, opening up the Amazon has made Brazil the largest foreign debtor of all developing countries.

The massacre of the Yanomami and the murder of Chico Mendes cost Brazil's reputation dear. They were denounced to the United Nations and the Organisation of American States for genocide in the 1990s, and NGOs and campaign groups continued to draw attention to their appalling indigenous rights record and abuses of power. Brazil got frightened and ashamed. When they hosted the 1992 Earth Summit, they showed off a whole infrastructure of specialized agencies for protecting the environment, from a special ministry down to state and municipal secretariats. Constitutional and legislative changes promised indigenous land demarcation and declared explicitly that private land titles on lands traditionally occupied by Indians were null and void. Environmental impact reports would be required before new development or industrial projects could go ahead. The world rejoiced, and Brazil obtained US$290 million in grants for forest and indigenous land protection.

But Brazil is a lumbering and corrupt giant, with a tongue that drips honey. The money was gratefully received. But none of it ever reached the *indígenas* and the national parks set up by the government were parks just on paper. The powerful and corrupt landowning oligarchy who rule the country, displayed their true colours only four years later, when they forced President Fernando Henrique Cardoso to pass a decree 1775, which revoked the law granting protection of indigenous lands, opening them up to loggers, miners and ranchers. An area the size of Rhode Island was cut from Macuxi indigenous territory in Roraima and handed over to 14 cattle ranchers from the National Institute for Colonisation and Agrarian Reform (INCRA). Further enclaves were created in the heart of the reserve for gold miners. Over the past decade, corrupt officials in the government's own environmental protection agency, Ibama, have been shown to have forged documents on a grand scale to allow the passage of illegally cut mahogany from indigenous reserves and national parks into Europe and the USA and attempts continue in Congress to open up indigenous areas to mining and reduce the size of the Yanomami territories.

Yet some progress was made. Significant areas of land have been marked out as indigenous territories; far more than in the USA or Canada both in real terms and as a percentage of national territory. Whether the indigenous peoples have any real sovereignty is another matter as their rights to the minerals beneath their land is by no means clear under Brazilian law. And in the Amanã Sustainable Development Reserve (SDR) was set up, linking two other reserves to form the world's largest protected rainforest area. The Amanã SDR surrounds Lake Amanã north of Tefé and covers 23,500 sq km. It is sandwiched between the Jaú National Park to the east and the Mamirauá SDR to the west, forming a 640-km long corridor. It is hoped that whole ecosystems will be preserved and that local inhabitants will be able to find sustainable work in the reserve's management.

Since he first came to power, Lula has promised much but has been stringently criticized by the Confederation of Amazon Indians for his policy towards them. He failed to demarcate a key indigenous reserve in Roraima, preferring to cut a deal with local politicians for political support. And although down briefly in the late 1990s, deforestation in 2003 was at an all time high thanks to a failure to curb illegal clearance by soya and cattle ranchers. The 2005 murder of the environmentalist and nun Dorothy Stang, by ranch owners in Para, showed that the problem of environmental destruction exists most acutely at a state level. It also brought widespread international condemnation. Once again Brazil was shamed into action.

The environment minister, Marina Silva, said the country could not 'give in to people committing acts of violence' and that the federal government would be 'putting the brakes on the predators.' There has been progress since. Immediately after the murder, large areas of national park were demarcated in Para, by the federal government. In 2005 deforestation in the Amazon slowed down by half – as much because of a fall in soya prices as because of federal policy. And in December 2006 Simão Jatene, the governor of Pará – long a conservative anti-environmentalist – announced the creation of nine new protected areas forming an ecological corridor between Brazil and the Guianas. Yet like all Brazil's national parks, these will exist on paper only – with no rangers and no organized monitoring. And all this good work could be offset by more destruction. On 6 June 2006 – World Environment Day – Lula announced plans to pave the road between Cuiabá and Santarém, in order to make the transport of soya beans cheaper and swifter. He claimed that the government was establishing strict environmental controls, and had created a 'sustainable forestry reserve' of 19 million ha (47 million acres) around the road and that the project 'will show how we can be Brazilian without being predators, as foreigners often say about Brazil'. But roads have always been associated with the arrival of squatters and the birth of towns in the Amazon and the sincerity of his promises remain to be seen.

Books

History and anthropology

Hemming, J, *Red Gold*, *Amazon Frontier* and *Die if You Must*, Pan. The little-known history of Brazil's indigenous people is alternately shocking and inspiring. This wonderful, scholarly and beautifully written account is as readable and exciting as Prescott's *Conquest of Peru* and will in time rank alongside it. A must for anyone with an interest in Brazil.
Reichel-Dolmatoff, G, *Rainforest Shamans*, Themis books. The best introduction to the philosophy of an Amazon people available in English.

Literature

Amado, J, et al, *Gabriela, Clove and Cinnamon*, *Dona Flor and her two Husbands* (Avon Books). Very poor translations of these captivating novels, almost all of which are set in Bahia, and which read like a cross between Poldark and Angelique. Romps through 19th- and 20th-century Bahia. Ripping yarns though not literary masterpieces. Over a long career Amado published many best sellers, most of which are available in English. He is often criticized for producing an overly optimistic, sexily tropical view of the country, and of Bahia, his home state.
Andrade, Mário de, *Macunaíma*. Written in the 1920s, this is a comic statement in picaresque form about Brazilian nationality, by the leader of modernism.
Ângelo, I, *The Celebration* (Avon Books). Much the best novel about the political, social and economic crisis at the end of the 1960s, the worst period of the military regime.
Buarque, C, *Turbulence* and *Budapest* (Bloomsbury). The first is a short, pacey allegory of modern Brazil, the second which has been recently translated, is a labyrinthine Borgesian magic realist novel set in Budapest. It was top of the

best sellers list in Brazil for many months – something unusual for literary fiction. Buarque is the son of a distinguished social historian and is most famous as a singer and composer.
da Cunha, E, *Rebellion in the Backlands* (University of Chicago Press). The book that inspired Mario Vargas Llosa and which is the country's most famous piece of sustained journalistic writing.
Freyre, Gilberto, *The Masters and the Slaves*, out of print. One of the central figures in the story of Brazil's struggle to define its identity. Controversial and sometimes viewed as implicitly racist, this account traces the psychology of Brazil to its sugar plantation past.
Guimarães Rosa, J, *The Jaguar and Other Stories* (Boulevard Books). Decent translations of Brazil's greatest novelist are hard to come by. There are none at all of his masterpiece, *Grande sertão, veredas: As trilhas de amor e guerra de Riobaldo*. Guimarães Rosa is, in a sense, the first great magic realist author, and is by far the most respected author within Brazil. He is credited with having invented a new kind of poetically colloquial literary Portuguese. This draws its inspiration from the mystical and lyrical language of the interior of Brazil, a region which was gradually cut off from the rest of the country. *The Jaguar* is little more than an introduction to his writing.
Hatoum, M, *The Brothers*. One of the most interesting of Brazilian contemporary writers who focusses on the experience of being Brazilian-Lebanese in the dangerous world of the early 20th-century Amazon. Wonderfully evocative.
Lins do Rego, J, *The Masters and the Slaves* (University of California Press). Highly influenced by Gilberto Freyre, this is an evocative account of childhood on a northeastern sugar plantation.

Lispector, C, *Family Ties*, *The Hour of the Star* and *Soulstorm* (University of Texas Press, Carcanet Press and New Directions). Brazil's other great modernist and the country's most highly revered woman's writer.

Llosa, M V, *The War of the End of the World* (Penguin). An enthralling dramatisation of the Canudos rebellion. Very hard to put down and beautifully structured.

Machado de Assis, J M, *The Posthumous Memoirs of Bras Cubas*, *Dom Casmurro* (Oxford University Press) and *Philosopher or Dog*,(Bloomsbury). At last some decent translations of Brazil's most acerbic and witty literary social commentator. With a black mother and white Portuguese-descended father, Machado de Assis was a bridge between the 2 Brazil's: the haves and the have nots.

Morley, H, *The Patriot* (London: Rex Collings). The diary of a girl's life in Diamantina, in Minas Gerais. Translated by the great American poet Elizabeth Bishop who lived in Brazil for many years. A delightfully intimate and frank portrait of small-town life.

Ramos, G, *São Bernardo* (Peter Owen) *Anguish* (Knopf, 1972) and *Barren Lives* (University of Texas Press, 1965). The greatest of the novelists of the 1930s and 1940s: a harsh realist.

Torres, A, *Blues for a Lost Childhood* (Readers International,1989). An idealistic Brazilian journalist leaves his rural town for Rio only to be crushed by the realities of the city. Sobering and not very cheerful reading.

Ubaldo Ribeiro, J, *The Lost Manuscript* (Bloomsbury). A panoramic historical novel, originally entitled *Long Live the Brazilian People*.

Poetry

Bandeira, M, *This Earth, that Sky: Poems by Manuel Bandeira* (University of California Press). The oldest member of the modernist movement, and one of Brazil's greatest poets, master of the short, intense lyric.

Drummond de Andrade, C, *Plantation Boy* (New York: Knopf). Perhaps Brazil's greatest poet, with a varied, lyrical, somewhat downbeat style.

Photography

Andujar, Claudia, *A vulnerabilidade do ser* (Cosacnaify). Wonderful evocative and masterful images that capture the poetry of Brazil's landscapes and people; often fused in a double exposure. Her Amazon images are startlingly original.

Bassit, José, *Imagens Fiéis*. A moving account of traditional religious life in the backlands of the northeast. Again, masterfully shot.

Salgado, S, *Migrations* (Aperture). The most recent volume from the world's most highly respected photojournalist renowned for transcendental images of the world's silent majority and their daily lives. Incredible.

Social comment

Bellos, A, *Futebol: The Brazilian Way of Life* (Bloomsbury, 2003). A loving look at the beautiful game, its history, its players, supporters and its legendary feats. Alex Bellos is one of the UK's leading Brazilian experts and was the *Guardian* correspondent based in Rio.

Castro, R, *Rio de Janeiro* (Bloomsbury, 2004). An anecdotal history and profile of Rio de Janeiro written by a Carioca.

Fausto, B, *A Concise History of Brazil* (Cambridge University Press). Dry as dust but the only readily available, reliable history of the country available in English.

Harvey, *Liberators* (Constable and Robinson, 2002). A wonderful romp through the Liberation of South America from Europe with a colourful section on imperial Brazil. How all history should be written.

McGowan, C and **Pessanha, R**, *The Brazilian Sound: Samba, Bossa Nova and the Popular Music of Brazil* (Temple University Press, 1998). An encyclopaedic survey of Brazilian popular music with interviews from many of the key players.

Page, J, *The Brazilians* (Da Capo Press,1995). One of the few popular books on Brazil which really gets under the country's skin. With excellent chapters on Carnaval, football, Brazilian society and character and plenty of information on Rio.

Travel writing

Davis, W, *One River*. A remarkable travel book: Hunter S Thompson meets George Forrest and Levi Strauss in the heart of the Amazon.

Fawcett, P, *Exploration Fawcett* (Weidenfeld & Nicholson, 2001). The diaries of the intrepid explorer who disappeared in Mato Grosso in the 1920s and whose descriptions of the table-top mountains there inspired Conan Doyle to write *The Lost World*. Some beautiful writing on the Amazon, Rio de Janeiro and the Andes.

Fleming, P, *Brazilian Adventure* (Pimlico, 1998). The sparkling, delightfully humorous account of a 1930s expedition in search of Colonel Percy Fawcett.

Robb, P, *A Death in Brazil* (Bloomsbury, 2004). A poetic odyssey through Brazil's history, culture and landscape.

Wildlife field guides

General

Kricher, J, *A Neotropical Companion* (Princeton University Press). A very clear, intelligent introduction to the ecosystems, biology and botany of the neotropical region.

Pearson, D and **Beletsky, L** *Brazil - Amazon & Pantanal* (Academic Press). By far the best introductory wildlife and botanical guide.

Birds

de la Peña, M and **Rumboll, M**, *Birds of Southern South America and Antarctica* (Harper Collins & Princeton University Press). A slim volume, but with comprehensive information on most of Brazil's non-neotropical species.

Dunning, J, *South American Birds: A Photographic Aid to Identification* (Harrowood Books, Pennsylvania, 1987). The best of the current photguides with more than 2700 species, over 1400 colour photographs.

Hilty, S and **Brown, W** *Birds of Colombia*. The best book for the northern Amazon region.

Ridgely, R and **Tudor, G**, *The Birds of South America, Volume 1 & II* (University of Texas Press & Oxford University Press, UK). One of the most important bird books of the century.

Sibley, D and **Alfred, A**, *Sibley's Birding basics* (Knopf, 2002). Very useful aid to bird identification giving clues through appearance, behaviour, flight and song. Invaluable for inexperienced bird wathchers.

Sick, H, *The Birds of Brazil* (Princeton University Press). Currently the only widely available book covering almost all Brazil's species (there are more species added almost monthly).

Souza, D, *All the Birds of Brazil* (Gráfica Santa Helena, 2002). Covering most Brazilian species and include illustrations, albeit rather poor ones. English and Portuguese.

Wheatley, N, *Where to Watch Birds in South America* (Princeton University Press). A little out of date but with an interesting list of places and useful bird inventories.

Zimmer, K and **Whittaker, A**, *Birds of Brazil* (Princeton University Press). The first comprehensive, modern illustrated field guide to the birds of Brazil. Originally due out in 2008. Now delayed until 2010.

Mammals
Eisenberg, J F and **Redford, K**, *Mammals of the Neotropics Vol 3: The Central Neotropics – Ecuador, Peru, Bolivia, Brazil.*
Emmons, L H, *Neotropical Rainforest Mammals: A Field Guide* (University of Chicago Press). Excellent illustrated field guides which between them cover pretty much everything in tropical Brazil.

Plants
Henderson, A, **Galeano, G** and **Bernal, R**, *A Field Guide to the Palms of the Americas* (Princeton University Press). A comprehensive illustrated guide. Well worth having.

Reptiles and amphibians
Bartlett, R D and **Pope Bartlett, P**, *Reptiles and Amphibians of the Amazon: An Ecotourist's Guide* (University of Florida Press). With 250 common species.

Contents

Footnotes

Basic Portuguese for travellers

Learning Portuguese is a useful part of the preparation for a trip to Brazil and no volume of dictionaries, phrase books or word lists will provide the same enjoyment as being able to communicate directly with the people of the country you are visiting. It is a good idea to make an effort to grasp the basics before you go. As you travel you will pick up more of the language and the more you know, the more you will benefit from your stay. ▶▶ See also *Language in Essentials, page 57*.

General pronunciation

Within Brazil itself, there are variations in pronunciation, intonation, phraseology and slang. This makes for great richness and for the possibility of great enjoyment in the language. A couple of points which the newcomer to the language will spot immediately are the use of the tilde (~) over 'a' and 'o'. This makes the vowel nasal, as does a word ending in 'm' or 'ns', or a vowel followed by 'm' + consonant, or by 'n' + consonant. Another important point of spelling is that for words ending in 'i' and 'u' the emphasis is on the last syllable, though (unlike Spanish) no accent is used. This is especially relevant in place names like Buriti, Guarapari, Caxambu, Iguaçu. Note also the use of 'ç', which changes the pronunciation of c from hard [k] to soft [s].

Personal pronouns

In conversation, most people refer to 'you' as *você*, although in the south and in Pará *tu* is more common. To be more polite, use *O Senhor/A Senhora*. For 'us', *gente* (people, folks) is very common when it includes you too.

Portuguese words and phrases

Greetings and courtesies

hello	*oi*
good morning	*bom dia*
good afternoon	*boa tarde*
good evening/night	*boa noite*
goodbye	*adeus/tchau*
see you later	*até logo*
please	*por favor/faz favor*
thank you	*obrigado* (if a man is speaking)
	/obrigada (if a woman is speaking)
thank you very much	*muito obrigado/muito obrigada*
How are you?	*Como vai você tudo bem?/tudo bom?*
I am fine	*vou bem/tudo bem*
pleased to meet you	*um prazer*
no	*não*
yes	*sim*
excuse me	*com licença*
I don't understand	*não entendo*
Please speak slowly	*fale devagar por favor*

What is your name?	Qual é seu nome?
my name is …	O meu nome é …
Go away!	Vai embora!

Basic questions

where is?	onde está/onde fica?
why?	por que?
how much does it cost?	quanto custa?
what for?	para que?
how much is it?	quanto é?
how do I get to … ?	para chegar a … ?
when?	quando?
I want to go to …	quero ir para …
when does the bus leave?/arrive?	a que hor sai/chega o ônibus?
is this the way to the church?	aquí é o caminho para a igreja?

Basics

bathroom/toilet	banheiro
police (policeman)	a polícia (o polícia)
hotel	o (a pensão, a hospedaria)
restaurant	o restaurante (o lanchonete)
post office	o correio
telephone office	(central) telefônica
supermarket	o supermercado
market	o mercado
bank	o banco
bureau de change	a casa de câmbio
exchange rate	a taxa de câmbio
notes/coins	notas/moedas
traveller's cheques	os travelers/os cheques de viagem
cash	dinheiro
breakfast	o caféde manh
lunch	o almoço
Dinner/supper	o jantar
Meal	a refeição
drink	a bebida
mineral water	a água mineral
soft fizzy drink	o refrigerante
beer	a cerveja
without sugar	sem açúcar
without meat	sem carne

Getting around

on the left/right	à esquerda/à direita
straight on	direto
to walk	caminhar
bus station	a rodoviária
Bus	o ônibus

bus stop	*a parada*
train	*a trem*
airport	*o aeroport*
aeroplane/airplane	*o avião*
flight	*o vôa*
first/second class	*primeira/segunda clase*
train station	*a ferroviária*
combined bus and train station	*a rodoferroviária*
ticket	*o passagem/o bilhete*
ticket office	*a bilheteria*

Accommodation

room	*quarto*
noisy	*barulhento*
single/double room	*(quarto de) solteiro/(quarto para) casal*
room with two beds	*quarto com duas camas*
with private bathroom	*quarto com banheiro*
hot/cold water	*água quente/fria*
to make up/clean	*limpar*
sheet(s)	*o lençol (os lençóis)*
blankets	*as mantas*
pillow	*o travesseiro*
clean/dirty towels	*as toalhas limpas/sujas*
toilet paper	*o papel higiêico*

Health

Chemist	*a farmacia*
doctor	*o coutor/a doutora*
(for) pain	*(para) dor*
stomach	*o esômago (a barriga)*
head	*a cabeça*
fever/sweat	*a febre/o suor higiênicas*
diarrhoea	*a diarréia*
blood	*o sangue*
condoms	*as camisinhas/os preservativos*
contraceptive (pill)	*anticonceptional (a pílula)*
period	*a menstruação/a regra*
sanitary towels/tampons	*toalhas absorventes/absorventes internos*
contact lenses	*lentes de contacto*
aspirin	*a aspirina*

Time

at one o'clock (am/pm)	*a uma hota (da manhã/da tarde)*
at half past two/two thirty	*as dois e meia*
at a quarter to three	*quinze para as três*
it's one o'clock	*é uma*
it's seven o'clock	*são sete horas*
it's twenty past six/six twenty	*são seis e vinte*

it's five to nine	*são cinco para as nove*
in ten minutes	*em dez minutos*
five hours	*cinco horas*
does it take long?	*sura muito?*

Days

Monday	*segunda feiro*
Tuesday	*terça feira*
Wednesday	*quarta feira*
Thursday	*quinta feira*
Friday	*sexta feira*
Saturday	*sábado*
Sunday	*domingo*

Months

January	*janeiro*
February	*fevereiro*
March	*março*
April	*abril*
May	*maio*
June	*junho*
July	*julho*
August	*agosto*
September	*setembro*
October	*outubro*
November	*novembro*
December	*dezembro*

Numbers

One	*um/uma*
two	*dois/duas*
three	*três*
four	*quatro*
five	*cinco*
six	*seis* ('*meia*' half, is frequently used for number 6 ie half-dozen)
seven	*sete*
eight	*oito*
nine	nove
ten	*dez*
eleven	*onze*
twelve	*doze*
thirteen	*treze*
fourteen	*catorze*
fifteen	*quinze*
sixteen	*dezesseis*
seventeen	*dezesete*
eighteen	*dezoito*

nineteen	*dezenove*
twenty	*vinte*
twenty-one	*vente e um*
thirty	*trinta*
forty	*cuarenta*
fifty	*cinqüe*
sixty	*sessenta*
seventy	*setenta*
eighty	*oitenta*
ninety	*noventa*
hundred	*cem, cento*
thousand	*mil*

Useful slang

that's great/cool	*que legal*
bloke/guy/geezer	*cara* (literally 'face')
biker slang for bloke/guy	*mano*
cheesy/tacky	*brega*
posh, spoilt girl/boy with rich parents	*patricinha/mauricinho*
in fashion/cool	*descolado*

Glossary

→ See also food glossary, page 46, and the Music and dance colour section.

azulejo	tile	ferroviária	train station
baía	bay	forró	music and dance style from northeast Brazil
bairro	area or suburb		
bandas	marching bands that compete during Carnaval	frevo	frenetic musical style from Recife
		gaúcho	cowboy, especially from Rio Grande do Sul
bandeirantes	early Brazilian conquistadors who went on missions to open up the interior		
		garimpeiro	miner or prospector
		igreja	church
barraca	beach hut or stall	ilha	island
berimbau	stringed instrument that accompanies capoeira	jangada	small fishing boats, peculiar to the northeast
biblioteca	library	jardim	garden
bilhete	ticket	lanchonete	café/deli
botequim	small bar, open-air	largo	small square
caboclo	rural workers of mixed descent	leito	executive bus
cachaça	cane liquor	litoral	coast/coastal area
cachoeira	waterfall	mata	jungle
caipirinha	Brazilian cocktail, made from cachaça, lime, sugar and ice	mercado	market
		Mineiro	person from Minas Gerais
câmbio	bureau de change	mirante	viewpoint
candomblé	African-Brazilian religion	mosteiro	monastery
capela	chapel	Paulista	person from São Paulo
capoeira	African-Brazilian martial art	ponte	bridge
Carioca	person from Rio de Janeiro	praça	square/plaza
carnaval	carnival	praia	beach
cerrado	scubland	prancha	surfboard
cerveja	beer	prefeitura	town hall
churrascaria	barbecue restaurant, often all-you-can-eat	rio	river
		rodoviária	bus station
empadas	mini pasties	rua	street
estrada	road	sambaquis	archaeological shell mounds
favela	slum/shanty town	sertão	arid interior of the northeast
fazenda	country estate or ranch	Sertanejo	person who lives in the sertão
feijoada	black-bean stew	vaqueiro	cowboy in the north

Acronyms and official names

FUNAI	Fundacao Nacional do Indio (National Foundation for Indigenous People)
IBAMA	Instituto Brasileiro do Meio Ambiente E Dos Recursos Naturais Renováveis (Brazilian Institute of Environment and Renewable Natural Resources)
MPB	Música Popular Brasileira
RAMSAR	Wetlands Convention

Advertisers' index

Acknowledgements

Thanks to the following people for updates: This book was updated with the assistance of: Gardenia Robinson (Bahia and Fortaleza), Lucy Bryson (Rio Grande do Sul and Santa Catarina), Daniel Egli (Upper Rio Negro). Chris Fuzinatto and the staff at Embratur in London and Julia Segatto at FSB. Raphael Robinson for invaluable research on things for the under-sixes, Jody Gillet, Michel Nicolau and David McLoughlin at Brazilian Music and Arts, Carlinhos Brown, Mariene de Castro, Erika Machado and Ju in Belo Horizonte, Coletivo Radio Cipo, Albery Albuquerque in Belém, Rodrigo in Belém, William Wisden, Jorge at Eco Dunas, Villa Kalongo in Jericoacoara, Daniel and Daniela at Mata Na'tiva in Trancoso, Klauber and Andrea from Portomondo in Porto Seguro, Orbita Tours in Ilhéus and Itacaré, Francisco França and family in São Paulo, Camila Belchior in São Paulo, Ale Ribeiro in São Paulo, Carlos at Cama e Café in Rio, Del in Maceió, Richard Dye of Trivium, Roy Funch in Lençóis, Vila Serrano in Lençóis, Maurício de Oliveira Junior in São Paulo.

Notes

Notes

Complete title listing

Footprint publishes travel guides to more than 150 destinations worldwide. Each guide is packed with practical, concise and colourful information for everybody from first-time travellers to travel aficionados. The list is growing fast and current titles are noted below. Available from all good bookshops and online
www.footprintbooks.com

(P) Denotes pocket guide

Latin America and Caribbean
Antigua & Leeward Islands (P)
Argentina
Belize, Guatemala &
  Southern Mexico
Bolivia
Brazil
Caribbean Islands
Dominican Republic (P)
Chile
Colombia
Costa Rica
Costa Rica, Nicaragua & Panama
Cuba
Cuzco & the Inca Heartland
Ecuador & Galápagos
Mexico & Central America
Nicaragua
Patagonia
Peru
Peru, Bolivia & Ecuador
South American Handbook

North America
Vancouver (P)
Western Canada

Africa
Cape Town (P)
Egypt
Kenya
Morocco
Namibia
South Africa Handbook

Middle East
Dubai (P)

Credits

Footprint credits

Editor: Nicola Gibbs
Map editor: Sarah Sorensen
Picture editor: Kassia Gawronski

Managing Director: Andy Riddle
Publisher: Patrick Dawson
Editorial: Felicity Laughton, Sara Chare,
Ria Gane, Jen Haddington, Alan Murphy,
Alice Jell
Cartography: Robert Lunn,
Kevin Feeney, Emma Bryers
Cover design: Robert Lunn
Design: Mytton Williams
Sales and marketing: Liz Harper,
Zoë Jackson, Hannah Bonnell
Advertising sales manager: Renu Sibal
Finance and administration:
Elizabeth Taylor

Photography credits

Front cover: jangada sail boats,
Dawn Fridmar, 4cornerimages
Back cover: portrait of samba
dancer at carnival parade city of
Rio_mediacolor's/Alamy

Manufactured in Italy by LegoPrint
Pulp from sustainable forests

Footprint feedback

We try as hard as we can to make each
Footprint guide as up to date as possible
but, of course, things always change. If you
want to let us know about your experiences –
good, bad or ugly – then don't delay, go to
www.footprintbooks.com and send in
your comments.

Publishing information

Footprint Brazil
6th edition
© Footprint Handbooks Ltd
February 2009

ISBN 978 1 906098 41 4
CIP DATA: A catalogue record for this
book is available from the British Library

® Footprint Handbooks and the Footprint
mark are a registered trademark of Footprint
Handbooks Ltd

Published by Footprint
6 Riverside Court
Lower Bristol Road
Bath BA2 3DZ, UK
T +44 (0)1225 469141
F +44 (0)1225 469461
www.footprintbooks.com

Distributed in the USA by Globe Pequot Press,
Guilford, Connecticut

Distance chart

Belém																	
2824	**Belo Horizonte**																
6083	4736	**Boa Vista**															
2120	716	4275	**Brasília**														
2942	1453	3836	1134	**Campo Grande**													
2941	1594	3142	1133	694	**Cuiabá**												
3500	1301	5128	1673	1298	1986	**Florianópolis**											
1610	2528	6548	2200	3407	3406	3838	**Fortaleza**										
5298	3951	785	3490	3051	2357	4443	5763	**Manaus**									
2108	2348	6770	2422	3534	3543	3662	537	5985	**Natal**								
3852	1712	5348	2027	1518	2206	476	4242	4563	4066	**Porto Alegre**							
2074	2061	6483	2135	3247	3255	3375	800	5698	297	3779	**Recife**						
4931	3584	2230	3123	2684	1990	3976	5396	1445	5533	4196	5243	**Rio Branco**					
3250	434	5159	1148	1444	2017	1144	2805	4374	2625	1553	2338	4007	**Rio de Janeiro**				
2100	1372	5794	1446	2568	2566	2682	1389	5009	1126	3090	839	4457	1649	**Salvador**			
806	2738	6120	2157	2979	2978	3537	1070	5305	1607	3891	1573	4968	3015	1599	**São Luís**		
2933	586	4756	1015	1014	1614	705	3127	3971	2947	1109	2660	3604	429	1962	2970	**São Paulo**	
3108	524	5261	1239	1892	2119	1597	2397	4476	2178	2001	1891	4909	521	1202	2607	882	**Vitória**

Distances in kilometres 1 kilometre = 0.62 miles

Map symbols

- ☐ Capital city
- ○ Other city, town
- International border
- Regional border
- ⊖ Customs
- Contours (approx)
- ▲ Mountain, volcano
- Mountain pass
- Escarpment
- Glacier
- Salt flat
- Rocks
- Seasonal marshland
- Beach, sandbank
- Waterfall
- Reef
- Motorway
- Main road
- Minor road
- Track
- Footpath
- Railway
- Railway with station
- ✈ Airport
- 🚌 Bus station
- Ⓜ Metro station

- --- Cable car
- Funicular
- Ferry
- Pedestrianized street
- Tunnel
- One way-street
- Steps
- Bridge
- Fortified wall
- Park, garden, stadium
- Sleeping
- Eating
- Bars & clubs
- Building
- Sight
- Cathedral, church
- Chinese temple
- Hindu temple
- Meru
- Mosque
- Stupa
- Synagogue
- Tourist office
- 🏛 Museum
- ⊠ Post office
- Police

- Ⓢ Bank
- @ Internet
- Telephone
- Market
- Medical services
- P Parking
- Petrol
- Golf
- Archaeological site
- National park, wildlife reserve
- Viewing point
- A Campsite
- Refuge, lodge
- Castle, fort
- Diving
- Deciduous, coniferous, palm trees
- Hide
- Vineyard, winery
- Distillery
- Shipwreck
- Historic battlefield
- 1 Detail map
- 1 Related map